Commercial Law

To Declan, Lauren and Daniel.

Commercial Law

Fidelma White

Dublin

Thomson Round Hall
2002

UNITED KINGDOM
Sweet & Maxwell
London

AUSTRALIA
Law Book Co.
Sydney

CANADA and USA
Carswell
Toronto

HONG KONG
Sweet & Maxwell Asia

NEW ZEALAND
Brookers
Wellington

SINGAPORE and MALAYSIA
Sweet & Maxwell Asia
Singapore and Kuala Lumpur

Contents

Detailed Contents

TABLE OF LEGISLATION

Pre-1922 Acts

Constitution of Ireland

Post-1922 Acts of the Oireachtas

Statutory Instruments

EUROPEAN UNION: TREATIES

EUROPEAN UNION: DIRECTIVES

European Union: Regulations

U.K. Acts

U.K. Statutory Instruments

Australia

Canada

Italy

New Zealand

United States

International Conventions

Table of Cases

PREFACE

Commercial law is an extensive subject which is difficult to define with precision. It is based largely on contract law, though it borrows from many other areas of law, including property, torts, equity and restitution. In common law jurisdictions, commercial law is transaction based, thereby excluding an examination of the institutions of commerce, such as partnerships and corporations. Moreover, commercial law is concerned primarily with the dealings of professional business persons, as opposed to consumers, although this distinction is not always recognised in legislation (*e.g.,* the Sale of Goods Act 1893) and can be difficult to draw. Despite such difficulties of definition, commercial law is a discrete subject with its own principles and objectives (see Chapter 1). At the heart of commercial law is the contract for the sale of goods. Surrounding a typical commercial sale of goods contract is a web of contracts and other legal arrangements and rights, including agency contracts, insurance contracts, carriage contracts, arrangements for finance, and intellectual property rights. This book explores the private law framework which facilitates these main areas of commercial activity.

The book was written with two types of reader in mind: the legal practitioner and the law student. It not only describes the current state of Irish commercial law but also critically analyses the law and considers options for reform. The "state of Irish commercial law" is a matter of concern. Much of Irish commercial law is rooted in nineteenth-century legislation (*e.g.* Bills of Exchange Act 1882, Factors Act 1889, Sale of Goods Act 1893, and Marine Insurance Act 1906). Modern commercial legislation is scarce and tends to be driven by external influences, such as the European Community (*e.g.* EC (Commercial Agents) Regulations 1994 and 1997) and the wider international trading community (*e.g.* Arbitration (International Commercial) Act 1998). Home-grown developments in commercial law have been largely at the initiative of our judiciary (*e.g.* the recognition of retention of title clauses in sale of goods contracts). This apparent lack of interest by our legislature is worrying. A good example of the poor state of our commercial law, both in terms of structure and content, is our sale of goods legislation. In terms of structure, there are three main sources of law: the Sale of Goods Act 1893, the Sale of Goods and Supply of Services Act 1980, and the EC Directive on certain aspects of consumer sale and associated guarantees. The Directive was due to be implemented in member states by January 1, 2002: at the time of writing, the Directive had not been implemented in Irish law. It is forecast that the Directive will be implemented by December 30, 2002 in the form of Regulations. These layers of legislation are untidy and the lack of clarity as to how the Directive and any national implementing measure relate to the pre-existing law causes uncertainty. In terms of content, there are many aspects of the legislation in need of review: the use of the term "merchantable quality" and its definition; the rules on the passing of property in unascertained goods; and the *nemo dat* exceptions, to name but a few. Any reform must, however, be contingent on the necessary empirical research being conducted. It is the author's view that the Government, in implementing the Directive, has missed an opportunity to review the whole of sales law. A more bold approach would have been to implement the Directive using primary legislation designed to fit with the pre-existing rules. Perhaps the neatest, though clearly not the easiest, solution would be to consolidate the three layers of rules identified above into one principal statute for the sale of goods. This statute could contain, in one part, the rules common to all domestic sales contracts and, in another part, the particular rules that apply to consumer sales. This approach would also allow the Government to implement the Law Commission's recommendation that the Vienna Convention be adopted in relation to international sales – a third part. At the same time, aspects of the Sale of Goods Acts 1893 and 1980 which are in need of review could be addressed.

There are some positive developments, though. In particular, the establishment of a *de facto* Commercial Court as a division of the High Court, following the recommendation of the Committee on Court Practice and Procedure in its 27th Interim Report in 2002, is to be welcomed. A Commercial Court staffed by judges with a particular expertise in commercial matters, hearing cases drawn from a dedicated "commercial list", will offer a more coherent and speedy approach to the resolution of commercial law disputes. It is hoped that the work of the Commercial Court will be facilitated by the introduction of new directions, rules, and electronic practices and procedures, appropriate to the Court.

At a personal level, I would like to take this opportunity to thank all those who contributed to the research and writing of this book, not least the many commercial law students who have asked questions and in doing so have inspired answers and indeed further questions. I am especially grateful to my colleagues in the Law Department at University College, Cork, in particular, Louise Crowley, Mary Donnelly, Shane Kilcommins and Darius Whelan. I would also like to thank my former colleague, and sometimes co-author, Rob Bradgate for all his encouragement and assistance. I was greatly assisted in the research which underlies this book by the efforts of Julia Emihk and the library staff of the Law Library at

University College, Cork. I would also like to thank the publishers, in particular Thérèse Carrick for commissioning the work, and Catherine Dolan, Dave Ellis, and Elina Talvitie for seeing the work through to publication. I must also acknowledge those who supplied standard form documentation and contracts included in the Appendices to the book, in particular the Grain and Feed Trade Association of London. Lastly, I would like to pay a special thanks to my husband Declan Flynn, who read and commented on draft chapters of the book. I am grateful to him, and my children, Lauren and Daniel, for their patience and support in the completion of the book.

While assistance was received from many quarters, any shortcomings, oversights and errors in the book are the responsibility of the author alone. Readers are reminded that this book is not intended as a substitute for legal advice and that no liability will be accepted in respect of any reliance on it. The book purports to be up to date as of June 1, 2002, although it has been possible to take account of some later developments at proof stage.

Fidelma White
Cork
November 2002

PART I

INTRODUCTION TO COMMERCIAL LAW

Chapter 1
INTRODUCTION

1.1 The Nature of Commercial Law

Commerce, or trade, is vital for the economy of a modern state. Many individuals earn their livelihood from trading, whether as entrepreneurs, agents, or employees. Moreover, the health of an economy is often judged by examining trade figures, for instance, by comparing the level of exports of commodities with the level of imports of commodities. Where exports exceed imports there is a trade surplus: this is taken as an indication of a healthy economy.[1] The purpose of this book is to examine the private law framework within which trade is conducted.[2]

It has been asked: does commercial law exist? Professor Goode answered this question in the following terms, in relation to English law:

> "If by commercial law we mean a relatively self-contained integrated body of principles and rules peculiar to commercial transactions, then we are constrained to say that this is not to be found in England."[3]

Similarly, when Irish commercial law is compared to the North American system, where there exists a Uniform Commercial Code,[4] or to

---

1 See, *e.g.* the External Trade statistics published by the Central Statistics Office: www.cso.ie.

2 The public law regulation of trade and business is outside the scope of this book. See, *e.g.* Central Bank and Financial Services Authority of Ireland Bill 2002; see further Crowley, "Reform of the Regulation of the Financial Services Industry – An Irish Viewpoint" (2002) 2 *Hibernian Law Journal* 105. In particular, see, in relation to banking regulation, Donnelly, *The Law of Banks and Credit Institutions* (Dublin, Round Hall Sweet & Maxwell, 2000) Part 1; in relation to insurance intermediaries, Buckley, *Insurance Law in Ireland* (Dublin, Oak Tree Press, 1997) Chapter 2; in relation to competition law, Maher, *Competition Law: alignment and reform* (Dublin, Round Hall Sweet & Maxwell, 1999); Massey & O'Hare, *Competition Law and Policy in Ireland* (Dublin, Oak Tree Press, 1996).

3 Goode, *Commercial Law* (London: Penguin, 2nd ed., 1995) p.1205.

4 The Uniform Commercial Code (UCC) is a model statute promoted by the National Conference of Commissioners on Uniform State Laws and the American Law Institute. The code's chief architect was Professor Carl Llewellyn. Its stated aim is "to simplify, clarify, and modernize the law governing commercial transactions; to permit the continued expansion of commercial practices through custom usage and agreement of the parties; to make uniform the law among the various jurisdictions" (s.1–102(2)). The first official text of the UCC was approved by its promoters in 1952 and has been revised on several occasions since. The UCC has been adopted in all the United States, except Louisiana which has a civil law system. It covers a wide range of commercial activities including: sales (Art. 2), leases (Art. 2A), negotiable instruments (Art. 3), bank deposits and collections (Art. 4), letters of credit (Art. 5), bulk transfers (Art. 6); warehouse receipts, bills of lading and other documents of title (Art. 7), investment securities (Art. 8); and perhaps most notably, secured transactions, sales accounts and chattel paper (Art. 9).

many civil law jurisdictions, where there are commercial codes, it is clear that Irish commercial law is neither integrated, nor is it peculiar to commercial transactions. Instead, it is to be found in numerous pieces of legislation, and the common law, and to a large extent is based on contract law and property law, though these subjects are not exclusively relevant to commercial law. Clearly, commercial law exists in Ireland, though setting its exact parameters is an almost impossible task.

1.1.1 Commercial law defined

Commercial law can be defined broadly or narrowly. In legal practice, commercial law tends to be defined broadly. A commercial law practitioner might deal with a variety of matters such as commercial contracts (ranging from contracts for the sale of goods and the supply of services; to agency, distribution and franchising agreements; to construction contracts); finance; intellectual property law; insurance law; competition law; property law; partnership law; company law and tax law. Commercial law textbooks may cover some but usually not all of the above. For academic purposes, it is widely accepted that at the heart of commercial law is the contract for the sale of goods.[5] More recently, it has been recognised that as the service market expands, contracts for the supply of services are of growing importance.[6] Agency law is also seen as a traditional commercial law subject. But beyond this, what constitutes commercial law and what topics should be included in a commercial law textbook depends greatly on the inclination of the individual author.

Professor Goode defined commercial law as:

> "that body of law which governs commercial transactions, that is, agreements and arrangements between professionals for the provision and acquisition of goods, services and facilities in the way of trade."[7]

1.1.1.1 Transaction-based

From this definition Goode identified four characteristics of commercial law. First, commercial law is based on transactions and not institutions. Hence, the focus of commercial law is on contracts and other

---

5 "The object of commerce is to deal in merchandise and, if we adopt this criterion, commercial law can be defined as the special rules which apply to contracts for the sale of goods and to such contracts as are ancillary thereto, namely, contracts for the carriage and insurance of goods and contracts the main purpose of which is to finance the carrying out of contracts of sale," Gutteridge, "Contract and Commercial Law" (1935) 51 *Law Quarterly Review* 91 at 91. See further Part III.

6 See generally Chapter 20.

7 Goode, "The Codification of Commercial Law" (1988) 14 *Monash Law Review* 135 at 141.

arrangements. Areas such as partnership and company law are usually considered separately from commercial law.[8]

1.1.1.2 Dealing between businesses

Second, commercial law is concerned primarily with the dealing of merchants, or professional business persons, as opposed to consumers. Broadly speaking, a consumer is a person who buys goods or services for his own personal use and not for the purpose of further trade.[9] Commercial law, as it developed from medieval times and into the twentieth century, was concerned with trade between merchants. This is not surprising, because it was not until the mid- to late twentieth century that the concepts of the consumer and the consumer society developed in Ireland.[10] For example, the Sale of Goods Act 1893 makes no distinction between commercial and consumer buyers. More recently, it has been recognised that consumers, because they are in a weaker bargaining position, may need protection. The first example of specific consumer protection legislation is the Consumer Information Act 1978.[11] Shortly thereafter came the Sale of Goods and Supply of Services Act 1980, which afforded

---

8 This contrasts with the approach of civil jurisdictions where company law is considered part of commercial law. On the relationship between company and commercial law, see Sealy, *Company Law and Commercial Reality*, (London, Sweet & Maxwell, 1984) Chapter 1. See generally, Twomey, Partnership Law (Dublin, Butterworths, 2000); Keane, *Company Law* (Dublin, Butterworths, 3rd ed., 2000); Forde, *Company Law in Ireland* (Dublin, Round Hall Sweet & Maxwell, 3rd ed., 1999); Courtney, *The Law of Private Companies* (Dublin, Butterworths, 2nd ed., 2002).

9 The term "consumer" is defined in various pieces of consumer protection legislation, see, *e.g.* Consumer Credit Act 1995, s.2. The phrase "dealing as a consumer" is defined in the Sale of Goods and Supply of Services Act 1980, s.3; see further 10.5.2.1. Unfortunately, these definitions are not entirely compatible.

10 Atiyah links the rise of the consumer society in the United Kingdom with the Industrial Revolution of the nineteenth century: the new technology of mass production; new marketing techniques, a new range of goods; the existence of surplus income due to wage increases and leisure time: see Atiyah, *The Rise and Fall of Freedom of Contract* (Oxford, Clarendon Press, 1979) pp. 572–581. In Ireland, the development of a consumer society occurred later in time. In contrast to the U.K., Ireland did not undergo an Industrial Revolution. By the 1950s, Ireland was still largely dependent on agriculture. High levels of unemployment and emigration resulted in a low standard of living: see Blackwell, "Government, Economy and Society" in Litton ed., *Unequal Achievement, The Irish Experience 1957–1982* (Dublin, Institute of Public Administration, 1982) p.43.

11 The Hire-Purchase Acts 1946 and 1960 (now repealed by the Consumer Credit Act 1995 which applies only to consumer hirers: s.2 and Part VI of the Act) applied to all hire-purchase arrangements and not specifically to consumer hirers. Nevertheless, a significant proportion of hirers were consumers and hence consumers benefited from this legislation. Other legislation not specifically directed at consumers, such as the Merchandise Marks Acts 1928–1970 and the Restrictive Practices Act 1953, indirectly benefited consumers.

various protections to consumers of goods and services.[12] Subsequently, the bulk of, if not all, consumer protection legislation has emanated from the European Community. Examples include: Council Directive 84/450 on misleading advertising;[13] Council Directive 85/374 concerning liability for defective products;[14] Council Directive 85/577 to protect the consumer in respect of contracts negotiated away from business premises;[15] Council Directives 87/102 and 90/88 concerning consumer credit;[16] Council Directive 90/314 on package travel, package holidays and package tours;[17] and Council Directive 93/13 on unfair terms in consumer contracts;[18] Council Directive 97/7 on distance contracts;[19] Council Directive 98/27 on injunctions for the protection of consumer interests;[20] and Council Directive 99/44 on certain aspects of consumer sales and associated guarantees.[21]

The question is: is consumer law a part of commercial law, or is it a distinct discipline with a different set of objectives and principles driving its development?[22] The difficulty arises, in part, because a lot of what can be classed as consumer law derives from commercial law: sale of goods law being the prime example. Part of the problem also centres on the legal definition of consumer. Consumer protection legislation emanating from the European Community defines a consumer as a *natural person* acting for purposes which are outside, or not related to, his trade, business or profession.[23] Domestic sale of goods and supply of services legislation however, does not exclude the possibility that a company, or other legal

---

12 See generally Part III.

13 See [1984] O.J. L250/17, implemented by the EC (Misleading Advertising) Regulations 1988, S.I. No. 134 of 1988.

14 See [1985] O.J. L210/29, implemented by the Defective Products Act 1991.

15 See [1985] O.J. L372/31, implemented by the EC (Cancellation of Contracts Negotiated away from Business Premises) Regulations 1989, S.I. No. 224 of 1989.

16 See [1987] O.J. L42/48 and [1990] O.J. L61/14, implemented by the Consumer Credit Act 1995.

17 See [1990] O.J. L158/59, implemented by the Package Holidays and Travel Trade Act 1995.

18 See [1993] O.J. L95/29, implemented by the EC (Unfair Terms in Consumer Contracts) Regulations 1995 and 2000, S.I. No. 27 of 1995 and S.I. No. 307 of 2000.

19 See [1997] O.J. L144/19, implemented by the EC (Protection of Consumers in respect of Contracts made by Distance Communications) Regulations 2001, S.I. No. 207 of 2001.

20 See [1998] O.J. L 166/51, implemented by the EC (Protection of Consumers' Collective Interests) Regulations 2001, S.I. No. 449 of 2001.

21 See [1999] O.J. L171/12, to be implemented by January 1, 2002: see further 13.11 and 14.7.

22 Some see consumer law as a specific application of general commercial law principles: see Reynolds "The Applicability of General Rules of Private Law to Consumer Disputes", in Andermann et al ed., *Law and the Weaker Party* (Abingdon, Professional Books, 1982) Vol. 2, pp.93–110. Cf. Sealy & Hooley, *Commercial Law: Text, Cases and Materials*, (London, Butterworths, 2nd ed., 1999) pp.16–17.

23 See, *e.g.* Council Directive 93/13 on unfair terms in consumer contracts, [1993] O.J. L95/29, Art. 2(b); and Council Directive 99/44 on certain aspects of consumer sales and associated guarantees, [1999] O.J. L171/12, Art. 1(2)(a).

association, may "deal as a consumer."[24] Therefore, the legal dividing line between commercial and consumer activity seems to depend on the context. Moreover, if the purpose of consumer law is to protect the weaker party, an argument could be made that small and medium size enterprises (SMEs) should be protected, as consumers, in their dealings with large multinational corporations. In some areas of law, such as competition law, SMEs are afforded separate treatment.[25] Commercial law has yet to make such a distinction.

Whether consumer law is recognised as separate from commercial law or as a component part of commercial law, it is important that a distinction is drawn between the two. Commercial law is about facilitating trade; consumer law seeks to regulate trade. Commercial law assumes that the parties meet on equal terms and can best protect their own interests; consumer law assumes that the consumer is the weaker party and in need of protection. The courts seem to have recognised this distinction. When we examine the law on implied terms in sale of goods contracts, for instance, we will see the courts taking a different approach depending on whether the buyer is a consumer or commercial buyer.[26] Equally, the legislature and the European Community make this distinction when they promote consumer protection legislation. Therefore, while commercial and consumer law may be inextricably linked, it is proper that they be considered as two separate doctrines of law. Hence, the focus of this book is on commercial law, to the exclusion of consumer law.[27] However, when we consider the law of sale of goods and supply of services, we will consider the distinction made when the buyer deals as a consumer or otherwise.

1.1.1.3 Contract and market practices

Third, according to Goode, commercial law is centred on contract and the usages of the market. While much of commercial law is founded on contract law, it is obvious that it extends into other areas including

---

24 Sale of Goods and Supply of Services Act 1980, s.3; *R&B Customs Brokers v. United Dominion Trust* [1988] 1 W.L.R. 321 (C.A.).

25 See, *e.g.* EC Commission Notice on Agreements of Minor Importance [2001] O.J. C368/12, which indicates, *inter alia*, that agreement between SMEs will not be caught by the Article 81 prohibition.

26 See generally Chapter 13.

27 See generally Harvey & Parry, *Law of Consumer Protection* (London, Butterworths, 6th ed., 2000); Bird, *Consumer Credit Law* (Dublin, Round Hall Sweet & Maxwell, 1998); Weatherill, *EC Consumer Law and Policy* (London, Longman, 1997); Howells & Wilhelmsson, *EC Consumer Law*, (Aldershot, Dartmouth, 1997); Cranston, *Consumers and the Law* (London, Weidenfeld & Nicolson, 2nd ed., 1984).

property,[28] tort, equity, restitution, and insolvency law. For example, where goods, the subject of a hire-purchase arrangement, are sold by the hirer to an innocent purchaser, the purchaser may be exposed to an action in conversion by the owner.[29] Where defective goods are sold to a consumer there may be a claim in contract against the seller[30] and a claim in tort, or under statute, against the manufacturer.[31] Where a principal/agent relationship is established, equity generally imposes strict fiduciary duties on the agent.[32]

The customs and usages of the market are also central to commercial law.[33] Commercial law often reacts to and adopts new market practices. For instance, the common law recognised that a bill of lading was a document of title because merchants treated it as a document of title.[34] More recently, judges have had to consider the legal significance of new commercial practices including the use of retention of title clauses in sale of goods contracts;[35] credit cards[36] and cheque guarantee cards;[37] and letters of comfort and letters of intent.[38] However, the recognition of trade custom and usage can be disputed and, even if accepted in broad terms, its exact definition can be unclear. To avoid such problems, trade organisations, particularly at an international level, have sought to codify certain trade usages and customs. The International Chamber of Commerce (ICC), based in Paris, dominates in this field. Two sets of ICC codified trade customs stand out in terms of their worldwide acceptance and use. First, the ICC produce *Incoterms*, a set of rules for the interpretation of commonly used price and delivery terms in international trade, such as FOB (free on board) and CIF (cost, insurance, and freight). These rules were first published in 1953 and are updated regularly. The current version

28 Commercial law relates principally to personal property law, *e.g.* goods, but land law cannot be excluded. Commercial finance is often secured on land by a mortgage or a charge, for instance. See further Chapter 3.

29 Sale of Goods Act 1893, s.25(2): see 19.1.1 and 19.8.

30 Sale of Goods Act 1893, ss.13–15: see generally Chapters 13 and 14.

31 See *Donoghue v. Stevenson* [1932] A.C. 562; and the Liability for Defective Products Act 1991: see further Chapter 16.

32 See 7.3.2.

33 Technically, a custom refers to a practice in a particular area, while a usage refers to a practice in a particular trade. Today, the terms are used interchangeably.

34 *Lickbarrow v. Mason* (1794) 5 Term Rep. 683: see further 31.2.3.

35 Retention of title clauses, now common in sale of goods contracts, were introduced into Irish and English law in the 1970s: see further 15.4.

36 *Re Charge Card Services Ltd* [1989] Ch. 497; [1988] 3 All E.R. 702 (C.A).

37 *Metropolitan Police Comr v. Charles* [1976] 3 All E.R. 112, at 121; [1977] A.C. 177 at 191; *Re Charge Card Services Ltd* [1989] Ch. 497; [1988] 3 All E.R. 702 (C.A.); *First Sport v. Barclays Bank* [1991] 3 All E.R. 789 (C.A.).

38 On letters of comfort, see *Kleinwort Benson Ltd v. Malaysian Mining Corpn Bhd* [1989] 1 All E.R. 785; [1989] 1 W.L.R. 379 (C.A.), see further 2.2.3 and 26.5; on letters of intent see *British Steel Corpn v. Cleveland Bridge and Engineering Co Ltd* [1984] 1 All E.R. 504.

is *Incoterms 2000*.[39] Second, the ICC produce the Uniform Customs and Practice for Documentary Credits (UCP) first published in 1933. The current edition is UCP 500, published in 1993. Bankers throughout the world use the UCP, through contractual incorporation. Other ICC uniform rules are the Uniform Rules for Collections,[40] the Uniform Rules for Demand Guarantees,[41] and the Uniform Rules for Contract Bonds.[42]

1.1.1.4 Typical and repetitive transactions

Last, commercial law is concerned with a large mass of transactions in which each participant is a regular player, so that transactions are typical, repetitive, and suitable for standardised treatment. In commercial law, standard form contracts[43] and documentation are regularly used to ease the administrative burden of doing business and to offer certainty as to terms and practices. This is especially the case in international trade.[44]

Commercial law is a pragmatic and responsive subject. Its main aim is to facilitate commerce.[45] As commercial practices change, so too should commercial law. Any attempt to define commercial law in exact terms or in relation to its exact content would run counter to the very nature of the subject. Therefore, rather than focusing on an exact definition or on the detailed content of commercial law, it is perhaps more useful to consider some more general matters, including the role and principles of commercial law.

1.1.2 The role of commercial law

The role of commercial law is widely accepted to be to facilitate trade, not to regulate it.[46] This is illustrated by the centre-piece of commercial legislation, the Sale of Goods Act 1893. The Act provides a legal framework within which contracts for the sale of goods can be concluded and performed. A significant proportion of the rules to be found in the 1893 Act are default rules, that is, they apply unless the parties have specified otherwise.[47] There are however, some important examples of the law intervening in the *private* arena of pure commercial law. Most notably, the Sale of Goods and Supply of Services Act 1980 regulates the use of

39 See also the ICC/UNCTAD Rules for Multimodel Transport Documents, ICC Publication No. 481, 1992.

40 ICC Publication No. 522, 1995.

41 ICC Publication No. 458, 1992.

42 ICC Publication No. 524, 1994.

43 See further 2.3.2.

44 See Part VI.

45 See 1.1.2.

46 See *e.g.* Irvine, "The Law: An Engine for Trade" (2001) 64 *Modern Law Review* 333.

47 There are also some mandatory rules in the 1893 Act, section 16 is an important example: see further 17.4.

exclusion clauses between businesses such that, for example, any clause which seeks to exclude or limit a seller's liability for breach of any of the statutory implied terms must be "fair and reasonable".[48] A second example is the EC Directive on self-employed commercial agents,[49] as implemented by the 1994 and 1997 EC (Commercial Agents) Regulations.[50] Where they apply, the Directive and Regulations modify the principal/agent relationship to protect commercial agents both during and following the termination of the agency relationship.[51] Nevertheless, a non-interventionist approach continues to dominate Irish commercial law. This can be seen, for example, in the Electronic Commerce Act 2000 which seeks to establish a minimalist framework within which e-commerce can develop.[52] Equally, the Arbitration (International Commercial) Act 1998 is based, in part, on the principle of party autonomy, and seeks to keep judicial intervention to a minimum.[53] The courts also seek to facilitate trade by pursuing a non-interventionist approach when dealing with business disputes. This is similar to the laissez-faire policy that applied traditionally in contract law.[54] It is assumed that the parties, being business persons, meet on equal terms. The autonomy of the parties is supreme and the courts are reluctant to interfere in the dealings of business. This approach is evidenced, for example, regarding the implication of terms in commercial contracts. In *Tradax (Ireland) Ltd v. Irish Grain Board Ltd*,[55] O'Higgins C.J. stated that the power to imply terms:

> "… must be exercised with care. The Courts have no role in acting as contract makers, or as counsellors, to advise or direct what agreement ought to have been made by two people, whether businessmen or not, who choose to enter into contractual relations with each other."[56]

This non-interventionist approach to commercial law contrasts sharply with the protectionist approach of the legislature and the judiciary in relation to consumers. Essentially, it is this difference of approach which divides commercial and consumer law.

1.1.3 Principles of commercial law

Leading commentators believe that commercial law is unified by certain common principles, including: freedom of contract; sanctity of the bargain;

48 1980 Act, s.22 and Schedule to 1980 Act: see further 10.5.2.2.
49 Directive 86/653/EEC, [1986] O.J. L 382/17.
50 S.I. No. 33 of 1994 and S.I. No. 31 of 1997.
51 See further Chapter 7.
52 See further 1.3.4.
53 See further 37.3.3.1.
54 See Atiyah, *The Rise and Fall of Freedom of Contract* (Oxford, Clarendon Press, 1979).
55 [1984] I.R. 1.
56 *Ibid.* at p.14.

flexibility; certainty; and fair dealing,[57] though the identification of these principles is not an easy task.[58] These principles all seek to facilitate trade. They can be used to enhance our understanding of commercial law and as guidelines when faced with problems not previously addressed by commercial law.

1.1.3.1 Freedom of contract and the sanctity of the bargain

First, commercial law is based on the related principles of freedom of contract and sanctity of the contract. As noted above, it is assumed that business people meet on equal terms and are therefore free to determine their respective rights and obligations. For instance, in *Tradax (Ireland) Ltd v. Irish Grain Board Ltd*,[59] with regard to implying terms into business contracts, McCarthy J. stated:

> "It is not the function of a court to write a contract for parties who have met upon commercially equal terms; if such parties want to enter into unreasonable, unfair or even disastrous contracts that is their business, not the business of the Courts."[60]

In a similar vein, Professor Schmitthoff has stated:

> "The basis of commercial law is the contractual principle of autonomy of the parties' will. Subject to the ultimate reservation of public policy, the parties are free to arrange their affairs as they like."[61]

1.1.3.2 Flexibility

Second, commercial law must be flexible to meet the changing needs of commerce. This principle underlies the judicial recognition of mercantile custom and usage. The most common means by which courts give effect to custom and usage is by implying a term into a contract. But not every trade custom or usage will receive judicial recognition. The trade custom

57 Professor Goode has identified eight principles which make up the philosophy of commercial law: (a) party autonomy (b) predictability (c) flexibility (d) good faith (e) the encouragement of self-help (f) the facilitation of security interests (g) the protection of vested rights (h) the protection of innocent third parties: Goode "The Codification of Commercial Law" (1988) 14 *Monash Law Review* 135 at 148–153.

58 See Sealy & Hooley, *Commercial Law: Text, Cases and Materials* (London, Butterworths, 2nd ed., 1999) p.6.

59 [1984] I.R. 1.

60 *Ibid.* at 26.

61 Schmitthoff, "The Concept of Economic Law in England" [1966] *Journal of Business Law* 309 at 315.

must be reasonable, consistent with the express terms of the contract and universally recognised in the trade as a legally binding custom.[62]

1.1.3.3 Certainty

Third, commercial law must provide certainty so that business people can make decisions based on an understanding of the legal consequences. In *Vallejo v. Wheeler,* Lord Mansfield said:

> "In all mercantile transactions the great object should be certainty: and therefore, it is of more consequence that a rule be certain, than whether the rule is established one way or the other. Because speculators in trade then know what ground to go upon."[63]

However, it should be noted that there is a certain tension between the principles of flexibility and certainty which is unavoidable. Ultimately, over a period of time, the principle of certainty has to give way to the principle of flexibility as commercial law develops to keep pace with commercial practice.

1.1.3.4 Fairness

Lastly, commercial law should encourage fairness between parties. While the common law does not recognise a general duty of good faith,[64] good faith, in the subjective sense of acting honesty,[65] is a requirement before certain rights can be exercised under the Bills of Exchange Act 1882[66] and the Sale of Goods Act 1893, for example.[67] There are also limited exceptions to the general rule. Insurance contracts and partnership contracts, for example, are contracts of good faith (*uberrimae fides*) requiring the parties to comply with a duty of disclosure during negotiations and performance of the contract.[68] Moreover, many contract law doctrines have been developed to ensure fair dealings between the parties: the doctrines of duress and undue influence, of mistake and misrepresentation, and the implication of terms in contracts can all be seen as an aspect of good faith in contract law. More recently, a requirement of good faith, in the objective sense, has been introduced into Irish law from

62 *Paxton v. Courtnay* (1860) 2 F&F 131; see further 2.3.4.3.

63 (1774) 1 Cowp. 143 at 153.

64 Nevertheless, this topic has generated great interest in academic circles: see e.g. Beatson & Friedmann ed., *Good Faith and Fault in Contract Law* (Oxford, Clarendon Press, 1997); Harrison, *Good Faith in Sales* (London, Sweet & Maxwell, 1997); and Brownsword, Hird and Howells eds., *Good Faith in Contract: Concept and Context* (Aldershot, Ashgate, 1999).

65 Bills of Exchange Act 1882, s.90; Sale of Goods Act 1893, s.62(2).

66 1882 Act, ss.12, 29(1), 31(2), 59(1), 60, 79(2), and 80.

67 1893 Act, ss.21–25, and s.47: see further Chapter 19 and 15.3.

68 On insurance, see Part V.

civil law, via the European Community, though the exact scope of this duty remains unclear. In particular, the E.C. directives on unfair terms in consumer contracts[69] and on self-employed commercial agents[70] impose good faith duties on the supplier of goods or services when dealing with a consumer where the terms are not individually negotiated, and on principals and commercial agents, respectively.

1.2 The Historical Development of Commercial Law[71]

The origins of modern commercial law can be traced back to the Middle Ages when trade was carried on at fairs. Merchants travelled across Europe to these fairs to buy and sell goods. At this time commercial law, or the *lex mercatoria* (the law merchant), was made up of the customs and practices of merchants, which were common throughout Europe. Where a dispute arose, it was settled quickly before a local merchant court, applying the *lex mercatoria*, and not the local law. The judge and jury would be merchants themselves. Hence, the *lex mercatoria* was international in character. It was characterised by a flexibility to adapt to the needs of merchants and was based on the principles of freedom of contract and the freedom of alienability of property. It was during this period that some of the most important features and concepts of commercial law were developed including the bill of exchange; the charterparty; the bill of lading; and the concepts of assignability; negotiability; and general average.

In the seventeenth and eighteenth centuries in England and Ireland, competition between different courts lead to the *lex mercatoria* being incorporated into the domestic common law.[72] Incorporation of the *lex mercatoria* occurred throughout Europe: in civil jurisdictions it occurred through codification, the most famous being the Napoleonic Code. This nationalisation of the *lex mercatoria* meant that commercial law lost its international character.

The nationalisation of commercial law through incorporation into the common law resulted, over time, in a mass of sometimes conflicting case law. In an attempt to simplify the law and make it more accessible, a

69 Council Directive 93/13, [1993] O.J. L95/29, implemented by the EC (Unfair Terms in Consumer Contracts) Regulations 1995 and 2000, S.I. No. 27 of 1995 and S.I. No. 307 of 2000; see further 2.3.5.3 and 10.5.3.

70 Directive 86/653/EEC, [1986] O.J. L382/17, as implemented by the 1994 and 1997 EC (Commercial Agents) Regulations, S.I. No. 33 of 1994 and S.I. No. 31 of 1997: see further Chapter 7.

71 See Holdsworths, *A History of English Law* (London, Methuen, Sweet & Maxwell, 1923–1966) Vol. 1, pp.526–573; Vol. 5, pp.60–154; and Vol. 8 pp.99–300; Schmitthoff, *Commercial Law in a Changing Economic Climate* (London, Sweet & Maxwell, 2nd ed., 1981) Chapters 1 and 2.

72 The process was started by Sir Edward Coke and completed by Sir John Holt (Chief Justice, 1689–1710) and Lord Mansfield (Chief Justice, 1756–1788).

process of codification was undertaken in the late nineteenth and early twentieth centuries in England and Ireland. But this codification did not involve one all-encompassing code, as in mainland Europe. Rather, certain areas of the common law were codified or consolidated into individual statutes.[73] Examples include the Bills of Exchange Act 1882, the Factors Act 1889, the Partnership Act 1890, the Sale of Goods Act 1893, and the Marine Insurance Act 1906.[74] It is perhaps an indication of the strength of this legislation that much of it is still in force today. However, it does beg the question as to whether legislation formulated in the nineteenth century is, or can be, suitable for the twenty-first century.

In constitutional and legal terms the next significant development was Irish independence in 1921. Although this represented a formal separation of the English and Irish legal systems, the influence of English commercial law continued. Broadly speaking, pre-1921 statutes applicable to Ireland continued in force, and pre-1921 case law continued to bind Irish courts.[75] While post-1921 legislation passed at Westminster has no force in Ireland, post-1921 English case law is considered persuasive, though not binding, precedent.[76]

1.3 Modern Influences on Irish Commercial Law[77]

It could be said, in relation to Irish commercial law, that not much has changed over the last 100 years or so. The major codifying statutes of the late nineteenth and early twentieth centuries – the Bills of Exchange Act 1882, the Factors Act 1889, the Partnership Act 1890, the Sale of Goods Act 1893, and the Marine Insurance Act 1906 – remain in force, with only

---

73 See Gutteridge, "Contract and Commercial Law" (1935) 51 *Law Quarterly Review* 91 at 117; Rodger, "The Codification of Commercial Law in Victorian Britain" (1992) 109 *Law Quarterly Review* 570; Arden, "Time for an English Commercial Code" (1997) 56 *Cambridge Law Journal* 516, esp. 518–522.

74 Two men dominated during this period, Sir Mackenzie Chalmers who drafted the Bill of Exchange Act, the Sale of Goods Act and the Marine Insurance Act, and Sir Frederick Pollock who drafted the Partnership Act.

75 See Byrne & McCutcheon, *The Irish Legal System* (Dublin, Butterworths, 4th ed., 2001) paras 2.64–2.65, and para 2.93. Provided there was no inconsistency with the Free State Constitution of 1922, the laws in force in the Irish Free State at the time of the coming into operation of the Constitution continued to be of full force and effect until repealed or amended by enactment of the Oireachtas: Art. 73 of the 1922 Constitution Act 1927. Similarly, Article 50 of Bunreacht na hEireann, 1937 provides that: "Subject to this Constitution and to the extent to which they are not inconsistent therewith, the laws in force in Saorstat Eireann immediately prior to the coming into force of this Constitution shall continue to be of full force and effect until the same or any of them shall have been repealed or amended by the Oireachtas"

76 See further 1.3.1.

77 See Goode, "Commercial Law in an International Environment: Towards the Next Millennium" in *Commercial law in the Next Millennium* (London, Sweet & Maxwell, 1998) Chapter 4.

the Sale of Goods Act 1893 being amended, though its basic framework stands unaltered. On the other hand, there have been some legislative developments, for example in the areas of intellectual property law[78] and arbitration.[79] But otherwise, the development of commercial law has been left to the judiciary to deal with on a case by case basis. The judicial recognition of retention of title clauses in sale of goods contracts is a good example of Irish judges responding to changes in commercial practice. However, such a case by case approach to commercial law development is limited and does not allow for the type of systematic law reform which may be needed.[80]

As in the past, Irish commercial law continues to be influenced by outside forces. This is to be welcomed. As an active member of an international trading community, Ireland cannot afford to be insular in its approach to commercial law and its development. Some of the major influences on Irish commercial law, external and otherwise, are considered below.

1.3.1 English Commercial Law

Until Irish independence in 1921, English and Irish commercial law were, practically speaking, one and the same. Today, that shared heritage means that English commercial law is still relevant within the Irish context. The major codifying statutes of the late nineteenth and early twentieth centuries remain in force in both jurisdictions, although subject to more recent amendments. English case law since 1921 in relation to this legislation and other areas of commercial law is considered persuasive authority in Ireland. Moreover, within the European Community context, Ireland and

78 On copyright, see the Commercial Property (Protection) Act 1927; Commercial Property (Protection) (Amendment) Acts 1929, 1957 and 1958; the Copyright Act 1963, and the Copyright and Related Rights Act 2000. On patents, see Commercial Property (Protection) Act 1927; the Patents Act 1964 and the Patents Act 1992. On trademarks, see the Commercial Property (Protection) Act 1927; the Trade Marks Act 1963; and the Trade Marks Act 1996. See generally, Part VII.

79 The Arbitration Acts 1954, 1980 and 1998: see further Part VIII.

80 For instance, in England, some call for codification of commercial law at a domestic level (see Goode, "The Codification of Commercial Law" (1988) 14 *Monash Law Review* 135 at 141; and Arden, "Time for an English Commercial Code" (1997) 56 *Cambridge Law Journal* 516) and at an international level Schmiotthoff, "The Codification of the Law of International Trade" [1985] *Journal of Business Law* 34. Codification is not without its critics: see, *e.g.* Goff, "The Future of the Common Law" (1997) 46 *International and Comparative Law Quarterly* 745. As regards a systematic reform of the law of sale of goods, see Stoljar, "Conditions, Warranties and Descriptions of Quality in Sale of Goods – I & II" (1952) 15 *Modern Law Review* 425 and (1953) 16 *Modern Law Review* 174; Lambiris, "Reform of the Law of Sale in Australia" (1996) 20 *Melbourne University Law Review* 690; the U.K. Law Commission Report No. 160 & the Scottish Law Commission Report No. 104, *Sale and Supply of Goods* (Cmnd. 137, 1987); Ontario Law Reform Commission, *Report on the Sale of Goods* (1979).

England are the only two common law jurisdictions and hence similar issues arise in both jurisdictions when it comes to implementing European Community measures.

English commercial law also has significant influence internationally. English commercial law, supported by the Commercial Court in London,[81] has a reputation for facilitating commerce and providing prompt justice. Consequently, many standard form contracts used in international trade are expressly made subject to English law. Furthermore, it has been estimated that about 50 per cent of litigants before the Commercial Court are foreign and almost 30 per cent of cases have no English litigants.[82]

However, other jurisdictions should not be forgotten, including other common law jurisdictions, such as Australia, Canada, New Zealand and the United States. For instance, the Sale of Goods and Supply of Services Act 1980 was clearly influenced by Canadian, and in particular, Ontario Law Reform Commission proposals.[83] Indeed, in a number of areas the courts of Australia, Canada and New Zealand, have been more adventurous than those of Ireland and England in developing the common law. For example, the courts of Canada and Australia have undertaken judicial reform of the law of privity.[84] The courts of Australia, Canada and New Zealand have all been more bold than their Irish and English counterparts in developing various common law doctrines to promote good faith dealings between contractors.[85] And, as the European Community extends its interests into matters commercial, consideration of the civil law approach to commercial law problems cannot be ignored.[86]

---

81 The Commercial Court acts as a division of the Queen's Bench Division in the High Court in London. The Commercial Court originated in 1895 following the creation of the "commercial list". The Commercial Court's rationale is to provide a court where there is greater familiarity with commercial disputes and to provide a procedure to enable commercial disputes to be resolved quickly and without undue formality. The court is staffed by judges with particular expertise in commercial law. See the Civil Procedures Act 1997 and the Civil Procedure Rules 1998 (S.I. No. 3132 of 1998, as amended) Part 58 and the Commercial Court Guide (2002) available at www.courtservice.gov.uk.

82 See Practice Statement: Commercial Court Procedures, 28 July 1989. See also Irvine, "The Law: An Engine for Trade" (2001) 64 *Modern Law Review* 333 at 333, where he notes that of the 72 trials heard in the Commercial List in the High Court during the last year, 44 involved foreign parties.

83 Whincup, *Consumer Protection Law in America, Canada and Europe* (Dublin, 1973).

84 *Trident General Insurance Co Ltd v. McNiece Bros Pty Ltd* (1988) 80 A.L.J.R. 574; *London Drugs v. Kuehne & Nagel* (1992) 97 D.L.R. (4th) 261. See the U.K. Contracts (Rights of Third Parties) Act 1999.

85 Mason, "Contract, Good Faith and Equitable Standards of Fair Dealing" (2000) 116 *Law Quarterly Review* 66.

86 See, *e.g.* a commercial agent's right to compensation to damage under French law: see further 7.6.3.2 (iv).

1.3.2 The European Community

Entry into the then EEC (European Economic Community) in 1973, led to dramatic changes in the Irish legal system generally. The European Community (EC) represents a new legal order distinct from, though closely linked to both international law and the legal systems of the member states.[87] The Community has supra-national institutions, with sovereign law-making powers.[88] Where there is a conflict between EC and domestic law, EC law prevails,[89] and provisions of EC law can be enforced at the suit of private parties before their national court.[90]

From a business perspective, the EC's major impact has been in the areas of regulation,[91] and, as noted above, consumer protection.[92] To the extent that consumer protection legislation encourages consumers to participate in the market and hence increases commercial activity, the EC has played an important role. As regards pure commercial law, the EC's influence has been limited, to date, to intellectual property law,[93] and commercial agents.[94] In 2001, the EC Commission published a Green Paper on European Contract Law.[95] One proposal put forward in the Green Paper is the harmonisation of contract law at an EC level. Such a development would clearly broaden the influence of the EC in the private rights of those involved in business.

1.3.3 A new *lex mercatoria*?

When the *lex mercatoria* was incorporated into various national systems, in the seventeenth and eighteenth centuries, it lost its international character and thereafter the different national systems of commercial law began to diverge. In the last 50 years or so, there has been a movement to

---

87 "We must conclude that this Community constitutes a new legal order in international law, for whose benefit the States have limited their sovereign rights within limited fields, and the subjects of which comprise not only the member States but their nationals:" *van Gend en Loos* (Case 26/62) [1963] C.M.L.R. 105 at 129.

88 Article 249 of the EC Treaty provides: "In order to carry out their task ... the Council and the Commission shall make regulations and issue directives, take decisions, make recommendations and deliver opinions."

89 *Internationala Handelsgessellschaft* [1972] 3 C.M.L.R. 255; see also Art 29.4.3° of the Constitution and *Doyle v. An Taoiseach* [1986] I.L.R.M. 693 (S.C.).

90 On the doctrine of direct effect, see *van Gend en Loos* (Case 26/62) [1963] C.M.L.R. 105; on the doctrine of indirect effect see *Marleasing SA v. La Comercial Internacional de Alimentación SA* (Case C106/89) [1990] ECR. I–4135, [1992] 1 C.M.L.R. 305; see also *Francovitch v. Italian State* (Cases C 6 & 9/90) [1992] I.R.L.R. 84. See generally McMahon & Murphy, *European Community Law in Ireland* (Dublin, Butterworths, 1989); *Lasok, Law and Institutions of the European Union*, (London, Butterworths, 7th ed., 2001).

91 In particular, in the areas of banking and insurance.

92 See Title XIV, Art 153, of the Treaty establishing the European Community, on consumer protection.

93 See Part VII.

94 See Chapter 7.

95 See http://europa.eu.int/comm/off/green/index_en.htm

re-internationalise certain aspects of commercial law. It is argued that international trade is better facilitated by a set of rules designed specifically with international trade in mind. Moreover, problems with conflict of laws can be avoided when parties select international law rules to govern their contracts and dealings, as opposed to national rules. Organisations exist whose purpose is to facilitate this process: the International Chamber of Commerce (ICC),[96] the United Nations Commission on International Trade Law (UNCITRAL),[97] the International Institute for the Unification of Private Law (Unidroit),[98] and the Hague Conference on Private International Law,[99] amongst others. But harmonisation at an international level is a slow process. It often takes ten years or more before agreement can be reached on a particular text. Once a text is agreed and promoted, the process of ratification and implementation by states can be even slower. Nevertheless, particular areas of commercial law are successfully *regulated* at an international level, including carriage of goods by sea,[100] and areas of banking, such as documentary credits.[101]

This process of harmonisation of international trade law has led some to talk of the development of a new *lex mercatoria*.[102] But much of what exists is not a new *lex mercatoria* in the true sense of an autonomous body of rules which exist independently of national legal systems. International harmonising measures, such as the 1980 Vienna Convention, and the Uniform Customs and Practice for Documentary Credits, UCP 500, only have legal effect because they have been incorporated into national law, or incorporated by parties into their contracts. So while there may be no new *lex mercatoria* within the strict meaning of the term, it is clear that at an international level there is a movement towards identifying common principles and practices to facilitate international trade. Ireland has adopted some of these measures, such as the Hague-Visby Rules under the

96 See 1.1.1.

97 Established in 1968, UNCITRAL is responsible for, *inter alia*, the 1980 Vienna Sales Convention and the 1985 Model Law on Arbitration: see 29.4.2 and 37.3.3, respectively. See further, Schmitthoff, "The Unification of the Law of International Trade" [1968] *Journal of Business Law* 105, "The Codification of the Law of International Trade" [1985] *Journal of Business Law* 34.

98 Based in Rome and established in 1926, Unidroit is responsible for, *inter alia*, the 1988 Conventions on International Factoring and International Finance Leasing and more recently has worked closely with UNICITRAL.

99 First held in 1893, the Hague Conference is most noted for the Hague Rules relating the carriage of goods by sea: see further 29.4.2 and Chapter 31.

100 See the Hague Rules, the Hague-Visby Rules and the Hamburg Rules: see further 29.4.2.

101 See, *e.g.* the UCP 500: see further Chapter 32.

102 See Lando, "The Lex Mercatoria in International Commercial Arbitration" [1985] *International and Comparative Law Quarterly* 747.

Merchant Shipping (Liability of Shipowners and Others) Act 1996,[103] and UNCITRAL'S Model Arbitration Law under the Arbitration (International Commercial) Act 1998.[104] Others, such as the 1980 Vienna Sales Convention, have yet to be adopted, despite a recommendation for adoption from the Law Reform Commission.[105]

1.3.4 E-Commerce

Perhaps the greatest challenge to commercial law in the twenty-first century is the need to respond to the use of technology as a means of doing business. In one sense, this is nothing new to commercial law which has always had to adapt to new technology: the telephone; telex and fax machine. But it would be wrong to underestimate the significance of the change brought about by the internet and e-mail, in terms of marketing and supplying goods and services worldwide.

At a European level, providing a legal framework for e-commerce is seen as central to the Single Market.[106] The EC has therefore produced directives on electronic commerce[107] and electronic signatures.[108] These have been implemented, in part, by the Electronic Commerce Act 2000.[109] The rationale for these measures is to bolster confidence in e-commerce. In keeping with the general role of commercial law, the intention is to facilitate e-commerce and not to regulate or limit its development. With this in mind, these measures address three main issues: freedom to provide services; liability of intermediary service providers; and the legal effect of electronic contracts and digital signatures.[110]

The E-commerce Directive seeks to establish a framework within which providers of information society services[111] will be free to supply services throughout the EC. It provides that member states may not make the provision of information society services subject to prior approval.[112]

---

103 See 31.2.

104 See 37.3.3.1.

105 Law Reform Commission, *Report on the United Nations (Vienna) Convention on Contracts for the International Sale of Goods 1980* (L.C.R. 42-1992).

106 At an international level, in 1996, UNCITRAL produced a Model Law on Electronic Commerce and, in 2001, UNCITRAL produced a Model Law on Electronic Signatures. For texts see www.uncitral.org.

107 Directive 2000/31/EC [2000] O.J. L178/1.

108 Directive 1999/93/EC [1999] O.J. L13/12.

109 Further regulations are being drafted to fully implement these EC measures.

110 See generally, Kelleher & Murray, *IT Law in Europe*, (London, Sweet & Maxwell, 1999); Kelleher & Murray, *Information Technology Law in Ireland*, (Dublin, Butterworths, 1997); Lloyd, *Information Technology Law* (London, Butterworths, 1997).

111 As defined in Directive 98/34/EC [1998] O.J. L204/37, as amended by Directive 98/48/EC [1998] O.J. L217/18.

112 Art. 4.

On the issue of liability, the Directive provides that a person who provides a service consisting of transmitting information, providing access to a communications network or storing information, shall not, without more, be liable for the information transmitted or stored.[113]

Many legal rules require the use of documents, written evidence, and signatures. Such requirements can impede the development of e-commerce unless they can be satisfied by electronic equivalents. In addressing this issue, the E-commerce Directive requires member states to ensure that their laws allow contracts to be concluded by electronic means.[114] Accordingly, the Electronic Commerce Act 2000 provides that an electronic contract shall not be denied legal effect solely because it is in electronic form or has been concluded by electronic means.[115]

Moreover, certain contracts and legal documents require a signature to have legal effect. Even where a signature is not legally required, it may be used to authenticate a document or message. There are a number of ways in which electronic documents and messages can be signed. Currently, the most effective form of electronic signature is based on encryption technology. Each user of the system is issued with a unique pair of corresponding keys: one private, one public. A message can be encrypted using a computer algorithm code: the private key. By encrypting a message using the private key, a person effectively signs the message, identifying himself as the sender or indicating his assent to the contents of the message. The message can then only be decrypted using a corresponding decoding algorithm: the public key. Should the sender dispute the authenticity of the message, it can be decrypted using the public key proving the origin of the message. The main difficulty associated with this technology is establishing a means of connecting a particular key with the person to whom it belongs.[116] The Electronic Signatures Directive, and the Electronic Commerce Act 2000, address this issue by allowing certification service providers to establish, without prior authorisation, and to act as third parties to certify the authenticity of a digital signature by confirming the identity of the holder of a particular key pair.[117] The equivalence between digital and hand-written signatures is recognised[118] and digital signatures based on such certificates are admissible as evidence in legal proceedings.[119]

EU legislation also seeks to encourage consumers to participate in the

113 Arts. 11–14. Under Art. 15, member states cannot require such service providers to monitor the information transmitted by or stored on their systems.

114 Art. 9.

115 2000 Act, s.19.

116 The confidential nature of this technology can also give rise to law enforcement and security problems.

117 Art. 3 and 2000 Act, s.29.

118 Art. 5 and 2000 Act, s.13.

119 Art. 5 and 2000 Act, s.22.

e-commerce market. For example, the E-commerce Directive contains provisions to enhance consumer confidence in e-commerce. It provides that information service providers must acknowledge a customer's order, electronically, without undue delay and provide certain information to the customers of such services.[120] This should be read alongside other consumer protection measures,[121] in particular, the Distance Selling Directive[122] and the EC (Protection of Consumers in Respect of Contracts made by means of Distance Communications) Regulations.[123]

While a European and international framework for e-commerce is being agreed, it is apparent that many important legal questions remain to be answered. Such basic issues as where and when a digital contract is formed, or when is a payment complete when made electronically, have yet to be addressed. These types of questions are not new however, and perhaps are best resolved on a case by case basis, before the courts. The courts can be expected to respond to this new technology as they have in the past: by seeking to facilitate commercial activity and by giving effect to commercial practices and reasonable expectations.

---

120 Arts. 5 and 6.

121 See Recital 11.

122 Directive 97/7/EC [1997] O.J. L144/19. See also Directive 2002/65 concerning the distance marketing of consumer financial services [2002] O.J. L271/16.

123 S.I. No. 207 of 2001.

CHAPTER 2

AN OUTLINE OF CONTRACT LAW

2.1 INTRODUCTION

As noted in Chapter 1, commercial law is centred on contracts and the law of contract. Contract is the medium through which the majority of commercial transactions and relationships are structured. When we examine sale of goods law, the law of agency, or insurance law, for example, much of the time is spent considering the specific rules which apply to sales, agency, and, insurance contracts. Where specific rules do not exist, the general rules of contract law apply. The aim of this chapter is to outline the principles of contract law.[1] Accordingly, this chapter will act as a foundation for the remainder of the book, much of which could be described as *applied* contract law.[2]

The majority of contracts, including commercial contracts, are entered into, performed and come to an end without any difficulty or dispute. A small minority lead to a dispute[3] but often this is resolved internally and privately between the parties, by negotiation or arbitration.[4] An even smaller number result in litigation. Ironically perhaps, it is this smaller number of cases that informs our knowledge and understanding of contract law.

2.2 CONTRACT FORMATION

A contract can be defined as a legally enforceable agreement or promise. In general, there are three requirements for the formation of a contract:

(i) agreement;
(ii) consideration; and
(iii) intention to create legal relations.

---

1 For a more detailed analysis the leading texts on Irish contract law are McDermott, *Contract Law* (Dublin, Butterworths, 2001); Friel, *Contract Law* (Dublin, Round Hall Sweet & Maxwell, 2nd ed., 2000); and Clark, *Contract Law in Ireland* (Dublin, Round Hall Sweet & Maxwell, 4th ed., 1998).

2 Indeed, much of what might be considered general contract law, was formulated with specific contracts in mind, such as sale of goods contracts, and later given general application.

3 Research in England has shown that, in the past, business persons have often been ignorant of contract law, although there are indications that such persons now have a greater awareness of legal principles, than formerly: Beale & Dugdale, "Contracts between Businessmen" (1975) 2 *British Journal of Law and Society* 45.

4 On dispute resolution see Part VIII.

2.2.1 Agreement

An agreement is a reasonably definite understanding between the parties. An agreement is made up of two parts, in law: (i) an offer on certain terms and (ii) an acceptance of the offer on those same terms.

2.2.1.1 Offer

An offer is any statement or conduct indicating a clear intention to contract on terms that are reasonably definite. A distinction is made in law between offers and invitations to treat, that is invitations seeking offers. Examples of invitations to treat include:[5]

(a) statements, reserving the right to negotiate further;
(b) displays of goods in shop windows[6] or on shelves;[7]
(c) price lists, circulars, and other advertisements;[8]
(d) requests for bids by an auctioneer;[9]
(e) requests for tenders.[10]

Offers are generally regarded as revocable until acceptance, hence offers can be withdrawn at any time up to acceptance.[11] However, to be effective, the withdrawal must be communicated to the offeree.

2.2.1.2 Acceptance

An acceptance is an expression by which the offeree indicates consent to be bound by the terms of the offer. An acceptance must be manifested in words or conduct, and this manifestation must be communicated to the offeror. Different rules apply depending on the means of communication.

---

5 The following are general rules. Where, for example, a display or advertisement indicates an intention to be bound to reasonably definite terms, it may constitute an offer: see, *e.g.* *Kennedy v. London Express Newspapers* [1931] I.R. 532; *R. v. Warwickshire County Council, ex parte Johnson* [1993] A.C. 583.

6 *Minister for Industry & Commerce v. Pim* [1966] I.R. 154.

7 *PSGB v. Boots Cash Chemists* [1953] 1 All E.R. 482 (C.A.).

8 *Grainger & Son v. Gough* (1896) A.C. 325 (H.L.).

9 A bid is an offer which the auctioneer accepts at the fall of the hammer: Sale of Goods Act 1893, s.58.

10 Tenders are offers, leaving the person who made the request for tender to choose whether to accept or not. But see *Harvela v. Royal Trust Bank of Canada* [1986] A.C. 207, [1985] 2 All E.R. 966 (H.L.).

11 A promise to keep an offer open can only be enforced where the promise is supported by consideration: see further 2.2.2.

(a) Oral acceptance and acceptance by telex must be received by the offeror. For example, where the offeror does not hear the offeree accepting the offer, due to a poor telephone line, there is no contract;[12]
(b) Acceptance by post is effective from posting.[13] Where the acceptance is lost in the post and never reaches the offeror, provided there is proof of posting, the contract is nevertheless concluded at the time of posting. Further, once an acceptance is posted, the offer cannot be withdrawn.
(c) Acceptance by fax or e-mail, if treated as instantaneous forms of communication like oral communications and telexes, probably requires receipt.[14] However, there is no direct case law on this point.[15]

It is sometimes said that silence cannot amount to acceptance;[16] but it seems that this is not an absolute rule. Normally silence will not provide an unequivocal indication of acceptance but in certain circumstances it may amount to acceptance.[17]

A distinction is drawn between acceptances and counter-offers. Where a person purports to accept an offer but, in doing so, alters the terms, this is viewed as a counter-offer. A counter-offer is treated as a new offer, terminating the original offer, which the offeror can choose to accept or reject.[18] Agreements, and in particular business agreements, are sometimes reached only after a process of negotiation. One party may offer to contract on one set of terms; the other party may seek to alter those terms. Where the parties use standard form documentation as part of this negotiating process, it is said that there is a *battle of forms*. To resolve the situation, the negotiating process is analysed in terms of offers and counter-offers. For instance, in *Butler Machine Tool v. Ex-Cell-O Corp*[19] the plaintiff quoted for the supply of goods to potential buyers subject to their standard terms of sale which included a statement that "these terms and conditions shall prevail over any terms and conditions in the buyer's order." One of the clauses in the seller's terms of trading was a price variation clause. The buyer placed an order on his own trading terms which did not include a

12 *Entores v. Miles Far East Crpn* [1955] 2 Q.B. 327; *Brinkibon v. SSS mbH* [1983] 2 A.C. 34 (H.L.).

13 *Kelly v. Cruise Catering Ltd* [1994] 2 I.L.R.M. 394, 397–398 (S.C.).

14 At what particular point a telex or fax is deemed to be received depends on each case. A fax might be received when it is printed by the offeror's machine, or when it should have been removed from the machine in the normal course of business, or when it is actually removed from the machine. On receipt of electronic communications, see Electronic Commerce Act 2000, s.21.

15 See *The Pamela* [1995] 2 Lloyd's Rep. 249.

16 *Felthouse v. Bindley* (1863) 1 New Rep. 401.

17 *The Leonidas D* [1985] 2 All E.R. 796, [1985] 1 W.L.R. 925 (C.A.).

18 *Brinkibon v. SSS mbH* [1983] 2 A.C. 34 (H.L.).

19 [1979] 1 All E.R. 965 (C.A.).

price variation clause. The buyer's order form had a tear-off slip at the bottom which was an acknowledgment of receipt of order which stated "we accept your order on the terms and conditions set out therein." The seller filled in the acknowledgment receipt and returned it to the buyer. A dispute arose and the question was whether there was a contract, and if so, on whose terms. The Court of Appeal found that the quotation was an offer, including a price variation clause. However, the buyer's order altered the terms under which they were willing to contract and so this was a counter-offer on new terms, with no price variation clause. The acknowledgment of receipt returned by the seller constituted an acceptance because by filling in the acknowledgment the seller was taken to have assented to the buyer's terms. This finding was despite the fact that the seller's terms of trading included the phrase that "these terms and conditions shall prevail over any terms and conditions in the buyer's order."

2.2.2 Consideration

Bar agreements in deeds, an agreement alone will not be enforced by the courts: it must be supported by "consideration". Essentially, consideration is that which is given in return for an agreement or a promise. For example, when a person purchases a can of cola, the consideration for the delivery of the can of cola is the payment of the price; and the consideration for the payment of the price is the delivery of the can of cola. As can be seen from this example, consideration may be the price paid under a contract but not necessarily. Indeed, one promise may be consideration for another promise. The doctrine of consideration is unique to the common law system and is complex, being based on a number of rules. These rules are outlined below.

2.2.2.1 Consideration must move from the promisee

Where two people, A and B, have an agreement, in order for A to enforce B's part of the agreement, A must show that he provided consideration for B's promise. In other words, consideration must move from the promisee (A, see diagram below).[20] Likewise, in order for B to enforce A's part of the agreement, B must show that he provided consideration for A's promise.

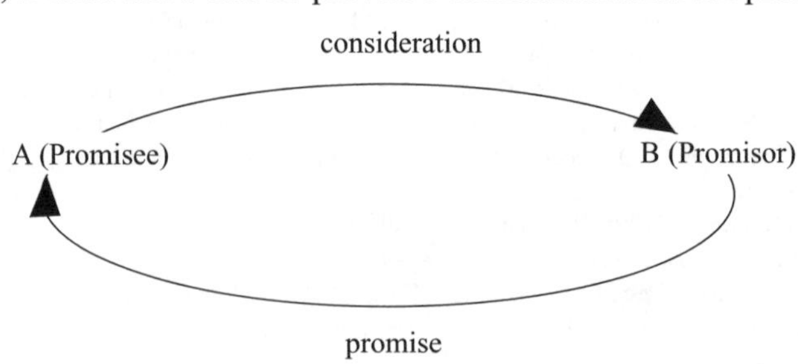

20 *Thomas v. Thomas* (1842) 2 Q.B. 851.

2.2.2.2 Adequacy of consideration irrelevant

In enforcing agreements, the courts are not concerned with the *adequacy*, or value, of consideration.[21] For example, it is not unusual to have a contract where the consideration is nominal, one cent or one euro, even though the actual value of the transaction is much higher.

2.2.2.3 Consideration must be sufficient

In the majority of commercial contracts, finding consideration to support an agreement or a promise does not cause a problem. However, problems can arise concerning the "sufficiency" of consideration and the variation of contracts.

(i) Past consideration is not sufficient

Consideration must be "sufficient" and past consideration is not sufficient consideration.[22] This means that consideration being provided for a promise must be given when the promise is made or after the promise is made but not *before* the promise is made. Consideration is past, for example, where goods are sold and, at some time subsequently, the seller gives a guarantee as to their quality.[23]

(ii) Performance of existing duty is not sufficient

Another aspect of this rule is that the performance of an existing duty is not sufficient consideration. The general rule is that where A is under a legal or contractual duty to B, performance of that duty (or a promise to perform that duty) is not consideration for a new promise from B. For example, assume that B agrees to pay A €100 to paint his house. Subsequently, they agree that A should get €150 for doing the job. When the job is completed, B refuses to pay the €150. Can A sue to enforce B's promise to pay €150? Because A was under a contractual duty to paint the house when B made his promise to pay €150, B's promise to pay €150 is not supported by sufficient consideration and so cannot be enforced. It follows, where A provides fresh consideration, by doing anything beyond his original promise, the new promise to pay €150 can be enforced. So, for example, if A agrees to complete the job earlier than scheduled in return for the €150, the €150 is payable.

The rule that the performance of an existing duty is not sufficient consideration has been undermined somewhat by the English case

21 *Westlake v. Adams* (1858) 5 C.B.N.S. 248.

22 *Eastwood v. Kenyon* (1840) 11 Ad. & El. 438.

23 *Roscorla v. Thomas* (1842) 3 Q.B. 234.

Williams v. Roffey Bros,[24] where it was held that A's performance of an existing duty was sufficient consideration where B derived a practical benefit from the performance. The case involved a contract to refurbish a roof and 27 flats. The defendant contractors sub-contracted joinery work to the plaintiffs costing £20,000, payable in stages. When the roof and nine flats had been completely refurbished and the remaining 18 flats partially refurbished, the plaintiffs approached the defendants seeking additional payments because they had under-estimated the costs and they were in financial difficulties. The plaintiffs had already received payments of £16,200. They were promised by the defendants that on completion of the work they would receive a further £10,300. The argument in favour of this payment was that the contractors needed the work finished and they would "never get the job finished without paying the money." When the work was completed, the plaintiffs sought the remainder of the money but the defendants refused to pay. The plaintiffs sued the defendants for their breach of promise. The issue was whether this promise was enforceable – was it supported by sufficient consideration?

The defendants argued that, because the plaintiffs were only doing what they had already promised to do, the promise to pay the additional amount was unenforceable. The Court of Appeal took what they referred to as a "pragmatic approach". They found consideration in various forms including the fact that the defendants could be assured that the work would be completed without the plaintiffs becoming insolvent.

More recent English authority suggests a return to the more traditional approach and seeks to limit *Williams v. Roffey Bros* to its facts. In *Re Selectmove Ltd*,[25] Selectmove owed tax to the Revenue. In July, the managing director of Selectmove offered to pay all future taxes as they fell due and arrears at the rate of £1,000 per month. The tax inspector did not accept this offer but said that he would have to talk to his superiors. Selectmove made some payments but some were late. In September, the Revenue demanded payment in full. To avoid insolvency, Selectmove argued, *inter alia*, that there was an agreement to pay existing and future taxes and that this promise to pay already existing debts was sufficient consideration because the Revenue would derive a practical benefit from it. However, the Court of Appeal held that the promise to pay an existing debt was not sufficient consideration. Consequently, the decision in *Williams v. Roffey Bros* was limited to contracts for the supply of services.

Subsequently, in *Truck & Machinery Sales v. Marubeni Komatsu*,[26] the Irish High Court declined to follow *Williams v. Roffey Bros*. There the defendant sold machinery to the plaintiff which was not paid for. In December 1993, the defendant sent a fax to the plaintiff's bank saying that

24 [1991] 1 Q.B. 1.
25 [1995] 2 All E.R. 531.
26 [1996] 1 I.R. 12.

it had reached an agreement with the plaintiff that if part of the money due was paid, it would wait for the balance. In July 1995, the defendant lost patience and its solicitor informed the plaintiff that if the balance due (over £2 million sterling) was not paid within 21 days it would petition the High Court to wind-up the plaintiff company. The plaintiff sought an injunction to stop this petition. One of its arguments was that the above fax reflected an agreement that the defendant would not pursue legal proceedings against the plaintiff. Following *Re Selectmove*, the High Court found that the promise to pay an existing debt was not good consideration.

(iii) Consideration to a third party

Another aspect of the rule, that consideration must be sufficient, concerns the question whether consideration to a third party, T, can be valid consideration for a contract between A and B. For instance, can performance of a duty owed to T be sufficient consideration for a promise between A and B. It seems, following the English case *New Zealand Shipping v. Satterthwaite*,[27] that this is possible. In that case, A (stevedores) had contracted with T (shipowners) to unload goods from T's ship. Some of the goods being unloaded belonged to B, who promised that he would not sue A for any damages caused during the unloading. It was held that B's promise not to sue was enforceable because it was supported by consideration (B received a benefit) from the promisee, and that consideration was the unloading of the goods, despite the fact that A was already obliged to unload the goods under his contract with T.

(iv) Variation of contract terms

A significant problem caused by the doctrine of consideration relates to the variation of contract terms. As noted above, consideration must be sufficient, and past consideration is not sufficient. This means that consideration being provided for a promise must be given when the promise is made or after the promise is made but not before the promise is made. Therefore, new contractual terms, or variations, cannot be incorporated into the contract after the contract is made, unless the promisee provides new consideration for the new term or variation. Hence, for every variation there must be fresh consideration. This difficulty can be avoided where the initial contract includes a term allowing one or both parties to vary the contract in specified circumstances: a "variation clause". Such a clause might allow the contract price to vary in accordance with market values, for example a "price variation clause".

27 [1975] A.C. 154. [1974] 1 All E.R. 1015 (P.C.).

(v) Waiver and estoppel

Even where a promise, such as a variation, is not supported by sufficient consideration, the promise may still bind the promisor under the doctrines of waiver and "promissory estoppel". At common law, where a party agrees not to insist on his strict legal rights, or represents that he will not insist on strict performance, he may be held to have waived his right to strict performance. In *Charles Rickards Ltd v. Oppenhaim*,[28] under a sales contract a car chassis was to be built and delivered by March 20. It was not delivered in time but the buyer continued to press for delivery until June 29 at which point he gave notice to the seller that he would not accept delivery if it was not made within four weeks. Delivery was not made until October at which time the buyer refused to accept it. The Court of Appeal found the buyer had waived the original delivery date, but by giving reasonable notice of his intention to insist on delivery, he was entitled to reject the goods when his four-week deadline was not satisfied.

A similar doctrine exists in equity whereby if one party promises that he will not insist on his strict contractual rights, he will not be allowed to retract that promise if the promise has been acted upon by the other party. The doctrine is referred to as equitable or "promissory" estoppel.[29] The exact scope of the doctrine is unclear but it would appear that the following requirements exist.

(a) The promisor must make an unambiguous statement, express or implied, that he will not insist on his strict legal rights.
(b) The promisee must have relied on that promise, perhaps acting to his detriment, but this is not clear.
(c) It must be inequitable to allow the promisor to retract his promise.

Where the doctrine applies, its effect is to suspend, not extinguish, contractual rights. Hence, the promisor can return to the original terms of the contract by giving reasonable notice. Significantly, promissory estoppel is said to operate as "a shield, not a sword", in that it creates no new rights of action for the promisee; it merely acts as a defence for the promisee.

2.2.3 Intention to create legal relations

The third requirement for the formation of a valid and enforceable contract is that there must be an intention to create legal relations between the

28 [1950] 1 K.B. 616, [1950] 1 All E.R. 520 (C.A.): see 11.2.4.1.

29 *Hughes v. Metropolitan Railway Co.* (1877) 2 App. Cas. 439, *Central London Property Trust Ltd v. High Tress House Ltd* [1947] K.B. 130, *Kenny v. Kelly* [1988] I.R. 457.

parties to the contract. This requirement causes little difficulty in a commercial context because, in relation to commercial transactions, there is a presumption that there is an intention to create legal relations.[30] However, this intention is only presumed and parties in commercial transactions may lack the necessary intention to create legal relations. For example, in *Kleinwort Benson Ltd v. Malaysia Mining Corporation Ltd*,[31] a creditor agreed a loan with a subsidiary company based on two letters of comfort provided by the parent company along the following lines:

> "It is our policy to ensure that the business of the subsidiary is at all times in a position to meet its liabilities to you under the loan agreement."

The subsidiary company went into liquidation and the creditors sought repayment from the parent company. The Court of Appeal held that the letters of comfort were not intended to create a contractual promise as to future conduct. The court took the view that letters of comfort are generally regarded as intended to create a moral but not a legal binding obligation.

2.2.4 Formalities

In general, where there is an agreement, supported by consideration and an intention to create legal relations, there are no requirements as to form for a valid and enforceable contract. The contract can be concluded orally, or in writing, or it may be implied from conduct. A written contract may be useful for evidential purposes but writing is not essential.

There are several important statutory exceptions to this general rule. For example, under section 2 of the Statute of Frauds (Ireland) 1695, contracts of guarantee[32] and contracts for the sale of land or an interest therein must be evidenced in writing and signed by the party to be charged, that is, sued. Similarly, under section 4 of the Sale of Goods Act 1893, a contract for the sale of goods of the value of £10 [€12.70] or more is not enforceable by action unless:

(i) the buyer accepts, and actually receives, part of the goods sold; or
(ii) the buyer gives something in earnest to bind the contract; or
(iii) the buyer has made part payment; or
(iv) there is a note or memorandum in writing of the contract and signed by the party to be charged, that is, sued.[33]

---

30 *Rose and Frank Co v. J.R. Crompton Bros* [1925] A.C. 445; [1924] All E.R. Rep 245 (H.L.).

31 [1989] 1 W.L.R. 379: see further 26.5. See also *British Steel Corpn v. Cleveland Bridge and Engineering Co Ltd* [1984] 1 All E.R. 504 on letters of intent.

32 See Chapter 26.

33 See 9.2.1.1.

Under the EC (Commercial Agents) Regulations 1994 and 1997,[34] which implement the EC Directive on self-employed commercial agents,[35] a "commercial agency" contract is not valid unless evidenced in writing.[36] Lastly, a variety of formal requirements apply to certain specific contracts entered into with consumers, in order to protect the consumer. Credit sales, contracts of hire-purchase and other hire contracts with consumers are all regulated by the Consumer Credit Act 1995.[37] Consumer buyers of goods or services are also protected by formal requirements in relation to contracts negotiated away from business premises, under the EC (Cancellation of Contracts Negotiated away from Business Premises) Regulations 1989,[38] and contracts concluded by means of distance communications, under the EC (Protection of Consumers in respect of Contracts made by means of Distance Communications) Regulations 2001.[39] Under these Regulations, for instance, certain information must be provided to the consumer, in written or other durable form, within a specified time. Failure to provide this information makes the contract unenforceable.[40]

2.2.5 Defects in formation

When contracts are being formed an event may occur, or, one party may do something which he should not do, which results in a defect in the formation of the contract. There are different types of defect; each having different consequences.

2.2.5.1 Effects of defects

A distinction is made between defects which render a contract void or voidable. A void contract is one that never existed, and hence never had any legal effect such that the parties do not owe, and never have owed, any legal obligations to each other. Any money paid under a void contract, or any property transferred, is returnable. In contrast, where a contract is found to be voidable, this means that the innocent party, that is, the party not responsible for the defect, has a choice: he can allow the contract to continue or he can rescind or set aside the contract. Where the contract is rescinded, it is set aside from the beginning and each party is required to

34 S.I. No. 33 of 1994 and S.I. No. 31 of 1997.

35 Directive 86/653/EEC, [1986] O.J. L382/17.

36 Article 13(2) and Reg. 5, 1994: see further 7.2.1.5.

37 Re credit sales see Part III of the Act; re hire-purchase see Part VI of the Act; and re other hire contracts see Part VII of the Act.

38 S.I. No. 224 of 1989, implementing Directive 85/577, [1985] O.J. L372/31: see 9.2.1.

39 S.I. No. 207 of 2001, implementing Directive 97/7, [1997] O.J. L144/19: see 9.2.1.

40 S.I. No. 224 of 1989 Reg. 4, and S.I. No. 207 of 2001, Regs 4 and 5.

return benefits received, as far as is possible. But until the contract is rescinded, it remains valid.

2.2.5.2 Defects

The main defects which render a contract void or voidable are: mistake; misrepresentation; and duress or undue influence. Each has a very particular meaning in law, leading to different consequences.

(i) Mistake

Mistake is a relatively narrow ground. For instance, if a purchaser of oats buys grain thinking it is old oats, where in truth it is new oats, this is not what would be categorised as a mistake, in law. When the law recognises a mistake, the contract is rendered void at common law.[41] For example, where two parties agreed to the sale of an item that does not exist, though both parties believed it to exist, it is said that they share a common mistake and the contract is void. The contract may also be void where the parties are at cross-purposes. In *Raffles v. Wichelhaus,*[42] there was a contract to buy cotton, shipped from Bombay on a ship called *Peerless*. There was in fact two ships called *Peerless*, both sailing from Bombay with cotton, one in October and the other in December. The buyer thought he was buying the October shipment, the seller thought that he was selling the December shipment. As a result, the parties were at cross-purposes and the contract was found to be void.

Problems can arise where A contracts with B, mistakenly believing him to be C. The issue is whether A intended to contract with B or C. Where the parties do not deal face to face, it is possible to establish that A intended to contract only with C, and hence there is no contract with B.[43] Where the parties deal face to face, the objective interpretation of the circumstances is that A intends to deal with the person before him.[44] In these circumstances, B will normally be responsible for A's "mistake" because he fraudulently misled him, and the contract will be voidable for misrepresentation.[45]

(ii) Misrepresentation

Where one party to a contract makes an untrue statement in relation to a

41 Equity may recognise a wider variety of mistakes making a contract voidable instead of void: see, *e.g. Solle v. Butcher* [1950] 1 K.B. 671.

42 (1864) 2 H. & C. 906.

43 *Cundy v. Lindsey* (1878) 3 App. Cas. 459 (H.L.).

44 *Phillips v. Brooks* [1919] 2 K.B. 243; *Lewis v. Avery* [1972] 1 Q.B. 198, [1971] 3 All E.R. 907; *cf. Ingram v. Little* [1961] 1 Q.B. 31, [1960] 3 All E.R. 332 (C.A.).

45 See further 2.2.5.2(ii) and 19.6.1.1.

material fact – a misrepresentation – before the contract is concluded, and this induces the other party to enter the contract, then the contract may be voidable for misrepresentation. The misrepresentation may be made fraudulently, negligently, or innocently. As well as being able to rescind the contract, the innocent party may be entitled to damages from the person making the misrepresentation.[46]

For example, in *Fenton v. Schofield*,[47] a vendor of land made a statement that over the previous four years a river running through the land had yielded 300–350 salmon a year and that he had spent £15,000 renovating the property. Both statements of fact were untrue and the vendor knew this. A purchaser paid £17,000 for the property on the strength of these statements. The plaintiff sued for fraudulent misrepresentation and was awarded damages based on the difference between what the land was worth and what it was represented to be worth. Similarly, in *Connor v. Potts*,[48] a seller of two farms described them as comprising 443 acres, which he believed to be true. The purchase price was calculated at £12.10s an acre, however there was in fact only 376 acres. Following a finding of innocent misrepresentation, it was held that the plaintiff was entitled to specific performance of the contract at a reduced price.

(iii) Duress or undue influence

The essence of contract law is that two parties freely consent to being bound to each other. Where consent is given only because pressure is put on a party, in the form of duress or undue influence, then this may lead to a defect in formation and the innocent party may be able to set aside the contract. Threats to a person's life, person or property have been recognised as constituting duress.[49] More recently, the courts have recognised the concept of "economic duress" which is particularly important in a commercial context. The equitable doctrine of undue influence is wider than the common law concept of duress and includes the situation where pressure is exerted without any threats. Equity gives further relief where a relationship between the parties is such that it gives rise to a presumption that one party exercised undue influence over the other. Such relationships include that of parent and child; and trustee and beneficiary. Other relationships, such as husband and wife, may be

46 Damages may be available at common law for fraudulent and negligent misrepresentation. Under the Sale of Goods and Supply of Services Act 1980, Part V which applies to sale of goods contracts, hire-purchase agreements; agreements for the letting of goods, and contracts for the supply of services, damages are also available for non-fraudulent misrepresentation: s.45.

47 (1966) 100 I.L.T.R. 69.

48 [1897] I.R. 534.

49 See, *e.g.* *Williams v. Baley* (1866) L.R. 1 H.L. 200.

included where the party challenging the transaction can show that they reposed trust and confidence in the other party.[50]

2.2.6 Rights of cancellation

There may exist a right to lawfully cancel a contract after its formation. Such a right is normally given as a form of consumer protection. For instance, under the EC (Cancellation of Contracts Negotiated away from Business Premises) Regulations 1989,[51] where a "trader"[52] contracts to supply goods or services to a "consumer"[53] on their "doorstep",[54] there is provision for a "cooling-off" period of seven days during which time the consumer can give notice of cancellation.[55] The consumer must be given written notice of this right, and failure to give such notice renders the contract unenforceable against the consumer.[56] On cancellation, any sums paid by the consumer are repayable by the trader, the consumer having a lien over the goods until such repayment.[57] Equally, any goods received are returnable.[58] Further rights of cancellation exists under the Consumer Credit Act 1995[59] and the EC (Protection of Consumers in respect of Contracts made by means of Distance Communications) Regulations 2001.[60]

2.2.7 Privity of contract

The doctrine of privity of contract provides that only the parties to the contract may sue to enforce the terms of the contract:

---

50 See, *e.g. Barclays Bank v. O'Brien* [1994] 1 A.C. 180.

51 S.I. No. 224 of 1989, implementing Directive 85/577, [1985] O.J. L372/31; see further Clark, *Contract Law in Ireland* (Dublin, Round Hall Sweet & Maxwell, 4th ed., 1998) p.191; Bird, *Consumer Credit Law* (Dublin, Round Hall Sweet & Maxwell, 1998) p.326.

52 Defined as "a natural or legal person who, for the transaction in question, acts in his commercial or professional capacity, or anyone acting in the name or on behalf of a trader:" Reg. 2(1).

53 Defined as "a natural person who, in transactions covered by these Regulations, is acting for purposes which can be regarded as outside his trade or profession": Reg. 2(1).

54 The regulations apply, subject to exceptions, to contracts concluded (i) during an excursion organised by the trader away from his business premises; (ii) during a visit by a trader to the consumer's home, or another consumer's home, or to the consumer's place of work, where the visit is unsolicited; (iii) following a solicited visit but where the goods and services supplied are other than those in respect of which the visit was requested. Additionally, the regulations apply to contracts in respect of which an offer was made by the consumer in circumstances similar to the above: Reg. 3(1).

55 Reg. 5.

56 Reg. 4. See further the Schedule as to the content and form of the notice.

57 Reg. 6(1) and (2): see generally 25.3.

58 Reg. 6(3).

59 See, *e.g.* s.58(5) with regard to hire-purchase arrangements.

60 S.I. No. 207 of 2001, Reg. 6, implementing Directive 97/7, [1997] O.J. L144/19.

> "… it has been decided that, where the foundation of the right of action is rested upon contract, no one can maintain an action who is not a party to the contract."[61]

However, sometimes contracts are made for the benefit of a third party. For example, in *Tweedle v. Atkinson*,[62] William Guy and John Tweedle contracted with each other that on the marriage of Tweedle's son to Guy's daughter, they would pay the son money. John Tweedle paid the sum as agreed, but William Guy did not and on his death, the sum was still outstanding. John Tweedle's son sought to recover the money from the deceased's estate but the court held that the action must fail because the son was not a party, or privy, to the contract. There are two main reasons for this doctrine. First, the third party is usually a gratuitous beneficiary and, as such, cannot enforce the promise even if it had been made to him because he has provided no consideration for it. Second, the courts have been keen to preserve the powers of the parties to control their contract – to end it or to alter it. If a third party acquired rights under their contract, this control would, at least, be diminished. Nevertheless, where a contract is made for the benefit of a third party, it seems unreasonable that the courts should override the clear intention of the parties in the name of this doctrine.

There are exceptions to the doctrine. The most important exception, in a commercial context, relates to the law of agency. Accordingly, where a person A enters a contract with another person T, on behalf of and with the authority of another person P, the contract which arises exists between P and T – A having no contractual rights or obligations under the contract.[63]

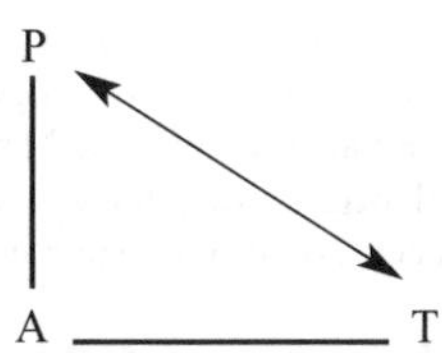

Another exception exists where a contractual right between X and Y is transferred or assigned to a third party Z. Despite the existence of various exceptions, the doctrine of privity has been strongly criticised,[64] and Ireland is part of a growing minority of jurisdictions which remain loyal to the doctrine. The civil law jurisdictions of the member states of the European Union, in general, recognise third party rights in contract law.[65]

61 *Murphy v. Bowen* (1866) I.R. 2 CL 506 per Monahan C.J. at 512.
62 (1861) 1 B. & S. 393.
63 See further Part II.
64 See, *e.g.* Friel, "The Failed Experiment with Privity", [1996] *Irish Law Times* 86.
65 See, *e.g.* "stipulation pour autrui" in French law: Art. 1121 of the Code Civil.

Equally, the American courts recognise an exception to the doctrine of privity which provides that where a contract expressly mentions third parties as intended beneficiaries of the contract, they are permitted to claim the envisaged benefits. Moreover, intended beneficiaries who are not expressly mentioned in the contract may be able to claim benefits under it.[66] More recently, in the U.K., the Contracts (Rights of Third Parties) Act 1999 modified the doctrine of privity of contract to enable a person who is not a party to a contract to enforce a term of the contract if:

(i) the contract expressly provides that he may do so; or
(ii) the term purports to confer a benefit on him and it appears that, on proper construction of the contract, the parties intended him to be able to enforce the contract.[67]

Reform may be on the agenda in Ireland also. The Law Commission, in its Second Programme (2000–2007) has identified privity of contract and the rights of third parties as a topic for examination. It is to be hoped that, as a result, the necessary legislation will be introduced to remedy this long-standing deficiency in the law of contract.

2.3 TERMS OF THE CONTRACT

Once a contract is properly formed, the contractual obligations of the parties are found in the terms of the contract. It is therefore important to be able to identify the terms of a contract and to classify them according to their status. Where contracts are in writing, this task may be less difficult than with oral contracts. In particular areas of commercial law, such as international trade, standard form contracts play an important role.[68] However, as noted above, there is no general legal requirement that contracts be recorded in writing and many commercial contracts are made informally, either face to face or over the telephone, by fax or e-mail.

2.3.1 Mere representations, representations and terms

In the negotiations which lead to the formation of a contract, parties may make numerous statements, either orally or in writing. A buyer may describe a particular type of product to perform a particular function; a seller may go to great lengths to highlight the features and advantages of his product over competitors' products. Not every word spoken between

---

66 See, *e.g. Ratzlaff v. Franz Foods* 150 Ark. 1003, 468 SW. 2d (1971).

67 1999 Act, s.1(1) and (2). The existing common law and statutory exceptions remain unaffected by this legislation.

68 See 2.3.2; see further Part VI.

the parties forms part of any subsequent contract. In the event of a dispute arising later, it may be necessary to determine the legal status of these various statements.

Generally, there are three categories of statement. The law distinguishes between mere representations, representations, and terms of the contract. The classification of statements is based on the intention of the parties, objectively assessed by a court. Mere representations, sometimes referred to as "mere puffs", are statements which are intended to have no legal effect. Mere representations probably include advertising claims and sales talk, which are usually exaggerated to entice a customer to purchase. For example, a statement by a car dealer that a car "will run forever," is most likely not intended to have legal effect and so is not actionable.

Other statements are either representations or terms of the contract, or both.[69] A representation is a pre-contractual statement of fact which encourages the other party to enter the contract, but it is not a term of the contract. In contrast, a term of the contract is any statement which is intended to have contractual effect and hence, is contractually binding on the parties. Determining whether a statement is a representation or a term of the contract depends on the intention of the parties. This in turn will depend on the court's view, based on the facts of the case. As a result, it is difficult to predict the status of any statement with certainty. Case law can be difficult to reconcile in this regard, but it does suggest that certain statements are more likely to be terms than representations, such as statements made close in time to the conclusion of the contract,[70] statements which are particularly important to the hearer,[71] and statements made by an expert to a non-expert.[72]

Representations and terms of the contract give rise to legal liability, if false.[73] Where a representation is factually false this may amount to a misrepresentation which renders the contract voidable, and damages may be payable.[74] Where a term of the contract is broken or breached, the innocent party can sue the person responsible for the breach, claiming damages, and may be able to terminate, or end, the contract.[75] The

69 Sale of Goods and Supply of Services Act 1980, s.44.

70 See *Routledge v. McKay* [1954] 1 All E.R. 885, [1954] 1 W.L.R. 615 (C.A.), *cf. Schawel v. Reade* [1913] 2 I.R. 81.

71 See *Bannerman v. White* (1861) 10 C.B.N.S. 844.

72 See *Dick Bentley Productions Ltd v. Harold Smith (Motor) Ltd* [1965] 2 All E.R. 65, [1965] 1 W.L.R. 623 (C.A.); *cf. Oscar Chess v. Williams* [1957] 1 All E.R. 325, [1957] 1 W.L.R. 370 (C.A.).

73 A person may be liable for the false statements of his agent (see generally Part II), and, where goods are supplied on credit to a person dealing as a consumer, the credit supplier will be liable for false statements made during negotiations by the supplier of goods: Sale of Goods and Supply of Services Act, s.14: see 9.2.2 and 13.10.

74 See 2.2.5.2(ii).

75 See 2.4.4.

classification between representations and terms is no longer as important as it once was. Liability for breach of contract is strict, so that an innocent party can claim damages for breach of a term of the contract even though the statement was made innocently, believing it to be true. Prior to 1980, damages were only available for misrepresentation where the false statement was made fraudulently,[76] or negligently.[77] However, the Sale of Goods and Supply of Services Act 1980[78] provides that damages are payable for non-fraudulent misrepresentation.[79] The maker of the statement can avoid liability if he can show that he had reasonable grounds to believe, and did believe, that the statement was true. This reduces the incentive that used to exist for an innocent party to argue that a statement was a term of the contract. But other distinctions remain. Where a term of the contract is breached, the innocent party may be able to terminate the contract. Termination is *prospective* in nature, releasing the parties from their future obligations to each other. In contrast, where there is a misrepresentation, the innocent party may be able to rescind the contract. Rescission is *retrospective* in nature, seeking to restore the parties to their pre-contractual positions. Furthermore, damages for breach of contract and misrepresentation are assessed differently, and the right to terminate may be lost more quickly than the right to rescind.

2.3.2 Individually negotiated or standard terms

The terms of a contract can be individually negotiated, whereby the parties negotiate each individual term, or standard in format. Standard form contracts developed in the nineteenth century. With the growth of mass production and mass distribution came the mass-produced or standard form contract. Today, standard form contracts are common in business because they offer many commercial advantages. For the business user, once the standard form contract has been drafted, it can be used repeatedly. As a result, standard form contracts save time, avoiding the cost of negotiations. For instance, junior employees can conclude contracts on standard terms. Standard form contracts can also be used by businesses to plan their business relationships. For example, risks can be allocated in the standard form contract and the business can arrange insurance on the basis

76 Using the tort of deceit: see McMahon & Binchy, *Law of Torts* (Dublin, Butterworths, 3rd ed., 2001), Chapter 35.

77 Under the authority of *Hedley Byrne & Co Ltd v. Heller & Partners Ltd* [1964] A.C. 465, [1963] 2 All E.R. 575 (H.L.).

78 This legislation is limited in its application to contracts for the sale of goods, hire-purchase agreements, other arrangements for the letting of goods, as defined, and contracts for the supply of services: 1980 Act, s.43; see further Chapters 9 and 20.

79 1980 Act, s.45(1). See further Clark, *Contract Law in Ireland* (Dublin, Round Hall Sweet & Maxwell, 4th ed., 1998), pp.252–255; *cf* Carey, "Misrepresentation and the Avoidance of Liability" (2001) *Commercial Law Practitioner* 131, esp. 136–137.

of that allocation. Moreover, standard form contracts can promote certainty as to the obligations under the contract. Many commercial contracts are made on standard terms promoted by trade or professional organisations. Standard terms of sale and purchase are quite common, as are standard terms in insurance, carriage, construction and banking contracts.

Some businesses will only contract on their standard terms, that is, on a "take-it-or-leave-it" basis. Such contracts are referred to as "contracts of adhesion". Businesses can afford to do this, for example, where they are the only supplier of a product, or where they are in a very strong market position. The use of adhesion contracts can be criticised on the basis that the contract is not based on "a meeting of the minds", instead it comes about because one party is in a position to dictate the terms of the contract, to which the other party "consents".[80] Nevertheless, such contracts are enforced because they accommodate the conduct of business. (See Appendix A for sample Standard Terms of Sale.)

2.3.2.1 Incorporation of terms by reference

The terms of a contract can derive from various sources: advertising, oral statements, letters, and standard terms printed in a master document or, more commonly, on the back of standard form documentation, such as order forms, receipt of order forms and invoices. Such terms may be incorporated into any contract "by reference", provided that the terms are introduced no later than the time when the contract is concluded. Any statement made after the conclusion of the contract will be unenforceable unless supported by further consideration.[81] Incorporation by reference can occur in three ways, by:

(i) signature;
(ii) notice; or
(iii) course of dealings.

(i) Signature

When a party signs a document containing a set of terms, he is *prima facie* bound by the terms, even if the party has not read the terms. In *L'Estrange v. Graucob Ltd*,[82] the plaintiff bought a machine on terms contained in a

80 Slawson, "Standard Form Contracts and Democratic Control of Lawmaking Power" (1971) 84 *Harvard Law Review* 529.
81 See 2.2.2.1(iv).
82 [1934] 2 K.B. 394.

document described as a "Sales Agreement". Some of the clauses were in "legible but regrettably small print". The plaintiff signed the "Sales Agreement" but did not read the terms. The court held that she was bound by the terms:

> "When a document containing contractual terms is signed then, ... the party signing is bound, and it is wholly immaterial whether he has read the document or not."[83]

This rule can operate harshly, especially in a consumer context, but it is justified by the objective approach to contract: a person who signs a document containing contractual terms appears to be assenting to those terms.

(ii) Notice

Standard terms set out in order forms, delivery notes, catalogues, or tickets, can be enforced without getting the signature of either party where the terms are made available or reasonable notice of the terms is given to the other party at the time the contract is made. Again, it usually does not matter whether the other party has read the terms. The rule of reasonable notice was established in a line of railway cases. In *Parker v. South Eastern Railways Ltd*,[84] the defendant railway company claimed that the plaintiff passenger was bound by terms printed on a cloakroom ticket, of which the plaintiff was ignorant. In order for the plaintiff to be bound by the terms on the ticket, the court set out the following rules.

(a) If the person receiving the ticket did not know there was writing on the ticket, he is not bound;
(b) If the person receiving the ticket knew there was writing on the ticket and knew that it contained terms, he would be bound;
(c) If the person receiving the ticket knew there was writing on the ticket but did not know it contained terms, nevertheless he will be bound if he was given reasonable notice of the terms.

Whether reasonable notice of the terms has been given will depend on the facts of the case, but the test is objective, so that, provided sufficient has been done to bring the terms to the notice of persons generally, no account is taken of subjective factors. Where the term to be incorporated is unusual,

83 *Ibid* at 403, per Scrutton L.J.; see further *Slattery v. C.I.E.* (1968) 106 I.L.T.R. 71.

84 (1877) 2 C.P.D. 416, [1874–1880] All E.R. 116; see also *Carroll v. An Post National Lottery* [1996] 1 I.R. 443.

then even more care must be taken to give reasonable notice, for example, by printing it in bold or larger print.[85]

(iii) Course of dealings

Lastly, where parties have contracted in the past and incorporated a standard set of terms, such past "course of dealings" may be enough to ensure that the standard terms are part of any future contract. However, there seems to be a requirement of *consistent* dealing before this argument will work.[86]

2.3.2.2 Statutory regulation of standard terms

The EC (Unfair Terms in Consumer Contracts) Regulations 1995, as amended,[87] represent a major departure in Irish contract law which traditionally has been non-interventionist in its general approach to contracts. Under these Regulations, any standard term in a contract between a business and a consumer which is "unfair" is void. Importantly, individual consumers, the Director General of Consumer Affairs, and others, can seek to enforce these Regulations. The Regulations are considered in detail below.[88]

2.3.3 Conditions, warranties, innominate terms and fundamental terms

Once the terms of the contract have been distinguished from mere representations and representations, they can be classified into four different categories: conditions, warranties, fundamental terms or innominate terms. Different consequences follow the breach of these different terms.

Traditionally, there were two classifications: conditions and warranties. A condition is a more important term of the contract when compared with a warranty. The difference between the two becomes apparent when you compare the effect of the breach of a condition with a breach of warranty. Where a term which is classified as a warranty is broken, the innocent party is entitled to damages only.

> **Example**: A promises to sell a book to B for €10 to be delivered the following day. However, the book is delivered two days later, in breach of contract. When the obligation as to the time of delivery is classified as a

---

85 *Interfoto Picture Library v. Stilletto Visual Programmes* [1988] 1 E.R. 348; see further *Western Meats Ltd v. National Ice and Cold Storage* [1982] I.L.R.M. 99.

86 *McCutcheon v. David MacBrayne Ltd* [1964] 1 All E.R. 430.

87 S.I. No. 27 of 1995 and S.I. No.307 of 2000.

88 See 2.3.5.3.

warranty, B is entitled to damages for any loss which results from A's breach. But B must accept and pay for the book, although delivered late.

However, where the term which is broken is classified as a condition, then the innocent party is entitled to damages and to terminate the contract.

Example: Assume the above facts, but during negotiations for the sale of the book, B states: "it is important that I get the book tomorrow because I have an exam the next day and I need it to study." In these circumstances, a court would be more likely to classify the term as to time of delivery as a condition. Accordingly, when A delivers the book late, there is a breach of condition and B can: (i) sue A for damages and (ii) refuse to perform his obligations under the contract, he can refuse to accept the book and pay for it, and (iii) he can terminate the contract.

The strict division between conditions and warranties can be criticised for being inflexible. For instance, where a term is classified as a condition, the innocent party can terminate the contract even though the effect of the breach might not be very serious.[89] Innominate or "intermediary" terms represent the middle ground between conditions and warranties.[90] Where an innominate term is breached, the effect depends on the seriousness of the breach. If the breach is not serious, the innocent party is limited to a claim in damages. In contrast, if the effect of the breach is serious, the innocent party can claim damages and terminate the contract. This flexibility gives a court more discretion to decide what is the fairest remedy in a given situation.

Fundamental terms are terms the breach of which amounts to total non-performance of the contract. For example, where there is a contract to deliver beans, and peas are delivered, it is said that there is a fundamental breach of contract.[91] The fundamental term was "invented" by English courts in an series of cases in the 1950s to control the use of widely drafted exclusion clauses. A number of cases have held that an exclusion clause can never excuse a fundamental breach of contract. However, this is not the position in English law and the position in Irish law is unsettled.[92]

Parties to a contract may seek to define their obligations by classifying the terms of a contract as conditions and warranties, for example. While courts seek to give effect to the intentions of the parties, they are not bound by such classifications. Where a term is identified as a "condition", a court might nevertheless find that the parties did not intend that the breach of the term would entitle the innocent party to terminate the contract.

89 See, *e.g. Cehave v. Bremer* [1975] 3 All E.R. 739.

90 See *Hong Kong Fir v. Kawasaki* [1962] 2 Q.B. 26; *Irish Telephone Rentals v. ICS Building Society* [1991] I.L.R.M. 880.

91 *Chanter v. Hopkins* (1838) 4 M. & W. 399.

92 See further 2.3.5.1(iv).

2.3.4 Express and implied terms

All terms of a contract are either express or implied. An express term is one expressed or stated, and agreed by the parties either by word of mouth or in writing. Express terms arise from the express wishes of the parties: one of the principles of contract law being to give effect to the intentions of the parties.

Into every contract, a court can imply further terms. In *Tradax (Ireland) v. Irish Grain Board Ltd*, it was stated that the power to imply terms:

> "must be exercised with care. The Courts have no role in acting as contract makers, or as counsellors, to advise or direct which agreement ought to have been made by two people, whether businessmen or not, who choose to enter into contractual relations with each other."[93]

> "It is not the function of the Court to rewrite a contract for parties met upon commercially equal terms; if such parties want to enter into unreasonable, unfair or even disastrous contracts that is their business, not the business of the Courts."[94]

These sentiments hold true in relation to commercial contracts, though where a party to the contract is a consumer there is now a substantial body of law which seeks to regulate the content of consumer contracts.[95] Generally, a court can imply a term on three different grounds: on the facts, in law, or based on trade custom and usage.

2.3.4.1 Implied by fact

Based on the express terms of a contract, a court may imply further terms into the contract to flesh out the contract or to give business effect to the contract.[96] For example, in *Gardner v. Coutts*,[97] land was sold, the vendor promising that the buyer would have first refusal if the vendor decided to sell adjoining land. The court implied a term whereby the vendor could not defeat the buyer's expectations by giving the land to a third party as a gift.

This is an important function of the courts, especially where the parties have failed to address all the necessary terms of the contract. The law in this area was re-stated in *Carna Foods v. Eagle Star*[98] where Lynch J., quoting MacKinnon L.J. in *Shirlaw v. Southern Foundries*[99] stated:

93 [1984] I.R. 1 at 14, per O'Higgins C.J.
94 [1984] I.R. 1 at 26, per McCarthy J.
95 See, *e.g.* 1.1.1 and 2.3.5.
96 *Luxor v. Cooper* [1941] A.C. 108.
97 [1967] 3 All E.R. 1064.
98 [1997] 2 I.L.R.M. 449 (S.C.).
99 [1939] 2 K.B. 206 at 227.

> "*Prima facie* that which in any contract is left to be implied and need not be expressed is something so obvious that it goes without saying: so that if while the parties were making their bargain an officious bystander were to suggest some express provisions for it in their agreement, they would testily suppress him with a common 'oh of course'."[100]

Lynch J. also quoted Lord Pearson in *Trollope v. NWMRHB*:[101]

> "An unexpressed term can be implied if and only if the court finds that the parties must have intended that term to form part of their contract: it is not enough for the court to find that such a term would have been adopted by the parties as reasonable men if it had been suggested to them: it must have been a term that went without saying, a term necessary to give business efficacy to the contract, a term which although not tacit, formed part of the contract which the parties made for themselves."[102]

2.3.4.2 Implied in law

Terms are implied in law where it is required by the Constitution, legislation, or the common law. For example, into every contract of employment the common law implies a term that the employee will not disclose confidential information;[103] and the Constitution implies a right to dis-associate.[104] Probably the most important terms implied by law, in a commercial context, arise from the Sale of Goods Act 1893 and Sale and Supply of Goods and Services Act 1980. Pursuant to this legislation, terms are implied into contracts for the sale of goods and the supply of services concerning the title of goods supplied,[105] and the quality of goods and services supplied, amongst others.[106]

2.3.4.3 Implied by usage

Lastly, a court can imply a term into a contract based on custom and usage.[107] Not every trade custom will receive judicial recognition. The trade custom must be reasonable, consistent with the express terms of the contract and universally recognised in the trade as a legally binding custom.[108]

---

100 [1997] 2 I.L.R.M.449 at 504.

101 [1973] 2 All E.R. 260 at 268 (H.L.).

102 [1997] 2 I.L.R.M. 449 at 504–505.

103 *Robb v. Green* [1895] 2 Q.B. 315.

104 *Educational Co. Ltd v. Fitzpatrick (No. 2)* [1961] I.R. 345.

105 See Chapter 12.

106 See Chapter 13 and Chapter 20.

107 Technically, a custom refers to a practice in a particular area, while a usage refers to a practice in a particular trade. Today, the terms are used interchangeably.

108 *Paxton v. Courtnay* (1860) 2 F. & F, 131; *O'Reilly v. Irish Press* (1937) I.L.T.R. 194; *O'Connaill v. The Irish Echo* [1958] 92 I.L.T.R. 156; see further 1.1.1.

2.3.5 Terms excluding or limiting liability

When two parties enter a contract they make mutual promises to perform certain duties and are legally obliged to perform their respective duties under the contract. Where a party fails to perform his duties under the contract, he may be in breach of contract and liable to the innocent party, in the form of a payment of damages. In this knowledge, parties, or more usually one party, may seek to exclude or limit their potential liability under a contract. This may be achieved using exclusion or limitation of liability terms or clauses. The same law applies to both types of clauses, often referred to as exclusion clauses.

Generally, at common law, the court will enforce an exclusion clause as long as it forms part of the contract and it is drafted to cover the situation. Between parties of equal bargaining strength, exclusion clauses allow the parties to allocate risk and plan their relationship. However, the use of exclusion clauses can be abused by a party in a stronger bargaining position, particularly where the other party is a consumer. As a result the common law developed rules to deal with widely drafted clauses. In addition, the Sale of Goods and Supply of Services Act 1980 contains special rules on the exclusion of liability for breach of the statutory implied terms, based on a distinction between commercial and consumer sales.[109] Moreover, the EC (Unfair Terms in Consumer Contracts) Regulations 1995, as amended, offer further protection for consumers from unfair terms, including exclusion clauses.[110]

2.3.5.1 Common law

Generally, at common law, a court will enforce an exclusion clause provided: (i) it is properly incorporated; and (ii) it is drafted to cover the situation.

(i) Incorporation

To be effective, the exclusion clause must form part of the contract, that is, it must be properly incorporated before the contract is concluded. The rules on incorporation of contract terms are examined above.[111] Indeed, many of these rules were developed with exclusion clauses in mind.

109 See 2.3.5.2 and 10.5.2. Similar rules apply under the Consumer Credit Act 1995 to hire-purchase and other hire contract: see Parts VI and VII of the 1995 Act.

110 See 2.3.5.3.

111 See 2.3.2.1.

(ii) Drafting

Clearly, the exclusion clause must be drafted to cover the situation which gives rise to liability in the first place. For example, an exclusion clause which provides: "In the event of liability arising for failing to supply soya beans of 'good quality,' any liability is limited to €500" may be effective where the goods supplied are not of "good quality", but it offers no protection for late delivery. A more widely drafted clause would be needed in such circumstances: for instance: "In the event of liability arising on *any grounds howsoever*, liability is limited to €500."

(iii) The *contra proferentem* rule

Where an exclusion clause is ambiguous, a court will interpret the exclusion clause against the party seeking to rely on it and in favour of the person against whom it is being enforced. This rule of interpretation is known as the *contra proferentem* rule. As a result, exclusion clauses must be drafted clearly and unambiguously. For example, an exclusion clause which provides: "The seller accepts no liability for defective delivery," is arguably ambiguous. Does "defective" refer to a defect in the goods or does "defective delivery" include late delivery? If the position is unclear, this clause will be construed against the party seeking to rely on it.

(iv) The doctrine of fundamental breach

Partly because of the fear that, in some contracts, parties were trying to exclude their liability for failure to perform even the most basic, or fundamental, terms of the contract, the courts developed the doctrine of fundamental breach. The issue is whether an exclusion clause can exclude liability for fundamental breach of contract. The courts have reacted to such clauses in two different ways by saying that:

(a) an exclusion clause can never excuse a fundamental breach, or

(b) an exclusion clause may excuse a fundamental breach depending on the construction of the clause.

In one line of English cases, the first position was preferred, but, in *Photo Production v. Securicor*,[112] the House of Lords adopted the second approach. There, the plaintiff had engaged the defendant security firm to make periodic visits during the night to its factory. An employee of the security firm on one of these visits lit a small fire which got out of hand

112 [1980] A.C. 827; see also *Suisse Atlantique* [1967] A.C. 361. See further *Western Meats Ltd v. National Ice and Cold Storage Co Ltd* [1982] I.L.R.M. 99 (H.C.).

and burnt down the factory and contents causing a loss of £615,000. The plaintiff sued, and the defendant sought to exclude its liability on the basis of a clause which provided that "under no circumstances" was the defendant

> "to be responsible for an injurious act or default by any employee ... unless the act could be foreseen and avoided by the due diligence of the defendants."

The Court of Appeal found that the defendant was in fundamental breach of contract by failing to do what in essence it had promised to do – keep safe the premises – and that an exclusion clause can never excuse such a fundamental breach. The House of Lords disagreed and found that the clause was completely clear; it covered the defendant's position and hence was effective. Therefore, under English law, there is no common law prohibition on the use of such clauses. Unfortunately, the position in Ireland is not so clear. The leading authority here is *Clayton Love v. B & I Transport*,[113] a case decided before the later English authorities setting out the above rule, which favours a stricter approach to the use of such clauses. However, its future application has been rendered uncertain by its age and the later English authority.[114]

2.3.5.2 Sale of Goods and Supply of Services Act 1980

The above rules apply to contracts in general. However, additional rules apply in particular areas. In a commercial context, the Sale of Goods and Supply of Services Act 1980 provides the most important source of such additional rules. The Sale of Goods Act 1893 and Sale of Goods and Supply of Services Act 1980 imply various terms as to title and the quality of goods and services supplied in contracts for the sale of goods and supply of services.[115] Liability for breach of some of these terms can never be excluded.[116] In other cases, liability for breach of the terms can never be excluded where the buyer deals as a consumer,[117] but otherwise "fair and reasonable" exclusion is permissible.[118] The detail of these rules is examined in Part III.

---

113 (1970) 104 I.L.T.R. 157 (S.C.).

114 See Clark, *Contract Law in Ireland* (Dublin, Round Hall Sweet & Maxwell, 4th ed., 1998) pp.157–159; and Friel, *The Law of Contract* (Dublin, Round Hall Sweet & Maxwell, 2th ed., 2000) pp.205–207.

115 See further Chapters 10, 13 and 20.

116 Liability for breach of 1893 Act, s.12, can never be excluded: 1893 Act, s.55(3), as substituted by the 1980 Act, s.22.

117 Defined in 1980 Act, s.3.

118 *E.g.* this rule applies to ss.13–15 of the 1893 Act: 1893 Act s.55(4), as substituted by the 1980 Act, s.22.

2.3.5.3 The EC (Unfair Terms in Consumer Contracts) Regulations

The Sale of Goods and Supply of Services Act 1980 regulates the exclusion of seller's liability for breach of the statutory implied terms only. All other terms in a sale of goods and a supply of services contract, whether exclusionary or not, are regulated by the common law,[119] and, in certain circumstances, by the EC (Unfair Terms in Consumer Contracts) Regulations 1995,[120] and 2000.[121]

The Regulations seek to implement the EC Directive on Unfair Terms in Consumer Contracts.[122] In essence, they seek to protect consumers from unfair contract terms. The 1995 Regulations are stated to apply to all contracts concluded after December 31, 1994.[123] Similar rules apply in all member states of the EC and decisions from other member states and the European Court of Justice will be important in interpreting the Directive and the implementing Regulations in Ireland. Under European law, the Regulations must be interpreted to give effect to the Directive,[124] and where this is not possible, the Directive, as a source of law, prevails over the Regulations.[125] Under the European doctrine of direct effect, an individual may be able to claim rights directly from the Directive against the state or any public body.[126] Further, if the state has failed to implement properly the Directive, an action may be taken in damages against the state.[127] Therefore, when advising on the Directive, as implemented in Ireland, it is vital to have a copy of the Directive, and the Regulations, at hand.

---

119 See 2.3.5.1 and 10.5.1.

120 S.I. No. 27 of 1995.

121 S.I. No.307 of 2000.

122 93/13/EEC, [1993] O.J. L95/29. For background to Directive see Duffy, "Unfair Contract Terms and the draft EC Directive" [1993] *Journal of Business Law* 67.

123 Reg. 1(2), 1995. The 1995 Regulations were adopted on February 1, 1995 and so claim to be retrospective in effect. On the issue of retrospective legislation, and other constitutional issues, see further Murphy, "The Unfair Contract Terms Regulations 1995: A red card for the State" [1995] *Irish Law Times* 156. The EC (Unfair Terms in Consumer Contracts) (Amendment) Regulations 2000 apply to contracts concluded after October 2, 2000: Reg. 1(3), 2000.

124 On the doctrine of indirect effect see *Marleasing SA v. La Comercial Internacional de Alimentación SA* (Case C106/89) [1990] E.C.R. I – 4135, [1992] 1 C.M.L.R. 305.

125 *Internationala Handelsgessellschaft* [1972] 3 C.M.L.R. 255; see also Art. 29.4.3° of the Constitution and *Doyle v. An Taoiseach* [1986] I.L.R.M. 693 (S.C.). See generally McMahon & Murphy, *European Community Law in Ireland* (Dublin, Butterworths, 1989); Lasok, *Law and Institutions of the European Union* (London, Butterworths, 7th ed., 2001).

126 On the doctrine of direct effect see *van Gend en Loos* (Case 26/62) [1963] C.M.L.R. 105.

127 See *Francovitch v. Italian State* (Cases C - 6 & 9/90) [1992] I.R.L.R. 84.

(i) Application

The Regulations apply to any term in a contract concluded between a seller of goods, or a supplier of services, and a consumer that has not been individually negotiated.[128] Hence, the Regulations are limited in their application to contracts for the sale of goods and the supply of services. Where a contract for the sale of an interest in land constitutes a sale of goods contract, the Regulations would seem to apply.[129] Contracts for the supply of services include financial services, such as insurance and investment contracts, and also come within the scope of the Regulations.

The First Schedule to the 1995 Regulations identifies contracts and terms excluded from the scope of the Regulations.[130] The excluded contracts are:

(a) contracts of employment;
(b) contracts relating to succession rights;
(c) contracts relating to rights under family law;
(d) contracts relating to the incorporation and organisation of companies or partnerships.

The excluded terms are any terms which reflect:

(a) mandatory, statutory, or regulatory provisions of Irish law;
(b) the provisions or principles of international conventions to which the member states or the Community are members.

This provision seeks to ensure that terms prescribed by law should not be considered unfair. Here, the assumption is that such provisions would not include any unfair terms.

A seller or supplier is defined as any person (natural or legal) who is acting for purposes related to his business. The phrase "for purposes related to his business"[131] would seem wider than the phrase "in the course of his business" used in the definition of "dealing as a consumer" in section 3 of the 1980 Act and in section 14 of the 1893 Act. However, "in the

128 Reg. 3, 1995; see also Arts 1 and 2, and the Recitals to the Directive.

129 See 9.2.5.

130 See Directive, Art. 1(2) and Recital 10.

131 Directive, Art. 2(c); Reg. 2, 1995. "Business" is further defined as including a trade, profession and the activities of any government department or local or public authority: Reg. 2, 1995.

course of a business" has been interpreted widely in Irish case law[132] and, in practice, there may be little or no difference between these two phrases. A consumer is defined as a natural person who is acting for purposes which are outside his business.[133] "Natural person" could include a sole trader or a partner, but clearly excludes any incorporated body.[134] This is narrower than the Irish definition of "dealing as a consumer" which is not expressly limited to natural persons. Although, again following Irish case law on the point,[135] it is difficult to envisage any person who is engaged in a business activity acting as "a consumer" as defined.

A term will always be regarded as having not been individually negotiated where it is drafted in advance and therefore the consumer has had no possibility to influence the term. Pre-formulated standard contracts are identified in particular in this context.[136] But there is no requirement that the contract as a whole be on standard terms. The Regulations apply to individual terms and expressly provide that the fact that a specific term has been individually negotiated does not preclude the application of the Regulations to the rest of the contract if an overall assessment indicates that it is a pre-formulated standard contract.[137] The burden of proving that a term was individually negotiated is on the seller/supplier.[138]

(ii) Content

The Regulations seek to control terms in contracts between sellers/suppliers and consumers in two ways, under the headings: (i) plain language, and (ii) unfair terms.

The Regulations require that in cases where all or certain terms offered to the consumer are in writing, the seller/supplier has an obligation to ensure that the terms are drafted in plain, intelligible language.[139] This provision raises a number of difficulties. It is not clear whether the requirement of plain, intelligible language is subjective or objective. It appears that this requirement applies to all terms and not just those which are not individually negotiated. Further, no sanction is provided for breach of this requirement in the Directive or Regulations, but where a non-negotiated term is not drafted in plain and intelligible language, it may be

132 In *re Henry O'Callaghan v. Hamilton Leasing (Ireland) Ltd and Access Refrigeration and Shop Fitting Ltd* [1984] I.L.R.M. 146; and *Cunningham v. Woodchester Investments and Inter-call Ltd*, unreported, High Court, Mc William J., November 16, 1984: see 10.5.2.1.

133 Directive, Art. 2(b); Reg. 2, 1995.

134 Cases C-541/99 and C-541/99, *Cape Snc v. Idealservice Srl*, and *Idealservice MN RE Sas v. OMAI Srl*.

135 *Supra*, note 132.

136 Directive, Art. 3(2); Reg. 3(4), 1995.

137 Directive, Art. 3(2); Reg. 3(5), 1995.

138 Directive, Art. 3(2); Reg. 3(6), 1995.

139 Directive, Art. 5; Reg. 5(1), 1995.

unfair. The Regulations also confirm the *contra proferentem* rule by providing that where there is doubt as to the meaning of a term, the interpretation most favourable to the consumer prevails.[140]

Most significantly, the Regulations provide that an *unfair term* in a contract concluded with a consumer by a seller or supplier shall not be binding on the consumer.[141] Hence, an unfair term is voidable, at the option of the consumer. Under the Regulations, a term is unfair if, contrary to the requirement of *good faith*, it causes significant imbalance of the parties' rights and obligations to the detriment of the consumer.[142] Further, under the Regulations, this assessment should take into account the nature of the goods or services and all the circumstances attending the conclusion of the contract and all other terms of the contract or of another contract on which it is dependent.[143]

It seems therefore that assessing fairness is a three-step process. First, you consider the balance of the parties' obligations under the contract. A term will only be unfair where it causes a *significant imbalance* in favour of the seller/supplier. So, for example, any term which gives significant rights to the seller/supplier without giving corresponding rights to the consumer may be unfair. Second, the imbalance must be "to the detriment of the consumer", and, third, the detriment must be contrary to the requirement of *good faith*. Some commentators argue that a term which causes a significant imbalance to the detriment of the consumer is necessarily "contrary to good faith". However, the House of Lords in *Director General of Fair Trading v. First National Bank*[144] took a different view, finding that a term will not be unfair merely because it causes an imbalance between the parties: the imbalance must also be contrary to the requirement of good faith.

To assist in determining whether a term satisfies the good faith requirement or not, the Second Schedule to the 1995 Regulations sets out guidelines,[145] similar to the fair and reasonable test under the Sale of Goods and Supply of Services Act 1980. Accordingly, when making an assessment of good faith, particular regard should be had to:

(a) the strength of the bargaining position of the parties;
(b) whether the consumer had an inducement to agree to the term;
(c) whether the goods or services were sold to the special order of the consumer; and

140 Directive, Art. 5; Reg. 5(2); see also Reg. 5(3), inserted by the 2000 Regulations.
141 Directive, Art. 6; Reg. 6, 1995; the remainder of the contract can continue to bind the parties provided the offending term can be severed.
142 Directive, Art. 3; Reg. 3(2), 1995.
143 Directive, Art. 4; Reg. 3(2), 1995.
144 [2001] 3 W.L.R. 1297.
145 Directive, Recital 16.

(d) the extent to which the consumer was treated fairly and equitably by the seller/supplier.

But a term shall not, of itself, be considered unfair by relation to the definition of the main subject matter of the contract, or to the adequacy of the price and remuneration under the contract, in so far as these terms are in plain, intelligible language.[146] It would seem that this provision is intended to prevent the courts making an assessment of the bargain itself (for example, was a fair price paid by the consumer for the goods or services), although price, for instance, is a factor which could be considered in making an assessment of fairness under Regulation 3(2). The House of Lords, in *Director-General of Fair Trading v. First National Bank*, has indicated that this provision should be given a narrow interpretation so as not to undermine the purpose of the Directive. The term in question was to be found in a standard loan agreement between the bank and a consumer. Clause 8 provided that should the borrower default on his repayments, interest was to be charged until payment, even after judgment. The House of Lords held that this term was not a "core term" of the contract and hence was subject to the fairness test. It further held that the term was fair.

The Third Schedule to the 1995 Regulations sets out an indicative, though not an exhaustive, list of terms which may be regarded as unfair.[147] This includes terms that have the object or effect of:

- excluding or limiting liability for death or personal injury by the consumer resulting from the act or omission of the seller/supplier;
- inappropriately excluding or limiting the legal rights of the consumer against the seller/supplier or other party regarding total or partial non-performance or inadequate performance by the seller/supplier of any obligations under the contract;[148]
- requiring any consumer who fails to fulfill his obligation to pay a disproportionately high sum in compensation;
- authorising the seller/supplier to terminate the contract on a discretionary basis where the consumer does not have the same right;
- excluding or hindering the consumer's right to take legal action or exercise any other legal remedy, particularly by requiring the consumer to take disputes exclusively to

146 Directive, Art. 4(2); Reg. 4, 1995.

147 Directive, Annex.

148 For example, including the option of setting-off a debt owed to the seller/supplier against any claim which the consumer may have against him.

> arbitration not covered by legal provisions, unduly restricting the evidence available to him or imposing on him a burden of proof which, according to the applicable law, should lie with another party to the contract.

This last term was the subject of a case before the European Court of Justice, *Océano Group Editorial SA v. Quintero & Ors*.[149] The defendants, all resident in Spain, had contracted to buy encyclopedias for private use from the plaintiff. The contracts contained a standard form jurisdiction clause in favour of the supplier's local forum, Barcelona, where none of the defendants were domiciled. It was held that this clause was unfair because, in terms of cost and convenience, it favoured the position of the supplier over that of the consumer. It should be noted that, in this case, it was enough that the defendants were required to litigate in the courts of a city where they were not domiciled although still in the country of their domicile. A similar outcome is even more likely where a consumer is required to litigate in a foreign country, in a foreign language, where the amount at stake is small thereby making it impractical to pursue a claim.

(iii) Enforcement

Where a term is unfair it is not binding on the consumer and so cannot be relied upon in any dispute resolution proceedings against the consumer.[150] The remainder of the contract can continue to bind the parties provided the offending term can be severed.[151] In many cases consumers are ignorant of their rights or they may lack the resources to enforce their rights. The Directive requires member states to ensure the protection of consumer interests by giving enforcement powers to "persons or organisations having a legitimate interest under national law in protecting consumers."[152] Accordingly, under the 1995 Regulations, the Director of Consumer Affairs,[153] and under the 2000 Regulations other "consumer organisations,"

149 (Joined Cases C-240/98 to C-244/98) [2000] I E.C.R. 4941; see also *Standard Bank London Ltd v. Apostolakis and another* [2001] Lloyd's Rep. Bank 240. See further Withers, "Jurisdiction clauses and the Unfair Terms in Consumer Contracts Regulations" [2002] *Lloyd's Maritime and Commercial Law Quarterly* 56.

150 Directive, Art. 6(1); Reg. 6(1), 1995.

151 Directive, Art. 6(1); Reg. 6(2), 1995.

152 Directive, Art. 7.

153 See Annual Reports of Director of Consumer Affairs for activities in this area. The types of contract which have been reviewed by the Director include insurance contracts, contracts with public utility companies (including mobile phone companies), airlines, car hires companies, ferry companies, house alarm contracts, and more recently, house building contracts. See further www.odca.ie for recent Annual Reports.

are given enforcement powers. The Director and other consumer organisations can obtain an order from the High Court prohibiting the use or continued use of any term adjudged unfair.[154] While there is no reported Irish case regarding the Directive and Regulations, the Director of Consumer Affairs has obtained from the High Court, on December 20, 2001, a declaratory order that 15 specified terms in standard form building contracts were unfair pursuant to the Directive and Regulations.[155] Where an injunction is granted against a business, it could have a detrimental effect, causing the business to cease using their standard terms, requiring new terms to be drafted and leading to bad publicity for the business.

2.3.6 The parol evidence rule

Generally, under the parol evidence rule, where a contract is reduced to writing, neither party can rely on evidence extrinsic to the written contract, whether oral or written, to add to or vary the terms of the written contract. The rationale for the rule is to promote certainty. It is assumed that where parties have gone to the trouble of reducing their agreement to writing, the written document represents fully their agreement and that the parties intend their relations to be governed by that written document and by it alone. The rule is, however, subject to many refinements and exceptions. For example, the rule only relates to evidence as to the *content* of a contract: it does not apply where evidence is introduced to show that the contract is not properly formed. Further, the rule only prevents a party relying on extrinsic evidence as to the *express* terms of a contract: intrinsic evidence can be introduced to show that the term ought to be implied.

2.4 The Discharge of Contractual Obligations

The obligations of the parties under a contract can be discharged, or brought to an end, in a number of ways:

- (i) by consent of the parties;
- (ii) by performance;
- (iii) under the doctrine of frustration; and
- (iv) sometimes, following a breach of contract.

2.4.1 Consent

Because the formation of a contract is based on the consent of the parties,

---

154 Reg. 8, 1995; see further Reg. 10, 1995 on investigation powers.

155 See www.lawsociety.ie/Buildagreements.htm See further Dorgan, "Safe as Houses" [2002] *Law Society Gazette* 12; Breslin, "What makes a term in a standard form contract unfair?" [2002] *Bar Review* 131.

parties are of course free to agree to terminate a contract, before or during performance, by mutual consent. However, as with formation of a contract, consideration is required. This is usually not a problem where both sides agree to terminate the contract when both still have obligations to perform: mutual promises represent sufficient consideration for each other. But where only one party is discharged, that party must supply some further consideration.[156]

2.4.2 Performance

Where parties perform their duties in accordance with the terms of the contract, their contractual duties are said to be discharged, or ended. However, performance must meet exactly with the terms of the contract, and where performance is less than is required by the contract, this can amount to a breach of contract. An illustration of this rule can be found in *Re Moore v. Landauer*,[157] where a sales contract required that tins were to be packed and delivered in cases of 30 tins. The correct total of tins was delivered but some cases contained only 24 tins. This was held to be a repudiatory breach of contract and the buyer did not have to pay or accept the goods.

Insignificant deviations from the terms of the contract may be allowed under the *de minimis* exception. What amounts to "insignificant" depends on each particular case. In *Wilensko v. Fenwick*,[158] sellers sold timber of specified measurements to the buyers. Just under one per cent of the timber failed to meet the exact specification and this was held to be a breach of contract. In contrast, in *Shipton Anderson & Co v. Weil Bros*,[159] where there was a contract for the sale of not more than 4,950 tons of wheat, an extra 55 pounds was delivered, an excess of 0.0005 per cent. The court found that this excess was so slight that the buyer could not argue that the seller had failed to perform his obligation under the contract. In commercial contracts, it seems likely that the *de minimis* exception will be narrowly construed, that is, only very slight variations will be allowed. To avoid this problem, an express term is often included in a commercial contract to allow for minor variations in performance. For example, in a contract to sell 10,000 tons of wheat, it would be advisable to include a term saying that the amount to be delivered is "in or about 10,000 tons" or "10,000 plus or minus a two per cent variation". In practice, most business persons would not seek to terminate a contract for slight variations; they would rather deal with a lesser, or excess, delivery by adjusting the contract price.

156 See variation of contract 2.2.2.1(iv).
157 [1921] 2 K.B. 519.
158 [1938] 3 All E.R. 429.
159 [1912] 1 K.B. 574.

2.4.3 The doctrine of frustration

Under this doctrine, the parties' obligations under a contract may be discharged by operation of the law.

2.4.3.1 Grounds for frustration

A contract is said to be frustrated where:

(i) it becomes impossible to perform the contract;
(ii) the purpose of the contract is not achievable; or
(iii) performance becomes illegal.

(i) Impossibility of performance

The occurrence of certain events between the time of the making of the contract and the performance of the contract can lead to the contract being frustrated. For instance, where the subject-matter of the contract is destroyed, the contract may be frustrated. In *Asfar v. Blundel*,[160] there was a contract for the sale of dates. The dates were on a barge which sank and were impregnated with river water and sewage. Physically the dates still existed, they were recovered from the river and could be used to distill alcohol. However, in a commercial sense, the dates – the subject-matter of the contract – were destroyed or perished, and hence the contract was frustrated. Equally, where a contract places a personal duty on a party, the death of that party may frustrate the contract.

The doctrine of frustration only relieves the parties from their respective obligations under the contract where the performance of the contract is impossible not merely impracticable. *Neville & Sons v. Guardian Builders Ltd*[161] illustrates this point. The defendant entered into a contract with the plaintiff whereby the plaintiff was to build houses on the defendant's land. A term of this agreement required the defendant to give the plaintiff permission (a licence) to enter the land. However, the defendant's land was landlocked and it had no access to a nearby road. The defendant sought to gain the necessary access by purchasing adjoining land owned by the county council. There were delays in buying the adjoining land, because the county council wanted to impose conditions on the sale to which the defendant would not agree. The plaintiff grew impatient and sought an order for specific performance. The plaintiff argued, in its defence, that the contract was frustrated. The Supreme Court stated that frustration of a contract takes place when a supervening event occurs without the default of either party and for which the contract makes no sufficient provision. Further, the frustrating event must so significantly

160 [1896] 1 Q.B. 123.
161 [1995] I.L.R.M. 1.

change the nature of the outstanding contractual rights and obligations from what the parties could reasonably have contemplated at the time of the contract's execution that it would be unjust to hold them to its stipulations in the new circumstances. In such a case, the parties are discharged from further performance of the contract and the court has the power to declare the contract at an end. On the facts, the court found that if the defendant had purchased the county council land, the building could start. However, the county council had insisted on certain conditions to the sale and the defendant was not happy to contract on those terms. This, according to the Supreme Court, should not be classified as a supervening event which significantly changes the nature of the outstanding contractual rights and obligations. The performance of the contract had become more onerous but was not frustrated. It is essential that the frustrating events are outside the control of the parties; you cannot have self-induced frustration.[162] In the *Neville* case, getting ownership of the county council land to give effect to the licence with the plaintiff was not outside the control of the defendant, and hence the contract was not frustrated.

(ii) Purpose frustrated

This is a narrow ground which is based on a series of cases involving the hiring of rooms to view the coronation of King Edward VII. Due to illness, the coronation was postponed. The rooms were still available but there was nothing to view and so the contracts were frustrated. Other cases illustrate the limits of this ground. For instance, where a property has been bought for redevelopment and it turns out that redevelopment cannot happen, or becomes more difficult, because the property is "listed," this has been held not to amount to frustration.[163] Also, a sales contract to export or import goods is not frustrated where there are export or import restrictions.[164] Moreover, the doctrine of frustration cannot be used to avoid a bad bargain.

(iii) Illegality

Where the performance of a contract becomes illegal, such as where a trade embargo is imposed after the contract is made, it is frustrated.

2.4.3.2 Effect of frustration

The effect of frustration is that the contract ends automatically, and the parties are discharged from all future obligations. In *Kearney v. Saorstat & Continental Shipping*,[165] the plaintiff's contract of employment ended when

162 *Herman v. Owners of SS Vicia* [1942] I.R. 304.
163 *AIP v. Walker* [1976] 3 All E.R. 509.
164 *CCGCIE v. Tradax* [1983] 1 Lloyd's Rep 250.
165 (1943) Ir. Jur. Rep. 8.

his ship sank. When he later died, his wife was unable to benefit from workman's compensation insurance which was dependent on the continued existence of an employment contract. Any obligations arising before the frustrating event are still effective in law.

It is said that the doctrine of frustration takes an all-or-nothing approach. There is no middle ground. Because of this strict rule, business persons often include express terms in their contracts specifying the effect of a supervening event. Conversely, the contract may provide that the contract will come to an end on the happening of certain events, whether or not these events would amount to frustration. Such clauses are referred to as *force majeur* clauses.

2.4.4 Breach of contract

A breach of contract does not discharge the contract, or either party. But, a breach may entitle the innocent party to terminate the contract and thus treat himself as discharged from his outstanding contractual obligations.

2.4.4.1 Actual and anticipatory breach

A contract is actually breached when the time for performance has arrived and

(i) there is a total failure to perform by a party, or
(ii) although there has been an attempt to perform, this does not comply with the exact terms of the contract.

There is a third type of breach: anticipatory breach. Here, a party, before the time for performance arrives, indicates that he will not perform his obligations under the contract. The innocent party has two options in the case of anticipatory breach. He can:

(i) accept the breach and thereby bring to an end the contract and sue for damages, or
(ii) not accept the breach, and continue to press for performance and so the contract is kept alive until the date of performance. If it is then actually breached, a claim for damages arises.

2.4.4.2 Strict liability

Generally, where a party does not do what he is required to do under the terms of the contract, his failure to properly perform is sufficient to establish liability. Liability is strict; it is not dependent on fault. However, in some areas, contractual liability is based on fault, such as with contracts for the supply of services under section 39(b) of the Sale of Goods and Supply of Services Act 1980.[166]

2.4.4.3 Remedies

Where a party fails to perform his contractual obligations, without lawful excuse, there is a breach of contract. There are a number of remedies available for a breach of contract including termination, damages, and specific performance.

(i) Termination

Breach of a term of the contract does not necessarily terminate the contract. Only where there has been a breach of a fundamental term or a condition, for example, is the innocent party entitled to treat the breach as a repudiation of the contract and terminate the contract.[167] The innocent party can accept or reject that repudiation. Where he accepts the repudiation, the contract is terminated and the parties' outstanding obligations under the contract are discharged. Or, the innocent party can choose to affirm the contract and pursue a claim in damages only. Where a warranty has been breached, the remedy is damages only. The parties are not discharged from their obligations under the contract: the contract continues.

(ii) Damages

Despite the principle *pacta sunt servante* (the sanctity of the bargain), where one party fails to perform his obligations under a contract the courts will rarely force performance. The common contract law remedy is damages, not an order for specific performance. Damages are available for every breach of contract whether the term breached is fundamental, a condition, an innominate term or a warranty. This contrasts with the discretionary nature of an order for specific performance.

(a) The compensation principle: An award of damages seeks to compensate the innocent party. It is said that the purpose of damages, in contract law, is to put the innocent party in the position he would have been in had the contract been performed. Following on from this compensation principle, a number of observations can be made. First, because damages are supposed to compensate, they are only payable where a party has suffered a loss. If no loss is suffered, the court may recognise that a legal

166 See 20.3.2.

167 See, *e.g. Athlone R.D.C. v. Campbell (No. 2)* (1913) 47 I.L.T.R. 142, *Dundalk Shopping Centre v. Roof Spray Ltd* [1990] I.L.R.M. 377.

right has been breached but because there is no loss, there is no need for compensation and so nominal damages – for example €1 – may be awarded. Second, the purpose of damages in contract law is to compensate the innocent party and not to punish the breaker of the contract, and so punitive damages are not available in contract law.

(b) Types of loss: Following a breach of contract, an innocent party can be compensated for physical injury; property damage; and more commonly in a commercial context, financial loss. Moreover, an innocent party can be compensated for his loss of expectation (sometimes referred to as loss of bargain); his reliance loss, and any consequential loss.

(c) Causation: A plaintiff can only recover damages if there is a causal link between the breach of contract and his loss. Where the loss is not caused by the breach of contract, no damages are available.

(d) Remoteness: When a contract is breached, a series of events can occur which cause the plaintiff loss. However, a defendant is not liable for every event which follows from a breach of contract. It is said that where the loss is too remote, or too far away from the breach, the defendant will not be liable. The rationale for this rule is that it would not be fair to make a defendant liable for every loss following a breach. If a defendant was liable for every last loss, then defendants in general might be reluctant to enter contracts, or would only enter contracts where they would charge a higher price to cover the possibility of being held liable for all losses.

The leading authority on contractual remoteness is *Hadley v. Baxendale.*[168] In that case, the plaintiff ran a mill. The shaft in the mill broke and had to be sent to the makers in Greenwich as a model for a new shaft. The defendant agreed to carry the shaft to Greenwich but in breach of contract, delayed its delivery for a few days, leaving the mill idle. The legal issue was whether the defendant should be liable for lost profits that resulted from the mill being idle because of the delay in delivery. The court held that this loss was too remote and it laid down the following test:

(a) the loss must arise *naturally* from the breach; and
(b) the loss must be such that it might reasonably be in the minds of the parties at the time they made the contract as the probable result of the breach.

In *Hadley v. Baxendale*, it appears that the defendant did not know that the mill would be kept idle until the new shaft arrived.

168 (1854) 9 Ex. 341.

(e) Mitigation: Where there has been a breach of contract, there is a duty placed on the innocent party to mitigate, or minimise, his loss. Where an innocent party pursues a claim for damages and the court finds that he has failed to take all reasonable steps to mitigate his loss, his damages will be reduced by an amount to arrive at a quantum, an amount, of damages as if he had mitigated his loss. For example, where a buyer of goods breaches a contract and there is a falling market, it is important that a seller of goods does not delay in trying to sell his goods, thereby increasing the value of his claim against the buyer. A seller is not required to act immediately. He is allowed time to assess the market and decide what is best to do, but the longer he delays, the more likely the court may find that he has failed to mitigate his loss. The converse rule applies to buyers.[169] Where a seller of goods breaches a contract by not delivering the goods, the buyer must at some reasonable point after the breach regard the contract as at an end and seek to mitigate his loss by purchasing substitute goods elsewhere. Again, where the market price of the goods is rising, the buyer cannot afford to delay.

(f) Measure of damages: The measure of damages, or the *quantum*, is the actual amount of money payable. Where the claim is for *expectation loss*, the measure is the difference in value between the performance rendered and the performance actually contracted for, or the cost of remedying the defective performance and bringing it up to the contractual standard. Where the claim is for *reliance loss*, the measure of damages is the cost of the action (inaction) on reliance on the contract.

(g) Time of assessment: The general rule is that the time you assess the amount of damages is the date of the breach. However, an innocent party is usually given some time after the breach to assess the position and decide what is best to do (in order to mitigate, for instance), and so damages are then assessed at the end of that time, rather than the day of the breach. At other times, the innocent party will not learn of the breach until days, or weeks, after it has occurred. In such circumstances, damages are assessed when the innocent party knew or should have known of the breach.

(h) Penalty clauses and liquidated damages clauses: The above rules, especially on remoteness and the measure of damages, can make it very difficult to predict what damages may be payable following a breach of contract. To avoid such uncertainty, commercial contracts often contain a clause providing that a fixed sum is payable on breach of contract: a "liquidated damages clause". Where the clause represents a reasonable

169 *Cullen v. Horgan* [1925] 2 I.R. 1.

pre-estimate of the loss, it will be enforced, but where the clause is excessive and acts as a sort of deterrent against breach, then it is called a "penalty clause" and the courts will not give effect to it. The leading authority for distinguishing the two is *Dunlop v. New Garage & Motor*,[170] where a four-stage test was established, the most important element being that a sum is a penalty where it is extravagant when compared with the greatest loss that could conceivably follow the breach.

In *Irish Telephone Rentals Ltd v. Irish Civil Service Building Society*,[171] the plaintiff was in the business of hiring out telephone equipment, particularly to large commercial enterprises. Under the rental contract, where a subscriber repudiated a rental contract, the subscriber was required to pay all accrued charges, all remaining rental due under the contract, but variable discounts were given for any rentals received immediately. The court found this excessive and said that the amount payable did not reflect the resulting loss. The above formula was said not even to attempt to assess the loss in a methodical way.

(iii) Specific Performance

An order for specific performance is only available where damages would not be sufficient to compensate the party. In most commercial contracts, damages will be sufficient compensation and hence specific performance has limited application in commercial dealings. Damages might not be sufficient compensation where there was a contract to sell unique goods,[172] for example. As noted above, there is no right to specific performance; the court has a discretion whether to grant it or not.

---

170 [1915] A.C. 79.

171 [1992] 2 I.R. 525; see also *O'Donnell & Co Ltd v. Truck and Machinery Sales Ltd*, unreported, Supreme Court, April 1, 1998.

172 See 14.5.

CHAPTER 3

ASPECTS OF PROPERTY LAW

3.1 INTRODUCTION

Much of commercial law involves the transfer of or dealing in property, whether through a contract for the sale of goods, the issue and transfer of negotiable instruments, or a grant of a licence to use a trade-mark. The purpose of this chapter is to introduce briefly the main types of property, some of the main concepts of property law including ownership and possession, and to consider how such rights can be transferred or otherwise dealt with, as under an attornment or a bailment.[1]

3.2 TYPES OF PROPERTY

All property can be classified as real or personal. Real property includes land and anything permanently attached to the land, such as buildings.[2] Personal property is all property except real property. Commercial law relates principally to personal property law, but land law cannot be excluded altogether. Commercial finance is often secured on land by a mortgage or charge, for instance.

Personal property is divided into two categories: chattels real (mainly leasehold interests in land)[3] and chattels personal (items which are not chattels real). Chattels personal sub-divide broadly into two classes: tangibles moveables (or choses in possession, such as goods or money) and intangibles moveables (or choses in action).[4] Intangible moveables comprise legal rights which have no tangible form in themselves, though they may be represented in the form of a document (documentary intangibles, such as bills of lading, and negotiable instruments). Documentary intangibles are notable because the document represents the

---

1 See further Sealy & Hooley, *Commercial Law: Text, Cases and Materials* (London, Butterworths, 2nd ed., 1999) Chapter 2; Goode, *Commercial Law* (London, Penguin, 2nd ed., 1995) Chapter 2. See generally, Bridge, *Personal Property Law* (London, Blackstone, 3rd ed., 2002); and Bell, *Modern Law of Personal Property in Ireland and England* (London, Butterworths, 1989).

2 See generally Lyall, *Land Law in Ireland* (Dublin, Round Hall Sweet & Maxwell, 2nd ed., 2000); Pearse & Mee, *Land Law* (Dublin, Round Hall Sweet & Maxwell, 2nd ed., 2000) and Wylie, *Irish Land Law* (Dublin, Butterworths, 3rd ed., 1997).

3 See generally, Wylie, *Landlord and Tenant Law* (Dublin, Butterworths, 2nd ed., 1998).

4 See *Colonial Bank v. Whinney* (1885) 30 Ch. D. 261 at 285, per Fry L.J.

property rights which can be transferred by transfer of the document itself. Rights which are not documentary intangibles are called pure intangibles (for example, debts, copyright and goodwill).

As Professor Goode has noted, when the differences between land and personal property are explored, it becomes apparent why the law treats the two types of property differently.[5] Land is considered immovable and permanent. For these reasons, it is susceptible to restrictions on transfer or use, such as are found in restrictive covenants and planning legislation, and its permanence facilitates the creation of multiple interests of long duration (for example, 999-year leases and life interests). As a result, the investigation of title in land and its transfer can be prolonged and complex. The unique character of land means that if a contract for the sale of land is not performed, the purchaser cannot usually be adequately compensated by an award of damages; an order of specific performance may be granted. In contrast, personal property is moveable, and more easily transferable. It tends to be of a shorter duration: for instance, goods may perish or be consumed; patents expire with the passage of time. Personal property is not usually unique: goods may be indistinguishable from other goods of the same class. Where under a contract for the sale of goods, the goods are not delivered, an award of damages will usually compensate the buyer. Orders for specific performance of sale of goods contracts are rare.[6]

The common law recognises two types of property rights over personal property: ownership, and possession of a limited interest. Each is examined below. All other rights exist in equity, such as the rights of a beneficiary under a trust or mere charges. All equitable proprietary rights suffer the same weakness: they can be overridden by a bona fide purchaser of the legal estate without notice of the equitable interest.[7]

3.3 Ownership

Honoré defines ownership "as the greatest possible interest in a thing which a mature system of law recognises."[8] Ownership is a bundle of rights and obligations including: "the right to possess; the right to use; the right to manage; the right to the income of the thing; the right to the capital, the right to security, the rights or incidents of transmissibility and absense of term, the prohibition of harmful use, liability to execution, and the incident of residuarity."[9] A person may be described as the owner of a thing and not

5 Goode, *Commercial Law* (London, Penguin, 2nd ed., 1995) pp.33–35.

6 See generally, Chapter 14.

7 See generally, Delany, *Equity and the Law of Trusts in Ireland* (Dublin, Round Hall Sweet & Maxwell, 2nd ed., 1999) pp.44–48.

8 Honoré, "Ownership" in Guest, ed., *Oxford Essays in Jurisprudence* (Oxford, Oxford University Press, 1961) p.107 at 108.

9 *Ibid.* at p.113. Cf. Eleftheriadis, "An Analysis of Property Rights" (1996) *Oxford Journal of Legal Studies* 31.

have all the above incidents of ownership. Where a person has the greatest possible interest in a thing, he may be described as the owner even though he has granted a lesser interest or interests to others. Where goods are leased for instance, ownership remains with the lessor while a lesser right to possession, for the term of the lease, is granted to the lessee.

3.3.1 Importance of ownership

Within the context of the sale of goods, for instance, ownership plays a pivotal role in a number of areas. It is generally assumed that the risk of accidental loss rests with the owner of goods, whether he is the seller or the buyer.[10] Ownership and the passing of property may be relevant also as to whether an unpaid seller can sue a buyer for the price of the goods.[11] More generally, the main significance of ownership is that it survives the insolvency of the person against whom it is asserted. For instance, if O's goods are stolen or wrongly detained by B, who becomes bankrupt, O can recover the goods from B's assignee in bankruptcy. The goods do not form part of B's estate on bankruptcy, and are therefore not available for distribution to B's creditors. Equally, where an unpaid seller of goods retains ownership in the goods, using a retention of title clause, the seller is entitled to reclaim the goods on the buyer's insolvency.[12]

3.3.2 Legal and equitable ownership

Ownership of personal property may be legal or equitable. Legal and equitable ownership may vest in the one person, or legal ownership may be vested in one person while equitable ownership may be vested in another, as where legal ownership to goods is held by a trustee on behalf of the beneficiary who has equitable ownership.[13]

Based on the concept of indivisibility of ownership, the common law did not recognise that legal title could be split between one person and another. Hence, the common law did not recognise the trust. Where property was conveyed to A upon trust for B, the common law regarded A as the legal owner and ignored the condition that A was to hold the property for B. This rigid rule was modified by equity which gave effect to the trust by insisting that A honour the condition upon which the property was conveyed to him. Hence, equitable ownership involves split ownership: with legal title vesting in A and beneficial ownership in B, thereby creating the relationship of trustee and beneficiary.

10 Sale of Goods Act 1893, s.20: see further Chapter 18.

11 Sale of Goods Act 1893, s.49: see further 15.2.1.

12 See 15.4.

13 See generally, Delany, *Equity and the Law of Trusts in Ireland* (Dublin, Round Hall Sweet & Maxwell, 2nd ed., 1999) Chapter 3.

3.3.3 Interest and title

A person's interest in property comprises the quantum of rights that person has over that property in relation to other persons. For instance, the owner of goods can be described as having an absolute interest in the goods, whereas a person who enjoys a specific right over goods, such as where a person has possession under a pledge or bailment, has only a *limited* interest.[14]

Interest can be distinguished from title. A person's title is a measure of the strength of that interest in relation to others. For example, if O is the owner of goods but T has taken possession of the goods, both are considered to have title to the absolute interest in the goods. O, as true owner, has the best title. T's *possessory* title is subordinate to O's, but is effective against all others not claiming under O's title or authority.[15]

3.3.4 Co-ownership

It is said that ownership of personal property is indivisible in the sense that legal title to an interest in a chattel can only be held or transferred entire. This contrasts with the position regarding land, where smaller legal titles can be carved out of a larger title. While a smaller legal title to a chattel cannot be carved out of it, there is nothing to prevent two or more persons from owning a chattel together as joint tenants or as tenants in common.[16] If two owners are joint tenants and one of them dies, the deceased's share passes automatically to the other by survivorship. In contrast, if two owners are tenants in common, the deceased's share forms part of his estate and passes under his will or on intestacy and not by way of survivorship to the other co-tenant.

Claims to co-ownership are a regular occurrence in commercial transactions. Particular problems can arise where one person holds a pool of assets to meet contractual claims of several others. For example, what is the position where two or more persons contract to buy goods forming part of a larger bulk in a store or warehouse and the seller becomes insolvent before delivery? This raises the fundamental difference between real and personal rights. The buyers may have a personal action against the seller, based on the sales contract, for failure to deliver. But where the seller is insolvent, this personal claim may be effectively worthless. A pre-paying buyer's position is best protected where the buyer can claim real or proprietary rights over the goods themselves. A buyer can claim a real or proprietary interest where he can show that the goods were "ascertained"

14 See, *e.g.* the Sale of Goods Act 1893, which refers to "the general property" and "a special property," the latter referring to a limited right to goods: s.62.

15 On conflicts of title to goods, see Chapter 19.

16 See, *e.g.* Sale of Goods Act 1893, s.1(1) on the co-ownership of goods.

and "appropriated" to each buyer individually or to them all collectively, as co-owners.[17]

3.3.5 Acquisition and transfer of legal and equitable ownership

Legal ownership can be acquired by a number of means: for instance, by taking possession of a thing which does not have an existing owner, such as a wild animal,[18] or by operation of the law on death or on insolvency.[19] In the commercial context, ownership is more usually acquired by creating or manufacturing a new thing, or by the consensual transfer of a thing by the existing owner. Generally, the manufacturer is considered the owner of the new thing, although the position is complicated where goods supplied to manufacture the new thing are supplied by another person subject to a reservation of title clause.[20] Consensual transfer may be by gift but more commonly is by sale for money consideration. At common law, there are strict rules governing the transfer of ownership in personal property. For example, the transferor must have legal title or the power to pass legal title,[21] and the transfer must be effected by the delivery of possession, or a grant by deed in the case of a gift, or otherwise by word of mouth.[22]

Equitable ownership may be acquired by a variety of means. For instance, by a transfer from someone who holds merely an equitable title; by an agreement to transfer legal or equitable ownership; by a defective transfer of legal ownership, or by a declaration of trust. In contrast to land, an agreement to sell goods is a mere executory contract and no property rights are created as a result.[23] The only way in which an outright disposition of goods can be effected in equity is by a declaration of trust. It should be noted that legal and equitable ownership can be transferred outright or by way of security.[24]

3.4 Possession

Possession is a legal concept, it has no equivalent in equity. Where a person agrees to hand over possession, no property rights are created in

---

17 See further 17.4.

18 There is no absolute property in wild animals and so they are not goods, though a qualified property can be obtained in them by lawfully taking them into possession. At this point, it appears that they can be bought and sold as goods: see *Kearry v. Pattinson* [1939] 1 K.B. 471; and *Hamps v. Derby* [1948] 2 K.B. 311. On the meaning of "goods", see 9.2.5.

19 Succession Act 1965; Bankruptcy Act 1988; Companies Acts 1963–2001.

20 See Webb, "Title and Transformation: Who Owns Manufactured Goods" [2000] *Journal of Business Law* 513; see further 15.4.

21 Re sale of goods, see Chapter 12.

22 *Flory v. Denny* (1852) 7 Exch. 581.

23 *Re Wait* [1927] 1 Ch. 606.

24 On security over personal property, see generally, Part IV.

law or in equity. The only remedy for failure to deliver under a contract would be for breach of contract. Further, possession is only relevant to chattels which are capable of physical possession, such as goods, money and documentary intangibles. Pure intangibles cannot be physically possessed.

3.4.1 Importance of possession

Possession is significant for a number of reasons. First, possession is *prima facie* evidence of ownership.[25] Second, possession may be relevant to the transfer of legal ownership, for example, as with a gift. Possession may also be relevant where there is a conflict of title over goods.[26] But, under a contract for the sale of goods, the transfer of property is not dependent on the transfer of possession.[27] Third, possession is the basis for certain remedies.[28] The plaintiff in an action for trespass, conversion or detinue must have been in actual possession of the chattel, or had an immediate right to possession, at the time of the interference alleged against the defendant.[29] Therefore, a legal owner of a chattel who lacks actual possession or an immediate right to possession, will not be able to sue.[30] Furthermore, it would appear that the plaintiff in an action in negligence for damage or loss to chattels must have either legal ownership of, or possessory title to the chattels at the time of the damage or loss.[31] Possession may also be relevant in cases of insolvency. For instance, where a buyer of goods goes insolvent while the goods remain in the possession of an unpaid seller, the seller is entitled to exercise a statutory lien over the goods, even where property has passed to the seller. Where the unpaid seller has lost possession of the goods, but the goods are not yet in the buyer's possession, but are in transit, the unpaid seller has a right of stoppage in transit.[32]

25 But see *Elliott v. Kemp* (1840) 7 M. & W. 306.

26 Sale of Goods Act 1893, s.25(1) and (2): see further 19.7 and 19.8.

27 Sale of Goods Act 1893, s.18, Rule 1: see further 17.2.1.

28 See generally, Palmer, "Possessory Title" in Palmer & McKendrick ed., *Interests in Goods* (London, Lloyd's of London Press, 2nd ed., 1998).

29 See generally, McMahon & Binchy, *Law of Torts* (Dublin, Butterworths, 3rd ed., 2000) Chapters 28, 29 and 30.

30 See, *e.g.* *Gordon v. Harper* (1796) 7 Term Rep. 9. Such a person may have an action in tort for any damage done to his reversionary interest in the chattel: *Mears v. London & South Western Rly Co* (1862) 11 C.B.N.S. 850; see Tettenborn, "Trust Property and Conversion: An Equitable Confusion" [1996] *Cambridge Law Journal* 36.

31 *The Aliakmon* [1986] A.C. 785 at 809, per Lord Brandon.

32 See the Sale of Goods Act 1893, ss.38–48; see further 16.3.

3.4.2 Types of possession

Possession, like ownership is a difficult concept to define with any precision. As Bell notes:

> "The truth is that 'possession' has no single meaning: it is used in different senses in different contexts. This is perfectly reasonable, for the essence of possession is control, but the degree of control required for a particular rule will depend on the purpose of that rule. This flexibility has its price, however, the price of uncertainty."[33]

Possession has three basic elements: (a) physical possession, (b) legal possession, and (c) the right to physical or to legal possession.[34] These elements can be found separately, or in combination.

Physical, or *de facto*, possession, or control, may be acquired by taking physical possession of a chattel itself or by taking possession of an object which gives physical control of the chattel, for example, by taking possession of the key to the warehouse where the chattel is stored. Once acquired, possession is deemed to continue unless it is acquired by someone else or it is abandoned.[35] Physical possession or control alone does not create legal possession. To constitute possession in law, physical control must be coupled with an intention to exclude others.

Legal possession is the state of being a possessor in the eye of the law. Normally legal possession co-exists with physical possession, making the exercise of control over the chattel lawful. However, legal possession may exist with or without physical possession and it may be with or without a rightful origin. The following example, from Pollock and Wright, explains the concept:[36]

> A tailor sends to JS's house a coat which JS has ordered. JS puts on the coat and then has both physical control and rightful possession in law.
> JS takes off the coat and gives it to a servant to take back to the tailor for some alterations. Now the servant has physical control … and JS still has the possession in law.
> While the servant is going on his errand, Z assaults him and robs him of the coat. Z is not only the physical master of the coat, but, so soon as he has complete control of it, he has possession in law, though a wrongful possession.

33 Bell, *Modern Law of Personal Property in Ireland and England* (London, Butterworths, 1989) p.34. See further Harris, "The Concept of Possession in English Law" in Guest ed., *Oxford Essays in Jurisprudence* (Oxford, Oxford University Press, 1961) Chapter 4; and Dias, *Jurisprudence*, (London, Butterworths, 5th ed., 1985) Chapter 13.

34 See Pollock & Wright, *An Essay on Possession in the Common Law* (Oxford, Oxford University Press, 1888) pp.26–28.

35 See Harris, "The Concept of Possession in English Law" in Guest ed., *Oxford Essays in Jurisprudence* (Oxford, Oxford University Press, 1961) p.73.

36 *Supra,* n.34. See further Battersby, "Acquiring Title by Theft" [2002] *Modern Law Review* 603.

Initially, JS has legal possession of the coat when he has ownership and physical possession of it. When he gives physical possession to the servant he maintains his legal possession because the servant does not have the intention to control, or to exclude others, necessary for legal possession. As possession is indivisible, JS loses legal possession when the thief steals it from the employee. At this point the thief has legal possession, though it is wrongful.

A right to physical or legal possession is what remains when the lawful possessor is wrongfully dispossessed. Hence, when the coat is stolen, JS is left with a right to possession or to legal possession. Similarly, when a bailee holds possession of a chattel for his own interest, as where he is asserting a lien, the bailor maintains a right to possession while the bailee has legal possession. But where the bailee holds possession for the bailor's interest, the bailor and bailee will share legal possession. It is said that the bailee has physical possession while the bailor has *constructive possession*. Constructive possession is a legal concept: there is no such thing as possession in equity in Irish law.

3.4.3 Acquisition and transfer of possession

The transfer of possession can be effected by a unilateral action (such as theft) or by operation of the law (as on death or insolvency). However, the most common form of transfer, in a commercial context, is the voluntary transfer effected by actual or constructive delivery.[37] Actual delivery occurs where the physical, or actual, possession of the chattel is delivered to the transferee. Constructive delivery occurs where the transferee is given actual control of the chattel though physical, or actual, possession is usually not transferred. The concept of constructive delivery is particularly important in the context of attornments and bailments, which are considered further below.

3.4.4 Attornment

Attornment is an important commercial application of the concept of constructive delivery. It is a process by which one party (the attornor) holding actual possession of a chattel, later undertakes to hold possession of the chattel for someone else (the attornee). The attornor must give his undertaking to the attornee[38] and once given, the attornee has constructive possession of the chattel. For example, section 29 of the Sale of Goods Act 1893, which deals with the seller's delivery obligations, provides that where goods at the time of the sale are in the possession of a third party, such as a warehouseman or carrier, there is no delivery by the seller to the

---

37 On delivery under sale of goods contracts see 11.2.1.

38 *Godts v. Rose* (1855) 17 C.B. 229.

buyer unless and until such third party acknowledges to the buyer that he holds the goods on the buyer's behalf. In effect, the third party (the attornor) attorns to the rights of the buyer (the attornee). However, for attornment to occur, the goods must be identifiable. Where the goods being sold are part of identified bulk, and hence are not separately identifiable, any acknowledgement by the warehouseman or carrier that he holds the goods on behalf of the buyer will not operate as an attornment so as to give constructive delivery to the buyer, but it may estop the warehouseman or carrier from denying that he holds the goods as described on the buyer's behalf.[39] This process has been described by Professor Goode as quasi-attornment.[40]

The difference between attornment and quasi-attornment is significant. With attornment, the attornee receives real or proprietary rights in the chattels. But with quasi-attornment, based on estoppel, the attornee is given a personal right of action in conversion if the attornor fails to release goods matching the contract description to the attornee, or to his order. This right of action in conversion suffers the same weakness of all personal rights when contrasted with real or proprietary rights: it may be effectively worthless on the attornor's insolvency.

3.4.5 Bailment[41]

A bailment is a transaction whereby one party (the bailor) delivers chattels to another party (the bailee) on terms which normally require the bailee to hold the chattels and eventually to redeliver the chattels to the bailor, or, to his order, that is, in accordance with his directions. The notable feature about a bailment is that there is no transfer of ownership in the chattels, merely possession. Further, this transfer of possession to the bailee is temporary in nature.[42] Everyday examples of bailment include leaving a coat in cloakroom for later collection; transporting goods with a carrier, or a contract of hire. Bailments can be contractual, for example, where you pay to leave your coat at a cloakroom, or gratuitous, for example, where you do not pay to leave your coat at a cloakroom.

There are three requirements for a bailment: (a) the bailee must receive

39 *Re London Wine Co (Shippers) Ltd* [1986] P.C.C. 121; *Maynegrain Pty Ltd v. Compafina Bank* [1982] 2 N.S.W.L.R. 141 (C.A.), reversed on another ground; see further Reynolds, "Attornment to agent of undisclosed principal" (1984) 4 *Oxford Journal of Legal Studies* 434.

40 Goode, *Proprietary Rights in Insolvency and Sales Transactions* (London, Sweet & Maxwell, 2nd ed., 1989) p.11.

41 See generally, Palmer, *Bailment* (London, Sweet & Maxwell, 2nd ed., 1991).

42 A bailment may be of a definite or indefinite duration. Where it is of an indefinite duration it may be determinable at the bailor's will or the bailee's will.

possession of the chattel;[43] (b) the bailee must consent to take possession of the chattel;[44] and, (c) the bailor must retain a superior interest to the chattel than that of the bailee. This last requirement is usually satisfied because the bailee receives a limited possessory interest in the chattels which is subordinate to the bailor's interest. This is because the bailee is required, at the end of the bailment period, to redeliver the chattels to the bailor or to his order.

Broadly speaking, bailments fall into two categories: bailments for reward (such as carriage contracts, hire contracts, hire-purchase contract) and gratutitous bailments (as where you lend a book to a friend without charge).[45] The basis of liability under a bailment is negligence.[46] The bailee must exercise due care in handling the goods in his possession. Traditionally, a different standard of care applied depending on whether the bailment was for reward or gratuitous. Where the bailment is for reward, the usual negligence standards applies; but where the bailment is gratuitous, it is thought that the bailee will only be liable for gross negligence.[47] Significantly for the bailor, when pursuing a claim in negligence, there is a reverse burden of proof, that is, contrary to the usual position, the bailee must prove that he was not negligent to avoid liability for any loss or damage caused to the chattels subject to the bailment.[48]

43 See, *e.g. Ashby v. Tolhurst* [1937] 2 K.B. 242, where the Court of Appeal held that when a car was parked in a private car park, the relationship of the car-park owner and the car owner was that of licensor and licensee, and not bailor and bailee, because the owner of the car park had not received possession of the car.

44 The issue of involuntary bailments, and whether they are bailments at all, is an area of uncertainty: see Palmer, *Bailment* (London, Sweet & Maxwell, 2nd ed., 1991) p.37; see further Bell, "The Place of Bailment in the Modern Law of Obligations" in Palmer and McKendrick ed., *Interests in Goods* (London, Lloyd's of London Press, 2nd ed., 1998) Chapter 19.

45 On the different types of bailment, see Palmer, *Bailment* (London, Sweet & Maxwell, 2nd ed., 1991) pp.125–131.

46 See *Sheedy v. Faughnan* [1991] I.L.R.M. 719 (H.C.); and *Scanlon v. Ormonde Brick Ltd* unreported, High Court, Barr J., July 21, 2000.

47 *Port Swettenham Authority v. TG Wu & Co Sdn Bhd* [1979] A.C. 580 (P.C.); cf. *Sutcliffe v. Chief Constable of West Yorkshire* [1996] R.T.R. 86 (C.A.). See further Bell, "The Place of Bailment in the Modern Law of Obligations" in Palmer and McKendrick ed., *Interests in Goods* (London, Lloyd's of London Press, 2nd ed., 1998) Chapter 19, p.477. See also position of gratuitous agents where the tradition distinguishing paid and unpaid agents has been removed: *Chaudrhy v. Prabakhar* [1988] 3 All E.R. 718 (C.A.); see further 7.3.1.2.

48 See *Sheedy v. Faughnan* [1991] I.L.R.M. 719 (H.C.); and *Scanlon v. Ormonde Brick Ltd* unreported, High Court, Barr, J., July 21, 2000.

PART II
AGENCY

Chapter 4

THE LAW OF AGENCY: AN INTRODUCTION

4.1 Introduction

Most businesses use intermediaries in their dealings with the outside world. Such intermediaries may be employed for a variety of reasons: they may possess a special skill or expertise; the business may need someone "on the spot"; or simply, the proprietor of the business cannot be responsible personally for all its dealings. Intermediaries can be engaged for a number of business purposes:

(i) to market goods or services,
(ii) to find and introduce customers,
(iii) to negotiate contracts, or
(iv) to negotiate and conclude contracts.

Many such intermediaries are referred to as agents. The need for agents is particularly acute where the business wishes to trade on an international basis.[1] Even at a domestic level, once a business develops from a single-person enterprise, the need for the use of agents is unavoidable. Where for instance, a sole trader joins with another to form a partnership, legislation provides that all partners are agents for the other partners and the firm.[2] Or, where the business is conducted through the medium of a company, which is in law a separate person from its shareholders, the company can only act through human agents. Hence, agents and the law of agency are central to the conduct of trade and commerce.

The word "agent" must be used with care. Not all those referred to as "agents" in commercial parlance are agents in *law*. For instance, an estate agent is not necessarily an agent in law; an "advertising agent" is usually not an agent in law. This is important because the law attaches special legal incidents to an agency relationship.[3] Conversely, a person who is an agent in law may not be called an agent, examples include company directors and brokers. Moreover, the concept of agency may be invoked by the courts, as a device or tool, to produce results which are (or are thought to be) commercially convenient or socially desirable.[4] Consequently, parties

---

1 See generally, Part VI. See also the Unidroit Convention on Agency in the International Sale of Goods (Geneva, 1983): www.unidroit.org.

2 Partnership Act 1890, s.5.

3 See 4.2 and Chapters 5, 6 and 7.

4 See Fridman, "Establishing Agency" (1968) 84 *Law Quarterly Review* 224 at 231.

may find that they have entered into an agency relationship without being aware of it.[5]

4.2 The Nature and Consequences of Agency

While many definitions of agency exist, few, if any, accurately reflect the complex nature of agency. For example, Bowstead & Reynolds define agency in the following terms:

> "Agency is the fiduciary relationship which exists between two persons, one of whom expressly or impliedly consents that the other should act on his behalf so as to affect his relations with third parties, and the other of whom similarly consents so to act or so acts."[6]

This definition focuses on the relationship of principal and agent, and the consent element of that relationship. Perhaps the majority of agency relationships fit this model but many do not. Instances of apparent authority,[7] and agency of necessity[8] are not based on consent between principal and agent. Arguably, cases of apparent authority fit within this consent model when consent is defined widely to include a "principal's objectively determined consent".[9] But agency of necessity arises by operation of the law without any form of consent being needed.

Another useful definition is provided by Fridman. Accordingly:

> "Agency is the relationship which exists between two persons when one, called the *agent*, is considered in law to represent the other, called the *principal*, in such a way as to be able to affect the principal's legal position in respect of strangers to the relationship by the making of contracts or the disposition of property."[10]

This definition focuses on the power of the agent to affect his principal's legal position in relation to third parties, thereby including those circumstances where the principal consents to the agent's actions and where consent is lacking, as in the case of apparent authority. Thus, in law, "agency" is the relationship that exists between two persons, the principal and the agent. Usually, the relationship of principal and agent arises by consent of the parties. This consent can form the basis of a contract – an

---

5 For a striking example see *First Sport v. Barclays Bank* [1991] 3 All E.R. 789; see further 5.3.1.1.

6 *Bowstead & Reynolds on Agency* (London, Sweet & Maxwell, 16th ed., 1996) para 1-001.

7 See 5.3.

8 See 5.6.

9 See *Bowstead & Reynolds on Agency* (London, Sweet & Maxwell, 16th ed., 1996) para 1-012.

10 See Fridman, *The Law of Agency* (London, Butterworths, 7th ed., 1996) p.11.

agency contract – or the agency may be gratuitous. But, agency is also a legal concept and two persons may be found to have "consented to" the creation of an agency relationship without realising it.

In general, no formality is required when appointing an agent. An agent can be appointed orally, in writing or by deed (usually called a power of attorney).[11] Under the Commercial Agents Directive,[12] as implemented in Ireland,[13] the agency agreement must be evidenced in writing,[14] and a commercial agent and his principal are each entitled to receive from the other, on request, a signed written statement of the terms of the agency contract, including any terms agreed after the creation of the agency contract.[15] These provisions cannot be waived.[16] Importantly, these provisions do not mean that the agency contract must be in writing.

Any person who is capable of consenting can act as an agent, even though he has limited or no contractual capacity himself. For instance, an adult principal can appoint a minor to act as his agent and because the actions of the agent are deemed to be those of the principal, contracts made by the minor will be fully binding on the adult principal. But, the contract between the adult principal and the minor agent may not be binding because of the agent's minority.

A number of consequences flow in law from the creation of an agency relationship. First, and arguably most importantly, the agent has power to affect the principal's legal position with third parties.[17] The most significant aspect of the agent's power in the commercial context is that, as an exception to the doctrine of privity, contracts made by the agent on behalf of the principal are treated in law as the principal's contracts and are directly enforceable by and against him. Therefore, where an agent (A) acting on behalf of a principal (P), negotiates and concludes a contract with a third party (T), the parties to that contract are P and T: P and T can sue each other for breach of contract. It is said that P steps into A's shoes and A disappears from the picture, in that A has no liability on the contract (though A's relationship with P may be based on contract – a separate

11 See further Powers of Attorney Act 1996.

12 Directive 86/653/EEC [1986] O.J. L382/17.

13 S.I. No 33/1994, and S.I. No 31 of 1997.

14 Art. 13(2) of the Directive and Regulation 5, 1994.

15 Art. 13(1) of the Directive.

16 Art. 13(1) of the Directive.

17 On the power/liability analysis of agency see, *e.g.* Seavey, "The Rationale of Agency" (1920) 29 *Yale Law Journal* 859; Montrose, "The Basis of the Power of an Agent in Cases of Actual and Apparent Authority" (1938) 16 *Can. Bar Rev.* 757; Dowrick, "The Relationship of Principal and Agent" (1954) 17 *Modern Law Review* 24; Fridman, "Establishing Agency"(1968) 84 *Law Quarterly Review* 224; Conant, "The Objective Theory of Agency: Apparent Authority and the Estoppel of Apparent Ownership" (1968) 47 *Nebraska Law Review* 678; Reynolds, "Agency: Theory and Practice" (1978) 94 *Law Quarterly Review* 224; McMeel, "Philosophical Foundations of the Law of Agency" (2000) 116 *Law Quarterly Review* 387.

agency contract – which gives rise to rights and responsibilities between the principal and the agent) (see diagram below).

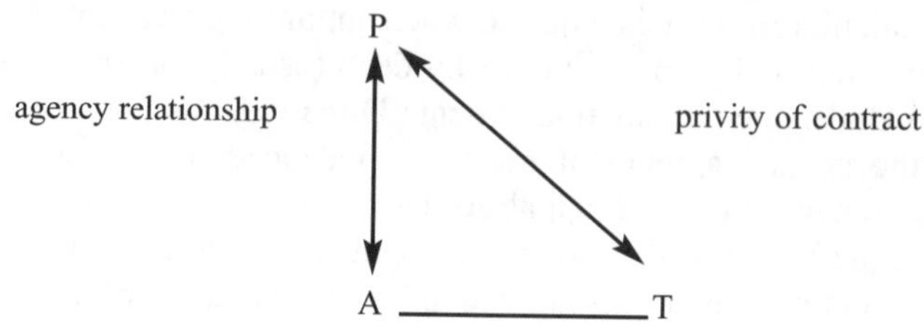

The agent may also make binding dispositions of the principal's property or acquire property on the principal's behalf; he may sign documentation on behalf of his principal;[18] and his statements may bind the principal, both in a contractual context and otherwise. The nature of this power and the effects of its exercise will be examined in detail in Chapters 5 and 6, respectively.

Second, the law gives the parties to an agency relationship certain rights, and imposes on them certain duties against each other. Significantly, the agent can occupy a fiduciary position *vis-à-vis* the principal. In return, the agent is given certain rights at common law and under the EC Commercial Agents Directive 1986,[19] as implemented in Ireland under the 1994 and 1997 Commercial Agents Regulations.[20] A detailed analysis of these rights and duties is provided in Chapter 7.

4.3 Identifying Agents

It is vital to be able to identify whether a person is an agent, or not, in order to advise parties of their legal rights and responsibilities. As noted above, not all those referred to as "agents" in commercial parlance are agents in law; and a person who is an agent in law may not be called an agent. To complicate the matter further, a person may be an agent with limited authority or power, such that in certain matters he is an agent with power to affect the legal position of his principal, while in others, he has no powers to affect the legal position of his principal and hence is not an agent.

The essential characteristic of an agent is the ability to affect the legal relations of his principal with third parties. Where this essential feature is lacking, the simple reference to someone as an agent has no legal consequence. In each case, regardless of the terminology used, a detailed examination of the role of the intermediary is vital to determine his legal

18 *Dundalk Football Club v. The Eircom League* [2001] 1 I.R. 434.
19 Directive 86/653/EEC [1986] O.J. L 382/17.
20 S.I. No. 33 of 1994, and S.I. No. 31 of 1997.

status. Some of the more common examples of agents encountered in business are identified below.

4.3.1 Company directors and other officers[21]

A company is a legal person but, as noted above, can only act through human agents. Primary authority to act on behalf of and in the name of the company rests with the board of directors as a whole. But under the company's articles of association, the board will usually delegate part or all of its functions to individual members of the board.[22] It is common for one or more executive directors to be appointed, with authority to run the company on a day-to-day basis. Accordingly, these directors are agents for the company.

The company secretary is another important company officer. It has been held, for example, that a company secretary has usual authority to sign contracts "dealing with the administrative side of [the] company's affairs."[23]

4.3.2 Partners

A partnership, unlike a company, has no separate legal identity from its members. Under the Partnership Act 1890, every partner is an agent for the firm and all the other partners for the purpose of the business of the firm, and every partner who does an act for carrying on in the usual way business of the kind carried on by the firm binds the firm and the other partners.[24] Hence, agency law and partnership law are intrinsically linked. Other principles of agency law are reflected in the Partnership Act 1890. For example, a person who is not a partner but allows himself to be held out as if he was, may be liable as a partner to any person who relies on such holding-out and extends credit to the firm.[25] This is akin to the liability of a principal based on apparent authority.[26]

21 See generally, Keane, *Company Law* (Dublin, Butterworths, 3rd ed., 2000); Forde, *Company Law in Ireland* (Dublin, Round Hall Sweet & Maxwell, 3rd ed., 1999); Courtney, *The Law of Private Companies* (Dublin, Butterworths, 2nd ed., 2002).

22 See Table A, Articles 80 and 110, First Schedule of Companies Act 1963.

23 *Panorama Developments (Guildford) Ltd v. Fidelis Furnishing Fabrics Ltd* [1971] 2 Q.B. 711.

24 Partnership Act 1890, s.5; see, *e.g. APD v. Walsh & ors* [1991] 2 I.R. 8.

25 Partnership Act 1890. s.14; see, *e.g. Nationwide Building Society v. Lewis* [1997] 1 W.L.R. 1181.

26 See 5.3.

4.3.3 Employees

An employee may be an agent if he possesses the ability to affect his principal's legal relations with third parties, but not all employees are agents. For example, the person at the cash register of a shop or supermarket is an agent for the employer for the purpose of concluding contracts of sale of goods[27] and receiving payment, though this power may be limited. Such a person may have no authority to accept cheques in payment without the authorisation of a supervisor, for example.

4.3.4 Other professionals

Professionals acting on behalf of clients may be agents with limited authority. For example, a solicitor may have authority to agree a settlement in the course of litigation, on behalf of a client. Similarly, an accountant may have authority to reach a settlement with the Revenue Commissioners regarding taxes due, on behalf of a client. Estate agents and auctioneers acting for prospective vendors of property are agents in law for the vendor, but they have very limited authority. In particular, they have no authority to enter into a contract of sale on behalf of the vendor unless they are expressly authorised to do so.[28] In *Law v. Roberts*,[29] it was held that where a contract of sale is made between a purchaser and an estate agent the onus of proving that the estate agent had authority to make the contract is on the purchaser. Insurance brokers and agents are agents in law, but the normal rules of agency are modified such that an agent working for an insurer may be deemed to be the agent of the insured for certain limited purposes.[30]

4.4 Types of Agent

Agents, of many different types, have been part of commercial life for hundreds of years.[31] Titles such as factors, brokers and mercantile agents[32] have dominated commercial life at different times; some have since faded into obscurity; others remain. In 1994, a new character, "the commercial agent" was introduced from mainland Europe into Ireland and England, following the implementation of the EC Directive on Self-employed

27 *PSGB v. Boots Cash Chemists* [1953] 1 All E.R. 482 (C.A.).
28 *Hamer v. Sharp* (1874) L.R. 19 Eq. 108; *Morrisey & Sons Ltd v. Nalty* [1976-7] I.L.R.M. 269.
29 [1964] I.R. 292.
30 See 27.5.
31 See, *e.g.* Fridman, *Law of Agency* (London, Butterworths, 7th ed., 1996) Introduction.
32 Mercantile agent is defined in section 1(1) of the Factors Act 1889 as an agent "having in the customary course of his business as such agent authority either to sell goods, or to consign goods for the purpose of sale or to buy goods, or to raise money on the security of goods."

Commercial Agents.[33] These different types are outlined below. A detailed analysis of the rights and obligations of "commercial agents" is provided in Chapter 7.

4.4.1 General and special agents

A general agent has general authority to act for the principal in a particular trade or class of transactions. In contrast, a special agent is authorised only to act in one particular transaction. This distinction is no longer as significant as it once was.

4.4.2 Factors and brokers

A factor is a commercial agent who handles the goods (or documents of title) of his principal in the course of finding a buyer or seller for them.[34] An example of a factor is an auctioneer selling furniture which is displayed in his showroom. Factor, in this technical sense, has dropped out of commercial usage. In modern business, the word "factoring" is used in the unrelated sense of assigning or discounting book-debts.[35] There is also a common practice of referring to dealers in certain goods and spare-parts as "factors", for example, "motor factors". Motor factors and others are not agents: they generally buy and sell goods in their own right. In contrast to a factor, a broker negotiates contracts for the sale and purchase of goods and other property on behalf of his principal without having possession of the goods. But, it should be noted that there are other types of brokers, such as stockbrokers and insurance brokers.

4.4.3 *Del credere* agents

A *del credere* agent negotiates contracts for a principal and guarantees to the principal that the third party will pay any sums due under the contract; this may be important where the third party is not known to the principal. The *del credere* agent charges the principal an extra commission for providing the guarantee.

---

33 Directive 86/653/EEC [1986] O.J. L382/17. The concept of "commercial agent" was described as "alien" to English law in one case: per Peter Gibson L.J. in *Imballaggi Plastici SRL v. Pacflex Ltd* [1999] 2 All E.R. (Comm) 249 at 255. A similar comment could be made in the Irish context.

34 There are five Factors Acts: 1823, 1825, 1842, 1877, and 1889. See further Chapter 19 on title conflicts in sale of goods transactions.

35 See Goode, *Commercial Law,* (London, Penguin, 2nd ed., 1995) Chapter 29, esp. pp.802-819.

4.4.4 Commission agents

A commission agent buys or sells property on behalf of a principal, but is not authorised to create privity of contract between the principal and the third party with whom he deals. Thus, *vis-à-vis* the third party, the agent contracts as principal and is therefore liable to the third party on the contract but *vis-à-vis* his principal, the agent owes the duties owed by an agent to his principal.[36] Today, this arrangement is more commonly used in civil law systems than in common law systems.

4.4.5 "Commercial agents"

The 1986 EC Directive on Self-employed Commercial Agents was drafted to protect the position of self-employed agents against exploitation by principals,[37] and to further the development of the internal market.[38] The Directive and the implementing Regulations define a "commercial agent" in the following terms:[39]

> "a self-employed intermediary who has continuing authority to negotiate the sale and the purchase of goods on behalf of another person, hereinafter called the principal, or to negotiate and conclude such transactions on behalf of and in the name of that principal."

There is also a list of exclusions from this definition, such that the term "commercial agent" does not include:

(a) company officers;
(b) partners of a firm;
(c) insolvency practitioners;
(d) unpaid commercial agent;
(e) commercial agents operating in a commodity exchange or market; and
(f) consumer credit agents and mail order catalogue agents, on the basis that their activities are secondary.[40]

---

36 *Ireland v. Livingstone* (1872) L.R. 5 H.L. 395.

37 Staughton L.J. in *Page v. Combined Shipping and Trading Co Ltd* [1997] 3 All E.R. 656 at 660 described commercial agents as "a down-trodden race" in need of protection against their principals.

38 See Recital 3.

39 Art. 1.2 and Regulation 2(1), 1994.

40 Art. 2; Regulation 2(1), 1994.

This definition is not straightforward and gives rise to a number of questions which will be examined in more detail in Chapter 7.[41]

4.5 AGENCY DISTINGUISHED

There is a variety of arrangements involving the use of representative intermediaries open to a business that wishes to market its goods or services. These include the use of employment contracts, agency contracts, a distribution network, a franchise network, or subsidiary companies where the business is a company. Some, but not all of these arrangements may amount to agency even though the representative may not be referred to as an "agent". For instance, a car dealer may be described as "sole agent" for a particular manufacturer, but in law the dealer is not usually an agent for the manufacturer. If he were an agent for the manufacturer, every time the dealer sold a car, it would be on the manufacturer's behalf, and the manufacturer would be entitled to any profits on the sale. Instead, in this context "sole agent" usually means "sole distributor", in which case the dealer acts on his own behalf but subject to certain obligations to the manufacturer under a distribution agreement.[42] The main alternatives to an agency arrangement are identified below and are contrasted with an agency arrangement under a number of headings.

4.5.1 Other marketing arrangements

The three main alternatives to an agency arrangement are:

(i) a distribution arrangement;
(ii) a franchising arrangement;
(iii) a subsidiary company, where the principal is a company.

A fourth alternative involves the use of employment contracts. As already noted, where an employee has the power to affect his employer's legal

41 For example, in *Parkes v. Esso Petroleum Co Ltd* [1998] Eu. L.R. 550 (H.C.), [1999] Tr. L.R. 232 (C.A.), the plaintiff was a licensee of a tied, self-service petrol station. The licence described him as an "agent" for the purpose of selling fuel on behalf of the petrol company and provided for him to receive commission on sales. At first instance, it was held that he was outside the Directive because he did not "negotiate" the sale of petrol, giving "negotiate" its ordinary meaning. The decision was upheld on appeal but on slightly different grounds. The Court of Appeal recognised that there could be negotiations without haggling over the price. The Court of Appeal emphasised that the petrol sales were self-service. Referring to the provisions on "secondary" activities in the Schedule to the U.K. Regulations, the court distinguished between "negotiated" and self-service sales, and found that, on the facts the plaintiff did not negotiate sales.

42 See 4.5.1.1.

relations with third parties, the employee is also an agent, with rights and responsibilities. Moreover, employment contracts are highly regulated to protect the interests of employees.[43] This relatively high degree of regulation can make the employment contract less attractive as a marketing mechanism than some of the arrangements set out below.

4.5.1.1 Distribution agreements[44]

A manufacturer or supplier of goods may use a network of distributors to market its products.

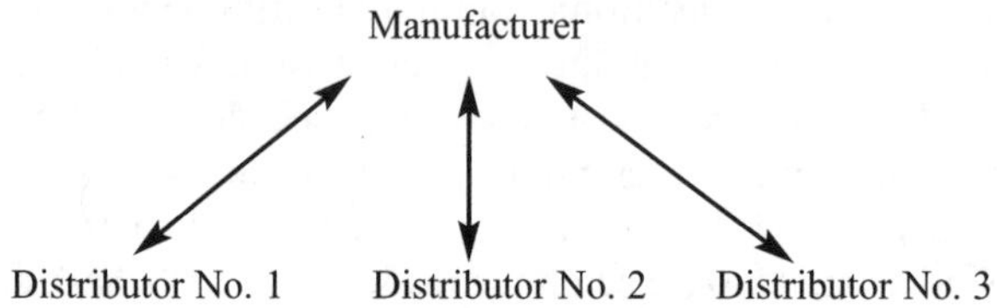

The relationship between the business and an individual distributor will generally be governed by a master agreement which imposes restrictions on both parties. For instance, the distributor may agree to purchase all its stock from the business and not to sell products of a rival business: this is commonly referred to as "exclusive purchasing." In return, the business may agree not to appoint other distributors in the same area: known as "a sole distribution arrangement;"[45] and the business may agree not to sell products in competition with the distributor within its area: known as "an exclusive distribution arrangement."[46]

Although the relationship between the business and an individual distributor is close, it does not amount to one of agency. When the business supplies goods to a distributor, they enter into a contract for the sale of goods, and the relationship of seller and buyer arises. When the distributor resells the goods, it does so on its own behalf, and it, rather than the business, will be liable to customers for performance of the contract of sale. The master agreement between the business and the distributor is not a sale of goods contract, but a contract governing the terms of their relationship, though it can contain terms of sale.

43 See Fennell & Lynch, *Labour Law in Ireland* (Dublin, Gill & Macmillan, 1993); Barnard, *EC Employment Law* (Oxford, Oxford University Press, 2nd ed., 2000).

44 See generally Bogaert & Lohmann ed., *Commercial Agency and Distribution Agreements: law and practice in the member states of the European Union* (The Hague, Kluwer, 3rd ed., 2000).

45 See, *e.g. Bob Bushell Ltd v. Luxel Varese SAS* unreported, High Court, O'Sullivan J., February 20, 1998.

46 It has been held that an agreement expressed to give the distributor the "sole right to sell" the suppliers' products has the same effect: *WT Lamb and Sons v. Goring Brick Company Ltd* [1932] 1 K.B. 710.

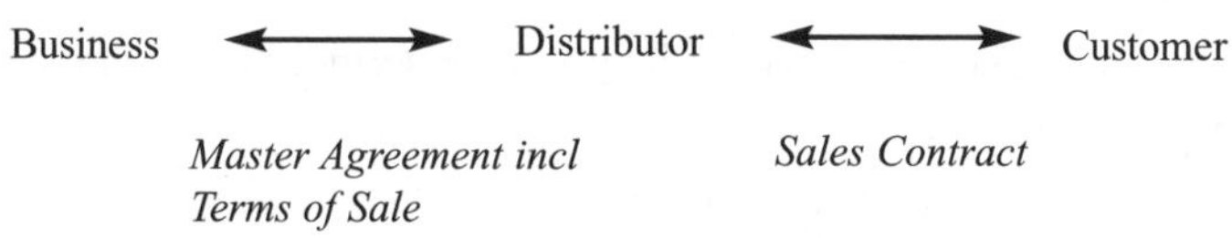

4.5.1.2 Franchising agreements[47]

As with a distribution arrangement, the relationship between a franchisor and a franchisee will be governed by a master agreement, but the relationship between franchisor and franchisee may be even closer than that between a manufacturer and its distributors.

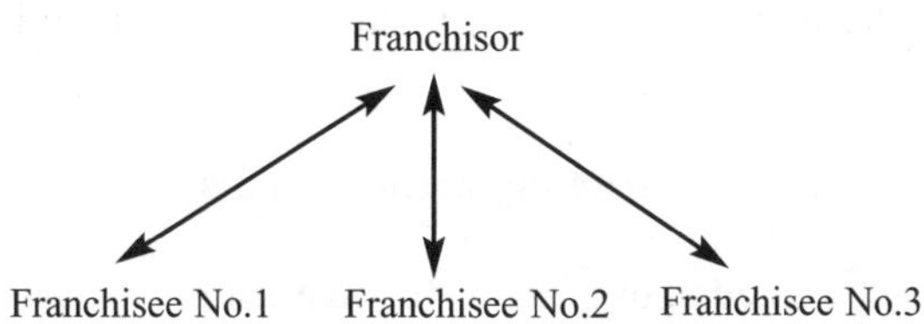

The master agreement between the franchisor and each individual franchisee will impose various restrictions on the parties. Basically, the franchisee will be given the right, or a licence, to use the franchisor's product or business idea and also its general style, including intellectual property rights such as copyrights and trade marks, in return for payment of a fee.[48] Indeed, the franchisee will generally be obliged to adopt the franchisor's style. The franchisee will also generally be obliged to purchase some or all of the products to be used in its business from the franchisor. The individual franchisee thus gets the benefit of appearing to be part of a large organisation and of the goodwill generated by the franchisor and other franchisees. However, once again, when goods are supplied from franchisor to franchisee the relationship is that of seller and buyer; and when the franchisee resells, it does so as seller on its own behalf and not as agent for the franchisor.

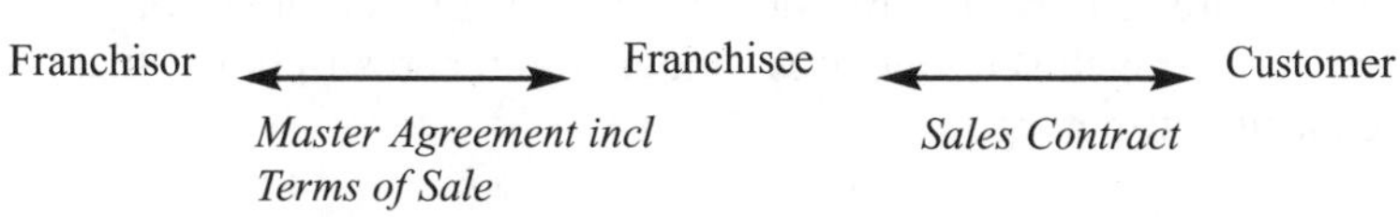

47 See generally Bogaert & Lohmann ed., *Commercial Agency and Distribution Agreements: Law and Practice in the Member States of the European Union* (The Hague, Kluwer, 3rd ed., 2000).

48 This can include an initial fee, and a proportion of annual turnover, usually payable regardless of whether profits are being made.

4.5.1.3 Subsidiary company

A company may choose to market its goods or services through a network of subsidiary companies.

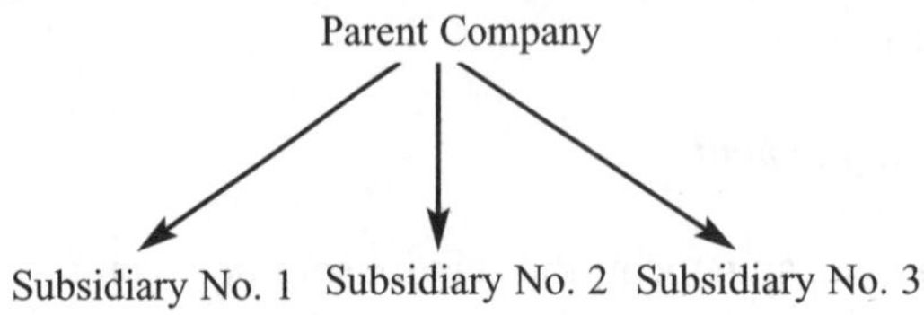

Parent and subsidiary companies are separate persons in law.[49] The relationship between parent and subsidiary will depend on the facts of the particular case. The subsidiary may be appointed to act as the parent company's agent; alternatively it may buy goods from the parent for resale on its own behalf.

4.5.2 The legal incidents of marketing arrangements

Each arrangement described above has distinctive features which, from a legal and commercial perspective, offers a business advantages and disadvantages. Hence, a business may need to be advised which arrangement would best suit its needs. Any such analysis would need to consider the following issues.

4.5.2.1 Control

Certain arrangements offer a business greater control over the intermediary than others. A business is likely to be able to exert greater control over agents than over independent intermediaries, such as distributors or franchisees. An agent sells goods on behalf of its principal; the contracts it makes are, in law, the principal's contracts. The principal is therefore entitled to control the terms of those contracts. A distributor and a franchisee are independent businesses, trading on their own behalf. Although the supplier may exert control over its distributor or franchisee through the terms of its agreements with them, the effectiveness of such limitations are controlled by domestic and EC competition law.[50] Generally, a franchisee operates under tighter restrictions than an independent distributor.

49 *Saloman v. Saloman & Co* [1897] A.C. 22.

50 See 4.5.2.5.

4.5.2.2 Product liability

It is important to be able to identify who is answerable to the ultimate customer for defects in the goods or services provided. Since the distributor and franchisee sell on their own behalf, they alone incur contractual liability to customers for the goods or services supplied. The manufacturer or franchisor is, in turn, liable to the distributor or franchisee, as supplier, but may be able to limit its liability by the terms of its contract with the distributor or franchisee. In contrast, when an agent sells on behalf of a principal, privity is established between principal and customer. The principal is therefore answerable to the customer for the goods or services and, if the customer is a consumer, the principal will be unable to limit its liability for breach of the statutory implied terms with regard to sale of goods contracts, for instance. However, even where sales are effected through a distributor or a franchisee, the supplier may incur liability directly to the end customer, or to any person damaged by defects in the goods, in the law of negligence; under the Liability for Defective Products Act 1991; or if it offers a guarantee, under the terms of that guarantee, under section 19 of the Sale and Supply of Goods Act 1980.[51]

4.5.2.3 Credit risk

Where the intermediary becomes insolvent, it must be established whether the business is entitled to claim payment direct from customers, or to claim monies received from customers. A business which markets goods or services through an agent must look for payment from the ultimate customers, not the agent. The business must therefore consider the creditworthiness of all the end customers introduced by its agent. A principal may authorise its agent to receive payments from customers. If the agent becomes insolvent, the principal can recover payment direct from any customer who has not already paid the agent. He may also claim in priority to the agent's other creditors any monies held by the agent which represent payments made to the agent by his customers.

In contrast, a distributor and a franchisee buy and resell on their own behalf and are therefore responsible for recovering the price from the end customers; the supplier need look only to the distributor or franchisee for payment. The failure of ultimate customers to pay for goods supplied may affect the viability of the distributor or franchisee, but if the distributor or franchisee becomes insolvent the supplier can neither claim payment direct from the ultimate customer nor establish a priority claim to monies due to the distributor or franchisee from their customers (except, possibly, under a reservation of title clause).[52]

---

51 See Chapter 16.

52 See 15.4.

4.5.2.4 Impact on prices

The choice of different arrangements may have an impact on prices. Since distributors and franchisees take the primary risk of customers' failing to pay for goods supplied, they will wish to increase their profit margin in order to reflect the increased risk (to cover bad debts).

As a result, the supplier must either:

(i) reduce its price to the distributor or franchisee, reducing its own profit margin; or

(ii) accept that the ultimate market price of its goods will increase (to cover the distributor's or franchisee's profit), thus possibly reducing the competitiveness of the goods or services being provided.

4.5.2.5 Competition law

Competition law may seek to regulate some of these arrangements. Prima facie, distributorship and franchise agreements may, by virtue of the restrictions undertaken by the parties to them, offend domestic and EC competition law.[53] However, there are special provisions in both EC law (the 1999 Regulation on Vertical Restraints)[54] and domestic law (the 1998 Category Certificate/Licence)[55] designed to deal with such agreements. Hence, distribution and franchise agreements must be carefully drafted in order to avoid contravention of competition law.

Agency agreements are less likely to contravene competition law. In 1962, the EC Commission issued a Notice saying that, in certain circumstances, agreements between commercial agents and their principals do not infringe Article 81(1) of the Treaty establishing the European Union. This Notice has been replaced by Chapter 2, Section II of the Commission Notice, Guidelines on Vertical Restraints, which accompanies the new Regulation on Vertical Restraints.[56] The Guidelines provide that an agency agreement will fall outside the Article 81(1) prohibition if the agent does not bear any, or only insignificant, risks in

53 In particular, Art. 81(1) of the EC Treaty, and section 4(1) of the Competition Act 2002: see further Maher, *Competition Law: Alignment and Reform* (Dublin, Round Hall Sweet & Maxwell, 1999); Massey & O'Hare, *Competition Law and Policy in Ireland* (Dublin, Oak Tree Press, 1996); Korah, *EC Competition Law and Practice* (Oxford, Hart, 7th ed., 2000); Whish, *Competition Law* (London, Butterworths, 4th ed., 2001).

54 See Regulation 790/99, [1999] O.J. L336/21, valid until May 31, 2010. This Regulation replaces three previous block exemptions on exclusive distribution, exclusive purchasing and franchising agreements. It is notable because it is capable of application to *all* vertical agreements, subject to its terms.

55 See the Category Certificate/Licence in respect of Agreements between Suppliers and Resellers, Decision No. 528, issued by the Competition Authority on December 4, 1998.

56 [1999] O.J. L336/21.

relation to contracts negotiated and/or concluded on behalf of the principal and in relation to market specific investments on behalf of the principal. Risk is assessed on a case-by-case basis and the Commission looks at the economic reality of the situation. The fact that a relationship may be regarded as one of agency in national law is irrelevant if the agent is taking too much financial risk. The Guidelines contain a non-exhaustive list of circumstances where the Article 81(1) prohibition will generally not apply. For example, Article 81(1) will probably not apply where the property in the contract goods bought or sold does not vest in the agent, or the agent does not itself supply the contract services and where the agent:

(a) does not maintain at its own cost or risk stocks of contract goods;
(b) does not create and/or operate an after-sales service;
(c) does not take responsibility for customers' non-performance of the contract.

The Guidelines also list obligations on the agent's behalf which generally will be considered inherent to the agency relationship, such as limitations on the territory in which the agent may operate, and the prices and conditions under which the agent sells or purchases the goods or services.

4.5.2.6 Termination and dismissal

Finally, important issues may arise on termination of the arrangement. In light of the 1994 and 1997 Commercial Agency Regulations, which implement the 1986 EC Directive on Self-employed Commercial Agents, it may be easier for a supplier to dismiss an unsatisfactory distributor or franchisee, than an agent.[57]

If the distribution or franchise agreement is not expressed to be for a fixed term, it will be for an indefinite term, terminable by notice from either party. If no notice period is specified in the agreement, it will be terminable by reasonable notice. What constitutes reasonable notice will differ from case to case and depend on the particular circumstances. For instance, in *Decro-Wall SA v. Marketing Ltd*,[58] it was held that 12 months' notice was required to terminate a distributorship agreement which had run for over two years; in *Aluminium Design Ltd v. Alcon Windows Ltd*,[59] it was held that one year's notice was appropriate in relation to a franchise agreement which had run for over ten years. In any case the agreement

57 See further Chapter 7.

58 [1971] 1 W.L.R. 361. See also *Irish Welding Co v. Philips Electrical (Ireland) Ltd* unreported, High Court, Finlay J., October 5, 1976; and *Barlo Farm Machines Ltd v. Case UK Ltd* unreported, High Court, McCracken J., October 24, 1996.

59 [1980] J.I. Soc. Eur. L 82 (H.C.).

may be terminated by either party without notice where the other has been guilty of a repudiatory breach of contract. Case law suggests that in view of the continuing relationship between the parties, the courts may be reluctant to find that a solitary breach justifies termination.[60]

60 See, *e.g.* *Decro-Wall SA v. Marketing Ltd* [1971] 1 W.L.R. 361; *Wickman Tools Ltd v. Schuler AG* [1974] A.C. 235.

CHAPTER 5

AUTHORITY AND POWER

5.1 INTRODUCTION

Two main theories dominate agency law: the consent theory and the power-liability theory.[1] The consent theory focuses on the "internal" relationship of principal and agent and the consensual nature of that relationship.[2] As noted in the previous chapter, the majority of agency relationships fit this model, but not all. Most authors now agree that the essence of agency is the agent's power to affect the principal's legal position in relation to third parties.[3] This theory focuses on the "external" nature of the principal's relationship with third parties, and thereby includes those cases where the principal does not consent but yet is bound by the actions of an agent.

A third doctrine is linked with agency, but must be distinguished: the doctrine of vicarious liability in tort law.[4] Under the doctrine of vicarious liability, an employer can be held liable for the torts of his employees acting in the course of their employment. In particular, an employer is vicariously liable for the fraudulent acts of his employee where he has put the employee in a position to commit the fraud and has held out the employee as acting on his behalf or in the course of his business.[5] This is essentially the same test as is used for the doctrine of apparent authority.[6] However, there are a number of important distinctions between these two doctrines. First, vicarious liability gives rise only to liabilities on the part

1 See generally, Seavey, "The Rationale of Agency" (1920) 29 *Yale Law Journal* 859; Montrose, "The Basis of the Power of an Agent in Cases of Actual and Apparent Authority" (1938) 16 *Can. Bar Rev.* 757; Dowrick, "The Relationship of Principal and Agent" (1954) 17 *Modern Law Review* 24; Fridman, "Establishing Agency" (1968) 84 *Law Quarterly Review* 224; Conant, "The Objective Theory of Agency: Apparent Authority and the Estoppel of Apparent Ownership" (1968) 47 *Nebraska Law Review* 678; Reynolds, "Agency: Theory and Practice" (1978) 94 *Law Quarterly Review* 224; McMeel, "Philosophical Foundations of the Law of Agency" (2000) 116 *Law Quarterly Review* 387.

2 See, *e.g. Bowstead & Reynolds on Agency* (London, Sweet & Maxwell, 16th ed., 1996) Art. 1.

3 See, *e.g.* Fridman, *The Law of Agency* (London, Butterworths, 7th ed., 1996) pp.10–11; Bradgate, *Commercial Law* (London, Butterworths, 3rd ed., 2000) p.126.

4 See generally, McMahon & Binchy, *Law of Torts*, (Dublin, Butterworths, 3rd ed., 2000) Chapter 43.

5 *Lloyd v. Grace Smith & Co* [1912] A.C. 716; *Armagas Ltd v. Mundogas Ltd* [1985] 1 Lloyd's Rep. 1; [1986] 2 All E.R. 385: see 5.7.

6 See 5.3.

of the employer; agency can give rise to rights and liabilities on the part of the principal. Second, vicarious liability is generally limited to the employer/employee relationship and does not extend to cover independent contractors, whereas an agent may be an employee or an independent contractor. Third, vicarious liability is only imposed where the employee is acting in the course of his employment; whereas a principal will be bound once an agent acts within his *authority*.

Therefore, this chapter concerns an agent's ability to legally bind his principal in relation to a third party. Sometimes we speak of an agent's *authority* to bind his principal but beyond the authority given to an agent by his principal, an agent may have power to bind his principal so that, strictly speaking, the agent's actions are *unauthorised*. In this part, the word authority is used to cover both these situations. An agent's authority can be categorised under the following five headings.

(i) "Actual" authority exists where the principal consents in advance to the agent's actions, giving the agent actual authority to act in a certain manner and bind the principal.[7]

(ii) "Apparent" authority exists where an agent appears to a third party to have authority, *whether he actually has it or not*; again the agent's actions will bind the principal. This type of authority can also be identified as a type of *power*, referred to above.[8]

(iii) "Usual" or "customary" authority pertains where an agent has authority which a person in his position usually, or customarily, has. This type of authority can be seen either to expand the scope of an agent's actual or apparent authority;[9] or to represent an independent head of authority.[10]

(iv) Authority by "ratification" occurs where although an agent does not have authority at the time when he acts on the principal's behalf, the principal later ratifies or adopts the agent's actions and is thus bound by them.[11]

(v) Agency of "necessity" arises where, due to an emergency situation, the agent is vested, by operation of the law, with authority to act in a way not actually authorised by the principal.[12]

For example, assume that a principal (P) appoints an agent (A) to buy a particular personal computer on his behalf, and instructs him to pay no more than €2,000 for it. A buys a computer as described from a third party

7 See 5.2.
8 See 5.3.
9 See 5.2.2 and 5.3.1.
10 See 5.4.4.
11 See 5.5.
12 See 5.6.

retailer (T) but pays €2,500 to T for it. An agent cannot have actual authority when he exceeds an express limit on his authority or where he does something expressly prohibited by his principal. Thus, in the circumstances described above, A has exceeded his actual authority, and accordingly is in breach of his duties to P.[13] P will not be bound to T unless T can rely on A's apparent authority. Alternatively, if P ratifies A's purchase the contract can be enforced by T and A's breach of duty is excused.

Unfortunately, judges and academics are not consistent in their use of terminology to describe agency. The same word can be used to mean different things and different words to mean the same thing. Actual authority is sometimes referred to as "real" authority, apparent authority as "ostensible" or "held-out" authority, and the boundaries between actual, apparent and usual authority are malleable.[14] Commercial lawyers must therefore be familiar with the full range of terminology in use.

5.2 Actual Authority

Actual authority is the authority which an agent *actually* has as a result of a consensual arrangement between the principal and agent. This consensual arrangement can form the basis of a contract, or the relationship between the principal and the agent can be gratuitous.

Actual authority is crucial as between the principal and the agent. If an agent acts outside his actual authority he is not entitled to payment of his remuneration or an indemnity from his principal. Moreover, he may be sued by his principal for breach of his duties as agent. However, if an agent acts within the scope of his actual authority, he is entitled to any remuneration due and an indemnity from his principal, and there is no breach of his duties as agent. Furthermore,

> "... actual authority can be express or implied. It is express when it is given by words such as when a board of directors pass a resolution which authorises two of their number to sign cheques. It is implied when it is inferred from the conduct of the parties and the circumstances of the case, such as when a board of directors appoint one of their number to be managing director. They thereby impliedly authorise him to do all such things as fall within the usual scope of that office."[15]

5.2.1 Express actual authority

An agent's express actual authority depends on the express words of appointment used by the principal, whether oral or written. Proof of the

13 See further 7.3 and esp. 7.3.1.1.

14 See 5.4.3.

15 *Hely-Hutchinson v. Brayhead Ltd* [1968] 1 Q.B. 549 at 583.

scope of an agent's express actual authority is therefore a matter of evidence of the words used and construction of those words, as a matter of law. Where words of appointment are ambiguous, the court will construe them in a way most favourable to the agent.[16] In practice, an agent if faced with ambiguous words of appointment should seek clarification from the principal. Where an agent is appointed by deed (usually called a power of attorney),[17] as where, for example, he is appointed to execute a deed, the words of the deed will be construed more strictly, in accordance with the rules applied to the construction of deeds.[18]

5.2.2 Implied actual authority

The scope of an agent's express actual authority may be broadened by implication. In the case of a written agency agreement, the normal principles of construction of written documents allow the implication of additional authority from the express words used, the usage of the trade and the course of business between the parties.

For example, assume that P instructs A, in writing, "to run a car sales business, for a four week period." In order to determine the extent of his implied authority, a court would seek to give effect to the intentions of the parties by (i) examining the express words used, (ii) enquiring what is the normal practice in the car trade, and, (iii) asking whether A had acted in this capacity previously and, if so, what powers had he. It is also common for agents to be given implied authority to do all that is incidental to carrying out the express wishes of his principal. A might thus be impliedly authorised to sell cars, buy cars, pay wages, and incur expenses in the day-to-day running of the business, but not, for example, to incur major capital expenditure, to raise finance by using the business as security, or to sell the business. It is important to remember that none of these specific powers were expressly granted to A by P, but are implied based on the express authorisation "to run a car sales business, for a four week period."

On the basis that it is common for the agent to be given implied authority to do all that is incidental to carrying out the express wishes of his principal, it has been held that an agent authorised to find a purchaser for property has implied authority to describe the property to prospective purchasers.[19] But an agent authorised to find a purchaser and conclude a contract does not have implied authority to receive the purchase money;[20] and an agent authorised to receive payment of money has no authority to accept payment in any other form or under any other arrangement.[21] It has

16 *Ireland v. Livingstone* (1872) L.R. 5 H.L. 395.
17 See further Powers of Attorney Act 1996.
18 *Midland Bank v. Rickett* [1933] A.C. 1.
19 *Mullens v. Miller* (1882) 22 Ch. D. 194.
20 *Mynn v. Joliffe* (1834) 1 Mood & R. 326.
21 *Pearson v. Scott* (1878) 9 Ch. D. 198.

been held that an agent instructed to sell a house and to be paid commission on the purchase price, has implied authority to make a binding contract and to sign an agreement of sale, as was then required.[22] But an agent instructed to find a purchaser did not have any implied authority to conclude a contract of sale.[23]

In other cases, an agent may have implied authority to do what is usual or customary for an agent in his particular trade or profession. Thus, for instance, cases have considered the "usual" authority of solicitors,[24] company directors[25] and secretaries[26] and ship's masters,[27] amongst others. A leading case on implied actual authority is *Hely Hutchinson v. Brayhead Ltd*[28] where the directors of a company allowed a director to act as managing director, though he was never actually appointed as such. The English Court of Appeal held that although he was never appointed, he had implied actual authority to act as managing director, in the circumstances.

Because an agent cannot have actual authority when he exceeds an express limit on his authority or where he does something expressly prohibited by his principal, a principal can prevent implied actual authority arising by expressly restricting his authority.

5.3 Apparent Authority

In the leading case of *Freeman and Lockyer v. Buckhurst Park Properties Ltd*,[29] Diplock L.J. explained that whereas actual authority is based on an agreement between the principal and agent, to which the third party is an outsider, apparent authority is based on a representation from the principal to the third party which does not directly concern the agent.

22 *Rosenbaum v. Belson* [1900] 2 Ch. 267.

23 *Hamer v. Sharp* (1874) L.R. 19 Eq. 108.

24 See *Kearney v. Cullen* [1955] I.R. 18, where it was held that in contentious business a solicitor not entered on the record cannot bind his client by accepting a cheque or other negotiable instrument. See also *Waugh v. HB Clifford & Son* [1982] 1 Ch. 374, [1982] 1 All E.R. 1095 (C.A.) where it was held that a solicitor conducting litigation usually has authority to compromise the action; and *United Bank of Kuwait v. Hammoud; City Trust v. Levy* [1988] 3 All E.R. 418, [1988] 1 W.L.R. 1051, (C.A.) where evidence from senior solicitors and the then President of the English Law Society was heard which established that an employed solicitor has usual authority to give undertakings to pay money out of funds in his control, provided the undertaking is given in connection with an underlying transaction.

25 See *Freeman and Lockyer v. Buckhurst Park Properties Ltd* [1964] 2 Q.B. 480; [1964] 1 All E.R. 630, (C.A.); and *Hely Hutchinson v. Brayhead Ltd* [1968] 1 Q.B. 549 (C.A.). See further below.

26 See *Panorama Developments (Guildford) Ltd v. Fidelis Furnishing Fabrics Ltd* [1971] 2 Q.B. 711; see further 5.4.1.

27 In *Grant v. Norway* (1851) 10 C.B. 665, it was held that a ship's master does not have usual authority to sign a bill of lading for goods not loaded.

28 [1968] 1 Q.B. 549 (C.A.); see 5.4.3.

29 [1964] 2 Q.B. 480; [1964] 1 All E.R. 630, (C.A.).

Apparent authority is based on estoppel:[30] if a principal makes a representation to a third party, that a person has authority and the third party relies on that representation, the principal is later estopped from denying that representation. Otherwise, a third party would be burdened with constantly having to confirm an agent's authority before dealing with him. In this sense, the doctrine of apparent authority favours third parties by allowing them to rely on appearances, and this, in turn, facilitates commerce in general, and, specifically, the ease with which transactions can be completed. However, a third party can only rely on appearances where they have been, in some way, corroborated by the principal. An agent may therefore have apparent authority to do things which he is not actually authorised to do. Where certain requirements are fulfilled, the principal will be bound by the agent's actions even though he did not actually authorise them. Moreover, as a form of estoppel, apparent authority can only make the principal liable under any contract made by his agent. It cannot give the principal an independent cause of action unless he ratifies his agent's unauthorised acts.[31]

Apparent authority usually coincides with an agent's actual authority but it can go further and it can:

(i) create authority where none existed;[32]
(ii) extend an existing agent's actual authority;[33]
(iii) create or extend authority despite an express restriction from the principal, unknown to the third party;[34]or
(iv) extend an agent's authority after termination of the agency.[35]

30 This was recognised in *Rama Corpn v. Proved Tin and General Investment Ltd* [1952] 2 Q.B. 147, [1952] 1 All E.R. 554; and approved in *Freeman and Lockyer v. Buckhurst Park Properties Ltd* [1964] 2 Q.B. 480; [1964] 1 All E.R. 630, (C.A.). This is not without its problems: see *Bowstead on Agency* (London, Sweet & Maxwell, 16th ed., 1996) para 8–029.

31 On ratification, see 5.5.

32 See, *e.g. Barrett v. Deere* (1828) Mood & M. 200 where A entered P's counting house and acted as if he was entrusted with P's business. A was a stranger to P and not an agent. Nevertheless it was held that payment of a debt to A was binding on P because P allowed A to enter his business premises and appear to be responsible for P's business.

33 See below, *e.g. First Energy v. Hungarian International Bank* [1993] 2 Lloyd's Rep. 194.

34 See, *e.g. Manchester Trust v. Furness* [1895] 2 Q.B. 539 where a charterparty provided that the ship's master, appointed by the ship owner, was to sign bills of lading on behalf of the charterers only. Despite this restriction, the ship owner was held liable on a bill of lading signed by the master because the third party was unaware of the restriction and was entitled to assume that the usual situation applied, that is, that the master was an agent for the owner.

35 See below, *e.g. Summers v. Salomon* (1857) 7 E. & B. 879.

5.3.1 Requirements for apparent authority

The leading case of *Freeman and Lockyer v. Buckhurst Park Properties Ltd*[36] sets out three requirements which must be fulfilled before a principal can be bound by an agent's apparent authority.

(i) There must be a representation that a person, the agent, has authority.
(ii) The representation must come from someone with authority to make that representation – usually, though not always, the principal.
(iii) The representation must be relied on by the third party.

Each requirement will be examined in detail below.

5.3.1.1 The representation

The representation that a person, the agent, has authority can be express or implied.[37] An express representation will be based on words, spoken or written. An implied representation can be based on previous dealings between the parties or on conduct. For instance, by placing a person, A, in a position and assenting to it, a principal may be taken to have represented to the world that A has the authority which an agent in that position usually has. In *Freeman and Lockyer v. Buckhurst Park Properties*,[38] the defendant company had power under its constitution to appoint a managing director but it never did so. However, A acted as if he had been appointed managing director. The other directors knew of this and did not object. A instructed the plaintiffs, a firm of architects, to do some work on behalf of the defendant company, but the company later refused to pay the plaintiffs' fee arguing that A had no authority to hire them. The architects sued for the fee. It was held in the Court of Appeal that the other directors knowingly acquiesced in A's conduct and hence had represented that A was authorised to act as managing director.[39] Moreover, the plaintiffs had relied on that representation – by entering a contract – and so the defendant company was now estopped from denying its representation and was liable to pay the fee.[40]

36 [1964] 2 Q.B. 480; [1964] 1 All E.R. 630, (C.A.).

37 Where a representation is made negligently, based on case law on estoppel from a related area, it would appear that the representation will only bind a principal where the principal owed a duty of care to the representee: see *Moorgate Mercantile Co Ltd v. Twitchings* [1977] A.C. 890, [1976] 3 W.L.R. 66; *Mercantile Credit Co Ltd v. Hamblin* [1965] 2 Q.B. 242, (C.A.), see further 19.4. There is no direct case law on this point in Ireland.

38 [1964] 2 Q.B. 480; [1964] 1 All E.R. 630, (C.A.).

39 On this analysis, a representation is made up of two elements: (i) the appointment of someone to a position *and* (ii) the acquiescence of the principal in the agent's actions. Thus, the appointment of someone to a position alone, does not amount to an representation: see further Brown, "The Agent's Apparent Authority: Paradigm or Paradox" [1995] *Journal of Business Law* 360.

40 See further 5.3.1.3.

An agent's power to bind his principal is not limited to contractual obligations, as was illustrated in the Irish case of *Kett v. Shannon & English*,[41] where the question of consent was at issue. Here the Supreme Court, approving *Freeman and Lockyer*, addressed the question of what amounts to a representation. The first defendant had bought a car from the second defendant garage owner but it proved defective and was returned for repair. In the meantime, the first defendant buyer got the loan of a car from the second defendant garage owner. When the buyer later returned to the second defendant's garage to collect his car it was not ready. The mechanic on duty said that the buyer could take another car. Two days later, the buyer negligently crashed into the plaintiff while driving the second loaned car. For the purpose of road traffic law, the issue was whether the first defendant buyer was driving with the consent of the second defendant garage owner, and, in particular, had the mechanic on duty authority to loan cars on behalf of the second defendant.

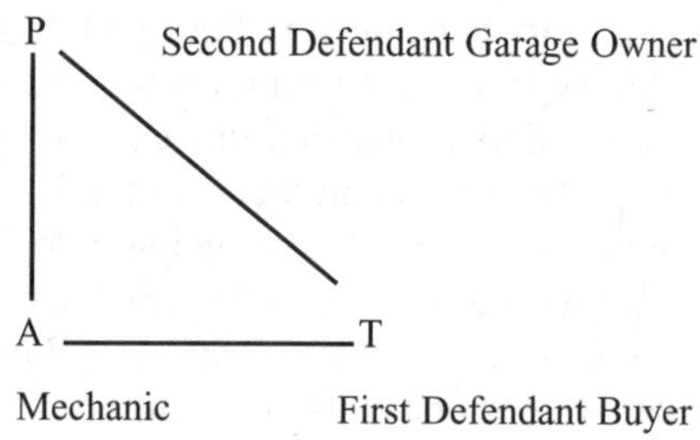

The Supreme Court found that the mechanic had no actual authority to loan cars to customers and that the second defendant garage owner, by simply leaving the mechanic in charge had made no representation to the buyer that the mechanic had authority to loan cars. Hence, there could be no apparent authority, and the second defendant was not liable. This case is clearly distinguishable from *Freeman and Lockyer*. In *Freeman and Lockyer*, the agent's conduct (acting as if he were managing director) was ongoing and the principal (the other directors) tacitly approved of the agent's conduct. In *Kett v. Shannon & English*, the principal was unaware of the mechanic's once-off exercise of power, and so was in no position to know or approve of this conduct. Clearly, if the mechanic had loaned cars in the past and the garage owner had not objected to such conduct, the argument in favour of a representation would have been stronger.

The issue of representation was also addressed in the Irish case *APD v. Walsh & ors*.[42] The plaintiff company was a drug distributor, the defendants were a firm of accountants, and the first defendant, W, was a partner within that firm. W became a shareholder and director of, and a financial advisor to the plaintiff company. The defendant firm audited the plaintiff's books

41 [1987] I.L.R.M. 364 (S.C.).
42 [1991] 2 I.R. 8 (H.C.).

and accounts. W advised the plaintiff to make loans to, and received loans from another company, T, an unlimited company operated by W. A number of different loan transactions were made on the advice of W. However, T became insolvent at a time when the plaintiff had £350,000 on deposit with the company. The plaintiff company sued the firm for losses caused by the investment advice of W, a partner of the firm. Under section 5 of the Partnership Act 1890, every partner is an agent of the firm and the other partners for the purpose of the business of the firm, and every partner who does an act for carrying on in the usual way business of the kind carried on by the firm binds the firm and the other partners. In defence, the firm argued that W had no authority to bind the other partners because the giving of investment advice was outside the ordinary course of business of a firm of accountants.

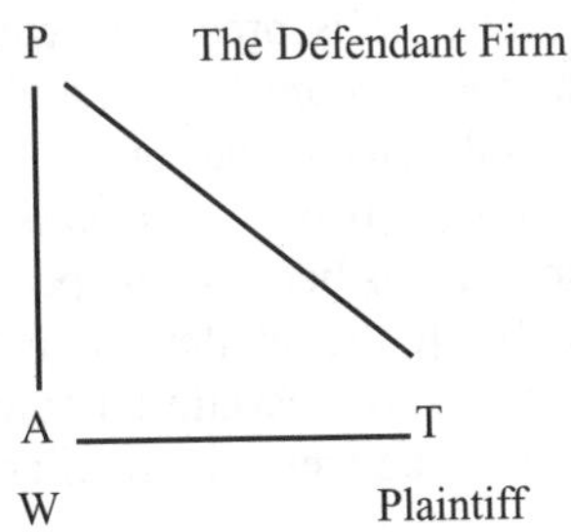

The High Court held that, in the circumstances, the giving of investment advice by one of the partners of the firm was in the ordinary course of the business. Further, it was held that the firm was aware that W was giving this advice because they audited the books and accounts of the company, and by not challenging the loan transactions, the firm represented that W had authority to give advice. This is similar to *Freeman and Lockyer* where the knowledge of a person's conduct followed by silence – *tacit approval* – constitutes a representation for the purpose of the doctrine of apparent authority.

A principal must be careful when an agency relationship is terminated to ensure that such termination is communicated to customers. Failure to do so can lead to a representation, based on a course of dealings, that the agent still has authority, as illustrated in *Summers v. Salomon*.[43] In this case, the defendant employed his nephew as manager to run his jewellery shop and regularly paid for the jewellery ordered by the nephew from the plaintiff for resale in the shop. The nephew left the shop, terminating the agency without notice. Subsequently, the nephew obtained goods from the plaintiff in the defendant's name and then disappeared. The defendant was held liable for the price of the goods because the defendant had represented

43 (1857) 7 E. & B. 879; see also *The Unique Mariner* [1978] 1 Lloyd's Rep. 438.

to the plaintiff, by his conduct, that his nephew was his general agent. Although the agency was terminated, what passed between the defendant and the nephew did not affect that representation and hence did not limit the defendant's liability. Only by giving the plaintiff notice of the termination of the agency would the representation be negatived.

The English case *First Sport v. Barclays Bank*[44] indicates the lengths to which a court will go to find a representation for the purpose of the doctrine of apparent authority. This case also illustrates the use of agency principles as a legal device or tool. Here, a person's cheque book and cheque guarantee card were stolen. The thief used them, by forging the signature, to purchase a pair of runners for £49.99 (the limit on the cheque guarantee card being £50.00). When the shop sought payment from the bank, the bank refused. The shop argued that the bank was bound, using the doctrine of apparent authority.

Normally when a cheque is presented with a guarantee card for the payment of goods, by the account holder, and accepted by the retailer, in accordance with the conditions on the card, a contract comes into existence between the retailer and the bank. Under this contract the bank becomes primarily liable to pay. This is because the person presenting the cheque is treated as making an offer to the retailer, *as agent of the bank*, that the bank will honour the cheque up to a certain amount and when accepted, there forms a unilateral contract between the retailer and the bank.[45]

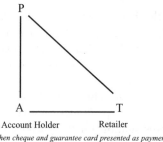

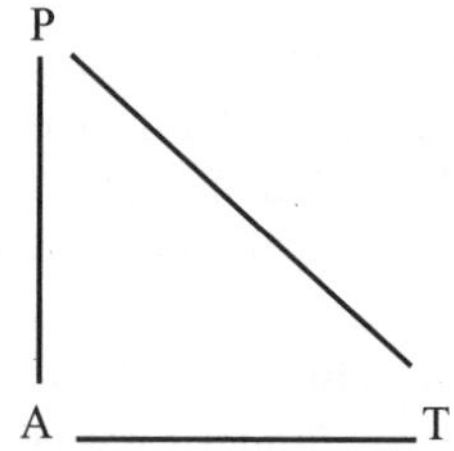

when cheque and guarantee card presented as payment

The issue in *First Sport v. Barclays Bank* was whether this agency analysis applied when the cheque and guarantee card was presented, not by the account holder, but by a thief. The Court of Appeal noted that the cheque guarantee card operated on condition that the signatures on the cheque and the card matched – which in this case they did. Moreover, the card, according to the court's interpretation, did not expressly provide that the cheque had to be signed by the authorised signatory. Clearly, the thief had no actual authority to bind the bank; only the authorised signatory had actual authority to bind the bank. The issue was whether the thief had apparent authority. The Court of Appeal held, despite a strong dissent from

44 [1991] 3 All E.R. 789 (C.A.).

45 *Metropolitan Police Comr v. Charles* [1976] 3 All E.R. 112 at 121; [1977] A.C. 177 at 191; and *Re Charge Card Services Ltd* [1987] Ch. 150.

Kennedy L.J., that the bank represented that the thief was its agent by the form of wording used on the guarantee card, in that it only required the signatures to match and hence, the retailer had only to concern himself with appearances. This representation was relied upon by the retailer and hence the bank was bound.

The case stretches the meaning of representation, arguable beyond all reasonable limits. Apparent authority must be based on a representation from the principal, and not the agent.[46] The bank was found to have made such a representation through the wording of the card, but that representation was passed to the retailer by the person in possession of the card. The decision comes close to allowing apparent authority to be based on the fraudulent actions of an apparent agent. The decision is clearly based on concerns about the efficacy of cheque guarantee cards,[47] but, it must be asked whether such a broad approach to the concept of representation has damaged the principles of law which underlie the doctrine of apparent authority?

5.3.1.2 By whom?

First, the representation is usually made by the principal. In *Freeman and Lockyer v. Buckhurst Park Properties*,[48] it was the board of directors, who had actual authority to act on behalf of the company, that made the representation, by allowing the director to act as *de facto* managing director. In *APD v. Walsh & ors*,[49] it was the firm, the collection of partners, that made the representation by allowing one of the partners to act as financial advisor to the plaintiff company.

Second, in general, apparent authority cannot be based on a representation by the agent that he is authorised. In the leading case, *Armagas Ltd v. Mundogas Ltd,*[50] the issue was whether the chartering manager (A) of the defendant company (P) had apparent authority to enter into a time-charter. T owned a ship and wished to charter it to P for three years. T dealt with A, who, as T knew, generally had no authority to enter such a transaction. However, A fraudulently claimed to have been given specific authority to enter the charter. T argued that P was bound on the basis that A had apparent authority to claim to have received actual authority to enter the contract. The House of Lords found that no representation by A could bind P.[51] Thus, where a third party deals with an

46 See 5.3.1.2.

47 Following this case, the wording on cheque guarantee cards is generally now altered such that the use of such cards are expressly restricted to persons to whom the card is issued.

48 [1964] 2 Q.B. 480; [1964] 1 All E.R. 630, (C.A.).

49 [1991] 2 I.R. 8.

50 [1985] 1 Lloyd's Rep. 1; [1986] 2 All E.R. 385, approved in Ireland in *Kett v. Shannon & English* [1987] I.L.R.M. 364; and *APD v. Walsh & ors* [1991] 2 I.R. 8.

51 In *United Bank of Kuwait v. Hammound: City Trust Ltd v. Levy* [1988] 1 W.L.R. 1051 at 1066, Lord Donaldson M.R. stated: "it is trite law that an agent cannot ordinarily confer ostensible

agent in a transaction which is not usual for an agent in his position, he will not normally be able to rely on the agent's own assertion that he has received actual authority to enter into the particular transaction since he cannot claim that the agent has apparent authority to claim authority. In such a situation the third party should seek confirmation of the agent's authority from the principal or someone who is authorised to manage the principal's business.

Ultimately, the representation must be made by someone with authority to make it. This is usually the principal, but not necessarily. In *Freeman and Lockyer v. Buckhurst Park Properties*, Diplock L.J. stated that an agent could make a representation about another person's authority but only if he had "actual" authority to do the very act that he represented the other person as having authority to do.[52] This approach has been criticised as unduly restrictive,[53] there seems no good reason why an agent who has apparent authority to do the act could not be able to represent that another person has authority to do the same act. Where the agent does not usually have authority to do the act himself, a third party is normally put on enquiry.[54]

Moreover, it would seem that a representation can come from the agent himself where he has actual or apparent authority to make representations about his own authority.[55] The issue will realistically only arise where it is claimed that an agent has apparent authority to make representations about his own authority, since it is not likely that a principal would give an agent actual authority to claim that he is authorised to do something that he is not actually authorised to do. In *City Trust Ltd v. Levy*,[56] the court had to decide if a firm of solicitors was bound by an undertaking given on its behalf by an assistant solicitor. As a matter of evidence, the court found that it was usual for such undertakings to be given only where there was an underlying transaction on behalf of the client. The assistant solicitor falsely told the third party that such an underlying transaction existed. The court found that the assistant solicitor had authority to communicate such information and the firm was bound. The assistant solicitor had no actual authority to make such false statements and so his authority to bind the firm must have been apparent, the representation being based on his own statement that there was an underlying transaction because it was usual for solicitors to make such statements.

A senior manager might have actual or apparent authority to make statements about the running of a business, including statements about the

authority on himself. He cannot pull himself up by his own shoe laces." These two cases were considered together by the Court of Appeal, because they involved very similar situations.

52 Applied in *Crabtree-Vickers Pty Ltd v. Australian Direct Mail Advertising and Addressing Co Pty Ltd* (1975) 133 C.L.R. 72 (H.C.).

53 See *Bowstead & Reynolds on Agency* (London, Sweet & Maxwell, 16th ed., 1996) para 8-021.

54 See, *e.g. Armagas Ltd v. Mundogas Ltd* above.

55 *The Rafaella* [1985] 2 Lloyd's Rep. 36.

56 [1988] 3 All E.R. 418 (C.A.); see further Stone, "Usual and Ostensible Authority – One Concept or Two?" [1993] *Journal of Business Law* 325.

authority of agents, including himself. For example, in *First Energy v. Hungarian International Bank*,[57] a senior manager was dealing with a client of the bank to arrange ad hoc finance, pending more general approval. The client knew that the manager could not approve the facility himself – he did not have the authority. Later, the senior manager alone wrote to the client in a manner signifying approval. However, the bank had not approved the loan and sought to repudiate it. The Court of Appeal held that although the senior manager did not have actual authority to approve the loan, he did have apparent authority to communicate approval and so the bank was bound. The court distinguished *Armagas* on the basis that the agent in *Armagas* had no apparent authority to claim that he was specifically authorised to enter the charter, whereas in this case the agent had a general apparent authority, by virtue of his position, to make representations and to communicate decisions from head office. The distinction is a fine one.[58]

However, anyone less than a senior manager would probably not have such authority. In *British Bank of the Middle East v. Sun Life Insurance of Canada*,[59] a third party got a guarantee, on behalf of the defendant company, from an unauthorised insurance agent. The third party wrote to the "general manager" of the company in London to enquire whether the agent was authorised. There was no general manager but his letter was answered by a "branch manager" who, without having any authority himself, stated that the agent had the necessary authority. It was found that a branch manager would normally have no authority to bind the company, and in this case the company was not bound. This decision might seem unfair on the third party who went to the effort of checking the authority of the agent. After all, how is the third party to know the usual authority of branch managers? On the other hand, the decision seems to be based, in part, on the fact that the third party wrote to the "general manager" but relied on the reply from a "branch manager" and that this inconsistency should have raised doubts in the third party's mind as to the reliability of the letter. Although there is no direct Irish authority on this point, it would appear from the above that cases where an agent has apparent authority based on his own representation will be rare and will be limited to situations where because of an agent's senior position or particular circumstances, it is usual for him to make such statements and it is not unreasonable for a third party to rely on those statements.

---

57 [1993] 2 Lloyd's Rep. 194.

58 See Brown, "The Agent's Apparent Authority: Paradigm or Paradox" [1995] *Journal of Business Law* 360.

59 [1983] 2 Lloyd's Rep. 9; see further Reynolds, "The Ultimate Apparent Authority" (1994) 110 *Law Quarterly Review* 21; and Brown, "The Agent's Apparent Authority: Paradigm or Paradox" [1995] *Journal of Business Law* 360.

Lastly, where an agent claims to have authority and a third party enters a contract in reliance on the agent's claim and it transpires that the agent is not authorised, a separate head of liability, known as breach of warrant of authority, allows the third party to sue the agent. This matter is considered in more detail in Chapter 6.[60]

5.3.1.3 Reliance

The third party must rely on the representation that the agent has authority and change his position as a result. Entering into a contract with the agent will be sufficient change of position. It seems that there is no further requirement of "detriment".[61] The third party must therefore know of the representation: constructive notice is insufficient.[62] Furthermore, a third party cannot claim to have relied on the representation if he knows the representation to be false. In certain circumstances, the court may find that the third party ought to be aware of the agent's lack of authority. In *Overbrooke Estates Ltd v. Glencombe Properties Ltd*,[63] T, the plaintiff, purchased property at an auction having relied on the auctioneer's statement which proved false. T alleged that P, the vendor, was liable for the statement on the basis of apparent authority, but failed. The auction particulars stated that the auctioneer had no authority to make such statements and T therefore could not claim to rely on any representation that he had authority.

5.4 Usual/Customary Authority

Usual and customary authority are similar concepts. In most cases they are types of actual or apparent authority.[64] But, based on case law,[65] it can be argued that there is a third separate type of authority, known as usual authority.[66]

60 See 6.4.5.

61 Based on *Freeman and Lockyer v. Buckhurst Park Properties* [1964] 2 Q.B. 480; [1964] 1 All E.R. 630, (C.A.) all that is needed is an alteration of position. The need for detriment is consistent with the strict requirements of an estoppel; see *Farquharson Bros & Co. v. King & Co.* [1902] A.C. 325. More recently, it was held that "The only detriment that has to be shown … is the entering into the contract;" per Gatehouse J. in *The Tatra* [1990] 2 Lloyd's Rep. 51 at 59.

62 For example, a statement in the Articles of Association of a company that it has power to appoint a managing director will not give rise to an estoppel as against a third party who has not read the Articles: *Rama Corpn v. Proved Tin and General Investment Ltd* [1955] 2 Q.B. 147.

63 [1974] 3 All E.R. 511.

64 See 5.4.1 and 5.4.2.

65 *Watteau v. Fenwick* (1893) 1 Q.B. 346.

66 See 5.4.3.

5.4.1 Usual authority

An agent (A) appointed to a position may either (i) implicitly be given, or (ii) appear to have the authority which an agent in that position usually has. In each case he may be said to have "usual authority". However in scenario (i) A's usual authority is a species of actual authority, whereas in scenario (ii) it is a species of apparent authority. This distinction may be important as between the principal and the agent. If A is appointed to a position but his authority is expressly limited so that it is less than an agent in that position would usually have, he may nevertheless have apparent authority to do what such agents may usually do, and third parties who are unaware of the limitation may rely on the appearance of authority.

For example, assume that A is appointed to act as company secretary to company P but is expressly told that he may not enter into any contract without the approval of the company's chief executive. A enters into a contract with T, who is unaware of the limitation on A's authority, for the supply to the company of a photocopier. P may be bound by the contract, notwithstanding the limitation on A's authority, under the doctrine of apparent authority, if it is within the usual authority of a company secretary.

Deciding what is usual for an agent in a particular position is a matter of evidence. For instance, in *Panorama Developments (Guildford) Ltd v. Fidelis Furnishing Fabrics Ltd*,[67] it was stated that a company secretary would have usual authority to sign contracts "dealing with the administrative side of [the] company's affairs", and on the facts it was held that a company secretary had actual implied usual authority to hire cars on behalf of the company.

5.4.2 Customary authority

An agent may also, impliedly or apparently, be authorised to do what is customary for agents in his particular trade. Such customary authority is a variety of usual authority and may be particularly important in the context of commercial transactions where particular markets – for instance, certain commodity markets – may have settled customs and practices.[68] It is illustrated in the case of *Dingle v. Hare*[69] where A, acting on behalf of the defendant, contracted to sell some manure and had warranted it. It was found that it was customary for agents in that particular trade to warrant manure, so the defendant was bound although he had not expressly authorised the warranty. A custom will only be recognised if it is certain, notorious and reasonable.

67 [1971] 2 Q.B. 711.

68 See, *e.g. Sheppard v. Murphy* [1867] I.R. 1 Eq. 490 regarding the customs of the London Stock Exchange and the usual authority of stockbrokers, at the time.

69 (1859) 7 C.B.N.S. 145.

5.4.3 Relationship between actual implied, apparent and usual authority

Where an agent is appointed to a position, the scope of his actual authority depends on (i) what he is expressly instructed to do and (ii) what is usual for an agent in that position. If no limitations are imposed by the principal on his authority, he may be held impliedly to have actual authority to do everything which an agent in his position is usually authorised to do. He may be said to have the usual authority of an agent in his position but his authority is actual. Thus if he acts in a way which is usual for an agent in his position, he binds the principal and acts in accordance with his duty as the principal's agent.

Even if express limitations are placed on an agent's actual authority, he may nevertheless appear to outsiders to have the authority which an agent in his position usually has. He may be said to have the *usual* authority of an agent in his position, but his authority is now only *apparent*. Thus if he acts in a way which is usual for an agent in his position, he will bind his principal but be liable to him for exceeding his actual authority.

Thus both *actual* and *apparent* authority can be described as *usual*. Moreover, in the first situation A will *appear* to have the authority which he *actually* has. This can cause confusion, as is illustrated by the decision in *Hely-Hutchinson v. Brayhead Ltd.*[70] A was appointed chairman of Brayhead Ltd. He also, with the acquiescence of the board of directors, acted as *de facto* managing director of the company, though he was never actually appointed as such. As part of a corporate financing deal, A gave an indemnity, on behalf of Brayhead, to the plaintiff, T. T sought to enforce the indemnity against Brayhead. The crucial issue was whether A had authority to give the indemnity so as to bind Brayhead. It was argued that A had both implied and apparent authority. Roskill J. at first instance refused to hold that A had implied authority to give an indemnity merely by virtue of being appointed chairman of Brayhead. However, he had apparent authority because he was allowed to act as, and appeared to be managing director. The Court of Appeal, in contrast, held that he had actual authority – not by virtue of his appointment as chairman, because a company chairman would not usually have authority to enter into such a contract, but because by allowing him to act as if he were managing director, the board of directors (acting on behalf of the company) had impliedly authorised A to do such things as a managing director would usually do. Of course, the company was bound to T in either case. But the difference between a finding of implied actual authority and apparent authority is crucial to the relationship between P and A. If A only had apparent authority, he would be liable to P for acting without consent.

---

70 [1968] 1 Q.B. 549 (C.A.).

5.4.4 Watteau v. Fenwick

There is some support for the existence of a separate category of usual authority, distinct from both actual and apparent authority, so that where an agent is appointed to a position, any acts that he does, which would be usual for a person in that position to do, are binding on the principal.[71] In *Watteau v. Fenwick*,[72] A was appointed to manage a public house, which he had previously owned. His name was still over the door as licensee. P expressly limited his actual authority by forbidding him to purchase anything other than bottled ales and mineral waters. In defiance of that prohibition, he bought cigars from T. In a very brief judgment, P was held liable for their price.

Clearly, A did not have actual authority: there was an express prohibition. Nor could this be a case of apparent authority, as T believed A to be owner of the business and was not aware of P, and so could not rely on any representation made by P. The correct basis of this decision is therefore unclear and various explanations have been offered; one is that an agent appointed to a position has power to bind his principal by doing acts which would be usual for an agent in his position.[73] The case is old and has been doubted but has not been overruled in Ireland or England, and hence could be significant.[74] This case has, however, been overruled several times in Canada.[75] It suggests that where a proprietor appoints a manager to run a business on his behalf, he may be bound by any acts of the manager which would be normal for a manager, or even a proprietor, of such a business, even though they have been expressly prohibited. But

71 See generally Stone, "Usual and Ostensible Authority – One Concept or Two?" [1993] *Journal of Business Law* 325, who argues for such a separate head of authority.

72 (1893) 1 Q.B. 346; see further Tettenborn, "Agents, Business Owners, and Estoppel" 57 (1998) *Cambridge Law Journal* 274.

73 Other explanations include: apparent authority, see Goodhart & Hamson, "Undisclosed Principals in Contracts" (1932) 4 *Cambridge Law Journal* 320 at 336, cf. Fridman, "The Demise of Watteau v. Fenwick: Sign-O-Lite Ltd v. Metropolitan Life Insurance Co." (1991) 70 *Can. Bar Rev.* 329; an analogy with vicarious liability in tort law, see Treitel, *The Law of Contract* (London, Sweet & Maxwell, 10th ed., 1999) pp.662–3, *cf.* Collier, "Authority of an Agent – *Wateau v. Fenwick* Revisited" [1985] *Cambridge Law Journal* 363 at 365; an extension of the doctrine of apparent ownership, see Conant, "The Objective Theory of Agency: Apparent Authority and the Estoppel of Apparent Ownership" (1968) 47 *Nebraska Law Review* 678, *cf.* Hornby, "The Usual Authority of an Agent" [1961] *Cambridge Law Journal* 239 at 246; estoppel by conduct, see Tettenborn, "Agents, Business Owners, and Estoppel" 57 (1998) *Cambridge Law Journal* 274, and Sealy & Hooley, *Commercial Law* (London, Butterworths, 2nd ed, 1999) p.117.

74 But see criticism of Bingham J. in *The Rhodian River* [1984] 1 Lloyd's Rep. 373.

75 See *McLoughlin v. Gentles* (1919) 46 O.L.R. 477; *Massey-Harris Co Ltd v. Bond* [1930] 2 D.L.R. 57; and *Sign-O-Lite Plastics v. Metropolitan Life Ins Co* (1990) 73 D.L.R. (4th) 541, at 548; see further Fridman,"The Demise of Watteau v. Fenwick: Sign-O-Lite Ltd v. Metropolitan Life Insurance Co." (1991) 70 *Can. Bar Rev.* 329.

if a third party is unaware of the existence of the principal, is it fair that he should be able to then fix that principal with the unauthorised acts of an agent? In order to avoid this outcome, the proprietor should ensure that third parties who deal with the business, such as suppliers and customers, are aware that he is the proprietor of the business, and of the scope of the manager's authority.

5.5 Ratification

Where an agent, purporting to act on behalf of a principal, enters into a transaction without the principal's prior actual authority, the principal can retrospectively approve the agent's actions and adopt the transaction. The principal is said to ratify the agent's actions and the result is as if the agent had, at all relevant times, acted with authority. This process of ratification can occur in two distinct circumstances:

(i) when a person acts without authority because he is not an agent at all, or,
(ii) when an appointed agent exceeds his authority.

5.5.1 Requirements for ratification

A principal can only ratify an agent's actions if the following seven conditions are met.

(i) The agent must purport to be acting for a principal.
(ii) The principal must have been in existence at the time when the agent purported to act on his behalf.
(iii) The principal must have been competent at the time when the agent purported to act on his behalf and at the time of ratification.
(iv) The principal must have been capable of being ascertained at the time when the agent purported to act on his behalf.
(v) A principal cannot ratify a nullity.
(vi) The principal must ratify within a reasonable time.
(vii) The principal cannot ratify unless aware of all the material facts.

5.5.1.1 Purported to be acting for a principal

The agent must have purported to be acting for a principal.[76] Hence, the existence of a principal must be disclosed to the third party. Where the principal is undisclosed,[77] that is, where the third party is not aware that the agent is acting for another party, the undisclosed principal can never ratify a contract.[78] So, for example, the owner of the public house in *Watteau v. Fenwick*[79] could not have enforced the contract made by the manager using the doctrine of ratification.

5.5.1.2 In existence

The principal must be in existence at the time when the agent purported to act on his behalf. This requirement caused problems in the past for promoters of companies who had to enter into contracts on behalf of the company before it was incorporated. Such contracts could not bind the company and the company could not later ratify such contracts.[80] Today, the issue of pre-incorporation contracts is addressed in companies legislation.[81]

5.5.1.3 Competent

The principal must be competent at the time when the agent purported to act on his behalf and when he seeks to ratify. Thus a company cannot ratify contracts which are *ultra vires* the company.

5.5.1.4 Capable of being ascertained

It is not enough that the agency is disclosed, the principal must be capable of being ascertained at the time when the agent purported to act on his behalf.[82] The principal does not have to be named or identified; rather there must be sufficient information to enable the third party to identify the

---

76 *Keighley, Maxstead & Co v. Durant* [1901] A.C. 240 (H.L.).

77 See 6.1.1 and 6.3.

78 For criticism of the rule that an undisclosed principal cannot ratify see Rochvarg, "Ratification and Undisclosed Principals" (1989) 34 *McGill Law Review* 286.

79 (1893) 1 Q.B. 346; see further Tettenborn, "Agents, Business Owners, and Estoppel" 57 (1998) *Cambridge Law Journal* 274.

80 *Kelner v. Baxter* (1866) L.R. 2 C.P. 174.

81 Companies Act 1963, s.37.

82 *Watson v. Swann* (1862) 11 C.B.N.S. 756; for criticism of this rule see *Bowstead on Agency* (London, Sweet & Maxwell, 16th ed., 1996) para 2–063. An important exception to this rule relates to marine insurance policies which can be taken out "for and on behalf of any person interested" and such persons can ratify even though not named in the policy: see *Hagedorn v. Olicerson* (1814) 2 M. & S. 485. See further Reynolds, "Some Agency Problems in Insurance Law" in Rose, ed., *Consensus Ad Idem* (London, Sweet & Maxwell, 1996), pp.82–83.

principal. One consequence of this rule is that if a contractor enters into a contract, such as a building or engineering contract, intending to sub-contract some of the work, sub-contractors appointed after the conclusion of the main contract cannot take advantage of exclusion clauses in the main contract, even if they were intended to have the benefit of them. In *Southern Water Authority v. Carey*,[83] for example, a contractor entered into a contract which contained exclusion clauses which purported to protect sub-contractors also. When the employer sued one of the sub-contractors in tort, the sub-contractor was unable to claim the benefit of the exclusion clauses because:

(i) they were not party to the main contract,
(ii) they had not authorised the main contractors to act on their behalf and,
(iii) being unascertainable to the employer at the time the contract was made, they could not later ratify the contract.

5.5.1.5 Cannot ratify a nullity

A principal can ratify acts which are both lawful and unlawful but cannot ratify a nullity. Thus it has been said that a principal cannot ratify a forged signature on a cheque,[84] while in *Presentaciones Musicales SA v. Secunda and another*,[85] it was held that a company could ratify the issuing of a defective writ. Where a contract is void for mistake, it cannot be ratified, though where a contract is voidable following a misrepresentation, it may be ratified.[86]

5.5.1.6 Reasonable time

A principal must ratify within a reasonable time from when the agent purported to act on the principal's behalf. What constitutes a reasonable time is a question of fact, depending on the circumstances of the case. Generally, a principal cannot ratify a contract after the time for its performance or the commencement of performance has arrived,[87] except perhaps, where such ratification benefits the third party.[88]

---

83 [1985] 2 All E.R. 1077.

84 *Brook v. Hook* (1871) L.R. 6 Exch. 89; see also *Athy Guardians v. Murphy* [1896] 1 I.R. 65.

85 [1994] 2 All E.R. 737; see further White & Bradgate, "Under Instruction" (1995) 92/33 *The Gazette* 22.

86 See 2.2.5.2.

87 *Metropolitan Asylums Board (Managers) v. Kingham* (1890) 6 T.L.R. 217.

88 *Bedford Insurance Co Ltd v. Instituto des Resseguros do Brazil* [1985] Q.B. 966.

5.5.1.7 Knowledge of all relevant circumstances

A principal cannot ratify unless he has full knowledge of all relevant circumstances. In *Brennan v. O'Connell*,[89] the defendant engaged an auctioneer to procure a purchaser for a farm. The auctioneer entered into a written contract of sale with the plaintiff and concluded the agreement without the defendant's authority. When the defendant was told of the sale, he said he was satisfied. However, when the defendant expressed his approval he did not know that the day after the sale there had been another inquiry about the farm, asking the price; and in response, the inquirer had simply stated that the price was "a lot of money". The plaintiff sought an order of specific performance, but the defendant argued that he was not bound because he did not have full knowledge of all the relevant circumstances when he purported to ratify. The Supreme Court held that the defendant's subsequent approval of the auctioneer's actions constituted ratification provided that at the time of the approval he knew of all facts which were known to the agent and which were objectively necessary for him to be aware in order to decide whether or not to ratify. The court found that the inquiry made was not of this type and so the ratification was effective and the defendant was bound. Moreover, it has been held that a principal with incomplete information may be taken to have ratified an agent's unauthorised action if it can be shown that he took a risk as to how circumstances might turn out.[90]

5.5.2 Method of ratification

The principal can expressly adopt the relevant transaction, or adoption can be implied from the facts. For instance, in *Barclay's Bank v. Breen*,[91] a solicitor was engaged by a bank to act on its behalf "in dealing with any legal formalities in connection with our proof of title and ultimate disposal of the property." The solicitor acted for the bank in the sale of the property, and issued a receipt for the deposit received. The solicitor was later paid the balance, some of which he paid to the bank before he became insolvent. The bank claimed the remainder of the balance not paid to them by the solicitor from the purchasers. The purchasers argued that they had paid the full price to the bank's agent, the solicitor. The Supreme Court, in granting specific performance of the sale, stated that even if the solicitor had no actual authority to receive monies as agent for the bank, the bank with knowledge of all the facts, had ratified the solicitor's acceptance of the money by itself accepting part of the deposit. Thus, a principal may be

89 [1980] I.R. 13.

90 *Marsh v. Joseph* [1897] 1 Ch. 213.

91 (1962) 96 I.L.T.R. 179.

taken to have ratified if he does any act which indicates an intention to adopt the contract. Indeed, he may also be bound (on the basis of estoppel) if he passively agrees to acts done on his behalf.[92]

5.5.3 The effect of ratification

The effect of ratification is that the agent is retrospectively deemed to have had authority, so that:

(i) the principal can sue, or be sued by, the third party on the contract made by the agent;
(ii) any liability the agent may have had to the third party for breach of warranty of authority is extinguished;[93]
(iii) the agent cannot be held liable to the principal for exceeding his authority; and
(iv) the agent is entitled to remuneration on the contract; to be indemnified against any expenses incurred by him; and to any other rights arising at law or under the contract.

The anomalous effect of ratification is illustrated by the case of *Bolton Partners v. Lambert*,[94] where it was held that if a third party makes an offer to an agent which the agent, without authority, accepts on the principal's behalf but the principal later ratifies the contract, the third party is bound by the contract even if he has purported to withdraw his offer before ratification. *Bolton Partners v. Lambert* can be criticised for favouring the position of the principal who has the option of accepting the third party's withdrawal of offer thereby avoiding contractual obligations or ratifying the agent's actions and creating contractual obligations. The position of the third party is irrelevant in these circumstances. The case was not followed in *Fleming v. Bank of New Zealand*,[95] and more recently was criticised by the Supreme Court of New South Wales in *NM Superannuation Pty Ltd v. Hughes*.[96] Under Article 15(2) of the 1983 Geneva Convention on Agency in the International Sale of Goods, a third party is allowed to withdraw before ratification if, at the time of contracting, he was unaware of the agent's lack of authority.[97] But *Bolton Partners v. Lambert* may not be as prejudicial to third parties as first appears. Where a principal ratifies an

92 *Spiro v. Lintern* [1973] 3 All E.R. 319.

93 See 6.4.5.

94 (1889) 41 Ch. D. 295; recently approved in *Presentaciones Musicales SA v. Secunda and another* [1994] 2 All E.R. 737.

95 [1900] A.C. 577 (P.C.).

96 (1992) 7 A.C.S.R. 105 at 115–117, per Cohen J.

97 See generally, Bonell "The 1983 Geneva Convention on Agency in the International Sale of Goods" (1984) 32 *American Journal of Comparative Law* 717; Evans, "Explanatory Report on the Convention on Agency in the International Sale of Goods" (1984) *Uniform Law Review* 74.

acceptance, the third party gets what he bargained for, in that a third party would assume he was bound from the time of the agent's (initially unauthorised) acceptance. Where a principal does not ratify, the third party has a right of action against the agent for breach of warranty of authority.[98] The only real prejudice is the uncertainty of waiting to see whether the principal will ratify or not.

5.6 Agency of Necessity[99]

According to *Bowstead*:[100]

> "A person may have authority to act on behalf of another in certain cases where he is faced with an emergency in which the property or interests of that other person are in imminent jeopardy and it becomes necessary, in order to preserve the property or interests, so to act."

5.6.1 Requirements for agency of necessity

There are four preconditions for agency of necessity to arise.

(i) It must be shown that the agent could not get instructions from the principal.[101]
(ii) The agent must have acted in the principal's interests and bona fide.[102]
(iii) The agent's actions must be reasonable.
(iv) There must have been some necessity or emergency which caused the agent to act as he did.

The traditional example of an agent of necessity is the master of a ship who acts in an emergency to save the ship or the cargo,[103] but the doctrine is not limited to these circumstances.[104] Developments in modern communications mean that in many cases the first requirement will not be

98 See 6.4.5.

99 This agency rises by operation of law. A second example of agency by operation of law is agency arising from cohabitation. There is a rebuttable presumption that a wife has authority to pledge her husband's credit for necessities (*e.g.* food and clothes) see *Bowstead on Agency* (London, Sweet & Maxwell, 16th ed., 1996) Art. 33.

100 *Bowstead on Agency* (London, Sweet & Maxwell, 16th ed., 1996) Art. 35.

101 *Springer v. Great Western Rly Co* [1921] 1 K.B. 257 at 265 per Bankes L.J.

102 *Prager v. Blatspiel, Stamp & Heacock Ltd* [1924] 1 K.B. 566 at 571–2 per McCardie J.

103 *Hawtayne v. Bourne* (1841) 7 M. & W. 595 at 599, per Parke B.

104 Case law has established that the doctrine extends to the carriage or storage of perishable goods or livestock on land: *Great Northern Rly Co v. Swaffield* (1874) L.R. 9 Exch. 132.

satisfied and hence there is not much use made of agency by necessity in modern times.[105]

5.7 Deceit and Agency

Where the agent acts within his actual or apparent authority, or where his actions are ratified, the principal is bound. Moreover, the principal will also be held liable for the agent's deceit or other misrepresentations if the agent was acting within the scope of his actual or apparent authority when he made the representation.[106] A principal will be liable even if he did not know of the agent's actions,[107] and even if the agent was acting for his own benefit and not for the benefit of the principal.[108] However, where an agent is party to a fraud committed against his principal, his knowledge of such fraud and of the surrounding facts and circumstances is not imputed to the principal. For example, in *United Dominion Trust (Ire) Ltd v. Shannon Caravans Ltd,*[109] an employee of a hire-purchase company designed a scheme whereby a third party could obtain finance to purchase a van. The defendant, Shannon Caravans, pretended that they owned the van, which they sold to the hire-purchase company who in turn let the van to the third party. The monies gained by the defendant were given to the third party, so the defendant never profited. When the third party failed to pay the instalments, the hire-purchase company discovered the true facts and sued the defendant.[110] In defence, the defendant argued that the hire-purchase company was bound by the deceit of its agent, the employee. The Supreme Court rejected this defence holding that the agent, and not the principal, was privy to the deceit and that the knowledge of that deceit could not be imputed to the principal.[111]

---

105 See *The Choko Star* [1989] 2 Lloyd's Rep. 42; see further Brown, "Authority and Necessity in the Law of Agency" (1992) 55 *Modern Law Review* 414; Reynolds, "Agency of Necessity" [1990] *Journal of Business Law* 505; Munday, "Salvaging the Law of Agency" [1991] *Lloyd's Maritime and Commercial Law Quarterly* 1.

106 *Lloyd v. Grace, Smith & Co* [1912] A.C. 716 (H.L.).

107 *Refuge Assurance Co Ltd v. Kettlewell* [1909] A.C. 243.

108 *Lloyd v. Grace, Smith & Co* [1912] A.C. 716 (H.L.).

109 [1976] I.R. 225.

110 The action was based on an alleged breach of a statutory implied term in the sales contract that the seller's had the right to sell: s.12 of the Sale of Goods Act 1893. See further Chapter 12.

111 See also *Wall v. New Life Assurance Co Ltd* [1965] I.R. 386; *Armagas Ltd v. Mundogas Ltd* [1985] 1 Lloyd's Rep. 1; [1986] 2 All E.R. 385.

CHAPTER 6

THE EFFECTS OF AGENCY

6.1 INTRODUCTION

The next two chapters consider the effects of an agency relationship between the parties, bearing in mind that agency is a tripartite relationship involving a principal, an agent and a third party.[1] Here, we focus on the relationship between the principal and the third party, and the relationship between the agent and the third party.[2] The relationship between the principal and the agent is examined, in detail, in the next chapter.

As noted in previous chapters, the essence of an agency relationship is the agent's power to affect the legal position of the principal in relation to third parties. This power can be exercised in many different ways but in the commercial context, the most significant aspect of an agent's power is his ability to affect the contractual relations of the principal with third parties. Accordingly, this chapter concentrates on this aspect of an agent's power.[3]

The typical agency scenario (the paradigm case) is where an agent, A, acting on behalf of a principal, P, and within the scope of the actual authority granted from P to A, concludes a contract with a third party, T, who knows that A is acting for P. The effect is that privity of contract is established between P and T: in effect P steps into the shoes of A, and A drops out of the picture.[4]

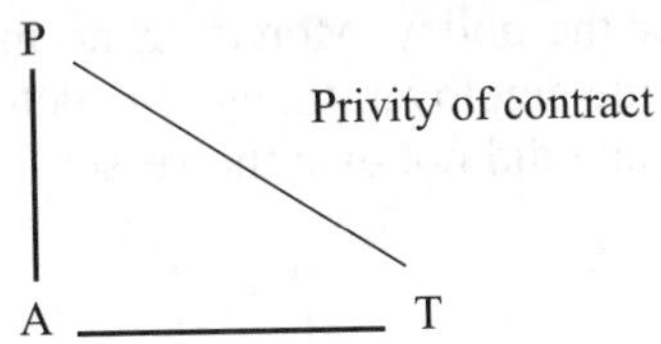

---

1 See 6.2 and 6.3.

2 See 6.3 and 6.4.

3 Other aspects of an agent's power include his ability to transfer property; to make settlements with third parties; and to make statements (see, *e.g.* *Kett v. Shannon & English* [1987] I.L.R.M. 364 (S.C.): see 5.3.1.1); on behalf of a principal. An agent's power to bind his principal depends on the agent having the necessary authority (*e.g.* actual, apparent or by ratification). But beyond these situations, a third party may acquire property rights against a principal in circumstances designed to protect third party transferees of property. For instance, "mercantile agents" have wide powers to make dispositions of their principals' property placed in their possession for the purpose of sale: see 19.2. Further, an owner of goods may be bound by a disposition under the doctrine of "apparent ownership:" see 19.4.

4 *Montgomerie v. United Kingdom Mutual Steamship Association* [1891] 1 Q.B. 370 (Q.B.D.).

It is said in this situation that the agency is disclosed, that is, the third party is aware that the agent is acting on behalf of a principal. The effects of the agency differ depending on whether the agency is disclosed or undisclosed.

6.1.1 Disclosed or undisclosed

As noted above, where the third party is aware that the agent is acting as an agent, and hence on behalf of someone else at the time of contracting, it is said that there is a disclosed agency. In contrast, where the third party believes that the agent is acting on his own behalf, and not for any other person at the time of contracting, there is an undisclosed agency. If the agency is disclosed, it is of no legal significance that the principal is not named. This distinction between disclosed and undisclosed agency is important as it affects:

(i) the principal's ability to ratify the agent's actions,[5] and,
(ii) the agent's personal liability to the third party.[6]

While the distinction is relatively easy to explain in theory, the position is more complex in practice, as illustrated by *Sui Yin Kwan v. Eastern Insurance*.[7] In this case, two crewmen were killed when their vessel was hit by a typhoon. Their personal representatives, the plaintiffs, sought compensation from the employers under, *inter alia*, an insurance policy. The employers, A Ltd, appointed RI Ltd as their general agents worldwide and to effect insurances, including workmen's compensation insurance, on the vessel. RI Ltd therefore effected workmen's compensation insurance with the defendant insurance company. RI Ltd was described as "the proposer" under the policy. Moreover, no mention was made of the fact that A Ltd was the employer, though the defendants did know that RI Ltd acted as agents and did not own the vessel.

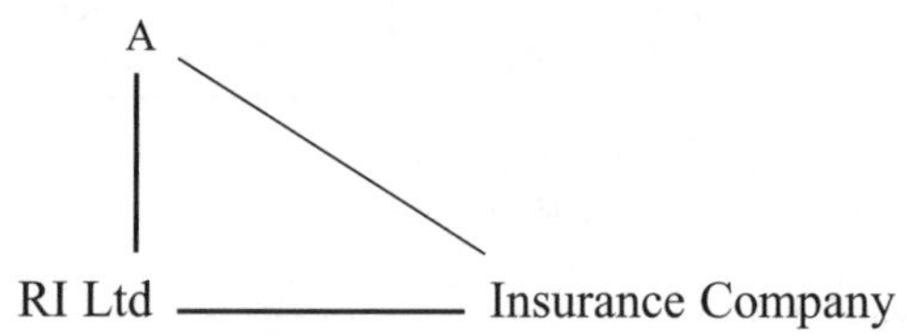

One of the first issues to be addressed was whether this was a case of disclosed or undisclosed agency. The Privy Council found that this was a

5 See 5.5.

6 See 6.4.3.

7 [1994] 2 A.C. 199; [1994] 1 All E.R. 213 (P.C.). See further Halladay, "Ability to Intervene as an Undisclosed Principal" [1994] *Lloyd's Maritime and Commercial Law Quarterly* 174; Reynolds, "When the undisclosed principal cannot intervene" [1994] *Journal of Business Law* 260; Tettenborn, "Insurers and Undisclosed Agency – Rough Justice and Commercial Expediency" [1994] *Cambridge Law Journal* 223.

case of undisclosed agency, despite the fact that the third parties knew that RI Ltd acted as agents and did not own the vessel, and that it was almost unheard of for a ship's crew to be the employees of the agents rather than the shipowners. This decision was based on a finding of fact, at first instance, that the judge was not satisfied that the third parties knew that the agents were not the employers of the crew.[8] The Privy Council went on to hold that as undisclosed principals, the principals were entitled to intervene and enforce the insurance contract. It can be noted that if the agency had been recognised as a disclosed agency in the first place, the outcome would have been the same.

6.2 Disclosed Agency

There are three particular scenarios which must be outlined to explain the effects of a disclosed agency on the parties. First, where an agent, with the principal's actual authority, concludes a contract on the principal's behalf with a third party and the agency is disclosed, a direct contractual relationship is created between the principal and the third party, and each party can sue the other on the contract (the paradigm case). The agent is not liable on this contract to either the third party or the principal.

Second, if an agent concludes a contract outside his actual authority, but within his apparent authority, the principal will be bound by the contract but cannot enforce it: as apparent authority is based on a form of estoppel it does not give rise to an independent cause of action.[9] Since apparent authority depends on a representation by the principal that the agent has authority, apparent authority can only arise where the (purported) agency is disclosed. The third party may also hold the agent personally liable for breach of warranty of authority,[10] or, in tort.[11]

Third, if an agent acts without the principal's actual authority, the principal can ratify his actions provided that the agent purported to act on his behalf; only a disclosed principal can therefore ratify an unauthorised contract. The effect here is the same as in the first scenario described above. Hence, a direct contractual relationship is created between the principal and the third party, and each party can sue the other on the

8 Lord Lloyd, delivering the judgment of the Board noted that this finding may have been "overgenerous" to the third party insurance company, see [1994] 2 A.C. 199 at 206–7; [1994] 1 All E.R. 213 at 220.

9 Markesinis & Munday submit that the same rule applies when an agent of necessity contracts on behalf of a principal: see Markesinis & Munday, *An Outline of the Law of Agency* (London, Butterworths, 4th ed., 1998) p.145. But agency of necessity, unlike apparent authority is not based on estoppel and it is hard to see why a principal should be prevented from bringing an action on the contract in these circumstances.

10 See 6.4.5.

11 See 6.4.6.

contract. The agent is not liable on this contract to either the third party or the principal.

It almost goes without saying that where an agent acts without authority, the principal will incur no liability to a third party.[12]

6.3 Undisclosed Agency

Where an agent contracts with a third party without disclosing that he is acting as an agent, so that the agency is undisclosed, the contract is initially between the agent and the third party and each may enforce the contract against the other. However, if the third party discovers the undisclosed principal's existence, the third party may enforce the contract against either the agent or the principal. Moreover, provided that the agent acted with actual authority, the undisclosed principal can intervene and enforce the contract against the third party.

The rule that the undisclosed principal may intervene and enforce the contract has often been described as anomalous.[13] From the third party's perspective, a complete stranger can appear and enforce the contract. It is best explained in terms of commercial convenience.[14] In particular, the doctrine prevents circuity of action: otherwise, the undisclosed principal could require the agent to lend his name to enforce the contract against the third party, and the undisclosed principal would have to indemnify the agent for any liabilities he incurs towards the third party.[15] It is far more straightforward to allow the undisclosed principal to enforce the contract directly against the third party using the doctrine of undisclosed agency. The doctrine operates in strictly defined circumstances which, to some extent, protect the position of third parties. These circumstances are detailed below.

---

12 *Wiltshire v. Sims* (1808) 1 Camp. 258; *Comerford v. Britannic Assurance Co Ltd* (1908) 24 T.L.R. 593.

13 See, *e.g.* Ames, "Undisclosed Principal – His Rights and Liabilities" (1909) *Yale Law Journal* 443; Seavey, "The Rationale of Agency" (1920) 29 *Yale Law Journal* 859; Goodhart & Hamson, "Undisclosed Principals in Contracts" (1932) 4 *Cambridge Law Journal* 320; Rochvarg, "Ratification and Undisclosed Principals" (1989) 34 *McGill Law Review* 286.

14 See, *e.g. Keighley Maxsted & Co v. Durant* [1901] A.C. 240 at 261–2, per Lord Lindley (H.L.); *Sui Yin Kwan v. Eastern Insurance* [1994] 2 A.C. 199 at 207; [1994] 1 All E.R. 213 at 220, per Lord Lloyd (P.C.).

15 See *Freeman and Lockyer v. Buckhurst Park Properties Ltd* [1964] 2 Q.B. 480 at 503; [1964] 1 All E.R. 630 at 644, per Diplock L.J. (C.A.).

6.3.1 Third party's right of election

Even where the undisclosed principal's existence is discovered, the agent remains liable on the contract and the third party may choose to enforce it against either the principal or the agent, but not both.[16] Once the third party elects to sue one party, his option to sue the other is extinguished. It seems that the third party will not be bound by an election unless he has unequivocally indicated his intention to hold one liable and release the other.

In *Clarkson, Booker Ltd. v. Andjel*,[17] A had failed to pay for airline tickets which he had purchased from T on behalf of an undisclosed P. Having discovered the existence of P, T wrote to both P and A requesting payment, and then served a writ on P. However, P was insolvent and T therefore sought payment from A. The Court of Appeal, while stating that this was a borderline case, found that serving a writ did not amount to an unequivocal election: T had never withdrawn the threat to sue A and was therefore free to pursue the action against A. This decision clearly favours the position of third parties.

6.3.2 Limitations on principal's right to intervene

The undisclosed principal's right to intervene and enforce the contract made on his behalf, is limited in several respects. These limitations go some way to rebalance a doctrine which at first sight seems to favour the position of the undisclosed principal over the third party.

6.3.2.1 Capacity

An undisclosed principal can only intervene if he was in existence and had the legal capacity to make the contract at the time it was made. This rule mainly affects pre-incorporation contracts made on behalf of companies.

6.3.2.2 Actual authority

An undisclosed principal can only intervene if the agent had actual authority to conclude the contract.[18] Hence, an undisclosed principal can never ratify a contract made without his prior consent.[19]

---

16 "... because the third party has only purported to make one contract with one person, to enter into a single obligation, these two rights of action are commonly said to be alternative." See Reynolds, "Election Distributed" (1970) 86 *Law Quarterly Review* 318 at 320.

17 [1964] 3 All E.R. 260 (C.A.).

18 *Keighley Maxsted & Co v. Durant* [1901] A.C. 240 (H.L.).

19 See 5.5.1.1.

6.3.2.3 Principal's intervention excluded

An undisclosed principal cannot intervene if such intervention is prohibited by the contract, either expressly or impliedly. It is more usual that the principal will be impliedly prohibited from intervening. This may happen if the language of the contract implies that no one, other than the agent, has an interest in it. However, it is not clear what language has this effect. Older case law suggests that where the contract relates to property and describes the agent as having *a proprietary interest* in the property, the agent may be taken impliedly to have undertaken that no one else has an interest in the contract so that an undisclosed principal will be excluded. In contrast, language describing the agent as a contracting party will not exclude an undisclosed principal's intervention.[20] Thus, an undisclosed principal was excluded in *Humble v. Hunter*, where an agent signed a contract to charter a ship as "*owner* of the good ship or vessel called *Ann*",[21] and in *Formby Bros v. Formby*, where an agent described himself as "owner" or "proprietor" of property.[22] But in *F Drughorn Ltd v. Rederiaktiebolaget Trans-Atlantic*, an undisclosed principal was allowed intervene where the agent signed a charterparty as "charterer."[23]

It is unclear whether this proposition remains good law. Subsequently, a principal was not excluded where an agent described himself as "tenant"[24] or "landlord",[25] and a more recent Privy Council decision declined to consider to what extent, if at all, cases such as *Humble v. Hunter* should still be regarded as good law. In *Sui Yin Kwan v. Eastern Insurance*,[26] a policy of workmen's compensation insurance was effected by agents on behalf employers, who were found to be undisclosed principals.[27] The Privy Council found that the agents had actual authority to effect the insurance; and that as the insurance contract was an ordinary commercial contract, the principal would be able to intervene unless intervention had been excluded in the insurance contract. The insurance contract described the agents as "the proposer/the insured". The Privy Council found that the language of the policy was not such as to exclude intervention. The policy did not exclude the possibility that the agents might be proposing insurance on behalf of another and it did not ask who the employer was. The Privy Council also stated *obiter dictum* that even if

20 See *F Drughorn Ltd v. Rederiaktiebolaget Trans-Atlantic* [1919] A.C. 203 (H.L.).

21 (1848) 12 Q.B. 310.

22 (1910) 102 L.T. 116.

23 [1919] A.C. 203. In *Epps v. Rothnie* [1945] K.B. 562 at 565, Scott L.J. suggested that *Humble v. Hunter* had been overruled by the *Drughorn* case.

24 *Danziger v. Thompson* [1944] K.B. 654.

25 *Epps v. Rothnie* [1945] K.B. 562.

26 [1994] 2 A.C. 199; [1994] 1 All E.R. 213 (P.C.).

27 See 6.1.1.

the agents had been named as employers, expressly or implied, this would not necessarily exclude intervention by the true principal.[28] The implication of this judgment is that, in commercial contracts, a court will be slow to exclude an undisclosed principal.[29]

6.3.2.4 Personal selection of agent

An undisclosed principal may be prevented from intervening if it can be shown that the third party contracted with the agent for personal reasons, for example, where it is clear that the third party intended to contract only with the agent due to some personal skill or due to the solvency of the agent. Thus, in *Greer v. Downs Supply Co.*,[30] the third party contracted with the agent so that he could set off a debt owed to him by A. The Court of Appeal refused to allow an undisclosed principal to intervene in these circumstances. A further example would be a contract to paint a portrait. An undisclosed principal could not intervene on such a contract because of the personal nature of the contract, in that it cannot be performed vicariously.[31]

It had been suggested that an undisclosed principal cannot intervene to enforce a contract where the benefit of the contract is unassignable, because of the contract's personal nature.[32] Arguably, insurance contracts (bar marine insurance) are personal contracts and hence are unassignable. However, the decision of the Privy Council in *Sui Yin Kwan v. Eastern Insurance*[33] rejected this view. There a policy of workmen's compensation insurance was effected by agents on behalf of employers, who were found to be undisclosed principals.[34] The defendant argued that a contract of insurance was a personal contract and hence incapable of assignment, and that the undisclosed principals could not intervene to enforce it. The Privy Council held that the insurance contract was not so personal a contract as to prevent an undisclosed principal from intervening, since, on the facts, the identity of the employer was a matter of indifference to the insurance company and not material to the risk. The decisive factor here seems to be that the court found that the insurance company would have granted cover on the same terms to the real principals.

---

28 *F Drughorn Ltd v. Rederiaktiebolaget Trans-Atlantic* [1919] A.C. 203 (H.L.) applied.

29 Markesinis & Munday conclude: "It will only be in exceptional cases that the undisclosed principal's intervention will be held inconsistent with the terms of the contract, and possibly only in cases where the agent can be construed to have contracted as the owner of the property." See Markesinis & Munday, *An Outline of the Law of Agency* (London, Butterworths, 4th ed., 1998) p.160.

30 [1927] 2 K.B. 28 (C.A.).

31 Lord Lloyd in referring to an undisclosed principal noted that "… intervention in such a case would be a breach of the very contract in which he seeks to intervene:" *Sui Yin Kwan v. Eastern Insurance* [1994] 2 A.C. 199 at 210; [1994] 1 All E.R. 213 at 223, (P.C.).

32 See generally, Goodhart & Hamson, "Undisclosed Principals in Contracts" (1932) 4 *Cambridge Law Journal* 320 at 323–4 and 338–341.

33 [1994] 2 A.C. 199; [1994] 1 All E.R. 213 (P.C.).

34 See 6.1.1.

6.3.2.5 Personal opposition to principal

In some cases it has been said that an undisclosed principal cannot intervene where the third party has personal reasons for not contracting with him.[35] However, it is clear that this rule can only apply where the personal element is "strikingly present" in the contract.[36] It is unlikely to apply in the context of ordinary commercial transactions. In *Dyster v. Randall & Sons*,[37] the plaintiff, P, knowing that the defendant would not sell certain property to him, engaged an agent, A, to conclude a contract without disclosing P's interest in the matter. The defendant unsuccessfully resisted P's attempt to enforce the contract. The court held that this was not a personal contract and so the identity of P was not material to it. It was noted that A could, in any case, have enforced the contract and re-sold the property to P.

While there is no positive obligation on an agent to disclose the existence or identity of a principal, if an agent positively misrepresents the position, for example, by claiming to be the principal, or by denying the principal's interest, if asked, an undisclosed principal cannot intervene,[38] because a third party can have the contract set aside for misrepresentation.

6.3.3 Principal enforces on the same terms as agent

If an undisclosed principal does intervene, he does so generally on the same terms on which the agent could have enforced the contract, so that a third party can raise any defences against the undisclosed principal which he would have had against the agent. These may include purely personal defences, such as rights of set-off available against the agent.[39]

6.4 Agent's Liability

Despite the general rule that where an agent concludes a contract on behalf of a principal, the contract is between the principal and the third party, an agent may be liable on, or be able to enforce a contract, either together with or to the exclusion of the principal, in the following circumstances.

35 See, *e.g. Said v. Butt* [1920] 3 K.B. 497 (K.B.D.); for a defence of this case see further Treitel, *The Law of Contract* (London, Sweet & Maxwell, 10th ed., 1999) p.675; and Williams "Mistake as to Party in the Law of Contract (Part II)" (1945) 23 *Can Bar. Rev*. 380.

36 *Said v. Butt* [1920] 3 K.B. 497 at 503.

37 [1926] Ch. 932 (C.D.).

38 *Archer v. Stone* (1898) 78 L.T. 34.

39 *Cooke & Sons v. Eshelby* (1887) 12 App. Cas. 271 (H.L.).

6.4.1 Agent is party to the contract

An agent will be liable on the contract where, on its proper construction, the agent is a party to the contract. This can occur where an agent contracts on behalf of himself and a principal. For instance, under partnership legislation, every partner is an agent of the firm, the firm being the

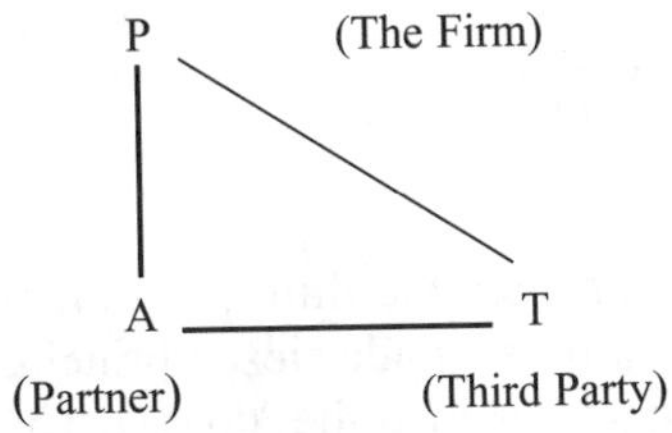

collection of all partners.[40] When a partner enters a contract, he does so as an agent of the firm, and also on his own behalf as a member of the firm. Or, the contract may expressly state that the agent is a party to the contract, so that the agent and the principal are both liable on the contract and can both enforce it. However, an agent may become a party to the contract in the absence of an express statement. Generally, where an agent signs a contract in his own name, he will be liable on it. Therefore, where an agent executes a contract in his own name, he should use clear words to indicate that he is acting in a representative capacity and not undertaking personal liability. Merely signing "A, agent" may not be enough; it would be better to sign "A, agent for P".[41]

6.4.2 Deeds

Generally, if an agent personally executes a deed, he is liable on it and able to enforce it to the exclusion of the principal[42] except where the deed is executed pursuant to a power of attorney.[43]

6.4.3 Bills of exchange[44]

An agent who signs a bill of exchange, such as a cheque, may become

---

40 Partnership Act 1890, s.5.

41 In *Sika Contracts Ltd v. BL Gill & Closegate Properties Ltd* (1978) 9 B.L.R. 11, a civil engineer signed a contract on behalf of a client using his own name and adding the words "chartered civil engineer". He was nevertheless held liable on the contract, because the additional words could be read merely as describing his profession and not the capacity in which he signed.

42 *Re International Contract Co, Pickering's Claim* (1871) 6 Ch. App. 525.

43 See further Powers of Attorney Act 1996.

44 See generally 23.3.

personally liable on it. A person will be liable on a bill of exchange if his name appears on the bill.[45] A principal will be liable on the bill if his signature is written on the bill by someone acting with his authority.[46] Therefore, where an agent signs a bill, he should use clear words to indicate that he is acting in a representative capacity and not undertaking personal liability. Merely signing "A, agent" is insufficient.[47] Where there is any ambiguity, the construction most favourable to the validity of the bill will be preferred.[48]

6.4.4 Undisclosed agency

In cases of undisclosed agency, the third party may elect to enforce the contract against the agent or the undisclosed principal. Equally, the agent may enforce the contract against the third party, if the undisclosed principal does not do so.

6.4.5 Warranty of authority

Where an agent purports to have authority to act on a principal's behalf, but in fact is unauthorised, we have seen that the agent's claim will not normally give rise to apparent authority. Apparent authority is normally based on a representation from the principal.[49] Third parties often deal only with agents and have no direct contact with principals. To require a third party to verify the agent's claim to authority would undermine the commercial convenience of the agency arrangement. Therefore, where an agent makes a false claim of authority, the agent may be liable to the third party for breach of warranty of authority.[50]

An agent will be liable if he falsely claims to have authority, even though his claim is wholly innocent. In contracting on behalf of a principal, an agent is taken impliedly to warrant, or promise, that he does have the principal's authority. If he has no such authority, he can be sued for breach of warranty of authority. An agent's warranty of authority is viewed as being collateral to the main contract.[51] The third party provides consideration for it by entering into the (supposed) main contract with the principal. Since the agent's liability is contractual, it is strict. Thus, in

45 Bills of Exchange Act 1882, s.23.

46 Bills of Exchange Act 1882, s.90(1).

47 Bills of Exchange Act 1882, s.26(1).

48 Bills of Exchange Act 1882, s.26(2).

49 See 5.3.1.2.

50 An agent may also be liable in tort in such circumstances: see 6.4.6.

51 A collateral contract also arises where an auctioneer enters into a collateral contract with a buyer whereby he warrants that he has authority to sell and that he knows of no defects in the principal's title, and whereby he can sue the buyer for the price. See Wedderburn, "Collateral Contracts" [1959] *Cambridge Law Journal* 58.

Yonge v. Toynbee,[52] solicitors were instructed by their client to defend an action. Unknown to them the agency was terminated due to their client's insanity; nevertheless they continued to act on his behalf and were held liable for breach of warranty of authority.

Damages for breach of warranty of authority are awarded to put the third party in the same position he would have been in had the warranty been true, and are assessed under the normal common law rules as set out in *Hadley v. Baxendale*.[53] They will therefore seek to put the third party in the same position as if he had had a contract with the principal, and will accordingly be limited to the amount that could be obtained from the principal. So, if the principal is bankrupt, the third party's damages against the agent are limited to the amount that could be recovered from the bankrupt principal. In order to sue an agent for breach of warranty of authority, the third party must establish that:

(i) the agent was purporting to act as an agent – if the agent was acting on his own behalf, or for an undisclosed principal, the agent is personally liable to the third party anyway;
(ii) the agent lacked authority;[54]
(iii) the agent expressed no doubts about his authority which would put the third party on notice to enquire further; and,
(iv) the third party relied on the agent's representation of authority.

Where there is any doubt about an agent's authority, the third party will probably seek to pursue the principal (on the supposed contract, on the grounds that the agent had actual or apparent authority) and the agent (for breach of warranty of authority), in the alternative.

---

52 [1910] 1 K.B. 215 (C.A.).

53 (1854) 9 Exch. 341.

54 Treitel argues that where an agent has actual or apparent authority or authority by ratification there is no breach of warranty of authority: Treitel, *The Law of Contract* (London, Sweet & Maxwell, 10th ed., 1999) p.683-4. Sealy & Hooley disagree. They argue that only where an agent has actual authority will he not be liable for breach of warranty of authority. Thus, where an agent has apparent authority or authority by ratification, the agent has no actual authority at the time of contracting and so is in breach of warranty of authority. However, because with apparent authority a third party can enforce the contract against a principal, the third party will suffer no loss. Equally, where a principal ratifies, the contract is enforceable by the third party against the principal and the third party will suffer no loss. See Sealy & Hooley, *Commercial Law* (London, Butterworths, 2nd ed., 1999) p.158–9.

6.4.6 Tortious liability

If an agent can be shown to have acted fraudulently, a notoriously difficult concept to prove, when he claimed to have authority, knowing that he had no authority, he may be liable to a third party in the tort of deceit.[55] Alternatively, an agent may be liable in negligence, under the ruling in *Hedley Byrne & Co Ltd v. Heller & Partners Ltd*,[56] if it can be shown that he was negligent in claiming to have authority. In either case, a third party may claim damages from an agent on a *tortious* basis. Such damages will seek to restore the third party to the position he was in before he entered the supposed contract with the principal. Since liability for breach of warranty of authority is strict, a third party will generally prefer to hold an agent liable on this basis, rather than in tort, unless the damages recoverable in tort are more favourable to him.

55 See generally, McMahon & Binchy, *Law of Torts* (Dublin, Butterworths, 3rd ed., 2000) Chapter 35.

56 [1964] A.C. 465.

CHAPTER 7

PRINCIPAL AND AGENT RELATIONS

7.1 INTRODUCTION

As noted in earlier chapters, "agency" is the relationship that exists between two persons, the principal and the agent, which usually arises by consent of the parties. This consent can form the basis of a contract – an agency contract that gives rise to rights and duties – or the agency may be gratuitous. Even where an agent agrees to act gratuitously, the relationship of principal and agent arises, giving rise to mutual rights and duties. This chapter examines these mutual rights and duties and concludes by considering the termination of the agency relationship. It is unclear whether non-consensual agencies, such as those based on apparent authority or necessity, give rise to the normal incidents of consensual agency relationships.[1]

7.2 REGULATION OF THE AGENCY RELATIONSHIP

In most cases, there are two levels of "regulation" of the agency relationship in Irish law.[2] The primary source of the parties' rights and duties is their agreement. The normal rules of construction will apply to give effect to the intentions of the parties when interpreting this agreement. Further, at common law, an agent is given three basic rights: to remuneration; to an indemnity and to a lien. The common law traditionally regarded agents as independent businesses and took the view that the agent was in a stronger position than the principal. Hence, the principal was in need of protection. As a result, the law imposed on agents extensive duties, partly because of the fiduciary nature of the agency relationship.

In addition, many agency agreements will now be subject to the EC (Commercial Agents) Regulations 1994[3] and 1997[4] (hereinafter "the

1 See Powell, *The Law of Agency* (London, Pitman, 2nd ed., 1961) pp.295–296, fn4; Dowrick, "The Relationship of Principal and Agent" (1954) 17 *Modern Law Review* 24 at 26–27, fn15.

2 An agent's rights and duties may derive from other sources such as tort law, statute or the law of restitution: see generally, Dowrick, "The Relationship of Principal and Agent" (1954) 17 *Modern Law Review* 24.

3 S.I. No. 33 of 1994; see further O'Mara, "New Regulations Establish Protection for Commercial Agents" [1994] *Commercial Law Practitioner* 162.

4 S.I. No. 31 of 1997. The 1997 Regulations were introduced to implement properly the Directive, in particular to enable Ireland to exercise its discretion under Article 17 of the Directive on the rights of an agent on termination of the agency agreement to "an indemnity" or "compensation for damage": see 7.6.3.2(iv).

Regulations"), which partly codify and partly modify the common law. The Regulations were passed to implement the EC Directive on Self-Employed Commercial Agents[5] and similar provisions apply in other member states.[6] The Regulations came into force on January 1, 1994 and apply both to agreements entered into after their commencement and to existing agreements.[7] Their main impact is to give agents more extensive rights than they enjoy at common law. However, although the Directive and Regulations apply to many commercial agency arrangements, they do not apply to all agencies, and it is therefore necessary to consider the common law rules applicable to agency alongside the Directive and Regulations.

7.2.1 Application of the Directive and Regulations

The Directive and Regulations apply to relations between "commercial agents" and their principals.[8] The Directive[9] and the Regulations[10] state that a "commercial agent" means:

> "a self-employed intermediary who has continuing authority to negotiate the sale and the purchase of goods on behalf of another person, hereinafter called the principal, or to negotiate and conclude such transactions on behalf of and in the name of that principal."

There are a number of exclusions from this definition and from the protection of the Directive. The Directive and Regulations provide a list of exclusions from the definition, such that the term "commercial agent" does not include:

(a) company officers;
(b) partners of a firm;
(c) insolvency practitioners.[11]

The Directive also provides that it shall not apply to commercial agents:

(a) whose activities are unpaid; or
(b) when they are operating in a commodity exchange or market.[12]

5 Directive 86/653/EEC [1986] O.J. L382/17.
6 See further Saintier, *Commercial Agency Law: A Comparative Analysis* (Aldershot, Ashgate, 2002); Randolph & Davey, *Guide to the Commercial Agents' Regulations* (Oxford, Hart, 2nd ed., 2002).
7 Reg. 3, 1994; Reg. 2, 1997.
8 Reg. 2(3), 1994.
9 Art. 1.2.
10 Reg. 2(1), 1994.
11 Art. 1(3) and Reg. 2(1)(a)–(c), 1994.
12 Art. 2(1).

Under the Regulations, these activities are excluded from the definition of commercial agent.[13]

Further, the Directive provides that member states have the right to specify that the Directive shall not apply to those persons whose activities as commercial agents are considered secondary by the law of the member state in question.[14] In implementing this provision, the Irish Regulations provide that there is a presumption that the activities of consumer credit agents and mail order catalogue agents for consumer goods are secondary.[15] This list is not described as exhaustive and therefore there may be other activities that might be considered secondary in Irish law. The English case of *Parkes v. Esso Petroleum Co Ltd*[16] is of interest in this regard. There, the plaintiff was a licensee of a tied, self-service petrol station. The licence described him as an "agent" for the purpose of selling fuel on behalf of the petrol company and provided for him to receive commission on sales. The issue was whether the plaintiff was a "commercial agent" as defined. The Schedule to the English implementing Regulations, as well as identifying mail order catalogue agents for consumer goods and consumer credit agents as being involved in activities which are secondary, also details factors which are relevant to considering whether an activity is secondary or not. One factor which indicates that an activity is secondary is where customers normally select the goods for themselves and merely place their orders through the agent.[17] The Court of Appeal emphasised that the petrol sales were self-service. By distinguishing between "negotiated" and "self-service" sales, the Court of Appeal found that, on the facts, the plaintiff did not negotiate sales, and hence was outside the protection of the Directive.

This definition, with its lists of exclusions, is not straightforward. While there are no reported Irish cases relating to the Directive, it has already given rise to a number of questions in United Kingdom and European Court of Justice case law. Many more questions remain unanswered. The critical features of a "commercial agent" are as follows.

7.2.1.1 Agency

The intermediary must be *an agent*, in law, acting "on behalf of another person" (the principal). For instance, in *AMB Imballaggi Plastici SRL v. Pacflex*,[18] it was held that the Directive and the relevant English

13 Reg. 2(1)(d) and (e), 1994.

14 Art. 2(2).

15 Reg. 2(1)(f) and 2(2), 1994.

16 [1998] Eu. L.R. 550 (H.C.); [1999] Tr. L.R. 232 (C.A.).

17 The Commercial Agents (Council Directive) Regulations 1993, S.I. 1993/3053 as amended, Sch 1, s.4(c).

18 [1999] 2 All E.R. Comm. 249 (C.A.).

Regulations did not apply where a person negotiates contracts for the supply of a manufacturer's products to a third party and then purchases the goods from the manufacturer and resells them in his own name to satisfy the contracts. This was not a true agency situation. Hence, the Directive and Regulations do not apply to marketing arrangements, such as distribution or franchising, other than agency arrangements.

It is unclear whether undisclosed agents, or agents working for unnamed principals, are protected by the Directive and Regulations. The definition refers to:

(a) intermediaries who have continuing authority to negotiate the sale and the purchase of goods *on behalf of another person*, and hence might exclude agents acting for undisclosed principals; and
(b) intermediaries who have continuing authority to … negotiate and conclude such transactions on *behalf of and in the name of that principal*, suggesting that the principal must be disclosed *and named*.

This internal inconsistency in the definition of a "commercial agent" makes interpreting the Directive more difficult. The rationale for protecting "commercial agents" is that they benefit the principal by building goodwill for him: where the principal is undisclosed or even unnamed, this is obviously not the case.

7.2.1.2 Continuing authority

The agent must have continuing authority, therefore the Directive and Regulations do not apply to agents acting in once-off transactions or if the agent is appointed for a specified number of transactions. An agent appointed for a fixed period would have continuing authority during that period and so would be protected.

7.2.1.3 Self-employed

The agent must be self-employed, and hence independent from the principal. But the reference to self-employed does not mean that the agent must be a natural person. The agent could be a sole intermediary, a partnership or a corporate body.[19]

19 "Self-employed" is derived from Articles 43–47 of the Treaty establishing the EC (which deal with freedom of establishment and freedom to provide services) and is consistent with EC law as including companies as well as individuals. See further *Cooney & Co v. Murphy Brewery Sales Ltd* unreported, High Court, Costello P., July 30, 1997; and *AMB Imballaggi Plastici SRL v. Pacflex* [1999] 2 All E.R. Comm. 249 (C.A.).

7.2.1.4 The transaction

The definition refers specifically to *negotiating, or negotiating and concluding* contracts for the *sale or purchase of goods*. On a strict reading of the definition, it would seem that an agent who merely *introduces* customers, sometimes known as a canvassing or introducing agent, is unprotected. Such agents normally have no power to bind their principal and hence are not agents in law. However, where such an agent has continuing authority to negotiate the sale or purchase of goods on behalf of his principal, even though in fact he merely effects introductions, it is arguable that he falls within the definition of "commercial agent". Where an "introducing agent" lacks such authority, he falls outside the scope of the Directive, clearly. Moreover, it may be that courts will interpret "negotiate" widely such that "introducing agents" generally will come within the definition of "commercial agent".

The meaning of *negotiate* was considered in *Parkes v. Esso Petroleum Co Ltd.*[20] The plaintiff was a licensee of a tied, self-service petrol station. The licence described him as an "agent" for the purpose of selling fuel on behalf of the defendant petrol company and he received commission on sales. At first instance, it was held that he was outside the protection of the Directive because he did not "negotiate" the sale of petrol, giving "negotiate" its ordinary meaning. The terms of sale, including the price, were set by the petrol company. The decision was upheld on appeal but on slightly different grounds. The Court of Appeal recognised that there could be negotiations without haggling over the price. The Court of Appeal emphasised that the petrol sales were self-service. Referring to the provisions on "secondary" activities in the schedule to the U.K. Regulations,[21] such activities being outside the protection of the Regulations, the court distinguished between "negotiated" and self-service sales, and found that, on the facts, the plaintiff did not negotiate sales.[22]

Moreover, the agent must be involved in the buying or selling of *goods*.[23] "Goods" would have to be interpreted in line with the EC Treaty and so may go beyond the definition in sales legislation where it is unclear whether certain items, such as computer software, are goods for the purpose of the relevant legislation.[24] For instance, it was held in *Tamarind*

20 [1998] Eu. L.R. 550 (H.C.); [1999] Tr LR 232 (C.A.). See further *Cooney & Co v. Murphy Brewery Sales Ltd* unreported, High Court, Costello, P., July 30, 1997.

21 The Commercial Agents (Council Directive) Regulations 1993, S.I. 1993/3053 as amended, Sch 1.

22 For criticism of the Court of Appeal's decision see Bradgate, *Commercial Law* (London, Butterworths, 3rd ed., 2000) p.179.

23 See 9.2.5.

24 On whether computer software is "goods" for the purpose of the sale of goods legislation, see *St Albans City and District Council v. International Computers Ltd* [1996] 4 All E.R. 481; *Saphena Computing Ltd v. Allied Collection Agencies Ltd* unreported, Court of Appeal, May 3, 1989; *Toby Construction Products Pty Ltd v. Computa Bar (Sales) Pty Ltd* [1983] 2 N.S.W.L.R. 48. There is no Irish case law on this issue. See further 9.2.5.

International Ltd v. Eastern Natural Gas (Retail) Ltd[25] that the Directive and U.K. Regulations applied to agents negotiating the sale of gas and electricity. Moreover, the Directive and Regulations have no application to agents dealing in services or land, thereby excluding travel agents and estate agents. Where the agent buys or sells goods and services together, a court would have to consider which aspect of the transaction (the goods or the service) dominated.[26] But given the rationale for the Directive, a court might well take a broad approach to the definition of goods.

7.2.1.5 Evidenced in writing

The Directive provides that member states may provide that an agency contract shall not be valid unless evidenced in writing.[27] The Regulations adopt this formal requirement.[28] While this may limit the protection afforded by the Directive, it must be noted that the agency contract is not required to be in writing, merely evidenced in writing.[29] The "evidenced in writing" requirement has been satisfied, in a different context, where the essential terms of the contract are evidenced in writing. Moreover, this evidence does not have to appear in a single document but could be provided in a series of documents.[30]

In *Moore v. Piretta*,[31] a sales agent entered into a series of agreements, commencing in January 1988, some written, some oral. The last such agreement was signed in February 1994 and took effect from January 1, 1994 and was terminable by either party giving six months notice. The principal terminated the agreement, by notice, and the agent sought to assert his right to an indemnity under the terms of the agreement and Article 17 of the Directive.[32] Article 17(1) refers to an agent's right to be indemnified or compensated for damage following the termination of the agency contract. The principal argued that any indemnity should be calculated with reference to the agency contract in existence at the time of termination. The court disagreed and found that the reference to "the agency contract" in Article 17(1) did not mean the contract at the date of termination but meant simply "the agency", the word contract adding nothing. Hence, where a previously oral agreement has been renewed, and that renewal is evidenced in writing, the agent's entitlement to an

25 [2000] 26 *Law Society Gazette*, Law Reports, 35.

26 See 9.3.6.

27 Art. 13(2).

28 Reg. 5, 1994.

29 See, *e.g. Godley v. Power* (1961) 95 I.L.T.R. 135; *Stinson v. Owens* (1973) 24 N.I.L.Q. 218; and *Black v. Kavanagh* (1973) 108 I.L.T.R. 91 re requirements of Statute of Frauds 1695.

30 On the doctrine of joinder of documents see *McQuaid v. Lynam* [1965] I.R. 564; and *Kelly v. Ross & Ross* unreported, High Court, McWilliam J., April 29, 1980.

31 [1999] 1 All E.R. 174 (Q.B.D.).

32 See 7.6.3.2(iv).

indemnity or compensation for damage under Article 17 should be based on the entire period of the agency and not just the written evidence period.

In some member states, such as Italy and France, there is provision for the registration of commercial agents.[33] It has been held that since the Directive is silent on the matter of registration, member states may require registration for administrative needs. However, the Directive precludes member states from making the protection of commercial agents or the validity of agency contracts conditional on registration.[34]

7.2.1.6 Territorial application

The Directive and the Regulations are silent on the issue of territorial application, but a recent European Court of Justice decision has addressed the matter.[35] In *Ingmar G.B. Ltd v. Eaton Leonard Technologies Inc*,[36] a written agency agreement was stated to be governed by Californian law though the agent was an English company with a territory of the United Kingdom and Ireland. The European Court of Justice held that the Directive applies whenever an agent undertakes activities in a member state, regardless of the fact either that the principal is established in a state outside the EU, or that the contract is expressly made subject to the law of a non-member state. Hence, the Directive and Irish Regulations should apply in all cases where the agent undertakes activities within Ireland, unless the contract is subjected to the law of another member state.

7.3 Agent's Duties

Beyond any duties imposed by contract, the law imposes a variety of duties on an agent, largely with a view to protecting the principal. In general, agents stand in a fiduciary position to their principals and hence quite onerous duties are imposed on agents in this position.[37] These duties may be modified where the Directive and Regulations apply. Moreover, many professionals, such as solicitors and auctioneers, are also required to comply with codes of practice promulgated by professional associations and self-regulatory bodies. The duties imposed on agents by these various sources overlap, though the precise relationship between them all can be unclear.

33 See, *e.g.* Italian Law No. 204 of May 3, 1985.

34 *Bellone v. Yokohama SpA* (Case C-215/97) [1998] 3 C.M.L.R. 975; affd in *Centrosteel Srl v. Adipol GmbH* (Case C-456/98) [2000] 3 C.M.L.R. 711.

35 The Commission has stated its view that Arts 17 and 18 of the Directive are mandatory in application: see the EC Commission Report on the Application of Article 17, COM(96) 364 final, p.10.

36 (Case C-381/98) [2000] All E.R. (D) 1759; [2001] All E.R. (EC) 57.

37 See 7.3.2

7.3.1 At common law

Three duties are imposed at common law: to obey instructions; to exercise reasonable skill and care; and to perform personally. Where the agency is contractual, these duties usually take effect as implied terms of the contract.

7.3.1.1 To obey instructions

An agent must obey his principal's lawful instructions. An agent is not obliged to obey instructions which require him to act illegally, and the duty of a professional agent to obey instructions may also be limited by rules of professional conduct. Where instructions are ambiguous, an agent will not be held liable where he acts on a reasonable interpretation of them,[38] though an agent should seek clarification, where possible.[39]

Where the agency is contractual, the agent is liable for breach of contract if he fails to act as instructed. For example, in *Turpin v. Bilton*,[40] an agent agreed to insure his principal's ship. He failed to do so and the ship was uninsured when lost. It was held that the agent was liable for breach of contract. An agent must follow, but not exceed, the terms of his authority. Where the agency is non-contractual, or gratuitous, the matter is less straightforward. In these circumstances, the agent will usually not be under a duty to act and so he cannot be liable for not acting, unless his failure to act gives rise to liability in tort.[41] Equally, where an agent acts under a unilateral contract he is under no duty to act.[42]

7.3.1.2 To exercise reasonable care

All agents are required to act with reasonable care. Where the agency is contractual, a term to exercise reasonable care will normally be implied in

38 *Ireland v. Livingstone* (1872) L.R. 5 H.L. 395.

39 *Woodhouse A.C. Israel Cocoa Ltd SA v. Nigerian Produce Marketing Co Ltd* [1972] A.C. 741 at 772 per Lord Salmon; *European Asian Bank AG v. Punjab & Sind Bank* [1983] 2 All E.R. 508 at 517 per Goff L.J.

40 (1843) 5 Man. & G. 455.

41 There is generally no liability in tort for negligent omissions though liability may be imposed on the basis of *Hedley Byrne v. Heller* [1964] A.C. 465; [1963] 2 All E.R. 575 (H.L.) for loss caused by a failure to warn, where the defendant has voluntarily assumed a responsibility to warn. Such an assumption may be found in cases where there is a particularly close relationship between plaintiff and defendant, as in the agency relationship: see, *e.g. Doolan v. Murray* unreported, High Court, Keane J., December 21, 1993 approving *Banque Financière de la Cité SA v. Westgate Insurance Co Ltd* [1989] 2 All E.R. 952 (C.A.) (no duty was found on the facts); see further *Bowstead on Agency* (London, Sweet & Maxwell, 16th ed., 1996) para. 6–027; *cf* Fridman, *The Law of Agency* (London, Butterworths, 7th ed., 1996) pp.156–157; Markesinis & Munday, *An Outline of the Law of Agency* (London, Butterworths, 4th ed., 1998) p.95.

42 *Carlill v. Carbolic Smoke Ball* [1893] 1 Q.B. 256.

the contract at common law. Where services are provided in the course of a business, a term to exercise reasonable care is implied by statute.[43] Where the agency is non-contractual, the duty to exercise reasonable skill and care arises in tort only. Hence, a contractual agent may be subject to concurrent duties in contract and tort unless either is modified or excluded by the contract. In such circumstances, the principal may choose to sue in contract or tort and take whatever procedural advantages may arise.[44] For example, in *Chariot Inns v. Assicurazioni Generali SPA*,[45] the plaintiff sought fire insurance from the defendant insurance company. The plaintiff stated that there had been no claims over the last five years, in response to a question in the proposal form, having taken the advice of his agent, an insurance broker. This statement was untrue. The insurance company repudiated liability for non-disclosure of a material fact and the plaintiff sought to recover damages from the insurance broker. The Supreme Court held that the broker was in breach of his contractual and tortious duty of care in advising the plaintiff not to disclose the relevant information in the proposal form. The broker was negligent for failing to protect the interests of the plaintiff and so damages were payable.

An agent's contractual and tortious duty of care can be limited or excluded by the agency contract.[46] However, clear words are needed to exclude liability for negligence. In *Henderson v. Merrett*,[47] contracts between "names" at Lloyd's and the agents who managed underwriting business on their behalf contained a term giving the agents "absolute discretion" in respect of the underwriting business. It was argued that this excluded both contractual and tortious duties of care. But the House of Lords found that this merely defined the agents' authority but did not exclude their duties to exercise reasonable care in exercising that authority.

The standard of care required is what is reasonable in the circumstances. This will vary depending on the particular facts of the case. Where the agent is a member of a profession,[48] he is expected to exercise the skill and care of a reasonably competent member of that profession. The standard of reasonable care may be lower where the agency is

43 Sale of Goods and Supply of Services Act 1980, s.39; see 20.2.3.

44 See *Kennedy v. AIB Ltd* [1998] 2 I.R. 48 (S.C.); *Henderson v. Merrett* [1995] 2 A.C. 145; [1994] 3 All E.R. 506 (H.L.): see further 20.3.2.1. It is unclear whether a third duty of care arises because of the agent's fiduciary position: this point was left undecided by the majority in *Henderson v. Merrett*, though Lord Brown-Wilkinson expressed the view that there is no separate fiduciary duty of care, at 205 and 543–4.

45 [1981] I.R. 199 (S.C.).

46 Where services are provided under contract, in the course of a business, see Sale of Goods and Supply of Services Act 1980, s.40 on exclusion of liability: see further 20.4. Where the services are provided on terms which are not individually negotiated, and the services are provided to a "consumer," see also the EC (Unfair Terms in Consumer Contracts) Regulations 1995 and 2000, S.I. No. 27 of 1995 and S.I. No. 307 of 2000: see further 2.3.5.3.

47 [1995] 2 A.C. 145; [1994] 3 All E.R. 506 (H.L.).

48 *Bolam v. Friern Hospital Management Committee* [1957] 2 All E.R. 118 per McNair J. at 121.

gratuitous, though not necessarily. In *Chaudrhy v. Prabakhar*,[49] the principal, an inexperienced driver, asked a friend to find a suitable car to buy, specifying that it must be one that had not been in an accident. The friend, who was not a mechanic, and was acting gratuitously, found and recommended a car. The principal bought the car and found later that it had been badly damaged in an accident and had been repaired. The friend (and agent) sought to rely on old case law which suggested that a lower standard of care applied to gratuitous agents.[50] The Court of Appeal held that the standard required of an agent is such as is reasonable in the circumstances. To determine what is reasonable, the court should consider whether the agent is paid or unpaid, the degree of skill possessed or claimed by the agent, and the degree of reliance placed by the principal on the agent. It was held that, on the facts, the agent did not exercise reasonable care.

7.3.1.3 To perform personally

Since an agent is often chosen for his personal qualities, the general rule is that he must perform his duties personally and cannot delegate performance (*delegatus non potest delegare*) unless delegation is authorised by the principal. In practice, delegation is quite common. For example, in relation to a company where the authority to act on behalf of the company is vested in the board of directors, the board usually delegates authority to individual directors, who in turn delegate to senior executives, who in turn delegate to junior executives and other employees. Accordingly, a long chain of delegation and authorisation can link the individual acts of a junior employee (such as a shop assistant) back to the board of directors, thereby legally binding the company.

Where delegation is authorised and the agent (A) employs a sub-agent (S), the agency agreement must be construed in order to determine whether the relationship of principal and agent is created between the principal (P) and S.

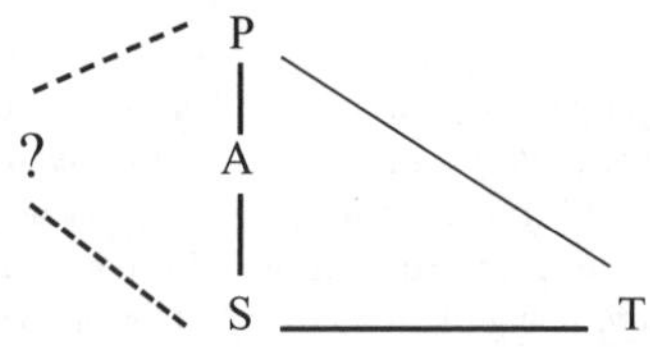

49 [1988] 3 All E.R. 718 (C.A.).

50 *Shiells & Thirne v. Blackburne* (1789) 1 Hy. Bl. 159; *Giblin v. McMullen* (1868) L.R. 2 P.C. 317).

The key is the agent's authority. Is A authorised to create privity of contract between P and S? Just because the agent has authority to delegate to S, does not mean that he has authority to create privity of contract between P and S. Generally, where delegation is authorised S will be the agent of the agent (A), so that there will be no legal relationship between P and S; A will remain liable to P for performance of his duties.[51] However, A can be authorised to create privity between P and S, as in *de Bussche v. Alt*[52] where P engaged A to sell a ship in India, China or Japan. A had no offices in Japan and so obtained P's consent to the appointment of a sub-agent, S, who had a presence in Japan. The Court of Appeal found that the delegation was authorised and that A was given express authority to create privity between P and S.

If there is no privity of contract between the principal and the sub-agent, the sub-agent generally owes no duty to account to the principal,[53] and he cannot be sued by the principal in contract for monies had and received.[54] But the general absence of an agency relationship between a principal and sub-agent does not mean that the sub-agent owes the principal no duties. The sub-agent may owe the principal a duty of care in tort law. For example, in *Henderson v. Merrett*,[55] Lloyd's "names" sued agents who managed syndicates of which the names were members. In some cases, the names were represented by "member's agents" who placed business, on behalf of the names, with "managing agents." The terms of the contracts made it clear that the managing agents were the agents of the members' agents who appointed them. Therefore, there was no agency relationship between the names and the managing agents. Nevertheless, it was held that the managing agents owed a duty of care, following the principle in *Hedley Byrne v. Heller*,[56] to the names because the managing agents provided professional services which they knew would be relied upon by the names. This case was described as "most unusual" by Lord Goff,[57] and an Irish court should consider whether, in more general terms, it is proper to allow a tort action to bypass the contractual structures put in place by the parties.[58] Furthermore, even where there is no agency relationship between a principal and a sub-agent, the sub-agent may still owe the principal fiduciary duties, as in

51 *Lockwood v. Abbey* (1845) 14 Sim. 437; *Calico Printers' Association v. Barclays Bank Ltd* (1931) 145 L.T. 51 (C.A.).

52 (1878) 8 Ch. D. 286 (C.A.).

53 *Lockwood v. Abdy* (1845) 14 Sim. 437.

54 *Robbins v. Fennell* (1847) 11 Q.B. 248.

55 [1995] 2 A.C. 145; [1994] 3 All E.R. 506 (H.L.).

56 [1964] A.C. 465; [1963] 2 All E.R. 575 (H.L.).

57 [1995] 2 A.C. 145 at 195; and [1994] 3 All E.R. 506 at 534.

58 Note, *e.g.* the comments of Keane J., in *Doolan v. Murray* unreported, High Court, Keane, J., December 21, 1993 that: "the general principle of caveat emptor, based as it is on the recognition by the law that parties should be left free to determine their obligations to each other, is not to be eroded by the inappropriate invocation of tortious liability."

Powell & Thomas v. Evan Jones & Co,[59] where it was held that the sub-agent will be liable to account to the principal if he makes a secret profit from his position.

7.3.2 In equity[60]

The traditional view on agents and fiduciary duties is outlined in the following statement from McCardie J.[61]

> "The position of principal and agent gives rise to particular and onerous duties on the part of the agent, and the high standard of conduct required from him springs from the fiduciary relationship between his employer and himself. His position is confidential. It readily lends itself to abuse. A strict and salutary rule is required to meet the special situation. The rules of English law as they now exist spring from the strictness originally required by Courts of Equity in cases where the fiduciary relationship exists."

As noted above, the concept of fiduciary duties was developed by the courts of equity and originally applied to trustees. It was later extended to cover analogous relationships of trust, including those involving agents and company directors. Fiduciary duties arise independently of any contract. They are imposed on the fiduciary automatically, as a matter of law, by virtue of the position he holds. Agents are normally subject to fiduciary duties because agents have the power to affect the legal position of their principals in relation to third parties, and principals normally place trust and confidence in the agent in the exercise of that power. Traditionally, fiduciary duties were applied strictly, partly as a deterrent to prevent fiduciaries being tempted to take advantage of their position.

In the past, fiduciaries of all types tended to be treated similarly. More recently, in England, and arguably in Ireland, there has been a tendency to reduce the force of fiduciary duties between parties in an essentially commercial relationship, such that the relationship of agency does not necessarily give rise to a fiduciary relationship,[62] or, the scope of the

---

59 [1905] 1 K.B. 11; see further Tettenborn, "Principals, Sub-Agents and Accountability" (1999) 115 *Law Quarterly Review* 655.

60 See generally, Finn, *Fiduciary Obligations* (Sydney, Law Book Co., 1977); Goff & Jones, *The Law of Restitution* (London, Sweet & Maxwell, 5th ed., 1998) Chapter 33; Sealy, "Fiduciary Relationships" [1962] *Cambridge Law Journal* 69 and "Some Principles of Fiduciary Obligations" [1963] *Cambridge Law Journal* 119; Jones, "Unjust Enrichment and the Fiduciary's Duty of Loyalty" (1968) 84 *Law Quarterly Review* 472 and "Restitution of Benefits Obtained in Breach of Another's Confidence" (1970) 86 *Law Quarterly Review* 463; Flannigan, "The Fiduciary Obligation" (1989) 9 *Oxford Journal of Legal Studies* 285 and (1990) 54 *Sask Law Review* 45.

61 *Armstrong v. Jackson* [1917] 2 K.B. 822, at 826 (K.B.D.).

62 Whether an agent is a fiduciary will depend on what he is authorised to do. For example, "if P appoints A to be his agent merely to sign a memorandum and places no particular trust in A, the doctrine of fiduciary relations and the incidents of agency which derive from this equitable doctrine would not apply": see Dowrick, "The Relationship of Principal and Agent" (1954) 17 *Modern Law Review* 24 at 31–32.

fiduciary duties, although they arise in equity, can be modified by contract.[63]

The core duties of a fiduciary are those of loyalty and fidelity.[64] These core duties have several aspects and an agent's fiduciary duties can be examined under four headings: to avoid conflicts of interest; not to make a secret profit; not to accept a bribe; and to account. These headings are not exclusive.[65] The duty not to accept a bribe can be viewed as an aspect of the duty not to make a secret profit, which, in turn, can be viewed as an aspect of the duty to avoid conflicts of interest. Moreover, these duties are prescriptive in nature: they tell the fiduciary what he must not do and not what he must do.[66]

Because these duties arise from the fiduciary nature of the relationship, independently of any contract, they may survive the termination of the contract, unless expressly or impliedly excluded by the contract. For example, in *A-G v. Blake*,[67] the Court of Appeal held that while a former employee of the Secret Intelligence Service did not owe a continuing duty of loyalty to this employers, he would continue to owe a separate fiduciary duty to maintain the confidentiality of information imparted to him in confidence, so long as that information had not become public knowledge. Another example, includes the duty to account, which has been held to apply after the termination of the agency.[68]

Where an agent is in breach of his fiduciary duties, a variety of remedies is available: proprietary and personal, at common law and in equity. For example, in particular cases, a principal may be entitled to sue for: damages in contract or in tort; an account of profits; rescission of the contract; an injunction; a declaration that property is held on constructive trust; a charge over property; an order for transfer of property, or other such orders. Such variety can, however, lead to uncertainty.[69] It is not always clear whether the principal's remedy is proprietary or personal. Some cases refer to agents and other fiduciaries holding property; "on constructive trust" for the principal, a proprietary remedy, while in others the agent is required to account for property, a personal remedy. There are two key advantages to a proprietary remedy over a personal remedy. First, with a

---

63 See, *e.g. Carroll Group Distributors v. G & JF Burke* [1990] I.L.R.M. 285 at 288, per Murphy J. See further *Kelly v. Cooper* [1993] A.C. 205; *Henderson v. Merrett* [1995] 2 A.C. 145, [1994] 3 All E.R. 506; *Triffit Nurseries v. Salads Etc Ltd* [1999] 1 All E.R. (Comm.) 110. See also Millett, "Equity's Place in the Law of Commerce" (1998) 114 *Law Quarterly Review* 214.

64 See *Bristol and West Building Society v. Mothew* [1998] Ch. 1 per Millett L.J. at 18

65 See Millett, "Equity's Place in the Law of Commerce" (1998) 114 *Law Quarterly Review* 214; *Arklow Developments v. Maclean* [2000] 1 W.L.R. 594.

66 *A-G v. Blake* [1998] 1 All E.R. 833 per Lord Woolf at 843.

67 [1998] 1 All E.R. 833 (C.A.).

68 *Yasuda Fire and Marine Insurance Co of Europe Ltd v. Orion Marine Insurance Underwriting Agency Ltd* [1995] Q.B. 174; see 7.3.2.4.

69 See, *e.g.* 7.3.2.2 and 7.3.2.3.

proprietary remedy, the principal can claim any enhanced value or profits gained as a result of the breach of duty, as where an agent has used a secret profit to purchase land which has increased in value. Second, with a proprietary remedy, the principal gains priority over the agent's unsecured creditors where the agent becomes insolvent, whereas a personal remedy would rank equally with other unsecured creditors.

7.3.2.1 To avoid conflicts of interest

> "It is a rule of universal application, that no one, having [fiduciary] duties to discharge, shall be allowed to enter into engagements in which he has, or can have, a personal interest conflicting, or which possibly may conflict, with the interests of those whom he is bound to protect."[70]

Hence, an agent must not allow his personal interests to conflict with those of the principal. This duty, which applies to all fiduciaries, is strictly applied. The fact that the agent acted in good faith and produced a benefit for his principal is irrelevant to the application of this rule.[71] English authority provides that this duty may be excluded by an express or implied term of the contract.[72] Whether an Irish court would allow such exclusion remains to be seen.[73]

Where the duty applies, there is a breach if, for instance, an agent instructed to buy property sells his own property to the principal[74] or if an agent instructed to sell property buys it for himself,[75] unless all the circumstances are disclosed to the principal and the principal consents to the transaction.[76] The agent cannot avoid the rule by dealing with the principal through a third party. In *McPherson v. Watt*,[77] an agent was instructed to sell property. He arranged for his brother to buy it for him. When the truth was discovered, the principal refused to complete and the court refused to grant an order for specific performance because of the agent's breach of duty.

Where an agent commits a breach of this duty, the principal may

70 Lord Cramworth L.C. in *Aberdeen Rly Co v. Blaikie Bros* (1854) 1 Macq. 461 at 471, (H.L.).

71 *Boardman v. Phipps* [1967] 2 A.C. 46 (H.L.).

72 See *Kelly v. Cooper* [1993] A.C. 205; *Henderson v. Merrett* [1995] 2 A.C. 145. In *Clarke Boyce v. Mauot* [1994] 1 A.C. 428, for example, the Privy Council held that a solicitor was entitled to act for both parties in a transaction even where their interests might conflict provided he obtained the informed consent of both parties to his so acting.

73 See further below.

74 See, *e.g. Armstrong v. Jackson* [1917] 2 K.B. 822 (K.B.D.).

75 See, *e.g. McPherson v. Watt* (1877) 3 App. Cas. 254 (H.L.).

76 *North & South Trust Co v. Berkeley* [1971] 1 W.L.R. 470 at 484–485. Where an agent buys his principal's property or sells his own property to the principal, the agent must also show that the price was fair and that he did not abuse his position: *Gibson v. Jeyes* (1801) 6 Ves. 266.

77 (1877) 3 App Cas. 254 (H.L.).

rescind the resulting contract. Normally, delay is a bar to rescission but in this case, time does not start to run until the breach is discovered. In *Oliver v. Court*,[78] the principal was able to rescind 13 years after the transaction. If the principal affirms the contract, he may require the agent to account for any profit he makes or claim damages.[79]

The above cases concern an agent placing himself in a position of conflict with his principal. Interesting questions arise where an agent places himself in a position where his duty to one principal may conflict with his duty to another principal. In the English case *Kelly v. Cooper*,[80] an estate agent, A, acted for two principals, P and X, who owned two adjacent properties. They both instructed A to sell their properties. A showed both properties to T, who agreed to buy X's property. T subsequently made an offer to P to buy his property. P, unaware that T had already agreed to buy X's property, accepted the offer. When P discovered that T had agreed to buy X's property, he argued that had he known that fact he would have been able to negotiate a higher price for his property because it was clear that T wanted both properties. P argued that A was in breach of his fiduciary duties in failing to disclose that T had agreed to buy X's property and in placing himself in a position where his duties to his two principals would conflict. He claimed damages for loss of the chance to negotiate a higher price. The Privy Council held that where an agent acts in pursuance of a contract, the scope of his fiduciary duties were determined by the contract. Since it was well known that estate agents might act for more than one principal, the agency contract in this case contained an implied term that the agent would be permitted to act for more than one principal, whose interests might compete, and to keep confidential information received whilst acting for other principals. On the facts, the contract could not include a term preventing the agent acting for other principals. This decision has wide implications because situations where an agent acts for more than one principal are increasingly common, as with financial advisors and solicitors, especially as firms become larger. In *Clarke Boyce v. Mauot*,[81] the Privy Council went a step further when it held that a solicitor was entitled to act for both parties in *the same transaction* even where their interests might conflict provided he obtained the informed consent of both parties to his so acting. The recognition, by English courts, of the ability of parties to contract out of the "no conflict rule" reflects modern commercial practice. Nevertheless, critics point to the danger of leaving everything to express and implied terms of the contract, thereby

---

78 (1820) 8 Price 127.

79 *Bentley v. Craven* (1853) 18 Beav. 75.

80 [1993] A.C. 205 (P.C.); see further Brown "Divided Loyalties in the Law of Agency" (1993) 109 *Law Quarterly Review* 206; and Reynolds "Fiduciary Duties and Estate Agents" [1994] *Journal of Business Law* 144.

81 [1994] 1 A.C. 428.

denying the importance of fiduciary obligations.[82] An Irish court faced with the questions raised above should be mindful of such criticism.

7.3.2.2 Not to make a secret profit

> "There is no dispute about the law, which is that an agent cannot without the knowledge of his principal make any profit for himself out of services rendered to his principal."[83]

This rule is strictly applied. It applies even to unpaid agents.[84] An agent must account to the principal for all profits made from his position. It is irrelevant that the agent acted in good faith, that the principal suffered no loss, that the agent made a profit which the principal could not, or that the principal actually benefited from the agent's actions. The strictness of the rule is illustrated by *Boardman v. Phipps*[85] where two agents for the trustees of an estate attended an annual general meeting of a company in which the estate had a minority interest. Later, they obtained information about share prices from the company. Using this information and acting honestly (but not having obtained the "informed consent" of all the trustees) the agents used their own money to bid for and eventually acquire the majority of shares in the company. Ultimately, the agents and the estate made a considerable profit on their respective shares. Nevertheless, by a majority of three to two, the House of Lords held that the agents were in breach of duty and were required to hand over their profits to the trust fund. The profits had been made by reason of their fiduciary position as agents and by reason of the opportunity and the information which had come to them while acting as agents.[86]

There will be a breach of this duty if, for instance:

(i) the agent receives a secret commission from a third party for negotiating a contract between the principal and the third party;

(ii) the agent profits from the use of the principal's property (for instance by investing money), or information which

---

82 See Brown, "Divided Loyalties in the Law of Agency" (1993) 109 *Law Quarterly Review* 206; and Reynolds, "Fiduciary Duties and Estate Agents" [1994] *Journal of Business Law* 144.

83 *Sherrard v. Barron* [1923] 1 I.R. 21, per Moore L.J. at 24.

84 *Turnbull v. Garden* (1869) 38 L.J. Ch. 331.

85 [1967] 2 A.C. 46 (H.L.).

86 Cf. *Peso Silver Mines Ltd (NPL) v. Cropper* (1966) D.L.R. (2d) 1; and *Consul Development Pty Ltd v. DPC Estates Pty Ltd* (1975) 5 A.L.R. 231; see further Jones, "Unjust Enrichment and the Fiduciary's Duty of Loyalty"(1968) 84 *Law Quarterly Review* 472.

he receives in his capacity as agent,[87] or otherwise from his position as agent.[88]

Where an agent breaches this duty, the principal may require him to account for the profit. The duty to account is personal. But where the profit is made using the principal's property, it appears that the principal's rights are proprietary, and the agent must hold any profits on constructive trust for the principal. The position with profits made using information received in the capacity of agent, or otherwise from the position of agent, is less clear. In *Boardman v. Phipps*,[89] it was held that the agent held the profits on constructive trust.[90] The case has been explained on the basis that confidential information is a form of trust property though the better view is that confidential information is not property.[91] The principal may also obtain an injunction restraining the agent from making further use of confidential information. Equity is sufficiently flexible to distinguish between an agent acting fraudulently and in good faith. For instance, in *Boardman v. Phipps*[92] the agents were allowed some payment for their expenditure.[93]

An agent may keep a profit only if it is disclosed to the principal who, with full knowledge, consents to his retaining it.[94]

7.3.2.3 Not to accept a bribe

A bribe is any payment or other inducement made to an agent by a third party which is secret from the principal. It is therefore a particular species of secret profit. In this context, "bribe" may not necessarily indicate corruption. If an agent receives a bribe, the principal may:

(i) dismiss the agent without notice;[95]
(ii) withhold any commission due to the agent on that

---

87 *E.g. Boardman v. Phipps* [1967] 2 A.C. 46 (H.L.).

88 *E.g. Hippisley v. Knee Bros* [1905] 1 K.B. 1 where A was instructed to sell property for P. A advertised the property and received a discount on the cost of advertising but charged P the full cost. It was held that A was in breach of his duty in keeping the discount.

89 [1967] 2 A.C. 46 (H.L.).

90 For criticism of this decision see Goff & Jones, *The Law of Restitution* (London, Sweet & Maxwell, 5th ed., 1998) p.736.

91 See Bradgate, *Commercial Law* (London, Butterworths, 3rd ed., 2000) p.201.

92 [1967] 2 A.C. 46 (H.L.).

93 In *Hippisley v. Knee Bros* [1905] 1 K.B. 1 the court found that the agent acted in good faith and so, although he was in breach of duty, he was allowed keep his commission on the transaction.

94 *Sherrard v. Barron* [1923] 1 I.R. 21.

95 See, *e.g. Boston Deep Sea Fishing and Ice Co v. Ansell* (1888) 39 Ch. D. 339 (C.A.); and *Bulfield v. Fournier* (1895) 11 T.L.R. 282.

transaction and recover any commission already paid;[96]

(iii) rescind the contract with the third party;

(iv) require either the agent or the third party to account for the amount of the bribe as money had and received;[97]

(v) claim damages (in the tort of deceit) for any loss he suffers as a result of payment of the bribe and entry into the consequent contract; the agent and third party are jointly and severally liable for such damages.[98]

Although the position is not clear, it seems that the principal cannot claim both damages and an account of the bribe.[99] However, the other remedies are cumulative. To allow a principal to recover the bribe and claim damages for his loss would allow double recovery and give the principal an undeserved "windfall",[100] but there is no reason the principal could not recover the bribe and then recover any excess loss in damages.

In *Lister v. Stubbs*,[101] it was held that a principal's claim to recover a bribe was a personal one, and so the bribe was not held on trust. In contrast, as noted above, where an agent makes a secret profit using his principal's property, or his position, the remedy is proprietary. This distinction between personal and proprietary remedies is significant. In particular, where the remedy is personal the funds cannot be traced into property into which they might have been converted and the principal cannot recover any profit made through the use of the funds, or acquire any preferential rights should the fiduciary become insolvent. Hence, an agent who obtains a bribe is merely obliged to account for its value whereas an agent who has earned a profit honestly holds the sum as a constructive trustee. *Lister* has been criticised for allowing the agent retain any profit made with the bribe thereby treating a dishonest agent more leniently than an honest one.[102] In *AG for Hong Kong v. Reid*,[103] the Privy Council found that *Lister* was

96 *Andrews v. Ramsey & Co Ltd* [1903] 2 K.B. 635.

97 *Lister & Co v. Stubbs* (1890) 45 Ch. D. 1, see further below.

98 *Arab Monetary Fund v. Hashim* [1993] 1 Lloyd's Rep. 543.

99 *Mahesan S/O Thambiah v. Malaysia Government Officers' Co-operative Housing Society Ltd* [1979] A.C. 374 (P.C.). For criticism of this decision see Tettenborn, "Recovering the Profits of Bribery" (1979) 95 *Law Quarterly Review* 68.

100 See Needham, "Bribery, Corruption and Restitution" (1979) 95 *Law Quarterly Review* 536.

101 (1890) 45 Ch. D. 1 (C.A.).

102 See, *e.g.* Millett, "Bribes and Secret Commissions" [1993] *Restitution Law Review* 7.

103 [1994] 1 A.C. 324; [1994] 1 All E.R. 1; see further Pearce, "Personal and Proprietary Claims against Bribees" [1994] *Lloyd's Maritime and Commercial Law Quarterly* 189; Oakley, "The Bribed Fiduciary as Constructive Trustee" (1994) 53 *Cambridge Law Journal* 31; Allen, "Bribes and Constructive Trusts" (1995) 58 *Modern Law Review* 87.

wrongly decided and instead recognised that agents hold the amount of the bribe on constructive trust for the principal, such that the principal can claim the amount of the bribe and any profits made with it. This decision can be welcomed for removing the arbitrary distinction between remedies imposed in circumstances where a fiduciary receives a bribe and earns a profit. While Privy Council decisions are not binding on Irish courts, and *Lister* is technically binding on Irish courts,[104] the decision in *AG for Hong Kong v. Reid* is of persuasive authority. But the Privy Council decision is not without its critics,[105] in particular, because of the Privy Council's failure to take proper account of the interests of the insolvent agent's unsecured creditors.[106]

Additionally, the payment of a bribe may give rise to criminal liability. At common law, an agent who accepts or agrees to accept a bribe may be guilty of conspiracy. Where it can be shown that the bribe was received or paid with a corrupt motive, the agent and briber will be guilty of an offence under the Prevention of Corruption Acts 1906 and 1916.[107]

7.3.2.4 To account

An agent must account to the principal for all property of the principal he receives in the course of the agency. He must therefore keep his own monies and property separate from those of the principal, unless mixing is authorised. If an agent wrongfully mixes his property with that of the principal, the principal may claim the whole of the mixed fund, unless the agent can establish any part of it as his own property.[108] Since the relationship between the principal and agent is generally fiduciary, the principal may trace his property in equity and thus claim any replacement assets if the agent wrongfully disposes of his property.

The duty to account is personal. An agent is not normally a trustee of the principal's property. This distinction is important in the case of an agent's insolvency. The existence of a trust will depend on the intentions of the parties. For example, where an agent sold goods on behalf of several principals on terms which permitted him to mix their goods such that it was impossible to connect any particular sale with any particular principal, it was held that the agent received payment on his own account, and not as

104 In *O'Mahoney v. Horgan* [1996] 1 I.L.R.M. 161, the Supreme Court departed from *Lister* on the issue of Mareva injunctions. This may indicate a willingness to overrule *Lister* on the substantive point, when the opportunity arises.

105 See Uff, "The Remedies of the Defrauded Principal after AG for Hong Kong v. Reid" in Feldman & Meisel ed., *Corporate and Commercial Law: Modern Developments* (London, Lloyd's of London Press, 1996) Chapter 13.

106 See Goode, "Proprietary Restitutionary Claims" in Cornish *et al* ed., *Restitution: Past Present and Future* (Oxford, Hart, 1998) Chapter 5.

107 See the 1906 Act, s.1(1). See the 1916 Act, s.2 for when a corrupt motive will be presumed.

108 *Lupton v. White* (1808) 15 Ves. 432.

trustee for the principals. The relationship of agent/principal was merely a debtor/creditor relationship.[109]

As part of this duty, an agent must keep complete records of transactions entered on the principal's behalf and make them available for inspection to the principal.[110] A court may make adverse inferences where the agent fails in this regard.[111] On termination of the agency, the agent must deliver up to the principal all books, accounts and other documents given to him by the principal or created in the course of the agency unless he is entitled to exercise a lien over it.[112] Moreover, the duty to account arises from the fiduciary nature of the relationship, independently of any contract, and hence it survives the termination of the contract, unless expressly or impliedly excluded by the contract.[113]

7.3.3 Under the Directive and Regulations

The Directive appears to restate an agent's common law duties, in broad terms. It provides that a commercial agent has a general duty to look after the interests of his principal and act dutifully and in good faith.[114] In particular, a commercial agent must:

(i) make proper efforts to negotiate and, where appropriate, conclude transactions he is instructed to take care of;
(ii) communicate to his principal all the necessary information available to him;
(iii) comply with reasonable instructions given by his principal.[115]

Importantly, the parties cannot derogate from these duties.[116] This contrasts with the common law position where case law suggests that an agent's duties, including his fiduciary duties, may be excluded by contract.[117] Nevertheless, the terms of the agency agreement will clearly be relevant in determining the exact requirements of the duties imposed by the Directive, such as the meaning of "proper efforts" and "necessary information".

---

109 *Triffit Nurseries v. Salads Etc Ltd* [2000] 1 All E.R. (Comm.) 737. See also *Carroll Group Distributors v. G & JF Burke* [1990] I.L.R.M. 285 and 15.4.1.3 in relation to retention of title clauses.

110 *Pearse v. Green* (1819) 1 Jac. & W. 135.

111 *Gray v. Haig* (1855) 20 Beav. 219.

112 *Gibbon v. Pease* [1905] 1 K.B. 810; see further 25.3.

113 *Yasuda Fire and Marine Insurance Co of Europe Ltd v. Orion Marine Insurance Underwriting Agency Ltd* [1995] Q.B. 174.

114 Art. 3(1).

115 Art. 3(2).

116 Art. 5.

117 See 7.3.2 *et seq*.

7.4 PRINCIPAL'S DUTIES

No duties similar to those placed on an agent are placed on a principal at common law, reflecting the common law position that principals, and not agents, need protection, as noted above.[118] For the first time, under the Directive and Regulations, good faith duties, similar to those placed on an agent, are placed on the principal.[119] The detail of these duties will have to be developed by case law. In particular, the Directive provides that a principal must:

> "(i) provide his commercial agent with the necessary documentation relating to the goods concerned;
>
> (ii) obtain for his commercial agent the information necessary for the performance of the agency contract, and in particular notify the commercial agent within a reasonable period once he anticipates that the volume of commercial transactions will be significantly lower than that which the commercial agent could normally have expected."[120]

The parties cannot derogate from these duties and so the information described above, which a principal might consider confidential, must be provided to the agent.[121]

7.5 AGENT'S RIGHTS

Other than the rights which may exist under an agency contract, an agent enjoys only limited rights at common law. These are greatly enhanced where the Directive and Regulations apply.

7.5.1 At common law

The agent has three basic rights at common law: a right to remuneration, a right to an indemnity, and a right to a lien.

---

118 It has been recognised, in insurance law, that an insurer owes the insured a duty of good faith, corresponding to the insured's duty of good faith: *Banque Financière de la Cité v. Westgate Insurance Co Ltd* [1990] 1 Q.B. 665, [1989] 2 All E.R. 952, (C.A.); affd [1991] 2 A.C. 249, [1990] 2 All E.R. 947 (H.L.). An argument could be made, by analogy, that a principal owes an agent a corresponding duty of good faith. However, attempts to place fiduciary duties on principals have proved unsuccessful: see, *e.g. Jirna Ltd v. Mister Donut of Canada Ltd* (1973) 40 D.L.R. (3d) 303 (S.C.).

119 Art. 4(1).

120 Art. 4(2).

121 Art. 5.

7.5.1.1 Right to remuneration

An agent is only entitled to remuneration if that has been agreed with the principal. In a commercial context, it is rare that an agent would agree to act gratuitously. The agreement as to remuneration can be express or implied. A right to remuneration will be implied on the same basis that other terms can be implied into contracts.[122] For instance, such a right would probably be implied where the agent is acting in the course of a profession or business, and would more easily be implied where the services have already been provided. Where it is agreed that an agent should be paid but the amount of remuneration is not agreed, the agent is entitled to a reasonable sum as a *quantum meruit*.[123]

An agent is entitled to be paid in accordance with the terms of the agreement. A well drafted agency agreement should deal with issues such as the method of payment, when remuneration is earned, and when it is payable. Remuneration may be by retainer and/or commission. Commission may be earned in differing circumstances, for instance, on conclusion or performance of the contract that the agent is instructed to negotiate and/or conclude. Where a commission is earned on an agent bringing about a result, he will only be entitled to payment if he is the effective cause of that result.[124] For instance, in *Stokes & Quirke Ltd v. Clohessy*,[125] the owners of a house instructed an auctioneer to sell it. The auctioneer found a buyer but before a formal agreement was signed, the sellers received a better offer from someone not known to the auctioneer who eventually bought the property. The auctioneer claimed commission but failed in the High Court where it was held that the agreement provided for commission only where the auctioneer introduced buyers who actually bought. In *Murphy, Buckley & Keogh Ltd v. Pye (Ire) Ltd*,[126] the seller of a factory appointed auctioneers as "sole agents" in the sale. However, the seller arranged a sale himself without telling the auctioneers. The auctioneers claimed a commission but lost in the High Court. It was held, first, that the sole agent had not effected a sale and hence was not entitled to commission. Second, the auctioneers were the sole agents but this did not prevent the seller from effecting a sale himself, merely from appointing

---

122 See 2.3.4.

123 *Way v. Latilla* [1937] 3 All E.R. 759 (H.L.), *Henehan v. Courtney* (1967) 101 I.L.T.R. 25. Failure to agree on the issue of remuneration may indicate that the parties have not reached an agreement. Nevertheless, where an agent has performed the service he may be entitled to a reasonable sum on a restitutionary basis.

124 *Millar, Son & Co v. Radford* (1903) 19 T.L.R. 575 (C.A.); *Judd v. Donegal Tweed Co Ltd* (1935) 69 I.L.T.R. 117. See generally, Markesinis & Munday, *An Outline of the Law of Agency* (4th ed., Butterworths, London, 1998) p.125 onwards, regarding case law on estate agency in particular.

125 [1957] I.R. 84 (H.C.).

126 [1971] I.R. 57 (H.C.).

any other agents.[127] Hence, where an agent is appointed "sole agent" to effect a contract, the principal commits a breach if a second agent is appointed; if the second agent then concludes a contract, the first agent would be entitled to damages, equal to the amount of commission of which he is deprived, for breach of that term.[128]

Where an agent is to be remunerated by commission it may be necessary to decide whether the principal may prevent him earning his commission, for instance, by refusing to perform a contract negotiated or concluded by the agent. In the absence of any express provision in the agency agreement, this depends on whether an appropriate term may be implied into the agency contract. For example, in *Cusack v. Bothwell*,[129] an auctioneer was instructed to find a buyer for lands at a certain price. The agent was to receive a commission of five per cent. He introduced a buyer but the seller refused to sell and pay the commission. The court awarded the auctioneer a sum equivalent to five per cent because he had done what was required of him. This ruling goes against some earlier English case law but appears to be supported in more recent case law. In the past, the courts have generally been reluctant to imply terms which would restrict a principal's right to deal with his own property. Thus, in *Luxor (Eastbourne) Ltd v. Cooper*,[130] the House of Lords refused to imply into a contract of estate agency a term that the principal should not refuse to sell to a buyer introduced by the agents. It has been observed that the House of Lords seemed to be influenced by the scale of the commission involved.[131] It was held that the agents had assumed the risk that the sale would not complete.[132] In *French & Co v. Leston Shipping Co Ltd*,[133] the House of Lords refused to imply a term which would prevent principal ship-owners selling the ship during the course of a charter party negotiated by the agent, where the effect of the sale was to deprive the agent of commission. Such a term would have restricted the principal's right to deal freely with his property. However, in *Alpha Trading v. Dunshaw-Patten*,[134] where agents were employed to negotiate a contract for the sale of cement and were entitled to commission on performance of the contract, the principals broke the contract negotiated with the third party (paying damages to the third party) in order to take advantage of a rising market. It was held that this was a breach of an implied term in the agency contract so that the agents were entitled to damages equal to the amount of commission of which they

127 Where an agent is appointed with "the sole right to sell" it has been held that the principal is in breach of contract if he sells in person: *Brodie Marshall & Co v. Sharer* [1988] 19 E.G. 129.

128 *Bentall, Horsley and Baldry v. Vicary* [1931] 1 K.B. 253.

129 (1943) 77 I.L.T.R. 18.

130 [1941] A.C. 108 (H.L.).

131 See Bradgate, *Commercial Law* (London, Butterworths, 3rd ed., 2000) p.183.

132 [1941] A.C. 108, per Viscount Simon LC at 120.

133 [1922] 1 A.C. 451 (H.L.); see also *Rhodes v. Forwood* (1876) 1 App. Cas. 256.

134 [1981] Q.B. 290.

had been deprived by the breach. This was not a risk which the agent had agreed to bear and the implication of this term was necessary to prevent the principal taking advantage of the agent and undermining the usefulness of commercial agency in general. It will probably be easier for such a term to be implied in a continuing contract rather than in a once-off contract. A well-drafted agency contract will seek to avoid such problems.

Lastly, an agent is only entitled to remuneration where he has acted within his authority. Where an agent acts without authority or exceeds the authority given to him, he is not entitled to be paid, even though the principal may be bound by the transaction, under the doctrine of apparent authority,[135] for example. Moreover, it seems that even where an agent has acted within his authority but has committed a serious breach of any of his duties to his principal, he loses his right to remuneration.

7.5.1.2 Right to an indemnity

An agent is entitled to be indemnified against any expenses and liabilities, contractual or tortious, necessarily incurred on behalf of the principal in performance of his duties when acting within the scope of his actual authority, or, if his actions are later ratified, or if the agency is one of necessity. Where the agent's actions are unauthorised, no right to indemnity arises. Where the agency is contractual, the right to indemnity will be an implied term of the contract; where the agency is gratuitous, the right will be restitutionary.

The right to indemnity does not cover any expenses or liabilities incurred due to the agent's own fault, nor any expenses or liabilities with regard to acts that the agent knew to be unlawful or illegal.[136] In one case, an auctioneer who sold goods on his principal's instructions, without knowing that the principal had no right to sell them, was entitled to an indemnity against liability to the true owner. The right to indemnity may also cover payments made by an agent even where there was no legal obligation to pay, where there is strong moral and professional pressure to pay.[137]

7.5.1.3 Right to a lien[138]

An agent is entitled to a lien over property – including papers – of the principal, in his possession, to secure payment of any remuneration or indemnity due to him. Most agents are entitled only to a particular lien – a right to retain property until sums related to that property or any related

135 See 5.3.

136 *Re Parker* (1882) 21 Ch. D. 408 (C.A.).

137 *Rhodes v. Fielder, Jones and Harrison* (1919) 89 L.J.K.B. 15 (K.B.D.).

138 See generally 25.3.

transaction are paid. However, some agents are entitled to a general lien, a right to retain any property of the principal to secure payment of any sums due from the principal, whether connected to that property or not. Factors, bankers, solicitors and stockbrokers are entitled to a general lien, for instance.

7.5.2 Under the Directive and Regulations

Where the Directive and Regulations apply, they modify the agent's right to remuneration and give him certain additional rights. The common law rights to indemnity and lien remain unchanged.

7.5.2.1 Right to commission

The Directive deals with a number of issues relating to remuneration. In particular, where an agent is paid wholly or partly by commission,[139] the Directive addresses the amount payable, when commission is earned, and when commission is payable.

In the absence of any agreement about the level of remuneration payable, a commercial agent is entitled to receive such remuneration as is customarily paid to a commercial agent dealing in the type of goods to which the agreement relates, in the area in which the agent operates. Where there is no custom, a reasonable sum is payable.[140] This is not unlike the common law position where, if it is agreed that an agent should be paid but the amount of remuneration is not agreed, the agent is entitled to a reasonable sum.[141]

A commercial agent is entitled to receive commission on transactions concluded during the agency:[142]

(i) which result from his actions;[143] and
(ii) which result from repeat orders of the same kind from customers introduced by the agent;[144] and
(iii) where the agent has the exclusive right to represent the principal in a specific geographical area or group of customers, on all contracts from customers belonging to that area or group.[145]

---

139 Any part of the remuneration which varies with the number or value of business transactions is deemed to be commission: Art. 6(2).

140 Art. 6.

141 *Henehan v. Courtney* (1967) 101 I.L.T.R. 25.

142 Art. 7 and Reg. 4, 1994.

143 Art. 7(1)(a).

144 Art. 7(1)(b).

145 Art. 7(2) and Reg. 4, 1994.

In *Georgios Kontogeorgas v. Kartonpak AE 1*,[146] the European Court of Justice had to interpret aspects of Article 7(2) of the Directive which deal with the situation where an agent represents a principal, exclusively or otherwise, in a specific area or to a specific group of customers – scenario (iii) above. The court made two important findings. First, the court found that where an agent is entrusted with a specific geographical area, he is entitled to commission on transactions concluded with customers belonging to that area even if they were concluded without any action on the part of the agent. The court also considered the phrase "customers belonging to that area." Where the customer is a legal person, whose seat is located outside the area in which its business and trading activities are carried on, the customer belongs to the area where its actual commercial activities are undertaken. This decision reflects the "real economic context" of the relationship between the agent and the customer.[147] Where the company carries on the business in several areas, it will be more difficult to identify the relevant area for the purposes of the Directive. Other factors would have to be considered, such as the place where the negotiations with the agent took place, or should, in the normal course of events, have taken place; the place where the goods were delivered; and the place where the customer who ordered the goods is located. The essential criterion is to avoid a single transaction from being regarded as attaching to the geographical area of two or more agents.

In comparison with an agent's rights at common law, these provisions are more generous. As noted above, where a commission is payable on an agent bringing about a result, he will only be entitled to payment, at common law, if he is the *effective cause* of that result.[148] This is similar to the first of the rights to commission under the Directive. However, unless the agency contract provides otherwise, an agent has no common law right to commission on repeat orders, or on orders received from customers within his specific area or group which he has not caused to happen. Where an agent has an exclusive right to a specific area or group, he would be entitled to damages for any breach of contract and the measure of damages would *prima facie* be the amount of lost commission.[149] Further provisions govern a commercial agent's right to commission on contracts entered into *after* termination of the agency. These are considered below.[150]

Broadly speaking, under the Directive, commission becomes due when either the principal or the third party perform their obligations under the contract. Where the principal fails to perform, commission is due when he

146 (Case C-104/95) [1996] ECR I-6643.

147 *Ibid.* para. 26.

148 *Judd v. Donegal Tweed Co. Ltd* (1935) 69 I.L.T.R. 117; *Stokes & Quirke Ltd v. Clohessy* [1957] I.R. 84 (H.C.); *Murphy, Buckley & Keogh Ltd v. Pye (Ire) Ltd* [1971] I.R. 57 (H.C.); see 7.5.1.1.

149 See 7.5.1.1.

150 See 7.6.3.2(ii).

should have performed, or, at the latest, when the third party should have performed had the principal not breached the contract.[151] The result is that, unlike the position at common law, arguably, a principal cannot deprive a commercial agent of commission by failing to perform the contract with the third party. However, no commission is payable where the contract is not performed "due to a reason for which the principal is not to blame."[152] Any commission already paid in such a case is refundable.[153] It is unclear what the reference to "blame" means. At common law, blame or fault is not relevant to liability for breach of contract: liability for breach of contract is usually strict. It seems clear that a principal should not be liable for commission where the contract is frustrated. But it is unclear whether lawful termination of contract by the principal, following, for example, a breach of contract by the third party, would entitle the agent to commission. Here, it could be argued that the principal was not "to blame" and so commission would not be payable. Moreover, it could be argued that where a principal breaches a contract but is not at fault, there is no commission payable. However, the more likely interpretation is that commission is payable whenever non-performance is as a result of the principal's breach.[154]

7.5.2.2 Right to information

The Directive requires the principal to provide the commercial agent with a detailed statement indicating the amount of commission due to him and how it is calculated.[155] A commercial agent can demand access to information and, in particular, to extracts of the principal's books – but not the full books – to check the amount of commission due.[156] Moreover, either party may require the other to provide a signed, written statement of the terms of the agency, including any variation.[157] At common law, the only right to information operates in favour of the principal and relates to an agent's duty to account to his principal. Hence, these rights to information in favour of the agent are alien to the common law, and only case law will determine their true extent.

---

151 Art. 10. Commission is payable not later than on the last day of the month following the quarter in which it became due: Art. 10(3). These provisions are mandatory: Art. 10(4).

152 Art. 11(1).

153 Art. 11(2).

154 *Bowstead on Agency* (16th ed., Sweet & Maxwell, London, 1996) para. 11–031.

155 Art. 12(1).

156 Art. 12 (2). Derogation from Art. 12(1) and (2) to the detriment of the commercial agent is not permitted: Art. 12(3).

157 Art. 13. Waiver of this right is not permitted: Art. 13(1).

7.6 Termination of the Relationship

Since the formation of an agency relationship depends on consent, the relationship of principal and agent can be terminated, at any time, by either party withdrawing consent. The relationship can also terminate automatically in certain circumstances, by operation of law. However, an agency may be irrevocable.[158] Even where an agency is revocable, termination of the relationship and of the agent's actual authority may leave the agent with apparent authority and may therefore not deprive him of power to bind the principal. In addition, as between the principal and the agent, termination of the agency may give rise to consequent, or secondary, rights, especially where the agency is contractual and termination amounts to a breach of contract. Once again, the general common law rules are modified by the Directive and Regulations.

7.6.1 Termination at common law

At common law, an agency, unless irrevocable, may be terminated automatically by operation of law, or by the act of either, or both, parties.

7.6.1.1 Termination by operation of law

An agency may be terminated, automatically, by effluxion of time; performance; frustration; or the bankruptcy or insanity of either party.

(i) Effluxion of time

Where an agency is expressed to be for a fixed period, the relationship and the agent's authority are automatically determined on expiry of that fixed period.

(ii) Performance

Where an agent is appointed to perform a particular task – for instance, to sell a particular item of property – the agency is terminated on performance of the task.

(iii) Frustration

A contractual agency may be terminated by any event which frustrates the contract. Thus, it will be terminated if performance becomes illegal or

---

158 An agency may be irrevocable where (i) the agent is given a "power with an interest," that is, where an agent is given power and a personal interest, as where P owes A money, and appoints A to act as his agent to sell property and thereby rise funds to pay the debt: see the Powers of Attorney Act 1996, s.20; or (ii) where a power of attorney is expressed to be "enduring" or irrevocable under Part II of the Powers of Attorney Act 1996.

impossible, for instance, because of the death of either party, or if a change in circumstances destroys the commercial purpose of the contract.[159] Where one of the parties is a company, the agency is similarly terminated by the winding up of the company.

(iv) Bankruptcy

The principal's bankruptcy terminates the agency and deprives the agent of authority (although there are a number of rules designed to protect agents and third parties in respect of acts done before they have notice of the bankruptcy).[160] An agent's bankruptcy will terminate the agency if it makes him unfit to continue to act.

(v) Insanity

The agency is automatically terminated by the insanity of either party. However, if an agent is appointed under an enduring power of attorney, the principal's insanity will not automatically terminate the agency.[161] Where an agent's authority is terminated by the principal's insanity, he may nevertheless continue to have apparent authority as against third parties who deal with him without knowledge of the termination;[162] However, there is also authority that if an agent continues to act he may incur personal liability for breach of warranty of authority.[163]

7.6.1.2 Termination by act of the parties

Since agency is a consensual relationship it can be terminated if either party withdraws consent.

(i) Mutual consent

Contractual and non-contractual agencies can be determined by the agreement of both parties.

(ii) Unilateral action

The agency relationship is terminated if either party withdraws consent to its continuance. Where an agent withdraws consent, he is said to "renounce" the agency. Where the principal withdraws consent, he is said

159 See 2.4.3.

160 See generally, the Bankruptcy Act 1988; see further, Forde, *Bankrupcy Law in Ireland* (Butterworths, Dublin, 1990).

161 See Part II of the Powers of Attorney Act 1996.

162 *Drew v. Nunn* (1879) 4 Q.B.D. 661.

163 *Yonge v. Toynbee* [1910] 1 K.B. 215; see 6.4.5.

to "revoke" the agent's authority. No formality is required for a renunciation or revocation.

Renunciation and revocation are effective even if in breach of contract. Thus, for instance, the authority of an agent appointed for a fixed term may be revoked before expiry of the term and the revocation will be effective to terminate the agent's actual authority. However, while the agency relationship may be effectively terminated, other liabilities may arise. For example, the agent may continue to have apparent authority, thereby binding the principal with third parties. Where possible, a principal should therefore publicise the termination of an agent's authority in order to draw it to the attention of those who have dealt with the agent in the past, thereby avoiding a representation that the agent continues to have authority from the principal.[164] Moreover, revocation or renunciation before the expiry of a fixed term may give rise to liability for breach of contract on the principal's or the agent's parts, respectively, unless justified by a prior breach by the other party.

Where an agent is appointed for an indeterminate period, the agency can be terminated in accordance with any provision in the agreement for termination by notice. In the absence of any express term, it will normally be implied that the agency can be terminated, by either party, on reasonable notice. What constitutes reasonable notice will depend on the facts of the particular case. In *Martin Baker Aircraft Co. Ltd v. Canadian Flight Equipment Ltd*,[165] where an agent agreed, in return for a commission, to promote the principal's products and not to sell competing products, it was held that twelve months' notice was required to terminate the agency.

Where an agent is appointed on a commission basis to perform a single task, this may be interpreted as a unilateral contract. If so, the principal may be entitled to withdraw the offer of commission and terminate the agency at any point before the agent has performed the specified task. However, in certain cases, a term, or a collateral contract, may be implied to restrict the principal's freedom to revoke the offer.[166] If the contract is unilateral, the agent is under no duty to act and can withdraw at any stage.[167]

Difficulties can arise where a principal ceases to trade during the currency of the agency agreement. Such cessation will amount to a repudiation of contract unless permitted by the agency agreement. Each case depends on the proper construction of the agency contract. In *Rhodes v. Forwood*,[168] P appointed A to act as agent for seven years or so long as P carried on the business. After four years, P sold the business and A's

---

164 See 5.3.1.1.

165 [1955] 2 Q.B. 556.

166 *Alpha Trading v. Dunshaw-Patten* [1981] Q.B. 290.

167 *Carlill v. Carbolic Smoke Ball* [1893] 1 Q.B. 256.

168 (1876) 1 App. Cas. 256.

authority was terminated. A claimed damages for breach of contract but failed. The court refused to imply a term that P would stay in business for the full term of the agreement, as this would restrict P's freedom to deal with his property. In contrast, in *Turner v. Goldsmith*,[169] P appointed A as agent for five years to sell shirts and other goods manufactured by P. P's factory burned down and P terminated the agency. A succeeded in a claim for damages because it was held that P could manufacture other goods, or provide A with shirts manufactured elsewhere.

7.6.2 Impact of the Directive and Regulations

A commercial agency agreement governed by the Directive and Regulations can be terminated in any of the ways described above. Where an agent is appointed initially for a fixed term but both parties continue to perform the contract after expiry of the term, the agency is treated as continuing as one for an indeterminate period, determinable by notice.[170] In the case of termination by notice, the notice required by the contract cannot be less than one month in the first year of the relationship, two months in the second and three months thereafter.[171] The parties cannot agree to shorter notice periods but they can agree to longer notice.[172] In the latter case, the notice to be observed by the principal must not be shorter than that to be observed by the agent.[173] In *King v. Tunnock*,[174] a long-standing agency was terminated without notice. In addition to his claim for compensation for damage following termination,[175] it was held that the agent was entitled to three months' notice and common law damages were payable to compensate him for this breach of contract.

Given that the purpose of the Directive is to protect commercial agents, it could be argued that dismissal of an agent with less than the above minimum notice periods should be ineffective. If accepted, this would mean that any agency terminated prematurely would continue until the relevant notice period had expired and the agent would be entitled to any commissions for that period. However, this argument was rejected in the Scottish case of *Roy v. MR Pearlman*.[176] In this case, the agency contract provided for termination by either party on six months' notice. The principal sought to terminate the contract summarily and it was held that, on the facts, the agent had accepted the principal's repudiation, thereby bringing the contract to an end. Because the Directive and relevant

169 [1891] 1 Q.B. 544 (C.A.).
170 Art. 14 and Art. 15(1).
171 Art. 15(2).
172 Art. 15(2) and (4).
173 Art. 15(4).
174 [2000] I.R.L.R. 569.
175 See 7.6.3.2(iv).
176 [1999] C.L.R. 36.

Regulations provided no remedy for failure to give proper notice, Lord Hamilton, the Lord Ordinary, concluded that the consequence of such failure was to be determined by domestic law. Therefore, failure to give notice gave rise to a claim in damages for breach of contract, but since A accepted the repudiation, the contract was terminated.

7.6.3 Consequences of termination

Where an agency relationship is terminated, in any of the ways described above, it will be necessary to consider

(i) what, if any, effect that termination has on the relationships of the principal and agent with third parties with whom the agent deals, and

(ii) what, if any, rights the principal and agent have against each other as a result of the termination.

7.6.3.1 Relations with third parties

An agent may continue to act even after his authority has been terminated. In such a case, the agent may incur liability to any third party with whom he deals for breach of his warranty of authority.[177] Since liability for breach of the warranty is strict, it is irrelevant that the agent is unaware of the termination of his authority – for instance, where it is brought about automatically by the principal's insanity.[178] However, where an agent continues to act after termination of his authority, the principal may also be held liable for the agent's actions since the agent may continue to have apparent authority, until the third party has notice that the agency has been terminated.[179]

7.6.3.2 Relations between principal and agent

Although either party may terminate the agency unilaterally by withdrawing consent to its continuance, where the agency is contractual, unilateral action may give rise to liability for breach of contract. Such rights of action, and other rights that may arise following termination, are considered below.

(i) Existing liabilities

Termination of agency, whether by operation of law or by action of one or both parties, does not affect existing liabilities. Thus, for instance, an agent

---

177 See 6.4.5.

178 *Yonge v. Toynbee* [1910] 1 K.B. 215.

179 *Drew v. Nunn* (1879) 4 Q.B.D. 661.

is entitled to any commission earned, and to any indemnity due in respect of liabilities incurred, before termination of the agreement.

(ii) Rights to commission

An agent may be entitled to commission on contracts performed after termination of the agency where they were entered into prior to termination. In certain circumstances, an agent may also be entitled to commission on contracts entered into after termination. This may be the case where the agreement entitles the agent to commission on "repeat orders".

In cases of commercial agency covered by the Directive and Regulations, an agent is entitled to commission on contracts concluded *after* the agency contract has terminated:

(a) if the transaction is mainly attributable to the commercial agent's efforts during the period of the agency contract and if the transaction is entered into within a reasonable time after termination; or

(b) if in accordance with the above the order of the third party reached the principal or agent before termination of the agency.[180]

As with rights to commission during the agency contract, these provisions greatly enhance a commercial agent's rights to commission after termination of the agency, not least by clarifying exactly when commission is earned.

(iii) Liability for breach of contract

Termination without notice will be justified where the other party has been guilty of a serious breach of contract. In other cases, termination without notice, or with less than the full notice required by the agreement, will terminate the agent's authority but may give rise to liability for breach of contract where the agency is contractual. Usually, this will be a claim against the principal by a dismissed agent. Where an agent is engaged under a bilateral contract and is dismissed in breach of contract, he may claim damages in respect of the loss of the opportunity to earn commission had the contract been performed. As with any claim for breach of contract, the claimant will have to show that the loss is not too remote and will have to mitigate his loss.[181] Where an agent is an employee, he may have an

180 Art. 8.

181 See 2.4.4.3(ii).

additional claim for a redundancy payment or for compensation for unfair dismissal in accordance with the general rules applicable to contracts of employment.[182]

(iv) Agent's right to compensation

In cases of commercial agency covered by the Directive, an agent is entitled, on termination of the agency, to be either *indemnified or compensated for damage*, at the option of the member state.[183] The main purpose of the Directive was to harmonise the laws of member states which were considered detrimental to the functioning of the single market.[184] But clearly, allowing member states the option of indemnity or compensation for damage undermines this purpose. In fact, all member states except France, the United Kingdom[185] and Ireland have opted for the indemnity system.[186] The 1994 Regulations failed to opt for one or the other and so, following a threat from the EC Commission that legal proceedings would be taken against Ireland, the 1997 Regulations provide that a commercial agent is entitled to compensation for damage suffered under Article 17(3).[187]

The concepts of indemnity and compensation derive from German and French law respectively, and an Irish court should be mindful of the origins of these provisions. In *Roy v. MR Pearlman*,[188] it was observed that in the interests of harmonisation it was appropriate to look to the national law upon which the Directive was based. It is thought that compensation for damage is a more generous measure than indemnity. Under the Directive, there is a one year cap on the amount of indemnity payable.[189] There is no maximum regarding the amount of compensation payable. It appears that the average award of compensation for damage in France is two years' commission; the average award in Germany is six months' commission.

Importantly, the right to compensation for damage is different from a claim for damages under the common law. An agent will be entitled to damages at common law if the agency is terminated in breach of contract. But, as noted above, any losses must not be too remote from the breach and an agent is under a duty to mitigate his loss. In contrast, the Directive

182 See generally Fennell & Lynch, *Labour Law in Ireland* (Gill & Macmillan, Dublin, 1993); Barnard, *EC Employment Law* (Oxford University Press, 2nd ed., Oxford, 2000).

183 Articles 17–20.

184 See Preamble of Directive.

185 In the U.K., parties can choose between indemnity or compensation for damage. In default of such choice, compensation for damage must be paid: Reg. 17 of S.I. No. 3053 of 1993, as amended (Reg. 17 of S.I. No. 483, as amended, for Northern Ireland).

186 See generally EC Commission Report on the Application of Article 17, COM(96) 364 final, published pursuant to Art. 17(6) of the Directive.

187 Reg. 2, 1997. Under Art. 19 of the Directive, parties cannot derogate from Art. 17.

188 *The Times,* May 13, 1999, Ct of Session; 2000 S.L.T. 727; [1999] 2 C.M.L.R. 1155.

189 Art. 17(2).

introduces a system of "no-fault" compensation under which, after termination, an agent is entitled to receive compensation for loss of his agency regardless of whether the principal is in breach of contract or not. This seems to recognise that the agent has a quasi-property interest in the agency. For instance, compensation is payable where the agency is terminated following the agent's death.[190]

While the position is unclear from the Directive and the Regulations, it would appear that an agent's right to common law damages and an agent's rights to compensation are two separate rights, designed to compensate for two different purposes. Common law damages are calculated to compensate the agent for losses, such as unearned commission, caused by the principal's breach of contract, while compensation is payable for the loss of interest in the agency.[191] Both can be claimed and accumulated, it seems. In *Duffen v. FRA BO SpA*,[192] a clause in the agency agreement between the principal, FRA, and the agent, D, provided for FRA, upon termination of the agreement, to pay D immediately the sum of £100,000 by way of liquidated damages. It was held that the clause was not a genuine attempt at estimating the loss that D would suffer as a result of a breach by FRA of its obligations under the agreement. Since £100,000 was payable irrespective of the unexpired term of the agreement, it would be possible for D to obtain a substantial windfall. The sum did not necessarily bear any relation to the loss D would sustain on termination and it was possible to terminate the agreement for the most trivial of reasons. Accordingly, the liquidated damages clause of the agreement was unenforceable.[193] However, it was held that it was open to D to claim compensation for damage under the U.K. Commercial Agents (Council Directive) Regulations 1993. It has been argued that this decision was based on a misunderstanding of the Directive.[194] The Directive provides that you cannot derogate from the indemnity/compensation provisions to the detriment of the agent, but there seems to be nothing to prevent the parties agreeing that an agent should receive more than would be payable under the indemnity/compensation system. In this context, the rule on penalty clauses should have no application.

Under Article 17(3) of the Directive, a commercial agent is entitled to compensation for damage suffered as a result of the termination of the agency relationship. Such damage is deemed to occur particularly where the termination takes place in circumstances which:

190 Art. 17.4.

191 *King v. Tunnock* [2000] I.R.L.R. 569; *cf Duffen v. FRABo SpA (No.2)* [2000] Lloyd's Rep. 180.

192 (1998) 17 Tr. L.R. 460 (C.A.).

193 *Dunlop Pneumatic Tyre Co Ltd v. New Garage and Motor Co Ltd* [1915] A.C. 79 applied.

194 Bradgate, *Commercial Law* (3rd ed., Butterworths, London, 2000) p.214.

(a) deprive him of commission which proper performance of the agency contract would have procured him whilst providing the principal with substantial benefits linked to the agent's activities; and/or
(b) prevents him from recouping the costs and expenses incurred in performing the agency contract.

These examples are not exhaustive.

The issue of "proper performance" was addressed in *Page v. Combined Shipping*.[195] There, the plaintiff contracted to act as agent, buying and selling commodities, for the defendants for four years in return for 50 per cent of the net profits. Under the terms of the contract, the principal effectively controlled the volume of business which the agent undertook. Six months later the defendants told the plaintiff that their parent company were planning to close down their trading activities. In response, the plaintiff terminated the agency arguing that the defendant's actions constituted a repudiatory breach of contract and that he had suffered "damage" which "proper performance" of the agency contract would have procured for him. At first instance, the judge dismissed the action saying that the defendants could have operated the agreement for four years such that the plaintiff made no money, hence he had suffered no damage. The Court of Appeal noted the good faith duties of the parties under Articles 3 and 4 of the Directive and held it was arguable that "proper performance" of the contract would not have allowed the defendants to reduce the trading to nil, or nearly nil, for the remaining period of the agreement. Rather, the plaintiff should be compensated for the loss of commission which "proper performance" would have procured if the contract had been performed in the *normal* manner in which the parties had intended.

Article 18 of the Directive provides that compensation is not payable where:

"(a) the principal has terminated the agency contract because of default of the agent which would justify immediate termination under national law;
(b) the agent has terminated the agency contract, unless termination is justified by circumstances attributable to the principal or on the grounds of age, infirmity or illness of the agent in consequence of which he cannot reasonably be expected to continue his activity;
(c) with the agreement of the principal, the agent assigns his rights under the agency contract to another."[196]

[195] [1997] 3 All E.R. 656, an interlocutory application only.
[196] Under Art. 19 of the Directive, parties cannot derogate from Art 18.

Moreover, Article 16 provides that nothing in the Directive affects national laws which provide for the immediate termination of the agency contract because of the failure of one party to perform his obligations under the contract, or where exceptional circumstances arise. Therefore, if a principal dismisses a commercial agent on grounds of a serious or repudiatory breach of contract by the agent, no compensation is payable. Conversely, if a commercial agent resigns, he loses his right to compensation unless his resignation is justified on one of the grounds listed in Article 18. The reference to "circumstances attributable to the principal" in (b) above may include not only those circumstances where an agent would be entitled to terminate the agency following the principal's serious or repudiatory breach of contract but also those circumstances which would not amount to a repudiatory breach of contract. This extended interpretation can be justified because (b) above, unlike (a), makes no reference to circumstances where "immediate termination" would be "justified."

It would seem that in all other circumstances, other than those listed in Article 18 above, compensation is payable. For instance, and unlike common law damages, compensation may be payable where the principal terminates by giving proper notice, unless the principal would have been justified in terminating without notice because of the agent's serious breach of contract. Compensation may also be payable where an agency terminates by effluxion of time. Under the Directive, compensation is payable on "termination," although it would seem unusual if compensation was payable where a fixed term contract expires and was renewed. Therefore it seems reasonable that compensation is due where a fixed-term contract expires without renewal. In *Moore v. Piretta PTA Ltd*,[197] it was held that the reference to "termination of the agency contract," in Article 17 should be read as "termination of the agency relationship" which would mean that no compensation is payable where the fixed term expires but the agency is renewed because in these circumstances the "relationship" continues. However, *Whitehead v. Jenks & Cattell Engineering Ltd*[198] involved a five-year agency contract, from January 1, 1993, which included a six-month notice period. On June 30, 1997, the principal wrote to the agent indicating that the contract would not be renewed on the same terms but indicating the possibility of a new contract. No new contract was agreed. The agent obtained a summary judgment to the effect that he was entitled to compensation on termination of the agency. The principal successfully appealed, seeking leave to defend, on the basis that he had an arguable case that the agency terminated by effluxion of time and hence no compensation was payable. The position remains uncertain. It seems that compensation is also payable on the closing-down or insolvency of the

197 [1999] 1 All E.R. 174.

198 [1999] Eu. L.R. 827 (Q.B.D.), leave to appeal granted.

principal's business. In *King v. Tunnock*[199] a long established agency was terminated when the principal decided to close the relevant part of the business. There, the agent was awarded a sum equal to two years' commission as compensation for damage.

In order to claim compensation under the Directive and Regulations, a commercial agent must deliver a written claim for compensation to the principal within one year of termination of the agency.[200] In *Hackett v. Advanced Medical Computer Systems*,[201] the plaintiff was an agent of A.M.C.S. within the terms of the Directive. The agency was terminated without notice and the plaintiff sought to claim compensation under Article 17. As a preliminary issue, there was a dispute as to whether the plaintiff had notified his principal of his intention within one year. The plaintiff relied on a letter from his solicitor indicating an intention to claim compensation arising out of the termination or, alternatively, the fact of service of the statement of claim as notice of his intention. A.M.C.S. argued that the letter was not sufficiently clear and the statement of claim was only for outstanding commission, not compensation under the Directive. It was held, giving judgment for the plaintiff, that in applying the requirements of the Directive, the court should avoid unnecessary formality. It was sufficient if the plaintiff had given notice that he intended to pursue claims under the Directive and it was not necessary to name any particular regulation or part thereof. The solicitor's letter was adequate to do this.

Neither the Directive nor the Regulations offer any guidance on the calculation of compensation. However, the practice of French courts provides guidance.[202] There the agency is treated as a "quasi-partnership" with the principal and the agent sharing a common aim. Both benefit from their "partnership"' and when the agency is terminated, the agent is entitled to compensation for his loss of the share of the business. There is no need to prove loss or to mitigate loss. In effect, the agent is paid for his "share" in the business. The practice of the French courts is to award a sum equal to two years' average commission. In *King v. Tunnock*,[203] a long established agency was terminated when the principal decided to close the relevant part of the business. The principal therefore derived no benefit after termination. It was held that this was irrelevant in assessing compensation. The circumstances where damage was deemed to occur under Article 17(3) were not exhaustive and it did not matter that the principal would not continue to enjoy "substantial benefits" from the agent's activities. Assessing compensation did not involve looking into the future to

199 [2000] I.R.L.R. 569; *cf. Duffen v. FRABo SpA* (*No. 2*) [2000] Lloyd's Rep. 180.

200 Art. 17(5).

201 [1999] C.L.C. 160

202 See Saintier "New Developments in Agency Law" [1997] *Journal of Business Law* 77; "Termination Rights of Commercial Agents" (1999) 20 *Company Lawyer* 149.

203 [2000] I.R.L.R. 569; *cf Duffen v. FRABo SpA* (No. 2) [2000] Lloyd's Rep. 180.

calculate future losses and there was no duty to mitigate those losses. The calculation was a backward-looking exercise. All the agent needed to prove was that after termination he lost the value of an agency asset which, prior to termination, existed. The agent was awarded the standard French sum (likened to a statutory redundancy payment) of two years' commission. This standard can be altered depending on the shortness or longevity of the agency term.[204] Also, the agent's entitlement to compensation for breach of the notice periods was treated as separate and added to this compensation amount.

(v) Restraint of trade

Because of the confidential nature of the relationship and the special relationship an agent is likely to develop with the principal's customers, the principal may wish to restrict the agent's activities after termination of the agency and to that effect may include a restrictive covenant in the agency agreement. Such a covenant is subject to the general rules of the common law and will only be valid provided it is not an unreasonable restraint of trade.[205] It must therefore protect a legitimate interest of the principal: normally the principal will have a legitimate interest in protecting his trade connections. In addition the covenant must be reasonable both in duration and geographical extent. What is reasonable will be a question of fact in each case. In cases of commercial agency covered by the Directive, similar restrictions can be imposed but the clause must be in writing and shall not apply for more than two years after termination of the agency.[206]

204 See EC Commission Report on the Application of Article 17, COM(96) 364 final p.5 and p.16.

205 See Clark, *Contract Law in Ireland* (Round Hall Sweet & Maxwell, Dublin, 4th ed., 1998) pp. 344–369; Friel, *The Law of Contract* (Round Hall Sweet & Maxwell, Dublin, 2nd ed., 2000) pp. 297–299.

206 Art. 20.

PART III

SALE OF GOODS AND SUPPLY OF SERVICES

CHAPTER 8

SALE OF GOODS AND SUPPLY OF SERVICES: AN INTRODUCTION

8.1 SUPPLY CONTRACTS AND THE ECONOMY

Contracts for the sale of goods and supply of services together represent the mainstay of commerce and trade, though goods and services can be supplied by other means.[1] Traditionally, sale of goods contracts have been considered the most important commercial transaction. They are certainly the most common. However, contracts for the supply of services have, more recently, increased in importance.[2] The health of an economy can be assessed with reference to the value and volume of such transactions.[3] Every day, for example, a vast number of sales occur, ranging from the relatively simple sale of goods to a consumer, to the more complicated sale of commodities in bulk between commercial traders. Whereas consumers buy goods for their own personal use and enjoyment, traders buy and sell goods with the intention of making a profit on the transaction. Regardless of the purpose of the transaction; the type of goods sold, their quantity, the status of the parties, or their respective locations, the same basic law of sale applies within Ireland.[4]

1 See further Chapter 9.

2 This is particularly so with the development of the financial services market. On contracts for the supply of services, see generally Chapter 20.

3 Indicators such as the trade surplus (the extent to which exports exceeds imports), and the Retail Price Index (which measures changes in the value and volume of retail sales) are regularly published by the Central Statistics Office for this purpose: see www.cso.ie.

4 See Forde, *Commercial Law* (Dublin, Butterworths, 2nd ed., 1997) Chapter 2. The leading English texts on sale of goods are Guest, ed., *Benjamin's Sale of Goods* (London, Sweet & Maxwell, 5th ed., 1997) and Adams, ed., *Atiyah's Sale of Goods* (Harlow, Pearson, 10th ed., 2001). See also Goode, *Commercial Law* (London, Penguin, 2nd ed., 1995) Parts 2 and 7; Bradgate, *Commercial Law* (London, Butterworths, 3rd ed., 2000) Parts III and V; and Sealy & Hooley, *Commercial Law* (London, Butterworth, 2nd ed., 1999) Parts III and IV.

8.2 Sources of Law

Contracts for the sale of goods are governed by the Sale of Goods Act 1893, as amended by Part II of the Sale of Goods and Supply of Services Act 1980.[5] Together this legislation is referred to as the Sale of Goods Acts 1893 and 1980.[6] The supply of services is regulated by Part IV of the Sale of Goods and Supply of Services Act 1980.[7] These Acts set out the rights and duties of the parties. However, neither are codes in that they do not contain all the rules applicable to these types of contracts. Much of the law can be found outside the Acts in the common law. Section 61(2) of the 1893 Act, provides that "The rules of the common law, including the law merchant ..." shall apply to contracts for the sale of goods, except insofar as they are modified by the Act. For instance, the common law rules on mistake,[8] frustration,[9] and damages[10] are modified in the legislation. Other relevant areas of the common law, including contractual formation, and privity remain untouched by the legislation. The phrase "common law" in section 61 is assumed to be a reference to "judge-made law" and hence does not exclude the rules of equity.[11]

Other legislation, such as the Bills of Sale (Ireland) Acts 1879 and 1883, the Factors Act 1889, the Companies Acts 1963–2001, the Bankruptcy Act 1988, the Electronic Commerce Act 2000, and the Competition Act 2002, may impact directly or indirectly on the sale of goods and supply of services.[12] In particular, where the buyer is a consumer, trade description legislation,[13] the Defective Products Act 1991 (which deals with manufacturers' and others' liability for defective products)[14] and the Consumer Credit Act 1995 (where goods are sold on credit terms) may be relevant.[15]

---

5 Part II of the 1980 Act amends the 1893 Act by substituting new sections, bearing the same number, for the original sections. The 1980 Act also inserts a new s.55A and an additional subsection (6) into s.61. It also contains a series of new provisions in ss.11–19.

6 1980 Act, s.9.

7 See generally Chapter 20. As to the remainder of the 1980 Act, Part I deals with preliminary and general issues; Part III with hire-purchase agreements, now repealed by the 1995 Consumer Credit Act; Part V with misrepresentation in sale and hire contracts and remedies; and Part VI contains miscellaneous provisions including provisions on unsolicited goods and directory enquiries.

8 1893 Act, s.6.

9 1893 Act, s.7.

10 1893 Act, ss.51–54.

11 This issue has not been directly addressed in a reported case in this jurisdiction or in England though there is authority to the contrary from New Zealand: see *Riddiford v. Warren* (1901) 20 N.Z.L.R. 572; and *Watt v. Westhoven* [1933] V.L.R. 458.

12 1893 Act, s.61.

13 Such as the Merchandise Marks Acts 1887–1970; the Consumer Information Act 1978; and the Trade Marks Act 1996. On trade marks, see further Chapter 36.

14 See 16.4.2.

15 See generally Bird, *Consumer Credit Law* (Dublin, Round Hall Sweet & Maxwell, 1998).

8.2.1 The history of sales law[16]

An awareness of the historical context of sale of goods law is important not only with regard to the interpretation of the legislation but also to explain past judicial decisions. According to Goode, the sale of goods is one of the earliest forms of business transaction, dating back to when money was first introduced to replace barter.[17] Modern sales law can be traced back to the common law of the eighteenth and nineteenth centuries. This was the period when contract law as we know it today was taking shape. The economic principle of *laissez-faire* prevailed, and politicians and judges were reluctant to interfere with the practices and expectations of merchants. Sales law reflected these policies. For instance, the basic principle of sales law was *caveat emptor* – let the buyer beware – and the implication of terms into the contract as to the quality of the goods or the seller's title to the goods was a slow and gradual process.[18]

By the end of the nineteenth century, a substantial body of sale of goods common law existed. Furthermore, the case law was not easily reconciled. To make sales law more accessible, there was a partial codification of this area.[19] Sir Mackenzie Chalmers, who drafted the legislation leading to the Bills of Exchange Act 1882, drafted the Sale of Goods Bill which was presented to Parliament in 1889. The Bill was not intended to alter the common law position at the time. However, it proved unsuccessful in this regard.[20] The Bill lapsed and was re-introduced in 1891. Following extensive amendments, the Bill emerged as the Sale of Goods Act 1893.[21] The Act is expressed to be: "An Act for codifying the law relating to sale

---

16 See Bridge, "The evolution of modern sales law" [1991] *Lloyd's Maritime and Commercial Law Quarterly* 52; Goode, *supra*, note 4, Chapter 6; and the Introduction to the First Edition of Chalmer's *Sale of Goods Act 1893* (London, Butterworths, 18th ed., 1981).

17 See Goode, *supra*, note 4, p.187, and see further Mann, *The Legal Aspects of Money* (Oxford, Clarendon Press, 5th ed., 1992).

18 See Goode, *supra*, note 4, pp.188–193.

19 Other areas of commercial law underwent similar treatment, including bills of sale – leading to the Bills of Sale (Ireland) Acts 1879 and 1883; bills of exchange – leading to the Bills of Exchange Act 1882; the operation of factors – leading to the Factors Act 1889; partnership – leading to the Partnership Act 1890; and marine insurance – leading to the Marine Insurance Act 1906. All this legislation continues in force in Ireland, and indeed in England, today.

20 *E.g.* the distinction between sales of specific goods and sales by description was not maintained, allowing the implication of implied terms to contracts for the sale of specific goods: see further Chapter 13.

21 The 1893 Act came into operation on January 1, 1894: 1893 Act, s.63.

of goods," although as noted above, it is not a code in the civil law sense of the word. Despite criticisms of the 1893 Act,[22] it remains in force in Ireland, subject to amendment by the Sale of Goods and Supply of Services Act 1980.[23] The 1980 Act, while making some important changes to the 1893 Act,[24] leaves undisturbed many of the fundamentals. Hence Irish sales law is still dominated by the 1893 Act.

When interpreting this type of codifying legislation, the proper approach was outlined by Lord Hershell in *Bank of England v. Vagliano Bros*,[25] in relation to the Bills of Exchange Act 1882:

> "... the proper course is in the first instance to examine the language of the statute and to ask what is its natural meaning, uninfluenced by any considerations derived from the previous state of the law, and not to start with inquiring how the law previously stood, and then, assuming that it was probably intended to leave it unaltered, to see if the words of the enactment will bear an interpretation in conformity with this view."

Following this line of reasoning, the purpose of a codifying statute is to remove the need to consult prior case law. Lord Hershell did observe that in exceptional cases reference to prior case law may be permissible. Where, for instance, the language of the statute is unclear or ambiguous, or where a term has acquired a technical meaning, case law prior to the statute can be examined for guidance. Although this approach is well established, it has often been ignored, and cases prior to the 1893 Act have been referred to for guidance.[26] In *Wallis v. Russell*,[27] Pallas C.B.

> "... protest[ed] against a principle of construction which, in relation to even a codifying statute, excludes from consideration the previous state of the law upon the matter which is the subject of the legislation."

---

22 See further 8.2.2.

23 The 1980 Act came into operation on December 30, 1980: 1980 Act, s.1(2).

24 The 1980 Act defines "merchantable quality", regulates the use of exclusion clauses in relation to the statutory implied terms; and includes a number of innovative provisions dealing with matters such as implied terms and motor vehicles, spare parts and servicing, guarantees, and buyer's remedies. Some of these amendments mirrored U.K. provisions at that time. See, *e.g.* the Supply of Goods (Implied Terms) Act 1973 on the exclusion of liability for breach of statutory implied terms (see now the Unfair Contracts Terms Act 1977) and the definition of "merchantable quality" (see now the Sale of Goods Act 1979, as amended).

25 [1891] A.C. 107 at 144.

26 The issue of the relevance of case law to a later statutory enactment has been addressed in a number of English cases. See, *e.g.* the Court of Appeal decision in *Rogers v. Parish (Scarborough) Ltd* [1987] Q.B. 933, where it was held that following the introduction of a statutory definition of "merchantable quality" the pre-existing case law on the meaning of merchantable quality should be ignored. Cf. the remarks of Lloyd L.J. in *Aswan Engineering Establishment Co v. Lupdine Ltd* [1987] 1 All E.R. 135 at 140; [1987] 1 W.L.R. 1 at 6.

27 [1902] 2 I.R. 585 at 590.

Following Irish independence in 1921, English case law dealing with the Sale of Goods Act 1893 and its successor, the Sale of Goods Act 1979, though not binding on Irish courts, is persuasive. Indeed, given the shortage of Irish case law in this area,[28] English case law is an invaluable source of guidance.

8.2.2 A critique of the legislation

The 1893 Act was an impressive feat of draftsmanship and was adopted as a model throughout the common law world.[29] The fact that it remains in force in Ireland, although amended, reflects its durability.[30] However, the 1893 Act has its flaws. First, the language of the statute is a major source of criticism. It is deceptively simple when compared with modern legislation.[31] In some instances, words and phrases are so concise that their meaning is ambiguous.[32] In other instances, words and phrases carry more than one meaning, depending on their context.[33] The language is rooted in the nineteenth century. For instance, "merchantable quality," a key concept in the legislation, is not a phrase in common usage today and hence there is a lack of common comprehension of this phrase.[34] Statutory definitions, and the lack thereof, is another source of criticism. Some statutory

28 For example, it appears that since amending legislation was introduced in 1980 in the form of the Sale of Goods and Supply of Services Act, there has been one reported judgment on the central provision of merchantable quality: see *O'Donnell v. Truck & Machinery Sales* [1997] 1 I.L.R.M. 466 (H.C.): see further 13.3.2.4 and 13.3.2.5. A second judgment has been recorded in note form: *McCullough Sales Ltd v. Chelthem Timber Co.* [1985] I.L.R.M. 217 (H.C.).

29 Not only in the Commonwealth but also in the United States. Regarding Australia, see Sale of Goods Act 1895 (S.A.); Sale of Goods Act 1895 (W.A.); Sale of Goods Act 1896 (Qld.); Sale of Goods Act 1896 (Tas.); Sale of Goods Act 1923 (N.S.W.); Sale of Goods Act 1958 (Vic.); Sale of Goods Act 1972 (N.T.); Sale of Goods Act 1975 (A.C.T.). Regarding New Zealand, see Sale of Goods Act 1908. Regarding the United States, see Uniform Sales Act 1906.

30 The primary legislation in the United Kingdom is the Sale of Goods Act 1979, as amended. This legislation remains closely based on the 1893 Act: further evidence of its durability.

31 See Goode, *supra* note 4, p.198. The provisions on the quality of goods supplied are, for example, superficially simple but actually highly complicated: see further Chapter 13.

32 See, *e.g.* Goode, *supra* note 4, p.199 on the meaning of "specific goods."

33 The word "condition" is used in two different senses in the 1893 Act: in its *suspensive sense*, *i.e.* that an obligation is dependant/conditional on the happening of an event (*e.g.* see s.18, rules 1 and 5, 1893 Act), and in its promissory sense, *i.e.* an important contractual promise, breach of which allows the innocent party to terminate the contract (e.g. ss.12–15, 1893 Act): see further Bradgate and White, "Rejection and Termination in Contracts for the Sale of Goods Contacts," in Birds, Bradgate & Villiers eds., *Termination of Contracts* (Chichester, Wiley Chancery, 1995).

34 This point was part of the criticism which lead to the phrase "merchantable quality" being replaced by the phrase "satisfactory quality" in the U.K.: see the Sale and Supply of Goods Act 1994.

definitions are showing their age.[35] Other various important concepts lack definition and so cause confusion. Examples include, "condition," "unascertained goods," and "deliverable state."[36] At a more general level, it must be questioned how a sales law, dominated by a nineteenth century statute can meet the needs of the twenty-first century? The 1893 Act was designed to meet the needs of merchant traders who dealt in relatively simple goods.[37] The nature of commerce has changed dramatically since. Commercial sales are more complex and, with the development of the consumer society,[38] it is argued that the legislation is ill-equipped to deal with consumer sales.[39]

The 1980 Act sought to meet some of these criticisms and to modernise sales law. For instance, while retaining the phrase, the legislation sought to clarify the meaning of "merchantable quality" by defining it.[40] The 1980 Act also prohibits the exclusion of the statutory implied terms where the buyer deals as a consumer and regulates their use in other circumstances.[41] Indeed, the provisions dealing with spare parts and servicing,[42] motor vehicles,[43] and guarantees[44] remain progressive.[45] Nevertheless, deficiencies remain. Recent reforms of the U.K. Sale of Goods Act, which is based closely on the 1893 Act, evidence some of these deficiencies. The continuing issue of archaic language and the expectations of consumers has led to the replacement of the requirement that goods be of "merchantable quality" with the requirement that goods be of "satisfactory quality," under the Sale and Supply of Goods Act 1994.[46] The *market overt* exception to the *nemo dat* rule was abolished in the Sale of Goods (Amendment) Act 1994,[47] and the problems associated with buying goods which form part of a bulk, caused by section 16 of the 1893 Act, have been addressed in the Sale of Goods (Amendment) Act 1995.[48] Furthermore,

---

35 For example, the issue whether computer software constitutes "goods," defined in s.62, remains unresolved: see further Chapter 9.

36 On the other hand, the flexibility provided by this lack of definition may have contributed to the legislation's longevity.

37 See further Bridge, "The evolution of modern sales law" [1991] *Lloyd's Maritime and Commercial Law Quarterly* 52.

38 See generally, Atiyah, *The Rise and Fall of Freedom of Contract* (Oxford, Clarendon Press, 1979) Chapter 17.

39 See 8.3; see further 13.3.2 on the definition of merchantable quality.

40 1893 Act, s.14(3) inserted by s.10 of the 1980 Act: see further 13.3.2.

41 1893 Act, s.55 inserted by s.22 of the 1980 Act: see further 10.5.2.

42 1980 Act, s.12: see further 13.8.

43 1980 Act, s.13: see further 13.9.

44 1980 Act, ss.15–19: see further Chapter 16.

45 See the Green Paper on Guarantees for Consumer Goods and After-Sales Services, COM(93)509, p.96.

46 The Sale and Supply of Goods Act 1994 also amends the rules on acceptance and buyer's remedies: see further Chapter 14.

47 See 19.5.

48 See 17.4.1.

European legislation, in the form of the EC Directive on Certain Aspects of the Sale of Consumer Goods and Associated Guarantees,[49] amends certain rules regarding consumer sales in the European Community. This legislation is expected to be implemented by regulations and will result in two sets of sales law – one for consumer buyers, as defined, and another for everyone else – where some of the rules are exclusive to consumer buyers while other rules are shared. It is unfortunate that the implementation of this Directive was not used as an opportunity to comprehensively review Irish sales law, with the recent U.K. reforms, amongst other issues, in mind.[50]

8.2.3 Standard terms of trade

As noted above, the primary sources of Irish sales law are the Sale of Goods Acts 1893 and 1980, supplemented by the common law. An important feature of this legislation is that many of the rules operate by default, that is, they apply unless the parties have agreed otherwise.[51] For example, many of the rules on delivery of the goods are default rules.[52] Again, the primary rule on the passing of property in specific goods is that property passes when the parties intend it to pass. Where no such intention is evident, rules of presumed intent are set out in section 18. This approach reflects the *laissez-faire* policy which dominated the late nineteenth century whereby the purpose of commercial law generally, and sales law in particular, was to provide a framework within which merchants could transact. Merchants were free to decide what suited them best, and only where they omitted to address a particular issue, such as the place of delivery, would the legislation step in to provide that the place of delivery is the seller's place of business.[53]

Following on from the above, today, in the commercial context, many sales of goods and supplies of services are governed by standard form contracts which contain detailed rules specific to the contract in question, the default rules in the legislation being inappropriate. These standard terms can either be drafted by one of the parties to the contract (usually the dominant party and the terms are offered on a "take-it-or-leave-it" basis)

49 After a long gestation period, the Directive was finally adopted on May 25, 1999. Art. 11 requires member states to implement the Directive by January 1, 2002. See further 13.11 and 14.7.

50 See White, "The EC Directive on Certain Aspects of Consumer Sale and Associated Guarantees: One Step Forward, Two Steps Back?" (2000) 7 *Commercial Law Practitioner* 3.

51 There are also some mandatory rules. One important mandatory rule is set out in s.16, which provides that no property can pass in unascertained goods until they become ascertained: see further 17.4.

52 See 1893 Act, ss.27–37: see further Chapter 11.

53 1893 Act, s.29(1).

and are "private" between the parties, or, adopted from a set of standard terms promoted by a trade organisation. In certain sectors of the economy, such as the oil trade or the grain trade, this latter type of standard form contract is prevalent.[54] Where a dispute arises in these circumstances, any resolution will usually revolve around the particular wording of the standard form contract in question, the legislation forming a backdrop to the dispute (see, *e.g*. GAFTA 100: see further Appendix B.).

8.3 Commercial and Consumer Transactions

As was noted above, the 1893 Sale of Goods Act was drafted with commercial traders in mind. The consumer, as an economic being, was not generally recognised at the time.[55] It took the combination of mass production and disposable incomes in the twentieth century to produce today's consumer society.[56] By the middle of the twentieth century, an awareness of the place of consumers in society, and more particularly in the economy, had developed. As a result, a variety of legislation has been enacted, starting with the Consumer Information Act 1978, to protect the weaker position of consumers.[57] Other examples of such legislation include the Sale of Goods and Supply of Services Act 1980, the European Community (Misleading Advertising) Regulations 1988,[58] the European Community (Cancellation of Contracts Negotiated away from Business Premises) Regulations 1989,[59] the Defective Products Act 1991, as

54 *E.g.* in international trade, GAFTA (the Grain and Feed Trade Association) and FOSFA (the Federation of Oil Seeds and Fats Association) promote standard form sales contracts, *e.g.* GAFTA 30 is a contract for North American wheat on *cif* terms, see further 30.3; FOSFA 24 is suitable for the sale of Canadian or American soya beans on *cif* terms.

55 It has been argued that the word *consommer* (to consume) was first used in its modern sense in the eighteenth century: see Ourliac, *Annales de la Faculté de Toulouse* (1979) 22.

56 See generally, Atiyah, *The Rise and Fall of Freedom of Contract* (Oxford, Clarendon Press, 1979) Chapter 17; and Blackwell, "Government, Economy and Society" in Litton ed., *Unequal Achievement, The Irish Experience* 1957–1982 (Dublin, Institute of Public Administration, 1982) 43. See further 1.1.1.

57 The Hire-Purchase Acts 1946 and 1960 (now repealed by the Consumer Credit Act 1995 which applies only to consumer hirers: s.2 and Part VI of the Act) applied to all hire-purchase arrangements and not specifically to consumer hirers. Nevertheless, a significant proportion of hirers were consumers and hence consumers benefited from this legislation. Other legislation not specifically directed at consumers, such as the Merchandise Marks Acts 1928–1970; and the Restrictive Practices Act 1953, indirectly benefited consumers.

58 S.I. No. 134 of 1988; implementing Council Directive 84/450: [1984] O.J. L250/17. Specific legislation exists in relation to particular products, *e.g.* tobacco – Directive 89/622 and S.I. No. 326 of 1991 – and medicine for human use – Directive 92/27 and S.I. No. 71 of 1993.

59 S.I. No. 224 of 1989 implementing Council Directive 85/577 [1985] O.J. L372/31.

amended,[60] the Consumer Credit Act 1995,[61] the Package Holidays and Travel Trade Act 1995,[62] the European Community (Unfair Terms in Consumer Contracts) Regulations 1995 and 2000,[63] the EC (Protection of Consumers in Respect of Contracts Made by Means of Distance Communications) Regulations 2001,[64] and the EC (Protection of Consumers' Collective Interests) Regulations 2001.[65] Today, the initiative for most, if not all, of this consumer-orientated legislation is the European Community,[66] and more can be expected in the future, hence increasing the divergence between commercial and consumer law.[67]

When dealing with the law on sale of goods and supply of services, the distinction between commercial and consumer transactions is material. Moreover, this distinction is more complex than it might appear at first. There are, in fact, three different classes of transaction which can be identified and distinguished from a legal perspective.

(i) There is the situation where one commercial trader deals with another commercial trader. This is a pure commercial transaction, in that only commercial interests are at stake. The general assumption here is that both parties, being of equal bargaining strength, can take care of their own interests.

(ii) Next, there is the situation where a commercial trader deals with a consumer. In these circumstances there are two interests to be balanced: those of the commercial trader and those of the consumer. The standard legislative response to this situation is to protect the consumer's interests from the assumed stronger position of the trader.[68]

---

60 Implementing Council Directive 85/374 [1985] O.J. L210/29, as amended by Council Directive 1999/34 [1999] O.J. L141/20, implemented by S.I. No. 401 of 2000, see further 16.4.2. There is further legislation dealing with unsafe products: see, *e.g.* Directives 87/357 (S.I. No. 265 of 1991) on unsafe products, 88/378 (S.I. Nos 32 of 1990 and 458 of 1994) on safety of toys and 92/59 (S.I. No. 197 of 1997) on general product safety.

61 Implementing Council Directive 87/102 [1987] O.J. L42/48, as amended by Council Directive 90/88 [1990] O.J. L61/14.

62 Implementing Council Directive 90/314 [1990] O.J. L158/59.

63 S.I. No. 27 of 1995, and S.I. No. 307 of 2000 implementing Council Directive 93/13 [1993] O.J. L95/29, see further 2.3.5.3 and 10.5.3.

64 S.I. No. 207 of 2001 implementing Council Directive 97/7 [1997] O.J. L144/19.

65 S.I. No. 449 of 2001, Council Directive 98/27 [1998] O.J. L166/51.

66 See generally, the European Commission's *Consumer Guide to the Single Market* (2nd ed., 1996). See further Council Directive 99/44 on certain aspects of consumer sales and associated guarantees [1999] O.J. L171/12, and Coucil Directive 2002/65 on the distance marketing of consumer financial services [2002] O.J. L271/16.

67 See 1.1.1. See the Treaty Establishing the European Community, Art. 95(3), for the legal basis of much of this legislation. See also Art. 153 on consumer protection.

68 This is the primary purpose of the raft of legislation mentioned above.

(iii) Finally, there is the situation where one consumer deals with another consumer. This is like scenario (i) above, in the sense that both parties can be assumed to have equal bargaining strength, and accordingly, can look after themselves.

There are a number of factors which complicate the above analysis further. First, the assumptions referred to above do not always hold true in practice. In relation to scenario (i), for instance, rarely are all commercial traders in positions of equal bargaining strength and so there will usually be a weaker party in commercial transactions. Should such a party be afforded protection in a manner similar to consumers in scenario (ii)? And, regarding scenario (ii), in some circumstances, the consumer may be in the stronger bargaining position. This leads to the second complicating factor: the definition of consumer. Consumer has been defined in a variety of ways at European Community level.[69] The more usual definition can be found in the Directive on the Protection of Consumers in Respect of Contracts Negotiated Away from Business Premises: a consumer is "a natural person who ... is acting for purposes which can be regarded as outside his trade or profession."[70] Under this definition, a business in the form of a company, for example, could never be a consumer.[71] Irish sale of goods and supply of services law, does not define "consumer", but it does define "dealing as a consumer" in section 3 of the Sale of Goods and Supply of Services Act 1980. Accordingly, a party is said to deal as a consumer in relation to another party if:

(a) he neither makes the contract in the course of a business, ... , and

(b) the other party does make the contract in the course of a business, and

---

69 See, *e.g.* the Council Resolution on a preliminary programme of the EEC for a consumer protection and information policy which defined consumer to include a purchaser or user of goods or services for personal, family or group purposes, as well as a person concerned with the various facets of society which may affect him either directly or indirectly as a consumer: a circular definition [1975] O.J. C92/1 at 2, para.3.

70 [1985] O.J. L372/31, Art. 2.

71 See *Cape Snc v. Idealservice Srl, and Idealservice MN RE Sas v. OMAI Srl*, Joined Cases C-541/99 and C-542/99. This definition is not without its difficulties: see *Bertrand v. Ott* C-150/77 [1978] E.C.R. 1431; *Patrice Di Pinto*, C-361/89 [1991] E.C.R. I-1189, [1993] 1 C.M.L.R. 399; *Shearson Lehmann Hutton Inc v. TVB Treuhandgesselschaft für Vermögensverwaltung und Beteilungem mbH* C-89/91 [1993] E.C.R. I-139; and *Bayerische Hypotheken- und Wechselbank AG v. Edgar Dietzinger* Case C-45/96 [1998] E.C.R. I-1199. See further Lewis, "The Protection of Consumers in European Community Law" 12 (1992) *Yearbook of European Law* 139; and Bamforth, "The limits of European Union consumer contract law" (1999) 24 *European Law Review* 410.

(c) the goods or services supplied ... are of a type ordinarily supplied for private use or consumption.[72]

Under this definition, and following an English line of authority,[73] arguably a business acting in the form of a company could be a consumer for the purposes of the legislation.

With regard to the law on the sale of goods and the supply of services, our starting point is that the provisions of both the Sale of Goods Act 1893 and the Sale of Goods and Supply of Services Act 1980 apply equally to commercial and consumer sales, as defined above. However, some provisions of the legislation apply only when the seller/supplier acts in the course of a business, regardless of the status of the buyer (scenarios (i) and (ii)).[74] Furthermore, the legislation restricts the ability of the seller/supplier to modify the liabilities imposed on him by the legislation where the buyer deals as a consumer (potentially scenarios (i), (ii) and (iii), though more commonly scenarios (ii) and (iii)).[75]

72 This definition is, for practical purposes, identical to the definition used in the U.K. Unfair Contract Terms Act 1977.

73 See *R&B Customs Brokers v. United Dominion Trust* [1988] 1 W.L.R. 321; *cf. O'Callaghan v. Hamilton Leasing* (Ireland) Ltd [1984] I.L.R.M. 146; *Cunningham v. Woodchester* Investments unreported, High Court, McWilliam J., November 16, 1984; *Stevenson v. Rogers,* [1999] 1 All E.R. 613: see further 10.5.2.1.

74 Such as s.14 of the 1893 Act: see further 13.3.1 and 13.4.1.

75 1893 Act, s.55 inserted by s.22 of the 1980 Act: see further 10.5.2.

CHAPTER 9

DEFINING AND DISTINGUISHING SALES CONTRACTS

9.1 INTRODUCTION

There are many ways of transferring possession and/or ownership of goods other than by selling them, such as by barter, gift, or hire. The popularity of these and other arrangements tends to rise and fall with changes in the social, economic and legal environment. For example, hire-purchase was very popular in the 1950s and 1960s, while today, the conditional sale arrangement is more prevalent. While many of these arrangements resemble a sale, there are fundamental differences, often technical and obscure, which a commercial lawyer must be familiar with. In this chapter, we first define "a contract for the sale of goods". The Sale of Goods Acts 1893 and 1980 only apply to contracts which come within the statutory definition. Other similar transactions are then defined and distinguished from a contract for the sale of goods, and reference is made to applicable legislation.

9.2 THE STATUTORY DEFINITION

Section 1(1) of the 1893 Act defines a contract for the sale of goods as:

> " ... a contract whereby the seller transfers or agrees to transfer the property in goods to the buyer for a money consideration, called the price."

The various elements of this definition: the contract; the parties; the property; the price; and the goods; are examined in more detail below.

Further, a contract of sale can be in one of two forms: a sale, or, an agreement to sell. This point is made in section 1(3):

> "Where under a contract of sale the property in the goods is transferred from the seller to the buyer the contract is called a sale; but where the transfer of the property in the goods is to take place at a future time or subject to some condition thereafter to be fulfilled the contract is called an agreement to sell."

Hence, a sale operates as an executed contract and a conveyance, in one. An agreement to sell, is merely a contract. Some further act or event is necessary before the property in the goods can vest in the buyer under the contract. But both are contracts of sale and come within the legislation. Section 62(1) provides that "sale" includes a bargain and sale, as well as a sale and delivery. This reinforces section 1 of the 1893 Act and makes the important point, a feature of Irish and English property law, that delivery is not a necessary element of a sales contract. Indeed, property can pass from the seller to the buyer without any delivery.[1]

9.2.1 The contract

Every contract for the sale of goods must be properly formed. The common law rules on agreement, consideration and intention to create legal relations apply.[2] For example, in *British Steel Corpn v. Cleveland Bridge and Engineering*,[3] the defendant entered into negotiations with the plaintiff to buy steel nodes. There was a clear indication that the parties intended to conclude a contract and, at the request of the defendant, the plaintiff began to manufacture the goods before a contract was agreed. Little was agreed between the parties, bar the price. When all the goods were delivered months later, the plaintiff claimed for the price and the defendant counter-claimed for late delivery. The court found that there was no contract between the parties and so the plaintiff could not argue that the defendant was in breach of the contract because of his failure to pay the price. But the court said that where there is no contract, the law imposes an obligation on the party who made the request to pay a reasonable sum, on a *quantum meruit* basis, for work done pursuant to the request. Following on from this analysis, the defendant would have no claim in contract if the nodes proved defective: a claim in negligence would be its only recourse. Again, in the commercial context, a "battle of the forms", whereby both parties seek to impose their standard terms of trade on the other party, can result in no agreement being reached and hence no contract being concluded, because the respective standard terms differ.[4]

Section 2 of the 1893 Act provides that capacity to buy and sell is regulated by the general law concerning capacity to contract and to transfer and acquire property. The legislation also includes rules on mistake which apply in specific circumstances.[5] Beyond these circumstances, the general law of mistake applies. The 1980 Act, in Part V, amends the common law

---

1 See further Chapter 17.
2 See generally Chapter 2.
3 [1984] 1 All E.R. 504.
4 See 2.2.1.2.
5 1893 Act, s.6; see further 18.3.1.

rules on misrepresentation in relation to, inter alia, contracts for the sale of goods.[6]

Specific provision is made for auction sales in the legislation. Section 58, reflecting the common law, provides that each lot is, *prima facie*, a separate contract.[7] Each new bid is an offer to buy cancelling any prior bids; a sale is complete on the "fall of the hammer", and until then any bid may be withdrawn.[8] An auction may be notified to be subject to a reserve price and a right to bid may be reserved by the seller (to "puff-up" the price).[9] Where no such right to bid is reserved, to bid is not lawful and the sale is fraudulent.[10] In practice, many auctions are conducted under special "conditions of sale", which may affect the application of section 58.[11]

Finally, pursuant to certain legislation, there may exist a right to lawfully cancel a contract after its formation. For instance, under the EC (Cancellation of Contracts Negotiated away from Business Premises) Regulations, 1989,[12] where a "trader"[13] contracts to supply goods or services to a "consumer"[14] on their "doorstep",[15] there is provision for a

---

6 Part V also applies to hire-purchase agreements; agreements for the letting of goods, as defined; and contracts for the supply of services: 1980 Act, s.43. Under s.44, rescission of the contract for innocent misrepresentation survives the incorporation of the misrepresentation into the contract, and the performance of the contract, at the discretion of the court. Section 45 imposes general liability in damages for non-fraudulent misrepresentation. Section 46 restricts the exclusion of liability for misrepresentation. This legislation corresponds to the U.K. Misrepresentation Act 1967 but the U.K. statute applies to contracts generally, including contracts for the sale of real property. See further Clark, *Contract Law in Ireland* (Dublin, Round Hall Sweet & Maxwell, 4th ed., 1998) Chapter 11; and Friel, *The Law of Contract* (Dublin, Round Hall Sweet & Maxwell, 2nd ed., 2000) Chapter 18.

7 1893 Act, s.58(1).

8 1893 Act, s.58(2).

9 1893 Act, s.58(4).

10 1893 Act s.58(3).

11 See generally, Harvey, *Auctions law and practice* (Oxford, Oxford Univeristy Press, 2nd ed., 1995).

12 S.I. No. 224 of 1989, implementing Directive 85/577, [1985] O.J. L372/31; see further Clark, *Contract Law in Ireland* (Dublin, Round Hall Sweet & Maxwell, 4th ed., 1998) p.191; Bird, *Consumer Credit Law* (Dublin, Round Hall Sweet & Maxwell,1998) p.326.

13 Defined as "a natural or legal person who, for the transaction in question, acts in his commercial or professional capacity, or anyone acting in the name or on behalf of a trader:" Reg. 2(1).

14 Defined as "a natural person who, in transactions covered by these Regulations, is acting for purposes which can be regarded as outside his trade or profession:" Reg. 2(1).

15 The regulations apply, subject to exceptions, to contracts concluded (i) during an excursion organised by the trader away from his business premises; (ii) during a visit by a trader to the consumer's home or another consumer's home or to the consumer's place of work, where the visit is unsolicited; (iii) following a solicited visit but where the goods and services supplied are other than those in respect of which the visit was requested. Additionally, the regulations apply to contracts in respect of which an offer was made by the consumer in circumstances similar to the above: Reg.3(1).

"cooling-off" period of seven days during which time the consumer can give notice of cancellation.[16] The consumer must be given written notice of this right, and failure to give such notice renders the contract unenforceable against the consumer.[17] On cancellation, any sums paid by the consumer are repayable by the trader, the consumer having a lien over the goods until such repayment.[18] Equally, any goods received are returnable.[19] Similar provision was made under section 50 of the Sale of Goods and Supply of Services Act 1980, whereby the Minister was empowered, by order, to provide that where contracts for the sale, hire, or hire-purchase of goods, or for the supply of services, of a class specified in the order, were entered into by a person in the course of their business elsewhere than at his place of business, there shall be a specified period within which the customer shall be entitled to withdraw from the contract. No orders were made under this provision, which was surpassed by the above Regulations and has since been repealed by the Consumer Credit Act 1995.[20] A further right of cancellation exists under the EC (Protection of Consumers in Respect of Contracts Made by Means of Distance Communications) Regulations 2001.[21]

9.2.1.1 Formalities

At common law, a contract for the sale of goods required no formalities. This position is reflected in the opening lines of section 3 of the 1893 Act, which provides that subject to the provisions of this Act, or any other Act, a contract of sale may be made in writing, by word of mouth, partly in writing and partly by word of mouth, or may be implied from the conduct of the parties.[22] But section 4(1) of the 1893 Act (which derives from the Statute of Frauds (Ireland) 1695) provides that a contract for the sale of goods of the value of £10 [€12.70] or more is not enforceable by action unless:

(i) the buyer accepts, and actually receives, part of the goods sold; or
(ii) the buyer gives something in earnest to bind the contract; or
(iii) the buyer has made part payment; or
(iv) there is a note or memorandum in writing of the contract and signed by the party to be charged.

16 Reg. 5.
17 Reg. 4. See further the Schedule as to the content and form of the notice.
18 Reg. 6(1) and (2): see generally 25.3.
19 Reg. 6(3).
20 See Sch. 2 of the 1995 Act. On the right of cancellation regarding hire-purchase contracts, see 1995 Act, s.58(5), for example.
21 S.I. No. 207 of 2001, Reg 6, implementing Directive 97/7 [1997] O.J. L144/19.
22 The provision also states that nothing in the section shall affect the law relating to corporations.

(i) Acceptance and receipt

Acceptance, in the context of section 4, has a different meaning than that of acceptance under sections 34 and 35 of the 1893 Act.[23] For the purposes of section 4, subsection (3) provides that there is an acceptance when the buyer does any act in relation to the goods which recognises a pre-existing contract of sale whether there be an acceptance in performance of the contract or not. In *Tradax (Ireland) v. Irish Grain Board*,[24] it was held that that the acceptance of 1,871 tonnes of grain out a total of 25,000 tonnes due under the contract constituted "acceptance and receipt" and so the contract was enforceable. Further, acceptance and receipt must be by the party to be sued, or his authorised agent, but not any other third party. In *Hopton v. McCarthy*,[25] the defendant, a coach-builder in Tipperary, orally ordered goods from the plaintiff, a timber merchant, based in London. The goods and the invoice were dispatched at the same time. On receipt of the invoice, the defendant wrote to the plaintiff, informing him not to send the goods because the price was far greater than he had expected. On arrival, the goods were stored by the rail carrier for collection by the defendant. It was held that the defendant was not bound because neither he, nor anyone else authorised by him, had accepted and received the goods.

(ii) Giving something in earnest

Clearly, payment of a deposit or some other sum would constitute giving something in earnest to bind the contract but this is covered under (iii) above,[26] so this phrase must mean something more. It has been suggested elsewhere that giving a business card or a credit card number over the telephone, for instance, would suffice.[27] In *Kirwan v. Price*,[28] an offer of payment for the sale of a horse was refused by the seller. It was argued that the offer of payment constituted giving something in earnest but this was rejected by the court.

(iii) Part payment

Part payment, or indeed full payment, by the buyer will render the contract enforceable, but the payment must be accepted, and not merely tendered. In *Kirwan v. Price*,[29] there was a dispute about the price for the sale of a horse. The plaintiff buyer offered £300 for the horse, while the defendant

---

23 See further 14.2.1.

24 [1984] I.R. 1 per Henchy J. and Griffin J. at 16 and 19.

25 (1882) 10 L.R. (Ir) 266.

26 See further below.

27 Clark, *Contract Law in Ireland* (Dublin, Round Hall Sweet & Maxwell, 4th ed., 1998) p.89.

28 [1958] Ir. Jur. 56.

29 *Ibid.*

seller was of the view that the price agreed was £350. The offer of £300 was refused by the seller. The court found, on these facts, that there was no part payment by the buyer and hence no enforceable contract. It would seem that though there is no Irish authority on the point, a part payment covers all of the goods under the contract, and not just a particular part or quantity of the goods, making the complete contract enforceable.[30] This is most certainly the case where the contract is not severable. Where the contract is severable, such as an instalment contract,[31] more doubt exists on this point.

(iv) A note or written memorandum

As noted above, section 4 derives from the Statute of Frauds (Ireland) 1695, and the requirement of a note or written memorandum evidencing the contract is the same under the Sale of Goods Act 1893 as under the Statute of Frauds.[32] The note or memorandum can take any form[33] or forms,[34] and it must contain the essential terms of the contact. At a minimum, it should identify the parties, the price, and the subject-matter of the contract and it must be signed by the party to be charged, that is, to be sued.[35]

Section 4 of the 1893 Act was repealed in the United Kingdom in 1954, following a recommendation of the Law Revision Committee.[36] A similar repeal is long overdue in Irish law for a number of reasons. First, the minimum figure of £10 [€12.70] is totally out of date due to inflation. As a result, the provision catches a whole range of transactions that were never intended to come within its scope.[37] Second, the provision derives

30 This conclusion is reinforced by the "in earnest provision". Express provision to the contrary exists in the U.S. under the Uniform Commercial Code, see U.C.C. 2–201(3)(c).

31 See 1893 Act, s.31(2), and 14.2.2.2.

32 See generally, Clark, *Contract Law in Ireland* (Dublin, Round Hall Sweet & Maxwell, 4th ed., 1998) Chapter 4; and Friel, *The Law of Contract* (Dublin, Round Hall Sweet & Maxwell, 2nd ed., 2000) Chapter 10. It is arguable that s.13 of the Statute of Frauds (Ireland) Act 1695 was impliedly repealed by s.4 of the Sale of Goods Act 1893, but s.13 was expressly repealed by the Statute Law Revision (Pre-Union Irish Statute) Act 1962, s.1 and Schedule.

33 For example, in *Tradax (Ireland) v. Irish Grain Board* [1984] I.R. 1, a telex and a letter which sought to repudiate the contract constituted a note or written memorandum because it contained, in sufficient detail, the terms of the contract.

34 Under the doctrine of joinder, any number of documents can be joined together to form the note or memorandum. See further *Kelly v. Ross & Ross* unreported, High Court, McWilliam J., April 29, 1980.

35 Again a fairly flexible approach is taken to this requirement. For instance, in *Casey v. Intercontinental Bank* [1979] I.R. 364, a letter typed on a solicitor's headed note-paper but not personally signed by the solicitor, was sufficient for the purpose of the Statute of Frauds. Also, a rubber-stamp or initials may be sufficient. *Cf. Kelly v. Ross & Ross* unreported, High Court, McWilliam J., April 29, 1980.

36 Law Reform (Enforcement of Contracts) Act 1954, s.1.

37 In the United States of America, the figure in the Uniform Commercial Code was raised to $500: see U.C.C. 2–201.

from a time when executory, as opposed to executed, contracts were treated with some suspicion by the law.[38] Fears of perjury and fraud on the courts lead to the requirement of written evidence for certain contracts if they were to be enforceable. Executory contracts no longer suffer from this secondary status when compared with executed contracts, and so the distinction maintained by section 4 is unfounded. Finally, when parties enter into contracts (whether executed or executory) they expect to be able to enforce the contract. The law should support this expectation and not hinder it by requiring out-of-date formalities to be complied with. Accordingly, this formal requirement in Irish sales law should be abolished and the common law position reinstated.

(v) Formal requirements under other legislation

There are special formal requirements in relation to particular types of sale of goods contracts. In particular, consumer buyers of goods benefit from a variety of formal requirements. For example, where the buyer is a consumer, credit sales, to be enforceable under the Consumer Credit Act 1995, must comply with various formal requirements designed to protect the consumer's interests.[39] Consumer buyers of goods are also protected by formal requirements in relation to contracts negotiated away from business premises under the EC (Cancellation of Contracts Negotiated away from Business Premises) Regulations 1989,[40] and contracts concluded by means of distance communications under the EC (Protection of Consumers in Respect of Contracts Made by Means of Distance Communications) Regulations 2001.[41] Under these Regulations, certain information, including written confirmation of the consumer's cancellation right under the Regulations, must be provided within a specified time. Failure to provide this information makes the contract unenforceable.[42] Under the Mercantile Marine Act 1955, a registered ship or a share therein must be transferred by a bill of sale satisfying the prescribed requirements, including registration.[43]

Bills of sale probably warrant mention at this early stage, though they are dealt with in more detail later in the book.[44] At common law, a bill of

38 See Atiyah, *The Rise and Fall of Freedom of Contract* (Oxford, Oxford University Press, 1979) Chapters 6 and 7 and pp.419–424.

39 1995 Act, Parts III, IV and V: see further Bird, *Consumer Credit Law* (Dublin, Round Hall Sweet & Maxwell, 1998) Chapter 3. Hire-purchase agreements with and other hire arrangements consumers, are treated similarly under this legislation (see 1995 Act, Parts VI and VII: see further Bird, *Consumer Credit Law* (Dublin, Round Hall Sweet & Maxwell, 1998) Chapter 6.

40 S.I. No. 224 of 1989, implementing Directive 85/577 [1985] O.J. L372/31: see 9.2.1.

41 S.I. No. 207 of 2001, implementing Directive 97/7 [1997] O.J. L144/19: see 9.2.1.

42 S.I. No. 224 of 1989, Reg. 4, and S.I. No. 207 of 2001, Regs 4 and 5.

43 1955 Act, ss.43–45.

44 See 25.6.1.

sale is a written instrument effecting a transfer of personal property.[45] This is the meaning used in relation to the transfer of ships under the Mercantile Marine Act 1955. For the purpose of the Bills of Sale (Ireland) Acts 1879 and 1883, the term "bill of sale" has a more restricted meaning and is used to describe documents that effect or record the transfer of ownership in goods without the corresponding transfer of possession. The 1879 Act applies to all bills of sale whether "absolute", effecting a complete transfer of ownership to the grantee, or by way of security only. The 1883 Act applies to bills by way of security only. The objective of the legislation is to prevent persons (the grantors) from giving the appearance of being creditworthy by retaining possession of goods which really belong to someone else, or over which someone else has a security interest. A variety of formalities, including registration, are prescribed to prevent such false appearances arising. Failure to comply with these formalities renders the transfer void against various persons, including the trustee in bankruptcy, the execution creditor, and even the parties themselves, in certain circumstances.

The Bills of Sale (Ireland) Acts 1879 and 1883 remained unaffected with the enactment of the Sale of Goods Act 1893.[46] However, sale of goods contracts are rarely caught by this legislation. Only where the sale of goods is made or evidenced by a written document and possession of the goods is retained by the seller will the Bills of Sale Act 1879 apply. Even then, section 4 of the 1879 Act exempts from the legislation, *inter alia*, "transfers of goods in the ordinary course of business of any trade or calling." Hence, practically all sales, except where the seller is a private person, are exempt from the legislation. Furthermore, the Bills of Sale Act 1883 should have no impact on a contract for the sale of goods. A sale of goods contract, by definition, involves a transfer of the absolute or general property, that is the ownership, in the goods. The 1883 Act only applies where ownership is transferred as security for a debt.[47]

(vi) Written contracts of sale

Where a contract of sale is reduced to writing, whether it is individually negotiated or on standard terms of trade, the contract will be governed by the ordinary rules of evidence which apply to written contracts. In particular, under the "parol evidence rule" where a document is intended by the parties to represent the entire agreement, further evidence cannot be

45 See Maguire, "The Bill of Sale: The Forgotten Relation?" (1997) *Commercial Law Practitioner* 3; Diamond, "Hire-Purchase Agreements as Bills of Sale (I) & (II)" (1960) 23 *Modern Law Review* 399 and 516.

46 1893 Act, s.61(3).

47 See 9.2.3 and the 1893 Act, s.61(4).

admitted to add to, vary, subtract from or contradict the written terms in the document. There are, however, many exceptions to this general rule.[48]

9.2.2 The parties

It is well established that the requirement in the statutory definition of a contract for the sale of goods that the property be transferred from one party to another means that there must be two distinct parties: a seller and a buyer. The seller and the buyer can be part-owners of the same goods,[49] but the same person cannot be both the seller and the buyer.

Under section 14 of the Sale of Goods and Supply of Services Act 1980, where goods are sold to a buyer, dealing as a consumer,[50] and a further agreement is entered into by the buyer with a finance house to repay the finance house the price paid by the finance house to the seller, the finance house is deemed to be a party to the sales contract.[51] In these circumstances, the finance house is jointly and severally liable to the buyer for any breach of the sales contract and for any misrepresentations made by the seller in relation to the goods. This extension of the finance house's liability is an important protection for consumer buyers where the seller is unable or unwilling to meet a claim against him by the buyer.

9.2.3 The transfer of property

The essence of a contract for the sale of goods is the transfer of property in the goods from the seller to the buyer. "Property" is defined in section 62 of the 1893 Act as meaning the general property in the goods, and not merely a special property.[52] In this sense, "property" means the absolute legal interest in the goods, or "ownership".[53] Where the intention of the parties is not to pass property or ownership, the contract is not a contract of sale within the meaning of the legislation. Section 61(4) of the 1893 Act provides that the legislation does not apply to any transaction in the form of a sale that is intended to operate by way of mortgage, pledge, charge or

48 See 2.3.6. See further Clark, *Contract Law in Ireland* (Dublin, Round Hall Sweet & Maxwell, 4th ed., 1998) pp.111–117; and Friel, *The Law of Contract* (Dublin, Round Hall Sweet & Maxwell, 2nd ed., 2000) pp.171–172.

49 1893 Act, s.1(1).

50 1980 Act, s.3; see further 10.5.2.1.

51 See further 13.10.

52 A special property, or a limited interest in goods is transferred, for instance, in a bailment arrangement where only a possessory interest in the goods is transferred from the bailor to the bailee: see further 3.4.5.

53 See 3.3. See further Battersby, "A Reconsideration of 'Property' and 'Title' in the Sale of Goods Act" [2001] *Journal of Business Law* 1; Ho, "Some Reflections on 'Property' and 'Title' in the Sale of Goods Act" (1997) 56 *Cambridge Law Journal* 571; Goode, "Ownership and Obligations in Commercial Transactions" (1987) 103 *Law Quarterly Review* 433; Battersby and Preston, "The Concepts of 'Property', 'Title' and 'Owner' used in the Sale of Goods Act 1893" (1972) 35 *Modern Law Review* 269.

other security.[54] Specific rules on the passing of property are set-out in sections 16–19 and are examined in detail in Chapter 17.

9.2.4 The price

The goods must be sold for "a money consideration, called the price." Money has been defined as "chattels issued by the authority of the law and denominations with reference to a unit of account and meant to serve as a universal means of exchange in the state of issue."[55] So, for instance, payment in the euro, or U.S. dollar, or by any legal instrument or device which can be used to represent money, such as bills of exchange, cheques, and credit cards, all qualify as money consideration under this definition. Some goods, or commodities, are commonly traded internationally in a particular currency: oil is sold in U.S. dollars, for instance. If the consideration for the goods under the contract is in any form other than money consideration, the contract will not be a contract of sale within the terms of the legislation. Where, for example, the consideration for the goods is other goods, as is the case with a contract of barter, the transaction falls outside the Sale of Goods Acts,[56] or where for example, money is traded for money, as is the case with a foreign exchange transaction, the Sale of Goods Acts have no application.

Section 8 of the 1893 Act provides for the setting of the price. Accordingly, the price can be fixed by the contract, or by an agreed manner, or it may be determined by the course of dealings between the parties.[57] Otherwise, a reasonable price is payable, and what is a reasonable price is a question of fact dependent on the circumstances of each case.[58] This section is not as straightforward as it first appears. It operates on the assumption that a contract of sale exists. However, where the parties have failed to agree on the price, this may indicate that the parties have yet to reach an agreement. It could be argued that this lack of certainty regarding such an important term of the contract undermines the existence of a contract. Support for this proposition can be found in *May & Butcher v. The King*,[59] where it was held by the House of Lords that an agreement for a sale of goods where the price and other details were to be agreed later was void for uncertainty. It was probably significant that this was an executory transaction (no part had been performed) and the agreement was not merely silent on the points in question but expressly stated that further agreement was required. Other cases can be distinguished. In *Foley v. Classique Coaches Ltd*,[60] for example, where the contract had been in other

54 See further Chapter 25.
55 See Mann, *The Legal Aspect of Money*, (Oxford, Clarendon Press, 5th ed., 1992) pp.8.
56 See further 9.3.1.
57 1893 Act, s.8(1).
58 1893 Act, s.8(2).
59 [1934] 2 K.B. 17n.
60 [1934] 2 K.B. 1. See further *Hillas & Co. Ltd v. Arcos Ltd* (1932) 147 L.T. 503.

respects performed, the Court of Appeal held that an agreement to sell petrol "at a price to be agreed by the parties in writing and from time to time" was a contract concluded with sufficient certainty to be binding, as the parties had displayed a clear intention to be bound. This contract also contained an arbitration clause under which a reasonable price could be set if there was no agreement as to the price.

9.2.5 The goods

Goods are defined in section 62 of the 1893 Act as including all chattels personal other than things in action and money. In Irish law, all property can be classified as real or personal. Real property includes land and anything permanently attached to the land, such as buildings.[61] Personal property is all property except real property.[62] Personal property divides into chattels real (mainly leasehold interests in land)[63] and chattels personal. Chattels personal are those items which are not chattels real. Chattels personal sub-divide broadly into two classes: tangibles moveables (or *choses in possession*) such as goods and money; and intangibles moveables (or *choses in action*).[64] Therefore, goods are a type of personal property, but excluded from the definition of goods under the Sale of Goods Acts are certain types of personal property: things in action, and money. Things in action (or *choses in action*) are legal rights that are intangible in form, such as debts, shares in a partnership or a company, and intellectual property rights – copyright, patents and trade marks. Goods in comparison are tangible, movable and visible in nature. Money, meaning legally recognised tender, is also excluded from the definition of goods. Money *in curia*, such as antique coins, is goods for the purpose of the legislation.

Certain items clearly come within the above definition and are well recognised as goods for the purpose of the Sale of Goods Acts. For example, ships, aircraft, motor vehicles and domestic animals are all

61 Where a building is sold for removal, or demolition and removal of the materials of which it is made, or where it is agreed that the building will be severed from the land and sold when severed, these are examples of contracts for the sale of goods, and not contracts for the sale of land or interests in land: see further note 75 and surrounding text. See generally Lyall, *Land Law in Ireland* (Dublin, Round Hall Sweet & Maxwell, 2nd ed., 2000); Pearse & Mee, *Land Law* (Dublin, Round Hall Sweet & Maxwell, 2nd ed., 2000) and Wylie, *Irish Land Law* (Dublin, Butterworths, 3rd ed., 1997).

62 See generally, Bridge, *Personal Property Law* (London, Blackstone, 3rd ed., 2002); Bell, *The Law of Personal Property in England and Ireland* (London, Butterworths, 1989).

63 See generally, Wylie, *Landlord and Tenant Law* (Dublin, Butterworths, 2nd ed., 1998).

64 See *Colonial Bank v. Whinney* (1885) 30 Ch. D. 261 at 285, per Fry L.J.

goods.[65] In *Brosnan v. Leeside Nursuries*,[66] Barrington J. stated *obiter* that he "would have no difficulty in accepting that potted dwarf chrysanthemums on a supermarket shelf are 'goods' for the purposes of the Sale of Goods Act 1893." The matter is not so straightforward in relation to other items though. Electricity, and other forms of energy, while clearly capable of being sold, have never been defined as goods for the purposes of the Sale of Goods Acts.[67] Also, there is no Irish authority on whether human remains and body parts, products and genetic material (such as organs, blood and sperm) are goods.[68] These items may be capable of being stolen.[69] In America, there is authority that the supply of a blood transfusion is a supply of services,[70] while in another case it was held that blood supplied by a blood bank was a sale of goods.[71]

Perhaps of more commercial significance is the status of computer software. Again, there is no Irish authority on this point. In *St Albans City and District Council v. International Computers Ltd*,[72] Sir Ian Gildewell stated *obiter* in the Court of Appeal that while a disk was clearly goods, a program or software, "being instructions or commands telling the computer hardware what to do," of itself was not. But where a disk carrying a program is supplied, or where hardware and software are supplied together, and the software program is defective, the supplier would be in breach of the statutory implied terms as to quality, under the Sale of Goods legislation.[73] In the *St Albans* case, as is common, the defective program was not sold or hired, it was simply copied from a disk onto the plaintiff's computer without delivery of the disk. The property in

65 There is no absolute property in wild animals and so they are not goods, though a qualified property can be obtained in them by lawfully taking them into possession. At this point, it appears that they can be bought and sold as goods: see *Kearry v. Pattinson* [1939] 1 K.B. 471; and *Hamps v. Derby* [1948] 2 K.B. 311.

66 [1998] 1 I.L.R.M. 312 at 317.

67 See Benjamin's *Sale of Goods* (London, Sweet & Maxwell, 5th ed., 1997) para. 1-084.

68 See Creagh, "Property in the Dead Body" [2000] *Bar Review* 301.

69 See *R v. Kelly & Lindsay* [1998] 3 All E.R. 741; see further Skene, "Proprietary rights in human bodies, body parts and tissue: regulatory contexts and proposals for new laws" [2002] *Legal Studies* 102.

70 *Perlmutter v. Beth David Hospital* 123 N.E. (2d) 792 (1955).

71 *Belle Bonfils Memorial Blood Bank v. Hansen* 579 P 2d 1158 (1978).

72 [1996] 4 All E.R. 481; for criticism of this decision see Hedley, "Quality of Goods, Information, and the Death of Contract" [2001] *Journal of Business Law* 114 at 119–120. In *Saphena Computing Ltd v. Allied Collection Agencies Ltd* [1995] F.S.R. 616 (C.A.), the court avoided classifying a supply of software which was adapted to the customer's needs because it was common ground that the law was the same whether it was a supply of services or a sale of goods. A contract to write a new program for a customer is clearly capable of being a contract for the supply of services: see *Salvage Association v. CAP Financial Services Ltd* [1995] F.S.R. 654.

73 In a New South Wales case, *Toby Construction Products Pty Ltd v. Computa Bar (Sales) Pty Ltd* [1983] 2 N.S.W.L.R. 48, the Supreme Court held that the transfer of property in hardware and software together was a sale of goods, but this case failed to address the issue of the supply of software alone, and particularly software adapted to specified requirements.

the disk remained with the supplier, while the plaintiff was licensed to use it. In these circumstances, the program was not "goods" so there were no statutory implied terms as to quality. But in the absence of any express terms, his Lordship held that there would be a term implied at common law that the program should be reasonably fit for its intended purpose.

The statutory definition of goods in section 62 of the 1893 Act includes emblements, industrial growing crops and things attached to or forming part of the land which are agreed to be severed before sale or under the contract of sale. Emblements are annual crops grown by agricultural labour; industrial growing crops are similarly cultivated but are not expected to mature within one year. Both emblements and industrial growing crops can be contrasted with naturally occurring crops or plants. Naturally occurring crops come under the heading "things attached to or forming part of the land." Provided there is an intention to sever any growing thing from the land before the sale or under the contract of sale, the transactions will probably be a sale of goods. So, for example, a contract to pick your own strawberries would be a contract to sell goods (emblements), and a contract to cut down your own Christmas tree would also be a contract for the sale of goods (industrial growing crops),[74] but a contract to extract minerals from land has been held to be a contract for the sale of an interest in land, rather than a contract for the sale of goods.[75] In contrast, a contract to sell minerals already extracted or severed would be a contract for the sale of goods.

The 1893 Act divides goods into categories: existing or future; and specific or unascertained. These categories have important implications regarding, *inter alia*, the passing of property and risk.[76]

9.2.5.1 Existing or future

Section 5 of the 1893 Act states that goods can be existing, that is, owned or possessed by the seller at the time of the sales contract, or future, that is, goods to be manufactured or acquired by the seller after the making of the sales contract. Therefore, a seller can enter into a contract to sell goods that do not exist because they have yet to be manufactured by him under the sales contract: future goods. Equally, a seller can enter into a contract to sell goods that are the property of another party: also future goods. There is no difficulty with either of these situations, provided that the seller manufactures the goods, or acquires the property in the goods, in time to

74 See Bradgate, R., *Commercial Law* (London, Butterworths, 3rd ed., 2000) p.233.

75 In *Morgan v. Russell* [1909] 1 K.B. 357, the defendant, a tenant of a plot of land, contracted to allow the plaintiff to enter the property and remove slag and cinders which lay on the land generally. The defendant's landlord refused the plaintiff entry onto the land, and the plaintiff sued for damages for breach of contract. It was held that the contract was not a sale of goods but a sale of an interest in land.

76 See further Chapters 17 and 18.

complete the sale with the buyer. Such sales of future goods operate as agreements to sell.[77]

9.2.5.2 Specific or unascertained

Section 62 of the 1893 Act provides that specific goods are goods identified and agreed upon at the time the contract is made. The implication is that all other goods are unascertained. With a contract for the sale of specific goods (for example, the car registration number, 03 C 1234), the seller is obliged to deliver the exact goods identified and agreed upon by the parties. The seller cannot deliver substitute or similar goods under the contract. In a contract for the sale of unascertained goods (for example, 10 bags of smokeless coal), the seller is entitled to supply any 10 bags of coal provided they comply with the description "smokeless." Thus, where goods are sold by a purely generic description, such as, 500 litres of heating oil, or a new VW Golf, they are unascertained goods.

There is an intermediate category, identified by Professor Goode as "quasi-specific" goods. Strictly speaking, and for the purposes of the legislation, these are unascertained goods, but from an identified source. For example, a contract to sell 500 tons of wheat out of a bulk cargo of 10,000 tons aboard the *M.V. Hopeful* is a contract for the sale of quasi-specific goods. Particular problems can arise with this type of sale where the goods are pre-paid and the seller becomes insolvent. These are considered further in Chapter 17.

Following from the above definitions, existing goods can be specific or unascertained, and future goods can be unascertained. It has been argued that future goods cannot be specific,[78] but this is probably not the better view. A contract whereby an antique dealer agrees to sell a specific item, yet to be bought by him, to a customer,[79] or a contract to purchase the first car off a particular production line, at a particular plant, at a specified future date, are both examples of contracts for the sale of future, specific goods, within the meaning of the legislation.

It is important to note that the relevant time for assessing the nature of goods, existing or future, specific or unascertained, is the time that the contract is made. In particular, in order for property to pass from the seller to the buyer, in unascertained goods, they must become ascertained at some time between the making of the contract and its completion. Nevertheless, the relevant time for assessing this initial classification is the time the contract was made.

77 See 9.2.

78 See Chalmers, *Sale of Goods Act 1979* (London, Butterworths, 18th ed., 1981) p.271; and Atiyah's *Sale of Goods* (Harlow, Pearson, 10th ed., 2001) pp.72–3.

79 See Bradgate, R., *Commercial Law* (London, Butterworths, 3rd ed., 2000) p.235.

9.3 Other Similar Transactions

It is important to distinguish a contract for the sale of goods from a number of other similar transactions, because only where a transaction is a contract for the sale of goods, as defined by the legislation, will the Sale of Goods Acts apply. Contracts for the sale of goods and other transactions, such as contracts of bailment and contracts for work and materials, share similar features. Sometimes, regardless of the classification of the transaction, as a contract for the sale of goods or something else, the outcome is the same. This prompted the House of Lords in *Young & Marten Ltd v. McManus Childs Ltd*[80] to express strongly views on the undesirability of drawing unnecessary distinctions between different types of contracts. Nevertheless, distinctions remain and need to be understood. In this part, six different transactions will be examined for the purpose of contrast with contracts for the sale of goods.

9.3.1 Contract of barter or exchange

The main distinguishing feature between a contract of barter or exchange and a contract for the sale of goods is the consideration. In a contract of sale, the consideration[81] for the transfer of the property in the goods must be money consideration whereas the traditional barter arrangement occurs where goods are exchanged in return for other goods.[82] Before money was coined, barter was the basic form of trade. Today, countertrade, whereby developing countries trade their native raw materials in exchange for manufactured goods, is probably a form of barter.[83] The exchange of trading stamps or other tokens for goods also appears to be a barter and not a sale.[84] Contracts of barter or exchange are governed by the common law.[85]

The legal issue becomes more complicated where goods are transferred in return for goods, plus money. A common example is where a second-hand car is traded in, in return for a new car plus money. Is this type of arrangement a sale of goods, or a contract of barter or exchange? In *Aldridge v. Johnson*,[86] there was an agreement to exchange 52 bullocks, valued at £192, with 100 quarters of barley valued at £215, with the difference in value (£23) to be made up in cash. The point was not disputed

80 [1969] A.C. 454.

81 1893 Act, s.1(1).

82 Similarly, goods can be supplied in consideration of work done, for the extinction of a right, or for any other valuable consideration. None of these examples constitute a sale of goods.

83 See further Schmitthoff's *Export Trade: the law and practice of international trade* (London, Sweet & Maxwell, 10th ed., 2000) Chapter 14.

84 Trading Stamps Act 1980 implies this interpretation and implies terms similar to the sales legislation: 1980 Act, s.8.

85 See *Benjamin's Sale of Goods* (London, Sweet & Maxwell, 5th ed., 1997) paras 1-035–1-039.

86 (1857) 7 E. & B. 885.

in the case, and the court treated the transaction as a sale of goods. More recent authority can be found in *Flynn v. Mackin & Mahon,*[87] where a car was traded for another car and £250. It was held that this was a barter because no value was, nor could be, placed on the goods. It would seem that if a value, even a notional value, can be placed on the goods, as was the case in *Aldridge v. Johnson*, the transaction will be a sale. Hence, in order for a buyer to benefit from the protection afforded by the sales legislation, such as the statutory implied terms as to quality, it is vital that some value be apportioned to the goods exchanged.

9.3.2 Gift

Again consideration, or the lack thereof, is the distinguishing feature between a contract for the sale of goods and a gift. With a gift of goods, there is no consideration provided for the transfer of the property in the goods, even though there may be a valid transfer of property where the gift is executed, that is, where the goods are delivered to the donee. Where the gift is executory (yet to be performed), the promise of a gift is not binding unless it is made by deed.

Goods are often supplied as part of a promotional scheme as "free offers" or "free gifts". The leading case in point is *Esso Petroleum Co. Ltd v. Customs & Excise Commissioners*,[88] where with the purchase of petrol the customer received a "free gift" (a coin). It was held by the House of Lords that the supply of the coin was not a gift because Esso was obliged to supply it once the petrol was purchased; but it was not a sale, either, because, it would seem, there was no money consideration provided for the coin. Rather, the supply of the coin was interpreted as a contract collateral to the sale of petrol.

9.3.3 Bailment[89]

A bailment is a transaction whereby one party (the bailor) delivers goods to another party (the bailee) on terms which normally require the bailee to hold the goods and eventually to redeliver the goods to the bailor, or in accordance with his directions. The notable feature about a bailment, when contrasted with a contract for the sale of goods, is that there is no transfer of property or ownership in the goods, merely possession, and further, this transfer of possession to the bailee is temporary in nature. Everyday examples of bailment include leaving a coat in a cloakroom for later

---

87 [1974] I.R. 101; see further Canton, "Sale of Goods and Barter" (1976) 39 *Modern Law Review* 589. See also *Clarke v. Reilly & Sons* (1962) 96 I.L.T.R. 96 where there were similar facts. Cf. *Connell Estates Agents v. Begej* [1994] 39 E.G. 123, where it was stated *obiter* that where domestic goods are supplied in part exchange for other goods, this is usually a sale.

88 [1976] 1 All E.R. 117.

89 See 3.4.5.

collection, or transporting goods with a carrier, or a contract of hire. Bailments can be contractual, for example, where you pay to leave your coat at a cloakroom, or gratuitous, for example, where you do not pay to leave your coat at a cloakroom.

The basis of liability under a bailment is negligence. The bailee must exercise due care in his handling of the goods in his possession, and significantly for the bailor, when pursuing a claim in negligence, there is a reverse burden of proof, that is, contrary to the usual position, the bailee must prove that he was not negligent to avoid liability for any loss or damage caused to the goods subject to the bailment.[90]

9.3.4 Lease/hire

A contract of hire, or a lease, is a type of bailment. Here, the owner of goods agrees to hire, or let, or lease the goods to a hirer. Under this arrangement, the hirer gets possession and use of goods during the hire period. In return, the hirer pays a rent, perhaps weekly or monthly, to the owner. At all times, the property in the goods remains with the owner. Where goods are very expensive, or where developments in technology render goods obsolete quicker than is usual, or where the hirer is not in a financial position to purchase the goods in question, hiring the goods may make commercial sense. The lease or hire agreement will usually impose various duties on the parties. For instance, the hirer may be given the right to quiet possession of the goods; and the owner may be given the right to repossess the goods in certain circumstances such as non-payment of the rent. The hirer, as bailee, will owe a duty to exercise reasonable skill and care in relation to the goods in his possession. Where the letting is financed by credit with a consumer hirer the arrangement is regulated under Part VII of the Consumer Credit Act 1995.

9.3.5 Hire-purchase

Hire-purchase can be defined as a transaction which initially involves a hiring, and hence a bailment, of goods from the owner (the bailor) to the hirer (the bailee), for a fixed period, in return for instalment payments or rent, and at the end of the hire period, the hirer is granted an option to purchase the goods in return for a final optional payment. The hirer is not legally obliged to purchase the goods: he has an option. In practice, however, this option is always exercised because the cost of the instalment payments will exceed the normal cost of hiring, and the final payment is usually nominal. Effectively, hire-purchase is a way to spread the cost of purchasing goods over a period of time (usually one to five years). The basic objective is to supply goods on credit terms. At the same time, the

90 See, for example, *Sheedy v. Faughnan* [1991] I.L.R.M. 719.

owner's interests are protected because, while he earns a rental income, he remains the owner of the goods until the final optional payment is made, and where the hirer defaults in any instalment payments, the owner can repossess his goods (although this right may be restricted by statute).[91]

Credit sales and conditional sales are similar arrangements. Both are subject to the Sale of Goods Acts. In a credit sale, the buyer is given credit, and payment is often by instalments. In this sense it is similar to hire-purchase. Indeed, similar legislation applies to consumer credit sales as to consumer hire-purchase, under the Consumer Credit Act 1995.[92] There is one important distinction between a credit sale and a hire-purchase arrangement. With a credit sale, the property in the goods passes to the buyer at the time of the contract, or, at least at the time of delivery of the goods. With a hire-purchase arrangement, the property in the goods does not pass until much later and only when the hirer exercises his option to purchase.

Section 19 of the 1893 Act allows the seller to impose a condition on the passing of property in the goods: a conditional sale. Conditional sales are very common today when goods are supplied on credit terms (where a conditional sale arrangement is also a consumer credit agreement, the Consumer Credit Act 1995 will apply).[93] The supplier will frequently include a clause in the sales contract known as a retention or reservation of title clause, whereby no property in the goods supplied under the contract can pass until the goods are paid for in full. This mechanism protects the seller's interests by retaining ownership until the price is paid, and the buyer has possession and use of the goods in the meantime.[94] Under a conditional sale, the price may also be paid by instalments. This method of payment and the delay in the passing of property are similar to hire-purchase arrangements.[95]

Consumers and traders alike may find all three arrangements (hire-purchase, credit sale, and conditional sale) difficult to distinguish. Hire-purchase is closest to a conditional sale arrangement: both offer the supplier protection against the default or insolvency of the hirer or buyer. This was recognised by the House of Lords in the late nineteenth century in *McEntire v. Crossley*.[96] Under the bills of sale legislation, as noted above,[97] a document recording the transfer of ownership in goods without

91 See generally Part VI of the Consumer Credit Act 1995; see further Bird, *Consumer Credit Law* (Dublin, Round Hall Sweet & Maxwell, 1998) Chapters 4 and 5.

92 See Parts III, IV and V of the Consumer Credit Act 1995; see further Bird, *Consumer Credit Law* (Dublin, Round Hall Sweet & Maxwell, 1998) Chapter 3.

93 *Ibid.*

94 See 15.4.

95 A contract under which the "buyer" will not become the owner of goods by paying instalments unless he exercises an option not to acquire the goods is a conditional sale, and is not hire-purchase: see *Forthright Finance plc v. Carlyler* [1997] 4 All E.R. 90.

96 [1895] A.C. 457; see further *Helby v. Matthews* [1895] A.C. 471.

97 See 9.2.1.1(v).

the transfer of possession is void against a trustee in bankruptcy, or an execution creditor unless certain formalities are complied with and the agreement is registered. Further, an agreement transferring the ownership of goods as security for a debt is void even between the parties themselves unless the statutory formalities are complied with and the agreement registered. In *McEntire v. Crossley*, the House of Lords held that the bills of sale legislation did not apply to conditional sale arrangements. The legislation only applied where the owner of goods transferred or granted a security interest in the goods. In a conditional sale arrangement, the seller retains ownership in the goods to protect his interests, and therefore the buyer/debtor has no security interest in the goods. This reasoning clearly applies to hire-purchase arrangements also.

Hire-purchase was devised because it offered suppliers of goods protection against the wrongful disposition of goods. Under the Factors Act 1889,[98] a person who "bought or agreed to buy" goods (B1), in certain circumstances, could dispose of them to a third party (B2) and pass good title in the goods to a third party even while the goods are still owned by the original supplier (S).

S ⟶ B1 ⟶ B2

In a conflict of title, or ownership, between S and B2, B2 could win if he could fit the transactions within the terms of the legislation. However, in *Helby v. Matthews*,[99] the House of Lords held that a hirer under a hire-purchase arrangement is not a person who has "... agreed to buy" goods under the Factors Act. Hence, the wrongful disposition by a hirer of goods (H) would not pass good title to a third party (T) thereby defeating the owner's (O) rights.

O ⟶ H ⟶ T

It was not until 1946 that the legislature turned its attention to hire-purchase and its regulation. The Hire-Purchase Act 1946, as amended, regulated all hire-purchase. This legislation is now repealed and only consumer hire-purchase is regulated by the Consumer Credit Act 1995.[100]

9.3.6 Contacts for the supply of goods and services

A contract for the sale of goods may be easily identifiable, as may be a contract for the supply of services, but what is the legal position where someone services your car and, in doing so, installs new spark plugs,

98 Section 9: see also s.25(2) of the Sale of Goods Act 1893 for a similar rule; see further 19.8.

99 [1895] A.C. 471.

100 See generally, Bird, *Consumer Credit Law* (Dublin, Round Hall Sweet & Maxwell, 1998).

brake-pads, oil and filters? Is this a contract for the sale of goods or a contract for the supply of services or something else? In these circumstances, the distinction is important because it can lead to different results. First, liability under the Sale of Goods Acts is strict; there is no need to prove fault. In contrast, liability for the supply of services, under Part IV of the Sale of Goods and Supply of Services Act 1980, is fault-based.[101] From a plaintiff's perspective, strict liability is to be preferred to having to prove that the defendant was at fault or negligent. Second, where the buyer of the goods is dealing as a consumer, any attempt to limit or exclude the statutory implied terms is void under the Sale of Goods Acts, whereas, under Part IV of the Sale of Goods and Supply of Services Act 1980, where the purchaser of the service deals as a consumer, a reasonable limitation or exclusion of the statutory implied terms is permitted.[102]

There are a number of different possible interpretations of the above example of the car-service. One approach is to ask whether one aspect of the transaction dominates: the sale element or the service element.[103] If one aspect dominates, such as in the above example, where the service element probably dominates, then the contract can be classed as a contract for the supply of services.[104] Another interpretation is that where goods and services are supplied at or around the same time, there may be two separate contracts: one of sale and one to supply services. A third analysis is to find that there is one contract, to supply services and materials/goods (sometimes referred to as a contract for work and materials). Such contracts are governed by Part IV of the Sale of Goods and Supply of Services Act 1980.[105]

The nature of the transaction will depend on the particular facts of the case and the intention of the parties, and accordingly case law, though useful as guidance, needs to be treated with care. For example, a contract to supply a meal in a restaurant has been held to be a sale,[106] but arguably there would be a difference between a meal in a fast-food restaurant and a meal in a gourmet restaurant because of the different levels of skill involved. A contract whereby the "buyer" provided the design and the "seller" built a ship's propeller was found to be a contract of sale.[107] If the seller had had more of a role in the design of the propeller, the outcome might have been different. A contract to build a ship and supply it was found to be a sale, but not a pure sale, because it had elements of a building

101 See 20.3.2.
102 See 20.4.
103 See *Robinson v. Graves* [1935] 1 K.B. 579.
104 *Myers v. Brent Cross* [1934] 1 K.B. 46.
105 See further Chapter 20.
106 *Lockett v. Charles* [1938] 4 All E.R. 170.
107 *Cammell Laird v. Manganese Bronze* [1934] A.C. 402.

(services) contract.[108] Both the application of hair dye,[109] and the administration of medicine by a veterinary surgeon,[110] have been held to be contracts for the supply of services.[111] A contract for professional services, such as with an accountant or a solicitor is usually a contract for services, though documents may be passed to the client and become his property.[112] A contract for a printer to print a book, the printer to supply the paper and ink has been held to be a contract for work and materials.[113] A contract for a painter to paint a picture was a contract for work and materials, but in the same case the court also said that a contract for a sculptor to produce a statue might be a sale of a finished product.[114]

108 *Hyundai v. Papadopoulos* [1980] 2 All E.R. 29.
109 *Watson v. Buckley, Osborne & Garrett* [1940] 1 All E.R. 174.
110 *Dodd & Dodd v. Wilson & McWilliam* [1946] 2 All E.R. 691.
111 It was argued unsuccessfully in *Carroll v. An Post National Lottery* [1996] 1 I.R. 443 that the supply of a lottery ticket was a supply of services.
112 *Lee v. Griffin* (1861) 1 B. & S. 272, per Blackburn J.
113 *Clay v. Yates* (1856) 1 H. & N. 73.
114 *Robinson v. Graves* [1935] 1 K.B. 579.

CHAPTER 10

THE TERMS OF THE CONTRACT

10.1 INTRODUCTION

As evidenced by the statutory definition,[1] the core objective of a contract for the sale of goods is the transfer of property (or ownership, or title)[2] in the goods from the seller to the buyer. The duty of the seller to pass good title and the rules on the passing of property, risk, and title conflicts are examined in Chapters 12, 17, 18 and 19, respectively. Moreover, the core duties of the parties to a contract for the sale of goods, or perhaps what could be called the fundamental terms of the contract, are set down in section 27 of the Sale of Goods Act 1893. Section 27 provides that it is the seller's duty to deliver the goods, and the buyer's duty to accept and pay for the goods "in accordance with the terms of the contract of sale". This phrase is packed with significance and accordingly requires closer examination. The logistics and the other aspects of delivery and the duties to accept the goods and to pay the price are considered in detail in Chapter 11.

In examining the terms of the contract of sale in a general sense, the first step is to distinguish statements that form part of the contract, that is, the terms of the contract, from other statements which have no contractual force, that is, representations. Having identified the terms of the contract of sale, these terms can be classified in a number of different ways for various purposes. One classification involves distinguishing between the express and implied terms of the contract. A second classification is based on the distinction between conditions and warranties. These classifications, and more, are considered further in this chapter.

1 1893 Act, s.1(1); see generally Chapter 9.

2 The words "property", "ownership" and "title" are used in different provisions of the legislation, without being fully defined. Strictly, they mean different things. For a scholarly analysis of the more precise meanings of these words and concepts: see Battersby, "A Reconsideration of 'Property' and 'Title' in the Sale of Goods Act" [2001] *Journal of Business Law* 1; Ho, "Some Reflections on 'Property' and 'Title' in the Sale of Goods Act" (1997) 56 *Cambridge Law Journal* 571; Goode, "Ownership and Obligations in Commercial Transactions" (1987) 103 *Law Quarterly Review* 433; Battersby and Preston, "The Concepts of 'Property,' 'Title' and 'Owner' used in the Sale of Goods Act 1893" (1972) 35 *Modern Law Review* 269. For present purposes, these words are being used more or less synonymously to mean the absolute legal interest in the goods being sold.

10.2 Mere Representations, Representations and Terms

In the discussions or negotiations that lead to the formation of a contract, the parties may make numerous statements, either orally, or in writing. Not every such statement forms part of the contract. In this context, there are three categories of statement: mere representations, representations, and terms of the contract.

Mere representations, sometimes referred to as "mere puffs", are statements which are intended to have no legal effect. Mere representations probably include advertising claims and sales talk, which is usually exaggerated to entice a customer to purchase. For example, a statement by a car dealer that a car "will run forever", is not intended to have legal effect and so is not actionable.

Other statements are either representations or terms of the contract, or both.[3] A representation is a pre-contractual statement of fact which encourages the other party to enter the contract[4] but it is not a term of the contract. It should be noted that where one party to a contract makes an untrue statement of fact before the contract is concluded, and this induces the other party to enter the contract, it may amount to a misrepresentation which may give rise to a right to rescind the contract or to claim damages.[5] In contrast, a term of the contract is any statement which is intended to have contractual effect and hence is contractually binding on the parties. Where a term of the contract is broken or breached, the innocent party can sue the person responsible for the breach, claiming damages and may also be able to terminate the contract.[6]

Determining whether a statement is a representation or a term of the contract depends on the intention of the parties. This in turn will depend on the court's view, based on the facts of the case. It is not always easy to predict whether a statement is a representation or a term of the contract. Older case law in this area is of limited value because these cases display a reluctance to impose contractual liability unless there was deceit or a clear contractual intention. For example, in *Oscar Chess Ltd v. Williams*,[7] an innocent statement that a car was a 1948 model, when in fact it was a 1939 model, was held not to have contractual effect.[8] Today, there is more

3 Sale of Goods and Supply of Services Act 1980, s.44.

4 In a sale of goods contract, statements which give rise to disputes are usually made by the seller to the buyer but they may be made by the buyer or a third party: for an example of a statement by a buyer see *Goldsmith v. Rodger* [1962] 2 Lloyd's Rep. 249.

5 See 2.2.5.2(ii) and 2.3.1; see further, Clark, *Contract Law in Ireland* (Dublin, Round Hall Sweet & Maxwell, 4th ed., 1998) Chapter 11, and Friel, *The Law of Contract* (Dublin, Round Hall Sweet & Maxwell, 2nd ed., 2000) Chapter 18.

6 On buyers' and sellers' remedies in sales contract, see Chapters 14 & 15.

7 [1957] 1 W.L.R. 370.

8 However, this case can be explained on the basis that the statement was made by a private seller to a motor dealer, who had the specialist knowledge and expertise to check these facts.

of a readiness to impose contractual liability regarding statements made at the time of the sale where there is evidence that they were intended to have contractual effect.

10.3 Express and Implied Terms

In any contract there will be express terms of the contract. Express terms include those aspects of the agreement that are manifested in words between the parties, either oral or written. Usually, and at a minimum, the express terms of a sale of goods contract would include a description of the goods, the quantity being bought, and the price to be paid. The ordinary rules of evidence apply to determine the express terms of the contract.[9] In many areas of commercial law, such as insurance, carriage and international trade, the express terms of a contract can be found in standard form contracts promoted by trade and professional associations.

Further to the express terms, a court may imply other terms into a contract. Terms can be implied "by fact", "by law" or "by custom". Terms implied by fact are those which although not expressed by the parties, must have been intended by the parties to have been included. For example, where something is so obvious that it goes without saying, and hence it is not expressed by the parties, it may be implied by a court.[10] Again, courts may imply a term to give "business efficacy" to the parties' agreement.[11]

Terms can also be implied by operation of the law: the common law, legislation, or the Constitution. In relation to the sale of goods, the statutory implied terms as to title,[12] and the quality of the goods,[13] are important examples of such terms.[14] Generally, these terms impose obligations on the seller of goods to supply goods that he has a right to sell and are of a certain quality, in order to meet the reasonable expectations of the buyer. Accordingly, these terms are usually viewed as affording some legal protection to the buyer of goods. These terms originated in the mercantile sales contract of the nineteenth century where their purpose was to ensure that when goods were supplied they were useable, and that contracts would meet the reasonable expectations of business persons. Today, the statutory implied terms have the additional purpose of protecting consumer buyers.

9 See, *e.g. Cotter v. Brewster* unreported, High Court, O'Donovan J., December 18, 1997.

10 *Shirlaw v. Southern Foundaries* (1926) Ltd. [1939] 2 K.B. 201, as per MacKinnon L.J. at 227. See further *Ward v. Spivack*, [1957] I.R. 40; *Carna Foods v. Eagle Star* [1997] 2 I.L.R.M. 499.

11 *Luxor (Eastbourne) Ltd v. Cooper* [1941] A.C. 108 as per Lord Wright at 137.

12 1893 Act, s.12: see further Chapter 12.

13 1893 Act, ss.13–15, and 1980 Act, ss.12–13: see further Chapter 13.

14 Similar terms are implied into hire and hire-purchase agreements under the Consumer Credit Act 1995; see also the implied terms under the Part IV of the Sale of Goods and Supply of Services Act 1980, see further Chapter 20.

These statutory implied terms have a number of distinctive features, which can aid a buyer in pursuing a claim against a seller for their breach. First, and unlike other terms which have to be proved in evidence, such as express terms, or terms implied by fact, the statutory terms arise automatically. Hence there is no evidential problems for the buyer. The existence of the statutory implied terms cannot be contested provided the requirements of the statutory provisions are met. This is of great practical advantage to the buyer. Second, it should be noted that liability for breach of the statutory implied terms is strict: the usual contractual standard. Therefore, even though the seller is not at fault, he will be liable for breach of the statutory implied terms. Again, from a buyer's perspective, it is easier to establish liability when it is strict rather than fault-based. Third, the exemption or exclusion of liability for breach of the statutory implied terms is regulated by statute, further increasing their protective force.[15] Broadly, some statutory implied terms can never be excluded.[16] Otherwise, where the buyer deals as a consumer, the effect of the statutory implied terms can never be negatived by the express terms in the contract; and in all other circumstances, only a fair and reasonable exclusion is allowed.

Lastly, a court can imply a term into a contract based on custom and usage.[17] Not every trade custom will receive judicial recognition. The trade custom must be reasonable, consistent with the express terms of the contract and universally recognised in the trade as a legally binding custom.[18]

10.4 Conditions and Warranties

The Sale of Goods Acts 1893 and 1980 divide terms of the contract into conditions or warranties. Section 62 of the 1893 Act, which reflects the common law, provides that a warranty means an agreement about the goods,[19] collateral to the main purpose of the contract, the breach of which gives rise to a claim for damages, but not the right to reject the goods and treat the contract as repudiated. Condition is not defined expressly in the legislation but by implication. Section 11(2) of the 1893 Act states:

> "Whether a stipulation in a contract of sale is a condition, the breach of which may give rise to a right to treat the contract as repudiated, or a

15 1893 Act, s.55 and 1980 Act, s.22; see 10.5.2.

16 These are 1893 Act, s.12 and 1980 Act ss.12–13.

17 Technically, a custom refers to a practice in a particular area, while a usage refers to a practice in a particular trade. Today, the terms are used interchangeably.

18 *Paxton v. Courtnay* (1860) 2 F. & F. 131; *O'Reilly v. Irish Press* (1937) 71 I.L.T.R. 194.

19 The reference to "agreement" in this phrase would seem inaccurate. A warranty is a term in an agreement, not an agreement.

> warranty the breach of which may give rise to a claim for damages but not to a right to reject the goods and treat the contract as repudiated, depends in each case on the construction of the contract."

When this provision is read in conjunction with the definition of warranty in section 62, the implication is that a condition is an important or central term of the contract, breach of which gives rise to a right to repudiate, or terminate, the contract, reject the goods and sue for damages. Section 11(1) of the 1893 Act provides that an innocent party may elect to treat the breach of a condition as a breach of warranty.

Many of the statutory implied terms are conditions, including those in sections 12(1)(a); 13(1), 14(2), 14(4) and 15(2) of the 1893 Act and section 13(2) of the 1980 Act. Others are identified as warranties: for example, section 12(1)(b) of the 1893 Act and section 12(1) of the 1980 Act.

It was thought that all terms in sales contracts were either conditions or warranties because the legislation refers only to these two types of term. This was the position even after the English case *Hongkong Fir Shipping Co. Ltd v. Kawasaki Kisen Kaisha Ltd*,[20] where a third type of contractual term was identified: the innominate or intermediate term.[21] An innominate term is a sort of hybrid combination of the condition and warranty, the effect of the breach of which depends on the seriousness of the breach. Only where the breach of such a term deprives the innocent party of substantially the whole benefit of the contract will the innocent party be able to repudiate the contract, otherwise his remedies are limited to a claim for damages. The existence of the classification of innominate term allows a court greater flexibility in determining the appropriate remedy following a breach of contract but brings with it uncertainty as to the parties' rights and liabilities. English case law has since recognised that innominate terms can exist in relation to sales contracts.[22] This is probably also the position in Ireland, although there is no direct authority on this point.[23] However, it must be remembered that any terms implied by the Sale of Goods Acts are expressly identified as either conditions or warranties, leaving no doubt as to the remedies available where such terms are breached. In contrast, the terms implied by section 39 of the Sale of Goods and Supply of Services Act 1980 in relation to contracts for the supply of services are not expressly identified as conditions or warranties but rather as undertakings and terms, and so arguably are innominate in nature.[24]

---

20 [1962] 2 Q.B. 26.

21 It is generally accepted that three classifications now exist, though this view is not universally accepted: see, *e.g.* Treitel, *The Law of Contract* (10th ed., London, Sweet & Maxwell, 1999) pp.738–743.

22 *The Hansa Nord* [1976] Q.B. 44.

23 See *Laird Bros v. Dublin Steampacket* (1900) 34 I.L.T.R. 9; *Taylor v. Smyth* [1990] I.L.R.M. 377; *Irish Telephone Rentals v. ICS Building Society* [1991] I.L.R.M. 880.

24 See further Chapter 20.

10.5 Exclusion Clauses

Contracts impose duties on the parties, as well as giving rights. Where a contractual duty is breached, legal, and hence financial, liability may arise. On entering a contract, parties aware of these potential liabilities often seek to limit or exclude their duties/potential liabilities by including an exclusion clause in the contract and getting the other party to the contract to agree to it.[25] Both parties are free to use exclusion clauses in this way although more frequently it is the party in the stronger bargaining position who will seek to include such clauses in their contracts. The legal response to exclusion clauses is varied. Increasingly, legal regulation has become more exact. The different layers of regulation are set out, in brief, below.

10.5.1 Common law regulation[26]

In a relatively minimal way, the common law regulates the use of exclusion clauses through its rules on incorporation of terms in a contract, and the construction of exclusion clauses, in particular, the *contra proferentem* rule and the doctrine of fundamental breach.

At common law, where two parties agree to a term in the contract, including an exclusion clause that favours one party over the other, the court will give legal effect to that term provided it is properly incorporated into the contract. The basic principle of freedom of contract prevails. Terms can be incorporated in three ways:

(i) when a document containing contractual terms is signed, the party signing is bound by those terms, and it is immaterial whether the document was read or not;[27]
(ii) by giving reasonable notice of the term to the other party,[28] and
(iii) by course of dealing between the parties.[29]

Further, and according to the *contra proferentem* rule, where the meaning of an exclusion clause is ambiguous and there are two or more possible meanings to the clause, the court will adopt the meaning most favourable to the party against whom the clause is being enforced.

25 The term "exclusion clause" includes clauses which seek to limit liability, e.g. "the seller will only be liable for any breach of contract up to a maximum figure of EUR 500," known as limitation of liability clauses, and clauses which seek to exclude a person's liability altogether, *e.g.* "the seller shall not be liable for any breach of contract howsoever caused."

26 See 2.3.5.1.

27 *L'Estrange v. Graucob Ltd* [1934] 2 K.B. 394.

28 *Thornton v. Shoe Lane Parking Ltd* [1971] 2 Q.B. 163; and *Carroll v. An Post National Lottery* [1996] 1 I.R. 443.

29 *McCutcheon v. David MacBrayne Ltd* [1964] 1 All E.R. 430.

Finally, and partly because of the fear that in some contracts parties were trying to exclude their liability for failure to perform even the most basic, or fundamental, terms of the contract, the courts developed the doctrine of fundamental breach. In English law, the position under this doctrine is that whether such an exclusion clause excusing fundamental breach will be enforced or not is a matter of construction of the clause in each individual case.[30] Therefore, there is no common law prohibition on the use of such clauses. Unfortunately, the position in Ireland is not so clear. The leading authority here is *Clayton Love v. B & I Transport*,[31] a case decided before the more recent English authorities setting out the above rule, which favours a stricter approach to the use of such clauses. However, its future application has been rendered uncertain by its age and the more recent English authority.[32]

10.5.2 The Sale of Goods and Supply of Services Act 1980

In addition to the common law position, the Sale and Supply of Goods Act 1980 regulates the use of exclusion clauses relating to the statutory implied terms in contracts for the sale of goods, and contracts for the supply of services.[33] Exclusion of liability in relation to any other terms of a sale or services contract, and in relation to all other types of contract, remained unaffected by this legislation.

With regard to the sale of goods, section 22 of the 1980 Act inserted a new section 55 in the 1893 Act on the exclusion of liability for breach of the statutory implied terms. Section 55(1) restates the common law position, as was originally stated in the 1893 Act, that any right, duty or liability which arises by implication of law may be negatived or varied by express agreement, or by the course of dealings between the parties, or by usage.[34] Section 55(1) is expressed to be subject to the subsequent provisions of the section. These subsequent provisions set out the rules on the exclusion of liability for breach of the implied terms found in sections 12–15 of the 1893 Act. Accordingly, section 12 on title can never be exempted: any attempt to exempt all or any of the provisions of section 12 shall be void.[35] In contrast, the implied terms in sections 13–15, on quality of goods supplied,[36] can never be excluded where the buyer deals as a

30 *Photo Production Ltd v. Securicor Transport Ltd* [1980] 2 W.L.R. 283.

31 (1970) 104 I.L.T.R. 157.

32 See Clark, *Contract Law in Ireland* (Dublin, Round Hall Sweet & Maxwell, 4th ed., 1998) pp.157–159; and Friel, *The Law of Contract* (Dublin, Round Hall Sweet & Maxwell, 2nd ed., 2000) pp.205–207.

33 The 1980 Act also applied to hire-purchase arrangements. The relevant provisions in relation to hire-purchase are now to be found in Part VI of the Consumer Credit Act 1995.

34 An express term seeking to negative an implied condition or warranty must do so clearly: s.55(2) and note also the *contra proferentum rule*, see 2.3.5.1(iii) and 10.1.4.1.

35 1893 Act, s.55(3); see Chapter 12.

36 See Chapter 13.

consumer, and in other cases, an exclusion clause shall not be enforceable unless it is shown that it is fair and reasonable.[37] These rules are stated not to apply to international sales contracts because the protectionist attitude which underlies these provisions does not extend beyond domestic sales into the international arena, where parties are assumed to be of a more equal bargaining strength and hence more able to protect their own interests.[38] Further, in relation to the terms implied by the 1980 Act, the 1980 Act contains rules on their exclusion. Liability for breach of section 12, which contains an implied warranty in relation to spare parts and servicing and section 13, which implies a condition on the sale of a motor vehicle, can never be excluded.[39]

Moreover, section 11 of the 1980 Act uses the criminal law to further protect the position of buyers, whether they deal as consumers or not. It is an offence for a person in the course of a business to display, or publish, or supply goods bearing, or otherwise furnish, a statement purporting to restrict the buyer's rights derived from the implied terms in sections 12–15 of the 1893 Act.[40] A seller may also be required to supply a declaration that the buyer's rights, by virtue of sections 12–15 of the 1893 Act, are in no way prejudiced by any statements which set out, limit or describe the rights of the buyer.[41] A person guilty of an offence under the 1980 Act is liable, on summary conviction, to a fine not exceeding £500 [€634.87], and/or imprisonment not exceeding six months; and on indictment, to a fine not exceeding £10,000 [€12,697.38], and/or imprisonment not exceeding two years.[42]

In relation to contracts for the supply of services, section 40 of the 1980 Act provides that the terms implied by section 39 may be excluded, except where the recipient of the service deals as a consumer, in which case it must be shown that the exclusion clause is fair and reasonable and has been specifically brought to the recipient's attention. There seems no principled reason why the rules on the exclusion of liability are more lax in relation to contracts for the supply of services. But in this regard, and in others,[43] contracts for the supply of services rank unfairly as the poor relation to sale of goods contracts, despite their growing importance to the economy.

---

37 Hence, the burden of proving the exclusion clause is fair and reasonable rests with the party seeking to enforce the clause.

38 1893 Act, s.61(6), as inserted by s.24 of the 1980 Act. See generally Part VI on international trade law.

39 1980 Act, s.12(3), and s.13(9) see further 13.8 and 13.9.

40 Statements to the effect that goods will not be exchanged, or that money will not be refunded, or that only credit notes will be given for goods returned will be likely to fall foul of this prohibition: 1980 Act, s.11(3).

41 1980 Act, s.11(4).

42 1980 Act, s.6. For information on the enforcement of this provision, see the Annual Reports of the Director of Consumer Affairs. Convictions under this provision are noted in the Annual Reports for 1990, 1991 and 1992. See generally www.odca.ie.

43 For instance, the use of retention of title clauses in sale contracts as a means of protecting the seller's financial interests cannot be extended to contracts for the supply of services: see further 15.4.

Two phrases warrant further consideration: "deals as a consumer" and "fair and reasonable."

10.5.2.1 Deals as a consumer[44]

This phrase is defined in section 3(1) of the 1980 Act. Accordingly, a party deals as a consumer in relation to another party if:

(i) he neither makes the contract in the course of a business; and
(ii) the other party does make the contract in the course of a business; and
(iii) the goods or services supplied are of a type ordinarily supplied for private use or consumption.[45]

Section 3(3) contains a presumption in favour of the consumer. It provides that it is for the party claiming that a person does not deal as a consumer to prove that he does not.

Section 3(1) has been considered in two Irish cases, of the same year, by the same judge. In *Re Henry O'Callaghan v. Hamilton Leasing (Ireland) Ltd and Access Refrigeration and Shop Fitting Ltd*,[46] a case not involving exclusion clauses, the plaintiff owned a take-away restaurant. He bought a drinks vending machine from the second-named defendant to be used in the restaurant. The purchase was financed by a leasing agreement between the plaintiff and the first-named defendant. The machine proved to be defective. The legal issue before the High Court was whether the plaintiff could maintain an action against the first-named defendant under sections 14 or 38 of the 1980 Act.[47] To do so, the plaintiff had to show that he was dealing as a consumer. In the High Court, McWilliam J., in a short judgment, held that the contract was made in the *course of the plaintiff's business* (contrary to paragraph (a) above) and hence the plaintiff did not deal as a consumer and his action was dismissed. McWilliam J. found that the purchase was made for the *purpose of the business* although he

44 See Bird, "Dealing as Consumer" [1999] *Commercial Law Practitioner* 10.

45 Section 3(2) provides that on a sale by competitive tender the buyer is not in any circumstances to be regarded as dealing as a consumer, but where the sale is by auction a buyer can deal as a consumer unless the goods are of a type defined by ministerial order or the auction is conducted by or on behalf of a person of a class defined by ministerial order. Orders could have been made in relation to the sale by auction of bloodstock; or auctions by personal representatives or liquidators, but no ministerial orders have been made under this provision. Hence, and in total contrast to the English position, buyers at auction can deal as consumers: see U.K. Unfair Contract Terms Act, s.12(2).

46 [1984] I.L.R.M. 146.

47 Section 14 of the 1980 Act deals with the joint liability of finance houses for the supply of defective goods; and section 38 (see now s.80, Consumer Credit Act 1995) dealt with letting agreements other than hire-purchase agreements and liability for defective goods thereunder.

recognised that the business was not involved in the re-sale or further dealing with the goods. Accordingly it would seem that in the course of a business does not require that the business is normally involved in dealing in goods of the type in question. It is sufficient that the contract is made for the purpose of the business. McWilliam J. also noted in relation to paragraph (c) above that because the goods were supplied for the purpose of the business they could not have been ordinarily supplied for private use and consumption.

In *Cunningham v. Woodchester Investments and Inter-call Ltd*,[48] the plaintiff was the bursar of a large agricultural college that sold a lot of its produce. Although the college was a non-profit making educational organisation, its annual turnover from the sale of its produce was about £1 million. It leased a telephone system from the defendant that proved faulty. In order to maintain the action, again under section 14 of the 1980 Act, the plaintiff had to be dealing as a consumer. Again, McWilliam J. in the High Court, held that the plaintiff was acting in the course of a business contrary to paragraph (a) of section 3(1) of the 1980 Act. The equipment was mainly used as part of the farming activity and regardless of what was done with the profits from this activity, McWilliam J. felt constrained to hold that this activity constituted carrying on a business. It would seem that an organisation with mixed activities, such as in this case, where the college was involved in educational and business activities, can be treated as acting in the course of a business with regard to some activities and not others. Further, the lack of a profit motive is not a bar to acting in the course of a business.

The U.K. Unfair Contract Terms Act 1977 contains an almost identical definition of dealing as a consumer in its section 12. There the leading case is *R&B Customs Brokers v. United Dominion Trust*,[49] where a small freight-forwarding company was managed by a husband and wife. The company bought a car for business and private use under a conditional sale agreement from the defendant finance company. It proved to be defective and the buyers wanted to reject the car. A clause in the agreement provided that the implied terms as to quality should not apply, although this clause was stated not to be effective against consumers. The defendant argued that the company was not dealing as a consumer since the car was bought *in the course of a business*, and accordingly the exclusion clause was enforceable. The Court of Appeal held that the company was dealing as a consumer and put forward the following test for *in the course of a business*. A contract is made in the course of a business if: (i) it is an integral part of the business; or (ii) there was a degree of regularity of similar transactions. On the facts, the court found that buying cars was not

48 Unreported, High Court, McWilliam J., November 16, 1984.

49 [1988] 1 W.L.R. 321; see also *Davies v. Sumner* [1984] 3 All E.R. 831.

integral to the freight-forwarding business and it was not regular enough either – a total of three cars had been bought over a period of five years. The end result is that in English law a company can deal as a consumer.

R&B Customs Brokers takes a different approach to the earlier Irish cases on the issue of dealing as a consumer. Because it defines buying *in the course of a business* narrowly, it therefore takes a broader view on when a buyer *deals as a consumer*. However, more recent English authority may undermine the decision in *R&B Customs Brokers*. In *Stevenson v. Rogers*,[50] the defendant sold his only boat, the *Jelle*, to another fisherman and replaced it with another boat. The Court of Appeal was asked to rule, as a preliminary issue, whether the sale of the *Jelle* was *in the course of a business* and so whether the merchantable quality provision, in the then section 14 of the U.K. Sale of Goods Act 1979, applied.[51] Having examined the legislative history of the phrase and relevant case law, including *R&B Customs Brokers*, the judge opted for a broad interpretation of the phrase *in the course of a business*. *R&B Customs Brokers* and *Stevenson v. Rogers* can be distinguished: the former concerned buying in the course of a business within the context of the Unfair Contract Terms Act, while the latter involved selling in the course of a business in the context of the Sale of Goods Act. The result in English law is that the same phrase has a different meaning depending on the context. In contrast, the broad meaning attributed to *in the course of a business* in *Stevenson v. Rogers* is more in line with the Irish case on dealing as a consumer. Ironically, this synthesis with Irish law means that fewer buyers will be afforded the status of consumer and hence will be less well protected under Irish consumer legislation.

10.5.2.2 Fair and reasonable

In a contract for the sale of goods where the buyer does not deal as a consumer, as defined, a seller's liability for breach of the implied terms in sections 13–15 of the 1893 Act may be excluded provided the exclusion is fair and reasonable. Regarding contracts for the supply of services, section 40 of the 1980 Act provides that the terms implied by section 39 may be excluded except where the recipient of the service deals as a consumer in which case it must be shown that the exclusion clause is fair and reasonable and has been specifically brought to the recipient's attention.

The phrase "fair and reasonable terms" is defined in the Schedule to the 1980 Act. The test of "fair and reasonable" is an objective one: is the term fair and reasonable having regard to the circumstances which were or

50 [1999] 1 All E.R. 613.

51 Section 14 of the UK Sale of Goods Act 1979 has since been amended by the Sale and Supply of Goods Act 1994 whereby goods sold in the course of a business must be of satisfactory quality, as defined.

ought reasonably have been, known to or in the contemplation of the parties when the contract was made?[52] The time for assessing whether the term is fair and reasonable is the time the contract is made, and not when the clause is relied upon.

Section 2 of the Schedule lists five particular factors that may be relevant to the test. An identical list of factors is provided in Schedule 2 of the U.K. Unfair Contract Terms Act 1977.[53] The factors are as follows.

(i) The relative bargaining strength of the parties, including alternative means by which the customer's requirements can be met. This suggests that where two parties are of equal bargaining strength, the clause will be more likely to be fair and reasonable. In *St Albans City and District Council v. International Computers Ltd*,[54] under a contract for the supply of computer software the defendant supplier sought to limit its liability to the cost of the software supplied or £100,000, whichever was the lesser. The suppliers effectively disclaimed liability for all other losses caused by the supply of defective software. The trial judge had estimated the loss to the plaintiff at GBP£1.3 million. In finding that the capping of liability was unreasonable, it was noted that the defendant was one of a limited number of companies which could meet the plaintiff's requirements; and all those companies dealt on similar terms. At the same time, the plaintiff was under severe time and financial constraints. Hence, the bargaining positions were extremely unequal.

(ii) Whether the customer received an inducement to agree to the term, or in accepting it had an opportunity of entering into a similar transaction with other persons, but without having to accept a similar term. In *Woodman v. Photo Trade Processing*,[55] a

52 1980 Act, Schedule, s.1.

53 The leading English case is *George Mitchell (Chesterhall) Ltd v. Finney Lock Seeds Ltd* [1983] 2 A.C. 803. This case was decided under the Supply of Goods (Implied Terms) Act 1973 which contained almost identical wording to the later 1977 Act. In this case, in a contract for the sale of seed, a clause limited the seller's liability to the contract price. The seed turned out to be wholly different and of an inferior type and the crop had to be ploughed into the ground causing a considerable loss to the plaintiff. The buyers were aware of the clause. The clause had been drafted by the seed supplier's trade association but the National Farmers' Union had failed to object to the clause. The court found the clause unreasonable. Crucial factors in coming to this finding included the facts that the defect was the result of the seller's negligence; sellers could insure against this type of loss; and when similar claims had arisen in the past, sellers had settled claims without relying on the clause. See further Adams & Brownsword, "The Unfair Contract Terms Act: A Decade of Discretion" (1988) 104 *Law Quarterly Review* 94.

54 [1996] 4 All E.R. 481 (C.A.), [1995] F.S.R. 686 (H.C.).

55 Unreported, County Court, May 17, 1981, cited in (1981) 131 N.L.J. 935.

clause in a contract for the processing of a photographic film that provided that in the event of loss the processor's liability would be limited to the cost of replacement of the unprocessed film, was held unreasonable. The film contained pictures from a family wedding. The court was influenced by the fact that the customer had little choice in entering the contract because few film processors accepted greater liability than the defendants.

(iii) Whether the customer knew or ought reasonably to have known of the existence and extent of the term. Although a clause may be incorporated into a contract by the customer signing the document containing the clause without reading it, this may render the clause unreasonable and hence unenforceable.

(iv) Where the term excludes or restricts liability if some condition is not complied with, whether it was reasonable at the time of the contract to expect that compliance with the condition would be practicable. In *RW Green v. Cade Bros Farms*,[56] a clause in a contract for the sale of seed potatoes required the buyer to notify the seller of any complaints within three to seven days of delivery. This clause was held to be unreasonable because many defects would not become apparent until the crop was harvested months later. Another clause in that contract limiting any damages to the contract price was found to be reasonable.

(v) Whether the goods were manufactured, processed or adapted to the special order of the customer.

10.5.3 The EC (Unfair Terms in Consumer Contracts) Regulations

The Sale of Goods and Supply of Services Act 1980 regulates the exclusion of a seller's liability for breach of the statutory implied terms only. All other terms in a sales contract, whether exclusionary or not, are regulated by the common law,[57] and the EC (Unfair Terms in Consumer Contracts) Regulations 1995 and 2000.[58] The Regulations seek to implement the EC Directive on Unfair Terms in Consumer Contracts.[59] In essence, they seek to protect consumers from unfair contract terms. The Regulations are examined in detail in Chapter 2.[60] The Regulations add

56 [1978] 1 Lloyd's Rep. 602.

57 See 2.3.5.1 and 10.5.1.

58 S.I. No. 27 of 1995, and S.I. No. 307 of 2000.

59 93/13/EEC [1993] O.J. L95/29.

60 See 2.3.5.3.

nothing to the protection afforded by the 1980 Act in relation to the exclusion of liability for breach of the statutory implied terms, but in relation to any of the other terms of a sales contract, whether they are exclusionary or not, the Regulations offer the only source of protection for consumers beyond the common law. As well as the "indicative and non-exhaustive list" of terms which may be "unfair" provided in Schedule 3 (the "grey list") clauses which:

(a) excuse the seller's liability for late-delivery; or
(b) allow the seller to deliver a greater or lesser quantity than the contract quantity; or
(c) excuse a party from liability where he is unable to perform that contract due to circumstances beyond his control (*force majeure clauses*); or
(d) extend the time for performance where a party isunable to perform that contract due to circumstances beyond his control;

must be assessed in terms of fairness, and if unfair are unenforceable.

CHAPTER 11

THE DUTIES OF THE PARTIES: TO DELIVER, ACCEPT AND PAY

11.1 INTRODUCTION

Part III of the Sale of Goods Act 1893, sections 27–37, is entitled "Performance of the Contract". The first provision of this Part, section 27 sets out the basic, or fundamental,[1] duties of the parties under a contract for the sale of goods. Section 27 provides that it is the seller's duty to deliver the goods in accordance with the terms of the sales contract, and the buyer's duty is to accept and pay for the goods in accordance with the terms of the sales contract. If either party fails in these basic duties, they will be in breach of the contract.

In this chapter, we are concerned with the meaning of delivery, and the various aspects of the seller's duty to deliver: the place of delivery, the cost of delivery, and the time of delivery, for instance. This involves an examination of many of the provisions in Part III of the 1893 Act. Many of the rules in Part III are default rules (the rules apply only where the parties have not provided otherwise).[2] Included in these provisions, in section 30, is a set of default remedies for the buyer where the wrong quantity of goods is delivered by the seller. The buyer's remedies for breach of the seller's title obligations under section 12 of the 1893 Act are dealt with in Chapter 12, and the buyer's remaining remedies for the seller's breach of contract, including breach of the delivery obligation, are covered in Chapter 13. In this chapter, we also consider the buyer's duties to accept the goods and to pay the price. The seller's remedies for the buyer's breach of contract, including breach of the obligations to accept the goods and pay the price, are covered in Chapter 15.

11.1.1 Section 28

Section 28 of the 1893 Act states that, unless otherwise agreed, the duties to deliver the goods and to pay the price are concurrent conditions. This is further explained in the provision in the sense that the seller must be ready

1 The legislation nowhere uses the term "fundamental duties," nor has case law identified section 27 as containing the fundamental duties of a sales contract. "Fundamental" is used in the sense of "core" or "basic."

2 See further 8.2.3.

and willing to give possession of the goods in exchange for the price, and the buyer must be ready and willing to pay the price in exchange for possession of the goods.

"Condition" is used in the law of contract to mean different things.[3] In sales law, it has two main meanings. First, a condition is an event upon which another event, an obligation, or a whole contract is dependent, or "conditional".[4] This can be referred to as the "suspensive" meaning of condition. Second, condition means a promise that is central to or goes to the root of the contract – the promissory sense.[5] In section 28, the word "condition" is used in its suspensive meaning, with each obligation dependent on the other.[6] The seller's duty to deliver is dependent on the buyer being ready and willing to pay the price, and the buyer's duty to pay the price is dependent on the seller being ready and willing to give possession of the goods. Of course, the seller does promise to deliver the goods and the buyer does promise to accept and pay for the goods, but these promises are more than conditions in the sense of terms of the contract; they are duties so basic that a seller who fails to deliver or a buyer who fails to accept or pay, has simply failed to perform the contract. It is in this sense that the duties described in section 28 can be referred to as fundamental terms of the contract. Furthermore, classifying these duties as conditions means that where either side fails to perform these basic obligations, the other side can not only sue for damages for breach of contract but also repudiate, or terminate the contract.[7]

While *cash on delivery* is what is envisaged in the legislation, in fact, these duties are frequently performed at different times, in accordance with the parties' agreement. Often goods are paid for in advance of delivery, and in other circumstances a buyer may be able to agree credit terms with a seller whereby the goods will be delivered, and indeed property may pass to the buyer, before the goods are paid for.[8]

11.2 The Duty to Deliver

The seller's duty is to deliver the goods in accordance with the terms of the contract.[9] The goods that are delivered must comply with all the terms of the contract, whether express or implied. Where the contract of sale is for

3 Stoljar, "The Contractual Concept of Condition" (1953) 69 *Law Quarterly Review*, 485 at 486–8 lists 12 different meanings of the word "condition."

4 See for example, 1893 Act, s.18, Rules 1 and 5, see further 17.2.1 and 17.4.2.

5 See for example, 1893 Act, ss.12–15, see further Chapters 12 and 13.

6 See further Bradgate & White, "Rejection and Termination in Contracts for the Sale of Goods" in Birds, Bradgate and Villiers eds., *Termination of Contracts* (Chichester, Wiley Chancery, 1995).

7 See 10.4.

8 See further Chapter 21 and Part IV generally.

9 See generally, Chapter 10.

specific goods, the seller must deliver those exact goods only.[10] Where the contract is for unascertained goods, the seller is obliged to deliver any goods that meet the contractual description. The goods must be delivered at the correct place, the correct time and in the correct quantity. The legislation contains detailed rules as to where to deliver, when to deliver and at whose expense delivery is to take place, for example. Generally, however, these default rules will be modified by the express terms of the contract, and the seller must have the right to sell the goods, and the goods must be of a sufficient quality as required by the statutory implied terms and any other express terms as to quality.

Delivery is defined simply as the "voluntary transfer of possession from one person to another."[11] Delivery, in this legal sense, is very different from the everyday meaning of the word where delivery usually involves some form of transportation from one place to another. In its legal meaning, no transport need be involved. A seller can fulfill his obligation to deliver by simply allowing the buyer to collect the goods being sold.

Delivery has both a practical and a legal significance. Practically, when the goods have been delivered to the buyer, and hence the buyer has possession of the goods, he can use the goods for his purposes even though he may not own the goods under the sales contract. The delivery of goods and the passing of property and risk in the goods are not necessarily linked.[12] From a legal perspective, once the seller has delivered the goods in accordance with the terms of the contract, he is entitled to demand payment of the price unless otherwise agreed.[13] Furthermore, the buyer must accept the goods. Failure to accept the goods gives rise to a right to sue for non-acceptance.[14] Finally, with delivery, the loss of possession by the seller terminates his lien over the goods as security for payment of the price.[15] On the other hand, where the seller fails to deliver the goods in accordance with the terms of the contract, he is in breach of contract. The buyer can sue for damages for non-delivery and, if the price has been pre-paid, claim a refund of the price on a restitutionary basis. Where there is a contract for the sale of specific goods which are unique, the buyer may claim specific performance of the contract, though in commercial contracts an order for specific performance is rarely made.[16]

10 Unless, of course, performance is excused under ss.6–7 of the 1893 Act: see 18.3.

11 1893 Act, s.62.

12 See Chapters 17 and 18.

13 See 11.1.1. A seller may not be able to sue for the price at this stage under s.49 of the 1893 Act though: see 15.2.1.

14 See 15.2.2.

15 See 15.3.1.

16 See 14.5.

11.2.1 Modes of delivery

The voluntary transfer of possession from one party to another, or delivery, can be effected in two ways: by actual delivery or constructive delivery.[17] "Actual delivery" involves the physical transfer of possession of the goods, whether by the seller sending the goods to the buyer, or the buyer taking possession of the goods from the seller.[18] "Constructive delivery" is concerned with the transfer of *control* over the goods, without the physical transfer of possession. Where the buyer already has the goods in his possession, as a bailee for instance, physical delivery is not necessary under the contract of sale. Here the buyer, by continuing in possession in his own right as buyer, and not as a bailee, notionally takes delivery. Or, where goods are represented by a document of title, such as a bill of lading covering goods at sea, the transfer of the document of title from seller to buyer, with the necessary intention, gives the buyer legal control over the goods, and so represents constructive delivery of the goods.[19] A third example concerns attornment.[20] Here the goods may be in the physical possession of the seller or a third party. If the person in possession acknowledges that he holds the goods for the buyer rather than for himself, he is said to *attorn* to the buyer. The effect of such an attornment is to put the buyer in constructive possession of the goods, with the person in physical possession of the goods acting as bailee on the buyer's behalf.[21] Finally, section 32(1) of the 1893 Act provides that where under the contract of sale the seller is authorised or required to send the goods to the buyer, delivery to a carrier, whether named by the buyer or not, for that purpose, *prima facie* constitutes constructive delivery to the buyer.[22]

11.2.2 Place of delivery

Unless the parties have agreed otherwise, the place of delivery is the seller's place of business if he has one, or if not, his residence.[23] So, unless otherwise agreed in the sales contract, a seller is under no obligation to transport the goods to the buyer. It is up to the buyer to take possession of the goods from the seller, at the seller's premises. If, however, the contract of sale is for specific goods that the parties know at the time of the sale to

---

17 See 3.4.2.

18 1893 Act, s.29(1) provides that it is a question depending on the terms of the contract whether the seller should send, or the buyer take possession of, the goods.

19 1893 Act, s.29(3).

20 See 3.4.4.

21 1893 Act, s.29(3).

22 This section is particularly important in relation to international sales contracts: see generally Chapter 30.

23 1893 Act, s.29(1).

be in some other place, then that other place is the place of delivery.[24] In many contracts, there will be an express term as to the place of delivery. Under an *fob* contract,[25] for example, the place of delivery is at the ship's rail when the goods are being loaded. Each contract will need to be examined to determine the proper place of delivery.

As noted above, under section 32(1) of the 1893 Act, where under the contract of sale the seller is required to send the goods to the buyer, delivery to a carrier, whether named by the buyer or not, for the purpose of transmission to the buyer, is *prima facie* deemed to be delivery of the goods to the buyer.[26] If, on the other hand, the carrier is the seller's agent, delivery to the carrier does not constitute delivery to the buyer. Further, under section 32(2) of the 1893 Act, unless otherwise authorised by the buyer, the seller is required to make a reasonable contract with the carrier on behalf of the buyer. If the seller fails to do so and the goods are damaged in transit, the buyer may decline to treat delivery to the carrier as delivery to himself and he can hold the seller responsible in damages.

A seller will frequently require the buyer, or someone with authority from the buyer, to sign a form acknowledging delivery, often called a delivery note. This note acts as a factual record that the goods were delivered and also can have legal implications for the remedies available to a buyer where it later transpires that the delivery is defective.[27]

11.2.3 Cost of delivery

All expenses of and incidental to putting the goods in a deliverable state[28] are borne by the seller, unless otherwise agreed.[29] But the legislation does not contain rules as to the expense of delivery itself. At common law, however, the expenses of and incidental to making delivery fall on the seller, and any expenses in relation to preparing for or receiving delivery fall on the buyer.[30] This rule can be varied by the parties, such as in contracts on *cif*,[31] *fob*, or "ex works" terms.[32]

---

24 *Ibid.*

25 A"free on board" contract, a type of international sales contract, see further 29.4.3 and 30.2.

26 See also 1893 Act, s.18, rule 5(2) on the passing of property in such circumstances; see further 17.4.2.2.

27 See 14.2.1.1.

28 Goods are in a "deliverable state" when they are in such a state that the buyer would under the contract be bound to take delivery of them: 1893 Act, s.62(4).

29 1983 Act, s.29(5).

30 *Benjamin's Sale of Goods* (London, Sweet & Maxwell, 5th ed., 1997) para 8–005.

31 "Cost, Insurance and Freight:" see further 29.4.3 and 30.3.

32 "Ex works" means the seller delivers when he places the goods at the disposal of the buyer at the seller's premises: see 29.4.3.

11.2.4 Time of delivery

As noted above, the time for delivery and the time for payment are often separated. The time of delivery can be expressed to be for a specific time, such as "8 a.m., next Monday," or, more usually, a time period within which delivery is to be made "during working hours, between 1 May and 7 May, this year." If the seller is obliged under the contract to send the goods to the buyer and no time is fixed, the seller is required to send them within a reasonable time.[33] Otherwise, if no time is fixed, a court would usually imply that the goods should be delivered within a reasonable time.[34] What is reasonable will depend on the circumstances of the case. A reasonable time for the delivery of perishable goods, will certainly be much shorter than a reasonable time for the delivery of durable goods. Moreover, a demand for or tender of delivery is only effective if made at a reasonable hour.[35]

11.2.4.1 Effect of late delivery

Late delivery can occur in two instances. There will be late delivery where: (i) a time for delivery is fixed (whether an exact time or a time period) and delivery occurs anytime beyond or outside that time; or (ii) where no time for delivery is fixed and the goods are not delivered within a reasonable time.

If goods are delivered late, the seller is in breach of contract and the buyer can sue for damages. However, if the duty to deliver at or within a specific time is classified as a condition, time is said to be "of the essence" and late delivery entitles the buyer to reject the goods, terminate the contract and sue the seller for damages, even if the delay is slight. Under section 10(1) of the 1893 Act, whether the time for delivery is "of the essence" or merely a warranty depends on the terms of the contract. However, it has been held that in ordinary commercial contracts for the sale of goods, the time for delivery is *prima facie* of the essence.[36] This is a presumptive rule that can be rebutted. It is also important to note that this rule is stated to apply to "ordinary commercial contracts" and not, for instance, to consumer contracts. Thus late delivery will generally allow a commercial buyer to terminate the contract, refuse to accept the goods, that is, reject the goods, and sue for damages, but under section 11(1) of the 1893 Act an innocent party may elect to treat the breach of a condition as a breach of warranty. So, rather than terminate the contract and reject the goods, the buyer may accept a late delivery of the goods in order to

33 1893 Act, s.29(2).

34 *Hick v. Raymond and Reid* [1893] A.C. 22.

35 1893 Act, s.29(4).

36 *Hartley v. Hymans* [1920] K.B. 475, per McCardie J. at 483–4.

preserve a good trading relationship, or because of a scarcity of the goods in the market, or because he bought the goods at a competitive price. In these circumstances, the buyer can still maintain an action for damages for late delivery if he so wishes.[37]

This strict rule, that stipulations as to time in commercial sale of goods contracts are conditions, is justified in that it provides certainty as to the parties' rights and obligations and hence facilitates trade. This is especially so in relation to "string transactions" where there is a series of sales contracts of the same goods, where the proper performance of each contract is dependent on the proper performance of the contract before it. Such "string" transactions are particularly common in large-scale commodity markets, such as the oil and grain trades. If an earlier delivery in the string of transactions is late, the risk is that all subsequent deliveries may be late also. Conversely, the time for payment is not generally of the essence.[38]

Where time is of the essence, the buyer may lose, or waive, his right to terminate the contract for late delivery by acting in such a manner as to lead the seller to believe that he intends to continue to perform the contract. This is what happened in the case of *Hartley v. Hymans*[39] where the contract was for the sale of yarn to be delivered between September and November 15. In fact, deliveries did not commence until late October and did not cease until March 13. All during this time, the buyer pressed the seller for delivery, until March 13, when the buyer wrote to the seller terminating the contract on the grounds of late delivery. The court found that the buyer was in breach of contract by terminating the contract. In pressing for delivery until March 13, he had waived his right to insist on prompt delivery.

A buyer who has waived the right to prompt delivery may set a new delivery date and make time of the essence afresh by giving reasonable notice. In *Charles Rickards v. Oppenhaim*,[40] under the sales contract a car chassis was to be built and delivered by March 20. It was not delivered in time but the buyer continued to press for delivery until June 29 at which point he gave notice to the seller that he would not accept delivery if it was not made within four weeks. Delivery was not made until October at which time the buyer refused to accept it. The Court of Appeal found that in giving the notice he had made time "of the essence" and was therefore entitled to reject the goods.

37 See 14.3.2.
38 1893 Act, s.10(1).
39 [1920] K.B. 475.
40 [1950] 1 K.B. 616.

11.2.5 Amount of delivery

Section 30 of the 1893 Act sets out details of the amount to be delivered and what happens if the wrong quantity is delivered. Essentially, unless the seller delivers the exact amount, barring minute differences under the *de minimis* doctrine, the buyer can reject the goods and terminate the contract. In *Shipton Anderson & Co v. Weil Bros*,[41] an excess of 55lbs of wheat over an agreed limit of 4,950 tons (that is, 0.0005% excess) was found to be so slight that the buyer could not reject. However, it seems likely that the *de minimis* rule will be narrowly construed. Further, section 31 provides that, unless otherwise agreed, the buyer is not obliged to accept delivery of the goods by instalments.[42]

11.2.5.1 Effect of delivery of wrong quantity

The remedies under section 30 are default remedies and are stated to apply subject to any usage of trade, special agreement, or course of dealing between the parties.[43] Section 30 applies in three sets of circumstances. First, where the seller delivers a lesser quantity than that contracted for, the buyer is given two options. He may (i) reject the quantity of goods delivered, or (ii) accept the quantity of goods delivered and pay for them at the contract rate, that is, the price payable is reduced proportionately to the quantity delivered.[44] In either case, the buyer also has the right to sue for damages for the seller's breach for non-delivery. Where the price is pre-paid, he is entitled to a refund of the full price under option (i), or to a refund of part of the price equal to the undelivered amount under option (ii).

Second, where the seller delivers a greater quantity than that contracted for, the buyer is given three options. He may (i) accept the contract quantity and reject the rest; or (ii) reject the whole quantity, or (iii) accept the whole quantity delivered and pay for them at the contract rate, that is, the price will be increased in proportion to the amount delivered.[45] Again, the buyer may be able to claim damages for the seller's failure to deliver the correct quantity, but option (iii) is effectively an offer for a new contract, and where the buyer accepts the greater quantity, it appears that he is precluded from claiming damages for delivery of the wrong quantity.

Finally, where the seller delivers goods he contracted to sell mixed with goods of a different description, the buyer is given two options. He may (i) accept the goods which match the contract description and reject the rest;

41 [1912] 1 K.B. 574.
42 See further 14.2.2.2 on remedies regarding defective deliveries in instalment contracts.
43 1893 Act, s.30(4).
44 1893 Act, s.30(1).
45 1893 Act, s.30(2).

or (ii) reject the whole quantity delivered.[46] In this context, contract description has the same meaning as in section 13 of the 1893 Act and arguably, following English case law, is narrowly defined.[47]

The exercise of these options will often be influenced by fluctuations in the market price of the goods and the general availability of substitute goods in the market. Where, for example, the seller delivers a lesser quantity than that contracted for, and the price of the goods has fallen since the contract was made, the buyer would be better advised to reject the whole delivery and buy substitute goods at the lower market price. Where, on the other hand, the price of the goods has risen, or there is a scarcity of similar goods in the market, the buyer might be better advised to take the lesser quantity, paying for them at the contract rate.

There is no mention of the buyer being able to treat the contract as repudiated where the wrong quantity is delivered, so general contract principles would appear to apply here. Accordingly, where a seller delivers the wrong quantity, and the goods are rejected by the buyer, it would seem that he is entitled to make a subsequent delivery of the correct quantity, which the buyer would be bound to accept unless the time for delivery had expired.[48]

The combination of the default remedies, and a narrow *de minimis* rule, can operate harshly on sellers where deliveries are made and they are not of the quantity contracted for. These default rules are frequently modified by the express terms of the sales contract. Rather than requiring delivery of an exact quantity, sales contracts often describe the quantity to be delivered in approximate terms, for example, "about 100,000 litres of white spirits" or in terms of a range, for example, "between 100,000 and 105,000 litres of white spirits" or "100,000 litres of white spirits, plus or minus 5%." The effect of expressing the quantity in terms of a range avoids the harsh effects of the above rules and is often more practical. Another way of dealing with such variations of quantity is to include a price variation clause whereby the price can vary in line with the quantity delivered, although outer limits on the maximum and minimum amount to be delivered would need to be agreed. Even without such express clauses, in practice, rather than exercise their strict legal rights under section 30 of the 1893 Act, commercial buyers will frequently agree with the seller to adjust the price in line with the variation in quantity delivered.

In the United Kingdom, the Law Reform Commission expressed concerns that unscrupulous buyers were using the strict rules in section 30 to reject goods and avoid a bad bargain, even for minute variations in the

46 1893 Act, s.30(3).

47 *Ashington Piggeries Ltd. v. Christopher Hill Ltd* [1972] A.C. 441 (H.L.): see further 13.2.4.

48 See further Bradgate & White, "Rejection and Termination in Contracts for the Sale of Goods" in Birds, Bradgate & Villiers eds., *Termination of Contracts* (Chichester, Wiley Chancery, 1995).

quantity supplied.[49] In response, the Sale and Supply of Goods Act 1994 amended the Sale of Goods Act 1979 such that where a buyer does not deal as a consumer, he cannot reject the whole quantity delivered where the excess or shortfall is so slight that it would be unreasonable for him to do so.[50] The onus is placed on the seller to establish that the excess or shortfall is so slight that rejection would be unreasonable.[51] It is expected that this modification will operate more favourably to sellers than the common law *de minimis* doctrine and hence a similar reform would be welcomed in Ireland.

11.2.6 Exclusion of the delivery obligation

The remedies available under section 30 of the 1893 Act are stated to be subject to any special agreement.[52] Hence, these remedies can be taken away by special agreement in the form of an exclusion clause. The exclusion of liability for breach of the delivery obligation is governed by the common law generally and the E.C. (Unfair Terms in Consumer Contracts Regulations) 1995 and 2000.[53] Clauses which excuse the seller's liability for late delivery; or allow the seller to deliver a greater or lesser quantity than the contract quantity; *force majeure* clauses, which excuse a party from liability where he is unable to perform that contract due to circumstances beyond his control; or clauses which extend the time for performance in such a case, are generally enforceable against commercial buyers, at common law, if properly incorporated and properly drafted. But such clauses must be assessed in terms of fairness, and if unfair are unenforceable against consumer buyers under the 1995 and 2000 Regulations.

11.3 The Duty to Accept and Pay the Price

In return for the seller making delivery, the buyer must accept the goods and pay the price in accordance with the terms of the contract, under section 27 of the 1893 Act. Where the buyer fails to accept the goods and/or pay the price, the seller may be able to sue for the price, under section 49 of the 1893 Act, or for non-acceptance under section 50 of the 1893 Act.[54] A buyer also has a duty to take delivery of the goods. Failure to do so gives the seller remedies under section 37 of the 1893 Act.[55] A buyer

49 Law Commission Report No. 160, paras 6.17–6.23.
50 1979 Act, s.30(2A).
51 1979 Act, s.30(2B).
52 1893 Act, s.30(4).
53 See 2.3.5 and 10.5.3.
54 See further 15.2.1 and 15.2.2.
55 See 15.2.3.

may be under further obligations under the terms of the contract. In international sales contracts, in particular, a buyer may have to give notice of readiness, or nominate a ship to carry the goods, to enable to seller to perform his obligations under the sales contract.

11.3.1 Acceptance

Acceptance is used in different parts of the Sale of Goods Acts with different meanings. Acceptance is defined in sections 34 and 35 of the 1893 Act, as amended by the 1980 Act, in relation to the buyer exercising the right to reject.[56] There, subject to a right to examine the goods under section 34, the buyer is deemed to have accepted the goods if he:

(i) intimates acceptance;
(ii) does any act inconsistent with the ownership of the seller; or
(iii) retains the goods without intimating rejection, without good reason.

But the buyer's duty to accept the goods under section 27 does not seem to fit with this definition. Rather, the buyer's duty to accept under section 27 can be expressed more clearly in the negative: the buyer is under a duty not to wrongfully reject the goods. Where the buyer wrongfully rejects the goods, he is in breach of contract.

Accepting the goods and taking delivery appear to be two different things, though the exact scope of each obligation is unclear. A buyer may accept goods but later fail to take delivery of them, and vice versa. The Act does not impose a positive duty to take delivery of the goods but it does contain sanctions where there is a failure to take delivery. Where the buyer fails to take delivery of the goods following a request from the seller, within a reasonable time, he is liable to the seller for any loss caused by his neglect or refusal to take delivery, and also for a reasonable charge for the care and custody of the goods.[57]

11.3.2 Payment

The buyer's duty to pay must be exercised in accordance with the terms of the contract, under section 27. The essence of a sales contract is the transfer of property in the goods in return for the price, so this obligation is fundamental. The amount, method, place and time of payment will usually be agreed in the contract. Where no price is fixed, a reasonable sum

56 See 1893 Act s.11, see further 14.2.1; see also 1893 Act s.4 and see further 9.2.1.1.
57 1893 Act, s.37.

is payable.[58] Although where no price is fixed, this may indicate that the parties have not concluded a binding contract. Normally, the buyer is bound to pay the full price unless a discount is agreed. The contract may allow a discount for early payment of the price or require interest at a specified rate to be paid for the late payment of the price. As a general rule, the payment of a lesser sum will not discharge the buyer's obligation to pay the balance, even if accepted in full settlement by the seller, because there will be no consideration for the seller's promise to forgo the residue of the debt.[59] But payment of a lesser sum, at a different time or place, or by a different method if made for the benefit of the seller will provide sufficient consideration, and discharge the debt.[60] Alternatively, the seller may be estopped from going back on his promise to forgo the residue under the doctrine of promissory estoppel.[61]

Unless otherwise agreed, the method of payment is cash, but contracts may provide for payment by negotiable instrument, such as by bill of exchange, cheque or promissory note, or by credit or debit card.[62] A contract should also define the place of payment. If this is not done, the general rule is that a debtor must seek out his creditor to make payment,[63] and payment will normally be due at the seller's place of business. Finally, as noted above, *cash on delivery* is the norm under section 28 of the 1893 Act, although in most commercial contracts this rule is displaced and the buyer is usually supplied the goods on credit terms. Even when a time for payment is fixed, and unlike the time for delivery, the time for payment is not deemed to be of the essence, unless a different intention appears from the contract.[64] So where payment is late, the seller may be able to claim interest[65] or damages for any losses caused by the late payment, but the seller cannot treat the contract as repudiated. However, the seller may be able to terminate the contract and resell the goods where:

(i) the goods are perishable; or
(ii) the seller gives the buyer notice that he intends to resell

58 1893 Act, s.8(2).

59 *Pinnel's Case* (1602) 5 Co Rep. 117a; *Foakes v. Beer* (1884) 9 App. Cas. 605. See further Clark, *Contract Law in Ireland* (Dublin, Round Hall Sweet & Maxwell, 4th ed., 1998) pp.58–60; Friel, *The Law of Contract* (Dublin, Round Hall Sweet & Maxwell, 2nd ed., 2000) pp.105–108.

60 *Ibid.*

61 See 2.2.2.3(v); see further Clark, *Contract Law in Ireland* (Dublin, Round Hall Sweet & Maxwell, 4th ed., 1998) pp.61–71; Friel, *The Law of Contract* (Dublin, Round Hall Sweet & Maxwell, 2nd ed., 2000) pp.122–130.

62 See generally Part IV.

63 *The Eider* [1893] P. 119.

64 1893 Act, s.10(1).

65 See further 21.2.1.

the goods and the buyer fails within a reasonable time to tender the price;[66] or

(iii) resale is authorised by the contract.[67]

Additionally, a seller can withhold delivery until the buyer is ready to pay,[68] and may exercise a lien over the goods until payment where he has possession of the goods.[69]

66 1893 Act, s.48(3): see further 15.3.3.

67 1893 Act, s.48(4): see further 15.3.3.

68 1893 Act, s.28.

69 1893 Act, s.41: see further 15.3.1.

CHAPTER 12

SELLER'S DUTIES I: IMPLIED TERMS AS TO TITLE

12.1 INTRODUCTION

The passing of property (title or ownership)[1] in the goods from the seller to the buyer is identified in the statutory definition as an essential ingredient in a sale of goods contract. But at common law, a seller's act of selling did not necessarily warrant that he had the right to sell.[2] Today, section 12 of the Sale of Goods Act 1893, as substituted by section 10 of the 1980 Act, implies various undertakings on the part of the seller as to title in contracts for the sale of goods.[3]

Section 12(1) implies one condition and two warranties. First, section 12(1)(a) implies a condition that the seller has the right to sell the goods, and in relation to an agreement to sell, that he will have the right to sell the goods at the time property is to pass.[4] Further, section 12(1)(b) implies a warranty that the goods are free and will remain free from any charge or encumbrance not disclosed to the buyer before the contract is made; and a second warranty that the buyer will enjoy quiet possession of the goods.[5]

Section 12(1) implies these undertakings "in every contract of sale, other than one to which subsection (2) applies." This provision is unique among the statutory implied terms with regard to its width of application. In contrast, section 13 of the 1893 Act applies only to sales by description;[6] while section 14 of the 1893 Act applies only to sales in the course of a business.[7] Again, unlike the other statutory implied terms, liability for breach of the section 12 undertakings can never be excluded.[8] Furthermore, the remedies for breach of these undertakings are more extensive than for the other implied terms.[9] As well as these legislative differences which set section 12 apart from the other implied terms, the courts tend to approach section 12 more strictly than the others.

1 See 12.1.1.
2 *Benjamin's Sale of Goods* (London, Sweet & Maxwell, 5th ed., 1997), para. 4-001.
3 Regarding hire-purchase arrangements, on implied terms as to title, see Consumer Credit Act 1995, ss.74 and 79.
4 See 12.2.
5 See 12.3.
6 See 13.2.
7 See 13.3 and 13.4.
8 See 12.4.
9 See 12.2.2

Section 12(2) allows the seller to limit the title he passes to the buyer under the contract of sale but requires disclosure to the buyer. Accordingly, where the sale is for a limited interest in goods, there is an implied warranty, under section 12(2)(a), that all charges or encumbrances known by the seller have been disclosed to the buyer before the contract is made, and there is an implied warranty under section 12(2)(b) that neither the seller, nor any third party, nor anyone claiming under them will disturb the quiet possession of the buyer. This provision would apply where a seller expressly or impliedly contracts to sell a limited title to goods. This provision would also apply, for instance, to sales by a sheriff who has seized goods in execution to satisfy a judgment debt,[10] or to sales by a landlord distraining on his tenant's goods[11] where the sheriff or landlord cannot be sure that the goods seized from a debtor or tenant are the debtor's/tenant's unencumbered property. Here, the buyer will get whatever title the debtor or tenant had to the goods. Again, where goods are found by a person and the owner cannot be traced, the person can sell his "finder's title" to the goods under this provision.[12]

In this chapter, we are interested in the various undertakings which make up the seller's duty to pass good title, in particular the right to sell under section 12(1); the remedies available where such undertakings are breached; and the rules on the exclusion of liability in relation to section 12.

12.1.1 The meaning of title

The words "property", "owner" and "title" are used in different provisions of the sales legislation without being fully defined. Strictly, they mean different things. "Property" is defined in section 62 of the 1893 Act to mean the general property in goods, and not merely a special property. A bailee, for example, could be described as having a special property, in that his property rights would extend to a right to possession of the goods but

10 The common law procedure *fieri facias*, is a method by which the sheriff or registrar of a county can seize a debtor's goods and have them sold, paying the proceeds to the judgment creditor, less the expenses of execution: see Dixon & Gilliland, *The Law Relating to Sheriffs in Ireland* (Dublin, 1888). The range of property subject to this procedure was extended by the Debtors (Ireland) Act 1840, s.20. However, under the Sale of Goods Act 1893, s.26(1) delivery to the sheriff of the *fieri facias* order shall not prejudice subsequent buyers in good faith for valuable consideration, unless they had notice of the *fieri facias* order. Hence the goods have to be actually seized by the sheriff to be bound by the order. See further R.S.C. 1986, Ord. 43; Forde, *Bankruptcy Law in Ireland* (Cork, Mercier Press, 1990) pp.14–17.

11 See Lyall, *Land Law in Ireland* (Dublin, Round Hall Sweet & Maxwell, 2nd ed., 2000) p.626; Wylie, *Landlord and Tenant* Law (Dublin, Butterworths, 2nd ed., 1998) para. 12.14–12.23; and Wylie, *Irish Land Law* (Dublin, Butterworths, 3rd ed., 1997) 17.064–17.066.

12 See Lyall, *Land Law in Ireland* (Dublin, Round Hall Sweet & Maxwell, 2nd ed., 2000) Chapter 2; Pearse & Mee, *Land Law* (Dublin, Round Hall Sweet & Maxwell, 2nd ed., 2000) pp.41–2; and Wylie, *Irish Land Law* (Dublin, Butterworths, 3rd ed., 1997) para. 4.022.

nothing more.[13] It has been suggested elsewhere[14] that "ownership" refers to the "absolute legal interest" in goods – the full collection of rights that can exist in relation to goods. Furthermore, when the legislation refers to "property", it refers to a title to absolute legal interest. As noted above, other, lesser qualities of title to goods can exist, such as possessory title which is based on a legal right to immediate possession of goods and nothing more. A person in possession of goods has title to them, possessory title, which can be sold, and the buyer will receive the same quality of title as the seller. Generally, a seller can transfer no better title than he holds.[15] Under section 12(1), the seller is required to transfer the best title to the goods, that is the absolute legal interest in the goods. Where the seller fails to do this, such that someone else has a better title than the buyer, the seller is in breach of contract.

12.2 The Right to Sell

The margin heading for section 12 refers to implied undertakings as to title, but the word "title" is only used in subsection (2) in relation to sales of limited interests in goods.[16] Section 12(1)(a) does not refer to the seller's title to the goods, nor does it require the seller to be "the owner" of the goods. Section 12(1)(a) simply requires that the seller has "the right to sell". Clearly, a thief does not have the right to sell goods that he has stolen and so he can be sued by a buyer for breach of section 12(1)(a), if he can be found. Where an owner authorises an agent to sell his goods, the agent has the right to sell, and the owner's title will be passed to the buyer.[17] However, it is arguable that, based on case law, where an owner of goods can be stopped by process of the law from selling the goods, he does not have the right to sell and is in breach of section 12(1)(a).[18] In *Niblett v. Confectioners' Materials Ltd*,[19] the defendant seller agreed to sell 3,000

13 See 3.4.5.

14 See Battersby, "A Reconsideration of 'Property' and 'Title' in the Sale of Goods Act" [2001] *Journal of Business Law* 1, and Battersby and Preston, "The Concepts of 'Property', 'Title' and 'Owner' used in the Sale of Goods Act 1893" (1972) 35 *Modern Law Review* 269. Cf. Ho, "Some Reflections on 'Property' and 'Title' in the Sale of Goods Act" (1997) 56 *Cambridge Law Journal* 571. See also Goode, "Ownership and Obligations in Commercial Transactions" (1987) 103 *Law Quarterly Review* 433.

15 See Chapter 19.

16 There may be an express term in the contract requiring that the seller be "the owner" of the goods being sold at the time the agreement is entered into, or some future time, such as delivery: see, *e.g. Barber v. NSW Bank* [1996] 1 All E.R. 906, [1996] 1 W.L.R. 641, (C.A.) where such an express term was identified as a condition.

17 See generally, Part II.

18 Ivamy, *Casebook on Sale of Goods* (London, Lloyd's of London Press, 4th ed., 1980) p.6.

19 [1921] 3 K.B. 387 (C.A.); see also *O'Reilly v. Fineman*, Ir. Jur. Rep. 36 and *The Irish Digest* 1939–1948 Col. 107.

cases of tinned condensed milk, to be shipped from New York to London, to the plaintiff buyer. When the goods arrived, one instalment of 1,000 cases were labeled, "Nissly". The well known Nestlé company obtained an undertaking from the seller not to deal further with any similar tins because it was admitted that any such dealing would infringe Nestlé's trademark. The plaintiff buyer, in order to deal with his tins, and avoid any potential problems with the Nestlé company, had to remove the labels from the tins, at considerable expense, and sell the goods for the best price obtainable. It was held by the Court of Appeal, that the buyer was entitled to damages because the seller did not have the right to sell the goods and so was in breach of the then section 12(1).[20]

Benjamin's Sale of Goods argues that this case does not lay down a general principle that a seller does not have the right to sell where the seller can be restrained from selling by process of the law.[21] According to the author, the words "right to sell the goods" mean that the seller has the power to vest full rights in the goods to the buyer, but the seller makes no promise about his own proprietary rights. For instance, where a seller without title sells goods in circumstances where the buyer acquires good title to the goods,[22] there would be no breach of section 12(1)(a). Similarly, the *ratio* of the *Niblett* case, according to the author, does not extend beyond the situation where the property rights which the seller purports to vest in the buyer are encumbered by a right vested in a third party, such as an intellectual property right, which affects the goods in the hands of the buyer.

The above assertion, from *Benjamin's Sale of Goods*, that there would be no breach of the right-to-sell condition under section 12, where a seller without title sells goods in circumstances where the buyer acquires good title to the goods under one or more of the exceptions to the *nemo dat* rule, must be questioned. There is no direct authority on this point though Atkin L.J. stated obiter in *Niblett v. Confectioners Materials Ltd*:[23] "It may be that the implied condition is not broken if the seller is able to pass to the purchaser a right to sell notwithstanding his own inability …" In contrast, Professor Goode argues that section 12 is breached in such a situation

20 It was further held, by Atkin L.J., that the seller was in breach of the warranty as to quiet possession under the then s.12(2) – see 12.3 below; and by Bankes and Atkin L.JJ., that the seller was in breach of the implied condition as to merchantable quality under s.14(2) – see 13.3.

21 *Benjamin's Sale of Goods* (London, Sweet & Maxwell, 5th ed., 1995), para 4-004.

22 Under any of the *nemo dat* exceptions, 1893 Act, ss.21–25; see further Chapter 19.

23 [1921] 3 K.B. 387 at 401. *Chitty on Contracts* (London, Sweet & Maxwell, 28th ed., 1999) Vol. 2, para. 43-061 also supports this viewpoint.

because, as against the true owner, the seller's disposition is unlawful, meaning that he has no right to sell.[24] This latter view is to be preferred. There is still a breach of the section 12 right-to-sell condition because the seller does not have the right to sell.

12.2.1 Timing

Section 12(1)(a) states that there is an implied condition on the part of the seller that in the case of a sale, the seller has the right to sell the goods, and in the case of an agreement to sell, he will have such right at the time when property is to pass. Therefore, a seller may be required to have the right to sell at two different times. First, where there is a sale, the seller must have the right to sell immediately, otherwise he will be in breach of section 12(1)(a). Second, where there is an *agreement to sell*, a seller who does not have the right to sell the goods when he concludes the sale agreement is not in breach of section 12(1)(a). Between the time of the agreement and the time for the passing of property under the contract, the seller must acquire the right to sell the goods. So, for example, a seller can contract to sell goods which he does not own, and provided that he acquires the right to sell them by buying the goods himself before property is due to pass under the first contract, he will not be in breach of section 12(1)(a).[25]

12.2.2 Remedies

The requirement to have the right to sell is identified in the legislation as a condition. Generally, where a condition is breached, the buyer may treat the contract as repudiated, reject the goods and sue for damages for any loss caused.[26] However, a buyer may lose the right to reject the goods where he is deemed to have accepted them under sections 34 and 35 of the 1893 Act.[27] Under section 35 a buyer will be deemed to have accepted goods where he (i) intimates acceptance; or (ii) does an act inconsistent with the ownership of the seller; or (iii) keeps the goods, without good and sufficient reason, without rejecting them. These standard rules on rejection and acceptance would appear not to apply to a breach of section 12. More particularly, where the breach consists of the seller's failure to pass good title to the goods sold, the buyer is *prima facie* entitled to recover the whole of the purchase price paid because of a total failure of consideration on the part of the seller.

24 See Goode, *Commercial Law* (London, Penguin, 2nd ed., 1995) p.298; *Atiyah's Sale of Goods* (Harlow, Pearson, 10th ed., 2001) p.104; Bradgate, *Commercial Law* (London, Butterworths, 3rd ed., 2000) p.358; see further *R v. Wheeler* (1991) 92 Cr. App. R. 279, and Brown, "The Scope of Section 12 and the Sale of Goods Act"(1992) 103 *Law Quarterly Review* 221.

25 See further 12.2.2 and the concept of "feeding title."

26 See generally, 10.4. On buyer's remedies see further Chapter 14.

27 See 14.2.1.

The leading case in this area is the English case of *Rowland v. Divall.*[28] There the defendant, S, bought a car, in good faith, from a thief, T, and resold it to the plaintiff, B1, a car-dealer, for £334. Two months later, the car-dealer, in turn, sold it on to a third party, B2, for £400.

O ⟶ T ⟶ S ⟶ B1 ⟶ B2

Another two months later, the police repossessed the car on behalf of the original owner, O. B1 returned the price of the car, £400, to B2, and then claimed £334 from S on the basis that there was a total failure of consideration because of the breach of section 12. S admitted liability for the breach but defended the claim by arguing that B1, and any subsequent buyers, obtained a benefit from the contract of four months' use of the car, and further, that B1 could not reject the car, because it had been repossessed by its owner. Despite these arguments, the Court of Appeal upheld B1's claim allowing a total refund of the price. The reasoning is not clear but it appears, in part, to be based on the notion that the whole object of a sale is to pass property and B1 did not get such property.[29] Further, the Court of Appeal held that because the breach had been so fundamental, there could be no acceptance in these circumstances. The rule in the legislation preventing rejection once the goods have been accepted[30] did not apply here because, according to Atkin L.J., the rule only applies to sales, and where no title is passed, as was the case here, the transaction is not a sale.[31]

This judgment seems unduly favourable to B1, who had use of the goods and yet was entitled to a full refund of the price. But it has been argued that the decision is fair because B1, as a car dealer, had no use for the car unless he had good title or property in the goods to enable him to resell the car.[32] Generally, this rule does seem to unjustly enrich a buyer by enabling him to claim a full refund of the price without account being taken of his use of the goods. Against this, such a buyer is always exposed to the risk of claims in conversion by the true owner,[33] and once the defect

28 [1923] 2 K.B. 500 (C.A.). Despite much criticism, see, *e.g. Benjamin's Sale of Goods* (London, Sweet & Maxwell, 5th ed., 1997) para 4–006; Goode, *Commercial Law* (London, Penguin, 2nd ed., 1995) p.223; *Atiyah's Sale of Goods* (Harlow, Pearson, 10th ed., 2001) pp.105–110, *Rowland v. Divall* was more recently approved, by the Court of Appeal, in *Barber v. NSW Bank* [1996] 1 All E.R. 906.

29 Atkin L.J. stated: " ... the buyer has not received any part of that which he contracted to receive – namely the property and right to possession – and, that being so, there has been a total failure of consideration;" [1923] 2 K.B. 500 at 507.

30 To be found in s.11(1)(c) of the original 1893 Act; see now s.11(3) of the 1893 Act, as substituted by s.10 of the 1980 Act.

31 Scrutton L.J. noted that B's inability to reject the car was a result of it being repossessed by the true owner and was therefore a direct consequence of the seller's breach.

32 See Treitel, *The Law of Contract* (London, Sweet & Maxwell, 10th ed., 1999) p.981.

33 See 19.1.1.

of title is discovered the buyer's title may be unmarketable. It has been suggested elsewhere that in claims under section 12, a buyer should be required to give credit to the seller for his use and enjoyment of the goods.[34] However, against this, it has been argued that there would be difficulties in assessing the value of such use. This argument is not particularly convincing. Courts, on a daily basis, place monetary valuations on a wide range of losses and injuries, and would appear sufficiently skilled to make such an assessment. More convincing perhaps is the argument which underlies the question: why should a seller who breached section 12 be paid by a buyer for the use of another party's goods?[35]

Rowland v. Divall was approved in Ireland in *United Dominion Trust (Ireland) Ltd v. Shannon Caravans Ltd.*[36] In this case, a third party bought a caravan from an English firm and took delivery of it but needed £3,300 to finance the purchase. The third party approached the plaintiff hire-purchase company (B) where he was told by a junior employee that the company could not provide hire-purchase financing for a purchase which had already taken place. The employee then devised a scam to get the money needed from the plaintiff company. The defendant, S, a dealer in caravans, agreed to purport to own the caravan and to supply it to the plaintiff finance house for £3,300. B then executed a hire-purchase agreement with the third party whereby the third party agreed to repay the plaintiff finance house by monthly instalments of £144.70, with an option to purchase for £2 at the end of the hire period. S, who did not profit from the transaction, immediately paid £3,300 to the third party, who used the money to complete the original purchase. The whole scheme was designed to finance the first sale. Difficulties arose when, after eight of the 36 monthly instalments due were paid, the third party became insolvent. The liquidator refused to make any further repayments or to deliver the caravan to the finance company because it was the property of the third party. B then discovered the true facts and turned to S to recover their loss: it sued for breach of section 12. In the High Court, in an action for consideration which had totally failed, B recovered £3,300 less the amount of instalments received from the third party. On appeal by S, the Supreme Court held that there was a breach of section 12 and a total failure of consideration. Moreover, B was entitled to a refund of £3,300 as S was not entitled to the benefit of the instalments paid by the third party.

As well as claiming a total refund of the purchase price, a buyer who has incurred further expenses may make a claim in damages. Where, for example, it transpires after several months that the seller of a car did not

---

34 See the U.K. Law Reform Committee 12th Report, *Transfer of Title to Chattels*, Cmnd. 2958 (1966); the U.K. Law Commission's Working Paper 85, *Sale and Supply of Goods* (1985) and the U.K. Department of Trade and Industry Report, *Transfer of Title: sections 21 to 26 of the Sale of Goods Act 1979* (1994).

35 See the U.K. Law Commission Report 160, *Sale and Supply of Goods* (1987).

36 [1976] I.R. 225 (S.C.).

have the right to sell it, the buyer, as well as reclaiming the price, may make a claim in damages for the cost of insurance, tax, maintenance, and even defending the action against the true owner.[37]

12.2.3 Feeding title

Even where there is a breach of section 12(1)(a), there is authority that the breach may be repaired by title being later fed through, provided that it is done before the buyer elects to treat the contract as repudiated and rejects the goods. In *Butterworth v. Kingsway Motors Ltd*,[38] the hirer, H, took goods, a car, on hire-purchase from the original owner, O. In breach of the hire-purchase agreement, H sold the car to A, before completing payments under the hire-purchase agreement. A resold the car to B, who resold it to the defendant, D, who resold it to the plaintiff, P, who used it for eleven months.

O ⟶ H ⟶ A ⟶ B ⟶ D ⟶ P

During this time, H continued to make the repayments under the hire-purchase agreement. However, eleven months after P bought the car, O repossessed it. P successfully recovered from D the price he had paid for the car. Eight days later, H made the last repayment under the hire-purchase agreement. It was held that when H made the last repayment, she acquired title and this title fed through to A and other subsequent purchasers. The court did not consider whether P would have succeeded had he made his claim after title was fed through, although Pearson J. did consider that it would be extraordinary if a buyer whose title had been fed in this manner could subsequently elect to treat the contract as repudiated and recover the purchase price.[39]

12.3 Free From Encumbrances and Quiet Possession

Section 12(1)(b) implies two further undertakings on the part of the seller. First, a warranty that the goods are free and will remain free until the time when property is to pass, from any charge or encumbrance not disclosed to the buyer before the contract is made. This provision is of little practical relevance. The rights of any person entitled to a charge or encumbrance

37 See, *e.g. Warman v. Southern Counties Car Finance Corpn Ltd* [1949] 2 K.B. 576, [1949] 1 All E.R. 711 (K.B.D.).

38 [1954] 2 All E.R. 694, [1954] 1 W.L.R. 1288. *Cf. West (HW) Ltd v. McBlain* [1950] N.I. 144 at 149 (K.B.D.).

39 *Cf. West (HW) Ltd v. McBlain* [1950] N.I. 144 for more literal reading of section 12.

over goods, such as a security interest in the goods, depends on them having possession of the goods. Without possession, the charge or encumbrance is equitable in nature, and would be overriden by a *bona fide* purchaser for value without notice of the charge or encumbrance.

Second, there is an implied warranty that the buyer will enjoy quiet possession of the goods except insofar as it may be disturbed by the owner or other person entitled to the benefit of any charge or encumbrance so disclosed.[40] For example, in *Rubicon Computer Systems Ltd v. United Paints Ltd*,[41] there was a contract to supply a computer system. Following installation and part-payment, a dispute arose. The supplier had installed a "time-lock," which when activated rendered the system unuseable. It was held, inter alia, that the supplier's installation of the "time-lock" constituted wrongful interference with the goods, and accordingly there was a breach of the buyer's right to quiet possession. Breach of this undertaking is not limited to physical interference with the goods. This part of the provision may overlap with section 12(1)(a). In *Niblett v. Confectioners' Materials Co. Ltd*, Atkin L.J. considered that the warranty as to quiet possession had been broken because the buyer had to strip off the labels before he could deal with the goods.

There will be a breach if the buyer is disturbed in possession by the wrongful acts of the seller, or any person claiming under him; or by the lawful acts of any other person, including the true owner.[42] However, there is authority that there will be no breach where the buyer's possession is disturbed by the wrongful acts of third parties,[43] although this is not expressed in the wording of the provision.

Unlike section 12(1)(a), the implied warranty as to quiet possession is a continuing warranty. This is illustrated by the English case, *Microbeads AC v. Vinhurst Road Markings Ltd*,[44] where a buyer was disturbed by a person who acquired a patent in relation to the goods, a road-marking machine, after they were sold to the buyer. There was no breach of the seller's right to sell because, at the relevant time, no such patent had been acquired and hence the seller did have the right to sell; but there was a breach of the warranty of quiet possession. Further, the buyer's right of action does not begin to run until he is disturbed, and under the Statute of Limitations 1957, he has six years from that time to pursue a section 12 action.[45]

40 Atkin L.J. in *Niblett v. Confectioners' Materials* [1921] 3 K.B. 387 at 403 states that: "Probably this warranty resembles the covenant for quiet enjoyment of real property by a vendor who conveys as benefical owner in being subject to certain limitations, and only purports to protect the purchaser against lawful acts of third persons and against breaches of the contract of sale and tortious acts of the vendor himself."

41 (2000) 2 T.C.L.R. 453.

42 *Mason v. Burningham* [1949] 2 K.B. 545 (C.A.).

43 *The Playa Larga* [1975] 1 W.L.R. 218 (C.A.).

44 [1975] 1 All E.R. 529, [1975] 1 W.L.R. 218 (C.A.).

45 Statute of Limitations 1957, s.11(1)(a) and (2)(a).

12.3.1 Timing

Unlike section 12(1)(a) where the requirement that the seller has a right to sell applies at different times, depending on whether the contract is a sale or an agreement to sell,[46] the implied warranties in section 12(1)(b) apply from the time of the contract, even with regard to an agreement to sell.

12.3.2 Remedies

The undertakings in section 12(1)(b) are warranties, breach of which gives rise to a right to claim damages[47] but not to reject the goods and treat the contract as repudiated.[48]

12.4 Exclusion of Liability

Section 55(3) of the 1893 Act, as substituted by section 22 of the 1980 Act, provides that any term exempting from all or any part of the provisions of section 12 shall be void. Therefore, no one can exclude or restrict the implied terms as to title regardless of whether the buyer is dealing as a consumer or not. In contrast with the rules on exclusion of liability in relation to the implied terms as to quality under sections 13–15 of the 1893 Act, a reasonable exclusion may be made where the buyer is not dealing as a consumer. This exclusionary rule in relation to section 12 illustrates the primacy, or fundamental nature, of section 12 amongst the implied terms. Of course, as noted above, section 12(1) does not apply where the sale is for a limited interest in the goods under section 12(2). Accordingly, the implied terms in section 12(1) can be effectively avoided where the seller sells a limited interest in goods and discloses this fact. As a result, there appears to be an inconsistency between section 12(2) and the rules on exclusion of liability under section 12 generally. The rules on the exclusion of liability for breach of the statutory implied terms, do not apply to international sale of goods contracts, as defined in section 61(6)(b) of the 1893 Act.[49]

---

46 See 13.2.1.

47 Under the Sale of Goods Act 1893, ss.53–54; see 14.3.

48 See generally 10.4.

49 See generally Chapter 29.

CHAPTER 13

SELLER'S DUTIES II: IMPLIED TERMS AS TO QUALITY

13.1 INTRODUCTION

As noted in earlier chapters, the core duties of the parties to a contract for the sale of goods are set down in section 27 of the Sale of Goods Act 1893. Section 27 provides that it is the seller's duty to deliver the goods, and the buyer's duty to accept and pay for the goods "in accordance with the terms of the contract of sale."[1] In this chapter, we are concerned with the seller's duty to deliver the goods in accordance with the statutory implied terms concerning the nature and quality of the goods supplied under a contract of sale. Where a seller fails to deliver goods in accordance with these terms, he will be in breach of contract. Moreover, because all the statutory implied terms in this area, bar one,[2] are classified as conditions of the contract, the buyer will be entitled to reject the goods, treat the contract as repudiated, and sue for damages for any resulting loss. These remedies place the buyer in a strong bargaining position. A buyer may waive his right to reject the goods and terminate the contract, and simply claim damages, or a buyer may lose his right to reject the goods if the buyer is deemed to have accepted them under sections 34 and 35 of the 1893 Act.[3] Of course, to be entitled to any of these remedies the buyer must prove that the loss sustained was *caused* by the seller's breach of contract,[4] and the loss must not be too remote from the breach.[5]

13.1.1 History of the implied terms

At common law, the basic principle of sales law was *caveat emptor* – let the buyer beware.[6] Generally, the seller did not impliedly warrant

1 See generally Chapter 10.

2 1980 Act, s.12; see further 13.8.

3 On buyer's remedies, see further Chapter 14.

4 See, *e.g. O'Regan v. Micro-Bio (Ireland) & Intervet* unreported, High Court, McMahon J., February 26, 1980 at pp.9–11 where a major issue was whether birds died because of the effect of being vaccinated with a defective vaccine or whether the birds were already infected with a disease before they were vaccinated. Expert evidence resolved the matter in favour of the plaintiff.

5 See generally 2.4.4.3(ii).

6 See Hamilton, "The Ancient Maxim Caveat Emptor" (1931) 40 *Yale Law Journal* 1133.

(promise) the quality of the goods he sold,[7] nor was he under a duty to disclose defects known to him.[8] Case law in relation to sale of goods, up to the seventeenth century, before the common law courts, concerned either breaches of express warranties, or actions in the tort of deceit. The later implication of terms into the sales contract as to the quality of the goods, and indeed, the seller's title to the goods,[9] was a slow and gradual process.[10]

The implied warranties of correspondence with description and sample in sales of unascertained goods were the first to be recognised at common law. Description here encapsulated not only identification in the modern narrow sense,[11] but also included quality and performance. At this time, a distinction was drawn between sales of specific goods and sales by description. With specific goods, the buyer was capable of examining the goods himself, or getting his own expert to examine the goods. As a result he was expected to rely on his own judgment to ensure that he got what he wanted. Such a sale did not attract an implied warranty, even as to latent defects – *caveat emptor*.[12] A buyer in these circumstances could ask the seller for an express warranty if he wanted the seller to undertake some responsibility in relation to the quality of the goods. In contrast, with sales by description, the buyer did not have any opportunity to examine the goods and the only means of ascertaining the quality of the goods was by reference to the contractual description by which they were sold. Hence, sales by description did attract an implied warranty of correspondence with description.[13]

In commercial sales, a further term was implied that they should be of merchantable quality under that description.[14] During the nineteenth century, the common law recognised that a buyer of goods expected them to meet a minimum standard of quality. As early as 1815, Lord Ellenborough stated, in relation to the sale of 12 bags of waste silk, that: "[t]he purchaser cannot be supposed to buy goods to lay them on a dunghill."[15] These expectations were given legal recognition when, even in

7 Co Litt 102, a; and no implied warranty as to quality as late as *Parkinson v. Lee* (1802) 2 East 314.

8 The common law was in stark contrast with the *lex mercatoria* on this point. The *lex mercatoria* required that the seller was under a strict duty of good faith, and if a seller sold goods to which he had no title, or, which were unmerchantable, the seller would be liable in damages to the buyer.

9 *Eichholz v. Bannister* (1864) 17 C.B.N.S. 708; *cf. Morley v. Attenborough* (1849) 3 Ex. 500. See generally Chapter 12.

10 See generally, Mitchell, "The Development of Quality Obligations in Sale of Goods"(2001) 117 *Law Quarterly Review* 645; and Goode, *Commercial Law* (London, Penguin, 2nd ed., 1995) Chapter 6, and pp.290–294.

11 See 13.2.4.

12 See, *e.g. Smith v. Hughes* (1871) L.R. 6 Q.B. 597.

13 See, *e.g. Jones v. Just* (1868) L.R. 3 Q.B. 197; see further Stoljar, "Conditions and Warranties on Sale" (1952) 15 *Modern Law Review* 425 at 434 for criticism of this judgment.

14 See, *e.g. Jones v. Bright* (1829) 5 Bing. 533.

15 *Gardiner v. Gray* (1815) 4 Camp. 144 at 145.

the absence of an express term about the quality of the goods being sold, the contract contained an implied term that the goods should be merchantable.

When goods were simple, supplied at local markets, and traded face to face, it was not unreasonable perhaps to place the burden on the buyer to ensure that he got what he wanted – *caveat emptor*. But with the industrial revolution in Great Britain, and developments in manufacturing and transportation, goods became more complex, and the market for goods expanded. Trading was often done at a distance. At this time also, sellers realised that it was in their commercial interest to promote the quality of their goods.[16]

When, in 1889, the Sale of Goods Bill was first presented to Parliament, this distinction between sales of specific goods and sales by description was intended to be preserved. However, following extensive amendment in Parliament, when the Sale of Goods Act was passed in 1894, the legislation deviated from the common law position in a number of respects, further eroding the principle *caveat emptor*. In particular, the distinction between the sale of specific goods and unascertained goods was not preserved. This allowed the courts to hold that a sale of specific goods could be by description,[17] and hence imported implied terms as to quality in sales of specific goods. Furthermore, the quality terms were elevated to the status of condition, rather than warranty.[18] In brief, the original 1893 Act provided, in section 13, that where there was a sale by description the goods had to correspond to that description. Section 14 only applied where the goods were sold by a seller who dealt in goods of that description. Section 14(1) required goods to be fit for the buyer's particular purpose, and section 14(2) required that where goods were bought by description they must be of merchantable quality. Otherwise, there was no implied warranty or condition as to the quality or fitness of the goods. Section 15 applied to sales by sample, requiring that the bulk correspond with the sample, that the buyer should have a right to inspect the goods, and that the goods should be merchantable. Finally, the above implied terms could be excluded by the agreement of the parties.

The widening of the phrase "sale by description" can be explained by reference to section 14(2) of the original 1893 Act, on merchantable quality, rather than section 13 on description. The merchantable quality

16 See Llewellyn, *Cases and Materials on the Law of Sales* (New York, Columbia Law School, 1929) 204.

17 See, *e.g. Varley v. Whipp* [1900] 1 Q.B. 513, where it was held that sale by description included the sale of a second-hand reaping machine (specific goods) that the buyer had not seen. Since that case, sale by description has been extended to circumstances where the goods have been seen and examined; see, *e.g. Grant v. Australian Knitting Mills Ltd* [1936] A.C. 85 (P.C.), where woollen underpants bought in a retail shop was a sale by description. See further 13.2.2.

18 See 10.4.

requirement only applied where goods were bought *by description* from a seller who dealt in goods of that description. Hence, to afford consumers greater protection under section 14(2), the phrase was extended to include the sale of specific goods. In *Grant v. Australian Knitting Mills Ltd*,[19] a consumer who bought woollen underpants and suffered severe dermatitis because there was excess sulphites, a chemical irritant, in the underpants which had not been washed out in the manufacturing process, would not have succeeded under section 14(2) without first finding that the sale was a sale by description.

13.1.2 The implied terms today

The Sale of Goods Act 1893, in its original form, governed Irish sales law for the majority of the last century. However, in the 1960s and 1970s, concerns were raised about the suitability of the 1893 Act to a modern society and economy. In particular, it was argued that the interests of consumers in sale transactions were not being protected.[20] In response to these concerns, the Sale of Goods and Supply of Services Act 1980 made some significant changes to the implied terms on quality and related areas. These changes were oriented more towards the consumer than commercial interests, and were similar to the provisions of the then new United Kingdom (U.K.) Sale of Goods Act 1979.[21] The implied conditions of correspondence with description under section 13, and sample under section 15, remained largely unchanged.[22] The application of section 14 was, it would seem, widened. Rather than section 14 applying only where goods were sold by a seller who deals in goods of that description, section 14 now applies where goods are sold in the course of a business.[23] In relation to merchantable quality in particular, the requirement that goods be bought by description, before the merchantable quality condition would

19 [1936] A.C. 85 (P.C.).

20 See Whincup, *Consumer Protection Law in America, Canada and Europe* (Dublin, National Prices Commission, Occasional Paper No. 9); National Consumer Advisory Council Report to Minister for Industry and Commerce (December 10, 1974) Chapters 1 and 2; and 309, Dáil Debates, Cols 1100–1106 (November 23, 1978).

21 The initial identical nature of English and Irish sales law (effectively from 1893–1973, though some minor changes started to appear from the 1950s), and the later similar nature of English and Irish sales law (1973 to date) has meant that English case law has always been a vital source of analysis and guidance for Irish courts.

22 New subsections (2) and (3) were included in section 13 to clarify that a sale could be a sale by description even though the goods are exposed for sale and selected by the buyer; and that the words on a label or other descriptive matter could form part of the description: see further 13.2.

23 See 13.3.1 and 13.4.1.

be implied, was dropped,[24] and merchantable quality was defined for the first time in section 14(3). The protection afforded by the implied terms was reinforced by the rules on the use of exclusion clauses which prohibited the seller from excluding liability for breach of the implied terms as to quality when the buyer was dealing as a consumer and, in other circumstances, allowed the seller to exclude or limit liability only where the exclusion was fair and reasonable.[25] It has been opined in the United Kingdom, with reference to their equivalent implied terms, that "it is now unrealistic to treat the basic principle of the law as *caveat emptor* rather than *caveat venditor*."[26] The same can be said of the Irish position.

Today, sections 13 and 14 of the Sale of Goods Act 1893, as substituted by section 10 of the Sale of Goods and Supply of Services Act 1980 imply three conditions relating broadly to the quality of goods supplied under a sale of goods contract. Section 15 of the 1893 Act, as substituted by section 10 of the 1980 Act, implies similar terms in contracts of sale by sample. Basically, section 13 requires that the goods supplied correspond with description; section 14(2) requires that the goods supplied are of merchantable quality; and section 14(4) requires that the goods supplied are fit for the buyer's particular purpose.[27]

Each provision offers the buyer greater protection than the one before; or, in other words, each provision places a heavier duty on the seller than the one before. For example, goods supplied may comply with their description under section 13, but they may still be unmerchantable under section 14(2).[28] And, goods may be merchantable under section 14(2) but

24 When in 1973 in the U.K., the condition of merchantability was no longer limited to sales by description, it was suggested that this might lead to a tendency to a narrower construction of s.13 in the future. Case law, such as *Ashington Piggeries Ltd v. Christopher Hill Ltd* [1972] A.C. 441 (H.L.) (see 13.2.4), supports this view.

25 Related areas of amendment included new implied terms on spare parts and after-sale services and motor vehicles (see 13.8 and 13.9); new rules on product guarantees (see Chapter 16); and changes to the buyer's remedies provisions allowing rejection of specific goods (old s.11(c) repealed), clarifying the buyer's right to examine before acceptance can be deemed; and clarification of deemed acceptance following retention of the goods (see generally Chapter 14).

26 *Atiyah's Sale of Goods* (Harlow, Pearson, 10th ed., 2001) p.138. See further Hedley, "Quality of Goods, Information and the Death of Contract" [2001] *Journal of Business Law* 114.

27 Terms, effectively identical to those implied by sections 13–15 of the 1893 Act, are implied into contracts of hire-purchase, and other hire agreements, with consumers, under the Consumer Credit Act 1995. Rules similar to those on exclusion of liability in sale of goods contracts also apply in relation to hire-purchase and other hire arrangements. These rules were originally introduced in Part III of the Sale of Goods and Supply of Services Act 1980, which amended the Hire-Purchase Acts 1946 and 1960. This legislation is now consolidated in Parts VI and VII of the Consumer Credit Act 1995, which apply only where the hirer is a consumer, as defined. Non-consumer hire-purchase and other hire agreements are governed by the common law.

28 Although these provision overlap and are progressive, they are also distinct. For example, it is possible for goods to be merchantable or fit for the buyer's particular purpose, and not to comply with description: see *Arcos Ltd v. E A Ronaasen & Son* [1933] A.C. 470 (H.L.); see further 13.2.4.

not fit for the buyer's particular purpose under section 14(4). However, the breadth of application narrows as you progress from section 13 to section 14. Where section 13 applies to all sales by description, section 14 only applies to sales in the course of a business. Hence, as you progress from section 13, through to sections 14(2) and 14(4), the provisions apply to a smaller number of sales but impose a higher standard of quality.[29]

These provisions are cumulative. They also overlap with each other such that the same circumstances may amount to a breach of two, or even all of the three provisions regarding the implied conditions. In practice, where the facts allow, a case is often pleaded as amounting to a breach of all three implied conditions: a belt-and-braces type argument. So long as the buyer succeeds in proving his claim under at least one of the implied terms, he will win the case. By pleading that all three conditions have been breached, a buyer can increase his chances of winning the case, in theory at least. Claims can also be brought at the same time for breach of an express term of the contract and/or misrepresentation.

13.2 Correspondence With Description

Section 13(1) of the 1893 Act provides that where there is a contract of sale by description, there is an implied condition that the goods shall comply with the description. This may seem like stating the obvious. It appears odd to state that it is an implied obligation of the contract to deliver goods matching the description, when such an obligation is surely an express obligation of the contract. This provision is best explained in its historical context,[30] and is not as straightforward as it appears.[31]

Compliance with description is particularly important in the sale of unascertained goods, in particular in a commercial context in relation to commodity sales where the buyer only has the description to rely on in order to ensure that he gets what he wants. In earlier case law, description included issues of quality and fitness.[32] Even today, an overlap exists between issues of quality and description because description is a factor relevant to merchantable quality under the statutory definition.[33] But today, more so than ever, description is interpreted narrowly, and, distinctly from issues of quality.[34]

29 For details see 13.2, 13.3 and 13.4.

30 See 13.1.1. See further *Atiyah's Sale of Goods* (Harlow, Pearson, 10th ed., 2001) pp.141–148.

31 It has been noted, with reference to s.13, that: "Conceptually this is one of the most troublesome provisions of the Act," see *Benjamin's Sale of Goods*, (London, Sweet & Maxwell, 5th ed., 1997) para 11-002. See also Goode, *Commercial Law* (London, Penguin, 2nd ed., 1995) p.303.

32 See 13.1.1

33 See 13.3.2.

34 See *Ashington Piggeries Ltd v. Christopher Hill Ltd* [1972] A.C. 441 (H.L.); see further 13.2.4.

13.2.1 Application

Unless excluded, section 13 applies to all sales whether the seller acts in the course of a business or otherwise. This contrasts with section 14 which applies only where the seller acts in the course of a business.[35] Therefore, where the seller acts in a private capacity (that is, not in the course of a business), section 13 is the buyer's main avenue of redress under the legislation.[36]

13.2.2 When is a sale a sale by description?

Clearly, where the goods being sold are not seen by the buyer, as is the case with sales of future or unascertained goods, there must be a description relied on by the buyer by which the goods can be identified and sold. So, a sale of future or unascertained goods will always be a sale by description.[37] But even where goods are seen by the buyer, there may be a sale by description.[38] The legislation provides that a sale shall not be prevented from being a sale by description because the goods are exposed for sale and selected by the customer.[39] Thus, sales from retail outlets where goods are packaged or labelled in some way and set out for display, such as in supermarkets, may be sales by description.[40]

In order for goods to be sold by description, the descriptive words must be influential in the sale. The circumstances must be such that the parties might reasonably expect the description to influence the buyer in his decision to buy the goods: an objective test. For instance, in *Egan v. McSweeney*,[41] the plaintiff purchased coal from the defendant for domestic use. When lit, some of the coal exploded causing injury. The plaintiff

---

35 See 13.3.1 and 13.4.1.

36 Further protection may be afforded by s.15 if the sale is a sale by sample. However, in practice, a person who sells by sample is unlikely to be a private seller, but would probably be dealing in the course of a business: see generally 13.5.

37 "The term 'sale of goods by description' must apply to all cases where the purchaser has not seen the goods, but is relying on the description alone .... The most usual application of that section no doubt is the case of unascertained goods ..." *Varley v. Whipp* [1900] 1 Q.B. 513 at 516 per Channel J.

38 Lord Wright in *Grant v. Australian Knitting Mills* Ltd [1936] A.C. 85 at 108 stated: "There is a sale by description even though the buyer is buying something displayed before him on the counter; a thing is sold by description, though it is specific, so long as it is sold not merely as a specific thing, but as a thing corresponding to a description, eg: woolen undergarments, a hot water bottle, a second hand reaping machine." See also *O'Connor v. Donnelly* [1944] Ir. Jur. Rep. 1 at 8, per Gavin Duffy J.

39 1893 Act, s.13(2).

40 The National Consumer Advisory Council had recommended that "sales by description should include self service sales": see Briefing Document in relation to the Sale of Goods and Supply of Services Act 1980.

41 (1956) 90 I.L.T.R. 40 (H.C.); see also *O'Connor v. Donnelly* [1944] Ir. Jur. Rep. 1 at 6; and *McDowell v. Sholedice* unreported, Supreme Court, July 31, 1969.

argued, *inter alia*, that there was a breach of the then section 14(2) of the 1893 Act, on merchantable quality, which only applied where goods were bought by description. Davitt P. found that this was a sale by description. He stated:

> "Whether it was made by word of mouth, or by means of a postcard, the plaintiff must have made known her requirements by describing them and by ordering two bags of coal. I think it is reasonably clear that what she wanted was coal and not coke, or turf, ...; and that she *relied* on her description to ensure that she got what she wanted."[42] [author's italics]

In the more recent English case of *Harlingdon and Leinster Enterprises Ltd v. Christopher Hull Fine Art Ltd*,[43] the importance of reliance was again highlighted.[44] There an oil painting, sold for £6,000 by the defendant art dealer, was described as being by Gabriele Münter, a German expressionist. This attribution was based on the painting's description in an art catalogue some years earlier. However, the seller emphasised that it had no expertise in this area of fine art and the seller appears to have made it clear that it considered that the buyer, who was also an art dealer, knew more about these matters than it did itself. The buyer had inspected the catalogue and the painting before the purchase. It was later discovered that the painting was a fake, worth about £50 to £100. The buyer sought to reject the goods on the basis that, inter alia, there was a breach of the implied condition as to description, under section 13(1) of the UK Sale of Goods Act 1979.[45] The majority of the Court of Appeal held, on the facts, that the parties could not reasonably have contemplated that the buyer was relying on the seller's attribution in view of the disclaimer by the seller and the relative expertise of the parties. Hence, the sale was not a sale by

---

42 (1956) 90 I.L.T.R. 40 at 41.

43 [1990] 1 All E.R. 737 (C.A.).

44 "The description must have a sufficient influence in the sale to become an essential term of the contract and the correlative of influence is reliance," per Nourse L.J., *ibid.* at 744. Although Nourse L.J. recognised that in theory a descriptive statement could be made a term of the contract without the buyer relying on it, he held that in practice the description could only have the necessary influence upon the sale if it was "within the reasonable contemplation of the parties that the buyer was relying on the description," *ibid.*, at 744.

45 For the purpose of this analysis, there is no difference between the U.K. provision and the Irish provision, on sales by description. The buyers also argued, unsuccessfully, breach of s.14(2) of the 1979 Act, on merchantable quality: see 13.3.2.3 and 13.3.2.4. Claims of this nature, it would seem, do not constitute mistake at common law. On mistakes as to quality, see Lord Atkin in *Bell v. Lever Brothers Ltd* [1932] A.C. 161 at 224, and *Leaf v. International Galleries* [1950] 2 K.B. 86. A claim for misrepresentation may be an option, although a claim based on breach of contract is usually to be preferred because of the difficulties of proving negligence or fraud in order to obtain more than the possibility of recission in equity. Damages for non-fraudulent misrepresentation may be available, but in lieu of recission and at the discretion of the court under the Sale of Goods and Supply of Services Act, s.45: see further 2.2.5.2(ii) and 2.3.1.

description. It has been suggested, following this case, that a seller could avoid liability under section 13 by simply disclaiming any knowledge or expertise as to the goods.[46] However, it should be noted that the contract in the *Harlingdon and Leinster* case was for the sale of fine art, an essentially speculative venture, and a similar disclaimer might not be effective in other circumstances.[47]

It can therefore be stated, as a general rule, that where descriptive words are used to refer to the goods being sold, and it is reasonable that the buyer would rely on those words, the sale will be a sale by description. In practice, the vast majority of sales will be sales by description. *Benjamin's Sale of Goods* gives an example of a sale not by description: "Specific goods may be sold as such ... where, though the goods are described, the description is not relied upon, as where the buyer buys the goods *such as they are*" [author's italics].[48] This statement was approved by Nourse L.J. in the *Harlingdon and Leinster case*.[49]

13.2.3 What words form part of the contractual description?

Case law makes clear that not every statement about the description, quality or fitness of the goods can be treated as a part of the contractual description. Some such statements may constitute mere representations, of no binding effect.[50] Even where a statement about the goods forms a part of the contract, it may not form part of the contractual description. It is not easy to predict what words or phrases will be construed as mere representation or terms of the contract, or ordinary terms of the contract or contractual words of description.[51] The legislation offers some assistance by providing that a reference to goods on a label or other descriptive matter accompanying the goods exposed for sale (such as a sales brochure, or other form of advertisement) may constitute or form part of a description. By way of illustration, the following have been held to form part of the description by which goods are sold: the date of shipment of goods,[52] a statement in a contract for the sale of 3,000 tins of fruit that the tins should

46 See Lawrenson "The Sale of Goods by Description - a Return to Caveat Emptor?" (1991) 54 *Modern Law Review* 122; see further Adams, "Consumer Sales" [1990] *Journal of Business Law* 433.

47 See Snaith, "A question of attribution" [1990] *New Law Journal* 1672; Hooley, "Sale by Description and Merchantable Quality" [1991] *Cambridge Law Journal* 33.

48 Benjamin's *Sale of Goods* (London, Sweet & Maxwell, 5th ed., 1997) para 11-011; see also Atiyah's *Sale of Goods* (Harlow, Pearson, 10th ed., 2001) p.149.

49 [1990] 1 All E.R. 737 at 744.

50 See 10.2.

51 1893 Act, s.13(3).

52 *Bowes v. Shand* (1877) 2 App. Cas. 455.

be packed in cases of 30 tins,[53] a statement in a contract for sale of wooden staves that the staves should be half an inch thick,[54] a statement as to the situation of goods,[55] and the markings on the goods.[56]

Conversely, in *Reardon Smith Line Ltd v. Yngvar Hansen-Tangen*,[57] Japanese shipbuilders contracted to charter a ship to the defendant, to be built to a detailed specification by the Osaka company, and known as Hull No. 354, until named. The defendant later sub-chartered the ship to the plaintiff, identifying the vessel as "Yard No. 354 at Osaka Zosen." The ship was in fact built elsewhere, under a different hull number. By the time the ship was built, the market had collapsed due to the oil crisis of 1974 and the charterer sought to reject the ship on the basis that it did not comply with its description. The House of Lords held that the words as to the identification of the vessel and the location of construction were of no legal significance.[58] Lord Wilberforce explained that the contractual description was concerned with words that identify "an essential part of the description of the goods."[59] In this case, the means of identification and the location of construction were not important to the parties, and hence, these did not form part of the contractual description of the goods.[60] Rather, the description of the goods was to be found in the specification.

Where there is a recognised trade description, goods should comply with the description in accordance with the standard generally accepted and applied in the trade.[61] For instance, in one case where there was a contract to supply safety goggles, there was no breach of contract when the seller supplied goggles made of "safety glass" that splintered in use. Safety glass had a technical meaning and did not guarantee that the goggles would be safe.[62]

Case law in this area must be treated with care. Each case must be looked at in the light of the language used and the surrounding circumstances. In particular, all the above cases are commercial in nature.

53 *Re Moore & Co Ltd and Landauer & Co's Arbitration* [1921] 2 K.B. 519 (C.A.): there was therefore a breach when the seller delivered the full quantity of tins but some were packed in cases of 24 tins. The buyer was entitled to reject the goods for breach of the implied condition as to description.

54 *Arcos Ltd v. E A Ronaasen & Son* [1933] A.C. 470.

55 *Macphearson Train & Co v. Howard Ross & Co* [1955] 1 W.K.L.R. 640.

56 *Smith Bros (Hull) Ltd v. Gosta Jacobsson & Co* [1961] 2 Lloyd's Rep. 522.

57 [1976] 3 All E.R. 570, [1976] 1 W.L.R. 989 (H.L.).

58 In other circumstances, such as where a particular shipyard has a good reputation, the location of construction might be of significance to the parties.

59 [1976] 3 All E.R. 570 at 577, [1976] 1 W.L.R. 989 at 999.

60 Further, because the shipbuilders had intended to build the ship at the particular yard identified, these words did not constitute a misrepresentation. In other circumstances, where a claim under s.13 of the 1893 Act is not possible, an action for misrepresentation may be available.

61 *Steels & Busks v. Bleecker Bik & Co* [1950] 1 Lloyd's Rep. 228.

62 *Grenfell v. Meyrowitz* [1936] 2 All E.R. 1313 (C.A.); see further 13.3.2.5 (i) on the issue of safety.

Older cases especially should be treated with caution. Modern case law has tended to adopt a more restrictive approach to identifying words of description. Accordingly, words "which were intended by the parties to identify the kind of goods to be supplied"[63] or which identify "an essential part of the description of the goods"[64] can be taken as part of the contract description.

13.2.4 What constitutes breach?

Once it is decided that a word or phrase forms part of the description by which the goods are sold, the goods must correspond exactly to that description, otherwise there will be a breach of the condition implied by section 13(1) enabling the buyer to reject the goods, terminate the contract and sue for damages.[65] It would seem that the more precise the contractual description of the goods, the more precisely they must correspond with the description. The issue of breach is a question of fact to be decided in each case. It should also be remembered that liability is strict and accordingly, the seller will be liable regardless of his responsibility for the breach.

Where the goods delivered are totally different from those contracted for, there is clearly a breach of contract.[66] However, in all other cases, it may be more difficult to decide whether goods correspond to their description or not. Since contractual description depends on the intentions of the parties, the test of compliance may be difficult to apply. Moreover, the parties may intend to describe the goods in broad terms or in minute detail. For instance, in *Ashington Piggeries Ltd v. Christopher Hill Ltd*,[67] Norwegian suppliers contracted to sell herring meal to buyers to be compounded and used as mink food. The meal supplied was treated with a preservative which reacted with the meal producing a toxin that made it fatal when fed to mink. The buyers argued that the meal supplied did not comply with its description. Four members of the House of Lords held that there was no breach of section 13 because the goods could still properly be described as "herring meal": contaminated herring meal is still herring meal; "herring meal" did not implicitly mean "non-toxic herring meal".

---

63 *Ashington Piggeries Ltd v. Christopher Hill Ltd* [1972] A.C. 441, per Lord Diplock at 503.

64 *Reardon Smith Line Ltd v. Hansen-Tangen*, [1976] 3 All E.R. 570, per Lord Wilberforce at 577.

65 On the doctrine of exact compliance, see 2.4.2.

66 For example, in *Fogarty v. Dickson* (1913) 47 I.L.T.R. 281 there was a breach of s.13 where winter wheat was supplied under a contract for "spring wheat;" and in *O'Connor v. McCowen & Sons Ltd* (1943) 77 I.L.T.R. 64, there was a breach of s.13 where there was a contract to sell turnip seed and cabbage seed was supplied. See further, *Chanter v. Hopkins* (1838) 4 Mee. & W. 399 at 404 where Lord Abinger C.B. stated: "if a man offers to buy peas of another, and he sends him beans, he does not perform his contract … the contract is to sell peas and if he sends him any thing else in their stead, it is a non-performance of it;" approved in *American Can Co v. Stewart* (1915) 50 I.L.T.R. 132.

67 [1972] A.C. 441 (H.L.).

Here the contamination was relevant to the issue of quality or fitness,[68] but it was made clear that not every statement about quality or fitness can be treated as part of the description. This case is notable for the narrow interpretation it gives to section 13 claims.

By way of example, courts have found a breach of section 13 where: Western Madras cotton was tendered for Long Staple Salem cotton,[69] a mixture of hemp and rape oil was tendered under a contract for foreign refined rape oil,[70] giant sainfoin was delivered under a contract for common English sainfoin seed,[71] winter wheat seed was supplied under a contract for the sale of spring wheat seed,[72] copra cake was contaminated with so large an admixture of caster bean as to render it poisonous,[73] meat and bone meal was contaminated with five per cent cocoa husks,[74] and a vaccine was sold under the description H-120 but was of greater potency than usual.[75] Again, it must be stressed that each case was decided on its own special facts.

Specifications which form part of the description are usually interpreted strictly. In *Arcos Ltd v. E A Ronaasen & Son*,[76] there was a sale of wooden staves, half an inch thick, for making cement barrels. In fact, only about five per cent of the goods conformed to this specification, with the remainder being not more than 9/16 of an inch thick. The goods were perfectly usable for making cement barrels and the court found that they were merchantable and reasonably fit for the purpose they were bought.[77] Nevertheless, the buyer was entitled to reject the goods because the court held that there was a breach of section 13. Lord Atkin stated:

> "If the written contract specifies conditions of weight, measurement and the like, those conditions must be complied with. A ton does not mean about a ton, or a yard about a yard. Still less when you descend to minute measurements does 1/2 inch mean about 1/2 inch. If the seller wants a margin he must and in my experience does stipulate for it …"
>
> No doubt there may be microscopic deviations which business men and therefore lawyers will ignore … But apart from this consideration the right

68 The buyer made a successful claim under s.14 of the 1893 Act: see further 13.4.2.

69 *Azemar v. Casella* (1867) L.R. 2 C.P. 677.

70 *Nichol v. Godts* (1854) 10 Exch. 191.

71 *Wallis Son & Wells v. Pratt & Haynes* [1911] A.C. 394 (H.L.).

72 *Fogarty v. Dickson* (1913) 47 I.L.T.R. 281.

73 *Pinnock Bros v. Lewis & Peat Ltd* [1923] 1 K.B. 690, where Roche J. described the goods as something "which could not properly be described as copra cake at all" at 697. Cf. *Ashington Piggeries Ltd v. Christopher Hill Ltd* [1972] A.C. 441.

74 *Robert A Munro & Co v. Meyer* [1930] 2 K.B. 312.

75 *O'Regan v. Micro-Bio (Ireland) & Intervet* unreported, High Court, McMahon J., February 26, 1980.

76 [1933] A.C. 470 (H.L.).

77 See 13.3.2.1 and 13.3.2.5 (ii).

> view is that the conditions of the contract must be strictly performed. If a condition is not performed the buyer has a right to reject.[78]

This case has been criticised on the basis that the goods were fit for their purpose and that the buyer's undenied reason for wanting to reject the goods was because the market price for such goods had fallen and they wanted to get out of a bad bargain.[79] Nevertheless, correspondence with description and fitness for purpose are two different concepts and should not be confused, and the strict application of the correspondence to description requirement can be justified, in the commercial context, on a number of grounds. First, it offers certainty and avoids any delays which would be caused by going to court to determine whether a deviation from the contract was significant or not. Second, in commodity sales, particularly at an international level, the goods are usually bought and re-sold, numerous times over, using the same description. If there is a dispute over conformity under the first contract, a court will not know what purpose the ultimate buyer has in mind for the goods and whether it is such as will entitle him to reject. Third, at an international level, sales contracts are frequently performed not by the parties themselves but by the respective banks whereby the goods are paid for against documents.[80] Banks in these circumstances are not to know whether goods that do not comply with the contract description are fit for their client's, or their client's sub-buyer's purposes. Hence, it is argued that the only workable rule in relation to correspondence with description is one of strict performance. Finally, the rule can be, and often is, contracted out of by using words of approximation. These same arguments cannot be applied blindly to the non-commercial context though.

Perhaps the real difficulty with section 13 in such circumstances, as has been noted elsewhere,[81] is that it is classified as a condition and consequently even a small deviation from the contractual description allows the buyer to reject the goods and terminate the contract. In the United Kingdom, under the Sale and Supply of Goods Act 1994 this position has changed, and a non-consumer buyer may no longer reject goods on the basis of a breach of the implied terms, including section 13, where the breach is so slight that rejection would be unreasonable. Barring microscopic deviations, which are excused under the *de minimis* doctrine,

---

78 [1933] A.C. 470 at 479–80

79 See, *e.g. Goode, Commercial Law* (London, Penguin, 2nd ed., 1995) pp.117–118. Similar criticism has been levelled at the decision in *Re Moore & Co Ltd and Landauer & Co's Arbitration* [1921] 2 K.B. 519: in *Reardon Smith Line Ltd v. Hansen-Tangen* [1976] 3 All E.R. 570, Lord Wilberforce stated that he found the decision in *Re Moore & Co Ltd and Landauer & Co's Arbitration* "excessively technical and due for fresh consideration by this House,"at 576.

80 See Chapter 32 on documentary credits.

81 See Bradgate, *Commercial Law* (London, Butterworths, 3rd ed., 2000) pp.275–276.

suppliers are therefore advised to contract for a variation in size, weight or other measurement of the goods delivered. Words of approximation, such as "about," "in or about", "approximately", or "plus or minus five per cent" can be used to avoid the harsh application of the strict compliance rule. Moreover, a price variation clause should be included in the supply contract to take account of any variations in delivery.[82]

13.2.4.1 False trade descriptions

False trade descriptions of goods are contrary to the provisions of the Merchandise Marks Act 1887[83] and constitute an offence under section 2 of the 1887 Act, as amended by the Consumer Information Act 1978. Further, section 17 of the 1887 Act, which appears to overlap with section 13 of the Sale of Goods Act 1893, provides that in a contract for the sale of goods to which a trade mark, or mark, or trade description has been applied, the seller shall be deemed to warrant[84] that the mark is genuine and not forged or falsely applied, or that the description is not a false trade description, as defined, unless the contrary is expressed in some writing signed by the seller and delivered at the time of the contract or sale to the purchaser. Hence, a person applying a false trade description may be criminally and civilly liable under the Merchandise Marks Act 1887, and also civilly liable under the Sale of Goods Acts 1893 and 1980. Breach of both pieces of legislation should be pleaded where possible.

13.2.5 Relationship between description and quality

As was seen above there can be a breach of section 13 on description and no breach of section 14 on quality,[85] and likewise there can be a breach of section 14 and no breach of section 13.[86] Hence, there is a conceptual difference between compliance with description and quality. In other circumstances though, there may be a breach of both sections 13 and 14

---

82 On problems with the variation of contracts see 2.2.2.3(iv).

83 This legislation was repealed in the U.K. by the Trade Descriptions Act 1968, although the repeal of s.17 of the 1887 Act was advised against by the final report of the Committee on Consumer Protection, Cmnd. 1781.

84 It is not clear from the legislation whether this "warranty" has the same meaning as under the Sale of Goods legislation, *i.e.* a minor term of the contract breach of which gives rise to a right to claim damages but not to terminate the contract, or whether it can be treated as a condition, thereby giving rise to the further right to reject the goods and terminate the contract, as is the case with s.13 of the 1893 Act. The latter construction would be preferable given the relationship between these two pieces of legislation on this point. A modern court could, of course, identify the promise implied in s.17 of the 1887 Act, as of innominate status: see generally 2.3.3 and 10.4.

85 *E.g. Arcos Ltd v. E A Ronaasen & Son* [1933] A.C. 470 (H.L.).

86 *E.g. Ashington Piggeries Ltd v. Christopher Hill Ltd* [1972] A.C. 441 (H.L.).

and so an overlap does exist. The application of these provisions also differs. Section 14 only applies where the seller sells in the course of a business,[87] and further, there are built-in exclusions of liability in relation to section 14 which have no application to section 13.[88]

The modern tendency, following *Ashington Piggeries Ltd v. Christopher Hill Ltd*, is to construe section 13 narrowly, leaving the issue of quality to be dealt with under section 14. However, the distinction between description and quality can be difficult to identify, depending on the circumstances. Where the defect relates to contamination, for instance, *Ashington Piggeries Ltd. v. Christopher Hill Ltd* suggests that contamination is a matter of quality, whereas previous case law supports the view that contamination can lead to non-compliance with description.[89] Arguably words of description may be phrased such that they comprise some element of quality, and in these circumstances the distinction between description and quality fades even more.[90] Ultimately, a buyer need only prove breach of any one of the implied conditions by the seller to have the full range of remedies available to him. Fine distinctions between matters of description and quality are of academic interest to the seller and buyer.

13.3 Merchantable Quality

Having stated the basic common law principle *caveat emptor* – let the buyer beware – in subsection (1), section 14 goes on to imply two conditions that protect the position of the buyer in relation to the quality of the goods supplied. The goods supplied must be: (i) of merchantable quality[91] and (ii) reasonably fit for the buyer's particular purpose.[92] These conditions effectively erode the principle *caveat emptor*, particularly where the buyer deals as a consumer where the conditions can never be excluded. Further to any express terms in the contract,[93] and the statutory

87 See 13.3.1.

88 See 13.3.1.

89 See *Pinnock Bros v. Lewis & Peat Ltd* [1923] 1 K.B. 690; and *Robert A Munro & Co v. Meyer* [1930] 2 K.B. 312; see further 13.2.4.

90 See, *e.g.* *Toepfer v. Warinco AG* [1978] 2 Lloyd's Rep. 569, "fine ground"soya meal.

91 See following text.

92 See 13.4.

93 Express terms as to description and quality are very common in commercial contracts, which may be standard form in nature, and less common, but not unusual, in consumer contracts: see generally, 2.3.2; see further, *e.g.* *Cotter v. Brewster* unreported, High Court, O'Donovan J., December 18, 1997. When drafting standard terms of trade it would be advisable to identify the terms as conditions, warranties or innominate terms.

implied terms, a term as to quality or fitness may also be implied by usage.[94]

Section 14(2) provides:

> "Where the seller sells goods in the course of a business there is an implied condition that the goods supplied under the contract are of merchantable quality, except that there is no such condition –
> (a) as regards defects specifically drawn to the buyer's attention before the contract is made; or
> (b) if the buyer examines the goods before the contract is made, as regards defects which that examination ought to have revealed."

13.3.1 Application

There are three issues concerning the application of section 14(2) of the 1893 Act.

13.3.1.1 In the course of a business

First, and unlike section 13, section 14 applies to sales "in the course of a business" only and hence not to sales in a private context. The status of the buyer is irrelevant for these purposes. This phrase is not defined in the legislation,[95] but it was interpreted for the first time recently by the Court of Appeal in *Stevenson v. Rogers*.[96] In this case, the defendant, a fisherman, sold his only boat, the *Jelle*, to another fisherman, and replaced it with another boat. The court was asked to rule, as a preliminary issue, whether the sale of the *Jelle* was "in the course of a business" and so whether the merchantable quality provision applied. Having examined the legislative history of the phrase and the relevant case law, the court opted for a broad interpretation of the phrase and found that the sale was "in the course of a

94 1893 Act, s.14(5). See, *e.g. Peter Darlington Partners Ltd v. Gosho Co Ltd* [1964] 1 Lloyd's Rep. 149, where canary seed was sold and according to the custom of the trade, the buyer was not entitled to reject the goods for impurities in the seed but was entitled to a reduction of the price.

95 "Business" is defined as including any profession and the activities of any state or local authority: 1980 Act. s.2(1),.

96 [1999] 1 All E.R. 613. See further Brown, "Sales of Goods in the Course of a Business" [1999] *Law Quarterly Review, 384*; de Lacy, "Selling in the Course of a Business under the Sale of Goods Act 1979" (1999) 62 *Modern Law Review* 776; Sealy, "When is a sale made 'in the course of a business'?" [1999] *Cambridge Law Journal* 176.

business."[97] This broad interpretation is in line with the interpretation of an identical phrase, used in the different context of the regulation of exclusion clauses, in the Irish cases *In re Henry O'Callaghan v. Hamilton Leasing (Ireland) Ltd and Access Refrigeration and Shop Fitting Ltd*,[98] and *Cunningham v. Woodchester Investments and Inter-call Ltd*.[99] Accordingly, goods may be sold in the course of a business even where the business is not normally involved in dealing in goods of the type, provided that the contract is made for the purpose of the business. So, for example, the sale by a solicitor of an old computer would be, following *Stevenson v. Rogers*, a sale in the course of a business and the implied terms in section 14 would place duties on the seller to ensure that the goods are of merchantable quality and fit for any particular purpose made known by the buyer.

Section 14 also applies where a sale is made by a person who, in the course of a business is acting as an agent for another,[100] as it applies to a sale by a principal in the course of a business, except where the agent's principal is not acting in the course of a business and either the buyer knows that fact or reasonable steps have been taken to bring this fact to the buyer's notice before the contract is made.[101] For example, where an auctioneer is engaged to act for a private seller, section 14 can be excluded where the auctioneer makes clear to the buyer that he is acting for a private seller. Otherwise, where a private person (a person not acting in the course of a business) sells goods to a commercial or a consumer buyer, *caveat emptor* applies.

13.3.1.2 Goods supplied

Second, the conditions implied in section 14 apply to the goods *supplied* under the contract, not merely the goods sold. Therefore, a defect in the packaging of the goods might render the goods unmerchantable, even if the

---

97 *Cf.* the narrow interpretations of the same phrase but in a different context in *Davies v. Sumner* [1984] 3 All E.R. 831, where the House of Lords held that a courier who sold the car he used in his business, was not selling the car in the course of a business for the purposes of the U.K. Trade Descriptions Act; and in *R & B Customs Brokers Ltd v. United Dominions Trust Co* [1988] 1 All E.R. 847, a case decided under the U.K. Unfair Contract Terms Act 1977, where the Court of Appeal held that a freight forwarding company which bought three cars over a period of five years was not acting in the course of a business when buying the cars. Both these cases can be distinguished from *Stevenson v. Rogers*: the former case concerned a criminal prosecution where the norm is to interpret such statutes restrictively; and the latter case involved determining whether the "buyer" was dealing as a consumer.

98 [1984] I.L.R.M. 146; see further 10.5.2.1.

99 Unreported, High Court, McWilliam J., November 16, 1984; see further 10.5.2.1.

100 Including an undisclosed principal in which case both principal and agent are liable for breach of the implied terms: *Boyter v. Thomson* [1995] 2 A.C. 628. See generally Chapter 6.

101 1893 Act, s.14(6).

packaging is returnable. In *Geddling v. Marsh,*[102] mineral water was sold to the plaintiff in a "returnable" bottle that was bailed to the plaintiff, that is, the bottle was not sold to the plaintiff.[103] The bottle burst and injured the plaintiff. The court held that the bottle was supplied under the sales contract and so the plaintiff could recover damages for breach of the merchantable quality requirement.

13.3.1.3 Built-in exemptions

Finally, as regards the application of the condition of merchantable quality, subsection (2) provides that the condition shall not apply in two circumstances. There is no implied condition as to merchantable quality where defects are disclosed in the sense of being specifically drawn to the buyer's attention before the contract is made. It has been suggested elsewhere that a seller would need to do more than include printed words in a written sales contract to satisfy this provision.[104] Personal intervention by the seller, or indeed any other person, drawing the buyer's notice to these printed words, would probably be required, and if a buyer undertakes to examine the goods before the contract is made, he loses the protection afforded by section 14(2) in relation to defects which that examination ought to have revealed. This provision only applies where an actual examination takes place. A buyer is not obliged to make any examination, but where an examination does occur, the seller will not be liable for any defects which *ought* to have been revealed by that examination, and not just for the defects actually revealed by the examination.[105] Where the examination is cursory, the buyer's right to complain about defects which a cursory examination could not reasonably be expected to reveal remains unaffected.[106] It would seem that the burden is on the seller to establish that either of these exemptions apply.

---

102 [1920] 1 K.B. 668; see further *Wilson v. Rickett, Cockerill & Co* [1954] 1 Q.B. 598 where Coalite sold included an explosive detonator. Even though there was nothing wrong with the Coalite, or even the detonator, the goods were found to be unmerchantable.

103 On bailment, see 3.4.5 and 9.3.3.

104 See *Atiyah's Sale of Goods* (Harlow, Pearson, 10th ed., 2001) p.163. Again, a sign nearby the goods being sold and stating that they are "shop-soiled" arguably would not satisfy this provision. Where a defect becomes known through course of dealings, see *Royal Business Machines v. Lorraine Corporation* 633 F. 2d 34, U.S. Ct. App. 7th Circuit (1980).

105 In *Thornett & Fehr v. Beers & Son* [1919] 1 K.B. 486, glue was being sold and the buyers were encouraged to open and inspect some barrels in which the glue was stored in the seller's warehouse. The buyers merely looked at the outside of the barrels before buying the glue. The buyers later claimed that the glue was unmerchantable but failed on the basis that they had examined the goods and so the implied term as to merchantable quality did not apply. This case was decided on a slightly different worded provision which refers to "defects which such examination ought to have revealed."

106 See *Godley v. Perry* [1960] 1 All E.R. 36 on 1893 Act, s.15.

13.3.2 Definition of merchantable quality

Quality in relation to goods is defined as including their state and condition.[107] Merchantable quality is defined in section 14(3) of the 1893 Act, a definition introduced by the Sale of Goods and Supply of Services Act 1980.[108] Section 14(3) states:

> "Goods are of merchantable quality if they are as fit for the purpose or purposes for which goods of that kind are commonly bought and as durable as is reasonable to expect having regard to any description applied to them, the price (if relevant) and all the other relevant circumstances ..."

As is common with the introduction of new legislative provisions, two important questions arise: has the law been changed, and how relevant is the earlier case law? Unfortunately, these questions remain unanswered in Ireland in relation to the definition of merchantable quality. When merchantable quality was first defined in the United Kingdom in 1973, there was conflicting case law as to whether the new definition represented a fresh beginning, without the need to refer to earlier case law,[109] or the earlier case law was still relevant to the meaning of merchantable quality.[110] While there is no Irish case law on this point, it seems that resort to the earlier case law will continue to be a feature of litigation in this area.[111]

There is, in fact, relatively little Irish case law on the detailed meaning of merchantable quality, as defined in the legislation. Hence, we have tended to rely on English case law for guidance in this regard. Care needs to be exercised, however, because the English and Irish definitions of merchantable quality, once introduced, never coincided. In particular, the

107 1893 Act, s.62. See further *Niblett v. Confectioners' Materials Ltd* [1921] 3 K.B. 387.

108 Before "merchantable quality" was defined in the U.K. in 1973, under the Sale of Goods (Implied Terms) Act 1973 and, in Ireland under the Sale of Goods and Supply of Services Act 1980, there was confusion in the case law as to the exact meaning of the phrase. There is authority to suggest that merchantable meant "usable" or "saleable," *i.e.* goods would be merchantable provided they would be used by a reasonable buyer for any purpose for which goods of that contract description were ordinarily used: arguably a commercially-orientated standard (see, *e.g. Jackson v. Rotax Motor & Cycle Co* [1910] 2 K.B. 937 (C.A.) and *BS Brown & Sons v. Craiks Ltd* [1970] 1 W.L.R. 752 (H.L.)). Alternatively, goods were merchantable where they were "acceptable" to a reasonable buyer, who was fully aware of all the facts including any hidden defects without any reduction of the price or other special terms: arguably a more consumer-orientated standard (see, *e.g. Henry Kendall & Sons v. William Lillico & Sons Ltd* [1969] 2 A.C. 31 (H.L.) per Lords Guest (at 108), Pearce (at 118), and Wilberforce (at 126). The statutory definition of merchantable quality in the U.K. was widely regarded as an amalgam of both tests: indeed, it is not clear how far the two tests differed.

109 See *Rogers v. Parish (Scarborough) Ltd* [1987] Q.B. 933 (C.A.).

110 See *Aswan Engineering Establishment Co. v. Lupdine Ltd* [1987] 1 All E.R. 135 (C.A.).

111 See further *Atiyah's Sale of Goods* (Harlow, Pearson, 10th ed., 2001) pp.158–159, and pp.167–172.

English definition of merchantable quality did not include an express reference to durability, whereas the Irish definition does. Furthermore, the change from a requirement of merchantable quality to a requirement of satisfactory quality (which does refer to durability, amongst a list of other factors) under section 14 of the United Kingdom Sale of Goods Act adds to this problem. To what extent will English case law on the meaning of satisfactory quality be of use in Ireland? The answer to this question will depend partly on whether, in English law, there is any real difference between merchantable and satisfactory quality,[112] and will need to take into account any initial differences between English and Irish law on the meaning of merchantable quality.

Despite the definition in section 14(3), the test of "merchantability" remains difficult to apply in many modern situations. A number of factors may be relevant, but it should be emphasised that each case will depend on its own facts. Case law also suggests that the courts may be applying the test of merchantable quality differently in "commercial" and "consumer" cases.[113] Considering the different contexts, this discriminatory approach can be justified.

Section 14(3) specifically mentions some factors to be taken into account in determining merchantability. However, it is clear that other factors may also be relevant. Merchantable quality has proved to be a flexible standard, and this partly explains its longevity. Goods can be of widely varying qualities, from relatively poor quality to top quality, and still be of merchantable quality, depending on the circumstances of the case and the application of a variety of factors. These factors are considered in more detail below.

13.3.2.1 Fitness for purpose or purposes

In *O'Regan & Sons Ltd v. Micro-Bio (Ireland) Ltd & Intervet Laboratories Ltd*,[114] the plaintiff company was in the business of rearing broiler chickens and it decided to vaccinate them against certain diseases. It bought a vaccine, Intervet H-120, and administered it according to the instructions. However, rather than immunising the chickens, an unusally high proportion of chickens died. Expert evidence was produced to the effect that this particular batch of vaccine was more potent than normal. The court found that the purpose of the goods was to vaccinate chickens, and

112 There is as yet only one reported first instance case on the meaning of satisfactory quality where the new provision was considered in any detail: in *Thain v. Anniesland Trade Centre* (1997) S.L.T. (Sh. Ct.) 102, the court referred to cases decided before 1994 as not "of much assistance." Subsequent cases have applied this new provision but without any discussion or analysis: see *Danka Rentals Ltd v. Xi Software* (1998) 17 Tr. L.R. 74; and *Albright & Wilson UK Ltd v. Biachem Ltd* [2000] All E.R. (D) 530 where pre-1973 cases were followed.

113 See 13.3.2.5 (ii).

114 Unreported, High Court, McMahon J., February 26, 1980.

that the evidence showed that the goods were not fit for this purpose. Hence the goods were unmerchantable.[115]

The question of fitness for purpose can be more complicated where goods have more than one common purpose. Section 14(3) requires goods to be fit for their *purpose or purposes*. Clearly, where goods have only one common purpose, the goods need only be fit for that one common purpose to be merchantable. But, where goods have more than one purpose, it is unclear from the statutory definition of merchantable quality whether the goods are merchantable when they are fit for any one common purpose, or whether they must be fit for all the purposes for which they are commonly bought. There is no Irish authority on this point. This question was addressed in the English case of *Aswan Engineering Establishment Co v. Lupdine Ltd*,[116] where it was held by the Court of Appeal that where goods have more than one common purpose they will be merchantable provided they are reasonably fit for any one of their common purposes. In this case, the plaintiff company bought waterproofing compound in plastic pails for export to Kuwait from the first defendant company. The first defendant, in turn, had bought the plastic pails from the second defendant. When the goods reached Kuwait, they were unloaded onto the quayside. The pails were stacked six high, and they remained there, in the intense heat, for a number of days. The plastic pails melted and the compound was lost. The plaintiff sued the first defendant and succeeded on grounds not specified in the report. The first defendant then claimed against the second defendant, *inter alia*, for breach of the implied condition as to merchantable quality. The court found that the pails were fit for most of the purposes for which they would be commonly bought, though they were unfit to be stacked six high in intense heat for a number of days. Therefore they were merchantable. This decision clearly favours the seller by placing the onus on the buyer to make known to the seller his purpose for buying the goods, thereby allowing the buyer to rely on section 14(4).[117] A prudent buyer will therefore (a) indicate the specific purpose for which he requires the goods, and, (b) include a term in the contract that the seller undertakes that the goods supplied are fit for *all* their common purposes so as to avoid the effects of the ruling in the *Aswan* case.

English law on this point has more recently been changed with the U.K. Sale and Supply of Goods Act 1994. This legislation amended the law in relation to implied terms and the remedy of rejection. In particular, goods must now be of *satisfactory quality*,[118] rather than merchantable quality,

115 The court also found a breach of ss.13(1) and 14(4).

116 [1987] 1 All E.R. 135. On this point there is no difference between the English statutory provision then in force and the current Irish legislation. See further *Sumner Permain & Co Ltd v. Webb & Co Ltd* [1922] 1 K.B. 55; and *Henry Kendall & Sons v. William Lillico & Sons Ltd* [1969] 2 A.C. 31.

117 See 13.4.

118 U.K. Sale of Goods Act 1979, s.14(2). See further *Thain v. Anniesland Trade Centre* (1997) S.L.T. (Sh. Ct.) 102.

and "fitness for all purposes for which goods of the kind in question are commonly supplied" is "in appropriate cases" an aspect of the quality of the goods.[119] It would seem that the intention behind this amendment was to reverse the decision in *Aswan*, such that a seller could not claim that goods were of satisfactory quality where they were fit for only one of their common purposes. However, this new legislation does not impose an absolute requirement that goods must be fit for all their common purposes. Arguably, goods which are fit for most of their common purposes but not for one particular common purpose may still be of satisfactory quality. This change goes some way to redress the balance in favour of buyers, following the *Aswan* case.

13.3.2.2 Durability

Goods, to be merchantable, must be reasonably durable, that is, in such a condition that they will remain fit for a reasonable time. An illustration of the requirement of durability can be found in the English case *Mash and Murrell v. Joseph I Emmanuel*[120] where sellers in Cyprus sold potatoes, c & f (cost and freight), bound for Liverpool. The potatoes, although sound when loaded, had deteriorated by the time the ship reached Liverpool. It was held that the goods were unmerchantable because the goods should have been loaded in "such a state that they could endure the normal journey and be in a merchantable condition on arrival."[121]

It should be noted, however, that the requirement that goods should be supplied in a reasonably durable condition relates to the time of supply.[122] If goods do break down or deteriorate earlier than would reasonably be expected, this may be evidence of a defect in the goods at the time of supply. If, however, it is shown that a breakdown or deterioration is due to some other factor, such as the way the goods are used by the buyer, rather than a defect present at the time of supply, the goods may not be unmerchantable. In order to avoid doubts and disputes, a buyer may expressly provide for durability by requiring the seller to give a product guarantee (sometimes called a warranty) covering the goods as regards certain defects, for an agreed period after delivery.[123]

13.3.2.3 Description

The description applied to goods will affect the standard that can be reasonably expected of them. For instance, a higher standard would be

119 U.K. Sale of Goods Act 1979, s.14(2B)(a).

120 [1961] 1 All E.R. 485, reversed by Court of Appeal on other grounds [1962] 1 W.L.R. 16n.

121 *Ibid.* at 488.

122 See 13.3.3.

123 See further Chapter 16.

expected from goods described as "brand new" or "deluxe," than those described as "second-hand", "seconds" or "shop-soiled".[124] In *Rogers v. Parish (Scarborough) Ltd*,[125] a buyer bought a "new Range Rover" for £16,000. The car suffered from a number of minor defects and was held to be unmerchantable. The Court of Appeal emphasised the importance of the descriptions "new" and "Range Rover:"

> "In the present case the car was sold as new. Deficiencies which might be acceptable in a second-hand vehicle were not to be expected in one purchased as new. Next, the description "Range Rover" would conjure up a particular set of expectations, not the same as those relating to an ordinary saloon car, as to the balance between performance, handling, comfort and resilience."[126]

It was further held in this case that the fact that the goods are repairable does not mean that the goods are merchantable.[127] Where, under a seller's or manufacturer's product guarantee, defective goods are replaced or repaired, this has no effect on the merchantability of the goods sold, as any rights under any such guarantees are additional to the buyer's statutory rights.[128]

It is not clear whether the reference to "description" in the definition of merchantable quality is a reference to all words of description, or merely to those words which form part of the contractual description, within the meaning of section 13. In *Harlingdon and Leinster Enterprises Ltd v. Christopher Hull Fine Art Ltd*,[129] the Court of Appeal, having decided that the sale was not a sale by description,[130] had to consider whether the court could take the "description" of the painting as by Münter into account in assessing merchantable quality. Nourse and Slade L.JJ. did not think it correct to take the description into account. To do so would be to give the description contractual effect which it was denied under section 13. While the point appears open in English law, there is a convincing argument that a non-contractual description should not be relevant in defining merchantable quality: otherwise, as has been stated elsewhere,[131] a mere

124 In *Bartlett v. Sidney Marcus Ltd* [1965] 2 All E.R. 753, for example, the plaintiff bought a second-hand car for £950. The dealers had informed the plaintiff that the clutch was defective, and they had offered to put it right and sell the car for £975. The defect was more serious than expected and cost £84 to be repaired. Nevertheless, the Court of Appeal held that the car was merchantable because it was sold as second-hand with a defective clutch.

125 [1987] Q.B. 933.

126 *Ibid*, per Mustill L.J. at 237. See also *Shine v. General Guarantee Corpn Ltd* [1988] 1 All E.R. 911 at 915 (C.A.); see further Brown, "Merchantable Quality and Consumer Expectations" (1988) 104 *Law Quarterly Review* 520.

127 *Cf. Millar of Falkirk v. Turpie* [1976] S.L.T. 66.

128 See generally Chapter 16. *Cf. Eurodynamics Ltd v. Automation Ltd* unreported, Queen's Bench Division, September 6, 1988 on computer software.

129 [1990] 1 All E.R. 737.

130 See 13.2.2.

131 See Hooley, "Sale by Description and Merchantable Quality" [1991] *Cambridge Law Journal* 33 at 35.

representation could become a condition of the contract by the back door. However, a closer reading of the provisions may suggest differently. It can be argued that the reference to "any description applied to" the goods, under section 14, is clearly wider than the description by which the goods are sold under section 13. Accordingly, in certain circumstances, such as a consumer sale where the manner in which the goods have been described and promoted may have a greater influence on the decision to buy, than in a commercial sale, it may be appropriate to take account of all descriptive words. Even in these circumstances, description is only one of the many factors relevant in assessing merchantable quality.

13.3.2.4 Price

While the adequacy of consideration is not relevant to the enforceability of a contract,[132] the price is relevant to the issue of merchantable quality. The same basic goods can be supplied for a wide range of prices: the higher the price, the greater the quality that can reasonably be expected. For example, in *Rogers v. Parish (Scarborough) Ltd*,[133] a car was bought for £16,000, whereas in *Bartlett v. Sidney Marcus Ltd*,[134] a car was bought at a "reduced price:" the standard of quality required in both these cases reflected this difference in price. However, where the purchase of goods is speculative in nature, price can be less useful as an indication of quality. In *Harlingdon and Leinster Enterprises Ltd v. Christopher Hull Fine Art Ltd*,[135] where a painting sold for £6,000 turned out to be a fake worth £50 to £100, it was held that the painting was of merchantable quality. Nourse L.J. found that the common purpose for buying a painting was aesthetic appreciation and possibly resale. He stated that "the question whether goods are reasonably fit for resale cannot depend on whether they can or cannot be resold without making a loss."[136] The painting could still be appreciated for what it was (rather than what it might have been) and it could be resold (although for £50 to £100) and hence it was merchantable.

A different approach to resale price seems to have been taken by Moriarty J. in *O'Donnell v. Truck Machinery Sales*.[137] The plaintiff sold machinery to the defendant who sued for the price in relation to some of the machinery supplied. The defendant counterclaimed, *inter alia*, that the machinery sold was in breach of sections 14(2) and 14(4) of the 1893 Act. Moriarty J. said he had little difficulty in finding no breach of these implied terms bearing in mind a number of factors, including "the relative prices

132 See 2.2.2.2.
133 [1987] Q.B. 933.
134 [1965] 2 All E.R. 753.
135 [1990] 1 All E.R. 737.
136 [1990] 1 All E.R. 737 at 745.
137 [1997] 1 I.L.R.M. 466 (H.C.).

obtained in resale in varying circumstances."[138] However, the cases can be distinguished. As noted above, *Harlingdon* involved the purchase of fine art, an essentially speculative venture where price and value are nebulous concepts. In contrast, *O'Donnell* involved the sale of machinery in respect of which price and value can more easily and accurately be assessed. In such circumstances, resale price may be of greater relevance in assessing merchantable quality.

13.3.2.5 Other relevant factors

The factors listed in the definition of merchantable quality – fitness for purpose, durability, description and price – are not exhaustive. Included in the definition is a catch-all phrase, whereby "all the other relevant circumstances" can be taken into account. The breadth of this phrase is illustrated in *O'Donnell v. Truck Machinery Sales*,[139] which involved the sale of mechanical shovels to the defendant company which was in the business of leasing and reselling heavy construction machinery. Moriarty J., in finding no breach of sections 14(2) and 14(4), stated:

> "it seems to me, construing the evidence in totality, … that given such factors as the relative prices obtained in resale in varying circumstances, the overall hire records, durability and income generated in favour of the [defendant] by those shovels which became part of the hire fleet, the relative incidence of repairs required and the apparent evaluation of the [shovels] in Ireland and other market places by other purchasers and users that neither term has been shown to be infringed."[140]

Two particular factors have been identified a number of times by case law, and in limited circumstances statute, as being relevant: safety; and what can be described as the non-functional factors of appearance and finish.

(i) Safety

Defects which render goods unsafe may be regarded as making them unmerchantable.[141] This factor has been emphasised in a number of English cases concerning motor cars. In *Bernstein v. Pamson Motors (Golders Green) Ltd*,[142] for example, a new Nissan Laurel car, bought for just under £8,000 seized up after three weeks and about 140 miles driving, due to a blob of sealant which blocked the oil supply. It was held that the car was

138 [1997] 1 I.L.R.M. 466 at 472–3.
139 [1997] 1 I.L.R.M. 466 (H.C.).
140 *Ibid*, at 473.
141 Safety is of course a key element under the Liability for Defective Products Act 1991, as amended. This legislation however is solely concerned with property damage and personal injury caused by defective products: see further 16.4.
142 [1987] 2 All E.R. 220; see further *Lee v. York Coach & Marine* [1977] R.T.R. 35.

unmerchantable. Though the defect was repairable, it had major consequences. The court emphasised the potentially disastrous consequences of the car seizing up while being driven at speed.

The safety of motor vehicles is addressed specifically in section 13 of the Sale of Goods and Supply of Services Act 1980. This provision implies a condition into every contract for the sale of motor vehicles[143] (except where the buyer is a person whose business it is to deal in motor vehicles) that at the time of delivery, it was free from any defect which would render it a danger to the public, including persons travelling in it.[144]

Although the legislation and case law has focused on safety in relation to motor vehicles, safety is clearly a factor in the consideration of merchantable quality in relation to all goods. In particular, safety will be an important factor in cases concerned with consumer goods.[145] Therefore, it is disappointing that safety is not expressly included in the general factors to be considered in assessing merchantable quality.

(ii) Minor and cosmetic defects

Goods that suffer from minor or cosmetic defects, what are sometimes called non-functional defects, may still be usable for their common purpose. Hence, it can be argued that because the goods are fit for their common purpose they are merchantable. In a commercial case, a court may be reluctant to hold goods unmerchantable, so as to allow the buyer to reject them, where the defect is minor. This was the finding in the English case of *Cehave v. Bremer*,[146] where it was held that a cargo of citrus pellets for cattle food that was overheated was "far from perfect." Nevertheless, the court found that the goods were merchantable as they could still be used for the buyer's purpose.[147]

In contrast, minor or cosmetic defects may be more important in the case of a consumer sale. For instance, in *Rogers v. Parish*,[148] the defects in a new Range Rover included misfiring, oil leaks, paint scratches and engine noise. These were categorised as minor by the Court of Appeal, but the car was nevertheless found to be unmerchantable. Mustill L.J. said that the purpose for which cars are bought would include:

143 For definition of "motor vehicle," see s.13(1).

144 See further 13.9.

145 On the safety of goods more generally see the Liability for Defective Products Act 1991; see further 16.4.

146 [1976] Q.B. 44; see also *Arcos Ltd v. E A Ronaasen & Son* [1933] A.C. 470.

147 Atiyah warns that it might be dangerous to read too much into this case because it was decided on its own peculiar facts and the merits of the case were all on the seller's side. For example, it emerged in court that the buyer, having sought to reject the cargo because it was unmerchantable, had arranged for an agent to purchase the same cargo, at a reduced price, for himself, and for the same use. See *Atiyah's Sale of Goods* (Harlow, Pearson, 10th ed., 2001) p.177.

148 [1987] Q.B. 933, [1987] 2 All E.R. 232 (C.A.).

> not merely the driver's purpose of driving the car from one place to another but of doing so with the appropriate degree of comfort, ease of handling and reliability and, one may add, pride in the vehicle's outward and interior appearance.[149]

Although there is no reported Irish case on the effect of minor or cosmetic defects in relation to merchantable quality, it is likely that an Irish court would be willing to take account of consumer expectations as to appearance, finish and freedom from minor defects.[150] Indeed, even in a commercial case, minor or cosmetic defects could render goods unmerchantable, especially if they were bought for resale rather than if they were bought as commodities or raw materials, which if defective would probably still have a commercial value.[151] But again, it is disappointing that factors such as freedom from minor defects, and appearance and finish, are not expressly included in the statutory definition of merchantable quality.[152]

13.3.3 Time for assessing merchantable quality

It seems most likely that the goods must be merchantable when the risk passes from the seller to the buyer: usually at delivery.[153] This was the finding in *Cordova Land Co. Ltd v. Victor Bros Inc.*,[154] where skins which were sold to be shipped from the United States to England, were found to

149 [1987] 2 All E.R. 232 at 237. In *Shine v. General Guarantee Corpn Ltd* [1988] 1 All E.R. 911 (C.A.), a car which had been submerged in water for 24 to 48 hours and hence was an insurance "write-off" was held by the Court of Appeal to be unmerchantable even though no specific defect or unroadworthiness was alleged. The decisive factor here seemed to be that a dealer gave evidence that if the full facts were revealed, the car would be worth £1,000 less than the price. Further in *Bernstein v. Pamson Motors (Golders Green) Ltd* [1987] 2 All E.R. 220, although the defect was minor, a blob of sealant in the lubrication system, and easily repairable, the consequences were very serious and hence the car was held to be unmerchantable. *Cf. Millars of Falkirk Ltd v. Turpie* [1976] S.L.T. 66 where a new car was sold with a leak in the power steering system. The defect would have cost £25 to repair and the seller offered to repair the leak, but the buyer refused the offer of repair and immediately sought to reject the car. The court found that the car was merchantable.

150 In *Marah v. Kellehers Ltd* unreported, High Court, Quirke J., December 3, 1998, see *Cork Examiner*, December 4, 1998, a defect in the paintwork of a car was held to constitute a breach of the implied condition as to merchantable quality.

151 See, *e.g. Jackson v. Rotax Motor & Cycle Co* [1910] 2 K.B. 937 (C.A.).

152 These factors are now included in the English definition of "satisfactory quality:" see s.14(2)(B)(b) and (c) of the U.K. Sale of Goods Act 1979.

153 *Benjamin's Sale of Goods* (London, Sweet & Maxwell, 5th ed., 1995) para 11-052. See further *Kendall v. Lillico* [1969] A.C. 31 (H.L.) where it was found that information as to repairability acquired after the sale and before the trial is also relevant to assessing merchantable quality. This case has been strongly criticised: see *Atiyah's Sale of Goods* (Harlow, Pearson, 10th ed., 2001) pp.139–140; Bradgate, *Commercial Law* (London, Butterworths, 3rd ed., 2000) p.296–7.

154 [1966] 1 W.L.R. 793.

be damaged on arrival. It was found that there could be no breach of the implied terms in the absence of evidence that the goods were defective at the time they were shipped.[155] Latent defects present at the time of delivery which manifest themselves after delivery may also render goods unmerchantable.[156] The fact that a defect in goods is not discoverable at the time of delivery does not prevent the goods from being unmerchantable. In *Bernstein v. Pamson Motors (Golders Green) Ltd*, it was stated that: "... the question of discoverability by itself [does not] affect the issue ... the question of whether a defect is latent or patent is immaterial."[157]

13.4 Fitness for Particular Purpose

Of all the implied terms in relation to quality, section 14(4) places the greatest burden on the seller. It states:

> "Where the seller sells goods in the course of a business and the buyer, expressly or by implication, makes known to the seller any particular purpose for which the goods are being bought, there is an implied condition that the goods supplied under the contract are reasonably fit for that purpose, whether or not that is the purpose for which such goods are commonly supplied, except where the circumstances show that the buyer does not rely, or that it is unreasonable for him to rely, on the seller's skill or judgement."

13.4.1 Application

As with section 14(2), the requirement that goods be fit for the particular purpose of the buyer, under section 14(4), applies only where the seller sells the goods *in the course of a business* and, it applies to goods *supplied* under the contract.[158]

13.4.2 Particular purpose

The reference to "particular" purpose means the purpose indicated by the buyer, rather than any special, or abnormal purpose. Where goods have only one purpose, this has been taken as the particular purpose. This broad interpretation has been pursued to protect the position of consumer buyers.

155 See also *Mash and Murrell v. Joseph I Emmanuel* [1961] 1 All E.R. 485, reversed by Court of Appeal on other grounds [1962] 1 W.L.R. 16n., where it was contemplated that the goods were to undergo a journey and it was held that the goods were not merchantable because they were not in such a state to endure the normal journey and be in a merchantable condition on arrival.

156 See 13.3.2.2.

157 [1987] 2 All E.R. 220 per Rougier J. at 226.

158 See 13.3.1.

For instance, food has been found to have the particular purpose of being eaten,[159] milk has been found to have the particular purpose of being drunk,[160] and a hot-water bottle has been found to have the particular purpose of being filled with hot water to warm a bed.[161] This broad interpretation of particular purpose is further supported by the words "whether or not that is the purpose for which such goods are commonly supplied." However, where goods are bought for their common or normal purpose, and this is found to be the buyer's particular purpose, the application of section 14(4) would appear to add little to the requirement that the goods should be of merchantable quality under section 14(2). In these circumstances, a buyer would be unlikely to succeed under section 14(4) if he could not establish a claim under section 14(2).[162]

The buyer's particular purpose can be made known expressly, by word of mouth or in writing, or impliedly. Where there has been a course of dealings between the same parties, the buyer may be held to have impliedly made his purpose known to the seller.[163]

The implied condition requires that the goods be reasonably fit for the purpose indicated by the buyer. This is therefore not an absolute standard, and in determining reasonable fitness, issues which are also relevant to merchantable quality, such as description and durability, may be relevant here.

Under section 14(4), goods must be *reasonably fit* for the particular purpose indicated by the buyer. The more precisely the buyer expresses his purpose, the more closely the goods must fit that purpose. Accordingly, a buyer should try to be as explicit as possible about the purpose for which the goods are being bought. However, case law suggests that courts may not always require buyers to be as explicit as possible, thereby placing a greater burden on sellers. For instance, in *Ashington Piggeries Ltd v. Christopher Hill Ltd*,[164] feeding compound was mixed by manufacturers to their buyers' formula. The feed contained herring meal sold to the manufacturers by Norwegian suppliers, which was contaminated by a toxic preservative, that proved fatal when fed to the buyer's mink. The manufacturers sued their suppliers for breach of the implied condition that goods must be fit for their particular purpose. Herring meal was commonly used as animal food and fertiliser. The Norwegian suppliers knew that the herring meal was to be used for animal feed, but not that it was to be used to feed mink. It was held that the manufacturers had sufficiently made

159 *Wallis v. Russell* [1902] 2 I.R. 585.

160 *Frost v. Aylesbury Dairy Co* [1905] 1 K.B. 609 (C.A.).

161 *Priest v. Last* [1903] 2 K.B. 148 (C.A.).

162 *Aswan Engineering Establishment Co. v. Lupdine Ltd* [1987] 1 All E.R. 135 per Nichols L.J. at 157.

163 *Manchester Liners Ltd v. Rea Ltd* [1922] 2 A.C. 74 (H.L.).

164 [1972] A.C. 441. See further *Henry Kendall & Sons v. William Lillico & Sons Ltd* [1969] 2 A.C. 31 (H.L.).

known the particular purpose for which the meal was bought. The making of mink food fell within the broader category of animal feed and was not an unforeseeable use. The toxin affected different species of animals in varying degrees, but was especially harmful to mink.

In contrast, in *Aswan Engineering Establishment Co. v. Lupdine Ltd*,[165] where pails were sold and used to store waterproofing compound which was lost when the pails were stacked six high in intense heat in Kuwait for several days, the Court of Appeal rejected the buyer's claim that the goods were not fit for their particular purpose.[166] Nicholls L.J. found that even if the particular purpose was "for export" this would not have been enough to find the sellers liable. Where the purpose is stated so broadly, section 14(4) adds little to the requirement of merchantable quality. Goods will be reasonably fit "for export" under section 14(4) if they are fit for export to most parts of the world. In order for the sellers to be liable under the facts in the *Aswan* case, the buyers would have to have stated their purpose more exactly, such as "for export to a hot climate," or "for export to Kuwait".

It would appear that there is no breach of section 14(4) where the failure of the goods to meet the particular purpose arises from an abnormal feature or idiosyncrasy not made known to the seller, either of the buyer, or in the circumstances of the use of the goods by the buyer. In *Slater v. Finning*,[167] the plaintiff owner of a fishing vessel, *Aquarius II*, wanted to upgrade the power of the engine, and accordingly the defendant installed a new camshaft. This proved unsatisfactory, causing excessive noise and wear and tear to parts of the camshaft. Two further replacement camshafts caused similar difficulties, and the plaintiff had to replace the whole engine with a different model. The plaintiff sued for breach of the implied term on fitness for particular purpose. It was accepted by both sides that the damage caused to the camshaft was caused by some unascertained force external to the engine and the camshafts themselves: an idiosyncratic feature of the vessel. Nevertheless, the plaintiff argued that he had made known the particular purpose for the camshafts, that is, to be installed in *Aquarius II*, idiosyncrasies included. The House of Lords rejected this notion that the defendant took the risk that *Aquarius II* might have unknown or unusual features and hence there was no breach of the relevant provision.

13.4.3 Reliance

Section 14(4) requires that (i) the buyer rely on the seller's skill and judgment and (ii) such reliance be reasonable. In many cases these

165 [1987] 1 All E.R. 135.

166 The claim for breach of merchantable quality also failed: see 13.3.2.1.

167 [1996] 3 W.L.R. 190. See further *Brady v. Cluxton* (1927) 61 I.L.T.R. 89 (H.C.); and *Griffiths v. Peter Conway Ltd* [1939] 1 All E.R. 685.

requirements will be satisfied easily: for instance, consumer buyers will generally be taken to rely on retailers;[168] and a person buying from a manufacturer will generally be taken to rely on the manufacturer.[169] Indeed, the provision, as amended in 1980, raises a presumption of reliance. So now, to avoid the application of section 14(4), the burden of proof is on the seller to show that the buyer did not rely, or that it was unreasonable for him to rely, on the seller's skill or judgment.

Difficulties may arise where goods are manufactured to a specification provided wholly or partly by the buyer. However, even in such a case, the buyer will rely on the seller to follow the specification, provide materials and actually manufacture the goods. In these circumstances, there may be a breach of the implied term if the finished article proves unfit for the buyer's purpose due to any defect within the area of the seller's responsibility. In the *Ashington Piggeries* case,[170] the buyers of the mink food gave the manufacturers/sellers detailed specifications as to how the mink food was to be compounded, but it was held that the buyers were entitled to rely on the manufacturers to ensure that the ingredients used would be fit for animal feed, including feeding to mink, which they were not.

In *Cammell Laird & Co Ltd v. Manganese Bronze & Brass Co. Ltd*,[171] the defendant agreed to build two ships' propellers for the plaintiff according to the plaintiff's specification. However, these specifications were silent on certain points, such as the thickness of the blades, and these matters were left to the defendant. One propeller was unsatisfactory due to defects in matters not covered by the specification. The House of Lords held that there was a breach of the implied condition as to fitness for particular purpose because "there was a substantial area outside the specification which was not covered by its directions and was therefore necessarily left to the skill and judgment of the seller."[172]

13.4.4 Time for assessing fitness

As with merchantability, it appears that the goods must be fit for the buyer's particular purpose when risk passes, usually on delivery. In *Viskasa Ltd v. Paul Kiefel GmbH*,[173] the Court of Appeal decided, for the purposes of the Brussels Convention on Jurisdiction and the Enforcement of Judgments in Civil and Commercial Matters 1968, that the obligations under a sales contract were performed at the time when the goods were supplied and therefore at the time of delivery. Where goods display defects

168 *Cf. Brady v. Cluxton* (1927) 61 I.L.T.R. 89 (H.C.).
169 *Henry Kendall & Sons v. William Lillico & Sons Ltd* [1969] 2 A.C. 31.
170 [1972] A.C. 441.
171 [1934] A.C. 402.
172 [1934] A.C. 402 at 414 per Lord Warrington.
173 [1999] 3 All E.R. 362.

within a shorter period of time than normal, this may evidence lack of fitness at delivery.

13.4.5 Relationship between merchantable quality and fitness for particular purpose

As noted above,[174] where goods have only one common purpose and they are bought for that common purpose, the implied conditions of merchantable quality and fitness for particular purpose will overlap. Where goods are not fit for their common purpose, buyers should plead a breach of sections 14(2) and 14(4). But where goods have more than one common purpose, as long as the goods are fit for one of their common purposes they will be merchantable, following the *Aswan* case, and only where the buyer makes known his particular purpose will he be able to plead breach of section 14(4).

Section 14(4) has no built-in exceptions, as section 14(2) has, in relation to defects specifically drawn to the buyer's attention or where the buyer examines the goods. But where a defect is drawn to the buyer's attention or where the buyer examines the goods, this may indicate that the buyer did not rely on the seller's skill and judgment, a necessary component of any section 14(4) claim.

13.5 Sale by Sample

Goods are frequently sold by reference to a sample. For example, in a commercial context, grain is usually bought on the basis that a sample of the grain is provided by the seller, for testing by the buyer. If the buyer is happy with the quality of the sample, he can buy the larger quantity by reference to the sample. In a consumer context, carpets are usually bought by reference to a sample. In both these examples, the buyer does not examine the actual goods being bought because it is more convenient to examine a sample. However, a sale is not a sale by sample simply because the buyer is shown a sample.

Section 15(1) provides that a sale is by sample where there is an express or implied term to that effect in the contract. Such express terms are more common in commercial sales. In general, it seems that in order for a contract of sale to be regarded as one by sample, the sample must be used to *define* the goods to be supplied.[175] There is no reason why a sale cannot

---

174 See 13.3.2.1 and 13.4.2.

175 A sale will be by sample where the sample "is to present to the eye the real meaning and intention of the parties with regard to the subject matter of the contract which, owing to the imperfections of language, it may be difficult or impossible to express in words. The sample speaks for itself:" per Lord MacNaghten in *Drummond v. Van Ingen* (1887) 12 App. Cas. 284 at 297 (H.L.).

be by sample and by description, in which case both sections 13 and 15 will apply.[176] Where a sample is provided to the buyer, the contract may therefore include a term making clear whether the sale is or is not a sale by sample within the meaning of the Act: for instance a provision that any sample provided is merely for the purposes of demonstration might prevent the sale being by sample.

Where goods are sold by sample, section 15 implies three conditions:

(i) that the bulk will correspond with the sample in quality;[177]
(ii) that the buyer will have a reasonable opportunity to compare the bulk with the sample,[178] and
(iii) that the goods will be free from any defect, rendering them unmerchantable, which would not be apparent on reasonable examination of the sample.[179]

These requirements largely mirror sections 13, 34 and 14(2) of the 1893 Act respectively and it would seem to add little to them.[180] However, section 15 is not limited like section 14, in that the seller does not have to be dealing in the course of a business. Further, where a sale is a sale by sample the rules on merchantable quality are different from those in ordinary sales. Under section 15(c), the condition implied is that the goods will be free from any defect which would not be apparent on reasonable examination of the sample, whether or not such examination was made.[181] Benjamin refers to this latter distinction as support for the proposition that purchases by consumers are less likely to be held to be sales by sample, because this rule would be inappropriate for consumers.[182] Indeed, most if not all of the case law in this area involves business sales.

13.6 Nature of Liability

Liability for breach of the implied terms in sections 13–15 of the 1893 Act is strict. This clearly favours the position of the buyer who does not have

176 1893 Act, s.13(1) provides that if the sale be by sample and by description, it is not sufficient that the bulk of the goods correspond with the sample if the goods do not correspond with the description.

177 See, *e.g. E & S Ruben Ltd v. Faire Bros & Co. Ltd* [1949] 1 All E.R. 215 where rubber was sold by sample for the manufacture of shoes. The sample was flat and soft while the goods delivered were crinkly and unsuitable for use in the buyer's machines. The court held that there was a breach of s.15 of the 1893 Act.

178 Normally this inspection will occur at the place of delivery, although the parties can agree otherwise: *Heilbutt v. Hickson* (1872) R. 7 C.P. 483. See further *Polenghi Bros v. Dried Milk Co. Ltd* (1904) 92 L.T. 64.

179 See, *e.g. Steel & Busks Ltd v. Bleecker Bik & Co Ltd* [1956] 1 Lloyd's Rep. 228 (Q.B.D.).

180 On s.34, see 14.2.1.

181 See, *e.g. Godley v. Perry* [1960] 1 All E.R. 36.

182 See further *Benjamin's Sale of Goods* (London, Sweet & Maxwell, 5th ed., 1997) para 11-092.

to prove fault or negligence on the part of the seller. Equally, it is no defence that the seller was unaware of the defect or that he took all reasonable care in relation to the goods. Where goods pass through a chain of supply from a manufacturer to a distributor to a retailer and finally to a consumer, it is the retailer/seller who will be liable, on the contract, to the consumer/buyer for any defects, even those caused by, say, the manufacturer. The doctrine of privity of contract limits a buyer's rights in such situations.[183]

A seller who is liable for breach of any of the implied terms as to quality may, in turn, have a claim for breach of the implied terms against his supplier, and so on up the chain of supply. However, the use of exclusion clauses which is permissible between a seller and a buyer who is not dealing as a consumer may mean that the full liability to the ultimate consumer cannot be passed back up the chain of supply. Moreover, this chain of liability may be broken where one of the parties becomes insolvent or cannot be located.

13.7 Exclusion of Liability

The implied terms in sections 13–15 of the 1893 Act cannot be excluded where the buyer deals as a consumer, and in other cases only a fair and reasonable exclusion is allowed.[184] In the commercial context, any attempt to reasonably exclude liability should use clear wording. For example, in *Robert A Munro & Co Ltd v. Meyer*,[185] the defendant agreed to buy goods "with all faults", but it was held by Wright J. that this clause did not excuse the seller for failure to supply goods which corresponded with their description, it merely protected the seller from the requirement to supply goods of merchantable quality.[186]

Moreover, a seller may seek to "exclude" liability under section 13, by preventing the sale from being a sale by description. In *Harlingdon and Leinster Enterprises Ltd v. Christopher Hull Fine Art Ltd*,[187] for example, the sale was not a sale by description because of the lack of reliance by the buyer on the seller. It is not clear if such "exclusion of liability" under section 13 is subject to section 55 of the 1893 Act which deals with exclusion of the statutory implied terms. In the *Harlingdon case*, Slade L.J. thought that there was no exclusion of section 13, and rather that the sale was simply not a sale by description,[188] but it has been held that a term in

183 For other remedies, including in tort law, see Chapter 16.
184 1893 Act, s.55(4), as substituted by the 1980 Act, s.22. See also 10.5.2.
185 [1930] 2 K.B. 312.
186 *Cf. Pinnock Bros v. Lewis & Peat Ltd* [1923] 1 K.B. 690.
187 [1990] 1 All E.R. 737 (C.A.).
188 *Ibid.*, at 753.

the contract "seen as sold" prevented it from being a sale by description and was subject to the rules on exclusion of liability in sales law.[189]

A seller may also seek to "exclude" liability under section 14(2) on the basis of the two built-in exemptions in that provision. There is no implied condition as to merchantable quality:

> (i) as regards defects specifically drawn to the buyer's attention before the contract is made; or
> (ii) if the buyer examines the goods before the contract is made, as regards defects which that examination ought to have revealed.[190]

This too, it would seem, would fall outside the rules on exclusion of liability.

13.8 Implied Warranty Regarding Spare Parts and Servicing

The five implied terms considered above – as to title, description, merchantable quality, fitness for particular purpose, and sale by sample – date back to the 1893 Act, although the Sale of Goods and Supply of Services Act 1980 did make some important amendments to the details of these provisions. The 1980 Act introduced two further implied terms in response to changes in the economy and society: an implied warranty as to spare parts and services,[191] and an implied condition regarding defects in motor vehicles.[192]

Section 12(1) of the 1980 Act provides that where there is an offer, description or advertisement by the seller representing that spare parts and servicing will be available from himself, or the manufacturer, then in the contract of sale there is implied a warranty that spare parts and adequate services will be made available. If a period is stated in the warranty, this must be complied with. If no period is stated, then these services must be available for a "reasonable period". The Minister may, after consultation, by order, specify what a reasonable period shall be for certain goods.[193] This power has not been exercised to date. Further, this warranty can never be excluded.[194]

It is important to note that there is no requirement on a manufacturer or

189 See *Hughes v. Hall* [1981] R.T.R. 430.
190 See 13.3.1.
191 See following text.
192 See 13.9.
193 1980 Act, s.13(2).
194 1980 Act, s.13(3).

retailer to offer spare parts or after-sales services. But where such an offer is made, this provision ensures that such a promise is elevated to warranty status, the breach of which gives right to a right to claim damages. In many areas of commercial sales activity, the offer of spare parts and after-sales services is an important factor on which the buyer relies in deciding whether to buy the goods or not. For instance, domestic appliances, such as refrigerators and washing machines, are commonly sold with such offers being made. Buying a brand of washing machine for which spare parts are readily available and which can be serviced locally is the preferred position of many consumers, but this provision applies to all sales whether the buyer is dealing as a consumer, or not.

13.9 Implied Condition Regarding Sale of Motor Vehicles

Motor vehicles must comply with all the implied terms as to description, merchantable quality, fitness for particular purpose and spare parts and after-sales services as described above. Moreover, the safety of motor vehicles is addressed specifically in section 13 of the Sale of Goods and Supply of Services Act 1980. This provision implies a condition into every contract for the sale of motor vehicles[195] (except where the buyer is a person whose business it is to deal in motor vehicles) that at the time of delivery, it was free from any defect which would render it a danger to the public, including persons travelling in it.[196] This implied condition can be avoided where (a) it is agreed that the vehicle is not intended for use in the condition in which it is sold, and (b) a document to this effect is signed by the parties and given to the buyer prior to or at delivery,[197] and (c) the above agreement is fair and reasonable.[198]

This section provides an exception to the doctrine of privity of contract in that it allows not only the buyer, but any person using the motor vehicle with the consent of the buyer, who suffers a loss, to sue the seller for breach of section 13(2). However, the generous lifting of the doctrine of privity of contract is diminished somewhat by the shorter than usual

195 For definition of "motor vehicle" see s.13(1).

196 See, *e.g.* *Glorney v. O'Brien* unreported, High Court, Lynch J., November 14, 1988, where a car bought for £250 soon after went out of control on a public road and crashed because of defective suspension. It was held that there was a breach of s.13 of the 1980 Act and damages were awarded for destruction of the property, physical injury and loss of earnings for several weeks.

197 1980 Act, s.13(5) states that where a document complying with the requirements of this section is not given, and an action is taken for breach of s.13, it shall be presumed that the defect existed at the time of delivery. Such an evidential presumption is of great benefit to any plaintiff. Furthermore, s.13(4) and s.13(6) provide that the Minister may make regulations prescribing the form(s) of this document: this power has never been exercised by the Minister.

198 1980 Act, s.13(3). On the meaning of fair and reasonable see Schedule to the 1980 Act; see further 10.5.2.2.

limitation period for such actions which, under section 13(8), is two years from the date on which the cause of action accrued. The buyer's right to sue for beach of section 13(2) remains unaffected at six years. Finally, in relation to the sale of motor vehicles, any term exempting from all or any of the provisions of section 13 shall be void.[199]

13.10 Liability of Finance Houses

One of the remaining notable provisions of the 1980 Act as regards sale of goods is to be found in section 14 which provides that where the buyer deals as a consumer and if, for the purpose of the sale, the buyer enters into an agreement with another person acting in the course of a business (a finance house) for the repayment to the finance house of the price paid to the seller, then the finance house is deemed to be a party to the sale, and the seller and the finance house are jointly and severally liable for any breach of contract or any misrepresentations. This provision is designed to deal with the common situation where the supply of goods is financed by credit and three parties are involved. Typically, the consumer will negotiate a sale of goods contract with a seller, and the seller arranges a contract with the consumer and a finance company to supply credit to the consumer to finance the sale. Usually the consumer has direct contact with the seller only who is responsible for negotiating the whole transaction. However, the seller and the finance house are really part of a "joint-venture", and on this basis the seller and finance house are made jointly and severally liable to the consumer buyer.

This dual target is only offered to buyers dealing as consumers. For example, in *O'Callaghan v. Hamilton Leasing (Ireland) Ltd*,[200] the plaintiff owned a take-away and he bought a vending machine through a finance house under a leasing agreement. Having paid two instalments, the machine proved to be defective and the plaintiff demanded a refund and damages for lost profits from the finance house. The defendant did not dispute that the machine was defective. However, it argued that since the plaintiff was not dealing as a consumer, it could not sue the finance company under section 14. The High Court held that the contract was made in the course of the plaintiff's business and hence he could not rely on section 14. The plaintiff had argued that he did not intend to further deal with the goods bought, but the court found that this was not sufficient to render him a consumer. It was enough that the goods were used for the purpose of the business.

199 1980 Act, s.13(9).
200 [1984] I.L.R.M. 146 (H.C.).

13.11 The EC Directive on Aspects of Consumer Sales and Associated Guarantees

One of the main purposes of the European Community remains the perfection of a single market, including a market where consumers can buy goods cross-border with confidence. This, the free movement of consumers, is the impetus for the European Commission's interest in the area of consumer sales that resulted in the EC Directive on Certain Aspects of Consumer Sales and Associated Guarantees.[201] The intention is to provide a European consumer sales law offering consumers a minimum standard of protection throughout the EC.[202] The Directive addresses a number of important aspects of sales law, including the quality of goods supplied under sales contracts.[203]

Member states had until January 1, 2002 to implement the Directive.[204] At the time of writing, the Directive had not been implemented in Irish law. It is expected that the Directive will be implemented by statutory instrument as opposed to primary legislation. Therefore, the following comments, as regards the quality provisions, are based on the wording of the Directive.

13.11.1 Application

The Directive mixes the "objective" and "subjective" approaches of previous consumer protection directives in determining its application. The Directive, similar to Directive 92/59 on General Product Safety,[205] takes an objective approach in that it focuses on the subject-matter of the contract,

201 Directive 1999/44/EC [1999] O.J. L171/12.

202 See Recitals 1–5 of the Directive.

203 Other aspects covered by the directive are remedies, and guarantees: see Chapters 14 and 16, respectively. See further Twigg-Flesner, "The EC Directive on Certain Aspects of the Sale of Consumer Goods and Associated Guarantees" [1999] *Consumer Law Journal* 177; Bradgate, "Harmonisation of Legal Guarantees: a Common Law Perspective" [1995] *Consumer Law Journal* 94; White, "The EC Directive on certain aspects of sale of consumer goods and associated guarantees: a step forward and two steps back?" [2000] *Commercial Law Practitioner* 3; Krümmel & D'sa, "Sale of consumer goods and associated guarantees: a minimalist approach to harmonised European Union consumer protection" (2001) 26 *European Law Review* 312; Twigg-Flesner, "A Response to EC Directive 99/44/EC on Certain Aspects of the Sale of Consumer Goods and Associated Guarantees - First Consultation of 2001" [2001] *Nottingham Law Journal* 91.

204 Art. 11.

205 [1992] O.J. L228/84.

the goods. Hence, the Directive applies to the sale of "consumer goods", defined as any tangible moveable item,[206] but the Directive, similar to Directive 93/13 on Unfair Terms in Consumer Contracts,[207] also takes a subjective approach by defining its application in terms of the parties involved. The Directive only applies to contracts for the sale of consumer goods between "sellers" and "consumers", as defined.[208] A "seller" is defined as "any natural or legal person who … sells goods in the course of his trade, business or profession",[209] A "consumer" is defined as "any natural person who … is acting for purposes which are not related to his trade, business or profession".[210]

Two points can be made about these definitions, first in the context of European Community law, and second in relation to Irish law. First, these definitions do not match exactly definitions to be found in related directives. For example, in the Directive on Unfair Terms in Consumer Contracts, a closely related directive, a "consumer" is defined as a natural person who is acting "for purposes which are outside his trade business or profession".[211] Do the words "not related to his trade, business or profession" (from the Consumer Sales Directive) correspond exactly in meaning to "outside his trade, business or profession" (from the Unfair Contract Terms Directive)? If so, why are different words used? Again, in the Unfair Terms in Consumer Contracts Directive, a "seller" is defined as a person who sells goods "for purposes related to his trade, business or profession" whereas the Consumer Sales Directive refers to selling goods "in the course of his trade, business or profession". Whether some of these terms are broader or narrower than the other terms is debatable. The result is a lack of clear understanding about their scope and any future attempts to consolidate these aspects of European Community private law will be dogged with such issues of definition and meaning.

When the Directive is compared with the current Irish position, similar problems of definition arise. For example, the Irish definition of "dealing as a consumer", like the Directive, mixes an objective and a subjective approach. Section 3 of the 1980 Act provides that, a party to a contract is said to deal as a consumer in relation to the other party if:

---

206 Art. 1(2)(b). Excluded from this definition are goods sold by way of execution or by authority of the law; water and gas where they are not put up for sale in a limited or set quantity, and electricity. Also, member states may provide that second-hand goods sold at public auction may be excluded: Art. 1(3).

207 [1993] O.J. L95/29.

208 Art. 1(4) provides that contracts for the supply of consumer goods to be manufactured or produced are within the scope of the Directive. This seems to conform to the domestic rules: see for example, *Cammell Laird v. Manganese Bronze* [1934] A.C. 402; and *Hyundai v. Papadopoulos* [1980] 2 All E.R. 29.

209 Art. 1(2)(c).

210 Art. 1(2)(a).

211 Art. 2(b).

"(i) he neither makes the contract in the course of a business …; and
(ii) the other party does make the contract in the course of a business …, and
(iii) the goods … supplied … are of a type ordinarily supplied for private use or consumption."

This definition mirrors the U.K.'s Unfair Contract Terms Act 1977 definition under which it has been held that a company can be a consumer,[212] whereas the Directive expressly limits "consumer" to "any natural person". On the other hand, the Irish definition limits the notion of consumer by reference to the type of goods sold, that is, goods of a type ordinarily supplied for private use or consumption. While earlier drafts of the Directive referred to consumer goods as any goods "normally intended for final use and consumption", this refinement was dropped from the final Directive and the definition of "consumer goods" has been broadened as a result. Against this, there is provision in the Directive for member states to exclude from the definition of "consumer goods", second-hand goods sold at public auction where consumers have the opportunity of attending the sale in person.[213] In Irish law, no distinction is made between new and second-hand goods, and the introduction of such a distinction would be a retrograde step for consumers.

Lastly, and in line with the definition of "seller" under the Directive, the implied terms in section 14 of the 1893 Act only apply where the seller sells goods in the course of a business, but the other implied terms (in sections 13, and 15 of the 1893 Act and section 13 of the 1980 Act) are not so restricted and offer consumer buyers protection where sales are not made in the course of a business.

The scope of application of the Directive relative to Irish law cannot be judged in isolation from the quality requirements imposed. A broad application catching a large number of "consumers" is of limited value when the quality standards required are low. However, it would be wrong to underestimate the importance of differences in application. Difference in application, in itself, will lead to confusion and complications in the settling and bringing of claims. Such confusion usually operates to the advantage of the seller, rather than the consumer buyer.

13.11.2 The quality obligation

The core requirement under the Directive is that "the seller must deliver goods to the consumer which are in conformity with the contract of sale."[214]

212 See *R & B Customs Brokers v. UDT Finance Ltd* [1988] 1 All E.R. 847; see further 10.5.2.1.
213 Art. 1(3).
214 Art. 2(1). Art. 2(3) provides that there will be no lack of conformity where, at the time the

This concept of conformity is modelled on the Vienna Convention on Contracts for the International Sale of Goods (1980).[215] Consumer goods are presumed[216] to be in conformity if they:

(i) comply with the description given by the seller and possess the qualities of the goods which the seller has held out to the consumer as a sample or model;
(ii) are fit for any particular purpose for which the consumer requires them and which he has made known to the seller at the time of the conclusion of the contract and which the seller has accepted;
(iii) are fit for the purpose for which goods of the same type are normally used; and
(iv) show the quality and performance which are normal in goods of the same type and which the consumer can reasonably expect, given the nature of the goods and taking into account any public statements on the specific characteristics of the goods made about them by the seller, the producer, or his representative, particularly in advertising or labelling.[217]

At first sight, these provisions may seem familiar to an Irish lawyer: paragraph (i) reflects section 13 of the 1893 Act on sales by description and section 15 of the 1893 Act on sale by sample; paragraphs (iii) and (iv) reflect section 14(2) of the 1893 Act on merchantable quality; and paragraph (ii) reflects section 14(4) of the 1893 Act on fitness for particular purpose. But a closer examination highlights subtle yet potentially significant differences between the Directive and the pre-existing Irish provisions.

13.11.2.1 Sales by description

Under the Directive, in all consumer sales, the goods must comply with the description given by the seller. There are two points of contrast here. First, in Irish law, the compliance with description requirement only applies to

contract was concluded, the consumer was aware, or could not reasonable be unaware of the lack of conformity, or if the lack of conformity has its origins in materials supplied by the consumer.

215 Art. 35; see further 29.4.2.

216 As a matter of evidence, such presumptions are rebuttable. Earlier drafts of the Directive used the word "deemed" rather than "presumed", which does not seem to leave room for any evidence to the contrary.

217 Art. 2(2).

"sales by description".[218] In fact, the large majority of all sales are "sales by description". Section 13(2) provides that a sale shall not be prevented from being a sale by description just because the goods are exposed for sale and selected by the buyer, as is the case with a self-service sale. The main determining factor appears to be that the buyer must have relied on the description in deciding to purchase the goods.[219] So, on this point, there may be little difference in practice between the Directive and the Irish provisions, but this is not the case in relation to the second point of contrast.

Under the Directive, the goods must comply with the description "given by the seller". In Irish law, where goods are "sold by description", they must comply with that description, that is, the description by which they are sold. That description may be given by the seller, or it may originate from other sources, such as information on the label or packaging placed there by the manufacturer. So long as the words identify the essential commercial characteristics of the goods sold, they will constitute words of description.[220] To give a similar level of protection to consumers under the Directive, sellers will have to be deemed to have adopted, in this instance, the manufacturer's description on the labelling or packaging. However, this construction may not be possible since public statements made by the manufacturer are expressly stated to be relevant to a later aspect of conformity (paragraph (iv)), and under Article 2(4) of the Directive a seller can exclude himself from liability for these statements in certain circumstances.

13.11.2.2 Fitness for purpose

Paragraph (c) requires that the goods be fit for the *purposes* for which goods of that type are normally used. In Irish law, goods are of merchantable quality if they are fit for the *purpose or purposes* for which goods of that kind are commonly bought. Where goods have more than one purpose, it has been held that they will be merchantable where they are fit for one of their common purposes.[221] Does the Directive's reference to purposes imply a higher standard requiring goods to be fit for all their normal purposes?

The Directive assesses fitness according to normal use. In contrast, the Irish provisions refer to the purposes for which the goods are commonly bought. Where goods are commonly bought for an abnormal use, they may

---

218 See 13.2.2.

219 See for example, *Egan v. McSweeney* (1956) 90 I.L.T.R. 40; and *Harlingdon & Leinster v. Christopher Hull Fine Arts Ltd* [1990] 1 All E.R. 737; see further 13.2.2.

220 *Ashington Piggeries Ltd v. Christopher Hill* [1972] A.C. 441; see further 13.2.3.

221 *Aswan Engineering v. Lupdine* [1987] 1 All E.R. 135; see further 13.3.2.1. This Court of Appeal ruling has since been reversed in the U.K. by the Sale and Supply of Goods Act 1994 under which goods must be fit for all their common purposes.

comply with the Irish provisions while breaching the Directive. Furthermore, merchantable quality requires goods to be fit for the purpose or purposes for which goods of that kind are commonly bought, as is reasonable to expect.[222] There is no mention of reasonableness in the Directive, where the requirement to be fit for normal purposes appears an absolute, and so an inflexible, requirement.

Most significantly, mechantable quality is assessed in Irish law by reference to a number of factors, of which fitness for purpose is one. Section 14(3) also mentions durability, description, price and other relevant circumstances.[223] The Directive focuses exclusively on fitness for purpose in paragraph (c). While fitness for purpose may be of major importance in a commercial context, it is of limited use for consumer buyers. Paragraph (d) is more expansive and requires goods to show the quality and performance which are normal in goods of the same type and as is reasonable to expect, given the nature of the goods and any public statements made about the specific characteristics of the goods. However, it is unclear how dominant consumer issues such as durability, price, safety, appearance and finish, and freedom from minor defects will fit into this legal framework.

13.11.2.3 Fitness for particular purpose

Under the Directive, goods must be fit for any particular purpose for which the consumer requires them, and which he has made known to the seller at the time of the conclusion of the contract, and which the seller has accepted. But under section 14(3) of the 1893 Act, there is no need for the seller to have accepted the buyer's particular purpose. However, a buyer cannot use section 14(3) where he did not rely, or it would be unreasonable to rely, on the seller's skill and judgment.

13.11.2.4 Defective installation

Article 2(5) of the Directive adds to the concept of conformity by including lack of conformity resulting from incorrect installation.[224] This is a useful addition for consumers where installation is often an important aspect of any purchase. The provision only applies where the installation forms part of the sales contract and the goods were installed by the seller or under his responsibility.[225] In these circumstances, the standard of liability is the contractual no-fault standard. This contrasts with the position in Irish law, where such installation would probably be subject to the rules in Part IV of

222 1893 Act, s.14(3); see further 13.3.2.1.
223 1893 Act, s.14(3); see further 13.3.2.
224 Otherwise, contracts for the supply of services are regulated at national level within the EC.
225 This provision also applies where the consumer was intended to install the goods and any incorrect installation is due to shortcomings in the installation instructions: Art. 2(5).

the Sale of Goods and Supply of Services Act 1980 on the supply of services. Here, the standard of liability is fault-based, and a consumer would have to prove negligence to be compensated.[226] Further, a supplier can exclude liability against a consumer so long as the exclusion is "fair and reasonable" and it must be specifically brought to the attention of the buyer to be effective.[227] The position under the Directive is clearly preferable from a consumer perspective.

13.11.2.5 Time for assessing conformity

Under the Directive, goods must conform to the sales contract at the time of delivery.[228] It would appear that the relevant time, in Irish law, for compliance with the implied terms, is when risk passes.[229] Sometimes delivery and the passing of risk coincide, but not always. Under the Sale of Goods Acts, the passing of risk is generally linked to the passing of property,[230] and property can pass before or after delivery.[231] For example, a contract of sale subject to a reservation of title clause would usually involve delivery of the goods to the buyer, but property (and hence risk) would not pass until the goods are paid for at a later date. Likewise, under section 18, rule 1 of the 1893 Act, in an unconditional contract for the sale of specific goods in a deliverable state, the property in the goods (and hence the risk) passes to the buyer when the contract is made, regardless of the time of payment or the time of delivery. Such differences in timing may lead to differences in results when a consumer seeks to enforce his legal rights under the Directive or under the Sale of Goods Acts, and, although Recital 14 of the Directive states that references to the time of delivery do not imply that member states have to change their rules on the passing of risk, the Directive effectively alters the rules on the passing of risk for non-conformity by linking it to delivery.

13.12 Review of Irish Law on Quality of Goods

Irish law on the sale of goods has gone through three distinct phases, each seeking to improve on what has gone before. The Sale of Goods Act 1893 sought to make the law more accessible by codifying the existing common law. The Sale of Goods and Supply of Services Act 1980 sought to modernise sales law and, in particular to protect the position of consumer

226 1980 Act, s.39; see further Chapter 20.
227 1980 Act, s.40 and the Schedule to the Act; see further Chapter 20.
228 Art. 2(1).
229 See *Benjamin's Sale of Goods* (London, Sweet & Maxwell, 5th ed., 1995) para 11–062; see 13.3.3 and 13.4.4.
230 1893 Act, s.20; see further Chapter 18.
231 1893 Act, ss.16–19; see further Chapter 17.

buyers. The EC Directive on Certain Aspects of Consumer Sales and Associated Guarantees seeks to protect consumer buyers of goods at a minimal European level.

In certain respects, it could be argued that our sales legislation remains largely unchanged since 1893, and accordingly is out of date. The basic quality requirement is "merchantable quality" an archaic phrase of little relevance to a modern consumer society. Moreover, the principal remedies for breach of the implied terms have also remained largely unchanged.[232] Against this, the Sale of Goods and Supply of Services Act 1980 has updated many other aspects of our sales law to meet changes in the economy and society, in particular to meet the needs of consumer buyers. Broadening the general application of section 14 by omitting the requirement that the goods be sold by a seller who deals in goods of that description, and more particularly in relation to merchantable quality, omitting the requirement that the sale must be by description, has afforded greater protection to consumer buyers. The detail in the definition of "merchantable quality" does a lot to give the phrase meaning – a benefit for both seller and buyer. The presumption of reliance in section 14(4) favours the buyer's position. The provisions on spare parts and after-sales services address new marketing practices.[233] The provisions on motor vehicles recognise the increased use of motor vehicles and the great potential for loss or injury which can be caused by the sale of defective motor vehicles. Perhaps most importantly, the provisions regulating the use of exclusion clauses do most to offer consumers protection in sale of goods transactions.[234]

Nevertheless, there is still room for further improvement. Of greatest concern appears to be the use of the phrase, and definition of, "merchantable quality". On the phrase itself, the criticism that its language is archaic and without meaning today, remains valid. Similar criticism in the United Kingdom led to proposals to change the requirement to "acceptable quality"[235] and later to "satisfactory quality",[236] each to be accompanied by a detailed definition. The U.K. Sale and Supply of Goods Act 1994 opted for "satisfactory quality". Apparently, it was felt by consumer groups that "satisfactory quality" imposed a higher standard than "acceptable quality". Some have argued that this change has been largely cosmetic to address the needs of the consumer lobby in the United Kingdom, with no real change being made to the meaning of

232 See generally, Chapter 14.

233 The same can be said for the provisions dealing with guarantees: 1980 Act, ss.15–19; see further Chapter 16.

234 See also 1893 Act, s.53(2) on new consumer remedies; see further 14.4.

235 Law Com. No. 160, Scot. Law Com. 104, Sale and Supply of Goods (1987).

236 D.T.I. Consultation Paper, Consumer Guarantees (1992).

"merchantable quality".[237] Against this, the phrase "satisfactory quality" does have a different flavour from the more commercially orientated "merchantable quality". This, in time, may lead to subtle differences of interpretation and hence changes to the law.

Whatever about semantics, the content of the definition of "merchantable quality" is clearly lacking. The omission from the definition of factors such as appearance and finish or freedom from minor defects is regrettable. While the definition of "merchantable quality" introduced in the 1980 Act may have succeeded in bringing that phrase out of the nineteenth century and into modern times without further amendments, this definition appears ill-equipped to deal with transactions in the present century.

With the implementation of the EC Directive on Certain Aspects of Consumer Sales and Associated Guarantees, a third layer of rules will exist in Irish sales law and, based on the above analysis, it is unclear how these rules will fit in with the existing rules in the Sale of Goods Acts or whether they will represent an improvement. It is perhaps unfortunate that the opportunity presented by the implementation of the EC Directive was not used to review Irish sale of goods law in its entirety.[238] A more bold, and in the author's view correct, approach would have been to implement the Directive using primary legislation designed to fit with the pre-existing rules. Perhaps the neatest, though clearly not the easiest, solution would be to consolidate the three layers of rules identified above into one principal statute for the sale of goods. This statute would contain in one part the rules common to all domestic sales contracts – such as on the passing of property – and in another part the particular rules which apply to consumer sales. This approach would also allow the Government to implement the Law Commission's proposal that the Vienna Convention be adopted in relation to international sales – a third part.[239] At the same time, aspects of the Sale of Goods Acts 1893 and 1980, which are in need of review, could be addressed. For instance, as noted in Chapter 9, section 4 of the 1893 Act dealing with formalities is well beyond its sell-by date.[240] In particular, in relation to quality, the phrase "merchantable quality" and its definition could also have been reconsidered.

237 See *Atiyah's Sale of Goods* (Harlow, Pearson, 10th ed., 2001) p.181; Bradgate, *Commercial Law* (London, Butterworths, 3rd ed., 2000) p.287; Bridge, "The evolution of modern sales law" (1991) Lloyd's *Maritime and Commercial Law Quarterly* 52 at 56–7. See further Adams & Brownsword, "Law Reform, Law Jobs, and the Law Commission No. 160" (1988) 51 *Modern Law Review 481*.

238 The Directive provided the imputus for a major overhaul of the German law of obligations contained in the Bürgerliches Gesetzbuch, for example. For other areas in potential need of reform see generally Chapter 14; and specifically 17.4.1.1; and 19.10.

239 See further 29.4.2.

240 See 9.2.1.1.

Chapter 14

BUYER'S REMEDIES

14.1 INTRODUCTION

A seller's basic duty under a sales contract is to deliver the goods in accordance with the terms of the sales contract.[1] Where a seller fails in this basic duty, by making a defective delivery, he will be in breach of the contract. In this context, the term "defective delivery" includes late delivery, non-delivery, defects in quality of the goods delivered, and defects in the quantity of the goods delivered.[2] The Sale of Goods Acts 1893 and 1980 provide remedies for the buyer where the seller makes a defective delivery. These remedies are the subject of this chapter, with one exception. The remedies for delivery of the wrong quantity are dealt with in Chapter 11 on Delivery.[3]

The distinction between conditions and warranties is fundamental in determining what remedies are available to an innocent party in relation to a breach of a sale of goods contract. Section 62 of the 1893 Act provides that a breach of warranty gives rise to a claim for damages, but not the right to reject the goods and treat the contract as repudiated. Condition is not defined expressly in the legislation but by implication. Section 11(2) of the 1893 Act states:

> "Whether a stipulation in a contract of sale is a condition, the breach of which may give rise to a right to treat the contract as repudiated, or a warranty the breach of which may give rise to a claim for damages but not to a right to reject the goods and treat the contract as repudiated, depends in each case on the construction of the contract."

Further, section 11(3) of the 1893 Act states:

> "Where a contract of sale is not severable, and the buyer has accepted the goods, or part thereof, the breach of any condition to be fulfilled by the seller can only be treated as a breach of warranty, and not as a ground for rejecting the goods and treating the contract as repudiated …"

---

1 Sale of Goods Act 1893, s.27: see generally Chapters 10 and 11.

2 On the seller's obligations as to title and remedies for breach of implied terms as to title, see Chapter 12.

3 See 11.2.5.1.

Hence, any defective delivery, whether a breach of condition or warranty, amounts to a breach of contract by the seller and entitles the buyer to damages for losses caused by the breach. In addition, where the seller commits a breach of a condition, or a serious breach of an innominate term,[4] the buyer may reject the goods and terminate the contract. Section 11(1) of the 1893 Act provides that where a condition is to be fulfilled by the seller, the buyer may waive the condition or elect to treat the breach of a condition as a breach of warranty. Hence, a buyer is not obliged to reject the goods following the breach of a condition: in practice, a buyer often opts to keep the goods and simply claim damages. Other remedies may be available under the general law of contract, including specific performance,[5] interest,[6] and rescission of the contract or damages for misrepresentation.[7]

One matter which is unclear from a reading of the statutory provisions, and indeed from case law, is whether an innocent buyer has three separate remedies on breach of a condition by the seller: (i) to terminate the contract; and (ii) to reject the goods; and (iii) to sue for damages; or whether the right to terminate and to reject are really one and the same right. This difficulty stems from the use of the word "and" in sections 11(2), 11(3) and 62 of the 1893 Act. For example, section 11(3) provides that if a contract is not severable, and the buyer has accepted the goods, or part of them:

> "the breach of any condition to be fulfilled by the seller can only be treated as a breach of warranty, and not as a ground for rejecting the goods *and* treating the contract as repudiated …" [author's italics]

Is the word "and" to be read disjunctively or conjunctively? In more practical terms, if the right to terminate and to reject are two separate rights, then an innocent buyer could reject the goods but not terminate the contract and continue to press for delivery in accordance with the terms of the contract: this is usually referred to as a right to cure. On the other hand, if the right to reject is really a practical exercise of the right to terminate, the buyer does not have this option,[8] or, as argued elsewhere in relation to English law, it is the seller who has the right to insist that he has the right

---

4 See 10.4.

5 See 14.5.

6 See 21.2.1.

7 See 2.2.5.2(ii), 2.3.1 and 14.6.

8 Judicial support for this view can be found in the dictum of Devlin J. that:"a right to reject is merely a particular form of the right to rescind, because it involves the rejection of goods"; see *Kwei Tek Chao v. British Traders and Shippers Ltd* [1954] 2 W.L.R. 365 at 375. This area is fraught with terminological difficulties and it is generally thought that Devlin J.'s reference to rescission was used in the sense of termination and not "recission ab initio".

to cure his defective delivery.[9] It is the author's view that based on an historical analysis of the legislation, an exact reading of the statutory provisions and a review of case law, the right to terminate and to reject are two separate rights, effectively allowing the buyer the right to request cure from the seller in certain circumstances.[10] This right to request cure applies to all buyers. Moreover, consumer buyers are given a statutory right to request cure under section 53(2) of the 1893 Act, as substituted by the 1980 Act.[11]

The rights to terminate the contract, reject the goods and sue for damages were provided for in the original 1893 Act. The 1980 Act made some important changes in relation to buyer's remedies. In general, these changes favoured the position of buyers by expanding their rights in certain circumstances. In particular, sections 34 and 35 of the 1893 Act, as amended by the 1980 Act, seek to extend the buyer's right to examine the goods before acceptance,[12] and section 53(2) of the 1893 Act, as amended by the 1980 Act, gives consumer buyers further rights to request cure and to reject the goods.[13] Nevertheless, deficiencies remain in this remedies regime. For instance, there is a lack of clarity in relation to the buyer's right to examine goods which should be addressed and could be extended further.[14] Moreover, the rules on partial rejection can operate harshly on buyers and probably should be relaxed.[15] Finally, it should be noted that provided a condition of the contract is breached, a buyer is entitled to reject the goods and terminate the contract regardless of whether the breach is serious or not. In other words, a buyer can reject the goods and terminate the contract for a minor breach provided that the term breached is properly classified as a condition of the contract.[16] The danger is that courts, faced

---

9 Goode, *Commercial Law* (London, Penguin, 2nd ed., 1995) pp.353–355 and pp.363–366. Some writers offer support for this view see, *e.g.* Treitel, *The Law of Contract* (London, Sweet & Maxwell, 10th ed., 1999) p.698; Carter, *Breach of Contract* (London, Sweet & Maxwell, 2nd ed., 1991) p.4; Davies, *Sale and Supply of Goods* (London, Longman, 1990) p.143. Other writers are more doubtful: see *Benjamin's Sale of Goods* (London, Sweet & Maxwell, 5th ed., 1997) para 12-031; *Atiyah's Sale of Goods* (Harlow, Pearson, 10th ed., 2001) p.508; Ahdar, "Seller cure in the sale of goods" [1990] *Lloyd's Maritime and Commercial Law Quarterly* 364; Apps, "The right to cure defective performance" [1994] *Lloyd's Maritime and Commercial Law Quarterly* 525.

10 See Bradgate & White, "Rejection and Termination in Contracts for the Sale of Goods" in Birds, Bradgate & Villiers eds., *Termination of Contracts* (Chichester, Wiley Chancery, 1995). Although this argument was made in relation to English law, it can also be made in relation to Irish law.

11 See 14.4.

12 See 14.2.1.

13 See 14.4.

14 See 14.2.1.

15 See 14.2.2.

16 Classifying the term as an innominate term avoids this outcome but the courts have no such discretion where the statutory implied terms under the Sale of Goods Acts are concerned.

with such circumstances, may hold that there was no breach of contract to avoid these extreme effects. This deficiency in the legislation has been addressed in the U.K. by the Sale and Supply of Goods Act 1994. Now, section 15A of the U.K. Sale of Goods Act 1979, as inserted by the 1994 Act, provides that where a breach of condition is so slight that rejection would be unreasonable, a buyer who does not deal as a consumer may not reject the goods but must treat the breach as a breach of warranty only. In contrast, the opportunity to reject in bad faith, as described above, still exists in Ireland.

The EC Directive on Certain Aspects of Consumer Sales and Associated Guarantees contains its own remedies regime for consumer buyers, as defined, which places the rights of repair and replacement before any right to reject the goods or get a reduction in the price.[17] The remedies available under the Directive will be examined, in detail, at the end of this chapter.[18]

14.2 The Right to Reject

A buyer can reject goods in four circumstances. First, where there is an express right to reject under the contract. For instance, some shops allow customers to return goods where they are not satisfied with them, offering their money back or a replacement. Such offers are, of course, additional to a buyer's statutory rights.[19] Second, the legislation provides a specific right where, for example, the seller delivers the wrong quantity.[20] Third, the legislation provides a general right to reject where the seller has breached a condition, and fourth, it would seem that the common law allows rejection for a serious breach of an innominate term.[21] A rejection in any other circumstance will not be justified and amounts to a breach of contract by the buyer for which the seller has remedies.[22] In practice, disputes about defective delivery and rejection involve claims and counterclaims of breach. For example, a buyer may reject goods, the seller can sue for non-acceptance, the buyer can reply that the rejection was justified because the seller was in breach by making a defective delivery, the seller may deny breach or claim that the buyer has lost the right to reject. Litigation can easily become protracted. Commercial traders more usually prefer to

17 Directive 1999/44/EC [1999] O.J. L171/12, to be implemented in member states by January 1, 2002: Art. 11.

18 See 14.7.

19 Sale of Goods and Supply of Services Act 1980, s.11: see 10.5.2.

20 See 11.2.5.1.

21 *The Hansa Nord* [1976] Q.B. 44. See also *Laird Bros v. Dublin Steampacket* (1990) 34 I.L.T.R. 97; *Taylor v. Smyth* [1990] I.L.R.M. 377; *Irish Telephone Rentals v. ICS Building Society* [1991] I.L.R.M. 880.

22 See generally Chapter 15.

negotiate their way out of such a dispute; consumers rarely have the resources to take legal proceedings.

Section 11(2) of the 1893 Act makes it clear that where there is a breach of a condition, the innocent party can repudiate or terminate the contract, reject the goods and claim for damages. If any price has been paid under the contract the buyer is also entitled to a refund of the price on the basis of a claim in restitution, for total failure of consideration.[23] Where the buyer claims such a refund, or makes an additional claim for damages for any additional losses caused by the breach, the assistance of the court will be needed, but where the price under the contract has not been paid, a buyer rejecting goods is essentially a self-help remedy.

Where a buyer wishes to reject goods, he must indicate his intentions clearly.[24] If a buyer seeks to reject goods, he does not necessarily have to physically return the goods to the seller. Rather he must make them available for collection at the delivery point.[25] Where the goods cannot be made available, for instance, because the goods have been consumed, rejection is not possible.[26]

On rejection, any property in the goods, and any risk associated with it, revest in the seller.[27] Where the buyer remains in possession following rejection, he would be liable as an involuntary bailee.[28] However, between delivery and rejection, it would seem that risk rests with the buyer. What then is the position when goods are damaged between delivery and rejection: can a buyer reject goods in these circumstances? Where the damage is caused by the very defect which the buyer complains of, for example, where a new car with defective brakes crashes into a wall, the buyer's right to reject is unaffected.[29] At the same time, where the defect is caused by the buyer's negligent usage he should be liable for that damage, and may be deemed to have accepted the goods.[30] However, the effect of accidental damage during his period is unclear. In *Head v. Tattersall*,[31] it was held that a buyer was entitled to reject a horse under an express right to reject in the contract, even though it had been accidentally injured after delivery but before rejection. It is unclear whether this case survives the 1893 Act and whether it applies to the statutory implied conditions.

---

23 1893 Act, s.54.

24 In *Lee v. York Coach and Marine* [1977] R.T.R. 35 (C.A.), the buyer's solicitor wrote to the seller indicating that the buyer had the right to reject and requesting that the seller repair the goods. It was held that the letter was insufficient to amount to a rejection of the goods. For a consumer's statutory right to reject and cure, see 14.4.

25 1893 Act, s.36.

26 See 14.2.1.2.

27 See generally Chapters 17 and 18.

28 See 3.4.5; see further Palmer, *Bailment* (London, Sweet & Maxwell, 2nd ed., 1991).

29 Bradgate, *Commercial Law* (London, Butterworths, 3rd ed., 2000) p.312.

30 See 14.2.1.

31 (1871) L.R. b7 Exch. 7.

The right to reject is a powerful sanction against the seller's breach of condition. In effect, the buyer is legitimately refusing to perform his part of the bargain. The buyer does not have to accept the goods and to pay for them. It is then up to the seller to keep or dispose of the goods for his own account. Where the goods are rejected because they are defective in quality or title, the seller may not be able to sell the goods to another buyer, or, if he is able to sell the goods he may have to do so at a discounted price taking into account the defect. Hence, the seller suffers the loss because of the defective delivery. Where the goods were made to the specific order of the buyer and they are rightfully rejected by the buyer, there may be no other market for the goods. Again the seller will suffer the loss. Moreover, the effect of lawful rejection is as if the seller had never delivered the goods. Unless the seller is entitled to and makes a replacement delivery, the buyer can sue for non-delivery and further can claim damages for any losses caused by the non-delivery,[32] but the legislation imposes restrictions on a buyer's right to reject.

14.2.1 Acceptance[33]

A buyer loses his right to reject if he is deemed to have accepted the goods under sections 34 and 35 of the 1893 Act.[34] These provisions must be read together. Section 34, as described in the margin, deals with the buyer's right to examine the goods. First, section 34(1) restricts the circumstances in which a buyer will be deemed to have accepted goods. It provides that where goods are delivered to the buyer and he has not previously examined them, he cannot be deemed to have accepted the goods until he has had a reasonable opportunity to examine the goods for the purpose of ascertaining whether they are in conformity with the contract. Reasonable opportunity, in this context, may include a reasonable time to see the goods

32 See 14.3.1.

33 The concept of "acceptance" is unique to sale of goods contracts. Other supply contracts, such as hire-purchase or barter, are governed by general principles of contract law. Thus a person who acquires goods under a hire-purchase contract, for instance, can reject the goods where there is a breach of condition, such as a statutory implied term, but he loses this right to reject where he affirms the contract. Crucially, a person can only affirm a contract where he is aware of the breach and the right to terminate. Further, affirmation is a matter of election. These general principles are more favourable than the rules which apply to buyers because where goods are supplied, other than under a sales contract with a latent defect, a person acquiring the goods cannot be deemed to have affirmed the contract until the defect becomes apparent and he elects to affirm the contract. A second difference involves the consequences of rejection under sales and other supply contracts. With a sales contract, where a buyer rejects goods he is entitled to a refund of the price on the basis of a total failure of consideration. But under other supply contracts, because a person may have had use of the goods before rejection there will not be a total failure of consideration and, in these circumstances, a person will be limited to a claim in damages.

34 1893 Act, ss.34 and 35, as amended by the 1980 Act, s.20. The rules on rejection and acceptance are modified for "consumer buyers" under s.53(2): see 14.4.

in operation.[35] Second, section 34(2) gives the buyer a right of examination in certain circumstances. It provides that, unless otherwise agreed, when the seller tenders goods for delivery, he is bound, on request, to afford the buyer an opportunity to examine the goods for the purpose of ascertaining whether they are in conformity with the contract. This right is made available to a buyer, but only on request by the buyer. When read in conjunction with section 35, it is unclear whether section 34 has a general or limited application. This matter is considered further below.

Section 35 outlines three ways in which a buyer will be deemed to have accepted goods, and thus lose the right to reject. Section 35 states:

> "The buyer is deemed to have accepted the goods when he intimates to the seller that he has accepted them, or, *subject to section 34 of this Act*, when he does any act in relation to them which is inconsistent with the ownership of the seller or when, *without good and sufficient reason*, he retains the goods without intimating to the seller that he has rejected them." [Author's italics identify insertions made by 1980 Act.]

Accordingly, a buyer is deemed to have accepted goods when:

(i) he intimates acceptance; or
(ii) he does any act inconsistent with the seller's ownership of the goods; or
(iii) without good and sufficient reason, he retains the goods without intimating rejection.

Section 35 is a recognition of the need for finality in sales contracts. There must come a time when the seller can consider the transaction closed and assume that he is safe from a claim for a refund. The circumstances which give rise to these deemed acceptances are examined further below. But first it is important to consider the relationship between sections 34 and 35, a matter which is far from clear.[36]

The second set of circumstances above, (ii), is expressly made subject to section 34. This reference to section 34 was inserted by the 1980 Act. The insertion was made to clarify the relationship between sections 34 and 35 following a decision of the English Court of Appeal which made section 35 dominant in relation to (ii) above. In *Hardy & Co. v. Hillerns and Fowler*,[37] it was held that a sale and part delivery to sub-buyers, without the original buyer having the opportunity to examine the goods, constituted an act inconsistent with the seller's ownership, thus barring rejection when the original buyer later discovered the non-conformity of the goods with

35 *Bernstein v. Pamsons Motors* (Golders Green) Ltd [1987] 2 All E.R. 220.

36 Gill, "Limitation on the right to reject goods for breach of condition under the Sale of Goods Act" [1987] *Irish Law Times* 136.

37 [1923] 2 K.B. 490; followed in *Ruben v. Faire* [1949] 1 K.B. 254.

the contract and immediately sought to reject. The problem was commonplace in commercial sales where the sub-buyer could exercise his right to reject while the original buyer could not, even though all parties involved were aware of the nature of the transactions. This case was distinguished in New Zealand despite very similar facts,[38] and the legislation was amended in the U.K.[39] and Ireland,[40] whereby the second set of circumstances in section 35, (ii) above, was made expressly subject to section 34. Hence, a buyer cannot be deemed to have accepted goods by doing any act in relation to the goods inconsistent with the seller's ownership of the goods, unless the buyer has been afforded the opportunity of examination as set out in section 34. While remedying one aspect of the difficult relationship between sections 34 and 35, this amendment may have led to other, unintentioned difficulties. For instance, from the above, it would seem that the section 34 right to examine does not apply to the first set of circumstances of deemed acceptance, (i) above, where the buyer intimates acceptance, and it is unclear whether section 34 applies to the third set of circumstances of deemed acceptance, (iii) above, by retaining the goods without rejecting them. Does the phrase "subject to section 34 of this Act" apply to the (ii) and (iii), or to (ii) only? And, why does it not apply to (i)?

On a literal reading of the provision,[41] and indeed applying the mischief rule of interpretation,[42] it can be argued that the right of examination only applies to (ii), and not to (i) or (iii). This interpretation is not unreasonable in the sense that a buyer who intimates acceptance under (i) above can be taken as impliedly waiving any right to examine the goods, and a buyer who retains the goods without rejecting them under (iii) above has had an opportunity to examine them, albeit for a limited time before he will be deemed to have accepted them.

There is further uncertainty concerning the application of section 34. The reference to section 34 in section 35 does not distinguish between subsections (1) and (2) of section 34. Taking a literal reading of the provision, the reference to section 34 would include all subsections of section 34. Does this mean, for example, that section 34, subsections (1) and (2) have no application to (i) above, where the buyer intimates acceptance? Such a reading would clearly be to the disadvantage of a buyer. Or, should the reference to section 34 in section 35 be read as a

---

38 *Hammer and Barrow v. Cola-Cola* [1962] N.Z.L.R. 723.

39 Misrepresentation Act 1967, s.4(2); see later Sale of Goods Act 1979, ss.34 and 35.

40 The Sale of Goods and Supply of Services Act 1980.

41 On the literal rule of statutory interpretation see Byrne & McCutcheon, *The Irish Legal System* (Dublin, Butterworths, 4th ed., 2001) pp.471–2. For application of the literal rule see, *e.g. The Inspector of Taxes v. Kiernan* [1981] I.R. 138.

42 On the mischief rule of statutory interpretation see Byrne & McCutcheon, *The Irish Legal System*, (Dublin, Butterworths, 4th ed., 2001) pp.473-4. For application of the mischief rule see, *e.g. Nestor v. Murphy* [1979] I.R. 326.

reference to section 34(1) only, on the basis that subsection (1) refers specifically to deemed acceptance, leaving subsection (2) to have general application in all cases? Similar questions can be put in relation to (ii) and (iii) above.

In fact, there is no reason why a buyer's right to examine goods, as defined in subsection (1) and (2) of section 34 should not apply to all three circumstances. The buyer's right to reject is the trump card in the pack of buyer's remedies and there is no good reason why before being deemed to have accepted goods, in whatever circumstances, the buyer should not be afforded the right to examine the goods to ensure that they are in conformity with the contract. It is ironic that a piece of legislation, that is, the 1980 Act, which was motivated by concerns to protect consumer interests, might have the effect of limiting the rights of buyers, including consumer buyers. In the United Kingdom, similar provisions have been amended to clarify the relationship between the buyer's right of examination and the rules on deemed acceptances.[43] There, under section 34 of the Sale of Goods Act 1979, as amended, there is a general right, unless otherwise agreed, that when the seller tenders delivery he is bound, on request, to afford a buyer the opportunity to examine the goods (the equivalent to our section 34(2)). Further, under section 35 of the Sale of Goods Act 1979, as amended, where goods are delivered, and the buyer has not previously examined them, he cannot be deemed to have accepted goods by intimating acceptance or by doing an act inconsistent with the seller's ownership, until he is given the opportunity to examine the goods. This right to an opportunity to examine does not apply where the buyer is deemed to have accepted the goods where he retains the goods beyond a reasonable time without intimating rejection. In this last set of circumstances, a right to examination seems unnecessary because, by virtue of retaining the goods for a period of time, the buyer is afforded the opportunity to examine them.

14.2.1.1 Intimation of acceptance

The buyer loses the right to reject the goods if he indicates to the seller that he accepts them. Such indication can be in any form, oral, written or by conduct, provided it is clear and unequivocal.[44] In order to take advantage of this provision, a seller may attempt to get the buyer to sign an "acceptance note" when the goods are delivered. The effect of such notes is not entirely clear and would depend on the circumstances of the case. For example, a mere "delivery note" or "acknowledgment of receipt" of

43 See the U.K. Sale and Supply of Goods Act 1994; see also Brown, "Acceptance in Sale of Goods" [1988] *Journal of Business Law* 56.

44 In *Varley v. Whipp* [1900] 1 Q.B. 513, the buyer's "grumbling" letter arranging a meeting with the seller to discuss a solution was held not to constitute acceptance.

the goods would not necessarily amount to acceptance in this context. Another area of uncertainty arises where the buyer asks for, or agrees to, repairs by the seller. This may amount to an intimation of acceptance.[45] In the U.K., following a recommendation of the Law Commissions,[46] any agreement in relation to repair does not of itself amount to acceptance.[47] While this appears to be the better approach, the position remains unsettled in this jurisdiction.[48]

If only part of section 35 is subject to section 34, as discussed above, then a buyer who intimates acceptance *before* having had a reasonable opportunity to examine the goods is deemed to have accepted the goods, and thus has waived the right of examination.[49] It seems unfair that a buyer, whether commercial or consumer, can be deemed to have accepted goods, for instance by signing a suitably worded acceptance note, without having had the opportunity to examine the goods, which may be very complicated and packaged, to determine whether they are in conformity with the contract. Again in the U.K., following a recommendation from the Law Commissions,[50] there can be no binding intimation of acceptance unless there has been a reasonable opportunity to examine the goods.[51] However, in commercial sales, parties are free to agree otherwise. Hence, the current position in the United Kingdom is more favourable to buyers, but this should not be over-estimated. First, what constitutes a reasonable opportunity of examination remains to be seen, and second, only obvious and immediate defects would be likely to be identified by such examination. More major defects might only become apparent over a period of time. In this context, the third scenario of acceptance – retention of the goods without intimating rejection – is relevant.[52]

14.2.1.2 An act inconsistent with the seller's ownership of the goods

It should be noted that this form of deemed acceptance is expressly stated to be subject to the buyer's right to examine the goods, under section 34. As noted above, this was not the position under the original 1893 Act and was amended by the 1980 Act. In many cases, property in the goods will pass on delivery, or soon after delivery.[53] Hence, it is difficult to see how

45 See also 14.2.1.2 on repairs.
46 *Sale and Supply of Goods*, Law Com. No. 160, Scot. Law Com. No. 104 (Cm. 137, 1987) para. 5.26–5.29.
47 U.K. Sale of Goods Act 1979, s.35(6).
48 See also 14.4 on consumer's right to seek cure.
49 *Hardy & Co. v. Hillerns and Fowler* [1923] 2 K.B. 490.
50 *Sale and Supply of Goods*, Law Com. No. 160, Scot. Law Com. No. 104 (Cm. 137, 1987) para. 5.20–5.24.
51 See U.K. Sale of Goods Act 1979, ss.34-35.
52 See 14.2.1.3.
53 See Chapter 18.

any act of the buyer could be "inconsistent with the seller's ownership". It has been suggested that this phrase means no more than "inconsistent with rejection".[54]

The law is unclear as to what constitutes an act inconsistent with the seller's ownership. There is authority that administrative acts, such as unloading or sorting goods,[55] or rebagging rejected goods is insufficient,[56] but even the most trivial act when done with knowledge of the seller's breach can constitute acceptance.[57] For instance, registering ownership of a defective car and advertising it for sale,[58] and the mere use of such a car,[59] have been held to constitute acceptance under this heading. It has also been held that incorporating goods so that they cannot be detached constitutes acceptance.[60] In general, the following may be regarded as acts inconsistent with the seller's ownership of the goods:

(i) using the goods more than is necessary in order to ascertain whether they conform to the contract;
(ii) incorporating or consuming the goods so that they cannot be returned;
(iii) attempting to repair the goods; in a commercial context, even asking the seller to repair the goods may amount to acceptance of the goods, particularly if the buyer does not make it clear that he reserves the right to reject;
(iv) any other dealing with the goods, such as reselling or making a gift of them.[61]

14.2.1.3 Retention of the goods

As noted above, this form of deemed acceptance appears not to be subject to the section 34 right of examination. Indeed, in the U.K., the Law Commissions recommended that the third ground of deemed acceptance –

54 See Goode, *Commercial Law,* (London, Penguin, 2nd ed., 1995) p.371–2. Further, in *Kwei Tek Chao v. British Traders and Shippers* [1954] 2 Q.B. 459, Devlin J. explained that the property in the goods initially passed conditionally, subject to the buyer's right to reject, such that the seller is left with a "reversionary interest." The buyer is deemed to accept where he does any act inconsistent with this interest: approved by the Court of Appeal in *Gill & Duffus SA v. Berger & Co Inc* [1983] 1 Lloyd's Rep. 622.

55 *Libau Wood Company v. H Smith & Sons Ltd* (1930) 37 Ll. L. Rep. 296 at 300.

56 *Dower & Co v. Corrie Maccol & Son* (1925) 23 Ll. L. Rep. 100 at 102.

57 *Gill v. Thomas Heiton & Co Ltd* [1943] Ir. Jur. Rep. 67.

58 *Armaghdown Motors Ltd v. Gray Motors Ltd* [1963] N.Z.L.R. 5.

59 *Lee v. York Coach and Marine* [1977] R.T.R. 35.

60 *Mechan & Sons Ltd v. Bow, M'Lachlin & Co Ltd* 1910 Sess. C. 758.

61 In international sales, the contract is often performed by delivery of documents. Here a buyer does not lose the right to reject by dealing with the documents. Rather the buyer has a right first to reject the documents, and then a second right to reject the goods for defects not apparent on the face of the documents: see 30.3.4.

retention – should *not* be made subject to the section 34 right of examination.[62] However, and perhaps as a concession, in assessing whether a reasonable time has elapsed, thereby barring rejection, an English court can consider whether a buyer has had a reasonable opportunity to examine the goods.[63]

Under this heading, the buyer loses the right to reject if, "without good and sufficient reason, he retains the goods without intimating to the seller that he is rejecting them."[64] Unlike the above two forms of deemed acceptance which, in themselves, have remained largely unchanged, this is different from the original provision of the 1893 Act and the position in the United Kingdom. Under the original 1893 Act, a buyer was deemed to have accepted goods when after the lapse of a reasonable time, he retained the goods without intimating rejection to the seller. The relevant United Kingdom provision is practically identical.[65] The key question in cases decided under the original 1893 Act or the English provisions is: for how long can a buyer hold goods and not lose the right to reject: what is a "reasonable time"? In addressing this question, what constitutes a "reasonable time" is a question of fact in each case.[66]

This time period can be very short as evidenced by *Gill v. Thomas Heiton & Co. Ltd*[67] where the plaintiff wholesalers sold a barge-load of turf to the defendant retailers. On delivery and shortly after unloading commenced, it was noted that the turf was unfit for resale. However, the unloading continued until the whole barge was unloaded. The following day the plaintiff was informed of the defective quality and the defendant sought to reject the goods. The plaintiff argued that the defendant had accepted the goods and demanded the price. The High Court held that the buyer had a right to reject goods for breach of condition, within a reasonable time. However, this right had not been exercised with sufficient promptness or in a manner consistent with the ownership of the seller, and so the plaintiff was limited to a claim in damages only.

In *Bernstein v. Pamsons Motors (Golders Green) Ltd*,[68] it was stated that a reasonable time is an objectively reasonable time to try out the goods, not necessarily a reasonable time to discover the defect. Here a new car seized up after three weeks driving and 142 miles due to a blob of

62 *Sale and Supply of Goods*, Law Com. No. 160, Scot. Law Com. No. 104, (Cm. 137, 1987) para. 5.25.

63 U.K. Sale of Goods Act 1979, s.35(5).

64 A contract could fix a time limit for rejection, but where the buyer is a consumer this clause would need to be fair in accordance with the E.C. (Unfair Terms in Consumer Contracts) Regulations 1995 and 2000, S.I. No. 27 of 1995, and S.I. No. 307 of 2000: see further 2.3.5.3 and 10.5.3.

65 Sale of Goods Act 1979, s.35.

66 1893 Act, s.56.

67 [1943] Ir. Jur. Rep. 67.

68 [1987] 2 All E.R. 220.

sealant in the lubrication system. It was held that the car was unmerchantable but the buyer was too late to reject and only had a claim in damages. Rougier J. emphasised, from the seller's point of view, "the commercial desirability of being able to close his ledger reasonably soon after the transaction is complete."[69] But he also stated "[w]hat is a reasonable time in relation to a bicycle will hardly suffice for a nuclear submarine",[70] thereby leaving a huge margin of discretion in deciding what constitutes a reasonable time for different goods. For instance, in a Canadian case, *Public Utilities Commission of City of Waterloo v. Burroughs Business Machines*,[71] based on similar statutory provisions, a computer system which was defective was rejected by the buyers after eight months. However, the buyers continued to use it for a further seven months. It was held that the buyer could reject the goods after 15 months, as the buyers had used their best efforts to make the computer function properly, and the goods were "complex and novel."

Later English case law seems to recognise that *Bernstein* was a harsh decision on its facts. For example, in *Truk (UK) Ltd v. Tokmakidis GmbH & ors*,[72] a buyer was entitled to reject a vehicle six months after delivery. The buyer bought the vehicle for resale – a fact known to the seller – and the defect was only discovered when found by a potential sub-buyer. At the same time, the court took a similar view to many points made in *Bernstein*. For example, it was accepted that what constitutes a reasonable time is a reasonable time to examine the goods and not a reasonable time to discover the defect. Also, it was noted that what is a reasonable time depends on the complexity of the goods. The court found that had the goods been bought for the buyer's own use, a period of one to two months might have been a reasonable time to examine the goods. However, when goods are bought for resale, defects are often not discovered until the goods are resold and hence a longer period of examination is required. This period comprises the anticipated time it takes to resell the goods (and not the actual time) plus another reasonable period to examine the goods by the sub-buyer.

Arguably, the current Irish position is more generous to the buyer in terms of the period of time during which he can hold the goods without being deemed to have accepted them under this third heading.[73] This is because of the inclusion of the phrase "without good and sufficient reason". Section 35 provides that a buyer is deemed to have accepted the goods when, "without good and sufficient reason", he retains the goods without rejecting them. Hence, an Irish court must concern itself with the

---

69 *Ibid.* p.230.

70 *Ibid.* p.230.

71 (1974) 52 D.L.R. 481.

72 [2000] 1 Lloyd's Rep. 543 (Q.B.D.); see also *Peakman v. Express Circuits Ltd* unreported, Court of Appeal, 1998.

73 See Gill, "Limitation on the right to reject goods for breach of condition under the Sale of Goods Act" [1987] *Irish Law Times* 136.

reason for a buyer retaining the goods. This is not required by the United Kingdom legislation. Taking the *Bernstein* case as an example, one of the reasons the car had travelled only 142 miles in three weeks before the defect became apparent was that the buyer, Mr Bernstein, had been ill for a period of that time. Could it not be argued that, under Irish law, this would be a "good and sufficient reason" for delaying in rejecting the goods?[74]

Other factors which may be relevant in deciding at what point a buyer loses his right to reject under this heading are as follows.

(i) The nature of the goods. If, for instance, the goods are perishable, the time for rejection may be relatively short; if the goods are complex, a longer time may be allowed to enable the buyer to try them out.[75]
(ii) The conduct of the parties. For instance, if the seller encourages the buyer to allow him to attempt repair, a court may be prepared to disregard the time taken to make that attempt.
(iii) The nature of the market. In a commercial context especially, where prices are volatile, the time for rejection will probably be shorter than in a more stable market.
(v) Any custom of the trade.

In general, even with the potentially more generous time period provided under Irish law, this part of section 35 can be criticised for the lack of certainty as to when acceptance will be deemed to occur. However, the alternatives are not without their own problems. In the United States, for example, "lemon laws" provide for fixed time periods for particular types of goods, hence providing certainty though lacking flexibility.[76]

Another option is the introduction of a long-term right to reject.[77] Such a right was present in the EC Commission's draft Directive on Consumer Sales, whereby a consumer buyer was given a one-year period in which to reject goods. This aspect of the Directive was removed during the legislative process and no long-term right to reject is provided in the final

---

74 It is not clear whether such an argument can be based on subjective factors, such as personal illness, or on objective factors only.

75 *Bernstein v. Pamsons Motors (Golders Green) Ltd* [1987] 2 All E.R. 220.

76 See Ervine, "Protecting New Car Purchasers: Recent United States and English Developments Compared" (1985) 34 *International and Comparative Law Quarterly* 342, for examples of the rigidity and complexity of such a system. In 1987, the English and Scottish Law Commissions rejected any notion of introducing such fixed time periods: see *Sale and Supply of Goods*, Law Com. No. 160, Scot. Law Com. No. 104, (Cm. 137, 1987) para. 5.14–5.19.

77 The English and Scottish Law Commissions recommended that there should be no general long-term right to reject: see *Sale and Supply of Goods*, Law Com. No. 160, Scot. Law Com. No. 104, (Cm. 137, 1987) para. 5.6– 5.19.

wording of the Directive.[78] Section 53(2) of the 1893 Act goes some way to provide a consumer buyer with a "longer-term" right to reject.[79] It seems right that any extension of rights in this area should be for the benefit of consumer buyers rather than commercial buyers. A commercial buyer may have an equality of bargaining power with the seller and so accept, as a business risk, that some goods may be defective. This risk can be factored into any pre-contractual bargaining. Further, a commercial buyer will be less at risk of post-contractual threats by the seller that the buyer should keep the goods, as the continuance of a good trading relationship may be in the interests of both parties. At worst, a commercial buyer will be better able to pursue litigation, if necessary. None of these factors apply to consumer buyers. Consumer buyers are normally in an inferior bargaining position: this can lead to the buyer keeping the goods and being satisfied with repair. Consumer buyers cannot be expected to pursue their rights through the litigation process, nor can they write off defects as business risks, nor are they in a position to resell defective goods. Rejection, and the longer-term right of rejection in section 53(2), are ideal consumer remedies. The right to reject is understandable and effective. It fulfills consumer expectations as a remedy for defective goods in which the buyer no longer has confidence. It also means that the consumer buyer need have no more dealings with the seller in whom he has lost confidence. Finally, it is claimed that the right to reject has the longer-term beneficial effect of keeping the quality of goods high. However, seller's interests must not be ignored in considering the right to reject and any extension of it.

As discussed above, this part of section 35 would appear not to be subject to the reasonable opportunity of examination under section 34. But durability is a factor in determining merchantable quality,[80] and where goods prove not to be durable at the time of the sale, although the right to reject may be lost through retention, a claim for damages is always available.

14.2.2 The rule against partial rejection

The rule against partial rejection is based on section 11(3) of the 1893 Act. It provides:

> "Where a contract of sale is not severable, and the buyer has accepted the goods, or part thereof, the breach of any condition to be fulfilled by the seller can only be treated as a breach of warranty, and not as a ground for rejecting the goods and treating the contract as repudiated, … "

Hence, where the contract is not severable, the buyer loses the right to reject if he accepts the goods or part of them. Thus, if only some or part of

78 See 14.7.

79 See 14.4.

80 1893 Act, s.14(3); see 13.3.2.2.

the goods delivered are defective the buyer must accept, or reject, all of them. There are two statutory exceptions to this "all or nothing" rule:

(i) where, under section 30(3), the seller delivers goods of the contract description mixed with goods of a different description, and
(ii) where, under section 11(3), the contract is severable.

These limited exceptions are discussed further below.

In practice, this rigid "all or nothing" approach is often not followed. Commercial contracts frequently make provision for partial rejection, as this is more in keeping with commercial reality, and even in the absence of a contractual right to partially reject the goods, a seller will often allow a buyer to reject part of the goods as part of a negotiated settlement. As a result, it would appear that the law is out of step with commercial practice. The position in the United Kingdom has been modified by the Sale and Supply of Goods Act 1994 to allow partial rejection in certain circumstances.[81] This right to partially reject is subject to two limitations. First, a non-consumer buyer should not reject at all where the breach is so slight that rejection would be unreasonable.[82] Second, where the buyer accepts some of the goods forming part of a "commercial unit," he is deemed to accept all the goods forming part of that unit.[83] For example, a pair of shoes would constitute a commercial unit such that a buyer could not reject one shoe only.[84] The introduction of a right to partially reject in Irish law should be considered.

14.2.2.1 Mixed description

Under section 30(3), where the seller delivers goods he contracted to sell mixed with goods of a different description, the buyer is given two options. He may (i) accept the goods which match the contract description and reject the rest – a form of partial rejection; or (ii) reject the whole quantity delivered. In this context, contract description has the same meaning as in section 13 of the 1893 Act and arguably, following English case law, is narrowly defined.[85]

---

81 U.K. Sale of Goods Act 1979, s.35A.
82 U.K. Sale of Goods Act 1979, s.15A.
83 U.K. Sale of Goods Act 1979, s.35(7).
84 *Sale and Supply of Goods*, Law Com. No. 160, Scot. Law Com. No. 104, (Cm. 137, 1987) para. 6.12.
85 See *Ashington Piggeries Ltd. v. Christopher Hill Ltd* [1972] A.C. 441 (H.L.): see further 13.2.

14.2.2.2 Severable contracts

Section 11(3) is expressed not to apply where the contract is severable, so that where the contract is severable the buyer may reject some goods notwithstanding that he has accepted other goods supplied under the contract. Hence, the first question to be addressed is whether there is one contract or several. This can be a difficult question to answer and will depend on the language and documents used in the formation of the contract(s). For example, a seller might send a customer a set of standard terms of sale and indicate that all orders are to be placed on those terms; or a seller and buyer might agree a common set of terms of trading in advance to govern all sales, a sort of master agreement. In these circumstances, each individual order is likely to be regarded as a new and separate contract. In contrast, where parties agree to supply a fixed quantity of goods over a period of time at the buyer's request, this is more likely to be interpreted as a single contract. Similarly, if a number of different items are ordered in one document, there is likely to be one contract.[86]

Once it is decided that there is a single contract, the second question is whether the contract is severable or not. An example of a severable contract is given in section 31(2) of the 1893 Act which refers to instalment deliveries. Accordingly, a contract is severable where the goods are to be delivered in separate instalments and are paid for separately. The courts have also interpreted contracts as severable in other circumstances, thereby allowing the application of more flexible rules. For instance, a contract was severable where the contract provided for the goods to be delivered in instalments, to be determined by the seller,[87] and as required by the buyer,[88] and where goods were to be paid for by monthly account.[89] The essence of a severable contract is that it is one contract, with the obligations under the contract, such as the delivery obligations or the payment obligations, being performed in several (two or more) parts. This can be contrasted with the position where several separate contracts exist. In the latter circumstances, defective performance under one contract has no legal effect on any other similar contracts. In contrast, with a severable contract, defective performance under one part can have legal consequences on the other parts and on the whole contract.

Where the contract is severable and the seller makes one or more defective deliveries, it may be necessary to decide whether the buyer can (i) reject the defective delivery, and/or (ii) terminate the contract and refuse future deliveries.

---

86 *E.g. Robert A Munro & Co Ltd v. Meyer* [1930] 2 K.B. 312: in this case a statement that each delivery should be treated as a separate contract did not take from the fact that, on its proper construction, there was one single, though severable, contract.

87 *Regent OHG v. Francesco of Jermyn St* [1981] 3 All E.R. 327.

88 *Jackson v. Rotax* [1910] 2 K.B. 937.

89 *Longbottom v. Bass Walker* (1922) W.N. 245.

(i) Rejection of the defective delivery

Where a contract is severable, acceptance of one instalment does not prevent the buyer rejecting another instalment. Hence, the usual rules on acceptance do not apply to severable contracts. But, although the position is not clear, the better view is that the buyer may not reject part of an instalment and accept the remainder: in these circumstances an "all or nothing" approach pertains.[90]

(ii) Termination of the contract

Section 31(2) provides that where the seller makes one or more defective deliveries under a severable contract, whether or not those breaches allow the buyer to terminate the whole contract depends on the terms of the contract and all the circumstances of the case. Hence, where the breach in relation to one or more instalments is sufficiently serious, this may amount to a repudiation of the whole contract and allow the buyer to terminate it.[91] Factors which may be taken into account in assessing the seriousness of the breach include: (i) the ratio of the breach to the contract as a whole; and (ii) the likelihood of the breach being repeated.[92]

The question whether the buyer is entitled to terminate the contract as a result of a breach by the seller may be crucial: if the buyer terminates in circumstances in which he is not entitled to do so he will be in breach of contract. However, the application of the test is difficult to predict, as the following cases illustrate, so that the commercial practitioner may not be able to advise the buyer with certainty as to his right to terminate the contract.

In *Maple Flock Co. Ltd v. Universal Furniture Products (Wembley) Ltd*,[93] the seller contracted to deliver 100 tons of rag flock in weekly instalments of 1.5 tons each. The first 15 deliveries were satisfactory and were accepted; the next was contaminated but the following two were acceptable. The buyer purported to terminate the contract for breach in relation to the sixteenth delivery. A further four satisfactory deliveries were tendered and rejected: the seller sued. The court held that, bearing in mind the ratio of the breach to the contract as a whole and the likelihood of the breach being repeated, the breach was not so serious as to justify termination. Therefore the buyer was in breach of contract. Again, in *Regent OHG v. Francesco of Jermyn St*,[94] the short delivery of one suit under a severable contract for the supply of 62 suits by instalments was held to be insufficient to amount to a repudiation of the whole contract. In

90 *Benjamin's Sale of Goods*, (London, Sweet & Maxwell, 4th ed., 1992) para. 12-038
91 *Warinco AG v. Samor SPA* [1977] 2 Lloyd's Rep. 582 per Donaldson J. at 588.
92 *Maple Flock Co. Ltd v. Universal Furniture Products (Wembley) Ltd* [1934] K.B. 148 (C.A.).
93 [1934] K.B. 148.
94 [1981] 3 All E.R. 327.

contrast, in *Robt A Munroe & Co Ltd v. Meyer*,[95] the seller contracted to deliver 1,500 tons of bonemeal in weekly instalments of 125 tons. After half the goods had been delivered, it was discovered that all the deliveries were contaminated with cocoa husks. In this case it was held that the buyer was entitled to terminate the contract.

These cases represent two different ends of the spectrum of degrees of seriousness of breach. In *Maple Flock*, the ratio was one defective delivery out of a total of about 67 deliveries and the likelihood of repeated breaches was low. In the *Munroe case*, the ratio was six defective deliveries out of a total of 12 and the likelihood of repeated breaches was high. The difficulty lies in determining the parties' rights when the degree of seriousness of breach is somewhere more in the middle of this spectrum.

Even where the buyer is entitled to terminate the contract under section 31(2), it is not clear whether this entitles him to reject goods from previous instalments already accepted. The language of the section refers to "repudiation" of the contract, suggesting that the buyer can terminate from the time of the breach only. But a buyer may be able to reject instalments already accepted if he can show that the acceptance was conditional on all remaining deliveries being acceptable.[96]

14.3 The Right to Damages

Any breach of contract by the seller entitles the buyer to claim damages in respect of any losses caused by the breach. Damages are assessed in accordance with the general rules of contract law;[97] the buyer must therefore show that his losses were caused by the breach in question, that they are not too remote to be compensatable and that he has taken reasonable steps to mitigate his loss. Further, any term in the contract fixing the amount of damages payable will be subject to the rule against penalties and will only be enforceable if it is a genuine pre-estimate of the loss. However, these rules are modified by the Sale of Goods Acts 1893 and 1980 and specific rules apply to claims for damages for non-delivery; late delivery; and breach of warranty.

14.3.1 Damages for non-delivery

Where the seller wrongfully neglects or refuses to deliver, he totally fails to perform his obligations under the contract and the buyer is released from his obligation to accept the goods and to pay for them. If the buyer has paid

95 [1930] 2 K.B. 312.

96 See *Atiyah's The Sale of Goods* (Harlow, Pearson, 10th ed., 2001) p.507; *cf.* 9th ed, 1995, p.455.

97 See generally 2.4.4.3.

the price, or any part thereof, in advance, and no goods are delivered, he can also reclaim the price as part of a restitutionary claim because there has been a total failure of consideration on the part of the seller.[98] Where the buyer has suffered additional losses because of the non-delivery, he may sue the seller for damages under section 51(1) of the 1893 Act.

14.3.1.1 The basic measure of damages

The basic measure of damages for non-delivery is provided for in section 51(2) of the 1893 Act as "the estimated loss directly and naturally resulting, in the ordinary course of events, from the seller's breach." This is, in effect, the first limb of the test established in the leading case on remoteness of loss in contract law, *Hadley v. Baxendale*,[99] and therefore it mirrors the common law position. The second limb of the *Hadley v. Baxendale* test, which deals with claims for unusual losses for which the seller is deemed to be responsible because of some particular facts known to the parties when the contract is made, is not reproduced in the legislation and so, in this regard, we must fall back on the common law.

14.3.1.2 The available market rule

The basic measure of damages is modified where there is an available market for goods of the contract description. In such circumstances, section 51(3) of the 1893 Act applies – the "available market rule". Indeed, while the available market rule is only a prima facie rule, in practice, it is applied more commonly than the basic rule.[100]

The available market rule provides that that the buyer's damages for non-delivery are prima facie the difference between the contract price and the market price for similar goods on the date(s) when the goods should have been delivered: an objective test.[101] The rationale for this rule is that the buyer is expected to take reasonable steps to mitigate his loss and, where there is an available market, he can mitigate by buying replacement goods in the market.

> **Example**: Assume that a contract for the sale of goods was concluded on January 1 and the contract price was €10,000. Assume that the delivery day was set for January 14, but no delivery was made on that day. If in January, the market in the goods in question was rising, due to high demand for the

98 1893 Act, s.54.

99 (1854) 9 Ex. 341.

100 The market price rule may be displaced where it would be inappropriate (see, *e.g. The Texaco Melbourne* [1994] 1 Lloyd's Rep. 473 (H.L.)) and it may not apply where the parties have contemplated that it would not provide adequate compensation for the breach (see *WL Thompson Ltd v. Robinson (Gunmakers) Ltd* [1955] Ch. 177 per Upjohn J.).

101 No account is taken of subjective factors personal to the buyer, such as lack of expertise which might result in him paying a higher price: see *Shearson Lehman Hutton Inc v. Maclaine Watson & Co. Ltd (No. 2)* [1990] 3 All E.R. 723.

goods and/or shortages of the goods, such that their market value on the 14th was €12,000, then the buyer's damages for non-delivery are prima facie the difference between the contract price (€10,000) and the market price for similar goods on the date when goods should have been delivered (€12,000), which is £2,000.

It is important to emphasise that the date of assessment is the date(s) when the goods ought to have been delivered: January 14 in the above example. If, say, the buyer in the above example had delayed in buying replacement goods and during that period of delay the market value of the goods continued to rise such that he had to pay €15,000 on February 1 for replacement goods. The cost of that delay (€3,000) would rest with the buyer.[102] It can be assumed that a court would show some flexibility in this regard and allow a buyer a couple of days, if necessary, to assess the situation and find a suitable replacement seller.

The available market rule has the advantage for a court that it is easy to apply. There is no requirement, as a condition of recovering damages, that the buyer enter into a substitute transaction. Even where it can be established that a market transaction would, because of volatility in the market, take time to arrange, damages will be assessed at the market value pertaining at the due delivery date, or thereabouts, and not at the date of any notional substitute transaction.[103]

Example: Assume the above facts but that the market in the goods is falling during the month of January, due to low demand for the goods and/or a glut in the market, such that the market value of the goods on January 14 is €8,000. In these circumstances, the buyer has suffered no loss because the same goods which would have cost him €10,000 under the contract, now cost €8,000, so the available market rule has no application in these circumstances. Here the seller's breach provides a welcome release from the contract for the buyer. Nominal damages would be available for the breach but, in practice, would not be worth pursuing.

It is generally accepted that resale value is irrelevant for fixing market value. In *Williams v. Agius*,[104] the buyer of a cargo of coal for 16s 3d per ton contracted to resell it at 19s per ton. By the time of the delivery date, the market price had risen to 23s 6d per ton and the seller failed to deliver. When the buyer sued for non-delivery, the seller argued that the damages

102 See, *e.g. Kaines (UK) Ltd v. Österreichische Warrenhandelsgesellschaft* [1993] 2 Lloyds Rep. 1: see further Bridge, "Market Damages in sale of goods cases – recent developments" [1994] *Journal of Business Law* 152.

103 *Shearson Lehman Hutton Inc v. Maclaine Watson & Co. Ltd (No. 2)* [1990] 3 All E.R. 723. The same can be said in relation to actions for non-acceptance by the buyer where a similar available market rule applies under s.50(3), see further 15.2.2; and in actions for breach of warranty of quality where a value rule also applies under s.53(5), see 14.3.2.1.

104 [1914] A.C. 510. But see further 15.3.1.3.

should be assessed with reference to the resale price and not the higher market value. The House of Lords disagreed, holding that the resale price was irrelevant. The buyer was entitled to be put in the same position he would have been in had the contract been properly performed, and in order to fulfill his resale contract he would have to buy substitute goods at market value. Equally, the sub-buyer would be entitled to damages with reference to the market value if the original buyer failed to deliver on the resale. It also appears that where the original buyer contracted to resell at a price higher than the market value, the resale price would be irrelevant.

In *Charter v. Sullivan*,[105] Jenkins L.J. sought to define "available market" in the following terms:

> "I … will content myself with the negative proposition that I doubt if there can be an available market for particular goods in any sense relevant to [the Sale of Goods Acts] unless those goods are available for sale in the market at the market or current price in the sense of the price, whatever it may be, fixed by reference to supply and demand as the price at which a purchaser for the goods in question can be found, be it greater or less than or equal to the contract price."

It would appear therefore that there is an "available market" for this purpose if there is an available source of supply from which the buyer could buy replacement goods at a price that fluctuates in line with supply and demand. The goods must also be available both in terms of geography and time. In *Cullen v. Horgan*,[106] the defendant seller based in Cahirciveen agreed in October to sell wool to the plaintiff in Dublin. No delivery date was fixed. Despite demands from the buyer, the seller failed to deliver the goods. During this time the market price of wool was rising. In an action for damages for non-delivery, the court held that the buyer was entitled to damages based on the difference between the contract price and the market price of the goods in the following January, the date by which the court found that delivery should have taken place. In determining the market price, there was no evidence of an available market for wool in Cahirciveen, where delivery was to take place. But the court took the market price in Cahirciveen to be the market price in Dublin, less the cost of carriage at the time of the defendant's failure to deliver.

It seems that there is no available market if the goods are unique or if demand for the goods exceeds supply. Where there is no available market, the measure of damages is prima facie, the difference in the contract price and the value of the goods at the date of delivery. In these circumstances, resale price may be used to set a value on the goods.[107] Moreover, where a

105 [1957] 2 Q.B. 117 at 128, per Jenkins L.J. *Cf. W L Thompson Ltd v. Robinson (Gunmakers) Ltd* [1955] Ch. 177.

106 [1925] 2 I.R. 1.

107 *Patrick v. Russo-British Grain Export Co.* [1927] 2 K.B. 535.

buyer cannot obtain substitute goods because there is no available market, a buyer may be able to buy goods of a superior quality, if, for instance, the goods are needed urgently to satisfy a sub-sale and claim the extra cost in any damages claim for non-delivery.[108]

In proceedings before a court, evidence will have to be produced of the market value or the value of the goods in question. Where goods are traded on a commodity market, for instance, evidence of the value of goods on a particular day can be readily established. In other circumstances, an auctioneer or valuer may need to be called as an expert witness in court, to give his opinion as to the value of the goods in question, at the relevant date. In many sales, particularly consumer sales, the value will be equivalent to the contract price.

14.3.1.3 Special damages

As noted above, where the buyer has contracted to resell the goods but the seller fails to deliver, generally no account is taken of the price at which the buyer contracted to resell.[109] A replacement purchase in the market will enable him to satisfy his resale contract. However, the market price rule does not prevent the buyer recovering special damages where they would be recoverable in accordance with general principles.[110] Thus, where the buyer loses a resale because he cannot satisfy his resale by buying in the market, special damages may be recoverable to compensate for the lost resale provided they are not too remote.

Authority for this proposition can be found in *Re R & H Hall & Co Ltd and W H Pim (Jnr) & Co Ltd's Arbitration*.[111] A buyer of a cargo of wheat for 51s 9d per quarter contracted to resell it at a profit for 56s 9d per quarter while the cargo was at sea. The seller failed to deliver. The market price of the goods at the date for delivery was 53s 9d. The House of Lords held that the damages could be assessed with regard to the resale price in order to take into account the lost profit provided certain requirements are complied with. Such damages are therefore recoverable where:

(i) the buyer contracts to resell the goods as *specific* goods (so that he cannot tender other goods to the sub-buyer by buying replacement goods in the market); and
(ii) the buyer does so before the seller's breach; and
(iii) the resale was foreseeable by the seller as a reasonable probability (in *Hall v. Pim* the resale was expressly provided for in the original sales contract); and
(iv) the resale price is not extravagant.

108 *Blackburn Bobbin Co v. Allen* [1918] 1 K.B. 540.
109 *Williams v. Agius* [1914] A.C. 510.
110 1893 Act, s.54.
111 (1927) 30 Ll. L. Rep. 159.

Other losses may be recovered as special damages, provided they are not too remote. For instance, where goods are bought for resale, the buyer may be able to claim damages for loss of goodwill or loss of future business.[112]

14.3.2 Damages for late delivery

Where time is of the essence,[113] late delivery constitutes a breach of condition and the buyer can reject the goods, terminate the contract and sue for damages for non-delivery as described above. A buyer can always choose to treat the breach of a condition as a breach of warranty,[114] and hence pursue a claim in damages only. Where time is not of the essence, the buyer's only remedy is to sue for damages.

14.3.2.1 Measure of damages

There are no special legislative rules as to the measure of damages for late delivery. Hence, the general common law rules will apply. Accordingly, where goods were intended for use in the buyer's business, he may recover damages for loss of profits caused by their non-availability, provided the loss is not too remote. Where the goods were to be used for some particularly lucrative purpose, the buyer will only be able to claim damages for such lost profits where this particular lucrative purpose was known to the seller at the time of the contract.[115] Where the goods were intended for resale, the basic measure of damages will be the difference in value of the goods between the contractual date of delivery and the actual date of delivery:[116] that is, the amount, if any, by which the value has fallen and the buyer has lost by the delay in reselling. If there is an available market for goods of the contract description, their value will be assessed by reference to the market price at the relevant date. It is not clear whether account can be taken of any actual resale by the buyer in fixing damages.[117] In practice, commercial buyers rarely seek damages for consequential

112 *Victoria Laundry (Windsor) Ltd v. Newman Industries Ltd* [1949] 2 K.B. 528 (C.A.).

113 See 11.2.4.

114 1893 Act s.11(2).

115 *Victoria Laundry (Windsor) Ltd v. Newman Industries Ltd* [1949] 2 K.B. 528 (C.A.).

116 *Heron II* [1969] 1 A.C. 350. See also *Croudace Construction v. Cawoods Concrete Products* [1978] 2 Lloyd's Rep. 55, where the goods, though delivered late, were used as originally intended. In this case, the measure of damages was assessed not by the difference in value but on the basis of the additional costs resulting from the late delivery.

117 See *Wertheim v. Chicoutimi Pulp Co* [1911] A.C.D. 301(P.C.), where it was held that account should be taken of the fact that the buyer had sold the goods at more than the market price current at the date of delivery. *Cf. Slater v. Hoyle and Smith* Ltd [1920] 2 K.B. 11 (C.A.), where the court refused to follow *Wertheim* and applied the simple "difference in value" rule.

losses caused by late delivery.[118] Sales contracts often exclude liability for such losses; a *force majeure* or other clause may extend the time for delivery; or a liquidated damages clause may exist to cover the situation.

14.3.3 Damages following rejection

Where there is a breach of condition, there are three options for the buyer:

(i) the buyer can reject the goods, terminate the contract and claim damages for any loss (and claim a refund of any price paid); or
(ii) the buyer may choose not to exercise his right to reject and terminate, and instead, he may treat the breach of condition as a breach of warranty and pursue a claim in damages only;[119] or
(iii) the buyer may lose his right to reject (by accepting the goods under sections 34 and 35) and be limited to a claim in damages only.

In the first case, where the buyer rejects the goods for breach of condition, the effect is as if the seller has not delivered. In these circumstances, the buyer may claim damages for non-delivery. Where the goods cause other losses to the buyer prior to rejection, for example, where the goods are defective and damage the buyer's other property, the buyer may claim damages for those losses in addition.

Damages in the second and third cases above are addressed in the next section on damages for breach of warranty.

14.3.4 Damages for breach of warranty

Under section 53(1), where the buyer retains the goods by choice ((ii) above) or by law ((iii) above) he may set up his claim for damages for breach of warranty against the seller's claim for the price and thus withhold some, or all of the price,[120] or he can sue for damages for breach of warranty.[121]

14.3.4.1 The measure of damages

Section 53(4) provides that the basic measure of damages for breach of warranty is "the estimated loss directly and naturally resulting, in the ordinary course of events, from the breach of warranty." As with section

118 See Beale and Dugdale, "Contracts between businessmen" (1975) 2 *British Journal of Legal Studies* 45.
119 1893 Act, s.11(1).
120 1893 Act, s.53(1)(a).
121 1893 Act, s.53(1)(b).

51(2), this is, in effect, the first limb of the test established in the leading case on remoteness of loss in contract law, *Hadley v. Baxendale*,[122] and again, as with section 51(2), there is no mention of the second limb of the *Hadley v. Baxendale* test, which deals with claims for unusual losses for which the seller is deemed to be responsible because of some particular facts known to the parties when the contract is made, and so, in this regard, we must fall back on the common law.

(i) Breach of warranty of quality

Section 53(5) is stated to cover the situation where there is a breach of warranty of quality, for example, where the goods delivered are unmerchantable. However, it is assumed that the provision applies to any claim where the goods are defective and for any claim for breach of any of the statutory implied terms. In these circumstances, the measure of damages is prima facie the difference between the value of the goods at the date of delivery and the value they would have had had they satisfied the warranty. In some cases, particularly consumer cases, this will often be the cost of repairing the goods. In commercial cases, rather than sue for breach of warranty, the parties more usually agree to a variation of the price.

While section 53(5) is commonly applied, it is a prima facie rule only, and can be displaced in certain circumstances. In *Bence Graphics v. Fasson*,[123] vinyl film was sold to a buyer who used it to manufacture decals bearing words or numbers of identification for containers in the shipping industry. In breach of warranty of quality, the film remained legible for much less than the industry standard of five years. The trial judge applied the prima facie value rule and awarded damages of over £500,000. The buyer's customers had complained, and although he had not compensated them, he remained open to such claims. The Court of Appeal overturned the award and held that the buyer's award should be limited to actual losses incurred following sub-sales, based on section 52(2). Here, sub-sales were within the reasonable contemplation of the parties, and so relevant to an assessment of damages.

(ii) Special damages

Special damages may also be recovered provided they are not too remote.[124] Additional damages may therefore be awarded for:

---

122 (1854) 9 Ex. 341.

123 [1997] 3 W.L.R. 205 (C.A.). See Bridge, "Defective goods and sub-sales" [1998] *Journal of Business Law* 259. For criticism of the decision see further, Treitel, "Damages for Breach of Warranty of Quality" (1997) 113 *Law Quarterly Review* 188.

124 1893 Act s.54.

(i) the buyer's lost profits as a result of being unable to use the goods;
(ii) loss of future orders or damage to goodwill;
(iii) damage to any property of the buyer;
(iv) personal injury suffered by the buyer;
(v) an indemnity against any damages payable by the buyer to his customer;
(iv) in a consumer case, disappointment.

14.4 A Consumer's Right to Request Cure

Section 53(2) of the 1893 Act provides an important right for the consumer buyer – a statutory right to request cure.[125] This right was introduced by the 1980 Act and is additional to any other rights that may exist for a buyer of goods. Where the seller of goods makes a defective delivery by breaching a condition of the contract, the buyer has, in the first place, a right to reject the goods. Normally, this right is lost where the buyer accepts the goods under section 34 and 35 of the 1893 Act, but this rule is modified in circumstances set out in section 53(2), for consumer buyers. This modification involves giving the consumer buyer a right to request the seller to cure the defect, by repair or replacement of the goods, and in default of this, the consumer buyer is given a second opportunity to reject the goods.

Section 53(2) operates as follows:

(i) where the buyer deals as a consumer;[126] and
(ii) there has been a breach of condition by the seller which, but for this provision, the buyer is required to treat as a breach of warranty (because he has accepted the goods); and
(iii) if the buyer acts promptly,[127] the buyer may request the seller:
 (a) to remedy the breach, or
 (b) to replace any defective goods;[128]
(iv) if the seller refuses, or fails to do so in a reasonable time, the buyer is entitled to:
 (a) reject the goods and repudiate the contract, or

---

125 See also 14.2.

126 See 1980 Act, s.3 for definition; see further 10.5.2.1.

127 The burden of proving that the buyer acted with promptness rests with the buyer: 1893 Act, s.53(3).

128 It would appear that the choice between repair or replacement, is at the buyer's, and not the seller's, discretion. Normally, where the contract is for the sale of *specific goods*, the only remedy will be repair. Replacement can only operate with the acquiescence of the buyer. With contracts for the sale of *unascertained goods*, both options are generally available but again the choice appears to be the buyer's, under s.53(2).

(b) have the defect remedied elsewhere and maintain an action for the cost against the seller.

This is potentially a powerful remedy for consumer buyers, and even from a seller's perspective is not without its positive aspects. The opportunity to repair or replace the goods free of charge is in keeping with what sellers and buyers often agree in practice. For the buyer, in particular, a second chance to reject has all the advantages of the standard right to reject. It places the buyer in a strong bargaining position; he is not left with defective goods on his hands; and he can purchase the same goods from another seller if he has lost confidence in the original seller. On the negative side, ideally consumer rights should be easy to understand and operate, and it can be questioned whether section 53(2) is easily understood, and hence often used, by consumer buyers.

It is important to note that it is the buyer, and not the seller,[129] who has this right to cure. Further, this right to cure is a right to request, not demand, cure. Where the seller refuses, or fails to cure the defective delivery, in a reasonable time, a consumer buyer is given a second chance to exercise his right to reject.

14.5 Specific Performance

Section 52 of the 1893 Act gives the court discretion to award specific performance in "any action for breach of contract to deliver specific or ascertained goods." Specific goods are defined in section 62 of the 1893 Act as goods that are identified and agreed upon at the time the contract is made.[130] It seems that there is no reason why, for this purpose, a contract to sell specific future goods should not be within the scope of the section so that where the seller contracts to sell goods which are in existence but yet to be acquired by him, the court would have discretion to grant a decree once he has acquired the goods. It may also be possible to argue that a contract to sell future goods to be manufactured, or possibly even grown,

129 A seller's right to cure exists under section 2-508 of the Uniform Commercial Code; the Vienna Convention makes provision for a seller's right to cure – Arts 34, 37, and 48 – and a limited buyer's right to cure – Art. 46. In the U.K. in 1983, the Law Commission in a Consultative Document promoted the introduction of a statutory right to cure in consumer contracts which would allow a seller to cure a defective delivery where refusal of cure would be unreasonable: Law Commission WP No. 85, "Sale and Supply of Goods" (1983). However, when the Law Commission's finally reported on the matter, it rejected the introduction of such a right on the basis that it might weaken the position of consumers; and would raise a number of consequential problems: *Sale and Supply of Goods*, Law Com. No. 160, Scot. Law Com. No. 104 (Cm. 137, 1987) esp. para 4.13. Cf. Ahdar, "Seller cure in the sale of goods" [1990] *Lloyd's Maritime and Commercial Law Quarterly* 364.

130 On the meaning of specific and ascertained goods, see 9.2.5.1 and 9.2.5.2.

by the seller is for "specific" goods for this purpose. Goods are "ascertained" for this purpose when they are identified in accordance with the agreement after the contract is made. The fact that a contract is initially for unascertained goods thus does not exclude the court's discretion under section 52, provided that the goods to be supplied have subsequently been identified. The English Court of Appeal decision in *Re Wait*[131] stands as authority, however, for the proposition that the court has no discretion to award specific performance of a contract for unascertained goods so long as the goods have not been ascertained. Although it is generally assumed that section 61(2) of the 1893 Act, which preserves and applies to sale of goods contracts the general rules of the common law, including the rules of equity, it was held in *Re Wait* that the court has no discretion to award specific performance of a sale contract outside the circumstances covered by section 52.[132]

Even if the buyer can establish that the court has a discretion to award a decree of specific performance, he must also persuade the court to exercise that discretion in his favour. The weight of authority shows that specific performance will rarely, if ever, be ordered where the goods to be supplied are "ordinary articles of commerce" which the buyer could obtain elsewhere.[133] In effect, therefore, specific performance will be ordered only where the goods to be supplied are "unique", and the courts have taken a very narrow view of what is "unique". Neither antique furniture,[134] nor ships[135] are necessarily unique. The basis for this approach is that where the goods are not unique, damages will enable the buyer to buy alternative goods in the market. It might be possible to argue for a more generous approach where the seller is insolvent so that damages will, for practical purposes, be worthless. In *Sky Petroleum*, the court ordered the seller to supply the buyer with petrol – plainly an ordinary article of commerce. It seems that the decision was influenced by the fact that if the seller defaulted, the buyer would be unable to find an alternative supplier and would be put out of business, so that damages would have been inadequate. However, this approach seems unlikely to succeed. In a later case, the

131 [1927] 1 Ch. 606 (C.A.) .

132 The more recent decision in *Sky Petroleum Ltd v. VIP Petroleum Ltd* [1973] All E.R. 953 in which Goulding J. granted an injunction to enforce a contract for the supply of petrol under a requirements contract suggests that there might be a wider discretion under the general law, but it seems that little reliance can be placed on the *Sky* case. In *Re London Wine Shippers Ltd* [1986] P.C.C. 121, Oliver J. suggested that the contract in *Sky* was not a sale contract at all, but a "long term supply contract under which successive sales would arise if orders were placed and accepted."

133 The only reported Irish case found by the author where specific performance was ordered is *Clarke v. Reilly* (1962) 96 I.L.T.R. 96 which involved a contract for the supply of a new car in return for a "trade-in" plus cash.

134 *Cohan v. Roche* [1927] 1 K.B. 169.

135 *CN Marine Inc v. Stena Line A/B and Reige Voor Maritem Transport (No. 2), The Stena Nauticaa* [1982] 2 Lloyd's Rep. 336; *cf. Behnke v. Bede Shipping Co Ltd* [1927] 1 K.B. 649.

English Court of Appeal refused specific performance of a contract to supply a machine weighing 220 tons and costing £287,500 even though it would take nine months for a replacement to be manufactured.[136] Moreover, in the context of the seller's insolvency, a court may be reluctant to grant specific performance where to do so would lift the plaintiff buyer out of the ranks of the seller's ordinary creditors and thus disturb the order for distribution of assets amongst the seller's creditors.

14.6 Other Remedies

Where the seller is guilty of misrepresentation, the buyer may claim damages or rescind the contract on the basis of the misrepresentation.[137] There may be advantages in pursuing a claim for misrepresentation rather than a claim for breach of contract. It would appear that delay alone will not bar the right to rescind for misrepresentation, whereas it may amount to acceptance and bar any right to reject the goods under the sales contract, but a court may be reluctant to allow rescission where the right to reject has been lost.[138] Also, unless the misrepresentation is fraudulent, a court may be inclined to exercise its discretion under Part V of the Sale of Goods and Supply of Services Act 1980 to award damages in lieu of rescission. In practice, both avenues should be pursued where possible.

Where the property in the goods has passed to the buyer and he is entitled to immediate possession of the goods, he may also be able to sue in the tort of conversion for any wrongful interference with the goods.[139] In such an action, the court has a discretion to order specific delivery of the goods, or to award damages based on the value of the goods. Where, for example, a seller refused to deliver, a claim in conversion may be available, alongside an action for non-delivery. But even where no action for non-delivery lies, for instance, where a third party interferes with the goods, such as a carrier who refused to deliver, a claim in conversion may exist.

14.7 The EC Directive on Consumer Sales

The EC Directive on Certain Aspects of Consumer Sales and Associated Guarantees,[140] adopted in May 1999, was to be implemented in member

136 *Societe des Industries Metalligurques SA v. The Bronx Engineering Co* [1975] 1 Lloyd's Rep. 465.

137 See 2.2.5.2(ii) and 2.3.1.

138 *Leaf v. International Galleries Ltd* [1950] 2 K.B. 86.

139 See generally, McMahon & Binchy, *Law of Torts* (Dublin, Butterworths, 3rd ed., 2001) Chapter 30.

140 Directive 1999/44/EC [1999] O.J. L171/12.

states not later than January 1, 2002. At the time of writing, the Directive had not been implemented in Irish law. It is expected that the Directive will be implemented by statutory instrument, as opposed to primary legislation. Therefore, the following comments, as regards the consumer buyer's remedies, are based on the wording of the Directive.[141]

14.7.1 The remedies regime

Article 3(1) identifies "the seller" as liable to the consumer for any lack of conformity.[142] In turn, Article 4 provides that where a final seller is liable under the Directive for a lack of conformity resulting from an act or omission of someone before him in the chain of distribution, the final seller can pursue contractual remedies against that person *under national law*. Hence, in Ireland, the doctrine of privity of contract will restrict a seller's right of redress under Article 4, such that the final seller can only sue the person immediately before him in the chain of distribution in contract law.

Article 3(2) outlines four remedies that may be available:

(i) repair;
(ii) replacement;
(iii) reduction in price;
(iv) rescission of the contract (that is, rejecting the goods and demanding a refund).[143]

Further, Article 7 provides that any contractual terms concluded between seller and buyer before any lack of conformity is brought to the seller's attention, which limit the above rights shall not bind the consumer. For instance, a clause that implies that the consumer was aware of any lack of conformity of the goods existing at the time of the contract would not be enforceable under this provision.

First, taking repair and replacement together, a consumer has the right to demand repair or replacement, free of charge,[144] unless this is impossible

141 For analysis of quality provisions of directive, see 13.11.

142 On the concept of "conformity", see 13.11.2.

143 Recital 15 of the Directive provides that member states may provide that any reimbursement to the consumer may be reduced to take account of the use the consumer had of the goods since they were delivered to him. This would be contrary to the current position in Irish law: see *Rowland v. Divall* [1923] 2 K.B. 100 and *United Dominions Trust (Ireland) Ltd v. Shannon Caravans Ltd* [1976] I.R. 225; see further 12.2.2.

144 This refers to the cost of bringing the goods into conformity, particularly the costs of postage, labour and materials: Art. 3(4).

or disproportionate. A remedy is disproportionate under this provision where it imposes costs on the seller, which relative to the other remedies, are unreasonable taking into account the value of the goods if there was no lack of conformity, the significance of the lack of conformity, and whether an alternative remedy could be performed without significant inconvenience to the consumer. Any repair or replacement must be completed within a reasonable time and without any significant inconvenience to the consumer.[145] These are the consumer's primary rights under the Directive.[146] While in practice, repair or replacement may be what the consumer is often satisfied with, making these rights the consumer's primary rights shifts the balance in favour of the seller when compared with domestic law on this point.[147] Under Irish law, a consumer's primary right for breach of any of the implied conditions is to reject the goods (and to demand a refund of the price, if the price has been paid). This right to reject is a powerful remedy and bargaining tool for the consumer. The right to "cure" (to request repair or replacement) under Irish law is secondary to the right to reject, and operates to provide a consumer buyer with a second chance to reject where the seller refuses to cure the defect or fails to do so in a reasonable time.[148]

Alternatively, under the Directive a consumer may require an appropriate reduction of the price or have the contract rescinded, in three circumstances.

(i) where the consumer is not entitled to repair or replacement; or
(ii) where the seller has not completed the repair or replacement within a reasonable time; or
(iii) where the seller has not completed the repair or replacement without significant inconvenience to the consumer.

Strictly speaking, the above right to a price reduction is a substantive right in law unlike anything that exists in Irish law. An apparently similar right exists under section 53(1)(a) of the 1893 Act, which permits a buyer with a claim for damages to "set up against the seller the breach of [contract] in diminution or extinction of the price": an essentially procedural self-help remedy.[149] However, as has been argued elsewhere, these two concepts can

145 Art. 3(3).

146 In the draft directive proposed by the Commission, consumers were given more optionality between remedies, including the right to reject the goods during the first year following delivery.

147 The introduction of a seller's right to cure was rejected by the English and Scottish Law Reform Commissions on the basis that it would operate to the disadvantage of buyers, especially consumers: *Sale and Supply of Goods*, Law Com. No. 160, Scot. Law Com. No. 104, (Cm. 137, 1987) para. 4.13.

148 See 14.4.

149 See 14.3.2.

lead to significantly different results.[150] Basically, section 53 operates a flat rate reduction, illustrated by the following examples.

> **Example 1**: Suppose that S contracts to sell goods to B for €100. The goods delivered are defective and are worth only €80. Assume that had the goods conformed to the contract they would have been worth *the same* as the contract price: €100. The buyer's damages at common law are the difference between the actual value of the goods delivered and their value had they conformed:[151] €20. After set-off, the buyer would pay £80.
>
> **Example 2**: Assume the same facts but that if the goods had conformed to the contract they would be worth *more* than the contract price: €120. The buyer's damages at common law are €40, and after set-off the buyer would pay €60.
>
> **Example 3**: Finally, assume that the goods are worth less than the contract price: €90. The buyer's damages at common law are €10, and after set-off the buyer would pay €90.

In contrast, price reduction is intended to prevent the seller receiving full payment where he has not performed in full. Accordingly, the price is reduced proportionately in the same ratio that the value of the goods as delivered bears to their value had they conformed to the contract.[152] Accordingly, the amount of price reduction varies depending on whether the buyer made a good bargain or a bad bargain because of fluctuations in the value of the goods.

> In **Example 1** above, the buyer has made neither a good nor a bad bargain because the value of the goods has remained the same as the contract price. Under a price reduction scheme, the buyer would pay a reduced price in the ratio that the actual goods bears to the value had they conformed to the contract: he pays 80/100 of the price, that is, €80. In these circumstances only, is there no difference between the two methods.
>
> In **Example 2** above where the buyer makes a good bargain because the price of the goods has risen since making the contract, the buyer would pay a reduced price in the ratio that the actual goods bears to the value had they conformed to the contract: he pays 80/120 of the price – €66.66.
>
> In **Example 3** above where the buyer makes a bad bargain because the price of the goods has fallen since making the contract, the buyer would

150 Twigg-Flesner & Bradgate, "The EC Directive on Certain Aspects of Consumer Sales and Associated Guarantees - all talk and no do?" [2000] *Web J.C.L.I.* <http://webjcli.ncl.ac.uk/2000/issue2/flesner2.html>

151 1893 Act, s.53(5).

152 This is, at least, how price reduction operates under the Vienna Convention, Art. 50.

pay a reduced price in the ratio that the actual goods bears to the value had they conformed to the contract: he pays 80/90 of the price – €89.

In the above examples the differences are small. In commercial transactions the difference could be very significant, but in consumer sales, where the contract price may be the best evidence of the value of the goods, there may be no effective difference between these two methods.

Perhaps of more practical significance is the provision in the Directive that a consumer is not entitled to have the contract rescinded if the lack of conformity is minor.[153] This would amount to an important change to Irish law in this area. Under Irish law, the right to rescind (terminate) a sales contract depends on whether the term that has been breached is a condition, an innominate term, or a warranty.[154] The implied terms as to quality (bar the provision on spare parts and after-sales service) are all classified as conditions "breach of which may give rise to a right to treat the contract as repudiated" as opposed to warranties, "the breach of which may give rise to a right to claim damages but not a right to reject the goods and treat the contract as repudiated".[155] Whether the breach of a condition is minor or not is irrelevant. Arguably, it is unfair on sellers to allow buyers to repudiate a contract for minor breaches, but the Irish position does place buyers, and particularly consumer buyers, in a stronger position than under the Directive.

14.7.2 Time limits

Article 5 provides that a seller is liable under Article 3 for any lack of conformity that becomes apparent within two years from the delivery of the goods, but under Article 7 member states may provide that in relation to second-hand goods, the seller and consumer may agree contractual terms which have a shorter time period for the liability of the seller, though such period cannot be less than one year. The six-year limitation period under Irish law is clearly much more generous to consumers, although the right to reject may be lost much sooner.[156]

The Directive also provides that member states may require consumers to inform sellers of any lack of conformity within two months from the date of discovery of the lack of conformity in order to benefit from their rights under the Directive.[157] Such a requirement would be particularly

---

153 Art. 3(6). In the U.K., a buyer's right to reject the goods and treat the contract as repudiated is restricted where the breach of condition is minor, under the Sale and Supply of Goods Act 1994, but this restriction applies only in relation to commercial contracts and not consumer contracts: see Sale of Goods Act 1979, s.15A.

154 See 10.4.

155 1893 Act, ss.11(2), 11(3) and 62.

156 See 14.2.1.

157 Art. 5(2).

onerous on a cross-border shopper and clearly operates to the advantage of sellers. Again, there is no such provision in Irish law.[158]

14.7.3 Burden of proof

Article 5(3) provides that any lack of conformity that becomes apparent within six months of delivery of the goods is presumed to have existed at the time of delivery. Currently, under Irish law, the burden to prove a breach of any of the implied terms is on the person alleging the breach, the buyer. Because "durability" is an element of merchantable quality, there may operate, in practice, a presumption that defects arising within a reasonable time after the sale were present at the time of the sale.[159] Nevertheless, the formal reversal of the burden of proof under the Directive, will greatly advantage the consumer buyer in pursuing a legal claim against a seller.

158 This is not to say that a consumer can delay in pursuing his rights. For example, he may lose the right to reject goods where without good and sufficient reason, the buyer retains the goods without intimating rejection to the seller (1893 Act, s.35); or to exercise his right to request "cure" under s.53(2), 1893 Act, he must act promptly.

159 See 13.3.2.2.

Chapter 15

SELLER'S REMEDIES

15.1 Introduction

Section 27 of the 1893 Act provides that the buyer's basic duties are to pay the price and accept the goods in accordance with the terms of the contract.[1] If the buyer indicates an intention to repudiate the contract, the seller may accept that repudiation and terminate the contract. The seller is then released from his obligations under the contract. Furthermore, the legislation provides the seller with a range of real and personal remedies for defective, or non-performance of the buyer's obligations. Where the buyer defaults on his basic duties under the contract, the seller has a personal action on the contract. But a personal remedy, such as a claim for damages, is against the person, natural or legal. Personal remedies are therefore of limited value where the defendant is insolvent: the claim may, in effect, be worthless. In contrast, a real remedy confers rights against property, not the person, and so is unaffected by insolvency. In these circumstances, a claimant has a far better chance of being compensated so long as the property exists. The detailed operation of these personal and real remedies is set out below.

The real remedies provided by the 1893 Act: the lien, the right of stoppage in transit, and the right of resale are of limited value in practice in modern trade and commerce, for reasons explained below. This weakness in the statutory scheme of real remedies, and the superior status of real rights in general, has led to the express inclusion of retention of title clauses in sale of goods contracts since the 1970s, as a means of protecting the seller's interests in sales contracts. The scope and legal effectiveness of such clauses will also be examined in this chapter.

15.2 Personal Remedies

The 1893 Act provides the seller with two types of right of action following the buyer's breach of contract. First, the seller can sue for the price under section 49 where the buyer fails to pay for the goods. Second, the seller can sue for damages under a number of headings.

---

1 See 11.3.

15.2.1 An action for the price

Section 49 of the 1893 Act provides that where the buyer wrongfully neglects or refuses to pay the price, a seller can sue for the price (i) if the property has passed to the buyer,[2] or (ii) even if the property has not passed to the buyer if the price is payable "on a day certain".[3] In order for the price to be payable "on a day certain", the date must be either fixed in the contract or the contract must provide a formula for the date to be fixed without reference to the actions of the parties. Where the contract provides for payment "X days after delivery", for example, this does not fix payment on a day certain.[4] In addition to a claim for the price, a seller can claim any interest due under the contract or otherwise,[5] and additional damages as a result of the failure to pay,[6] or the failure to take delivery at the proper time.[7]

If the seller cannot fit within the above provisions, he will be limited to a claim for damages for non-acceptance, under section 50 of the 1893 Act. From the seller's point of view a claim for the price has advantages over a claim for damages for non-acceptance: it is a liquidated claim so there is no need to prove causation or loss and there is no duty to mitigate. There are also procedural advantages to such claims.[8]

15.2.2 Damages for non-acceptance

Section 50 provides that where the buyer wrongfully neglects or refuses to accept and pay for the goods, the seller can sue the buyer for damages for non-acceptance. Where the seller cannot sue for the price, this is his only remedy. A claim for damages for non-acceptance mirrors the buyer's claim for damages for non-delivery, and is governed by similar principles.[9] The standard rules of damages claims apply: the seller must prove that his loss was caused by the buyer's breach; the seller will not be compensated for losses that are too remote; and he is under a duty to mitigate his loss. The measure of damages is the estimated loss directly and naturally resulting,

---

2 1893 Act, s.49(1).

3 1893 Act, s.49(2).

4 In *Henderson and Keay Ltd v. A M Carmichael Ltd* [1956] S.L.T. (Notes) 58 (O.H.) "prompt payment cash against invoice" was held not to be "a day certain."

5 See the EC Directive on Combating Late Payment in Commercial Transactions, Directive EC/35/2000, [2000] O.J. L200/35: see further 21.2.1.

6 1893 Act, s.54.

7 1893 Act, s.37: see 15.2.3. Under s.22 of the Courts Act 1981, a court has a discretion to order the payment of interest on damages for breach of contract; see further Courts and Courts Officers Act 1995, s.50.

8 See Orders 13 and 37 of the Superior Court Rules on the summary summons procedure: see further 37.4.1.1.

9 See 14.3.1.

in the ordinary course of events, from the buyer's breach.[10] Where there is an available market for the goods of the contract description, the measure of damages is, prima facie, the difference between the contract price and the market price of the goods at the date when they should have been accepted, or if no time was fixed for acceptance, at the time of the refusal to accept. This rule seeks to ensure that the seller mitigates his loss by finding an alternative buyer for the goods in the market. So, where the market price exceeds the contract price, the seller is prima facie entitled to no damages.

The existence of an "available market" is assessed in a similar manner as with a claim for non-delivery.[11] But in a seller's claim, there will only be an available market for the purposes of a claim for damages for non-acceptance where there are sufficient (potential) buyers to buy the contract goods, so that there will be no market where supply exceeds demand. However, simply because the seller manages to sell the goods to another buyer does not in itself mean that "the second customer was a substitute customer, that, had all gone well, the [seller] would not have had both customers, both orders, both profits."[12]

Where there is an available market, the actual price at which the seller sells is irrelevant for assessing damages. Where the seller actually sells for a price greater than the market price,[13] his damages are still assessed by reference to the market price. Nevertheless, in practice, the resale price may provide strong evidence of the market price.[14] If there is no available market, the seller will be entitled to damages to compensate him for the profit he would have made had the contract been performed, that is, had the buyer accepted and paid for the goods.[15] Again, the seller must mitigate his loss by seeking alternative buyers. Where goods are unique, they may need modification to make them saleable in which case the cost of reasonable modifications can be recovered in any damages claim. In any case, a seller may also recover special damages in respect of other losses caused by the buyer's breach, including the cost of storing the goods and the cost of advertising or modifying them for sale, provided such losses are not too remote.[16]

10 1893 Act, s.50(2).

11 See 14.3.1.2.

12 *Re Vic Mill* [1913] 1 Ch. 465 at 473 *per* Hamilton L.J.

13 *Campbell Mostyn (Provisions Ltd) v. Barnett Trading Co* [1954] 1 Lloyd's Rep. 65.

14 In *Shearson Lehman Hutton Inc v. Maclaine Watson & Co Ltd (No. 2)* [1990] 3 All E.R. 723, Webster J. held that if the seller offers the goods for sale on the day of the breach, there is an available market if there is one actual buyer at a fair price.

15 *W L Thompson Ltd v. Robinson (Gunmakers) Ltd* [1955] Ch. 177; *cf. Charter v. Sullivan* [1957] 2 Q.B. 117.

16 1893 Act, s.54.

15.2.3 Damages for failure to take delivery

A distinction must be made between a buyer failing to accept and pay for the goods, and a buyer failing to take delivery. Where a buyer delays in taking delivery though he ultimately accepts and pays for the goods, the seller cannot claim for non-acceptance, or the price, but he may have incurred losses due to the delay in taking delivery. Under section 37, where the seller is ready and willing to deliver the goods and he requests the buyer to take delivery and the buyer fails to take delivery of the goods within a reasonable time, the buyer is liable to the seller for any loss caused by his failure to take delivery and also the buyer must pay the seller a reasonable charge for the care and custody of the goods. A seller's rights under section 37 are without prejudice to his rights under sections 49 and 50, above.

15.3 Real Remedies

Personal claims on the contract, such as the right to sue for the price or damages for non-acceptance, will be of little use where the buyer is insolvent and unable to pay. Sections 38–48 of the 1893 Act therefore give the seller three real remedies which offer some measure of protection against the buyer's failure to pay or inability to pay due to insolvency. They are:

(i) a lien over the goods;
(ii) a right to stop the goods in transit; and
(iii) a right to resell the goods and terminate the original contract.[17]

These rights arise automatically, by implication of the law, although they can be augmented by the express terms of the contract. They are available to an unpaid seller only. For these purposes, a seller is "unpaid" until he has received payment in full for the goods.[18] So, for example, where goods are sold on credit, a seller remains unpaid until the whole price is paid or tendered. Where the seller has received conditional payment, such as a cheque, the seller is unpaid until the condition is fulfilled: accordingly where the seller is paid by a cheque which is dishonoured, the seller is "unpaid".[19] "Seller" is defined in section 38(2) as including any person who is in the position of seller, such as an agent. If, for example, the seller

17 1893 Act, s.39(1).
18 1893 Act, s.38(1)(a).
19 1893 Act, s.38(1)(b).

has used an agent to sell the goods and the agent has paid the price to the seller, the agent is entitled to exercise any of the rights of an unpaid seller.[20]

Where the buyer has both possession of and property in the goods, the seller's remedies are limited to a personal right of action on the contract against the buyer. In this case, the seller has lost all rights against the goods for the price. Any attempt to enforce the seller's right to the price by repossessing the goods would amount to a breach of section 12 of the 1893 Act and constitute the tort of conversion.[21] Where property in the goods has not passed to the buyer, the seller can protect his interests by withholding delivery, or stopping the goods in transit, and reselling the goods because he is still the owner,[22] although these actions may amount to a breach of contract.[23] The real remedies under the legislation protect the seller by giving him express rights, in defined circumstances, to withhold delivery, in the form of a lien and a right of stoppage in transit and a right of resale. These real rights apply even where the property in the goods has passed to the buyer. As noted above, these rights are of limited value in modern commercial sales because the conditions of their operation, set out below, are not usually met. As a result, sellers have resorted to the use of retention of title clauses in their sales contracts to protect themselves from non-payment by buyers.

20 *Ireland v. Livingstone* (1872) L.R. 5 H.L. 395. This statutory definition of "seller" is not so wide as to include a buyer who has rejected the goods and is seeking to use the unpaid seller's rights to reclaim the price paid to the seller. Where a buyer has paid for goods which he seeks to reject, for lack of conformity with the contract, he should be mindful of the seller's solvency. On rejection, property in the goods revests in the seller. Where a buyer rejects goods and the seller is insolvent, the buyer will not be able to get a refund of the price. In these circumstances, a buyer would be advised to retain the goods, even though defective.

21 See Chapter 12 and 20.1.1: see further McMahon & Binchy, *Law of Torts* (Dublin, Butterworths, 3rd ed., 2001) Chapter 30.

22 1893 Act, s.39(2) refers to the situation where the property in the goods has not passed to the buyer. Here, the unpaid seller is stated to have a right of withholding delivery similar to and co-extensive with his rights of lien and stoppage where property has passed. Strangely there is no reference to the right of resale where property has not passed. For criticism of the drafting of this provision in general, see *Atiyah's Sale of Goods* (Harlow, Pearson, 10th ed., 2001) pp.447–450.

23 Whether such action amounts to a breach of contract depends partly on the nature of the goods being sold. Where there is a contract to sell unascertained goods that have not been appropriated in a contractual or proprietary sense (on contractual appropriation see 30.3.1.2; on proprietary appropriation see 17.4.2), the seller can resell those particular goods without breaching the original contract. Where there is a contract to sell specific goods, or where the contract is for the sale of unascertained goods which have been contractually appropriated to the contract, the seller will be under a personal obligation to deliver those particular goods though no property will have passed to the buyer. Any resale of those particular goods constitutes a breach of the original contract unless the legislation affords the seller protection under ss.38–48 of the 1893 Act.

15.3.1 Lien

A lien is a right to retain possession of the goods as security for payment of the price.[24] It is available to an unpaid seller where:

(i) the goods are sold without any stipulation as to credit; or
(ii) the goods are sold and any credit period allowed has expired; or
(iii) the buyer becomes insolvent.[25]

The existence of a lien is based on possession. A lien will be lost where possession is lost and a seller does not regain his lien merely because he obtains possession of the goods again.[26] Hence, the lien is lost where, for instance, the seller delivers the goods to the buyer, his agent, or an independent carrier or bailee for transmission to the buyer without reserving the right of disposal.[27] On the other hand, a seller may exercise his lien notwithstanding that he is in possession of the goods as agent or bailee for the buyer.[28] However, where a seller agrees to hold goods as agent or bailee for the buyer, he may be taken to have waived his lien. The exercise of a right of lien does not itself terminate the contract. Failure of the buyer to pay the price at an agreed time is not a breach of condition that entitles the seller to terminate.[29] A seller, of course, loses his lien where the goods are paid for in full.

The statutory lien is of little practical value in modern commercial circumstances when goods are normally supplied on credit terms and they come into the buyer's possession before the expiry of the credit period. But because a lien operates until the price is paid in full, it may be useful in relation to instalment deliveries, under one severable contract, where a seller may be able to withhold delivery of an instalment until earlier instalments are paid for.[30]

24 See 25.3. It seems that an unpaid seller's lien in contracts for the sale of goods depends entirely on the legislation: see *Transport & General Credit Corpn Ltd v. Morgan* [1939] 2 All E.R. 17 at 25 per Simonds J. At common law, a lien does not confer a power of sale though the unpaid seller is given an express right of resale, in certain circumstances: see 15.3.3.

25 1893 Act, s.41; s.62(3) provides that a person is deemed to be insolvent within the meaning of this Act who either has ceased to pay his debts in the ordinary course of business, or cannot pay his debts as they become due.

26 *Valpy v. Gibson* (1847) 4 C.B. 837; *Pennington v. Motor Reliance Works Ltd* [1923] 1 K.B. 127. But a seller who exercises his right of stoppage in transit does in effect regain his lien: see 15.3.2.

27 1893 Act, s.43.

28 1893 Act, s.41(2).

29 See 15.2.1 and 11.3.2.

30 See 14.2.2.2 and *Longbottom v. Bass Walker* (1922) W.N. 245 (C.A.). See further s.42 on part deliveries: "Where an unpaid seller has made part delivery of the goods he may exercise his right of lien or retention over the remainder, [unless the lien has been waived]."

15.3.2 Stoppage in transit

The seller loses his lien over the goods when he delivers them to anyone other than his own agent, such as the buyer himself, the buyer's agent or an independent carrier for transmission to the buyer. However, if the buyer becomes insolvent while the goods are in transit, the unpaid seller is allowed to stop them, retake possession of them and reassert his lien over them.[31] It makes no difference whether the property in the goods has passed or not.[32]

This right can only be exercised while the goods are in transit and not once the transit ends. Goods are in transit when they have passed out of the possession of the seller into the possession of an independent carrier,[33] but have not yet reached the possession of the buyer.[34] There has been little difficulty with determining when transit begins.[35] The more vexed question concerns the termination of the transit. Section 45 contains detailed rules concerning the duration of transit. For example, the transit is deemed to have ended where the buyer or his agent obtains delivery of the goods before their arrival at the appointed destination,[36] or where the carrier wrongfully refused to deliver the goods to the buyer or his agent.[37]

This right is exercised by the seller taking actual possession of the goods from the carrier or by giving notice of his claim to the carrier.[38] The right of stoppage in transit is of limited value where the transit is brief in duration.

15.3.3 Right of resale

A seller who has exercised his right of lien or stoppage in transit may, in

31 1893 Act , ss.44–45.

32 1893 Act, s.39. Where property in the goods has not passed, the seller, as owner, has the power to stop the goods. The legislation gives the seller the legal right to repossess the goods and resell them in defined circumstances.

33 In New Zealand, it was held that the Post Office was not a carrier for these purposes and there was no right of stoppage where goods are consigned by post: *Postmaster-General v. W H Jones & Co (London) Ltd* [1957] N.Z.L.R. 829.

34 See 1893 Act, s.45(1); cf. s.32(1) which provides that delivery of goods to a carrier is prima facie delivery to the buyer. Section 32 deals with the seller's general duty to deliver under the contract and s.32(1) is an example of *constructive delivery* (see 11.2.1). But it is only actual delivery to the buyer which terminates the right of stoppage: *Ex parte Rosevear China Clay Co Ltd* (1879) 11 Ch. D. 560 at 569.

35 Where the carrier is the seller's agent, the transit has not commenced and there is no question of exercising a right of stoppage: in these circumstances, the seller can exercise his statutory lien instead.

36 1893 Act, s.45(2).

37 1893 Act, s.45(6).

38 1893 Act, s.46.

certain circumstances, resell the goods.[39] The consequences of such a resale are that:

(i) the original contract of sale is terminated and the seller may claim damages from the buyer for any losses he suffers as a result of the buyer's breach of contract: for instance, the difference between the original contract price and the amount realised on the resale; and
(ii) the resale passes a good title to the goods to the second buyer to whom the goods are resold, even if property in the goods had already passed to the first buyer.[40]

The right of resale is available under the legislation where:

(i) the goods are perishable; or
(ii) the seller gives the buyer notice that he intends to resell the goods and the buyer fails within a reasonable time to tender the price;[41] or
(iii) resale is authorised by the contract.[42]

In these cases where the seller resells, he does so for his own benefit and therefore is entitled to any profit on the resale.[43]

15.4 Retention of Title Clauses

Ideally, from a seller's perspective, the best position to be in is to be paid before possession of, and the property in the goods passes to the buyer. The danger when property passes before payment is that the buyer (i) may decide not to pay, or (ii) may not be able to pay due to insolvency. Even when mere possession passes before payment, the seller is at a disadvantage because he cannot exercise his real remedies under the legislation. However, today it is common to allow buyers credit. In these circumstances, the buyer will usually have possession of, and even property in the goods before payment is effected. In modern commercial circumstances, the statutory rights of lien, stoppage in transit and resale

39 1893 Act, s.48. Otherwise, a seller may resell goods where property has not yet passed to the buyer (although this may give rise to contractual liability for non-delivery of specific goods), or where the buyer refuses to accept and pay for the goods the seller may treat the contract as repudiated and resell the goods.

40 1893 Act, s.48(2).

41 1893 Act, s.48(3).

42 1893 Act, s.48(4).

43 *R v. Ward Ltd v. Bignall* [1967] 1 Q.B. 534 (C.A.). *Cf. Gallagher v. Shilcock* [1949] 2 K.B. 765.

offer the seller very limited protection against the buyer's failure to pay the price. Alternatively, the seller's rights to sue for the price and for damages for non-acceptance are personal rights: they may be worthless if the buyer is insolvent.

"Insolvent" means that a person has ceased to pay his debts in the ordinary course of business or cannot pay his debts as they fall due.[44] Where a debtor becomes insolvent, an insolvency practitioner can be appointed to take over the management of the debtor's property and distribute it to discharge the debtor's liabilities.[45] Where an individual becomes insolvent, he can be declared bankrupt, and his property can be collected and distributed by an official assignee.[46] Where a company becomes insolvent, the business may be wound up by a liquidator. Alternatively, a secured creditor may have the right to appoint a receiver whose job it is to take over the management of the company and to realise sufficient assets to pay the appointing creditor. Sometimes the actions of a receiver will have the effect of "turning the company around", but often the appointment of a receiver is a precursor to the appointment of a liquidator. A final alternative involves the appointment of an examiner. The examination process involves placing the company under the protection of the court for a certain period so that the examiner can assess whether the company can be rescued or is "terminally insolvent". While the examination process is ongoing, an unpaid seller with a retention of title clause is prohibited from recovering his goods without the consent of the examiner.[47] Again, the appointment of an examiner may have the effect of rescuing the company, but it may be the precursor to the appointment of a liquidator.

On insolvency, debts are paid following a statutory scheme of order, which is basically the same regardless of the type of insolvency proceedings. Creditors are ranked into separate classes for the purpose of this scheme. The costs of the insolvency procedure itself, the claims of preferential creditors, such as unpaid taxes and social welfare contributions to the Revenue Commissioners and employees' wages, and secured creditors, such as banks or other creditors with charges or mortgages over the debtor's property must be paid before any claims of unsecured creditors. Moreover, no creditor can be paid unless all the creditors in the prior class are paid in full. Where there are insufficient funds to meet all

---

44 1893 Act, s.62(3).

45 See generally Keane, *Company Law* (Dublin, Butterworths, 3rd ed., 2000) Parts V and VIII; Forde, *Company Law in Ireland* (Dublin, Round Hall Sweet & Maxwell, 3rd ed., 1999) Chapters 16–18; Lynch Marshall & O'Farrell, *Corporate Insolvency and Rescue: Law and Practice* (Dublin, Butterworths, 1996); Courtney, *The Law of Private Companies* (Dublin, Butterworths, 2nd ed., 2002) Chapters 14–19.

46 See the Bankruptcy Act 1988; see further Forde, *Bankruptcy Law in Ireland* (Dublin, Butterworths, 1990).

47 Companies (Amendment) Act 1990, s.5(2)(e).

the claims within a class, each creditor receives a rateable proportion of the amount due to him. Therefore, the personal claims of an unpaid seller, who is usually an ordinary unsecured creditor, will rank behind those of the buyer's preferential and secured creditors. In most cases the unpaid seller will only receive a small percentage of the sum due to him. In many cases he will receive nothing.

Thus, a seller may require additional protection against the buyer's inability to pay. He may, for instance, require the buyer to organise a guarantee from some creditworthy third party, such as a bank. However, it may not be easy to find a guarantor and there are formalities to be complied with: for instance, the guarantee contract must be evidenced in writing.[48] The simplest option will often be to retain property in the goods. In appropriate cases, the seller may lease the goods to the buyer; alternatively, they may be supplied on hire purchase terms. However, leasing and hire purchase are inappropriate where the goods are supplied to the buyer for resale or for use in manufacturing. A further alternative is for the seller to supply the goods under a conditional sale agreement, retaining title to them until they are paid for. It is now common for commercial sale contracts to contain a "retention of title clause" whereby the seller retains title to the goods supplied until they are paid for in order to protect himself against the buyer's failure to pay the price.[49] From a commercial perspective, the retention of title clause operates like an extended version of the real rights of lien and stoppage in transit but unlike the real remedies, the retention of title must be expressly provided for.[50] Such clauses are often complex and must be drafted with care.

Retention of title by the seller is sanctioned by sections 17 and 19 of the 1893 Act. Section 17 provides that property passes when the parties intend it to pass; section 19 provides that the seller may reserve the right of disposal of the goods until certain conditions are met.[51] At its simplest, a sale subject to a retention of title clause is essentially a conditional sale agreement. However, whereas traditionally goods were only supplied on conditional sale terms where it was expected that they would be retained by the buyer in the form in which they were supplied, retention of title clauses are used in contracts even where it is expected from the outset that the goods may be resold, consumed or used in a manufacturing process before they are paid for.

A seller will not normally seek to enforce a retention of title clause unless the buyer is insolvent. A successful claim under a retention of title clause will remove the assets claimed by the seller from the pool of assets available for distribution to other creditors. Insolvency practitioners will

48 See generally 26.2.

49 Although less common, such clauses are found in sales contracts with consumers also.

50 See *Atiyah's Sale of Goods* (Harlow, Pearson, 10th ed., 2001) p.447, pp.469–480.

51 See generally Chapter 17.

therefore seek to resist a seller's claim under a retention of title clause, if at all possible. One standard argument put forward by insolvency practitioners is that the clause was not properly incorporated into the sales contract. There are three ways in which a term can be incorporated in a contract: (i) by signature; (ii) by giving reasonable notice; and (ii) by course of dealings.[52] A retention of title clause will prima facie be incorporated in the contract where the buyer signs a document containing the clause, even if the buyer does not read the clause.[53] A retention of title clause may also be incorporated where the clause is made available, or reasonably notice of the clause is given, to the buyer at the time the contract is made.[54] In *Sugar Distributors Ltd v. Monaghan Cash and Carry*,[55] the parties had been trading since 1974, though the retention of title clause was first included on the seller's invoices in 1977, about 15 months before this dispute arose. In addressing the incorporation point, Carroll J., in the High Court, noted that such clauses were becoming very common. She also referred to evidence of the managing director of the buyer company that although he never read the small print on the invoices, he did notice a change in the form and size of the invoices. He further stated that it would have made no difference to him if he had read the new invoice. It was held that despite the finding that the sellers failed to prove that the clause was drawn to the special attention of the buyers, reasonable notice of the clause had been given and hence it was properly incorporated into the sales contract. Finally, where the parties have contracted in the past and incorporated a retention of title clause, this past "course of dealings" may be enough to ensure that the clause is part of future contracts. However, there seems to be a requirement of "consistent dealing" before this argument will work.[56]

Indeed, where the goods being sold are unascertained, section 19(1) of the 1893 Act allows the seller to reserve his title to the goods when appropriating them to the contract.[57] It would seem that, even in breach of contract – most likely breach of section 12(1)(b) of the 1893 Act on warranty of quiet possession[58] – a seller can subsequently protect himself

---

52 See 2.3.2.1.

53 *L'Estrange v. Graucob Ltd* [1934] 2 KB.

54 *Parker v. South Eastern Railways Ltd* (1877) 2 C.P.D. 416; *Thornton v. Shoe Lane Parking Ltd* [1971] 2 Q.B. 163; *Interfoto Picture Library v. Stilletto Visual Programmes* [1988] 1 E.R. 348 re unusual terms; *Western Meats Ltd v. National Ice and Cold Storage Ltd and Anor* [1982] I.L.R.M. 99.

55 [1982] I.L.R.M. 399. See also *Kruppstahl AG v. Quitmann Products Ltd* [1982] I.L.R.M. 551; *cf. Union Paper Co. v. Sunday Tribune (In Liquidation)* unreported, High Court, Barron, J., April 27, 1983, where it was held that the relevant clause was not incorporated because the defendant company had never been supplied with any documentation setting out the retention of title clause.

56 *McCutcheon v. David MacBrayne Ltd* [1964] 1 All E.R. 430.

57 On appropriation of unascertained goods, see 17.4.2.

58 See 12.3.

up to the time of the appropriation of the goods to the contract by reserving title.[59] He may be liable in damages for breach of contract, but against this he can repossess his goods and resell them if the buyer becomes insolvent. The measure of damages for breach of section 12(1)(b) would appear to be the value of the goods repossessed which may be more or less than the contract price depending on fluctuations in the market.[60] It might seem pointless to impose a retention of title clause on appropriation where, having recovered the goods the seller then has to pay to the buyer their value as damages, but this strategy might be useful where a seller is owed other sums by the buyer, in which case he can set off those other sums against the damages claim.

There is now a substantial body of case law and extensive academic literature surrounding retention of title clauses.[61] Nevertheless many aspects of the law relating to retention of title clauses are unclear. It must be remembered that each case was decided on its particular facts and based on the interpretation of each individual clause. Accordingly, case law is less of a guide than usual.

15.4.1 Types of claim

Retention of title clauses can be broken down into various types of claims. For instance, a "simple clause" seeks to retain title to the goods supplied under the contract until their price is paid – an original goods claim. Clauses can also include claims of ownership over any new product manufactured using the original goods supplied – a manufactured products claim; and/or claims to the proceeds of sale of the original or manufactured goods – a proceeds claim. Retention of title clauses also provide that the above claims over goods (original; manufactured products; or proceeds) will be extinguished in one of two circumstances: (i) when the contract price is paid; or (ii) when all sums due (not just those due under the particular sales contract) from the buyer to the seller are paid. The latter stipulation is referred to as a "current account" or an "all sums due" or "all monies" clause. All retention of title clauses are a combination of the above claims. A "simple clause", for example, is a combination of a claim to original goods until the contract price is paid. Alternatively, the seller could retain title in original goods until all sums due were paid. More complex clauses will seek to retain title in a wider range of circumstances. For instance, a seller may use a current account clause which lays claim to goods supplied, proceeds of sale of the goods supplied, products

59 See Bradgate, "The Post-Contractual Reservation of Title" [1988] *Journal of Business Law* 477.

60 See 12.3.2 and 14.3.4.

61 See, *e.g. McCormack, Reservation of Title Clauses* (London, Sweet & Maxwell, 2nd ed., 1995); Wheeler, *Reservation of Title Clauses: Impact and Implications* (Oxford, Clarendon Press, 1991).

manufactured from the goods supplied and proceeds of sale of those new products. Some of these claims may succeed while others may fail.

15.4.1.1 Simple clauses

A "simple clause" might state: "The seller reserves ownership of the goods supplied under this contract until the price is paid in full."

It is now settled that a simple clause which retains title to the goods supplied until they are paid for is legally effective.[62] It had been argued by insolvency practitioners that such a retention of title clause involved more than a simple agreement between the parties as to the passing of property. The real purpose of such a clause, it was argued, was to protect the seller against non-payment by the buyer, and accordingly the clause was a form of security against non-payment. Based on this analysis, the true construction of a sales contract subject to a simple retention of title clause involved the property in goods passing to the buyer and the buyer granting back to the seller a mortgage or charge over the goods to the value of the debt. It was further argued that such a mortgage or charge was unenforceable due to lack of registration under the relevant legislation.[63] In practice, retention of title clauses are never registered in this way partly because the process would be administratively cumbersome, requiring a separate registration for each individual clause. This rather complicated charge argument was definitively rejected by the courts in Ireland and England in the 1980s. However, it is essential that the clause retains legal title: it has been held that a clause which retained "equitable and beneficial ownership" of goods supplied allowed the legal title to pass to the buyer subject to the grant back to the seller of an equitable charge, which was void for lack of registration.[64]

European Community law also sanctions the use of "simple clauses". The EC Directive on combating late payment in commercial transactions provides, in Article 4:

> "that the seller retains title to goods until they are fully paid for if a retention of title clause has been expressly agreed between the buyer and the seller before the delivery of the goods."

The Irish Regulations implementing this Directive do not include any specific provision on retention of title clauses because national law is already in compliance with Article 4.

62 *Frigoscandia Ltd v. Continental Irish Meat Ltd* [1982] I.L.R.M. 396; *Clough Mill v. Martin* [1984] 3 All E.R. 982.

63 Where individuals grant security interests over goods, they must be registered under the Bills of Sale (Ireland) Acts 1879 and 1883: see 25.6.1. Where companies grant security interests they must be registered under the Companies Act 1963: see 25.6.2.

64 *Re Bond Worth Ltd* [1980] 1 Ch. 228.

Claims under a "simple clause" can be divided into two types: (i) claims to original goods *in their original form*; and (ii) claims to original goods *which have entered a manufacturing process*.

(i) Goods in their original form

Under a simple clause the seller retains title to goods supplied under the contract in which the clause appears until the sum due under that contract – the contract price – is paid. Where the seller relies on such a clause, an insolvency practitioner will therefore require the seller to prove that the price is unpaid and to identify that the goods in stock, in the insolvency practitioner's possession, are the original goods supplied by the seller under the particular contract in respect of which he claims. In many cases, this may be difficult. Sellers should therefore be advised that, wherever possible, the goods they supply should be identifiable with the contract of supply, by using markings on the goods themselves or the packaging. To facilitate this identification process, the retention of title clause may require the buyer to store the seller's goods separately from other similar goods.

In *Bernard Somers v. James Allen (Ireland) Ltd*,[65] the respondent supplied animal feed to a company subject to a simple retention of title clause. On appointment of the receiver, the goods were identifiable and had not been used in the manufacturing process. The applicant receiver sought the assistance of the court and argued that a simple retention of title clause was not effective where it was known that the goods would be used in a manufacturing process. It was held by Carroll J., in the High Court, that as long as the goods still existed in the same state in which they were supplied, and as long as they had not been mixed with other goods or transmuted into a manufactured product, then a simple clause would be effective.

(ii) Original goods from a manufacturing process

Where goods supplied under a sales contract, subject to a simple retention of title clause, enter a manufacturing process, there is the risk that they will change their form such that they cannot be identifiable as the goods originally supplied. However, if the goods supplied can be identified as the original goods supplied and removed from the manufacturing process, the seller may retain title to them by means of a simple clause. In *Hendy Lennox v. Grahame Puttick Engines Ltd,*[66] diesel engines supplied by the seller were incorporated into generator sets. The court found that the

65 [1985] I.R. 340; [1984] I.L.R.M. 437; appealed to the Supreme Court, unsuccessfully, on separate point: [1985] I.R. 340; [1985] I.L.R.M. 624.

66 [1984] 1 W.L.R. 485.

engines were still identifiable and could be removed without doing damage to them or other components and so title was retained.

Where the manufacturing process results in the seller's goods being irreversibly incorporated into a new product, or losing their identity, the seller's title to the original goods will be extinguished as they will cease to exist as an independent item. For instance, in *Borden v. Scottish Timber Products Ltd*,[67] where a seller supplied resin, his title was extinguished when the resin was used to manufacture chipboard. In *Peachdart Ltd*,[68] leather was supplied to manufacture handbags. It was possible to identify which handbags were made from the supplier's leather. However, it was held there that there is a presumption that property passes to the buyer as soon as the goods enter a manufacturing process that will result in the loss of their identity, in this case, once the leather was first cut.

Generally, where goods supplied by the seller are incorporated into realty, or the land, they will become part of the realty and therefore the property of its owner if the annexation is such as to make them a fixture. In order to determine whether something has become a fixture or not, courts usually consider two things: the degree of annexation and the object of annexation.[69] In *Re Galway Concrete Ltd (In Liquidation)*,[70] machinery was bought and installed as plant. The contract provided that the machinery was to remain the property of the suppliers until the price was paid in full. Payment was to be by instalments. The purchasing company went into liquidation before the full price was paid, so the suppliers sought to rely on the retention of title clause. The liquidator argued that the machinery had been substantially incorporated into the premises defeating the clause. The High Court held that although the machinery had become affixed to the premises, it was for the purpose of the company's trade and so was in the nature of a tenant's fixture which could be removed.[71] Hence the suppliers were entitled to regain possession and assert ownership as against the purchasers.

15.4.1.2 Manufactured products claims

In order to overcome the above problem of the original goods supplied losing their identity in a manufacturing process, retention of title clauses have been drafted to claim title to the products manufactured using the original goods supplied. However, it will generally be assumed that new

---

67 [1981] Ch. 25.

68 [1984] 1 Ch. 131.

69 *Holland v. Hodgson* (1872) L.R. 7 C.P. 328.

70 [1983] I.L.R.M. 402.

71 See Lyall, *Land Law in Ireland* (Dublin, Round Hall Sweet & Maxwell, 2nd ed., 2000) pp.623–625; Pearse & Mee, *Land Law* (Dublin, Round Hall Sweet & Maxwell, 2nd ed., 2000) pp.33–37; and Wylie, *Irish Landlord and Tenant Law* (Dublin, Butterworths, 2nd ed., 1998) Chapter 9.

products manufactured by the buyer will be the buyer's property, since to recognise them as belonging to the seller would allow him to take the benefit of the buyer's labour and of any other goods or materials used in their manufacture. Where the seller's retention of title clause lays claim to such manufactured products, it will normally give him no more than a charge over the manufactured product to secure the sums owed to him, which if not registered is not enforceable.[72]

In *Kruppstahl AG v. Quitman Products Ltd*,[73] steel was supplied for a manufacturing process subject to a retention of title clause. On liquidation of the buyer, the seller claimed ownership of (i) some unworked steel, and (ii) some worked steel. It was held by the High Court that the original steel remained the property of the seller but regarding the steel used in the manufacturing process, the seller's interest amounted to a charge on the steel which was unenforceable for lack of registration under the Companies Act 1963.

15.4.1.3 Proceeds claims

If the buyer resells the goods before paying for them, the seller's rights over the goods will normally be extinguished because the sub-buyer will take a good title to the goods by virtue of section 25(2) of the 1893 Act.[74] In order to overcome this problem, the seller may seek to claim an interest in the proceeds of the resale. In *Aluminium Industrie Vaasen BV v. Romalpa Aluminium*,[75] the Court of Appeal held that, in certain circumstances, the seller was entitled to trace his goods into the proceeds of their resale. A claim to proceeds will only be worthwhile where, as in the *Romalpa* case itself, the proceeds of resale are received after commencement of the insolvency; if they are received before the insolvency they are likely to be lost in the buyer's bank account which, almost certainly, will be overdrawn (thus defeating any attempt to trace).

A seller's claim to proceeds will only succeed if the seller can show that the relationship between himself and his buyer is fiduciary, thereby establishing a right to trace in equity. The establishment of a fiduciary relationship will depend on the wording and construction of the particular retention of title clause and the other provisions of the contract in which it appears. In *Romalpa*, the seller sold aluminum foil to the buyer subject to a retention of title clause which provided that:

(i) the foil should be stored in such a way as to identify it as the seller's property;

72 See further Webb, "Title and Transformation: Who Owns Manufacturer Goods?" [2000] *Journal of Business Law* 513.

73 [1982] I.L.R.M. 551; see further *Clough Mill v. Martin* [1984] 3 All E.R. 982.

74 See further 19.8.

75 [1976] 1 W.L.R. 676.

(ii) products made from the seller's foil were to belong to the seller and be stored so as to make them identifiable as such;
(iii) that until resale, the buyer was to hold manufactured products in the capacity of "fiduciary owner" for the seller; and
(iv) on demand the buyer should "hand over" to the seller claims against its customers who bought manufactured products.

The buyer went into receivership without paying for a quantity of foil. However, prior to the receivership, the buyer sold a quantity of foil and it was paid for after the appointment of a receiver. The seller claimed the proceeds of sale from the receiver. The contract contained no express provision to cover such a situation. Counsel for the receiver conceded that the buyer held the foil as bailee for the seller, and the Court of Appeal held, in light of that concession and the provisions of the contract, that (i) a right for the buyer to sell foil must be implied and (ii) the relationship between the seller and buyer was fiduciary so that on a resale of the foil the seller could trace into the proceeds of sale.

In order to establish such a relationship, clauses will often state that the buyer holds the goods as bailee for the seller and when he re-sells them he does so as agent for the seller. But bailees and agents are not necessarily fiduciaries.[76] To add to the impression, the seller often requires separate storage of goods and separate bank accounts for proceeds, and separate financial accounts. However, despite these and similar attempts, the courts today are reluctant to recognise a fiduciary relationship between a buyer and a seller when in truth the relationship is really one of debtor and creditor. If this were a real fiduciary relationship, the buyer would be obliged to hand over all profits on resale to the seller.

There is no reported English case where a claim for proceeds of sale has succeeded since *Romalpa*. Subsequent English cases have refused to find the requisite fiduciary relationship. For instance, in *Re Andrabell Ltd*,[77] the fact that the buyer was allowed credit and so could use the proceeds of sale in his own business negated the existence of a fiduciary relationship. Moreover, the buyer did not have to store the seller's goods or the proceeds of sale separately. In *Compaq Computers v. Abercorn*,[78] a comprehensively drafted clause which included all the magic phrases – buyer stored goods as bailee and agent for seller; buyer to account in full for proceeds and keep proceeds in separate bank account – was interpreted as creating a charge over the proceeds of resale. In *Tatung v. Galex*,[79] the judge, at odds

76 See 7.3.2.

77 [1984] 3 All E.R. 407, see Farrar & Chai, "Romalpa Revisited – Again" [1985] *Journal of Business Law* 160.

78 [1991] B.C.C. 484: see Sealy, "Retention of Title – Rule in Dearle v. Hall" (1992) *Cambridge Law Journal* 19.

79 (1988) 5 B.C.C. 325. See further *E Pfeiffer v. Arbuthnot* [1988] 1 W.L.R. 150 and *Re Weldtech* [1991] B.C.C. 16.

with *Romalpa*, said that even where a fiduciary relationship exists, the clause may amount to a charge over proceeds. Generally it seems that the courts regard imposition of a fiduciary relationship as unreal, in that such a relationship would entitle the unpaid seller to the whole of the proceeds of the buyer's resale, including any profit element. Instead, a clause which makes an express claim to proceeds of resale is likely to be regarded as an assignment of future book-debts, or a charge on the proceeds of resale which will require registration as a charge or bill of sale.

Although *Romalpa* type claims were initially successful in Ireland,[80] the more recent authority in Irish law, *Carroll Group Distributors v. G & JF Burke*,[81] has taken a different approach which is more in line with subsequent English case law.[82] In *Carroll Group Distributors v. G & JF Burke*, the plaintiff supplied goods to the defendant, subject to a retention of title clause, and four weeks credit. The clause provided, *inter alia*, that the goods were to remain the property of the supplier until all sums due were paid. It gave the buyer the express right to resell the goods; where goods were resold the clause provided that the buyer did so on their own account and not as agent for the supplier; and the buyer undertook to keep all proceeds of such resale "in trust" for the supplier and in a separate bank account. The buyer went into liquidation and the supplier sought to trace into the proceeds of sale of the goods. No such separate bank account was ever created and the court found that the supplier was probably aware of this fact. Murphy J., in the High Court, in dismissing the plaintiff's claim, held that had this system operated, the buyer would have sums in a bank account in excess of the supplier's claim, partly because of the mark-up in price. As such, the bank account would be a source of funds to which the supplier could have recourse to discharge monies due though he would not be entitled to all the monies in the account. On the basis of this analysis, the court found that this possessed all the characteristics of a mortgage or charge which was void for non-registration under section 99 of the Companies Act 1963. It is unclear from the judgment to what extent this case is limited to its facts, or represents a shift away from the relative ease at which fiduciary relations were found to exist in the context of sale of goods contracts in Ireland. In particular, the aspect of the retention of title clause that provided that when the buyer resold the goods, it did so on his own account and not as agent for the supplier seems to be the basis for the

80 See, *e.g. Re Sugar Distributors Ltd* [1982] I.L.R.M. 399; *SA Foundaries Du Lion v. International Factors Ltd* [1985] I.L.R.M. 66; *Re WJ Hickey Ltd* [1988] I.R. 126. This line of cases has been referred to as being based on "the automatic fiduciary relationship proposition:" see McCormack, *Reservation of Title Clauses* (London, Sweet & Maxwell, 2nd ed., 1995) p.88.

81 [1990] I.L.R.M. 285.

82 See De Lacy, "The Anglocisation of Irish Retention of Title" [1990] *Irish Law Times* 279.

court's finding that no fiduciary duty was imposed by the clause. Therefore, although there is precedent for such a claim succeeding, the courts in Ireland and England seem unlikely to uphold a seller's claim to an interest in the proceeds of the buyer's resale, and an insolvency practitioner can be expected to contest strongly any such claim.

15.4.1.4 All sums due clauses

Where a seller relies on a "simple clause", the seller is only entitled to claim the goods so long as sums remain due under the contract under which the particular goods were supplied. This is not problematic where the seller and buyer transact on a once-off basis. However, where the parties trade more frequently or where there is a continuous trading relationship between the parties, problems of identification can arise for the seller seeking to pursue a claim based on a simple retention of title clause. As noted above, when pursuing a claim based on a simple retention of title clause, the seller must prove that the price under the particular contract is unpaid and he must identify that the goods in stock, in the insolvency practitioner's possession, are the original goods supplied by the seller under the particular contract in respect of which he claims. Further, the fact that sums may be due under other contracts is irrelevant.

In order to avoid, in part, these identification problems, a seller may use an "all sums due" clause[83] which provides that as long as any sum is outstanding, whether under the relevant supply contract or otherwise, no property in any goods supplied can pass from the seller to the buyer. However, once the account between the seller and buyer is cleared, that is, all sums owing are paid, property in any goods supplied, up to that point in time, will pass to the buyer.

In *Armour v. Thyssen*,[84] the only reported case which addressed this type of clause directly,[85] the House of Lords held that an all sums due clause was effective to prevent title passing to the buyer until its conditions were fulfilled and it therefore seems that such a clause does not create a charge. However, the reasoning in the *Armour* case has been criticised.[86] Moreover, the case was argued and (technically) decided on a point of Scots law, so the effectiveness of all sums due clauses cannot be regarded as conclusively settled. Insolvency practitioners still tend to resist claims

83 Also referred to as "all monies due", "all debts due", "all liability" or "current account" clauses.

84 [1990] 3 All E.R. 481.

85 "All sums due" clauses were used in a number of Irish cases with success but the "all sums" aspect of the clauses was not directly in issue: see, *e.g.* *Re Interview Ltd* [1975] I.R. 382; *Frigoscandia Ltd v. Continental Irish Meat Ltd* [1982] I.L.R.M. 396; *Kruppstahl AG v. Quitman Products Ltd* [1982] I.L.R.M. 551.

86 See, *e.g.* Bradgate, "Retention of Title in the House of Lords: Unanswered Questions" (1991) 54 *Modern Law Review* 726.

under all sums due clauses, arguing that such clauses allow property to pass to the buyer subject to a charge back in favour of the seller. They should therefore be used with care. Moreover, an all sums due clause does not always avoid the need for goods to be identifiable: if the buyer's account with the seller is clear at any time, property in all goods supplied prior to that time will pass to the buyer so that it will be necessary to differentiate between goods supplied before and after that date.

Where a seller enforces a claim under an all sums due clause, he may repossess goods for which the buyer has already paid. It is not clear whether, in such a case, he may retain the money paid for those goods. The House of Lords, in *Armour v. Thyssen*, declined to consider this issue.[87] A similar issue was addressed in *Clough Mill v. Martin*[88] which involved a simple clause under which the seller retained title to all the goods supplied under a particular contract until he received payment for all that contract consignment.[89] The members of the Court of Appeal realised that this wording could give rise to two problems. First, what if the buyer only paid for some of the contract goods before becoming insolvent: should the supplier be allowed to repossess all the goods supplied including those already paid for? Second, who is entitled to any profit on resale by the seller after repossession, should the goods be resold for more than their original contract price? Two Law Lords considered this problem. According to Goff L.J., the position differed depending on whether the contract of sale remained in force or not. Where the contract still existed, the seller would be restricted by an implied term in the contract so that he could resell only so much as was necessary to discharge the unpaid balance of the price. If he sold more, he would be accountable to the buyer for the excess. In contrast, after termination of the contract, the seller would be free from this implied term and would be able to repossess and resell any of the goods in the buyer's possession. However, the seller would have to refund the buyer any part of the price paid and attributable to the goods resold, on the basis that there was a total failure of consideration for which he had been paid, although he could set-off any sum to be so repaid against any damages suffered due to the buyer's breach of contract. Lord Donaldson M.R. suggested a slightly different solution. Based on a close analysis of the clause in question, he found that the seller could repossess and resell the goods "until" he had been paid in full. Any resale thereafter was accountable to the buyer. These two analyses produce identical results in all cases bar one: where the seller resells at a profit. With Lord

87 [1990] 3 All E.R. 481 at 486. But see Goodhart & Jones, "The Infiltration of Equitable Doctrine into English Commercial Law" (1980) 43 *Modern Law Review* 489.

88 [1984] 3 All E.R. 982.

89 Though Goodhart has questioned the appropriateness of applying an analysis of simple clauses to all sums due clauses: see Goodhart, "Clough Mill v. Martin - A Comeback for Romalpa" (1986) 49 *Modern Law Review* 96.

Donaldson's analysis, the profit would belong to the buyer; with Goff L.J., the profit rests with the seller. In favour of Lord Donaldson's analysis, it might seem fairer that the seller should not be allowed make a windfall profit, and that any profit should go to benefit the general body of the buyer's creditors. However, it has been argued that Goff L.J.'s analysis is more conceptually correct.[90] Since the goods repossessed by the seller are the seller's property, because of the retention of title clause, he should be entitled to retain any profit on resale. If his interest is limited to the balance of the unpaid price, he would appear more like a charge holder than an owner of the goods.

15.4.2 Reform

As noted above, where a retention of title clause succeeds, the effect is to reduce the pool of assets available for distribution to the buyer's creditors. In effect, an unpaid seller, as an unsecured creditor, can jump the queue on insolvency by the insertion of a retention of title clause in the sales contract. This inequity between creditors within the legislative framework on insolvency has led a number of jurisdictions to reconsider the law in this whole area.

In Ireland and England, proposals for change have been made but not implemented. For example, in 1989, the Irish Law Reform Commission reported on the problems of retention of title clauses in the context of debt collection.[91] The Commission proposed that retention of title clauses should not be enforceable unless evidenced in writing and signed by the buyer; and that such clauses would not be deemed to create any form of charge over the goods unless expressly stipulated at the time the contract was concluded by the parties. It further proposed the establishment of a system of registration of retention of title clauses,[92] while at the same time not ruling out, at some future date, a more comprehensive registration system for other types of security interests in goods. Neither the register for retention of title clauses nor the more comprehensive register have been established. In the United Kingdom, also in 1989, Professor Diamond, in his *Review of Security Interests in Property*,[93] recommended that

90 See further Bradgate, "Retention of Title in the House of Lords: Unanswered Questions" (1991) 54 *Modern Law Review* 726, at 731–2.

91 Law Reform Commission Report on Debt Collection (2) Retention of Title (L.R.C. 28 – 1989).

92 To deal with the burden of registration, the Commission recommended that the legislation should allow the registration of a single retention of title agreement covering the repeated supply of goods for a period not exceeding five years; and retention of title clauses to secure payment of a sum of less than £500 should be exempt from registration.

93 London, H.M.S.O., 1989. Earlier recommendations for change in this area were made by the Report of the Crowther Committee on Consumer Credit (Cmnd. 4596, 1971); and the Cork Committee Report on Insolvency Law and Practice (Cmnd. 8558, 1982).

legislation should clarify that retention of title clauses are security interests taken by a seller of goods. But he drew a distinction between, on the one hand, "simple" and proceeds clauses, which would be subject to a simplified "notice filing" requirement,[94] and, on the other hand, wider clauses such as "all sums due" and "manufactured products" clauses, which would be regarded as creating a charge and need to be registered for each individual transaction. Nothing has been done to implement the Diamond proposals.[95]

In other jurisdictions, legislation has been introduced to address these problems. Most notably, Article 9 of the United States Uniform Commercial Code (U.C.C.) provides a uniform system of control of all personal property security interests based on substance not form. Distinctions between different types or forms of security interest are removed in favour of one form of security interest. Retention of title clauses are treated as security interests and so they do not prevent title passing to the buyer under the sales contract. If a seller wishes to make a retention of title clause, as a form of security interest, effective against third parties, he must perfect it by making a valid filing of a "financial statement". Such filing is effective for five years but can be continued. More recently, in New Zealand, under the Personal Property Security Act 1999, a similar uniform approach to security interests in personal property, including retention of title clauses, is taken.[96]

In Ireland, like in the United Kingdom, because no legislation has been introduced, despite recommendations, the use and efficacy of retention of title clauses is a matter which has been left to the judiciary to determine. In seeking to balance the interests of all the parties involved, the judiciary appear to have drawn a line in the sand: certain types of retention of title clauses will succeed ("simple" and "all sums due" clauses) while others will not ("products" and probably "proceeds" clauses). Unfortunately, the rationale for this line in the sand is not apparent or well reasoned. For instance, the Court of Appeal in *Clough Mill v. Martin* referred to the plain wording of the clause to uphold the "simple" aspect of the clause on the basis that it represented the intentions of the parties, but later refused to give effect to the wording in the part of the clause claiming ownership of the manufactured products on the basis that such an outcome could not

94 These he classed as purchase money securities which would not require individual registration but instead the creditor could register in advance a notice that the named debtor may have created a security interest in favour of a named creditor.

95 See further U.K. Law Commission, *Consultation Paper on the Registration of Security Interests* (No. 164, 2002); and D.T.I. Consultation Document, *Company Law Review: Proposals for Reform of Part XII of the Companies Act 1985* (1994).

96 See Webb, "The PPSA - A New Regime for Secured Transactions" [2000] *New Zealand Law Review* 175. See also, *e.g.* in Canada, the Ontario Personal Property Security Act 1967, based on Article 9 of the U.C.C.; see further 25.6.3.

have been intended by the parties. It would appear that nothing less than legislation, along the lines of Article 9 of the U.C.C. will properly resolve the matter.

CHAPTER 16

PRODUCT GUARANTEES, AFTER-SALE SERVICES, AND PRODUCT LIABILITY

16.1 INTRODUCTION

Where a contract of supply can be classified as a sale of goods contract, the statutory implied terms as to the quality of the goods supplied offer a buyer, and in particular a consumer buyer, many advantages when seeking compensation for defects in quality.[1] First, the statutory implied terms arise automatically, avoiding problems of proof. Second, liability for breach of the statutory implied terms is strict. Therefore, even though the seller is not at fault, he may be liable for breach of the statutory implied terms. Finally, the exemption or exclusion of liability for breach of the statutory implied terms by the seller is regulated by statute, further increasing their protective force.[2] In particular, where the buyer deals as a consumer, liability for breach of the statutory implied terms can never be excluded. Finally, an award of damages for breach of the statutory terms, or indeed any contractual terms, may include damages for personal injury, or even death, property damage, and financial loss, including the reduced value of the defective goods themselves. Nevertheless, a buyer's contractual remedies,[3] whether based on the express terms of the contract or the statutory implied terms, have their limitations. The principal limitation derives from the doctrine of privity of contract.[4] Accordingly, a buyer's remedies under a sales contract are enforceable against the seller of the goods only.

A standard chain of supply contracts is illustrated in the diagram below. The manufacturer sells to a distributor, who in turn sells to a retailer, who in turn sells to the customer.

1 On statutory definition of sale of goods contract, see Chapter 9; on defects in quality, see Chapter 13; and on buyer's remedies, see Chapter 14. It should be noted that similar, though not identical terms may be implied in contracts for the supply of services, see Chapter 20; and in consumer contracts of hire and hire-purchase, see Parts VI & VII of the Consumer Credit Act 1995.

2 1893 Act, s.55 and 1980 Act, s.22; see further 10.5.2.

3 See Chapter 14.

4 See 2.2.7; see further Friel, *Contract Law* (Dublin, Round Hall Sweet & Maxwell, 2nd ed., 2000) Chapter 9; and Clark, *Contract Law in Ireland* (Dublin, Round Hall Sweet & Maxwell, 4th ed., 1998) Chapter 17.

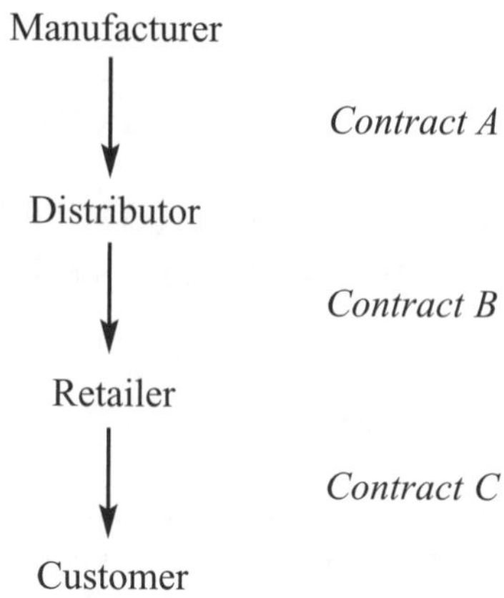

The customer, in the above diagram, cannot sue, in contract law, the distributor or the manufacturer because he has no contractual relations with these parties. The customer can only sue the retailer, in contract law, under Contract C. Liability can be passed back up the chain of distribution in the sense that the retailer may be able to sue the distributor for breach of Contract B, and, the distributor may be able to sue the manufacturer for breach of Contract A. However, this chain of liability can be broken because of the different rules on the exclusion of liability in sales contracts. Where the buyer deals as a consumer, no exclusion is allowed but, where the buyer deals otherwise, a fair and reasonable exclusion is allowed.[5] Therefore, valid exclusion clauses in Contracts A and B may prevent actions based on those contracts from succeeding.

Even where privity of contract exists between two parties, as between the retailer and the customer in the above diagram, there may be more practical limitations to taking a claim in contract law. Where the seller operates at a distance from the buyer, perhaps in another country, a buyer may be reluctant to pursue his contractual remedies against the seller because of the legal complexities of conflict of laws issues[6] and of the more practical logistics involved. More significantly, where the seller becomes insolvent, there is often little point in a disappointed buyer pursuing his contractual remedies against the seller, because even if

5 See 10.5.2.

6 Conflicts of laws issues include what law governs a contract (what is the "proper law"?) and in what jurisdiction should a dispute be heard (what is the "proper forum"?). See further the Contractual Obligations (Applicable Law) Act 1990, implementing the Rome Convention on the Law Applicable to Contractual Obligations 1980, [1980] O.J. L266/1; and the EC (Civil and Commercial Judgments) Regulations 2002, S.I. No. 52 of 2002, implementing Council Regulation EC/44/2001 on jurisdiction and the recognition and enforcement of judgments in civil and commercial matters. See generally, Binchy, *Irish Conflict of Laws* (Dublin, Butterworths, 1986); see also Dicey and Morris, Conflict of Laws (London, Sweet & Maxwell, 13th ed., 2000).

successful in his claim, he will rank along with the other unsecured creditors at the end of the queue of creditors in insolvency.

Fortunately, there are other bases on which a disappointed buyer can seek compensation for defects in quality and other potential defendants, perhaps closer at hand to the buyer. These other bases are the subject of this chapter. When goods are sold, they may be accompanied by a product guarantee, often written, from the manufacturer, offering various remedies, such as repair or replacement if the goods prove defective. The nature of such guarantees and the extent to which they are regulated in Irish law will be considered in the next section of this chapter. Moreover, a buyer may be compensated for losses caused by defective products at common law under principles established in *Donoghue v. Stevenson,*[7] and/or under the provisions of the Liability for Defective Products Act 1991. Liability for defective products is considered in the last section of this chapter.

16.2 Product Guarantees[8]

As noted above, when goods are sold there is often a document accompanying the goods, from the manufacturer guaranteeing the quality of the goods and offering remedies, such as repair, or replacement of the goods, on certain terms, should the goods prove defective. Such documents are commonly referred to as "product guarantees", "manufacturer's guarantees" or "warranties."[9] Usually, for the product guarantee to operate, a standard form accompanying the goods needs to be completed by the buyer, including details of the product, where it was bought and when, and the name and address of the buyer, and returned to the manufacturer. Manufacturers and others[10] use product guarantees to increase their sales of a product. Product guarantees are an indication of the manufacturer's confidence in the quality of the goods supplied.[11] Therefore, the interplay between the statutory implied terms as to quality and the use of product guarantees is very important, especially in a consumer society.

Product guarantees can be provided for free, and hence act as an incentive to the buyer to buy a particular product, rather than a similar

7 [1932] A.C. 562.

8 Product guarantees must be distinguished from financial guarantees which operate as a form of personal security: see Chapter 26.

9 Warranty in the sense described herein must be distinguished from contractual warranties which in general contract law are terms of a contract of less importance than conditions: see 10.4.

10 Any person in the chain of distribution can offer such a product guarantee including an importer, a distributor and a retailer, but the vast majority of product guarantees appear to be offered by manufacturers: see further below.

11 See further Priest, "A Theory of the Consumer Product Warranty" (1981) 90 *Yale Law Journal* 1297.

product without an accompanying guarantee, or they can be bought and paid for. Often, a manufacturer will combine the two: he may offer a "free" guarantee for a limited period, say one year, and also offer the buyer the option to extend the period of the guarantee, for a price. Where guarantees are bought and paid for, they are commonly referred to as "extended warranties". Such warranties are often linked to insurance policies taken out with a third party[12] and are offered as an optional addition to the product itself. Extended warranties are common, for instance, in the motor trade.

At common law, the legal status of product guarantees is uncertain. The main problem derives from the doctrine of privity of contract. Usually, guarantees are offered by manufacturers, but, as is common, where a buyer purchases goods from a retailer, there is no privity of contract between the buyer and the manufacturer. Hence, any guarantee offered by a manufacturer cannot be enforced by the buyer, as a contract, against the manufacturer. Furthermore, the buyer's rights under the contract, principally relying on the statutory implied terms, are enforceable against the seller of goods only. Various arguments can be made to avoid this problem but without certainty. For instance, it can be argued that the guarantee represents a collateral contract between manufacturer and consumer: collateral to the sales contract between the retailer and the consumer. Where there has been no payment for the guarantee, the success of this argument will depend, in part, on the influence the guarantee had on the consumer in deciding to buy the goods. Accordingly, it can be argued that the consideration for the guarantee is provided by the buyer entering the main contract.[13] Or, depending on the circumstances, it can be argued that the guarantee represents a unilateral contract[14] to which no formal acceptance, nor further action, is needed by the consumer.

Ireland, unlike the United Kingdom,[15] for example, avoids this uncertainty, to a large extent, by regulating the use of guarantees by statute.[16] The importance of guarantees in the marketing of goods and in the competition between manufacturers on quality and service was recognised

---

12 On insurance, see generally Part V.

13 On collateral contracts, see generally, Friel, *Contract Law* (Dublin, Round Hall Sweet & Maxwell, 2nd ed., 2000) pp.170–171; and Clark, *Contract Law in Ireland* (Dublin, Round Hall Sweet & Maxwell, 4th ed., 1998) pp.117–119.

14 *E.g. Carlill v. Carbolic Smoke Ball Co* [1892] 2 Q.B. 484; affd [1893] 1 Q.B. 256.

15 But see U.K. DTI Discussion Document on Consumer Guarantees (1992) which proposed that a manufacturer should be civilly liable for the performance of his guarantee to the consumer; a retailer should be jointly liable to the consumer for a manufacturer's guarantee; and manufacturers and importers should be jointly liable for the "satisfactory quality" of goods. These proposals were never implemented and have since been over-taken by the EC Directive on Consumer Sales: see 16.2.3.

16 For the legal position in other member states of the E.U. on product guarantees, see the EC Commission, Green Paper on Guarantees for Consumer Goods and After-Sales Services, COM(93)509 final, pp.44–49, therein referred to as "commercial guarantees."

by the Sale of Goods and Supply of Services Act 1980 which regulates guarantees in sections 15–19, and the related topic of after-sales services in section 12.[17] In doing so, the legislation seeks to increase the protection afforded to buyers, and in particular consumer buyers, who are the main target of product guarantees.

16.2.1 Definition and form of guarantee

"Guarantee" is defined in section 15 as meaning

> "any document, notice or other written statement, howsoever described, supplied by a manufacturer or other supplier, other than a retailer, in connection with the supply of any goods and indicating that the manufacturer or supplier will service, repair or deal with the goods, following purchase."

Therefore, oral guarantees are outside the scope of the legislation: the guarantee must be in written form, as is usually the case. The definition makes it clear that the guarantee can be supplied by anyone in the distribution chain, including a manufacturer, distributor, wholesaler, or importer, other than the retailer.[18] Moreover, guarantees, as defined, cover more than sales contracts and include any supply of goods arrangement. Lastly, the guarantee must refer to the manufacturer or supplier offering to service, repair or deal with the goods, following purchase. "Dealing" in section 15 can be taken to include replacing and also refunding the price on a return of the goods. Where a product guarantee does not come within this definition, a buyer must rely on the common law and hence is severely disadvantaged. Interestingly, the definition makes no reference to whether the guarantee is provided freely or not, and hence it can be assumed that the Irish legislation, unlike the more recent EU legislation,[19] applies to both free guarantees and extended warranties.

Minimum requirements in relation to the form of a guarantee are set out in section 16. For instance, the guarantee must:

(a) be clearly legible;
(b) state clearly the name and address of the supplier;
(c) state clearly its duration;
(d) state clearly the procedure for presenting a claim, and this procedure shall not be more difficult than ordinary commercial procedures; and
(e) state clearly what the supplier undertakes to do and what charges apply,[20] if any.

---

17 On after-sales services, see 16.3.

18 On retailer liability for guarantees, see 1980 Act, s.17(1); see further 16.2.2.

19 See 16.2.3.

20 Such as the cost of carriage.

Failure to comply with the above formalities is an offence,[21] but although not stated, presumably does not affect the existence of the guarantee.

16.2.2 Liability under a guarantee

Under sections 17–19 of the 1980 Act, both the seller and the manufacturer/supplier may be liable under a guarantee to the buyer. Section 17 deals with seller's liability. Accordingly, where the seller of goods delivers a guarantee to the buyer, howsoever it is delivered, the seller is liable to the buyer for the observance of the terms of the guarantee.[22] Guarantee documents are often included within the packaging of goods and so may not be available to the consumer for inspection before they are purchased, brought home and opened. Nevertheless, it would seem that such a guarantee document would be delivered within the meaning of section 17. It has been argued that it is unfair on the seller to make him liable for another's guarantee, but a seller can avoid liability by expressly excluding himself at the time of delivery of the goods.[23] Moreover, where a seller provides his own written "undertaking" or guarantee to service, repair or otherwise deal with the goods, it is presumed that he will not be liable under any supplier's guarantee.[24] This presumption is, of course, rebuttable. The main purpose of these provisions is to provide buyers, and in particular consumer buyers, with more grounds on which to remedy the supply of defective goods, and indeed, more persons to assert such rights against. Finally, the rights of a buyer under section 17 are additional to a buyer's rights under section 19,[25] and indeed any other rights a buyer might have under the Sale of Goods Acts 1893–1980, in particular the statutory implied terms, or at common law.[26]

Section 19 deals with manufacturers' and other suppliers' liability.[27] It provides that a buyer can maintain an action against any manufacturer or supplier who has failed to observe the terms of the guarantee as if the manufacturer or supplier had sold the goods to the buyer and had committed a breach of warranty.[28] In effect, the terms of any guarantee are given contractual effect as if they were warranties. Hence, where a term of the guarantee is breached, a buyer can maintain an action for damages

21 1980 Act, s.16(6) and s.2(6) for penalties.

22 1980 Act, s.17(1).

23 1980 Act, s.17(1).

24 1980 Act, s.17(2). Such a guarantee or "undertaking" is made subject to ss.16, 18 and 19 of the 1980 Act: s.17(3).

25 1980 Act, s.17(4).

26 1980 Act, s.18.

27 Manufacturer expressly includes importer for the purpose of s.19(1): see 1980 Act, s.19(1).

28 1980 Act, s.19(1). Where a guarantor is liable to an owner in damages, the court may at its discretion afford the guarantor the opportunity to perform those obligations under the guarantee to the satisfaction of the court: 1980 Act, s.19(2).

against the manufacturer/supplier for breach of warranty, as under section 53 of the 1893 Act, but he cannot reject the goods or terminate the contract.[29] As an alternative to a claim in damages, section 19(1) provides that a court may order a seller or manufacturer/supplier to take such action as is necessary to observe the terms of the guarantee: an order of specific performance. As is the case at common law, such an order would not be made where damages will offer sufficient compensation to the buyer.[30] Importantly, for the purposes of section 19(1), "buyer" includes all persons who acquire title within the duration of the guarantee, such as the donee of a gift, or other successor in title. This means that the guarantee is not personal in nature but attaches to the goods.

Section 18 deals with the exclusion of a buyer's rights under a guarantee. It provides first, that the rights under any guarantee shall not exclude or limit a buyer's rights at common law and under statute and, second, that any provision in a guarantee which imposes obligations on a buyer which are additional to his obligations under the contract shall be void.[31] Furthermore, any provision which purports to make the guarantor or his agent, the sole authority to decide whether goods are defective, or whether the buyer is otherwise entitled to present a claim, shall be void.

Therefore, sections 17 and 19 detail the nature of liability under a guarantee and section 18 makes clear that the purpose of a guarantee is to augment the rights of buyers and others and not to diminish their rights at common law and under statute. Nevertheless, there are two main limitations to these provisions. First, it is vital to appreciate that the statutory provisions contain no legal obligation to offer a guarantee in the first place. Only where a manufacturer or other person decides to offer a guarantee, does the legislation apply. Second, the legislation does not prescribe a minimum promissory content for guarantees. This can be contrasted with the position in Greece and Spain, for example, where suppliers are obliged to offer guarantees of certain minimum content, for certain types of goods, such as new consumer durables, or motor cars.[32]

16.2.3 Product guarantees under the Consumer Sales Directive

The EC Directive on Certain Aspects of Consumer Sales and Associated Guarantees,[33] as well as dealing with issues of quality of goods and remedies for breach of the quality standard,[34] also addresses the issue of guarantees in Article 6, in a manner not unlike the Irish legislation. Earlier

29 See 14.3.4.

30 See 14.5.

31 1980 Act, s.18(1).

32 See EC Commission, Green Paper on Guarantees for Consumer Goods and After-Sales Services, COM(93) 509 final, p.46

33 Directive 1999/44/EC, [1999] O.J. L171/12.

34 See 13.11 and 14 7.

proposals for European legislation in this area considered the possibility of a "European guarantee" (a uniform guarantee throughout the European Union), but this idea was not followed-up in the Directive.[35] The directive was due to be implemented by member states by January 1, 2002.[36] At the time of writing, the Directive had not been implemented in Irish law. It is expected that the Directive will be implemented by Statutory Instrument, as opposed to primary legislation. Therefore, the following comments, as regards guarantees, are based on the wording of the Directive.

"Guarantee" is defined in the Directive as any undertaking by a seller or producer[37] to the consumer, given without extra charge, to reimburse the price paid, or to replace, repair or otherwise handle the goods if they do not meet the specifications set out in the guarantee documentation or relevant advertising.[38] Hence, this definition, unlike the Irish definition, is limited to free guarantees.

Article 6(1) provides that a guarantee shall be binding on the offerer, under the conditions laid down in the guarantee statement and the associated advertising.[39] This reference to "laid down in the guarantee statement" suggests that for a guarantee to come within the provisions of the Directive it must be in written form. The inclusion of advertising is a useful addition. In reality, consumers rarely have access to guarantee documents prior to purchase and the only knowledge a consumer may have is through advertising. It is through such advertising that a consumer's confidence and expectations about a product are built-up. Hence, it is only right that guarantee statements in advertising be placed on the same footing as express statements in guarantee documents.[40] Further, Article 6(3) provides that on request by a consumer, the guarantee shall be made available in writing or feature in another durable form available and

35 See EC Commission, Green Paper on Guarantees for Consumer Goods and After-Sales Services, COM(93)509 final, p.99

36 Art. 11.

37 Producer means manufacturer or importer: Art. 1(2).

38 Art. 1(2).

39 It is not apparent from a reading of the Directive what measure of damages a consumer would be entitled to receive where he does not receive full and proper satisfaction under the guarantee. Irish law opts for the contractual measure (broadly, the difference between the purchase price and the value of the goods in their defective state); though the tortious measure (broadly, for any loss that is reasonably foreseeable, which may include the cost of putting the defect right and for other economic loss suffered) may reflect more the consumer's idea of what is fair.

40 A similar approach is taken regarding advertising and the holiday trade: see Art. 3(2) of Council Directive 90/314 on Package Travel, Package Holidays and Package Tours; and the Package Holidays and Travel Trade Act 1995.

accessible to the consumer. Both of these provisions go further than the current Irish rules on guarantees.

However, in other respects the Directive does not go as far as the Irish provisions or other national provisions on guarantees. First, and like the Irish position, the Directive's approach is voluntary. The decision to offer a guarantee is a decision for the supplier, based on his assessment of the market. Second, the Directive makes the offerer of the guarantee liable. This contrasts with the Irish position of joint liability of seller and manufacturer, unless the seller expressly excludes himself from liability at the time of the sale.[41] Although this places a heavy burden on sellers to be familiar with all guarantees offered by manufacturers, from a consumer perspective, the two targets in Irish law are better than the one target, the offerer, under the Directive. The Irish position makes it easier for the consumer to invoke his rights arising under the manufacturer's guarantee, by offering a local target.[42] Third, although not stated expressly, it would seem from the definitions in Article 1(2) that a guarantee would be enforceable only by the consumer buyer. Again, this falls short of the Irish position where under section 19 of the 1980 Act, the guarantee runs with the goods for the benefit of all persons who acquire title within the duration of the guarantee.[43]

Article 6(2) contains minimum requirements as to the form of the guarantee, similar to the Irish provisions.[44] Article 6(5) states that a guarantee that infringes any of the requirements under the Directive is nevertheless enforceable by a consumer.

16.3 After-Sale Services

After-sale services refer, strictly speaking, to services not connected with honouring a guarantee. The offering of after-sale services is, like the offering of guarantees, a particular phenomenon of our modern consumer society. Suppliers offer after-sale services to gain a competitive edge. Normally, after-sale services are offered by the retailer himself, or by firms specialising in such services. Rarely would a manufacturer provide such services directly to consumers, although the manufacturer is vital to these arrangements, especially in the provision of spare parts. The European Community, in their original proposals on the Consumer Sales Directive, considered legislating in this area but later, on grounds of subsidiarity,

---

41 1980 Act, ss.17 and 19; see 16.2.2.

42 In 1992, the Department of Trade and Industry in the U.K. made proposals that a retailer should be jointly and severally liable with the manufacturer for the manufacturer's guarantee to a consumer. Nothing has come of these proposals since: See D.T.I., Discussion Document on Consumer Guarantees (1992).

43 1980 Act, s.19(1).

44 See 16.2.1.

decided not to.[45] The Irish Sale of Goods and Supply of Services Act 1980 does not fail in this regard, although the provision on after-sale services can best be described as minimal.

Section 12(1) of the 1980 Act provides that in a contract for the sale of goods there is an implied warranty that spare parts and an adequate after-sale service will be made available by the seller in such circumstances as are stated in an offer, description or advertisement by the seller, on a manufacturer's behalf or on his own behalf, for such stated period or, if no period is stated, for a reasonable period. Section 12(2) provides that the Minister can by order define, in relation to a class of goods, what such a reasonable period is. This power has never been exercised. Any terms seeking to limit this provision are void under section 12(3).

The Irish provisions can be described as minimalist in that there is no obligation placed on sellers or others to offer after-sale services. It is only where the seller makes such an offer that the legislation comes into play by making any such offers contractually binding, in the form of warranties, breach of which gives rise to a right to claim damages but not to reject the goods or terminate the contract. In contrast, in Spain, a royal decree fixes at seven years the duration of the obligation to keep spare parts available in relation to household appliances.[46]

16.4 Product Liability[47]

As well as contractual liability under the sales legislation and any guarantees on offer, a supplier of goods may find himself liable to a buyer, or other consumer, for losses caused by defective goods in tort law, either at common law or under the Liability for Defective Products Act 1991.

16.4.1 At common law

The common law basis of liability is the seminal case of *Donoghue v. Stevenson*[48] where the consumer of the contents of an opaque bottle of ginger beer succeeded in suing the manufacturer for personal injury caused because the bottle contained the remains of a decomposing snail. Accordingly, in certain circumstances, a manufacturer, or indeed anyone in

45 See EC Commission, Green Paper on Guarantees for Consumer Goods and After-Sales Services, COM(93) 509 final, p.100.

46 See EC Commission, Green Paper on Guarantees for Consumer Goods and After-Sales Services, COM(93) 509 final, p.50.

47 See further McMahon & Binchy, *Law of Torts* (Dublin, Butterworths, 3rd, ed., 2001) Chapter 11; Garvey, "Developing the Law Concerning Product Liability" [1995] *Commercial Law Practitioner* 61.

48 [1932] A.C. 562; see also *Kirby v. Burke and Holloway* [1944] I.R. 207 (H.C.); *Power v. Bedford Motors* [1959] I.R. 391 (S.C.) .

the chain of distribution, owes a duty of care to the ultimate consumer or user of his product, and may be liable in negligence, if as a result of negligence in the manufacture or distribution of the product, the product is defective and causes loss or injury to the consumer or user. Prior to *Donoghue v. Stevenson*, a manufacturer's only liability was in contract law to the immediate purchaser of the product, unless the product was inherently dangerous or the manufacturer was guilty of fraud.[49] The decision in *Donoghue v. Stevenson* represented a recognition by the judiciary of the changes brought about by mass production and standardised products. As a result, many products are supplied pre-packaged with no opportunity for inspection between manufacture and purchase by the consumer. Hence, products should leave the manufacturer, and others in the distribution chain, in a fit state suitable for consumption or use.[50] The rationale for such tortious liability is that a manufacturer of a defective product is an appropriate person to bear the cost of any losses caused by the defective product because he is responsible for the defect in the first place, and, furthermore, he is in a good position to spread the cost of any losses, through price increases and insurance.

The major advantage of a claim in tort law is that it is unrestricted by the doctrine of privity of contract. Accordingly, for example, it is not only the immediate purchaser from the manufacturer who can take a claim in tort law against the manufacturer, but any purchaser of the product, howsoever distant from the manufacturer. Equally, any intermediate, or end consumer or user of the product can sue the manufacturer, such as the recipient of the product as a gift. Even a third party bystander injured by the product may have a right of action against the manufacturer.

At the same time, there are a number of difficulties in taking a claim in tort law. First, tortious product liability is based on proving negligence on the part of the manufacturer, or other defendant. When compared with the strict liability of contract law, this is a serious disadvantage. The burden of proving negligence can weigh heavily on a plaintiff. Expert evidence will probably be necessary and usually be expensive. However, the principle *res ipsa loquitur* may be used to transfer the burden of proof onto the defendant.[51] Second, the plaintiff will have to prove that the defect in the product caused the loss and that the loss was not too remote,[52] but similar issues of causation and remoteness arise in contract claims also.[53] A final

49 McMahon & Binchy, *Law of Torts* (Dublin, Butterworths, 3rd, ed., 2001) pp.251–2.

50 "The essential point [is] that the article should reach the consumer or user subject to the same defect as it had when it left the manufacturer." Per Lord Wright in *Grant v. Australian Woolen Mills Ltd* [1936] A.C. 85 at 106–7 (P.C.).

51 *Fleming v. Henry Denny & Sons Ltd* unreported, Supreme Court, July 29, 1955.

52 On the doctrine of causation, see McMahon & Binchy, *Law of Torts* (Dublin, Butterworths, 3rd, ed., 2001) Chapter 2; on the doctrine of remoteness see McMahon & Binchy, *Law of Torts* (Dublin, Butterworths, 3rd, ed., 2001) Chapter 3.

53 See 2.4.4.3(ii).

and major potential limitation relates to the type of loss that can be compensated for under tort law. Traditionally, tort law provided compensation for physical injury and damage to property but not for pure financial loss. This changed with the decision in *Hedley Byrne v. Heller*[54] Nevertheless, it may be difficult to get damages in respect of the reduced value of the defective product itself, or the cost of repairs even where this is necessary to make the product safe.[55]

16.4.2 The Liability for Defective Products Act 1991, as amended

The Liability for Defective Products Act 1991 was enacted to give effect to the 1985 EC Directive on Product Lability.[56] The 1985 Directive has since been amended by Council Directive 1999/34/EC,[57] implemented in Ireland by the EC (Liability for Defective Products) Regulations 2000.[58] The purpose of this amendment was to extend the meaning of "product" to include primary agricultural products, largely as a result of various "food scares" in Europe. Significantly, liability under this legislation is strict.[59] The Directive[60] seeks to harmonise the law on product liability throughout the European Community in order to facilitate the free movement of goods

54 [1964] A.C. 465; see further *McShane v. Johnston*, [1997] 1 I.L.R.M. 86.

55 *Junior Books Ltd v. Veitchi* [1983] 1 A.C. 520 (H.L.); *Ward v. McMaster* [1985] I.R. 29; cf. *Murphy v. Brentwood DC* [1991] 1 A.C. 398 (H.L.). See further McMahon & Binchy, *Law of Torts* (Dublin, Butterworths, 3rd, ed., 2001) pp.273–4.

56 Directive 85/374/EEC, [1985] O.J. L210/29. Where legislation seeks to implement an EC measure, it is important to bear in mind a number of doctrines of EC law. For example, where an Act of the Oireachtas seeks to implement an EC measure, such as a directive, under the doctrine of supremacy, the EC measure is paramount should a conflict between the two measures arise: *Internationala Handelsgessellschaft* [1972] 3 C.M.L.R. 255; see also Art 29.4.3° of the Constitution and *Doyle v. An Taoiseach* [1986] I.L.R.M. 693 (S.C.) . Moreover, Irish courts are required, where possible, under the doctrine of indirect effect, to interpret national law to comply with EC law: *Marleasing SA v. La Comercial Internacional de Alimentación SA* (Case C106/89) [1990] E.C.R. I - 4135, [1992] 1 C.M.L.R. 305. Further, under the Treaty of Rome, the Court of Justice (E.C.J.) is the sole interpreter of the Treaty and other EC measures, and an Irish court is bound by the interpretation of the E.C.J.: Treaty of Rome, Art. 234; see also *Benedetti v. Munari* (Case 52/76) [1977] E.C.R. 163.

57 [1999] O.J. 1 L141/20.

58 S.I. No. 401 of 2000, commenced December 4, 2000. See further the EC Commission Green Paper on Liability for Defective Products, COM (1999) 396 final, July 28, 1999.

59 A similar principle of strict liability was adopted by the courts in the United States, and was embodied in s.402A of the Second Restatement of Torts (1964), but the Third Restatement (1997) represents a shift away from strict liability towards a more negligence-based system. See Pelly, "Is European Products Liability More Protective than the Restatement (Third) of Torts: Products Liability - Parts I and II?" [2001] *Irish Law Times* 314 and [2002] *Irish Law Times* 9.

60 Reference to "the Directive" refers to the 1985 Directive as amended.

and to enhance competition. However, the level of harmonisation is not uniform because the Directive includes optional provisions.[61]

Under the Act an "injured party" can sue the "producer" for damages in tort, for "damage" caused by a defect in his "product".[62] As is usual, the onus is on the injured party to prove the damage, the defect, and a causal link between the two.[63] "Injured party" is defined as: "a person who has suffered damage caused ... by a defect in a product or, if he has died, his personal representative ... or dependants".[64] This includes any buyer of the product, recipient of the product as a gift, consumer or user of the product or even an innocent bystander injured by the product. The defendant in all these claims is the "producer". Producer is defined in the legislation as including:

> (a) the manufacturer or producer of a finished product, or any raw material, or of a component part of a product;
> (b) any person who, by putting his name, trade mark or other distinguishing feature on the product, has held himself out to be the producer of the product,
> (c) any person who has imported the product into a Member State from a place outside the European Communities in order, in the course of any business of his, to supply it to another.[65]

Where there is more than one defendant for the same damage, liability is joint and several.[66]

Importantly, the types of damage which can be compensated for under this legislation is more limited than in contract law. "Damage" under the legislation means: "death or personal injury, or loss of, damage to, or destruction of, any item of property, other than the defective product itself".[67] Therefore, any damage to, or loss in value of, the product itself cannot be compensated for under this legislation; and pure economic losses cannot be compensated for under this legislation. In contrast, in a claim in contract law, an award of damages for breach of the statutory implied terms, or indeed any contractual terms, may include damages for death, personal injury, damage to other property, and any other economic loss, including the reduced value of the defective goods themselves.

61 See, *e.g.* the development risks defence in Art. 15(1)(b); see further Howells, "Implication of the Implementation and Non-Implementation of the E.C. Product Liability Directive" (1990) 41 *Northern Ireland Legal Quarterly* 22.

62 1991 Act, s.2(1); Directive, Art. 1.

63 1991 Act, s.4; Directive, Art. 4.

64 1991 Act, s.1; Directive, Art. 2.

65 1991 Act, s.2(2); Directive, Art. 3.

66 1991 Act, s.8; Directive, Art. 8.

67 1991 Act, s.1; Directive, Art. 2.

"Product" is defined as meaning all moveables, including primary agricultural products that have not undergone initial processing, and includes electricity.[68] A product is defective, for the purposes of the Act, if it fails to provide the safety which a person is entitled to expect, taking all circumstances into account, including:

(i) the presentation of the product;
(ii) the use to which it could reasonably be expected that the product would be put; and
(iii) the time when the product was put into circulation.[69]

The circumstances listed above are not exhaustive and other relevant circumstances might include any instructions or warning issued with the product.

A major advantage of this legislation in relation to product liability at common law is that, under the Act, liability is strict. Nevertheless, the legislation provides a series of defences for the producer. So, for example, a producer is not liable under the Act if he proves that:

(i) he did not put the product into circulation, or
(ii) having regard to the circumstances, it is probable that the defect which caused the damage did not exist at the time when the product was put into circulation by him or that the defect came into being afterwards, or
(iii) the product was neither manufactured by him for sale or for any form of distribution for an economic purpose nor manufactured or distributed by him in the course of his business, or
(iv) the defect concerned is due to compliance by the product with any requirement imposed by or under any enactment or any requirement of the law of the European Communities, or
(v) the state of scientific and technical knowledge at the time when he put the product into circulation was not such as to enable the existence of the defect to be discovered,[70] or
(vi) in the case of the manufacturer of a component or the producer of a raw material, the defect is attributable entirely to the design of

68 1991 Act, s.1, as amended; Directive, Art. 2, as amended.

69 1991 Act, s.5; Directive, Art. 6. This last circumstance allows a court to consider the "state of the art" at the time the product was put on the market. See further s.5(2) which provides: "A product shall not be considered defective for the sole reason that a better product is subsequently put into circulation."

70 Known as the "development risks defence": an optional provision in the Directive. This defence is particularly important regarding high-tech products including new drugs.

> the product in which the component has been fitted or the raw material has been incorporated or to the instructions given by the manufacturer of the product.[71]

Additionally, any defences available in a tort action, such a contributory negligence or *volenti non fit injuria*, are available in a claim under this legislation.[72] However, liability under this legislation cannot be limited or excluded by any contract terms or notice or other provision.[73]

Finally, the limitation period for actions under the Act is three years from the date of the damage or injury.[74] Where such damage or injury is not immediately apparent, the limitation period starts to run from the date on which the injured party became aware or should reasonably have become aware of the damage, the defect and the identity of the producer. However, a final cut-off point for producers is provided for in the legislation and no claim can be brought more than 10 years after the product was put into circulation.[75]

Fears that the introduction of strict liability would lead to a flood of claims, as in the United States, have so far proved unfounded. In fact, there is no reported Irish case law on this legislation and English case law has only started to emerge in the last couple of years.[76] The decision in the English case *A v. The National Blood Authority*[77] is therefore welcome, not least because it relies on the wording of the Directive, as opposed to the implementing U.K. legislation, the Consumer Protection Act 1987. The plaintiffs received blood transfusions or products which had been infected with Hepatitis C from blood donors. The virus itself was not identified until May 1988 and a screening test was not available for it until the mid-1990s, although in May 1988 there were two procedures (known as surrogate tests) which were possible indicators of the presence of the virus. These were introduced in the U.S.A. in 1986 but were never used in the United Kingdom. The High Court held that the plaintiffs should succeed in their claim under the relevant legislation because there was a defect (a virus in the blood) which caused damage (a virus in the patient). The court confirmed that the factors listed in Article 6 were not exhaustive and that all relevant circumstances were to be considered in assessing whether a defect existed. However, it ruled that the avoidability of the risk of infection was not a relevant factor in establishing if a product is defective

---

71 1991 Act, s.6; Directive, Art. 7.

72 1991 Act, s.9.

73 1991 Act, s.10; Directive, Art. 12.

74 1991 Act, s.7; Directive, Art. 10.

75 1991 Act, s.7(2).

76 See Deards & Twigg-Flesner, "The Consumer Protection Act 1987: Proof at Last that it is Protecting Consumers" [2001] *Nottingham Law Journal* 1.

77 [2001] 3 All E.R. 289; see further Howells & Mildred, "Infected Blood: Defect and Discoverability – A First Exposition of the EC Product Liability Directive" (2002) 65 *Modern Law Review* 95.

(this factor may be relevant in relation to the development risk defence though). On the facts, it was found that doctors knew of the risk, but society in general did not know of the risk. Such a risk could not then be accepted by consumers unless they were warned, which they had not been. The infected blood products were therefore defective. It was further held that the development risk defence did not apply because the existence of the defect was discoverable at the relevant time, either by surrogate testing or screening. It would appear therefore that this defence will only operate if either there is no test available to discover the defect at all, or the defect has been discovered but this information is not "accessible" to the defendant.

CHAPTER 17

THE PASSING OF PROPERTY

17.1 INTRODUCTION

The legal objective of a contract for the sale of goods is the transfer of property in the goods from seller to buyer. This is recognised by the statutory definition of a contract of sale, and it is one of the features which distinguishes sale from other, apparently similar, transactions involving the transfer of possession and use of goods.[1] In this chapter, the rules which determine when property passes from the seller to the buyer are examined. The related topic of risk, and its passage, is considered in the next chapter.

17.1.1 The meaning of property

"Property" is defined by the legislation as "the general property in goods and not merely a special property."[2] A distinction is drawn, in Irish and English law, between *the* property in goods, and *a* property, or a special property, in the same goods.[3] A pledgee of goods, for instance, has a property in the goods which comprises the right to possess the goods until payment of the relevant debt.[4] In contrast, it seems that the property, or the general property means the *absolute interest* in the goods; for practical purposes it can be regarded as meaning "ownership".[5] Ownership comprises a bundle of rights, described by Sir Fredrick Pollock as "the entirety of powers of use and disposal allowed by law."[6] The legislation

---

1 1893 Act, s.1; see generally Chapter 9.

2 1893 Act, s.62.

3 Chalmers, *Sale of Goods* (London, Butterworths, 18th ed., 1981) p.269.

4 See 25.2. Other persons with a special property include a bailee and someone with a lien (see 3.4.5 and 25.3): see further Bell, *Modern Property Law in England and Ireland* (London, Butterworths, 1989) p.6.

5 See *Fitzpatrick v. Criminal Assets Bureau* [2000] 1 I.R. 217 at 234–5; see further Battersby, "A Reconsideration of 'Property' and 'Title' in the Sale of Goods Act" [2001] *Journal of Business Law* 1, and Battersby and Preston, "The Concepts of 'Property', 'Title' and 'Owner' used in the Sale of Goods Act 1893" (1972) 35 *Modern Law Review* 269. Cf. Ho, "Some Reflections on 'Property' and 'Title' in the Sale of Goods Act" (1997) 56 *Cambridge Law Journal* 571. See also Goode, "Ownership and Obligations in Commercial Transactions" (1987) 103 *Law Quarterly Review* 433.

6 Pollock, "Some General Legal Notions" Part VII reprinted in Goodhart, *Jurisprudence and Legal Essays* (London, Macmillan, 1961) p.97; see also 3.3.

refers at different times to "property",[7] "title",[8] and "owner,"[9] but nowhere clearly defines and distinguishes these terms.[10] For the purposes of this chapter, these terms will be used synonymously.

17.1.2 The consequences of ownership

The transfer of property has important practical and legal consequences. Primarily, as the owner of goods, a person has the absolute legal right to use them in any way he thinks fit, subject to general legal restrictions, such as the criminal law and the law of tort.[11] An owner of goods may keep, use, or consume the goods himself, or he may dispose of them. He can sell the goods, mortgage them, or transfer them otherwise, such as by way of gift or under a will. An owner can even destroy the goods if he wishes. Moreover, where a third party interferes with the owner's rights, the torts of conversion, trespass and negligence may offer relief.[12] However, ownership has its downside. Where the goods are accidentally lost or damaged, for example, it is the owner who is "at risk", that is, who bears the risk of such loss.[13] In particular, where S sells goods to B, but before delivery, they are accidentally lost or damaged:

(i) where property has passed to B, he will have to accept any damaged goods and pay the full price, bearing the cost of any loss himself; but
(ii) where property has not passed to B, S will have to bear the cost of any loss; where the goods sold were specific, B can sue S for damages for non-delivery; where the goods sold are unascertained, S will have to buy replacement goods in time for the delivery date or else face an action for damages for non-delivery.

Such loss can be protected against, or covered, by an insurance policy on the goods, provided, of course, that the person who is at risk knows that he is at risk and takes out the necessary insurance cover.[14]

The passing of property is relevant in a number of other circumstances. First, a claim for the price, under section 49(1), depends on the property

7 *E.g.* 1893 Act, s.1 and ss.16–18.
8 *E.g.* 1893 Act, ss.21–25.
9 *E.g.* 1893 Act, s.21, s.24, s.25.
10 See Battersby and Preston, *supra* note 5; and further Ho, *supra* note 5.
11 Professor Birks gives an extreme example: a man cannot justify shooting another by saying that he was merely using his own weapon; "The Roman Law Concept of Dominium and the Idea of Absolute Ownership" [1985] *Acta Juridica* 1, at 1.
12 On conversion see 19.1.1; see generally McMahon & Binchy, *Law of Torts* (Dublin, Butterworths, 3rd ed., 2000) Chapters 11, and 28–30.
13 See further Chapter 18.
14 See generally Part V.

having passed to the buyer.[15] Where property has not passed, a seller may only be entitled to sue for non-acceptance and hence is required to mitigate his loss.[16] Second, the passing of property is important in resolving title conflicts, that is, where two or more people claim to be the owner of, or have the better title to, the goods in dispute.[17] For example, assume that S agrees to sell goods to B, and delivers them, but before paying for them B sells them to X:

(i) if property has passed to B, S will be unable to recover the goods from X; but
(ii) if no property has passed to B, at the time of the sale to X, S may be able to recover them.

This is because of the general rule that only the owner of goods can dispose of them to another person so as to pass good title – *nemo dat non quad habet*. However, there are exceptions to this general rule which may protect X even if B was not the owner of the goods at the time of the sale to X.[18] Finally, matters of ownership and the passing of property are relevant when a business becomes insolvent, as can be seen in relation to reservation of title clauses.[19] In particular, where S sells goods to B and pays for them before they are delivered, and S becomes insolvent before the goods are delivered:

(i) if property has passed to B he can assert his rights over the goods and demand possession of them;
(ii) but if no property has passed to B, he is left as an unsecured creditor in S's insolvency to pursue a refund of the price and an action for damages for non-delivery.

On the other hand, where S sells goods to B and delivers them, but before B pays for them B becomes insolvent:

(i) if property has passed to B, S is left as an unsecured creditor in B's insolvency to pursue an action for the price; but
(ii) if no property has passed to B, S is entitled to assert his property rights and repossess the goods.

---

15 See 15.2.1.

16 See 15.2.2.

17 See generally Chapter 19.

18 See further 19.2–19.9.

19 See 15.4.

17.1.3 The statutory rules

Because of the legal and commercial importance of ownership or property in goods, the legislation contains detailed rules governing various aspects of its transfer including: the time when property is transferred from seller to buyer, in sections 16–19, the subject-matter of this chapter; the issue of risk, in section 20, covered in Chapter 18; and the effect of a purported transfer by someone who is not the owner of the goods, in sections 21–26, dealt with in Chapter 19. There are no equivalent provisions in the legislation dealing with other supply contracts, such as hire-purchase arrangements and contracts for work and materials. It seems that under such contracts, property in goods passes at common law when the parties intend it to pass. Some contracts, such as hire-purchase contracts, may include an express provision dealing with the passing of property, but in the absence of such provision the parties' intention must be inferred from the circumstances of the case. Ultimately, the end result will often be the same as under the statutory rules of the Sale of Goods Acts 1893–1980.

The statutory rules on the passing of property are based on rules developed at common law prior to the 1893 Act, and they have remained unchanged since 1893. Perhaps surprisingly, the passing of property is not related to the delivery of the goods or the payment of the price. This means that the rules often operate contrary to consumer, and even commercial, expectations. Instead, the legislation contains rather technical and complicated rules depending largely on the type of goods sold: specific, unascertained or future.

The basic rule is found in section 17 which provides that property passes when the parties intend it to pass. Section 17(2) provides that: "[f]or the purpose of ascertaining the intention of the parties regard shall be had to the terms of the contract, the conduct of the parties and the circumstances of the case."[20] Sometimes the parties include an express term in the contract on the passing of property, such as a reservation of title clause.[21] This is sanctioned under section 19(1), which provides that the seller may reserve the right of disposal of the goods until certain conditions are fulfilled. Parties can make the passing of property conditional on the occurrence of any event but payment of the price is the common condition placed on the passing of property. Section 19(2) provides a statutory example of an implied reservation of the right of disposal in the context of international trade. Where goods are shipped and under the bill of lading the goods are deliverable to the seller or his agent, the seller is prima facie deemed to have reserved the right of disposal. A reservation of the right of

20 Although s.17 is expressed to apply to contracts for the sale of specific or ascertained goods, it is well established that s.17(2), as a matter of common law, applies to unascertained goods also.

21 See 15.4.

disposal can be implied from other circumstances. For example, an express term about the passing of risk may indicate that property is not intended to pass until the goods are paid for because property and risk normally pass together, but in many cases, consumer and commercial, the parties never address their minds to the issue of the passing of property.

Where the parties' intention is not clear, a series of rules of presumed intent are set out in section 18. Because these are rules of presumed intent, they can be excluded or negatived, expressly or impliedly, by the contrary intention of the parties. But significantly, both sections 17 and 18 are subject to section 16 which is mandatory in application: section 16 can never be excluded or varied by the parties agreement. Section 16 is limited to the sale of unascertained goods and provides that property cannot pass until the goods are first ascertained.

17.2 Specific Goods

Specific goods are defined as goods which are identified and agreed upon at the time the contract is made.[22] Under a contract for the sale of specific goods, the seller must deliver the specific goods identified and agreed upon and cannot, without the consent of the buyer, tender substitute goods. The first three rules in section 18 contain presumptions of intention as to the passing of property in specific goods. These presumptions can, of course, be rebutted where a contrary intention appears. A contrary intention would be indicated, for instance, where a retention of title clause delaying the passing of property until payment of the price was incorporated in the contract.[23] Other indicators of a contrary intention might include an agreement as to the passing of risk, which normally passes with property.[24] Accordingly, if risk has passed this may indicate that property has passed; and if risk has not passed this may indicate that property has not passed.[25] However, the exact opposite inferences can be drawn. For example, in *Re Anchor Line Ltd*,[26] it was inferred that property had not passed because there was a specific clause in the contract placing risk on the buyer, and the court found that if property had passed, such a clause would have been unnecessary. Therefore, drawing an inference as to the passing of property, based on an agreement about the passing of risk, will depend on the circumstances of the case: no hard and fast rules apply. Other examples of a contrary intention can arise in contracts to sell goods and land together,

22 1893 Act, s.62.

23 See 15.4.

24 See generally Chapter 18.

25 See, *e.g. Underwood Ltd v. Burgh Castle Brick and Cement Syndicate* [1922] 1 K.B. 343; see 17.2.1.

26 [1937] Ch. 1 (C.A.).

where the usual inference is that property passes on conveyance,[27] or in contracts for the sale and installation of goods, where property normally does not pass until the installation is complete.[28]

17.2.1 Specific goods in a deliverable state

Rule 1 provides:

> "Where there is an unconditional contract for the sale of specific goods, in a deliverable state, the property in the goods passes to the buyer when the contract is made, and it is immaterial whether the time of payment or the time of delivery, or both, be postponed."

There are a number of pre-conditions to the operation of this rule. First, the reference to "unconditional contract" seems to require no more than that there is no condition in the contract as to the passing of property, such as a retention of title clause.[29] Second, the goods must be in a deliverable state. "Deliverable state" is defined in section 62(4) of the 1893 Act as "such a state that the buyer would under the contract be bound to take delivery of them." "Deliverable state" has been given a restricted meaning. It is clear that goods may be in a deliverable state and defective.[30] Goods will not be in a deliverable state if the seller has agreed to do something to the goods before delivery under the contract. For example, if a car is sold provided that the seller fits a new exhaust, the car is not in a deliverable state until the exhaust is fitted. Another example can be found in *Underwood Ltd v. Burgh Castle Brick and Cement Syndicate*,[31] where the plaintiff seller agreed to sell an engine weighing 30 tons "free on rail." The engine was bolted and cemented to the ground. Under the sales contract, the seller had to remove the engine from its base, dismantle it and load it aboard the train. On loading, it was damaged. The issue was whether property, and hence risk of loss, had passed to the buyer. It was held that property had not passed when the contract was made because the engine was not in a deliverable state when the contract was made: rule 1 did not apply.[32] The

27 *Commissioner of Stamps v. Queensland Meat Export Co Ltd* [1917] A.C. 624.

28 *Clarke v. Bulmer* (1843) 11 M&W 243.

29 Earlier case law (*Varley v. Whipp* [1900] 1 Q.B. 513) had suggested that a contract which contains "conditions", *i.e.* important terms, was not unconditional, but, for instance, section 12 of the 1893 Act implies a condition into all domestic sales and can never be excluded, so that all such contracts contain conditions in this sense and so "unconditional" must mean something else here.

30 If this were not so, property would never pass in defective goods. Hence, defects in goods do not prevent property passing; if a buyer rejects the goods, property revests in the seller.

31 [1922] 1 K.B. 343 (C.A.).

32 The judges were also of the view that there was sufficient contrary intention to be inferred from the facts that some element of risk was involved in dismantling the engine, such that property (and risk) was not intended to pass on sale.

Court of Appeal laid down the following test for deliverable state:

> "A deliverable state does not depend upon the mere completeness of the subject matter in all its parts. It depends on the actual state of the goods and the state in which they are to be delivered by the terms of the contract."[33]

Finally, property passes in specific goods at the time of the contract, regardless of the time of delivery or payment. In *Clarke v. Micheal Reilly & Sons*,[34] on March 1, 1961 the parties agreed to supply a new car in return for a trade-in, plus the balance in cash. The plaintiff paid the money. The defendant's sales representative stated that delivery of the new car would take 14–21 days. The plaintiff then asked if he could use the old car until delivery of the new car, and the sales representative agreed. Before the new car was delivered, the old car was involved in an accident and the defendant sought to repudiate the contract. The court found that when the contract was concluded on March 1, the property in the old car, being specific goods in a deliverable state, had passed to the defendant. The defendant permitting the plaintiff to continue to use the old car indicated that the parties had intended the defendant to become the owner once the agreement was concluded. After March 1, the plaintiff was only a bailee of the old car. Consequently the plaintiff was entitled to specific performance of the contract to purchase the new car, even though the trade-in car had been damaged. This case is not without its critics,[35] and it has been argued that a court would be fully justified in finding on these facts a contrary intention that property should not pass until delivery. There are good policy reasons for holding that the "seller" in such circumstances should bear the risk because he has possession of the goods and is more likely to have insurance cover. This decision seems to have been influenced by an admission by the defendant that they would have regarded a resale by the plaintiff of the car to a third party as a breach of contract. But, while this may be correct, it does not affect the passing of property.

This case illustrates the dangers associated with splitting property and possession. Risk of loss of, or damage to, the goods normally passes with property.[36] Thus, where rule 1 applies risk will pass to the buyer when the contract is made, even though delivery is delayed. Where goods are accidentally lost or damaged before delivery, the buyer will bear the loss. The seller is in possession as a bailee and will therefore be liable in negligence for any loss, but unless he is responsible for the delay, he will

33 [1922] 1 K.B. 343 per Banks L.J. at 345.

34 (1962) 96 I.L.T.R. 96 (Circuit Court).

35 *Atiyah's Sale of Goods* (Harlow, Pearson, 10th ed., 2001) p.320.

36 1893 Act, s.20; see Chapter 18.

not be liable for any pure accidental damage or loss. This can operate harshly for consumer buyers: goods bought but not yet delivered will most likely not be covered by the buyer's household insurance, and because property and risk have passed to the buyer under rule 1 the goods cannot be insured by the seller for lack of an insurable interest.[37]

17.2.2 Specific goods not in a deliverable state

Where the goods are not in a deliverable state at the time of the contract, rule 2 provides:

> "Where there is a contract for the sale of specific goods and the seller is bound to do something to the goods, for the purpose of putting them into a deliverable state, property does not pass until the thing is done, and the buyer has notice thereof."

Thus, for example, where B buys a car on condition that a new exhaust is fitted, property in the car will not pass until S has fitted the new exhaust *and* B has notice of that fact.[38] The notice requirement gives the buyer some opportunity to prepare himself for ownership, including the opportunity to insure the goods, but it should be noted that the legislation does not require the seller to give notice; merely that the buyer *has* notice. This difference means that the buyer is less well protected than he would be if the seller had to *give* notice.

17.2.3 Do an act to ascertain the price

Rule 3, which is of limited application, provides:

> "Where there is a contract for the sale of specific goods in a deliverable state, but the seller is bound to weigh, measure, test, or do some other act or thing with reference to the goods for the purpose of ascertaining the price, the property does not pass until such act or thing be done and the buyer has notice thereof."

Here, again, the goods must be in a deliverable state, as defined in section 62(4), and some act must be done by the seller (and not the buyer or a sub-buyer,[39] for example) for the purpose of ascertaining the price. In these

37 See 27.3.1.

38 *Cf. Anderson v. Ryan* [1967] I.R. 34 which involved an agreement to sell a car. The High Court found, we can assume under section 17 of the 1893 Act, that it was the intention of the parties that the property would not pass until certain repairs were done and paid for.

39 *Nanka-Bruce v. Commonwealth Trust* [1926] A.C. 77 (P.C.).

circumstances, property passes when the act is done and the buyer has notice of the act.

17.3 Goods on Approval or on Sale or Return

Goods may be delivered to a potential buyer in order for him to evaluate their suitability for his purposes, or to try to resell them under terms which allow him to return them if they prove unsuitable or unsaleable. In such cases, the goods are said to be delivered "on approval" or "on sale or return" terms, respectively. Such arrangements have obvious advantages for the potential buyer, who avoids the risk of buying goods that he cannot use or resell. However, there are also advantages for the seller in that the seller has some protection against a buyer's failure to pay and his insolvency.

Strictly, where goods are delivered on approval, or on sale or return terms, there may, at the time of delivery, be no contract of sale. Instead there will be an agreement under which the buyer effectively has an option to buy the goods if they are approved or resold. It is important to emphasise that although under such arrangements there is initially no contract of sale, the goods must be delivered at the request of the potential buyer and there will often be a detailed contract between the parties. If the delivery is not requested by the buyer, the goods are unsolicited and the buyer may be entitled to treat them as an unconditional gift under section 47 of the Sale of Goods and Supply of Services Act 1980.

The sale on approval, and the sale or return agreement may contain detailed provisions dealing with the buyer's right to return the goods and the passing of property in them.[40] In the absence of any express or implied agreement as to the passing of property, section 18, rule 4 provides that property in the goods passes to the buyer in one of four circumstances:

(i) when the buyer signifies his approval or acceptance of them to the seller;

(ii) when the buyer does any other act adopting the transaction. A buyer will be deemed to have adopted the transaction by dealing with the goods, such as reselling or pledging them. However, it has been held that a buyer does not adopt the transaction where he is prevented by circumstances outside his control from returning the goods – for instance because they are accidentally damaged or destroyed.[41]

---

40 A retention of title clause for example: see *Weiner v. Gill* [1906] 2 K.B. 574.

41 *Elphick v. Barnes* (1880) 5 C.P.D. 321.

(iii) when the buyer retains the goods, without rejecting them, beyond the time limit fixed for their return. Unless agreed otherwise,[42] all that is required to give notice of rejection is a clear indication that the buyer rejects the seller's offer.[43]

(iv) when no time limit for their return is fixed, on the expiry of a reasonable time. What is reasonable will depend on the circumstances of the case. A shorter time will be allowed for perishable goods than durables, for instance.

The buyer will be a bailee of the goods for the seller from the time when they are delivered to him until he either returns them or buys them. Of course, rule 4, like the other rules, is a rule of presumed intent and can be excluded by the agreement of the parties. Hence, a seller can agree to sell goods on approval or on sale or return, subject to a retention of title clause, such that no property in the goods would pass until they are paid for.

17.4 Unascertained Goods

The category of unascertained goods is not expressly defined in the legislation, but section 62 of the 1893 Act does define specific goods as goods which are identified and agreed upon at the time the contract is made. The implication is that all other goods are unascertained, sometimes known as "fungibles." So, a contract to sell a car, registration number, 02 C 1234, is a contract to sell specific goods. In contrast, a contract to sell 10 bags of smokeless coal is a contract to sell unascertained goods because although the goods are described, the actual goods to be used to fulfill the contract have not been specifically identified at the time the contract is made. Accordingly, the seller is entitled to supply any 10 bags of coal provided they comply with the description "smokeless". Furthermore, there is an intermediary category, identified by Professor Goode as "quasi-specific" goods.[44] Strictly speaking, and for the purposes of the legislation, these are unascertained goods, but from a source identified when the contract is made. For example, a contract to sell 500 tons of wheat, out of a bulk cargo of 10,000 tons aboard the *MV Hopeful*, is a contract for the sale of quasi-specific goods, as is a contract to buy 99 bottles of wine from

42 The terms of an effective rejection notice may be prescribed in the agreement and could include the requirement that the goods be actually returned; or made available for return, or simply that notice of rejection be given by the specified date.

43 See *Atari Corpn (U.K.) Ltd v. Electronics Boutique Stores* (U.K.) Ltd [1998] 2 W.L.R. 66 (C.A.); see further Adams, "Sale or Return Contracts: Shedding a Little Light" (1998) 61 *Modern Law Review* 432; Brown, "The Sale of Goods and Sale or Return Transactions" [1998] *Law Quarterly Review*, 198; and Rotherham "Sale or Return Contracts: the right to reject" [1998] *Cambridge Law Journal* 451.

44 Goode, *Commercial Law* (London, Penguin, 2nd., ed., 1995) pp.217–222.

a total of 100 held in the seller's warehouse.[45] It is important to note that the relevant time for assessing the nature of goods, whether specific or unascertained, is the time the contract is made. In order for property in unascertained goods to pass from the seller to the buyer, the goods must first become ascertained at some time between the making of the contract and its completion. Nevertheless, the relevant time for determining this initial classification is the time the contract was made.[46]

The passing of property in unascertained goods usually involves two statutory provisions: section 16, and section 18, rule 5, of the 1893 Act. Although, once the goods are ascertained, property can pass by common intention of the parties under section 17.

17.4.1 Section 16

Section 16 of the 1893 Act provides that: "where there is a contract for the sale of unascertained goods no property in the goods is transferred to the buyer unless and until the goods are ascertained."

This rule cannot be excluded or varied by the terms of the contract or the intention of the parties. Where the goods to be used in performance of the contract are not identified at the time the contract is made, no property in any goods can pass to the buyer until the goods to be used are identified in some way, when they are said to be "ascertained": " … for how can we speak of someone having bought goods if we cannot tell what it is that he has bought."[47]

It is important to note that this rule is phrased in the negative: "no property in the goods is transferred to the buyer unless and until…." Section 16 does not provide the rules on when property is transferred. For this, reference must be had to sections 17 and 18 of the 1893 Act.

It has been said that goods are ascertained when they are "identified in accordance with the agreement after [the] contract ... is made."[48] An illustration of this rule, and the resulting injustice, can be found in *Re Wait*.[49] Wait bought 1,000 tons of wheat to be loaded on the *MV Challenger*. Wait then resold 500 tons of the cargo to a buyer who paid for that part of the cargo in advance. However, before the ship reached its destination, Wait became bankrupt. It was held that the buyer was unable

45 See 9.2.5.2.

46 As happened in *Re Stapylton Fletcher Ltd* [1994] 1 W.L.R. 1181, for example: see 17.4.1.1.

47 Goode, *Proprietary Rights and Insolvency in Sale Transactions* (London, Sweet & Maxwell, 2nd ed., 1989) p.17; these sentiments were echoed more recently by Lord Mustill *in Re Goldcorp Exchange Ltd* [1995] 1 A.C. 74 at 90; [1994] 2 All E.R. 806 at 814 (P.C.) , when he said: " … common sense dictates that the buyer cannot acquire title until it is known to what goods the title relates. … It makes no difference what the parties intend if what they intend is impossible: as is the case with an immediate transfer of title to goods whose identity is not yet known."

48 *Re Wait* [1927] 1 Ch. 606, per Atkin L.J. at 630.

49 [1927] 1 Ch. 606.

to claim any part of the cargo. He owned no part of the goods because he had agreed to buy unascertained goods (albeit from an identified source and hence quasi-specific) which had not been separated from the bulk and hence not identified with the buyer's contract. The fact that the goods were unascertained prevented property passing; and it also prevented the buyer obtaining a decree of specific performance.[50] A claim to an equitable interest in the cargo was also unsuccessful, the court finding that the mere fact of a sale or an agreement to sell part of a specified bulk did not give the buyer an equitable interest in the goods.[51] The result was that the buyer was left as an unsecured creditor to claim repayment of the price.

As can be seen from the above case, section 16 can cause problems where part of a bulk is sold. Certain commodities, such as oil and grain, are commonly traded in this manner and so trade in these commodities are particularly affected by this rule.[52] Following *Re Wait*, in order for the part of a bulk being sold to be ascertained, it must be physically separated from the bulk. It seems that a momentary separation, even if followed by a reunion of the part and the bulk, will suffice for the purposes of section 16. Moreover, it has been held that goods can be ascertained by exhaustion. In *The Elafi*,[53] the seller agreed to sell to a buyer, B, 6,000 tons of copra from a larger quantity aboard *The Elafi*. The rest of the cargo was sold to other buyers. B subsequently agreed to buy a further 500 tons from one of these other buyers. All but 6,500 tons, due to be delivered to B, was discharged at Hamburg. The *Elafi* sailed to Karlshamn where the remaining 6,500 tons

---

50 1893 Act, s.54; see 14.5.

51 Per Atkin L.J., pp.635–6; approved more recently in *Re Goldcorp* [1995] 1 A.C. 74 at 91; [1994] 2 All E.R. 806 at 814–5. Hence, it is widely accepted that the legislation contains a complete statement of the proprietary rights conferred by a sale of goods contract: no equitable interest can be created merely by virtue of a sale contract. This is despite the fact that it is well established that equitable rights can arise in relation to the transfer of other types of property such as land or book-debts (*Tailby v. Official Receiver* (1888) 13 App. Cas. 523). Of course, the parties to a sale of goods contract can *expressly agree* to create equitable rights, and indeed include such an agreement as a term of the sales contract, but this is strictly speaking, in Atkin L.J.'s terminology "dehors the contract of sale." See, *e.g. Re Kayford Ltd* [1975] 1 All E.R. 604; [1975] 1 W.L.R. 279; *McCann v. Irish Board Mills Ltd* [1980] I.L.R.M. 216, but it should be noted that *Re Wait and Re Goldcorp Exchange* both concerned sales of unascertained goods, and hence the cases could be limited to these circumstances. Lord Mustill's comments in *Re Goldcorp Exchange* related to wholly unascertained goods only, while Atkin L.J.'s comments in *Re Wait* were strictly speaking *obiter*, and Lord Hamworth M.R., who agreed with Atkin L.J. in the result in *Re Wait*, seems to have concerned himself with sale of unascertained goods only. Accordingly, it is not conclusively settled that a contract of sale, in itself, can never give rise to an equitable interest before the passing of property. However, the creation of an equitable interest normally depends on the contract being specifically enforceable (*Holroyd v. Marshall (1862)* 10 H.L. Cas. 191). Because courts rarely order specific performance of sales contracts (see 14.5), such an equitable interest would only arise in exceptional cases.

52 See 17.4.1.1.

53 [1982] 1 All E.R. 208.

was damaged by the intrusion of sea water. It was held that the goods were ascertained by exhaustion at Hamburg when all but the 6,500 tons due to B were removed and further that property in the goods passed to B at that time. Hence when the cargo was damaged at Karlshamn, B was the owner of the goods and was able to sue the carrier, in negligence, for the damage to his goods.[54]

Section 16 can have adverse consequences not only for pre-paying buyers of part of a bulk commodity, but also for pre-paying consumer buyers of unascertained goods, where the seller becomes insolvent. For instance, in *Re London Wine Co (Shippers) Ltd*,[55] the company sold wine to customers as an investment. For convenience, the company stored the wine on behalf of the customers. The customers paid the price, storage charges and insurance costs. In return, the customers were given "certificates of title" which described the customers as the "sole and beneficial owners" of the wine in question. All the wine sold was kept together, and boxes were not labelled or earmarked to the different sales contracts. Following the company's insolvency, the issue was whether the property in the wine had passed to the various customers, and in particular, had the goods been ascertained. In general, the court found that the goods had not been identified with the separate contracts and hence the goods had not been ascertained. Three categories of claim were made by the customers but all failed:

(i) One customer, for example, argued that although he had bought a quantity of generic goods by description, it so happened that the quantity he bought was the only wine of that description in the company's possession at that time, and hence the goods were ascertained.
(ii) Another group of customers argued that between them they bought all of the stock of one type of wine, so that the property passed to them because it was ascertained by exhaustion.
(iii) A third group of customers, who had not purchased the total stocks of the wine they bought, had received acknowledgments (attornments) from the company or the warehouse that an appropriate quantity of wine was held on their behalf.

All these claims failed because none of the goods described above had been ascertained. Furthermore, the court found that the "certificates of title" were of no value in relation to "goods."[56]

54 *Margarine Union GmbH v. Combay Prince Steamship* [1967] 2 Lloyd's Rep. 315; [1969] 1 Q.B. 219.

55 [1986] P.C.C. 121.

56 Similarly, a vehicle log book or registration document is not a document of title; the person named therein need not be the owner but is the person "by whom the vehicle is kept:" see *Fitzpatrick v. Criminal Assets Bureau* [2000] 1 I.R. 217 (S.C.). A "bill of lading" is the only

A similar example is *Re Goldcorp Exchange Ltd*.[57] There, the company had invited members of the public to invest in gold and other precious metals. Purchasers paid the price and received a certificate of ownership detailing, *inter alia*, the amount bought and giving them the right to call for delivery of the gold on giving seven days notice. Goldcorp also made assurances about the physical presence of the gold sold which was not stored separately for each contract but as part of a larger bulk. Goldcorp promised that it would have enough gold in stock to satisfy demand and to ensure this, the stock would be audited monthly by a respectable firm of accountants. However, Goldcorp went into receivership, and there was a conflict of ownership between the customers of Goldcorp and a bank who had a floating charge over the assets of Goldcorp. The Privy Council held that the customers were purchasers of unascertained goods which were never ascertained and so they had no property rights in the gold.

In contrast, in *Re Stapylton Fletcher Ltd*,[58] a first instance decision, the court found in favour of the buyers because of the unique circumstances of the case. Here, two companies, S Ltd and E Ltd, which subsequently came under the same ownership, traded in wine. The general practice was that customers bought wine and left it in storage (in the company warehouses or a bonded warehouse) for a rental. In particular, where E Ltd sold wine, the wine was removed from the general trading stock and stacked in a different part of the warehouse, by type and vintage, but it was not marked with individual customers' names. However, an index card system, described as 100 per cent accurate, kept track of customers and their stock of wine. Moreover, the trading and customer stocks were separately identified in the company financial accounts, in an insurance policy and also in a debenture document. Subsequent to the take-over of E Ltd, the wine was moved to a different premises, the trading and customer stocks of wine were mixed and the card index lost. With S Ltd, some wine sold was individually allocated to customers, but otherwise there was no identification of wines to customers. Some wines sold had not even left the French vineyards.

Both companies went into receivership. At the time of the appointment of the receiver, a number of different claims were brought by customers of the companies. It was held that where stock was separated from company

---

document recognised at common law to represent the goods while they are in transit: see 31.2.3.

57 [1995] 1 A.C. 74; [1994] 2 All E.R. 806 (P.C.). See further McKendrick, "Unascertained Goods: Ownership and Obligation Distinguished" (1994) 110 *Law Quarterly Review* 509; Sealy, "Contract to Sell Unascertained Goods - No Passing of Property, No Equitable or Restitutionary Relief" [1994] *Cambridge Law Journal* 443.

58 [1994] 1 W.L.R. 1181; see further Campbell, "Passing of Property in Contracts for the Sale of Unascertained Goods" [1996] *Journal of Business Law* 199.

trading stock and stored as "customer's stock", then it was ascertained for the purpose of section 16.[59] The stock still in France had not been ascertained. The court, approving *Re Wait*, held further that a contract for sale, in itself, does not create any equitable rights in the goods, and any claims based on estoppel would have no effect on the rights of the debenture holder. Finally, various other arguments based on the establishment of constructive trusts, agency principles and the duties of fiduciaries also failed.

These cases represent the difficult problem a court faces in deciding between customers claiming a proprietary interest and creditors on insolvency. Where the goods being sold are not ascertained for the purposes of section 16, a pre-paying buyer will have no proprietary claim to the goods bought under the contract and he will see his price, along with the remaining assets of the insolvent seller, being used to pay the creditors of the seller. The buyer, as an unsecured creditor of the seller seeking a refund of the price and any damages for non-delivery, will rank at the bottom of the list of creditors to be paid.

17.4.1.1 Reform of section 16

The above case law illustrates how the operation of section 16 can lead to injustice. First, section 16 is mandatory; it cannot be contracted out of. Second, it applies equally to wholly unascertained goods and quasi-specific goods, even though the latter category are identified as to their source. In particular, where the seller becomes insolvent, a pre-paying buyer of part of a bulk is left as an unsecured creditor with no likely opportunity to recoup any price paid in advance. It has been noted elsewhere that section 16 operates contrary to most people's expectations, including buyers and sellers, commercial and consumer.[60] It also leads to anomalous results. For example, it may not apply where the proportion of a bulk being bought is represented as a fraction, such as a half share, but does apply where the proportion is expressed as an amount, such as 500 tons out of 1,000. Where one buyer purchases the whole bulk under several contracts, the goods will be ascertained but where two or more buyers purchase the whole bulk there is no ascertainment. Finally, it seems that separation of the part being bought from the bulk for a moment, even where the part is later returned to the bulk, will suffice for section 16.

Because of these and other perceived defects in the law,[61] an identical section 16 of the U.K. Sale of Goods Act 1979 was amended by the Sale

59 Property then passed in the wine by common intention under section 17, and not under section 18, Rule 5, the buyers sharing ownership in the wine as tenants in common.

60 Goode, "Ownership and Obligations in Commercial Transactions" (1987) 103 *Law Quarterly Review* 433 at 447–451.

61 See the Law Commission and the Scottish Law Commission, Sale of Goods Forming Part of a Bulk, (Law Com. No. 215; Scot. Law Com. No. 145) (H.C. 807, 1993).

of Goods (Amendment) Act 1995. The amendment relates to the sale of quasi-specific goods only, which have been paid for. Accordingly, a pre-paying buyer of a specified quantity out of an identified bulk is recognised as having a proprietary interest in the goods in the form of an undivided share in the bulk and he becomes a tenant in common with the other owners.[62] The amendment is complicated and includes rules on dealing with the bulk and the consequences of a shortfall in the bulk. If the buyer's portion is ever removed from the bulk, it will be ascertained for the purposes of section 16, allowing property to pass to the buyer. While this reform is not without its critics,[63] it does raise the question whether such, or similar reform would be appropriate in an Irish context.

Ownership in common is also used in the United States to address this problem. There the Uniform Commercial Code, section 2-105(4) provides:

> "An undivided share in an identified bulk of fungible goods is sufficiently identified to be sold although the quantity of the bulk is not determined. Any agreed proportion of such a bulk or any quantity thereof agreed upon by number, weight or other measure may to the extent of the seller's interest in the bulk be sold to the buyer who then becomes an owner in common."[64]

For the reasons given above, the author is of the view that reform of section 16 is overdue.

17.4.2 Section 18, rule 5

Subject to section 16, and unless a different intention appears, section 18, rule 5(1) provides that under a contract for the sale of unascertained goods, property passes to the buyer when goods of the contract description in a deliverable state are "unconditionally appropriated to the contract" by one party with the consent of the other. It seems that "description" here has the same meaning as under section 13 of the 1893 Act, where description defines the essential commercial characteristics of the goods. Thus, in order for property to pass, the goods appropriated under the contract must correspond to the contract description. "Deliverable state" is defined in section 62(4) as meaning goods in such a state that the buyer would under the contract be bound to take delivery of them.[65] The unconditional appropriation must be with the assent of the other party. Rule 5(1) states

62 A tenancy in common in an identified bulk may arise at common law if the goods of two owners are mixed: *Indian Oil Corpn Ltd v. Greenstone Shipping* [1988] Q.B. 345, [1987] 3 All E.R. 893; *Aldridge v. Johnson* (1857) 7 E. & B. 885.

63 See Bradgate & White, "Sale of Goods Forming Part of a Bulk: Proposals for Reform" [1994] *Lloyd's Maritime and Commercial Law Quarterly* 315; Ulph, "The Sale of Goods (Amendment) Act 1995: co-ownership and the rogue seller" [1996] *Lloyd's Maritime and Commercial Law Quarterly* 93.

64 This provision seems to have caused little difficulty and there are few reported cases on it.

65 See further 17.2.1.

that such assent can be express or implied and can be given either before or after the appropriation is made, but the key to the passing of property in unascertained goods under rule 5(1) is the phrase "unconditional appropriation".

17.4.2.1 Unconditional appropriation

It is said that goods are "unconditionally appropriated" to the contract if they have been "irrevocably attached or earmarked" for use in its performance.[66] Generally, this requires the seller to do some act which puts the goods out of his control, so that he cannot use them in the performance of another contract. The simplest way in which this happens is by delivery to the buyer. The different aspects of "unconditional appropriation" are best illustrated using case law.

In *Aldridge v. Johnson*,[67] the plaintiff agreed to purchase a quantity of barley from the defendants and sent 200 sacks to the defendants to fill. The defendants filled 155 sacks and then emptied them before becoming insolvent. It was held that the goods had been unconditionally appropriated when the barley was placed in the sacks and property had passed at that stage. Emptying the sacks was of no legal consequence. Pearson J. explained this as an example of "constructive delivery" when the defendant sellers placed the goods in the plaintiff buyer's sacks. The buyer had consented in advance, as is usually the case, to this unconditional appropriation. *Aldridge v. Johnson* was distinguished in the later English case *Carlos Federspiel & Co SA v. Charles Twigg & Co Ltd*.[68] Following this case, it can be said that, generally, the act of unconditional appropriation is the last act the seller has to do in performance of the sales contract. There, Twigg agreed to manufacture and sell *fob* (free on board, meaning that it was the seller's responsibility, under the sales contract, to load the goods aboard the ship)[69] a quantity of bicycles to a buyer, Federspiel, in Costa Rica. The buyer paid for the goods in advance. The bicycles were placed in crates marked with the buyer's name. Twigg then became insolvent and the receiver refused to deliver the goods to the buyer. The issue before the court was: who owned the goods; and in particular, had they been unconditionally appropriated to the contract? It was held that the goods had not been "unconditionally appropriated" to the buyer's contract. Packaging the goods and marking the buyer's name on them was not sufficient, in this case, to constitute unconditional appropriation. Such conduct was considered merely an aspect of the internal administration of

66 *Atiyah's Sale of Goods* (Harlow, Pearson, 10th ed., 2001) p.329. Unconditional appropriation which leads to the passing of property must be distinguished from contractual appropriation: 30.3.1.2.

67 (1857) 7 E. & B. 885; see also *Langton v. Higgins* (1859) 4 H.& N. 402.

68 [1957] 1 Lloyd's Rep. 240.

69 See further 30.2.

the seller's business. Rather, the act of appropriation will often be the last act a seller will perform, which in this case would have involved placing the goods on board the ship. Hence the receiver was entitled to remove the bicycles from the crates and sell them to another customer, leaving the buyer an unsecured creditor.

It is important to remember that before goods can be "unconditionally appropriated" to a contract, they must first be ascertained under section 16. In *Healy v. Howlett & Sons*,[70] the plaintiff, a fish exporter based in Ireland, agreed to sell 20 cases of mackerel to the defendant, a fishmonger based in London. The plaintiff had two other customers for mackerel and so he dispatched 190 cases of mackerel by train to satisfy all three contracts. The plaintiff gave instruction to the railway company to divide the consignment into three lots for the three customers at Holyhead. However, the train was delayed before the defendant's boxes were earmarked and by that time, they had deteriorated and were not merchantable. The defendant refused to pay and it was held that no property in the goods had passed to him. The goods would not be unconditionally appropriated until they were separated into the three lots and prior to that time they were part of a larger bulk, and hence unascertained. Even if only 20 cases had been loaded, it would seem that the goods would not have been unconditionally appropriated any sooner. The goods, when loaded, were consigned to S's order; hence loading would not constitute unconditional appropriation which was not due to occur until the goods reached Holyhead. In contrast, in *Wardar v. Norwood*,[71] the defendant contracted to sell 600 cartons of frozen kidneys out of 1,500 cartons held in cold storage. The sellers provided the plaintiff buyers with a delivery note to obtain the goods. The buyer's representative (a carrier) arrived at the cold store at 8 a.m. to find 600 cartons stacked on the pavement awaiting collection. It was held that the goods were unconditionally appropriated, at the latest, at 8 a.m. when the representative presented the delivery note in respect of the goods which were on the pavement awaiting collection.[72]

A final example is *Hendy Lennox Ltd v. Graham Puttick Engines Ltd*,[73] which involved, *inter alia*, the sale of generators. It was held that the goods had been "unconditionally appropriated" to the buyer's contract, with their consent, when the goods were ready for delivery and once invoices and delivery notes, identifying the particular items to be delivered, were received by the buyers from the sellers. At this point, the sellers could no

70 [1917] 1 K.B. 337; see also *Spicer-Cowan Ireland Ltd v. Play Print Ltd* unreported, High Court, Doyle J., March 13, 1980; and *Cronin v. IMP Midleton Ltd* unreported, High Court, Carroll J., January 31, 1986.

71 [1968] 2 Q.B. 663; [1968] 2 All E.R. 602 (C.A.) .

72 The court declined to consider whether the goods had been unconditionally appropriated before presentation of the delivery note, such as when they were removed from the cold store and placed on the pavement.

73 [1984] 1 W.L.R. 485.

longer substitute for them other goods without the buyer's consent. However, it would appear that merely setting the goods to one side in the seller's premises and placing the buyer's name on them would not be enough to amount to unconditional appropriation.

17.4.2.2 Delivery to a carrier

A statutory example of unconditional appropriation can be found in section 18, rule 5(2). Accordingly, where the seller delivers goods to the buyer or an independent carrier or bailee for transmission to the buyer, he is to be taken as having unconditionally appropriated the goods to the contract unless he reserves a right of disposal of the goods. Thus, if a seller puts goods in the post for delivery to a buyer he will be taken to have unconditionally appropriated them to the contract. Conversely, if a seller gives goods to an independent carrier but makes them deliverable to himself or his agent, he has retained control over them and they are not unconditionally appropriated to the contract.

17.4.2.3 Ascertainment and unconditional appropriation

While the concepts of ascertainment and unconditional appropriation are theoretically different, in many cases, the same act will both ascertain the goods to be used in performance of the contract and unconditionally appropriate those goods to the contract. For instance, we have noted that where there is a contract for the sale of goods forming part of an identified bulk, the contract goods may be ascertained by exhaustion, as in *The Elafi*. Generally, there will be no need for any further act of appropriation since the seller cannot fulfill the contract by delivering any other goods. However, there is no hard and fast rule: in some cases the goods may be ascertained but no property will pass because they are not unconditionally appropriated to the contract, as in the *Carlos Federspiel* case.

17.5 Future Goods

Section 5(1) of the 1893 Act states that goods can be existing, that is, owned or possessed by the seller at the time of the sales contract, or future, that is, goods to be manufactured or acquired by the seller after the making of the sales contract. Therefore, a seller can enter into a contract to sell goods that do not exist because they have yet to be manufactured by him under the sales contract: future goods. A seller can enter into a contract to sell goods that are the property of another party: also future goods. There is no difficulty with either of these situations, provided that the seller manufactures the goods, or acquires the property in the goods in time to complete the sale with the buyer. Such sales of future goods operate as agreements to sell.[74] It was noted earlier that future goods could be described as specific.[75] However, for the purpose of the rules on the passing of property, goods must be either future (sections 17 and 18, rule 5), or specific (sections 17 and 18, rules 1–3).

Where the contract is for future goods sold by description, in the absence of any indication of the parties' intention, section 18, rule 5 applies and provides that property passes when goods of that description and in a deliverable state are "unconditionally appropriated" to the contract with the consent of the other party. Thus where a manufacturer contracts to sell goods to be manufactured by him, property will pass when goods of the contract description are unconditionally appropriated to the contract by one party with the consent of the other. The case of *Carlos Federspiel & Co SA v. Charles Twigg & Co Ltd*,[76] discussed above, is an example of property in future goods failing to pass for lack of unconditional appropriation. Up to the moment of unconditional appropriation, the goods remain the property of the seller. Say, for example, M, a manufacturer, receives an order for goods from a customer, C1. He manufactures goods for the contract but, before they are delivered, receives another order for similar goods from another customer, C2. Provided that the goods already manufactured have not been unconditionally appropriated to C1's contract, M is free to appropriate them to the contract with, and deliver them to, C2, although, as a result, M may incur liability to C1 for late delivery.

74 See 9.2.

75 See 9.2.5.2, for example, where an antique dealer agrees to sell a specific item, yet to be bought by him, to a customer, or where there is a contract to purchase the first car off a particular production line, at a particular plant, at a specified future date. For the purposes of the passing of property, these goods would be classified as future goods. This must be so, because if they were classified as specific goods, property would pass under section 18, rule 1 when the contract was made and this would render the seller in breach of section 12 of the 1893 Act. Because the sale of future goods operates as an agreement to sell, the parties cannot have intended that property would pass at the time of the contract.

76 [1957] 1 Lloyd's Rep. 240.

CHAPTER 18

THE PASSING OF RISK

18.1 INTRODUCTION

All commercial undertakings involve risk. Where credit is provided, for instance, the creditor takes a risk that the debtor will not pay the sums due.[1] In the context of sale of goods transactions, where goods yet to be acquired are sold at a fixed price, the seller takes the risk that the market price of goods will rise; while the buyer takes the risk that the market price will fall. At common law, the risk of defects in goods rests with the buyer: *caveat emptor*. But, today, that risk has greatly shifted because of the statutory implied terms and the rules on the exclusion of liability for breach of these terms.[2] Indeed, where the buyer deals as a consumer, the risk that the goods do not comply with the statutory implied terms rests with the seller.[3]

"Risk" in the context of this chapter is more limited in meaning.[4] While "risk" is not defined in the legislation, it is accepted that risk refers to damage to or loss of the goods. This damage or loss can be caused by fire, or the sinking of a ship on which the goods are being carried or by theft, for example. The damage or loss can be accidental or caused by third parties. Hence, "risk" is concerned only with events causing damage to or loss of the goods which is not attributable to the act or fault of the seller or buyer.

If goods are damaged whilst at the seller's risk, the seller may not be able to require the buyer to accept them in performance of the contract of sale. Therefore, where goods are damaged or lost, the seller may have to repair them or find replacement goods in order to perform his contract. Such repair or replacement will be at his expense. Where the contract is for the sale of specific goods, replacement is not an option without the consent of the buyer. If he is unable to repair or replace the goods within the time for performance of the contract, he may incur liability for late or non-delivery, unless he is excused by the contract on the grounds of impossibility. If, on the other hand, the goods are damaged whilst at the buyer's risk, the buyer must accept and pay for them under the contract of

1 On credit and security, see Chapter 24.
2 See generally Chapter 13.
3 Where the buyer does not deal as a consumer, some of that risk can be passed back to the buyer through the use of exclusion clauses.
4 See further Sealy, " 'Risk' in The Law of Sale" (1972) 31 *Cambridge Law Journal* 225.

sale, unless he is excused by the contract on the grounds of impossibility.

The party who bears the risk of damage to or loss of goods therefore bears the risk that they may have to be replaced or repaired and may wish to insure against that risk. It has been held that a person who bears the risk of damage to or loss of property has sufficient interest in that property to insure it.[5] Moreover, the party who bears the risk of damage or loss is still bound by his contractual obligations, regardless of any damage or loss, and will be in breach of contract for any failure to perform his contractual obligations unless such performance is excused. Performance of contractual obligations can be excused on the grounds of impossibility, under the doctrine of frustration. The doctrine of mistake may also provide an excuse for non-performance. Instances of these common law doctrines, excusing performance, are to be found in sections 6 and 7 of the 1893, and the operation of these provisions is linked to the passing of risk.

18.2 The General Rule on the Passing of Risk

The basic common law rule is that the owner of property bears the risk of its damage, deterioration or destruction: *res peruit domino*. Section 20 of the 1893 Act reiterates this rule:

> "Unless otherwise agreed, the goods remain at the seller's risk until the property in them is transferred to the buyer, but when the property in them is transferred to the buyer the goods are at the buyer's risk whether delivery has been made or not."

Hence, we say, risk passes with property. In order to determine when risk passes, the different rules on the passing of property examined in the previous chapter must be applied, depending on whether the goods sold are specific, unascertained or future. Where, for example, specific goods are sold, but possession is retained by the seller under section 18, rule 1, property passes at the time the contract is made and hence, under section 20, risk passes to the buyer at the time of contract, regardless of delivery. Where unascertained goods are sold, no property or risk can pass until the goods are ascertained, under section 16, and then property and risk can pass in accordance with the intention of the parties, under section 17, or when the goods are unconditionally appropriated to the contract, under section 18, rule 5. Where goods are supplied on approval or on sale or return, no property or risk passes until the buyer "adopts" the transaction, under section 18, rule 4. Conversely, where a seller supplies goods subject to a retention of title clause, possession of the goods may pass to the buyer,

---

5 *Inglis v. Stock* (1885) 10 App. Cas. 263.

but property and risk will remain with the seller until the goods are paid for.

Healy v. Howlett & Sons[6] is an illustration of this general rule in operation. There, the plaintiff, a fish exporter based in Ireland, agreed to sell 20 cases of mackerel to the defendant, a fishmonger based in London. The plaintiff had two other customers for mackerel and so he dispatched 190 cases of mackerel by train to satisfy all three contracts. The plaintiff gave instruction to the railway company to divide the consignment into three lots for the three customers at Holyhead. However, the train was delayed before the defendant's boxes were earmarked and by the time this was done at Holyhead, the fish had deteriorated. The defendant refused to pay and it was held that no property and hence no risk had passed in the goods to him. Property and risk would not pass until the goods were ascertained and unconditionally appropriated to the contract.[7]

Another illustration of the general rule being applied can be found in *Clarke v. Micheal Reilly & Sons*[8] where the plaintiff bought a new car in return for a trade-in and the balance in cash.[9] Delivery of the new car was delayed and the plaintiff was allowed to use the old car in the meantime. But before the new car was delivered, the old car was involved in an accident. The court found that property in the old car, and hence risk, had passed when the contract was concluded, the old car being specific goods.[10] Consequently, the plaintiff was entitled to specific performance of the contract to purchase the new car, even though the trade-in car had been damaged.

Because, generally, risk is linked to property, and not possession, and because the rules on the passing of property are technical and not always in keeping with people's expectations, a person can find himself at risk without being aware of this fact, without any practical control over the goods and without insurance. However, the general rule that risk passes with property can be modified, and in certain circumstances the issue of possession may be relevant to the passage of risk.

18.2.1 Exceptions to the general rule

The rule in section 20 may be displaced by express or implied agreement. In addition, it is subject to a number of exceptions or modifications. The contract may contain an express provision as to the passing of risk that contradicts the general rule. This possibility is expressly recognised by section 20 which is a default rule. For example, where goods are sold and

6 [1917] 1 K.B. 337.

7 See 17.4.

8 (1962) 96 I.L.T.R. 96 (Circuit Court); see 17.2.1.

9 The court seems to have assumed that the transaction was a sale of goods as opposed to a contract of exchange: see further 9.3.1

10 1893 Act, s.18, Rule 1.

the seller retains title to the goods, the agreement often states that risk passes to the buyer with possession of the goods, and requires the buyer to insure the goods. But even where the contract contains no express provision as to the passing of risk, it may be possible to find an implied term governing the subject. For instance, in international sale contracts, it is implied, by custom, that risk usually passes on shipment, although property usually does not pass until a later date.[11]

The general rule can also be displaced by an implied agreement based on the facts of the case. In *Sterns Ltd v. Vickers Ltd*,[12] the plaintiffs owned 200,000 gallons of white spirit held in a storage tank by a third party bailee. They agreed to sell 120,000 gallons of the spirit to the defendant buyers and gave the buyers a delivery warrant or order addressed to the bailee to enable them to collect the spirit. The buyers delayed in taking delivery, and when they did collect the spirit, it was found that it had deteriorated in quality during the continued storage. It was held that the spirit was at the buyers' risk from the time they were provided with the means to obtain delivery, despite the fact that no property had passed to the buyers during this time because the goods remained unascertained.

In contrast, *Head v. Tattersall*[13] is a case where although property had passed, risk remained with the seller. The plaintiff bought a horse from the defendant on the basis that it had hunted with the Bicester and Duke of Grafton's hounds and he was given a week to return the horse if it did not match the contract description. During this week the horse was accidentally injured and the plaintiff sought to return the horse having discovered that it had not hunted with the Bicester and Duke of Grafton's hounds. It was held that the plaintiff was entitled to return the horse and claim a refund of the full price. Further, the risk was held to be with the seller, although property had probably passed to the buyer subject to a right to reject. Similar facts today would probably lead to the same outcome but in a different manner, under section 18, rule 4 on sale on approval, where property would not pass, and hence risk would not pass, until the expiry of the fixed time: one week.

It has been argued elsewhere[14] that the ruling in *Head v. Tattersall* illustrates a broader principle of sales law, not spelt out in the legislation, but implied from the rules on acceptance and rejection, that when risk passes to the buyer, it does so conditionally, subject to his right to reject the goods. The rules on acceptance and rejection do not distinguish between accidental damage or other damage causing the goods to be unmerchantable, for example.[15] So, where a buyer rejects goods, any

11 See 30.2.5 and 30.3.6.

12 [1923] 1 K.B. 78 (C.A.).

13 (1870) L.R. 7 Ex. 7.

14 *Atiyah's Sale of Goods* (Harlow, Pearson, 10th ed., 2001) pp.352–353.

15 Similarly, accidental damage will not prevent a buyer returning goods delivered on approval or sale or return terms: *Elphick v. Barnes* (1880) 5 C.P.D. 321.

property revests in the seller, and risk is also thrown back on the seller. During this time, the buyer will be a bailee of the goods and hence must take reasonable care of them.

Unlike the Sale of Goods Acts 1893, the EC Directive on Consumer Sales[16] is silent on issues of risk.[17] For instance, it is not clear who bears the risk of loss of, or damage to the goods when they are returned to the seller for repair under the provisions of the Directive. It has been suggested that the logic of *res peruit domino* would require that, as between seller and consumer buyer, the buyer should bear the risk of loss while the goods are in transit to the seller, unless they are collected by the seller's agent. While the goods are in the seller's possession, the seller should be liable for negligent loss or damage to the goods as a bailee; and the seller should owe a duty of care to the buyer in returning the goods after repair, although the buyer would remain at risk for purely accidental loss.[18] Moreover, Member States in implementing the Directive, may provide that any refund due to the buyer following "recission of the contract" may be reduced to take account of the buyer's use of the goods.[19] It is not clear whether such reduction could extend to accidental damage to the goods while in the buyer's possession.

18.2.1.1 Delayed delivery

Section 20 also provides that where delivery is delayed through the fault of either buyer or seller, the goods are at the risk of the party at fault as regards any damage or loss that might not have occurred but for such fault. Where the damage or loss is caused otherwise than by the seller's or buyer's fault, this provision has no application. This modification to the general rule is illustrated in *Demby Hamilton & Co Ltd v. Barden*[20] where there was an agreement to sell 30 tons of apple juice, to correspond with an agreed sample. The sellers crushed the apples and put the juice in barrels to await collection but the goods were not appropriated to the contract. The goods were to be collected at the rate of one truckload per week by third parties to whom the goods had been sub-sold, at the direction of the buyer. The buyer delayed in giving such directions: only two deliveries being made within the contract period. The remainder of the juice went putrid. It was held that although property had not passed to the buyer, the buyer should bear the risk of deterioration because it had resulted from his delay.[21]

16 Directive 1999/44/EC, [1999] O.J. L171/12; see further 13.11; 14.7 and 16.2.3.

17 Recital 14.

18 Bradgate, *Commercial Law* (London, Butterworths, 3rd ed., 2000) p.399.

19 Recital 15.

20 [1949] 1 All E.R. 435 (K.B.).

21 It is not clear, from this case, on which party the burden of proving that the delay caused the deterioration rests.

18.2.1.2 Duties of bailees[22]

Section 20 finally provides that nothing in this section shall affect the duties or liabilities of either seller or buyer as a bailee or custodier of the goods for the other party. Where, for example, under a retention of title clause, property and risk is retained by the seller but the buyer has possession and use of the goods, the buyer will be a bailee of the goods.[23] Similarly, where property and risk has passed to the buyer, but the seller remains in possession of the goods, the seller will be a bailee of the goods.

A bailee is required to take reasonable care in his custody of the goods. Hence, generally, a bailee is only liable for loss caused by his negligence. Where the loss is wholly accidental and could not have been avoided by taking reasonable care, the bailee will not be liable. Against this, there is a reverse burden of proof: it is the bailee who must prove that he exercised reasonable care. Moreover, a bailee is strictly liable under the terms of the bailment. Thus if a bailee agrees to store goods at one premises, he is strictly liable for any loss if he stores the goods at another premises.

If the buyer fails to take delivery at the time fixed in the contract, it can be argued that the seller is an involuntary or gratuitous bailee and hence owes the buyer a lower duty of care than a voluntary bailee. Against this, the Acts allow the seller to charge a reasonable sum for his care of the goods,[24] and the preferred view seems to be that he should be regarded as a voluntary bailee.[25] The seller must take reasonable care of the goods although, as noted above,[26] the buyer will bear the risk of loss to, or damage of the goods caused by the delay in collecting the goods but not caused by the seller's negligence. It appears that where a person fails to take reasonable care of the goods under a bailment, the innocent party is entitled to sue for damages, but cannot refuse to accept the goods or refuse to pay. In this regard, section 20 merely preserves the common law liability that would arise under a bailment.

18.2.1.3 Goods damaged in transit

Transit involves further risks for goods. Sections 32 and 33 deal with the allocation of risk when goods are damaged in transit to the buyer and provide a statutory modification to the general rule on the passing of risk.

Section 32(1) provides that where, under the sale contract, the seller is

---

22 See also 3.4.5.

23 A person who receives goods on approval or on sale or return is also a bailee of the goods until adoption of the transaction or return of the goods. But, a careless act that damages the goods may amount to adoption, causing property and risk to pass to the buyer: see 17.3.

24 1893 Act, s.37.

25 See *Benjamin's Sale of Goods* (London, Sweet & Maxwell, 5th ed., 1997) para 6–019; *Chalmer's Sale of Goods* (London, Butterworths, 18th ed., 1981) p.158.

26 See 18.2.1.1.

authorised or required to send the goods to the buyer, delivery to a carrier for transmission to the buyer is prima facie deemed to be delivery to the buyer. It is as if the carrier were the buyer's agent. Such delivery satisfies a seller's section 27 obligation to deliver the goods to the buyer. Such delivery may pass property and therefore risk in the goods unless property and risk have already passed or unless the seller has reserved his right of disposal.[27] Hence, prima facie, the buyer is at risk during transit. This presumption can be rebutted. For instance, where the carrier is the seller's agent, the seller will be at risk until the goods reach the delivery point, or under international sales contracts, risk passes from seller to buyer when the goods pass the ship's rail, so if goods are damaged while in transit to the port of departure they are at the seller's risk.[28]

Where, under section 32(1), the seller makes a contract of carriage on behalf of the buyer, section 32(2) provides that he must make a reasonable contract having regard to the nature of the goods and the other circumstances of the case. If he fails to do so and the goods are lost or damaged in transit, the buyer may decline to treat delivery of the goods to the carrier as delivery to himself, thus throwing the risk of loss during transit back onto the seller. Alternatively, the buyer may claim damages from the seller in respect of the damage caused by this breach. What is a reasonable contract will depend on all the circumstances of the case. For example, where goods are perishable, a slow or long means of transit may be unreasonable. In one case,[29] a seller contracted to sell goods "free on rail" and the seller contracted with the railway company that the goods would be carried at the owner's risk. It transpired that the goods could have been carried at the carrier's risk for the same price, subject to an examination. The court found that the contract was unreasonable.

Where the transit involves carriage by sea, section 32(3) provides that the seller must give the buyer such information so as to enable him to insure the goods. If the seller fails to do so, the goods are at the seller's risk while in transit.

Finally, where the seller agrees to deliver the goods at his own risk at a place other than where they were sold, section 33 provides that, unless otherwise agreed, the buyer must take any risk of deterioration in the goods necessarily incidental to the transit. Under this provision, a buyer is only at risk for deterioration caused by the ordinary risks of transit. Such risks are greatly reduced today, as opposed to when the provision was drafted, due to improvements in the speed and methods of transportation.[30] Moreover, a seller remains liable for any deterioration caused by his own neglect.

27 1893 Act, s.19(1).

28 See 30.2.5 and 30.3.6.

29 *Thomas Young & Sons v. Hobson* (1949) 65 T.L.R. 365 (C.A.) .

30 See Goode, *Commercial Law* (London, Penguin, 2nd ed., 1995) p.265.

18.3 Impossibility

As noted above, if goods to be sold are lost or damaged so as to become unmerchantable for instance, whilst at the seller's risk, he will be unable to insist on the buyer accepting them under the contract and may have to repair or replace them. Where the contract is for specific goods, replacement is not possible without the buyer's consent, so that the seller may be unable to perform the contract, and in any case the delay involved in arranging repair or replacement may put the seller in breach of contract. But sections 6 and 7 of the 1893 Act contain rules broadly analogous to the general common law rules of mistake and frustration which may excuse the seller from liability if performance becomes impossible. These rules apply in limited circumstances: where "specific" goods have "perished". Where they apply, the general common law rules on mistake and frustration are displaced. Where the facts of the case fall outside sections 6 and 7, the common law doctrines of mistake and frustration apply.

18.3.1 Section 6

Section 6 provides that:

> "Where there is a contract for the sale of specific goods and the goods without the knowledge of the seller have perished at the time the contract is made, the contract is void."[31]

Section 6 is an instance of the doctrine of common mistake as to the existence of the subject-matter. It applies where goods have perished before the contract is made. Further, the goods must have perished without the knowledge of the seller. Where a seller seeks to sell goods that he knows do not exist, he can be sued for non-delivery. The effect of section 6 is that the contract is void. Because the contract is void, no contract ever existed and the parties have no legal obligations to each other: the seller has no obligation to deliver, and the buyer has no obligation to accept and pay.

18.3.2 Section 7

Section 7 provides that:

> "Where there is an agreement to sell specific goods and subsequently the goods, without any fault on the part of the seller or buyer, perish before the risk passes to the buyer, the agreement is avoided."

---

31 This provision is said to be based on *Couturier v. Hastie* (1856) 5 H.L. Cas. 673, (H.L.).

Section 7 is an instance of the doctrine of frustration caused by the destruction of the subject-matter of the contract. It applies where goods perish after the contract is made, but before risk passes to the buyer. Normally, where specific goods are sold, property and hence risk passes when the contract is made, under section 18, rule 1 and section 20. Accordingly, this provision has very limited application and will apply only where rule 1 is displaced by rules 2 or 3 or a contrary intention, or where section 20 is displaced. Moreover, the perishing must take place without any fault on the part of the seller or the buyer. At common law, frustration cannot be self-induced, and the same rule applies under section 7. Therefore, for example, if goods are totally destroyed due to the negligence of the seller in their storage, the buyer can sue for non-delivery. The effect of section 7 is that the contract is avoided. The initial existence of the contract is not affected, but from the perishing event, the contract is avoided, that is, the parties cease to have any contractual obligations to each other: the seller does not have to deliver and the buyer does not have to accept and pay. If the price is paid in advance, the buyer can claim a refund, otherwise losses lay where they fall.

In practice, in commercial contracts, the types of events that come within section 7 or otherwise frustrate a contract are often covered by express provision in the contract: *force majeure* clauses.[32] Rather than rely on the rules in section 6 and 7, or the relevant common law rules, commercial traders often seek to negotiate their way out of such a situation to maintain a good trading relationship, rather than enforce their strict legal rights.

18.3.3 Specific goods

Sections 6 and 7 apply to specific goods only. Specific goods are defined as goods which are identified and agreed upon at the time the contract is made.[33] However, *Howell v. Coupland,*[34] decided before the 1893 Act, seems to give an extended meaning to specific goods. There, the seller contracted to sell 200 tons of potatoes to be grown on specified fields. Due to disease, only 80 tons were produced on those fields The buyer took delivery of, and paid for the 80 tons, and sued for non-delivery in respect of the shortfall. The Court of Appeal treated the contract as one for the sale of "specific things;" crop failure made delivery impossible; and the seller's non-performance was excused. A similar contract was considered in *Sainsbury Ltd v. Street.*[35] There the sellers contracted to sell the crop of barley, estimated at 275 tons, to be grown on a particular field. There was a bad harvest and the field produced only 140 tons. However, the price of

32 See 2.4.3.

33 1893 Act, s.62.

34 (1876) 1 Q.B.D. 258 (C.A.).

35 [1972] 3 All E.R. 1127; [1972] 1 W.L.R. 834.

barley rose substantially and the sellers sold the barley to another buyer at a higher price than agreed with the first buyer. The first buyer sued for non-delivery and the sellers argued that the contract was avoided under section 7, following *Howell v. Coupland*. It was held that the contract was not for the sale of specific goods and so sections 6 and 7 had no application. *Howell v. Coupland* was not overruled: it survived the Act as an example of a sale subject to a contingency to be fulfilled,[36] or as a rule of common law, preserved by section 61(2), of the 1893 Act.

Deciding that the case is outside the scope of sections 6 and 7 can provide more flexibility. In *Sainsbury v. Street*, the court found that the parties must have intended that, in such circumstances, the seller should offer the buyer the option of buying the goods actually produced on the terms originally agreed. Accordingly, the seller would not be liable for any shortfall. In these circumstances, all depends on the construction of the contract. Where on the proper construction of the contract, the seller promises to produce a certain quantity, he will be liable for any shortfall. In contrast, the risk of partial or total failure to produce a certain quantity may be placed on the buyer where he contracts to pay the contract price regardless of the amount produced.

It was noted earlier that specific goods could be described as future.[37] For example, where an antique dealer agrees to sell a specific item, yet to be bought by him, to a customer, or where there is a contract to purchase the first car off a particular production line, at a particular plant, at a specified future date, these would appear to be contracts for the sale of specific goods to which sections 6 and 7 would apply. There is no judicial pronouncement on this issue. Where such goods are not specific for the purposes of section 6 and 7, a court would have to apply the common law rules of mistake and frustration, or decide the case based on the presumed intention of the parties. It is clear, however, that a contract for the sale of unascertained goods falls outside the scope of sections 6 and 7. The rationale for sections 6 and 7 is that a seller's non-performance can be excused because it is impossible due to circumstances beyond his control, but where unascertained goods are being sold, a seller may be able to buy replacement goods to perform the contract. Where the seller agrees to sell goods from an identified source, such as a ship, and the source is totally destroyed, the contract may be frustrated at common law:[38] section 7 has no application.

36 1893 Act, s.5(2).

37 See 9.2.5.2.

38 But it has been held that where a seller contracts to sell all of the goods from a named bulk to several buyers, and only part of the bulk is destroyed, the seller cannot argue that any of the contracts are frustrated: *The Super Servant Two* [1990] 1 Lloyd's Rep. 1 (C.A.).

18.3.4 Perishing of goods

There is no statutory definition of "perishing". Clearly, where goods have been totally destroyed, they can be regarded as having perished, but total destruction is not necessary. An item is generally regarded as having perished if it has "so changed as to become an unmerchantable thing which no buyer would buy and no honest seller would sell."[39] However, cases on the meaning of "perishing" are not easy to reconcile. In *Asfar v. Blundell*,[40] an insurance law case, dates which were impregnated with river water and sewage when the barge on which they were carried sank were found to have perished, even though they still existed, were recovered from the river and could be used to distil alcohol. The court said: "[the] test is whether, as a matter of business, the nature of the thing has been altered."[41] In contrast, in *Horn v. Minister of Food*,[42] it was held *obiter* that rotten potatoes, unfit for consumption, could still be described as "potatoes" and had not perished.

While *Asfar v. Blundell* seems the better view,[43] it does raise a problem caused by equating perishing with merchantable quality. Normally, where a seller delivers unmerchantable goods, the buyer can reject the goods, claim a refund of any price paid and sue for damages for non-delivery and any consequential loss. However, if the unmerchantable goods are deemed to have perished, the seller may be able to avoid any liability (other than to refund any price paid), under sections 6 and 7. In order to avoid this result, a court might adopt a restrictive approach to perishing, such as in *Horn v. Minister of Food*, or a court might seek to treat sections 6 and 7 as rules of presumed intent which could be excluded by contrary intention,[44] although the wording of sections 6 and 7 do not favour this latter approach. An example of a finding of contrary intention can be found in the Australian case of *McRea v. Commonwealth Disposals Commission*.[45] The defendants advertised for sale "an oil tanker lying on the Jourmand Reef." The plaintiff agreed to buy the tanker and its contents for £285. He went to considerable expense to fit-out a salvage operation and when he went to the advertised location there was no tanker there, and no reef. In fact, no such tanker ever existed. The High Court held that the equivalent of section 6 had no application. Instead, the court found that the defendants had

39 *Asfar & Co v. Blundell* [1896] 1 Q.B. 123 per Lord Esher at 128

40 [1896] 1 Q.B. 123.

41 *Ibid.* at 127.

42 [1948] 2 All E.R. 1036.

43 *Benjamin's Sale of Goods* (London, Sweet & Maxwell, 5th ed., 1997) para 1-127; Goode, *Commercial Law* (London, Penguin, 2nd ed., 1995) pp.271–272.

44 See, *e.g. McRea v. Commonwealth Disposals Commission* (1950) 84 C.L.R. 377; see further *Atiyah's Sale of Goods* (Harlow, Pearson, 10th ed., 2001) pp.94–98; Benjamin's *Sale of Goods* (London, Sweet & Maxwell, 5th ed., 1997) para 1-130.

45 (1950) 84 C.L.R. 377.

contracted to sell a ship and as a term of that contract they had promised that the ship existed. Hence, the defendants were liable for breach of contractual promise that there was an oil tanker at the specified location.[46]

Goods may be treated as having "perished" when they are stolen, or even when part of the goods is stolen. In *Barrow, Lane and Ballard Ltd v. Phillip Phillips & Co*,[47] the sellers contracted to sell 700 bags of nuts. It was held that the contract was void under section 6 when it was discovered that 109 of the bags had been stolen before the contract was made. Cases decided under analogous rules at common law (not strictly cases concerned with specific goods) suggest a more flexible approach. Accordingly, where part of the contract goods are lost:

(i) the seller cannot be held liable for non-delivery in respect of the lost goods:[48]
(ii) the seller must offer the remaining goods to the buyer:[49]
(iii) the buyer cannot be required to take the reduced quantity.[50]

Similar, more equitable results could be reached under the statutory rules only where the rules are treated as subject to a contrary intention.

18.4 Risk, Loss and Insurance

While the general rule links risk with property, and not possession, risk can be placed with someone who has neither property nor possession. In these circumstances, and in the absence of insurance cover, difficulties can arise as illustrated by *The Aliakmon*.[51] There a buyer agreed to buy a cargo of steel coils carried by sea on terms which meant that risk passed to the buyer on shipment, when the goods passed the ship's rail, while property and the right to possession was retained by the seller until payment, under a retention of title clause. The coils were damaged in transit due to

46 Atiyah identifies three possible interpretations of the facts of *McRea* and similar cases:
(i) the contract might be subject to an implied condition precedent that the goods exist: if it turns out that the goods do not exist, no contract comes into being and no party incurs any liability; or
(ii) the seller might promise that the goods exist, if they do not, the seller is liable to the buyer for breach of contract; or
(iii) the buyer might assume the risk or chance that the goods do not exist, in which case the buyer bears the risk of non-existence: see *Atiyah's Sale of Goods* (Harlow, Pearson, 10th ed., 2001) p.94.

47 [1929] 1 K.B. 574.

48 *Howell v. Coupland* (1876) 1 Q.B.D. 258 (C.A.).

49 *Sainsbury Ltd v. Street* [1972] 3 All E.R. 1127; [1972] 1 W.L.R. 834.

50 *Barrow, Lane and Ballard Ltd v. Phillip Phillips & Co* [1929] 1 K.B. 574.

51 [1986] A.C. 785, [1986] 2 All E.R. 145 (H.L.).

negligent storage. The risk of this loss fell on the buyer under the sales contract. However, the House of Lords held that in order to sue in negligence for damage to goods, the plaintiff must either have property in the goods or the immediate right to possession. As a result, the buyer was unable to sue the carrier for breach of the carriage contract. This ruling applies equally to domestic sales, so that where goods are damaged during a land transit, the buyer who bears the risk but has no property is unable to sue the carrier.

There are ways of avoiding such difficulty. The sale contract could include a term that requires the seller to sue the carrier on the buyer's behalf, or to assign his right to sue, though this may be impractical. Alternatively, insurance cover for the goods once the buyer is at risk is the safest option but this is only realistic where the buyer is aware that he is at risk. As can be seen from above, the rules on the passing of risk are technical,[52] and not always in keeping with people's expectations and so frequently, a person may be at risk without knowing it. Moreover, such insurance shifts the cost onto the buyer when it is the carrier, or other person in actual possession, who is responsible for the goods.

Consumers are even less likely to insure goods, than commercial persons, because of an understandable failure to appreciate how the rules on the passing of risk operate. Therefore, they are in a more vulnerable position. For instance, to borrow an example,[53] where a consumer buys a specific sofa to be delivered the following day, the consumer will be at risk from the time the contract is made, the goods being specific.[54] If, without any negligence on the part of the seller, the sofa is destroyed by a fire overnight, the buyer will have to bear the risk of that loss.[55] In practice, to maintain goodwill, sellers in these circumstances may not force a buyer to pay for goods but nevertheless a seller has a legal right to press for such payment.[56] Contrast the position where a consumer buys a sofa by description, and hence unascertained goods, for delivery the following day. Assume that the following day, three sofas, matching that contract description, are loaded in a van for delivery to three different customers. If the van crashes, damaging the goods, while the three sofas are on board, the seller will be at risk because the goods remain unascertained.[57] However, if the van crashes, damaging the goods, after two sofas have been delivered, the remaining sofa will be ascertained by exhaustion and

52 Atiyah has described the "technical legal position" as "grotesque": see *Atiyah's Sale of Goods*, (Harlow, Pearson, 10th ed., 2001) p.354.

53 Bradgate, *Commercial Law* (London, Butterworths, 3rd ed., 2000) p.400.

54 Applying s.18, rule 1 and s.20 of the 1893 Act.

55 Standard household policies would probably not cover goods lost in these circumstances, though supplier's insurance can cover goods even after property and risk has passed to a buyer, where "property in trust or on commission" is covered: *Waters and Steel v. Monarch Fire* and Life Assurance Co (1856) 5 E. & B. 870.

56 1893 Act, s.49.

57 1893 Act, s.16 and *Healy v. Howlett & Sons* [1917] 1 K.B. 337.

property and risk will have passed to the buyer.[58] As in the above examples, where the strict legal rules are applied, the outcome is arbitrary and hence unfair. To avoid such outcomes, a court might seek to find an implied intention that property and/or risk should not pass until delivery. Linking risk with possession would avoid many of the problems highlighted above.

58 1893 Act, s.16 and *The Elafi* [1982] 1 All E.R. 208.

CHAPTER 19

TITLE CONFLICTS

19.1 INTRODUCTION

It is a fundamental rule of property law that no one can transfer a better title than he himself has: *nemo dat quod non habet*.[1] This, or a similar basic rule applies to sales of goods, land, and to other forms of property, to gifts, and to bailments such as contracts of hire and hire-purchase. In relation to goods, the basic rule is restated in section 21 of the 1893 Act: "Subject to the provisions of this Act, where goods are sold by a person who is not the owner thereof, ... the buyer acquires no better title to the goods than the seller had ..."

Over time, a number of common law exceptions to the basic rule were developed in order to protect bona fide purchasers and thus encourage commercial activity by reinforcing the security of sale transactions. These exceptions are now set out in sections 2, 8 and 9 of the Factors Act 1889 and sections 21–26 of the Sale of Goods Act 1893, and are the subject of this chapter.[2]

The more widely these exceptions are interpreted by the courts, the more the position of the bona fide purchaser will be protected, and the more the general principle of *nemo dat* will be side-lined. In truth, while the *nemo dat* principle is the starting point in describing Irish law, the exceptions in the Factors Act and the Sale of Goods Act effectively render this general rule more commonly honoured in the breach.[3] Thus if a person (S) purports to sell goods which he does not own, his buyer (B) will get no

1 *e.g. Cundy v. Lindsay* (1878) 3 App. Cas. 459 (H.L.); see generally Chapter 3.

2 See also the Consumer Credit Act 1995, s.70 which provides that where goods of any class or description are let under a hire-purchase agreement to a dealer who deals in goods of that class or description, and the dealer later sells the goods when ostensibly acting in the ordinary course of his business, the sale shall be valid as if the dealer were expressly authorised by the owner to make the sale, provided that the buyer (defined as a consumer buyer: 1995 Act, s.2) acts in good faith and without notice of the dealer's lack of authority.

3 As noted by Lord Denning in *Bishopsgate Motor Finance Corpn Ltd v. Transport Brakes Ltd* [1949] 1 K.B. 322 (C.A.) at 336–7:"In the development of our law, two principles have striven for mastery. The first is for the protection of property: no one can give a better title than he himself possesses. The second is for the protection of commercial transactions: the person who takes in good faith and for value without notice should get a better title. The first principle has held sway for a long time, but it has been modified by the common law itself and by statute so as to meet the needs of our time."

title to them unless he can rely on one of the statutory exceptions to the *nemo dat* rule. Such a situation can arise in a number of ways.

(i) S may be a thief who stole the goods from their rightful owner (O), or may have purchased the goods from a thief.[4]
(ii) S may have agreed to buy the goods under a contract containing a reservation of title clause, so that title has not passed to him at the time he resells to B.
(iii) S may have already sold the goods to O, but remained in possession of them after the transfer of property to O.
(iv) S may have possession of the goods under a hire purchase agreement.
(v) S may have obtained the goods from O by deception, under a contract that, as a result, is voidable.

In each case, B may find that, having bought goods, they are claimed by another person, O, who asserts that he is the true owner of the goods, or has a prior right to possession of them, and was dispossessed of them by the wrongful act of S or of a third party. B may be entirely innocent, but O will generally seek to recover the goods from B by suing in conversion; hence the conflict of title between O and B. The court's function, in applying the *nemo dat* principle and the exceptions thereto, is to decide between two parties, both of whom are innocent, who shall bear the consequences of a fraud or deception.

19.1.1 The tort of conversion[5]

An owner, or a person with an immediate right to possession of goods, such as a pledgee or a lienee,[6] who is wrongfully deprived of possession, may sue in the tort of conversion any person who deprives him of possession or who, without his authority, deals with the goods intending to assert a right to them inconsistent with his right. Provided the defendant has this intention, liability in the tort of conversion is strict. So, a defendant may be liable even though he was unaware of the plaintiff's right to the goods or honestly believed that he himself was their true owner.

4 1893 Act, s.24(1) provides that where goods have been stolen and the offender is prosecuted to conviction, the property in the goods revests in the original owner. In these circumstances, the exceptions to the *nemo dat* rule are of no use to an innocent purchaser; however, the purchaser can recover damages from the seller for breach of the implied terms as to title in s.12 of the 1893 Act: see, *e.g. York St Flax Spinning Co v. Harbison* (1911) 45 I.L.T.R. 248. In contrast, under s.24(2) where goods are obtained by fraud or other wrongful means not amounting to larceny, the property in the goods shall not revest in the original owner, by reason only of the conviction. See further Larceny Acts 1916–1990.

5 See McMahon & Binchy, *Law of Torts* (Dublin, Butterworths, 3rd ed., 2001) Chapter 30.

6 See generally Chapter 25.

In practice, O will generally seek to recover the goods from B, the person in possession. If he can do so lawfully, O is entitled to recover the goods without court action. However, if B resists O's claim, O will need to bring an action in conversion. In his defence, B can rely on any of the exceptions to the *nemo dat* rule. If he succeeds, B will acquire a title to the goods superior to that of O and therefore be able to resist O's claim. The goods may have changed hands several times via a chain of transactions before coming into B's hands. In order to dispute O's entitlement to the goods, B must therefore examine each of the transactions in the chain in order to see if any fall within any of the *nemo dat* exceptions. It is vital to appreciate that if any of the transactions in the chain fall within any of the *nemo dat* exceptions, all subsequent parties in the chain will have a good defence to O's claim.

> **Example**: W, a thief, steals O's car and sells it to X. W has no right to the goods and, prima facie, can pass no greater right to X. X then resells the car to Y in circumstances which bring that sale within one of the *nemo dat* exceptions, so that Y will acquire a title to the car superior to that of O. Y then sells the car to Z who resells it to S. Finally, S sells the car to B.
>
> O → W → X → Y → Z → S → B
>
> The title acquired by Y will be transferred, via the sales to Z, S and B, allowing B to resist O's claim.

Even if O's claim against B fails because B can rely on one of the *nemo dat* exceptions, O may still succeed against other, earlier, parties in the transaction chain who are unable to rely on a *nemo dat* exception. Thus, in the example above, where the sale from X to Y falls within a *nemo dat* exception, the title acquired by Y in that transaction will give him, Z, S and B a defence to O's conversion claim; however, X has no such defence and thus may be liable to O.

19.1.2 Section 12

Where B cannot rely on any of the *nemo dat* exceptions he will be forced to surrender the goods, or pay their value, to O. In these circumstances, B has a claim against S, his vendor, for breach of the implied terms in the contract of sale that S should have had the right to sell the goods and that B should enjoy quiet possession of them, under section 12 of the 1893 Act.[7] Where such a claim succeeds, according to the leading case of *Rowland v. Divall*,[8] there will be a total failure of consideration and B will be entitled to a full refund of any price paid, from S, irrespective of any beneficial enjoyment B may have had of the goods in question. B will therefore join

7 See Chapter 12.

8 [1923] 2 K.B. 500.

S in the proceedings as a third party. S will have a similar claim against his vendor, Z, and so on. Each party involved in the transaction chain can thus be joined in the action, and liability can be passed back up the chain. In theory, liability could be passed back in this way to W, the original wrongdoer. However, in practice, W will often be untraceable or unable to satisfy any judgment.

19.1.3 Good faith and without notice[9]

The exceptions in the Factors Act 1889 and in sections 22–25 of the 1893 Act operate only where the buyer of goods acts in good faith and without notice of the rogue's defect in title.[10] It has been argued that the good faith and notice requirements in this context have more to do with commercial convenience and expediency than with broader notions of justice, fairness, and reasonableness associated with the principle of good faith, and hence the scope of good faith in these specific rules is limited.[11] Section 62(2) provides that a thing is deemed to be done in "good faith" when it is in fact done honestly, whether it be done negligently or not.[12] Therefore good faith simply requires the buyer to act honestly: a subjective test.

"Notice" is not defined in the legislation. But it is generally accepted that "constructive notice" has no role in commercial transactions,[13] and that notice in this context means "actual notice".[14] However, the concept of actual notice is far from simple. Actual notice is not the same as actual knowledge. Actual notice is assessed objectively. In deciding what facts a buyer has notice of, a court may draw inferences from the facts. For instance, a buyer will be treated as having notice of facts to which it can be shown he deliberately turned a blind eye.[15] Moreover, a buyer will be treated as having actual notice of facts if he knows of circumstances which

9 See generally Ulph, "Good Faith and Due Diligence" in Palmer & McKendrick eds., *Interests in Goods* (London, L.L.P., 2nd ed., 1998); Harrison, *Good Faith in Sales* (London, Sweet & Maxwell, 1997) Chapter 8.

10 A good faith requirement also exists in relation to s.26 of the 1893 Act on writs of execution and s.47 of the 1893 Act on the effect of a sub-sale or pledge by a buyer on an unpaid seller's real rights.

11 O'Connor, *Good Faith in English Law* (Aldershot, Dartmouth, 1990) Chapter 3; see further Beatson & Friedmann eds., *Good Faith and Fault in Contract Law* (Oxford, Clarendon, 1995) and Brownsword, Hird & Howells eds., *Good Faith in Contract: Concept and Context* (Aldershot, Ashgate, 1999).

12 This definition is taken from s.90 of the Bills of Exchange Act 1882. "Good faith" is not defined in the Factors Act 1889.

13 See, in a different context, the statement by Lindley L.J. in Manchester *Trust v. Furness* [1895] 2 Q.B. 539 at 545.

14 See *Worcester Works Finance Ltd v. Cooden* [1972] 1 Q.B. 210 at 218; [1971] 3 All E.R. 708 at 712 per Lord Denning (C.A.).

15 See *London Joint Stock Bank v. Simmons* [1892] A.C. 20 regarding negotiable instruments.

"must lead a reasonable man applying his mind to them, and judging from them, to the conclusion that the fact is so."[16]

There is, in fact, a degree of overlap between the concepts of "good faith" and "notice".[17] Evidence of facts which would make a reasonable person suspicious may be taken as evidence of lack of good faith, or as evidence that the buyer must have had notice of the rogue's defect of title, or both. Furthermore, under section 2 of the Factors Act 1889[18] and arguably under section 25(2) of the 1893 Act,[19] there is a requirement that the disposition to the buyer seeking to rely on the exception to the *nemo dat* rule must have been "in the ordinary course of business". This requirement overlaps with the concepts of good faith and notice such that circumstances that would make a reasonable buyer suspicious may mean that the disposition is not in the ordinary course of business.

Under all the exceptions, bar section 23 of the 1893 Act, the burden of proving good faith and lack of notice lies on the person seeking to rely on the exception: the buyer. Where circumstances are suspicious, the court will examine carefully a claim of good faith and lack of notice and consequently the evidential burden of proof will be harder to discharge.

19.2 Exception No. 1 – The Factors Act 1889

Section 21(2)(a) of the Sale of Goods Act 1893 provides that nothing in the 1893 Act shall affect the provisions of the Factors Acts, or any enactment enabling the apparent owner of goods to dispose of them as if he were the true owner thereof. Accordingly, innocent purchasers of goods will plead both the Factors Act and the Sale of Goods Act where possible. There are five Factors Acts in all: the first dating from 1823; the latest, from 1889,[20] is still in force and contains exceptions to the *nemo dat* principle in sections 2, 8 and 9. Despite its title, the seller of goods does not need to be a "factor", a commercial agent who handles the goods (or documents of

16 Per Lord Tenderden in *Evans v. Truman* (1830) 1 Mood. & R. 10 at 12.

17 The relationship between good faith and notice, in the context of negotiable instruments, was referred to by Lord Herschell in *London Joint Stock Bank v. Simmons* [1892] A.C. 201 at 221: "regard to the facts of which the taker of such instruments had notice is most material in considering whether he took in good faith. If there be anything which excites the suspicion that there is something wrong in the transaction, the taker of the instrument is not acting in good faith if he shuts his eyes to the facts presented to him and puts the suspicion aside without further inquiry." This comment is equally applicable to sale of goods transactions.

18 19.2.1.3.

19 19.8.2.

20 The five are the Factors Acts 1823; 1825; 1842; 1877; and 1889.

title) of his client in the course of finding a buyer or seller for them.[21] The Act uses the term "mercantile agent" instead of the now obsolete "factor". Section 2 provides that good title passes to a bona fide purchaser where goods are sold by a mercantile agent where he is in possession of the goods with the owner's consent and sells them in the ordinary course of business.[22] Sections 8 and 9 of the 1889 Act are almost identical to section 25 of the Sale of Goods Act 1893.[23]

19.2.1 Dispositions by mercantile agents

Section 2(1) of the Factors Act 1889 Act provides:

> "Where a mercantile agent is, with the consent of the owner, in possession of goods or of documents of title to goods, any sale, pledge, or disposition of the goods made by him when acting in the ordinary course of business of a mercantile agent, shall, subject to the provisions of this Act, be valid as if he were expressly authorised by the owner of goods to make the same; provided that the person taking under the disposition acts in good faith, and has not at the time of the disposition notice that the person making the disposition has not authority to make the same."

Hence, where the facts of a case come within this provision, the mercantile agent (MA) can give a good title to the goods to (B), thereby defeating any prior claim of (O) over the goods.

O ———→ MA ———→ B

The different aspects of this provision will be examined in detail under the following headings.

19.2.1.1 Mercantile agent

Mercantile agent is defined in section 1(1) of the 1889 Act as an agent:

> "having in the customary course of his business as such agent authority either to sell goods, or to consign goods for the purpose of sale or to buy goods, or to raise money on the security of goods."

---

21 A common example of a factor is an auctioneer selling furniture that is displayed in his showroom. A factor can be contrasted with a broker who is an agent who buys and sells without handling the goods. Factor, in this technical sense, has dropped out of commercial usage. In modern business, the word "factoring" is used in the unrelated sense of assigning or discounting book-debts: see Goode, *Commercial Law* (London, Penguin, 2nd ed, 1995) Chapter 29. There is also a common practice of referring to dealers in certain goods and spare-parts as "factors," for example, "motor factors."

22 See 19.2.1.3.

23 See 19.7 and 19.8.

Hence, a mercantile agent must have a business and must, in the course of that business, deal with goods belonging to his principal, by selling, buying or raising finance on them. But beyond that the statutory definition is of limited use: what sort of business must the mercantile agent have; and how much business must the mercantile agent do? The statutory definition has been considered in a number of cases from which the following statements can be supported.

First, it is important to stress that a mercantile agent must be an agent, albeit with limited authority, and not merely a servant or an employee.[24] Second, to be a mercantile agent a person must have a business or at least be acting in a business capacity with the owner of goods. For instance, in *Budberg v. Jerwood*,[25] the owner entrusted a necklace to a Dr de Wittchinsky, a lawyer, to sell. The necklace was eventually sold to Jerwood. The owner sought to recover her necklace, while Jerwood claimed that Dr de Wittchinsky acted as a mercantile agent. The court found that the relationship between Dr de Wittchinsky and the owner was not a business relationship: there was no mention of remuneration and Dr de Wittchinsky was acting as a friend. Third, a person whose principal business does not involve selling goods, for instance, can sell as a mercantile agent. Section 2(1) does not require that the seller's "ordinary business" be that of a mercantile agent, but that the sale in question must have been made in the ordinary course of his business.[26] It was held in *Astley Industrial Trust Ltd v. Miller*[27] that a car hire company, when it sold second hand cars, was acting as a mercantile agent. Fourth, it has been held that a person can be a mercantile agent where he works for only one principal.[28] Finally, a person can be a mercantile agent in respect of a transaction even though he never acted as one before.[29] The essential issue is whether, in the case in question, the owner of goods gave them to a person to deal with in a manner usual for a mercantile agent. Where the person who obtains the goods is not a mercantile agent at the time he obtains them, the fact that he becomes a mercantile agent later while still

24 *Cole v. North Western Bank* (1875) L.R. 10 C.P. 354 on earlier Acts; and *Lowther v. Harris* [1927] 1 K.B. 393 (K.B.D.) on 1889 Act.

25 (1934) 51 T.L.R. 99 (K.B.D.).

26 *Weiner v. Harris* [1910] 1 K.B. 285.

27 [1968] 2 All E.R. 36 (Q.B.D.). The argument based on s.2(1) of the Factors Act 1889 failed in this case because the mercantile agent did not have possession of the goods as mercantile agent: see 19.2.1.2. In this case, a firm called Droylesden had a car-hire business but it also dealt in cars. It did not own its hire-cars but let them on hire-purchase from Astley. One such car hired from Astley was subsequently sold by Droylesden to Miller. It was held that since Droylesden had possession of the car as hirer and not as a motor dealer, s.2(1) did not apply to the transaction and Miller had to return the car to Astley or pay its value. *Cf. Belvoir Finance Ltd v. Harold G Cole Ltd* [1969] 2 All E.R. 904, [1969] 1 W.L.R. 1877.

28 *Hyman v. Flewker* (1863) 13 C.B.N.S. 519, on earlier Acts; and *Lowther v. Harris* [1927] 1 K.B. 393 (K.B.D.) on 1889 Act.

29 *Mortgage Loan & Finance Co v. Richards* (1932) S.R. (N.S.W.) 50.

in possession of the goods will not bring the case within the Factors Act unless the owner later consents to his possession as mercantile agent.[30]

19.2.1.2 In possession of goods or documents of title

The Act provides that the agent is in possession where the goods, or documents of title are in his actual possession or are held "by any other person subject to his control or for him or on his behalf"[31] – constructive possession. It has been held that the mercantile agent must have possession at the time of the disposition to B.[32] It is insufficient that the mercantile agent was in possession at some earlier time, such as when showing the goods to the innocent purchaser.

Section 2(1) refers to the goods or documents of title to the goods. Similarly, section 25(1) of the 1893 Act – seller in possession – and section 25(2) of the 1893 Act – buyer in possession – refer to the goods or the documents of title thereto. In this context, documents of title include not just those documents recognised at common law as documents of title, namely bills of lading, but are defined to include many other documents, that have no relevance to title, including

> "… any bill of lading, dock warrant, warehouse-keeper's certificate, and warrant or order for the delivery of goods, and any other document used in the ordinary course of business as proof of the possession or control of goods, or authorising or purporting to authorise, either by endorsement or by delivery, the possessor of the document to transfer or receive goods thereby represented."[33]

Documents of title fall into two classes: acknowledgments and orders. An acknowledgment is signed usually by a person in physical possession of the goods (such as a bailee) noting that he is holding the goods on a particular person's behalf. An order is signed usually by the owner or other person entitled to possession of them, directing another person such as a bailee or carrier, who has possession of the goods, to deliver the goods as directed. These documents (bar a bill of lading) do not confer rights of ownership on their holders, rather they give the holder power to control the right of disposal of the goods which they represent. It has been held that a motor car registration document, or log book, is not a document of title for the purposes of the 1889 Act.[34] Instead, its purpose is to record the "keeper" of a vehicle for taxation and other purposes.

30 *Heap v. Motorists' Advisory Agency* [1923] 1 K.B. 577.
31 1889 Act, s.1(2).
32 *Beverley Acceptances Ltd v. Oakley* [1982] R.T.R. 417.
33 1889 Act, s.1(4).
34 See *Bishopsgate Motor Finance Corp v. Transport Brakes Ltd* [1949] 1 K.B. 322; see further *Fitzpatrick v. Criminal Assets Bureau* [2000] 1 I.R. 217 (S.C.).

19.2.1.3 In possession with consent of owner

The reason for protecting innocent buyers dealing with mercantile agents is the appearance created by the agent's possession of the goods to which the owner has consented. Accordingly, section 2(1) requires that the mercantile agent must have possession with the consent of the owner. Consent is presumed in the absence of evidence to the contrary.[35] Hence, the burden of proof is on the owner to show that he did not consent to possession.

Provided that the mercantile agent has been in possession of the goods with the owner's consent, it is irrelevant that the owner withdraws consent prior to the mercantile agent's disposition of them, so long as any bona fide purchaser has no notice of the withdrawal.[36] Provided the owner has given consent to the mercantile agent's possession, it is also irrelevant that the mercantile agent obtained his consent by deceiving him,[37] but it has been held that this exception to the *nemo dat* principle does not apply where the goods or documents of title to them were stolen from the owner.[38]

19.2.1.4 Possession as mercantile agent

The nature of the owner's consent must be such that the seller, for instance, has the goods as mercantile agent for one of the purposes listed in section 1 of the 1889 Act such as to sell, as opposed to repair the goods or simply hold the goods under a bailment. But it has been held that consent for sale is not strictly necessary. Consent may be for any purpose connected with or preparatory to sale such as for display purposes or to get offers.[39]

---

35 1889 Act, s.2(4).

36 1889 Act, s.2(2). Moreover, a consent to possession of the goods carries with it deemed consent to the possession of any documents of title in relation to the goods which the agent has obtained by reason of his having or having had possession of the goods: 1889 Act, s.2(3).

37 *Folkes v. King* [1923] 1 K.B. 282 (C.A.). In *Pearson v. Rose Young Ltd* [1951] 1 K.B. 275 (C.A.), it was held that consent obtained by fraud was still consent for these purposes. However, based on a rather strained interpretation of s.2, and on the facts of this case, the court found that no title passed under s.2 in this case. A car had been delivered to a dealer with instructions to obtain offers but with no authority to sell. The dealer, however, sold the car and the innocent purchaser claimed title under s.2 of the 1889 Act. However, the court found that the necessary consent was lacking: the "goods" in s.2 referred to the car plus registration book, and the owner had not consented to the dealer having possession of the registration book – it had been unintentionally left with the dealer when the owner was called away in haste on a bogus errand. See also *Stadium Finance Ltd v. Robbins* [1962] 2 Q.B. 664 (C.A.).

38 *National Employers Mutual General Insurance Association Ltd v. Jones* [1990] 1 A.C. 24 (H.L.): see further 19.8.2.

39 In *Pearson v. Rose Young Ltd* [1951] 1 K.B. 275 at 288; see further "Notes" (1951) 67 *Law Quarterly Review* 6.

19.2.1.5 Disposition in the ordinary course of business

To pass good title to the bona fide purchaser, the mercantile agent must have sold or otherwise disposed of the goods "in the ordinary course of business". This means that he "is acting at the time, and in the manner, and possibly in other respects, as though he had authority and occasion" to dispose of the goods.[40] What is in the ordinary course of business is a question of fact. For instance, did the sale occur during normal business hours, at a usual business location, or was the price at a substantial undervalue? It has been held, for example, that the sale of a second-hand car off the pavement in London's Warren Street was in the ordinary course of the second-hand car business: in Warren Street and its neighbourhood there was a well-established street market for cash dealing in used cars.[41] In contrast, it has been held that the sale of a car without registration documents[42] or an ignition key[43] would not be in the ordinary course of business. However, these are not absolute rules and there may be circumstances where the sale of a car without registration documents would be in the ordinary course of business: as where the car has been recently purchased and the new registration documents have not yet been received.[44]

19.2.1.6 Good faith and without notice

To avail of this exception to the *nemo dat* principle, like other exceptions, the person who deals with the mercantile agent must act in good faith and without notice of the agent's lack of authority. In particular, the requirements of good faith and lack of notice are closely tied with the "ordinary course of business" requirement, such that any departure from the ordinary course of business may suggest dishonesty and put the disponee on notice that the circumstances are suspicious. Under section 2(1), the burden of proof is on the disponee to show good faith and lack of notice.[45] But, against this, the equitable doctrine of constructive notice is not sufficient to constitute notice of no authority to engage in commercial transactions in goods.[46]

---

40 *Oppenheimer v. Attenborough & Son* [1908] 1 K.B. 221 at 232 per Buckley L.J.

41 *Newtons of Wembley v. Williams* [1965] 1 Q.B. 560.

42 *Pearson v. Rose Young Ltd* [1951] 1 K.B. 275.

43 *Stadium Finance Ltd v. Robbins* [1962] 2 Q.B. 664 (C.A.).

44 *Astley Industrial Trust Ltd v. Miller* [1968] 2 All E.R. 36 (Q.B.D.).

45 *Heap v. Motorists' Advisory Agency Ltd* [1923] 1 K.B. 577. Atiyah notes that the reasons given in this case are not convincing, though the result seems sensible: *Atiyah's Sale of Goods* (Harlow, Pearson, 10th ed., 2001) p.389. It is not difficult for a buyer to prove his good faith, hence the U.K. Law Reform Committee recommended the endorsement of this case: Twelfth Report of the Law Reform Committee, Transfer of Title to Chattels, Cmnd 2958 (1966), para. 25. Cf. the position under s.23 of the 1893 Act: 19.6.3.

46 See, in a different context, the statement by Lindley L.J. in *Manchester Trust v. Furness* [1895] 2 Q.B. 539 at 545.

19.2.2 The effect of section 2(1)

Where all the above requirements are satisfied, the effect of a disposition by a mercantile agent is as if the agent was expressly authorised to dispose of the goods. Hence the owner of goods is bound by the disposition even where the agent lacks any form of authority. The original owner's title is extinguished and the bona fide purchaser or disponee acquires a good title and is protected against any claims by the original owner.

This exception to the *nemo dat* principle was devised in the nineteenth century when commercial conditions were very different from today. Nevertheless, the basic rationale for this exception seems fair. An owner who consents to an agent having possession of his goods is in a better position to assess the trustworthiness of that agent than a third party dealing with the agent. Therefore, the owner should bear the risk of the agent's dishonesty. However, in modern conditions, it is doubtful whether this highly technical rule provides adequate protection to third parties who deal with agents.

19.3 Exception No. 2 – Agency

In the Sale of Goods Act 1893, the first two exceptions to the *nemo dat* rule are based on agency principles and are to be found in section 21. There is some overlap between these first two exceptions. Section 21 provides:

> "... where goods are sold by a person who is not the owner thereof, *and who does not sell them under the authority or with the consent of the owner*, the buyer acquires no better title to the goods than the seller had ..." [author's italics].

In addition, section 61 preserves the common law rules of agency. Hence, and unsurprisingly, an owner will be bound by any disposition of his goods by an agent acting with his authority or consent. As noted in an earlier chapter, an agent may have a number of types of authority.[47] Where an agent has any type of authority recognised by law, whether actual, express or implied, apparent, usual, or authority by ratification for instance, the owner will be bound by any disposition of his goods. However, where an agent exceeds his authority or consent, any disposition will not bind his principal, and the principal will be able to recover the goods from a

[47] See generally Chapter 5.

purchaser. Moreover, in these circumstances, the agent may be liable to his principal for breach of the agency agreement and to any third party for breach of warranty of authority.[48] But, in many cases, the agent will be a mercantile agent within the meaning of the Factors Act 1889 and thereby have wide powers to dispose of his principal's goods.[49]

19.4 Exception No. 3 – Estoppel

The second agency exception is also found in section 21 of the 1893 Act:

> "… where goods are sold by a person who is not the owner thereof, and who does not sell them under the authority or with the consent of the owner, the buyer acquires no better title to the goods than the seller had, *unless the owner of the goods is by his conduct precluded from denying the seller's authority to sell.*" [author's italics].

The words in italics reproduce a common law exception to the general *nemo dat* rule that a person who buys from someone other than the owner may acquire a title to the goods where the owner is precluded or estopped from denying the seller's right to sell the goods.[50] The exception may apply in two different types of case:

- (i) where the owner represents that the seller is the owner's agent, as in cases of apparent authority; and
- (ii) where the owner represents that the seller is the owner of the goods, sometimes referred to as "apparent ownership".

In each case the owner will be prevented from recovering his goods, and the buyer will acquire title to them, provided the seller's dealing in the goods is consistent with the appearance created by the owner's conduct.

Although section 21 refers only to the owner's "conduct", it is clear that in both cases above the owner's representation may be by words or by conduct. Common to all estoppels, the representation must be one of fact; it must be unambiguous, and it must be acted upon. However, this estoppel

---

48 See 7.3 and 6.4.5.

49 See 19.2.

50 As noted by Atiyah, this provision merely throws us back on the common law doctrine of estoppel because it gives no indication when the owner is by his conduct precluded from denying the seller's authority to sell: *Atiyah's Sale of Goods* (Harlow, Pearson, 10th ed., 2001) p.371. It has been suggested that this provision operates separately from common law estoppel: see *Shaw v. M.P.C* [1987] 1 W.L.R. 1332 (C.A.), but this was rejected and Atiyah's view was endorsed by the New South Wales Court of Appeal in *Thomas Australia Wholesale Vehicle Trading Co Pty Ltd v. Marac Finance Australia Ltd* [1985] 3 N.S.W.R. 452, esp 470.

exception has generally been narrowly interpreted.[51] For instance, it has been held that the owner's representation will only estop him if it was voluntarily made. So, where O surrendered his car to a robber, and at gunpoint completed a document stating that he had sold the car to the robber, O was not estopped from denying the robber's right to sell the car.[52] Moreover, merely parting with possession of goods, even if voluntarily, is insufficient to give rise to an estoppel.[53] There are so many circumstances where an owner of goods may allow another in possession of them that it cannot be claimed that such conduct amounts to an unambiguous representation that the person in possession is the owner or has the authority of the owner to sell. Generally, a positive representation that the seller has the right to sell is required. This point is illustrated in *Central Newbury Car Auctions Ltd v. Unity Finance Ltd*[54] where shortly after signing hire-purchase proposal forms and making a cash payment, a fraudster obtained possession of a car and its registration book from the plaintiff. The fraudster then purported to sell the car and it was, in turn, re-sold to the defendant. The plaintiff refused the hire-purchase proposal, traced the car and sued the defendant in conversion. In its defence, the defendant argued that by giving the fraudster possession of the car and registration book, the plaintiff was estopped from denying his authority to sell the car. This argument was rejected on the basis that merely parting with possession does not give rise to an estoppel. The court held further that even though the plaintiff owner might have been careless or negligent in not checking the credentials of the fraudster, the position would be unchanged.[55]

---

51 An example of how narrowly this exception has been interpreted in England is illustrated in *Shaw v. M.P.C* [1987] 1 W.L.R. 1332 (C.A.) where it was held that the word "sold" in the second line of s.21(1) does not include where there is an agreement to sell. In this case, an overseas student who was about to leave Britain for home entrusted possession of his car to a rogue (Mr London) and signed papers which would have estopped him from denying London's authority to sell. London delivered the car to Shaw, pursuant to an agreement to sell and then disappeared. Shaw claimed to be entitled to the car under the estoppel exception but the Court of Appeal held otherwise because there was no sale – only an agreement to sell. See further Gill, "Transfer of Title to Goods by a Non-Owner" [1987] *Irish Law Times* 276.

52 *Debs v. Sibec Developments Ltd* [1990] R.T.R. 91.

53 *Farquharson Bros & Co v. King & Co* [1902] A.C. 325 (H.L.) ; *Jerome v. Bentley & Co* [1952] 2 All E.R. 114 (Q.B.D.). Note, these cases are effectively reversed where the person in possession is a mercantile agent under s.2 of the Factors Act 1889: see 19.2.1; and where the person in possession has contracted to buy goods under s.9 of the 1889 Act and s.25(2) of the 1893 Act: see 19.8.

54 [1957] 1 Q.B. 371 (C.A.). See also *Mercantile Bank of India v. Central Bank of India* [1938] A.C. 287 (P.C.) where it was held that entrusting a person with documents of title to goods was no different from entrusting them with the goods and hence could not give rise to an estoppel.

55 "It cannot be that ownership is lost on the basis of enduring punishment for carelessness." [1957] 1 Q.B. 371 per Morris L.J. at 394.

In theory, at least, estoppel may be based on an owner's negligence,[56] but it seems that the owner's negligence in dealing with his property will not estop him from recovering it from an innocent buyer unless he owes a duty of care. It is clear from the above case, and others, that English courts have been reluctant to find that an owner of goods owes a duty of care to the world at large which would be broken merely by entrusting his goods to another. Even where it could be proved that an owner owed a duty of care to a particular purchaser, rather than to the world at large, there are still legal hurdles to pursuing a claim of estoppel by negligence. The purchaser would have to prove that (i) the duty of care was breached and (ii) the breach of duty was the proximate and effective cause of the purchaser entering into the transaction by which he obtained the goods. Again, English case law indicates a reluctance to go down this path. For instance, in *Moorgate Mercantile Co Ltd v. Twitchings*,[57] the plaintiff was a hire-purchase company that supplied a car to the defendant on the usual hire-purchase terms. The defendant defaulted on the agreement and purported to sell the car to another, who in turn sold the car again.

H.P. Co./Plaintiff ➞ Twitchings/Defendant ➞ X ➞ Y

Under the standard hire-purchase arrangement, the hirer does not acquire title to the goods until all the instalments and other sums due are paid. Hence, applying the *nemo dat* principle, the defendant, not being the owner of the goods, could not pass good title to the goods. Against this it was argued that the plaintiff, through their negligent conduct, had represented that the defendant had the right to sell. At the time of the sale by the defendant, there was a private and voluntary registration system operating in England in relation to hired cars, known as Hire Purchase Information (H.P.I.).[58] H.P.I. keep records of the ownership of goods, mainly motor vehicles, let on hire-purchase or credit-sale terms. This registration system was designed to deter the unauthorised dealing in hired goods. Most hire-purchase companies, including the plaintiff, participated in this scheme.

56 A similar concept of estoppel by negligence exists in other areas of law, such as in relation to negotiable instruments but appears to be very limited in its operation in relation to goods: see further below.

57 [1977] A.C. 890, [1976] 3 W.L.R. 66. See also *Mercantile Credit Co Ltd v. Hamblin* [1965] 2 Q.B. 242 (C.A.) where the court found a duty of care but no negligence; and moreover found, even if negligence was established that the proximate and real cause of the innocent purchaser parting with its money was found to be the fraud of a dealer and not the actions of the owner. Estoppel by negligence was also applied in *Coventry Shepherd & Co v. Great Eastern Rly Co* (1883) 11 Q.B.D. 776 where the defendants negligently issued two delivery orders relating to the same goods. The person to whom they were issued was thereby able to represent to the plaintiff (to whom he had pledged the goods) that the goods were in fact available after they had been disposed of.

58 In Irish context see, *e.g.* the Irish Credit Bureau: www.oasis.gov.ie/personal_finance/irish _credit_bureau.html.

However, the plaintiff failed to register the hire-purchase arrangement with the defendant thereby facilitating the subsequent re-sales. It was argued that this negligent failure gave rise to a representation that the defendant had authority to sell and that the plaintiff was estopped from denying the defendant's authority to sell. It was held by a majority that this failure did not amount to estoppel by negligence and that the purchaser did not get good title.[59]

Therefore, under English law at least, it seems that it will very rarely be possible for a buyer to establish a title to goods on the basis of estoppel by negligence.[60] In contrast and in principle, Irish courts do not appear to show the same reluctance to recognise a duty of care to avoid economic loss and to compensate for pure economic loss.[61] It could be argued, for example, that where an owner knew a person to be a rogue likely to obtain money by fraud, he would owe a duty to the world at large not to give the rogue possession of his goods or documents of title thereto, or other signed documents which would facilitate a fraud.[62] If he did give the rogue possession of his goods, it could be argued that he was in breach of his duty to the world at large and that any economic loss to an innocent purchaser from the rogue was caused by and sufficiently proximate to the owner's breach of duty.

19.5 Exception No. 4 – Market Overt[63]

By a long-established exception to the *nemo dat* rule, section 22 of the 1893 Act provides:

> "Where goods are sold in market overt, according to the usage of the market, the buyer acquires a good title to the goods, provided he buys them in good faith and without notice of any defect or want of title on the part of the seller."

Accordingly, the sale must take place in an open, public, and legally constituted market, established by Royal Charter, statute or custom. For instance, any sale from a shop, as defined,[64] in the City of London

59 It was said that the plaintiff's failure to register with H.P.I. was "at worst, careless in respect of [its] own property, and it was not a breach of any duty to other parties" [1977] A.C. 890 at 926, [1976] 3 W.L.R. 66 at 91 Lord Fraser.

60 *Moorgate Mercantile Co Ltd v. Twitchings* [1977] A.C. 890, [1976] 3 W.L.R. 66.

61 See, *e.g. McShane v. Johnston* [1997] 1 I.L.R.M. 86; see further McMahon & Binchy, *Law of Torts* (Dublin, Butterworths, 3rd ed., 2000) Chapter 10.

62 See *Mercantile Credit Co Ltd v. Hamblin* [1965] 2 Q.B. 242 (C.A.).

63 See Smith, "Valediction to Market Overt" (1997) XLI *The American Journal of Legal History* 225; and Davenport & Ross, "Market Overt" in Palmer & McKendrick, eds., *Interests in Goods* (London, LLP, 2nd ed., 1998) Chapter 14.

64 See Davenport & Ross, "Market Overt" in Palmer & McKendrick, eds., *Interests in Goods* (London, LLP, 2nd ed., 1998) Chapter 14.

constitutes, by custom, a sale in a *market overt*.[65] Though Irish case law on the point is scarce, it has been held that the old Prussia Street cattle market in Dublin was a *market overt*.[66] A list of such *markets overt* does not exist for consultation; the issue of whether a particular market qualifies or not can be addressed only in the context of a dispute in relation to a sale in a particular market. Nevertheless, it seems clear that a private market or a car-boot sale would not qualify as a *market overt*.[67] Section 22 expressly provides that the sale must be in accordance with the customs or usages of the market. So, for example, if a car was bought in what is normally an antiques market, this would not qualify under the above exception. Moreover, the sale must take place between sunrise and sunset. Finally, and common to many of the *nemo dat* exceptions, the buyer must act in good faith and without notice of any defect in the seller's title to the goods.

This exception was said to derive from the ancient *lex mercatoria*,[68] and has been part of the common law since the fifteenth century, a time when the only trading in goods occurred in open markets and neither people nor goods were very mobile. It sought to represent a compromise between the interests of the owners of goods and the traders and buyers at such markets. Where goods were stolen, the onus was placed on the owner to go to the nearest market to seek his goods. If an owner failed in this endeavour and the goods were sold at market, the buyer took a good title, hence encouraging trading at markets. Today, the same rationale does not hold good. Indeed, in England, the equivalent of section 22 was referred to as a "thief's charter" because of the perception that the market overt exception facilitated the "fencing" or "laundering" of stolen goods.[69] Following strong lobbying by fine art dealers and others, the market overt exception was repealed in England under the Sale of Goods (Amendment) Act 1994.[70]

In Ireland, this exception is in need of immediate review. Either we abolish the exception, the approach favoured in England, or, as has been suggested elsewhere,[71] we extend the principle to all sales from retail premises. Extending the scope of this exception to all sales from retail premises would further protect innocent purchasers of goods and facilitate

65 *Case of Market Overt* (1596) 5 Co. Rep. 83b, discussed by Scrutton J. in *Clayton v. Le Roy* [1911] 2 K.B. 1031. See further Pease, "Market Overt in the City of London" (1915) 31 *Law Quarterly Review* 270.

66 *Ganly v. Ledwidge* (1876) I.R. 10 C.L. 33; and *Delaney v. Wallis* (1883) 14 L.R. I.R. 31.

67 *Lang v. Jones*, *The Times*, March 6, 1990.

68 Scrutton J. in *Clayton v. Le Roy* [1911] 2 Q.B. 1031 at 1038–9.

69 See, *e.g. The Times*, July 25, 1994, p.5.

70 See also D.T.I. Consultation Document, *Transfer of Title: Sections 21 to 26 of the Sale of Goods Act 1979* (1994). See further the Twelfth Report of the Law Reform Committee, Transfer of Title to Chattels, Cmnd. 2958 (1966); and Professor Diamond's *Review of Security Interests in Property* (London, HMSO, 1989).

71 See the Twelfth Report of the Law Reform Committee, *Transfer of Title to Chattels*, Cmnd. 2958 (1966).

commercial transactions generally. If the principle was extended, it has been noted that the original owner of goods would not be left without a remedy: an owner would have a right of action in the tort of conversion against the retailer, and may have insurance cover in relation to the goods. However, an action in conversion may be of little practical value and not all owners will have such insurance cover. More significantly, the extension of the *market overt* exception might be viewed as encouraging crime and, for that reason alone, would probably meet with strong opposition.

As part of any review, empirical research is needed.[72] What is the extent of the problem of stolen goods? How much property, and what kind of property (excluding cash) is stolen? How much is recovered? To what extent does stolen property find its way into the hands of innocent purchasers? Where do innocent purchasers buy such property: in *markets overt*, from standard retail premises, or at public auction? Most significantly, how much stolen property is insured against theft? The subject-matter of many of the cases on title conflicts are cars which are usually insured for theft, as are valuable items stolen from homes and elsewhere. Is it not a reasonable policy to favour the position of innocent purchasers against the interests of insured original owners? But to what extent do insurance companies pursue their subrogation rights,[73] and what effect would a change in the law have on insurance premia?

19.6 Exception No. 5 – Voidable Title

Section 23 of the 1893 Act provides:

> "When the seller of goods has a voidable title thereto, but his title has not been avoided at the time of the sale, the buyer acquires a good title to the goods, provided he buys them in good faith and without notice of the seller's defect in title."

Accordingly, where a person (B) buys goods from a seller (S) who has only a voidable title to the goods, but his title has not been avoided at the time of the sale to B, B may nevertheless acquire a good title to the goods provided he buys them in good faith and without notice of S's defect in title.

72 See Atiyah, "Law Reform Committee: Twelfth Report" (1966) 29 *Modern Law Review* 541.

73 See, *e.g. National Employers Mutual General Insurance Association Ltd v. Jones* [1990] 1 A.C. 24 (H.L.); see further 19.8.2.

19.6.1 Voidable

This section applies only where S's title is voidable. Hence, it can apply in two main situations:

(i) where S acquired the goods under a transaction which was voidable as a result of, most commonly, misrepresentation, or more rarely duress, undue influence, or drunkenness; or
(ii) where S's title is defective because one of his predecessors in title acquired the goods under a voidable contract.

In *Anderson v. Ryan*,[74] the owner of a Mini car, D, answered an advertisement from X which offered a Sprite car for sale. D and X met, exchanged cars,[75] and X left with the Mini. X did not own the Sprite car, which had been stolen, and X ultimately pleaded guilty to a charge of obtaining the Mini by false pretences. X later sold the Mini to the defendant, and the defendant in turn sold it to the plaintiff.

D ⟶ X ⟶ Defendant ⟶ Plaintiff

O ⟶ S ⟶ B1 ⟶ B2

It was held, in the High Court, that the contract of exchange was voidable as a result of X's fraudulent misrepresentation of an existing fact, that the Sprite was his property to sell. Hence, X acquired a voidable title to the car. This title had not been avoided by D at the time of the sale to the defendant. Accordingly, the defendant acquired a good title to the car under section 23, which he was able to pass to the plaintiff.

As the High Court in *Anderson v. Ryan*[76] noted, section 23 does not apply where S has no title at all, such as where goods are stolen. Furthermore, it cannot apply where the contract under which S acquired the goods:

(i) purported to transfer only possession of the goods; or
(ii) was an agreement to sell under which property is to pass at a later date; or
(iii) was wholly void, as opposed to voidable, since a void contract has no legal effect at all.[77]

---

74 [1967] I.R. 34.

75 This was a pure contract of exchange, with no money being paid: see 9.3.1.

76 [1967] I.R. 34 at 38.

77 *Cundy v. Lindsay* (1878) 3 App. Cas. 459 (H.L.) an example of a contract rendered void on grounds of mistake of identity.

19.6.1.1 Void or voidable contracts

Where B claims to have acquired a good title under section 23, the original owner (O) may argue that the contract under which he transferred the goods to S was not merely voidable but was wholly void, typically on the grounds of mistake. Where S contracts to buy goods, and, by falsely claiming to be someone else, persuades O to give him credit, or to accept a cheque, there is clearly a misrepresentation by S, which makes the contract voidable; however, O may seek to argue that the contract is void on the grounds of mistake of identity. The authorities show that the distinction between a contract which is void (on the grounds of an operative mistake of identity) and one which is merely voidable for misrepresentation is a fine one, and difficult to draw.

In *Ingram v. Little*,[78] S, presenting himself as PGM Hutchinson, bought a car from O and sought to pay by cheque. To assure O of his identity, he also gave an address which O checked in the telephone directory. It turned out that the S was not who he claimed and the cheque was stolen. The car had subsequently been sold to B. The Court of Appeal found that the contract was void for mistake. This is an exceptional case and the favoured position of the law is to be found in *Lewis v. Averay*.[79] There O sold a car to a person claiming to be a famous actor, RA Green, for a cheque signed RA Green. It was held that the contract was voidable for misrepresentation. Applying the prima facie presumption, O intended to contract with the person in front of him – there was no mistake. However, the person in front of him misrepresented who he was.

As a result, it seems that O will only succeed in arguing that the contract was void if he can establish that:

(i) he intended to contract with someone other than the actual buyer, and
(ii) the identity of the other contracting party was a vital feature of the contract.[80]

Where O and S deal face to face, it will generally be presumed that O intends to contract with the person before him and O will find it difficult to establish that he intended to deal with someone else.

78 [1961] 1 Q.B. 31 (C.A.).

79 [1972] 1 Q.B. 198. Lord Denning in *Lewis* went so far as to say that *Ingram* was wrongly decided.

80 It has been suggested that the crucial factor in *Ingram* was that the seller checked the telephone directory, proving that the seller intended to deal with Hutchinson: see Treitel, *The Law of Contract* (London, Sweet & Maxwell, 10th ed., 1999) p.276.

19.6.2 Avoiding title

B will succeed in a conflict of title with O, where S has a voidable title and the title has not been avoided at the time of the sale between S and B. Therefore, O should take immediate steps to rescind the contract with S, in order to recover the goods and prevent their sale to a bona fide purchaser who may be protected by section 23. He may do so without court proceedings merely by notifying S of his intention to avoid the contract between them or by retaking possession of the goods. However, where S is untraceable, O may be able to rescind the contract by taking other steps to recover his property, such as notifying the police. In *Car and Universal Finance Co Ltd v. Caldwell*,[81] Caldwell was induced to sell his car to Norris by fraud. The car was re-sold a number of times: first to Motobella, and finally to the plaintiff. When Caldwell discovered the fraud, he had immediately notified the police and the Automobile Association but was unable to communicate with Norris, who had disappeared. The Court of Appeal found that Caldwell had avoided the first contract of sale to Motobella by his actions, and so Caldwell was entitled to the car. The court left open the question whether the law would be the same where the innocent party's inability to communicate with the other party is not due to the fact that the latter is deliberately keeping out of the way. In practice, the decision in *Caldwell* will be of limited application because, in the same circumstances, a third party may get a good title under section 25(2) of the 1893 Act.[82]

19.6.3 Good faith and without notice

As with the other *nemo dat* exceptions, the buyer must act in good faith and without notice of the seller's defect in title. However, the burden of proof under section 23 is different from the other exceptions. It has been held that, under section 23, it is for the original owner to prove that the purchaser did not act in good faith.[83] Requiring an owner to prove a third party's bad faith is clearly more difficult than requiring a third party to prove his good faith: all the relevant evidence is in the hands of the third party. The U.K. Law Reform Committee recommended the reversal of this burden of proof, though its recommendation was never implemented.[84] Any review of the law in Ireland would need to address this issue.

81 [1965] 1 Q.B. 525 (C.A.).

82 See further 19.8.

83 *Whitehorn Bros v. Davison* [1911] 1 K.B. 463.

84 Twelfth Report of the Law Reform Committee, Transfer of Title to Chattels, Cmnd. 2958 (1966), para. 25.

19.7 Exception No. 6 – Seller in Possession[85]

Possession can give the impression of ownership. However, possession and property are two separate concepts,[86] and we have seen how property in goods can pass before or after physical possession passes.[87] For this reason, section 25 of the 1893 Act, which mirrors sections 8 and 9 of the Factors Act 1889, is designed to protect persons who deal with sellers or buyers in possession of goods but who no longer, or do not yet, own the goods. These provisions have many features in common, and so case law under any one of these provisions may have relevance to the others.

The legislation gives a seller a statutory lien over goods in his possession to secure payment of the price.[88] So long as the price remains unpaid, the seller can withhold delivery and retain possession. Where an unpaid seller entitled to a lien over the goods sells them a second time, the second buyer (B2) takes a good title to the goods superior to the first buyer's (B1's) title, even where property has passed to B1 under section 18, rule 1, for instance.[89]

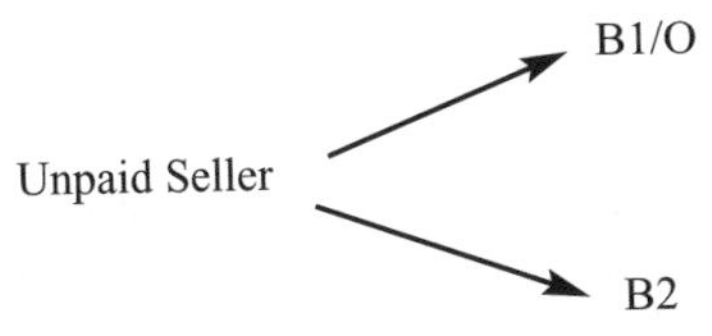

Such a resale may be in breach of contract with B1, enabling B1 to sue the seller, but the legislation allows the seller, in certain circumstances to terminate the contract with B1, in which case the seller can sell without incurring liability for breach of contract.[90] If the seller remains in possession after he has been paid, he has no statutory rights of resale under the legislation. But if he sells the goods he may still pass a good title to the second buyer: either because property in the goods remains with the seller, or even where property has passed to the buyer, under section 25(1) of the 1893 Act.

Section 25(1) states:

> "Where a person having sold goods continues or is in possession of the goods, or of the documents of title to the goods, the delivery or transfer by that person, or by a mercantile agent acting for him, of the goods or

85 See also Factors Act 1889, s.8.
86 See Chapter 3.
87 See Chapter 17.
88 1893 Act , ss.41–43; see 15.3.
89 1893 Act, s.48(2).
90 1893 Act, s.48(3) and s.48(4).

documents of title under any sale, pledge or other disposition thereof, to any person receiving the same in good faith and without notice of the previous sale, shall have the same effect as if the person making the delivery or transfer were expressly authorised by the owner of the goods to make the same."

This provision covers the situation where a person (S), who has contracted to sell goods, retains possession of them after the contract of sale and thus appears to own the goods, even if property in them has in fact already passed to the buyer (B1). Other people (B2) may therefore deal with S as if he were still the owner of the goods – for instance, by agreeing to buy the same goods, or to take security over them. Section 25(1) may protect such a person, B2, who deals with a seller who remains in possession of goods after selling them.

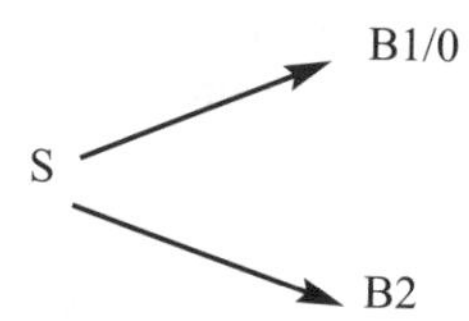

It is important to note that this provision deals with the situation where property has passed to B1 under the sale from S, such that B1 becomes the owner (O) and a conflict of title arises between B1/O and B2. Where the property has not passed to B1 under the first contract of sale, S may continue to deal with the goods as owner himself. If S resells the goods to B2, a second buyer, B2 will acquire property in the goods and a title superior to that of B1. S may incur liability to B1 for failure to deliver where the contract with B1 is for specific goods, or where the contract with B1 is for the sale of unascertained goods if S cannot deliver goods which match the contract description by the delivery date. Hence, section 25(1) only applies where the seller has "sold" (not "agreed to sell") goods.

Section 8 of the Factors Act 1889 is similar to section 25(1) of the 1893 Act, but is a little broader because it seeks to validate the transfer of property under any agreement to sell, pledge, or otherwise dispose of the goods, as well as under an actual sale, pledge or other disposition. Both provisions are usually pleaded together, if possible.

19.7.1 The requirements of section 25(1)

The different aspects of section 25(1) must all be present for the provision to operate to give B2 priority over B1/O. These requirements are as follows:

(i) there must be a sale from S to B1;
(ii) after the sale, S must "continue or be in possession";

(iii) S must deliver or transfer the goods to B2 under any sale, pledge or other disposition; and
(iv) B2 must receive the goods in good faith and without notice.

19.7.1.1 Sale

The original transaction between S and B1 must be a sale within the statutory definition of the 1893 Act.[91] Moreover, as noted above, the transaction must be executed such that property has passed to B1. Where the transaction between S and B1 is an agreement to sell, section 25(1) will not apply.

19.7.1.2 Continues or is in possession

Following the sale from S to B1, S must remain in possession of the goods. Section 1(2) of the Factors Act provides that a person shall be in possession of goods or documents of title to goods where they are "in his actual custody or are held by any other person subject to his control or for him or on his behalf."[92] S may therefore be in actual physical possession of the goods or constructive possession of the goods, as where the goods are physically held by a bailee, on behalf of S.

It now seems clear that the provision applies regardless of the capacity in which S remains in possession of the goods.[93] In *Pacific Motor Auctions Property Ltd v. Motor Credits (Hire Finance) Ltd*,[94] a dealer, S, transferred cars to B1, a finance company, under a financing arrangement, but retained possession as B1's agent. It was held that the seller in possession exception applied. In *Worcester Works Finance Ltd v. Cooden Engineering Ltd*,[95] S transferred ownership of a car to B1, a finance company, representing that it was to be let to a particular customer who in fact did not exist. S therefore remained in possession of the car and it was held that the continuity of physical possession was sufficient to satisfy this exception to the *nemo dat* rule. It was also stated that the possession need not be lawful. This case was approved in Ireland by the High Court, in *Hanley v. ICC Finance*.[96] This case involved an arrangement whereby the defendant purchased a car from the seller, Huet Motors Ltd, and then leased the car back to a company wholly owned by the seller. At the end of the leasing

91 See Chapter 9.
92 See 19.2.1.2.
93 Earlier case law required that S remained in possession as seller: *Staffs Motor Guarantee Ltd v. British Wagon Co Ltd* [1934] 2 K.B. 305; *Eastern Distributors v. Goldring* [1957] 2 Q.B. 600.
94 [1965] A.C. 867 (P.C.). See also *Mitchell v. Jones* (1905) 24 N.Z.L.R. 932.
95 [1972] 1 Q.B. 210 (C.A.).
96 [1996] I.L.R.M. 463 (H.C.); see further Byrne & Binchy *Annual Review of Irish Law* 1995 (Dublin, Round Hall Sweet & Maxwell, 1997) pp.535–536.

period, the seller was to re-purchase the car. The defendant initially retained the car's registration book but it was returned to the lessee for the purpose of allowing it to tax the car. While in the lessee's possession, the plaintiff purchased the car. Subsequently, the lessee went into liquidation.

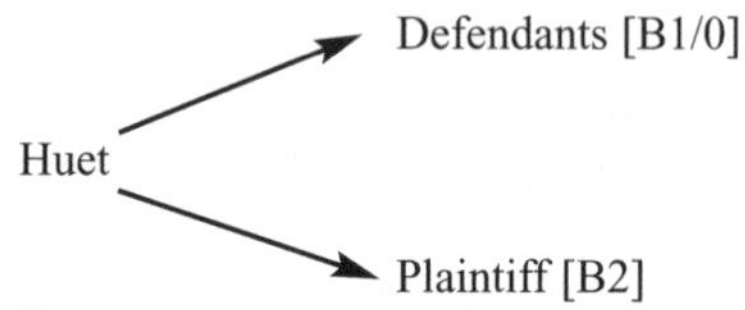

The court found that at all relevant times the car was in the possession of Huet Motors: the leasing to a wholly owned subsidiary was a device used to provide a system of cash-flow. Accordingly, Huet could and did give good title to the car to the plaintiff under section 25(1).

Section 25(1) applies where S continues or is in possession. A literal reading of this provision would suggest that once S had possession in any circumstances, he could pass good title to B2. This would expose B1 to extensive risk if, for example, S sold a car to B1 and B1 took possession of it but later returned it to S for repair or service. However, there is authority that once possession is lost by S and later regained, section 25(1) will not apply.[97] In *Worcester Works Finance Ltd v. Cooden Engineering Ltd*, it was noted that the reference to "is in possession" was designed to refer to future goods not in the seller's possession at the time of the transaction, and so that otherwise the seller's possession must be continual and unbroken.

19.7.1.3 Delivery or transfer under any sale, pledge or other disposition

B2 takes priority over B1 provided the goods (or documents of title), are delivered or transferred under any sale, pledge or other disposition. There are two issues to consider under this heading. First, the provision appears to require that the goods be delivered or transferred to B2 if he is to get priority over B1. In *Nicholson v. Harper*,[98] a merchant owned wine stored with the defendant warehousemen. He sold some wine to the plaintiff who left the wine in the possession of the warehousemen, giving them no notice of their purchase nor receiving any delivery orders or acknowledgments of their claim. Subsequently, the original seller pledged all his wine to the warehousemen and later became insolvent. It was held that property in the wine had passed to the plaintiff under the first sale and that the warehousemen obtained no title under section 25(1). Although the

97 *Mitchell v. Jones* (1905) N.Z.L.R. 932.

98 [1895] 2 Ch. 415. This case was followed in New Zealand in *New Zealand Securities & Finance Ltd v. Wright Cars Ltd* [1976] 1 N.Z.L.R. 77.

merchant was a seller who had retained possession, there had been no delivery or transfer of possession to the warehousemen after the sale.[99]

Nicholson v. Harper was rejected in Australia in *Gamer's Motor Centre (Newcastle) Pty Ltd v. Natwest Wholesale Australia Pty Ltd*,[100] a case concerning the buyer in possession exception, where it was held that it was already well established at the time of the Sale of Goods Act 1893 that physical transfer of possession was not necessary. The law recognised the concept of "constructive delivery" where physical possession remained unaltered while the right to possession was transferred. It has been noted that the *Gamer* decision appears inconsistent with the line of authority starting with *Pacific Motor Auctions Property Ltd v. Motor Credits (Hire Finance) Ltd*[101] where continuity of physical possession is stressed. However, there are a number a good reasons to prefer the approach of the *Gamer* decision. The other exceptions to the *nemo dat* rule, such as section 2 of the Factors Act, or estoppel, or section 23 of the 1893 Act appear to protect a buyer from the moment of the sale to him, provided he has paid the price or acted to his prejudice so as to constitute himself as a bona fide purchaser for value. None of these provisions appear to require actual physical delivery. Moreover, the second buyer is protected even where he has only agreed to buy and the property has not yet passed to him. In these circumstances it would seem odd to insist on actual physical delivery.

Second, the second transaction is not limited to being a sale but can include a pledge or other disposition. "Other disposition" has been given a wide meaning but the disposition to B2 must involve the creation of a *proprietary*, rather than of a mere *possessory*, interest.[102] In *Worcester Works Finance Ltd v. Cooden*,[103] the defendant sold a car to a rogue who paid by cheque which was later dishonoured. The rogue sold the car to the plaintiff finance company but kept possession of the car as he had induced the finance company to accept a hire-purchase proposal for the benefit of an accomplice. Subsequently, the defendant, with the consent of the rogue,

99 It has been argued that there was no delivery either actual or constructive in this case: the goods were always in the possession of the warehousemen, first as bailees for sellers and then in their own right, and there was nothing beyond the disposition itself to indicate any change in the nature of their possession: *Gamer's Motor Centre (Newcastle) Pty Ltd v. Natwest Wholesale Australia Pty Ltd* (1987) 163 C.L.R. 236 (H.C.). It has been further argued that a better explanation for the decision may be that although constructive delivery may suffice, there must be some voluntary act of delivery over and above the disposition: Bradgate, *Commercial Law* (London, Butterworths, 3rd ed., 2000) p.424.

100 (1987) 163 C.L.R. 236 (H.C.): approved in *The Saetta* [1994] 1 All E.R. 851; and *Michael Gerson (Leasing) Ltd v. Wilkinson* [2001] 1 All E.R. 148, where the Court of Appeal accepted that constructive delivery will suffice for the purposes of the seller in possession exception. See further Skelton, "Dispositions to Recipients in Good Faith" [1994] *Lloyd's Maritime and Commercial Law Quarterly* 19.

101 [1965] A.C. 867 (P.C.). See also *Mitchell v. Jones* (1905) 24 N.Z.L.R. 932.

102 *Worcester Works Finance Ltd v. Cooden* [1972] 1 Q.B. 210 (C.A.).

103 [1972] 1 Q.B. 210 (C.A.).

retook possession of the car. It was held that the defendant was protected against the plaintiff's claim. From the defendant's perspective, the rogue was a seller who remained in possession and the retaking by the defendant was a "disposition" by the rogue in that it amounted to a rescission of the contract between them, and it therefore revested property in the defendant.

A similar, wider provision in the Factors Act 1889 protects B2 even though he receives possession of the goods under an agreement for sale, pledge or other disposition.[104]

19.7.1.4 Good faith and without notice

Finally, and as with the previous exceptions, B2 will only take priority where he receives the goods in good faith and without notice of S's defect in title. The burden of proof under section 25 is on B2 to prove that he acted in good faith and without notice of S's rights.

19.7.2 The effect of section 25(1)

Where all the above requirements are satisfied, section 25 provides that the transfer to B2 has the same effect as if S were authorised by the owner of the goods, B1/O, to make it. S is thus treated as if he were B1's agent, and B1 is therefore bound by S's dealings with the goods. Where B2 buys the goods, and the requirements of section 25(1) are satisfied, B2 gets title to the goods, extinguishing B1's title. Where B2 takes the goods under "any other disposition," the nature of B2's interest will depend on the nature of the disposition. Where, for example, B2 takes the goods under a pledge, B1 will own the goods subject to the pledge. It appears that where B2 takes the goods under a conditional sale, as in a contract with a retention of title clause, B2 will acquire no title until the condition is fulfilled.[105]

19.8 Exception No.7 – Buyer in Possession[106]

Section 25(2) of the 1893 Act states:

> "Where a person having bought or agreed to buy goods obtains, with the consent of the seller, possession of the goods or the documents of title to the goods, the delivery or transfer by that person, or by a mercantile agent acting for him, of the goods or documents of title, under any sale pledge or other disposition thereof, to any person receiving the same in good faith and without notice of any lien, or other right of the original seller in respect

---

104 See also the Factors Act 1889, s.8.

105 *Re Highway Foods International Ltd*, [1995] B.C.C. 271; [1995] 1 B.C.L.C. 209.

106 See also the Factors Act 1889, s.9.

> of the goods, shall have the same effect as if the person making the delivery or transfer were a mercantile agent in possession of the goods or documents of title with the consent of the owner."

This provision covers the situation where a person who has agreed to buy goods (B1) takes possession of them before title passes to him and, by being in possession of the goods may appear to be the owner of the goods. If he resells or otherwise disposes of them before property passes to him, a title or priority dispute may then arise between S, the person who sold the goods to B1, and B2, the person to whom B1 transferred them.

S ⟶ B1 ⟶ B2

Section 25(2) may protect B2 in such a case. Provided that the requirements of the provision are fulfilled, the disposition by B1 has the same effect as if he were a mercantile agent in possession of the goods with the consent of their owner, allowing B2 to take priority over S.

Section 9 of the Factors Act 1889 is to the same effect as section 25(2) but is a little broader because it seeks to validate the transfer of property under any *agreement* to sell, pledge, or other disposition of the goods, as well as under an actual sale, pledge or other disposition. Both provisions are usually pleaded together, if possible.

19.8.1 Requirements for section 25(2)

There are a number of pre-requisites before section 25(2) will apply. They are:

(i) B1 must have bought or agreed to buy goods;
(ii) B1 must be in possession of the goods with the consent of S;
(iii) B1 must deliver or transfer the goods under any sale, pledge or other disposition; and
(iv) B2 must receive the goods in good faith and without notice.

19.8.1.1 Bought or agreed to buy

B1 must have bought or agreed to buy the goods. Section 25 only applies where B1 acquired possession of the goods under a sale or agreement for a sale; it thus applies in the common commercial situation where S sells goods to B1 subject to a reservation of title pending payment.[107] It does not apply where B1 acquired the goods under a hire purchase contract,[108] an

107 For example of conditional sale, see *Lee v. Butler* [1893] 2 Q.B. 318 (C.A.).

108 *Helby v. Matthews* [1895] A.C. 471; *cf. Lee v. Butler* [1893] 2 Q.B. 318 (C.A.).

agency agreement,[109] a sale or return agreement,[110] or a contract for work and materials,[111] although a person who acquires goods from B1 in any of these circumstances may acquire a good title to them by virtue of other exceptions to the *nemo dat* rule.

Section 25(2) also applies where B1 has bought goods under a contract which is voidable at the instance of S, and may protect B2 even though he acquires the goods after S has avoided B1's title.[112] Rescinding a voidable contract therefore does not guarantee that the dispossessed owner will be able to recover his property.

19.8.1.2 Possession with consent of seller

B1 must be in possession of the goods, or the documents of title to them, with the consent of S. So, a thief cannot pass good title under section 25(2). This is similar to the requirement of consent in section 2 of the Factors Act.[113] At the time of the disposition to B2, B1 must be in actual or constructive possession of the goods, or of documents of title to them. Provided that B1 acquired possession of the goods with S's consent, it is irrelevant that S withdraws consent prior to B1's disposition of them. Provided S has given actual consent to B1's possession, it is also irrelevant that B1 obtained his consent by deceiving him[114] But, it has been held that this exception to the *nemo dat* principle does not apply where the goods or documents of title to them were stolen from the owner.[115]

The notion of constructive possession and delivery has been recognised in this context. It has been held that where S, at the request of B1, himself delivers goods directly to B2, this is enough to bring B2 within the protection of section 25(2).[116] Accordingly, B1 is in constructive possession at the time of his direction to S and there is a constructive delivery from B1 to B2 that is sufficient for this provision to operate.

109 *Shaw v. MPC* [1987] 1 W.L.R. 1332; see further Thornely, "Thieves, Rogues, Innocent Purchasers, and Legislative Tangles" [1988] *Cambridge Law Journal* 15.

110 *Weiner v. Harris* [1910] 1 K.B. 285. In practice, it may not matter whether a person who takes goods on sale or return comes within s.25(2) of he 1893 Act and s.9 of the 1889 Act because if he sells or pledges the goods, he does an act adopting the transaction under section 18, rule 4 of the 1893 Act and the property passes to him and any sub-buyer or pledgee is hence protected: see 17.3.

111 *Dawber Williamason Roofing v. Humberside* CC (1979) 14 B.L.R. 70.

112 *Newtons of Wembley Ltd v. Williams* [1965] 1 Q.B. 560.

113 See 19.2.1.2.

114 In *Pearson v. Rose Young Ltd* [1951] 1 K.B. 275, the owner of a car was tricked by an agent into parting with the car and its registration book. It was held that consent obtained by fraud was still consent for these purposes.

115 *National Employers Mutual General Insurance Association Ltd v. Jones* [1990] 1 A.C. 24 (H.L.): see further 19.8.2.

116 *Four Point Garage Ltd v. Carter* [1985] 3 All E.R. 12.

19.8.1.3 Deliver or transfer under any sale, pledge or other disposition

B1, or a mercantile agent acting for him, must deliver or transfer the goods, or documents of title to them, to B2 under a sale, pledge or other disposition. This requirement is identical to that under section 25(1) above.[117] A similar, wider, provision in the Factors Act 1889 protects B2 even though he receives possession of the goods under an agreement for sale, pledge or other disposition.[118]

19.8.1.4 Good faith and without notice

Finally, and as with the previous exceptions, B2 must act in good faith and without notice of any rights of S. As noted above, the burden of proof under section 25 is on B2 to prove that he acted in good faith and without notice of S's rights.

19.8.2 The effect of section 25(2)

Where the requirements of section 25(2) are satisfied, the disposition by B1 to B2 has the same effect as if B1 "were a mercantile agent in possession of the goods with the consent of the owner." These words have been interpreted in Northern Ireland and England as requiring that B1 must act in the way in which a mercantile agent acting in the ordinary course of business would act in disposing of the goods.[119] In *RF Martin Ltd v. Duffy*,[120] the plaintiff sold equipment to the owner of a restaurant under a contract whereby title was to remain with the seller until the goods were paid for. Subsequently, the owner sold the entire restaurant, including the lease for it and the equipment, to the defendant. The plaintiff claimed that the defendant could have no title to the goods under section 25(2) because the goods had not been sold by the restaurant owner as a mercantile agent. This was also the finding of the court: the business had been sold as one lot, without a separate valuation for the goods in question. Hence the goods had not been sold in a way in which a mercantile agent acting in the ordinary course of business would act in disposing of the goods. So, for instance, where goods are sold in unusual circumstances, such as outside normal business hours, or at an unusual location, a court might find that

117 See 19.7.1.3.

118 Factors Act 1889, s.9. It was suggested in Benjamin's *Sale of Goods* (London, Sweet & Maxwell, 4th ed., 1992) 5-128 that a sub-purchaser when in possession under a sale with a reservation of title clause might be able to rely on the wider wording of s.9. However, in *Re Highway Foods International Ltd* [1995] B.C.C. 271; [1995] 1 B.C.L.C. 209 it was held that in such a situation the original seller could claim title to the goods. See now *Benjamin's Sale of Goods* (London, Sweet & Maxwell, 5th ed., 1997) 5-151.

119 *RF Martin Ltd v. Duffy* [1985] N.I. 417; and *Newtons of Wembley Ltd v. Williams* [1965] 1 Q.B. 560.

120 [1985] N.I. 417.

this is not in the ordinary course of business and so the exception would not apply. However, this seems to read into the statute a meaning which is not there, and it is not clear whether an Irish court would adopt such an interpretation. Indeed, the Australian courts have rejected such an interpretation.[121]

It has also been held in England that since a disposition by a mercantile agent is only binding on the owner of goods if the agent is in possession of them with the consent of the owner, section 25(2) only applies where B1 is in possession with the consent of the owner.[122] Thus if S steals goods from O and sells them to B1, a resale by B1 to B2, and any subsequent resales, are not within the provision, since B1, although in possession with the consent of his seller is not in possession with the consent of the owner. This difficulty is caused by the fact that section 25(2) refers to "the seller" (in line 2) and "the owner" (in the last line). The suggestion that these words be given their literal meaning, such that the seller and the owner may be two separate persons was rejected in *National Employers Mutual General Insurance Association Ltd v. Jones*.[123]

In *National Employers Mutual General Insurance Association Ltd v. Jones*, the plaintiff was the insurer of a car which had been stolen and resold five times, and ultimately found in the possession of the defendant, Jones. The plaintiff, as insurer, was subrogated to the rights of the owner,[124] and sought the return of the car from Jones.

Owner (Insurers) ➤ Thief ➤ B1 ➤ B2 ➤ B3 ➤ B4 ➤ Jones

Jones argued that he had title to the goods based on a literal reading of section 9 of the Factors Act 1889 and section 25 of the Sale of Goods Act 1979 (previously section 25(2) of the 1893 Act). Using section 25(2) as a model and inserting the relevant parties, the defendant argued that he received good title because:

> "Where a person [B4] having bought or agreed to buy goods obtains, with the consent of the seller [B3], possession of the goods …, the delivery or transfer by that person [B4], …, of the goods …, under any sale pledge or other disposition thereof, to any person [Jones] receiving the same in good faith and without notice…, shall have the same effect as if the person making the delivery or transfer [B4] were a mercantile agent in possession of the goods or documents of title with the consent of the owner."

121 *Gamer's Motor Centre (Newcastle) Pty Ltd v. Natwest Wholesale Australia Pty Ltd* (1987) 163 C.L.R. 236.

122 *National Employers Mutual General Insurance Association Ltd v. Jones* [1990] 1 A.C. 24 (H.L.); see further Thornely, "Thieves, Rogues, Innocent Purchasers, and Legislative Tangles" [1988] *Cambridge Law Journal* 15; Battersby, "The Sale of Stolen Goods: A Dilemma for the Law" (1991) 54 *Modern Law Review* 752.

123 [1990] 1 A.C. 24 (H.L.).

124 On doctrine of subrogation in insurance law, see 28.2.2.

This analysis seeks to identify the seller (in line 2) as B3 and the owner (in the last line) as the original owner/insurer. So, although a thief could not pass good title under section 25(1) because he had not "bought or agreed to buy goods", a sub-buyer from a thief could. The House of Lords unanimously rejected this literal interpretation. Based on an analysis of the legislative history and the policy underlying that history, it was held that section 25(2) only applies where the person [here B4] is in possession with the consent of *the owner*: an impossibility where the goods have been stolen from the owner. Surprisingly, this was the first time such an argument, based on a literal interpretation of the provisions, had been advanced in England. There is one New Zealand decision,[125] and one Canadian decision[126] also opposed to the literal interpretation. There is no Irish authority on the point.

Where B2 buys the goods, and the requirements of section 25(1) are satisfied, B2 gets title to the goods, extinguishing B1's title. Where B2 takes the goods under "any other disposition", the nature of B2's interest will depend on the nature of the disposition. Where, for example, B2 takes the goods under a pledge, B1 will own the goods subject to the pledge. It appears that where B2 takes the goods under a conditional sale, as in a contract with a retention of title clause, B2 will acquire no title until the condition is fulfilled.[127]

19.9 Exception No. 8 – Sales Under Special Powers of Sale or Orders of the Court

Section 21(2)(b) of the 1893 Act provides that nothing in the Act shall affect the validity of any contract of sale under any special common law or statutory power of sale or under the order of a court of competent jurisdiction. This provision speaks for itself. Such powers are numerous. Examples of special common law powers include a pledgee's right to sell goods pledged to him;[128] and an agent of necessity's power of sale.[129] Statutory powers include those of unpaid sellers of goods,[130] unpaid hoteliers,[131] landlords who have distrained upon their tenant's goods,[132]

125 *Elwin v. O'Regan and Maxwell* [1971] N.Z.L.R. 1124 (S.C.).

126 *Brandon v. Leckie* (1972) 29 D.L.R. (3d) 633, Alberta Supreme Court.

127 *Re Highway Foods International Ltd* [1995] B.C.C. 271; [1995] 1 B.C.L.C. 209.

128 *Re Hardwick* (1886) 17 Q.B.D. 690; see further 25.2.3.

129 See further 5.6.

130 See further 15.3.3.

131 See Hotel Proprietors Act 1963, s.8.

132 See Lyall, *Land Law in Ireland* (Dublin, Round Hall Sweet & Maxwell, 2nd ed., 2000) p.626; Wylie, *Landlord and Tenant Law* (Dublin, Butterworths, 2nd ed., 1998) para. 12.14–12.23; and Wylie, *Irish Land Law* (Dublin, Butterworths, 3rd ed., 1997) 17.064–17.066.

sheriffs and bailiffs who sell goods of debtors seized under writs or warrants of execution,[133] and those relating to pawns under the Pawnbrokers Act 1964.[134] A sale may also be made by an officer of the court, either under the court's inherent powers or on foot of a court order. For example, where parties are arguing over the ownership of perishable goods, to avoid the goods perishing and hence losing their value, a court may order the sale of the goods, leaving the parties to fight over the proceeds of sale.[135]

19.10 Reform

While the *nemo dat* principle itself is clear and simple to apply, the same cannot be said for the exceptions to it. There is no discernible policy linking the exceptions. There is considerable overlap between the exceptions, and it is clear from the above analysis that the law in this area is outdated, highly technical and in many regards in need of review. In Ireland, the law has remained unchanged since the Factors Act 1889 and the Sale of Goods Act 1893, while in England, there have been five occasions when reform of the law was proposed, but in only one case was a proposal implemented.

The one case where a reform proposal was implemented concerned the repeal of the market overt exception under the U.K. Sale of Goods (Amendment) Act 1994.[136] As noted above,[137] this exception is in need of immediate review in Ireland, but whether we follow the English precedent, and abolish the rule, or as has been suggested elsewhere,[138] we extend the principle to all sales from retail premises, any decision should not be made without first conducting the necessary empirical research, as indicated above.[139]

133 The common law procedure *fieri facias* is a method by which the sheriff or county registrar can seize a debtor's goods and have them sold, paying the proceeds to the judgment creditor, less the expenses of execution: see Dixon & Gilliland, *The Law Relating to Sheriffs in Ireland* (Dublin, 1888). The range of property subject to this procedure was extended by the Debtors (Ireland) Act 1840, s.20. However, under the Sale of Goods Act 1893, s.26(1) delivery to the sheriff of the *fieri facias* order shall not prejudice subsequent buyers in good faith for valuable consideration, unless they had notice of the *fieri facias* order. Hence the goods have to be actually seized by the sheriff to be bound by the order. See further R.S.C., Ord. 43; Forde, *Bankruptcy Law in Ireland* (Cork, Mercier Press, 1990) pp.14–17.

134 See the Pawnbrokers Act 1964, ss.29–31.

135 See Rules of the Superior Courts, Ord. 50, r.3.

136 See also D.T.I. Consultation Document, *Transfer of Title: Sections 21 to 26 of the Sale of Goods Act 1979* (1994).

137 See 19.5.

138 See the Twelfth Report of the Law Reform Committee, *Transfer of Title to Chattels*, Cmnd. 2958 (1966).

139 See 19.5.

The other suggestions for reform include the following. It has been suggested that it might be possible to apportion the loss which occurs when an innocent owner and an equally innocent bona fide purchaser are left in a conflict of title.[140] However, in 1966 the U.K. Law Reform Committee rejected this proposal pointing out that where there was a chain of transactions, the apportionment of such losses would be difficult.[141] The Law Reform Committee produced its own set of proposals the same year including a proposal to abolish the distinction between contracts void for mistake and voidable for fraud.[142] Accordingly, illogical distinctions based on cases like *Ingram v. Little*,[143] and *Lewis v. Averay*,[144] would be removed and in both cases the bona fide purchaser would be protected. This result is achieved by s.2-403 of the U.S. Uniform Commercial Code.

The Committee also recommended:

(a) the reversal of the decision in *Car and Universal Finance Co Ltd v. Caldwell*[145] thereby restating the old law and requiring communication before a voidable contract can be avoided;[146]

(b) the reversal of the decision in *Newtons of Wembley v. Williams*,[147] and that the legislation should be clarified such that a buyer in possession can pass good title without requiring him to act as a mercantile agent;[148] and

(c) in relation to section 23, the reversal of the burden of proof of bad faith and notice from the owner,[149] onto the innocent buyer, in keeping with the other exceptions.[150]

The Committee's set of proposals was rejected for fear that they would encourage dishonesty by facilitating the disposal of stolen goods.[151]

While each of these individual proposals is worthy of consideration,

140 *Ingram v. Little* [1961] 1 Q.B. 31 at 38 (C.A.) per Lord Devlin.

141 See Twelfth Report of the Law Reform Committee, *Transfer of Title to Chattels*, Cmnd. 2958 (1966).

142 See Twelfth Report of the Law Reform Committee, *Transfer of Title to Chattels*, Cmnd. 2958 (1966), para. 15.

143 [1961] 1 Q.B. 31 (C.A.).

144 [1972] 1 Q.B. 198 (C.A.).

145 [1965] 1 Q.B. 525 (C.A.); see 19.6.2.

146 Twelfth Report of the Law Reform Committee, *Transfer of Title to Chattels*, Cmnd. 2958 (1966), para. 16.

147 [1965] 1 Q.B. 560; see 19.8.2.

148 Twelfth Report of the Law Reform Committee, *Transfer of Title to Chattels*, Cmnd. 2958 (1966), para. 23.

149 *Whitehorn Bros v. Davison* [1911] 1 K.B. 463.

150 Twelfth Report of the Law Reform Committee, *Transfer of Title to Chattels*, Cmnd. 2958 (1966), para. 25.

151 For Professor Atiyah's criticisms of the Report see Atiyah, "Law Reform Committee: Twelfth Report" (1966) 29 *Modern Law Review* 541.

wider proposals for reform were made by Professor Diamond, inspired by the U.S. Uniform Commercial Code (U.C.C.).[152] The Diamond Review was primarily concerned with reform of the law relating to security interests over personal property. The review recommended that all security devices (including conditional sales and hire-purchase) should be treated alike, and that non-possessory securities should require registration. Professor Diamond stated that such reform would necessitate:

> "a clear statement of the rights of innocent purchasers of the goods subject to the security interest ... It would be an unacceptable hindrance to trade if buyers from dealers in such goods, whether at the manufacturing, wholesale or retail level, were expected to search the register of security interests."[153]

Amongst a set of proposals,[154] Professor Diamond recommended that there should be a general principle that applies wherever the owner of goods has entrusted goods to, or acquiesced in their possession to another person, so that any disposition of the goods by the possessor to an innocent purchaser would confer a good title on the purchaser.[155] This principle would only apply where the disposition was in the ordinary course of business and would not extend to a sale of consumer goods.[156] Such a broad principle would cover cases currently arising under sections 23 and 25 of the 1893 Act and many of the agency and apparent ownership cases. The advantage of such a wide sweeping reform is that it is based on a coherent policy and it avoids the detailed and over-technical rules which require courts to distinguish transactions which may have similar practical effects.

152 See Professor Diamond's *Review of Security Interests in Property* (London, H.M.S.O., 1989). The other reform proposal came in 1971, when the Crowther Committee on Consumer Credit recommended the removal of certain technical distinctions which the law draws between similar supply arrangements, such as conditional sales and hire-purchase, allowing the innocent purchaser the same protection in each case: Report of Crowther Committee on Consumer Credit, Cmnd. 4596 (1971).

153 Paras 13.5.1 and 13.5.2.

154 Professor Diamond also recommended that ss.8–9 of the Factors Act, largely duplicating section 25 of the 1893 Act should be repealed (para. 13.6.10), as should the decision in *Car and Universal Finance Co Ltd v. Caldwell* [1965] 1 Q.B. 525 (C.A.) (para. 13.6.6): see 19.6.2. He also proposed that recission of a voidable contract should have no effect on an innocent purchaser, who would be protected unless the dispossessed owner had repossessed the goods (para. 13.6.6).

155 Para. 13.6.3.

156 Para. 13.6.4. The Department of Trade and Industry (D.T.I.) followed up the Diamond proposals in 1994 when they sought views on their main proposal to replace the detailed exception in ss.21–25 of the Sale of Goods Act 1979 with a broad principle, similar to Professor Diamond's, that where the owner of goods has entrusted them to or acquiesced in their possession by another person, an innocent purchaser of the goods should acquire a good title to them which might be limited to dispositions in the ordinary course of business, or extend to all sales of consumer goods: see D.T.I. Consultation Document, *Transfer of Title: Sections 21 to 26 of the Sale of Goods Act 1979* (1994).

Nevertheless, the lack of empirical research makes it very difficult to justify any proposals for change of a fundamental character.[157] In particular, one question which is vital to address is the likelihood of the original owner of lost or stolen goods being protected by an insurance policy. Where this is the case, there seems good reason to give greater protection to bona fide purchasers than at present.

157 See Atiyah, "Law Reform Committee: Twelfth Report" (1966) 29 *Modern Law Review* 541.

CHAPTER 20

CONTRACTS FOR THE SUPPLY OF SERVICES

20.1 INTRODUCTION

Contracts for the sale of goods have traditionally been considered the backbone of commercial activity and indeed continue to remain so. More recently, contracts for the supply of services have increased in prominence, though many services are provided in the course of other commercial transactions. Agency contracts,[1] carriage contracts,[2] and warehousing contracts, are all contracts for the supply of services that are often ancillary to commercial sale of goods contracts, for example. Contracts for services cover a wide range of activities from contracts for professional services (such as contracts for the services of engineers, medics, and solicitors) to contracts for leisure services (such as contracts for the provision of holidays, hotel accommodation and entertainment). Construction and related contracts are also important types of service contract. More everyday contracts for the supply of services include contracts for the servicing and repair of domestic appliances and motor vehicles, and contracts for the dry-cleaning of clothes. A major growth area involves contracts for the supply of financial services.[3] Another more recent development involves the growing provision of such services at a distance, using electronic means such as the internet.[4]

As with all contracts, the starting point for examining the rights and obligations of the parties is the express terms of the contract. Some services contracts are standard form contracts promoted by the various

---

1 See generally Part II.

2 On carriage of goods by sea contracts, see Chapter 31.

3 For instance, London is well established internationally as a centre for the provision of financial services: see further Clarke, *How the City of London Works* (London, Sweet & Maxwell, 4th ed., 1995). More recently, other cities have sought to establish themselves as centres for financial services. Note the establishment of the International Financial Services Center (I.F.S.C.) in Dublin, as such an example.

4 See Directive 2000/31 on certain aspects of information society services, in particular electronic commerce, in the Internal Market [2000] O.J. L178/1. The main objective of the Directive is to ensure the free movement of information society services between member states. See further the Electronic Commerce Act 2000. See also the European Communities (Protection of Consumers in respect of Contracts made by means of Distance Communications) Regulations 2001 S.I. No. 207 of 2001, implementing Council Directive 97/7: [1997] O.J. L144/19. See further Directive 2002/65 concerning the distance marketing of consumer financial services [2002] O.J. L271/16.

professional bodies.[5] In relation to construction contracts, for instance, a significant body of case law exists to define the obligations of the parties.[6] Beyond the express terms of the contract, certain terms may be implied at common law. For example, in agency contracts where it is agreed that an agent should be paid, but the amount of remuneration is not expressly agreed between the parties, it is implied that a reasonable sum will be payable.[7] Moreover, Part IV of the Sale of Goods and Supply of Services Act 1980 implies a set of four terms, related to the quality of service, into every contract for the supply of services where the supplier is acting in the course of a business.[8] This legislation also deals with the exclusion of liability for breach of these statutory implied terms.[9]

While sale of goods legislation has provided a relatively detailed code since 1893, contracts for the supply of services were regulated by the common law only until the 1980 Act. Part IV of the 1980 Act was intended to codify the existing common law regarding the quality of services supplied,[10] and to bolster the protection of recipients of services by regulating the use of exclusion clauses. It is not as comprehensive a code as the Sale of Goods Acts 1893–1980 though, with only four sections in it. On the one hand, this legislation can be viewed as flexible: terms such as reasonable care and merchantable quality leave a discretion to courts to determine, on the facts of any particular case, whether there has been a breach of contract. On the other hand, the implied terms as to quality may have the effect of focusing the mind of the supplier of services on the minimum standards required by law, and may strengthen the position of the recipients of services, in particular, consumers, when confronted with a dispute over the quality of services provided. Lastly, in particular areas, there may be further regulating legislation and rules such as the Solicitors Acts 1954–1994, as amended, or the Investment Intermediary Act 1995, or the Irish Bankers' Federation Code of Ethics and Practice.[11] These more specific forms of regulation are beyond the scope of this work. In this chapter, we examine the provisions of Part IV of the Sale of Goods and Supply of Services Act 1980.

5 With regard to building and construction services, a variety of standard form contracts are promoted by the R.I.A.I. (Royal Institute of Architects of Ireland); the C.I.F. (Construction Industry Federation); and the Law Society of Ireland, for example.

6 See, *e.g. Chitty on Contracts*, Vol. 2 (London, Sweet & Maxwell, 28th ed., 1999) Chapter 37.

7 *Henehan v. Courtney* (1967) 101 I.L.T.R. 25: see generally 2.3.4 and 7.5.1.1.

8 1980 Act, s.39; see 21.3.

9 1980 Act, ss.40–41; see 21.4. Sections 39 and 40 are made mandatory in application by s.42 of the 1980 Act, which deals with conflict of laws issues. See similarly, 1893 Act, s.55A regarding sale of goods contracts.

10 See, *e.g. Brown v. Norton* [1954] I.R. 34 at 56, where it was stated that when there is an agreement to purchase a dwellinghouse in the course of construction the work which remains to be done "will be carried-out in a good and workmanlike manner and with sound and suitable materials."

11 See generally www.ibf.ie.

20.2 Application of Part IV of the 1980 Act[12]

It is important to understand the circumstances in which Part IV of the 1980 Act applies. There are two prerequisites: first, the contract must be classified as a contract for the supply of a service; and second, the supplier must be acting in the course of a business.

A contract for the supply of a service is not defined in the legislation but may be taken to include the following:

(i) a simple supply of services contract, such as a consultation with a solicitor,[13] the application of hair dye,[14] or the administration of medicine by a veterinary surgeon;[15] and

(ii) a contract for work and materials, as where a printer prints a book,[16] or where a mechanic repairs a car;[17] and

(iii) a contract for the supply of services which involves the supply of a finished item or goods.[18]

The lack of a statutory definition can lead to uncertainty. For example, in *Carroll v. An Post National Lottery*,[19] a Lotto agent, authorised by the defendant to sell Lottery tickets, incorrectly entered the numbers selected by the plaintiff, a player in one of the National Lottery games. As a result, the plaintiff failed to win approximately a quarter of a million pounds. The plaintiff argued, *inter alia*, that the supply of the lottery ticket by the defendant was a contract for the supply of a service, and that the defendant

12 On distinguishing sale of goods and supply of services contracts, see 9.3.6.

13 A contract for professional services, such as with a solicitor or an accountant is usually a contract for services though documents may be passed to the client and become his property: *Lee v. Griffin* (1861) 1 B. & S. 272, *per* Blackburn J.

14 *Watson v. Buckley, Osborne & Garrett* [1940] 1 All E.R. 174.

15 *Dodd & Dodd v. Wilson & McWilliam* [1946] 2 All E.R. 691.

16 In *Clay v. Yates* (1856) 1 H. & N. 73, a contract for a printer to print a book, the printer to supply the paper and ink was held to be a contract for work and materials. In *Robinson v. Graves* [1935] 1 K.B. 579, a contract for a painter to paint a picture was found to be a contract for work and materials but in the same case, the court also said that a contract for a sculptor to produce a statue might be sale of finished product.

17 In *Stewart v. Reavells Garage* [1952] 2 Q.B. 545, a contract to repair the braking system of a car whereby the garage supplied new lining for the brake drums was found to be a contract for work done and materials supplied.

18 In *Hyundai v. Papadopoulos* [1980] 2 All E.R. 29, it was held that a contract to build a ship and supply it was a sale but not a pure sale because it had elements of a building (i.e. service) contract. Accordingly, if the process of manufacture forms part of the contract, the contract can be divided into two sub-contracts: (1) a contract whereby the supplier is to construct the ship – a service contract; and (2) a contract whereby the seller agrees to supply the finished ship – a sale of goods contract. *Cf. Cammell Laird v. Manganese Bronze* [1934] A.C. 402 where the "buyer" provided the design and the "seller" built a ship's propeller, was found to be a contract of sale.

19 [1996] 1 I.R. 433.

failed to supply the service with due skill, care and diligence, and hence there was a breach of section 39 of the 1980 Act.[20] The High Court held that the contract between the plaintiff and the defendant was a contract to sell a lottery ticket which confers rights and obligations on the parties, but was not a contract for the supply of a service. Accordingly, the provisions of the 1980 Act had no application. This decision has been criticised for its narrow interpretation of a service contract,[21] but the decision would appear to be correct, though the reasons for this decision are not clearly stated. A contract to purchase a lottery ticket cannot be easily classified as one of the nominate contracts which exist, such as a contract for the sale of goods, or supply of services. Instead it is more like a "hybrid" with characteristics of more than one type of nominate contract.[22] For instance, it would share some features of a sale of goods contract in that there would be a claim for non-delivery if the buyer paid and received no ticket. Further, there would be implied terms that the seller had the right to sell the ticket, and that the ticket was "fit for purpose", though these terms would not arise under the Sale of Goods Acts 1893 and 1980 but at common law. The situation under which the lottery ticket was sold in the *Carroll* case did involve some aspect of a service being provided to the player, in that, under the "rules of the game" the Lotto agent was deemed to be acting on behalf of the player when entering the numbers into the National Lottery computer. Hence, the Lotto agent was the player's agent, for those purposes, and like any agent, was providing a service. It could be argued that because the player provided no consideration to the Lotto agent in return for this service, the service was provided gratuitously, and hence Part IV of the 1980 has no application: there must be a *contract* for the supply of a service for Part IV to apply. On the other hand, it could be argued that the consideration provided by the player to a third party, here the National Lottery, is sufficient consideration for the supply of services, following the English case of *New Zealand Shipping v. Satterthwaite*.[23] But in both cases the agency relationship would be between the plaintiff and the Lotto agent, and not the defendant. Either way, the judge was correct to identify that the contract with the defendant was not a contract for a service, but a sale of a lottery ticket which gave rise to rights and obligations between the parties. This type of contract is probably best described as *sui generis*.

The legislation expressly excludes from the application of Part IV meteorological or aviation services provided by the relevant Minister and anything done under a contract of service, such as an employment or apprenticeship contract.[24] Further, the legislation provides that reference to

20 See further 20.3.

21 Clark, *Contract Law in Ireland* (Dublin, Round Hall Sweet & Maxwell, 4th ed., 1998) p.181.

22 See, *e.g. Hyundai v. Papadopoulos* [1980] 2 All E.R. 29.

23 [1975] A.C. 154.

24 1980 Act, s.2.

the supply of services includes reference to the rendering or provision of a service or facility and to offer to supply.[25]

As with certain provisions under the sales legislation,[26] Part IV of the 1980 Act only applies where the supplier is acting "in the course of a business". Hence this legislation has no application to the supply of services in a non-business or private context. The status of the recipient of the service is irrelevant for these purposes: he may be a business or a private recipient. This phrase is not defined in the legislation,[27] but it was interpreted recently, for the first time, in the context of a sale of goods contract by the Court of Appeal in *Stevenson v. Rogers*.[28] It is reasonable to assume that this phrase would carry the same meaning whether in a sale of goods or a supply of services context. In that case, the defendant, a fisherman, sold his only boat, the *Jelle*, to another fisherman, and replaced it with another boat. The court was asked to rule, as a preliminary issue, whether the sale of the *Jelle* was "in the course of a business" and so whether the merchantability quality provision applied. Having examined the legislative history of the phrase and the relevant case law, the court opted for a broad interpretation of the phrase and found that the sale was "in the course of a business".[29] This broad interpretation is in line with the interpretation of an identical phrase used in the different context of the regulation of exclusion clauses in the Irish cases of *Re Henry O'Callaghan v. Hamilton Leasing (Ireland) Ltd and Access Refrigeration and Shop Fitting Ltd,*[30] and *Cunningham v. Woodchester Investments and Inter-call Ltd*.[31] Accordingly, services may be provided *in the course of a business* even where the business is not normally involved in providing services of that type. So, for example, where a hardware retailer, whose main business is selling hardware, also provides DIY advice under a contract, it is

25 1980 Act, s.2.

26 Principally, the 1893 Act, s.14.

27 "Business" is defined as including any profession and the activities of any state or local authority: 1980 Act, s.2(1).

28 [1999] 1 All E.R. 613. See further de Lacy, "Selling in the Course of a Business under the Sale of Goods Act 1979" [1999] *Modern Law Review*, 776; Sealy, "When is a sale made 'in the course of a business'?" [1999] *Cambridge Law Journal* 176; Brown, "Sales of Goods in the Course of a Business" [1999] *Law Quarterly Review*, 384.

29 *Cf.* the narrow interpretation of the same phrase but in a different context in *Davies v. Sumner* [1984] 3 All E.R. 831, where the House of Lords held that a courier who sold the car he used in his business was not selling the car in the course of a business for the purposes of the U.K. Trade Descriptions Act; and in *R & B Customs Brokers Ltd v. United Dominions Trust Co.* [1988] 1 All E.R. 847, a case decided under the U.K. Unfair Contract Terms Act 1977, where the Court of Appeal held that a freight forwarding company which bought three cars over a period of five years was not acting in the course of a business when buying the cars. Both these cases can be distinguished from *Stevenson v. Rogers*: the former case concerned a criminal prosecution where the norm is to interpret such statutes restrictively; and the latter case involved determining whether the "buyer" was dealing as a consumer.

30 [1984] I.L.R.M. 146.

31 Unreported, High Court, McWilliam J., November 16, 1984; see 10.5.2.1.

arguable, following *Stevenson v. Rogers*, that the supply of DIY advice would be provided in the course of a business and the implied terms in section 39 would place further duties on the retailer than already exist under the contract and at common law.

While the statutory implied terms only apply where the supplier is acting in the course of a business, it may be that similar terms would be implied at common law where the supplier of the service is not acting in the course of a business, though the quality of service required may be lower when it is provided in a non-business context. Nevertheless, it has been held that even a gratuitous supplier of services is subject to a duty of care in negligence requiring him to exercise reasonable skill and care.[32]

Lastly, it should be noted that for Part IV of the 1980 Act to apply, there must be a contract. Under the Sale of Goods Acts 1893 and 1980, the consideration for the goods must be a money consideration but there is no similar requirement under Part IV of the 1980 Act for contracts for the supply of services. Hence the consideration for the service provided can be in any form – money, other services or otherwise – provided that it is sufficient.[33]

20.3 Implied Terms as to Quality

Section 39 of the 1980 Act implies four terms into every contract for the supply of services where the supplier is acting in the course of a business. They are:

(a) that the supplier has the necessary skill to render the service;
(b) that he will supply the service with due skill, care and diligence;
(c) that, where materials are used, they will be sound and reasonably fit for the purpose for which they are required; and
(d) that, where goods are supplied, they will be of merchantable quality.

Significantly, section 39 implies "terms" into the service contract, not conditions or warranties, as is the case with the sales legislation.[34] Accordingly, these terms are what can be described as "innominate terms".[35] An innominate term is a sort of hybrid of a condition and a

32 *Chaudhry v. Prabhakar* [1988] 3 All E.R. 718 (C.A.).

33 See 2.2.2.3.

34 See 10.4.

35 *Hong Kong Fir Shipping Co. Ltd v. Kawasaki Kisen Kaisha Ltd* [1962] 2 Q.B. 26. It is generally accepted that three classifications of term exist – condition, warranty and innominate term: See, *e.g.* *Chitty on Contracts*, Vol. 2 (London, Sweet & Maxwell, 28th ed., 1999) 12-020 and 12-034–12-040. But this view is not universally accepted: see, *e.g.* Treitel, *The Law of Contract* (London, Sweet & Maxwell, 10th ed., 1999) pp.738–743.

warranty, the effect of the breach of which depends on the seriousness of the breach. Only where the breach of such a term deprives the party not in default of substantially the whole benefit of the contract will the innocent party be able to repudiate the contract, otherwise his remedies are limited to a claim for damages. The existence of the classification of innominate term allows a court greater flexibility in determining the appropriate remedy following a breach of contract but brings with it uncertainty as to the party's rights and liabilities. In *Irish Telephone Rentals v. ICS Building Society*,[36] this classification of innominate term was recognised in relation to supply of service contracts. There, the court found a breach of section 39 of the 1980 Act, and, applying the reasoning of the *Hong Kong Fir* case,[37] the court held that the breach was such as to allow the defendant to terminate the contract.

The four terms arise automatically and, unlike the express terms of the contract, have the advantage that they do not need to be proved in evidence. Moreover, these four terms are cumulative and a dissatisfied recipient of a service may argue that any one or more of these terms have been breached. Case law on the exact meaning of these separate provisions is minimal and hence the following analysis includes references to common law authorities and English case law under the Supply of Goods and Services Act 1982 where similar provisions apply.

20.3.1 Necessary skill

The first term requires that the supplier of the service has the necessary skill to render the service. This may involve ensuring that the supplier is properly trained and educated. Because the legislation provides that reference to the supply of services includes reference to offer to supply,[38] where a supplier offers services and he does not have the necessary skill to provide the service, there may be a breach of section 39, though no service has actually been provided.

20.3.2 Due skill, care and diligence

The second implied term requires that the supplier supply the service with due skill, care and diligence. Where the supplier fails to exercise due skill, care and diligence, he will be liable for all proximate losses caused by the breach of contract.[39] This requirement means that liability under section 39(b) of the 1980 Act is equivalent to the common law negligence standard

36 [1991] I.L.R.M. 880; see 21.3.4. See further *Laird Bros v. Dublin Steampacket* (1900) 34 I.L.T.R. 9; and *Taylor v. Smyth* [1990] I.L.R.M. 377.

37 *Hong Kong Fir Shipping Co Ltd v. Kawasaki Kisen Kaisha Ltd* [1962] 2 Q.B. 26.

38 1980 Act, s.2.

39 See 2.4.2.2.

and hence fault must be proved. This compares with the strict liability standard under the sale of goods legislation. From a plaintiff's perspective, strict liability is to be preferred to fault-based liability. With the burden of proof on the plaintiff, proving negligence can be onerous and expensive.

What constitutes due skill, care and diligence will depend on the facts of the case and the standards of reasonable conduct prevailing at the time. In general, the supplier is expected to exercise "the ordinary skill of an ordinary competent man exercising that particular art."[40] Where a supplier of a service claims any particular skill, expertise or specialism, that claim may raise the standard of care expected of the service provider.[41]

There are various authorities illustrating what is reasonable in a particular trade or profession, in particular circumstances. For example, carpet-layers have been held to be in breach of contract where they left the carpet in such a condition that it constituted a danger to anyone using the premises.[42] In contrast, in another case, carpet-layers were found not to be in breach of contract where they failed to lay a carpet such that the pattern on the carpet was centralised.[43] Again, for example, it has been held that the general duty owed by a solicitor to his client is to show him the degree of care to be expected in the circumstances from a reasonably careful and skilful solicitor.[44] Usually a solicitor will meet this standard if he follows a common practice among the members of his profession,[45] but where the common practice has inherent defects, which ought to be obvious to any person giving the matter due consideration, the fact that the practice is shown to have been widely and generally adopted does not make the practice any the less negligent.[46] Hence, a solicitor was found in breach when he failed to discover a mortgage on a property, being bought by his client, because he failed to make the appropriate pre-contract searches in the Companies Office.[47] Exceptionally, professional standards may be higher than the law requires. In *United Mills Agencies Ltd v. Bray & Co*,[48] it was recognised that it was common practice within the insurance broker's profession to issue cover notes as soon as possible after insurance cover was obtained. However, the court held that there was no legal duty on the defendant broker to issue a cover note. Further, it has been held that an insurance broker owes his client a duty to ensure that the necessary

40 *Bolam v. Friern Hospital Management Committee* [1957] 2 All E.R. 118 per McNair J. at 121.

41 *Duchess of Argyll v. Beuselinck* [1972] 2 Lloyd's Rep. 173.

42 *Kimber v. William Willett Ltd* [1947] K.B. 570; [1947] 1 All E.R. 361 (C.A.).

43 *C.R.C. Flooring Ltd v. Heaton* unreported, Court of Appeal, October 8, 1980; see Lawson, "The Quality of Services Supplied: Guidance from the Court of Appeal" [1984] *New Law Journal* 39.

44 *Roche v. Peilow* [1986] I.L.R.M. 189 (S.C.) per Henchy J. at 196–7.

45 *Daniels v. Heskin* [1954] I.R. 73.

46 *O'Donovan v. Cork County Council* [1967] I.R. 173 at 193.

47 *Roche v. Peilow* [1986] I.L.R.M. 189 (S.C.).

48 [1951] 2 Lloyd's Rep. 631; followed in *Curtis t/a Agencies Transport Ltd v. Corcoran Insurances Ltd* unreported, High Court, Pringle J., July 13, 1973.

information is furnished to the insurers so as to protect the interests of his client. Hence, a broker was found to be in breach of contract with his client when he advised the client not to disclose certain information and the insurance company subsequently repudiated the insurance contract for non-disclosure.[49]

There are a number of cases dealing with the contractual duty of tour operators and travel agents.[50] For instance, it has been held that a tour operator discharged its duty of care under section 13 of the U.K. Supply of Goods and Services Act 1982, which implies a similar reasonable skill and care requirement as Part IV of the 1980 Act, if the tour operator checked that local safety standards were complied with. The duty did not extend to excluding from the accommodation offered in its brochure hotels whose safety standards were below U.K. standards, provided that these lack of standards were not such that a reasonable holiday-maker would decline to go there.[51] In *McKenna v. Best Travel and ors*,[52] the plaintiff argued, *inter alia*, that the defendants, a tour operator and a travel agent, were in breach of section 39 of the 1980 Act. The plaintiff purchased a holiday in Cyprus through the second defendant and organised by the first defendant. An "add-on mini-cruise", which included a trip to Bethlehem, was advertised in the brochure but could only be purchased in Cyprus from a representative of the first defendant. While visiting Bethlehem, a stone was thrown at the bus in which the plaintiff was travelling and she sustained physical injuries. The plaintiff argued that there was a breach of contract in that she had received no warning as to the possible danger inherent in travelling to certain parts of Israel. Lavan J., in the High Court, found that, as regards the duty to exercise due skill, care and diligence, the routes were checked daily and no warning had been issued for the route on the morning in question. The fact that nothing like this had ever happened before seemed to indicate that the defendants had exercised the due care required. For these reasons, the defendants were held not to have breached the implied terms under the Act.[53]

Where the service involves the provision of advice, it may be difficult

---

49 *Chariot Inns Ltd v. Assicurazioni Generali SPA et al* [1981] I.R. 199 (S.C.).

50 See also the Package Holidays and Travel Trade Act 1995 implementing EC Directive 90/314 [1990] O.J. L158/59. See further Grant & Urbanowicz, "Tour operators, package holiday contracts and strict liability" [2001] *Journal of Business Law* 253.

51 *Wilson v. Best Travel* [1993] 1 All E.R. 353 (H.C.).

52 Unreported, High Court, Lavan J., December 17, 1996; [1998] 3 I.R. 57 (S.C.).

53 In the High Court, the defendants were held liable based on negligence in tort law; this decision was reversed by the Supreme Court. Barron J. stated: "The defendants in this case were not insurers that nothing would happen to injure the plaintiff. Their obligation stops at taking all reasonable steps to ensure the safety and well-being of their customers." [1998] 3 I.R. 57 at 60.

to establish liability, especially if the advice is speculative in nature.[54] In *Luxmore-May v. Messenger May Baverstock*,[55] auctioneers were retained to research two paintings for a client who intended to sell them. The auctioneers consulted Christie's, but failed to attribute the paintings to Stubbs. As a result, the paintings were sold for less than one hundredth of the price they fetched when sold five months later when attributed to Stubbs. The auctioneers were not found liable because the valuation of paintings by unknown artists "pre-eminently involves an exercise of opinion and judgment … it is not an exact science."[56] In *Stafford v. Conti Commodity Services Ltd*,[57] a similar finding was reached in relation to a broker's advice on a commodity futures market.

The supplier of a service does not normally promise that the service will be fit for any particular purpose or achieve a particular result.[58] However, a supplier may expressly undertake to achieve a particular result, or it may be possible to imply such a term in a case. In *Greaves & Co Contractors Ltd v. Baynham, Meikle & Partners*,[59] contractors were engaged by an oil company to build a warehouse to store barrels of oil and they sub-contracted the design of the building, including the floors, to a firm of structural engineers. The engineers were informed that stacker trucks carrying barrels of oil would be running over the floor. After the warehouse opened, cracks started to appear in the floor, caused by the weight and vibrations of the trucks. On the facts of the case, it was held that there was an implied term that if the work was completed in accordance with the design, the floor would be reasonably fit for use by loader stacker trucks. Indeed, in a construction or similar contract, it may be that a term that the finished product will achieve its purpose will generally be implied at common law.[60]

54 For example "the valuation of land by trained, competent and careful professional men is a task which rarely, if ever, admits of a precise conclusion. Often beyond certain well-founded facts so many imponderables confront the valuer that he is obliged to proceed on the basis of assumptions. Therefore he cannot be faulted for achieving a result which does not admit some degree of error." Per Watkins J. in *Singer and Friedlander Ltd v. John D Wood & Co* (1977) 243 *Estates Gazette* 212 at 213.

55 [1990] 1 All E.R. 1067, [1990] 1 W.L.R. 1009 (C.A.).

56 [1990] 1 All E.R. 1067, per Slade L.J. at 1076.

57 [1981] 1 All E.R. 691.

58 "The law does not usually imply a warranty that he will achieve the desired result, but only a term that he will use reasonable care and skill. The surgeon does not warrant that he will cure the patient. Nor does the solicitor warrant that he will win the case." Per Lord Denning M.R. in *Greaves & Co Contractors Ltd v. Baynham, Meikle & Partners* [1975] 3 All E.R. 99 at 103 (C.A.).

59 [1975] 3 All E.R. 99 at 103 (C.A.).

60 *IBA v. BICC Construction Ltd* (1980) 14 B.L.R. 9 (H.L.).

20.3.2.1 Liability in contract and tort

The standard imposed by Part IV of the 1980 Act is the same as that imposed in the tort of negligence. Hence, the same act may give rise to liability in both contract and tort. This may have advantages for the recipient of the service, because although the limitation period in contract and tort is six years, the limitation period in contract law runs from the date of the breach whereas the limitation period in tort runs from the date of the damage.[61]

There are two views on the issue of concurrent liability in contract and tort. One view prefers to leave the rights and duties of parties who are in contractual relations to be governed by the terms of the contract, and opposes the imposition of any further tortious duty. For instance, in *Tai Hing Cotton Mill Ltd v. Liu Chong Hing Bank Ltd*,[62] Lord Scarman stated:[63]

> "Their Lordships do not believe that there is anything to the advantage of the law's development in searching for liability in tort where parties are in contractual relationships. This is particularly so in a commercial relationship."

A second view is that where the requirements of a tortious duty of care are satisfied, such a duty should be imposed even where the parties are in contractual relations. There is strong support for this second view in Ireland and in England,[64] though the position is far from resolved.[65]

In *Finlay v. Murtagh*,[66] a case concerning an action against a solicitor for not prosecuting a claim within the period allowed by the Statute of Limitations, the question was raised whether the action was based in contract or tort. Henchy J. (with whom O'Higgins C.J. and Parke J. agreed) stated:[67]

> "… It is undeniable that the client is entitled to sue in contract for breach … But it does not follow that, because there is privity of contract between them, and because the client may sue the solicitor for breach of contract,

---

61 Statute of Limitations Act 1957, s.11(1) as amended by Statute of Limitation (Amendment) Act 1991, s.3(2); see also *O'Donnell v. Kilsaran Concrete Ltd* [2002] 1 I.L.R.M. 551. See further Brady & Kerr, *The Limitation of Actions* (Dublin, Incorporated Law Society of Ireland, 2nd ed., 1994).

62 [1986] A.C. 80 (P.C.).

63 [1986] A.C. 80 at 107.

64 *Henderson v. Merrett Syndicates Ltd* [1995] 2 A.C. 145, [1994] 3 All E.R. 506 (H.L.); see further below.

65 See McMahon & Binchy, *Law of Torts* (Dublin, Butterworths, 3rd ed., 2000) 1.109–1.116 and 10.16–10.49.

66 [1979] I.R. 249. See also *Wall v. Hegarty* [1980] I.L.R.M. 124 9 (H.C.); *Chariot Inns Ltd v. Assicurazioni Generali SPA et al* [1981] I.R. 199 (S.C.); and *Roche v. Peilow* [1985] I.R. 232 (S.C.). *Cf. Madden v. Irish Turf Club* [1997] 2 I.L.R.M. 148 where the plaintiff's contract with the defendant was said to erect "a barrier so as to prevent such close and direct relations to occur as is necessary to give rise to a duty of care between the plaintiff and the defendants" per O'Flaherty J. at 155.

67 [1979] I.R. 249 at 256.

> that he is debarred from suing also for the tort of negligence. … The coincidence that the solicitor's conduct amounts to a breach of contract cannot affect either the duty of care or the common law liability for its breach …"

In the more recent English case of *Henderson v. Merrett Syndicates Ltd*,[68] it was held that managing agents (and hence suppliers of a service) acting for "names" in the Lloyd's insurance market owed both a tortious and a contractual duty of care to the names for whom they acted. The names were free to pursue their claims either in contract or in tort, taking whatever procedural advantages. Hamilton C.J., in the Irish Supreme Court, in *Kennedy v. AIB Ltd*,[69] approved *Henderson v. Merrett* and stated:[70]

> "… where a duty of care exists, whether such duty is tortious or created by contract, the claimant is entitled to take advantage of the remedy which is most advantageous to him subject only to ascertaining whether the tortious duty is so inconsistent with the applicable contract that, in accordance with ordinary principle the parties must be taken to have agreed that the tortious remedy is to be limited or excluded."

However, Hamilton C.J.'s approval of *Henderson v. Merrett* is undermined by the fact that he then quotes an arguably inconsistent proposition of law from an earlier Court of Appeal decision[71] and states:

> "The cases clearly establish that when parties are in a contractual relationship their mutual obligations arise from their contract and are to be found expressly or by necessary implication in the terms thereof and that obligations in tort which may arise from such a contractual relationship cannot be greater than those to be found expressly or by necessary implication in the contract."[72]

Two separate issues need to be identified in relation to concurrent liability in contract and tort. First, it is clear that there can be concurrent liability enabling a plaintiff to take any procedural advantages which may be

68 [1995] 2 A.C. 145, [1994] 3 All E.R. 506 (H.L.). Lord Goff of Chieveley in the course of his speech in *Henderson v. Merrett* distinguished *Tai Hing Cotton Mill Ltd v. Liu Chong Hing Bank Ltd* when he stated at p.526: "the issue in Tai Hing was whether a tortious duty of care could be established which was more extensive than that which was provided for under the relevant contract".

69 [1998] 2 I.R. 48 (O'Flaherty and Denham JJ. concurring). See also *Tulsk Co-operative Livestock Mart Ltd v. Ulster Bank Ltd* unreported, High Court, Gannon, J., May 13, 1983.

70 At p.56: approved in *Pat O'Donnell & Co Ltd v. Truck Machinery Sales Ltd* [1998] 4 I.R. 191 (S.C.); [1997] 1 I.L.R.M. 466 (H.C.).

71 *National Bank of Greece SA v. Pinios Shipping Co* (No3) [1988] 2 Lloyd's Rep. 126 where Lloyd L.J. stated: "But so far as I know it has never been the law that a plaintiff who has the choice of suing in contract or tort can fail in contract yet nevertheless succeed in tort."

72 [1998] 2 I.R. 48 at 56.

available. The second issue is the extent to which contractual and tortious liability coincide. It seems clear, from Hamilton C.J.'s first statement above, that through the use of contractual provisions the tortious duty of care can be limited or excluded. Further, based on Hamilton C.J.'s second statement above, it seems clear that a defendant's tortious liability can never exceed his contractual liability. The difficulty with these propositions of law is that they are based on two conflicting authorities. Further consideration by the Supreme Court is needed to clarify this important issue.

20.3.2.2 Sub-contracting

A person who has contracted to supply a service may use third-party sub-contractors to fulfill his obligations under the main contract.

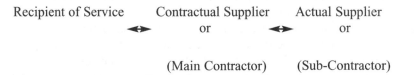

Recipient of Service ↔ Contractual Supplier or (Main Contractor) ↔ Actual Supplier or (Sub-Contractor)

Such an arrangement is often anticipated in the main contract and is the norm in construction contracts and package holiday contracts, for instance. If the service performed does not reach the required standard of care, it may be necessary to consider the liability of the contractual supplier (the main contractor) and the actual supplier (the sub-contractor).

With regard to the liability of the sub-contractor, if he is negligent he may be liable to the recipient of the service in the tort of negligence. Moreover, if the main contractor was acting as an agent for the recipient of the service when arranging the sub-contract, there may be a direct contractual link between the recipient and the sub-contractor, under which the sub-contractor will owe a contractual duty of care.

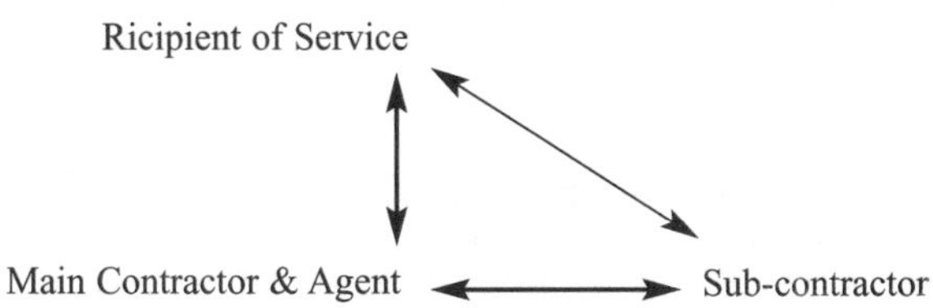

With regard to the liability of the main contractor, it will be necessary to determine whether the main contractor's undertaking was one to perform the service or merely one to act as the recipient's agent and arrange for others to perform the service (see diagrams above). Which it is depends on the proper construction of the contract. If it is the latter, the main contractor's only obligation is, as agent, to exercise reasonable care when selecting sub-contractors.[73] Where, however, the main contractor's obligation is to perform the service, the main contractor undertakes that the service will be performed with due care, skill and diligence, so that if the sub-contractors perform negligently, the main contractor will be personally liable for any losses suffered by the recipient of the service.[74]

20.3.3 Materials will be sound and fit

Section 39(c) provides that where materials are used, they must be sound and reasonably fit for the purpose for which they are required. What constitutes materials, and what distinguishes materials from goods under paragraph (d), is unclear. Clearly, materials will come within the statutory definition of goods under the Sale of Goods Acts[75] but because different words are used in this context, it must be assumed that a different meaning should apply. It could be that goods and materials would be distinguished not, using legal definitions but by giving those words their ordinary, everyday meaning.[76] So, for example, where a person is engaged to fit a shower unit, arguably the shower unit represents the goods being supplied while items such as the sealant and glue would constitute materials. Furthermore, it is not clear what the difference between "sound and reasonably fit for the purpose for which they are required" means when compared to our understanding of merchantable quality. Again, arguably it must mean something different, because different words are used; but in practice there may be little difference between the standard of quality required for materials under implied term (c) and for goods under implied term (d).

In *McKenna v. Best Travel and ors*,[77] the plaintiff argued in the High Court, *inter alia*, that the defendants, a tour operator and a travel agent, were in breach of section 39 of the 1980 Act. While visiting Bethlehem, a stone was thrown at the bus in which the plaintiff was travelling and she sustained physical injuries. In particular, the plaintiff argued that the bus used was not fitted with reinforced glass and hence there was a breach of

73 *Wilson v. Best Travel* [1993] 1 All E.R. 353 (H.C.); see also *Wong Mee Wan v. Kwan Kin Travel* [1996] 1 W.L.R. 38 (P.C.).

74 See further the Package Holidays and Travel Trade Act 1995 implementing EC Directive 90/314 [1990] O.J. L158/59, under which the organiser is liable to the consumer for the proper performance of the obligations under the contract, irrespective of whether such obligations are to be performed by the organiser, the retailer, or other suppliers of services without prejudice to any remedy the organiser may have against the retailer or those other suppliers of services: 1995 Act, s.20(1).

75 1893 Act, s.62; see further 10.2.5.

76 Along the line of the literal rule of statutory interpretation, see, *e.g. Inspector of Taxes v. Kiernan* [1981] I.R. 117.

77 Unreported, High Court, Lavan J., December 17, 1996; [1998] 3 I.R. 57 (S.C.).

section 39(c) which required that where materials are used they will be sound and reasonably fit for the purpose for which they are required. Lavan J. stated that no evidence has been adduced that the use of reinforced glass was common or recommended practice and hence this argument failed.

20.3.4 Merchantable quality

Section 39(d) provides that where goods are supplied under a supply of service contract, there is an implied term that they will be of merchantable quality within the meaning of section 14(3) of the 1893 Act.[78] Accordingly,

> "Goods are of merchantable quality if they are as fit for the purpose or purposes for which goods of that kind are commonly bought and as durable as is reasonable to expect having regard to any description applied to them, the price (if relevant) and all the other relevant circumstances ..."

Hence where goods are supplied under a sale of goods contract or a supply of services contract, the same quality standard – merchantable quality – applies. However, significantly, the remedies following breach of this identical quality standard may differ depending on whether the goods were supplied under a sale or service contract. As noted above, under a sale of goods contract, the implied term as to merchantable quality is a condition which if breached allows the innocent party to terminate the contract, reject the goods and sue for damages. In a contract for the supply of a service, the term as to merchantable quality is an innominate term and the effect of its breach depends on the seriousness of the breach. Where the breach is serious, the innocent party can repudiate the contract and sue for damages, but where the breach is minor, the innocent party's remedy is limited to a claim in damages.

An example of a serious breach of this term can be found in *Irish Telephone Rentals v. ICS Building Society*.[79] In 1982, the defendant hired a telephone system from the plaintiff, whereby the hire contract provided that the agreed rent was paid during the continuance of the contract "for the hire of the installation and for maintenance of same in good working order." The "installation" included the provision of a switchboard, an operator's console, and telephone sets. By 1985, because of an increased volume in the defendant's business, the system started to prove defective. In 1988, and following numerous complaints, the defendant terminated the contract, claiming that there was a breach of condition by the plaintiff entitling it to terminate. The plaintiff counter-claimed that the termination was wrongful and that the defendant was in breach of contract. It was held in the High Court that there had been a breach of an express term of the contract in that the plaintiff failed to provide installations during the

78 See further 13.3.2.

79 [1991] I.L.R.M. 880.

continuance of the hiring in good working order. Moreover, the court found that the contract entered into by the parties was a contract for the supply of a telecommunications service, and that the plaintiff entered into the contract in the course of its business. Hence, Part IV of the 1980 Act applied. In particular, section 39 of the 1980 Act implied a term that any goods supplied under the service contract must be of merchantable quality. The court held that because the goods supplied were not fit for the purpose of providing a reasonably efficient telephone system they were not merchantable and therefore there was also a breach of section 39 of the 1980.

Where goods are supplied under a contract for the supply of services, there are no statutory implied terms requiring the goods to correspond with any description or to be fit for any particular purpose made known, or to correspond with any sample, as would be the case with a contract for the sale of goods under sections 13, 14(4) and 15 of the 1893 Act. This means that when compared with contracts for the sale of goods, goods supplied under contracts for the supply of services do not have to satisfy the same high quality standard, and hence recipients of goods under contracts for the supply of services are less well protected than if the contract was classified as a sale of goods contract. To avoid this inequity, a court might be inclined to identify the contract in question as a contract for the sale of goods, or while holding it to be a contract for the supply of services, it could imply similar terms at common law.

20.4 Exclusion of Liability

Section 40 states that any term implied by section 39 can be excluded (expressly, or by course of dealings, or by usage) except where the recipient of the service deals as a consumer, in which case the express term limiting or excluding liability must be fair and reasonable and must be specifically brought to the attention of the buyer to be effective.[80] Hence, other than where the recipient of the service deals as a consumer, the common law rules on exclusion clauses prevail.[81] Where the recipient deals

80 It has been held that a standard arbitration clause found in a contract for the supply of holiday services is not an "express term" within s.40 of the 1980 Act and it is therefore irrelevant whether or not is was brought to the consumer's attention: *Carroll v. Budget Travel & Counihans Travel* unreported, High Court, Morris J., December 7, 1995. *Cf. McCarthy and Others v. Joe Walsh Tours Ltd* [1991] I.L.R.M. 813.

81 See 2.3.5.1.

as a consumer, as defined,[82] any express exclusion must be fair and reasonable, as defined,[83] and specifically brought to his attention. The requirement of "specifically brought" to the recipient's attention appears to add little to the common law requirement of reasonable notice[84] as illustrated by *Carroll v. An Post National Lottery*.[85] Here, the plaintiff failed to win approximately a quarter of a million pounds because a Lotto agent, acting under the authority of the defendant, incorrectly entered the numbers selected by the plaintiff for one of the National Lottery games. While the High Court found that the contract between the plaintiff and the defendant was not a contract for the supply of a service, it held further that the exemption printed on the playslip to the effect that the Lotto agent was at the time the player's agent was brought to the plaintiff's attention as required by section 40.

Whereas the statutory implied terms under the sales legislation can never be excluded where the buyer deals as a consumer, this is not the case with contracts for the supply of services. There seems no principled reason why the rules on the exclusion of liability are more lax in relation to contracts for the supply of services, but in this regard, as in others,[86] contracts for the supply of services rank unfairly as the poor relation to sale of goods contracts, despite their growing importance to the economy.

---

82 1980 Act, s.3(1) provides that a party deals as a consumer in relation to another party if:
(a) he neither makes the contract in the course of a business; and
(b) the other party does make the contract in the course of a business; and
(c) the goods or services supplied are those ordinarily supplied for private use or consumption.

See *In re Henry O'Callaghan v. Hamilton Leasing (Ireland) Ltd and Access Refrigeration and Shop Fitting Ltd* [1984] I.L.R.M. 146 and *Cunningham v. Woodchester Investments and Intercall Ltd* unreported, High Court, McWilliam J., November 16, 1984. See further 10.2.5.1.

83 Schedule to 1980 Act. Section 2 of the Schedule lists five particular factors that may be relevant to the fair and reasonable test:
(a) the relative bargaining strength of the parties, including alternative means by which the customer's requirements can be met;
(b) whether the customer received an inducement to agree to the term, or in accepting it had an opportunity of entering into a similar transaction with other persons, but without having to accept a similar term;
(c) whether the customer knew or ought reasonable have known of the existence and extent of the term;
(d) where the term excludes or restricts liability if some condition is not complied with, whether it was reasonable at the time of the contract to expect that compliance with the condition would be practicable;
(e) whether the goods were manufactured, processed or adapted to the special order of the customer.

See further 10.5.2.2.

84 See 2.3.5.1.

85 [1996] 1 I.R. 433.

86 For instance, the use of retention of title clauses in sale contracts as a means of protecting the seller's financial interests cannot be extended to contracts for the supply of services: see further 15.4.

20.4.1 Statement purporting to restrict rights of recipient

As with the sale of goods legislation,[87] section 41 of the 1980 Act makes it an offence for any person in the course of a business to display, publish, or otherwise furnish a statement to the effect that the rights conferred by section 39 are restricted or excluded. A person guilty of an offence under the 1980 Act is liable, on summary conviction, to a fine not exceeding £500 [€634.87], and/or imprisonment not exceeding six months; and on indictment to a fine not exceeding £1,000 [€1,269.74], and/or imprisonment not exceeding two years.[88]

87 1980 Act, s.11.

88 1980 Act, s.6. In the Director for Consumer Affairs' Annual Report for 1990, for example, it was noted that there was one breach of the Sale of Goods and Supply of Services Act 1980 in respect of a sign purporting to restrict the rights of buyers/recipients. It is not clear whether this was a breach in relation to a sale of goods (1980 Act, s.11) or a supply of services (1980 Act, s.41): see www.odca.ie for more recent Annual Reports.

PART IV

FINANCE

CHAPTER 21

FINANCE: AN INTRODUCTION

21.1 PAYMENT METHODS

Where a person acquires goods or services, unless the goods or services are supplied as a gift or under a contract of barter or exchange,[1] the person will have to pay for the goods or services. Payment is usually in the form of a money payment,[2] although alternatives exist. For instance, under the doctrine of set-off, where one person, X, is owed a sum of money from another person, Y, and subsequently Y supplies goods to X under a contract of sale, the price of the goods owed by X to Y can be set off against the pre-existing debt, to reduce or cancel the debt.[3]

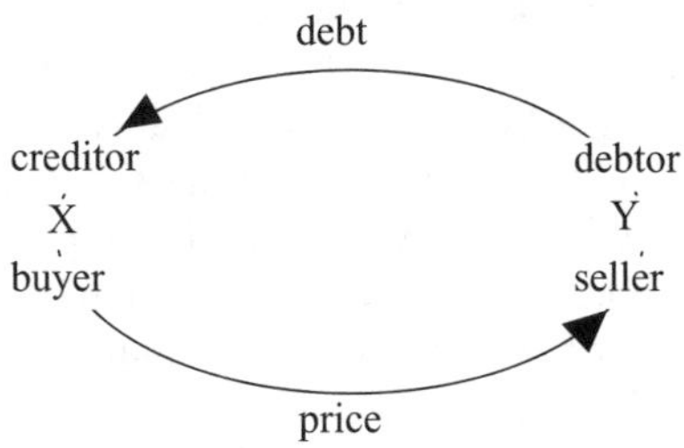

The most obvious form of money payment is cash. However, today, even within a consumer context, the use of cash as a payment mechanism is decreasing with the growth in the use of alternative mechanisms, including debit cards, credit cards, and various forms of funds transfers, such as credit transfers (for example, standing orders) and debit transfers (for example, direct debits).[4] Within the commercial context, where sums involved can be large, and parties frequently do not deal face to face, cash payment is impractical. Therefore, commercial law has developed a number of payment methods to suit the needs of the commercial community. There are three main forms of payment methods:

1 See further 9.3.

2 See generally, Mann, *The Legal Aspects of Money* (Oxford, Clarendon Press, 5th ed., 1992).

3 See generally, Derham, *Set-Off* (Oxford, Clarendon Press, 3rd ed., 2002); Wood, *English and International Set-Off* (London, Sweet & Maxwell, 1989).

4 See 23.7; see further Donnelly, *The Law of Banks and Credit Institutions* (Dublin, Round Hall Sweet & Maxwell, 2000) Chapters 12 and 13; Breslin, *Banking Law in the Republic of Ireland* (Dublin, Gill & Macmillan, 1998) Chapter 17.

(a) the buyer may make a promise, separate from the supply contract, to pay at a later date, as where he gives a promissory note;[5]
(b) the buyer gives an order to a third party to make payment, as where he gives a bill of exchange;[6]
(c) the buyer may arrange for a third party to make payment or to give an undertaking to make payment at a later stage, as where the buyer arranges a letter of credit.[7]

Moreover, the majority of these mechanisms can only operate with the assistance of a financial institution, such as a bank.

21.2 The Time for Payment – Credit and Security

Under the Sale of Goods Act 1893, for example, the basic rule is that delivery of the goods and payment of the price are concurrent conditions, that is, the seller must be ready and willing to give possession of the goods in exchange for the price, and the buyer must be ready and willing to pay the price in exchange for possession of the goods.[8] While *payment* on delivery is what is envisaged in the legislation, in fact these duties are frequently performed at different times, in accordance with the parties' agreement. Goods may be paid for in advance of delivery, and in other circumstances, a buyer may be able to agree credit terms with a seller whereby the goods will be delivered, and indeed property may pass to the buyer, before the goods are paid for. The relative bargaining strength of the parties and the level of competition in the market will determine whether payment is deferred or not.

There is a natural tension between the buyer of goods or the recipient of services, and the supplier when it comes to the time of payment. The buyer/recipient will want to defer payment for as long as possible, but under a contract of sale, for example, the buyer will want possession of, or even property in, the goods as soon as possible to enable him to use the goods or deal with them further. A buyer may be unable to pay for the goods at the time of delivery and may need to be able to use or otherwise deal with the goods to finance the purchase. Even where a buyer has the financial resources to pay on delivery, any delay in payment will improve the buyer's cash flow to the benefit of the business generally. The seller, on the other hand, will be reluctant to part with possession of, or property in, the goods until payment. This is based largely on the fear that the buyer may be unwilling, or unable in an insolvency situation, to pay for the

5 See 23.5.
6 See 23.3.
7 See Chapter 32.
8 See 1893 Act, s.28; see further 11.1.1.

goods. To avoid this possibility a seller may seek to retain possession of, or property in, the goods until payment. Even where the seller is confident of the buyer's willingness and ability to pay, a seller may seek to minimise the credit period afforded to a buyer, in order to limit the risk of non-payment and increase the general cash flow of his business. Commercial law has reacted to these tensions by providing a range of mechanisms to meet the competing needs of the parties.

Where the supplier is in a strong bargaining position, he may be able to demand immediate payment, or even payment in advance. Otherwise, immediate or early payment can, in effect, be achieved where the supplier of goods sells the goods to a finance house which pays immediately, and it is the finance house which supplies the goods on credit terms to the recipient. This arrangement is common in hire-purchase[9] and equipment leasing.[10] Alternatively, a supplier can supply goods or services directly to the buyer and subsequently sell the right to be paid to a third party for an immediate cash payment. This is referred to as *discounting receivables*.[11] Today, however, the majority of commercial contracts for the sale and supply of goods and services are agreed on credit terms. Where a supplier grants credit, he may seek some form of security to protect against the buyer's non-payment.[12] A supplier could ask for a third-party guarantee of payment from a creditworthy source; or under a sale of goods contract, a supplier could seek security over the property itself by retaining title in the goods by supplying them on hire-purchase,[13] or under a conditional sale arrangement, such as through the use of a retention of title clause.[14]

21.2.1 Late payment of commercial transactions

Until recently, any agreement between the supplier of goods or services and the buyer in relation to the granting of credit and the cost of that credit, including any interest payable on late payment, has been a matter for private negotiation between the parties, regulated only by market forces. While parties remain free to agree terms of credit, in the absence of such agreement, or where their agreement falls short of certain minimum standards, the EC (Late Payment in Commercial Transactions) Regulations 2002, implementing the EC Directive on combating late payment in commercial transactions, regulate the payment of interest in the case of late payment and related matters. The rationale for this legislation is a recognition that late payment is a breach of contract which has been made

9 See 9.3.5.

10 See 24.3.1.3.

11 See Goode, *Commercial Law* (London, Penguin, 2nd ed., 1995) Chapter 29, esp. pp. 800–819.

12 See generally Chapters 24, 25 and 26.

13 See 9.3.5.

14 See 15.4.

financially attractive to debtors in most Member States by low interest rates on late payments and slow procedures for redress. This legislation is intended to reverse this pattern by encouraging prompt payment of commercial debts, including by providing compensation to creditors for costs incurred.

Broadly speaking, the Directive applies to payments made as remuneration for almost all commercial transactions in the public and private sectors. A "commercial transaction" means a transaction between undertakings or between undertakings and public authorities for the purposes of providing goods or services for remuneration. Excluded from the Regulations are, *inter alia*:

(a) contracts made before August 7, 2002;
(b) claims for late payment interest of less than €5.00;
(c) transactions with consumers.

It is an implied term of every commercial transaction that interest is payable in relation to late payments. A payment is late when it exceeds the "relevant payment date". The "relevant payment date" means:

(a) the date specified in the contract; or
(b) where the contract does not specify a date -
   (i) 30 days after the date of receipt of the invoice; or
   (ii) where the date of receipt of the invoice is uncertain, or the purchaser receives the invoice before the goods, 30 days after the receipt of the goods or services; or
   (iii) where there is a procedure for acceptance or verification of the goods and the invoice arrives earlier than, or on, the date of such procedure, 30 days after the latter date.

Unless otherwise agreed in the contract, the rate of interest payable is specified to be the interest rate applied by the European Central Bank to its most recent refinancing operation, plus seven percentage points. Where a contract purports to waive or vary the above provisions in a manner which is "grossly unfair" to the supplier, application can be made to the Circuit Court, or an arbitrator, where the waiver or variation can be found to be unenforceable. Further, it is an implied term of every commercial contract that where interest is payable, the supplier is entitled to compensation towards the relevant recovery costs. Whether the Directive and the implementing Regulations actually succeeds in changing the culture of late payments remains to be seen.

The following chapters examine some of the main private law aspects of commercial finance mentioned above. In particular, the relationship between banks and their customers is considered in Chapter 22. Chapter 23 examines the use of various payment methods including bills of exchange and cheques. The use of letters of credits is examined in Part VI on International Trade in Chapter 32, and the area of credit and security is explored in Chapters 24, 25 and 26.

CHAPTER 22

BANKER/CUSTOMER RELATIONS

22.1 INTRODUCTION

Banks and other financial institutions play a central role in commercial activity. Banking activity underpins all commercial activity by facilitating the payment for goods and services, and by providing credit facilities. As well as supporting commercial activity in this way, the provision of banking services to commercial and private customers is a commercial activity in itself. In subsequent chapters we will examine various payment methods and the provision of credit and security in a commercial context, but first, in this chapter, we examine briefly the private law aspects of the banker/customer relationship, in particular the nature of that relationship, the legal incidents which arise from that relationship and the termination of that relationship.[1]

As a preliminary to the examination of the banker/customer relationship, it is important to understand what the terms "bank" or "banker", "banking" and "customer" mean. These terms have been defined for a number of different purposes, but there is no single, all-purpose definition for each of these terms. For example, both the Bills of Exchange Act 1882 and the Cheques Act 1959 refer to "bankers", but neither offer a comprehensive definition of the term. The 1882 Act defines a banker as "a body of persons whether incorporated or not who carry on the business of banking", without offering any definition of the "business of banking".[2] For regulatory purposes, "a banking business" has been defined as:

> "(i) the business of accepting, on own account, sums of money from the public in the form of deposits or other repayable funds whether or not involving the issue of securities or other obligations, howsoever described, or
> (ii) the business aforesaid and any other business normally carried on

---

1 The business of banking is highly regulated, a topic outside the scope of this book. See the Central Bank and Financial Services Authority of Ireland Bill 2002: this Bill lapsed with the dissolution of the 28th Dáil in 2002, but was quickly reintroduced by the 29th Dáil. See generally, Donnelly, *The Law of Banks and Credit Institutions* (Dublin, Round Hall Sweet & Maxwell, 2000) Part I; Breslin, *Banking Law in the Republic of Ireland* (Dublin, Gill & Macmillan, 1998) Part I.

2 1882 Act, s.2.

> by a bank which may include the granting of credits on own account ..."[3]

This statutory definition reflects the common law definition of banking, which also focuses on the acceptance of deposits. In *Re Shields Estate*,[4] it was stated by Holmes L.J. that: "The real business of the banker is to obtain deposits of money which he may use for his profit by lending it out again." Similarly, Diplock L.J. in the Court of Appeal, in *United Dominions Trust Ltd v. Kirkwood*[5] was of the view that the essential characteristic of banking was the acceptance of deposits. But Lord Denning M.R. and Harman L.J., relying on expert opinion, agreed that the essential characteristic of banking was the collection and payment of cheques. Diplock L.J. was "inclined to agree" that "to constitute the business of banker today", the banker must also pay cheques drawn on him and collect cheques on behalf of customers. Since these cases were decided, significant changes have occurred in the provision of banking services. In particular, the use of cheques as a means of making payment has declined and is expected to continue do so, as alternative payment methods involving the use of credit and debit cards and electronic funds transfers have developed. Any modern definition of banking should take such developments into account.

Modern banking is notable both in terms of the range of institutions which offer banking services, and the range of services on offer. As well as the two main banks, Allied Irish Bank and Bank of Ireland, which dominate the Irish market, there are a number of other banks and other credit institutions such as building societies, as well as credit unions, competing for business and private customers. More recently, retailers, such as Tesco and Marks & Spencer, have entered the financial services market. Further, at a commercial level, merchant banks offer banking services exclusively to business customers. Merchant banks do not generally have a branch network, but operate from a small number of offices, usually centrally located. Discount houses also offer specialist financial services to the commercial community, by buying at a discount bills of exchange, for example. Other finance houses provide credit facilities by financing transactions such as hire-purchase, equipment leasing and by factoring debts.

The range of banking services has also expanded beyond the acceptance of deposits and the making of loans, and the collection and payment of cheques and other payment orders. Traditionally, banks have

3 Central Bank Act 1971, s.2, as amended by the Central Bank Act 1997, s.70: see further Breslin, "The Central Bank Act 1997: The New Definition of Banking Business" [1997] *Commercial Law Practitioner* 160.

4 [1901] 1 I.R. 173 at 182.

5 [1966] 2 Q.B. 431, [1966] 1 All E.R. 968, see also *Re Roes' Legal Charge* [1982] 2 Lloyd's Rep. 370.

provided credit references for customers and facilities for the safe storage of documents and valuables. Today, banks also provide advice on investment and tax, and offer a variety of services, including stockbroking and insurance services. The method of delivering these services has also changed radically with a move away from the branch to electronic, telephone and internet banking.[6] Moreover, in relation to their business customers, banks provide a further range of services including factoring of debts, discounting of bills, and letter of credit facilities.

As with the term "banker", the term "customer" is used in the Bills of Exchange Act 1882 and the Cheques Act 1959 but the Acts offer no definition. It may be important to identify a customer in order to determine whether a bank can rely on the statutory defences available to banks under these Acts when paying and collecting cheques.[7] The classification of a person as a customer is also important because, at common law, certain incidents attach to the banker/customer relationship, taking effect as implied terms of the contract. At common law, it has been held that a person becomes a customer as soon as he opens an account with a bank.[8] Indeed, it may be that a person becomes a customer earlier in time when the bank agrees to open the account.[9] However, it should be noted that many banking services, such as loan or credit card services, are offered to persons who do not have a deposit or current account with the bank and hence are not, strictly speaking, customers. More generally, therefore, a customer can be defined as any person who has a contractual relationship with a bank under which the bank provides financial services to the person. Even in these latter circumstances, some of the common law incidents of the banker/customer relationship may apply.

22.2 Nature of the Banker/Customer Relationship

The banker/customer relationship is based on contract, although other aspects of the law including agency, equity, property, restitution and tort play an important role. While many banking services, such as loans, ATM cards and credit card facilities, are provided on the basis of standard form contracts drafted by the bank,[10] the legal incidents of the banker/customer relationship derive from the common law, as implied terms of contract,

6 See Directive 2002/65 on the distance marketing of consumer financial services [2002] O.J. L271/16. See generally, Donnelly & McDonagh, "Maintaining Standards in Electronic Banking: How Does Ireland Measure Up?" [2000] *Commercial Law Practitioner* 211; Donnelly, "Electronic Banking and the Consumer: What Price Convenience?" [1997] *Commercial Law Practitioner* 132.

7 See 1882 Act, ss.60 and 80, and 1959 Act, ss.1 and 4: see further 23.4.4.

8 *Ladbroke & Co v. Todd* (1914) 30 T.L.R. 433.

9 *Woods v. Martins Bank* [1959] 1 Q.B. 55, [1958] 3 All E.R. 166.

10 See Donnelly, *The Law of Banks and Credit Institutions* (Dublin, Round Hall Sweet & Maxwell, 2000) Chapter 7, Part I.

when a customer opens an account. These legal incidents are based on mercantile expectations and banking practice.[11] To date, legislative regulation of the banker/customer relationship has been minimal.[12] What legal regulation does exist, exists largely at a consumer level. In particular, where banking services are provided to a "consumer" pursuant to a standard form contract, the European Communities (Unfair Terms in Consumer Contracts) Regulations 1995 and 2000 apply.[13] Otherwise, a number of codes of practice operate in different sectors of the financial services industry. In particular, the Irish Bankers' Federation (IBF), the representative body for all the leading banks, has issued a Code of Ethics and Practice which includes codes of practice for personal customers on transparency in credit charges and on mortgage arrears; for small business customers; and on competition practices.[14] Importantly, the codes themselves have no legal force, though they are used by the Ombudsman for Credit Institutions in performing his dispute resolution function in relation to "individual customers".[15]

As noted above, the opening of an account gives rise to the banker/customer relationship. Essentially, the relationship of banker/customer is that of debtor/creditor.[16] Accordingly, when a customer opens a deposit or current account, the customer lends the money deposited to the bank, and in return acquires contractual rights to repayment. Repayment may be due at a specified date, as with certain fixed-term savings accounts, or on demand as with the more usual deposit and current accounts. Where an account is overdrawn, the relationship is reversed with the bank becoming the creditor and the customer becoming the debtor.

Importantly, and as a consequence of the usual debtor/creditor relationship between the bank and the customer, when a customer deposits money with a bank, the customer ceases to own the money and it becomes

11 *Hare v. Henty* (1861) 10 C.B.N.S. 65 at 77.

12 But see recommendations of Implementation Advisory Group on the Establishment of a Single Regulatory Authority for the Financial Services Sector (Dublin, Stationery Office, June 1999), and Central Bank and Financial Services Authority of Ireland Bill 2002: this Bill lapsed with the dissolution of the 28th Dáil in 2002, but was quickly reintroduced by the 29th Dáil.

13 S.I. No. 27 of 1995 and S.I. No. 307 of 2000; see further 2.3.5.3; see also the Consumer Credit Act 1995. See further the Data Protection Act 1988, and the European Communities (Data Protection) Regulations 2001 S.I. No. 626 of 2001; the Criminal Justice Act 1994, and the Equal Status Act 2000. See also the Data Protection (Amendment) Bill 2002 which lapsed with the dissolution of the 28th Dáil in 2002: see further www.dataprivacy.ie

14 See generally www.ibf.ie

15 The term "individual customers" is defined broadly to include a partnership, an unincorporated body not consisting entirely of bodies corporate, and a company having an annual turnover of €1.3 million or less in the financial year prior to the year in which the complaint is made.

16 *Foley v. Hill* (1848) 2 H.L.C. 28.

the property of the bank. Therefore, for example, when the bank makes payment in accordance with the customer's instructions it does so from its own resources first; subsequently it reimburses itself for the amount paid out by debiting the customer's account and thereby reducing its debt to the customer. Equally, if the bank becomes insolvent, the customer has no real or proprietary rights in relation to the money deposited; rather, the customer becomes an unsecured creditor of the bank.[17]

22.3 Bank's Duties

As stated above, on the opening of an account the relationship of banker/customer arises and a number of legal incidents follow. In particular, various duties are implied into the contract between the bank and the customer.[18] The bank's main duties are examined briefly below.

22.3.1 To honour customer's mandate

It is an implied term of the banker/customer contract that the bank will honour the customer's instruction to make payments to third parties: the customer's mandate.[19] Such instructions can be given in various forms: by cheque; or by other written order, such as a direct debit mandate or standing order; or by use of a debit card. Where a payment is made in accordance with the customer's mandate, the bank is entitled to reimburse itself by debiting the customer's account, but if a bank makes a payment without the customer's mandate, the bank has no authority, at common law, to debit the account.[20] Failure by a bank to honour the customer's mandate and to make payment, where the necessary funds are available,[21] is a breach of contract and the customer can sue the bank for damages for any loss caused. Moreover, where a cheque is returned unpaid, the wording on the cheque, such as "refer to drawer", may be defamatory, thereby allowing the customer to sue for damages for defamation.[22]

The demand for payment must be made at the branch where the account is drawn.[23] If a bank pays a cheque elsewhere, it is treated as buying the

17 Today, deposit protection legislation seeks to afford some protection to depositors: see the European Communities (Deposit Guarantee Schemes) Regulations 1995 (S.I. No. 168 of 1995) which seek to implement the EC Directive on Deposit Guarantee Schemes, Directive 94/19 [1994] O.J. L135/5.

18 See *Joachimson v. Swiss Bank Corpn* [1921] 3 K.B. 110 (C.A.).

19 See further *Kinlan v. Ulster Bank* [1928] I.R. 171 at 185 (S.C.) on the bank's duty to repay.

20 This rule is modified by statute which protects banks paying cheques: see Bills of Exchange Act 1882, s.60 and s.80, and the Cheques Act 1959, s.1: see further 23.4.4.

21 *Marzetti v. Williams* 1 B. & Ad. 415.

22 *Pike v. Hibernian Bank* [1950] I.R. 195; *Kinlan v. Ulster Bank* [1928] I.R. 171 at 183 (S.C.); *Jayson v. Midland Bank Ltd* [1968] I Lloyd's Rep. 409 (C.A.).

23 *Joachimson v. Swiss Bank Corpn* [1921] 3 KB 110 (C.A.).

cheque, which it then presents for payment on its own behalf. The bank is entitled to refuse payment where there are insufficient funds to honour the order,[24] or, if a cheque is "stale". Normally, a cheque is regarded as stale if it is presented for payment more than six months after it is drawn.

A bank's duty to honour its customer's mandate is restricted in certain circumstances. For example, a person with a claim against another can apply to the High Court for a *Mareva* injunction freezing the respondent's assets, including any bank accounts, to prevent the respondent moving assets out of the jurisdiction and hence frustrating any judgment which may be obtained against him.[25] If a *Mareva* injunction is granted and a bank is served with notice of the injunction, any dealing with the bank account in accordance with a customer's mandate, contrary to the terms of the injunction, will constitute contempt of court. A bank's duty to obey its customer's mandate may also be restricted if the bank exercises its right to combine accounts. Where a customer holds more than one account with the same bank, the bank has an implied right to combine those accounts. This right is usually exercised where one account is overdrawn and the other is in credit. By combining the accounts, the bank may reduce or cancel the customer's overall indebtedness to the bank. As a result, a bank can dishonour a payment order such as a cheque, where the account on which the cheque is drawn is in credit, if the customer holds a second overdrawn account and the combination of these two accounts is insufficient to make payment.[26] This right of combination can operate in favour of the customer where he draws a cheque on an account without sufficient funds to make payment and the customer holds a second account which if combined with the first will provide the necessary funds.

22.3.2 To obey customer's countermand

As a corollary to the above implied term, it is an implied term of the banker/customer contract that a customer can always withdraw his mandate, for example, by "stopping" or "countermanding" a cheque.[27] Notice of the countermand must be clear and unambiguous,[28] and it must given to the branch on which the cheque is drawn.[29] To be effective, a countermand must be brought to the actual (not constructive) notice of the bank, and hence it is not effective until it reaches the teller or ledger clerk

---

24 *Marzetti v. Williams* 1 B. & Ad. 415.

25 See further 37.4.1.2.

26 *Re European Bank, Agra Bank Claim* (1872) 8 Ch. App 41.

27 Bills of Exchange Act 1882, s.75. It is not clear whether a customer can countermand a cheque supported by a cheque guarantee card: see *First Sport Ltd v. Barclays Bank plc* [1993] 3 All E.R. 789; see further 23.4.1 and 5.3.1.1.

28 *Westminster Bank v. Hilton* (1926) 43 T.L.R. 124.

29 *London Provincial & South Western Bank v. Buszard* (1918) 35 T.L.R. 142.

for example. In *Curtice v. London City & Midland Bank*,[30] a customer sought to stop a cheque by writing a letter to the bank, which due to the bank's error was not removed from the bank's letter-box until after the cheque had been paid. The Court of Appeal held that the cheque had not been effectively countermanded.

22.3.3 Bank's duty of care

A bank owes the customer a duty of care in the performance of its functions, including the paying and collecting of cheques.[31] This general duty arises at common law as an implied term of the contract and also may be implied under section 39 of the Sale of Goods and Supply of Services Act 1980.[32] A concurrent duty in tort may also arise.[33] A bank may incur further duties of care, either in contract or tort, if it provides further services to its customer. For example, if it stores valuables in a safe-deposit box on behalf of a customer, it will be liable as a bailee of the goods; or if it offers advice or provides a credit reference, the bank owes a duty to exercise reasonable care in giving the advice,[34] or providing the reference,[35] under normal tortious principles.

A bank may undertake to act as agent for a customer, in which case certain legal incidents of the principal/agent relationship, including a duty of care, may arise.[36] For example, in *Irish Nationwide Building Society v. Malone*,[37] a loan offered by the plaintiff required the borrowers to have mortgage protection insurance. The borrowers filled in the relevant forms, forwarded them to the plaintiff and paid an "administration fee." The plaintiff delayed in sending the forms to the insurance company and there were no policies in place when the defendant's husband died. The Supreme Court found that the plaintiff had acted as agents for the borrowers when it agreed to arrange insurance in return for an administration fee. The plaintiff's duty of care as agent required more than simply forwarding the application form to the insurers; they were under an obligation to pay "close attention to the progress of the matter until it is completed or

30 [1908] 1 K.B. 293 (C.A.).

31 See, *e.g.* *Tulsk Co-operative Livestock Mart Ltd v. Ulster Bank* unreported, High Court, Gannon, J., May 13, 1983; *Towey v. Ulster Bank* [1987] I.L.R.M. 142 where delays in obtaining payment of cheques amounted to negligence.

32 See Chapter 20.

33 See 20.3.2.1.

34 *Hedley Byrne v. Heller & Partners* [1964] A.C. 465, [1963] 2 All E.R. 575 (H.L.); *Tulsk Co-operative Livestock Mart Ltd v. Ulster Bank* unreported, High Court, Gannon, J., May 13, 1983; *Towey v. Ulster Bank* [1987] I.L.R.M. 142. But there is no general duty to advise recognised in Irish law: see *Kennedy v. AIB* [1998] 2 I.R. 48 (S.C.), and *Bank of Ireland v. Lennon* unreported, High Court, Lavan, J., February 17, 1998.

35 *Spring v. Guardian Assurance plc* [1994] 3 W.L.R. 354.

36 On principal/agent relations, see generally Chapter 7.

37 Unreported, Supreme Court, December 10, 1998.

abandoned."[38] Even when the plaintiff had allowed the borrower to draw down the loan, requiring them to sign an acknowledgment that that there was no mortgage protection in place, the court held that this was not sufficient to relieve the plaintiff of its obligations: "[the plaintiff] still remained under an obligation to remain in touch with the [borrowers] and the [insurance company] to ensure as far as possible that the matter was progressing and was not sliding into inertia."[39]

Importantly, such duties of care are not limited to customers.[40] For example, in *Potterton v. Northern Bank Ltd*,[41] it was held that a bank which dishonours a cheque owes a duty of care to the payee when notifying the reason for dishonour. Hence, a bank could be liable where the stated reason for dishonour misleads the payee in relation to the prospects of the cheque being paid and the drawer's solvency.

22.3.4 Bank's fiduciary duties[42]

Normally, a bank is not in a fiduciary position with its customers because the funds deposited with it are the bank's property and not the customers. However, a bank may incur extra duties. For example, if it acts as a trustee it will owe fiduciary duties to any beneficiaries. Moreover, the law may impose obligations on a bank, in the form of a constructive trust, where there has been a breach of trust by a trustee or other fiduciary (usually a customer of the bank) and the bank has been involved in the breach in some way.[43]

22.3.5 Bank's duty of confidentiality

The leading authority on a banker's duty of confidentiality is *Tournier v. National Provincial and Union Bank of England*.[44] In this case, a customer got into financial difficulties. In the course of a conversation between the bank manager and the customer's employer, the bank manager disclosed that the customer's account was overdrawn and that the customer was involved in gambling. The customer lost his job as a result. It was held that

---

38 *Ibid*., at p.12 of transcript.

39 *Ibid*., at p.13 of transcript.

40 *Macken v. Munster & Leinster Bank* (1961) I.L.T.R. 17; *Hedley Byrne v. Heller & Partners* [1964] A.C. 465, [1963] 2 All E.R. 575 (H.L.); *Securities Trust v. Hugh Moore & Alexander* [1964] I.R. 417.

41 [1993] 1 I.R. 413; see further Ellinger, "Bank's Liability for Information Respecting Dishonour of Cheque" [1995] *Journal of Business Law* 583.

42 See Breslin, "Banks as Fiduciaries" [1998] *Commercial Law Practitioner* 47.

43 *Barnes v. Addy* (1874) 9 Ch. App. 244; see generally Delany, *Equity and the Law of Trusts in Ireland* (Dublin, Round Hall Sweet & Maxwell, 2nd ed., 1999) Chapter 8; Ashe & Reid, "Equity and the Pursuit of Hot Money - Warning to Banks" [1997] *Commercial Law Practitioner* 188.

44 [1924] 1 K.B. 461 (C.A.).

the bank was in breach of its duty of confidentiality by disclosing this information. In referring to the extent of a bank's duty of confidentiality, Lord Atkin stated:

> "It clearly goes beyond the state of the account, that is whether there is a debit or credit balance, and the amount of the balance. It must at least extend to all transactions that go through the account, and to the securities, if any, given in respect of the account; and in respect of such matters it must, I think, extend beyond the period when the account is closed, or ceases to be an active account … [T]he obligation extends to information obtained from other sources than the customer's actual account if the occasion upon which the information was obtained arose out of the banking relations of the bank and its customers …"[45]

Hence, the duty of confidentiality is extensive, covering all information, from whatever source,[46] concerning the banker/customer relationship. The duty may extend to other persons who, because of the bank's actions, have come into possession of confidential information. In *National Irish Bank v. RTÉ*,[47] the Supreme Court found that, in principle, an injunction could be granted in such circumstances, although, in this case, which concerned allegations of bank-assisted tax evasion, the public interest demanded disclosure and the injunction was refused.

However, a number of exceptions to this duty were recognised in the *Tournier* case, which would justify the disclosure of information. The exceptions are:

(i) where disclosure is compelled by law;
(ii) where there is a public duty to disclose the information;
(iii) where the bank's own interest requires disclosure;
(iv) where disclosure is expressly or impliedly authorised by the customer.

The first two exceptions are clearly connected, though the second exception is somewhat vague.[48] Disclosure may be compelled by law in a variety of circumstances, for example, to assist in the detection of crime.[49]

---

45 [1924] 1 K.B. 461 at 485.

46 This point was not unanimous. Scrutton L.J. stated that the duty did not apply to "knowledge derived from other sources": [1924] 1 K.B. 461 at 481.

47 [1998] 2 I.R. 465 (S.C.).

48 Paget cites *Arab Foreign Bank v. Banker's Trust Co* [1988] 1 Lloyd's Rep. 259 as the only reported English case on public interest disclosure: see *Paget's Law of Banking* (London, Butterworths, 11th ed., 1996) at p.122.

49 See particularly the Criminal Justice Act 1994 in relation to money laundering: see further Reid, "Cleaning up the Financial System: Money Laundering and the Criminal Justice Act 1994: A New Regime for Banks" [1994] *Commercial Law Practitioner* 279.

Indeed, it has been noted that the range of statutory exceptions to the duty of confidentiality are so extensive now[50] that the duty has been seriously undermined.[51] The second exception was considered in *National Irish Bank v. RTÉ*.[52] There the Supreme Court held that the public interest demanded public disclosure of customer names who availed of an investment scheme offered by the bank, the primary purpose of which was to evade tax. The bank had argued that such disclosure would be in breach of the banker's duty of confidentiality to these customers, and that disclosure of the names to the relevant authorities would be sufficient. The Supreme Court disagreed and found that the public interest in disclosure outweighed the bank's duty of confidentiality. The case has been criticised for blurring the distinction between "public curiosity" and "genuine public interest".[53]

The third exception is also potentially controversial. It clearly covers the situation where a bank is a party to legal proceedings and is required to disclose information in its pleadings to support its case. In *Tournier v. National Provincial and Union Bank of England*, Bankes L.J. gave the example of a bank's action for loan enforcement, where the bank would have to make known to the court details of the amount owed by the customer.[54] English authority suggests that the exception is wider, though. In *Suderland v. Barclays Bank*,[55] it was held that a bank was entitled to disclose to a customer's husband that the customer's account was overdrawn in order to protect its commercial reputation when the customer unjustifiably complained that her cheques were being dishonoured. More recently, it was suggested in *Christofi v. Barclays Bank plc*[56] that it was for the bank to decide what was in its own best interest.

Under the fourth exception, a customer can expressly or impliedly consent to disclosure. The question of implied consent can cause problems. One area where a customer impliedly gives consent is where the customer gives the name of his bank as a referee. The IBF's Code of Practice for Personal Customers provides that a bank will not respond to third-party inquiries about a customer's financial position without the express consent of the customer.

As banks have developed the range of financial services available, such as insurance and stockbroking, usually offered through the use of

50 See further, *e.g.* The Bankers' Book of Evidence Act 1879, as amended; Companies Act 1990, s.10 and *Glackin v. TSB* [1993] 3 I.R. 55; and the Taxes Consolidation Act 1997, as amended.

51 See Donnelly, *The Law of Banks and Credit Institutions* (Dublin, Round Hall Sweet & Maxwell, 2000) p.149; and Donnelly, "The Erosion of the Bankers' Duty of Secrecy" [1996] *Commercial Law Practitioner* 226.

52 [1998] 2 I.R. 465 (S.C.).

53 See Donnelly, *The Law of Banks and Credit Institutions* (Dublin, Round Hall Sweet & Maxwell, 2000) p.160.

54 [1924] 1 K.B. 461 at 473 (C.A.).

55 [1938] 5 *Legal Decision Affecting Bankers* 163.

56 [1999] 2 All E.R. (Comm.) 417

subsidiary companies, banks have sought to share information about customers with their subsidiaries. The issue of how the duty of confidentiality operates within the context of a banking group arose in *Kennedy v. AIB*.[57] The issue before the court was whether the two defendants, Allied Irish Bank and Allied Irish Finance, should be treated as a single entity, thus entitling them to share customer information without breaching the banker's duty of confidentiality. While Murphy J. noted that this was an "interesting and important point for all banking groups",[58] he did not find it necessary to resolve the issue in the case before him. The decision of the Court of Appeal in *Bank of Tokyo v. Karoon*[59] suggests that disclosure by a bank to a separate company, even a wholly owned subsidiary, would involve a prima facie breach of the banker's duty of confidentiality. Whether such type of disclosure comes within the third exception is unclear, and the preferred option for a bank is to get its customer's express consent to such activity.

22.4 Customer's Duty of Care

A customer owes a duty of care to its bank, although this duty is not extensive.[60] A customer owes a duty to take reasonable care in drawing cheques so as not to facilitate fraud, and the customer is liable to the bank for any loss caused to the bank for breach of that duty. For example, in *London Joint Stock Bank Ltd v. Macmillan and Arthur*,[61] a customer drew cheques by filling in the amount in figures and signing the cheques, leaving a clerk to insert the necessary wording. The customer drew a cheque for £2, while the clerk fraudulently inserted the words "one hundred and twenty pounds" and inserted the figures "1" before, and "0" after, the figure "2". The court held that the customer was negligent and the customer failed in an action to recover the extra £118 paid out by the bank on the altered cheque. Subsequently, in *Greenwood v. Martin's Bank Ltd*,[62] it was held that a customer owed a duty of care to its bank to inform the bank of any fraud relating to his account, of which he is aware.

English authority suggests that this duty of care will not be extended further. In *Tai Hing Cotton Mill Ltd v. Liu Chong Hing Bank Ltd*,[63] a clerk working for the plaintiff company over a six-year period fraudulently drew cheques by forging the managing director's signature and obtained a sum of HK$5.5 million. In 1978, a new accountant began checking bank

57 Unreported, High Court, Murphy, J., May 18, 1995.
58 *Ibid.*, at p.31 of transcript.
59 [1986] 3 All E.R. 468; see also *Chemical Bank v. McCormack* [1983] I.L.R.M. 350.
60 See further Gill, "The Duties of a Customer to his Bank" (1986) 4 *Irish Law Times* 47.
61 [1918] A.C. 77.
62 [1933] A.C. 51 (H.L.).
63 [1986] A.C. 80, [1985] 2 All E.R. 947 (P.C.).

statements against the company accounts and the fraud was discovered. The company sought to recover the monies paid by three banks on the strength of the forged signatures. In their defence, the banks argued that the plaintiff company had been negligent in failing to check bank statements and hence the plaintiff was estopped from denying that the bank statements were accurate. The Privy Council held that a customer's duty of care was limited to that identified in *London Joint Stock Bank Ltd v. Macmillan and Arthur* and *Greenwood v. Martin's Bank Ltd*. Where a bank requires a customer to check bank statements, this should be made an express term of the contract; the Privy Council refused to imply such a term. Any such express term should be clear and unambiguous if the banks were to make the bank statements conclusive evidence of the state of the customer's account. Each of the three banks did have express terms requiring the customer to check statements, but the Privy Council found that the terms were not sufficiently clear to prevent a challenge to the statements or to impose such a duty of care. Moreover, the insertion of any new terms would require sufficient notice to the customer, from which the court could infer the customer's consent, and would have to be supported by new consideration moving from the bank to the customer.[64]

22.5 Termination of the Banker/Customer Relationship

The banker/customer relationship may be terminated in a number of ways, by the customer, the bank, or the operation of the law. The relationship may terminate automatically, under the terms of the banker/customer contract, as where the customer holds a fixed term deposit account and the term expires. In such circumstances, neither the customer nor the bank can unilaterally terminate the relationship before expiry of the fixed time, although in practice banks allow customers to terminate prematurely on payment of a penalty. Otherwise, the relationship can be terminated unilaterally. For example, a customer can always close an account where the sum deposited is payable on demand. However, the customer must also indicate an intention to terminate the relationship. Equally, the bank can terminate the relationship. However, because payments in and out of a customer's account take a number of days to process, a bank can only terminate the relationship by giving reasonable notice to the customer as a means of avoiding the dishonouring of cheques, for example.[65] What is reasonable will depend on the facts of the case. The customer may need to be given sufficient time to rearrange his banking affairs. In *Prosperity Ltd v. Lloyds Bank Ltd*,[66] one month's notice was held to be insufficient

64 See 2.2.2.3

65 *Joachimson v. Swiss Bank Corpn* [1921] 3 K.B. 110 (C.A.).

66 (1923) 39 T.L.R. 372.

because the customer was an insurer who had directed clients to make payments directly into his bank account. However, the court did not order that the account be kept open; damages were awarded instead. Where the account is in overdraft without prior approval from the bank or the account is being used for unlawful purposes, the bank can close the account without giving notice.[67] Because the banker/customer relationship is personal, it will automatically terminate where the customer dies[68] or becomes insolvent. Clearly, termination of the banker/customer relationship also involves termination of the customer's mandate to the bank.

67 *Blighty v. Norton* (1862) 3 B. & S. 305.
68 See Bills of Exchange Act 1882, s.75(2).

CHAPTER 23

NEGOTIABLE INSTRUMENTS, BILLS OF EXCHANGE AND OTHER PAYMENT MECHANISMS

23.1 INTRODUCTION

A supplier will generally be reluctant to supply goods or services without some assurance of payment which will protect him against the customer's failure to pay both through unwillingness (including, for instance, where liability is disputed on grounds of allegedly defective performance), and inability (as where the customer becomes insolvent). The customer on the other hand will want to withhold payment at least until the contract is performed, in order to assure himself of satisfactory performance, and will often want credit, so that he is not obliged to pay immediately even on completion of the supplier's performance. There are a number of ways in which these competing needs may be satisfied. The seller may take real or personal security from the buyer or may protect himself by reserving title to goods supplied until the price is paid.[1] In addition, commercial practice has developed a number of payment mechanisms which may be used to satisfy the needs of both parties. These payment mechanisms will often be more convenient than cash, offering a further advantage. Amongst the most important, from a legal perspective, are bills of exchange. Although their use today is limited mainly to the commercial sphere, and in particular, international trade, the law on bills of exchange forms the basis of our understanding of a range of other payment mechanisms, including cheques. Therefore, this chapter concentrates on bills of exchange while considering briefly a number of other mechanisms, such as cheques, promissory notes, bank drafts, automated payments and electronic fund transfers. Documentary credits and performance bonds are especially important in international transactions and are dealt with in Chapter 32 in Part VII on International Trade.

1 On real and personal security, see Chapters 24–26; on retention of title clauses in sale of goods contracts, see 15.4.

23.2 Negotiable Instruments

Bills of exchange, promissory notes and cheques are contractual documents but are distinct and valuable in that they are all negotiable instruments. An instrument is a document which evidences title to a legal right, such as a right to enforce a debt. Negotiable instruments have three features which distinguish them from other contractual rights. First, merely being in possession of a contractual document does not normally allow the holder to enforce the contract. Only the parties (or their assignees) to the contract can enforce it by action, under the doctrine of privity of contract. However, the lawful holder of a negotiable instruments can enforce it by action. Second, as an instrument which evidences title to a legal right, a property right, it can therefore be transferred. Generally rights under a contract can only be transferred by formal assignment.[2] However, a *negotiable* instrument can be transferred without formal assignment, either simply by delivery to the transferee, or, by delivery and indorsement with the name of the transferee. The transferee is then able to enforce the legal obligation evidenced by the instrument. Third, the transferee of a negotiable instrument, unlike other contractual assignments where the transferee takes subject to equities, may take it free of any defects in the transferor's title and defences which could have been set up against the transferor.[3]

23.3 Bills of Exchange

A bill of exchange is an order by one person (the *drawer*) to another person (the *drawee*) to pay a sum of money to a person (the *payee*). The bill need not name a payee: instead it may be payable simply to "bearer." If a payee is named, the payee may be the drawer or a third party. The sum ordered to be paid by the bill may be payable immediately or at a future date. The payee may enforce the bill himself by presenting it for payment in accordance with its terms, or may sell (or "discount") it to a third party, transferring it to the third party in return for an immediate cash payment. The transferee will then enforce the bill in due course, or may in turn himself transfer it. In this way, the bill can be used like paper currency, and indeed it performed a like function before national and regional currencies were established. Eventually, the holder of the bill could be a complete stranger to the drawee, the bill having being transferred numerous times.

A bill contains an *unconditional* contractual undertaking to pay a sum of money to the payee.[4] The unconditional nature of the undertaking gives

2 See, *e.g. Supreme Court of Judicature* (Ireland) Act 1877, s.28(6).

3 See *Belfast Banking Co v. Doherty* (1879) 4 L.R. (Ir.) 124 at 134.

4 *Walek v. Seafield* [1978] I.R. 167; Nova (Jersey) *Knit Ltd v. Kammgarn Spinnerei GmbH* [1977] 2 All E.R. 463 (H.L.).

the bill a second characteristic, in addition to negotiability, which makes it attractive to business as a payment mechanism. Hence, the undertaking to pay contained in the bill is largely independent of any underlying transaction, so that the bill can be enforced regardless of any alleged breaches in the underlying contract.[5] The drawer and drawee are parties to the bill and are liable to honour the payment undertaking. The drawee is the person primarily liable to honour the bill; however, liability depends on signature. The drawer is therefore immediately liable on the bill but the drawee is only liable on it if it is presented to him for acceptance and he accepts the obligation it contains by signing it. A bill only has to be presented for acceptance if it is drawn payable "X days after sight" (when presentation for acceptance is needed to fix the date when it is payable) but a bill generally will be presented for acceptance, since acceptance will make the drawee liable to honour it and thus increases its value. If the drawee fails to accept the bill when presented to him, it is dishonoured by non-acceptance.

Today, bills of exchange are used mainly in a commercial context. For example, S agrees to sell goods to B: B wants credit but S wants immediate payment. S may agree with B that B will accept a bill of exchange drawn on him by S for the price. S will therefore draw a bill on B naming himself as payee, and present it to B for acceptance. S will not supply the goods until the bill is accepted. On B's acceptance, S can discount the bill to a bank or discount house in return for an immediate cash payment. A discounter will pay less than the full face value of the bill to take account of both (i) the fact that the bill is not immediately payable and (ii) the risk that the bill will be dishonoured on presentation for payment. The value of the bill to a discounter will therefore depend on the creditworthiness of B. S will take this fact into account when fixing the price under the contract of sale, which will therefore be higher than if B were to pay on delivery. Alternatively, a bill of exchange can be used as "security" for a loan. Assume that C agrees to make a loan to D. In order to secure repayment, C may require D to accept a bill of exchange for the amount of the loan plus interest; or, where the loan is repayable by instalments, C may require D to accept a series of bills of exchange payable at future dates for the amounts of the instalments. C can then discount the bill(s) for immediate cash payment.

Because the value of a bill of exchange depends on the creditworthiness of the drawee, its value may be increased if drawn on and accepted by a respected and creditworthy institution, such as a bank. In the first example above, therefore, B may agree with his bank that it will accept a bill of exchange for the price of goods sold by S. S will therefore reduce the price

---

5 The only exception to this general rules is where the breach gives rise to a total failure of consideration for which the bill was given or a partial failure in a quantified amount: *Nova (Jersey) Knit Ltd v. Kammgarn Spinnerei GmbH* [1977] 2 All E.R. 463 at 480 (H.L.).

to reflect the increased marketability and value of a bill accepted by B's bank. B will, of course, have to pay his bank for providing this facility.

The law relating to bills of exchange is contained in the Bills of Exchange Act 1882.[6] The 1882 Act, like the Sale of Goods Act 1893, was a consolidating statute which sought to codify the pre-existing case law on bills of exchange, cheques and promissory notes. The proper approach to interpreting the Bills of Exchange Act 1882 and other codifying legislation was outlined by Lord Hershell in *Bank of England v. Vagliano Bros*:[7]

> "...the proper course is in the first instance to examine the language of the statute and to ask what is its natural meaning, uninfluenced by any considerations derived from the previous state of the law, and not to start with inquiring how the law previously stood, and then, assuming that it was probably intended to leave it unaltered, to see if the words of the enactment will bear an interpretation in conformity with this view."

Following this line of reasoning, the purpose of a codifying statute is to remove the need to consult prior case law. Lord Hershell did observe that in exceptional cases reference to prior case law may be permissible.

23.3.1 Defining a bill of exchange

The 1882 Act defines a bill of exchange as

> "an unconditional order in writing addressed by one person to another, signed by the person giving it, requiring the person to whom it is addressed to pay on demand or at a fixed or determinable future time a sum certain in money to or to the order of a specified person, or to bearer."[8]

An instrument which does not comply with these conditions is not a bill of exchange.[9] Each element of this definition is significant and is examined in further detail below.

23.3.1.1 An unconditional order in writing

A bill of exchange must contain an order, or a demand to pay, as opposed to a mere request. An instrument in the form: "You will oblige your humble servant by paying ...," was held to be a mere request and hence not a bill of exchange.[10] Moreover, the order must be unconditional in the sense that

---

6 See also the Cheques Act 1959; and the Consumer Credit Act 1995, s.41.

7 [1891] A.C. 107, at 144.

8 1882 Act, s.3(1).

9 1882 Act, s.3(2).

10 *Little v. Slackford* (1828) 1 M. & M. 171.

there must be no condition on the drawee's liability to pay: an order to pay dependent on a contingency, such as "provided the goods are satisfactory" or "if X is made redundant", is not a bill of exchange.[11] The unconditional nature of the order to pay gives the bill of exchange one of its most important commercial features. As noted above, generally the undertaking to pay in a bill is separate from any underlying commercial contract in connection with which the bill is drawn.[12] Thus, if B buys goods and accepts a bill drawn on him by S for the price, B cannot avoid liability on the bill on the grounds of an (alleged) breach of the underlying contract of sale. In *Walek v. Seafield,*[13] the plaintiff had obtained judgment on foot of the bill dishonoured by the defendant. The defendant sought a stay on the judgment because they were bringing a counterclaim for fundamental breach of contract. The defendant was refused the stay because the court recognised that the undertaking to pay in a bill was separate from the underlying commercial contract.

The only formality is that a bill of exchange must be in writing though, in practice, bills are similar in form. "Writing" is defined to include print,[14] and bills are normally drawn on standard printed forms.[15]

23.3.1.2 Addressed by one person to another, signed by the person giving it

The bill must be addressed by one person to another, and hence the drawer and the drawee must be different persons. As noted above, there is no reason why the drawer cannot draw a bill in favour of himself and hence the drawer and payee can be the same person.

Until signed by the drawer, a bill is not valid. However, a person may sign through an agent, as where a director of a company signs on behalf of the company. Generally, a person who signs a bill is liable on it, and so an

---

11 In *Bavins v. London & South Western Bank* [1900] 1 Q.B. 270, the instruction on a cheque read: "Pay to X provided the receipt form at the foot is duly signed and dated." This did not constitute a cheque/bill of exchange. Further, an instrument payable on a contingency is not a bill of exchange even if the contingency actually occurs: 1882 Act, s.11.

12 There is one exception to this general rule which applies where there is a failure of consideration under the underlying commercial contract: see *Nova Jersey Knit Ltd v. Kammgarn Spinnerei GmbH* [1977] 2 All E.R. 463 (H.L.).

13 [1978] I.R. 167 approving *Nova Jersey Knit Ltd v. Kammgarn Spinnerei GmbH* [1977] 2 All E.R. 463 (H.L.). See also *Terex Equipment Ltd v. Truck and Machinery Sales Ltd* [1994] 1 I.L.R.M. 557.

14 1882 Act, s.2.

15 See further Electronic Commerce Act 2000, s.12.

agent should be careful to make clear the capacity in which he is signing the bill, in order to avoid personal liability.[16] "Signature" is not defined in the 1882 Act. In a different context, "signature" has been given a wide meaning.[17] A rubber-stamp or initials are widely used and may be sufficient.

23.3.1.3 Requiring the person to whom it is addressed to pay on demand or at a fixed or determinable future time

Essentially, there are three options as to the time of payment under a bill of exchange. First, a bill may be payable on *demand*.[18] For instance, a bill of exchange payable "at sight" or "on presentation" is payable on demand and the drawee is required to pay as soon as the bill is presented.[19] A cheque is a bill of exchange payable on demand.[20] Second, a bill may be drawn payable at a *fixed future date*, and third, a bill may be drawn payable at a *determinable future date*, for example, "90 days after date" – in which case it is payable 90 days after the date in the bill – or "90 days after sight" – in which case it is payable 90 days after presentation for acceptance.[21] Such a bill must be presented for acceptance in order to fix the date for payment. A bill payable "90 days after acceptance" would not be valid, since it would not contain an *unconditional* order to pay because the payment obligation would be dependent on acceptance by the drawee.[22] Bills payable at a fixed or determinable time in the future and referred to as "time bills" are generally used as a form of finance allowing the acceptor a period of credit before payment becomes due. In *Creative Press v. Harman*,[23] the instrument was payable "on or before the 1st day of November 1970." The question was whether an instrument which gives the option of earlier payment satisfied the definition of being payable at a fixed or determinable future date. The court held that the instrument satisfied the statutory definition because the option to pay earlier did not alter the nature of the unconditional promise to pay at the time fixed in the instrument.[24]

16 1882 Act, s.26.

17 For instance, in *Casey v. Intercontinental Bank* [1979] I.R. 364, a letter typed on a solicitor's headed note-paper but not personally signed by the solicitor, was sufficient for the purpose of the Statute of Frauds. *Cf. Kelly v. Ross & Ross* unreported, High Court, McWilliam J., April 29, 1980. See further Electronic Commerce Act, s.13.

18 1882 Act, s.10.

19 1882 Act, s.10(1)(a).

20 1882 Act, s.73: see further 23.4.

21 1882 Act, s.11.

22 1882 Act, s.11, but see *Hong Kong & Shanghai Banking Corpn Ltd v. GD Trade Co Ltd* [1998] C.L.C. 238.

23 [1973] I.R. 313.

24 This decision followed the Supreme Court of Canada decision in *John Burrows Ltd v. Subsurface Surveys Ltd* [1968] S.C.R. 607; *cf. Williamson v. Rider* [1963] 1 Q.B. 89 where "on or before" was not acceptable; and *Claydon v. Bradley* [1987] 1 All E.R. 522 where "by" was not acceptable.

23.3.1.4 A sum certain in money[25]

The sum payable must be expressed with certainty. In *Barlow v. Broadhurst*,[26] an instrument which stated: "Pay B after deduction of what he owes me" was held to be not for a sum certain. Moreover, a bill of exchange may order payment in instalments, with interest at a specified rate or in foreign currency at a stated rate of exchange.[27] Where the sum payable is expressed in words and figures and there is a discrepancy between the two, the words prevail over the figures.[28]

23.3.1.5 To or to the order of a specified person, or to bearer[29]

There are three options as to the manner in which a bill of exchange is payable: all qualify as bills within the definition. First, a bill may be payable to a named person – "pay F White" – this bill is transferable. Second, the addition of the words "or order" – "pay F White or order" – confirms that the bill is transferable, although the bill is transferable even without those words unless it is expressed to be payable to "F White only". Therefore, a bill made payable to "F White or order" is payable to F White or any person nominated by F White. Last, a bill may be drawn payable "to bearer". This bill is payable to whomsoever has possession of it and is also transferable. A bill payable to a named payee is transferable by delivery and indorsement; a bearer bill is transferable by simple delivery. An instrument which is payable neither to bearer nor to a named payee, such as "to cash" or "to wages", is not a valid bill of exchange. A bill payable to a non-existent or fictitious payee is treated as a bearer bill and is thus transferable by delivery without indorsement.[30] The case law on this point is complex, but essentially a payee is "fictitious" for this purpose even though there is a real person with the same name as that given for the payee, provided that the drawer of the bill did not intend that person to receive payment of the bill.[31]

23.3.1.6 Other information[32]

In addition to the details required by section 3 of the 1882 Act, a bill of exchange may contain other information. For instance, a bill may be dated with the date when it is drawn. Although this is common, an undated bill

---

25 1882 Act, s.9.

26 (1820) 4 Moor C.P. 471.

27 1882 Act, s.9.

28 1882 Act, s.9(2).

29 1882 Act, s.7.

30 1882 Act, s.7(3).

31 See *Bank* of *England v. Vagliano Bros* [1891] A.C. 107; *Clutton v. Attenborough*[1897] A.C. 90; *cf Vinden v. Hughes* [1905] 1 K.B. 795 [1897] A.C. 90.

32 1882 Act, s.3(4).

is valid unless it is made payable "x days after date",[33] in which case a date must be included to fix the date of payment. However, if no date is stated, any holder may complete the bill by inserting the date, and if the bill comes into the hands of a holder in due course, the date so inserted is deemed to be correct. A bill may also include a statement of the place(s) where it is drawn and/or payable.

23.3.1.7 Incomplete bills

A bill which does not comply with the requirements of section 3 of the 1882 Act is not a valid bill of exchange: the bill can be described as "incomplete" or "inchoate". However, any person in possession of an incomplete bill has prima facie authority to complete it.

23.3.2 Transfer of bills of exchange

A significant number of bills of exchange are not presented for payment by the original payee but are transferred to a third party (usually in return for payment) who may present the bill themselves or transfer it again to another party. Prima facie, all bills of exchange are transferable unless their transferability is restricted by the parties. A bill payable "to X only", or crossed "not transferable" or "not negotiable" is not transferable. The method by which a bill is transferred depends on whether it is a bearer bill or an order bill. A bearer bill can be transferred by simple delivery.[38] Delivery means the transfer of possession, actual or constructive, from one person to another.[39] In contrast, an order bill is transferred by indorsement and delivery.[40] In order to indorse a bill, the payee must sign his name, either on the reverse of the bill or on a slip of paper attached to the bill and known as an "allonge".[41] The indorsement may be general, special or restrictive.

A "general" indorsement consists merely of the payee's signature. Its effect is to convert an order bill into a bearer bill, so that after a general indorsement, the bill can be transferred by simple delivery.[42] However, any holder can convert a generally indorsed bill back into an order bill by writing the name of a person as transferee/payee above the indorser's

33 1882 Act, s.12.
34 1882 Act, s.3(2).
35 1882 Act, s.20.
36 1882 Act, s.8(1).
37 1882 Act, s.8(2).
38 1882 Act, s.31(2).
39 1882 Act, s.2.
40 1882 Act, s.31(3).
41 1882 Act, s.32(1).
42 1882 Act, s.34(1).

signature.[43] A "special" indorsement consists of the payee's signature together with the name of a person to whom the bill is to be transferred, for example, "pay F White" printed above the indorsor's signature. This converts a bill into an order bill. A "restrictive" indorsement limits the further transfer of the bill, either by prohibiting further transfer or by indicating that it is transferred in order to be dealt with in a particular way.[44] For instance, the bill in the example above might be indorsed by the payee "pay F White only," in which case F White cannot further transfer the bill. In the absence of a restrictive indorsement, there is (in theory) no limit to the number of times a bill may be transferred.

23.3.2.1 Forged and unauthorised signatures

An order bill can only be transferred by indorsement with the signature of the payee or last indorsee. This makes an order bill more secure against theft than a bearer bill. The legislation provides that a forged or unauthorised signature has no effect, and the transferee acquires no title to the bill through a forged or unauthorised indorsement.[45] The distinction between a forged indorsement and one which is merely unauthorised is unclear and may be difficult to draw, but it is clear that an unauthorised indorsement can, while a forged indorsement cannot, be ratified.[46] However, a forged indorsement is not wholly ineffective. A person who takes a bill as a result of a forged indorsement can enforce the bill against the person who transferred the bill to him (the forger) but not against persons who became parties to the bill before the forgery. Further, a person who takes a bill as a result of forged indorsement may be able to retain it as against the true holder if the holder is estopped from setting up the forgery or unauthorised signature. In addition, where a bill is drawn payable to a non-existent or fictitious payee, it is treated as a bearer bill so that it can be transferred without indorsement.[47] A person to whom such a bill is indorsed can therefore acquire title to it and enforce it, notwithstanding the fact that the signature on the bill is a "forgery" since his title to the bill does not depend on the signature.

23.3.3 Holders

The person entitled to enforce a bill of exchange by presenting it for payment or by taking enforcement proceedings if it is dishonoured, is called the holder of the bill. Only payment to the holder of a bill can

43 1882 Act, s.34(2).
44 1882 Act, s.35.
45 1882 Act, s.24.
46 1882 Act, s.24.
47 1882 Act, s.7(3).

discharge the payer's liability on the bill. The holder of a bearer bill is the bearer; the holder of an order bill is the payee or indorsee in possession of it.[48] As a result of this definition, a thief can be the holder of a bearer bill. The thief has no title to the bill and so can be refused payment if the theft is known, but as a holder, the thief can transfer the bill to a third party who may qualify as a holder in due course and hence take a perfect title to the bill.

The 1882 Act recognises three classes of holder, each with different rights:

(i) holders;
(ii) holders for value; and
(iii) holders in due course.

Since "holder" status depends, at least in part, on possession of the bill,[49] only one person can be a holder of a bill at any time. Having decided who is the holder, it will then be necessary to classify the holder into one of these three classes above in order to decide what rights he enjoys and what, if any, defences can be raised against him if he seeks to enforce the bill. The basic distinction between the three classes relates to the giving of consideration for the bill.

23.3.3.1 Mere holders

A mere holder is a person in possession of the bill where no value has ever been given for the bill. Every person whose signature appears on the bill is prima facie deemed to have become a party to it for value.[50] And every holder is rebuttably presumed to be a holder in due course.[51] Where these presumptions are rebutted, the mere holder has fewest rights. He is entitled:

(a) to transfer the bill;
(b) to insert the date in the bill if it has been omitted; and
(c) to present the bill for payment.

However, he cannot benefit from the negotiable aspect of the bill, and so his rights are subject to prior equities and defects.

48 1882 Act, s.2.
49 1882 Act, s.2.
50 1882 Act, s.31(1).
51 1882 Act, s.32(2).

23.3.3.2 Holders for value[52]

Since liability on a bill of exchange is contractual, a person against whom a holder seeks to enforce the bill can deny liability if he received no consideration for the bill. However, a holder for value can overcome this objection. A holder will be a holder for value if he, or any previous holder,[53] provided consideration for the bill. For this purpose, consideration is defined widely to include any consideration which would be sufficient to support a simple contract, or an antecedent debt or liability of the person against whom the bill is to be enforced.[54] This appears to be an exception to the rule that past consideration is not sufficient consideration.[55]

> **Example**: Black sells 20 suits to Brown for €1000. One month after delivery, Brown accepts a bill of exchange for €1000 in favour of Black. Black is a holder for value, Brown's existing debt providing consideration for the promise of payment contained in his acceptance of the bill. Black subsequently transfers the bill to White as a birthday present. White is also a holder for value, since Brown provided value for it.

23.3.3.3 Holders in due course[56]

A holder for value can enforce the bill even though the person against whom he enforces it received no consideration for his promise to pay. However, other defences may be raised against a holder for value; for instance, that the bill was obtained by fraud or duress. A holder in due course, however, can enforce the bill free from all defences and defects in title or his predecessors in title: in these circumstances the bill is truly negotiable. Every holder is rebuttably presumed to be a holder in due course.[57] A holder in due course is defined in section 29(1) of the 1882 Act as:

> "a holder who has taken a bill complete and regular on the face of it, under the following conditions, namely,
>
> (a) that he became the holder of it before it was overdue and without notice that it had previously been dishonoured, if such was the fact;

---

52 1882 Act, s.27.

53 1882 Act, s.27(2).

54 1882 Act, s.27(1).

55 See 2.2.2.3.

56 1882 Act, s.29.

57 1882 Act, s.32(2).

(b) that he took the bill in good faith[58] and for value, and that at the time the bill was negotiated to him he had no notice of any defect in the title of the person who negotiated it."

The meaning of "holder in due course" was one of the issues which arose in *Shield Life Insurance Co Ltd & O'Callaghan v. Ulster Bank.*[59] In this case, the defendant bank argued that it was a holder in due course and hence that it held the bill free from any previous defects in title. Two separate frauds had been perpetrated by an insurance broker, O'Callaghan. With regard to the first fraud, Mrs Murphy drew a cheque on her bank in favour of the plaintiff, Shield Life, which she gave to O'Callaghan for transmission to the plaintiff. O'Callaghan indorsed the cheque with the name of his own company and took the cheque to his own bank, the defendant bank, where he lodged some of the proceeds to his office account and the remainder to his client account. He later withdrew the amount from his client account. In an action for conversion by the plaintiff, Shield Life, the defendant bank argued that it was a holder in due course because it took the cheque in good faith for value. While assuming that the defendant bank had given value for the cheque when it credited the amount of the cheque to its customer's account before receiving payment through the clearing system,[60] the court found that the bank was not a holder in due course for three reasons. First, to be a holder in due course, a person must first be a holder as defined in section 2 of the 1882 Act, which "means a payee or indorsee of a bill … or the bearer thereof." Bearer, in turn, "means the person in possession of the bill … which is payable to bearer." The court found that the defendant did not come within any of these definitions. The payee was the plaintiff, Shield Life, and therefore there could be no bearer, and the cheque had not been properly indorsed to the bank and so the bank was not an indorsee. Second, there was an irregularity on the face of the cheque, because it had not been indorsed by the payee before being transferred. Third, the absence of an indorsement meant that the bank had notice of the defect in title of the person negotiating the cheque.

Once a bill has come into the hands of a holder in due course, all prior defects in title are cured. Subsequent holders can therefore enforce the bill against all persons who became party to it before it came into the hands of the holder in due course, free of all defects in title, even if they are aware of them. The only exception is that a person who acquires a bill through a

58 1882 Act, s.90 defines good faith as an action done honestly, whether it is done negligently or not. It has been held that a holder will not have acted in good faith if he has been wilfully blind and deliberately avoided having notice of possible defects: *Jones v. Gordon* (1877) 2 All Cas. 616; *Bank of Ireland v. EBS* [1998] 2 I.L.R.M. 451 (S.C.).

59 [1995] 3 I.R. 225; see further Donnelly, "Cheque Fraud: Modern Treatment and Future Trends" [1997] *Commercial Law Practitioner* 216.

60 See further 23.4.4. See further *Underwood v. Barclays Bank* [1924] 1 K.B. 775.

holder in due course cannot take free of defects if he was party to the conduct which gave rise to the defect.[61]

23.3.4 Liability on a bill of exchange

The general rule is that every person who puts his name to a bill, as drawer, acceptor or indorser, becomes liable on it and the bill can be enforced against him by persons to whom it is subsequently transferred. In addition, a person who transfers a bearer bill may be liable in certain circumstances if it is dishonoured. The person primarily liable is the acceptor or, if the drawee fails to accept, the drawer. Other parties are only liable if the person primarily liable fails to honour the bill.

23.3.4.1 Capacity[62]

No one can be held liable on a bill unless he has the capacity to incur contractual liability. So, for example, an infant or minor will not be liable on a bill. Equally, a company may lack the necessary capacity if its Memorandum and Articles of Association do not provide for the exercise of such powers. Generally, a trading company will have implied power to draw, accept and indorse bills of exchange. Where a party lacks capacity, he cannot be held liable on the bill but the bill remains valid and fully enforceable against other parties.

23.3.4.2 Signature[63]

A person's liability on a bill prima facie depends on him having signed it. Difficulties arise if a person whose signature appears on a bill claims that it was placed there without his authority. The signature may be forged or unauthorised.[64] A person whose signature on a bill is forged incurs no liability unless he is estopped from asserting the forgery, as, for instance, if, having become aware that his signature on the bill had been forged, he stood by while the person seeking to enforce the bill gave value for it. If the drawer's signature on the bill is forged, there is no bill of exchange at all. In the case of unauthorised signatures, a person incurs no liability on a bill through an unauthorised signature unless (i) he is estopped from denying the signor's authority or (ii) he subsequently ratifies the signature. An agent who signs a bill on behalf of his principal may incur personal liability on it if he signs his own name, unless his signature clearly indicates that he signs as agent and does not undertake personal liability.[65]

61 1882 Act, s.29(3).
62 1882 Act, s.22.
63 1882 Act, s.23.
64 1882 Act, s.24.
65 1882 Act, s.26(1).

23.3.4.3 Delivery[66]

Every contract on a bill is incomplete and revocable until the bill is delivered. The only exceptional case, where liability is complete without delivery, is if the drawee of a bill notifies the person entitled to payment that he accepts the bill. "Delivery" means the transfer of possession, actual or constructive, from one person to another.[67] Delivery may be conditional: for instance, if a person orders goods and gives the seller a bill of exchange for the price, he may deliver the bill conditionally on delivery of the goods.

Since delivery is necessary to complete liability on a bill, a person who signs a bill and then loses it, or has it stolen, is prima facie not liable on it. However, it is rebuttably presumed that a bill has been delivered by every signatory to it and if the bill comes into the hands of a holder in due course, it is irrebuttably presumed that it has been delivered by all prior parties to it.[68] Hence, the transferability of bills is promoted.

23.3.4.4 The undertakings given by parties to the bill

Each person who becomes a party to a bill by signing and delivering it gives certain contractual undertakings relating to its payment. In addition, each party is bound by certain estoppels relating to existing facts and events prior to his becoming a party to the bill.

(i) Acceptor

The acceptor is the party primarily liable on the bill. By accepting the bill, he undertakes that at maturity he will honour the bill in accordance with the terms of his acceptance. In addition, as against a holder in due course, he is estopped from denying:

(a) the drawer's existence, capacity and authority to draw the bill;
(b) the genuineness of the drawer's signature; and
(c) the payee's existence and capacity to indorse the bill.[69]

(ii) Accommodation party

A person may accept a bill in order to increase its marketability by lending the value of his name to the bill to increase its marketability. Such a person is referred to as "an accommodation party".[70]

66 1882 Act, s.21.
67 1882 Act, s.2.
68 1882 Act, s.22(2).
69 1882 Act, s.54.
70 1882 Act, s.28.

> **Example**: If A wishes to borrow money from B, he may draw on C and get C to accept a bill in favour of B for the amount of the loan. Effectively C acts as guarantor of the loan; he is then an accommodation party and the bill is an accommodation bill.

Where a person accepts a bill as an accommodation party, the drawer, and not the acceptor, is primarily liable on the bill. Thus if C is called on to pay the bill he may seek reimbursement from A.

(iii) Drawer

The drawer's liability can be described as secondary in that the drawer does not undertake to pay the bill. Instead, the drawer undertakes that on presentation the bill will be accepted and paid and that, if not, he will compensate the holder or any indorsee who pays the bill, provided that the necessary dishonour proceedings are taken. The drawer's undertaking to pay compensation following dishonour will normally include the value of the bill, plus interest and the cost of enforcement.[71] As against a holder in due course, he is estopped from denying the existence of the payee and his capacity to indorse the bill.[72]

(iv) Indorser

Each person who indorses the bill becomes party to it and gives the same undertakings as the drawer.[73] He is estopped, as against a holder in due course, from denying the genuineness and regularity of the drawer's signature or of any indorsements prior to his own.[74] In addition, as against subsequent indorsees, he is estopped from denying that the bill was valid and that he had a good title to it at the time of his indorsement.[75]

> **Example**: A draws a bill of exchange on B, payable to C. It is stolen by D, who forges C's indorsement and transfers it to E, who transfers it to F.
>
> A B C D E F
>
> Since no title to a bill is conferred by a forged signature, F has no title to the bill as against A, B and C; however, both D and E are bound as indorsers and both are estopped from denying that they had a good title to it at the time of their indorsements. F can therefore enforce the bill against D or E; similarly if E pays F, E can enforce the bill against D.

71 1882 Act, s.57.
72 1882 Act, s.55(1).
73 1882 Act, s.55(2)(a).
74 1882 Act, s.55(2)(b).
75 1882 Act, s.55(2)(c).

Any other person who signs a bill is liable on it as if he were an indorser.[76]

(v) Signature without recourse

The drawer and indorsers of the bill can avoid liability on it by drawing/indorsing it "without recourse," in which case he will add the words "without recourse" or "sans recours" after his signature to indicate to future parties that he accepts no liability for the bill being honoured.

(vi) Transferor of a bearer bill

A bearer bill can be transferred by delivery, without signature, and hence the transferor of a bearer bill does not become a party to the bill. However, a person who transfers a bearer bill by simple delivery gives the following warranties to the transferee:

(a) that the bill is genuine as it purports to be;
(b) that he has the right to transfer it;
(c) that he is not aware of any facts which make the bill worthless.[77]

If the holder of a bearer bill signs it, he becomes a party to the bill and is liable as an indorser.

23.3.5 Procedures for enforcement of a bill of exchange

Unless a bill is an accommodation bill, the person primarily liable to honour it is the drawee. However, if he fails to honour it, either by refusing to accept or pay it, the holder may take steps against any prior party to the bill to enforce their undertakings with regard to the bill, as described above. The 1882 Act prescribes certain steps which the holder must take on dishonour if he is to enforce the bill against anyone other than the drawee; generally failure to take the prescribed steps will release some or all previous parties from liability on the bill.

23.3.5.1 Presentation of the bill

Generally, the holder must present the bill (unless it is a demand bill):[78]

(i) for acceptance, and
(ii) for payment.

---

76 1882 Act, s.56.
77 1882 Act, s.58
78 1882 Act, s.39.

A bill payable "X days after sight" must be presented for acceptance to fix the date of payment,[79] and it must be presented within a reasonable time.[80] If the bill is not presented within a reasonable time, the drawer and any prior indorsers are released from liability.[81] Where a bill expressly stipulates that it must be presented for acceptance, or where a bill is drawn payable elsewhere than at the residence or place of business of the drawee, it must be presented for acceptance.[82] Otherwise, presentation for acceptance is not required.[83] The statutory rules on acceptance are set out in sections 39–44 and are very detailed. For example, where required, presentation must be to the drawee or his authorised representative (often a bank).[84] Presentation may be excused in certain circumstances, as where presentation is impossible despite the exercise of reasonable diligence.[85] But presentation is not excused because the holder believes that the bill will not be accepted on presentation.[86]

All bills of exchange must be presented for payment in accordance with the statutory rules.[87] If not properly presented, the drawer and any prior indorsers are released from liability.[88] Generally, presentation for payment must take place at the correct time and place. For instance, where the bill is a "time bill," it must be presented for payment on the day the bill falls due.[89] Where the bill is a demand bill, it must be presented for payment within a reasonable time of its issue to make the drawer liable, and a reasonable time after its indorsement to make the indorser liable.[90] Presentation for payment may be excused in limited circumstances, as where presentation is impossible despite the exercise of reasonable diligence,[91] but otherwise failure to present for payment at the proper time and place operates to release prior parties.

---

79 1882 Act, s.39(1).

80 1882 Act, s.40(1). On what constitutes "reasonable time," see s.40(3).

81 1882 Act, s.40(2).

82 1882 Act, s.39(2).

83 1882 Act, s.39(3).

84 1882 Act, s.41(1).

85 1882 Act, s.41(2).

86 1882 Act, s.41(3).

87 1882 Act, s.45-46.

88 1882 Act, s.45.

89 1882 Act, s.45(1).

90 1882 Act, s.45(2). On what constitutes "reasonable time," see s.45(2). There is a difference, for example, in what is reasonable for an ordinary holder presenting a cheque for payment and for a banker presenting a customer's cheque for payment, with the ordinary holder being given more time: *Royal Bank of Ireland v. O'Rourke* [1962] I.R. 159 (S.C.) where it was held that a bank presenting a cheque for payment was not bound to present the cheque for payment on the day it received it, but had until post time the following day to transmit it to the paying bank. See also *Brennan v. Bank of Ireland* unreported, High Court, Murphy, J., May 23, 1985; *cf. Barclays Bank plc v. Bank of England* [1985] 1 All E.R. 385.

91 1882 Act, s.46(2).

23.3.5.2 Notice of dishonour

Once presented, the drawee must deal with the bill of exchange either by discharge,[92] or by dishonour. If the drawee fails to accept the bill as drawn,[93] or, having accepted it, fails to pay it,[94] the bill is dishonoured by non-acceptance or non-payment, as appropriate. In that case, the holder can enforce the undertakings given by the drawer or indorsers, but in order to do so he must, within a reasonable time, give notice of dishonour to every previous party to be held liable.[95] The legislation contains detailed rules on the timing and content of the notice. Notice of dishonour is excused in certain circumstances,[97] but generally failure to notify any party of dishonour in accordance with the legislative rules will release that party from liability on the bill,[98] unless the bill is subsequently negotiated to a holder in due course. A notice of dishonour given by one party to another protects not only the person giving the notice but also all intermediate parties in the liability chain.[99]

> **Example**: A draws a bill on B, payable to C. C indorses it in favour of D who presents it to B. B refuses payment and D gives notice of dishonour to A and C. He can then take enforcement proceedings against either C or A; if he takes proceedings against C, C can in turn take proceedings against A, relying on the notice given by D.

23.3.6 Defences to liability on a bill of exchange

A person against whom it is sought to enforce a bill of exchange may raise a number of defences in order to seek to avoid liability. The validity of some of these defences depends on whether the relationship between the person seeking to enforce the bill and the person against whom the bill is to be enforced is immediate or remote. The relationships between drawer and drawee, drawer and payee, and indorser and indorsee are all immediate. All other relationships are remote. Thus the relationship between a person to whom a bill is indorsed and the original acceptor of the bill is remote.

First, as against an immediate party, a person may avoid liability on a bill by showing that his undertaking on the bill is voidable on the grounds of duress, misrepresentation or undue influence. These are personal

92 See 23.3.7.

93 1882 Act, s.43.

94 1882 Act, s.47.

95 1882 Act, s.48, esp. s.49(12) on reasonable time. See further *Royal Bank of Ireland v. O'Rourke* [1962] I.R. 159 (S.C.).

96 1882 Act, s.49.

97 1882 Act, s.50.

98 1882 Act, s.48.

99 1882 Act, ss.49(3) and (4).

defences and cannot be raised against a remote party who is a holder in due course. Further, as against an immediate party, a person may avoid liability by showing that there is a total failure of the consideration for which that undertaking was given; there may be such a failure as a result of a breach of the underlying contract. This is also a personal defence. Second, a person may deny liability to the person seeking to enforce the bill by showing that that person has no title to it, because it was stolen, for example, or by showing that he is not a party to the bill on the grounds that his signature on the bill was forged or placed there without his authority. Third, a person may deny liability by showing that there is no valid bill, because the statutory requirements for a valid bill are not fulfilled. Fourth, a person other than the acceptor may avoid liability by showing that the required proceedings were not taken on dishonour. And lastly, a person may avoid liability by showing that the bill has been materially altered without his consent.[100] If a bill is materially altered and the alteration is apparent, the bill is wholly avoided as against all persons who became party to the bill before the alteration, unless they consent to it. Where the alteration is not apparent, a holder in due course may enforce the bill against persons who became party to it prior to the alteration in accordance with its original terms. An altered bill may be enforced as altered against any person who becomes party to it after the alteration.

23.3.7 Discharge of the bill

The person primarily liable on a bill of exchange is the drawee/acceptor. However, if he fails to honour the bill, the holder may either:

(i) seek to enforce his undertaking on the bill by legal action; or
(ii) enforce the bill against one of the other parties liable on it, providing the appropriate proceedings have been taken on dishonour.

If anyone other than the drawee/acceptor pays the bill, all subsequent parties are discharged from liability but the bill generally remains enforceable against prior parties.

An indorser who pays a bill may either:

(i) cancel all endorsements subsequent to his own and re-issue it for value; or
(ii) enforce the bill against a previous party.

If the drawer pays the bill, he may enforce it against the drawee/acceptor, unless it was an accommodation bill.

100 1882 Act, s.64(2).

> **Example**: A draws a bill on B, payable to C. C transfers the bill to D by indorsing it and D transfers to E in the same way. If B fails to honour the bill on presentation, E should give notice of dishonour to D, C and A. He may then enforce it against any of them. If he enforces it against C, as indorser, D is discharged but C may either (i) cancel D's indorsement and re-issue the bill or (ii) enforce the bill against A or B.

The undertakings contained in the bill therefore remain enforceable until the bill is discharged.

A bill may be discharged in the following ways. First, by payment in due course by or on behalf of the drawee/acceptor. A payment is only "in due course" if made:

(i) on or after maturity;
(ii) to the holder; and
(iii) in good faith without notice of any defect in the holder's title.[101]

Second, a bill can be discharged by the acceptor becoming the holder of the bill because any legal action by the holder against himself would be impossible.[102] Third, a bill may be discharged by the holder renouncing his rights either on the bill as a whole or against one or more individual parties.[103] Fourth, a bill may be discharged by cancellation of the bill or of the liability of one or more parties.[104] And lastly, a bill may be partially discharged where it is materially altered without the assent of all parties liable on the bill.[105]

23.4 Cheques

The use of cheques is now in decline with the rise in the use of other payment mechanisms including automated payments, such as direct debits and standing orders. Nevertheless, it would appear that cheques remain the single most used payment method and are particularly important in business-to-business payments.[106]

---

101 1882 Act, s.59(1).
102 1882 Act, s.61.
103 1882 Act, s.62.
104 1882 Act, s.63.
105 1882 Act, s.64.
106 Payments Systems of the European Union (European Monetary Institute, 1998) p.277; see further www.ecb.int.

23.4.1 Cheques defined

A cheque is defined by section 73 of the Bills of Exchange Act 1882 as "a bill of exchange drawn on a banker payable on demand." It follows therefore that a valid cheque must satisfy the requirements for a valid bill of exchange.[107] In general, the law applicable to bills of exchange applies equally to cheques, although there are rules which apply specifically to cheques and not bills of exchange.[108] However, cheques are used very differently from other types of bills of exchange. Commonly cheques are used to withdraw cash or to pay a third party: they are rarely negotiated.

A cheque is an order from a customer to his bank to pay money in accordance with the terms of the cheque. As noted in Chapter 22, the bank makes the payment out of its own funds and recoups the amount by debiting the customer's account, hence reducing its indebtedness to the customer.[109] Unlike other bills of exchange, a cheque is not accepted by the drawee, so that the bank on which it is drawn is under no obligation to the payee to honour the cheque. Instead, primary liability on a cheque falls on the drawer. This is modified where a cheque is supported by a cheque guarantee card, in which case the bank does come under an obligation to the payee, but that obligation is based on the undertaking contained in the card rather than any undertaking in the cheque itself.[110] However, the drawee bank is, in all cases, under an obligation to its customer to honour cheques drawn by him so long as there are sufficient funds in his account to meet the cheque.[111] Where a bank wrongfully dishonours a cheque when there are funds available,[112] the bank is liable to the customer for breach of contract and the customer can sue the bank for damages for any loss caused. Moreover, where a cheque is returned unpaid, the wording on the cheque, such as "refer to drawer," may be defamatory thereby allowing the customer to sue for damages for defamation.[113]

23.4.2 Obtaining payment

A payee can obtain payment of the sum ordered in the cheque in three different ways. First, as a bill of exchange, a cheque can be presented to the drawee for cash payment. Hence, a payee can personally present the cheque for payment at the bank branch where it is drawn, that is, the branch where the drawer holds his account. This may be impractical for the payee, so secondly, as an alternative, a payee can use his own bank to act

107 See 23.3.1.

108 See Part III of the 1882 Act and the Cheques Act 1959.

109 *Foley v. Hill* (1848) 2 H.L.C. 28.

110 *First Sport Ltd v. Barclays Bank plc* [1993] 3 All E.R. 789: see also 5.3.1.1.

111 See 22.3.1.

112 *Marzetti v. Williams* 1 B. & Ad. 415.

113 *Pike v. Hibernian Bank* [1950] I.R. 195; *Kinlan v. Ulster Bank* [1928] I.R. 171 at 183 (S.C.); *Jayson v. Midland Bank Ltd* [1968] I Lloyd's Rep. 409 (C.A.).

as agent to present the cheque for payment on his behalf. In such circumstances, the cheque is presented through the clearing system, and the cheque is credited to the payee's account by his own bank. Third, a cheque may be transferred to a third party for an immediate cash payment. In effect, the third party buys the cheque and presents it for payment on its own behalf. However, the choice of payment may be limited by a crossing on the cheque, affecting its transferability.

23.4.3 Crossing cheques

As a bill of exchange, a cheque is a negotiable instrument and hence is transferable. However, such transferability exposes the holder or payee to the risk of theft or fraud. Crossings or other markings on a cheque can restrict its transferability, and hence make it more secure. Different forms of crossing have different legal effects. Three forms of crossing are covered in the 1882 Act: a general crossing; a special crossing; and a not-negotiable crossing. A further type of crossing, "account payee," has no legislative basis in Ireland.

The simplest form of crossing is a general crossing. This is effected by drawing two parallel lines across the face of the cheque; the words "and company" or "& Co" can be inserted between the lines.[114] As a result, the cheque must be presented for payment through a bank account; it cannot be cashed. Alternatively, a cheque can be specially crossed. This involves inserting the name of a particular bank between the parallel lines,[115] and the effect is that the cheque can only be presented for payment at the bank named. In addition, generally or specially crossed cheques can be marked or crossed with the words "not negotiable." This type of crossing negatives the negotiability of the cheque, that is, if the cheque is transferred, the transferee can obtain no better title than the transferor. Importantly, such a crossing does not prevent the cheque from being transferred.[116]

In order to make cheques more secure, the practice has developed of generally crossing a cheque and putting the words "account payee" or "account of F White" between the two parallel lines. The intention is to ensure that the cheque can be lodged into the payee's or F White's account only. The legal effect of this type of crossing is unclear,[117] and has been addressed by legislation in the United Kingdom. There, under the Cheques Act 1992, such a crossing has the effect of rendering the cheque non-transferable and valid only as between the parties thereto.[118] Similar legislation is awaited in Ireland.

---

114 1882 Act, s.76(1).

115 1882 Act, s.76(2).

116 1882 Act, s. 81; see also *Shield Life Insurance Co Ltd & O'Callaghan v. Ulster Bank* [1995] 3 I.R. 225.

117 *National Bank v. Silk* [1891] 1 Q.B. 435.

118 The 1992 Act inserted a new s.81(a)(1) into the 1882 Act.

23.4.4 The clearing system

There are in fact a number of clearing systems to deal with different types of payment orders.[119] The cheque clearing system is operated by the Irish Paper Debit Clearing Company Ltd,[120] but not all cheques are cleared through the Irish Paper Debit Clearing Company Ltd: some cheques can be collected locally. As noted above, a cheque can be presented for payment at the bank branch where it was drawn, that is, at the drawer's branch. In these circumstances, the cheque can be cleared internally at the branch, and payment can be received in one business day, without the need of the services of the Irish Paper Debit Clearing Company Ltd. Similarly, if a cheque is presented for payment at a different branch of the same bank on which it is drawn, payment can be made through the bank's internal collection system without the need to utilise the clearing system operated by the Irish Paper Debit Clearing Company Ltd. However, where a payee lodges a cheque with his own bank, a bank different from the bank on which the cheque is drawn, the payee's bank acts as his agent in presenting the cheque for payment.[121] This presentation is operated through the clearing system. Today, presentation of a cheque for payment involves a bilateral exchange of cheques between members of the Irish Paper Debit Clearing Company Ltd. Settlement of the cheques exchanged each day is made on a multilateral net basis,[122] and takes place through members' accounts held at the Central Bank. The whole process is slow, taking from three days to complete if the cheque is honoured and up to five days where the cheque is dishonoured. For example, on Day 1, the payee lodges the cheque at his bank (the collecting bank) and the receipt of the cheque is noted on the payee's bank records. On Day 2, the collecting bank sends the cheque to its clearing department, where all cheques are sorted and bundled and sent to the clearing departments of the banks on which they are drawn (the paying bank). At the close of business, each paying bank pays the value of cheques received to the collecting bank. As part of this process the paying bank can off-set any amounts due from the collecting bank that day. By the close of business, the cheque is "cleared for value",

119 The systems are operated by five companies: the Irish Paper Debit Clearing Company Ltd for cheques; the Irish Paper Credit Clearing Company Ltd for credit transfers; Irish Retail Electronic Clearing Company (IRECC) for electronic debits and credits; and the Irish Real Time InterBank Settlement Company Ltd (IRIS) which deals with high-value funds transferred on a "real time gross settlement basis", and Laser Card Services Ltd. All of these bodies are members of the Irish Payment Services Organisation: see further www.ipso.ie

120 The members of this company include the main banks, and the Central Bank. Where a non-member bank wishes to use the system, it must engage a member bank to act as agent on its behalf.

121 On presentation of bills of exchange for payment, see 1882 Act, s.45: see 23.3.5.1. See further *Royal Bank of Ireland v. O'Rourke* [1962] I.R. 159.

122 The amount due from Bank A to the other members of the system is set off against the amount due to Bank A from the other members of the system.

that is, the cheque's value is credited to the payee's account. On Day 3, the clearing department of the paying bank sends the cheque to the payor's branch of the bank. If there are enough funds in the payor's account, the account is debited with the amount of the cheque and this transaction is backdated to Day 2 of the process. At this point, the cheque is "cleared for fate," that is, the cheque has been paid and the payee can withdraw the amount from his account.

Because of the high volume usage of cheques, and because most cheque payments involve two banks, the collecting and the paying bank, cheques are particularly susceptible to theft and fraud. As a result, legislation offers collecting and paying banks protection where cheques are forged provided generally that the paying bank acts in good faith and in the ordinary course of business,[123] or that the collecting bank acted in good faith and without negligence.[124]

23.5 Promissory Notes

A promissory note is a promise to pay a sum of money. Bank notes are promissory notes; notes other than bank notes are no longer widely used other than in international transactions. They may be used as a form of security for a loan, the lender requiring the borrower to provide a promissory note for the amount of the loan.[125] A promissory note is defined as:

> "an unconditional promise made in writing by one person to another signed by the maker, engaging to pay on demand or at a fixed or determinable future time, a sum certain in money to, or to the order of, a specified person or to bearer."[126]

A valid note must comply with all aspects of this definition. A note must be distinguished from an I.O.U., which is a mere acknowledgement of a debt rather than a promise to pay. The definition of a promissory note is similar to that of a bill of exchange, and the law relating to bills and notes is largely similar. It follows that a note can be transferred and negotiated in the same way as a bill. The law relating to notes is contained in Part III of the Bills of Exchange Act 1882. The main difference between bills and notes is that a note is never accepted: it is a promise, rather than an order, to pay. And since, unlike a bill, a note is not accepted, liability to honour a note falls on the maker and any indorser.

123 1882 Act, ss.60 and 80, and the Cheques Act 1959, s.1.

124 Cheques Act 1959, s.4; see further *Shield Life Insurance Co Ltd & O'Callaghan v. Ulster Bank* [1995] 3 I.R. 225.

125 Their use is restricted by the Consumer Credit Act 1995, s.41.

126 1882 Act, s.83.

23.6 Bank Drafts

A bank draft is a draft drawn by a bank on itself requiring it to pay a specified amount to a named payee. A bank draft does not qualify as a bill of exchange because the drawer and the drawee/acceptor are not separate persons.[127] However, although bank drafts are not bills of exchange or cheques, they are made subject to the Cheques Act 1959.[128] Bank drafts are commonly used where the payee wishes to be as certain of payment as may be possible. Because the draft is drawn on a bank, there is little doubt as to payment, unless the bank becomes insolvent. Bank drafts can also be used by persons who do not hold a current account or have cheque book facilities.

23.7 Automated Payments and Electronic Fund Transfers

Developments in technology have led to huge changes in modern banking practices. Traditional payment methods, such as cheques, are in decline, while automated payments and electronic fund transfers are on the increase. Moreover, banking services are being provided directly to the office or the home via telephone or the internet rather than in person at the bank's branch office. While these developments might be expected to speed up the banking process, the result is not necessarily so, although they do offer convenience and security. There is as yet very little legal authority on the legal implications of these developments.[129] For example, it is not clear a when is payment complete and hence thus incapable of being countermanded.[130]

Automated payments comprise standing orders, direct credits and direct debits. Payments may be initiated either by the payer or the payee. Credit transfers are initiated by the payer and include standing orders, used for regular repeat payments, such as savings; and direct credits, used by a business to order its bank, using one form, to pay several payees, such as salary payments to employees. In contrast, direct debits are initiated by the payee, who obtains authority from the payer to order the payer's bank to make such payments as the payee may demand from time to time. Direct debits are used for regular payments where the amount may differ, such as utility bills and mortgage repayments at a variable rate. Automated payments offer convenience all around. Payments are made directly from

---

127 1882 Act, s.3: see 23.3.1.2.

128 1959 Act, s.1(2).

129 See generally Donnelly, *The Law of Banks and Credit Institutions* (Dublin, Round Hall Sweet & Maxwell, 2000) Chapter 12.

130 *Ibid.* pp.324–328.

the payer's bank to the payee's bank via the clearing system. Where repeat payments have to be made, as with standing orders or direct debit mandates, one written authority is all that is needed. Automated payments also reduce the potential for fraud. Except in the case of direct debits, the instruction goes directly from the payer to his bank with no risk of the payee altering the amount of the order. Also, the risk of loss or theft of the order is minimal when compared with cheques.

Electronic fund transfers (EFT) describes a number of different systems in which the instruction to a bank to make a payment to the credit of a particular payee, or to debit a particular account, is given by electronic means, normally using a computer system.[131] Examples include the use of automated teller machines (ATMs) used for cash withdrawals, and electronic fund transfers at point of sale (EFTPOS) used for the payment of goods or services (Laser cards). These latter two mechanisms offer convenience and security to consumers, though they are of limited use to business customers as payment mechanisms.

131 See further UNCITRAL's Legal Guide on Electronic Funds Transfers (1987): see www.uncitral.org.

CHAPTER 24

COMMERCIAL CREDIT AND SECURITY

24.1 CREDIT

Most businesses rely on credit facilities. A business which does not have sufficient capital to finance its spending must obtain credit facilities, usually from fellow traders and/or financial institutions. Moreover, and generally, as a business expands so too does its need for credit facilities.[1]

24.1.1 Types of credit

Credit has been defined as "the provision of a benefit (cash, land, goods, services and facilities) for which payment is to be made by the recipient in money at a later date."[2] Credit, therefore, can be provided by several different types of arrangements and can be classified in a number of ways. Two important classifications involve distinctions between loan and sales credit; and between fixed term and revolving credit.

Loan credit involves the advance of money; sales (or supplier) credit involves a deferment of a payment obligation under a supply contract. A loan is a payment of money by a creditor to a debtor as a means of benefiting and enriching the debtor, upon condition that the money paid, plus any interest and charges, shall be repaid by the debtor to the creditor at a specified rate over a specified period. Examples include bank loans and overdrafts. In contrast, a deferment of a payment obligation occurs where the buyer of goods or the recipient of services obtains the benefit of the goods or services without having to pay the price immediately and/or in full. Examples include conditional sales and hire-purchase arrangements.[3] The practical effect of these two types of credit is the same: the debtor/buyer receives a benefit without having to incur immediate expenditure and hence a drain on capital resources. However, loan and sales credit have, historically, been treated differently by the law. The courts have tended to regarded price deferment mechanisms as different

---

1 According to the U.K. Cork Report on Insolvency Law and Practice, "credit is the lifeblood of the modern industrialised economy" (Cmnd. 8558, 1982) para 10.

2 Goode, *Commercial Law*, (London, Penguin, 2nd ed., 1995) p.637.

3 On the distinctions between contracts for the sale of goods, conditional sales and hire-purchase arrangements, see generally 9.3.5.

from loan and security arrangements. However, the Consumer Credit Act 1995 applies to both types of arrangement.[4]

A business that wishes to purchase goods or services on credit therefore has a choice of sources of credit. It may obtain the goods or services on credit from the supplier, or it may obtain loan credit from a third party, such as a bank, and use that credit facility to finance the purchase. Loan credit has the advantage of flexibility: the loan can be used for any purpose (although in some cases the debtor may be contractually obliged to use the loan for a particular purpose). On the other hand, loan credit may appear to be more expensive, because a debtor will have to pay for the credit facility through the payment of interest on the amount of the loan. However, a debtor will generally also have to pay for sales credit since the amount actually paid to the creditor will be increased to compensate the supplier for the fact that he is deprived of the use of the price to be paid for the credit period; and to cover the risk of non-payment.

The second classification is based on the distinction between fixed-term and revolving credit. Under a fixed-term credit arrangement, a fixed amount is drawn by the debtor and is repaid over a stated period. The arrangement comes to an end on completion of the repayments. Examples include a personal loan and a hire-purchase arrangement. Alternatively, credit can be provided using a revolving facility. In such circumstances, the debtor is not given a fixed amount but an upper credit limit is set, as with overdraft or credit card facilities, for example. The debtor can make one or more drawings of any amount provided that at any time the total amount outstanding does not exceed the fixed upper limit. He is not obliged to use the full facility. Each drawing reduces the amount of the credit facility, and as the debtor repays amounts to the creditor the facility is replenished.

24.1.2 Consumer Credit Act 1995[5]

The Consumer Credit Act 1995 regulates the credit industry involved in the supply of credit to consumers, defined as a natural person acting outside his trade, business or profession.[6] Business credit agreements therefore fall outside the ambit of the Act. The Act applies to all credit agreements (whether loan or sales credit), hire-purchase agreements and consumer-hire agreements.[7] There are also Parts in the 1995 Act on moneylending,[8] housing loans,[9] and pawnbrokers.[10] The Act imposes controls on

4 See 24.1.2.

5 The 1995 Act, bar one provision, came into operation on May 13, 1996: S.I. No. 121 of 1996. This legislation seeks to implement EC legislation in the area including Directive 87/102 [1987] O.J. L42 and Directive 90/88 [1990] O.J. L61.

6 1995 Act, s.2(1).

7 1995 Act, s.3(1).

8 1995 Act, Part VIII.

9 1995 Act, Part IX.

10 1995 Act, Part XV.

advertising and contains provisions regulating individual credit agreements including:

(a) the formation and form of agreements;
(b) termination of agreements;
(c) default by the debtor;
(d) enforcement by the creditor.

Consumer credit is not within the scope of this book and will not be considered further.[11]

24.2 Security

Before a creditor will be willing to advance credit to a debtor, he will want to be satisfied that the debt will be repaid. If the potential debtor is a creditworthy business, the creditor may be happy, on the basis of the strength of the debtor's business alone, that the debt will be repaid. However, creditworthiness may be difficult to assess, especially in times of recession. Equally, a harmonious trading relationship in the past may give rise to a confidence on the creditor's part that all debts due will be paid. Creditors less sure of their debtors' willingness to pay can use various contractual mechanisms to encourage prompt payment, such as offering discounts for early payment, and/or charging interest for late payment.[12]

Non-payment of a debt can occur where the debtor refuses to pay or is unable to pay. A debtor may refuse to pay when, for example, he alleges that the creditor is in breach of contract. To enforce payment, the creditor may ultimately have to resort to legal proceedings. More serious perhaps, is a creditor's fear that the debtor will be unable to pay the debt. A debtor who is unable to pay his debts is insolvent.[13] Where a debtor becomes insolvent, an insolvency practitioner can be appointed to take over the management of the debtor's property and distribute it to discharge the debtor's liabilities. Where an individual becomes insolvent, he can be declared bankrupt, and his property can be collected and distributed by an official assignee.[14] Where a company becomes insolvent, the business may be wound up by a liquidator. Alternatively, a secured creditor may have the

---

11 See further, Bird, *Consumer Credit Law* (Dublin, Round Hall Sweet & Maxwell, 1998); Donnelly, *The Law of Banks and Credit Institutions* (Dublin, Round Hall Sweet & Maxwell, 2000) Chapter 16.

12 On the late payment of commercial debts, see 21.2.1.

13 For example, the Sale of Goods Act provides that "a person is deemed to be insolvent … who has either ceased to pay his debts in the ordinary course of business or cannot pay his debts as they fall due …":1893 Act, s.62(3).

14 See the Bankruptcy Act 1988; see further Forde, *Bankruptcy Law in Ireland* (Dublin, Butterworths, 1990).

right to appoint a receiver whose job is to take over the management of the company and to realise sufficient assets to pay the appointing creditor. Sometimes the actions of a receiver will have the effect of "turning the company around", but often the appointment of a receiver is a precursor to the appointment of a liquidator. On insolvency, debts are paid following a statutory scheme of order, which is basically the same regardless of the type of insolvency proceedings. Creditors are ranked into separate classes for the purpose of this scheme. The costs of the insolvency procedure itself, the claims of preferential creditors, and secured creditors are paid before any claims of unsecured creditors. Moreover, no creditor can be paid unless all the creditors in the prior class are paid in full. Where there are insufficient funds to meet all the claims within a class, each creditor receives a rateable proportion of the amount due to him. Therefore, the ordinary unsecured creditor will rank behind those of the buyer's preferential and secured creditors. In most cases, the unsecured creditor will only receive a percentage of the sum due to him, in the form of a "dividend"; in many cases he will receive nothing. A creditor can minimise the risk of a debtor's insolvency by taking security for payment of a debt: the security exists to reinforce the performance of the personal obligation to pay the debt.

24.2.1 Types of security

It has been noted that the ingenuity of the commercial community is well illustrated by the variety of arrangements it has developed to fulfill a creditor's desire for security.[15] Essentially, security can be real (or proprietary) or personal.

Real security gives the creditor real, proprietary rights over some or all of the debtor's assets. Such proprietary rights can be based on an agreement between the parties, as where a person pledges his goods to another as security for a loan; or they may arise by operation of the law, as with an unpaid seller's lien.[16] Moreover, real securities can be possessory, in the sense that it depends on the creditor having possession of the property over which the security exists. Examples of possessory security include pledges and liens. Alternatively, real security can be non-possessory, that is, it is not dependent on possession by the creditor, as where the creditor has a mortgage or charge over the debtor's property but the debtor remains in possession of the property. The detailed rights of a creditor with real security vary depending on the type of security, but essentially all real security allows the creditor to retain or take possession of the property in question, and ultimately to have it sold and the proceeds applied to satisfy his debt.[17] In contrast, personal security involves a third

15 Bradgate, *Commercial Law* (London, Butterworths, 3rd ed., 2000) p.488.

16 See 15.3.1.

17 See further Chapter 25.

party to the contract between the debtor and the creditor entering into a separate contract with the creditor and undertaking responsibility for the debt if the debtor defaults, as is the case under a contract of guarantee; or indemnifying the creditor against losses caused by the debtor's failure to perform.

Real security protects against the debtor's insolvency by providing the creditor with real rights over the debtor's assets, offering the creditor priority if the debtor becomes insolvent. The effectiveness of personal security will depend on the creditworthiness of a third party such as a guarantor. For this reason, a personal security is often reinforced by requiring the guarantor to grant real security over his assets to secure the guarantee.

24.2.2 Formalities and registration of security interests

Possession of property gives the impression of ownership. Where a debtor is allowed to retain possession of property over which he has granted security rights to a creditor, he may appear to other third-party creditors to be more creditworthy than he actually is. In order to protect subsequent creditors from advancing credit facilities to a debtor who looks sound because he has possession of property, even though that property is subject to a security interest in favour of an earlier creditor, there are various statutory controls. These statutory controls are needed regarding non-possessory security only, such as mortgages and charges. With possessory security, the creditor's security interest is dependent on possession of the property which is securing the debt, by the creditor, and hence no false impressions of wealth on the debtor's behalf are created.

The statutory controls in relation to non-possessory security require the registration of security interests as a means of providing third parties with notice of them. Where the debtor is an individual, the bills of sale legislation lays down various requirements as to form and registration.[18] Where the debtor is a company, registration requirements for company charges are set out in the Companies Act 1963.[19] Moreover, there exists a number of separate registers setting out different rules for specific types of property.[20] The detail of this statutory control is examined further in Chapter 25.

24.3 Quasi-Security

A number of other arrangements are available to provide a creditor with

18 Bills of Sale (Ireland) Acts 1879–1883: see further 25.6.1.

19 1963 Act, s.99: see further 25.6.2.

20 See, *e.g.* Agricultural Credit Act 1978 regarding security over farming stock and machinery; and the Patents Act 1992, s.85, and the Trade Marks Act 1996, s.28 regarding security over intellectual property.

"security" against the debtor's non-payment or insolvency. In particular, a seller who supplies goods on credit terms can protect his interests by utilising the rules on passing of property.[21] Reservation of ownership under a conditional sale, hire purchase or similar arrangements allow the supplier to retake the goods if the debtor fails to pay and gives him priority over the debtor's other creditors if the debtor becomes insolvent. The practical effect of these arrangements is therefore to grant the supplier security. However, the courts have tended not to regard them as security devices so that they avoid the formality and registration requirements which apply to some security interests, such as mortgages and charges. For this reason, such devices can be referred to as "quasi-security."

24.3.1 Retention of title devices

A supplier of goods on credit terms can secure himself against the buyer's inability to pay by supplying the goods under an arrangement by which he reserves ownership of the goods until their price is paid. Such arrangements include hire-purchase agreements, conditional sale arrangements and finance leases.

24.3.1.1 Hire-purchase[22]

For example, under a hire purchase agreement, the owner/creditor retains property in the goods until all the instalments and the final option payment are paid by the hirer/debtor. If the hirer/debtor becomes insolvent before this time, the owner/creditor can reclaim his property before it is realised to meet the claims of other creditors.

24.3.1.2 Conditional sale arrangements

Similarly, under a conditional sale, property in the goods does not pass to the buyer until the condition is met: typically, until the price is paid in full. Hence the seller can demand redelivery if, before paying for the goods in full, the buyer becomes insolvent. A sale subject to a reservation of title clause is a conditional sale, expressly sanctioned by section 19(2) of the Sale of Goods Act 1893.[23] It is now standard practice for sellers to include a clause to the effect that the property in the goods will not pass from the seller to the buyer until the price is paid. If the buyer/debtor becomes insolvent before the price has been paid, the seller/creditor can demand the redelivery of his goods. Again the goods cannot be realised to meet the claims of other creditors because they are the property of the seller. A

21 See Chapter 17.

22 On the distinction between sale of goods contracts and hire-purchase arrangements, see 9.3.5.

23 See generally 15.4.

number of attempts have been made to challenge the effectiveness of reservation of title clauses and argue that they create registrable charges. It is now settled that a simple clause which reserves title in goods until their price is paid does not create a charge.[24] The seller may even reserve property in goods supplied as security for payment of other debts.[25] Attempts to claim rights over property other than the goods supplied may be construed as creating a charge, however.[26]

24.3.1.3 Finance leases[27]

Under a lease, the owner of goods (the lessor) transfers possession of the goods to a hirer (the lessee), for use by the lessee, in return for payment, while retaining ownership.[28] Since ownership is retained, the lessor can repossess the goods if the lessee defaults, and is thus effectively granted some security against the lessee's default and insolvency.

Leases can be classified as operating leases or finance leases. An operating lease usually involves goods being hired out to a series of different lessees in return for payment of rental; it can be used for a variety of arrangements – anything from the hire of a car for a day, to a five-year lease of an aeroplane. The owner/lessor is often responsible for such things as maintenance and repair of the goods. A finance lease, on the other hand, is viewed as a financial tool where the retention of ownership is nominal. Here the goods (usually equipment) are acquired by the owner/lessor and hired out for a period equivalent to the working life of the equipment, to one lessee, who is responsible for their maintenance. The rental is calculated so that the owner/lessor will recoup the cost of the goods and a profit. In effect, therefore, the lessor provides financial assistance to the lessee to acquire the goods while the lease provides the lessor with security against the lessee's default. Commercially, such an arrangement achieves much the same effect as a secured credit sale of the goods, but it is not recognised at law as creating a security interest.

24.3.1.4 Sale with a right to re-purchase

Sale with a right to re-purchase involves a transaction whereby X sells goods to Y, payment to be by instalments. X and Y also agree that if Y

24 *Frigoscandia Ltd v. Continental Irish Meat Ltd* [1982] I.L.R.M. 396; *Clough Mill v. Martin* [1984] 3 All E.R. 982, [1985] 1 W.L.R. 111.

25 *Armour v. Thyssen Edelstahlwerke GmbH* [1990] 3 All E.R. 481; see further 15.4.1.4.

26 See generally 15.4.

27 See also the Unidroit Convention on International Finance Leasing (1988) at www.unidroit.org See further, Davies, Security Interests in Mobile Equipment (Aldershot, Ashgate, 2002); Schmitthoff's *Export Trade* (London, Sweet & Maxwell, 10th ed., 2000) pp.235–237; Goode, *Commercial Law* (London, Penguin, 2nd ed., 1995) Chapter 28.

28 On the distinction between sale of goods contracts and leases, see 9.3.4.

defaults on the instalments, X has the right to purchase back the goods, setting off the amount outstanding against the re-purchase price. Although this resembles a mortgage arrangement, if genuine, it will be regarded as a sale. It has been held that there are three points of distinction between a sale and a mortgage or charge:

(i) under a sale the vendor is not entitled to get back the subject-matter of the sale by returning the purchase price; in the case of a mortgage or charge, the mortgagor is entitled, until he has been foreclosed, to recover the subject-matter of the mortgage or charge on payment of the debt;
(ii) if a buyer resells the subject-matter of the sale at a profit, that profit is his; a mortgagee who realises the subject-matter of the mortgage for a sum greater than is sufficient to repay himself, must account to the mortgagor for the surplus;
(iii) a buyer who resells the goods at a loss must bear that loss; but a mortgagee who realises the subject-matter for a sum insufficient to satisfy his debt is entitled to look to the mortgagor to make good the balance.[29]

24.3.2 Use of assets as quasi-security

There are a number of arrangements which may be used by a business that wishes to raise finance using its assets as security, but without entering into formal legal security arrangements.

24.3.2.1 Sale and lease-back

Instead of agreeing a mortgage, an owner may sell goods to a finance house for the purpose of raising funds, and then take them back under a lease, hire purchase, or conditional sale agreement. He thus has use of the goods and use of their capital value. The effect is very similar to a mortgage of the goods to secure a loan: ownership of the goods is transferred; the original owner gets their cash price, the equivalent of the mortgage advance; the price, together with a payment to cover the finance house's charges, is repaid by instalments; the reservation of title under the hire purchase or other agreement is equivalent to security over the goods. A genuine sale and lease-back is a valid transaction and is not regarded as a disguised mortgage. Under a variant on this arrangement, the goods are leased back not to the original owner but to his nominee. Alternatively, the owner may sell the goods to a dealer who then sells them to a finance house which leases them back to the original owner on hire-purchase: a refinancing transaction.

---

29 *Re George Inglefield Ltd.* [1933] Ch. 1 at 27, per Romer L.J.

24.3.2.2 Discounting of receivables

Just as a business may use its tangible property to obtain financial accommodation in a quasi-security arrangement, it can use its intangible property in the same way. It may sell its receivables (future debts and other obligations owed by third parties) to a creditor in return for an immediate cash payment. Since the creditor is providing a cash advance against future receivables, it will pay less than the full face value of the debts, which are thus said to be "discounted"; it may also discount to cover the risk of non-payment. The borrower may be required to guarantee payment of the assigned debts.

> **Example**: A company, X Ltd., wishes to borrow money from Y Ltd using its receivables as security. However, X Ltd has already given its bank a debenture to secure a loan, and that debenture restricts its power to make further secured borrowings. X may achieve its objective by selling its receivables at a discount to Y Ltd, guaranteeing payment by the debtors.

This has the same effect as a secured loan: X Ltd gets money at a cost (the discount on the sale) while Y Ltd pays money but is guaranteed to get it back, in full, at a later date. X Ltd effectively avoids the restrictions placed on its borrowing in the debenture.

A genuine discounting arrangement does not create a charge, even though its effect is to provide security for a cash advance.[30]

24.3.3 Bills of exchange

Because a bill of exchange creates a contractually binding obligation to pay money which is separate from any underlying contract in connection with which it is given, bills may be used as an alternative to, or to reinforce, other security. For instance, a creditor providing a loan to a debtor may require the debtor to accept bills of exchange for the instalments of the loan; if there is doubt about the debtor's ability to meet the repayments, the creditor could require the debtor to have the bills accepted by some creditworthy third party, such as a bank.[31]

24.3.4 Set-off agreements

It is common in commercial contracts, where there is a payment obligation on one party, to find a provision which allows that party to set off against the sum he is obliged to pay under the contract any amount owing to him by the other. This contractual right of set-off can operate in a similar

30 *Lloyds and Scottish Finance Ltd. v. Cyril Lord Carpets Sales Ltd.* [1979] 129 N.L.J. 366, [1992] B.C.L.C. 609.

31 See generally 23.3.

fashion to a security, but in law it does not create a security interest. It establishes no rights over the creditor's assets but is merely an entitlement to set-off one personal obligation against another: it therefore does not need to be registered.

CHAPTER 25

REAL SECURITY

25.1 INTRODUCTION

The provision of real security involves the creditor obtaining proprietary rights over property of the debtor. Real security confers two basic rights on the secured creditor: the right of *pursuit* and the right of *preference*.[1] Accordingly, a secured creditor can:

(a) follow the property, its products and proceeds into the hands of third parties other than those obtaining title under the *nemo dat* rules,[2] and
(b) claim the property or the proceeds of its sale to satisfy his claim in priority to the claims of other creditors.[3]

Real security therefore gives the debtor an incentive to pay the debt in order to recover his property unencumbered. This may be particularly powerful if the property in question is worth more (to the debtor) than the amount of the debt. In this chapter we examine the main forms of real security: pledges, liens, mortgages and charges, in relation to personal property and, in particular, goods.[4] Essentially, pledges and liens are based purely on the common law idea of possession.[5] A mortgage involves the transfer of ownership and can be legal or equitable. A charge, recognised only in equity, is a type of encumbrance on property and may exist in fixed or floating form.[6] We also consider briefly the current system of statutory control regarding the granting of security over personal property and the question of reform.

As noted in Chapter 24, real security may be classified as consensual or

---

1 See Goode, *Commercial Law* (London, Penguin, 2nd ed., 1995) p.673.

2 See Chapter 19.

3 Except, of course, where another creditor has a security or other real right ranking in priority to that of the secured creditor in question.

4 See further Bridge, *Personal Property Law* (Oxford, Oxford University Press, 2nd ed., 1996) Chapter 7; Donnelly, *The Law of Banks and Credit Institutions* (Dublin, Round Hall Sweet & Maxwell, 2000) Chapters 19 and 20; Breslin, *Banking Law in the Republic of Ireland* (Dublin, Gill & Macmillan, 1998) Chapter 37; Forde, *Commercial Law* (Dublin, Butterworths, 2nd ed., 1997) Chapter 5.

5 See 3.4, although there is such a thing as an equitable lien, see 25.3.1.3.

6 Many of the authorities on mortgages and charges involve land; nevertheless, they may be relevant in relation to personal property, except where the rules of real and personal property diverge.

non-consensual; and possessory or non-possessory. Real security is consensual where it is created by the agreement of creditor and debtor. Examples include pledges, mortgages and charges. It is non-consensual where it arises by operation of the law, as is the case with liens. Possessory security depends on the creditor having possession of the property: types of possessory security include pledges and liens, whereas with non-possessory security the creditor's security interest is not dependent on possession, *e.g.* mortgages and charges. Non-possessory security will be preferable where the debtor needs access to the property to be used as security, for instance, plant and machinery, and is therefore not in a position to transfer possession of it. However, non-possessory securities tend to be subject to a higher degree of statutory control, especially in order to protect third parties. Where a debtor is left in possession of property which is in fact subject to a security interest in favour of a creditor, other potential creditors may believe him to be the unencumbered owner of that property and thus be misled as to his creditworthiness. In order to avoid the creation of this false impression, non-possessory securities generally have to be registered.[7] Further statutory controls are imposed to protect the debtor.[8]

25.2 Pledge[9]

A pledge is a type of real security which involves a debtor (the pledgor) delivering goods to a creditor (the pledgee) who has the right to retain possession of the goods as security until payment of a debt or until discharge of another obligation upon an express or implied undertaking that the goods shall be restored to the pledgor as soon as the debt or other obligation is met. The debt may arise at the time the pledge is created, or it may be pre-existing or, indeed, a future debt. A pledge is therefore a consensual, possessory form of security. Pledges are commonly used in commerce; for example, where a buyer of goods under an international sale contract pledges a bill of lading to a bank as security for an advance of money to pay for them.[10] In the consumer context, the most common type of pledge is a "pawn."[11]

7 Bills of Sale (Ireland) Acts 1879–1883; Companies Act 1963; see further 25.6.

8 See 25.6.1.2 on formalities regarding bills of sale.

9 See Palmer & Hudson, "Pledge" in Palmer & McKendrick eds., *Interests in Goods* (London, Lloyd's of London Press, 2nd ed., 1998) Chapter 24.

10 See generally Part VI.

11 Pawns and pawnbrokers are regulated by the Pawnbrokers Act 1964, as amended by the Consumer Credit Act, 1995, Part XV.

25.2.1 Possession

Since a pledge involves the transfer of possession to the pledgee, it gives the pledgee a special property in the goods.[12] The pledgee is a bailee of the goods for the pledgor and therefore owes the pledgor a duty of care.[13] The pledgee's possession of the goods can be actual or constructive.[14] However, if the creditor has only a contractual right to seize the goods to secure a debt, the contract will amount to a security bill of sale or a charge which will be void unless the relevant registration and formality requirements, under the bills of sales or companies legislation, are satisfied.[15] In *Dublin City Distillery Ltd v. Doherty*,[16] for example, the plaintiff company borrowed money from the defendant, and in return the company sought to provide security over whiskey which was stored in the company's warehouse in Great Brunswick Street. The security was arranged by entering the defendant's name against the whiskey in their stockbook. The company also gave an invoice and a document stating that the whiskey was to be delivered to the defendant or his assigns. However, the warehouse could only be accessed by an official from the company and an excise officer acting together. The excise officer was not informed of this transaction. The court had to decide whether the security was a pledge or a charge. It was held that a valid pledge had not been created because no change had occurred in the character of the company's possession of the goods sufficient to complete an agreement to pledge something by actually putting the pledgee in possession of the goods.

Actual possession of the goods brings with it the expense of storage and insurance, so the pledgee should make express provision in the pledge agreement that such costs are to be met by the pledgor. As a bailee of the goods, the pledgee is liable for loss of or damage to the goods caused by his negligence and the burden of proof is reversed so that the pledgee/bailee must prove that he was not negligent.[17] Today, it is far more usual for the pledgee to have constructive possession of the goods, for example, by holding the keys to the warehouse where the goods are stored or by having possession of a bill of lading which is recognised as a document of title to the goods while the goods are at sea.[18] Equally, an attornment by the pledgor or his bailee would suffice.[19]

The main limitation of this type of security is that it is dependent on

---

12 *Carter v. Wake* (1877) 4 Ch. D. 605; *Sewell v. Burdick* (1884) 10 App. Cas. 74.

13 *Coggs v. Bernard* (1703) 2 Ld. Raym. 909.

14 *Dublin City Distillery Ltd v. Doherty* [1914] A.C. 823; *Official Assignee of Madras v. Mercantile Bank of India* [1935] A.C. 53.

15 See 25.6.1.

16 [1914] A.C. 823.

17 On bailment, see 3.4.5.

18 See 31.2.3.

19 On attornment, see 3.4.4.

possession (actual or constructive) and so is not applicable to intangible property which cannot be possessed in the physical sense. Other means of security, such as a mortgage or charge, fulfill this function. Moreover, if the pledge agreement allows the pledgor to retain some control over the goods, the pledgee's security may be destroyed. A provision stating that the pledgor may repossess the goods whenever he likes would take precedence over the pledge. However, if the pledgee redelivers the goods to the pledgor for a limited purpose and on terms that the pledge is to continue, the pledge is not destroyed. For instance, where a bill of lading is pledged with a bank as security for an advance of the price of the goods, the bank may release the bill of lading to the buyer for the limited purpose of collecting the goods. The pledgee's possession must be lawful; where goods are taken by force or the pledgor's consent to the pledge is obtained by fraud or misrepresentation, the pledgor is not bound.

The pledgee's special property in the goods is a disponable interest which can be assigned or sub-pledged,[20] and delivery by the pledgee to a third party does not destroy the pledge or enable the pledgor to sue the pledgee or sub-pledgee in the tort of conversion. However, the pledgee cannot sub-pledge the goods for a sum greater than the original debt, as this would prejudice the pledgor's right to repossess the goods on payment of the debt. If the pledgee purports to deal with the *general property* in the goods – for instance by pledging them – he commits a breach of contract *vis-à-vis* the pledgor and is liable in damages for any loss the pledgor suffers as a result. However, the pledge continues. The pledgor can sue the pledgee in conversion if he first pays the debt secured by the pledge. The pledgor can deal with his general property in the goods while the pledge continues and may therefore sell the goods subject to the pledge. The buyer may then recover possession of the goods by redeeming the pledge. Where the pledgee refuses to permit the pledgor's transferee to redeem the pledge, he will be liable in conversion.[21]

25.2.2 Creation and formation

As a form of consensual security, a pledge is created by the agreement of the parties. Registration is not required: the very fact of possession is sufficient evidence of the pledge and puts third parties on notice of the pledgee's interest. No formality is required for creation of a pledge. However, it is standard banking practice to require the pledgor to sign a document such as a "letter of pledge". A letter of pledge may include terms by which:

20 *Donald v. Suckling* (1866) L.R. 1 Q.B. 585.

21 *Franklin v. Neate* (1844) 13 M. & W. 481. On the tort of conversion and sale of goods contracts, see 19.1.1; see generally, McMahon & Binchy, *Law of Torts* (Dublin, Butterworths, 2001, 3rd ed.) Chapter 30.

(a) the pledgor agrees that the pledgee is to have a pledge over all goods or documents of title delivered by the pledgor or his agent into the possession of the pledgee or his agent;
(b) the credit provided is a revolving facility, the pledgor agrees that the goods and documents are pledged as continuing security for the payment of all sums owed by the pledgor from time to time;
(c) the pledgor agrees that in the case of his default in repayment of any sum or sums on demand, the pledgee has the right to immediate actual possession of the goods and to sell the goods or any part of them, [X] days after the default;
(d) the pledgor agrees to keep the goods fully insured to their full value, with such persons as the pledgee may approve and provide proof of such insurance, the customer further agrees to notify the insurers of the pledgee's interest in the goods;
(e) the pledgor agrees to pay all the costs of storage of the goods;
(f) all risk of loss of or damage to the goods remains, at all times, with the pledgor whether the goods are in his possession, the pledgee's possession or the possession of a third party.

25.2.3 Power of sale

If the debt is not paid by the date fixed by the pledge agreement, the pledgee can sell the goods.[22] If no date is stipulated, the pledge must be redeemed within a reasonable time. A sale by the pledgee must be reasonable in that the goods must be sold at a reasonable price. The pledgee must account to the pledgor for any monies received on the sale in excess of the debt after the costs of selling have been reimbursed.[23] If the sale fails to meet the debt in full, the pledgee may pursue the pledgor personally for the amount outstanding.[24]

25.2.4 Termination of the pledge

In the normal course of events, the pledgee's interest terminates when the underlying debt is paid, thereby releasing the security. A pledgee may also waive his rights by, for example, returning the goods to the possession of the pledgor and hence terminate the pledge. Or, a pledge may be terminated where the pledgee breaches an important term of the pledge agreement, for instance, by intentional destruction of the goods. This will rarely occur. Dealing with the goods does not destroy the pledge. Use of the goods by the pledgee may not amount to a breach, at least where use

22 *Exp. Hubbard* (1866) 17 Q.B.D. 699; *Re Morritt* (1886) 18 Q.B.D. 222.
23 *Halliday v. Holgate* (1868) L.R. 3 Ex. 299.
24 *Jones v. Marshall* (1889) 24 Q.B.D. 269.

does not adversely affect the goods, although use may be a breach if the goods are adversely affected. In *Cooke v. Hadden*,[25] the pledge was destroyed when the pledgee of champagne started drinking it! Generally, pledges are not affected by lapse of time. Thus the pledgee's rights under the pledge remain even if the debt secured by the pledge is time barred. Equally, the pledgor can reclaim the goods on payment of the barred debt. However, lapse of time may amount to a waiver.

25.3 Lien

A lien is a relatively primitive form of real security. Essentially, it entitles a person (the lienee) who has provided goods to or services for another (the lienor), to retain possession of the lienor's goods or documents until the charges for the goods or services have been paid.[26] The lienee is said to have a right of retention: hence, it is a "self-help remedy".[27] While the goods are in the lienee's possession, he is a bailee of those goods; hence if the goods are lost or damaged as a result of his negligence, he will be liable for that loss and the burden of proving that he was not negligent rests with him.

25.3.1 Types of lien

Liens derive from many sources including the common law, contract, equity, statute and maritime law. A lien may also be described as general or specific (particular): the former being the rarer case.

25.3.1.1 Common law lien

The common law has recognised that practitioners of certain trades or callings (especially those pursuing "common callings")[28] may have a lien over their customers' property. This is a non-consensual form of security which arises by operation of the law. Examples of common law liens include a ship's master's lien on cargo for freight or on luggage for passage,[29] an innkeeper's (or hotelier's) lien over a guest's belongings for sums due,[30] and, a repairer's lien over goods repaired for the cost of the

25 (1862) 3 F. & F. 229.

26 *Re Barrett Apartments Ltd* [1985] I.R. 350 at 357, [1985] I.L.R.M. 679 at 681 per Henchy J. (S.C.).

27 *Tappenden v. Artus* [1964] 2 Q.B. 185.

28 In medieval times, certain "service providers" were obliged to render services to the public on demand, such as the common callings of innkeepers, ferrymen, and common carriers. Accordingly, they were entitled to a lien for their services.

29 *The Princess Royal* (1859) 5 Ir. Jur. (n.s.) 74; *Belfast Harbour Commissioners v. Lawther* (1866) 17 Ir. Ch. R. 54.

30 See now Hotel Proprietors Act 1963, s.8. The 1963 Act repeals the Innkeepers Act 1878: 1963 Act, s.13 and Second Schedule.

repair. As Professor Bridge notes, it is hard to imagine this common law entitlement being extended to new relationships,[31] although statute law has recognised such new relationships. For example, under the European Communities (Cancellation of Contracts Negotiated away from Business Premises) Regulations 1989,[32] where a "trader"[33] contracts to supply goods or services to a "consumer"[34] on their "doorstep",[35] there is provision for a "cooling-off" period of seven days, during which time the consumer can give notice of cancellation.[36] On cancellation, any sums paid by the consumer are repayable by the trader, the consumer having a lien over the goods until such repayment.[37]

Possession of the goods by the lienee is essential both for the creation and continued existence of a common law lien.[38] Generally, the lienee must have an immediate right to possession so that if payment is tendered, at any time, the goods can be immediately returned to the lienor, their owner. Hence, a lien, unlike a pledge, cannot be transferred,[39] and is in this respect weaker than a pledge interest.[40] If the lienor retains some control over the goods, the lien may be overridden unless it is clear that the lienor's control is subject to the superior rights of the lienee. In *Forth v. Simpson*,[41] for example, a race-horse trainer who claimed a lien over some horses failed because the owner had been given a right to take the horses away to race whenever he wished. This case can be compared with *Allen v. Smith*,[42] where an innkeeper's lien was held to continue, despite the fact that a guest who had brought with him two horses and stayed several months at an inn without paying, regularly took the horses out of the stables for exercising and away for several days, because he had the intention of returning.

31 Bridge, *Personal Property Law* (Oxford, Oxford University Press, 2nd ed., 1996) p.134.

32 S.I. No. 224 of 1989, implementing Directive 85/577 [1985] O.J. L372/31; see further Clark, *Contract Law in Ireland* (Dublin, Round Hall Sweet & Maxwell, 4th ed., 1998) p.191; Bird, *Consumer Credit Law* (Dublin, Round Hall Sweet & Maxwell, 1998) p.326.

33 Defined as "a natural or legal person who, for the transaction in question, acts in his commercial or professional capacity, or anyone acting in the name or on behalf of a trader". Reg. 2(1).

34 Defined as "a natural person who, in transactions covered by these Regulations, is acting for purposes which can be regarded as outside his trade or profession": Reg. 2(1).

35 The Regulations apply, subject to exceptions, to contracts concluded (i) during an excursion organised by the trader away from his business premises; (ii) during a visit by a trader to the consumer's home, or another consumer's home, or to the consumer's place of work, where the visit is unsolicited; (iii) following a solicited visit but where the goods and services supplied are other than those in respect of which the visit was requested. Additionally, the regulations apply to contracts in respect of which an offer was made by the consumer in circumstances similar to the above: Reg. 3(1).

36 Reg. 5.

37 Reg. 6(1) and (2).

38 *ESSI v. Crown Shipping (Ireland) Ltd* [1991] I.L.R.M. 97.

39 *Legg v. Evans* (1840) 6 M. & W. 36.

40 *Donald v. Suckling* (1866) L.R. 1 Q.B. 585.

41 (1843) 13 Q.B. 680.

42 (1862) 12 C.B.N.S. 638.

Although the common law lien is non-consensual, the terms of a contract may prevent a lien arising if it appears that the parties intended that the goods should not be retained until payment. An agreement excluding a lien may be express or implied. So, for example, where the owner of the goods is given credit and not expected to pay immediately, it may be argued that the intention of the parties overrides the operation of a common law lien. For instance, in *Wilson v. Lombard Ltd*,[43] a car mechanic was held to have no lien over a car because the cost of repair was to be charged to the customer's account.

25.3.1.2 Contractual lien

A right of lien may be reserved by contract and any provider of services may find it useful to include such a lien in its contracts of supply as a means of reinforcing its common law rights. Such a term may be implied following a course of dealing or trade custom, but it is preferable that it be expressly provided for. A contractual lien should include an express right to sell.[44] For example, in *De Lorean Motor Car Ltd v. Northern Ireland Carriers Ltd*,[45] the plaintiff car manufacturer agreed with the defendant carriers that they would carry cars from the plaintiff's factory to the Belfast dockyard. A clause in the agreement provided that the defendant would have a "general lien" over the goods carried "for moneys whatsoever due from" the plaintiff. The agreement also conferred a power of sale on the defendant if it was not paid on time. The court found the lien to be effective.[46]

25.3.1.3 Equitable lien

Possession is not necessary for an equitable lien. For instance, the vendor of land has a lien to secure the purchase price,[47] and the purchaser has a lien to secure repayment of the price if the transaction falls through.[48] The seller of intangible property, including shares, debts and intellectual property, also has an equitable lien over the property to secure the price, but the unpaid seller of goods has no such lien.[49] Where a creditor is given a non-possessory equitable lien over goods not in his possession, this will amount

43 [1963] 1 W.L.R. 1294.

44 See 25.3.2.

45 [1982] N.I. 163.

46 However, a stipulation in an agreement with an agent, purporting to confer a lien will only be effective if the agent has authority from the owner/principal to confer a lien: *ESSI v. Crown Shipping (Ireland) Ltd* [1991] I.L.R.M. 97; on agency generally, see Part III.

47 *Shaw v. Foster* (1872) L.R. 5 H.L. 321.

48 *Re Barrett Apartments Ltd* [1985] I.R. 350, [1985] I.L.R.M. 679 (S.C.).

49 *Transport and General Credit v. Morgan* [1939] 2 All E.R. 17.

to a security bill of sale which will be void if not formed and registered in accordance with the bills of sale legislation.[50]

25.3.1.4 Statutory lien

Certain statutes grant creditors liens or similar rights. The most important example of a statutory lien is to be found in sections 41–43 of the Sale of Goods Act 1893 which provide that a seller of goods who has not been paid has the right to retain the goods even though property in the goods has passed to the buyer.[51]

25.3.1.5 General or specific liens

A lien may be general or specific (particular). A general lien allows the creditor to retain possession of any property of the debtor until any debt due from the debtor is paid. Solicitors, bankers, factors, insurance brokers and stockbrokers have all been recognised as having general liens over their client's papers for all sums owing for professional services rendered as a matter of usage.[52] The lien is general in that it is not confined to services provided in relation to the papers in question. A specific or particular lien, on the other hand, only allows the creditor to retain possession of goods or documents as security for payment of debts which relate to the property retained. For instance, a warehouseman has a specific lien over goods for warehouse charges relating to those goods; and a repairer can retain possession of the goods repaired until he is paid for the work done on them. If a repairer has provided services in the past and released possession of the goods to the owner, the lien which is lost with possession cannot be revived by attaching the unpaid bill to a later lien arising as a result of later services provided.[53]

Although some general liens are recognised at common law, most common law and statutory liens tend to be specific, while general liens are usually the creation of contract. Where parties are in a continuing trading relationship, a general lien will usually be preferred by the parties. A general lien offers the lienor greater and more flexible security but also offers advantages to the lienee. If the lienee has only a particular lien, he may be reluctant to release property until debts relating to that property are paid, thus restricting the lienor's trading ability, as he will have to pay for each transaction as it is completed in order to regain possession of the goods. If the lienee has a general lien, he will be more willing to release

50 See 25.6.1.

51 See 15.3.1.

52 See, *e.g.* O'Callaghan, "Safeguarding Solicitors' Fees" [1996] *Commercial Law Practitioner* 167.

53 *Hatton v. Car Maintenance* [1915] 1 Ch. 621.

goods to the lienor without immediate payment, as long as he has possession of some of the lienor's other goods or will have possession of more of the lienor's goods at some future date. A contract provision granting a general lien is perfectly valid even if the lienee would have only a particular lien at common law.

25.3.2 Power of sale

At common law, a lien does not confer a right of sale,[54] and such an act amounts to conversion and also surrenders the lien.[55] However, a number of statutes give lienees powers of sale, including the Sale of Goods Act 1893.[56] Moreover, a lienee may reserve a right of sale by contract, and in view of the limited rights of sale under the general law this will generally be advisable. Where the lienee has a contractual right of sale, no particular method of sale is prescribed but the sale must be reasonable. If the goods are sold at an undervalue, this may amount to an unreasonable sale. If the proceeds of the sale exceed the debt, the lienee must account to the lienor for this surplus. If, however, the sale fails to satisfy the debt, the lienee may pursue a personal action against the lienor for the remaining balance. Statute does prescribe formalities in certain areas: for example, an unpaid seller of goods must give reasonable notice of the sale, unless the goods are perishable.[57]

25.3.3 Termination of the lien

A lienee's interest in the goods terminates on payment of the debt, though a lien may terminate in other circumstances also. For example, a lien will terminate where the lienee loses possession of the goods. In *Pennington v. Reliance Motor Works Ltd*,[58] car mechanics returned a repaired car before payment and without asserting a lien. When the car was later returned to their possession for other work, they sought to assert their lien for work previously done, but it was held that by initially returning the goods any potential lien had been destroyed. A lien will also terminate where the lienee waives his right by returning the goods to the lienor or where, for instance, alternative security is provided. Moreover, where the lienee breaches a term on which he holds the goods, the lien will terminate and the immediate right of possession will revest in the lienor. There would be

54 *Thames Iron Works Co v. Patton Derrick Co* (1860) 1 J. & H. 93; *Somes v. British Empire Shipping Co* (1859) 28 L.J.Q.B. 220.

55 *Mulliner v. Florence* (1878) 3 Q.B.D. 484. On the tort of conversion and sale of goods contracts, see 19.1.1; see generally, McMahon & Binchy, *Law of Torts* (Dublin, Butterworths, 3rd ed., 2001) Chapter 30.

56 See 15.3.3.

57 Sale of Goods Act, s.48(3).

58 [1923] 1 K.B. 127.

a breach if, for example, the lienor tenders payment of the debt and this is wrongly refused by the lienee; or if the immediate right to possession passes to a third party. This restricts the lienee's ability to re-deliver the goods to the lienor on payment, and hence constitutes a breach of his obligations under the lien. However, it has been held that the lienee is entitled to do what is reasonably incidental to his obligation under the lien, so that in *Chesham Automobile Supply Ltd v. Beresford Hotel (Birchington) Ltd*,[59] a lienee, intending to exercise a right of sale, could send the goods to be repaired without losing his lien. As with pledges, generally liens are not affected by lapse of time and limitations of actions do not affect a lienee's rights even if the debt is time barred. Equally, the lienor can reclaim the goods on payment when the debt is barred, but again, such a lapse of time may amount to a waiver.

25.4 Mortgage

A mortgage is a non-possessory form of real security, which involves the transfer of ownership of property to a creditor (the mortgagee) by way of security upon condition that the property will be transferred back to the debtor (the mortgagor) when the sum secured is paid.[60] The mortgagor may retain possession of the mortgaged property – though there is no requirement that this must be so – an advantage where the mortgaged property must be used by the mortgagor in its business. The mortgagor has the right to recover ownership of the mortgaged property – known as the "equity of redemption" – on payment of the debt secured by the mortgage. Any property can be mortgaged, including real and personal, tangible and intangible, present and future, property.[62] This gives it an advantage over a pledge which cannot be granted over intangible or future property.

25.4.1 Legal or equitable

A mortgage can be either legal or equitable. A legal mortgage involves the transfer by way of security of legal ownership of the property. An equitable mortgage is created where:

(i) the mortgagor transfers the equitable ownership or confers an equitable interest in the property;

59 (1913) 29 T.L.R. 584.

60 *Keith v. Burrows* (1876) C.P.D. 722.

61 *Santley v. Wilde* [1899] 2 Ch. 474; *Carter v. Wake* (1877) 4 Ch. D. 605.

62 For mortgages of real property, see generally Lyall, *Land Law in Ireland* (Dublin, Round Hall Sweet & Maxwell, 2nd ed., 2000) Chapter 23; Pearce & Mee, *Land Law* (Dublin, Round Hall Sweet & Maxwell, 2nd ed., 2000) Chapter 18; and Wylie, *Irish Land Law* (Dublin, Butterworths, 3rd ed., 1997) Part V.

(ii) the mortgage is of equitable property – this includes a mortgage of future property to be acquired by the mortgagor, such as a mortgage of future book debts;
(iii) the parties enter into a contract to create a mortgage at a future date; or
(iv) there is a defective execution of a legal mortgage, as for example where the parties fail to comply with any necessary formalities.

In the cases of the binding agreement and the defective execution, (iii) and (iv) above, equity looks on that as done which ought to be done, and decrees that a valid equitable mortgage has been granted, which can, by the equitable remedy of specific performance, be inflated into a legal mortgage.

25.4.2 Formalities

Generally there is no prescribed form for a mortgage of personalty.[63] The manner of transfer will depend on the type of property being transferred. No formality is required for the transfer of goods; property passes when the parties intend it to pass.[64] However, it will generally be advisable for the mortgage to be in writing. If the mortgagee does not take possession of the mortgaged property, a written transfer by way of mortgage will have to comply with the formal requirements set down by the bills of sale legislation if granted by an individual or other non-corporate association.[65] In the case of intangible property, transfer is usually by assignment in writing;[66] in the case of a mortgage of a debt, notice should be given to the debtor to perfect the assignment to make the assignment a legal, as opposed to an equitable assignment and to fix priority as against any other assignee of the debt in accordance with the rule in *Dearle v. Hall*.[67]

25.4.3 Enforcement

A mortgagee generally has four rights as a means of enforcing the mortgage:

(i) a right of foreclosure which terminates the mortgagor's right of redemption;
(ii) a right to take possession of the mortgaged property; where the

63 *Flory v. Denny* (1852) 7 Ex. 581.
64 Sale of Goods Act 1893, s.17: see further Chapter 17.
65 See 25.6.1.
66 See, *e.g.* Patents Act 1992, s.79 and s.85; Trademarks Act 1996, ss.28–29.
67 (1828) 3 Russ. 1.

mortgage is a security bill of sale, the mortgagee has a special statutory right of seizure;[68]

(iii) an implied power of sale;

(iv) the right to apply to the court for an order for sale or the appointment of a receiver.

These rights are generally amplified and reinforced by express provisions in the security instrument. The mortgagor's equity of redemption prevents the mortgagee claiming outright ownership and compels him to allow the mortgagor to redeem the mortgaged property, by tender of the amount due plus interest. But the mortgagor's equity of redemption is extinguished by foreclosure and sale.

25.4.3.1 Foreclosure

If the debtor fails to redeem the mortgage within a reasonable time after the debt has become due, the mortgagee can apply for a court order for foreclosure. The effect of foreclosure is to end the mortgagor's equity of redemption, leaving the mortgagee outright owner of the property. In the case of an equitable mortgage, a further court order for the transfer to the mortgagee of the legal property is necessary. The debt secured by the mortgage is extinguished: the mortgagee is deemed to have taken the property in satisfaction of the debt. Hence, foreclosure may give the mortgagee a windfall where the value of the asset exceeds the debt. In practice, foreclosure is not granted: possession and sale are the preferred remedies.[69]

25.4.3.2 Possession

In principle, a mortgage gives a mortgagee the right to possession once the mortgage is executed. In practice, the exercise of this right is largely useless and so mortgage agreements usually permit the mortgagor to remain in possession. This right to remain in possession depends on the mortgagor's observance of the terms of the mortgage agreement. Hence, where a mortgagor defaults, he may have to surrender the right to remain in possession. Where the mortgage is a security bill of sale under the Bills of Sale Act 1879 (Amendment) Act 1883,[70] an implied right of seizure (and sale) arises but this right must be exercised within certain limits.[71] For example, the goods must be held at the mortgagee's premises for five days before they are sold in order to give the mortgagor the opportunity to reinstate himself under the bill of sale.[72]

68 See 25.6.1.4.

69 *Bruce v. Brophy* [1906] 1 I.R. 611.

70 See 25.6.1.

71 *Re Morritt* (1886) 18 Q.B.D. 222.

72 1883 Act, ss.7 and 13.

25.4.3.3 Power of sale

The mortgagee has a power of sale where it is expressly or impliedly included in the contract of mortgage; or where the mortgage is a security bill of sale under the Bills of Sale Acts. A well drafted mortgage will include an express power of sale. In the absence of an express power, a right of sale may be implied. There is extensive authority supporting the existence of a common law right to sell under a mortgage of intangible property.[73] The position of a mortgagee of goods is unclear: there is authority that a legal mortgagee in possession of goods has a common law power of sale if the mortgagor defaults,[74] but this was queried in *Deverges v. Sandman, Clark & Co*,[75] so that an express power should be reserved. The position of an equitable mortgagee is unclear, and an equitable mortgagee wishing to sell should seek the assistance of the court. Where the mortgage is a security bill of sale under the bills of sale legislation, the mortgagee has a power of sale subject to restrictions imposed by the legislation.[76]

Although a mortgagee exercising a power of sale sells for his own benefit rather than on behalf of the mortgagor, he is nevertheless under a duty of care to obtain a reasonable price. It appears that this duty may be excluded by a carefully drafted term in the mortgage.[77] If sale of the mortgaged property realises more than is required to pay the debt, the mortgagee must account to the mortgagor for the surplus.

25.5 Equitable Charge

An equitable charge involves the debtor (chargor) granting the creditor (chargee) the right to have designated property of the debtor appropriated to discharge a debt. It involves no transfer of possession or ownership of the property;[78] the debt is satisfied by the proceeds of sale of the property which can be transacted voluntarily by the chargor or result from an application by the chargee for a court order. As a mere encumbrance without any conveyance or assignment, a charge exists only in equity or under statute. A charge can be created over any class of property, including goods, intangible property and property to be acquired by the debtor. Although charges can be conferred by an individual, they are most often utilised by companies to secure loans.

---

73 See, *e.g. Deverges v. Sandman*, Clark & Co. [1902] 1 Ch. 579.

74 *Re Morritt* (1886) 18 Q.B.D. 222.

75 [1902] 1 Ch. 579.

76 See 25.6.1.4.

77 *Bishop v. Bonham* [1988] 1 W.L.R. 742 at 752.

78 *Re Bond Worth Ltd* [1980] Ch. 228.

25.5.1 Fixed or floating

Equitable charges can be fixed or floating. A fixed (or specific) charge is one which attaches to the property as soon as the charge is created or the chargor acquires the rights over the property to be charged, whichever is the later. The chargor cannot dispose of the property free of the charge without the chargee's consent, unless the debt secured by the charge is paid. Any person can create a fixed charge. Charges created by an individual are subject to the bills of sale legislation; those created by companies are subject to the companies legislation.

The floating charge which is not dedicated to any particular asset(s) but floats over a designated class of assets, present or future, allowing the chargor to deal with those assets free from the charge as long as it remains floating, is a more flexible instrument.[79] The security fund is therefore constantly changing, but if, for example, a receiver is appointed to the chargor, or the chargor goes into liquidation, the charge *crystallises*, that is to say it attaches to those assets then owned by the chargor which correspond with the description specified in the charging instrument, limiting the chargor's right to deal with them. Details of the circumstances in which a floating charge will crystallise should be provided for in the charging instrument.[80] Because of formal requirements imposed by the bills of sale legislation (in particular, the goods which comprise the bill must be listed in a Schedule) it is difficult, if not impossible, for an individual or non-corporate association to create a floating charge over property to be acquired in the future. Hence, only a company can create a floating charge.

The obvious advantage of the floating charge is that it leaves the chargor free to use and deal with the charged property. The danger for a creditor taking a floating charge as security is that before crystallisation the chargor's freedom to deal with the property, including by selling it or using it as security to raise further loans, may reduce the security fund below the amount due to be repaid. As a result, floating charges tend to be used to supplement fixed charges. For example, a lending institution will usually take a fixed charge over certain assets of a company (for example, by way of a legal mortgage on its premises, plant and machinery) and then a floating charge over the remainder of its assets.

---

79 A floating charge has been described as a "dormant" security which permits the debtor company to deal with the charged assets until default or other prescribed event which causes the charge to "crystallise:" *Government Stock Investment Co. v. Manila Railway Co.* [1897] A.C. 81 at 86 per Lord Macnaghten.

80 On the effect of automatic crystallisation clauses see *Re Brightlife* [1986] B.C.L.C. 418. *Cf.* Keane, *Company Law* (Dublin, Butterworths, 3rd ed., 2000) p.239. See further Forde, *Company Law in Ireland* (Dublin, Round Hall Sweet & Maxwell, 3rd ed., 1999) pp.624–626; Courtney, *The Law of Private Companies* (Dublin, Butterworths, 1994) pp.596–7.

25.5.2 Debentures

A charge may be created by contract or trust, but a commercial charge is generally created by contract. A charge created by a contract is often referred to as a "debenture." The Companies Act 1963 defines debenture as including debenture stock, bonds and any other securities of a company whether constituting a charge on the assets of the company or not,[81] but the term can be used more generally to refer to a type of instrument, which creates a charge on a company's assets. Lending institutions such as banks, have their own printed form of debenture which will normally contain:

(i) an undertaking by the company to repay on demand all monies owing, including interest and charges;

(ii) an undertaking by the company to create
  (a) a fixed charge over assets X,Y and Z, and
  (b) a floating charge over the company's remaining assets, present and future;

(iii) an undertaking by the company to create no mortgage or charge that would rank in priority to or *pari passu* with the floating charge created herein;

(iv) provision that the monies secured by the debenture become payable on the happening of any of the following events:
  (a) a written demand for payment by the bank,
  (b) the commencement of winding-up proceedings in respect of the company, or
  (c) the cessation of business by the company;

(v) power for the bank to appoint a receiver in certain circumstances, usually at any time after it has demanded payment of the monies secured and whether or not they have become due;

(vi) an undertaking by the company to provide the bank quarterly, or on demand, with up-to-date financial records, including a trading account, profit and loss account, and balance sheet representing the true position of the company and duly audited, to enable the bank to review the financial situation and health of the company;

(vii) an undertaking by the company to insure all its assets to their full value with such persons as the bank may approve, and provide proof of such insurance.

25.6 Statory Control

Non-possessory securities – mortgages and equitable charges – are subject to a high degree of statutory control, which requires the registration of

81 1963 Act, s.2.

security interests as a means of providing third parties with notice of them. The basic rationale is to protect creditors from advancing credit facilities to debtors who look sound because they have possession of property even though that property is subject to a security interest in favour of an earlier creditor. Hence, statutory control is needed regarding non-possessory security, but not for possessory security. Where the debtor is an individual, the bills of sale legislation lays down various requirements as to form and registration. Where the debtor is a company, security interests in the form of a charge (including mortgages) must be registered under the Companies Act 1963. Moreover, there are various statutes which establish separate registers and which set out different rules for specific types of property, including:

(a) the Mercantile Marine Act 1955;
(b) the Agricultural Credits Act 1978;
(c) the Patents Act 1992;
(d) the Trade Marks Act 1996;
(e) the Industrial Designs Act 2001.

For the purpose of this book, the two most important systems of regulation are those in the bills of sale legislation and the Companies Act 1963, both of which are examined further below.

25.6.1 Bills of sale[82]

Broadly speaking, a bill of sale is an instrument in writing whereby one party transfers property in goods to another party but remains in possession. There are two types of bills of sale:

(i) an absolute bill, and,
(ii) a conditional bill, more usually called a "security bill."

A bill is absolute if given otherwise than as security for payment of money; a bill is conditional or a security bill if it is given to secure a money payment.

25.6.1.1 Application of the legislation

The bills of sale legislation provides for a public registration system for bills of sale to protect third parties who are contemplating taking security in return for credit. The potential creditor has the opportunity to examine the register to see if other prior security interests exist, before advancing

82 See generally, Maguire, "The Bill of Sale: the Forgotten Relation?" [1997] *Commercial Law Practitioner* 3.

the credit. The legislation also seeks to protect the debtor from poor deals and oppressive enforcement measures by requiring bills to be in a prescribed form and restricting enforcement procedures. The courts have been astute to prevent creditors evading the statutory controls; therefore where an individual or other non-corporate entity, such as a trading partnership, gives security over goods, the bills of sale legislation comes into play and the transaction must be considered in order to decide if the legislation applies.

The governing legislation in this jurisdiction is:

(a) the Bills of Sale (Ireland) Act 1879 (which applies to absolute bills of sale); and
(b) the Bills of Sale (Ireland) Act 1879 Amendment Act 1883 (which applies specifically to security bills of sale).

The 1879 and 1883 Acts must be read together regarding bills of sale given by way of security for a money payment. A transaction comes within the scope of the Acts if five conditions are met:

(i) there must be a document, hence oral transactions are not affected by the legislation;[83]
(ii) the document must be a bill of sale as defined by the legislation;[84]
(iii) the document must relate to personal chattels as defined in the legislation, so that security over intangible property is excluded;[85]
(iv) the document must confer on the transferee a right to seize or take possession of the goods; and,
(v) this right to possession must derive from the document.

The legislation does not apply when security is given by a company. Section 17 of the 1883 Act provides that a bill of sale does not include a debenture issued by a company and indeed no other form of company security comes within the remit of this legislation. Further exclusions are found in section 4 of the 1879 Act, including assignments for the benefit of creditors and marriage settlements which involve security, and transfers of goods in the ordinary course of business of any trade or calling.

83 1879 Act, s.4; *Charlesworth v. Mills* [1892] A.C. 231; *Newlove v. Shrewsbury* (1888) 21 Q.B.D. 41.
84 1879 Act, s.4.
85 1879 Act, s.4.

25.6.1.2 Formalities

Section 9 of the 1883 Act makes a security bill of sale void unless made in a deed in the form prescribed in the Schedule to the Act, though minor departures from the prescribed form have been tolerated.[86] The bill must include:

(i) the names, addresses and description of the parties;
(ii) the consideration given by the creditor;
(iii) the details of the repayment – amount, interest, time and manner;
(iv) the details of insurance;
(v) the enforcement terms; and
(vi) a reasonably detailed inventory of the chattels affected.[87]

Non-compliance not only means that the security interest cannot be enforced, but also that the underlying loan is void.

25.6.1.3 Registration and attestation

The 1883 Act requires that all security transactions covered by the Acts must be attested and registered within seven days,[88] and for an absolute bill, if necessary, the registration must be renewed every five years.[89] Attestation must be made by at least one credible witness.[90] The bill, together with its due execution and attestation and certain personal details of the maker of the bill and the witness, have to be filed in the Central Office of the High Court. If the bill of sale is not duly attested and registered in compliance with the legislation, it is void and not enforceable.[91] Registration is also important because if two or more bills of sale have been given, they will take priority in the order in which they were registered.[92] However, this position is modified where an absolute bill is followed by a security bill. If a grantor first gives an absolute bill followed by a security bill over the same goods, the absolute bill will take priority notwithstanding that the security bill was first registered.[93]

86 *Re Morritt* (1886) 18 Q.B.D. 222; *Thomas v. Kelly* (1888) 13 App. Cas. 506.
87 1883 Act, s.4.
88 1879 Act, s.8, and 1883 Act, s.8.
89 1879 Act, s.11.
90 1879 Act, s.8, and 1883 Act, s.10.
91 1883 Act, s.8.
92 1879 Act, s.10.
93 1883 Act, s.5.

25.6.1.4 Enforcement

The 1883 Act gives the creditor limited powers to seize and sell personal chattels secured by the bill of sale. The secured chattels may be seized by the creditor on five grounds:[94]

(i) if the debtor is in default, or fails to comply with any obligations necessary to maintain the security;
(ii) if the debtor becomes bankrupt, or suffers the goods to be distrained for rent, rates, or taxes;
(iii) if the debtor fraudulently removes or allows the goods to be removed from an agreed premises;
(iv) if the debtor fails to comply with a written request for his last receipts of rent, rates and taxes; or,
(vi) if execution has been levied against the debtor's goods.

If seized, the goods cannot be removed from the debtor's premises for five days and in that time the debtor can apply to the court for relief.[95]

25.6.1.5 Practical use of bills of sale

The extensive formality and registration requirements mean that, in practice, in spite of the draconian effect of failure to comply, the vast majority of bills of sale are not registered. Coupled with the statutory restrictions on enforcement procedures, the formal requirements of the legislation mean that mortgages and charges of goods by individuals are little used.

25.6.2 Companies Act 1963

The Companies Act 1963, section 99 requires certain charges (including mortgages) created by a limited company to be registered with the Registrar of Companies. Unlike the bills of sale legislation, the Companies Act protects only third parties, not the debtor company itself. Companies are considered to be in a sufficiently strong bargaining position to protect themselves.

25.6.2.1 Registration

Section 99 of the Companies Act 1963 sets out a list of classes of charges which must be registered. Particulars of a registrable charge, together with the instrument by which the charge was created or evidenced, must be registered at the Companies Registration Office within 21 days of its

94 1883 Act, s.7.
95 1883 Act, ss.7 and 13.

creation. The duty to register the charge is imposed on the company but in practice, to ensure registration, the secured creditor usually registers the charge. When registration is completed, the Companies Registrar issues to the applicant a certificate of registration which is conclusive evidence of registration. The register of charges is a public register, available for consultation by the public.[96] Any person contemplating advancing loan or credit facilities on the basis of security offered by a limited company should inspect the register for prior registered charges. Non-compliance with the registration requirements mean that the security is void *against the liquidator and any creditor* of the company so that against them the creditor is unsecured, but it remains valid against all other persons: so it continues to bind the company and any purchaser of the charged assets.

25.6.2.2 Priority

Registration of a charge is required to perfect the chargee's security. Where there are two or more charges over the same property, priority depends primarily on the date of creation of the charge. As between two similar charges, priority depends on the date of creation so that, provided it is registered within the 21-day period, the first created charge has priority over the second, even if the latter is the first registered.

> **Example**:
> Charge 1: registered June 10, 2002 – created June 5, 2002
> Charge 2: registered June 21, 2002 – created June 1, 2002
> Here, Charge 2 has priority.

Where a fixed charge is created over property covered by a prior floating charge, the normal rule is varied so that the later fixed charge may have priority because it is regarded as having being completed under an implied licence from the holder of the floating charge. In order to avoid this, the chargee may include in the floating charge a "negative pledge" clause providing as follows: "The company undertakes not to create any mortgages or charges on any of its assets which would rank in priority to or pari passu with the floating charge." This clause will only be binding upon a subsequent chargee if he has actual notice of it.[97] Registration of the charge at the Companies Office is not itself notice that the charge contains a negative pledge clause. One way to avoid this outcome is to recite the clause in the documentation used when registering the charge.

96 See www.cro.ie.

97 *Welch v. Bowmaker (Ireland) Ltd* [1980] I.R. 251 (S.C.).

25.6.3 Reform of personal property security law

Like the English law of real security,[98] the Irish law of real security can be criticised.[99] The law is highly compartmentalised, depending on who or what is creating the security interest and what type of property the security interest is being created over. Different registers exist with different rules as to form, priorities and enforcement. As a result, transactions of a similar nature are treated very differently. Therefore, it can be argued that the law is unnecessarily complex and uncertain. There have been repeated calls in the United Kingdom for a functional approach to this issue, based on Article 9 of the U.S. Uniform Commercial Code.[100] For example, Professor Diamond in his Review of Security Interests in Property proposed a single system which would apply to all consensual securities, including hire-purchase, conditional sale and retention of title agreements,[101] pledges, and leases for three years or more. The company charges system would be abolished and all non-possessory securities would be perfected by a "notice filing" system – rather than the current transaction system – whereby the creditor would have to register a financial statement putting on the record the name of the debtor and the type of property affected. Registration would not be compulsory but priority would be determined by filing. The Article 9 model is not perfect;[102] nevertheless, it provides a useful point of contrast at which to start to consider Irish law in this area, a project which, from a lawyer's perspective, is long overdue. At the same time, it must be noted that there is little political appetite for reform in this area. Moreover, credit institutions, and in particular banks, seem content to continue with the system as is.

---

98 See, *e.g.* The Crowther Report on Consumer Credit (Cmnd. 4596, 1971); The Cork Committee on Insolvency and Practice (Cmnd. 8558, 1982); *The Diamond Review of Security Interests in Property* (D.T.I., 1989).

99 See Donnelly, "Reforming Personal Property Security Law" (2002) 22 *Dublin University Law Journal* 50.

100 For revised version of Article 9, see www.nccusl.org. Other jurisdictions have followed this approach: see, *e.g.* the Personal Property Security Acts adopted in Ontario in 1967 (see now Ontario Personal Property Security Act 1989); Manitoba in 1973; British Columbia, Alberta, Ontario, New Brunswick and Saskatchewan in 1993; and Yukon in 1995. See further Ziegel, "The New Provincial Chattel Security Regimes" (1991) 70 *Canadian Bar Review* 681, and "Canadian Perspectives on Chattel Security Law Reform in the United Kingdom" (1995) 54 *Cambridge Law Journal* 430. See also the New Zealand Personal Property Securities Act 1999; see further Webb, "The PPSA – A New Regime for Secured Transactions" [2000] *New Zealand Law Review* 175.

101 However, in some instances "purchase money security interests" such as hire purchase, conditional sale and some retention of title agreements would be given special treatment.

102 See Gilmore, "The Good Faith Purchase Idea and the Uniform Commercial Code: Confessions of a Repentant Draftsman" (1981) 15 *Georgia Law Review* 605; Donnelly, "Reforming Personal Property Security Law" (2002) 22 *Dublin University Law Journal* 50; McCormack, "Personal Property Security Law Reform in England and Canada" [2002] *Journal of Business Law* 113.

CHAPTER 26

PERSONAL SECURITY

26.1 INTRODUCTION

Personal security is provided by means of contracts of suretyship, whereby one person, the surety, agrees to be answerable for the debt of another, the principal debtor. It therefore involves a tri-partite relationship between creditor, principal debtor and surety. It should be noted that the debtor is not a party to the contract of surety.

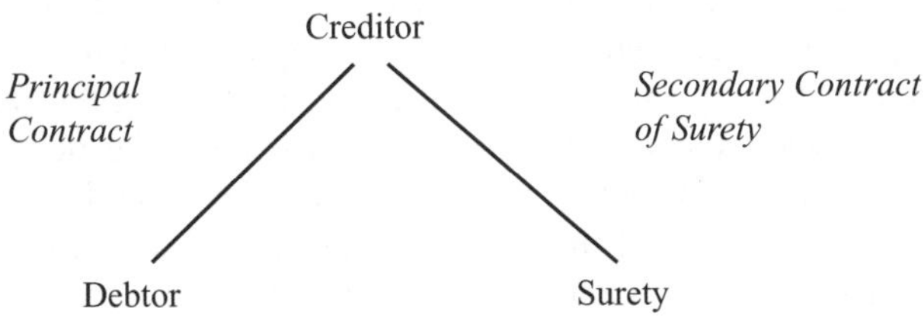

A contract of surety gives the creditor a personal right of action against the surety, but no real rights over any property. Its value thus depends entirely on the creditworthiness of the surety. However, the surety may be required to reinforce his personal undertaking by providing real security to secure his performance: for instance, he may be required to mortgage his house.

Contracts of suretyship take two forms: guarantees and indemnities. A guarantee is an undertaking, given by a third party, to answer for another's default.

> **Example**: X will loan money to Y, subject to Z providing security by guaranteeing the loan. The guarantor, Z, will only become liable under the guarantee if the principal debtor, Y, defaults.

The guarantee is based on the debtor's default, so it is referred to as a secondary obligation; the primary obligation to pay lies with the principal debtor. The secondary liability of a surety under a guarantee can be compared with the surety's primary liability under an indemnity. Like a guarantee, an indemnity is a personal security undertaking given by a third party, but under an indemnity the surety's obligation is independent of the debtor/creditor relationship. It is therefore a primary liability, not dependent on the debtor's default.[1] The difference between indemnities and guarantees can be illustrated by example.

> **Example**: If X says to Y: "Supply goods to Z and if he does not pay, I will", X's undertaking is a contract of guarantee, as payment by X is conditional on Z's default. But if X says to Y: "Supply goods to Z and I will see you paid", this is a contract of indemnity because X's liability to pay is not contingent on Z's default.[2]

This distinction between guarantees and indemnities is not always easy to identify.[3] This is not helped by the fact that judges and commentators sometimes use the terms interchangeably. In seeking to distinguish the two, a court will examine the facts of each case to determine the intention of the parties. For instance, in *Commodity Banking Company v. Meehan*,[4] a company wholly owned by the defendant owed £36,000 to the plaintiff. The defendant acknowledged the debt and indicated to the plaintiff that the company was insolvent. The defendant agreed that he would personally repay the debt by instalments but he refused to sign a guarantee to this effect. It was held that the agreement to repay the debt constituted an indemnity rather than a guarantee because the defendant agreed to repay the monies due even if the company as principal debtor did not.[5]

Guarantees and indemnities are often used to reinforce each other. A standard provision in a contract for guarantee might state:

> "Without prejudice to the guarantee herein given, the guarantor agrees to indemnify the Bank against any loss or damage which the Bank may suffer as a result of providing the debtor, named above, with credit facilities."

or,

> "[The guarantor] undertakes, as a separate and independent obligation, that all sums due under the guarantee, shall be recoverable by the creditor from [the guarantor], as principal debtor and/or by way of indemnity."

A clause such as the latter is known as a "principal debtor clause". Its main purpose is to exclude the rules by which a guarantor is discharged, for instance where the creditor agrees to give the borrower extra time for

1 See, *e.g. Gulf Bank KSC v. Mitsubishi Heavy Industries Ltd* (No. 2) [1994] 2 Lloyd's Rep. 145.

2 *Birkmyr v. Darnell* (1704) 1 Salk 27.

3 Another distinction which may need to be drawn, but is less difficult to establish, relates to the distinction between contracts of guarantee and contracts of insurance: see, *e.g. Seaton v. Heath* [1899] 1 Q.B. 782; *International Commercial Bank v. ICI* [1991] I.L.R.M. 726; *Hong Kong and Shanghai Banking Corpn v. Icarom plc* unreported, Supreme Court, July 31, 1992. On contracts of insurance, see generally Part V.

4 [1985] I.R. 12. See also *Yeoman Credit v. Latter* [1961] 2 All E.R. 294 (C.A.).

5 The plaintiff's claim in this case failed for lack of consideration: see further 26.2.2.

repayment,[6] or to preserve the guarantor's liability where the borrower's obligations are void from the outset or are later discharged. In this chapter, we concentrate on the use of guarantees as a form of personal security, making brief reference to indemnities where relevant, before looking at some alternatives to guarantees, including letters of comfort.

26.2 GUARANTEES[7]

A guarantee can be used to secure both fixed debts and revolving debts. For example, before agreeing to sell goods on credit terms, a seller, unsure of the potential buyer's creditworthiness, may require that a creditworthy third party guarantee payment of the price. Similarly, a bank contemplating providing loan or overdraft facilities, may require a creditworthy third party to guarantee repayment. Common instances of the use of guarantees include a parent guaranteeing a bank loan for a son or daughter; and a parent company guaranteeing a loan to a subsidiary company.[8] A *del credere* agent who arranges an international sale of goods contract guarantees payment by the buyer.[9] Guarantees are used not only to secure the repayment of a loan or overdraft, but also can be given to guarantee tender or performance of a contract. Such transactions are known as performance guarantees or bonds but they do not comply with the strict legal meaning of guarantees.[10]

26.2.1 Types of guarantee

Guarantees can be classified in several ways: as once-off or continuing; and as a demand or a conditional guarantee. Guarantees can also be classified according to whether they were requested by the debtor or the creditor.

---

6 See 26.2.6.1.

7 See further Donnelly, *The Law of Banks and Credit Institutions* (Dublin, Round Hall Sweet & Maxwell, 2000), Chapter 17; Breslin, *Banking Law in the Republic of Ireland* (Dublin, Gill & Macmillan, 1998) Part VI; Andrews & Millett, *Law of Guarantees* (London, Sweet & Maxwell, 3rd ed., 2001); Breslin, "Guarantees Under Attack" [1996] *Commercial Law Practitioner* 243.

8 On the limitations of companies giving guarantees, see generally doctrine of *ultra vires*. In particular, see Companies Act 1963, s.60 and Companies Act 1990, s.31. See generally, Keane, *Company Law* (Dublin, Butterworths, 3rd ed., 2000); Forde, *Company Law in Ireland* (Dublin, Round Hall Sweet & Maxwell, 3rd ed., 1999); Courtney, *The Law of Private Companies* (Dublin, Butterworths, 2nd ed., 2002).

9 See 4.4.3.

10 See further 26.4. and 32.3.

26.2.1.1 Once-off or continuing

A guarantee may secure a single, "once-off" obligation, such as the price under a sale contract, or a loan for a fixed sum. Alternatively, it may secure a continuing obligation, such as rental instalments due under a lease or an equipment hire contract, or sums due under a revolving credit facility such as an overdraft. A "once-off" guarantee secures the single transaction until the debtor's obligation has been discharged. A continuing guarantee imposes a continuing obligation on the surety; if it secures a revolving facility it continues so long as the facility remains available, and the amount of the guarantor's liability will vary in accordance with the extent of the debtor's borrowing.[11] A creditor will usually require a guarantee of a revolving facility to include a provision that the guarantee will continue despite intermediate discharge of the debt,[12] for example:

> "The guarantor's liability under the guarantee will be of a continuous nature and apply to the balance outstanding from time to time and shall not be terminated by any intermediary payment or satisfaction of the debt owed by the debtor."

The effect of such a provision is that the guarantor remains liable throughout the period of the credit facility, and is not released merely because the debtor's account is cleared from time to time.

26.2.1.2 Demand or conditional

Under a conditional guarantee, the guarantor's obligation to pay is conditional on the happening of a specified event, such as the production of a written statement that the principal debtor is in default or a court judgment in favour of the creditor, so the clause might take the following form:

> "The guarantor undertakes that, if the debtor defaults in the payment due to the creditor, he, the guarantor, will pay that sum to the creditor on the production of a written statement that the principal debtor is in default."

In contrast, under a demand guarantee the guarantor must pay on first demand by the creditor. An "on demand" clause could be drafted along the following lines:

> "The guarantor undertakes that, if the debtor defaults in the payment due to the creditor, he, the guarantor, will pay that sum to the creditor on demand."

---

11 But see *Bank of Ireland v. McCabe* unreported, Supreme Court, December 19, 1994.

12 On discharge, see 26.2.6.

Under a demand guarantee, the surety's liability arises as soon as a demand is made. However, if the guarantee also contains what is termed a "principal debtor" clause, the surety's liability is not even contingent on a demand being made.[13] Banks most often use demand guarantees so as to avoid disputes. But other financial institutions, such as insurance or surety companies often agree to conditional guarantees.

26.2.1.3 Requested by debtor or creditor

Guarantees can also be classified according to whether they are requested by the debtor or the creditor. Where the guarantee is requested by the creditor, there is no contractual relationship between surety and debtor; this has important consequences for the guarantor's rights.[14] In hire purchase agreements, where a finance company supplies goods on hire purchase to a debtor introduced by a dealer from whom the finance company buys the goods, the following situations can arise. The finance house (the creditor) may require that a third party acts as guarantor for the debtor, so that the debtor must ask a parent or friend to provide the guarantee; or the finance house may agree with the dealer that the dealer will guarantee payment by all debtors he introduces.

26.2.2 Formation of a guarantee

Guarantees must conform to the general requirements for the formation of a contract: there must be an agreement, supported by consideration (unless made by deed) and an intention to create legal relations. These general requirements are modified in some respects. For example, where the guarantee is of a future debt or transaction, the creditor provides consideration for the guarantor's promise by making the loan to the principal debtor, and the agreement will usually recite that the guarantee is given in consideration of the loan. A guarantee of an existing debt may be expressed to be in consideration of the creditor's forbearance to sue the principal debtor; otherwise it must be made by deed, since the loan itself would be past consideration.[15] For instance, in *Fullerton v. Provincial Bank of Ireland*,[16] the defendant bank informed the debtor that his account was overdrawn. In response, the debtor offered the title deeds to his property as security. It was held that, although the bank had never expressly agreed not to sue, their restraint in not calling in the overdraft immediately constituted sufficient consideration. This contrasts with the approach of the court in

13 *MS Fashions v. Bank of Credit & Commerce International SA* [1993] 3 All E.R. 769; *cf. Re Bank of Credit & Commerce International SA (No. 8)* [1994] 3 All E.R. 565.

14 See 26.2.4.

15 On the doctrine of consideration generally, see 2.2.2.

16 [1903] A.C. 309; see also *Blandford & Houdret Ltd v. Bray Travel Holdings Ltd* unreported, High Court, Gannon J., November 11, 1983.

Commodity Banking Company v. Meehan[17] where a company wholly owned by the defendant owed £36,000 to the plaintiff. The defendant agreed that he would personally repay the debt by instalments. The company was insolvent at the time of this promise. It was held that the promise was not legally binding because there was no consideration to support it. The court found that there was no express or implied request for forbearance from legal action. The reason that the bank had not sued was not because of the defendant's promise but because any legal action would be fruitless because of the company's insolvency.

More recent pronouncements from the Supreme Court suggest a willingness to find consideration to support guarantees. In *First National Commercial Bank plc v. Anglin*,[18] the defendant guarantor argued that he executed a guarantee in September 1989 as security for monies lent the previous February and hence the consideration for the guarantee was past and the guarantee unenforceable. The Supreme Court found, on the facts, that the guarantee had been executed before the loan and that the issue of past consideration did not arise. The Supreme Court also questioned the relevance of a past consideration argument even if the defendant had signed the guarantee when he argued that he did. The court was of the view that the loan was made expressly on the basis that a guarantee would be given and that the guarantee extended to present and future indebtedness of the principal debtor.[19]

Moreover, the guarantee, to be enforceable, must be evidenced by a note or memorandum in writing and signed by the guarantor or other authorised person.[20] In *Bank of Ireland v. McCabe*,[21] the defendant had signed an earlier guarantee, but in relation to a new loan no separate or new guarantee was signed. The court held that the earlier guarantee applied only to a previous loan and hence there was no enforceable guarantee to support the new loan.

26.2.2.1 Revocability of the guarantor's undertaking

A guarantee may be a unilateral or a bilateral contract. If the creditor agrees that, in consideration of the surety's guarantee, it will provide credit to the debtor, the contract is bilateral. More often, the creditor will not actually promise to advance credit. In that case the contract is unilateral: the surety's undertaking is that *if* the creditor advances credit, the surety will guarantee the debt. The creditor accepts that offer, and provides

17 [1985] I.R. 12. See also *Provincial Bank of Ireland v. Donnelly* [1934] N.I. 33, approved in *Riordan & Mulligan v. Carroll* [1996] 2 I.L.R.M. 263.

18 Unreported, Supreme Court, June 27, 1996.

19 See similarly *Pao on v. Lau Yiu Long* [1980] A.C. 614 (P.C.).

20 Statute of Frauds (Ireland) 1695, s.2; see further 2.2.4. Importantly, the Statute of Frauds does not apply to contracts of indemnity.

21 Unreported, Supreme Court, December 19, 1994.

consideration for the surety's promise, by advancing the credit. Where the contract is unilateral, the surety can revoke its offer at any time before it is accepted. Once credit is advanced, the surety is bound. In some cases, however, such as where the surety guarantees a revolving credit facility, the correct analysis may be that the surety's undertaking is a standing offer which the creditor accepts each time it makes a new advance to the debtor. In that case, the surety can at any time revoke its offer and thus terminate its liability in respect of future advances; it remains liable in respect of advances made before revocation. The terms of the guarantee will normally require the surety to give notice before revoking the offer in this way. Whether a continuing guarantee is revocable in this way depends on the construction of the contract. The undertaking is revocable where the consideration provided by the creditor is severable. Where the creditor's consideration is entire – for instance where the surety guarantees payment of rent if the creditor accepts the debtor as a tenant – the surety is irrevocably bound once its offer is accepted.

26.2.2.2 Duress and undue influence

If the surety's undertaking is obtained by duress, undue influence or misrepresentation *by the creditor*, the guarantee will be voidable.[22] Unlike contracts of insurance, contracts of suretyship are not contracts of *utmost good faith*, that is, the creditor is not under a legal duty to disclose all materials facts to the guarantor.[23] However, it has been recognised that a creditor owes a limited duty to disclose unusual features of the principal contract unknown to the surety. In *Levett & ors v. Barclays Bank*,[24] the debtor convinced the plaintiffs to let him use their Treasury stock as short-term security for a loan from the defendant bank, the stock to be returned before maturity. The bank forwarded a standard memorandum of deposit to the plaintiffs where the transaction was presented as one of security. However, between the debtor and the bank, the loan facility letter made it clear that the stock would be used to repay the loan. This fact was not told to the plaintiffs. The debtor was untrustworthy and the bank had to use the stock to reduce the debtor's debt. The plaintiffs successfully sought a return of the proceeds of the stock. At first instance, it was held that a creditor was under a duty to disclose to the surety contractual arrangements made between the debtor and the creditor, which make the terms of the

22 See, *e.g. Lloyds Bank Ltd v. Bundy* [1975] Q.B. 326; *National Westminster Bank plc v. Morgan* [1985] A.C. 686; *Bank of Nova Scotia v. Hogan* unreported, High Court, Keane J., December 21, 1992; [1997] 1 I.L.R.M. 407 (S.C.); *Carroll v. Carroll* [1998] 2 I.L.R.M. 218.

23 On the distinction between insurance contracts and contracts of guarantee, see *Seaton v. Heath* [1899] 1 Q.B. 782; *International Commercial Bank v. ICI* [1991] I.L.R.M. 726; *Hong Kong and Shanghai Banking Corpn v. Icarom plc* unreported, Supreme Court, July 31, 1992. On contracts of insurance, see generally Part V.

24 [1995] 2 All E.R. 615.

principal contract something materially different in a potentially disadvantageous respect from those which the surety might naturally expect.

(i) Improper conduct by the debtor

The guarantee may also be invalidated by duress, undue influence or misrepresentation by the debtor if:

(a) the debtor was acting as the creditor's agent – for instance, in obtaining the surety's agreement to the transaction; or
(b) the creditor has actual or constructive notice of the debtor's improper conduct.

In *Barclays Bank v. O'Brien*,[25] the House of Lords held that where a wife gave a guarantee to secure her husband's debt, and the guarantee was not to the wife's advantage (as, for instance, where the secured debt was the sole liability of the husband),[26] there was a substantial risk of the husband committing a wrong which would allow the wife to set the transaction aside. The creditor would have constructive notice of the debtor's conduct unless the creditor took reasonable steps to ensure that the guarantee had been properly obtained. In this case, the husband had misrepresented the amount and duration of the loan to his wife. The same rule applies where surety and debtor are cohabitees, and the creditor is aware of the personal relationship between them, or in any other relationship where the creditor is aware that the guarantor reposes trust and confidence in the principal debtor.[27] To avoid being fixed with such notice, the creditor should inform the surety of the nature of the transaction and of the risks involved and of the advisability of obtaining independent advice. In *Royal Bank of Scotland plc v. Etridge and ors*,[28] the House of Lords sought to indicate clear, simple and practically operable minimum requirements for procedures to be followed when a bank is obtaining security. In particular, a bank would satisfy the minimum requirements by taking steps to bring to a wife's attention the risks of standing as surety for her husband if it insisted that the wife attend a private meeting with a representative of the bank where:

25 [1993] W.L.R. 786.

26 *Cf Ulster Bank Ireland Ltd v. Fitzgerald* unreported, High Court, O'Donovan J., November 9, 2001.

27 See, *e.g. Credit Lyonnais v. Burch* [1997] 1 All E.R. 144 (C.A.) where the relationship of surety and principal debtor was that of employee and employer.

28 [2001] 4 All E.R. 449, [2001] 2 All E.R. (Comm.) 1061; see further Donnelly, "Undue Influence, Misrepresentation and Guarantees: What is a Bank to do?" [1999] *Commercial Law Practitioner* 167; Breslin, "Undue Influence: Guarantor's Equitable Right or Creditor's Contractual Obligation?" [2002] *Commercial Law Practitioner* 35.

(a) she was told of the extent of her liability as surety;
(b) she was warned of the risk she was running; and
(c) she was urged to take separate legal advice.

To be safe, a bank could insist that she take separate legal advice. The House of Lords also set out the minimum content of the legal advice that a solicitor advising the wife should give. Where the guarantee is not for the sole benefit of the debtor – as, for instance, where a wife guarantees a loan made to her and her husband jointly and secures the guarantee by giving a mortgage over her property – the creditor is not fixed with constructive notice of improper conduct by the debtor.[29]

The Irish position is less clear-cut. In *Bank of Ireland v. Smyth*,[30] the defendant's wife gave her consent to a deed of charge in favour of the plaintiff bank over lands owned by her husband (as required by section 3(1) of the Family Home Protection Act 1976). When the bank sought possession of the lands following the husband's default, the defendant's wife argued that her consent was invalid because she had not understood that in the event of default the family home could be sold. The Supreme Court held that because the defendant's wife was not "fully informed," her consent was invalid and hence the relevant conveyance was incapable of creating a valid mortgage over the family home. The matter of the enforceability of guarantees and improper conduct by the debtor was considered by the Supreme Court in *Bank of Nova Scotia v. Hogan*.[31] The case actually involved an allegation that the bank itself had exercised undue influence over the surety, but the case was dismissed for lack of evidence supporting the claim. However, Murphy J., speaking *obiter* for the Supreme Court, appears to have approved the reasoning of the *O'Brien* decision. A definitive judgment is awaited.

26.2.3 Relations between the guarantor and the creditor

Unless agreed otherwise, the guarantor's liability is coterminous with that of the principal debtor, so that the guarantor is not liable unless the debtor defaults, and where the debtor pays the secured debt in full, the guarantee terminates. If the debtor defaults, it is not necessary for the creditor to sue or even to make a claim against the principal debtor before calling on the guarantor, unless the contract of guarantee expressly so provides.[32] It is unlikely that a bank would agree to such a provision.

29 *CIBC Mortgages plc v. Pitt* [1993] W.L.R. 802.

30 [1993] 2 I.R. 102; see further Sanfey, "Consenting Adults: the Implications of Bank of Ireland v. Smyth" [1996] *Commercial Law Practitioner* 31.

31 [1997] 1 I.L.R.M. 407.

32 *AG v. Sun Alliance and London Insurances Ltd* [1985] I.L.R.M. 522 (S.C.). In *Holl v. Hadley* (1828) 5 Bing. 54 the contract required the creditor to use "the utmost efforts and legal proceedings" against the debtor, and thus, it was held that the creditor was obliged to sue the principal debtor.

26.2.3.1 Nature of the guarantor's liability

The extent of the guarantor's liability depends on the construction of the contract, but usually the guarantor's responsibility is not merely to pay a sum of money to the creditor if the principal debtor fails to do so, but to procure the debtor's performance. In *Moschi v. Lep Air Services Ltd*,[33] freight forwarders agreed to relinquish their lien over the debtor's goods in return for the debtor's agreement to pay £40,000 in instalments. The appellants guaranteed performance of the debtor's obligation. The debtor defaulted and the creditors, treating this as a repudiation of the agreement, terminated the contract and claimed against the appellants. The appellants argued that termination of the contract with the principal debtors released them from liability. The House of Lords held that the undertaking to guarantee was not to pay the instalments on the debtor's default, but to procure performance by the debtor of his obligations under the contract, so that the guarantors were liable for damages equal to the amount the debtor would have paid, plus interest.

26.2.3.2 Invalidity of the principal contract

The effect on the surety's liability of invalidity or unenforceability of the main contract depends on the construction of the surety contract and whether it is classified as a guarantee or an indemnity. Since a guarantee is ancillary to the main contract, if the principal contract is void and unenforceable, so too is the contract of guarantee. This point is illustrated by the case of *Coutts & Co v. Browne-Lecky*,[34] where a guarantee of a minor's overdraft at a bank could not be enforced due to the Infants Relief Act 1874 which provided that the infant was not liable to repay the loan. In contrast, if the surety is properly construed as an indemnity, the surety incurs primary liability so that he remains liable even though the principal contract is unenforceable against the principal debtor. To avoid any uncertainty over classification of the surety, an express provision should be included that the surety shall be liable even in circumstances where the principal debtor is not.[35]

If the surety contract itself is void or voidable, it is irrelevant that it is an indemnity rather than a guarantee. In *Associated Japanese Bank (International) v. Credit de Nord*,[36] the defendant guaranteed payment of rentals due to the plaintiff under a sale and lease-back arrangement of machinery and undertook that they would be liable as "sole or principal debtor." In fact, the machinery which was the subject of the sale and lease-

33 [1973] A.C. 331.
34 [1947] K.B. 104.
35 See *Heald v. O'Connor* [1971] 1 W.L.R. 497.
36 [1989] 1 W.L.R. 255.

back contract did not exist. It was held that the guarantee contract itself was void *ab initio* for mistake, so that the plaintiff could recover nothing under the guarantee. In addition, the court found that on the construction of the contract there was an express (or at least implied) condition precedent to the guarantee agreement that the machinery existed.

26.2.4 Relations between the guarantor and the debtor

The guarantor has two basic rights against the principal debtor: a right to indemnity, and a right of subrogation. Where there is a contract between surety and debtor, these may be supplemented by express or implied provisions of the contract.

26.2.4.1 A right to indemnity

If the guarantee is given at the request of the debtor, the guarantor has an implied contractual right to be indemnified by the debtor against all liabilities he incurs, including the sum paid and any interest which has accrued from the date of payment.[37] This is an example of the general rule that if one party incurs expenditure or liabilities at another party's request or with his authority, then that party is entitled to be compensated or indemnified, since the request or authority implies a promise to compensate or indemnify the creditor.[38]

The guarantor's right of indemnity is often restricted by the contract of guarantee, for example:

> "The guarantor undertakes not to pursue a claim for indemnity in competition with the creditor in the insolvency of the principal debtor until the creditor has received payment in full."

The effect of such a provision is that the guarantor cannot pursue his right of indemnity, and hence reduce the pool of assets available to satisfy the creditor's claim, until the creditor's claim has been satisfied. Where a guarantor entitled to indemnity is sued on the guarantee, he may claim indemnity from the debtor in third party proceedings.

26.2.4.2 A right of subrogation

Where the guarantor discharges the debt which he has guaranteed, he is entitled to step into the shoes of the creditor and, under the doctrine of subrogation, pursue any claims against the debtor which the creditor had,

37 *Re Fox Walker & Co, ex parte Bishop* (1880) 15 Ch. 400.

38 *Re a Debtor* [1937] 1 All E.R. 1 at 7–8, *per* Greene L.J.; see further *Owen v. Tate* [1976] Q.B. 402 (H.L.).

including enforcing securities held by the creditor for the debt, whether made before or after the guarantee. The doctrine of subrogation arises by operation of the law to prevent the debtor being unjustly enriched.[39] It is available whether the guarantee was given at the request of the debtor or the creditor. For the purposes of subrogation, although the payment of the debt extinguishes the debt, any other securities are kept alive for the benefit of the guarantor who is entitled to have them transferred to him together with any judgment obtained by the creditor. The guarantor ranks in the same priority as the creditor. The guarantor can only claim a right to subrogation to securities or other rights of the creditor where he has paid the debt in full: a proportionate right of subrogation does not exist.[40]

As noted above, under the doctrine of subrogation, the guarantor is entitled to step into the shoes of the creditor. Therefore, a guarantor's rights cannot be more extensive than the rights which the creditor would have had. This point is illustrated in *Re Chipboard Ltd (in liquidation)*,[41] where the Minister for Finance gave two guarantees as security for bank loans to Chipboard Ltd which subsequently became insolvent. The bank loans were in fact secured in two ways: first, by a charge in favour of the bank over the assets of the company, including book debts; and second, by the Minister's guarantees. The Minister's guarantees were, in turn, secured by a charge on the company's assets, excluding the book debts. The charge in favour of the bank entitled the bank to interest at the current rate of simple interest. The charge in favour of the Minister entitled him to interest set at five per cent above the bank's lending rate. The guarantees supplied by the Minister were called upon by the bank, and the Minister paid. The Minister then sought to exercise his right to be subrogated to the securities held by the bank: the charge over the company's assets, including the book debts. It was held that the fact that the Minister had other securities himself did not preclude him from exercising his right of subrogation,[42] but because he had opted to exercise his right of subrogation he was limited to the rate of interest specified in the bank's charge – a lesser rate than his own charge.

26.2.5 Rights against co-guarantors

Where two or more guarantors are liable for the same obligation to the same amount, the extent of the liability is shared equally between them, unless otherwise agreed. So, where one guarantor has paid the full guaranteed amount, he is entitled to claim reimbursement from his co-guarantor in an equitable action for contribution (the debtor and any other co-guarantors should be joined as co-defendants in the action to avoid

39 *Highland Finance v. Sacred Heart College* [1992] 1 I.R. 472.

40 *Re Sass* [1896] 2 Q.B. 12.

41 [1994] 3 I.R. 164.

42 *Cf. Bank of Ireland v. Daly* [1978] I.R. 79; and *Highland Finance v. Sacred Heart College* [1992] 1 I.R. 472.

multiplicity of actions).[43] The guarantees need not be created by the same instrument, and indeed the fact that each guarantor is unaware of the other's existence does not affect the right to contribution. Where the guarantees cover the same obligation but in different amounts, each guarantor must contribute in proportion to their respective liabilities.

26.2.6 Discharge of the guarantor

A guarantee is usually discharged where the creditor does any act which alters the guarantor's rights, or the debtor is discharged from liability.[44]

26.2.6.1 Where the guarantor's rights are altered

Unless otherwise agreed, any acts or omissions by the creditor which alter or extinguish the guarantor's rights (for example, by releasing a co-guarantor,[45] or giving the debtor more time)[46] operate to discharge the guarantee.[47] In *Holme v. Brunskill*,[48] it was held that if the alteration was not obviously insubstantial or non-prejudicial to the guarantor, the guarantor should be discharged from liability, unless he consents otherwise. This test clearly favours the guarantor who does not have to prove actual loss or damage. In *MacEnroe v. AIB*,[49] the plaintiff agreed to guarantee loans advanced to a company whether "on foot of … current account or otherwise", subject to a limit of IR£75,000. At the time of the guarantee, the company had two bank accounts, both overdrawn. After the guarantee was executed, a third account was opened and this fact was known to the guarantor. It was agreed between the bank and the company that this third account could not be set off against the debts in the other two accounts. The plaintiff argued that the opening of the third account altered the guarantee contract, and therefore he should be discharged from liability. The Supreme Court held that the opening of the account was not a "material variation" of the guarantee and hence the guarantor was not discharged. It has been argued that this difference in terminology between

43 In *Re PMPA (Longmile) Ltd* [1993] 1 I.R. 190. See further *Bank of Ireland v. O'Shea* unreported, High Court, Denham J., July 31, 1992.

44 See further *Bank of India v. Trans Continental Commodity Merchants Ltd* [1982] 1 Lloyd's Rep. 506 at 514–5, per Bingham J. (H.C.); [1983] 2 Lloyd's Rep. 298 (C.A.).

45 *Ward v. National Bank of New Zealand* (1883) 8 App. Cas. 755.

46 *Prendergast v. Devey* (1821) 6 Madd. 124; *Munster & Leinster Bank v. France* (1889) 24 L.R. I.R. 82.

47 *Holme v. Brunskill* (1878) 3 Q.B.D. 495; *MacEnroe v. AIB* [1980] I.L.R.M. 171 (S.C.); *ADM Ltd v. Kavanagh* unreported, Supreme Court, May 10, 2002.

48 (1878) 3 Q.B.D. 495.

49 [1980] I.L.R.M. 171 (S.C.).

"not obviously insubstantial or non-prejudicial to the guarantor" and "material alteration" means that an Irish court will be less sympathetic to guarantors seeking release from their obligation following an alteration of the guarantee contract.[50] To avoid discharge following a "material alternation," the guarantee should include a provision such as:

> "The guarantor agrees and consents to any alteration, variation, amendment or extinction of his rights to indemnity and subrogation made by the creditor."

26.2.6.2 Discharge of the debtor

Under a contract of guarantee, because a guarantor's liability is coterminous with that of the debtor, the guarantor's liability is discharged if the debt is paid, or the debtor is discharged from liability, or the liability to pay is extinguished by operation of the law. If, on proper construction of the guarantee, the guarantor is responsible for the procurement of the debtor's performance, the guarantor is not released if the creditor terminates the principal contract in response to a serious breach of contract by the debtor.[51] The debtor's primary liability in debt is converted into a liability in damages, and this secondary obligation is also guaranteed. Under a contract of indemnity, since the surety's liability is independent of the debtor's, discharge of the debtor does not necessarily release the surety.

26.3 Letters of Credit[52]

Letters of credit or documentary credits are used as a means of securing payment in international sales contracts. They are used, especially under an international contract, to give a seller of goods an assurance of payment: the buyer arranges for a bank to give the seller an undertaking to pay the price if certain conditions are fulfilled. They thus resemble a guarantee. However, the bank's undertaking under a letter of credit is generally a primary obligation, independent of the underlying contract and the seller looks to the bank rather than to the buyer for payment.

26.4 Performance Guarantees[53]

Performance guarantees (sometimes referred to as bank guarantees or

50 Donnelly, *The Law of Banks and Credit Institutions* (Dublin, Round Hall Sweet & Maxwell, 2000) at p.443.
51 *Moschi v. Lep Air Services Ltd* [1973] A.C. 331: see 26.2.3.1.
52 See generally Chapter 32.
53 See generally 32.3.

performance bonds) are not guarantees in the strict common law sense, in that they are not secondary obligations which come into operation on the debtor's default, but are primary autonomous obligations. They are undertakings by a bank or similar institution to pay money, used in a similar way to letters of credit to provide an assurance of payment or performance of another obligation.

26.5 Letters of Comfort

A letter of comfort may be used as an alternative to a guarantee. The use of letters of comfort has become more common recently as a means of reassuring potential creditors that their loan or credit facilities will be repaid, without actually guaranteeing repayment. It is usually given by a parent company to support an advance of credit facilities to its subsidiary by a lending institution.

A typical comfort letter provides:

(i) a statement of the awareness of a parent company of the advances made to the subsidiary;
(ii) a promise that the parent company will not, without the lender's consent, relinquish or reduce control of the subsidiary before repayment; and
(iii) words of comfort, stating how far the parent company is prepared to go in supporting its subsidiary, often beginning "it is our intention" or "it is our policy".

Whether the words of comfort in (iii) above have contractual effect depends on the construction of the letter. Despite the presumption, in commercial dealings, that parties intend their agreements to have legal effect,[54] it seems that generally letters of comfort will be regarded as not intended to be binding.[55] In *Kleinwort Benson Ltd v. Malaysia Mining Corporation Ltd*,[56] a creditor agreed a loan with a subsidiary company based on two letters of comfort provided by the parent company (who had been unwilling to guarantee the loan) along the following lines: "It is our policy to ensure that the business of [the subsidiary] is at all times in a position to meet its liabilities to you ..." The subsidiary company went into liquidation and the creditors sought repayment from the parent company.

---

54 See 2.2.3.

55 See, *e.g.* *Kleinwort Benson Ltd v. Malaysia Mining Corporation Ltd* [1989] 1 W.L.R. 379 (U.K.); *Commonwealth Bank of Australia v. TLI Management Pty Ltd* [1990] U.K. 510 (Aust.); *Toronto-Dominion Bank v. Leigh Instruments Ltd* (*Trustee of*) (1998) 81 A.C.W.S. (d) 117 (Can.); and *Bank of New Zealand v. Ginivan* [1991] 1 N.Z.L.R. 178 (N.Z.).

56 [1989] 1 W.L.R. 379; approved in *Re Atlantic Computers plc* [1995] B.C.C. 696. See further Brown, "Letters of Comfort: Placebo or Promise"[1990] *Journal of Business Law* 281.

The Court of Appeal held that the letters of comfort were not intended to create a contractual promise as to future conduct. The court did not consider the possibility that the letters contained an *implied* future promise, but took the view that letters of comfort are generally commercially regarded as intended to create a moral but not a legally binding obligation. As a result, a letter of comfort represents a poor substitute for a binding personal security undertaking, and creditors may be reluctant to advance credit on the basis of letters of comfort alone. However, where a parent company is unwilling to provide a guarantee, a letter of comfort may be the only "security" available to the creditor.

Part V

PRINCIPLES OF INSURANCE LAW

CHAPTER 27

THE INSURANCE CONTRACT

27.1 INTRODUCTION

Commerce involves risk. A buyer under a sales contract may not pay; or goods delivered by the seller may be defective. Commercial contracts may deal with certain aspects of risk and distribute them between the parties to the contract. Exclusion clauses are generally used for this purpose.[1] For example, an exclusion clause which excludes or limits the seller's liability for the supply of defective goods effectively throws the risk of such loss on the buyer. Equally, section 20 of the Sale of Goods Act 1893 deals with the allocation of risk for accidental loss or damage to the goods between seller and buyer under a sales contract.[2] Similarly, the use of insurance contracts involves the allocation of risk, but to a third party – the insurer. Broadly speaking, in return for a premium, the insurer takes over certain risks from the insured. Should these risks ever materialise, the insurer will compensate or "indemnify" the insured for any loss or damage caused, under the terms of the insurance contract.

Insurance allows the cost of risk to be spread over a range of persons. For example, a manufacturer may take out product liability insurance. The premium paid by the manufacturer for the insurance cover is part of the cost of producing the product and hence will be reflected in the price of the product, thereby spreading the cost of the insurance among the manufacturer's customers. Where the manufacturer makes a claim, or several claims, under his insurance contract, the premium on renewal will most likely increase. In such circumstances, this increase in cost can be absorbed by the manufacturer or, more commonly, is passed on to the customer through a price increase, perhaps making the product less competitive when compared with its rivals.

Many of the risks of commercial activity can be insured against, and a prudent business person will therefore consider putting in place such insurance cover. Some forms of insurance are compulsory. For example, where you drive a motor vehicle you are required to have third party motor

1 See generally 2.3.5; and regarding exclusion clauses in sale of goods contracts see 10.5.

2 See generally Chapter 18.

liability insurance.[3] Certain professions, such as solicitors,[4] may be required by legislation or by rules of professional conduct to have minimal professional liability insurance cover. Other forms of insurance which a business may consider taking out include: property insurance,[6] public liability insurance,[7] product liability insurance,[8] employers' liability insurance,[9] business interruption insurance[10] and bad debt insurance. Each type of insurance is a topic for study in its own right but in this part we concentrate on the main principles of insurance law.

27.2 The Nature of Insurance Contracts

A contract of insurance has been defined as one "under which a sum of money becomes payable on an event which is uncertain as to its timing or its happening at all."[11] More generally, a contract of insurance is a contract under which one party (the insurer) agrees, in return for a consideration

---

3 See Road Traffic Act 1961, as amended, and various regulations made thereunder. See Buckley, *Insurance Law in Ireland* (Dublin, Oak Tree Press, 1997) Chapter 8, and Buckley, *Insurance Law in Ireland Vol. Two* (Dublin, Oak Tree Press, 2002) and O'Regan Cazabon, *Insurance Law in Ireland* (Dublin, Round Hall Sweet & Maxwell, 1999) Chapter 12C.

4 See the Professional Indemnity Insurance Regulations 1995 (S.I. No. 312 of 1995), as amended, made under the Solicitors (Amendment) Act 1994, s.26.

5 See O'Regan Cazabon, *Insurance Law in Ireland* (Dublin, Round Hall Sweet & Maxwell, 1999) Chapter 12F; Buckley, *Insurance Law in Ireland* (Dublin, Oak Tree Press, 1997) Chapter 12.

6 See Buckley, *Insurance Law in Ireland* (Dublin, Oak Tree Press, 1997) Chapter 15, and Buckley, *Insurance Law in Ireland Vol. Two* (Dublin, Oak Tree Press, 2002); and O'Regan Cazabon, *Insurance Law in Ireland* (Dublin, Round Hall Sweet & Maxwell, 1999) Chapter 12E.

7 See Buckley, *Insurance Law in Ireland* (Dublin, Oak Tree Press, 1997) Chapter 10, and Buckley, *Insurance Law in Ireland Vol. Two* (Dublin, Oak Tree Press, 2002); and O'Regan Cazabon, *Insurance Law in Ireland* (Dublin, Round Hall Sweet & Maxwell, 1999) Chapter 12F.

8 See O'Regan Cazabon, *Insurance Law in Ireland* (Dublin, Round Hall Sweet & Maxwell, 1999) Chapter 12F; and Buckley, *Insurance Law in Ireland* (Dublin, Oak Tree Press, 1997) Chapter 11.

9 See Buckley, *Insurance Law in Ireland* (Dublin, Oak Tree Press, 1997) Chapter 14, and Buckley, *Insurance Law in Ireland Vol. Two*, (Dublin, Oak Tree Press, 2002); and O'Regan Cazabon, *Insurance Law in Ireland* (Dublin, Round Hall Sweet & Maxwell, 1999) Chapter 12F.

10 See Buckley, *Insurance Law in Ireland* (Dublin, Oak Tree Press, 1997) Chapter 16, and Buckley, *Insurance Law in Ireland Vol. Two* (Dublin, Oak Tree Press, 2002).

11 *Fuji Finance v. Aetna* [1994] 4 All E.R. 1025 at 1031, following *Prudential Insurance Co v. IRC* [1904] 2 K.B. 658; reversed on different grounds [1996] 4 All E.R. 608 (C.A.). See also *Seaton v. Heath* [1899] 1 Q.B. 782, at 792–3, approved in *International Commercial Bank plc v. Insurance Corporation of Ireland plc & Meadows Indemnity Co Ltd* [1991] I.L.R.M. 726 (H.C.), unsuccessfully appealed to the Supreme Court on a separate point: unreported, Supreme Court, July 31, 1992. See further *Rafter v. Solicitors Mutual Defence Fund Ltd* unreported, High Court, McCracken J., May 20, 1999.

known as the premium, to assume the risk of an uncertain event to which the other party (the insured) is exposed and in which the insured has an interest, and on the occurrence of the event insured against, to pay the insured a sum of money or provide some other benefit with a monetary value.[12]

Insurance contracts can be classified in different ways. There is an important distinction between indemnity and contingency insurance. Indemnity insurance involves the insurer undertaking to insure against a risk that may never occur, and payment under indemnity insurance seeks to indemnify or compensate the insured for the loss sustained. Examples include property insurance and product liability insurance. In contrast, contingency insurance (often referred to as assurance) involves the payment of a fixed sum on the happening of an event. An example of contingency insurance is a policy of life insurance, under which a fixed sum is payable on the death of the insured. Here, death is certain to happen; the uncertainty relates to the timing.

Another important distinction is between first and third party insurance. Commonly, insurance on one's own life or property will be first party, in that the insured is protecting his own interest in his life or property. In contrast, liability insurance, such as public liability insurance or product liability insurance will be third party, in that the insured is protecting himself from claims by third parties that they have suffered loss for which he is legally responsible. These two types of insurance can be combined in a single contract, as is usual with motor insurance. A "fully comprehensive" motor policy will provide compulsory third party insurance cover and will also provide the insured with first party cover for damage to his vehicle.

The insurance industry is now highly regulated.[13] The main purpose of this regulation is twofold:

(i) to supervise the operation of the insurance industry; and
(ii) to ensure that insurers do not become insolvent, thereby causing substantial losses to policy-holders.

Regulation includes a requirement that a person cannot carry on business in the State as an insurer or an insurance intermediary without a licence from, or the authorisation of the relevant body. Major changes to insurance regulation are due under proposals to establish a single Financial Services

12 For example, a standard term in a comprehensive motor policy is to provide a substitute car while the insured's car is being repaired.

13 See, *e.g.* Insurance Act 1936, the Insurance Act 1989, Investment Intermediaries Act 1995, Investor Compensation Act 1998, and Insurance Act 2000 amongst others. There is a significant body of EC legislation in this area also. See further, Crowley, "Who Regulates the Insurance Industry" [2001] *Commercial Law Practitioner* 241.

Regulator, covering banking, insurance and other financial services.[14] The focus of this Part of the book is not on the public law regulation of the insurance industry, but on the private law aspects of insurance contracts: formation; terms; and issues of liability.[15]

While the insurance industry is highly regulated, the same cannot be said for the insurance contract. Most insurance contracts are standard form contracts produced by the insurer and are commonly "sold" on a "take-it-or-leave-it" basis. The main source of regulation in this area is the European Communities. (Unfair Terms in Consumer Contracts) Regulations 1995[16] and 2000,[17] which seek to implement the European Community Directive on Unfair Terms in Consumer Contracts.[18] Further, the Insurance Act 1989 empowered the Minister to prescribe codes of conduct to be observed by insurers in their dealings with proposers and policyholders renewing policies.[19] However, following discussions with the Irish Insurance Federation (IIF), the representative body for insurers, the Minister declined to exercise his authority to prescribe codes of conduct: instead the IIF introduced its own voluntary codes of conduct and statements of insurance practice.[20] Importantly, these codes have no force of law. Moreover, both the EC (Unfair Terms in Consumer Contracts) Regulations and the IIF codes apply in a non-commercial context only. Lastly, under the Insurance Act 1989,[21] the Minister may make regulations requiring pre-contractual disclosure of certain information by insurers and insurance intermediaries in relation to life assurance and non-life

14 See the Central Bank and Financial Services Authority of Ireland Bill 2002: this Bill lapsed with the dissolution of the 28th Dáil in 2002, but was quickly reintroduced by the 29th Dáil. See further Crowley, "Reform of the Regulation of the Financial Services Industry: An Irish Viewpoint" (2001) 2 *Hibernian Law Journal* 105.

15 See generally, Buckley, *Insurance Law in Ireland* (Dublin, Oak Tree Press, 1997) and Buckley, *Insurance Law in Ireland Vol. Two* (Dublin, Oak Tree Press, 2002); O'Regan Cazabon, *Insurance Law in Ireland* (Dublin, Round Hall Sweet & Maxwell, 1999); Corrigan & Campbell, *A Casebook of Irish Insurance Law* (Dublin, Oak Tree Press, 1995). Leading English texts include *Birds' Modern Insurance Law* (London, Sweet & Maxwell, 5th ed., 2001); *MacGillivray on Insurance Law* (London, Sweet & Maxwell, 9th ed., 1997); Clarke, *Policies and Perceptions of Insurance*, (Oxford, Clarendon Press, 1997); and *Ivamy on General Principles of Insurance Law* (London, Butterworths, 6th ed., 1993).

16 S.I. No. 27 of 1995.

17 S.I. No. 307 of 2000.

18 93/13/EEC [1993] O.J. L95/29; see further 2.3.5.3. See Director of Consumer Affairs Annual Reports from 1996 onwards for work in relation to insurance contracts generally: see www.odca.ie.

19 1989 Act, s.61.

20 For text of Codes, see www.iif.ie.

21 1989 Act, ss.43B, 43D and 43E (inserted by the Insurance Act 2000).

insurance.[22] However, there is no sanction for failure to meet these requirements and any subsequent insurance contract is still enforceable.

27.3 Formation

An insurance contract,[23] like any other contract, is subject to the general rules of contract law.[24] For example, to be properly formed there must be an agreement, supported by consideration and accompanied by an intention to create legal relations. However, specialised rules have developed in relation to insurance contracts, and indeed in relation to particular types of insurance contract. In this regard we will consider, in relation to the formation of insurance contracts, the requirement of an insurable interest, the rules as to form, and the position as regards misrepresentation and the duty to disclose.

27.3.1 Insurable interest

It is a requirement of every insurance contract that the insured has an "insurable interest" in the event insured against. Where there is no such insurable interest, the insurer may be able to avoid liability at common law, or the contract may be void by statute.[25] The requirement of an insurable interest is based on the notion that the insured should have an economic interest or a proximate legal relationship with the subject matter insured. Accordingly, an insured would have an insurable interest in his own life, or in his own property, but not in the property of others. This requirement seeks to prevent "a mischievious kind of gaming"[26] which might follow if an insured could obtain insurance cover for an event in which he had no such interest.

The concept of insurable interest is also closely related to indemnity insurance.[27] Under indemnity insurance, the insured must have suffered a loss to be indemnified, but where the insured has no interest in the event insured against he cannot have suffered a loss to be compensated. In

22 See Life Assurance (Provision of Information) Regulations 2001 (S.I. No 15 of 2001) and the Life Assurance (Provision of Information) (Amendment) Regulations 2002 (S.I. No 161 of 2002).

23 The descriptions "insurance contract" and "insurance policy" are commonly used interchangeably. Strictly, an insurance contract is likely to comprise more than the policy, that is the document called by that name, and to include the proposal form and other documentation.

24 See generally Chapter 2.

25 See the Life Assurance Act 1774; the Life Assurance (Ireland) Act 1886; and the Gaming and Lotteries Act 1956.

26 Life Assurance Act 1774, s.1.

27 See 28.2.

modern times, Irish courts have adopted a liberal interpretation of the requirement of an insurable interest.

27.3.1.1 Life assurance

In relation to life assurance, the position is relatively straightforward, being governed by the Life Assurance Act 1774, which was extended to Ireland by the Life Assurance (Ireland) Act 1886. This legislation requires the insured under a policy of life assurance to have an insurable interest in the life insured.[28] This requirement applies at the time when the policy is effected and not when a claim is made.[29] Where such an interest is lacking, the legislation provides that the policy is void,[30] but it has been held that the effect is to render the policy illegal.[31] It is clear that a person has an insurable interest in his own life (despite the lack of a financial interest) as do most close relatives.[32] Moreover, a creditor may have an insurable interest in the life of his debtor, and an employer may have an insurable interest in the life of his employee and *vice versa*. To ensure compliance with this requirement, the legislation also requires that the name of the person for whose benefit the policy is made shall be inserted in the policy and failure to do so renders the policy illegal.[33] Moreover, the interest, and therefore the sum claimed, is restricted by the value of the interest.[34]

The exact application of this legislation remains unsettled. The 1774 Act is expressly stated not to apply to insurance on "ships, goods, or merchandise",[35] but its application to other types of insurance is unclear. The 1774 Act is entitled:

> "Act for regulating insurances upon Lives, and for prohibiting all such Insurances, except in cases where the persons insuring shall have an Interest in the Life or Death of the Person insured."

This title would suggest that the legislation is concerned with life assurance only. However, the preamble states that "whereas it hath been found by experience that the making of insurances on lives *or other events* where the assured shall have no interest hath introduced a mischievous kind of gaming", and section 2 of the Act provides:

28 1774 Act, s.1.
29 *Dalby v. India and London Life Assurance Co* (1854) 15 C.B. 365.
30 1774 Act, s.1.
31 *Harse v. Pearl Life* [1903] 2 K.B. 92.
32 See, *e.g.* Assurance Companies Act 1909 and the Insurance Act 1936.
33 1774 Act, s.2.
34 *Hebdon v. West* (1863) 3 B. & S. 579; *Fuji Finance Inc v. Aetna Insurance Co Ltd* [1996] 4 All E.R. 608.
35 1774 Act, s.4.

> "It shall not be lawful to make any policy or policies on the life or lives of any person or persons, *or other event or events* without inserting in such policy or policies the person's or persons' name or names interested therein."

These latter two provisions arguably extend the scope of the 1774 Act beyond life assurance. The problem is compounded further in Ireland because the Life Assurance (Ireland) Act 1886, which applies the 1774 Act to Ireland, appears to limit expressly the application of the 1774 in Ireland. The 1886 Act is entitled an "Act to amend the Law relating to Life Assurances in Ireland" and having recited the title of the 1774 Act, the 1886 Act provides in section 2 that: "This Act … shall apply to all Policies of Insurance upon lives entered into upon and after [the commencement date]."

Judicial reaction and academic opinion[36] on the application of the 1774 Act has been varied. For example, in *Re King, Robinson v. Gray*, Lord Denning M.R. stated:[37]

> "When a policy of fire insurance of a building … is taken out, the names of all the persons interested therein … must be inserted in the policy. No person can recover thereon unless he is named therein and then only to the extent of his interest. This is clear from the Life Assurance Act 1774, s.2, s.3, and s.4, which by their very terms apply to policies on "any other event" as well as life."

Similarly, in *M.I.B.I. v. P.M.P.A.*,[38] the Supreme Court proceeded on the basis that the 1774 Act had a wide application. In that case, the court found that the insurance of a motor vehicle was insurance of "goods" within the meaning of section 4 of the 1774 Act which removes such insurances from the scope of the Act. The court found that because the policy was one of indemnity insurance, there was still a requirement to have an insurable interest. However, in *Church & General v. Connolly and McLoughlin*,[39] the High Court held, following a detailed examination, that the 1774 Act did not apply to fire insurance and indeed that its application was limited to life policies.

English courts have also struggled with this matter. In *Mark Rowlands Ltd v. Berni Inns Ltd*,[40] the plaintiff was the freeholder of premises and the

---

36 See, *e.g. MacGillivray on Insurance Law*, 8th ed., para. 153 which supported the application of the 1774 Act to real property insurance, while the current edition of *MacGillivray on Insurance Law* (London, Sweet & Maxwell, 9th ed., 1997) takes an opposing view at para 1–155.

37 [1963] 1 All E.R. 781 at 790; [1963] Ch. 459 at 485.

38 [1981] I.R. 142 (S.C.).

39 Unreported, High Court, May 7, 1981; see also *Brady and ors v. The Irish Land Commission* [1921] 1 I.R. 56.

40 [1985] 3 All E.R. 473 (C.A.).

defendant was the tenant of the basement. The question was whether fire insurance taken out by the plaintiff enured for the benefit of the defendant, although his name did not appear on the policy. The Court of Appeal held that the policy did not infringe section 2 of the 1774 Act, because the Act was not intended to apply to indemnity insurance. More recently, the Privy Council in *Sui Yin Kwan v. Eastern Insurance*[41] followed the ruling of the Court of Appeal in *Mark Rowlands Ltd v. Berni Inns Ltd.* The Privy Council noted that in *Re King* the point was not argued; Lord Denning's comments were *obiter* and were not reflected in the judgments of the other two members of the court. In finding that the Life Assurance Act 1774 is limited in its application to life policies, their Lordships stated that they were giving the legislation a meaning which corresponded with the obvious legislative intent. These later Court of Appeal and Privy Council decisions suggest that the proper construction of the 1774 Act is that it is limited in its application to life assurance policies. These findings, coupled with the provisions of the 1886 Act, suggest that the High Court was correct in its findings in *Church & General v. Connolly and McLoughlin.* But, the matter awaits a definitive resolution.

27.3.1.2 Marine insurance

Marine insurance is governed by the Marine Insurance Act 1906, the last of the major commercial codifying statutes of the late nineteenth and early twentieth centuries. Like the Sale of Goods Act 1893, the Act was intended largely to restate the pre-existing common law position. Consequently, many of its provisions are reflected in the general law or applied by analogy to non-marine insurance cases. Marine insurance is commonly effected at Lloyd's of London, an organisation which dominates in this area of business.

In marine insurance, "every person has an insurable interest who is interested in a marine adventure,"[42] including where he stands in any legal or equitable relation to the adventure "or to any insurable property at risk therein."[43] The insured must have acquired an interest by the time of the loss, provided that at the time the policy was effected, he had an expectation of acquiring an interest.[44] There is a marine adventure where:

(a) any ship goods or other moveables are exposed to maritime perils;
(b) the earning or acquisition of any freight, passage money, commission, profit or other pecuniary benefit, or the security of any advances, loan, or other disbursements, is endangered by the exposure of insurable property to maritime perils;

41 [1994] 1 All E.R. 213 (P.C.).
42 1906 Act, s.4.
43 1906 Act, s.5.
44 1906 Act, s.4(2).

(c) any liability to a third party may be incurred by the owner of or other person interested in or responsible for insurable property, by reason of maritime perils.[45]

"Maritime perils" is defined widely to include:

> "perils consequent on or incidental to the navigation of the sea, that is to say, perils of the sea, fire, war perils, pirates, rovers, thieves, captures, seizures, restraints, and detainments of princes and peoples, jettisons, barratry and any other perils, either of the like kind or which may be designated by the policy."[46]

27.3.1.3 Other insurance

With regard to other forms of insurance, the Gaming and Lotteries Act 1956 requires a sufficient interest at the time the contract is made to prevent the contract being one of wager,[47] and the common law requires an insurable interest at the time of the loss (the essence of indemnity).[48] The requirements of the Gaming and Lotteries Act 1956 are less stringent than those of the common law. Accordingly, a contract will be a contract of insurance and not a wager provided the insured has an interest in, or an expectation of acquiring an interest in the subject matter of the contract.

The classic definition of an insurable interest in relation to property insurance was given by Lord Eldon in *Lucena v. Crauford*,[49] where it was defined as:

> "a right in the property, or a right derivable out of some contract about the property, which in either case may be lost upon some contingency affecting the possession or enjoyment of the party."

This is a narrow definition of insurable interest. The House of Lords, in accepting this definition, rejected a broader definition which would recognise a person as having an insurable interest in an event where he has a factual expectation of loss on the happening of that event.[50] The narrow test was strictly applied in *Macaura v. Northern Assurance Co Ltd*.[51] The appellant, M, was a major shareholder and a major creditor of a company

---

45 1906 Act, s.3(1).

46 1906 Act, s.3(2).

47 1956 Act, s.36.

48 It appears that the common law requirement of an insurable interest may be waived by clear words in the policy: *Prudential Staff Union v. Hall* [1947] K.B. 685.

49 (1806) 2 Bos. & Pul. 269 at 321, (H.L.).

50 This broader test was expressed by Lawrence J. in *Lucena v. Crauford* (1806) 2 Bos & PNR 269 at 302 and adopted by the Canadian Supreme Court in *Constitution Insurance Co of Canada v. Kosmopoulos* (1987) 34 D.L.R. (4th) 208.

51 (1925) 59 I.L.T.R. 45; [1925] A.C. 619 (H.L.).

which owned a quantity of timber. The timber was stored on M's property, and M took out insurance over the timber in his own name. When the timber was destroyed by fire, M sought to claim on the insurance. Clearly, the fire caused M loss in a certain sense, but the court held that he did not have an insurable interest. M did not own the timber or have a contractual right to it.

It is clear that any person who owns property – legally or beneficially, solely or jointly – has an insurable interest in it. Moreover, any person who is exposed to legal liability in relation to the property, such as a bailee of goods or other person at risk of loss, has an insurable interest.[52] As stated earlier, Irish courts have been less strict in their requirement of an insurable interest. For instance, in *Carrigan Ltd & Carrigan v. Norwich Union*,[53] a house and its contents were insured against fire. The house was owned by the first plaintiff company but insured by the second plaintiff (as in *Macaura*). The second plaintiff was noted as the proposer of the insurance policy. Having examined the detailed arrangement of the company and the insurance policy, the court recognised that the second plaintiff had a "substantial beneficial ownership" in the company and so an insurable interest in the property.

27.3.1.4 Insurance of third party interests

Where a policy of insurance is effected by a person with a limited interest in, or with no interest in the subject matter insured, the question arises as to whether a third party with an interest in the subject matter can benefit under the policy. Such a third party is caught by the privity of contract rule which provides that only the parties to the contract can enforce it against each other. There are, however, exceptions to this rule, in particular under the law of agency.[54]

In relation to insurance on goods, it is clear that an insured who has an interest in the goods can recover to the extent of his interest. So, for example, a bailee of goods, such as a warehouseman or a carrier, can insure goods owned by another against any damage caused to the goods for which he may be liable. Since a bailee's liability is based on negligence, any damage accidentally caused will not be recoverable by the bailee. The question then arises whether the owner of the goods can recover under the policy. The answer depends on whether, on the proper construction of the policy, it extends to cover the owner's interest. In *Northern British and Mercantile Insurance Co v. Moffat*,[55] for example, it was held that a

52 *Inglis v. Stock* (1885) 10 App. Cas. 263.

53 Unreported, High Court, Lynch J., December 11, 1987; see also *James and Others v. The Royal Insurance Co.* (1875) 9 I.L.T.R. 194.

54 Other exceptions relate to the use of trusts; and statutory exceptions, such as under the Road Traffic Act 1961.

55 (1871) L.R. 7 C.P. 25.

warehouse company's policy on goods in their possession which covered "goods in trust or on commission for which they are responsible" only covered the bailee's interest in the goods. In contrast, in *Waters and Steel v. Monarch Fire and Life Assurance Co*,[56] a policy held by a bailee covering goods "in trust or on commission" was held to cover the owner's interest in the goods. In *Church and General Insurance Co & Patrick Connolly and ors*,[57] Costello J. stated: "The law permits a person with a limited interest in a property to insure not only his interest but the interest which others may have in the same property …"[58] In this case, the High Court found that the defendants, as tenants at will, held an insurable interest in the property destroyed and that they were entitled to be indemnified under an insurance contract effected by them. Moreover, it was held that they were entitled to be indemnified not only in respect of the loss they sustained to their limited interest, as tenants at will, but also in respect of the loss to the owners of the property, despite the fact that the owner's interest was not noted on the policy, because, in effecting the insurance, it was the insured's intention to cover the interests of the owner.

If the policy is construed to cover the interest of the third party as well as of the insured, a second question arises: can the third party enforce the contract himself or can he require the named insured to enforce the policy for his benefit? If the insured does claim, he will hold any proceeds for the third party either on trust or subject to a duty to account. It is well established that a third party can enforce a contract of insurance made in his name and with his prior authority under agency law principles: this is a case of disclosed, authorised agency.[59] The third party may not be named in the policy, but it seems that provided he can show that he authorised the named insured to obtain insurance on his behalf, the third party may be able to enforce the insurance as an undisclosed principal.[60] Problems can arise, however, because insurance contracts are contracts of *utmost good faith* and an insured is obliged to disclose all material facts;[61] in many cases the identity of the insured party will be a material fact. Even if the third party did not authorise the insurance in the first place, he may, again under agency principles, be able to take the benefit of the insurance by ratifying the contract.[62] This would require that the named insured (the agent) purported to act on behalf of the third party (the principal); and that the

56 (1856) 5 E.& B. 870.

57 Unreported, High Court, Costello J., May 7, 1981.

58 *Ibid.* at p.11.

59 See 6.2.

60 In *Sui Yin Kwan v. Eastern Insurance* [1994] 1 All E.R. 213 (P.C.), it was held that a contract of insurance was not so personal as to prevent an undisclosed principal from enforcing it. An undisclosed principal would be entitled to the benefit of the contract unless expressly excluded by the terms of the contract: see 6.3.2.3.

61 See 27.3.3.1.

62 See 5.5.

third party, if not named in the policy, is identifiable as a member of a class of persons protected by and referred to in the policy.[63] Even where these requirements are satisfied, a third party will generally only seek to ratify when he wants to claim on a policy. But it was held in *Grover & Grover v. Matthews*[64] that an insurance contract, other than one for marine insurance, cannot be ratified after the loss insured against has occurred. More recently, however, in *National Oilwell (UK) Ltd v. Davy Offshore Ltd*,[65] it was stated *obiter* that there is no general rule prohibiting ratification after loss.

27.3.1.5 Assignment

Where a person disposes of insured property, any insurance contract lapses for lack of insurable interest. However, in theory, the insurance policy may be assigned at the same time as the property, thereby ensuring no lapse of an insurable interest, provided the necessary formalities are complied with. This is subject to the general rule that contractual rights and obligations of a personal nature are not assignable. Otherwise, for example, under the Supreme Court of Judicature (Ireland) Act 1877, contractual rights under an insurance contract can be assigned provided the assignment is absolute, in writing, and written notice is given to the insurer.[66] However, compliance with these requirements may be impractical in a commercial context, and commonly the new owner of property effects a new insurance contract in relation to the property, rather than taking an assignment of an existing policy.

In contrast, life assurance and marine insurance contracts are frequently assigned. Life assurance policies are assignable in a number of ways,[67] including under the Policies of Assurance Act 1867. The assignment must be made in writing and can be made by an indorsement on the policy or under a separate instrument.[68] The Act further requires that written notice of the date and purport of such assignment be given to the insurer.[69] Similarly, the Marine Insurance Act 1906 expressly provides that a marine insurance contract is assignable, by indorsement or other customary manner, unless it contains terms expressly prohibiting assignment.[70] The Act allows assignment after loss has occurred,[71] so that a *cif* seller can

63 See 5.5.1.
64 [1910] 2 K.B. 401.
65 [1993] 2 Lloyd's Rep. 582.
66 1877 Act, s.28(6).
67 Trainor, "Assignability of Life Policies as Security for Bankers' Advances" [1994] *Commercial Law Practitioner* 127.
68 1867 Act, s.5.
69 1867 Act, s.3.
70 1906 Act, s.50.
71 *Ibid.*

tender shipping documents, including the insurance policy, after the goods have been lost, thereby allowing the buyer to claim on the insurance contract.[72]

27.3.2 Formation and form

As noted above, insurance contracts are subject to the general law of contract and hence there must be an agreement, supported by consideration, and an intention to create legal relations. Otherwise, there are no other formal requirements and, provided the above requirements are satisfied, an insurance contract may be concluded orally.[73] In practice however, standard formation procedures tend to be followed. An applicant for insurance fills in a "proposal form" provided by the insurer, containing details relevant to the risk to be insured against. This form usually constitutes an offer by the applicant which the insurer can accept or refuse. This offer is usually subject to the insurer's standard terms which are expressly incorporated by reference. An insurer can accept the applicant's offer unconditionally, or subject to conditions, such as "no insurance is effective until the premium is paid." This would probably constitute a counter-offer which the applicant could accept, by paying the premium, or refuse.

Marine insurance is the exception to the above general rule that there are no formal requirements in effecting an insurance contract. The Marine Insurance Act 1906 provides that a contract of marine insurance is inadmissible in evidence unless embodied in a marine policy.[74] Moreover, the policy must specify the name of the insured or his agent,[75] and must be signed by the insured or his agent.[76] The policy may take the form in the First Schedule to the 1906 Act,[77] but since 1982, Lloyd's of London and the marine insurance companies have used new forms of policies. The practice of effecting insurance at Lloyd's is also different from the norm. An applicant for insurance or a proposer does not deal directly with Lloyd's but through a Lloyd's broker. It is the broker's job to present a "slip" containing the details of the insurance required to Lloyd's underwriters (who act on behalf of syndicates) seeking their initials in order to underwrite a percentage, or all, of the risk. In *General Reinsurance v. Fannia Patria*,[78] it was held that, on initialling, each underwriter was bound to the insurance contract for that amount, thereby overruling

72 On cif contracts, see 30.3.

73 Insurance contracts must be stamped, generally by the insurer (Stamp Duties Consolidation Act 1999, s.2), but failure to stamp does not invalidate the contract.

74 1906 Act, s.22.

75 1906 Act, s.23.

76 1906 Act, s.24.

77 1906 Act, s.30.

78 [1983] 1 Lloyds Rep. 287.

previous case law which suggested that an underwriter could withdraw up until the final initialling. Once full cover is obtained in this way, the policy is prepared by the broker and submitted to the Lloyd's Policy Signing Office for checking and signing.

Most indemnity insurance is fixed term, commonly one year. When insurance contracts are renewed, a new contract is concluded, again on the insurer's standard terms. Generally, there is no requirement to complete another proposal form, and the offer to renew is made by the insurer. When an insurance contract has expired, it appears that there is no new insurance in place until the insured accepts the insurer's offer. In practice, insurers allow a number of "days of grace" after expiry of the old insurance, whereby if the premium is paid within this period the policy is renewed and continuous cover is provided. In contrast, life assurance is probably an entire contract without the need for renewal. But life assurance policies usually provide that insurance cover will lapse if the premium is not paid. Again, it is usual for insurers to operate a period of grace for late payment of the premium.

Insurers are not obliged to accept proposals for insurance or to renew policies that have expired. Indeed, an insurer may cancel an insurance policy where the contract provides for such a right. In *Carna Foods Ltd v. Eagle Star Insurance Co (Ireland) Ltd*,[79] the Supreme Court held that in exercising these rights, insurers were under no implied contractual obligation to give reasons for their decisions to the insured.

27.3.3 Misrepresentation and non-disclosure

As noted above, in the first instance, it is the insurer's decision to accept or refuse the applicant's offer, made in the proposal form. This decision to accept or refuse insurance is based largely on the answers and statements provided by the applicant in the proposal form. Hence, these statements are very important. Commonly, the proposal form will contain a term which provides that these statements form the basis of the contract (a "basis of the contract" clause)[80] thereby converting such statements into important terms of the contract, known as warranties.[81] Where such statements take effect as warranties, any false statement will be a serious breach of contract allowing the insurer to repudiate the contract.

Even where a statement does not take effect as a term of the contract, any false statement may amount to a misrepresentation. Similar to other contracts, where one party to an insurance contract makes an untrue

79 [1997] 2 I.L.R.M. 499 (S.C.); [1995] 1 I.R. 526 (H.C.).

80 On the fairness and hence enforceability of such clauses in consumer contracts, see further 27.4.4.1.

81 See further 27.4. This classification is at odds with the general law of contract where important contractual terms are referred to as "conditions": see 2.3.3, and as regards sale of goods contracts, see 10.4.

material statement, a misrepresentation, before the contract is concluded, and this induces the other party to enter the contract, then the contract can be avoided.[82] So, for example, where an applicant for insurance makes a false statement in the proposal form, the insurer can avoid any subsequent liability. In relation to marine insurance, this position has been put on a statutory basis,[83] reflecting the common law. Accordingly, a representation is material if it would influence the judgment of a prudent insurer in fixing the premium or determining whether he will take the risk or not.[84] And, a statement may be a matter of fact, expectation or belief.[85] A statement as to expectation or belief is true if it is made in good faith, that is, honestly.[86]

In the majority of cases, an insurer's right to rescind the contract for misrepresentation is of little significance because, in one important regard, insurance contracts are different from most other contracts when it comes to pre-formation statements. Unlike the majority of contract types, insurance contracts are contracts of *utmost good faith* (*uberrimae fides*) and the parties owe each other a duty of utmost good faith.[87] While the law recognises that this duty of good faith is mutual,[88] most legal actions involve the insured's duty of good faith to the insurer. For example, the duty of good faith comprises a duty not to make fraudulent claims,[89] and, perhaps more importantly, it comprises a duty of disclosure on the parties. In particular, the insured is under a strict legal duty to actively disclose certain matters to the insurer (usually on the proposal form). Where the insured fails in this duty, the insurer can avoid the contract and liability is repudiated. The rationale for this aspect of the duty of disclosure is that in order to assess the risk, the insurer must be informed of all material facts, and it is the insured who has the best knowledge of these facts.[90]

27.3.3.1 Insured's duty of disclosure

The insured's duty of disclosure has been strictly applied. The duty extends beyond answering the specific questions in the proposal form. For instance, following a list of detailed questions, the proposal form usually

82 See 2.2.5.2(ii).

83 Marine Insurance Act 1906, s.20.

84 1906 Act, s.20(2).

85 1906 Act, s.20(3).

86 1906 Act, s.20(5); *Economides v. Commercial Union Assurance plc* [1997] 3 All E.R. 636 (C.A.).

87 See O'Rourke, "A Look at Utmost Good Faith" [1998] *Commercial Law Practitioner* 140. Other contracts which have been recognised as contracts of good faith include partnership agreements and family arrangements.

88 *Carter v. Boehm* (1766) 3 Burr. 1905 at 1909; *Fagan v. General Accident Fire & Life Assurance Corporation plc* unreported, High Court, Murphy J., February 19, 1993; upheld by the Supreme Court, unreported, Supreme Court, October 14, 1998.

89 See 28.1.1.

90 See *Abbott v. Howard* (1832) Hayes 381.

asks whether there is any other information relevant to the proposed insurance. Failure to answer this question fully may enable the insurer to avoid the insurance contract. In essence, the insured is required to disclose all material facts known to him.

Under the Marine Insurance Act 1906, the insured must disclose facts which are known to him, and the insured is deemed to know every fact which, in the ordinary course of business, ought to be known to him – constructive knowledge.[91] It has been held by the Court of Appeal that this rule applies to non-marine insurance.[92] However, this rule cannot apply to private individuals because a private individual, acting in a non-business capacity, cannot be deemed to know anything "in the ordinary course of business". Therefore, in relation to private individuals, an insured is probably only required to disclose all material facts *actually* known to him, provided he does not deliberately shut his eyes to obvious facts. In *Keating v. New Ireland Assurance*,[93] the Supreme Court made it clear that the burden was on the insurer to prove that the material facts alleged were known by the insured at the time of the alleged failure to disclose. In this case, the plaintiff and her husband entered into a life assurance contract with the defendant insurer. The plaintiff's husband disclosed that months previously he had undergone a medical examination and treatment for what he believed to be an epigastric discomfort – in fact, the examination revealed a condition of angina but there was no evidence that the doctors told the husband of this condition. The plaintiff's husband died subsequently, and the plaintiff sought to claim on the policy. The insurer sought to avoid the policy for non-disclosure of the angina. The Supreme Court held that the state of knowledge of the husband was a matter of fact, and the onus was on the insurer to prove that the deceased was aware of the angina: it was not sufficient to show that he ought to have been aware.

27.3.3.2 What is material?

The insured is required to disclose all *material* facts known to him. In assessing what is material, it is irrelevant that the insured did not think the information material, nor is it an excuse that the insured acted with *good faith*. The standard for assessing materiality is that of a prudent insurer. The common law duty of disclosure was codified in section 18(2) of the Marine Insurance Act 1906 which provides that: "Every circumstance is material which would influence the judgment of a *prudent insurer* in fixing the premium or determining whether he will take the risk."[94]

This test was adopted by Kenny J. in the Supreme Court in *Chariot Inns*

91 1906 Act, s.18(1).
92 *PCW Syndicates v. PCW Reinsurers* [1996] 1 All E.R. 774.
93 [1990] 2 I.R. 383.
94 See also *Joel v. Law Union & Crown Insurance Co* [1908] 2 K.B. 863.

Ltd v. Assicurazioni Generali SpA.[95] The plaintiff company, whose principal shareholder was a Mr Wootton, made a claim under an insurance policy following a fire at the plaintiff's premises in Ranelagh. The defendant insurers sought to avoid liability because the plaintiff had failed to disclose the fact that the plaintiff had been paid £8,000 by another insurer in relation to property damage at another premises on Leeson Street. The plaintiff had stored furniture there which had been damaged. The Leeson Street premises was owned and insured by Consolidated Investments Ltd, also controlled by Mr Wootton. The proposal form for the insurance on the Ranelagh premises asked for details of claims experience over the last five years. The plaintiff answered "none": this was technically correct as the claim had been made by Consolidated Investments Ltd and not the plaintiff. The Supreme Court held that the mere fact that Mr Wootton was a director of Consolidated Investments Ltd and the plaintiff company would not of itself make a fire at the property of Consolidated Investments Ltd a material fact. However, it was material that goods belonging to the plaintiff company were damaged by a fire at Consolidated Investment Ltd, and so the insurance could be avoided by the insurers. While the plaintiff was literally correct in response to the question regarding claims over the last five years, the fact that the plaintiff ultimately got money following the fire at Leeson Street was a matter which would reasonably affect the judgment of a prudent insurer in deciding whether to take the risk or how to fix the premium.

There are signs that the courts have recognised the potential harshness of the strict application of this rule and are willing to limit its application in defined circumstances. For instance, the burden is on the insurer to prove what a prudent insurer would require and while expert witnesses are usually called to assist, ultimately the court sets the standard. In *Aro Road v. Insurance Corporation*,[96] Carroll J. in the High Court was of the opinion that the fact that a Mr Mansfield, the managing director and main shareholder of the plaintiff insured company, was in 1962 convicted on 10 counts of receiving stolen goods and sentenced to 21 months' imprisonment, was not material. However, she deferred to expert opinion and found that the insurers could repudiate the contract for non-disclosure of these facts. On appeal to the Supreme Court, Carroll J.'s deference to expert opinion was criticised and her ruling overturned. The case involved the transportation of goods by the plaintiff insured company, using CIE as the carrier. The carriage and insurance arrangements were made over the telephone, with CIE acting as agents for the defendant insurers. In

95 [1981] I.R. 199; see further Kilcommins & Lind, "Making sense of the cases on 'materiality' and 'the duty of disclosure' in Irish insurance law" [1998] *International Journal of Insurance Law* 263.

96 [1986] I.R. 403; see further Kelleher, "Expert Evidence in Ireland" (1996) 14 *Irish Law Times* 42.

arranging the insurance, CIE were described as acting in "an informal and perfunctory manner".[97] CIE did not require the completion of a proposal form by the insured, and the only enquiries made were as to the name and address of the consignee of the goods and the nature and value of the goods. The insurance cover was then described over the telephone. Subsequently, two insurance certificates were issued by CIE, as agents for the insurer, and the premium was collected. When some of the goods were damaged, the insured claimed on the policy and the insurers sought to repudiate the contract for non-disclosure. In finding for the plaintiff, the Supreme Court first emphasised that assessing the standard of a prudent insurer is a matter for the court. Second, while recognising the general principle of utmost good faith and the insured's duty of disclosure, the Supreme Court also noted that exceptions to this principle exist. For example, a contract might expressly or by implication exclude the requirement of full disclosure, as in the case of "over-the-counter insurance", such as flight insurance sold just before boarding, where full disclosure is made impossible or impractical. The court found that the facts of this case also fitted into the category where the manner in which the insurance was effected showed a failure or unwillingness to give the insured company the opportunity to make full disclosure before the insurance was effected.[98] Hence, liability could not be avoided. The Supreme Court also noted that petty convictions from 20 years earlier need not be recounted because they were not material.

Again in the Supreme Court, in *Kelleher v. Irish Life Assurance*,[99] the insurers were held to have waived their right to full disclosure due to the nature and circumstances of insurance effected in 1985. In this case, life assurance was marketed as a "special promotional offer". A whole series of questions on the application form concerning the health, activities and history of the life to be insured were crossed out, thereby indicating that no answers from the applicants for life assurance were required. A declaration of health was made on the application form by the insured, which concerned the insured's work record and any medical treatment in the previous six months. The insurers unsuccessfully sought to repudiate liability on the basis of, *inter alia*, non-disclosure of a material fact that the insured had undergone treatment for cancer in 1981.

Materiality has been interpreted, more recently, by the House of Lords in *Pan Atlantic Insurance v. Pine Top*.[100] There the House of Lords held, by a bare majority, that a fact is material where it would affect the mind of the

---

97 *Ibid.* at 410.

98 See also *Kreglinger and Fernau v. Irish National Insurance* [1956] I.R. 116 (H.C.) where it was recognised that while the burden to disclose is on the insured, this does not relieve the insurer from making proper enquiries.

99 [1993] 3 I.R. 393.

100 [1995] 1 A.C. 501, [1994] 3 All E.R. 581, confirming earlier authority in *CTI v. Oceanus Mutual Underwriting Association* [1984] 1 Lloyd's Rep. 476 (C.A.).

prudent insurer in accepting the risk even where it would not alter his actual decision. This decision has been criticised as being too favourably disposed to the position of insurers,[101] and it remains unclear whether it would be followed in Ireland. The House of Lords did qualify the above test by holding that an insurer could only avoid a policy on the grounds of non-disclosure of a material fact if the non-disclosure did *actually* induce him to enter the contract. This establishes a two-stage test: the second stage being subjective. Provided that the fact in question would have "influenced" the decision of a prudent insurer, it is irrelevant that it would have made no difference to the actual decision of the insurer, if it did in fact induce entry into the actual contract. Moreover, it seems that the second stage requires only that the non-disclosure should have been an inducement for the insurer, not necessarily the decisive inducement. And, in an appropriate case, once it is shown that the fact not disclosed was material, the insurer may be able to rely on a presumption of inducement without adducing evidence of the effect of the non-disclosure on him.[102]

The duty of disclosure continues up to the time of formation of the contract, so that if the material facts change between completion of the proposal form and acceptance by the insurer, the insured must disclose the facts.[103] However, there is no duty of disclosure during the currency of the insurance contract, unless there is an express contractual provision requiring such disclosure.[104] Because renewal of insurance involves a new contract, a new duty of disclosure arises, even though there is usually no proposal form.[105]

---

101 See generally Clarke, "Failure to Disclose and Failure to Legislate: Is it Material I & II" [1988] *Journal of Business Law* 206 & 298; see more specifically Clarke, "Insurance Contracts and Non-disclosure" [1993] *Lloyd's Maritime and Commercial Law Quarterly* 297; Insurers – Influenced but not yet Induced [1994] *Lloyd's Maritime and Commercial Law Quarterly* 473; Hird, "Rationality in the House of Lords" [1995] *Journal of Business Law* 194; Bird & Hird, "Misrepresentation and Non-disclosure in Insurance Law - Identical Twins or Separate Issues" [1996] *Modern Law Review* 285.

102 *St Paul Fire & Marine (UK) Ltd v. McConnell Dowell Constructors Ltd* [1996] 1 All E.R. 96 (C.A.), see further Hird, Pan Atlantic – Yet more to Disclose [1995] *Journal of Business Law* 608; and Hamilton, "The Duty of Disclosure in Insurance Law" [1996] *Juridical Review*, 212; Kilcommins, "The Duty of Disclosure Revisited" [1997] *Juridical Review* 125; Hamilton, "The Duty of Disclosure Revisited: A Reply" [1997] *Juridical Review* 132.

103 *Canning v. Farquhar* (1886) 16 Q.B.D. 727; *Locker & Woolf Ltd v. Western Australia Insurance Co Ltd* [1936] 1 K.B. 408 (C.A.).

104 *Pim v. Reid* (1843) 6 M. & G. 1; see further O'Regan Cazabon, "Insurance Contracts – The Duty to Disclose: is it of a continuing nature?" [1999] *Irish Insurance Law Review* 68. A term requiring further disclosure in the standard policy might provide: "It is a condition precedent to our obligation to make payment under this Policy that any facts known to the insured, and any changes affecting the risk since inception of the Policy or last renewal date (whichever is the later) must be disclosed to the insurer. Failure to disclose such facts or changes may mean that the Policy will not provide you with the cover you require, or may invalidate the Policy altogether."

105 *Latham v. Hibernian Insurance Co Ltd* unreported, High Court, Blayney J., March 22, 1991; *Pan Atlantic Insurance Co v. Pine Top Insurance Co* [1995] 1 A.C. 501.

The Irish Insurance Federation has issued a number of voluntary codes of practice, including one on non-life and another on life insurance. Both codes seeks to soften the strict legal effects of the duty of disclosure. In relation to the duty of disclosure, the code on non-life insurance, for example, provides:

> "1. Proposal Forms
>
> (a) If the proposal form calls for the disclosure of materials facts a statement should be included …
>   (i) drawing attention to the consequences of failure to disclose all material facts and explaining that these are facts that an insurer would regard as likely to influence the assessment and acceptance of a proposal;
>   (ii) warning that if the signatory is in any doubt about whether certain facts are material, these facts should be disclosed …
>
> (c) Those matters which insurers have commonly found to be material should, as far as practicable, be the subject of clear questions in the proposal form.
>
> (d) Insurers should avoid asking questions which would require knowledge beyond that which the signatory could reasonably be expected to possess."
>
> "3. Claims
>
> (a) An insurer shall not repudiate liability to indemnify a policyholder:
>   (i) on grounds of non-disclosure of a material fact which a policyholder could not reasonably be expected to have disclosed …
>
> 4. Renewals
>
> Renewal notice shall contain a warning about the duty of disclosure including the necessity to advise changes affecting the policy which have occurred since the policy inception or last renewal date, whichever was the later."

As noted above, these codes have no legal effect and apply only to proposers and insured persons in their private capacity.[106] In relation to

106 See also the Office of Insurance Ombudsman Annual Reports from 1993 onwards: see further www.ombudsman-insurance.ie. Many of the complaints referred to the Ombudsman relate to the insured's duty of disclosure. The Ombudsman's decision whilst binding on insurers who participate in the scheme is not binding on the complainant who has further recourse to the courts.

business policies, the full rigours of the common law duty of disclosure continue to apply.

27.4 The Terms of the Contract

The insurance contract comprises terms derived mainly from the proposal form and the policy document. The effect of breach of any of these terms will depend on their classification. It would appear that there are four classifications of terms in insurance law: warranties; conditions; terms descriptive of the risk; and innominate terms.

27.4.1 Warranties

In contrast to the general law, "warranties" are important terms of an insurance contract, breach of which allows the innocent party to terminate the contract (and hence equivalent to a condition in the general law of contract)[107] whereas "conditions" are less important terms, breach of which gives rise to a claim for damages only (and hence equivalent to a warranty in the general law of contract).[108] However, in *The Good Luck*,[109] the House of Lords held, in relation to a marine insurance contract,[110] that breach of a warranty automatically discharged the insurer from liability without the insurer having to take any positive action to terminate the contract because fulfillment of the warranty was a condition precedent to liability. It appears that this ruling is not limited in application to marine insurance contracts, and it represents a significant change in what was understood to be the conventional legal position.[111] Whether the case will be followed in Ireland remains to be seen. A party can always waive a breach of a warranty, as where, for example, an insurer accepts a premium or renews a policy after becoming aware of the insured's breach of warranty.

The contract may identify various terms as warranties, but, while courts seek to give effect to the intentions of the parties, they are not bound by such classifications. Where a term is identified as a "warranty", a court might nevertheless find that the parties did not intend that the breach of the term would entitle the innocent party to terminate the contract.

107 See 2.3.3.

108 See 2.3.3.

109 [1992] 1 A.C. 233; [1991] 3 All E.R. 1: see further Birds, "Insurance Contracts" in Birds, Bradgate & Villiers eds., *Termination of Contracts* (Chicester, Wiley Chancery, 1995).

110 See 1906 Act, s.33(3) on warranties in marine insurance.

111 See Kerr L.J.'s speech in *State Trading Corporation of India Ltd v. Golodetz* [1989] 2 Lloyd's Rep. 277 at 287; *The Good Luck* [1992] 1 A.C. 233 at 262–3; [1991] 3 All E.R. 1 at 16 per Lord Goff; and *Hussain v. Brown* [1996] 1 Lloyd's Rep. 627.

The exact effect of a breach of warranty depends on whether the warranty is classified as a warranty as to past or existing fact, or a continuing promissory warranty relating to the future. A statement in a proposal form may be construed as a warranty of existing fact at the time the contract is made. If the statement is false at that time, there is a breach of warranty at that time and the insurer is discharged from liability: in effect, the risk under the policy never attaches. Unless the breach is waived, the insurer must refund any premiums paid, but provided the statement as to existing fact is true at the time it was made, there is no breach if circumstances subsequently change. However, in practice, insurance contracts frequently impose a duty on the insured to notify the insurer of any change in circumstances.

In contrast, where the warranty is classified as a continuing promissory warranty, the insured is treated as promising that the circumstances described will continue to exist, so that any change in circumstances will constitute a breach of contract, allowing the insurer to terminate the contract from the date of the breach. For example, in *The Good Luck*,[112] a contract of marine insurance on a ship included a warranty that the ship would not go into certain prohibited high-risk areas in a war zone.[113] It was found that the warranty was breached and the insurer was discharged from liability when the ship entered the prohibited area. For a warranty to be continuing or to relate to the future, it must be expressed in very clear language. For instance, it has been held that a warranty that the insured's plant and machinery "are properly fenced and guarded" was not a continuing warranty;[114] and where a proposal form asked "Are the premises fitted with any kind of intruder alarm?" and the proposer answered "Yes" and provided details, the court held that this amounted to a warranty of existing fact only.[115] In contrast, where insurance was sought in relation to the demolition of a mill and the proposal form asked: "Are any explosives used in your business?" and the proposer answered "No", it was held that this was a continuing warranty relating to the future.[116]

27.4.1.1 Basis of the contract clauses[117]

It is the practice of insurance companies to incorporate answers to questions in the proposal form into the insurance contract, along with

---

112 [1991] 3 All E.R. 1.

113 The prohibited area was the Persian Gulf during the Iran-Iraq conflict.

114 *Woolfall & Rimmer v. Moyle* [1942] 1 K.B. 66, [1941] 3 All E.R. 304 (C.A.); followed in Ireland in *Re Sweeney & Kennedy's Arbitration* [1950] I.R. 85.

115 *Hussain v. Brown* [1996] 1 Lloyd's Rep. 627 (C.A.).

116 *Beauchamp v. National Mutual Indemnity Insurance Co Ltd* [1937] 3 All E.R. 19.

117 See further Hasson, "The basis of the contract clause in insurance law" (1971) 34 *Modern Law Review* 29.

other terms of the policy, and furthermore to require that the insured warrant or promise the veracity of the answers. This is effected by a "basis of the contract clause" whereby the answers are said to form the basis of the contract and are converted into warranties or conditions precedent to liability,[118] regardless of their materiality to the risk. For example:

> "It is a condition precedent to our obligation to make any payment under this Policy that the answers in any proposal and declaration for this insurance are true and complete to the best of your knowledge and belief, and any such proposal and declaration shall be the basis of this contract and are deemed to be incorporated therein."

Therefore, where an answer turns out to be false, the contract can be terminated and/or liability denied. The way in which this practice operates in favour of insurers is well illustrated in *Keenan v. Shield Insurance Co Ltd*,[119] where a private residence and contents were insured. The contract had a "basis of the contract clause" in it, and the insurers sought to repudiate liability on the basis that the answer to Question 8 was not true or complete. Question 8 asked whether the insured had ever sustained any loss or damage by any of the risks or liabilities he had insured against. The insured answered "No" although the insured had received £53 in respect of fire damage to a pump within the previous year. Despite this relatively unimportant inaccuracy, the High Court found that the answer was not true and complete and the insurer was able to repudiate liability.

In *Keating v. New Ireland Assurance*,[120] the Supreme Court was critical of the use by insurers of basis of the contract clauses. While recognising that freedom of contract was the fundamental philosophy at the time, the Supreme Court emphasised that such clauses would have to be drafted in exceptionally clear language and fully explained to the insured. Moreover, such clauses would be read in line with the *contra preferentem* rule, that is, against the drafter of the clause. In *Keating v. New Ireland Assurance*, the defendant insurer failed to meet the required standard and therefore it could not avoid the policy. A term that "[t]he policy is conditional on true and full disclosure" was interpreted to mean the insured was under a duty to disclose only what was within his knowledge. A requirement for anything more would have to be clearly expressed, without ambiguity.

Freedom of contract remains the dominant philosophy where the insured is acting in the course of a business. However, where the insured is a consumer, a standard form insurance contract, including any "basis of the contract" clause therein, is now subject to the EC (Unfair Terms in Consumer Contracts) Regulations 1995[121] and 2000.[122] The Regulations

118 See further 27.4.3.
119 [1987] I.R. 113.
120 [1990] 2 I.R. 383.
121 S.I. No. 27 of 1995.
122 S.I. No. 307 of 2000.

seek to implement the European Community Directive on Unfair Terms in Consumer Contracts.[123] The Regulations seek to control terms in contracts between sellers of goods/suppliers of services, including insurers, and consumers in two ways.

First, the Regulations require that in cases where all or certain terms offered to the consumer are in writing, the seller/supplier has an obligation to ensure that the terms are drafted in plain, intelligible language.[124] The Regulations also confirm the *contra proferentem* rule by providing that where there is doubt as to the meaning of a term, the interpretation most favourable to the consumer prevails.[125]

Second, and most significantly, the Regulations provide that an *unfair term* in a contract concluded with a consumer by a seller/supplier shall not be binding on the consumer.[126] Hence, an unfair term is voidable at the option of the consumer. Under the Regulations, a term is unfair if, contrary to the requirement of good faith, it causes significant imbalance of the parties' rights and obligations to the detriment of the consumer.[127] But the effect of these Regulations in relation to insurance contracts may be significantly limited because the Regulations provide that a term shall not, of itself, be considered unfair by relation to the definition of the main subject matter of the contract, or to the adequacy of the price and remuneration under the contract, in so far as these terms, sometimes referred to as "core terms", are in plain, intelligible language.[128] Arguably, many of the terms in insurance contracts could be described as "core terms", being terms which define the subject-matter of the contract, that is, what is insured and the level of cover, and hence would not be subject to the Regulations.[129] This analysis would limit the application of the Regulations to more ancillary terms, such as those in relation to claims procedure.[130] However, the House of Lords, in *Director-General of Fair Trading v. First National Bank*,[131] has indicated that this provision should be given a narrow interpretation so as not to undermine the purpose of the

123 Directive 93/13 [1993] O.J. L95/29: see 2.3.5.3. See further Adams, "Basis of the Contract Clauses and the Consumer" [2000] *Journal of Business Law* 203.

124 Reg. 5(1), 1995; Directive, Art. 5.

125 Reg. 5(2); Directive, Art. 5; see also Reg. 5(3), inserted by the 2000 Regulations.

126 Reg. 6, 1995; Directive, Art. 6; the remainder of the contract can continue to bind the parties provided the offending term can be severed.

127 Reg. 3(2), 1995; Directive, Art. 3.

128 Reg. 4, 1995; Directive, Art. 4(2).

129 Early attempts by the insurance industry to have certain terms listed as "core" and "non-core" were successfully resisted by the Director of Consumer Affairs: see Office of the Director of Consumer Affairs, Annual Report 1995–1996. Only a court of law can make such a definitive distinction.

130 Terms imposing obligations on the insured generally fall into two classes: "risk-related" terms, and "claims process" terms: see Birds, "Insurance Contracts" in Birds, Bradgate & Villiers, eds., *Termination of Contracts* (Chicester, Wiley Chancery, 1995) p.87.

131 [2000] 2 All E.R. 759 (C.A.).

Directive. Accordingly, the enforceability of basis of the contract clauses in consumer insurance contracts seems questionable.

In relation to basis of the contract clauses, the Irish Insurance Federation's voluntary Codes of Practice on non-life and life insurance provide: "Neither the proposal form nor the policy shall contain any general provision converting the statements as to past or present fact in the proposal form into warranties … " Of course, these codes have no legal effect and apply only to proposers and insured persons in their private capacity.

27.4.2 Terms descriptive of the risk

On relatively rare occasions, and as an alternative to classifying a term as a warranty, arguably to avoid the harshness of the effect of breach, a court may classify a term as a term "descriptive of the risk" covered by the contract. Where a term is descriptive of the risk, the insurance cover is suspended while the term is not complied with, but the insurance contract cannot be terminated. For example, in *Farr v. Motor Traders' Mutual Insurance Society*,[132] the plaintiff insured two motor vehicles used as taxis with the defendant. The plaintiff stated in the proposal from that the taxis would only be used for one shift per day. For a short time, one taxi was used for two shifts. The taxi was later damaged while being used for one shift per day. The defendant sought to avoid liability on the basis that the plaintiff was in breach of warranty. The Court of Appeal held that the term was merely descriptive of the risk and not a warranty. Since the term was being complied with when the damage occurred, liability could not be avoided. Whether a term is descriptive of the risk depends on the proper construction of the contract and, as noted above, a clause may be descriptive of the risk even though it is referred to as a warranty.

27.4.3 Conditions

An insurance policy may contain various terms, referred to as conditions, relating to the insured's duties in relation to claims procedure, taking reasonable care to avoid liability and not making any admission of liability. The effect of a breach of such terms depends on their proper classification as a condition, or otherwise.

A condition may be described as a condition precedent to liability. Where the condition is not met, no liability arises. A condition may be precedent to all liability, or more usually, as where the condition relates to ancillary matters, such as claims procedure, to a particular liability under the contract. Where a condition is not stated to be precedent to liability,

132 [1920] 3 K.B. 669 (C.A.).

breach of the condition will only entitle the innocent party to a claim for damages.

27.4.4 Innominate terms

In general contract law, the strict division between conditions and warranties was criticised for being inflexible. For instance, where a term is classified as a condition, the innocent party could terminate the contract even though the effect of the breach might not be very serious.[133] This led to the recognition, or rediscovery, of "innominate" or "intermediary" terms which represent a middle ground between conditions and warranties.[134] Where an innominate term is breached, the effect depends on the seriousness of the breach. If the breach is not serious, the innocent party is limited to a claim in damages. In contrast, if the effect of the breach is serious, the innocent party can claim damages and terminate the contract. This flexibility gives a court more discretion to decide what is the fairest remedy in a given situation. While insurance law has always deviated from general contract law on the classification of contractual terms, the Court of Appeal has recently recognised that terms in insurance contracts may be classified as innominate.[135] This is to be welcomed for the same reasons that it was a welcome development in general contract law. However, whether an Irish court will follow the lead of the Court of Appeal in recognising such terms in insurance contracts remains to be seen.

27.5 Insurance Intermediaries

Most insurance is effected not directly with the insurer but indirectly through intermediaries: independent brokers, insurer's agents and employees. As noted above, where insurance is effected with Lloyd's of London, the business must be conducted through a Lloyd's broker. The Insurance Act 1989, as amended,[136] defines an "insurance intermediary" as:

> "any person who, on a professional basis –
>
> (a) assists or offers to assist third parties in the placing or taking-up of insurance, or

133 See, *e.g Cehave v. Bremer* [1975] 3 All E.R. 739.

134 See *Hong Kong Fir v. Kawasaki* [1962] 2 Q.B. 26; *Irish Telephone Rentals v. ICS Building Society* [1991] I.L.R.M. 880.

135 *Alfred McAlpine plc v. BAI (Run-Off) Ltd* [2000] Lloyd's Rep. 437; see further Yeo, "Of co-operation clauses and uberrima fides in insurance contracts" [2002] *Lloyd's Maritime and Commercial Law Quarterly* 39.

136 By Part 2, Chapter 1 of the Insurance Act 2000.

(b) gives or offers to give advice regarding insurance policies to third parties, but does not include an insurance undertaking or an employee of an insurance undertaking … [137]

The 1989 Act, as amended,[138] also defines an insurance agent as an insurance intermediary acting for a limited number (no more than four) of insurance undertakings.[139] More specifically, a "tied insurance agent" means an insurance agent who undertakes to refer all proposals of insurance to a particular insurance undertaking.[140] In contrast, the Insurance Act 1989, as amended,[141] provides that an insurance broker is an insurance intermediary acting with the freedom of choice whereby he is in a position to place insurance with at least five insurance undertakings.[142]

It is not always clear whether such intermediaries are agents, in law, for the insurer or the insured. The Investment Intermediaries Act 1995, as amended,[143] goes some way to resolve this issue. For example, an insurance agent is deemed to be acting for the insurer to whom a proposal of insurance is being made when he completes or helps the proposer to complete a proposal for insurance.[144] Hence, the insurer is responsible for any errors or omissions in the completion of the proposal form. Moreover, an insurer is responsible for the acts or omissions of its "tied agents" in relation to insurance contracts as if the agent was an employee of the insurer and hence is to be treated as acting on behalf of the insurer.[146] Again, where a premium is paid to an insurance intermediary in respect of renewal of a policy offered by the insurer, or in respect of a proposal accepted by the insurer, the premium is treated as having being paid to the insurer when it is paid to the intermediary.[147] Hence, the intermediary is an agent for the insurer as regards the receipt of monies for premium payments. But other than in these circumstances identified by legislation, it is necessary to establish whether the intermediary is an agent for the insurer or the insured. Brokers are normally regarded as agents for the insured. However, this is only a general rule and it has been held that a

137 1989 Act, s.2, as amended by Insurance Act 2000, s.3. This definition corresponds to the definition in the Investment Intermediaries Act 1995, s.2, as amended by the Insurance Act 2000, s.16.

138 1989 Act, s.2, as amended by Insurance Act 2000, s.3.

139 This definition corresponds to the definition in the Investment Intermediaries Act 1995, ss.2 and 25C, as amended by the Insurance Act 2000, s.16 and 22.

140 Investments Intermediaries Act 1995, s.2 and s.25D, as amended by the Insurance Act 2000, s.16 and s.22, respectively.

141 1989 Act, s.2, as amended by Insurance Act 2000, s.3.

142 This definition corresponds to the definition in the Investment Intermediaries Act 1995, ss.2 and 25B, as amended by the Insurance Act 2000, s.16 and 22.

143 By Part III of the Insurance Act 2000.

144 1995 Act, s.25E(1).

145 1995 Act, s.25E(2).

146 1995 Act, s.25E(3).

147 1995 Act, s.25G(1).

broker may be deemed an agent for the insurer to issue cover notes or to receive information if the facts suggest that he has authority to do so.[148] Therefore, identifying who the principal is – insurer or insured – is vital in determining the rights and liabilities of the parties. This is the case, for example, in relation to the duty of disclosure. It is well established that information known to an agent can be imputed to his principal where the agent has authority to receive information on behalf of the principal. Hence, where the agent is acting for the insurer, disclosure of material facts to the agent will satisfy the insured's duty of disclosure,[149] and if an agent of the insurer knows that a statement in the proposal form is false, that knowledge can be imputed to the principal and the insurer may be deemed to have waived any breach of warranty.[150] On the other hand, where the agent is acting for the insured, as is the usual case with brokers, disclosure to the broker will not satisfy the insured's duty of disclosure. Where the insured discloses information to the broker and the broker fails to pass this on to the insurer, or advises the insured not to pass this information on to the insurer, the insured will be in breach of his duty of disclosure to the insurer, but may have a claim in negligence against the broker.[151]

Once the principal and agent have been identified, the legal consequence of this relationship depends, in the first instance, on the general principles of agency law.[152] However, in some respects, these general principles are modified and their application is not always clear. Broadly speaking, an agent owes his principal a variety of fiduciary duties: in particular, a duty to obey instructions; and a duty to exercise reasonable skill and care.[153]

All agents are required to act with reasonable care. Where the agency is contractual, a term to exercise reasonable care will normally be implied in the contract, at common law. Where services are provided in the course of a business, a term to exercise reasonable care is implied by statute.[154] Where the agency is non-contractual, the duty to exercise reasonable skill and care arises in tort only. Hence, a contractual agent may be subject to concurrent duties in contract and tort unless either is modified or excluded by the contract. In such circumstances, the principal may choose to sue in contract or tort and take whatever procedural advantages may arise.[155]

148 See, *e.g. Stockton v. Mason* [1978] 2 Lloyd's Rep. 430.

149 *Ayrey v. British Legal and United Provident Assurance Co* [1918] 1 K.B. 136.

150 *Wing v. Harvey* (1854) 5 De G.M. & G. 265.

151 *Chariot Inns Ltd v. Assicurazioni Spa and Coyle Hamilton* [1981] I.R. 199.

152 See Part II, esp. 7.3 on agent's duties.

153 See 7.3.

154 Sale of Goods and Supply of Services Act 1980, s.39; see 20.2.3.

155 See *Kennedy v. AIB Ltd* [1998] 2 I.R. 48 (S.C.); *Henderson v. Merrett* [1995] 2 A.C. 145; [1994] 3 All E.R. 506 (H.L.): see further 20.3.2.1. It is unclear whether a third duty of care arises because of the agent's fiduciary position: this point was left undecided by the majority in *Henderson v. Merrett* though Lord Brown-Wilkinson expressed the view that there is no separate fiduciary duty of care, at 205 and 543–4.

In *Chariot Inns v. Assicurazioni Generali SPA*,[156] the plaintiff sought fire insurance from the defendant insurer. In response to a question on the proposal form, and having taken the advice of his agent, an insurance broker, the plaintiff stated that there had been no claims over the last five years. This statement was untrue. The insurer repudiated liability for non-disclosure of a material fact, and the plaintiff sought to recover damages from the insurance broker. The Supreme Court held that the broker was in breach of his contractual duty of care, and his tortious duty of care in advising the plaintiff not to disclose the relevant information in the proposal form. The broker was negligent for failing to protect the interests of the plaintiff and so damages were payable. Again, in *Latham v. Hibernian & Sheridan*,[157] the plaintiff sought insurance for business premises from the first defendant insurers, Hibernian. Prior to renewal of the policy, the plaintiff was arrested and charged with receiving stolen goods. The broker knew of this but failed to advise the plaintiff that the information should be disclosed on renewal. As a result of the broker's negligence, the policy was avoided, but the broker was held responsible for breach of his duty to the insured. Beyond a broker's duty to advise on the duty of disclosure, a broker also has duties in relation to obtaining cover,[158] explaining the contents of policy, and exploring alternatives: all to a reasonable standard of fellow brokers.[159]

An agent's contractual and tortious duty of care can be limited or excluded by the agency contract.[160] However, clear words are needed to exclude liability for negligence. In *Henderson v. Merrett*,[161] contracts between "names" at Lloyd's and the agents who managed underwriting business on their behalf contained a term giving the agents "absolute discretion" in respect of the underwriting business. It was argued that this excluded both contractual and tortious duties of care. However, the House of Lords found that this merely defined the agents' authority and did not exclude their duties to exercise reasonable care in exercising that authority.

156 [1981] I.R. 199.

157 Unreported, High Court, Blayney J., December 4, 1991.

158 In *Irish Nationwide Building Society v. Malone* unreported, Supreme Court, December 10, 1998, it was held that the normal duties of an insurance agent required close attention to the progress of the matter until the policy had been effected or abandoned.

159 *Curtis t/a Agencies Transport Ltd v. Corcoran Insurances Ltd* unreported, High Court, Pringle J., July 13, 1973; *Chariot Inns v. Assicurazioni Generali SPA* [1981] I.R. 199.

160 Where services are provided under contract, in the course of a business, see Sale of Goods and Supply of Services Act 1980, s.40 on exclusion of liability: see further 21.4. Where the services are provided on terms which are not individually negotiated, and the services are provided to a "consumer," see also the European Communities (Unfair Terms in Consumer Contracts) Regulations 1995 (S.I. No. 27 of 1995).

161 [1995] 2 A.C. 145; [1994] 3 All E.R. 506.

Chapter 28

LIABILITY IN INSURANCE LAW

28.1 Insurance Claims

Where the insured sustains a loss caused by a risk insured against, the insured is entitled to enforce the insurance contract and claim the benefit promised by the insurer. The benefit is frequently, but not necessarily, in the form of a monetary payment. The insurer may provide some other benefit with a monetary value, such as repairing or replacing damaged property. Similarly, today, a standard term in a comprehensive motor policy is to provide a substitute car while the insured's car is being repaired. The relevant term in a standard insurance policy might provide:

> "We [the insurers] agree subject to the terms and conditions contained in or endorsed on the Policy to indemnify you [the insured] by payment, reinstatement, repair or replacement for any event insured against in the Sections shown in the enclosed Schedule, occuring during any period of insurance."

The insurance contract commonly imposes obligations on the insured when it comes to making claims. For example, an insured is usually under a duty to promptly notify the insurer of any claims, and under a liability insurance contract, the insured is required not to make any admission of liability. The respective terms in a standard insurance policy might provide:

> "You [the insured] must immediately notify us [the insurer] of any event which may give rise to a claim under the Policy;
> You [the insured] must not admit deny negotiate or settle a claim without our [the insurer's] written consent."

The policy normally describes such terms as conditions precedent to liability and therefore, where they are not complied with, the insurer can avoid liability for a particular claim. To avoid the harsh effect of classifying these terms as conditions precedent, a court may classify them as mere conditions, breach of which gives rise to a claim for damages but does not avoid liability, unless the terms are clearly drafted.[1] Alternatively, a court might classify the terms as innominate.[2] Moreover, where there is

1 On conditions precedent and mere conditions, see 27.4.3.

2 See 27.4.4.

any ambiguity, the term can be interpreted in accordance with the *contra preferentem* rule, that is, against the party who drafted it.

28.1.1 Fraudulent claims

The duty of good faith requires the insured to make a full disclosure of all material facts when making a claim under the policy.[3] Where an insured makes a fraudulent claim, such as where he fails to disclose all the circumstances of the loss, or he exaggerates the loss,[4] he is therefore in breach of this duty. The Marine Insurance Act 1906 provides that breach of the duty of good faith allows the insurer to avoid the contract.[5] In the English case, *The Litsion Pride*[6] it has been held that this means that the contract may be avoided ab initio. On the basis that the 1906 Act sought to codify the common law, this ruling would apply to non-marine insurance also and, if followed in Ireland, would mean that a fraudulent claim would allow the insurer to avoid liability for a valid claim if made before the fraudulent claim. The harshness of this rule can be justified on the basis that the practice of making fraudulent claims needs to be strongly discouraged.

28.1.2 Cover

In order to claim under an insurance contract, the insured must establish that the risk insured against is the proximate cause of his loss.[7] However, where the contract contains exclusions to liability, as is common, the burden shifts to the insurer to prove that the insured's loss was caused by one of the excluded risks.[8] Whether or not a particular risk is covered by the contract depends on the construction of the contract. The interpretation of insurance contracts is made more difficult by the variety of drafting styles and language used. In general, as with other contracts, in interpreting an insurance contract, a court will first seek to ascertain the intention of the parties.[9] Moreover, any ambiguity in the language used will be construed

3 See *Fagan v. General Accident Fire & Life Assurance Corporation plc* unreported, High Court, Murphy J., February 19, 1993; upheld by the Supreme Court, unreported, October 14, 1998; see also *Superwood Holdings plc v. Sun Alliance and London Insurance plc and ors* [1995] 3 I.R. 303 (S.C.) on contractual duty to co-operate re claims: see further McDermott, "Good Faith in Insurance Claims" [2001] *Commercial Law Practitioner* 56. See generally 27.3.3.

4 See, *e.g. Fagan v. General Accident Fire & Life Assurance Corporation plc* unreported, High Court, Murphy J., February 19, 1993; upheld by the Supreme Court, unreported, October 14, 1998.

5 1906 Act, s.17.

6 [1985] 1 Lloyd's Rep. 437.

7 Marine Insurance Act 1906, s.55(1); see further *Marsden v. City and County Assurance* (1865) L.R. 1 C.P. 232; *The Kanchenunga* [1990] 1 Lloyd's Rep. 391.

8 *Gorman v. The Hand in Hand Insurance Co* (1877) I.R. 11 C.L. 224.

9 *Rohan Construction Ltd v. Insurance Corporation of Ireland Ltd* [1988] I.L.R.M. 373 (S.C.).

in accordance with the *contra preferentem* rule, that is, against the party who drafted the contract, the insurer.[10] More specifically, McCarthy J. in *Keating v. New Ireland Assurance Co. plc*[11] set out a number of "clear" principles that must be applied when construing insurance contracts:

1. Parties of full age and competence are, subject to any statutory impediment, entitled to contract as they wish.
2. Whilst acknowledging the right of parties to express the pre-contract representations as being the basis of the contract, same must be read in light of the actual terms of the contract subsequently executed. The contract, so to speak, takes over from the proposal.
3. If insurers desire to found contract upon any particular warranty, it must be expressed in clear terms without any ambiguity.
4. If there is any ambiguity, it must be read against the person who prepared it.
5. Like any commercial contact, such a policy must be given a reasonable interpretation.[12]

McCarthy J. stated that these principles applied to insurance contracts of the kind with which the court was then concerned,[13] contracts of life assurance concluded for non-business purposes. However, the last principle above, which equates the contract in question with other commercial contracts, suggests that these principles may have a wider application and may apply to business as well as non-business insurance contracts.

Where the insurance contract is subject to the European Communities (Unfair Terms in Consumer Contracts) Regulations 1995 and 2000,[14] the Regulations require that in cases where all or certain terms offered to the consumer are in writing, the seller/supplier has an obligation to ensure that the terms are drafted in plain, intelligible language.[15] This provision raises a number of difficulties. It is not clear whether the requirement of plain, intelligible language is subjective or objective. Further, no sanction is provided for breach of this requirement in the Directive or Regulations. The Regulations also confirm the *contra proferentem* rule by providing

10 *Ibid.*

11 [1990] 2 I.R. 383 (S.C.).

12 *Ibid.* at 394–5.

13 *Ibid.* at 394.

14 S.I. No. 27 of 1995; and S.I. No. 307 of 2000, implementing the EC Directive on Unfair Terms in Consumer Contracts 93/13/ EEC [1993] O.J. L95/29: see 2.3.5.3 and 27.4.1.1.

15 Reg. 5(1), 1995; Directive, Art. 5.

that where there is doubt as to the meaning of a term, the interpretation most favourable to the consumer prevails.[16]

28.2 The Principle of Indemnity

As noted in Chapter 27, an important distinction in insurance law is between indemnity and contingency insurance. Contingency insurance involves the payment of a fixed sum on the happening of an event, such as death or illness. In contrast, indemnity insurance, such as property insurance and liability insurance, involves the insurer undertaking to insure against a risk that may never occur, and payment under indemnity insurance seeks to indemnify or compensate the insured for the loss sustained. The insurance contract usually sets a ceiling on the amount payable, but does not define the exact amount. The basic principle is that an insured is entitled to be indemnified, no more or no less:

> "The contract of insurance is a contract of indemnity and of indemnity only and … this contract means that the assured, in case of a loss against which the policy has been made, shall be fully indemnified, but shall never be more than fully indemnified."[17]

Three sets of rules seek to ensure that the principle of indemnity is applied. The rules involve the measure of loss, the insurer's right of subrogation, and the rules relating to double insurance. The insurer's right of contribution is closely related and is also considered below.

28.2.1 The measure of loss

If a valid claim is made by an insured under an insurance contract, the insurer is obliged to satisfy it. The amount payable is governed by the terms of the contract, so, for example, where the contract sets a maximum amount payable, as is usual, if the insured's loss is greater than the maximum, the insured must bear the risk of that extra loss. Moreover, insurance contracts commonly include an excess clause whereby the insured agrees to bear the risk of the first part of the loss, say €100, himself. Where the loss is less than €100, the insured must bear the risk of that loss completely. Therefore, under a third party liability insurance contract, such as a public liability policy, for example, the amount payable by the insurer is the amount required to indemnify the insured against third party claims, subject to any ceiling fixed in the contract and any excess

16 Reg. 5(2); Directive, Art. 5; see also Reg. 5(3), inserted by the 2000 Regulations.

17 *Castellain v. Preston* (1883) 11 Q.B.D. 380 per Brett L.J. at 386 (C.A.); see also *Vance v. Forster* (1841) I.R. Cir. Rep. 47 and *St Albans Investment Co v. Sun Alliance & London Insurance Ltd & ors* [1983] I.R. 363.

clause. However, with property insurance, the measure of loss can be more complicated and the rules differ depending on whether the property insured is goods or land, and whether the claim is for total or partial loss.

28.2.1.1 Total loss

In relation to goods, the measure of loss in the case of total loss is the market value of the goods at the time of the loss. Hence, where the goods are not new, the insurance contract will not provide sufficient funds to purchase new goods unless the contract provides for replacement on a "new for old" basis. Such provision will normally cost more in terms of the premium payable.

With insurance on land, such as buildings insurance, two basic measures of damage can be used: market value or reinstatement cost.[18] Depending on the state of the property market, one measure can be significantly greater than the other. For example, in a period of high building costs, market value may be much lower than reinstatement cost, and so an insured should obtain cover for reinstatement in such circumstances. An insurance contract should clearly indicate which measure is to be used, and where such a clear indication does not exist, the market value measure prevails. In the leading case, *St Albans Investment Co v. Sun Alliance & London Insurance Ltd & ors*,[19] the plaintiff purchased a building in Glasgow, in 1977 for £15,000 with the intention of development. The plaintiff insured the building against fire with the first defendant for £250,000 and with the second defendant for £50,000. Before the policies issued, the building was destroyed by fire. Shortly thereafter, policies issued in what was described as standard form. The plaintiff sought to claim under both policies for the full £300,000, as the cost of rebuilding premises similar to those destroyed would be in excess of this figure. The plaintiff argued that it was the intention of the parties that the insurance contracts would include a reinstatement clause to cover the rebuilding costs. Alternatively, the plaintiff argued that the standard fire policies issued extended to the cost of rebuilding. The defendants argued that they would never have offered such cover, particularly because of the age of the building being insured. In the High Court, it was held that there was no agreement as to reinstatement or rebuilding, and the plaintiff was only entitled to be indemnified for his loss and was not entitled to recover on the basis of an agreement for reinstatement. In the Supreme Court, Griffin J. and Hederman J. concurred that the trial judge was correct in

---

18 Other measures are available but should be clearly expressed in any insurance contract. For example, the indemnity can be calculated on the basis of the cost of a similar premises; or on the basis of the cost of erecting a modern premises which would provide the same facilities as the destroyed premises: see, *e.g. Reynolds v. Phoenix Assurance Co Ltd.* [1978] 2 Lloyd's Rep. 440.

19 [1983] I.R. 363.

taking market value at the time of destruction as the measure of damages necessary to put the plaintiff in the position it would have been in had the fire not occurred.

As an alternative to a simple indemnity policy, insurance on property can be effected by means of a *valued* policy, as is common with marine insurance.[20] Accordingly, the parties agree a value on the property and in the case of total loss, that agreed sum is payable, provided that the sum is not so excessive as to amount to a breach of the duty of good faith. In this way, the valuation operates like a liquidated damages clause in a contract,[21] or the sum assured in a contingency policy.

28.2.1.2 Partial loss

In the case of partial loss, where goods or premises are damaged but not totally destroyed, the measure of loss is essentially the cost of repair, subject to a deduction for betterment if the repair leaves the property better than it was before the loss and subject to any maximum ceiling.[22] Because premiums for property insurance are set with the value of the property in mind, a person seeking insurance may be tempted to understate the value of the property and thereby reduce the cost of the insurance, on the basis that total loss of the property is unlikely to occur, and in the case of partial loss he will be sufficiently covered. In order to avoid such under-insurance, insurance contracts usually contain "average clauses," for instance:

> "Where a sum insured is stated as being subject to Average, if the property so covered is, at the time of any loss or damage to it by any insured peril, collectively of greater value than the declared sum insured then the insured will be regarded as his own insurer for the difference, and will bear a proportionate share of the loss."

Therefore, where there is under-insurance, the insured will not recover the full amount of his loss, even if the amount of loss is less than the sum insured. Instead he will receive the proportion of his actual loss which bears the same relationship to his actual loss as the sum insured bears to the actual value of the property. For example, if a building worth €100,000 is insured for €50,000, and suffers damage €30,000, the insured will only recover 50 per cent of his loss, €15,000. A similar principle applies to marine insurance, by statute.[23]

With a valued policy, in the case of partial loss, the insured will be entitled to recover the proportion of the cost of the repair which bears the

20 Marine Insurance Act 1906, s.27; *cf. Brodigan v. The Imperial Live Stock and General Insurance Co Ltd* (1927) 61 I.L.T.R. 193.

21 2.4.4.3.(ii)(h).

22 *Vance v. Forster* (1841) I.R. Cir. Rep. 47.

23 Marine Insurance Act 1906, s.81.

same relation to the cost of the repair as the policy value bears to the actual value of the property prior to the loss.[24]

Where an insurer refuses or fails to satisfy a valid claim, he is in breach of contract and the insured has an action in damages against the insurer. The measure of damages is prima facie the amount of the claim.

28.2.2 The doctrine of subrogation

Essentially, subrogation is the right of the insurer, having indemnified the insured, to pursue any claims the insured might have had against another party in relation to the insurance claim, thereby allowing the insurer to diminish his loss, and in turn place legal responsibility on the person at fault.[25] While the right arises at common law, most modern insurance contracts will make express provision for this right allowing the insurer to take and defend proceedings in the insured's name and requiring the insured to provide assistance to the insurer.[26] The right of subrogation operates in the same way as an implied assignment of the right of action. The insurance contract may even require the insured to expressly assign his right of action allowing the insurer to bring proceedings in his own name and entitling him to retain all that he recovers.

In *Doyle v. Wicklow County Council*,[27] Griffin J. stated that:

> "it is beyond question that all claims of the insured arising out of any ground of legal responsibility vest in the insurer by subrogation. The value of all benefits received by the insured from claims which have been satisfied before payment under the policy ought to be deducted from the indemnity at the time of payment; equally, after the insurers have paid the insured under the policy, they have an equity in respect of all the insured's claims."[28]

The doctrine of subrogation is linked with the general principle of indemnity that the insured should be fully indemnified, but no more or no less.[29] There are two main elements to this doctrine. First, and following from the principle of indemnity, where an insured has been indemnified under an insurance contact, the insured must account to the insurer for any

24 *Elcock v. Thomson* [1949] 2 K.B. 755, [1949] 2 All E.R. 381.

25 The doctrine of subrogation is not limited to insurance law: see Goff & Jones, *The Law of Restitution* (London, Sweet & Maxwell, 5th ed., 1998) Chapter 3.

26 The relevant term in a standard insurance policy might provide: "The insurer may take over and conduct in the insured's name, with complete and exclusive control of the defence or settlement of any claim; and the insurer may take legal proceedings in the insured's name against any other parties to recover any payment we have made under this Policy. This will be at our own expense and for our own benefit."

27 [1974] I.R. 55 (S.C.).

28 *Ibid.* at 72.

29 *Castellain v. Preston* (1883) 11 Q.B.D. 380.

benefits received from a third party, before or after payment under the insurance contract. For instance, in *Castellain v. Preston*,[30] the owner of property which was insured against fire contracted to sell it for a fixed price. Between the exchange of contracts and completion of the sale, it was damaged by fire, but the sale went ahead and the vendor was paid in full. The purchaser sought to claim against the insurer but that claim was defeated because the insurance contract was with the vendor, not the purchaser, and the insurance contract "did not run with the land." Having paid the vendor under the insurance contract, the insurer sought to recover the purchase price from him. To ensure that the vendor did not "profit" from the circumstances, the court held that the insurer was subrogated to the insured in respect of the purchase monies.

The second element of the insurer's right of subrogation is more important in practice. Accordingly, where the insured suffers loss as a result of the wrongful action of a third party, the insurer, having indemnified the insured, can pursue any claims the insured might have had against that third party. Many of the cases in international trade law, such as where the insured's goods are damaged at sea by the carrier's negligence, involved the insurer being subrogated to the rights of the insured to sue the carrier.[31] This right only arises where the insured is fully indemnified by the insurer.[32] If an insured has not been fully indemnified, he is entitled to bring a claim against the third party on his own behalf.[33] Where an insurer fails to exercise his right of subrogation, the insured may sue a third party, although any moneys recovered will be held on behalf of the insurer, under the principle of indemnity and the first element of the doctrine of subrogation. The insurer's right of action under the doctrine of subrogation is identical to that of the insured. The insurer is subject to the same defences as the insured, for example, and the insurer can be in no better position than the insured. Lastly, the insured must not do anything to prejudice the insurer's right of action, and if he refused to allow his name to be used in proceedings, the insurer may commence an action in his own name and join the insured as a co-defendant.

The right of subrogation arises in relation to all types of insurance but, in practice, they are frequently not exercised in relation to motor insurance.

30 (1883) 11 Q.B.D. 380.

31 See 31.4.

32 *Driscoll v. Driscoll* [1918] 1 I.R. 152.

33 *Commercial Union Assurance Co v. Lister* (1874) 9 Ch. App. 483. However, it was recognised by the House of Lords that subrogation rights may be affected by the terms of the insurance contract in *Napier & Ettrick v. Kershaw* [1993] A.C. 713, [1993] 1 All E.R. 385 which dealt with the effect of an excess clause in an insurance contract. In this case, it was held that under the excess clause the insured had agreed to bear the first part of the loss up to a set amount. Therefore, where an insurer indemnifies the insured under the contract, and subject to the excess, for damage caused by a third party, an insurer has priority to claim sums from the third party who caused the loss before the insured can seek to recover the excess amount: see further Buckley, "Subrogation - Have Insurers' Rights been Extended" [2000] *Commercial Law Practitioner* 22.

This is as a result of "knock-for-knock" agreements between motor insurers.[34] Under such agreements, where two vehicles, which are insured comprehensively, are involved in a collision, each insurer will pay its own insured and not seek to exercise its right to subrogation, regardless of the responsibility of the two drivers involved. The benefits of such agreements outweigh any costs: there is no need to investigate claims or take legal proceedings and in the longer term it appears that an insurer's losses and gains balance each other out.

28.2.3 Double insurance and the doctrine of contribution

Not infrequently, the insured's loss may be covered by more than one insurance contract. For instance, an insured may insure the same risk with two separate insurers or the same risk may be insured under two separate contracts of insurance with the same insurer, as where a business takes out public liability insurance and product liability insurance. If so, the insured is entitled to claim under either or both insurance contracts until he is fully indemnified. But, importantly, the law precludes double recovery, as this would be contrary to the principle of indemnity.

Where a risk is insured against with more than one insurer and the insured makes a claim and recovers against only one insurer, that insurer can seek a pro rata contribution from any other insurers under the equitable doctrine of contribution.[35] Again, the insurance contract usually modifies this right to contribution by including a "rateable proportion clause", for example: "If at the time of a claim there is any other Policy covering any events insured under this Policy we shall be liable only for our proportionate share."Accordingly, any one insurer is protected from paying more than his "share" of the loss, thereby forcing the insured to pursue claims against each insurer for their proportion of the loss.

Double insurance and the doctrine of contribution only operates where the same subject-matter is covered by two or more separate insurance contracts, in relation to the same risk. For example, in *Hibernian Insurance v. Eagle Star Insurance* and *Guardian Royal Exchange Assurance*,[36] Hibernian insured a Hillman Imp car owned by a Mrs Gent; her husband was a named driver on the policy. This insurance contract was amended to cover a red Alpine car on the day it was driven and crashed by the insured's husband. Following the road accident between the insured's husband and a third party, the third party successfully sued the insured, amongst others. Consequently, Hibernian indemnified the insured and then sought contribution, first against Eagle Star, the insurers of the owners Talbot (Ireland) Ltd, of the red Alpine car, and second against Guardian Royal

34 See further Lewis, "Insurers' Agreements not to Enforce Strict Legal Rights" (1985) 48 *Modern Law Review* 275.

35 A similar doctrine of contribution arises between two or more sureties of a debt: see 26.2.5.

36 Unreported, High Court, February 17, 1987.

Exchange, who were the insurers of the husband's employer in respect of vehicles in their custody. In relation to the claim against Eagle Star, the insurance contract covered any property owned by Talbot and any driver, where the driver had Talbot's permission. On the facts, these conditions were satisfied and so Eagle Star were liable for 50 per cent of the third party's claim: the subject-matter insured by Hibernian and Eagle Star was the same. Regarding the Guardian Royal Exchange claim, the court found, on the facts, that the vehicle was not in the custody of the employers and so there was no liability: in this case the subject-matter insured by Hibernian and Royal Guardian Exchange was different.

Again, in *Zurich Insurance Co. v. Shield Insurance Co.*,[37] an employee of Quinnsworth was injured when travelling in a car driven by another employee, as a passenger during the course of his work. The plaintiff, Zurich Insurance, which provided motor insurance cover for personal injury to Quinnsworth, indemnified the insured under the contract. Zurich then sought to claim a 50 per cent contribution from the defendant, Shield Insurance, which provided employee liability cover to Quinnsworth. The defendant argued that the doctrine of contribution applies only where the two insurance contracts cover the same risk, the insured in each policy is the same person, and the interest of the insured in the risk is the same. Gannon J., in the High Court, noted that under the plaintiff's motor insurance policy, there were a number of insured parties, named and unnamed companies, including Quinnsworth, which were insured against the risks of the driving of their cars, which might arise vicariously or otherwise. In contrast, the defendant's employers' liability insurance policy was issued to Quinnsworth and/or associated and subsidiary companies, and this contract covered only liability of Quinnsworth to its employees. In comparing the two insurance contracts, Gannon J. further noted that although Quinnsworth was the insured under both contracts, the interests of Quinnsworth being protected were not the same and the risks covered were not the same, though the same set of events could give rise to liability under both contracts. Hence, the plaintiff's claim for contribution failed. This decision was upheld by the Supreme Court.

Similarly in *Re Kelly's Carpetdrome*,[38] the insured was the liquidator of Kelly's Carpetdrome who obtained insolvency insurance which provided a type of blanket cover over the activities of liquidators and the property over which they were appointed. The properties in question were destroyed by fire and the insurers wanted only to pay 50 per cent of the indemnity claiming, under their right of contribution (as expressed in the contract), that another insurance contract existed which covered the loss. The other contract was insurance cover taken out by third-party tenants, noting the interest of the owners of the properties in question, with Lloyd's. The

37 [1988] I.R. 174.

38 Unreported, High Court, Barrington J., April 14, 1985.

liquidator first tried to make a claim against Lloyd's but Lloyd's denied liability for non-disclosure. The liquidator then argued that the only relevant insurance contract was the insolvency policy with the insurer. In the High Court, Barrington J, found that the legal interests of the owner and tenant were different and hence this was not a case of double insurance. Accordingly, the insurer was liable for the full sum although it would be subrogated to any rights the liquidator might have against the tenants.

Part VI

INTERNATIONAL TRADE LAW

CHAPTER 29

INTRODUCTION TO INTERNATIONAL TRADE

29.1 INTRODUCTION

When we examined contracts for the supply of goods and services in Part III, we were concerned predominately with domestic supply contracts. Today, businesses must consider trading not only on the domestic market but also internationally. An international market benefits both the individual business and the general economy. An international market provides a business with a second market, which is particularly important when the domestic market is in recession. Moreover, the health of the general economy can be assessed with reference to levels of international trade. Where exports exceed imports there is said to be a trade surplus, an indication of a strong economy.[1]

International trade involves the provision of goods and services. The establishment of the International Financial Services Centre (IFSC) and the International Arbitration Centre in Dublin are examples of Ireland's attempt to export financial and arbitration services; but, the international sale of goods remains the most important export for Irish business and the Irish economy.[2] In this Part, we look at the special problems which international sale of goods transactions pose and examine how Irish commercial law has adopted to resolve these problems and meet the needs of the international trading community. The focus is on the private law of international trade,[3] and not the public law aspects of international trade, which include international agreements between states regarding tariffs, quotas, and other mechanisms to regulate inter-state trade, such as the General Agreement on Tariffs and Trade (GATT).[4]

There are, in fact, very few Irish cases regarding international trade law.

---

1 The trade surplus is regularly assessed and published by the Central Statistics Office: see www.cso.ie.

2 For example, in 2001 Ireland exported a total of €92,523m worth of goods: of this total €20,419m was to the United Kingdom; €15,695 was to the USA; €11,718 was to Germany; and €5,614m was to France. See further External Trade Figures at www.cso.ie.

3 See generally, Schmitthoff's *Export Trade: the Law and Practice of International Trade* (London, Sweet & Maxwell, 10th ed., 2000); Forde, *Commercial Law* (Dublin, Butterworths, 2nd ed., 1997) Chapter 11.

4 See further Jackson, *The Jurisprudence of GATT and the WTO* (Cambridge, Cambridge University Press, 2000); Petersmann ed., *International Trade Law and the GATT/WTO Dispute Settlement System* (London, Kluwer, 1997); Emilou & O'Keeffe, *The European Union and World Trade Law: After the GATT Uruguay Round* (Chicester, Wiley, 1996).

This is an area where English commercial law has dominated internationally, and continues to do so, although perhaps to a lesser extent than in the past. For instance, many of the standard form contracts used in international trade are produced by organisations and associations based in London. For example, the Lloyd's of London marine policy and the Institute of London Underwriter's Clauses are used throughout the world when effecting marine insurance contracts.[5] These contracts commonly choose English law as the proper law of the contract, with any disputes to be resolved by arbitration in London, or before the High Court in London.[6] Therefore, because of the close links, historical and otherwise, between the Irish and English legal systems, English case law in the area of international trade is an important source of guidance when it comes to describing and analysing Irish international trade law.

29.2 When is a Sale International?

In determining whether a sale is international, the law concentrates on the place of business of the parties to the contract and not whether the goods are dispatched and delivered in different countries. This is the approach of Irish and international sales law. For example, section 61(6)(b) of the Sale of Goods Act 1893,[7] which permits the exclusion of a seller's liability for breach of the statutory implied terms in international sales contracts, defines a contract for the international sale of goods as:

> "a contract of sale of goods made by the parties whose place of business (or, if they have none, habitual residences) are in the territories of different States and in the case of which one of the following conditions is satisfied:
> (i) the contract involves the sale of goods which are at the conclusion of the contract in the course of carriage or will be carried from the territory of one State to another; or
> (ii) the acts constituting offer and acceptance have been effected in territories of different States; or
> (iii) delivery of the goods is to be made in the territory of a State other than that within whose territory the acts constituting the offer and acceptance have been effected."

5 On marine insurance, see further Chalmers' *Marine Insurance Act 1906* (London, Butterworths, 10th ed., 1993); Hardy Ivamy, *Marine Insurance* (London, Butterworths, 4th ed., 1985); *Templeman on Marine Insurance* (London, Pitman, 6th ed., 1986); and *Schmitthoff's Export* Trade (London, Sweet & Maxwell, 10th ed., 2000) Chapter 19.

6 Statistics evidence the international influence of English law and the High Court in London. For example, out of the 72 trials heard in the Commercial List in the High Court during one year, 44 involved foreign parties: see Irvine, "The Law: An Engine for Trade" (2001) 64 *Modern Law Review* 333 at 333. And, in a Practice Statement on Commercial Court Procedures, on July 28, 1989, it was stated that about 50 per cent of litigants before the Commercial Court were foreign and almost 30 per cent of cases had no English litigants.

7 Inserted by the Sale of Goods and Supply of Services Act 1980, s.24.

This two-part test requires first that the parties' place of business be in different jurisdictions and second some further element of an international character, such as that the goods are, at the conclusion of the contract, in the course of carriage or will be carried from one jurisdiction to another, or that the offer and acceptance have been effected in different jurisdictions. Article 1 of the Vienna Convention on the International Sale of Goods (1980),[8] defines a sale as international solely in terms of the parties' place of business. So, under both regimes, although the goods may never leave a jurisdiction, where the parties to the sales contract have their places of business in different jurisdictions, a commercial lawyer must be able to assess what effect this international character has on the parties' rights and obligations.

29.3 Special Problems and Solutions Regarding International Trade

Based on the above definitions of an international sales contract, the primary problem for a seller and buyer is that the parties operate in different jurisdictions. This can cause problems when it comes to negotiating the contract, in particular where different languages are involved. However, an agent can be engaged to deal with negotiations and any language problems, and to provide a "person on the spot."[9]

An international sale of goods very often involves a sea transit. Because of the usual perils of sea transit, and the fact that the time between dispatch of the goods by the seller and actual delivery to the buyer can be substantial, there is an increased risk of loss of, or damage to the goods while in transit. The sales contract, and subsidiary contracts, such as contracts of insurance, carriage and warehousing, will normally address this issue of risk.

Payment in relation to international sale transactions can also raise problems. Where the sale is on credit terms, how can the buyer's creditworthiness be assessed and how best can the seller ensure payment of the price? Moreover, fluctuations in currency due to exchange rates can render unprofitable what was once considered a good deal. Some of these problems may be dealt with by appropriate contractual terms, such as a price variation clause in the sales contract. Contracts can also provide for payment in a strong currency, while a documentary letter of credit can be used to provide a reliable paymaster.

International sales transactions may also raise conflict of laws problems: what is the proper law of the contract, where is the proper forum for dispute resolution and under what procedures can a judgment be

8 See further 29.4.2.

9 On agency, see generally Part II.

enforced abroad? Again, a well-drafted contract will include proper law and proper forum clauses and the rules of private international law, as are found in the Rome Convention and elsewhere,[10] seek to address these and similar issues. A commercial lawyer needs to be aware of these special problems and the means of getting around them. In this Part, international sale contracts are examined in Chapter 30; contracts for the carriage of goods by sea are the subject of Chapter 31; and documentary credits are examined in Chapter 32.[11]

29.4 Sources of International Trade Law

International trade law is a mixture of common law and statute, international conventions, rules, terms and customs. A preliminary point to be considered when dealing with problems arising out of an international sales transaction is what law governs the contracts. A well-drafted contract will normally contain an express choice of law clause. If not, the question will be decided in accordance with rules of private international law designed to identify the proper law of the contract.[12] In this Part, we examine the Irish law of international trade.

29.4.1 Domestic legislation

The two principal pieces of domestic legislation which are relevant to this area are the Bills of Lading Act 1855, and the Sale of Goods Acts 1893 and 1980. A bill of lading is a document issued to the shipper of goods, by the ship's master, when goods are received on board. The bill is then forwarded to the person collecting the goods at the destination. On

[10] The Rome Convention on the Law Applicable to Contractual Relations 1980 [1980] O.J. L266/1, incorporated into Irish law by the Contractual Obligations (Applicable Law) Act 1991. See also Council Regulation 44/2001 on jurisdiction and the recognition and enforcement of judgments in civil and commercial matters [2001] O.J. L12/1, which came into force on March 1, 2002, and the European Communities (Civil and Commercial Judgments) Regulations 2002 (S.I. 52/2002). The above Regulation (the Brussels I Regulation) supersedes the Brussels Convention (1968), incorporated into Irish law by the Jurisdiction of Courts and Enforcement of Judgments Act 1998, in EC member states other than Denmark: see Art. 68 of the Brussels I Regulation.

[11] Other important aspects of international trade law, such as carriage of goods by road and air, insurance, in particular marine insurance, and conflicts of law are outside the scope of this work. On carriage by road and air see *Schmitthoff's Export Trade* (London, Sweet & Maxwell, 10th ed., 2000) Chapter 17 & 18; and Forde, *Commercial Law* (Dublin, Butterworths, 2nd ed., 1997) Chapter 11; on insurance see *Schmitthoff's Export Trade* (London, Sweet & Maxwell, 10th ed., 2000) Chapter 19; *Chalmers' Marine Insurance Act 1906* (London, Butterworths, 10th ed., 1993); Hardy Ivamy, *Marine Insurance* (London, Butterworths, 4th ed., 1985); *Templeman on Marine Insurance* (London, Pitman, 6th ed., 1986); on conflict of laws, see Binchy, *Irish Conflict of Laws* (Dublin, Butterworths, 1986); see also Dicey and Morris, *Conflict of Laws* (London, Sweet & Maxwell, 13th ed., 2000).

[12] See further Binchy, *Irish Conflict of Laws* (Dublin, Butterworths, 1986); see also Dicey and Morris, *Conflict of Laws* (London, Sweet & Maxwell, 13th ed., 2000).

production of the bill, the ship's master is required to hand over the goods shipped. In this way, the bill acts as a receipt for the goods. The 1885 Act seeks to make the bill of lading more efficacious in two ways. First, under section 1, where a consignee named in a bill of lading, or his indorsee, acquires property in the goods upon or by reason of such consignment or indorsement, he also acquires any contractual rights against the carrier of the goods under the contract of carriage evidenced in the bill of lading.[13] Second, under section 3, the bill of lading is made conclusive evidence of the goods shipped, subject to certain conditions.[14]

The Sale of Goods Acts 1893 and 1980, examined in detail in Part II of this book, apply whether the sale of goods is domestic or international, provided the statutory definition of a sale of goods contract is met.[15] Hence, many of the rules which apply to domestic and international sales are shared. However, the legislation does address specific issues relevant to international sales, in certain provisions, in particular in relation to the passing of property and risk.[16]

29.4.2 International harmonising measures[17]

It is argued that international trade is better facilitated by a set of legal rules designed specifically with international trade in mind. Moreover, problems with conflict of laws can be avoided when parties select international law rules to govern their contracts and dealings, as opposed to national rules. Some of these international rules have been incorporated into Irish law,[18] or they may be adopted contractually by the parties themselves.[19]

One of the first areas of law to be successfully regulated at an international level was the carriage of goods by sea contract. Traditionally, a carrier of goods by sea was strictly liable for their safe delivery, subject only to what were known as the "common law exceptions". These comprised loss of, or damage to the goods caused by act of God, public enemy, or inherent vice. With the development of the principle of freedom of contract in the nineteenth century, sea carriers took advantage of their

13 See 31.4.

14 See 31.2.2.

15 See Chapter 9.

16 See further Chapter 30 and in particular 30.2.4, 30.2.5, 30.3.5, and 30.3.6.

17 See generally, Schmitthoff, "The Unification of the Law of International Trade" [1968] *Journal of Business Law* 105, "The Codification of the Law of International Trade" [1985] *Journal of Business Law* 34; *cf.* Hobhouse, "International Conventions and Commercial Law: the Pursuit of Uniformity" [1990] *Law Quarterly Review* 530.

18 *e.g.* the Hague-Visby Rules 1968/1979 and the Merchant Shipping (Liability of Shipowners and Others) Act 1996; see further 31.2.

19 *e.g.* the Uniform Customs and Practices relating to Documentary Credits (UCP); see further Chapter 32.

superior bargaining power and introduced clauses which sought to limit their common law liability, and more. In some jurisdictions, legislation was introduced to regulate the use of such clauses.[20] However, it soon became apparent that an international response was needed. Following discussions between representatives of shipowners, shippers, underwriters and bankers from the major shipping jurisdictions, the Maritime Law Committee of the International Law Association drafted a set of rules at a meeting held in the Hague in 1921. The draft rules were the subject of negotiation and amendment, and were finally adopted as an international convention by the major trading nations in 1924, and became known as the Hague Rules. The Hague Rules regulate various aspects of the carriage of goods by sea contract, between shipper and carrier, including the use of exclusion clauses. The Hague Rules were adopted in Ireland by the Merchant Shipping Act 1947. The rules have been amended and updated twice: first in 1968 under what are known as the Hague-Visby Rules, and again in 1978 under the Hamburg Rules. Currently, the Hague-Visby Rules apply in Ireland, under the Merchant Shipping (Liability of Shipowners and Others) Act 1996.[21]

In the last 50 years or so, there has been a general movement to re-internationalise certain aspects of commercial law. Organisations exist whose purpose is to facilitate this process: the International Chamber of Commerce, (ICC); the United Nations Commission on International Trade Law (UNCITRAL); the International Institute for the Unification of Private Law (Unidroit); and the Hague Conference on Private International Law, amongst others.[22] For example, UNCITRAL produced the Hamburg Rules, referred to above. UNCITRAL is also responsible for the Vienna Convention on the International Sale of Goods.

The Vienna Convention came into effect on January 1, 1988.[23] Ireland has not acceded to the Convention despite a recommendation, in 1991, from the Law Reform Commission to do so.[24] It is therefore not part of Irish law. Nevertheless, parties to a sales contract can expressly adopt the Convention, or conflict of laws rules may result in the application of the Convention, so it is advisable for a commercial lawyer to have a working

20 *e.g.* the U.S. Harter Act 1893; or the New Zealand Shipping and Seamen Act 1908.

21 See 31.2.

22 See 1.3.3.

23 The Vienna Convention superseded two earlier Conventions, The Hague Convention Relating to Uniform Law on the International Sale of Goods (ULIS) and the Hague Convention Relating to a Uniform Law on the Formation of Contracts for the International Sale of Goods (UFL) 1964. Ireland did not accede to these Conventions.

24 Law Reform Commission, Report on the United Nations (Vienna) Convention on Contracts for the International Sale of Goods 1980 (L.R.C. 42-1992). See generally, Feltham, "The United Nations Convention on Contracts for the International Sale of Goods" [1981] *Journal of Business Law* 346; Nicholas, "The Vienna Convention on International Sales Law" [1989] *Law Quarterly Review* 201; Lee, "The United Nations Convention on Contracts for the International Sale of Goods: OK for the UK?" [1993] *Journal of Business Law* 131.

knowledge of the Convention. To date, the Convention has been ratified by 63 states, including 12 members of the EU and many of Ireland's trading partners.[25] Because there is now a significant body of case law interpreting the Convention,[26] and the number of ratifications of the Convention is ever-increasing, the case for Irish accession is even stronger now than in 1991.

The Convention covers issues such as its application, contract formation, rights and duties of the parties, risk and remedies, but not the passing of property. The obligations of the parties under the Convention are largely similar to those under domestic law but there are greater differences in relation to contract formation and remedies. Some notable features of the Convention, with regard to the formation of contracts, when compared with Irish law, include the following:

(i) An offer can be irrevocable if:
   (a) it indicates, whether by stating a fixed time for acceptance or otherwise, that it is irrevocable; or
   (b) it was reasonable for the offeree to rely on the offer as being irrevocable and the offeree has acted in reliance on the offer.

(ii) Acceptance does not become effective until it reaches the offeror, and may be withdrawn if the withdrawal reaches the offeror before or at the same time as the acceptance would have become effective. So, mere despatch of acceptance does not bind the offeree, but it suffices to prevent the offeror from revoking the offer.[28]

(iii) An acceptance containing additional or different terms, which does not materially alter the terms of the offer, may constitute an acceptance, unless the offeror objects.[29]

Notable features in relation to breach of contract and remedies include the fact that:

25 See www.uncitral.org. For example, the USA ratified the Vienna Convention and it entered into force on January 1, 1988 but subject to a reservation under Art. 95 that it would not be bound by Art. 1(1). This narrows the application of the Convention by providing that where the governing law of a contract is deemed to be US law under the rules of conflict of laws, US domestic law and not the Convention will apply. The major exception is the UK where the Government has indicated that it will ratify the Convention once parliamentary time can be found for the necessary legislation: see DTI Consultation Document, United Nations Convention on Contracts for the International Sale of Goods (June 1989); DTI Consultation Document, United Nations Convention on Contracts for the International Sale of Goods (September 1997).

26 Case law is published in summary form by UNCITRAL as "Case Law on Uncitral Texts" or CLOUT: see www.uncitral.org. See also Schlectriem ed., *Commentary on the UN Convention on the International Sale of Goods* (CISG) (Oxford, Oxford University Press, 1998).

27 Art. 16(2).

28 Arts. 16(1), 18(2) and 22.

29 Art. 19.

(i) There is no mention of conditions or warranties, instead the Convention uses a concept similar to fundamental breach to determine whether the innocent party may terminate the contract.[30]
(ii) The seller may have a right to "cure" defective performance.[31]
(iii) The buyer may have a right to demand specific performance, replacement or repair of the goods.[32]
(iv) There is a two-year time limit from physical delivery for rejection.[33]
(v) There is a right to partial rejection.[34]
(vi) Where defective goods are delivered, the buyer can claim a reduction in price in proportion to the defect.[35]
(vii) Where the contract has been avoided and the innocent party makes a substitute transaction, then the innocent party can recover the difference between the contract price and the substitute transaction provided the substitute transaction was made in a reasonable manner and within a reasonable time after avoidance.[36]
(viii) The passage of risk is not linked to property but to control.[37]

29.4.3 Standard form contracts, terms and customs

International sales contracts are often concluded using standard form contracts which contain detailed rules specific to the contract in question. These standard terms can be adopted from a set of standard terms promoted by an trade organisation, such as GAFTA (the Grain and Feed Trade Association) or FOSFA (the Federation of Oil Seeds and Fats Association). For instance, GAFTA 79 (see Appendix C) is a contract for the sale of United Kingdom and Ireland grain on *cif* terms; FOSFA 24 is suitable for the sale of Canadian or American soya beans on *cif* terms.[38] Where a dispute arises in these circumstances, any resolution will usually revolve around the particular wording of the standard form contract in question, with the sale of goods legislation forming a backdrop to the dispute.

Alternatively, the terms of sale can be negotiated by the parties to the contract and hence are "private" to the parties, but they may incorporate established trade terms into the contract. The most authoritative document

30 Art. 25; see further O'Neill, "Contracts for the International Sale of Goods" [1999] *Irish Business Law* 82.
31 Arts. 34, 37 and 48.
32 Art. 46.
33 Art. 39(2).
34 Arts. 51–2.
35 Art. 50.
36 Art. 75.
37 Arts. 67–9.
38 *CIF* is cost, insurance and freight; see further below and 30.3.

defining these terms is the ICC's International Rules for the Interpretation of Trade Terms (INCOTERMS).[39] INCOTERMS have no legal force in Irish law and must be expressly adopted contractually by the parties to have legal effect. They allow many of the parties' obligations, such as the method of delivery of the goods sold, the different duties of the parties, the calculation of the purchase price and incidental charges, to be defined by use of short-hand terms. The definitions in INCOTERMS reflect commercial practice, and hence they are revised periodically: the latest revision dates from 2000. The following are examples of some of the terms defined in INCOTERMS.

(i) *Ex works* – means the seller delivers when he places the goods at the disposal of the buyer at the seller's premises. This involves minimum duties on the seller's part and this is reflected in the price. The buyer must therefore arrange the collection and transport of the goods.
(ii) *Free Alongside Ship (fas)* – means the seller delivers when the goods are placed alongside the vessel at the named port of shipment. All costs associated with placing the goods alongside the ship are born by the seller. The buyer must make the shipping arrangements.
(iii) *Free on Board (fob)* – means that the seller delivers when the goods pass the ship's rail. The seller bears the cost of the stevedore company for loading, for example, but gets it back in the price.
(iv) *Cost and Freight (c & f)* – means that the seller delivers when the goods pass the ship's rail. The seller must pay the costs and freight necessary to bring the goods to the named port of destination.
(v) *Cost, Insurance and Freight (cif)* – as above but the seller also has to procure marine insurance.
(vi) *Delivered Ex Ship* – means the seller delivers when the goods are placed on board the ship, not cleared for import, at the port of destination.
(vii) *Delivered Ex Quay* – means the seller delivers when the goods are placed at the disposal of the buyer, not cleared for import, on the quay at the named port of destination.

The adoption of these terms helps avoid disputes as to their exact meaning and they also have the advantage of being neutral.

As well as standard contract and trade terms, certain trade customs may govern an international trade transaction. In particular, in the area of payment the ICC's Uniform Customs and Practices for Documentary Credits (UCP 500) dominate. Again, these customs have no force of law in Ireland but must be expressly adopted by the parties to the contract.[40]

39 For text of INCOTERMS, see www.iccwbo.org.
40 See further Chapter 32.

29.5 A Typical Transaction

An international trade transaction involves a number of related contracts with the sales contract at the centre. The following outlines a typical international trade transaction.

(i) The parties enter into an international sale of goods contract. The contract will detail the respective responsibilities of the seller and buyer, including who is responsible for transport, insurance and other arrangements, and the method of payment.

(ii) Depending on the sales contract, either the seller or the buyer will have to make the shipping arrangements. This may involve getting an export licence, obtaining insurance cover, transporting the goods to the port, warehousing the goods at the port, booking space on board a ship, clearing customs and getting the goods loaded on board. Freight forwarders can be engaged to make the necessary shipping arrangements which usually involves entering into several contracts, such as an insurance contract, various carriage contracts by road, rail and sea, a warehousing contract, and a contract with a stevedore company to load the goods.

(iii) Depending on the terms of the sales contract, the buyer may have to make payment, or set up an agreed payment mechanism, such as a documentary letter of credit.

(iv) When the shipper (the seller or buyer identified in the sales contract) delivers the goods to the ship's master, on loading, he will be issued with a document called a bill of lading.[41] This document is needed to obtain possession of the goods at the port of destination and so it will be forwarded to the shipper's agent (where the shipper is the buyer) or the seller's consignee (the buyer) on payment of the price. Alternatively, goods may be shipped without a sales contract in place. Where goods are sold while in transit, the bill of lading, and other shipping documents, are forwarded to the buyer on payment of the price to facilitate taking possession at the port of destination.

(v) When the goods arrive at the port of destination they need to be collected from the ship by the buyer. The buyer may have to make arrangements for the collection of the goods, the clearance of customs and payment of any customs duties and their transportation to the buyer's premises.

41 Other documents, such as a waybill, may be used instead of a bill of lading, but bills are still commonly used and problems of international trade cannot be understood without an understanding of bills of lading.

Chapter 30

INTERNATIONAL SALE CONTRACTS

30.1 Introduction

Although governed by the general law of sale of goods,[1] international sale contracts contain trade terms which are not customary in domestic trade and which define many of the obligations of the parties.[2] Most of these terms are defined by the ICC's INCOTERMS.[3] The most common trade terms are "free on board" or *fob*, and "cost, insurance and freight" or *cif*. These two contract types are the subject of this chapter, although there are several variants to these basic terms, all of which place different rights and duties on the parties to the sales contract.[4]

30.1.1 The distinction between fob *and* cif *contracts*

Each of these common types of contract is recognised by custom as having different legal incidents. Classification of the contract therefore affects the rights and duties of the parties, and matters such as the passing of property and risk. Unfortunately, the distinctions between these different types of contract are not entirely clear-cut. There is a well-recognised overlap between *fob* and *cif* contracts and the parties may vary the standard incidents of a particular contract so that a contract labelled *fob* may in fact be more like a *cif* contract. In order to determine the rights and liabilities of the parties, it will therefore be necessary to look beyond the labels to consider whether the standard incidents of that type of contract have been varied. For instance, in *McKelvie v. Wallace Bros Ltd*,[5] there was stated to be a *cif* contract for the purchase of coal from Glasgow. However, there was no requirement as to an insurance policy, and the cargo had been unloaded and accepted before the bill of lading was tendered to the buyer. The court held that because of these facts, the usual incidents of a *cif* contract with regard to the passing of property did not apply. Again, in *The*

---

1 See generally Part III.

2 See Sassoon, "The Origin of FOB and CIF Terms and the Factors Influencing their Choice" [1967] *Journal of Business Law* 32.

3 See 29.4.3.

4 See generally, Bridge, *The International Sale of Goods* (Oxford, Oxford University Press, 1999); *Schmitthoff's Export Trade: the law and practice of international trade* (London, Sweet & Maxwell, 10th ed., 2000) Part One; Forde, *Commercial Law* (Dublin, Butterworths, 2nd ed., 1997) Chapter 11.

5 [1919] 2 I.R. 250.

Julia,[6] a contract stated to be on *cif* terms provided that the sellers:

(i) were entitled to substitute a delivery order at the port of destination for a bill of lading; and
(ii) were liable for the condition of the goods on arrival.

It was held that the contract was not a *cif* contract but an *ex ship* contract because the express terms were inconsistent with the normal incidents of a *cif* contract. In examining these two common terms, we will concentrate on the obligations of the parties, and the passage of property and risk.

30.2 *Fob* Contracts

As noted above, *fob* stands for "free on board". The abbreviation is usually followed by the name of a port – for instance "*fob* Cork" – which is the port of shipment. At its most basic, the *fob* contract requires the seller to supply the goods and place them on board a ship at the named port at his own expense – hence, from the buyer's perspective, "free on board".[7] The price naturally includes an element to cover this cost, but the advantage for the buyer is that he does not have to concern himself with loading the goods as this, and sometimes more, is the seller's responsibility. The buyer must pay the cost of carriage and insurance of the goods during transit.

The popularity of *fob* contracts fluctuates depending on political and economic factors. For example, because carriage is the responsibility of the buyer, the seller will prefer to contract on *fob* terms when shipping space is scarce, as was the case during the First and Second World Wars, when *fob* contracts proved popular. Further, when the cost of carriage and insurance is high, or subject to fluctuation, sellers will prefer to contract on *fob* terms.

30.2.1 Types of *fob* contracts

The *fob* contract is flexible: the parties may vary many of its incidents without changing its nature as an *fob* contract. Three basic types have been recognised:

(i) the strict, or "classic" *fob* contract;
(ii) the *fob* contract with additional duties; and,
(iii) the modern *fob* contract.[8]

---

6 [1949] A.C. 293.

7 *Wimble Sons & Co v. Rosenberg* [1913] 1 KB 279.

8 *Pyrene and Co Ltd v. Scindia Navigation Co Ltd* [1954] 2 Q.B. 402 at 424 per Devlin J.

30.2.1.1 The strict or classic fob *contract*

Under a strict or classic *fob* contract, the buyer is obliged to nominate the ship. When it arrives, it is the seller's duty to place the goods on board under a contract of carriage which the seller makes with the carrier for the account of the buyer. The seller receives the bill of lading which names him as consignor, or is made out to his order, and he transfers it to the buyer, usually on payment of the price. The carriage contract is therefore originally between the seller and the carrier.

30.2.1.2 Fob *with additional services*

An *fob* with additional services is similar to the classic *fob*, in that the seller enters into a contract of carriage with the carrier, places the goods on board and transfers the bill to the buyer, but the seller will have accepted additional duties, such as nominating the ship and/or arranging the insurance of the cargo. As a result, this type of contract may closely resemble a *cif* contract.

30.2.1.3 Modern fob contracts

With modern *fob* contracts, the buyer himself makes the carriage contract in advance, either directly or through his agent, for example, a freight forwarder, so it is the buyer who nominates the ship, and when it arrives at the port, the seller must place the goods on board in exchange for a mate's receipt. The mate's receipt is forwarded to the buyer and is used to obtain the bill of lading. Hence, the bill goes directly to the buyer, usually through his agent, and does not pass through the seller's hands. Today, this type of contract has replaced the classic *fob* contract as the norm.

30.2.2 Relations with the carrier

Under a classic *fob* contract and an *fob* with additional services contract, the contract of carriage is initially made by the seller but may be transferred to the buyer when the bill of lading is transferred.[9] Whether the seller makes the contract as agent for the buyer or as a principal depends on the contract between the seller and buyer. This may have important implications for the nature of the seller's liability to the buyer. For instance, if he acts as principal, failure to obtain shipping space in accordance with the contract of sale will amount to non-delivery, whereas if he acts as agent, he will only incur liability if he fails to exercise reasonable care in obtaining shipping space.[10]

9 See further 31.4.

10 On agent's duties, see 7.3.1.2.

Under the modern *fob* contract, the contract of carriage is between the buyer and the carrier; however, the seller needs the assistance of the carrier to load the goods and fulfil his obligations under the sale contract, and a court may find that contractual relations exist between the seller and the carrier on the terms of the contract of carriage, to facilitate this process.[11] This means that relations between the seller and the carrier may be governed by the terms of the contract of carriage, which may be significant if the goods are damaged by the carrier during loading whilst at the seller's risk.[12] In that case, therefore, the seller may have an action against the carrier, but the carrier will be protected by the terms of the contract of carriage. This is illustrated in *Pyrene and Co Ltd v. Scindia Navigation Co Ltd*,[13] an example of a modern *fob* contract. The seller had contracted to sell a fire tender *fob* London to the Indian Government. The buyer made the shipping arrangements in advance. During loading, and before the goods passed the ship's rail, the goods were dropped and damaged. The goods were therefore at the seller's risk,[14] and the seller sued the carrier for the damage. The carrier sought to rely on a limitation of liability clause in the contract of carriage. It was argued that the seller was not bound by the limitation of liability clause because of lack of privity of contract between the seller and the carrier. The court held that although the buyer had made the contract of carriage, it must have been intended to bind and benefit the seller and had therefore been made on his behalf. The buyer was obliged under the sales contract to load the goods and he must therefore be in contractual relations with the carrier. Alternatively, the court could imply a contract between the seller and the carrier, on terms identical to the carriage contract, based on the fact of delivery of the goods to the carrier and lifting the goods on board.

30.2.3 Obligations of the parties

The duties of the seller and the buyer depend on two factors: the classification of the contract as a classic, additional duties or modern *fob*, and the remaining terms of the contract. Unless there is provision to the contrary, the basic duties of the parties are as follows.

Generally, under a classic *fob* contract, the buyer must:

- (i) nominate a ship;
- (ii) notify the seller of the nomination, so that the seller can fulfil his obligations in time;
- (iii) pay the price.

11 See *Pyrene and Co Ltd v. Scindia Navigation Co Ltd* [1954] 2 Q.B. 402.
12 See 30.2.5.
13 [1954] 2 Q.B. 402.
14 See 30.2.5.

And, the seller must:

(i) make a reasonable contract;[15]
(ii) load conforming goods;
(iii) load the goods at the proper time (time is prima facie of the essence in sales contracts);[16] and
(iv) load the goods at his expense.

Under an *fob* contract with additional duties, the duties of the parties are the same as under a classic *fob* contract except that the seller must perform the extra duties imposed on him by the contract, such as arranging insurance.

Under a modern *fob* contract, the buyer must:

(i) make the contract of carriage; and
(ii) pay the price.

And, the seller must:

(i) load conforming goods on the ship nominated by buyer;
(ii) load the goods at his expense;
(iii) provide the necessary information so that the buyer can insure the goods;[17] and
(iv) transfer the relevant shipping documents, usually a mate's receipt, so that the buyer can obtain the bill of lading and collect the goods at their destination.

Some of these duties are examined in more detail below.

30.2.3.1 Nomination

Where the buyer is obliged to nominate a ship, as under strict or modern *fob* contracts, he must nominate an "effective or suitable ship". A ship is suitable if it is ready, willing and able to carry the goods from the port of shipment to the destination. The ship will not be effective or suitable if, for example, it does not arrive in time to enable the seller to perform his obligations, or at all; or if perishable goods are being transported and the ship is not equipped with cold stores; or if oil that needs heating is being transported and the ship does not have heating coils. Failure to nominate a suitable ship entitles the seller to terminate the contract, thereby releasing him from his obligation to perform and allowing him to seek damages from

15 Sale of Goods Act 1893, s.32(2).
16 See 11.2.4.
17 Sale of Goods Act 1893, s.32(3).

the buyer for non-acceptance.[18] However, where the goods have not been loaded, property will generally not have passed from seller to buyer, so the seller will not be able to sue for the price of the goods.[19]

Time for nomination is usually of the essence, that is, it is a condition of the contract. The seller may treat the contract as repudiated if the buyer fails to nominate a ship in the specified time, or if no time is specified, within a reasonable time.[20] Where a contract provides for a "shipment period" – for example, "shipment in August or September" – the buyer must nominate a suitable ship at a time which will allow for shipment during the period. Equally, the seller must load within the specified shipment period.

If the buyer's nomination is ineffective – for instance, because the nominated ship is delayed – he may be able to nominate a substitute ship provided he can still give sufficient notice of the replacement nomination to comply with the contract. He must do so as soon as possible and at his expense. If, however, there are specified time limits, a substitution can only be made within these limits, unless trade custom can be proved to the contrary. If the buyer is entitled to make a substitute nomination, failure by the seller to accept it may put the seller in breach of contract.[21] It is not clear who bears the costs of storage of the goods or risk of their deterioration while awaiting arrival of the substitute vessel; the contract should therefore contain express provisions to determine (i) whether the buyer is entitled to make a substitute nomination, and (ii) the consequences of such a substitution.

30.2.3.2 Notify the nomination

The contract will usually require the buyer to give notice, within a stated time, of the probable readiness of the ship to load, so that the seller can have the goods ready for loading. This is customary in the oil trade. This requirement to give notice will usually be a condition of the contract. In *Bunge Corpn v. Tradax Export SA*,[22] an *fob* buyer was required to give "at least fifteen consecutive days notice" of probable readiness of their ship to load the goods. The notice given was five days short. The House of Lords held that the stipulation as to time was a condition, so that breach allowed the seller to terminate the contract.

18 *Bunge Corpn v. Tradax Export SA* [1981] 2 All E.R. 513.

19 See 15.2.1.

20 *Bunge Corpn v. Tradax Export SA* [1981] 2 All E.R. 513.

21 *Agricultores Federatos Argentinos v. Ampro* [1965] 2 Lloyd's Rep. 157.

22 [1981] 2 All E.R. 513.

30.2.3.3 To provide information for insurance purposes

Section 32(3) of the Sale of Goods Act 1893 provides:

> "Unless otherwise agreed, where goods are sent by the seller to the buyer by a route involving sea transit, under circumstances in which it is usual to insure, the seller must give such notice to the buyer as may enable him to insure them during their sea transit, and, if the seller fails to do so, the goods are at his risk during such sea transit."

This provision applies to a classic or a modern *fob* contract, where the seller is under no duty to insure, but not if the seller is himself responsible for obtaining insurance cover under an additional duties *fob* contract. If the seller fails to provide the necessary information, risk does not pass to the buyer on loading, as is normal,[23] but remains with the seller during transit. Since the seller may not have insurance to cover loss of the goods during transit, he will probably have to bear any such loss himself. He should therefore be advised of the importance of providing the buyer with the necessary information. This will normally include the details of the ports of loading and delivery and of the nature and value of the goods.

30.2.3.4 To make a reasonable contract

Section 32(2) of the Sale of Goods Act 1893 states:

> "Unless otherwise authorised by the buyer, the seller must make such contract with the carrier on behalf of the buyer as may be reasonable having regard to the nature of the goods and the other circumstances of the case. If the seller omits to do so, and the goods are lost or damaged in course of transit, the buyer may decline to treat delivery to the carrier as a delivery to himself, or may hold the seller responsible in damages."

This provision applies to classic and additional duties *fob* contracts. What is reasonable depends on the nature of the goods and other circumstances, so that a reasonable contract would make provision for refrigeration for frozen food, or heating coils for certain types of oil. A contract which allows for excessive deviation may be unreasonable. In *Thos Young & Sons v. Hobson & Partners*,[24] where the seller made a contract for carriage at the consignee's risk, though the goods could have been carried at the carrier's risk for no extra cost, it was held that the seller was in breach of this provision.

---

23 See 30.2.5.

24 [1949] 65 T.L.S. 365.

30.2.3.5 To load conforming goods

Goods must conform with both the express and implied terms of the contract, including those implied by the Sale of Goods Acts 1893 and 1980.

(i) Description

It has been held that in international sales contracts, statements as to country of origin and the date of loading form part of the contract description for the purposes of section 13 of the Sale of Goods Act 1893.[25] In *Bowes v. Shand*,[26] the contract was for "600 tons of Madras rice to be shipped at Madras during March and April." The cargo tendered was shipped during February. It was held that the buyer could reject the goods for breach of section 13 because the shipment period formed part of the description. Although the "excessively technical" nature of what constitutes part of the contractual description has been criticised,[27] it seems that this criticism will not apply in relation to international sales, in particular the sale of bulk commodities. A seller seeking to avoid this "excessively technical" approach may include in the sale contract terms which restrict the scope of the description – for instance, by expressly stating that statements as to date of loading do not form part of the contract description – or limit the right of rejection. Such exclusions in an international sales contract are subject to the general law of contract, including the doctrine of fundamental breach,[28] but are not subject to any statutory regulation under the sales of goods legislation,[29] or otherwise.

(ii) Quality and fitness for purpose

The merchantability and fitness for purpose of goods, under sections 14(2) and 14(4) of the Sale of Goods Act 1893,[30] is assessed when the goods are loaded and risk of loss passes to the buyer, as this is the time of delivery under an *fob* contract. However, in order to be merchantable, it has been held that the goods must be fit when loaded to survive the transit under normal conditions.[31] Deterioration during transit will therefore be the seller's responsibility if it occurs because the goods were not merchantable on loading.

---

25 See 13.2.

26 (1877) 2 App. Cas. 455.

27 See *Reardon Smith Line Ltd v. Yngvar Hansen-Tangen* [1976] 3 All E.R. 570 at 576 *per* Lord Wilberforce; see further 13.2.

28 See 2.3.5.

29 Sale of Goods Act 1893, s.61(6).

30 See 13.3 and 13.4.

31 *Mash & Murrel v. Emmanuel* [1961] 1 All E.R. 485.

30.2.4 Passing of property

As with domestic sales of goods, property passes when the parties intend it to pass,[32] and the seller may reserve a right of disposal.[33] Where the goods are specific, property may pass at the time of the contract.[34] However, no property can pass so long as the goods remain unascertained.[35]

Where the goods are ascertained, it is presumed in *fob* contracts, on the basis of trade practice, that property passes on shipment when the goods pass the ship's rail, unless title is retained until some condition is fulfilled, for example, until the goods are paid for. Every case must be assessed on its own facts and the time when property passes depends on:

(i) the intention of the parties,
(ii) the wording of the bill of lading, and,
(iii) the surrounding circumstances.

Although the normal rule is that property passes on loading, it has been held that an *fob* seller may reserve title until payment.[36] If the seller takes the bill of lading in his own name, he is prima facie taken to have reserved a right of disposal under section 19(2) of the Sale of Goods Act 1893. This provision applies to *fob* contracts. If the seller takes the bill in his own name and has not received full payment at the time of shipment, he may be taken to have impliedly reserved title under this provision. However, section 19(2) raises only a rebuttable presumption and a court may hold, on examination of all the facts of the case, that even though the seller takes the bill in his own name, property passes on loading. For example, in *The Parchim*,[37] the seller took the bill in his own name but it was held on examination of all the facts of the case that property passed on loading. Conversely, in *Kronprinsessan Margareta*,[38] the seller took a bill in the buyer's name but retained possession of it. It was held that property had not passed because it was retained by the seller. In order to avoid disputes, the contract should contain express provisions as to the passing of property and if the seller wants to reserve title to guard against non-payment by the seller, he should expressly so provide.

30.2.5 Passing of risk

Under an *fob* contract, the general rule is that risk passes on loading when

32 Sale of Goods Act 1893, s.17: see 17.1.3.

33 Sale of Goods Act 1893, s.19: see 15.4 and 17.1.3.

34 Sale of Goods Act 1893, s.18, Rule 1: see 17.2.

35 Sale of Goods Act 1893, s.16: see 17.4. See, *e.g. Carlos Federspiel & Co v. Twigg & Co Ltd* [1957] Ll. L.R. 240.

36 *Mitsui & Co Ltd v. Flota Mercante Grancolombiana SA* [1989] 1 All E.R. 951 (C.A.).

37 [1918] A.C. 157 (P.C.).

38 [1921] A.C. 486 (P.C.).

the goods pass the ship's rail.[39] The seller thus bears the risk of loss or damage prior to loading; the buyer bears the risk of loss during the voyage. If the goods are damaged during the loading process, allocation of the risk of that damage will depend whether the goods had crossed the ship's rail before it occurred. This general rule applies even if property does not pass on loading – for example, if the cargo is part of a larger bulk, and so unascertained,[40] or if the seller reserves ownership.[41]

The buyer may therefore be at risk before owning the goods, but for insurance purposes, once the goods are at the buyer's risk, he has an insurable interest in them and can therefore insure the cargo against loss or damage.[42] Once the bill of lading is transferred to the buyer, he may enforce the contract of carriage against the carrier and sue for any damage to the goods which occurs during the voyage, including damage which occurred before transfer of the bill of lading.[43]

Conversely, the seller must bear the risk of loss or damage prior to loading even if loading is delayed. This is illustrated in *Cunningham v. Munro*,[44] where the contract was for the sale of bran *fob* Rotterdam, for October shipment. The seller delivered the cargo to the port on October 14, but the buyer could not find shipping space until two weeks later and nominated a ship loading at Rotterdam on October 28, by which time the bran had deteriorated due to overheating. The buyer refused to accept it on loading. It was held that he was entitled to reject the goods: the bran was at the seller's risk until it passed the ship's rail.

30.2.5.1 Exceptions to the general rule

By using the trade term "free on board", the parties are taken to have intended that risk is to pass on loading. This presumed intention may be excluded by an express provision in the contract. For example, the buyer may delay the passing of risk by contracting for the goods to be sold "free on board stowed": risk will then not pass until the goods are properly stowed. Alternatively, there is some authority that if the buyer instructs the seller to deliver the goods to the port prematurely and they deteriorate as a result, for instance as a result of a subsequent delay in loading, the buyer must bear the risk of that deterioration.[45] Moreover, the Sale of Goods Act

39 *Pyrene and Co Ltd v. Scindia Navigation Co Ltd* [1954] 2 Q.B. 402.

40 Sale of Goods Act 1893, s.16: see 17.4.

41 Sale of Goods Act 1893, s.19: see 15.4 and 17.1.3.

42 *Inglis v. Stock* (1885) 10 App. Cas. 263: see generally Part V.

43 See 31.4.

44 [1922] 28 Com. Cas. 42.

45 *Cunningham v. Munro* [1922] 28 Com. Cas. 42.

1893 provides instances where the passage of risk is delayed. First, the risk of loss remains with the seller if he fails to give the buyer the information necessary for the buyer to insure the goods.[46] However, in order to insure the goods, the buyer needs only to know the ports of loading and destination, and the nature and value of the goods. As a result, the only information an *fob* buyer normally needs from his seller in order to arrange insurance is the details of the port of loading where that is chosen by the seller.[47] Second, risk may also remain with the seller if he fails to make a reasonable carriage contract on behalf of the buyer allowing the buyer to refuse to treat delivery to the carrier as delivery to himself.[48]

30.3 *CIF* CONTRACTS

Under a *cif* contract, the seller is responsible for supplying the goods, insuring them and shipping them: hence "cost, insurance and freight." A *cif* contract therefore involves the seller entering into not only a sales contract but also, at a later date, insurance and carriage contracts. The seller therefore fixes a price to cover all these costs and it is he who carries the risk of fluctuations in insurance and freight costs. This type of contract is now more common than the *fob* contract. Hybrids can occur by intention or default.

Under a *cif* contract, the seller undertakes to be responsible for the transportation of, and insurance cover for the goods, to a named port of destination (the port named in the contract, *e.g.* "*cif* Cork" is the port of destination), while the buyer agrees to pay, not against delivery of the goods but against the tender of the shipping documents. The seller fulfils his part of the bargain by tendering the correct documents; he does not have to ensure the arrival of the goods, but is under a negative duty not to prevent their being delivered; he can therefore demand payment on tender of the documents.

A *cif* contract is a contract for the sale of goods; however, from a business point of view, it can be said that the purpose of a *cif* contract is not a sale of the goods themselves, but a sale of the documents relating to the goods.[49] The effectiveness of the *cif* contract depends on the transfer of the documents which gives the buyer control and rights over the goods. From the buyer's point of view, it is advantageous because he obtains the means to take delivery of the goods, the means to dispose of the goods in

46 Sale of Goods Act 1893, s.32(3): 30.2.3.3.

47 *Wimble, Sons & Co v. Rosenberg & Sons* [1913] 1 K.B. 279.

48 Sale of Goods Act 1893, s.32(2): 30.2.3.4.

49 In *Arnhold Karberg & Co v. Blyth Green Jourddin & Co* [1915] 2 K.B. 379, a *cif* contract was described as "not a sale of goods but a sale of documents relating to the goods" per Scrutton J. at 388. See also *Michel Freres Société Anonyme v. Kilkenny Woollen Mills* (1929) Ltd [1961] I.R. 157.

order to resell them or to secure a bank advance using them as security before they actually arrive at their destination, and the right to enforce the contract of carriage and the contract of insurance and recover the value of the goods if they are lost or damaged during transit. From the seller's perspective, a *cif* contract allows him to accommodate the buyer; he secures increased profits by providing carriage and insurance, he retains the right of disposal until payment, and he is not answerable for loss or damage to the goods during carriage.

30.3.1 The seller's obligations

Unless there is provision to the contrary, the seller's duties under a *cif* contract are:

(i) to ship goods which conform to the contract;
(ii) to procure a contract of carriage, under which the goods will be delivered to the destination contemplated in the contract;
(iii) to arrange for an insurance contract, upon the terms current in the trade, which will be available for the benefit of the buyer;
(iv) to make out an invoice;
(v) where necessary, to appropriate goods to the contract; and,
(vi) to tender the shipping documents to the buyer so that he may know what freight he has to pay in order to obtain delivery of the goods if they arrive,[50] or to recover for their loss if they are lost on the voyage.

30.3.1.1 To ship the goods

The seller need not actually ship the goods himself. He can fulfil his obligations under a *cif* contract by allowing his supplier to ship goods which comply with the contract terms within the relevant shipping period, as his agent; or, by appropriating to the buyer's contract goods which comply with the contract terms, already shipped by him or his agent provided they were shipped within the relevant shipping period. Indeed, a seller can fulfil his obligations under a *cif* contract by buying goods already afloat which comply with the contract terms and were shipped within the relevant shipping period by a third party, and then appropriating them to the buyer's contract. If one method becomes impossible, the general rule is that the seller must use another. So if the seller intended to ship the goods himself but cannot, he is expected, for instance, to buy compatible goods afloat.

50 Freight may be pre-paid by the seller; if not, the invoice should be discounted for the amount of freight due, so that the buyer does not pay for freight twice: once to the seller under the *cif* contract and again to the carrier.

30.3.1.2 To appropriate the goods to the contract

Unless the contract is for specific goods, the seller must appropriate goods to the contract. Here the word "appropriation" is used not in its proprietary sense but rather in its contractual sense. In this context, appropriation means that the goods are nominated, or earmarked for the buyer's contract: property only passes when goods are unconditionally appropriated.[51]

Some sales contracts expressly require that a notice of appropriation be sent to the buyer so that he can in turn deal with the goods. Once this happens, the goods cannot be used for any other contract, and if they are, the buyer can sue the seller for breach of contract. Conversely, the seller cannot substitute other goods for those appropriated to the contract without the buyer's consent. Usually, appropriation occurs on service of notice of appropriation or when the shipping documents are tendered. A buyer should contract for service of notice of appropriation, as this enables him to make arrangements to resell or pledge the goods.

30.3.1.3 To tender the shipping documents

The contract normally requires the seller to tender the following:

(i) a bill of lading,
(ii) an insurance policy, and
(iii) an invoice.

The first two documents ensure that if the goods are lost or damaged during transit, the buyer will generally have a right of action against either the carrier or the insurer. The invoice contains a description of the goods and a statement of the price; it may be needed to clear the goods through customs.

These basic requirements may be varied by the express terms of the contract, either by imposing qualifications on the basic documents to be tendered or by requiring the tender of additional documents. Buyers should be as specific as possible in defining in the sales contract the shipping documents to be tendered. In practice, buyers usually demand that the shipping documents include the following:

(i) A full set of clean, shipped, transferable, bills of lading covering the whole transit (bills are usually issued in triplicate);
(ii) An assignable marine insurance policy on the usual terms covering only the goods being sold, for the whole transit. The buyer could also require that the insurance be taken out with a

51 Sale of Goods Act 1893, s.18, Rule 5; see 17.4.

company which meets its approval; that the policy covers "all risks;" or that the goods be insured to an agreed valuation.

(iii) An invoice, identifying the goods in accordance with the sales contract description, inclusive of the *cif* price. If freight is not pre-paid by the seller, the invoice should be discounted for the amount of freight due. Where a letter of credit is being used to finance the transaction, the description in the invoice and the letter of credit should correspond.[52]

The buyer can reject the documents tendered if they do not correspond to the contract requirements. The more specific the buyer's requirements, therefore, the greater the scope for rejection. So, using the above example of shipping documents required, the buyer could reject the tender if:

(i) the bill is not clean, that is, it is claused;
(ii) the bill is a received for shipment, as opposed to a shipped, bill;[53]
(iii) the bill tendered is a straight consigned bill, and hence is not transferable;
(iv) anything less than an insurance policy, such as an insurance certificate or a cover note, is tendered;
(v) the insurance contract fails to cover the whole transit or the usual risks; or,
(vi) the invoice does not identify the goods being sold.

The bill of lading will identify the goods. However, it will generally give the buyer no guarantee that the goods shipped are of the required quality. The buyer will, therefore, often require additional documents, such as certificates of origin, quality or inspection, or export or import licences to be tendered.

Where the seller is consigning the goods to himself, or is in a particularly strong position, or where there is a good trading relationship established between the buyer and the seller, the contract may provide for the tender and acceptance of other, perhaps lesser or more convenient documents, such as delivery orders instead of a bill of lading or an insurance certificate instead of a policy.

30.3.1.4 Time of tender

If a time for tender is specified it must be strictly complied with; late tender allows the buyer to reject the documents and terminate the contract.[54]

52 Uniform Customs and Practice for Documentary Credits (UCP 500), Art. 37(c): see further 32.2.

53 A received for shipment bill can be tendered where the words "since shipped" and a date is attached, thus effectively turning the bill into a shipped bill.

54 *Toepfer v. Lenersan - Poortman NV* [1980] 1 Lloyd's Rep. 143 (C.A.); *cf Sanders v. Maclean* (1883) 11 Q.B.D. 327 (C.A.) .

Where there is no stipulation as to the time for tender, the documents must be forwarded with reasonable despatch. It is unclear whether failure to do so gives the buyer the right to reject the documents and terminate the contract. However, the buyer may be able to serve notice fixing a time for tender and making time of the essence. The contract should normally fix a time for tender and expressly deal with the consequences of late tender.

30.3.1.5 A right to re-tender?

There is some authority that a seller who has tendered defective documents may re-tender, if he can do so within the contract period.[55] In contrast, in *Kwei Tek Chao v. British Traders and Shippers Ltd*,[56] Devlin J. was of the opinion that a buyer was entitled to reject documents which do not conform with the contract *and* terminate the contract. Accordingly, the position is unclear and the contract should therefore contain an express provision to deal with this possibility.

30.3.2 The buyer's obligations

The general rule[57] that delivery of the goods and payment of the price are concurrent obligations is displaced in *cif* contracts where, unless otherwise agreed, the buyer must be ready and willing to pay the price against tender of the documents.[58] Provided that the documents accord with the contract, the buyer must accept them and pay the price: rejection of the documents and non-payment of the price is a breach of contract which allows the seller to terminate the contract and sue for damages. The buyer can therefore only avoid payment at this stage if:

(i) the contract on its true construction is not a *cif* contract, but rather some type of arrival contract where the seller is responsible for the good's arrival;[59] or,
(ii) the shipping documents do not conform with the requirements of the sales contract.[60]

30.3.2.1 Where the goods are lost

Even if the goods are lost in transit, the seller is still entitled to tender the

55 *Borrowman, Phillips & Co v. Free and Hollis* (1887) 4 Q.B.D 500.
56 [1954] 2 Q.B. 459.
57 Sale of Goods Act 1893, s.28: see generally Chapter 11.
58 *Biddel Bros v. E Clement Horst Co* [1911] 1 K.B. 214.
59 See *e.g. The Julia* [1949] A.C. 293: see further 31.1.1.
60 See 30.3.1.3.

documents and claim the purchase price. This rule applies even if at the time of tender the seller knows that the cargo has been lost.[61] Generally this causes no hardship to the buyer who has a remedy against the insurers or the carrier. However, the rule applies even where the buyer has no such right, for instance because the goods are lost without fault on the part of the carrier due to an uninsured risk. The buyer must then bear the loss, because he is at risk from shipment. For example, in *Groom v. Barber*,[62] on August 20, the seller appropriated to the buyer's contract the cargo of a named ship. In fact, unknown to the buyer, the ship was sunk by a submarine on August 6. On August 21, the sinking became public knowledge and the buyer rejected the tender and refused to pay. It was held that the buyer was obliged to pay, even though the contract of sale provided that war risks were for the buyer's account and so the policy of insurance did not cover loss of the cargo due to enemy action.

30.3.2.2 Where the goods are defective

The buyer must accept and pay for the documents even if the goods themselves are defective. The buyer may have a separate right to reject the goods themselves on arrival.[63]

30.3.3 The seller's remedies

If the buyer fails to perform any of his obligations, the seller has the usual remedies of a seller under the Sale of Goods Acts 1893 and 1980, as amended by any express terms of the contract. In particular, if the buyer wrongfully rejects the documents or the goods, the seller can terminate the contract and sue the buyer for non-acceptance.[64]

30.3.4 The buyer's remedies

The buyer's remedies depend on whether the seller has breached a condition of the contract, in which case he can reject the goods and sue for damages; or a warranty, in which case he must accept the goods but has a claim in damages.[65] Breach of a condition under a *cif* contract gives the buyer, in effect, two rights to reject:

(i) he can reject the documents when they are tendered, and

61 *Manbre Saccharine v. Corn Products* [1919] 1 K.B. 198; and *State Trading Corporation of India v. Golodetz* [1988] 2 Lloyd's Rep. 182.

62 [1915] 1 K.B. 316.

63 See 30.3.4.2.

64 See generally Chapter 15.

65 See 10.4. and Chapter 14.

(ii) he can reject the goods when they are landed and when after examination they are found not to be in conformity with the contract.[66]

30.3.4.1 Right to reject the documents

A buyer can reject documents which do not comply with the contract: for instance, if the bill is claused, showing that the goods were not in good condition when loaded; or if the bill is dated outside the shipment period; or if the bill discloses deficiencies in quantity; or if an insurance certificate is tendered instead of a policy. This right to reject the documents is lost if the buyer (or bank where payment is through a letter of credit)[67] takes up the documents, even though inaccurate, and pays the price without objection. For example, in *Panchaud Freres SA v. Establissments General Grain Co*,[68] the contract of sale was for a quantity of Brazilian maize, *cif* Antwerp, shipment June/July 1965. The maize was actually loaded during August, but the seller tendered a bill of lading falsely dated July 31, and a certificate of quality from loading supervisors stating that they had drawn samples on 10 and 12 August. This certificate formed part of the shipping documents which were taken up and paid for by the buyer, so the fact of late shipment was apparent. The buyer nevertheless accepted the documents. They were therefore precluded from complaining of the late shipment.

Moreover, if a defect in the goods is apparent on the face of the documents the buyer who accepts the documents will also be unable to reject the goods themselves on arrival for that defect. It is therefore vital that the buyer, or the bank, checks the documents carefully to ensure they conform to the contract before accepting them.

If the documents do correspond to the contract, the buyer cannot reject them on the grounds of defects in the goods, and if the buyer does reject documents in such a case he will be in breach of contract. In *Berger & Co Inc v. Gill & Dufus SA*,[69] the buyers rejected a tender of documents and tried to justify their rejection on the grounds that the goods, when delivered, did not correspond to the contract description. The House of Lords held that they could not do so and were in breach of contract; however, the fact that the goods would not have conformed to the contract could be taken into account by the court when assessing damages.

66 *Kwei Tek Chao v. British Traders and Shippers Ltd* [1954] 2 Q.B. 459.

67 See 32.2.

68 [1970] 1 Lloyd's Rep. 53.

69 [1984] A.C. 382; see further Treitel, "Rights of rejection under c.i.f. sales" [1984] *Lloyd's Maritime and Commercial Law Quarterly* 565.

30.3.4.2 Right to reject the goods

A buyer who has accepted documents may still reject the goods if, on arrival, they do not comply with the terms of the contract. However, he may only do so for defects not apparent from the documents, so if a buyer accepts documents which show that the goods were damaged on loading, he cannot then reject the goods when they arrive on that ground.[70]

The buyer will be deemed to have accepted the documents if he deals with them before the goods arrive – for instance, by using them to resell or pledge the goods. A buyer who deals with the documents in this way therefore loses the right to reject the goods themselves for defects apparent from the documents.[71] Any rejection must be clear and unequivocal.

30.3.4.3 Damages

Even where the buyer has lost the right to reject the goods – for instance because he accepted documents which indicated that the goods were defective – he may nevertheless claim damages for the seller's breach of contract. In practice, the buyer will generally not reject the goods after acceptance of the documents. He, or his bank, will have paid the price on presentation of the documents, and rejection of the goods will therefore leave him in the position of having to pursue the seller to recover the price. It will generally be better for the buyer to accept the goods and then bring a claim for damages for breach of warranty.

Damages will be assessed in accordance with the general rules for buyer's claims for breach of warranty so that the basic measure will be the difference between the value which goods corresponding with the contract would have had, and the actual value of the goods delivered.[72] Where the market value of the contract goods falls between the date of tender of the documents and the date of delivery of the goods, the buyer may therefore find that a claim in damages leaves him worse off than if he had rejected the documents. Where a defect in the documents is concealed by the fraud of the seller (or his predecessors in title), the buyer can claim additional damages to cover any loss he could have avoided if the defect had been apparent on the documents and he had rejected them.[73]

30.3.5 Passage of property

Again, the basic rule is that property passes when the parties intend it to

---

70 *Kwei Tek Chao v. British Traders and Shippers Ltd* [1954] 2 Q.B. 459.

71 See 14.2.1.

72 See 14.3.4.

73 *Kwei Tek Chao v. British Traders and Shippers Ltd* [1954] 2 Q.B. 459.

pass,[74] and no property can pass in unascertained goods.[75] Under a *cif* contract, property usually passes when the buyer (or the bank when a letter of credit is being used)[76] receives the shipping documents and pays the price, and the buyer thus acquires the right of disposal.[77] However, this is only a presumption, so that if, for example, the contract is for specific goods, property could pass when the contract is made; or on shipment if the goods are then ascertained;[78] or when the notice of appropriation is given (though this would be rare). Where the bill of lading is made to the seller's order, he is presumed to have reserved title.[79] Express provisions dealing with passing of property will generally avoid disputes and uncertainty.

30.3.6 Passage of risk

The general rule that risk passes with property is displaced with *cif* contracts.[80] Risk of loss of, or damage to the goods usually passes when the goods pass over the ship's rail, and the goods travel at the buyer's risk, although the seller is responsible for the payment of freight and the insurance premium. If the seller sells goods already afloat, risk passes when the seller tenders the documents, but does so retrospectively as from shipment, so that the buyer bears the risk even of any loss which has already occurred prior to the tender of the documents.[81] He is protected by the availability of actions against either the carrier or the insurers. However, where any loss is not covered by the insurance contract or the carriage contract, the buyer will have to bear that loss personally. For instance, in *Manbre Saccharine v. Corn Products*,[82] goods were lost when a ship sank during World War I. The insurance contract, which covered the usual terms when it was taken out, did not cover "war risks" and therefore the buyer would have had to pay for the goods while receiving nothing. In fact, the buyer escaped liability because the seller tendered the wrong documents. Furthermore, section 32(2) of the Sale of Goods Act 1893 applies to *cif* contracts, so that risk of loss may rest with the seller unless he makes a reasonable contract of carriage.[83]

---

74 Sale of Goods Act 1893, s.17 and 18: see 17.1 and 17.2.

75 Sale of Goods Act 1893, s.16: see 17.4.

76 See generally Chapter 32.

77 *The Miramichci* [1915] P. 71.

78 See *e.g. McKelvie v. Wallace Bros Ltd* [1919] 2 I.R. 250.

79 Sale of Goods Act 1893, s.19(2): see 15.4 and 17.1.3.

80 Sale of Goods Act 1893, s.20: see Chapter 18.

81 *Comptoir d'Achat et de Vente du Boerenbond Belge SA v. Luis de Ridder Limitada* [1949] A.C. 293, [1949] 1 All E.R. 269 (H.L.). See further Felthem, "The Appropriation to a CIF contract of goods lost or damaged at sea" [1975] *Journal of Business Law* 273.

82 [1919] 1 K.B. 198.

83 See 30.2.3.4. Generally, section 32(3) of the Sale of Goods Act 1893 (see 30.2.3.3) has no application to *cif* contracts because under a *cif* contract the seller is responsible for arranging carriage and insurance: see *Law and Bonar v. British American Tobacco Co. Ltd.* [1916] 2 K.B. 605

CHAPTER 31

CARRIAGE OF GOODS BY SEA

31.1 INTRODUCTION

International sales contracts often require the goods to be shipped, so it is important for a commercial lawyer to have an understanding of contracts for the carriage of goods by sea.[1] Depending on the terms of the sale contract, it may be the seller's or the buyer's duty to arrange shipment of the goods.[2] For the purposes of this chapter, the person who arranges the carriage will be referred to as "the shipper".

In *Heskell v. Continental Express*,[3] Devlin J. outlined the standard practice when shipping goods. First, the shipper or his agent (a freight forwarder) needs to determine when a suitable ship is sailing to the particular port, book space on the ship for the goods with the carrier or his agent (a loading broker), and deliver the goods to the port. On delivering the goods to the carrier, the shipper receives a mate's receipt for the goods and, using this, fills in the details on the bill of lading. Next, the bill of lading is presented to the carrier or his representative, perhaps the master of the ship, who checks the details on the bill (dates, ports of shipment and destination, description, quantity of goods and apparent condition, etc.) against the goods and, if there are no discrepancies, signs the bill, making any necessary amendments, and issues it to the shipper, in return for the mate's receipt. The shipper forwards the bill, by post, to the person responsible for collecting the goods, the consignee. The consignee may be a buyer, or someone acting for the shipper. If the former, the shipper usually only transfers the bill in return for payment of the price. Finally, the consignee presents the bill of lading to the carrier at the destination: the master usually will not release the goods without presentation of the bill. In practice, one way around this is through the use of an indemnity, whereby the consignee agrees to indemnify the carrier against any claims that may arise due to the carrier handing over the goods without presentation of the bill of lading.

Important changes have occurred in practice since *Heskell*. For instance, mates' receipts are not often used today. Instead, goods are

1 See generally, *Schmitthoff's Export Trade: The Law and Practice of International Trade* (London, Sweet & Maxwell, 10th ed., 2000) Chapter 15; Forde, *Commercial Law* (Dublin, Butterworths, 2nd ed., 1997) Chapter 11.

2 See generally Chapter 30.

3 [1950] 1 All E.R. 1033.

usually forwarded to the port with a Standard Shipping Note (see Appendix D) or, if necessary, a Dangerous Goods Note (see Appendix E) containing details of the goods which, when signed, is issued to the shipper as a receipt. Also, it is more common now for the carrier to prepare the bill of lading by computer from the details given by the shipper when booking space on the ship. Indeed, the use of bills of lading has declined, especially when the voyage is short, where they have been replaced by the sea waybill (see Appendix G).[4] Moreover, the development of containerisation and the use of multimodal transport (combining carriage by road, rail and sea, for example, rather than just from port to port), and, multimodal or combined transport documents, has given rise to new legal questions.[5] For example, are such documents documents of title? The bill of lading was recognised as a document of title following commercial practice.[6] It could be argued that today, commercial practice recognises the use of multimodal transport documents as documents of title, and hence they should also be recognised as documents of title at common law.[7] The question remains unanswered. Nevertheless, and despite their decreasing use, bills of lading still play a vital role in shipping transactions and therefore warrant further examination (see Appendix F).

31.2 Bills of Lading

A bill of lading is a transport document with unique characteristics. It has three functions:

(i) it evidences the contract of carriage,
(ii) it is a receipt for the goods, and
(iii) it is a document of title.

We will examine each of these functions in more detail.

31.2.1 Evidence of the contract of carriage

The contract of carriage is concluded between the shipper and the carrier, or through their agents, usually before the goods are shipped; often when

4 See 31.3.1.

5 See Ramberg, "The Combined Transport Operator" [1968] *Journal of Business Law* 132; Diplock, "The Combined Transport Document" [1972] *Journal of Business Law* 269; Faber, "The Problems arising from multimodal transport" [1996] *Lloyd's Maritime and Commercial Law Quarterly* 503. See also U.N. Convention on International Multimodal Transport of Goods (1980). See further 31.3.1.

6 *Lickbarrow v. Mason* (1794) 5 T.R. 683: see further 31.2.3.

7 For example, INCOTERMS recognises the use of multimodal transport documents and the UCP 500 also recognises such documents by allowing banks to accept them under documentary credit arrangements: see generally 32.2.

the shipper books space on the ship for his goods; perhaps on loading of the goods; or acceptance for loading by the carrier.[8] Hence, the bill of lading cannot be the contract: but it can evidence the contract. The terms and conditions of carriage are detailed on the back of modern standard form bills, so when the bill is issued or signed by the master it evidences a contract that was previously concluded. More recently, a "short form" bill has been promoted: here the terms and conditions of carriage are not printed on the back of the short form bill, which is issued to the shipper, but are incorporated by reference to the carrier's standard terms which are available for inspection.[9]

To regulate the shipment of goods, rules were developed by the international shipping community which set out the duties and liabilities of the parties to the carriage contract.[10] Today, three different sets of rules (each an amendment to its predecessor) are in force:

(a) the Hague Rules, 1924;[11]
(b) the Hague-Visby Rules, 1968/1979;[12] and
(c) the Hamburg Rules, 1978.[13]

Currently, the Hague-Visby Rules are incorporated into Irish law by the Merchant Shipping (Liability of Shipowners and Other) Act 1996.[14]

31.2.1.1 Application

Article X of the Hague-Visby Rules and sections 31, 33 and 34 of the Merchant Shipping (Liability of Shipowners and Other) Act 1996 provide

8 *Sewell v. Burdick* (1884) 10 App. Cas. 74 at 105 per Lord Bramwell; *Heskell v. Continental* Express [1950] 1 All E.R. 1033.

9 See Williams, "Waybills and Short Form Documents: A lawyer's view" [1979] *Lloyd's Maritime and Commercial Law Quarterly* 297. On incorporation of standard terms, see generally 2.3.2.1.

10 See 29.4.2.

11 The Hague Rules were incorporated into Irish law by the Merchant Shipping Act 1947, s.13 and the Second Schedule. This legislation is now repealed by the Merchant Shipping (Liability of Shipowners and Other) Act 1996, s.3 and the Fourth Schedule. By 1977, when the Hague-Visby Rules came into effect, there were more than 60 ratifications and accessions to the Hague Rules. Many states, including the U.S.A. (see the Carriage of Goods by Sea Act, 1936) remain loyal to the Hague Rules.

12 At the time of writing, 28 states, including Ireland and the U.K. (see the Carriage of Goods by Sea Act 1971) have adopted the Hague-Visby Rules.

13 At the time of writing, 28 states have signed the Hamburg Rules, including Germany and France, though the remaining signatories are said to represent a total of little more than five per cent of world trade, being developing counties in the main: see Wilson, *Carriage of Goods by Sea* (Harlow, Longman, 4th ed., 2001) pp.120–121. See generally, Tetley, "The Hamburg Rules – A commentary" [1979] *Lloyd's Maritime and Commercial Law Quarterly* 1; Waldron, "The Hamburg Rules – A Boondoggle for Lawyers?" [1991] *Journal of Business Law* 305.

14 1996 Act, Part IV and the Third Schedule. The 1996 Act came into force on February 6, 1997: S.I. No. 215 of 1997

for the application of the Rules.[15] Section 31 states that the Rules shall have the force of law in the State,[16] while Article X provides that the Rules apply:[17]

> "to every bill of lading relating to the carriage of goods between ports in two different states if:
> (a) the bill of lading is issued in a Contracting State, or
> (b) the carriage is from a port in a Contracting State, or
> (c) the contract contained in or evidenced in the bill of lading provides that the rules of this Convention or legislation in any State giving effect to them are to govern the contract whatever may be the nationality of the ship, the carrier, the shipper, the consignee, or any other interested party."

The Rules clearly envisage an international carriage of goods between ports in two different states, but section 34 of the 1996 Act extends the operation of the Rules to cover coastal trade. It would also appear that the Rules do not apply to contracts of carriage where a waybill, or other non-transferable document, is issued because these do not constitute documents of title.[18] However, section 33(1)(b) of the 1996 Act extends the application of the Rules to any receipt which is a non-transferable document which expressly provides that the Rules are to govern the contract as if the receipt was a bill of lading. Further, section 33(2) extends the application of the Rules to a contract of carriage under a bill of lading or receipt of deck cargo and live animals, although deck cargo and live animals are excluded from the definition of goods under Article I(c) of the Rules.

15 The application of the Hague-Visby Rules is considerably wider than that of the Hague Rules. Essentially, under the Merchant Shipping Act 1947, the Hague Rules only applied when goods were shipped from an Irish port, that is, outward voyages only. In other circumstances, parties could expressly adopt the Hague Rules using what is known as a "clause paramount".

16 See *Morviken* [1983] 1 Lloyd's Rep. 1 (H.L.), where under English law, the Hague-Visby Rules were held to apply despite a choice of law clause in favour of Dutch law. See further Jackson, "The Hague-Visby Rules and forum, arbitration and choice of law clauses" [1980] *Lloyd's Maritime and Commercial Law Quarterly* 159; Mann, "Uniform Statutes in English Law" (1983) 99 *Law Quarterly Review* 376, cf. Diamond, "The Hague-Visby Rules" [1978] *Lloyd's Maritime and Commercial Law Quarterly* 225; Morris, "The Scope of the Carriage of Goods by Sea Act 1971" (1979) 95 *Law Quarterly Review* 59.

17 See generally, Wilson, *Carriage of Goods by Sea* (Harlow, Longman, 4th ed., 2001) pp.176–180.

18 See also Art. I(b) which defines a contract of carriage as a contract covered by a bill of lading or any similar document of title, and see the 1996 Act, s.33(3). The Hague Rules were also limited in their application to bills of lading, and in *Burns & Laird Line Ltd v. Hugh Mack & Co Ltd* (1944) 78 I.L.T.R. 56, it was held that the Hague Rules had no application where goods are not sent under a bill of lading but are shipped under a non-transferable receipt. The application of the Hamburg Rules is wider again, not being limited to contracts of carriage under bills of lading, for example: Arts 1 and 4. See generally Wilson, *Carriage of Goods by Sea* (Harlow, Longman, 4th ed., 2001) pp.213–214.

31.2.1.2 Duties of the parties

The Rules set out the duties of the parties. For example, the Rules require the carrier:

> "(i) to exercise due diligence, before, and at the beginning of the voyage to, make the ship seaworthy, properly man, equip and supply the ship and generally make the ship fit and safe for the reception, carriage and preservation of the goods;[19]
>
> (ii) to properly and carefully load, handle, stow, carry, keep, care for and discharge the goods carried;[20] and
>
> (iii) on demand from the shipper, to issue a bill of lading showing leading marks of identification; either the number of packages or pieces, or the quantity, or weight; and the apparent order and condition of the goods."[21]

The shipper, on the other hand, is required not to ship dangerous goods without informing the carrier.[22]

31.2.1.3 Exclusion and limitation of liability

The carrier's liability for breach of the carriage contract is excluded in certain circumstances, and can be limited in others. Importantly, Article IV, rule 2 states that the carrier has no liability for loss or damage arising or resulting from, *inter alia*, act, neglect or default of the master, mariner, pilot, or the servants of the carrier in the navigation or in the management of the ship; fire, unless caused by the actual fault or privity of the carrier; perils of the sea; act of God; act of war; act of public enemies; seizure under legal process; quarantine restrictions; act or omission of the shipper; strikes; riots; saving or attempting to save life or property at sea; wastage in bulk or weight arising from inherent defect of the goods; insufficient packing; insufficient marks; latent defects; and any other cause arising without the actual fault or privity of the carrier. Moreover, any deviation in saving or attempting to save life or property at sea, or any reasonable deviation is not a breach of contract and the carrier is not responsible for any loss or damage resulting therefrom.[23]

In relation to the limitation of liability, unless the nature and value of the goods has been declared before shipment and entered on the bill of lading, the carrier's liability is limited under Article IV, Rule 5. The

---

19 Art. III, rule 1.

20 Art. III, rule 2.

21 Art. III, rule 3.

22 Art. IV, rule 6.

23 Art. IV, rule 4.

financial limit is linked to "the special drawing right" defined by the International Monetary Fund, a variable sum which tracks inflation, and is calculated on the basis of package or weight.[24]

Lastly, and in order to protect the position of shippers, Article III, rule 8 provides that any clause relieving or lessening the liability of the carrier, as set out in the Rules, shall be null and void.

31.2.1.4 Limitation period

The limitation period for claims is one year from the delivery of the goods or when they should have been delivered.[25]

31.2.2 A receipt

It has been stated that a ship must "deliver what she receives, as she receives it."[26] This means that if the goods are lost or damaged while in transit, the carrier may be liable. For a shipper or his consignee to pursue such a claim, it is necessary to know the quantity and condition of the goods on receipt by the carrier or on shipment. Also, if a shipper is planning to deal with goods while they are at sea, by selling or pledging them, for instance, he will require some form of evidence that proves that the goods exist and provides details as to the quantity and condition of the goods. Written records are relied on as evidence for these purposes, the most important being the bill of lading. A bill of lading can be either:

(i) a "received for shipment" bill – that is, a bill of lading evidencing the quantity and condition of the goods when they are received for shipment, or,
(ii) a "shipped" bill - that is, a bill of lading which evidences the quantity and condition of the goods on shipment.

As noted above, when the Hague-Visby Rules apply, the shipper is entitled to demand from the carrier a bill of lading showing, *inter alia*:

(i) leading marks of identification;
(ii) either the number of packages or pieces, or the quantity, or weight; and
(iii) the apparent order and condition of the goods.[27]

---

24 Art. IV, rule 5, and 1996 Act, s.36. Under the Hague Rules liability was limited to £100 per package or unit. It was partly because this financial limit could not be justifed, given the rate of inflation since 1924, that the Hague Rules were revised.

25 Art. III, rule 6.

26 *FC Bradley & Son Ld v. Federal Steam Navigation Co Ltd* (1927) 27 Ll. L. Rep. 395 at 396 per Lord Sumner.

27 Art. III, rule 3.

In return, the shipper is deemed to have guaranteed to the carrier the accuracy of any information supplied by him for incorporation in the bill, and the shipper is required to indemnify the carrier against any loss, damages or expenses arising from any such inaccuracies.[28] A shipper should therefore always demand a bill with these details, but a carrier can refuse to issue a bill with such information where he has reasonable grounds for suspecting that the information supplied is inaccurate or where he has no reasonable means of checking.[29]

The evidential status of the bill of lading is addressed at common law, as amended by the Bills of Lading Act 1855; and under the Hague-Visby Rules, as adopted by the Merchant Shipping (Liability of Shipowners and Others) Act 1996. In considering the evidential status of the bill of lading, distinctions need to be drawn between statements as to quantity and statements as to apparent condition; and the status of the bill in the hands of the shipper and the status of the bill in the hands of a consignee.

31.2.2.1 Bills covered by the Hague-Visby Rules

The Hague-Visby Rules provide that a bill of lading is prima facie evidence of the quantity and apparent condition of the goods at the time of loading.[30] As this raises only a presumption, the carrier can produce evidence to dispute any statements in the bill.[31] However, proof to the contrary is inadmissible when the bill of lading is transferred to a third party acting in good faith. In these circumstances, the bill is conclusive evidence as to the quantity and apparent condition of the goods. A transferee's position is better than that of the original shipper because, unlike the original shipper, he has no information as to the state of the goods on loading other than what is stated in the bill.

31.2.2.2 At common law, as amended

This position is dealt with at common law, as amended by section 3 of the Bill of Lading Act 1855. In the hands of the original shipper, statements in the bill as to quantity and condition are prima facie evidence. However, once the bill comes into the hands of a third party, statements as to the condition of the goods are binding on the carrier. If a bill states that the goods are loaded in "good order and condition", the carrier is estopped

28 Art. III, rule 5.
29 Art. III, rule 3.
30 Art. III, rule 4.
31 *Smith v. Bedouin Steam Navigation Co* [1896] A.C. 70.

from denying the truth of this statement.[32] This estoppel operates only in favour of a transferee who takes the bill for value in good faith and relies on it. However, if the bill is claused, that is, there is an annotation on the bill to the effect that the goods are in some way defective, the carrier can raise evidence to prove the condition of the goods loaded.

The position as regards statements as to *quantity* is different. It was decided in *Grant v. Norway*,[33] that a ship's master had no authority to sign a bill where goods were not actually loaded. Hence, where the bill overstates the quantity loaded or states that no goods were loaded at all, the carrier may dispute the statement in the bill as to the amount shipped. Today, it is widely recognised that *Grant v. Norway* is inconsistent with general agency principles,[34] and indeed the courts have gone to great lengths to avoid its strict application.[35] Section 3 of the Bills of Lading Act 1855 was intended to solve the problem of *Grant v. Norway* by providing that the bill should: "… be conclusive evidence of such shipment as against the master or other person signing the same …" However, section 3 is fundamentally flawed. It does not make the bill conclusive evidence against the carrier, only against the master or other signatory against whom there is usually no cause of action, since such people are rarely contractually liable. Even if the master was personally liable, he does not have the same deep pocket as the carrier.

Many of the problems caused by *Grant v. Norway* have been addressed by the Hague-Visby Rules. As noted above, under Article III, rule 4, a bill of lading is prima facie evidence of the quantity and condition of the goods at the time of loading against the carrier, while proof to the contrary is inadmissible when the bill is transferred to a third party acting in good faith. However, there are gaps in this provision – where no goods at all are shipped, for example, or where there is a "weight and quantity unknown" clause.[36] In light of this unsatisfactory position, in the United Kingdom, the Carriage of Goods by Sea Act 1992 abolished the rule in *Grant v. Norway*, and following the rationale of section 3 of the 1855 Act, provides that a bill of lading, representing goods that are received or shipped, in the hands of a lawful holder is conclusive evidence of such receipt or shipment as against the carrier.[37] A similar provision can be found in the U.S. Federal

32 *Compania Naviera Vasconzada v. Churchill and Sim* [1906] 1 K.B. 237.

33 (1851) 10 C.B. 665.

34 See, *e.g. Lloyd v. Grace Smith & Co* [1912] A.C. 716 where the House of Lords held that a firm of solicitors was responsible for the fraud of its agent; see further Reynolds, "Warranty of Authority" (1967) *Law Quarterly Review* 189.

35 The master may be held liable for breach of warranty of authority: see *Rasnoimport v. Guthrie & Co Ltd* [1966] 1 Lloyd's Rep. 1, and 6.4.5; or possibly for negligent mis-statement.

36 See, *e.g. New Chinese Antimony Co Ltd v. Ocean Steamship Co Ltd* [1917] 2 K.B. 664. See further Debattista, "The Bill of Lading as a Receipt – missing oil in unknown quantities" [1986] *Lloyd's Maritime and Commercial Law Quarterly* 97.

37 1992 Act, s.4.

Bills of Lading Act 1916.[38] The U.K. Carriage of Goods by Sea Act is not without its critics;[39] it too leaves gaps. For instance, the provision applies only to bills of lading as defined by the Act, and not to other non-transferable documents. Hence, a straight-bill, waybill or delivery order can never be conclusive evidence. Clearly, the abolition of the rule in *Grant v. Norway* is long overdue in Ireland, but any reform should be made in light of experience abroad.

31.2.3 A document of title[40]

In *Lickbarrow v. Mason*,[41] a bill of lading was recognised as a document of title, because in practice it was treated as such. By recognising trade custom in this way, the court was facilitating trade. Professor Goode identified three requirements for a document to be recognised as a document of title at common law:

(i) it must be issued by a bailee of the goods, so that it operates as an advance attornment to any transferee;
(ii) it must relate to identified goods; and
(iii) there must be a custom recognising that transfer of the document transfers constructive possession or control of the goods.[42]

The bill of lading thus symbolises the goods and proper transfer of the bill effects a transfer of property in, or ownership of the goods.[43]

31.2.3.1 Transfer of property

The time when property passes depends on:

(i) the intention of the parties,
(ii) the wording of the bill, and,
(iii) the surrounding circumstances.

---

38 1916 Act, s.22.

39 See, *e.g.* Bradgate & White, "The Carriage of Goods by Sea Act 1992"(1993) 56 *Modern Law Review* 188.

40 See Dromgoole & Baatz, "The Bill of Lading as a Document of Title" in Palmer & McKendrick eds., *Interests in Goods* (London, Lloyd's of London Press, 2nd ed., 1998) Chapter 22.

41 (1794) 5 T.R. 683.

42 Goode, *Proprietary Rights and Insolvency in Sales Transactions* (London, Sweet & Maxwell, 2nd ed., 1989) p.61. Note that a wider category of documents of title is recognised by the Factors Act for the purposes of that Act: see the Factors Act 1889, s.1(4): see further 20.2.1.2. See also Tettenborn, "Transferable and negotiable documents of title – a redefinition?" [1991] *Lloyd's Maritime and Commercial Law Quarterly* 538.

43 *Bateman v. Green* (1868) I.R. 2 C.L. 166.

(i) Intention

The basic rule is that property in goods passes when the parties intend it to pass.[44] So, for example, when a bill is assigned to a bank as security for a loan, the transfer does not pass property in the goods to the bank because the necessary intention is lacking. Instead, the bank has a security interest in the goods represented by the bill.[45]

(ii) Wording

Bills of lading can be classified under three headings:

(a) bearer bills;
(b) straight bills; or
(c) order bills.

Where no consignee is named in the bill, the bill is a "bearer bill" which may be transferred by simple delivery, so that any person can present the bill at the port of destination and seek delivery of the goods. This type of bill is rarely used due to the danger of theft and the potential for fraud. If, on the other hand, the bill is made out to a named consignee, it is known as a "straight consigned bill". Such a bill cannot be transferred, and only the named consignee can seek delivery of the goods at the port of destination. This type of bill is useful where the shipper has no intention of selling the goods while at sea, as when he is shipping goods to himself. Lastly, the most common type of bill in use is known as an "order bill," where a bill is made out to a named party and the words "or order" are included: for instance, "to Fidelma White, or order". The inclusion of the two words "or order" makes the bill transferable, so where it is contemplated that the goods may be sold or pledged while afloat, these words should be included. The bill is transferred by indorsement and delivery of the bill, and often the goods are sold numerous times over with the bill being indorsed and delivered each time. On transfer of an order bill, the carrier attorns that he holds the goods as bailee for the benefit of the transferee and subject to his directions.[46]

Where goods are shipped and the bill of lading provides that the goods are deliverable to the seller or his agent, the seller is prima facie to be taken to have reserved the right of disposal.[47] Usually, the seller retains the right

44 Sale of Goods Act 1893, ss.17–18.

45 See, *e.g. Sewell v. Burdick* (1884) 10 App. Cas. 74; see further Sale of Goods Act 1893, s.62 on the definition of "property".

46 See 3.4.4 and 3.4.5.

47 Sale of Goods Act 1893, s.19(2).

of disposal, or title, until the goods are paid for. This presumption can however be rebutted.

31.3 Other Transport Documents

Despite the unique legal status of the bill of lading, it may not always be necessary or practical to use a bill: other transport documents will suffice.

31.3.1 Waybills[48]

With short voyages, the ship may arrive at the port of destination before the bill of lading. There is no implied term in the contract of carriage that the bill must arrive before the ship: this must be expressly contracted for. Where the ship is expected to arrive before the bill of lading (for instance, due to a short voyage, or because the bill is delayed in the banking system where a letter of credit is being used to finance the transaction),[49] the seller should expressly provide for the substitution of a letter of indemnity. However, the carrier may not be happy to accept an indemnity against liability, especially from a stranger. The use of sea waybills avoids these problems. The waybill performs some of the functions of a bill of lading, in that it both:

(i) evidences the carriage contract, and,
(ii) acts as a receipt.

However, unlike a bill of lading, a waybill is not a document of title. Therefore, there are no means of selling the goods while at sea. As the possibility of sale is unlikely during a short voyage, this is not a great disadvantage. Indeed, the waybill has several advantages over a bill of lading. With a waybill:

(i) there is no need for the consignee to produce the waybill to obtain delivery of the goods, so delays in collection due to the late arrival of the documents can be avoided, along with consequent storage charges;
(ii) a lot of the detailed checking at either end of the voyage which is associated with bill of lading, is avoided, and,

48 See generally, Tetley, "Waybills: The Modern Contract of Carriage of Goods by Sea" [1983] *Journal of Maritime Law and Commerce* 465; Humphries & Higgs, "Waybills: A Case of Common Law Laissez Faire in European Commerce" [1992] *Journal of Business Law* 453; and Faber, "The problems arising from multimodal transport" [1996] *Lloyd's Maritime and Commercial Law Quarterly* 503. See also CMI Uniform Rules for Sea Waybills (1990).

49 See generally Chapter 32.

(iii) the waybill can be given to the shipper as soon as the carrier has taken charge of the goods, so that it can be used immediately to obtain payment under a letter of credit or as security for a bank loan.

Waybills are widely used in container transport.

31.3.2 Delivery order

The delivery order is most often used in the transportation of bulk cargoes (oil or grain, for instance) to break up the bulk into smaller consignments. A delivery order is an undertaking by the shipper (merchant's delivery order) or by the carrier (ship's delivery order) that the goods will be delivered to the person named therein, or to the holder of the order.

31.3.3 Mate's receipt

This is a temporary form of receipt, given by the mate of a ship, for goods which have been received on board. This receipt is usually handed to the carrier or his loading broker in exchange for the bill of lading. As noted above, the use of mates' receipts has declined in modern international trade.[50]

31.4 Actions Against the Carrier

Under a contract of carriage, the carrier is contractually responsible for the care of the goods during transit. If the shipper retains ownership of the goods during the transit and, on discharge, it materialises that some or all of the goods have been lost or damaged, the shipper has a contractual right of action against the carrier on the terms of the contract of carriage. Problems arise, however, where the goods are sold while in transit. Under standard international sale contracts, the buyer bears the risk of loss from the time of shipment, but although he may have transferred to him a document of title representing the goods, and as a result have constructive possession or ownership of the goods, because he is not privy to the contract of carriage he would appear to have no contractual recourse against the carrier. In these circumstances, the buyer can pursue a claim under a number of different heads, including section 1 of the Bills of Lading Act 1855, and at common law.[51] There are, however, many deficiencies in the current position.

50 See 31.1.

51 Since goods are normally covered by insurance against loss and damage while in transit, the problems of liability and title to sue are largely faced by insurers and not traders, as a result of the doctrine of subrogation in insurance law: see generally 28.2.2.

31.4.1 Section 1 of the Bill of Lading Act 1855

The Bills of Lading Act 1855 was passed to remedy the above privity of contract problem by conferring on the buyer a contractual right of action. Section 1 provides:

> "Every consignee of goods named in a bill of lading, and every endorsee of a bill of lading to whom the property in the goods therein mentioned shall pass, upon or by reason of such consignment or endorsement, shall have transferred to and vested in him all rights of suit, and be subject to the same liabilities in respect of such goods as if the contract contained in the bill of lading had been made with himself."

As early as 1890, the Act received its first of many criticisms.[52] One problem is that the Act transfers rights of suit where "the property" passes to a consignee or an indorsee. But, the House of Lords in *Sewell v. Burdick*[53] held that a pledgee of goods, in this case a bank, did not acquire "the property".[54] Therefore, the bank did not have a right of action against the carrier. Strong doubts were also expressed about the position of mortgagees. The underlying rationale for this decision was a reluctance to make holders of bills as security liable for freight and other charges under the contract of carriage. The overall effect of this judgment was that anything less than an out and out transfer of full or general property will not suffice for the purpose of section 1.

A second problem is caused by the wording of the provision which requires that property must pass "... upon or by reason of such consignment or endorsement ..." The exact meaning of this phrase has been the subject of much litigation. For instance, in *McKelvie v. Walker*,[55] the defendant bought a cargo of coal from Glasgow which was delivered and paid for. The charterparty under which the goods were shipped provided for the payment of demurrage should there be any delay in unloading; the bill of lading contained a similar clause. A day after the goods were unloaded, the bill of lading arrived and was presented to the buyer. Because there was a delay in unloading, the carrier sought to hold the defendant liable under the contract of carriage, for demurrage. It was held, on the facts, that property passed to the buyer before the ship left port and so because the Bills of Lading Act operates to transfer such rights and

52 Carver, "On some defects in the Bills of Lading Act 1855" (1890) XXIII *Law Quarterly Review* 289. See also O'Ceidigh, "Privity and Contracts for the Carriage of Goods by Sea" [1991] *Gazette* 25.

53 (1884) 10 App. Cas. 74 (H.L.).

54 The bank's security interest amounts to a "special" property, and not the general property: see Sale of Goods Act 1893, s.62.

55 [1919] 2 I.R. 250. See also *The San Nicholas* [1976] 1 Lloyd's Rep. 8; *The Elafi* [1981] 2 Lloyd's Rep. 679; *The Sevonia Team* [1983] 2 Lloyd's Rep. 640; *The Delfini* [1990] 1 Lloyd's Rep. 252.

liabilities where property passes "upon or by reason of consignment or endorsement" only, the bill did not transfer the rights and liabilities under the carriage contract to the buyer.

Several interpretations of the phrase "... upon or by reason of such consignment or endorsement..." have been offered. According to the narrowest interpretation, it means that property must pass at the same time as consignment or indorsement,[56] whereas according to the widest interpretation, it is sufficient that property pass:

> "from the shipper to the consignee or indorsee under a contract in pursuance of which the goods are consigned to him under the bills of lading or in pursuance of which the bill of lading is indorsed in his favour."[57]

The more recent authority, *The Delfini*,[58] takes a middle view allowing the indorsee to sue even though the indorsement was not the immediate cause of the passing of property, as long as the indorsement played an essential causal role in its transfer.[59] Thus if property passes before, or independently of consignment or indorsement, section 1 does not apply. This is what happened in *The Delfini* where the relevant indorsement took place 11 days after the completion of delivery and was in no way linked to the passing of property.[60] This is a particular problem where the voyage is short, and where there are long chain sales transactions, as in the case of the oil trade. Similarly, no right of action would arise where goods are shipped in bulk, and no property can pass until the buyer's goods are separated from the bulk, usually at the port of destination;[61] or where, as in *The Aramis*,[62] a buyer of goods forming part of a bulk receives no goods at all; or where, as in *The Aliakmon*,[63] the bill is indorsed subject to a retention of title clause, whereby property passes on payment of the price. Lastly, section 1 of the Bills of Lading Act is limited in its application today, because it applies only where bills of lading are consigned or indorsed. Where other shipping documents are used, such as waybills, multimodal transport documents or delivery orders, a buyer must resort to other causes of action, and not always with success.

---

56 *Scrutton on Charterparties* (London, Sweet & Maxwell, 19th ed., 1984) p.27; now in its 20th ed., 1996.

57 Carver, *Carriage by Sea* (London, Stevens, 13th ed., 1982) para. 98; see also *The San Nicholas* [1976] 1 Lloyd's Rep. 8; *The Sevonia Team* [1983] 2 Lloyd's Rep. 640.

58 [1990] 1 Lloyd's Rep. 252; see further Treitel, "Passing of Property under CIF Contracts and the Bills of Lading Act 1855" [1990] *Lloyd's Maritime and Commercial Law Quarterly* 1.

59 *Ibid.*, per Lord Purchas at p.261, per Mustill L.J. at p.274; and per Woolf L.J. at p.275.

60 The goods had been released against an indemnity given by the indorsee to the carrier.

61 Sale of Goods Act 1893, s.16; see 17.4.

62 [1989] 1 Lloyd's Rep. 213.

63 [1986] A.C. 785; [1986] 2 All E.R. 145 (H.L.).

31.4.2 An implied contract

It is long established that where a consignee takes delivery of goods from the carrier by presenting the bill of lading and paying outstanding charges, a contract on the terms of the bill of lading may be implied between consignee and carrier.[64] Such contracts are often referred to as "Brandt contracts" after the leading case of *Brandt v. Liverpool, Brazil and River Steam Navigation Co Ltd.*[65] In this case, the plaintiff was a pledgee, and therefore had no cause of action under section 1 of the 1855 Act. In order to alleviate the position of pledgee, especially banks, the court implied a contract, on the same terms as those evidenced in the bill of lading, based on the fact that the consignee presented the bill, paid freight, and took delivery of the goods. The pre-conditions for finding an implied contract seem to include that: the holder of the bill must have some interest in the property; the actions of the parties must in some way be construed as offer and acceptance; and sufficient consideration must be provided. However, despite the relative ease with which these requirements may be satisfied,[66] in some cases it may still be impossible to establish an implied contract.

In *The Aliakmon*,[67] the bill was indorsed to the buyer, to whom risk passed, but the seller retained property in the goods. The buyer presented the bill as agent for the seller thereby negativing the possibility of a contract between himself and the carrier. In *The Aramis*,[68] freight was prepaid and so the Court of Appeal refused to imply a contract on the mere basis that the buyer presented the bills and took delivery. These actions were explicable by reference to the parties' existing obligations under the contracts of carriage and sale. Moreover, it seems that a contract will not be implied where there is no delivery, as, for example, where the ship sinks.[69]

While *The Aramis* clearly limits the scope of implied contracts, later case law suggests a willingness to use this device. In *The Captain Gregos*

64 *Cock v. Taylor* (1811) 12 East 399; *Stindt v. Roberts* (1845) 17 L.J. Q.B. 166; *Allen v. Coltart* (1883) 11 Q.B.D 782. While this point has not been judicially considered in Ireland, contracts have been implied between parties originally outside the bargain see, *e.g. Fox v. Higgins* (1912) 46 I.L.T.R. 222 (H.C.).

65 [1924] 1 K.B. 575.

66 For example, in *The Gudermes* [1991] 1 Lloyd's Rep. 456 at 468, Hirst J. states: "Once an intention to contract is found no problem on consideration arises, since there would be ample consideration in the bundle of rights and duties which the parties would respectively obtain and accept." See further [1993] 1 Lloyd's Rep. 311.

67 [1986] 2 All E.R. 145; see further Adams & Brownsword, "'The Aliakmon' and the Hague Rules" [1990] *Journal of Business Law* 23.

68 [1989] 1 Lloyd's Rep. 213; see further Treitel, "Bills of lading and implied contracts" [1989] *Lloyd's Maritime and Commercial Law Quarterly* 162.

69 *The Aramis* [1989] 1 Lloyd's Rep. 213 at 230 per Stuart-Smith L.J.

(No. 2)[70] a shipment of oil was sold by X, who was named in the bill as consignee, to Y, who in turn sold the oil to BP. BP wished to claim against the plaintiff carrier for short-delivery. On the facts it was found that there was no direct contract between BP and the carriers, yet at Rotterdam, the operation of discharging the oil into BP's refinery was said to involve "active co-operation" leading to a "direct relationship". Against this background, the court implied a contract "to give business reality to the transaction between them and to create the obligation which, as we think, both parties plainly believe to exist."[71] However, in *The Gudermes*,[72] the plaintiff had bought a shipment of oil from the shippers. The original vessel was not equipped with heating coils and the operators of the terminal at the destination rejected the oil on the basis that it would clog their pipes. The plaintiff had to arrange trans-shipment to another vessel with heating-coils in order to off-load the cargo. The plaintiff argued that, as a result of the trans-shipment, there was implied between the original carrier and himself a contract based on the bill of lading. The Court of Appeal refused to imply a contract despite the extensive co-operation regarding the trans-shipment. It stated that a contract will only be implied if the parties' actions are "consistent only with there being a new contract implied, and inconsistent with there being no such contract."[73]

31.4.3 An assignment of contractual rights

Where contract rights are vested in the shipper, those rights may be assigned to the consignee as choses in action under section 28(6) of the Supreme Court of Judicature (Ireland) Act 1877, for example. However, technicalities as to form, notice and procedure make this an unpopular option. Moreover, an assignment requires the shipper's co-operation.

31.4.4 An action in tort

A consignee who bears the risk of loss of or damage to goods may be able to sue the carrier in tort. Such an action will, however, only succeed if the consignee had property in, or an immediate right to possession of the goods at the time when the damage occurred.[74] In *The Aliakmon*,[75] a retention of title clause meant that the consignee did not have ownership, and, at the relevant time, when the damage occurred, did not have the

70 [1990] 2 Lloyd's Rep. 395; see further Clarke, "The Consignee's Right of Action against the Carrier of Goods by Sea" [1991] *Lloyd's Maritime and Commercial Law Quarterly* 5.

71 *Ibid.* at 402.

72 [1993] 1 Lloyd's Rep. 311; White & Bradgate, "The Survival of the Brandt-Liverpool Contract" [1993] *Lloyd's Maritime and Commercial Law Quarterly* 483.

73 [1993] 1 Lloyd's Rep. 311 at 320 per Staughton L.J.

74 See *Margarine Union v. Cambay Princes* [1969] 1 Q.B. 219.

75 [1986] 2 All E.R. 145.

immediate rights of possession because the cargo was in the carrier's possession.[76] Even where the consignee acquires property, there may be problems in identifying whether he had property when the loss or damage due to negligence occurred. This problem is exacerbated in string transactions. Where goods are resold in bulk, no property will pass while the goods remain unascertained.[77] Also, suing in tort allows the parties to evade the contract terms which usually incorporate the Hague Rules, including the rules on the exclusion and limitation of liability.

31.4.5 An action under the rule in *Dunlop v. Lambert*

Known as the rule in *Dunlop v. Lambert*,[78] in certain situations the shipper may enforce his right of action against the carrier for the benefit of the consignee where the latter bears the risk of loss or damage to the goods.[79] The shipper is accountable to the consignee for any damages recovered. However, the scope of this rule has been restricted by the decision in *The Albezero*,[80] where the House of Lords held that where section 1 of the 1855 Act applied, this rule could no longer be utilised. In this case, the right of action under section 1 was time-barred. It is not clear whether the rule survives in other cases.

31.4.6 Reform?

Despite this plethora of options, there exists a number of circumstances where third parties may find difficulties in bringing a claim against the carrier. First, where the cargo remains part of a larger bulk, no property can pass until the goods are ascertained.[81] This will not usually occur until discharge, and so property cannot pass *upon or by reason* of consignment or indorsement of the bill of lading, and hence section 1 of the 1855 Act has no application. Moreover, the buyer cannot pursue an action in tort because to do so, the buyer must own, or have an immediate right to possession of the goods at the time of the loss. Further problems arise where, as is the case in short voyages, the vessel arrives before the bill of lading. Again, section 1 may not apply because the property may have

76 It seems that constructive possession will not suffice to found a claim in tort: see Treitel, "Bills of Lading and Third Parties" [1986] *Lloyd's Maritime and Commercial Law Quarterly* 294.

77 Sale of Goods Act 1893, s.16; see 17.4.

78 (1839) 6 Cl. & F. 600.

79 *The Sanix Ace* [1987] 1 Lloyd's Rep. 465.

80 [1977] A.C. 774, applied in relation to a construction contract in *Linden Gardens Trust Ltd v. Lenesta Sludge Disposals Ltd* [1993] 3 All E.R. 417 (H.L.).

81 Sale of Goods Act 1893, s.16; see, *e.g. The Gosforth* S. en S. 1985 Nr. 91; see further Davenport, "Ownership of Bulk Cargoes" [1986] *Lloyd's Maritime and Commercial Law Quarterly* 4.

passed independently of the indorsement of the bill.[82] Section 1 also does not apply to protect pledgees, such as banks, and it is limited in its application to bills of lading. The alternatives to an action under the Bills of Lading Act also have their limits. For example, where a retention of title clause makes the buyer an agent for the seller, no contract can be implied between the buyer and the carrier,[83] and where the vessel is lost, an implied contract cannot be argued, as this is dependent on presentation of the bill by the buyer to the carrier, and delivery of the goods to the buyer.

The basic problem is the doctrine of privity of contract;[84] the specific problem is the Bills of Lading Act 1855. A recognition that these deficiencies in the law were damaging English commercial law internationally, led to the enactment of the U.K. Carriage of Goods by Sea Act 1992.[85] This Act repealed the 1855 Act, thereby breaking the link between the passing of property and the transfer of contractual rights and liabilities. Broadly speaking, under the 1992 Act, the lawful holder of a bill of lading, or the person entitled to delivery under a sea waybill, or a ship's delivery order, has transferred to him all rights of suit under the contract of carriage as if he had been a party to the contract.[86] These rights of suit are transferred notwithstanding that the goods have ceased to exist or where the goods cannot be identified, for instance because they are unascertained.[87] The 1992 Act is not without its critics. It is a cautious response to the problem which succeeds in remedying some of the major defects of the 1855 Act.[88]

An alternative approach to reform is to address the wider issue of privity of contract. While Irish and English courts have persistently, if sometimes reluctantly, limited the range of persons who can enforce a contract, the American courts have shown themselves more willing. For instance, American courts recognise an exception to the doctrine of privity which provides that where a contract expressly mentions third parties as intended beneficiaries of the contract, they are permitted to claim the envisaged benefits. Moreover, intended beneficiaries who are not

82 *The Delfini* [1990] 1 Lloyd's Rep. 252.

83 *The Aliakmon* [1986] 2 All E.R. 145.

84 See further Adams & Brownsword, "'The Aliakmon' and the Hague Rules" [1990] *Journal of Business Law* 23.

85 See U.K. Law Commission Report, Rights of Suit in Respect of Carriage of Goods by Sea (Law Com No. 196; Scot Law Com No. 130, 1991); Beatson & Cooper, "Rights of suit in respect of carriage of goods by sea" [1991] *Lloyd's Maritime and Commercial Law Quarterly* 196; Bradgate & White, "The Carriage of Goods by Sea Act 1992" 56 (1993) *Modern Law Review* 188.

86 1992 Act, s.2.

87 1992 Act, s.5(4).

88 See *e.g.* Bradgate & White, "The Carriage of Goods by Sea Act 1992" (1993) 56 *Modern Law Review* 188. See also *The Berge Sisar* [1998] 3 W.L.R. 1353; [1998] 2 Lloyd's Rep. 475, [1999] Q.B. 863; see further Reynolds, "The Carriage of Goods by Sea Act 1992 Put to the Test" [1999] *Lloyd's Maritime and Commercial Law Quarterly* 161.

expressly mentioned in the contract may be able to claim benefits under it.[89] More recently, in the U.K., the Contracts (Rights of Third Parties) Act 1999 modifies the common law rule of privity of contract to enable a person who is not a party to a contract to enforce a term of the contract, including by taking the benefit of an exclusion or similar clause if:

(i) the contract expressly provides that he may do so; or
(ii) the term purports to confer a benefit on him and it appears that, on proper construction of the contract, the parties intended him to be able to enforce the contract.[90]

Although there appears to be no political appetite for reform of the Bills of Lading Act 1855, reform may be on the agenda in relation to the doctrine of privity of contract generally. The Law Commission, in its Second Programme (2000-2007) has identified privity of contract and the rights of third parties as a topic for examination. It is to be hoped that within this wider study, the particular position of third parties in relation to contracts for the carriage of goods by sea will be fully addressed and the necessary legislation introduced to remedy this long-standing deficiency in the law.

89 See, *e.g. Ratzlaff v. Franz Foods* 150 Ark. 1003, 468 SW. 2d (1971).
90 1999 Act, s.1(1) and (2). The existing common law and statutory exceptions remain unaffected by this legislation.

CHAPTER 32

DOCUMENTARY CREDITS AND PERFORMANCE BONDS

32.1 INTRODUCTION

In international trade transactions the normal risks with regard to payment are magnified. Where parties trade on a regular basis, the seller may be willing to grant credit to the buyer. In order to guard against a buyer who is unwilling or unable to pay, due to insolvency, the seller may retain property in the goods until payment of the price. However, given the complications of enforcing rights abroad, a seller may be reluctant to part with possession of, or control over the goods until he has received payment or some assurance of performance by the seller. Equally, a buyer may be unwilling to pay until he has received some assurance of the seller's performance. A number of options exist to meet the needs of the parties in this situation, including the use of documentary credits and performance bonds: the subject of this chapter.[1]

A further alternative is for the seller to require payment by bill of exchange.[2] If the bill is accepted, the seller has some protection against the buyer's non-performance because of the independent nature of the payment undertaking in the bill. Commonly, the seller draws a bill of exchange on the buyer for the price of the goods. The bill is presented to the buyer for acceptance with the other shipping documents and hence is known as a "documentary bill". The buyer can then accept the bill, promising to pay at some future date. If the buyer fails to accept the bill of exchange, he may not retain the bill of lading, and no property will pass to him.[3] In this way, a documentary bill serves the interests of the seller and buyer. The presentation of the bill with the shipping documents gives the buyer an assurance of the seller's performance before he accepts the bill; and the retention of property until the bill is accepted protects the seller. Where the bill provides for payment at a later date, the buyer gets credit while the seller can discount the bill for immediate payment. Bills of exchange do not provide complete assurance of payment, however: the buyer may fail to honour the bill on maturity, even after acceptance, and enforcing a bill abroad carries with it the usual difficulties. A seller may therefore require the buyer to arrange for the bill to be accepted by a bank

1 See generally, *Schmitthoff's Export Trade: The Law and Practice of International Trade* (London, Sweet & Maxwell, 10th ed., 2000) Part Two.

2 See Chapter 22.

3 Sale of Goods Act 1893, s.19(3).

or other financial institution. Alternatively, a seller may require a buyer to arrange payment through a documentary credit, also known as a banker's commercial credit, or a letter of credit. Such an arrangement gives the seller an assurance of payment from a reliable paymaster, a bank or other financial institution, preferably within his own jurisdiction. A similar assurance of the seller's performance can be obtained through the use of a performance bond.

32.2 Documentary Credits[4]

Where, under the contract of sale, payment is to be by documentary credit, the buyer is required to enter an arrangement with a bank whereby the bank gives an undertaking that, provided certain conditions are met, the bank will pay the seller. The conditions that are normally to be fulfilled relate to the presentation by the seller of shipping documents for the goods being sold. Once the credit is opened, the seller can ship the goods and present the documents required under the sales contract to the bank. Provided the documents correspond with the instructions given to the bank by the buyer, the bank will pay the seller. The bank's undertaking to pay can take several forms. For example, the bank may agree to pay the seller cash immediately on presentation of the shipping documents, or at some fixed date, such as, 90 days, thereafter. Alternatively, the bank may agree to accept bills of exchange drawn on it by the seller (an acceptance credit). Or, the bank may agree to discount bills drawn by the seller on the buyer (a negotiated credit). Here, the seller will normally indorse such bills "without recourse".[5]

Significantly, the bank's undertaking to pay is recognised as creating an obligation independent or autonomous of the underlying sales contract. Therefore, a seller looks first to the bank for payment and cannot look to the buyer for payment unless the bank defaults. As a result, a documentary credit gives a seller an almost certain promise of payment.[6] At the same time, the bank will only pay on presentation of the shipping documents showing that the goods have been shipped in apparent good condition and insured, and hence that the seller has performed his part of the sales contract.

4 Described as "the life blood of international commerce" in *Harbottle v. National Westminster Bank Ltd* [1978] Q.B. 146 at 155 per Kerr L.J. See generally, Gutteridge & Magrah, *Law of Bankers' Commercial Credits* (London, Europa, 8th ed., 2001).

5 See 22.3.4.4(v).

6 In *Mitsui & Co Ltd v. Flota Mercante Grancolombiana SA* [1989] 1 All E.R. 951, [1988] 1 W.L.R. 1145 (C.A.), it was stated that "even the most copper-bottomed letter of credit sometimes fails to produce payment" per Staughton L.J. at 957 and 1153. In that case, it was held that a seller who had retained title on shipment, still retained title even though he had received 80 per cent of the price with the balance secured by a documentary credit.

32.2.1 Sources of law

Documentary credits are not regulated by statute. The relevant law is found in the common law which is largely based on commercial practice. The majority of documentary credits are made expressly subject to the Uniform Customs and Practices relating to Documentary Credits (UCP), promoted by the International Chamber of Commerce (ICC).[7] The UCP is revised periodically in keeping with commercial practice: the current version is UCP 500 (1993).[8] More recently, there has been an increase in the volume of litigation involving documentary credits.[9] This is not surprising given the sums of money involved and the widespread use of documentary credits. In response to this trend, in 1997 the ICC instituted a special dispute resolution procedure known as DOCDEX. In effect, this is a specialist arbitration service, which may be used to resolve disputes concerning documentary credits.

32.2.2 Types of credit

The UCP defines a documentary credit as:

> "any arrangement, however named or described, whereby a bank (the 'Issuing Bank') acting at the request and in accordance with the instructions of a customer ('the Applicant')
>
> (i) is to make payment to or to the order of a third party ('the Beneficiary') or is to pay or to accept and pay bills of exchange (Draft(s)) drawn by the Beneficiary, or
> (ii) authorises another bank to effect such payment, or to accept and pay such bills of exchange (Draft(s)), or
> (iii) authorises another bank to negotiate,
>
> against stipulated document(s), provided that the terms and conditions of the credit are complied with."[10]

There is a range of different documentary credits which fit within this definition. There is one important exception worth noting. "Standby credits" are not true documentary credits in that the bank's obligation to pay only arises on default of the debtor: standby credits are therefore a type of guarantee. They were developed in the United States as a means of getting around the legal restrictions on the enforceability of guarantees.

---

7 See generally, www.iccwbo.org

8 See Ellinger, "The Uniform Customs and Practice for Documentary Credits – the 1993 Revision" [1994] *Lloyd's Maritime and Commercial Law Quarterly* 377.

9 See Preface to UCP 500.

10 UCP, Art. 2.

They are, however, governed by the UCP and the rules applicable to documentary credits.

32.2.2.1 Revolving credits

Where two parties trade with each other on a continuing basis, rather than opening a new credit for each transaction, the buyer may request the bank to operate a revolving credit whereby the bank undertakes to pay the seller sums due from time to time, up to an agreed credit limit.

32.2.2.2 Transferable credits

With a transferable credit, the seller (the beneficiary) may request the bank to make the credit available to a third party, in whole or in part. The seller can thereby use the credit to pay his supplier or other creditors.[11]

32.2.2.3 Back to back credits

A back to back credit is a credit used by the seller to pay his supplier. Under this arrangement, two credits are established: the first in favour of the seller, and, the second "back to back" with the first, in favour of the seller's supplier. The first credit finances the second credit.

32.2.2.4 Revocable and irrevocable credits

The distinction between revocable and irrevocable credits is very important in practice. Where the credit is revocable, the bank can withdraw its undertaking to the seller to pay at any time before payment is due, and the bank is under no obligation to notify the seller of its withdrawal.[12] Accordingly, a revocable credit offers the seller little security of payment, because he can ship the goods and later find that the credit has been withdrawn and he has no rights against the bank. His only remedy is against the buyer for the price, or for damages for breach of contract. The UCP 500 provides that all credits are presumed to be irrevocable unless expressly stated to be revocable.[13] This reverses the previous position. With an irrevocable credit, once the bank has advised the seller that the irrevocable credit is opened, the bank's undertaking cannot be withdrawn, even where the buyer requests withdrawal, except in the case of clear evidence of fraud by the seller.[14] Therefore, a seller will seek to demand that the buyer opens a irrevocable credit.

11 UCP, Art. 48(a) and Art. 54.

12 *Cape Asbestos Ltd v. Lloyds Bank Ltd* [1921] W.N. 274.

13 Art. 6(c).

14 *Discount Records Ltd v. Barclays Bank Ltd* [1975] 1 W.L.R. 315; see further 32.2.4.2.

32.2.2.5 Confirmed and unconfirmed credits

The distinction between confirmed and unconfirmed credits also important in practice. Where a bank has no branch in the seller's jurisdiction, it will normally arrange for a bank within the seller's jurisdiction to act as its agent by notifying the seller that the credit is opened. The seller will present the shipping documents to that bank and that bank may make the payment. The bank which opens the credit is known as the "issuing bank", while the bank which notifies the seller of the opening is referred to as the "correspondent bank". Generally, the correspondent bank undertakes no obligation to the seller, merely acting as an agent between the issuing bank and the seller. This arrangement is referred to as an unconfirmed credit.

A seller will prefer if a bank within his jurisdiction provides an undertaking as to payment. A confirmed credit involves the correspondent bank notifying the seller that the credit is opened, but also *confirming* the issuing bank's undertaking. The seller therefore has two undertakings as to payment: one from the issuing bank and another from the confirming bank, the latter being within the seller's jurisdiction. A confirmed credit is more costly than an unconfirmed credit to arrange, because the confirming bank will want to be paid for adding its confirmation. A confirming bank which makes payment is entitled to reimbursement from the issuing bank. A correspondent bank will normally only confirm a credit that is irrevocable.

32.2.3 A typical documentary credit transaction

The stages in a typical documentary credit transaction are as follows.

- (i) The seller and buyer enter into a contract for the sale of goods. The sales contract will specify that payment is to be by documentary credit and the type of credit required.
- (ii) The buyer instructs his bank to open the required credit, and as to the documents to be presented by the seller to obtain payment. The opening of the credit is an extra cost for the buyer.
- (iii) Where the bank has no branch in the seller's jurisdiction, it will instruct a correspondent bank in the seller's jurisdiction to notify the seller that the credit is opened and as to the documents to be presented by the seller to obtain payment. Where the credit is confirmed, the correspondent bank will be asked to confirm the issuing bank's undertaking.
- (iv) The seller is notified by the relevant bank that the credit is opened.
- (v) Provided the credit conforms with the sales contract, the seller ships the goods in conformity with the sales contract.
- (vi) The seller presents the documents specified by the sales contract and the terms of the credit to the relevant bank. These documents

usually comprise a clean shipped bill of lading, an insurance policy, and an invoice. Additional documents, such as certificates of quality or origin may be required. Provided that the documents are in order, the seller is entitled to payment under the documentary credit.

(vii) The bank may hold the shipping documents pending payment by its customer, the buyer. Or it may release the documents allowing the buyer the deal with the goods, in return for the buyer giving the bank some security over the goods.

Some of these stages are examined in more detail below.

32.2.3.1 Opening the credit

Where the sales contract provides for payment by documentary credit, it is the buyer's duty to open a credit. The credit must conform with the terms of the sales contract. The contract should specify the type of credit required. The contract may also specify a particular bank, otherwise the choice of bank is the buyer's choice.

The time for opening of the credit may cause difficulties. If the sales contract fixes a date for opening, then the credit must be opened by that date. If the credit is to be opened "immediately," it must be opened within a reasonable time.[15] Where no time is fixed, the credit is generally required to be opened before the time fixed by the sales contract for shipment of the goods.[16] But this is only a general rule. One of the few Irish cases concerned with the operation of a documentary credit is *Tradax (Ireland) Ltd v. Irish Grain Board Ltd*.[17] This is an unusual case in that the seller and buyer agreed to payment by documentary credit without realising fully the nature of this payment mechanism and, therefore, without addressing properly a variety of issues including the identity of the bank which was to issue the letter of credit, notification of opening, and the documents to be presented. The contract was for the sale of grain, in two lots, to be available for delivery during April–June 1978. The entire contract was to be paid for by a letter of credit "maturing" on May 1, 1978. Deliveries were made from April 7 to April 21, at which point the seller refused to make any more deliveries on the ground that the buyer had failed to furnish letters of credit and hence was in breach of contract. On April 24, the buyer's bank issued two letters of credit in favour of the seller to enable the seller to obtain payment on May 1. The seller was notified of the opening of the credit on the same day. It was argued by the seller that the court should imply a term

15 *Garcia v. Page & Co Ltd* (1936) 55 Ll. L. Rep. 391.

16 *Pavia & Co SpA v. Thurmann Nielson [*1952] 2 Q.B. 84; *Ian Stach Ltd v. Baker Bosley Ltd* [1958] 2 Q.B. 130, [1952] 1 All E.R. 492 (C.A.).

17 [1984] I.R. 1.

in the sales contract that the letters of credit should have been opened before the start of the shipment period. The Supreme Court refused to imply such a term, particularly in light of the express terms of the contract which required the credit to "mature" or become payable on May 1. This case highlights the importance of the parties addressing, in the sales contract, the main issues in relation to the documentary credit including: the type of documentary credit; when it is to be opened; notification of the opening; the identity of the bank; and the documents to be presented.

32.2.3.2 The buyer's instructions

The buyer's instructions to the bank form the basis of the contract with the bank. Such instructions are usually given on the bank's standard form. It is vital that the buyer's instructions are clear and unambiguous and this is confirmed by the UCP.[18] The instructions will include what documents are to be presented by the seller to obtain payment; and an undertaking by the buyer to reimburse the bank, and a grant to the bank of a charge over the goods as security for payment, unless the buyer has put the bank in funds prior to payment.

32.2.3.3 Presenting documents: the doctrine of strict compliance

Once the credit is opened, the bank will arrange for the seller to be notified of the fact. When notified, the seller can ship the goods, and present the shipping documents as described in the sales contract and under the terms of the credit to the bank for payment. In light of the autonomous nature of documentary credits, and perhaps to tip the scales back in favour of the buyer, the doctrine of strict compliance provides that a seller is only entitled to payment when he presents documents which correspond exactly with the terms of the credit. Where documents do not *exactly* correspond, the bank is entitled to reject the documents and refuse to pay. This rule is strictly applied, in practice. For example, in *JH Rayner & Co Ltd v. Hambros Bank*,[19] the terms of the credit required the seller to present a bill of lading covering "machine shelled groundnut kernels". When the shipping documents were presented to the bank, the bill referred to "coromandel groundnuts". Even though there was evidence that it was well known that these two were the same, it was held that the bank was entitled to reject the documents and refuse to pay. This rule relieves a bank from any responsibility to look beyond the terms of the credit and the documents presented. The rule of strict compliance is modified where the UCP is

18 Art. 5; any ambiguity may be interpreted in favour of the beneficiary: see, *e.g. Credit Agricole Indosuez v. Muslim Commercial Bank Ltd* [2000] 1 Lloyd's Rep. 275.

19 [1943] 1 K.B. 37.

adopted in relation to quantity of goods shipped, for example. Under Article 39(b), a bank will not reject the bill of lading provided the quantity shipped is within a tolerance of plus or minus five per cent of the contract quantity.

The UCP provides that the bank has:

> "... a reasonable time, not to exceed seven banking days following the receipt of the documents, to examine the documents and determine whether to take up or refuse the documents and to inform the party from which it received the documents accordingly."[20]

This seven-day period is a maximum, and in certain cases the time for making a decision will be shorter. In deciding what is a "reasonable time", a court will consider the current practices of local banks operating in the same market, the nature and complexity of the credit, and the amount of technical language used.[21] For example, in *Bankers Trust Ltd v. State Bank of India*,[22] where the documents concerned ran to 967 pages, there was evidence that London clearing banks would normally take three working days to make and notify a decision. It would appear that a court may also take into account subjective factors, such as the size of the bank and the expertise of its staff, so that a bank which takes longer than the norm, will not automatically be found to have taken an unreasonably long time.[23]

If the bank rejects the documents, the seller may re-present them,[24] or he may contact the seller and request that the seller instruct the bank to accept them. However, having agreed payment by documentary credit, he cannot present the documents directly to the buyer for payment. As noted above though, the credit operates as conditional payment, so that when the bank fails to pay, for instance due to insolvency, the buyer's obligation under the sales contract is revived, and the seller can claim payment directly from the buyer.[25]

Where a bank accepts documents and pays for the goods, the bank will look to the customer to reimburse it and pay any fees due. It may retain the shipping documents as security for payment. However, without the documents, in particular the bill of lading, the buyer cannot deal with the goods, and so a bank may release the documents in return for a charge over the goods to secure payment, or under a trust receipt, whereby the buyer

---

20 UCP, Art. 13(b) and Art. 14(d).

21 *Bankers Trust Ltd v. State Bank of India* [1991] 2 Lloyd's Rep. 443, see further Bennett, "Documentary Credits: A Reasonable Time for What?" [1992] *Lloyd's Maritime and Commercial Law Quarterly* 169; and *Hing Yip Hing Fat Co Ltd v. Daiwa Bank Ltd* [1991] 2 H.K.L.R. 35, see further [1992] *Lloyd's Maritime and Commercial Law Quarterly* 26.

22 [1991] 2 Lloyd's Rep. 443.

23 *Bankers Trust Ltd v. State Bank of India* [1991] 2 Lloyd's Rep. 443; *Hing Yip Hing Fat Co Ltd v. Daiwa Bank Ltd* [1991] 2 H.K.L.R. 35.

24 UCP, Art. 14(d).

25 *Alan v. El Nasr* [1972] 2 Q.B. 189.

acknowledges that he receives the goods as trustee for the bank and that, if he resells them, he holds the proceeds as trustee for the bank.

Where a bank does not follow the instructions of its customer and accepts documents which do not strictly comply with the credit, the bank is in breach of contract with its customer. A customer could refuse to take the documents from the bank or to pay the bank, leaving the bank with the goods, and sue the bank for damages.

32.2.4 The contracts

A documentary credit arrangement involves a number of contracts between the parties, including:

(a) the underlying sales contract between seller and buyer;
(b) the contract between the buyer/customer and the issuing bank to arrange the documentary credit;
(c) the agency contract between the issuing bank and any correspondent bank;
(d) the contract between the issuing bank and the seller whereby the bank undertakes to pay against presentation of the stipulated shipping documents.

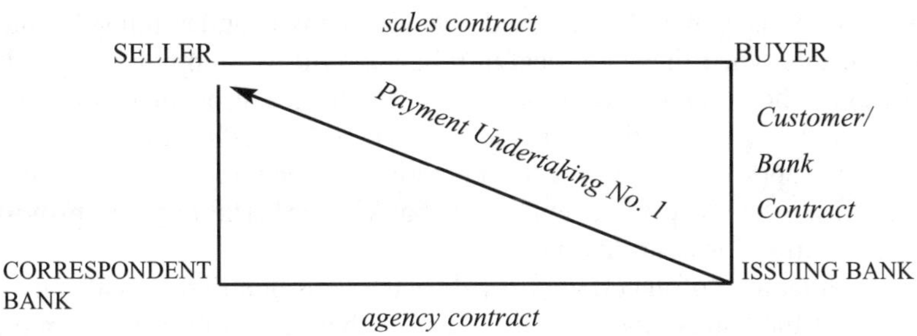

Where the credit is confirmed, a further contract exists: the contract between the confirming bank and the seller whereby the confirming bank undertakes to pay against presentation of the stipulated shipping documents.

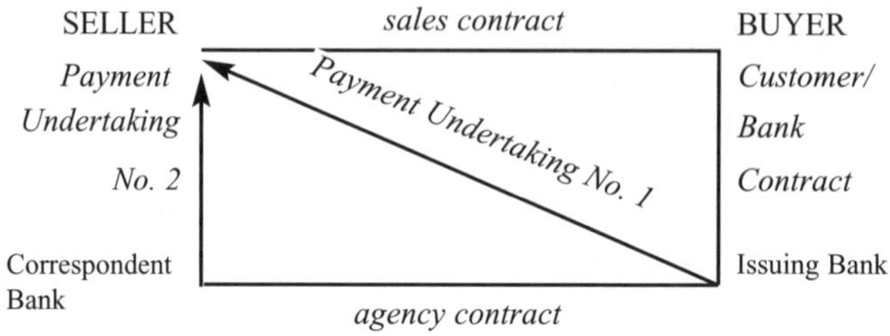

32.2.4.1 The bank's contractual undertaking

The main advantage offered by documentary credits lies in the issuing and confirming banks' undertakings to pay the price if certain conditions are fulfilled. These undertakings are treated as independent and autonomous.[26] A number of questions remain unanswered about the operation of documentary credits. However, this uncertainty seems to have little impact on their utility and popularity in international trade. For example, it is not clear when a bank's undertaking under an irrevocable credit becomes binding. It is generally accepted that the bank's undertaking becomes irrevocable when the seller acts in reliance on it by shipping the goods;[27] however, there is some legal authority that the credit becomes binding at the earlier stage when the seller is notified that the credit is opened.[28] While the latter approach may reflect commercial expectations, it is difficult to see how the buyer accepts the bank's undertaking or provides consideration for it, at this stage.

Another area of uncertainty involves the consideration provided by the seller for the banks' undertakings. Clearly, there are enforceable contracts between the buyer and the issuing bank; and between the issuing and the correspondent/confirming banks. The seller is a stranger to these contracts. Any consideration provided by the seller is under the sales contract with the buyer; this would be past consideration in relation to any contract with the relevant banks. It could be argued, in the light of the decision in *New Zealand Shipping v. Satterthwaite (The Eurymedon)*[29] that the seller provides consideration when he ships the goods under the sales contract. Alternatively, it may be that the seller provides no consideration in return for the bank's undertaking.[30] It is assumed that should such a matter come

26 UCP, Art. 9(a) and (b).

27 *Urquhart Lindsay & Co Ltd v. Eastern Bank Ltd* [1922] 1 K.B. 318.

28 *Dexters Ltd v. Schenker & Co* (1923) 14 Ll. L. Rep. 586.

29 [1975] A.C. 154, [1974] 1 All E.R. 1015 (P.C.); see further 2.2.2.1(iii).

30 It has been suggested that contracts created by documentary credits should be regarded as *sui generis* and enforceable without consideration: see, *e.g. Benjamin's Sale of Goods* (London, Sweet & Maxwell, 5th ed., 1997) para. 23–115.

before an Irish or English court, the court would uphold the binding nature of the bank's undertaking because of the commercial importance of documentary credits.

32.2.4.2 The autonomy of the bank's undertaking

As noted above, the undertakings given by the issuing and confirming banks are recognised as autonomous, by commercial practice and the courts, from the underlying sales transaction. The UCP provide:

> "Credits, by their nature, are separate transactions from the sales or other contract(s) on which they may be based and banks are in no way concerned with or bound by such contract(s) even if any reference whatsoever to such contract(s) is included in the credit."[31]

A seller will look first to the bank for payment, and only on default by the bank can the seller turn to the buyer. As a result, a bank must honour its undertaking to pay, provided the relevant conditions are met, regardless of any problems which might arise under the sales contract, as for example, where the seller is in breach of the sales contract. A court will not grant the buyer an injunction to prevent the seller drawing on the credit in such a situation;[32] nor will it grant a buyer an injunction against the bank making payment.[33] For example, in *Discount Records Ltd v. Barclays Bank Ltd*,[34] there was a contract for the sale of records. When the goods were delivered, they were found to be very different from those described in the sales contract. The buyer sought an injunction to prevent the bank paying under the credit. The court refused to grant an injunction stressing the separation of the payment obligation under the sales contract and under the documentary credit. The court noted that the commercial value of the documentary credit system lies in the certainty of payment created by the credit. If a court were to allow the payment obligation to be revoked, that certainty would be undermined.

Similarly, in *GPA Group plc v. Bank of Ireland and EUROCONTROL*,[35] the plaintiff leased aircraft worldwide while the second defendant, EUROCONTROL, was responsible for the collection of route charges. EUROCONTROL detained five GPA aircraft because of failure by the

---

31 UCP, Art. 3.

32 *Hamzeh Malas Inc v. British Imex Industries* [1958] 1 Q.B. 542.

33 *Discount Records Ltd v. Barclays Bank Ltd* [1975] 1 W.L.R. 315.

34 [1975] 1 W.L.R. 315.

35 [1992] 2 I.R. 408 (H.C.); see also *GPA Group plc v. Bank of Ireland and EUROCONTROL* unreported Supreme Court, November 9, 1995, where the Supreme Court observed that while letters of credit were irrovocable and must be paid when documents are in order and the terms of the credit satisified, that does not mean that a dispute cannot arise between the parties other than the bank.

lessee to pay route charges. EUROCONTROL agreed to release the aircraft to GPA in return for a letter of credit from GPA in the sum of US$3,000,000 for the benefit of EUROCONTROL. A letter of credit was drawn on the first defendant bank which provided for payment on presentation of a demand certificate either:

(i) signed by the officers of both GPA and EUROCONTROL; or
(ii) signed by the officers of EUROCONTROL and attaching a final and binding court order of a competent jurisdiction for the amount claimed [in respect of which the] time for appeal shall have passed.

Subsequently, GPA argued that the lessee, and not GPA, was responsible for route charges and therefore GPA sought assurance that EUROCONTROL would not seek payment under the letter of credit. EUROCONTROL refused to make such an assurance. The bank received a demand certificate, duly signed by EUROCONTROL officers and attaching a consent order of the English High Court against the lessee purportedly in compliance with the letter of credit. GPA argued that the demand certificate did not comply with the letter of credit and was granted an interim injunction restraining the bank from making payment. However, a permanent injunction to restrain payment was refused. The High Court stated that when a letter of credit is issued and confirmed by a bank, the bank is obliged, save in the case of fraud, to pay if the documents are, on their face, in order. The court found that the documents were prima facie in order and the terms of the letter of credit were satisfied. The High Court also stated that the honouring of a letter of credit should not be lightly prohibited by the courts. The court also noted that the policy of the courts was to require immediate compliance with a demand for payment. Furthermore, the bank's obligation cannot be affected by disputes between its customer and third party beneficiaries under the letter of credit.

There are two exceptional cases where payment may be withheld:

(i) where there is clear evidence of fraud on the part of the beneficiary;[36] and
(ii) where the credit itself is void or illegal.[37]

36 *United City Merchants Ltd v. Royal Bank of Canada* [1983] 1 A.C. 168.

37 *E.g.* void for mistake as in *Power Curber International Ltd v. National Bank of Kuwait* [1981] 1 W.L.R. 1233. There is some authority that the credit may be rendered illegal where the underlying contract is illegal and the credit is tainted by that illegality: *Group Josi Re v. Walbrook Insurance Co Ltd* [1994] 4 All E.R. 181, affd [1996] 1 All E.R. 791 at 803 per Staughton L.J. (C.A.).

An injunction to prevent payment on the grounds of fraud is very rarely granted. For example, in *United City Merchants Ltd v. Royal Bank of Canada*,[38] the sales contract and the credit required the goods to be shipped by December 15, 1975. The sellers presented a bill of lading showing that the goods were shipped on December 15, but unknown to them, the bill had been altered by shipping brokers, the shipment actually taking place on December 16. The defendant bank refused to accept the shipping documents. The House of Lords emphasised that the documentary credit was separate from the underlying sales transaction. It held that the bank was in breach of its undertaking to pay because the documents on their face conformed to the credit and it was irrelevant that the buyer could reject the goods under the sales contract. The bank could only reject the documents if there was clear evidence of fraud to which the seller was a party and of which the bank was aware.

An interim injunction is granted on the balance of convenience,[39] and in the case of a documentary credit, this requirement will rarely be satisfied because if the bank pays where it has knowledge of clear evidence of the seller's fraud, it will be in breach of its contract with the buyer, its customer, who therefore has a remedy in damages against the bank.[40] The rationale for this approach it that the commercial value of documentary credits would be undermined if payment could be withheld easily.

32.3 Performance Bonds[41]

Performance bonds are used to secure the performance of a wide range of contractual and other obligations. For instance, with an international sale of goods, financed by documentary credit, the buyer may require some assurance that the goods will be shipped and can therefore require the seller to arrange a performance bond, so that, in default of shipment, the

38 [1983] 1 A.C. 168; see further, Ellinger, "Fraud in Documentary Credit Transactions" [1981] *Journal of Business Law* 258; Schmitthoff, "Fraud in Documentary Credit Transactions" [1982] *Journal of Business Law* 319; Todd, "Sellers and Documentary Credits" [1983] *Journal of Business Law* 468.

39 *Campus Oil Ltd v. Minister for Industry & Commerce* [1983] I.R. 88; *American Cyanamid Co v. Ethicon Ltd* [1975] 1 All E.R. 504.

40 See, *e.g. Czarnikow Rionda Sugar Trading Inc v. Standard Bank of London Ltd* [1999] 1 All E.R. Comm. 890.

41 See generally, White, "Performance Bonds: Surety Bonds and Demand Guarantees Distinguished" [1998] *Commercial Law Practitioner* 35; Coleman, "Performance guarantees" [1990] *Lloyd's Maritime and Commercial Law Quarterly* 223; Williams, "Performance Bonds: use and usefulness" [1983] *Lloyd's Maritime and Commercial Law Quarterly* 423; Arora, "The Legal Position of Banks in Performance Bond Cases" [1981] *Lloyd's Maritime and Commercial Law Quarterly* 264. See also the ICC Uniform Rules for Demand Guarantees (ICC No. 458, 1991) at www.iccwbo.org ; see further Goode, "The new ICC Uniform Rules for Demand Guarantees" [1992] *Lloyd's Maritime and Commercial Law Quarterly* 190.

sum fixed in the bond will become payable. The person who arranged the bond is called the "account party" while the recipient of the bond is called the "payment party." The essential feature of a performance bond is that it is provided by a creditworthy institution such as a bank, offering the payment party/beneficiary a guarantee of performance and in default, monetary compensation from the reliable paymaster. While performance bonds perform the function of guarantees, they have been treated by the courts as broadly analogous to documentary credits.[42]

32.3.1 When is a bond payable?

The terms of the bond will determine when it becomes payable. A bond may only be payable when the account party is in default under his contract with the beneficiary. However, in these circumstances it must be shown that the account party is in default. Alternatively, a bond may provide that it is payable on production of a certificate from a third party, such as a surveyor or valuer, stating that the account party is in default. This avoids problems of the bank becoming involved in whether the account party is in breach of contract with the beneficiary or not. A further alternative is for the bond to provide that it is payable on demand. This is most advantageous for the beneficiary and the bank: the bond is payable on demand and there is no question as to whether the demand is justified or not. But from the account party's point of view, a demand bond leaves itself open to an unjustified demand. The account party's position is further exacerbated by the autonomous nature of performance bonds.

32.3.2 The autonomy of the undertaking

The autonomous nature of performance bonds and the danger for account parties of demand bonds is illustrated by the case *Edward Owen Engineering Ltd v. Barclays Bank International*.[43] Under a contract for the sale of glasshouses to a Libyan buyer, the buyer was required to pay by documentary credit and the seller was required to arrange a performance bond, payable on demand, to guarantee his performance. The buyer failed to arrange the credit, and the seller refused to ship the goods. The buyer then made a demand under the performance bond and the Court of Appeal held that the seller could not get an injunction to prevent the bank paying. The bank had given an undertaking to pay on the buyer's demand and was obliged to fulfill that undertaking, which was autonomous from the

42 *Cf.* Debattista, "Performance Bonds and Letters of Credit: a Cracked Mirror Image" [1997] *Journal of Business Law* 289.

43 [1978] 1 Q.B. 179. See further Penn, "Performance bonds: are bankers free from the underlying contract?" [1985] *Lloyd's Maritime and Commercial Law Quarterly* 132; Lawson, "Performance Bonds – Irrevocable Obligations" [1987] *Journal of Business Law* 259.

underlying contract of sale. This case was approved by the Irish Supreme Court in *Celtic International Insurance v. Banque Nationale de Paris*.[44] The case involved a construction contract between Mahon & McPhillips Ltd, a customer of the defendant bank, and the South Eastern Health Board, whereby the defendant undertook to pay to the plaintiff a sum of money, if demanded, provided that such a claim was accompanied by a certificate from the South Eastern Health Board indicating that the sum of money was owing to them. Subsequently, a receiver was appointed to Mahon & McPhillips and the benefit of the construction contracts was assigned to another construction company. The Health Board issued the necessary certificate and made a call on the performance bond, but the defendant refused to pay. The Supreme Court held that a bank which gives a performance guarantee must honour it according to its terms. The bank should not be concerned with the relations between the parties to whom the guarantee is given and the party whose performance is guaranteed, nor as to whether the party to whom the guarantee is given has performed his contractual obligations or is in default. The bank must make payment pursuant to the guarantee on demand if this has been stipulated. The only exception to this rule being where it is clear that there has been fraud on behalf of the peron to whom the guarantee is given.

Where a bank makes payment under a bond, the bank is entitled to reimbursement from the account party. In the above case, the account party may be able to recover payment from the beneficiary under the sales contract, but may be forced to take proceedings to do so and may have to do so outside the jurisdiction.

Because of the autonomous nature of performance bonds, a court will not grant an injunction to prevent a beneficiary claiming payment, or a bank from making payment, provided the conditions of the bond are met. Again, the major exception to the autonomous nature of performance bonds is where the bank has clear evidence of fraud on the part of the beneficiary.[45] So, for example, if a bond provides for payment on condition that the beneficiary certifies that certain conditions are satisfied and the beneficiary seeks payment by falsely certifying that they are so satisfied, the court may restrain the beneficiary from seeking payment and, where the bank is aware of the falsity of the beneficiary's statement, may restrain the bank from making payment.[46]

Where a bond is payable when the account party is in breach of contract, it appears that the beneficiary is entitled to seek payment without

44 [1995] 2 I.L.R.M. 518.

45 *Edward Owen Engineering Ltd v. Barclays Bank International* [1978] 1 Q.B. 179. See further, Seung Chong, "The Abusive Calling of Performance Bonds" [1990] *Journal of Business Law* 414; *cf.* Chandran "Performance Bonds and Unconscionability in Singapore" [2000] *Commercial Law Practitioner* 170.

46 *Kvaerner John Brown Ltd v. Midland Bank plc* [1998] Com. L.C. 446.

proof of loss. However, where the account party recovers more than his actual loss, he may be liable to refund the excess to the account party.[47]

47 *Cargill International Sugar SA v. Bangladesh Sugar & Food Industries.*

PART VII

INTELLECTUAL PROPERTY LAW

CHAPTER 33

AN INTRODUCTION TO INTELLECTUAL PROPERTY LAW

33.1 WHAT IS INTELLECTUAL PROPERTY?[1]

As noted in Chapter 3, all property can be classified as real or personal. Real property includes land and anything permanently attached to the land, such as buildings. Personal property is all property except real property.

Personal property divides into chattels real (mainly leasehold interests in land) and chattels personal. Chattels personal sub-divide broadly into two classes:

(a) tangibles moveables (or choses in possession, such as goods or money); and
(b) intangibles moveables (or choses in action).[2]

Intangible moveables comprise legal rights which have no tangible form in themselves, though they may be represented in the form of a document, and are known as *documentary intangibles*. Examples include bills of lading and negotiable instruments. Documentary intangibles are notable because the document represents the property rights which can be transferred by transfer of the document itself. Rights which are not documentary intangibles are called *pure intangible*. Examples include, debts, goodwill and intellectual property rights.

When we study the law on sale of goods, for instance, we are concerned with tangible personal property. When we study intellectual property law, we are concerned with pure intangibles. Like goods, intellectual property can be traded, by outright disposition such as an assignment for a cash payment, or by the owner permitting others to exploit his property, either exclusively or jointly with him, for instance by granting a licence or licences to one or more persons to exploit the property. Like goods, intellectual property can be charged,[3] or gifted away, though statute may

1 See generally Vaver, "Intellectual Property: the State of the Art" (2000) 116 *Law Quarterly Review* 621; Cornish, *Intellectual Property* (London, Sweet & Maxwell, 4th ed., 1999) Chapter 1.
2 See *Colonial Bank v. Whinney* (1885) 30 Ch. D. 261 at 285, per Fry L.J.
3 See Hackett, "Taking Security over Intellectual Property Rights in Ireland" [1994] *Commercial Law Practitioner* 50.

require certain formalities to be complied with. Both types of property represents a valuable asset to any business.[4]

Property which is *intellectual property* is so classified because it can in some way be attributed to the creative mind. Accordingly, patent law protects inventions; copyright law protects creations of the mind such as literary works of fiction, and musical compositions and recordings, for example. Trade marks are protected as symbols used by customers to distinguish between competing goods and services. Other forms of intellectual property include design rights, performers' rights, trade secrets and other confidential information.

Therefore, intellectual property comprises legal rights: these rights are intangible, that is they have no physical form, and exist only because they are recognised by law, either statute or the common law; and generally they relate to the creative process. Intellectual property rights, as intangible rights, must be distinguished from the tangible property to which they may relate. For example, if I write a book, I, as author, initially own the copyright in the book.[5] When a person buys a published copy of my book, that person owns the book in its physical form, the goods, and he can use it, or sell it, or burn it. But I, as author, remain the owner of the copyright in the book.

While intellectual property rights confer some positive rights on the right holder, the rights granted are predominately negative in nature. They include rights to stop others doing certain "restricted acts" without the permission of the rights holder: to stop pirates, counterfeiters, imitators and in some cases third parties who have arrived at the same idea. Moreover, intellectual property rights are not prerequisites to exploitation: an invention can be exploited without registering a patent, though registration provides temporary protection against imitators. Equally, intellectual property rights do not provide immunity against breach of other parties' rights (including intellectual property rights) and other public liabilities.

Intellectual property rights underpin much modern commercial activity. For instance, when a business manufactures and markets a product, it may need advice on a complex network of interlocking intellectual property rights. It may patent the product and market it under a trade name which it may protect by registering the trade mark or by the law of passing off. Its own corporate name may also be protected by a trade mark. Instructions for the use of the product may be protected by copyright; and its marketing plans may be regarded as confidential. A business therefore needs to know:

4 See Donnelly, "Transferring Intangibles: Possibilities and Pitfalls" [2000] *Commercial Law Practitioner* 58.

5 Unless it is assigned, in advance: see 34.7.

(i) what intellectual property rights it has;
(ii) what, if anything, it must do to protect those rights;
(iii) how they may best be exploited;
(iv) what action it may take against anyone who infringes those rights;
(v) how it may avoid infringing the rights of others.

33.2 Why Protect Intellectual Property?

The legal protection of monopoly rights in intellectual property is generally justified on two grounds. First, since the work of an author or inventor is the product of his personality or labour, it deserves protection on the ground that he is entitled to reap the fruits of his labour and to control what he has created (the moral rights ground). Alternatively, the law grants authors and inventors rights to exploit their work in order to provide an incentive for them, and others, to create and invent. This is essentially a pragmatic argument: society as a whole benefits from inventions and creative works and should therefore encourage their production. Without protection for the inventor/creator, competitors would be able to copy his invention/creation and, free from the labour and costs which the inventor/creator bears, would be able to undercut his prices, depriving him of profits and discouraging others from inventing (the economic rights ground).

Both theories recognise the need to balance the rights of the owner of intellectual property rights, which are monopolistic in nature, with those of society as a whole. The law therefore contains a system of checks and balances designed to balance the rights of the property owner with those of potential competitors and of the public at large. Intellectual property law is therefore closely linked to competition law.

33.3 Intellectual Property and Competition Law[6]

Since intellectual property law grants monopoly rights, there is obviously a tension between it and competition law. Two sets of rules restrict the anti-competitive effects of intellectual property law: (i) those within intellectual property law itself, and (ii) those imposed by competition law, both domestic and European.

Within intellectual property law, various rules restrict its anti-competitive effects. For instance, the monopoly rights granted by intellectual property may be limited in time, as with patents and copyright.

---

6 Maher, *Competition Law: alignment and reform* (Dublin, Round Hall Sweet & Maxwell, 1999) Chapter 9; Massey & O'Hare, *Competition Law and Policy in Ireland* (Dublin, Oak Tree Press, 1996) Chapter 11; Korah, *EC Competition Law and Practice* (Oxford, Hart, 7th ed., 2000) Chapter 9; Whish, *Competition Law* (London, Butterworths, 4th ed., 2001) Chapter 19.

The monopoly granted to the owner is often qualified by allowing "permitted acts" by third parties: there is the concept of "fair dealing" in copyright law,[7] and in trade mark law there are limits on the effects of a registered trade mark.[8] Moreover, the law may permit third parties to obtain licences to exploit intellectual property without the consent of the owner, as is the case with patents and the compulsory licensing regime.[9]

As regards competition law and allied principles, at European level, Articles 28–30, and, 81 and 82, of the Treaty of Rome and, at a domestic level, the Competition Act 2002,[10] which is modelled closely on Articles 81 and 82 of the Treaty, regulate further the exercise of intellectual property rights. These provisions limit the scope of national intellectual property laws where they give rise to a conflict with the policies underlying the above provisions.

33.3.1 Articles 28–30

Articles 28–30 deal with the free movement of goods within the internal market. They prohibit national measures which impose quantitative restrictions on imports from other member states, or have equivalent effect. Hence, national intellectual property law may breach this prohibition. However, restrictions are allowed, *inter alia*, for "the protection of industrial and commercial property."[11] The European Court of Justice (ECJ) has interpreted these provisions as permitting the existence of intellectual property rights but not their unfettered exercise, which is governed by the rules on free movement of goods.[12] In particular, under the doctrine of exhaustion of rights, when goods are first placed on the market in any member state by, or with the consent of the owner of the relevant intellectual property rights, his rights are "exhausted" so that he cannot use them to control trade in those goods within the Community.[13] This prevents intellectual property rights from being used to partition the internal market.

33.3.2 Articles 81 and 82

Article 81 prohibits agreements, decisions and concerted practices which may affect trade between member states and which have as their object or

7 Copyright and Related Rights Act 2000, Part II, Chapter 6: see 34.9.

8 Trade Marks Act 1996, s.15: see 36.6.5.

9 Patents Act 1992, ss.70–75: see 35.5.

10 See Competition Act 2002 (Commencement) Order 2002 (S.I. No. 199 of 2002). The 2002 Act repeals the Competition Act 1991, as amended: 2002 Act, s.48.

11 Art. 30; Art. 295 further states: "This Treaty shall in no way prejudice the rules in Member States governing the system of property ownership."

12 *Grundig & Consten v. Commission* [1996] E.C.R. 299.

13 *E.g. Deutsche Grammophon Gessellschaft mbH v. Metro* [1971] E.C.R. 487 (copyright); *Centrafarm BV v. Winthrop BV* [1974] E.C.R. 1183 (trade marks); *Pharmon BV v. Hoechst AG* [1985] E.C.R. 2281 (patents).

effect the prevention, restriction or distortion of competition within the common market. Section 4 of the Competition Act 2002 contains a similar prohibition within a domestic context.[14] Many agreements relating to the exploitation of intellectual property would *prima facie* fall foul of Article 81. However, under Article 81(3), exemption from this prohibition can be granted on an individual or block basis. In particular, block exemptions exist in relation to:

(a) certain categories of vertical agreements and concerted practices, including distribution agreements;[15]
(b) research and development agreements;[16] and
(c) technology transfer agreements, such as patent licences and know-how licences.[17]

Provided that the agreement is drafted in compliance with the relevant block exemption, it will be enforceable.

Article 82 and section 5 of the 2002 Act[18] seek to prevent the abuse of a dominant position in the market. Intellectual property rights may enable a business to acquire a dominant position in the market. Importantly, however, mere ownership or assertion of intellectual property rights is not *per se* abuse.[19] It has been held, for instance, that it is not abuse for an intellectual property rights holder to refuse to licence others to exploit his rights; or to refuse to do so on reasonable terms.[20] In contrast, an abuse of a dominant position was found in *RTÉ v. Commission*.[21] There RTÉ, the State-owned broadcasting organisation in the Republic of Ireland, and U.K. broadcasting organisations and their subsidiaries published weekly magazines which contained weekly television listings for all RTÉ, BBC and ITV programmes. Another company, Magill, started to publish these listings, until RTÉ and the other broadcasting organisations obtained injunctions preventing publication on the basis that such publication breached their copyright in the listings.[22] The ECJ found that these restrictions on publication were an abuse of a dominant position and were prohibited.

14 The 2002 Act, s.4 replicates the Competition Act 1991, s.4.
15 Reg. 2790/99, until May 31, 2010: [1999] O.J. L 336/21.
16 Reg. 2659/2000, until December 31, 2010: [2000] O.J. L304/7.
17 Reg. 240/96, until March 31, 2006: [1996] O.J. L31/2.
18 The 2002 Act, s.5 replicates the Competition Act 1991, s.5.
19 *E.g. Parke, Davis v. Centrafarm* [1968] E.C.R. 55.
20 *CICRA v. Renault* [1988] E.C.R. 6039; *Volvo v. Veng* [1988] E.C.R. 6211; *Philips Electronics N.V. v. Ingram Ltd* [1999] F.S.R. 112.
21 [1995] 1 E.C.R. 743.
22 *RTÉ v. Magill TV Guide* [1990] I.L.R.M. 534.

33.4 European and International Aspects of Intellectual Property Law

If intellectual property is to be fully exploited in global markets it must be capable of being protected internationally. Measures have therefore been designed to harmonise intellectual property laws throughout the EU and on a more international basis.[23] In some cases, these measures seek to harmonise the substantive laws of states, in others merely to secure a degree of international co-operation and mutual recognition of intellectual property rights. Many of these regional and international harmonising measures have been incorporated into Irish domestic law – the subject of this Part of the book. The following chapters explore the areas of copyright, patents, trade-mark and passing-off, in Irish law.[24]

Where Irish law seeks to implement EC harmonising measures, it is important to bear in mind a number of doctrines of EC law. For example, where an Irish measure, such as an Act of the Oireachtas or a Statutory Instrument, seeks to implement an EC measure, such as a regulation or a directive, the EC measure is paramount should a conflict between the two measures arise: the doctrine of supremacy.[25] Moreover, Irish courts are required, where possible, under the doctrine of indirect effect, to interpret national law to comply with EC law.[26] Therefore, a lawyer advising a client,

23 *E.g.* on copyright see the Berne Copyright Convention 1886, as amended by the Paris Act 1971; the Universal Copyright Convention 1952; the W.I.P.O. Treaties on copyright and on performers' rights 1996 and various E.C. Directives: see Chapter 34; see further Clark & Smith, *Intellectual Property Law in Ireland* (Dublin, Butterworths, 1997) Chapter 20; see generally Clark, *Irish Copyright and Design Law* (Dublin, Butterworths, 2001) Part 1. On patents, see the Paris Convention 1883; the Strasbourg Convention 1963; the Patent Co-operation Treaty 1970; the European Patent Convention 1973; the Community Patent Convention 1989: see further Chapter 35; and Clark & Smith, *Intellectual Property Law in Ireland* (Dublin, Butterworths, 1997) Chapter 2. On trade marks, see the Paris Convention for the Protection of Industrial Property 1883, as amended, including: the Madrid Protocol on International Registration of Marks, 1989, and various EC Regulations and Directives: see Chapter 36; see further Clark & Smith, *Intellectual Property Law in Ireland* (Dublin, Butterworths, 1997) Chapters 26 & 27. See also the WTO's Agreement on Trade Related Aspects of Intellectual Property (TRIPs Agreement) 1994.

24 See generally, Clark & Smith, *Intellectual Property Law in Ireland* (Dublin, Butterworths, 1997); Clark, *Irish Copyright and Design Law* (Dublin, Butterworths, 2001); *Cornish, Intellectual Property* (London, Sweet & Maxwell, 4th ed., 1999). Excluded from consideration is the law relating to confidential information, such as trade secrets, also considered a species of intellectual property: see further Lavery, *Commercial Secrets* (Dublin, Round Hall Sweet & Maxwell, 1996); Clark & Smith, *Intellectual Property Law in Ireland* (Dublin, Butterworths, 1997) Chapter 23; McMahon & Binchy, *Law of Torts* (Dublin, Butterworths, 3rd ed., 2001) pp.998–1012; Keane, *Equity and the Law of Trusts in the Republic of Ireland* (Dublin, Butterworths, 1988) Chapter 30.

25 *Internationala Handelsgessellschaft* [1972] 3 C.M.L.R. 255; see also Art 29.4.3° of the Constitution and *Doyle v. An Taoiseach* [1986] I.L.R.M. 693 (S.C.).

26 *Marleasing SA v. La Comercial Internacional de Alimentación SA* (Case C106/89) [1990] E.C.R. I–4135, [1992] 1 C.M.L.R. 305.

and a court faced with a dispute, needs to have access to both the national implementing measure and the underlying European legislation to determine the applicable law. Further, under the Treaty of Rome, the ECJ is the sole interpreter of the Treaty and other EC measures, and following a preliminary reference to the ECJ under Article 234 to determine the meaning of a particular provision, an Irish court is bound by the interpretation of the ECJ.[27] Where the ECJ has not pronounced on a particular matter, it may be useful for an Irish court to consider the decisions of courts in other member states of the EU and not just English case law.

As regards international measures, there may be obligations on Irish courts or other bodies to have "notice" of the decisions and opinions of international bodies. For example, under the Patents Act 1992, judicial notice and notice by the Controller of Patents, Designs and Trade Marks shall be taken of, *inter alia*, the European Patent Convention (EPC), the Washington Patent Co-operation Treaty (PCT), any other international agreements, and decisions or opinions of "a competent authority" under the EPC.[28]

27 *Benedetti v. Munari* (Case 52/76) [1977] E.C.R. 163.
28 1992 Act, s.129.

Chapter 34

COPYRIGHT

34.1 Introduction

The notion of copyright (a right to copy) dates back to the invention of the printing press and was originally a monopoly right to copy, or print, given to the King's printers and then to the Stationers' Company.[1] The Stationers' Company established the practice of allowing its members, stationers or printers, to register the fact that an individual member had possession of the manuscript of a book, usually under a contract with the author, and that the manuscript had been read by the censor. In time, this register came to represent a printer's sole right to print a particular book. Therefore, historically, copyright was used as form of control and censorship.[2] The rights of the author were not, initially at least, part of this legal equation. It was not until the Statute of Anne 1709 that the author of a book was given a statutory property right to print, that is, a publishing right, for a period of 14 years from first publication, renewable for another 14 years if the author was still alive at the end at that first period.[3]

Today, copyright is a property right which is defined principally within the terms of the Copyright and Related Rights Act 2000.[4] Copyright is different from other intellectual property rights, such as patents and trademarks, in that it arises automatically and is not dependent upon registration. In *Phonographic Performance (Ireland) Ltd v. William Cody and Princes Investments Ltd*,[5] Keane J. was of the opinion that the author's right to copyright derives from Articles 40.3.2° and 43 on private property, in the Constitution. Hence, the right cannot be abolished but is regulated

---

1 Blagden, *The Stationers Company – A History* (London, Allen & Unwin, 1960).

2 For more modern examples of copyright being used as a means of censorship, see Akdeniz, "Copyright and the Internet" [1997] *New Law Journal* 965.

3 See Clark & Smith, *Intellectual Property Law in Ireland* (Dublin, Butterworths, 1997) Chapter 9; and Tompson "Scottish Judges and the Birth of British Copyright" [1992] *Juridical Review* 18.

4 The 2000 Act was enacted on July 10, 2000, and, barring four minor provisions, came into effect from January 1, 2001: S.I. Nos. 404–411 of 2000 and S.I. No. 427 of 2000. U.K. copyright law continued to apply in Ireland until 1927 when the Industrial and Commercial Property (Protection) Act was enacted (Part VI covered copyright, the remainder dealing with patents, designs and trademarks). Part VI of the 1927 Act, as amended, remained in force until the Copyright Act 1963 repealed it. The 1963 Act was modelled on the U.K. Copyright Act 1956.

5 [1994] 2 I.L.R.M. 241 at 247, reversed on other grounds in the Supreme Court, [1998] 2 I.L.R.M. 21.

by legislation. Section 17 of the 2000 Act further identifies copyright as a property right.

The Copyright and Related Rights Act 2000 repealed the vast majority of the earlier legislation[6] and sought to meet our obligations under various EC Directives[7] and international treaties[8] and to consolidate the law into one piece of legislation. The 2000 Act was intended to update, improve and make more accessible the law in this area. Broadly speaking, the 2000 Act deals with:

(a) copyright, including moral rights, in Part II;
(b) performers' rights, including moral rights, in Parts III and IV;
(c) databases in Part V; and
(d) the jurisdiction of the Controller of Patents, Designs and Trade Marks in Part VI.

---

6 2000 Act, s.10 and the Second Schedule. The 2000 Act repealed, *inter alia*, all of the Copyright Act 1963 other than s.59; the Performers' Protection Act 1968; the Copyright (Amendment) Act 1987; ss.2-3 of the Intellectual Property (Miscellaneous Provisions) Act 1998; the EC (Legal Protection of Computer Programs) Regulations 1993; and the EC (Term of Protection of Copyright) Regulations, 1995.

7 Such as the EC Directive on Rental and Lending Rights (92/100/EEC); the EC Directive on Copyright Applicable to Satellite Broadcasting and Cable Retransmission (93/83/EEC); and the EC Directive on Databases (96/9/EC). Failure to implement these Directives on time led to proceedings being commenced in relation to the Satellite and Cable Directive under the then Art. 169 by the Commission: Case C-212/98 [2000] E.C.D.R. 201. See also the EC Directive on Copyright in the Information Society (2001/29/EC) [2001] O.J. L167/10. See further Vinje "Should we begin digging Copyright's Grave?" [2000] *European Intellectual Property Review* 551; Hugenholtz, "Why the Copyright Directive is Unimportant, and Possibly Invalid" [2000] *European Intellectual Property Review* 499; Hart, "The Copyright in the Information Society Directive: An Overview" [2002] *European Intellectual Property Review* 58, and the EC Directive on Artists' Resale Rights (2001/84/EC) [2001] O.J. L272/32, which will require a further legislative response. Where the 2000 Act seeks to implement an EC measure, it is important to bear in mind a number of doctrines of EC law. For example, where an Act of the Oireachtas seeks to implement an EC measure, such as a directive, under the doctrine of supremacy, the EC measure is paramount should a conflict between the two measures arise: *Internationale Handelsgesellschaft* [1972] 3 C.M.L.R. 255; see also Art. 29.4.3° of the Constitution and *Doyle v. An Taoiseach* [1986] I.L.R.M. 693 (S.C.). Moreover, Irish courts are required, where possible, under the doctrine of indirect effect, to interpret national law to comply with EC law: *Marleasing SA v. La Comercial Internacional de Alimentación SA* (Case C-106/89) [1990] E.C.R. I–4135, [1992] 1 C.M.L.R. 305. Further, under the Treaty of Rome, the Court of Justice (ECJ) is the sole interpreter of the Treaty and other EC measures, and an Irish court is bound by the interpretation of the ECJ: Treaty of Rome, Art. 234; see also *Benedetti v. Munari* (Case 52/76) [1977] E.C.R. 163.

8 Such as the Berne Convention 1886 (Paris Act 1971); the Rome Convention 1961; the Agreement on Trade Related Aspects of Intellectual Property Law (TRIPs) 1994; and the WIPO Copyright and, Performances and Phonograms Treaties 1996: see further Clark & Smith, *Intellectual Property Law in Ireland* (Dublin, Butterworths, 1997) Chapter 20.

In this chapter, we concentrate on copyright, the database right, and moral rights. Reference is made to the related area of industrial design and to performers' rights. The jurisdiction of the Controller of Patents, Designs and Trade Marks (hereinafter "the Controller") is also considered briefly.

34.2 The Subject-Matter of Copyright

Under the first statute in this area, the Statute of Queen Anne 1709, copyright protected literary or written works for a maximum of 28 years from first publication. Over the centuries, this protection has been expanded dramatically in terms of both subject-matter and time.[9]

Section 17(2) of the 2000 Act provides that copyright subsists in:

(a) original literary, dramatic, musical or artistic works;
(b) sound recordings, films, broadcasts or cable programmes;
(c) the typographical arrangement of published editions; and
(d) original databases.

An important general distinction is drawn between ideas and the expression of ideas. Copyright law protects the expression of ideas only.[10] Section 17(3) provides that copyright protection shall not extend to ideas and principles which underlie any element of a work. Moreover, copyright cannot subsist in a literary, dramatic or musical work, or an original database, unless it is recorded in writing or otherwise,[11] and copyright cannot subsist in a sound recording until the first fixation of the sound recording is made.[12]

34.2.1 Original literary, dramatic, musical or artistic works

For a work to be "original", it has been held that it must be a product of the author's labour, skill and capital, and not a copy of someone else's work.[13] However, the *original* requirement in copyright law must not be confused with the novelty requirement in patent law.[14] There is no novelty

9 For a critical analysis of this expansion see Breyer, "The Uneasy Case for Copyright: a Study of Copyright in Books, Photocopies, and Computer Programs" (1970) 84 *Harvard Law Review* 281; cf. Tyerman, "The Economic Rationale for Copyright Protection for Published Books: a Reply to Professor Breyer" (1971) 18 *UCLA Law Review* 1100; see also Laddie, "Copyright: Over-strength, Over-regulated, Over-rated?" [1996] *European Intellectual Property Review* 253.

10 *University Press Ltd v. University Tutorial Press Ltd* (1916) 2 Ch. 601 at 608–9.

11 2000 Act, s.18(1).

12 2000 Act, s.19.

13 *MacMillan & Co Ltd v. K&J Cooper* (1924) 40 T.R.L. 186 at 188 (P.C.); *University Press Ltd v. University Tutorial Press Ltd* (1916) 2 Ch. 601.

14 See 35.2.2.

requirement in copyright law,[15] so that if two authors independently produced the same musical work, such as an ad jingle, both would enjoy copyright in their creation."Literary work" is defined in section 2 of the 2000 Act as meaning: "a work, including a computer program,[16] but does not include a dramatic or musical work or an original database, which is written, spoken or sung".

"Written" is defined as including any form of notation or code, whether by hand or otherwise and regardless of the method or medium in or on which it is recorded.[17]

Dramatic or musical works, and original databases are excluded from this definition because they are protected in their own right.[18] The protection of computer programs, as a literary work, may seem to strain the concept of literary work, but it is based on the fact that a program for a computer can be represented in written form.[19] There is, however, an overlap between copyright law and patent law regarding computer programs. The Patents Act 1992 provides that a program for a computer, *as such*, is not patentable,[20] but where a computer program can be used to produce a technical effect it can be patented.[21]

Under the Copyright Act 1963, "literary work" indicated a work which was expressed in print or writing.[22] Case law provides many examples of what constitutes and what does not constitute a literary work. For example, books,[23] newspaper reports,[24] and law reports,[25] have been protected by copyright as literary works. The work does not need to have literary merit: exam papers,[26] and business letters,[27] have also been protected as literary

15 *University Press Ltd v. University Tutorial Press Ltd* (1916) 2 Ch. 601 at 608–9.

16 See further the Software Directive, Directive 91/250/EEC, [1991] O.J. L122/42.

17 2000 Act, s.2(1).

18 See further below.

19 This view is frequently opposed: see, *e.g.* Gordon, "The Very Idea! Why Copyright Law is an inappropriate way to protect computer programs" [1998] *European Intellectual Property Review* 10. See also Arreidge, "Copyright Protection for Computer Programs" [2000] *European Intellectual Property Review* 563.

20 Patents Act, s.9(2); see further 35.2.4.

21 See further Cohen, "The Patenting of Software" [1999] *European Intellectual Property Review* 607; Newman, "Patentability of Computer-Related Inventions in Europe" [1997] *Commercial Law Practitioner* 81.

22 *University Press Ltd v. University Tutorial Press Ltd.* (1916) 2 Ch. 601 at 608; *RTE & others v. Magill TV Guide* [1990] I.L.R.M. 534.

23 *Folens v. O'Dubhghaill and Joyce* [1973] I.R. 255.

24 *Hall v. Crosbie & Co* (1931) 66 I.L.T.R. 22.

25 *Hodges v. Walsh* (1840) 2 I.R. Eq. R. 266.

26 *University Press Ltd v. University Tutorial Press Ltd* (1916) 2 Ch. 601.

27 *British Oxygen Co Ltd v. Liquid Air Ltd* [1925] Ch. 383.

works. In contrast, it has been held that names,[28] titles,[29] and words[30] are not generally protected by copyright.[31]

An attempt was made in the case of *Gormley v. EMI Records*[32] to extend the meaning of literary work beyond a work which is expressed in print or writing. In this case, a woman claimed that her copyright in a literary work, under the Copyright Act 1963, had been infringed. As a child in the early 1960s, the plaintiff's teacher had recorded her and other children telling stories from the Bible. These tapes were discovered years later and extracts were produced on cassette tapes by the defendant and sold. The issue before the court was whether the plaintiff's oral recitation of the story was a "literary work" of which she was the author and hence entitled to copyright protection. The High Court and the Supreme Court referred to the leading case on the meaning of the phrase "literary work," *University Press Ltd v. University Tutorial Press Ltd*,[33] which concerned the copyright in examination papers. There, Peterson J. found that a literary work "covers work which is expressed in print or writing, irrespective of the question of whether the quality or style is high."[34] "Writing" was defined in section 2(1) of the 1963 Act as including "any form of notation, whether by hand or by printing, typewriting or other process." Following this case, the High Court and Supreme Court rejected the plaintiff's submissions. In the High Court, Costello J. held that the plaintiff's story telling was essentially oral and not literary. He also found that it lacked originality, and hence was not protected by copyright. In the Supreme Court, Barron J. agreed that the writing or the symbols which comprise the notation must be capable, without more, of being understood. The new definition of "literary work" in the 2000 Act expressly includes, in the definition of literary work, a work which is written, spoken or sung. Arguably, however, the decision in *Gormley* would not be any different under this wider definition because in that case, the teacher had provided the underlying form of words of the stories to the children and hence any copyright in these words would vest in the teacher.[35] The spoken word, including the Dublin accent which characterised the stories, could be protected under the heading of performers' rights.[36]

28 *Exxon Corporation v. Exxon Insurance Consultants International Ltd* [1982] R.P.C. 69, no copyright in the name "Exxon."

29 *Dicks v. Yates* (1881) 18 Ch. D. 76, no copyright in the novel title "Splendid Misery."

30 *Wombles Ltd v. Wombles Skips Ltd* [1975] F.S.R. 488, no copyright in the word "Wombles."

31 Such a name, title or word may be a registered trademark and may be protected at common law by the tort of passing off: see generally Chapter 36.

32 [1998] 1 I.L.R.M. 124 (H.C.); [1999] 1 I.L.R.M. 178 (S.C.).

33 (1916) 2 Ch. 601.

34 (1916) 2 Ch. 601 at 608.

35 See further Clark, *Irish Copyright and Design Law* (Dublin, Butterworths, 2001) Part I, Chapter 2, para. 82-91.

36 See further 34.14.

"Dramatic work" includes not only plays and sketches but also choreographic works and works of mime.[37] The essential requirement for a dramatic work appears to be that the work must be presented with dramatic scenery or dramatic effect,[38] but "dramatic work" has been held to exclude unscripted or ad-lib works.[39]

"Musical work" is defined for the first time in section 2 of the 2000 Act, though in the past, the lack of definition seems to have caused little difficulty. Musical work is defined as: "a work consisting of music, but does not include any words, or action, intended to be sung, spoken or performed with the music". Words of a song which are written, spoken or sung may be protected as "literary" works; while actions performed may be protected as "dramatic" works.[40]

Lastly, the definition of "artistic works" in section 2 of the 2002 Act is lengthy, and includes, for example, photographs, paintings, drawings, sculptures, works of architecture, and works of artistic craftsmanship, irrespective of their artistic quality. In *Green v. Independent Newspaper & Freeman's Journal*,[41] a "commonplace" drawing of Santa Claus on a poster was protected as an artistic work.

34.2.2 Sound recordings, films, broadcasts or cable programmes

The category of subject-matter, including sound recordings, films, broadcasts and cable programmes, is referred to as "neighbouring" or "related" rights. Neighbouring rights can be distinguished from literary, dramatic, musical or artistic works in that they do not arise by virtue of authorship. Rather, neighbouring rights tend to be entrepreneurial in nature, and exploitative of literary, dramatic, musical or artistic works. "Sound recording" is defined in section 2 of the 2000 Act and means:

> "a fixation[42] of sounds, or of the representation thereof, from which the sounds can be reproduced, regardless of the medium on which the recording is made, or the methods by which the sounds are reproduced".

This definition is technology neutral and covers a fixation of sounds, or a recording on audio tape, compact disc, semiconductor chip, or by any other means not yet developed. In the case of *Gormley v. EMI Records*,[43] the

37 2000 Act, s.2.

38 *Fuller v. Blackpool Winter Gardens* [1895] 2 Q.B. 429.

39 *Tate v. Fullbrook* [1908] 1 K.B. 821 where it was held that there was no copyright in an unscripted dramatic incident using a fire-cracker.

40 See also 34.14 regarding performers' rights.

41 [1899] 1 I.R. 386.

42 "Fixation" is defined in s.2 of the 2000 Act as meaning: "the embodiment of sounds or images or any combination of sound or images, or the representation thereof, from which they can be perceived, reproduced, or communicated through a device."

43 [1999] 1 I.L.R.M. 178; see 34.2.1.

plaintiff claimed copyright infringement under the 1963 Act, when a recording of her oral recitation as a child of Bible stories was produced and sold on cassette tapes. The recording was made by the plaintiff's teacher. The defendant had recognised that the teacher had copyright in the sound recording of the childrens' stories and as a consequence it entered into an agreement with the teacher whereby the defendant agreed to pay royalties to the teacher on the sale of the tapes that it had produced.

"Film" is defined in section 2 as meaning: "a fixation[44] on any medium from which a moving image may, by any means, be produced, perceived or communicated". The Copyright Act 1963 had covered cinematographic film only, though this definition had been interpreted to include film on video.[45] The new definition, which is technology neutral, removes any doubt in this regard because it is wide enough to cover film on video-tape, compact disc or "by any other means", as well as film for television or otherwise. Moreover, there is authority that the reproduction of a "still" photograph from a cinematographic film is also a breach of copyright.[46]

"Broadcast" means:

> "a transmission by wireless means, including by terrestrial and satellite means, for direct public reception or for presentation to members of the public of sounds, images, or data or any combination of sounds, images or data, or the representations thereof, but does not include MMDS service".

Hence the content of radio and television broadcasts are protected by copyright provided they are by wireless means and are for public reception, so that RTE has copyright in its broadcasting of a programme. This protection is not afforded to the providers of MMDS services who are protected under a separate heading of cable programme services.

"Cable programme" means: "any item included in a cable programme service". "Cable programme service" is defined, in turn, as meaning:

> "a service, including MMDS, which consists wholly or mainly of sending sounds, images or data or any combination of sounds, images or data, or the representation thereof, by means of a telecommunications system ..."[47]

The key distinction between a broadcast and a cable programme service involves the means of delivery: a cable service uses the telecommunications system. Hence, services provided over the telephone and fax, the distribution of information using a modem and the use of WAP technology would appear to come within this definition. In these

44 *Supra*, note 42.

45 *Universal City Studios and ors v. Mulligan*, unreported, High Court, Laffoy J., November 28, 1997.

46 *Spelling-Goldberg v. BPC Publishing* [1981] R.P.C. 283.

47 2000 Act, s.2(1).

circumstances, copyright protects the content, sounds, images and text sent in this way.

34.2.3 Typographical arrangement of published works

As well as copyright in a literary work such as a book, where an edition of the book is first published in the State, or is first published by an editor who is a qualified person,[48] there is copyright in the typographical arrangement of that edition. "Typographical arrangement" refers to the layout and presentation of a particular edition of a book, including details such as print type and size, and the placement of illustrations. Accordingly, each new edition may attract new copyright protection.

34.2.4 Databases

Under the 2000 Act, databases may be protected by copyright under Part II, or by a new property right[49] known as the database right, under Part V, depending on the originality of the work. These rights are independent of each other (though a database protected by copyright can also benefit from the protection offered by the database right) and of any copyright or other intellectual property rights which might exist in the individual contents of the database.[50] The database right is described as *sui generis*,[51] and affords lesser protection than copyright. These provisions seek to implement the EC Database Directive.[52] A database means:

> "a collection of independent works, data or other materials, arranged in a systematic or methodical way and accessible by whatever means but excludes computer programs used in the making or operation of a database".[53]

Simply put, a database is a compilation of information, such as a telephone directory, a dictionary, or an encyclopaedia, in whatever form, printed or digital, for example.[54] The Preamble of the Database Directive gives an indication of the breadth of this definition when it refers to the term "database" as including a wide variety of materials whether literary, artistic, musical or other collections of works or other materials, and such

---

48 34.5.
49 2000 Act, s.321(1).
50 2000 Act, s.17(3) and s.321(3); Directive, Arts. 3(2) and 13.
51 See Chapter III of Database Directive 96/9/EC, [1996] O.J. L77/20.
52 Directive 96/9/EC, [1996] O.J. L77/20; see further Rowland, "The E.C. Database Directive: an Original Solution to an Unoriginal Problem?" [1997] 5 Web J.C.L.I., http://webjcli.ncl.ac.uk/1997/issue5/rowlands5.html
53 2000 Act, s.2(1); Directive, Art. 1(2).
54 See Recital 14 and Art. 1(2).

materials may consist of texts, sound, images, numbers, facts or data.[55] However, the data must be arranged systematically or methodically, and be individually accessible, thereby excluding recordings on whatever medium, such as cinematographic film (a collection of still photographs) and musical compilations on CD.[56] The above definition also makes it clear that the Directive does not cover any computer programs used in the making or operation of a database. Such computer programs are protected in their own right, as literary works, under section 17 of the 2000 Act and the Software Directive.[57]

Where the database is "original", it will receive copyright protection.[58] "Original database" is defined as: "a database in any form which by reason of the selection or arrangement of its content constitutes the original intellectual creation of its author".[59] For example, the conventional encyclopaedia or anthology would most likely be an example of an "original database", because of the extent of the author's intellectual input. Importantly, the copyright in a database supplements any copyright which may exist in the contents of the database.[60] So, for example, with regard to an anthology of poetry, the individual poems may be protected by copyright, and the collection or anthology may be protected by a separate copyright. The owner of copyright in a database is the author, and the author of a database is identified as the natural person or group of persons who created the database.[61]

Prior to the 2000 Act, databases of very low originality received copyright protection in Irish law. For example, in *RTÉ v. Magill TV Guide*,[62] Lardner J. found that the weekly schedule of television listings was a result of "skill and judgment", and so was entitled to copyright protection.[63] It would appear that this position has changed with the 2000 Act. Where the database is of low originality, it will not receive copyright protection but may receive a lower level of protection, known as the database right, under Part V of the 2000 Act.

Under Part V, where a database has involved "a substantial investment" in obtaining, verifying or presenting the contents of a database, the maker has rights to do certain acts, known as "restricted acts", and to restrict others from doing those acts.[64] "Substantial investment" is defined broadly:

---

55 Recital 17.

56 Recital 19.

57 Directive 91/250/EEC [1991] O.J. L122/42.

58 2000 Act, s.17(2)(d); Directive, Art. 3.

59 2000 Act, s.2(1); Directive, Art. 3(1).

60 Arts. 3(2) and 13.

61 2000 Act, s.21(g), Directive Art. 4(1).

62 [1990] I.L.R.M. 534.

63 Note the Court of First Instance's indirect criticism of the low level of literary content necessary in Ireland: *RTÉ v. Commission* [1991] 4 C.M.L.R. 586.

64 2000 Act, s.321; Directive, Art. 7.

"investment" includes any investment, whether of financial, human or technical resources:[65] while "substantial" means substantial in terms of quantity or quality or a combination of both.[66]

Restricted acts comprise mainly extraction[67] or re-utilisation[68] of the contents of the database.[69] Lawful users[70] cannot be prevented from extracting or re-utilising insubstantial parts of the contents of the database,[71] but repeated and systematic extraction or re-utilisation of insubstantial parts of the contents of the database which conflicts with the normal exploitation of the database is prohibited as unreasonably prejudicing the legitimate interests of the maker.[72] Certain acts are permitted in relation to the database right including:[73]

(a) in relation to non-electronic databases, fair dealing by a lawful user for research and private study;[74]
(b) fair dealing by lawful users for educational purposes;[75]
(c) anything done in relation to public administration.[76]

It is the maker of the database, and not the author, (these may be the same person though not necessarily) who enjoys the database right, because it is the maker who has made the necessary investment in the database.[77] However, such makers, if natural persons, must be nationals of a member state or habitually resident in the Community or, if legal persons, must have their registered office or principal place of business in the Community.[78] The database right lasts for 15 years from the end of the year

65 2000 Act, s.320(1); Recital 40.
66 2000 Act, s.320(1); Directive, Art. 7(1).
67 "... the permanent or temporary transfer of all or a substantial part of the contents to another medium by any means in any form": 2000 Act, s.320; Directive Art. 7(2).
68 "...making available to the public all or a substantial part of the contents of a database by the distribution of copies, by renting, by on-line or by other forms of transmission": 2000 Act, s.320; Directive Art. 7(2).
69 2000 Act, s.324; Directive, Art. 7.
70 Defined as "any person who, whether under a licence to undertake any of the acts restricted by any database right in the database, or otherwise, has a right to use the database": 2000 Act, s.320(1).
71 2000 Act, s.327; Directive, Art. 8(1).
72 2000 Act, s.324(3); Directive, Art. 7(5).
73 Directive, Art. 9.
74 2000 Act, s.329.
75 2000 Act, s.330.
76 2000 Act, ss.331–336.
77 2000 Act, s.322–323; Directive, Preamble 41 and Art. 7.
78 Directive, Art. 11.

in which the database was created.[79] Any substantial alternations to the database will re-commence this period.[80]

34.2.5 Miscellaneous copyright

The 2000 Act recognises a number of other types of copyright. For example, Chapter 19 of Part II of the 2000 Act deals with government and Oireachtas copyright. Under section 191, the copyright in a work made by an officer or employee of the government or the State, in the course of his duties, is owned by the government. Such copyright expires 50 years from the end of the calendar year in which the work was made.[81] The copyright in any Bill or enactment vests in the Houses of the Oireachtas, and lasts also for 50 years from the end of the calendar year in which the work was made available.[82] There is also provision for recognising the copyright of international organisations,[83] and the copyright in legal notes issued by the Central Bank is recognised and vests *perpetually* in the Bank.[84]

34.3 The Period of Protection

As noted above, since copyright was first recognised by statute, the tendency has been to extend the subject-matter protected by copyright and the duration of copyright. In terms of duration, copyright in a literary work was protected for a maximum of 28 years under the Statute of Anne 1709. Under the Copyright Act 1963, copyright in a literary work was protected for the lifetime of the author plus 50 years. This period of protection was in compliance with the Berne Convention for the Protection of Literary and Artistic Works, under which the minimum period of protection was for the lifetime of the author plus 50 years. The intention was to afford protection for the author and the first two generations of his descendants. However, according to the EC Commission, increased average lifespan in the Community meant that this protection was no longer adequate.[85] Accordingly, this period was further extended by the EC Term of Protection Directive,[86] to the lifetime of the author plus 70 years.[87] This

79 2000 Act, s.325; Directive Art. 10.

80 2000 Act, s.325(3); Directive, Art. 10(3).

81 2000 Act, s.191(4).

82 2000 Act, s.192.

83 2000 Act, Part II, Chapter 20, s.196.

84 2000 Act, s.200(1).

85 See Recital 5 of EC Directive on Term of Protection, Directive 93/98/EEC, [1993] O.J. L290/9.

86 Directive 93/98/EEC, [1993] O.J. L290/9.

87 The equated to the lengthiest period of protection afforded within the EC, which was set by German law, at the time.

general expansion of copyright protection is not without its critics.[88] The effect of such lengthy periods of protection, it is argued, is to reduce cheaper public access to copyright works. Many critics argue that the periods are too long when compared with the protection afforded by other intellectual property rights, such as patent law where the period of protection is 20 years.[89] Moreover, it is argued that certain works, such as academic and scientific texts, or computer programs, have a much shorter commercial life – three to five years on average – and do not need such extended protection. Nevertheless the periods of protection have gained an international acceptance,[90] and there is no indication of any shortening of these period in the near or medium term future.

The periods of protection have not changed with the 2000 Act.[91] The periods vary depending on the subject-matter being protected. For example, the copyright in:

(a) literary, dramatic, musical or artistic works or original databases, expires 70 years after the death of the author, irrespective of when the work was first lawfully made available to the public;[92]
(b) a film expires 70 years after the last of the following persons dies:
  (i) the principal director;
  (ii) the author of the screenplay;
  (iii) the author of the dialogue; or
  (iv) the author of the music specifically used in film;[93]
(c) a sound recording expires:
  (i) 50 years after the sound recording is made; or
  (ii) where it is first lawfully made available to the public in the period referred to above, 50 years after the date of such making available.[94]

88 See, *e.g.* Cornish, "The International Relations of Intellectual Property" (1993) 53 *Cambridge Law Journal* 46; Ricketson, "The Copyright Term" [1992] *International Review of Industrial Property and Copyright* 753.

89 See 35.4.

90 See, *e.g.* U.S. Copyright Term Extension Act 1998.

91 2000 Act, Part II, Chapter 3, which implements the EC Term of Protection Directive 92/98/EEC, [1993] O.J. L290/9.

92 2000 Act, s.24; Directive, Art. 1.

93 2000 Act, s.25; Directive, Art. 2.

94 2000 Act, s.26; Directive, Art. 3.

34.4 Identifying the Owner of Copyright

Generally, the creator of the work, such as the author of a literary work, owns the copyright in that work. Sometimes, however, the creator is not easily identified and there are exceptions to this general rule. In three provisions, Chapter 2, in Part II of the 2000 Act, deals with the issue of authorship and ownership of copyright.

Section 21 states that the author means the person who creates a work and includes, in the case of:

(a) a sound recording, the producer;
(b) a film, the producer and the principal director;
(c) a broadcast, the person making the broadcast, …;
(d) a cable programme, the person providing the cable programme service in which the programme is included;
(e) a typographical arrangement of a published edition, the publisher;
(f) a computer-generated work, the person by whom the arrangements necessary for the creation of the work are undertaken;
(g) an original database, the individual or group of individuals who made the database; and
(h) a photograph, the photographer.

Section 22 addresses the issue of "joint-authorship", that is, where the contribution of each author is not distinct from that of the other author(s). For example, a film is treated as a work of joint authorship, unless the producer and the principal director are the same person.[95]

Section 23 contains exceptions to the general rule that the owner of copyright is the creator. In particular, where a copyright work is produced by an employee in the course of employment, copyright vests in the employer unless specified to the contrary in the employment contract. A qualification to this exception applies in relation to a work[96] made in the course of employment with a newspaper or periodical proprietor. In such circumstances, while copyright in the work vests in the employer (the newspaper or periodical proprietor), the author may use the work for any purpose, other than for the purpose of making available that work to newspapers or periodicals. Other exceptions to the general rule relate to government and Oireachtas copyright, and copyright of international organisations.[97]

Where a work is commissioned, copyright vests in the author of the work in the usual way. Thus if an independent contractor is commissioned to produce a work, such as a report or a computer program, he will own the

95 2000 Act, s.22(2).
96 Other than a computer program: 2000 Act, s.23(2).
97 2000 Act, s.23(1).

copyright in that work. In order to avoid this, the person commissioning the work may require the contractor to agree to assign to him the copyright in the work.

As a result of these provisions, ownership of copyright can exist in "layers", with different owners owning copyright in different aspects of a work, for different periods of protection. The example of a film is useful to illustrate this point. Assume that a production company wishes to make a film based on a novel. The first copyright to consider is that of the author of the novel. Is the novel still protected by copyright, and if so, who owns the copyright: the author or his assigns? If the novel is protected by copyright, the owner will have to assign various rights, including the film and allied rights[98] to the production company to enable to film to be made. In return, the owner of the copyright in the novel may receive a lump sum, or a share in the profits of the film, if any, or a combination of both.[99] Once the production company have secured the film rights, the novel will need to be adapted and a screenplay produced. Copyright in the screenplay exists because the screenplay would usually be considered an original literary work. Ownership of the copyright in the screenplay would vest initially in the author of the screenplay, unless:

(i) the author is an employee of the production company, in which case copyright would vest in the employer, or
(ii) the author assigns the copyright, in advance, in return for a fee or a share in the profits of the film, to the production company.

When the film is made, it will be protected by copyright, and that copyright is initially owned by the producer and the principal director. If a soundtrack for the film is needed, there are two options. Already existing music can be used, though if the music or its recording is protected by copyright, the permission of the copyright owners of the music and sound recordings will need to be sought and paid for. Alternatively, and often more conveniently and cheaply, an original soundtrack can be composed, preferably by one person. In these circumstances, the copyright in such a musical work vests first in the composer, unless:

(i) the music is composed in the course of employment with the production company, in which case copyright would vest in the employer, or
(ii) the composer assigns the copyright in advance to the production company, in return for a fee or a share in the profits of the film.

98 As part of the reproduction right (see 34.6) other rights include: foreign language rights; serialisation rights; electronic publishing rights; talking book rights; and adaptation rights.

99 Such a deal is often negotiated through the author's publisher or literary agent.

Where any sound recordings of the music are made, a separate copyright exists in favour of the maker of the recording, the producer. Furthermore, any posters used to promote the film (usually stills from the film) will be protected by copyright in the film.[100]

34.5 Formalities and Qualification for Protection

There is no registration requirement for copyright protection in Ireland, under the 2000 Act, or indeed in many parts of the world.[101] Copyright is acquired automatically, provided the statutory requirements are met. So, for example, copyright cannot subsist in a literary, dramatic or musical work, or an original database, unless it is recorded in writing or otherwise.[102] Copyright cannot subsist in a sound recording until the first fixation of the sound recording is made.[103]

Chapter 18 of Part II of the 2000 Act deals with the issue of qualification for copyright protection. For instance, for a work to qualify for copyright protection, the author must be a qualifying person, defined as including:

(a) an Irish citizen,
(b) a citizen, or subject of, or an individual domiciled or ordinarily resident in the State, or in any country, territory, state or area to which the relevant provisions of the Part extends;
(c) a body incorporated under Irish law;
(d) a partnership or body unincorporated under Irish law.

Additionally, section 184 provides that a work shall qualify for copyright protection where it is first lawfully made available to the public:

(a) in the State, or
(b) in any country, territory, state or area to which the relevant provisions of this Part extends.[104]

100 See 2000 Act, s.39(1)(c); see also *Spelling-Goldberg v. BPC Publishing* [1981] R.P.C. 283.

101 There is a copyright registry in the U.S.A. It is advisable in order to obtain full international copyright protection under the Universal Copyright Convention 1952 to use the symbol © with the name of the author and the date of first publication. This common marking is not needed to secure protection in any member state of the Berne Union, such as Ireland.

102 2000 Act, s.18(1).

103 2000 Act, s.19.

104 2000 Act, ss.188–189.

34.6 The Rights of a Copyright Owner

The rights of a copyright owner are outlined in section 17 and Chapter 4 of Part II of the 2000 Act. The 2000 Act reproduces many of the rights which existed under the previous legislation, but modifies them and introduces some new rights. This aspect of copyright law has been totally reorganised as a result.

Section 17(1) provides:

> "Copyright is a property right whereby, ..., the owner of the copyright in any work may undertake ... certain acts in the State, being acts which are designated by the Act as acts restricted by copyright in a work of that description."

Section 37 expands on this provision by listing three broad categories of "restricted acts". It provides that:

> "... the owner of the copyright in a work has the exclusive right to undertake or authorise others to undertake all or any of the following acts, namely:
>
> (a) to copy the work;
> (b) to make available to the public the work;
> (c) to make an adaptation of the work."

The right to copy, or the "reproduction right,"[105] is developed further in section 39 of the 2000 Act which provides that copying, in relation to any work, includes:

(i) storing the work in any medium;
(ii) the making of copies which are transient or incidental to some other use of the work.[106]

Moreover, copying in relation to an artistic work includes making a copy in three dimensions of a two-dimensional work and vice versa. Copying in relation to a film, television broadcast or cable programme includes making a photograph of the whole or a substantial part of any image forming part of the film, broadcast or programme.[107] And copying in

105 2000 Act, s.39(2).

106 2000 Act, s.39(1)(a); but see 2000 Act, ss.80–82 which permit, *inter alia*, making back-up copies of computer programs, and making copies of computer programs to achieve interoperability between computer programs.

107 2000 Act, s.39(1)(c).

relation to a typographical arrangement of a published edition includes making a reprographic copy of the arrangement.[108]

Section 40 spells out the nature of the making available right as including:

(a) making available copies of a work over the internet;
(b) performing, showing or playing a copy of the work in public;
(c) broadcasting a copy of the work;
(d) including a copy of the work in a cable programme service;
(e) issuing copies to the public;[109]
(f) renting copies of the work;[110]
(g) lending copies of the work without payment of remuneration to the owner of the copyright in the work.[111]

The right to make an adaptation of a work is considered further in section 43 and, for example, in relation to a literary or dramatic work, film, sound recording, broadcast, cable programme or typographical arrangement of a published edition includes:

(i) a translation, arrangement or other alternation of the work;
(ii) a version of a dramatic work which is converted into a non-dramatic work, and vice versa;
(iii) a version of a work in which the story or action is conveyed wholly or mainly by means of pictures in a form suitable for reproduction.[112]

However, where a person proposes to play a sound recording in public or include a sound recording in a broadcast or a cable programme service, he may do so without the prior consent of the copyright owner provided he agrees to pay royalties to the relevant licensing body, and he complies with the relevant statutory provision.[113]

108 2000 Act, s.39(1)(d).

109 Known as the distribution right. While a copyright holder can control distribution, this is limited by the European "doctrine of exhaustion," recognised by the 2000 Act, s.41, whereby once a work has been put into circulation in the E.E.A. by or with the consent of the copyright owner, the subsequent distribution within the E.E.A. cannot be prohibited or controlled: see generally 33.3.1.

110 Known as the rental right, see further 2000 Act, s.42.

111 Known as the lending right, see further 2000 Act, s.42.

112 2000 Act, s.43(2).

113 2000 Act, s.38.

34.7 Dealing in Copyright

Sections 17(1) and 120(1) of the 2000 Act specify that copyright is personal or moveable property and therefore it can be can be traded, by outright disposition such as an assignment for a cash payment, or by the owner permitting others to exploit his property by granting a licence. Equally, like other forms of property, it can be charged or gifted away. However, such dealings must comply with statutory formalities to be fully effective. Chapter 8 of Part II of the 2000 Act covers dealings in copyright works.[114] Section 120(1) provides: "The copyright in a work is transmissible by assignment, by testamentary disposition or by operation of the law …"

An assignment may be whole or partial. In the latter case, the assignment may relate to one or more but not all of the acts which a copyright owner can undertake, the "restricted acts," or it may relate to a part, but not whole of the period of copyright protection.[115] An assignment may also be described as partial where it is limited geographically. Future copyright can also be assigned by the prospective owner of a work not yet created.[116] This occurs frequently, for example, where an established author assigns the future copyright in a book as yet unwritten. An assignment, whether whole or partial, must be in writing and signed by the assignor.[117] "Writing" is defined as including any form of notation or code, whether by hand or otherwise and regardless of the method or medium in or on which it is recorded.[118] There is also authority to support the notion of an equitable assignment of copyright where, for example, the strict legal formalities have not been complied with,[119] or where there is an agreement to assign copyright in an existing work at some time in the future.[120] Because there is no public registration system with regard to copyright, an assignee is taking a risk that there is no prior assignment which would take priority over his. If there is, then the assignee has a personal cause of action against the assignor, but has no proprietary claims over the copyright.

Assignment of copyright must be distinguished from a licence agreement in relation to a copyright work. With an assignment, the copyright owner transfers all or part of his property rights in the copyright

114 See further Beatty, "Transmission of Copyright and Moral Rights" [2001] *Commercial Law Practitioner* 27.

115 2000 Act, s.120(2).

116 2000 Act, s.121.

117 2000 Act, s.120(3).

118 2000 Act, s.2(1).

119 *Brooker v. John Friend Ltd* [1936] N.Z.L.R. 743; *Wah Sang Industrial Co v. Takmay Industrial Co* [1980] F.S.R. 303; *Batjak Production Inc v. Simitar Entertainment* (UK) [1996] F.S.R. 139.

120 *Western Front Ltd v. Vestron* [1987] F.S.R. 66; *Wah Sang Industrial Co v. Takmay Industrial Co* [1980] F.S.R. 303; *Batjak Production Inc v. Simitar Entertainment* (*U.K.*) [1996] F.S.R. 139.

work. This transferred right may, in turn, be transferred. With a licence agreement, no property in the copyright work is transferred, but the licensee is given permission to undertake some or all the "restricted acts" in relation to the work. Section 37(2) states: "The copyright in a work is infringed by a person who without the licence of the copyright owner undertakes ... any of the acts restricted by copyright." This permission may be personal to the licensee and if so, cannot be transferred.

A licence can be contractual or gratuitous,[121] and if contractual, it can be express or implied. It may be implied, for example, where plans produced by an architect to secure planning permission, once completed and paid for, can be used for another purpose by the person who commissioned the plans, including the construction of a building.[122] Moreover, a licence can be exclusive or non-exclusive. Under the 2000 Act, an exclusive licence is defined as a licence in writing and signed by a copyright owner which authorises the licensee, to the exclusion of all other persons, including the copyright owner, to undertake "restricted acts" in relation to the work. Otherwise, there are no statutory formalities, though it is advisable that any licence be in writing. A licence granted by the owner of copyright is binding on every successor in title except a purchaser in good faith for valuable consideration without notice, actual or constructive.[123]

The licensing of copyright works is beneficial both to the copyright owner, as it generates a source of income, and to the general public as it facilitates wider access to copyright works. There are a variety of means of securing licences. For example, in relation to literary works, such as a book, an author may engage a literary agent to negotiate and procure a publishing contract. Another means of securing licensing agreements is through the use of collecting societies. There are a number of different collecting societies operating in Ireland on behalf of copyright owners. Their function is to grant licences and collect royalties, on a collective basis.[124]

The major collecting societies operate in the music industry[125] and are:

(a) The Irish Music Rights Organisation (IMRO);
(b) The Mechanical Copyright Protection Society (MCPS);
(c) Phonograph Performance Ireland Ltd (PPI).

---

121 For example of gratuitous licence, see *Trumpet Software Property Ltd v. Ozemail Pty Ltd* (1996) 34 I.P.R. 481.

122 *Blair v. Oxborne and Tompkins* [1971] 1 All E.R. 468 (C.A.); *cf. Stovin Bradford v. Volpoint Properties* [1971] 3 All E.R. 570 (C.A.).

123 2000 Act, s.120(4) and (5).

124 On the role of Controller regarding licence schemes and terms, see 2000 Act, Part II, Chapter 16; see further 34.12.

125 Other collecting organisations exist, *e.g.* regarding the licensing of literary works and published editions: see the Irish Copyright Licensing Agency; see further (1997) 3 *Irish Intellectual Property Review* 28.

IMRO takes an assignment of the public performance rights in the music of its copyright owner members, that is, composers and music publishers. It then grants licences in return for royalties in respect of the public performance of such music to bodies such as television and radio broadcasters, and pubs, clubs and other venues where music is performed in public.[126] MCPS collects royalties in respect of the music used on sound recordings on behalf of composers and music publishers from record companies, video, film and advertising companies, and broadcasting organisations. PPI grants licences in respect of public performances and broadcasting of sound recordings (as opposed to the music contained thereon). Other rights are licensed individually by the copyright owner or his agent.

Concerns have been expressed in the past about the operation of such bodies.[127] In particular, a collecting society is usually entitled to exclusively represent its members and hence enjoys a monopoly position. This raises concerns in relation to competition law.[128] To address some of these concerns, the 2000 Act requires a "licensing body"[129] to register and to maintain registration for as long as it operates as a licensing body. Failure to register is a criminal offence.[130] The Register of Copyright Licensing Bodies is maintained by the Controller of Patents, Designs and Trade Marks and it must contain information prescribed under the 2000 Act, such as details of the scales of charges to be levied and the class of rightholders represented.[131] This Register provides information to the public and hence is intended to bolster confidence in the operation of licensing bodies generally.

34.8 INFRINGEMENT[132]

As noted above, section 37(2) provides: "The copyright in a work is infringed by a person who without the licence of the copyright owner undertakes, ... any of the acts restricted by copyright." Further, section

126 See generally www.imro.ie.

127 For example, allegations have been made that charges are arbitrary and are imposed retrospectively by bodies that enjoy a monopoly position: see, *e.g.* 199 Dáil Debates, Col 1463 onwards (February 14, 1963); and 136 Seanad Debates, Cols 1090 onwards (June 9, 1993); and 464 Dáil Debates, Cols 806–812, (April 23, 1996).

128 See Clark & Smith, *Intellectual Property Law in Ireland* (Dublin, Butterworths, 1997) paras 15.51–15.74; Carney & Balding, "The Application of E.C. Competition Law to Copyright Collecting Societies" [1999] *Irish Law Times* 53.

129 "Licensing body" means "a society or other organisation which has as it main object … the negotiating or granting … of copyright licences, and whose objects includes the granting of licences relating to works of more than one copyright owner;" 2000 Act, s.149(1).

130 2000 Act, s.181.

131 2000 Act, Chapter 17, ss.175–180.

132 See 2000 Act, Part II, Chapters 4 & 5.

37(3) states that: "References to the undertaking of an act restricted by copyright in a work shall relate to the work as a whole or to any substantial part of the work and to whether the act is taken directly or indirectly." Hence, infringement is broadly defined and can relate to the work as a whole or to a substantial part of the work, and it can be direct or indirect. Infringement may also be secondary in nature. The concept of "secondary infringement" is dealt with in Chapter 5 of Part II of the 2000 Act and includes:

(a) dealing with infringing copy;[133]
(b) providing the means for making an infringing copy;[134]
(c) permitting use of premises for infringing performances;[135]
(d) permitting use of apparatus for infringing performances.[136]

Section 38 provides an exception to infringement by allowing the playing of a sound recording in public, or the inclusion of a sound recording in a broadcast or cable programme service without the prior permission of the copyright owner, provided a payment is made to the relevant licensing body and the statutory provision is complied with.

While the whole area of copyright owners' rights, restricted acts, and infringement has been restructured by the 2000 Act, many aspects of the previous legislation remain intact. As a result, case law on infringement under the 1963 Act may still be relevant. For example, a common infringement is copying or "reproduction". With the advances in reproduction technology, high-quality copies can be made quickly and cheaply. Nevertheless, it has been held that an infringing copy need not be identical to the copyright work to constitute infringement. For instance, in *Education Co. of Ireland v. Fallon*,[137] there was infringement of a literary work, a book, even though verbal and structural changes were made. In *House of Spring Gardens Ltd v. Point Blank Ltd*,[138] the defendants sought to avoid liability for copyright infringement by re-designing a bullet-proof vest which the plaintiffs had sold to the Libyan Government. However, the resulting product was held by the Supreme Court to have been a substantial reproduction of the original work and hence infringement was proved.

133 Dealing includes: selling; renting; lending; or offering to sell, rent or lend; importing; having possession of; 2000 Act, s.45.

134 Providing the means include making; selling, renting or lending; or offering to sell, rent or lend; importing or having possession of an article specifically designed for making copies; 2000 Act, s.46.

135 2000 Act, s.47.

136 2000 Act, s.48.

137 [1919] 1 I.R. 62.

138 [1984] I.R. 611 (S.C.).

The distinction between an infringing copy, and something which is similar, but only by coincidence, was addressed in the leading English case of *Francis Day & Hunter Ltd v. Bron.*[139] There the Court of Appeal held that two elements must be present for infringement to be established:

(i) sufficient objective similarity between the copyright work and the alleged infringing work or a substantial part thereof; and
(ii) evidence that the copyright work is the source of the infringing work (a causal link).

The issue of how to prove sufficient objective similarity between a plaintiff's original work and the defendant's alleged infringing work was addressed in *Ravenscroft v. Herbert*[140] where four principal factors were identified:

(i) the volume of the material taken, bearing in mind that quality is more important than quantity;
(ii) how much of the material taken is protected by copyright and how much is not;
(iii) whether the defendant intended to take the plaintiff's work to save himself labour; and
(iv) the extent to which the plaintiff's work and the defendant's work are in competition.

As a matter of evidence though, proving infringement can be difficult. The case of *News Datacom v. David Lyons*[141] involved the alleged copying of the plaintiff's decoder and smart card in order to view Sky TV. The smart card contained an algorithm which enabled the decoder to descramble the television signal. The smart card was changed periodically and new cards were distributed to subscribers to maintain the security of the system. In 1993, the defendant produced a card which could decode the television signal. The plaintiff applied for an injunction to prevent the defendant producing their card, claiming that the plaintiff's algorithm was so complex that it could only be reproduced by copying. Flood J. rejected the plaintiff's claim, relying on the decision of *Megarry V.C. in Thrustcode Ltd v. WW Computing.*[142] There it was made clear that two different programs can lead to the same result, and simply because the programs produced the same result did not mean that one was a copy of the other. Better evidence was needed, such as written evidence of the programs.

The copyright owner[143] or his assignee, and an exclusive licensee are

139 [1963] Ch. 587.
140 [1980] R.P.C. 193.
141 [1994] 1 I.L.R.M. 450.
142 [1983] F.S.R. 502.
143 2000 Act, s.127(1).

entitled to bring infringement proceedings.[144] The right of a copyright owner and an exclusive licensee are concurrent.[145] Infringement proceedings under the 2000 Act are frequently coupled with a related cause of action, such as an action for breach of contract, passing-off, or trade-mark infringement. A plaintiff will seek to pursue as many causes of action as possible in the hope of success.[146]

34.9 Permitted Acts in Relation to Copyright

The 2000 Act contains a number of permitted acts in relation to copyright works, in other words, defences to infringement: some old, some new. Their purpose is to balance the rights of copyright owners and other users. The effect of the 2000 Act has been to expand the number and scope of these permitted acts thereby facilitating wider public access to copyright works.

The main "permitted act" is referred to as "fair dealing" and this applies to all works under the 2000 Act. "Fair dealing" is defined, for the first time in the 2000 Act, as: "making use of a work … for the purpose and to an extent which will not unreasonably prejudice the interests of the owner of the copyright."[147] For example, "fair dealing" with a work for the purposes of research or private study, shall not infringe copyright.[148] Fair dealing with a work for the purposes of criticism or review, shall not infringe copyright where accompanied by an acknowledgment.[149]

Further permitted acts or defences exist in relation to education,[150] prescribed libraries and archives,[151] public administration,[152] designs,[153] computer programs,[154] original databases,[155] and typefaces, amongst others.[156] Under the heading of education, for instance, copyright in a work is not infringed where it is copied in the course of instruction or examination.[157] Under the heading of public administration, copyright in a work is not infringed by anything done for the purpose of parliamentary or judicial proceedings. And under the heading of computer programs, it is

144 2000 Act, s.135(1).
145 2000 Act, s.135(2).
146 See, *e.g. House of Spring Gardens Ltd v. Point Blank Ltd* [1984] I.R. 611.
147 2000 Act, s.50(4).
148 2000 Act, s.50.
149 2000 Act, s.51.
150 2000 Act, ss.53–58.
151 2000 Act, ss.59–70.
152 2000 Act, ss.71–77.
153 2000 Act, ss.78–79.
154 2000 Act, ss.80–82.
155 2000 Act, s.83.
156 2000 Act, ss.84–85.
157 2000 Act, s.53.

not infringement of the copyright in a computer programs to make a back-up copy of the program which is necessary for the purpose of lawful use.[158]

34.10 Remedies on Infringement

Where a person's copyright has been infringed, the legislation offers a variety of civil remedies and criminal sanctions, both supported by strong presumptions of ownership in copyright works.[159]

Section 127 of the 2000 Act provides that infringement of copyright in a work is actionable by the copyright owner. Furthermore, section 135(1) provides that an exclusive licensee has the same rights and remedies in respect of matters occurring after the grant of the licence as if the licence had been an assignment. Where infringement proceedings are brought by a copyright owner, or an exclusive licensee, in respect of which they have concurrent rights, the owner or the licensee cannot, without the leave of the court, bring proceedings unless the other party is joined as a plaintiff or added as a defendant.[160]

The remedies available for breach of copyright include damages, or an account of profits, and injunctions.[161] Additionally, a successful party will normally be awarded costs against the other party.

Under section 128(1), a court may award such damages as, having regard to all the circumstances, it considers just. Damages are awarded on the basis of compensation for loss suffered as a result of infringement. A plaintiff seeking damages must prove that the infringement caused the loss suffered (such as loss of profit on sales, loss of licence income, and losses resulting from damage to product reputation). However, the 2000 Act provides that where the infringement is innocent, no damages can be awarded.[162] In addition to or as an alternative to compensatory damages, a court may award aggravated and/or exemplary damages where, for example, the breach of copyright is flagrant.[163]

Alternatively, a plaintiff can seek an account of profits. The rationale behind this remedy is to ensure that the infringer does not profit from his wrongful conduct.[164] Rather than seeking damages based on the plaintiff's loss, the plaintiff can elect to require the infringer to account for the profits made on the infringing activities. This remedy is useful where it is difficult to measure the plaintiff's loss, or where an account of profits yields a larger

---

158 2000 Act, s.80(1); on "lawful user" see 2000 Act, s.80(2).

159 2000 Act, Part II, Chapters 9–15.

160 2000 Act, s.136.

161 2000 Act, s.127(2). See further Brennan & Hennessy, "Forensic Accounting and Intellectual Property Infringement" [2001] *Commercial Law Practitioner* 112.

162 2000 Act, s.128(2).

163 2000 Act, s.128(3).

164 *House of Spring Gardens Ltd v. Point Blank Ltd* [1984] I.R. 611.

sum to the plaintiff than a damages claim, as where the infringer makes sales to customers who are not customers of the copyright owner, or where sales are made at a higher price than that offered by the copyright owner. Discovery has particular importance in this context. Plaintiffs are normally awarded discovery of the infringer's documents relating to profits sufficient to allow the plaintiff to elect between damages or an account of profits. With an account of profits, the infringer cannot be required to pay more than the profits it actually made. The innocent infringer defence does not apply in relation to a claim for an account of profits.

As well as granting interlocutory and perpetual injunctions,[165] to prevent further infringement, a court can grant orders of delivery-up;[166] and powers of seizure following a court order[167] or otherwise[168] may be conferred. Such powers are very important when piracy of copyright works is alleged.

The 2000 Act contains strong presumptions of ownership in favour of copyright holders to facilitate the taking of civil and criminal legal proceedings.[169] For instance, copyright is presumed to exist in a work until the contrary is proved,[170] and the plaintiff is presumed to be the owner, or exclusive licensee, until the contrary is proved.[171]

Beyond the civil remedies available to a copyright owner or exclusive licensee, the 2000 Act prescribes specific criminal offences.[172] Moreover, the 2000 Act provides for substantial financial sanctions for copyright offences: up to £1,500 [€1,904.61] and/or 12 months' imprisonment on summary conviction; and up to £100,000 [€126,973.81] and/or five years' imprisonment on indictment.[173]

---

165 See further 37.4.1.2 and 37.4.1.3.

166 2000 Act, s.131; see further 2000 Act, s.138 for six-year time limit on this remedy.

167 2000 Act, s.132.

168 2000 Act, s.133.

169 2000 Act, Part II, Chapter 12, s.139. These presumptions were first introduced in the Intellectual Property (Miscellaneous Provisions) Act 1998, ss.2–3, which sought to comply with international obligations, in particular under the TRIPs Agreement 1994. See further Newman, "Practical and Constitutional Impact of the Presumptions in the Intellectual Property (Miscellaneous Provisions) Act 1998" (1998) 2(3) *Irish Intellectual Property Review* 2.

170 2000 Act, s.139(2).

171 2000 Act, s.139(3).

172 2000 Act, Part II, Chapter 13.

173 2000 Act, s.140(7) and (8).

34.11 Moral Rights[174]

The above rights and legal protections are largely based on providing and protecting the financial or economic interests of "authors".[175] The 2000 Act, in Chapters 7 and 11 of Part II, recognises for the first time in Irish law the moral rights of authors. Accordingly, even after the transfer of an author's economic rights, the author's moral rights remain. This aspect of the legislation seeks to implement our international obligations under the Article 6*bis*(1) of the Berne Convention for the Protection of Literary and Artistic Works (Paris Act 1971).[176]

The author of a work[177] has the following moral rights recognised by the 2000 Act:

(a) the paternity right, that is, the right to be identified as the author of a work;[178]
(b) the integrity right, that is, the right to object to derogatory treatment of a work;[179]
(c) the right not to have work falsely attributed to him, as author;[180] and
(d) a right to privacy in photographs and film when commissioned for private or domestic purposes.[181]

There is, as yet, no reported Irish case law on the moral rights of authors, though case law from other jurisdictions is informative. For example, in *Snow v. Eaton Centre*,[182] the plaintiff sculptor had been granted an order for the removal of Christmas decorations from a snow geese sculpture by him which had been commissioned by the defendant shopping centre because the decorations distorted the sculpture in a prejudicial manner contrary to his integrity right. In *Clark v. Associated Newspapers Ltd*,[183] a mock diary column in the defendant newspaper which purported to be written by the well-known politician Alan Clark, and which carried his photograph, was held to amount to false attribution of the work to the plaintiff politician.

174 See Vaver, "Moral Rights: the Irish Spin" (1999) 3(3) *Irish Intellectual Property Review* 3.
175 2000 Act, s.21; see 34.4.
176 These rights may also be protected by the Constitution, the common law of contract, passing-off and defamation.
177 "Work" for the purpose of the moral rights provisions, is defined as meaning: a literary, dramatic, musical, or artistic work, or film: 2000 Act, s.2(1).
178 2000 Act, s.107 and exceptions listed in s.108. See further *Rowe v. Walt Disney Productions* [1987] F.S.R. 38, a French case.
179 2000 Act, s.109 and exceptions and qualifications provided for in ss.110–111.
180 2000 Act, s.113.
181 2000 Act. s.114.
182 [1982] 70 C.P.R. 105; see also *Morrison Leahy Music Ltd v. Lightbound* [1993] E.M.L.R. 144; *Pasterfield v. Denham* [1999] F.S.R. 168.
183 [1998] 1 All E.R. 959.

The paternity right, the integrity right and the right to privacy in photographs and film exist for the same period of time as the relevant economic rights.[184] In contrast, the right not to have the work falsely attributed subsists 20 years after the death of the person on whom it is conferred.[185] While the economic rights which comprise copyright are *personal property* which can be sold or licensed, moral rights are *personal rights* and hence cannot be assigned or transferred,[186] except by devolution on death.[187] Significantly, though, they can be waived.[188] Any waiver must be in writing and signed by the person waiving the rights.[189] The waiver may relate to a specific work or works, or to works generally. It can relate to existing or future works.[190] The waiver may be conditional or unconditional, revocable or irrevocable.[191] Sections 137 and 138 provide that a breach of moral rights is actionable, as a breach of statutory duty owed to the author. Damages, injunctive relief and other remedies are available.

34.12 The Controller[192]

Although there is no registration requirement for copyright, the Controller of Patents, Designs and Trademarks does have a role to play in relation to copyright. As noted above, the Controller has a new role in the establishment and maintenance of a register of copyright licensing bodies, which must contain information prescribed under the 2000 Act, such as details of the scales of charges to be levied and the class of rightholders represented.[193] A "licensing body"[194] is required to register and to maintain registration for as long as it operates as a licensing body: failure to register is a criminal offence.[195]

The Controller continues to have a dispute resolution function in relation to licensing bodies and persons requiring licences, under a number

---

184 2000 Act, s.115(1).
185 2000 Act, s.115(2).
186 2000 Act, s.118.
187 2000 Act, s.119.
188 2000 Act, s.116.
189 2000 Act, s.116(2).
190 2000 Act, s.116(3)(a).
191 2000 Act, s.116(3)(b).
192 See generally, 2000 Act, Part VI.
193 2000 Act, Chapter 17, ss.175–180.
194 "Licensing body" means "a society or other organisation which has as it main object … the negotiating or granting … of copyright licences, and whose objects includes the granting of licences relating to works of more than one copyright owner;" 2000 Act, s.149(1).
195 2000 Act, s.181.

of headings, including where there is a licensing scheme[196] and where there is no licensing scheme.[197] For example, where a licensing scheme is in operation and a dispute arises between the operator of the scheme and a person requiring a licence, or an organisation claiming to represent such a person, the scheme can be referred to the Controller who may confirm or vary the scheme, as he thinks fit.[198] Where there is no licensing scheme, the terms on which a licensing body proposed to grant a licence may be referred to the Controller by a prospective licensee, and the Controller may confirm or vary the terms as he thinks fit.[199] As noted above,[200] where a person proposes to play a sound recording in public, or include a sound recording in a broadcast or a cable programme service, he may do so without the prior consent of the copyright owner, provided he agrees to pay royalties to the relevant licensing body, and he complies with the relevant statutory provision.[201] Where an agreement cannot be reached as to payment, the proposed agreement can be referred to the Controller for resolution in relation to the amount and terms of payment.[202]

Further, the 2000 Act provides that where an author has transferred his rental right, he nonetheless retains a right to equitable remuneration for the rental.[203] Where an agreement about the amount of equitable remuneration cannot be reached, a reference can be made to the Controller to determine the amount payable.[204]

34.13 Industrial Designs

Industrial designs are relevant to copyright law because of the relationship between the legal protection of industrial designs and copyright in artistic works. The governing legislation is the Industrial Designs Act 2001,[205] which seeks, *inter alia*, to implement an EC Directive on the legal

196 2000 Act, ss.150–156. A "licensing scheme" means a scheme specifying (a) the classes of case in which the operator of the scheme is willing to grant licences, and (b) the terms on which such licences may be granted in those classes of case: 2000 Act, s.149(1).

197 2000 Act, ss.157–161.

198 2000 Act, s.152.

199 2000 Act, s.158.

200 See 34.6.

201 2000 Act, s.38.

202 2000 Act, s.38(4)

203 2000 Act, ss.124–125.

204 2000 Act, s.126.

205 The Industrial Designs Act 2001 was enacted on November 27, 2001, and was commenced on July 1, 2002: see S.I. No. 275 of 2002. See also the Industrial Design Regulations 2002, S.I. No. 280 of 2002.

protection of designs.[206] Broadly speaking, this legislation is expansionist in nature: for instance, it widens the definition of industrial design and extends the period of protection. Importantly, registerable designs can now have dual protection under copyright law and by registration as a design. "Design" is defined as:

> "the appearance of the whole or a part of a product resulting from the features of, in particular, the lines, contours, colour, shape, texture or materials of the product itself or its ornamentation".[207]

"Product" means:

> "any industrial or handicraft item, including parts intended to be assembled into a complex product,[208] packaging, get-up, graphic symbols and typographic typefaces, but excluding computer programs".[209]

These definitions substantially expand the meaning of design. For example, there is no longer a requirement for "eye appeal" or aesthetic character or industrial applicability, as under the previous legislation.[210] The inclusion of colour, texture and "materials of the product itself" clearly goes beyond earlier law, also. The definition of product is broader than the definition of "article" under the previous legislation, and permits the registration of designs for products which have no other function than to carry the design. So, designs for packaging, get-up and graphic symbols are registerable.

A design to be registered, and hence protected, must be *new* and have *individual character*.[211] A design is "new" where: "… no design identical to it has been made previously available to the public before the filing date …"[212]

206 Directive 98/71/EC, [1998] O.J. L289/28; see further Shortt, "Implementation in Ireland of the E.C. Directive on Legal Protection of Designs" (1999) 3(3) *Irish Intellectual Property Review* 16; McGovern, "Protection of Designs – The Current Position and the Future" [2000] *Irish Business Law* 92. The 2001 Act also enables the State to ratify the Hague Agreement concerning the International Registration of Industrial Designs (1999) which provides an international register of design, maintained by the WIPO in Geneva. An international application for registration of a design may be filed, designating the countries where design registration is sought and this takes effect in each designated country as if the application was filed nationally. See also the Community Design Regulation, adopted December 12, 2001, Regulation 6/2002 [2002] O.J. L3/1 which provides for a Community-wide registration system for designs, similar to the trade mark regime. This Regulation entered into force on March 6, 2002.

207 2001 Act, s.2(1); Directive, Art. 1(a).

208 2001 Act, s.2(1); Directive, Art. 1(c).

209 2001 Act, s.2(1); Directive, Art. 1(b).

210 Industrial and Commercial (Property) Act 1927, s.3 and *Allibert SA v. O'Connor* (1981) F.S.R. 613. See generally, Shortt, "The Law on Industrial Design in Ireland" (1998) 2(2) *Irish Intellectual Property Review* 5.

211 2001, s.11; Directive, Art. 3(2).

212 2001 Act, s.12(1); Directive, Art. 4.

Designs are deemed to be identical if their features differ only in immaterial details.[213] A design will have "individual character" if:

> "the overall impression it produces on the informed user differs from the overall impression produced on such a user by a design which has been made available to the public before the filing date … "[214]

A design will be deemed to have been "made available to the public" if it has been:

> "published following registration or otherwise, or exhibited, used in trade or otherwise disclosed, except where these events could not reasonably have become known in the normal course of business to the circles specialising in the sector concerned, operating within the EEA …"[215]

Significantly, "universal novelty" is now required; previously local novelty only was required.[216] But disclosure in confidence to a third party will not destroy novelty.[217]

A design right does not subsist in features of appearance of a product which are solely dictated by technical function,[218] and a design right does not subsist in a design which is contrary to public policy and morality.[219]

The author or owner of a design is the person who created it, unless the design is created in the course of employment, in which case the owner is the employer, unless there is an agreement to the contrary.[220] On registration,[221] the term of protection is initially five years, renewable for further five-year periods, up to a maximum of 25 years.[222] The previous maximum was 15 years.[223] The rights of the design owner are stated to be the exclusive right to use the design and to prevent any unauthorised use.[224] In particular, "use" includes the making, offering, putting on the market, importing, exporting or the using of a product in which the design is incorporated or to which it is applied, or stocking such a product for those purposes. There is no requirement that the design be applied to a product

213 2001 Act, s.12(2); Directive, Art. 4.
214 2001 Act, s.13; Directive, Art. 5. See also Recital 13.
215 2001 Act, s.2(1); Directive, Art. 6.
216 1927 Act, s.64.
217 2001 Act, s.2(7); Directive, Art. 6(1).
218 2001 Act, s.16; Directive, Art. 7.
219 2001 Act, s.21(1)(a); Directive, Art. 8.
220 2001 Act, ss.17–19.
221 On registration see 2001 Act, Part II, Chapters 3 and 4.
222 2001 Act, s.43; Directive, Art. 10.
223 1927 Act, s.70.
224 2001 Act, s.42(4); Directive, Art. 12. See further 2001 Act, Part II, Chapters 7 and 8 on infringement of design rights and remedies, respectively.

for infringement to occur. There is also a litany of "permitted acts", in relation to a design right including:

(i) acts done privately and for non-commercial purposes;
(ii) acts done for experimental purposes;
(iii) acts of reproduction for the purpose of making citations or of teaching …[225]

A design, if registered, may be declared invalid on a number of stated grounds including if:

(i) it does not fall within the definition of design;
(ii) it is not new or does not have individual character;
(iii) it has been made available to the public prior to filing;
(iv) it is functional;
(v) the holder of the design is not entitled to it under the law of the member state concerned;
(vi) the design is in conflict with a prior design.[226]

Article 17 of the Design Directive provides that a design registered in a member state shall also be eligible for protection under the law of copyright.[227] However, section 79 of the Copyright and Related Rights Act 2000 contains two important exceptions from copyright protection.[228] Section 79(1) provides that copyright infringement will not arise by the making of an object in three dimensions of a two dimensional work (namely, to make a product from a drawing) if the object would not appear to a non-expert to be a reproduction of the work. Section 79(2) provides that reproducing an object in three dimensions shall not be infringement of copyright in the work of two dimensions where:

(i) the lines, contours, colours, shape, texture and materials of the product itself or its ornamentation that appear in the work and are applied to objects, are wholly or substantially functional, and

(ii) the object is one of a number, in excess of 50, of identical objects which have been manufactured and made commercially available by the owner of the copyright.

Moreover, the 2001 Act amends the Copyright and Related Rights Act

225 2001 Act, s.48; Directive, Art. 13.
226 2001 Act, s.47; Directive, Art. 11.
227 *Cf.* 1927 Act, s.172 which provided that copyright did not subsist in designs capable of being registered and which were intended to be industrially multiplied.
228 Repeating the provisions of the Copyright Act, 1963, s.14(7), as amended.

2000 to the effect that copyright in a design registered under the 2001 Act expires 25 years after filing, or the date of expiry of copyright under the 2000 Act, whichever is the sooner.[229]

Probably the most controversial aspect of the draft Directive concerned the proposed "repair clause", which was intended to liberalise the motor car spare-parts trade. This clause would have allowed third-party companies to supply spare parts for motor cars in return for a fair and reasonable contribution to motor vehicle manufacturers. However, agreement could not be reached on the issue and, as a result, Article 14 of the Directive includes a "standstill clause". Accordingly, until the Directive is amended, member states must maintain in force their existing laws relating to the use of designs for spare parts. The Directive further requires the Commission, within three years, to analyse this issue and within another year to bring forward proposals for any changes needed in relation to spare parts.[230]

34.14 Performers' Rights

Since copyright protects *expressions* which are fixed in some medium, performances, such as a singer's rendition of a song, or an actor's performance in a role, are not protected by copyright. For the first time in Irish law, Parts III and IV of the 2000 Act provide for a regime of rights, exceptions and sanctions in respect of performers' rights and rights in performances which is broadly parallel to those provided in Part II in relation to copyright.

"Performance" means a performance of any actors, singers, musicians, dancers or other persons who act, sing, deliver, play in, interpret, or otherwise perform literary, dramatic, musical or artistic works or expressions of works of folklore, which is a live performance given by one or more individuals, and shall include a performance of a variety act or any similar presentation.[231] The key requirement relates to the live nature of the activity. So, for example, in *Gormley v. EMI Records*,[232] the rendition of the Bible stories could be protected by performers' rights.

Performers' rights include:

(i) the exclusive right to authorise or to prohibit the making of a copy of a recording of a performance: the reproduction right;[233]

229 2001 Act, s.89.
230 Art. 18.
231 2000 Act, s.202(1).
232 [1998] 1 I.L.R.M. 124 (H.C.); [1999] 1 I.L.R.M. 178 (S.C.).
233 2000 Act, s.204.

(ii) the exclusive right to authorise or to prohibit the making available to the public of copies of a recording of a performance;[234]
(iii) the exclusive right to authorise or to prohibit the issuing of copies of a performance to the public: the distribution right;[235]
(iv) the exclusive right to authorise or to prohibit the renting or lending of copies of a recording of a performance;[236]
(v) a right to equitable remuneration from the owner of the copyright in a sound recording of a performance for its exploitation.[237]

These rights expire 50 years after the performance takes place or in relation to a recording of a performance, 50 years after the recording is first made available to the public.[238] The moral rights of performers are recognised in Part IV of the 2000 Act.

---

234 2000 Act, s.205.
235 2000 Act, s.206.
236 2000 Act, s.207.
237 2000 Act, s.208.
238 2000 Act, s.291.

CHAPTER 35
PATENTS

35.1 INTRODUCTION[1]

Broadly speaking, patents protect inventions and thereby seek to encourage inventiveness. The rights given to the owner of a patent reward his effort. Without this protection, once an invention is made public, it could be taken apart, imitated and produced more cheaply by a competitor. The central issue in patent law is the balance between the rights of inventors – noting the importance of research, development and invention for society in general – and the greater public access to inventions. Patent law, while protecting inventions for a specified period – 20 years – recognises the need to maximise the number of inventions in the public domain for the purpose of increasing scientific and technological progress. Ensuring public access to inventions, even if their use is restricted, is also maximised by the requirement of disclosure in the patent application,[2] and the compulsory licensing of inventions which have not been used within the given period.[3]

The governing legislation is the Patents Act 1992.[4] The 1992 Act repealed the Patents Act 1964, as amended,[5] and enabled ratification of the

1 See further Clark & Smith, *Intellectual Property Law in Ireland* (Dublin, Butterworths, 1997) Chapters 1-8.

2 See 35.3.

3 See 35.5.

4 The 1992 Act was enacted on February 27, 1992 and came into force on August 1, 1992: S.I. No. 181 of 1992. It has been amended by the Intellectual Property (Miscellaneous Provisions) Act 1998, ss.4–5. For unsuccessful challenge to the constitutionality of these provisions in the 1998 Act, *see Controller of Patents, Designs and Trade Marks v. Ireland* unreported, High Court, Kelly J., July 31, 1998 and February 18, 1999; see further Byrne, "Intellectual Property (Miscellaneous Provisions) Act 1998" [1999] *Irish Law Times* 297. In the Patents Office Annual Report for 2000, it is indicated that High Court and Supreme Court proceedings in relation to this matter are still pending: see www.patentoffice.ie for 2000 Annual Report. Previously, U.K. patent law continued to apply in Ireland until 1927, when the Industrial and Commercial Property (Protection) Act was enacted (Part II covered patents, the remainder dealing with copyright, designs and trademarks). The 1927 Act, as amended, remained in force until the Patents Act 1964 repealed it. The 1964 Act was modelled on the U.K. Patents Act 1949, thought it went further by introducing provisions of the Strasbourg Convention on the Unification of Certain Points of Substantive Law on Patents for Inventions (1963).

5 1992 Act, s.5 and the First Schedule.

European Patents Convention (EPC) 1973,[6] and the Washington Patent Co-operation Treaty (PCT) 1970,[7] both of which attempt to provide international uniformity in this area and to facilitate an applicant who wishes to file patent applications in a number of jurisdictions.[8] In particular, the EPC, which is not limited to EU states, established the European Patent Organisation which administers the European Patent Office (EPO).[9] The aim of the EPC is to enable a patent applicant to secure patent rights in a number of European jurisdictions by way of a single application to a centralised office, the EPO, designating some or all of the 24 contracting states,[10] including Ireland.[11] Prior to the EPC, separate applications had to be made to the national Patent Office of each jurisdiction where protection was sought. Where protection was sought in a large number of jurisdictions, the procedures were slow and expensive. Where a "European patent" is granted, it operates not as a unitary patent but as a bundle of national patents in the states designated by the applicant,

6 Proposals to revise the EPC were made at Munich in November 2000. The revised Convention would have to be ratified by Contracting States before it would enter into force, a process which could take four or five years.

7 The P.C.T. is administered by the World Intellectual Property Organisation in Geneva and it provides a procedure for filing a single international patent application, designating up to 116 countries but not for granting a patent. In 2000, the Irish Patents Office, as receiving agent under the P.C.T., received 169 international applications: Patents Office, Annual Report 2000, p.5; see www.patentsoffice.ie See further Clark & Smith, *Intellectual Property Law in Ireland* (Dublin, Butterworths, 1997) paras 2.58–2.69.

8 Other international treaties in this area include: the Paris Convention 1883, the Strasbourg Convention 1963, the Community Patent Convention (CPC) 1989, and the Agreement on Trade Related Aspects of Intellectual Property Law (TRIPs) 1994. Prior to 1992, the main international element to Irish patent law was the Paris Convention which provides that nationals of Convention states have the same rights to obtain patents as Irish nationals, and which also provides for a right of priority derived from the first patent application filed in a Convention state. In 2000, 357 applicants, out of a total of 1,079, claimed priority under the Paris Convention: Patents Office, Annual Report 2000, p.6. The CPC was intended to provide for a unitary and autonomous patent effective throughout the EC. Article 29 of the Irish Constitution had to be amended to enable Ireland to ratify the CPC because the CPC provides for a common appeals court. But the CPC has not come into effect and has been surpassed by the draft Regulation on a Community Patent System: COM (2000) 412. See further Clark & Smith, *Intellectual Property Law in Ireland* (Dublin, Butterworths, 1997) Chapter 2.

9 The EPO is based in Munich, with offices in the Hague and Berlin: see www.epo.org. Applications can be filed at any of these locations or at the national Patent Office of a contracting state. In 2000, the Irish Patents Office received 123 such applications: Patents Office, Annual Report 2000, p.6.

10 Since July 1, 2002.

11 Unlike the CPC, an amendment to the Constitution was not deemed necessary to enable Ireland to ratify the EPC. The constitutionality of the 1992 Act can be questioned to the extent that the EPC provides for Boards of Appeal which hear appeals against decisions of Examining and Opposition Divisions of the EPO, and hence exercise a judicial function (see *Voest Alpine* [1987] O.J. EPO 447; *Merrell Dow Pharmaceuticals v. Norton* [1996] R.P.C. 76 at 82). However, support for the constitutionality of the 1992 Act is evidenced in the judgment of Keane J. in *ACW v. Ireland* [1994] 3 I.R. 232 at 243.

subject to national patent law.[12] Section 128 of the 1992 Act empowers the Minister by order to give effect to any amendment of the EPC or the PCT, or any international treaty, convention or agreement relating to patents to which the state is or proposes to become a party. This wide-ranging power would enable the Minister, by statutory instrument, to give effect to any revision of the EPC, for example.

The wording of the 1992 Act closely follows that of the EPC and the PCT. Section 129 of the 1992 Act provides that judicial notice and notice by the Controller of Patents, Designs and Trade Marks shall be taken of, *inter alia*, the EPC, the PCT, any other international agreements, and, decisions or opinions of "a competent authority" under the EPC. The European Patent Office enlarged Board of Appeal would be a "competent authority" for these purposes.[13] Irish courts may also be expected to look to the decisions of other European jurisdictions which have similar legislation. The U.K. Patent Act 1977 does not follow as faithfully the wording of the above Conventions and hence English case law may be less persuasive as a result.

35.2 What is Patentable?

The 1992 Act contains new criteria as to what is patentable.[14] Section 9(1) of the 1992 Act provides that: "an invention is patentable if it is susceptible to industrial application, is new and involves an inventive step." Hence, there are three conditions to patentability:

(i) susceptible to industrial application;
(ii) novelty; and
(iii) inventive step.

"Invention" itself is not defined in the legislation.

35.2.1 Industrial application

"Industrial application" is defined in section 14 of the 1992 Act: "an invention is susceptible to industrial application if it can be made or used in any kind of industry, including agriculture."[15] European Patent Office (EPO) guidelines[16] provide that the word "industry" should be given a

12 1992 Act, s.119; see further Clark & Smith, *Intellectual Property Law in Ireland* (Dublin, Butterworths, 1997) paras 2.32–2.57.

13 *John Wyeth's and Schering's Applications* [1985] R.P.C. 545.

14 Chapter II of the 1992 Act conforms with the E.P.C., Arts. 52–57; and the Strasbourg Convention 1963, Arts. 1–5.

15 See also E.P.C., Art. 57.

16 C IV 4.1.

broad meaning and includes any physical activity of a "technical character", that is, an activity which belongs to the useful or practical arts, as opposed to the aesthetic arts. Importantly, "industry" is not limited to the use of a machine or the manufacture of an item, but includes a process, and a substance or composition.

35.2.2 Novelty

The term "new" is explained in section 11(1) of the 1992 Act which states: "an invention shall be considered to be new if it does not form part of the state of the art."[17] The "state of the art" comprises everything made available to the public, *worldwide*, including by means of written or oral description, by use, or otherwise – absolute novelty is required.[18] If an invention is made available to the public before the date of filing of the patent application (the priority date), there is no novelty. An example of something made available to the public would be where a product or process is described in a published journal, no matter how obscure the journal. In contrast, an example of something not available to the public would be such a description in an internal company memorandum. An example of a borderline case is *Monsanto Co (Brignac's) Applicators*[19] where a patent was sought for the process of colouring nylon. The granting of the patent was successfully opposed on the basis that a prior company had printed brochures about the process which it had given to salesmen which in turn were expected to be passed on to potential customers. Therefore, it is vital that a patent application is filed before there is any public disclosure of the invention such as putting it on the market, or describing it in a publication, or exhibiting it.

Sometimes the information in the public domain will not be exactly the same as the information which forms the basis of the patent, but if the information available anticipates discovery, it will prevent the registration of the patent.[20] In *Windsurfing International v. Tabur Marine*,[21] the applicants were the holders of a patent for the manufacture of windsurfing boards. They discovered that the defendants were manufacturing such boards and took an action for infringement. The defendants successfully argued that the original patent should never have been granted because the invention has been anticipated by a 12-year-old boy in 1958 who had used a similar though less sophisticated device while on holiday and also by an

17 See also E.P.C., Art. 54(1).

18 1992 Act, s.11(2).

19 [1971] R.P.C. 153.

20 See *Wavin Pipes v. The Hepworth Iron Co.* [1982] F.S.R. 32 on the meaning of "published" under the Patents Act 1964.

21 [1985] R.P.C. 59.

article published in 1966 which discussed the exciting new sport of sailboarding which was similar to wind-surfing.

The legislation does provide that certain disclosures will not be prejudicial to novelty, such as disclosures in breach of confidence, or, under certain conditions, the display of the invention at specified international exhibitions.[22]

35.2.3 Inventive step

The concepts of "novelty" and "inventive step" are separate criteria but they are related. The issue of "inventive step" only arises if there is novelty.[23] Both involve looking at the state of the art. "Inventive step" is defined in section 13 of the 1992 Act which provides that: "an invention qualifies if, having regard to the state of the art, it is not obvious to a person skilled in the art."

The courts have developed a number of tests for "inventive step".[24] For example, in the *Windsurfing* case, based on similar wording from the U.K. Patents Act, Oliver L.J. stated that in assessing what is inventive and what is "obvious", the court has to identify the inventive process and then it has to:

> "assume the mantle of the normally skilled but unimaginative addressee in the art at the priority date and to impute to him what was, at that date, common knowledge in the art in question."[25]

The court must then identify the differences between the inventive step and the generally known matter and ask itself whether those differences constitute steps which would be obvious to the skilled but unimaginative addressee or whether the step involves some level of inventiveness.[26] In the *Windsurfing* case, the only differences provided by the holders of the patent involved changing the shape of the boom and sail and this, according to the court, would have been obvious to the reasonably knowledgeable addressee.

In *Rawls v. Irish Tyre & Rubber Services Ltd*,[27] the High Court summarised the test for distinguishing invention from workshop improvement and hence what is "obvious" as follows:

> "Has the improvement been a commercial success? Has it supplied a want? Has the problem awaited solution for many years and is the device novel

22 1992 Act, s.12.

23 EPO Guidelines, C IV 9.1.

24 See further Cole, "Inventive Step" [1998] *European Intellectual Property Review* 214 and 267.

25 [1985] RPC 59 at 73–74.

26 See also EPO Guidelines, C IV 9.3.

27 [1960] I.R. 11 at 30.

> and superior to that which has gone before? Is it used and is it widely used in preference to alternative devices? It is apparent that mere simplicity of the device is no objection, and a very slight advance, something approaching a scintilla, will suffice to support the invention. Moreover an *ex post facto* approach and analysis of the invention is to be guarded against, because it is easy to say after the event, that the whole thing was perfectly obvious in the popular sense of the word."

35.2.4 Exceptions

There are a number of exceptions to patentability listed in sections 9 and 10 of the 1992 Act.[28] Section 9(2) provides the following exceptions:

(a) a discovery, a scientific theory, or a mathematical method;
(b) an aesthetic creation;
(c) a scheme, rule or method of performing a mental act, playing a game or doing business, or a program for a computer;
(e) the presentation of information.

These things are only excluded to the extent that a patent application or a patent relates to that thing *as such*:[29] anything more than "that thing as such" may be patentable. So, for example, while a discovery is not patentable, a person who discovers a naturally occurring substance and a practical use for it may patent *the use of that thing*. This distinction is not always easy to apply.

Section 9(4) excludes from patentability a method of treatment for the human or animal body by surgery or therapy, and a diagnostic method practised on the human or animal body. Importantly, this provision is stated not to apply to a product, and in particular a substance or a composition (such as a drug), for use in any such method.

These exceptions are not patentable for a variety of reasons. Some exceptions do not come within the meaning of "invention". For instance, it has been held that a discovery and an invention are two different things:

> "discovery adds to the amount of human knowledge, but it does so only by lifting the veil and discovering something which had been unseen or dimly seen. Invention also adds to human knowledge, but not merely by disclosing something. Invention necessarily involves also the suggestion of an act to be done, and it must be an act which results in a new product, or a new result, or a new process, or a new combination for producing an old product or an old result."[30]

28 The Minster may modify this list under the 1992 Act, s.9(5).
29 1992 Act, s.9(3).
30 *Reynolds v. Herbert Smith & Co Ltd* (1903) 20 R.P.C. 123 at 126 per Buckley J.

Many of the exceptions listed above are not patentable because they are protected by another area of intellectual property law. So, for example, copyright law may protect an aesthetic creation, such as a literary, dramatic, musical or artistic work; a scheme, rule, or method of performing a mental act, playing a game, or doing business; or a program for a computer.[31] However, the boundaries between patent law and copyright law overlap, and patent and copyright protection can exist in the same product. For example, the rules of a board game may be protected by copyright while the apparatus of the game, that is, the board and the pieces can be patented; or computer software *as such* is not patentable but computer software which produces a technical effect can be patented.[32]

Section 10 contains two further exceptions to patentability. Section 10(a) provides that inventions contrary to public order or morality shall not be patentable.[33] However, section 10(a) states that inventions will not be regarded as contrary to public policy or morality only because they are prohibited by law. Hence, an invention contrary to Irish law is not necessarily contrary to public order and morality.[34] The words "public order or morality" are very general and hence open to wide interpretation. However, EPO guidelines suggest that this exception will be invoked rarely.[35] The guidelines provide that this exception is designed to prevent the patenting of inventions likely to induce riot or public disorder or to lead to criminal or generally offensive behaviour. Examples given of things that would be excluded under this exception are letter-bombs and anti-personnel mines. In applying this exception, the EPO ask whether it is probable that the public in general would regard the invention as so abhorrent that the grant of patent rights would be inconceivable. This test was applied in *Harvard/Onco-mouse*.[36] In Harvard, a genetically engineered mouse, Onco-mouse, was developed which was more susceptible to carcinogens and therefore more useful in medical research. Previously, a large number of mice had to be produced to provide a sufficient number with cancer. Onco-mouse saved time and effort and was less cruel to a larger number of mice. Onco-mouse was patented in the

31 See 34.2.1.

32 See further Cohen, "The Patenting of Software" [1999] *European Intellectual Property Review* 607; Newman, "Patentability of Computer-Related Inventions in Europe" [1997] *Commercial Law Practitioner* 81.

33 See also EPC, Art. 53(a).

34 Under the 1964 Act, which had a similar exception, applications for contraceptives were refused by the Irish Patent Office. Today, a product such as an abortifacient for human use could be manufactured in Ireland under a European patent, for export to states where its use is not prohibited.

35 C-IV, 3.1–3.3.

36 [1989] O.J. EPO 451; [1990] O.J. EPO 476; [1992] O.J. EPO 589. See further *Moore v. Regents of the University of California*, 249 Cal. Rptr. 494 (1988); 271 Cal. Rptr. 46 (1990); Warren, "A Mouse in Sheep's Clothing: The Challenge to the Patent Morality Criteria Posed by 'Dolly'" [1998] *European Intellectual Property Review* 445.

U.S.A. and an application was made to the EPO. The Board of Appeal required the Examining Division to balance the moral and environmental factors.[37] It was acknowledged by the Board that there was cruelty to Onco-mouse but, from a moral perspective, this factor was outweighed by the fact that Onco-mouse was being used to search for a prevention for cancer in humans and by the fact that there was little danger of environmental damage since the animals could not reproduce their artificial genetic make-up. The Division held that the patent should be granted.[38]

Section 10(b) excludes from patentability a plant or animal variety or an essentially biological process for the production of plants or animals other than a microbological process or the products thereof.[39] Therefore, genetically modified organisms can be patented. This exception applies to varieties only, and a plant or animal treated by a patentable process can be patented.[40] While not patentable, plant variety rights do arise under the Plant Varieties (Proprietary Rights) Act 1980, as amended.[41] The criteria for protection are that the variety must be distinct, uniform, stable, and new.[42] The minimum period of protection is set at 25 years under this legislation.[43]

Further exceptions to patentability are to be found in the EC Directive on the Legal Protection of Biotechnological Inventions,[44] as implemented in the EC (Legal Protection of Biotechnological Inventions) Regulations 2000.[45] While not addressed directly in the Patent Act 1992, the EC Directive puts beyond doubt the legal position that biotechnological inventions, including an element isolated from the human body, are patentable under national laws.[46] However, exceptions to patentability are listed in Articles 4, 5, and 6. For example, Article 5 of the Directive, and

---

37 [1990] O.J. EPO 476.

38 [1992] O.J. EPO 589.

39 See also E.P.C., Art. 53(b).

40 *Hybrid Plants/Lubrizol* [1990] E.P.O.R. 173.

41 See Plant Varieties (Proprietary Rights) (Amendment) Act 1998. The 1980 and 1998 Acts seek to implement the International Convention for the Protection of New Varieties of Plants (O.P.O.C. Convention) (1961, as revised in 1972, 1978, and 1991). See further Clark & Smith, *Intellectual Property Law in Ireland* (Dublin, Butterworths, 1997) 3.21–3.37.

42 1980 Act, s.5 and First Schedule, as amended; U.P.O.V. Convention, Art. 5.

43 1998 Act, s.15.

44 Directive 98/44/EC [1998] O.J. L213/13. A Dutch legal challenge to the Directive failed: see Case C-377/98; see further Moore, "Challenge to the Biotechnology Directive" [2002] *European Intellectual Property Review* 149; Scott, "The Dutch Challenge to the Bio-Patenting Directive" [1999] *European Intellectual Property Review* 212. See further Duffy, "Biotechnology and its Patenting under the New EC Directive" (1998) 2 *Irish Intellectual Property Review* 23; Nott, "You Did It! The European Biotechnology Directive at Last" [1998] *European Intellectual Property Review* 347.

45 S.I. No. 247 of 2000, which came into operation on July 30, 2000: see further Crowley, "Ireland's Answer to Europe's Call for Patent Protection for Biotechnological Inventions" [2001] *Commercial Law Practitioner* 51.

46 See Arts. 1, 3 and 5(2) of the Directive and Reg. 4, 2000.

Regulation 5(1) state that the human body and the simple discovery of an element from the human body are not patentable. Article 6 of the Directive and Regulation 6(1) provide that inventions contrary to public order and morality are not patentable. In particular, excluded from patentability are:

(a) processes for cloning human beings;
(b) processes for modifying the germ line genetic identity of human beings;
(c) uses of human embryos for industrial or commercial use; and
(d) process for modifying the genetic identity of animals which are likely to cause them suffering without producing substantial medical benefits.[47]

35.3 Obtaining a Patent

As with trademarks, for example, the legal rights of a patent holder derive from registration.[48] A patent can be obtained for any patentable invention provided the proper statutory procedure is followed. Under the 1992 Act, the Patents Office[49] and the Controller of Patents, Designs and Trademarks continue to administer the registration scheme.[50] Detailed rules govern the application, examination and grant process.[51] Each part of the process must be completed within prescribed time limits and fees are payable at various stages. In addition, an applicant will usually pay professional fees to a patent agent who assists the applicant through this technical and complex process, making it even more expensive.[52] The process is outlined below.

35.3.1 Application[53]

An Irish patent application must be filed at the Irish Patents Office on a standard form, with the appropriate fee. The application must contain:[54]

47 Art. 6(2) of the Directive; Reg. 6(2), 2000.

48 See 1992 Act, Part VII, ss.84–89 regarding the Register.

49 Based in Kilkenny: S.I. No. 293 of 1998. See generally www.patentsoffice.ie

50 1992 Act, s.6, as amended by the Intellectual Property (Miscellaneous Provisions) Act 1998.

51 1992 Act, ss.18–35; and the Patent Rules 1992, S.I. No. 179 of 1992; see further Clark & Smith, *Intellectual Property Law in Ireland* (Dublin, Butterworths, 1997) Chapter 4.

52 Re patent agents, see 1992 Act, ss.105–109. Importantly, professional privilege has been extended to communications with patent agents "in relation to any matter concerning the protection of an invention, patent, design, or technical information or any matter involving passing-off:" 1992 Act, s.94. At the end of 2000, 30 individuals and five partnerships were registered as Patent Agents: Patents Office, Annual Report 2000, p.7.

53 In 2000, 1,079 applications for patent were received by the Irish Patents Office; a total of 6,844 applications were pending at December 31, 2000. The bulk of these applications were awaiting the submission of evidence of novelty: Patents Office, Annual Report 2000, p.5.

54 1992 Act, s.18. All these requirements need not be complied with on the date of filing.

(i) a request for the grant of the patent;
(ii) a specification, that is a detailed technical description of the invention, including one or more claims for the patent, that is a detailed description of what the invention does;[55]
(iii) any plans and drawings referred to in the specification and claims;[56] and
(iv) an abstract, or a concise summary of the specification.

The "priority date" is an important concept in patent law.[57] This date fixes the time at which the prior art is to be considered for the purpose of assessing the novelty of the invention. The priority date is usually the date of filing the application. In order to claim early priority, an inventor can pay the official filing fee and provide documentation containing:

(i) a request for grant of a patent; and
(ii) the identity of the applicant;
(iii) a description of the invention.[58]

Provided he files the claims and an abstract within 12 months from the date of filing, the application will proceed with priority given from the date of filing.[59]

35.3.2 Examination

Within about four weeks of filing, brief particulars of the application are published in the Patents Office Journal. This is the only information publicly available until the application is published. This occurs as soon as practicable after the expiry of 18 months from the date of filing.[60]

An applicant has two options at this stage. An applicant may submit to the Controller a statement that an application for the same invention has been made elsewhere, such as in the U.K., or, in another State under the EPC. In addition, there must subsequently be filed evidence of novelty of the invention in the form of either an official search report issued on the

55 The claims must define the matter for which protection is sought, be clear and concise and supported by the description: 1992 Act, s.20. The scope of protection conferred by the patent is determined by the claims, hence, patent agents may draft claims to obtain the widest protection for the invention, so that a patent cannot be avoided by making minor changes. On the other hand, a claim may need to be drafted narrowly in order to distinguish the invention from the state of the art.

56 The description must be sufficiently clear and complete for it to be carried out by a person skilled in the art: 1992 Act, s.19(1). See *Rawls v. Irish Tyre and Rubber Services Ltd* [1960] I.R. 11.

57 1992 Act, ss.25–27.

58 1992 Act, s.23.

59 Patent Rules 1992, Rule 19: S.I. No. 179 of 1992.

60 Earlier publication can be requested: 1992 Act, s.28.

relevant patent application or the grant of a patent.[61] Alternatively, an applicant can proceed by means of a search report requested from the Irish Patent Office,[62] subject to the payment of the appropriate fee.[63] The request and fee must be submitted within 21 months from filing. When completed, a search report is sent to the applicant who has two months to advise the Controller whether the application is to be withdrawn or maintained. If maintained, the search report is published and the applicant has four months within which to make amendments to the application or to advise the Controller that no amendments are being made. If this is not done, the Controller may refuse the application.[64] A limited examination is then carried out by the Patent Office under section 31 of the 1992 Act to determine whether the application complies with the legislation. The onus is placed on the applicant and his agent to ensure that the necessary requirements of patentability,[65] novelty,[66] inventive step,[67] industrial application,[68] clear and complete disclosure in the specification,[69] and clear and complete claims are complied with.[70] Failure to comply with these requirements could lead to revocation of the patent under section 58.[71]

35.3.3 Grant[72]

If all statutory formalities have been complied with, the Controller will request payment of a grant fee. Failure to pay within the time limit will mean that the application is deemed to be withdrawn.[73] Once the grant fee and any renewal fees have been paid, a certificate of grant of a patent will be issued.

61 1992 Act, s.30.
62 The search is actually carried out by the U.K. Patent Office.
63 1992, Act, s.29. The aim of the search report is to identify, from prior literature, the relevant prior art.
64 1992 Act, s.29(4).
65 1992 Act, s.9.
66 1992 Act, s.11.
67 1992 Act, s.13.
68 1992 Act, s.14.
69 1992 Act, s.19.
70 1992 Act, s.20.
71 See 35.4.
72 In 2000, when 1,079 applications for patent were received by the Irish Patents Office, and a total of 6,844 applications were pending at December 31, 2000, 456 patents were granted: Patents Office, Annual Report 2000, p.5. The number of patent in force on December 31, 2001 was 26,844: Patents Office, Annual Report 2000, p.7.
73 1992 Act, s.31(3).

35.4 Patent Owner's Rights

Once granted, a patent gives the owner a monopoly right to exploit the invention, that is a right to prevent others from exploiting the invention: a negative right.[74] Importantly, a patent does not authorise use; it is not a prerequisite to exploitation; and it does not provide immunity against breach of other parties' rights (including intellectual property rights) and other public liabilities.

Section 36 of the 1992 Act provides for an increase in the term of the patent, from 16 years under the 1964 Act, to 20 years from the date of filing of the patent application.[75] There is no provision for the extension of the period. Moreover, there is new provision for a short-term patent, of ten years duration. Less strict rules as to patentability apply: the invention must be new, susceptible to industrial application and *not clearly lacking* an inventive step.[76]

Section 79 of the 1992 Act provides that the rules of law applicable to the ownership and devolution of personal property shall apply in relation to patent applications and patents, subject to the Act. A patent and a patent application is personal property and therefore, for example, can be assigned, licensed,[77] or charged by way of a mortgage.[78] Any changes in ownership or in an interest in a patent application, once published, or a patent must be recorded on the Register of Patents.[79] Failure to comply means that any document which has not been recorded will only be admitted as evidence of ownership or interest in court if the court so directs.[80]

Where a patent application or a patent is owned by two or more persons, there is a presumption that they hold the property as tenants in common in equal shares.[81] With a tenancy in common, the deceased's share forms part of his estate and passes under his will or on intestacy. One co-owner cannot assign any share in, or licence, the patent, without the consent of all the other co-owners.[82]

74 1992 Act, Part II, Chapter VI, ss.40–46.

75 Subject to the payment of renewal fees payable in respect of the third and each subsequent year calculated from the date of filing of the patent application: Patent Rules 1992, Rules 33 and 34, S.I. No. 179 of 1992. Under the 1992 Act, s.29 where a patent has lapsed following failure to pay a renewal fee, application can be made by the patentee within three years of the patent lapsing, for restoration of the patent.

76 1992 Act, s.63–67. In 2000, the Irish Patents Office, 641 applications for short-term patents, out of a total of 1079 application, were received; 158 were granted: Patents Office, Annual Report 2000, p.7.

77 See 35.5. Note the constitutional protection afforded to private property under Articles 40.3.2° and 43.

78 1992 Act, s.85.

79 1992 Act, s.85.

80 1992 Act, 85(7).

81 1992 Act, s.80.

82 1992 Act, s.80(3).

Under the 1992 Act, there is no opportunity for pre-grant opposition which was available under the 1964 Act. However, there is provision in the legislation for the revocation of a patent, at any time during its life, by the High Court or the Controller, on stated grounds, which include: that the subject-matter of the patent is not patentable;[83] or that the owner of the patent is not entitled to it.[84]

35.5 LICENCES

A patent owner may not wish, or be in a position, to exploit fully the patent. In such circumstances, a patent owner may licence the patent. Licences are dealt with in Part IV of the 1992 Act. There are two types of licence: voluntary or compulsory.

A voluntary licence involves the patent owner applying to the Controller, at any time after the grant of the patent, to indicate that licences as of right are available regarding the patent.[85] On application for a licence of right, the patent owner must satisfy the Controller that he is not precluded by contract from granting licences on the patent. The Controller must give notice to anyone listed on the register as having an interest in the patent, such as another licencee, or a mortgagee. Once a licence of right is entered on the Register, any person may obtain a licence on terms to be agreed between the parties, or in default, on terms settled by the Controller.[86]

A licence is usually granted in return for a royalty payment. A licence is commonly limited in terms of its duration and its geographical scope. A licence may be exclusive or non-exclusive in nature. A third type of licence, a sole licence, must be distinguished from an exclusive licence. An exclusive licence gives the licensee exclusive rights over the patent: a third party, including the owner, cannot use the patent.[87] A sole licensee means that the licensee is the only licensee, but it does not exclude the owner from utilising the patent. A non-exclusive licence means that any number of persons including the owner, can exploit the patent. The E.C. Block Exemption on certain categories of technology transfer agreements exempts from the provision of Article 81 of the Treaty of Rome certain patent and know-how licences, drafted in compliance with the Block Exemption.[88]

---

83 1992, s.58(a).

84 1992 Act, s.58(e). See generally, 1992 Act, ss.57–62; see further Clark & Smith, *Intellectual Property Law in Ireland* (Dublin, Butterworths, 1997) Chapter 7.

85 The fees for renewal of a patent indicating that licences as of right are available are halved: 1992 Act, s.68(2)(d).

86 1992 Act, s.68(2)(a).

87 1992 Act, s.2.

88 Reg. 240/96 [1996] O.J. L31/2.

While there is no positive obligation placed on patent owners to exploit the patent, the compulsory licence provisions seek to ensure such exploitation. A compulsory licence cannot be applied for until after three years from the date of publication of the grant of the patent.[89] The grounds on which such an application can be made are set out in section 70 and include:

(i) insufficient domestic working;
(ii) failure to meet reasonable demand;
(iii) refusal to grant licence on reasonable terms.

35.6 Infringement and Remedies

Section 40 of the 1992 Act prohibits direct infringement,[90] while section 41, a new provision, prohibits indirect infringement. Infringement must occur in the State for the provisions of the 1992 Act to apply. A third party does not infringe where he has the consent, express or implied, of the owner of the patent. In *Betts v. Willmott*,[91] for instance, it was held that following the sale of a product, there is an implied licence to use or re-sell. There is also an implied right to repair a patented product provided that such repair does not amount to the manufacture of a new product.[92]

Section 40 classifies infringement according to whether the invention is a product, a process, or the product of a process. For example, direct infringement in relation to a product arises by making, offering, putting on the market, using, importing or stocking the product for those purposes. In *Hoffman-Law Roche v. Harris Pharmaceutical Ltd*,[93] the concept of infringement, under equivalent wording under the Patent Act 1964,[94] was extended to include possession with the intention of using the product for trade purposes, and for securing of a profit. Whether this extended scope of infringement exists under the 1996 Act remains to be seen.

Indirect, or contributory, infringement, under section 41,[95] occurs where any person supplies or offers to supply any of the means relating to an essential element of the invention for putting the invention into effect, but indirect infringement does not occur where the "means" are "staple commercial products" except where the supply or offer is made for the purpose of inducing the person supplied to do an act which constitutes a

89 1992 Act, s.70.
90 See C.P.C., Art. 25.
91 (1871) L.R. 6 Ch. 239.
92 See further *Solar Thompson Engineering Co Ltd v. Barton* [1977] R.P.C. 537.
93 [1977] F.S.R. 200.
94 That is, making, using, exercising or vending the invention, 1964 Act, s.25.
95 See C.P.C., Art. 26.

direct infringement.[96] There is no definition of "staple commercial product" though it may include generally available raw materials and goods suitable for uses, some of which would not amount to infringement.[97]

Sections 42 and 43 limit the extent to which infringement proceedings can be taken by providing a number of exceptions to infringement. Acts which do not amount to infringement include:

(i) acts done privately for non-commercial purposes;[98]
(ii) acts done for experimental purposes;[99]
(iii) extemporaneous preparation of a medicine in a pharmacy for individual cases;[100]
(iv) acts which cannot be prevented under the Treaty of Rome.[101]

Under section 44, protection is provided from the date of first publication of the specification.[102] Hence, acts which occur prior to publication cannot constitute infringement. But a patent must be granted before proceedings for infringement can commence.[103]

Infringement proceedings may be taken by a patent owner or by a licensee. However, before a licensee can take proceedings, the licensee must first request the patent owner to take proceedings and the patent owner must fail to do so within two months of the request. The patent owner must then be joined as a defendant in the proceedings, but is not liable for costs unless he enters an appearance and takes part in the proceedings.[104]

The scope of protection given by a patent is determined by the patent claim or claims and how a court interprets those claims. Prior to 1992, interpretation of claims was governed at common law. The English House of Lords adopted a "purposive" interpretation, as opposed to a literal

96 1992 Act, s.41(2).

97 See Baillie, "Contributory Infringement in the US" (1980-81) 10 *Journal of Chartered Institute of Patent Agents* 56.

98 1992 Act, s.42(a).

99 1992 Act, s.42(b).

100 1992 Act, s.42(c).

101 See *Internationala Handelsgessellschaft* [1972] 3 C.M.L.R. 255; see also Art. 29.4.3° of the Constitution and *Doyle v. An Taoiseach* [1986] I.L.R.M. 693 (S.C.). For example, where the owner of a patent has consented to goods made in accordance with his patent being placed on the market within the E.C., the doctrine of exhaustion of rights may prevent him from complaining of the import of goods which would otherwise infringe his patent: see, *e.g. Merck & Co Ltd v. Stephar BV* [1981] E.C.R. 2063.

102 That is, 18 months from the earliest priority date, or 18 months after the date of application where no priority is claimed. See further 1992 Act, s.56(3) under which damages can be reduced if it would not have been reasonable to expect from a consideration of the published application, that the patent would be infringed; see also E.P.C. Art. 67.

103 1992 Act, s.56.

104 1992 Act, s. 68(3).

interpretation, of patent claims and this was approved by the Irish High Court in *Wavin Pipes Ltd v. The Hepworth Iron Co. Ltd.*,[105] but the 1992 Act contains a Protocol on Interpretation in the Second Schedule, which derives from Article 69 of the EPC. Accordingly, the Protocol provides that in interpreting a patent, a court should adopt a middle ground between a strict literal interpretation and a more liberal interpretation, thereby providing fair protection of the patent owner and a reasonable degree of certainty for third parties. Whether this marks a departure from the pre-1992 position remains to be seen.[106]

The burden of proving infringement, as is normal, rests on the patent owner or the licensee. However, this burden can shift. If the invention is a process for obtaining a new product, and if the same product is produced, there is a presumption that such a product is made using the patented process, unless the defendant can prove to the contrary.[107]

Section 47 provides for a series of remedies for infringement of a patent, including injunctive relief, an order for delivery up or destruction of the infringing product, damages or an account of profits, and a declaration that the patent is valid and has been infringed. There is a restriction on recovery of damages for "innocent" infringement,[108] and in certain cases where the specification of the patent has been amended.[109] There is also provision in the legislation for a third party to seek a declaration of non-infringement.[110] These remedies are only available from the High Court, except regarding a short-term patent, where proceedings can be taken before the Circuit Court.[111]

Lastly, a person aggrieved by groundless threats of infringement proceedings may seek an injunction to restrain such threats and damages.[112] A mere notification of the existence of a patent is not a threat.[113]

105 [1982] FSR 32.

106 In *Kastner v. Rizla* [1995] R.P.C. 58, the Court of Appeal held that the purposive interpretation should continue to be applied until there is a contrary judgment from the House of Lords.

107 1992 Act, s.46(1).

108 1992 Act, s.49(1).

109 1992 Act, s.49(3).

110 1992 Act, s.54.

111 1992 Act, s.66(4).

112 1992 Act, s.53.

113 1992 Act, s.53(4).

Chapter 36

TRADE MARKS AND PASSING-OFF

36.1 Introduction

Image and reputation are important to business: brand names are especially valuable as an element of goodwill.[1] They attract custom and are marketable commodities in their own right. The law seeks to protect reputation and brand names through the registration of trade marks and the tort of passing-off. To bring a passing-off claim, a trader must show that he has an established reputation, and that he is being damaged by the defendant's conduct. Trade mark registration allows the trade mark owner to prevent others using that mark without having to show that the trade mark owner has a reputation or that he has suffered damage. A trade mark can therefore be obtained for a wholly new product or business.

Marks can be traced back to Roman times when manufacturers of pottery impressed their mark on the pottery to indicate the maker. Today, trade marks are used by manufacturers and others, primarily, as an indication of origin,[2] so that customers can identify their goods or services and distinguish them from competitors' goods or services.[3] Some marks are so successful that the mark becomes synonymous with the product – Hoover, Biro and perhaps Ballygowan.[4] The danger for manufacturers and other owners of trademarks is that a competitor may use an identical or a similar mark in relation to a competing product in an attempt to take custom and trade from the owner of the mark. If allowed, the competitor would benefit from the success of the mark and at the expense of the owner of the mark.

1 See Dawson, "Trade Mark Law and the Creation and Preservation of Well-Known Brands" (1998) 49 *Northern Ireland Legal Quarterly* 343.

2 See, *e.g.* Recital 10 of the EC Directive on Trade Marks: Directive 89/104/EEC, [1989] O.J. L40/1.

3 See generally, Schechter, "The Rational Basis of Trade Mark Protection" (1927) *Harvard Law Review* 813; Gielen, "Harmonisation of Trade Mark Law in Europe: The First Trade Mark Harmonisation Directive of the European Council" [1992] *European Intellectual Property Review* 263.

4 Once a trade mark becomes commonly known as the name of the product, it loses its trade mark function and is vulnerable to attack and removal from the register. As a result, it is advisable when displaying trade marks to use the designation "TM" or "registered trade mark" accompanied by a description of the goods/services to emphasise the separate function of the trade mark.

Trade marks are protected by statute, the Trade Marks Act 1996,[5] and by the common law tort of passing-off.[6] The 1996 Act was introduced to meet our obligations under various EC measures,[7] and a number of international agreements,[8] and to update the law in this area. In brief, the 1996 Act is notable because:

(i) it introduces a new, wider, definition of a mark;
(ii) it introduces the collective mark and the Community mark;
(iii) there is a new test for assessing registrability;
(iv) there are new grounds for refusal of registration and infringement, in particular the scope of protection extends beyond the exact goods/services, to dissimilar goods/services;
(v) there are new rules dealing with comparative advertising.

---

5 The 1996 Act was enacted on March 16, 1996 and came into effect from July 1, 1996: S.I. No. 199 of 1996. The implementation date set down by the Trade Mark Directive, which the Act sought to implement, was December 31, 1992: Directive 89/104/EEC, Art. 16 [1989] O.J. L40/1. This lateness gave rise to questions of direct effect, and, state liability under Art. 226 of the Treaty of Rome and *Francovich v. Italian State* (Cases C-6 & 9/90) [1992] I.R.L.R. 84. Prior to the 1996 Act, the Trade Marks Registration Act 1875 established the first register. This legislation was succeeded by the 1905 Trade Marks Act and in turn by the Commercial Property (Protection) Act 1927, which created an Irish register of trade marks and established the office of Controller of Patents, Designs and Trade Marks. The legislation was updated by the Trade Marks Act 1963 – similar to the then English position. The 1963 Act was repealed by the Trade Marks Act 1996, s.5.

6 See 36.7.

7 In particular, the EC Directive on Trade Marks: Directive 89/104/EEC [1989] O.J. L40/1; and the EC Regulation on the Community trade mark: Regulation 40/94/EC [1994] O.J. L11/1. Where the 1996 Act seeks to implement an EC measure, it is important to bear in mind a number of doctrines of EC law. For example, under the doctrine of supremacy, the EC measure is paramount should a conflict between the two measures arise: *Internationale Handelsgesellschaft* [1972] 3 C.M.L.R. 255; see also Art. 29.4.3° of the Constitution and *Doyle v. An Taoiseach* [1986] I.L.R.M. 693 (S.C.). Moreover, Irish courts are required, where possible, under the doctrine of indirect effect, to interpret national law to comply with EC law: *Marleasing SA v. La Comercial Internacional de Alimentación SA* (Case C-106/89) [1990] E.C.R. I–4135, [1992] 1 C.M.L.R. 305. Further, under the Treaty of Rome, the European Court of Justice (ECJ) is the sole interpreter of the Treaty and other EC measures, and an Irish court is bound by the interpretation of the ECJ: Treaty of Rome, Art. 234; see also *Benedetti v. Munari* (Case 52/76) [1977] E.C.R. 163.

8 The Madrid Protocol relating to the International Registration of Marks (1989); and the Paris Convention for the Protection of Industrial Property (1883), as revised. The Protocol relating to the Madrid Agreement operates under the aegis of the WIPO. The Protocol permits trade mark owners to make, through their national trade mark offices, a single application to the WIPO in which they can seek protection for their marks in any or all countries party to the Protocol. The Madrid Protocol was ratified on July 22, 2001 and came into force on October 19, 2001: Trade Marks (Madrid Protocol) Regulations, S.I. No. 346 of 2001.

36.2 REGISTRABILITY: WHAT IS A TRADE MARK?

A trade mark can be registered if it complies with the statutory definitions and requirements. The definition of trade mark has been simplified and widened by the 1996 Act to mean: "…any sign capable of being represented graphically which is capable of distinguishing goods or services of one undertaking from those of other undertakings."[9] The word "sign" is not defined but may be expected to be interpreted widely to include a three-dimensional sign, a hologram, and a sensory sign such as music, a sound,[10] smell,[11] taste, feel or gesture.[12] The requirement that the sign must be capable of being represented graphically is a practical one to enable parties to establish the scope of protection by, for example, carrying out searches of the Register.[13]

The requirement that the mark must be "capable of distinguishing goods or services of one undertaking from those of other undertakings" was an aspect of the previous 1963 Trade Marks Act, and hence case law under the 1963 Act is informative in this regard. For example, in *Waterford Glass Ltd v. Controller of Patents Designs and Trade Marks*,[14] despite the geographical significance of the word "Waterford", registration was allowed in relation to cut-glass crystal because the mark had been used continually since 1952 and had achieved 100% factual distinctiveness. In *Application of Mothercare Ltd*,[15] an objection to registering the mark "Mothercare" in relation to women's and children's clothing, on the basis that it referred to the character or quality of the goods, was rejected. Kenny J. stated:

> "There is some element of descriptiveness in the word, but it would apply to so many domestic goods that I think that the word must be regarded as having no direct reference to the character or quality of the goods."

Equally, in *Miller Brewing Company v. Controller of Patents Designs and Trade Marks*,[16] the words "High Life" were held not to bear any direct reference to the commodity of beer, its quality or character and hence was

---

9 1996 Act, s.6(1): Directive, Art. 2.

10 In the U.S.A., there has been an application to register the sound of the start of a Harley Davidson. In 2000, the Irish Patents Office registered its first "sound mark": Patents Office, Annual Report 2000, p.10.

11 See, *e.g.* the U.S. case, *Re Clark* [1991] E.I.P.R. 119, where a smell ("a fresh floral fragrance reminiscent of plumeria blossoms") was registered as a mark for yarn and thread. In the U.K., the scent of Chanel No. 5 has been registered.

12 In the U.K., there has been an application to register the gesture of tapping the side of one's nose twice.

13 See 36.4 on registration process.

14 [1984] F.S.R. 390; [1984] I.L.R.M. 565 (S.C.).

15 [1968] I.R. 359 at 363 per Kenny J.

16 [1988] I.L.R.M. 259 (S.C.).

registrable as a trade mark. In *Seven-Up v. Bubble-Up*,[17] the applicants, Bubble-Up, to support their claim that the phrase was *capable of distinguishing*, adduced evidence that the use of the mark to date did distinguish their product from others. Reference was made to the U.S.A. where the two marks "Seven-Up" and "Bubble-Up" were registered without causing confusion. The court held that the mark was registrable. Importantly, the onus is on the applicant to prove registrability.

Prior to the 1996 Act, it was possible to register marks used or proposed to be used in the course of trade in *goods* only. Providers of services who had a "mark" were clearly at a disadvantage. The above definition makes clear that under the 1996 Act, "marks" in relation to both goods and services are registerable.[18]

The 1996 Act provides further that: "… a trade mark may, in particular, consist of words (including personal names), designs, letters, numerals, or the shape of goods or of their packaging."[19] The reference to "in particular" indicates that this list is not exhaustive. "Words", "names", "designs" or devices,[20] "letters" and "numerals" were all previously registrable provided the other statutory requirements were satisfied, but the inclusion of "the shape of goods or of their packaging" is new and widens the definition of a trade mark.[21]

The 1996 Act recognises a number of *types* of trade mark: some old some new. The legislation retains the concept of "certification mark," that is, a mark indicating that the goods or services are certified by the proprietor as to origin, material, mode of manufacture of goods or performance of services, quality, accuracy or other characteristics.[22] A well-known example is "the Wool Mark". The concept of "collective mark" is introduced by the Act. A collective mark can be used to distinguish goods or services of members of an association which owns the mark from another association.[23] There are detailed provisions on the

17 [1990] I.L.R.M. 204 (H.C.).

18 In 2000, the Patents Office received 4,781 trade mark applications, of which 1702 related to services: Patents Office, Annual Report 2000, p.10.

19 1996 Act, s.6(2); Directive, Art. 2.

20 The Trade Marks Act 1963, s.2 defined a mark as including a "device, brand, heading, label, ticket, name, signature, word, letter or numeral, or any combination thereof ..."

21 *Cf. Coca Cola Trade Marks* [1986] R.P.C. 421; [1986] 1 W.L.R. 695 where under earlier U.K. legislation similar to the Irish 1963 Act, the plaintiff sought to register the shape of a bottle as a mark. The bottle had originally enjoyed the protection of a registered design but this had expired in the 1940s. The House of Lords refused registration because it held that the function of trade mark registration was to protect the mark and not the article which was marked. In support of widening the definition of mark to include "the shape", see *Reckitt & Colman Products v. Borden Inc* [1990] R.P.C. 341 where it was recognised that certain shapes are distinctive to consumers, *e.g.* the Jif get-up (a plastic lemon containing lemon juice). See further *Philips Electronics NV v. Remington Consumer Products Ltd* [1999] R.P.C. 809.

22 1996 Act, s.6(3) and s.55; see further Second Schedule to Act.

23 1996 Act, s.6(3) and s.54; see further First Schedule to Act.

registration of each in the First and Second Schedules of the 1996 Act.

The 1996 Act also makes provision for the Community trade mark, thereby seeking to implement the EC Regulation on the Community trade mark.[24] Since January 1, 1996, it has been possible to apply for a single EC-wide mark as an alternative to national registration. The main advantage of the Community trade mark is that it saves cost and time because one application can lead to registration in all member states. The substantive law governing what marks can be registered, and the rights of Community trade marks, is broadly similar to that contained in the E.C. Directive on Trade Marks[25] and the 1996 Act.

36.3 Grounds for Refusal

While widening the definition of a trade mark, the 1996 Act at the same time extended the grounds for refusal of registration. Given that trade mark registration grants the owner monopoly rights, it is not surprising that there are limits on what is registrable. Grounds for refusal are either absolute or relative. The absolute grounds involve an inherent defect in the trade mark applied for and are not related to any prior rights. In contrast, the relative grounds do not involve any inherent defects in the trade mark applied for but relate to the existence of earlier rights.

The absolute grounds for refusal include that:

(i) the sign does not satisfy the section 6(1) definition;
(ii) the trade mark is devoid of distinctive character;
(iii) the mark consists exclusively of signs or indications which may serve, in trade, to designate the kind, quality, quantity, intended purpose, value, geographical origin, the time of production of the goods or of rendering of services, or other characteristics of goods or services;
(iv) the mark consists exclusively of signs or indications which have become customary in the current language or in the bona fide and established practice of the trade;
(v) the sign consists exclusively of the shape which results from the nature of the goods, or, is necessary to obtain a technical result,[26] or gives a substantial value to the goods;
(vi) the mark is contrary to public policy or morality;
(vii) the use of the mark is prohibited by law.[27]

24 Regulation 40/94/EC [1994] O.J. L 11/1; 1996 Act, ss.56–57.
25 Directive 89/104/EEC [1989] O.J. L 40/1.
26 See, *e.g. Philips Electronics NV v. Remington Consumer Products Ltd* [1999] R.P.C. 809.
27 1996 Act, s.8, ss.62 and 63; Directive, Art. 3.

Under the heading "relative grounds for refusal", a trade mark will not be registered if, for example:

(i) the mark is *identical* with an earlier trade mark, and the goods or services for which the trade mark is applied are *identical* with the goods or services for which the earlier trade mark is protected;[28]

(ii) because the trade mark is *identical* with an earlier trade mark and would be registered for goods or services *similar* to those for which the earlier trade mark is protected, and there exists a likelihood of confusion on the part of the public, which includes the likelihood of association of the later mark with the earlier mark;[29]

(iii) because the trade mark is *similar* to an earlier trade mark and would be registered for goods or services *identical* with or *similar* to those for which the earlier trade mark is protected, and there exists a likelihood of confusion on the part of the public, which includes the likelihood of association of the later mark with the earlier mark;[30]

(iv) the trade mark is *identical* with or *similar* to an earlier trade mark, and is to be registered for goods or services which are *not similar*, to those for which the earlier trade mark is protected, where the earlier trade mark has a reputation in the State and the use of the later trade mark would take unfair advantage of, or be detrimental to, the distinctive character or reputation of the earlier trade mark.[31]

36.4 The Registration Process

As with patents, the legal rights of a trade mark owner derive from registration.[32] Marks can be registered in one of 42 classes: 34 in relation to goods (for example, Class 01 – Chemical Products; Class 02 – Paints; Class 03 – Bleaching Preparations) and eight for service marks (for example, Class 35 – Advertising and Business Management; Class 36 – Insurance and Financial Affairs; Class 37 – Building Construction, Repair and Installation Services).[33] The classification is not entirely logical and a business may have to register in more than one class where the goods or services are thought to be similar. Detailed rules and procedures, beyond

28 1996 Act, s.10(1); Directive Art. 4(1)(a).
29 1996 Act, s.10(2)(a); Directive, Art. 4(1)(b).
30 1996 Act, s.10(2)(b); Directive, Art. 4(1)(b).
31 1996 Act, s.10(3); Directive, Art. 4(3) which is mandatory and Art. 4(4)(1) which is optional. See also 1996 Act, ss.11 and 12, and s.52(2): Directive, Art. 4.
32 See 1996 Act, s.7(1) and Part IV concerning the Register and other administrative provisions.
33 1996 Act, s.39.

the scope of this book, regulate the registration process.[34] The following outlines the registration process.[35]

36.4.1 Application

Applications for Irish trade marks are made to the Controller of the Patents Office.[36] Applications for a Community Trade Mark can also be filed through the Irish Patents Office and are then forwarded to the Office for Harmonisation in the Internal Market (OHIM), Alicante, Spain.[37]

When filing an Irish trade mark application, there are certain minimum formalities required to secure a "filing date."[38] This is usually the eventual date of registration under the 1996 Act,[39] and an infringement action can be taken from this date.[40] To secure a filing date, documents must be filed which:

(i) indicate that registration of a trade mark is sought and the name and address of the person seeking registration;
(ii) contain a representation of the mark for which registration is sought;
(iii) indicate the goods or services which relate to the mark.[41]

Filing fees must be paid on application or within one month of the date of filing, otherwise the application is treated as abandoned.[42] Where priority is sought under the Paris Convention,[43] then the application must be filed within six months from the date of filing of the first Convention application.[44]

34 1996 Act, ss.37–46; and the Trade Mark Rules, S.I. No. 199 of 1996.

35 For more detail see Clark & Smith, *Intellectual Property Law in Ireland* (Dublin, Butterworths, 1997) Chapter 33.

36 1996 Act, s.37(1). The Patents Office is based in Kilkenny: S.I. No. 293 of 1998; see further www.patentsoffice.ie

37 In 2000, 73 application for Community Trade Marks were filing through the Irish Patents Office. Under Art. 39(3) of Regulation 40/94 on the Community Trade Mark, a national trade marks office can search C.T.M. applications and convey the results of its search to O.H.I.M.

38 1996 Act, s.38.

39 1996 Act, s.45(3).

40 1996 Act, 13(3) and (4); see further 36.5.

41 Trade Mark Rules, S.I. No. 199 of 1996, rule 12.

42 Trade Mark Rules, S.I. No. 199 of 1996, rule 12(5).

43 The Paris Convention for the Protection of Industrial Property (1883), as revised; see 1996 Act, ss.60–65.

44 1996 Act, s.40(1).

36.4.2 Examination

Once an application is filed, there is no statutory time-limit within which the application must be examined by the Patents Office.[45] The purpose of the examination is two-fold:

(i) to ensure the necessary formalities of the 1996 Act and the Trade Mark Rules have been complied with; and
(ii) to consider whether the substantive requires of the 1996 Act and the Trade Mark Rules have been complied with, including whether the application should be refused on the absolute or relative grounds specified in the 1996 Act.[46]

If, following the examination, it is found that any of these requirements have not been met, then an official action issues to the applicant allowing the applicant to make representations or to amend the application. Again, there are no statutory time-limits and in practice there is a dialogue between the applicant and the relevant examiner. Where the applicant has failed to respond, or to satisfy the examiner that the requirements have been met, the application is refused.[47] Where the requirements are met, the application is accepted and proceeds to publication.

36.4.3 Publication

Once an application is accepted following examination, it is published or advertised in the Patents Office Journal, a fortnightly publication.[48] This allows third parties to oppose the application before registration. The 1996 Act includes a three-month opposition period which is not extendible.[49] There are no specified grounds for opposition. Hence, the grounds for opposition are the same as those which apply generally in relation to the refusal of registration: the absolute and relative grounds of refusal. Where an opposition is filed (with the relevant fee), the applicant must file, within three months, a counter-statement. If a counter-statement is not filed, the application is deemed withdrawn. If a counter-statement is filed (with the relevant fee), there follows a period in which both sides must file their evidence supporting their claims with the Office, by way of statutory declaration. When the evidence is complete, both parties are invited to a hearing at which they are usually represented by their trade mark agents or

45 During 2000, 3,200 applications were examined; the length of time between filing and the initial examination rose in 2000 from 14 weeks at the end of 1999 to 20 weeks by the end of 2000, partly due to high staff turnover: Patents Office, Annual Report 2000, p.10.

46 1996 Act, s.42.

47 1996 Act, s.42(3).

48 1996 Act, s.43.

49 Trade Mark Rules, S.I. No. 199 of 1996, rule 18(1).

counsel.[50] Following the hearing, a decision is made and notified to the parties.[51]

36.4.4 Registration

If there is no opposition, or if any opposition is decided in favour of the applicant, then upon payment of the final registration fee, a certificate of registration will issue.[52] A mark is registered initially for 10 years, renewable indefinitely for further periods of 10 years on payment of a renewal fee.[53] In legal proceedings, registration is prima facie evidence of the validity of the trade mark.[54]

36.5 Owners' Rights and Dealing in Trade Marks

Section 7(1) of the 1996 Act provides that a registered trade mark is a property right obtained by registration under the 1996 Act, and the owner shall have the rights and remedies provided for by the Act.[55] Further, section 26 describes a registered trade mark[56] as personal property and therefore, like other forms of personal property, it can be can be traded by outright disposition such as an assignment, or by the owner permitting others to exploit his property by granting a licence. Equally, it can be charged or gifted away. However, such dealings must comply with statutory formalities to be fully effective. Provision is made for the co-ownership of registered trade marks.[57]

Section 47 provides that the duration of a registered trade mark is 10 years from the date of registration (usually the filing date). Registration can be renewed indefinitely for further periods of 10 years, provided the prescribed renewal fee is paid,[58] but a trade mark may be revoked on a number of stated grounds, including that, within five years of registration, the trade mark has not been put to genuine use in the State and there are no proper reasons for non-use.[59]

---

50 On trade mark agents, see 1996 Act, Part V. At the end of 2000, there were 120 individuals and six partnerships entered on the Register of Trade Mark Agents: Patents Office, Annual Report 2000, p.12.

51 This decision can be appealed to the High Court: 1996 Act, s.79. Six notices of appeal to the High Court and one to the Supreme Court were filed during 2000: Patents Office, Annual Report 2000, p.10.

52 1996 Act, s.45.

53 1996 Act, ss.47–48.

54 1996 Act, s.76.

55 Note the constitutional protection afforded to private property under Articles 40.3.2° and 43.

56 A trade mark application is also treated as personal property: 1996 Act, s.31(1).

57 1996 Act, s.27.

58 1996 Act, s.48.

59 1996, Act, s.51; Directive, Arts. 10, 11 and Art. 12.

Section 28 states that a registered trade mark, or an application,[60] is transmissible by assignment, testamentary disposition or otherwise, in the same way as other personal property, with or without the goodwill of a business. This provision removes the limitations on assignment which had existed under the earlier legislation, whereby an assignment of a trade mark which did not include goodwill had to be advertised.[61] Further, the Controller had power to compel the assignment of a number of identical or similar trade marks *en bloc* if he considered that separate assignment could lead to confusion in the public mind. These restrictions on assignment no longer exist.

An assignment can be whole or partial. It may be partial, or limited, in that it applies to some but not all of the goods or services for which it is registered; or it applies to use of the trade mark in a particular manner or a particular locality.[62] But, to be effective, the legal assignment must be in writing and signed by or on behalf of the assignor.[63] Equitable assignment of a trade mark may also be effected in which case there is no written requirement. A trade mark may also be subject to an equitable charge, created in the same way as over other personal property.[64]

A trade mark can also be licensed. This aspect of trade mark law is of particular interest to those engaged in character merchandising, franchising and similar activities. Licensing is dealt with expressly for the first time in the 1996 Act.[65] The Trade Marks Act 1963 did not deal specifically with licensing: it covered the issue of registered users. The 1963 Act took a very restricted view of an applicant's entitlement to register a mark which is to be used not by the applicant but a licensee. Basically, the legislation contemplated that an application should be made by the undertaking which was using or intending to use the mark itself. There was provision for the registration of a "registered user" of a trade mark, but this was highly regulated, requiring proof of a prescribed control relationship between the parties.[66] Moreover, a registered user would not be registered if the purpose of the application was to facilitate "trafficking" in the mark.[67] There are no

60 1996 Act, s.31(1). Under the 1963 Act, an assignment of a pending trade mark application was not permitted: *Western States Bank Card Association v. The Controller* unreported, High Court, Parke J., March 1, 1978.

61 Trade Marks Act 1963, s. 39(7).

62 1996 Act, s.28(2).

63 1996 Act, s.28(3).

64 1996 Act, s.28(5).

65 See generally, 1996 Act, ss.32–36; Directive, Art. 8.

66 Trade Mark Rules, 1963, rules 83–90.

67 Trade Marks Act 1963, s.36(1); see further *Holly Hobbie Trade Mark* [1984] R.P.C. 329, where the House of Lords refused applications, accompanied by licence agreements, to register a trade mark comprising a likeness of a fictional character in respect of an extensive range of goods. The relevant provision was however described as "an anachronism: a consumer buying goods bearing an image of the character is not deceived into thinking that the goods were produced by the originator of the character (though he may well infer that they were made under licence ..." U.K. White Paper, "Reform of Trade Mark Law" (Cmnd. 1203, 1990) p. 27.

similar provisions in the 1996 Act. The approach of the 1996 Act is to leave the contractual arrangements between the parties to their discretion on the basis that the trade mark owner will exercise due control over the licensee to protect the integrity of his trade mark.

The 1996 Act provides that a licence to use a trade mark can be general or limited.[68] It can be limited, for instance, when it applies to some but not all of the goods or services for which it is registered; or when it applies to use of the trade mark in a particular manner or a particular locality.[69] A licence may be also be exclusive or non-exclusive in nature. A third type of licence, a sole licence, must be distinguished from an exclusive licence. An exclusive licence gives the licensee exclusive rights over the trade mark: a third party, including the owner, cannot use the trade mark.[70] A sole licensee means that the licensee is the only licensee, but it does not exclude the owner from utilising the trade mark. A non-exclusive licence means that any number of persons including the owner, can exploit the trade mark. To be effective, the licence must be in writing and signed by, or on behalf of the grantor.[71] In the absence of a written agreement, the purported licensee is in fact an infringer. A licensee may be entitled, under sections 34 and 35, to bring infringement proceedings in his own name.

There is provision under section 29 for the recording of certain transactions, such as assignments,[72] licences, and grants of security,[73] on the Register.[74] The Register is open for public inspection. Failure to record a registrable transaction brings with it a number of disadvantages. First, until an application to record a registrable transaction is made, it is ineffective against a person acquiring a competing interest in ignorance of the transaction.[75] Second, a licensee may be unable to bring infringement proceedings in his own name. Third, a person may not be unable to recover damages or an account of profits.[76]

Any assignment or licence agreement must be considered in light of domestic and European competition law.[77] In particular, while there is no EC block exemption for trade mark licence agreements, a number of block exemptions may be relevant including:

---

68 1996 Act, s.32(1).

69 1996 Act, s.32(2).

70 1996 Act, s.33(1).

71 1996 Act, s.32(3).

72 An equitable assignment will not be registered: 1996 Act, s.30.

73 1996 Act, s.29(2).

74 See further rule 45 of the Trade Mark Rules 1996 (S.I. No. 199 of 1996). In 2000, for example, there were 73 applications under section 29 dealt with, leaving 117 application pending at the end of that year: Patents Office, Annual Report 2000, p.12.

75 1996 Act, s.29(3)(a).

76 1996 Act s.29(4).

77 See 33.3.

(i) the EC Block Exemption on Certain Categories of Vertical Agreements and Concerted Practices;[78] and
(ii) the EC Block Exemption on Certain Categories of Technology Transfer Agreements.[79]

36.6 Infringement and Remedies

Both the civil and criminal law are used to protect the position of trade mark owners and licensees. It is not possible to commence infringement proceedings before the date of publication of the registration of the trade mark,[80] though the effective date of registration is the filing date. Damages can therefore be claimed from this date. Equally, no offence can be committed prior to the date of publication.[81]

The legislation provides that infringement proceedings can be brought by the owner of a registered trade mark and/or a licensee.[82] Under section 35, an exclusive licensee can take infringement proceedings in his own name. However, under section 34, before any other type of licensee can take proceedings, the licensee must first request the trade mark owner to take proceedings, and the trade mark owner must fail to do so within two months of the request.[83] The trade mark owner must then be joined as a defendant in the proceedings, but is not liable for costs unless he takes part in the proceedings.[84]

Section 13 states that the owner of a registered trade mark has exclusive rights in the trade mark and such rights are infringed by the use of the trade mark in the State without the owner's consent. Section 14 specifies various infringing acts, which mirror the relative grounds for refusal set out in section 10.[85] Accordingly, a person infringes a registered trade mark if that person uses in the course of trade[86] a sign which:

(i) is *identical* with the trade mark, in relation to goods or services which are *identical* with those for which it is registered;[87]
(ii) because the sign is *identical* with the trade mark and is used in relation to goods or services *similar* to those for which the trade

78 Reg 2790/99, [1999] O.J. L336/21.
79 Reg 240/96, [1996] O.J. L31/2.
80 1996 Act, ss.13(3) and 13(4)(a).
81 1996 Act, ss.13(3) and 13(4)(b).
82 1996 Act, s.13, s.18, s.34 and s.35.
83 1996 Act s.34(3).
84 1996 Act, s.34(4) and (5).
85 See 36.3.
86 In *British Sugar plc v. James Robertson & Sons Ltd* [1996] R.P.C. 281, it was held that infringement included non-trade mark use.
87 1996 Act, s.14(1); Directive Art. 5(1)(a).

mark is registered, there exists a likelihood of confusion on the part of the public, which includes the likelihood of association of the sign with the trade mark;[88]

(iii) because the sign is *similar* to the trade mark and is used in relation to goods or services *identical* with or *similar* to those for which the trade mark is registered, there exists a likelihood of confusion on the part of the public, which includes the likelihood of association of the sign with the trade mark;[89]

(iv) is *identical* with or *similar* to the trade mark, and is used in relation to goods or services which are *not similar* to those for which the trade mark is registered, where the trade mark has a reputation in the State and the use of the sign takes unfair advantage of or is detrimental to the distinctive character or reputation of the trade mark.[90]

"Use" of a sign includes:

(i) affixing it to goods or packaging;
(ii) offering or exposing goods for sale, putting them on the market or stocking them for those purposes under the sign, or offering or supplying services under the sign;
(iii) importing or exporting goods under the sign;
(iv) using the sign on business paper or in advertising.[91]

Clearly, this is not an exhaustive list.

36.6.1 Identity and similarity

When taking infringement proceedings, it may be necessary to establish that a sign and a mark are *identical or similar*, or that the goods or services to which the sign and mark relate are *identical or similar*. Issues of the identical nature of signs and marks, and goods and services, may give rise to little room for argument. This point is often conceded by the defendant. However, it would appear that signs and marks, and goods and services, do not have to be one hundred per cent identical to lead to infringement. Issues of identity, and similarity, are a matter of degree and are to be understood in the light of case law, because there are no statutory definitions of these terms.

In *British Sugar v. Robertson*,[92] a leading English case which addressed

88 1996 Act, s.14(2)(a); Directive, Art. 5(1)(b).
89 1996 Act, s.14(2)(b); Directive, Art. 5(1)(b).
90 1996 Act, s.14(3); Directive, Art. 5(2). This provision was optional under the Directive.
91 1996 Act, s.14(4); Directive, Art. 5(3).
92 [1996] RPC 281.

the issues of identity and similarity, the plaintiff had registered the word "Treat" as a trade mark in relation to dessert sauces in 1992. The plaintiff alleged infringement by the defendant for using the sign "Robertson's Toffee Treat" in relation to a toffee spread. The court found, first, that this was not a case of infringement where the sign and the mark are identical, and the goods to which the sign and the mark relate are identical (infringement scenario (i) above) because the defendant's spread was primarily intended to be used as a jam and that would not be regarded, for the purposes of trade, as identical to a dessert sauce. Considering infringement under the next heading where the sign and the mark are identical, and the goods to which the sign and the mark relate are similar (infringement scenario (ii) above), the court found that that the mark and the sign ("Treat" and "Robertson's Toffee Treat" respectively) were identical by severing the words "Robertson's Toffee" from the defendant's sign as "external added matter".[93] This approach of pruning away whole words has be criticised as being unsound and unjust.[94]

Turning the issue of similarity between the defendant's goods and those covered by registration, Jacob J. listed six factors to be used in determining similarity:

(1) their respective uses;
(2) their respective users;
(3) their physical nature;
(4) the respective trade channels through which they reach the market;
(5) if consumer items, where the goods are likely to be found in the supermarket and, in particular, if they might be placed on the same shelf; and
(6) the extent to which the goods are in competition, having regard also to their categorisation by the marketing industry.

On the facts, the goods were found to have different uses. They were physically different – one was spooned while the other was spread. They were not found side by side in the supermarket and were not in direct competition. They were also categorised separately for marketing purposes. Hence, no infringement was found.

93 *Origins Inc v. Origin Co* [1995] F.S.R. 280; *Saville Perfumery Ltd v. June Perfect Ltd* (1942) 58 R.P.C. 147.

94 Newman, "Trade Marks Act 1996 – Recent U.K. Case Law (Part II)" [1997] *Irish Law Times* 2.

36.6.2 Non-origin association

Where the sign and the mark are identical, and the goods or services to which the sign and the mark relate are identical, there is infringement (infringement scenario (i) above). This is the most straightforward type of infringement to establish, there being no requirement to prove any likelihood of confusion.

However, where the sign and mark are *identical* in relation to goods or services which are similar (infringement scenario (ii) above);[95] or where the sign and mark are *similar* in relation to goods or services which are *identical or similar* (infringement scenario (iii) above),[96] there is a further requirement to prove that *there exists a likelihood of confusion on the part of the public, which includes the likelihood of association of the sign with the trade mark*. This phrase has been the subject of a number of cases before the Irish and English courts and the European Court of Justice (ECJ). Broadly speaking, at issue was the point whether *likelihood of association* is an alternative to *likelihood of confusion* and hence proof of either one would lead to infringement, or *whether likelihood of association* is an element of *likelihood of confusion*, requiring proof of *likelihood of confusion* to establish infringement.

Under the Trade Marks Act 1963, the use of a sign which was "confusingly similar" to a registered trade mark was an infringement. The test was whether similarities between the sign and the mark would lead a substantial number of customers to either:

(i) mistake the defendant's goods for those of the trade mark owner; or
(ii) assume that the defendant's goods and the goods of the trade mark owner were somehow connected or shared a common origin – known as "origin association".

It would appear that both these types of infringement are included in the 1996 Act. There is a third potential type of infringement, known as "non-origin association". This was not recognised by the 1963 Act, as evidenced in *Coca Cola v. Cade Ltd*.[97] There, the Supreme Court held that the sign "Cada-Cola" used for beverages would not be confused with the Coca-Cola trade mark, and hence there was no infringement even though the sign "Cada-Cola" would bring to mind the Coca-Cola trade mark and there was, as a result a "non-origin association". A question which was raised in relation to the EC Directive on Trade Marks, and hence the Irish Trade

95 1996 Act, s.14(2)(a); Directive, Art. 5(1)(b).
96 1996 Act, s.14(2)(b); Directive, Art. 5(1)(b).
97 [1957] I.R. 196.

Marks Act 1996 was whether "non-origin association" would constitute infringement?

In *Wagamama v. City Centre Restaurants plc*,[98] an attempt was made to interpret the relevant U.K. provisions, based on the EC Directive on Trade Marks, to include "non-origin association". The plaintiff ran a popular Japanese restaurant, registering its name as a trade mark in relation to restaurant services. The defendant opened an Indian restaurant calling it "Raja Mama's", the first of a chain. The plaintiff argued that the relevant U.K. provision should be widely interpreted, following Benelux law, to include non-origin association, that is, if the sign called to mind the registered trade mark, there is infringement. Laddie J. rejected the broad view, finding that the concept of *likelihood of association* is not an alternative to that of *likelihood of confusion*, but an element of it. On the facts, and applying the narrow view, the court found that there was an infringement because the public would confuse the two and assume that they were connected. The former law on "confusing similarity" was applied without comment. The reasoning of the English court in *Wagamama* has since been followed broadly by the ECJ in *Sabel v. Puma*,[99] and *Canon v. MGM*.[100]

In *Smithkline Beecham plc v. Antigen Pharmaceutical Ltd*,[101] the plaintiff alleged, *inter alia*, trade mark infringement of a number of its registered trade marks, including "Solpadeine" when the defendant marketed an analgesic called "Solfen". McCracken J. stated that while he did not have to determine whether there was a likelihood of association between the sign and the mark at the interlocutory stage, there was a serious issue to be tried. He further stated, *per curium*, that the concept of association under the new Act would seem wider than the meaning of "confusion" under the previous legislation.

36.6.3 Domain names

The right to use a particular internet domain name which resembles a business's trading name or trade mark is vital to any business wishing to use the internet as a marketing tool. Two main types of trade mark disputes

98 [1995] F.S.R. 713.

99 C-251/95, [1997] E.C.R. I–6191, [1998] 1 C.M.L.R. 445. See further Carboni, "Confusion Clarified" [1998] *European Intellectual Property Review* 107; Gielen, "The Benelux Perspective" [1998] *European Intellectual Property Review* 109; and Kamp, "Protection of Trade Marks: The New Regime - Beyond Origin?" [1998] *European Intellectual Property Review* 364; Lambert, "Likelihood of Confusion and Likelihood of Association under EC Trade Mark Law" [1998] *Irish Law Times* 218.

100 C-39/97 [1999] 1 C.M.L.R. 77. See further Wagner "Infringing Trade Marks: Function, Association and Confusion of Signs According to the EC Trade Marks Directive" [1999] *European Intellectual Property Review* 127.

101 [1999] 2 I.L.R.M. 190 (H.C.).

have arisen in recent years concerning the use of domain names. First, there have been a number of disputes between domain name pirates and persons claiming to be entitled to prevent use of the domain name by the pirate. Second, disputes have arisen between parties who argued that they were each entitled to use the disputed domain name.[102]

Domain name pirates operate by obtaining domain name registration for a domain name, which in some way resembles the trading name or trade mark of a business, and then offering for sale the domain name to that particular business. For example, the domain name "burgerking.co.uk" was offered for sale to Burger King for GBP£25,000 plus VAT; while BT.org was offered for sale to British Telecommunication plc for GBP£4,700 plus VAT.[103] In the leading case of *British Telecommunications plc v. One in a Million Ltd*,[104] the defendant had registered internet domain names identical or similar to several well-known business organisations, including "bt.org" and "marksandspencer.com", and then sought to sell them. The Court of Appeal found that the registration of the domain names constituted passing-off[105] and trade mark infringement,[106] and granted a final injunction restraining the defendant from continuing its activities and ordered it to assign the registration of the disputed domain name to the relevant plaintiffs. As a result of such disputes, many domain name registries have tightened up their allocation procedures.[107] For instance, the Irish registry will allocate a domain name only if it is shown that the organisation applying for it has a legal right to it.[108]

The second type of dispute may arise between parties who may be each entitled to use the disputed trade/domain name. For example, in *Avnet v. Isoact*,[109] the plaintiff was a distributor of electronic components and computer software which it sold by catalogue and on a web-page. It also advertised goods from other suppliers. It was the holder of the trademark "Avnet" in relation to advertising services (Class 35). The defendant had a

102 Other causes of action may assist in dealing with domain name disputes including injurious falsehood, unjust enrichment, defamation and passing-off. On passing-off, see 36.7.

103 See *British Telecommunications plc v. One in a Million Ltd* [1998] 4 All E.R. 476; [1998] F.S.R. 265.

104 [1998] 4 All E.R. 476, [1998] F.S.R. 265; see further Thorn & Bennett, "Domain Names - Internet Warehousing" [1998] *European Intellectual Property Review* 468; Carey, "Trade Marks and the Internet" [1998] *Commercial Law Practitioner* 115.

105 See further 36.7

106 Under the equivalent of section 14(3) of the 1996 Act (infringement scenario (iv), above).

107 The U.S. response included the Anticybersquatting Consumer Protection Act 1999, see Marray "The US Anticybersquatting Consumer Protection Act 1999 and its implications for Irish Users of the.com Registry" [2000] *Irish Law Times* 78.

108 For further information on the IE Domain Registry (IEDR) see http:www.domainregistry.ie

109 [1998] F.S.R. 16; see further Hurdle, "Domain Names – The Scope of a Trade Mark Proprietor's Monopoly" [1998] *European Intellectual Property Review* 74. See also *Pitman v. Nominet* [1997] 38 I.P.R. 341; *Prince plc v. Prince Sports Group Inc* [1998] F.S.R. 21; *Local Ireland Ltd & Nua Ltd v. Local Ireland On-Line Ltd* unreported, High Court, Herbert J., October 2, 2000; see further Dodd, "Passing-off, Domain Names and Injunctive Relief" [2001] *Commercial Law Practitioner* 79.

very different business as an internet service provider, providing services mainly to the aviation industry, including a facility to allow customers to advertise on the customer's own web-page. The defendant used the name "Aviation Network" and had a website with the address www.avnet.co.uk. The plaintiff sued the defendant, arguing that the defendant's use of the above domain name infringed its registered trade mark, alleging that the services provided by the defendant were identical to the plaintiff's advertising services. The defendant counter-claimed for rectification of the trade mark register on the basis that the plaintiff did not use the mark for advertising services. The judge dismissed the plaintiff's claim on the basis that the service provided by the defendant as an internet service provider, was not in substance the same as providing advertising services. Therefore there was no infringement of the plaintiff's trade mark.

36.6.4 Comparative advertising[110]

Comparative advertising is the practice of referring, expressly or implied, to a well-known rival product or service and its trade mark in the context of an assertion of the superior qualities of the advertised product or service. The 1996 legislation sanctions the practice of comparative advertising, in defined circumstances. Section 14(6) provides that the infringement provisions shall not be construed as preventing the use of a trade mark in order to identify the goods or services of a trade mark owner.[111] This reverses the former position where trade mark protection prevented the use of trade marks in advertising issued to the public in the course of trade.[112] Section 14(6) seeks to facilitate the identification of competitors' goods and services in advertising but there is a proviso. Section 14(6) states that:

> "any such use, otherwise than in accordance with honest practices in industrial or commercial matters, shall be treated as infringing the

110 See generally, EC Directive on Comparative Advertising, Directive 97/55 EC [1997] O.J. L290/18; see further Spink & Petty, "Comparative Advertising in the European Union" (1998) 47 *International and Comparative Law Quarterly* 855. See also EC Directive on Misleading Advertising, 84/450/EEC [1984] O.J. L250/17, implemented in the EC (Misleading Advertising) Regulations 1988, S.I. No 134 of 1988. The Government view is that the Sale of Goods Acts and the Misleading Advertising Regulations are sufficient in relation to the implementation of the 1997 Directive because the practice of comparative advertising is not prohibited under their terms. At the time of writing, this view had been communicated to the European Commission and a response is awaited. Note also the overlap with torts of passing-off (see 36.7), libel and malicious falsehood: see McMahon & Binchy, *Law of Torts* (Dublin, Butterworths, 3rd ed. 2001) Chapters 31, 34 and 35; Clark & Smith, *Intellectual Property Law in Ireland* (Dublin, Butterworths, 1997) Chapter 24.

111 Section 14(6) does not derive from any single provision in the Directive but draws from Arts. 5(5) and 6(1).

112 1963 Act, s.12(1)(b).

> registered trade mark if the use without due cause takes unfair advantage of or is detrimental to, the distinctive character or reputation of the trade mark."

In practice, a court when faced with this provision will have to strike a balance between allowing comparative advertising in the interests of consumers, and protecting the property of owners of registered trade marks. The phrases *honest practices in industrial or commercial matters* is clearly open to wide interpretation, but case law suggests that an objective "reasonable man" test will be applied to determine what is *honest*. In *Barclays Bank v. RBS Advanta,*[113] the defendant was about to launch a new credit card on the market. Its mail-shot to potential customers included promotional material listing 15 ways why its credit card was better than other cards. Some other cards were named, including Barclaycard Standard Visa. The plaintiff sought an injunction preventing the use of the promotional material on the basis that it infringed their trade mark "Barclaycard", and that it suggested that Barclaycard was an inferior product rather than explaining that, for example, Barclaycard charges were higher because they offered extra services. In refusing an injunction, Laddie J. applied a reasonable audience test and asked would a reasonable audience think the promotional material passes the proviso. He found that the defendant's use complied with the proviso. The promotional material suggested that the defendant believed that its credit card was better – it was not unreasonable – and the promotional material did not suggest that the plaintiff's card possessed no features which were better than the defendants.

36.6.5 Defences to infringement

There are limits on the effect of a registered trade mark and these operate as defences to infringement. Section 15 provides for a number of such defences.[114] For example, a registered trade mark is not infringed:

(a) by the use of another registered trade mark;[115]
(b) by a person who, acting in accordance with "honest practices in industrial and commercial matters,"
    (i) uses his own name or address;
    (ii) uses indications of the kind, quality, quantity, intended

113 [1996] R.P.C. 307, approved in *Vodafone Group plc v. Orange Personal Communications Services Ltd* [1997] F.S.R. 34.
114 Directive, Art. 6.
115 1996 Act, s.15(1).

purpose, value, geographical origin, the time of production of the goods or services;

(iii) uses the mark where it is necessary to indicate the intended purpose of the goods or service, in particular as accessories or spare parts.[116]

The phrase *honest practices in industrial or commercial matters* is clearly open to wide interpretation but, as noted above, case law suggests that an objective "reasonable man" test will be applied to determine what is honest.[117]

In addition, and in keeping with the doctrine of exhaustion under EC law,[118] the owner of a registered trade mark cannot complain that his rights are infringed when the mark is used on goods which have been put on the market in the European Economic Area by the owner or with his consent.[119] However, the owner may complain of infringement where he has "… legitimate reasons … to oppose further dealings in the goods", for instance where the goods have been altered after being first marketed.[120]

A defendant in infringement proceedings may challenge the validity of the registration of the plaintiff's mark, on the grounds that it should not have been registered.[121] Where such a challenge succeeds, the mark will be declared invalid and removed from the register.

36.6.6 Remedies

Both the civil and criminal law are used to protect the position of trade mark owners and licensees. As regards civil remedies, the legislation provides that where a registered trade mark is infringed, the owner and/or a licensee can sue for damages or an account of profits, an injunction, or otherwise.[122] Usually, a plaintiff will seek an injunction to prevent the defendant from continuing to use the mark, and damages for any losses caused by the defendant's use of the mark, or an account of profits. Additionally, a successful party will normally be awarded costs against the other party.

Damages are awarded on the basis of compensation for loss suffered as a result of infringement. A plaintiff seeking damages must prove that the

---

116 1996 Act, s.15(2).

117 *European Ltd v. Economist Newspapers Ltd* [1996] F.S.R. 431; *Cable & Wireless plc v. British Telecommunications plc* [1998] F.S.R. 383.

118 See 33.3.

119 1996 Act, s.16(1); Directive, Art. 7(1). See further Davidoff, *A&G Imports & Levi-Strauss v. Tesco*, Joined Cases C414/99, C415/99 and 416/99 approving *Silhouette International v. Hartlauer* C-355-96 [1998] 2 C.M.L.R. 593.

120 1996 Act, s.16(2); Directive, Art. 7(2).

121 1996 Act, s.52; Directive Arts 3 and 4.

122 1996 Act, s.18 and s.34.

infringement *caused* the loss suffered (such as loss of profit on sales, loss of licence income, and losses resulting from damage to product reputation). Importantly, innocent infringement is no defence to a claim for damages.[123]

Rather than seeking damages based on the plaintiff's loss, the plaintiff can elect to require the infringer to account for the profits made on the infringing activities. This remedy is useful where it is difficult to measure the plaintiff's loss, or where an account of profits yields a larger sum to the plaintiff than a damages claim, as where the infringer makes sales to customers who are not customers of the trade mark owner, or where sales are made at a higher price than that offered by the trade mark owner.

As well as granting interlocutory and perpetual injunctions[124] to prevent further infringement, the legislation also provides for orders for erasure of an infringing sign,[125] for delivery-up of infringing goods,[126] and for the disposal of infringing goods,[127] and grants various search and seizure powers to facilitate the taking of infringement proceedings.[128]

Criminal remedies are provided for in sections 92–95, which cover matters such as fraudulent use of a trade mark, including counterfeiting,[129] falsification of the Register,[130] and falsely representing a trade mark as being registered.[131]

Lastly, there is provision to deal with groundless threats of infringement proceedings. A person so threatened can apply for:

(a) a declaration that the threats are unjustified;
(b) an injunction against the continuance of the threats;
(c) damages in respect of any loss sustained as a result of the threats.[132]

Mere notification that a trade mark is registered or that an application for registration has been made, does not constitute a threat. The jurisdiction conferred by section 24 relates to the *threat* of proceedings. Once an action is commenced, the section 24 jurisdiction is spent and the court is seized

123 *Gillette UK Ltd v. Edenwest Ltd* [1994] R.P.C. 279.
124 See further 37.4.1.2 and 37.4.1.3.
125 1996 Act, s.19.
126 1996 Act, ss.20–22.
127 1996 Act, s.23.
128 1996 Act, s.25
129 1996 Act, s.92.
130 1996 Act, s.93.
131 1996 Act, s.94.
132 1996 Act, s. 24.

of the matter. Hence, it has been held that a party threatening proceedings may pre-empt a section 24 application by issuing proceedings.[133]

36.7 Passing-Off[134]

While section 7(1) of the 1996 Act makes it clear that a registered trade mark is a property right which derives from registration, section 7(2) provides that the common law of passing-off remains unaffected by the 1996 Act. In many cases, the same act may amount to infringement of a trade mark and passing-off, and there is nothing to prevent the owner of a registered trade mark suing for trade mark infringement and passing-off in the alternative.

Broadly speaking, passing-off involves one trader representing his goods or services to be those of another, so as to mislead the public and thereby cause an appreciable risk of detriment to the other trader. This risk is two-fold: first, the other trader may lose customers to the trader who is passing off his goods or services; and second, where the passing-off involves goods or services which are inferior to those of the other trader, the reputation of the other trader may be damaged. For example, in *Jameson v. Dublin Distillers Co Ltd*,[135] the plaintiff, John Jameson & Son, produced whiskey of a high reputation. The defendant acquired a business known as William Jameson & Co which also produced whiskey, but whose sales had been falling for some years. In 1898, the defendant decided to sell their whiskey under the name "Jameson's Whiskey" omitting the prefix "William." It was held that the defendant had unlawfully passed off their product as that of the plaintiff because the evidence showed that the name of "Jameson's Whiskey" had become so identified with the plaintiff that its use without qualifying words by the defendant to show that it was their whiskey was likely to mislead purchasers into believing that the whiskey was made by the plaintiff.

In *Reckitt & Colman Products v. Borden Inc*[136] (the jif-lemon case), Lord Oliver outlined three essential features of passing-off which the plaintiff must establish:

133 *Symonds Cider v. Showerings (Ireland) Ltd* [1997] 1 I.L.R.M. 481. *Cf. Trebor Bassett Ltd v. The Football Association* [1927] F.S.R. 211.

134 See generally, McMahon & Binchy, *Law of Torts* (Dublin, Butterworths, 3rd ed., 2001) Chapter 31; Clark & Smith, *Intellectual Property Law in Ireland* (Dublin, Butterworths, 1997) Chapter 24.

135 [1900] 1 I.R. 43.

136 [1990] 1 W.L.R. 491 at 499, approved by Laffoy J. in *DSG Retail Ltd v. World Ltd* unreported, High Court, January 13, 1998; see also *Erven Warnick Besloten Vennootschap v. J. Townend & Sons (Hull) Ltd* (the "Advocaat" case) [1979] A.C. 731 at 741, applied in numerous Irish cases including *Falcon Travel Ltd v. Owners Abroad Group plc* [1991] 1 I.R. 175 (H.C.); *An Post v. Irish Permanent plc* [1995] 1 I.R. 140 (H.C.); *Smithkline Beecham plc v. Antigen Pharmaceuticals Ltd* [1999] 2 I.L.R.M. 190 (HC).

(i) a goodwill attaching to the goods/services which in the minds of the public is associated with an identifying "get-up" (brand name, trade description, individual features, labelling or packaging) and which is distinctive specifically of the plaintiff's goods/services;
(ii) that the defendant made a misrepresentation (intentional or otherwise) which leads or is likely to lead the public to believe that the goods/services offered by the defendant are in fact offered by the plaintiff; and
(iii) proof that the plaintiff has suffered or is likely to suffer as a result of the erroneous belief engendered by the defendant's misrepresentation.

36.7.1 Goodwill

Goodwill has been defined as:

> "the benefit and advantage of the good name, reputation connection of a business. It is the attractive force which brings in custom. It is the one thing which distinguishes an old established business from a new business at its start."[137]

It is clear from case law that the necessary goodwill can be established quite quickly. In *Stannard v. Reay*,[138] for example, the plaintiff and defendant both established chip-shops under the name "Mr. Chippy", but the plaintiff did so three weeks earlier than the defendant. The court, in granting an injunction against the defendant, held that the plaintiff had built up trade very quickly and therefore could be said to have established the necessary goodwill.

The geographical scope of a business reputation or goodwill can be extensive. In *Chelsea Man Menswear v. Chelsea Girl*,[139] the plaintiff sold clothes under the label "Chelsea Man Menswear" in Leicester, Coventry and London. The defendant wanted to expand into menswear under the label "Chelsea Man". The plaintiff sought an injunction to prevent the defendant doing so. The defendant argued that if an injunction was granted, it should be limited to the areas where the plaintiff operated. The court stated that clothes and people travelled and hence goodwill was not limited to a particular geographical area. It was also noted that the plaintiff might want to expand its business in the future. As a result, a country-wide injunction was granted. Goodwill can also be protected across international boundaries. In *Maxim v. Dye*,[140] the owners of Maxim's in Paris got an injunction to prevent a Norwich bistro opening in the same name. Again,

137 *Inland Revenue v. Muller's & Co's Margarine Ltd* [1901] A.C. 217.
138 [1967] R.P.C. 589.
139 [1987] R.P.C. 189.
140 [1977] F.S.R. 364.

in *C&A Modes Ltd v. C&A Waterford Ltd*,[141] the plaintiff was a well-known British chain-shore which operated in England and Northern Ireland. The defendant, an Irish company, used the letters "C&A" with the intention of leading customers to connect their business with that of the plaintiff. Although the plaintiff did not have a store in the Republic of Ireland, there was evidence that a large number of people travelled from the Republic to Northern Ireland to shop at the plaintiff's store there. Therefore, goodwill was established and the action for passing-off succeeded.

36.7.2 Misrepresentation causing confusion

It is clear that imitation of a product alone without confusion is insufficient to base a passing-off action. In *Adidas Sportsschuhfabricken Adi Dassler KG v. Charles O'Neill*,[142] the plaintiff was a well-known German sports gear company which used the distinctive three stripes on its goods. The plaintiff sought an injunction to prevent the defendant's use of three strips on its sportsgear. It was held that the defendant's conduct did not constitute passing-off, because the defendant was a well established sportsgear manufacturer and its goods were boxed with its name marked clearly thereon.

The tests for determining confusion is the likely impression on the passing or unwary customer.[143] It is no defence to claim that an observant person making a careful examination of the goods or services would not have been confused. For example, in cases involving packaged goods, the court will consider the "get-up" of the goods and, in many cases, Irish courts have focused on the packaging rather than the names and content. For instance, in *Polycell Products v. O'Carroll*,[144] an injunction was granted in relation to an adhesive product in packaging similar in colour and design to the plaintiff's product even though the names of the products were reasonably different: "Polycell" and "Clingcell". Again, in *United Biscuits v. Irish Biscuits*,[145] the two products in question were "Cottage Creams" and "College Creams". Despite a similarity in names and type, the plaintiff's action for passing-off failed because the packaging was very different and therefore there was no risk of confusion.

Whether there is confusion is a matter of evidence. In *Muckross Park Hotel Ltd v. Randles*,[146] the plaintiff purchased the "Muckross Hotel" in Muckross, Co. Kerry, near Killarney, refurbished it and reopened it under

141 [1976] I.R. 198 (S.C.).

142 [1983] I.L.R.M. 112 (S.C.); cf. *Gabicci v. Dunnes Stores Ltd* unreported, High Court, Carroll J., July 31, 1991.

143 *Singer Manufacturing Co v. Loog* (1882) 8 A.C. 15 at 18; *An Bord Trachtála v. Waterford Foods plc* [1994] F.S.R. 316 (H.C.).

144 [1959] Ir. Jur. Rep. 34.

145 [1971] I.R. 16.

146 [1995] 1 I.R. 130.

the name "Muckross Park Hotel". Shortly thereafter, the defendant commenced construction on the "Muckross Court Hotel" outside Killarney, but not in Muckross itself. There was evidence of some confusion caused. The court stated that the essential question was whether the similarities were "calculated to lead to confusion"; such a calculation may be difficult to make but in the circumstances, the court found that the necessary likelihood of confusion was established.[147]

Likelihood of confusion was established in *Guinness Ireland Group v. Kilkenny Brewing Company Ltd*,[148] where the defendant was engaged in a different type of business from the plaintiff. An injunction was granted against the use of the name "Kilkenny Brewing Company" by the defendant, a company whose purpose was to hold land, on which was situated a micro brewery, rather than to be a trading company for the business carried on at the micro brewery. There was evidence, from three persons "very experienced in the licensed trade" that consumers would be likely to get the impression that the defendant brewed "Kilkenny Irish Beer," the plaintiff's product.

In *Smithkline Beecham plc v. Antigen Pharmaceutical Ltd*,[149] the court had to consider who would be confused. The defendant marketed an analgesic called "Solfen" which the plaintiff claimed would be likely to be confused with their product "Solpadeine." Neither product was sold on the open shelf, but under the supervision of a pharmacist. The plaintiff was concerned that a customer with an imperfect recollection might ask for a pain-killer called "Sol-something" and that confusion would occur. It was found that such confusion would be that of the pharmacist, or the carelessness of the pharmacist in not asking further questions, rather than any confusion on the part of the customer. Nevertheless, it was held that there was a serious question to be tried in relation to the risk of confusion and passing-off, though McCracken J. acknowledged that the case was very much weakened because the goods were not available on open shelves.

36.7.3 Damage

The requirement of damage is an area of uncertainty.[150] Earlier cases suggest that there is no need to prove actual damage: the assumption is that

147 See also *An Post v. Irish Permanent plc* [1995] 1 I.R. 140 where the plaintiff who had promoted a savings scheme for many years under the name "Savings Certificates" obtained an interlocutory injunction against the defendant promoting a financial product under the same name.

148 [1999] 1 I.L.R.M. 531 (H.C.).

149 [1999] 2 I.L.R.M. 190 (H.C.).

150 See further Carty, "Dilution and Passing-Off: Cause for Concern" [1996] *Law Quarterly Review* 632; and Coughlan, "The Requirement of Damage in Passing Off" [1991] *Irish Law Times* 138.

confusion in the minds of the public of itself causes damage.[151] However, *Stringfellow v. McCain Foods GB Ltd*[152] suggests a move away from this traditional position. There, the plaintiff was the owner of a nightclub "Stringfellows". The defendant manufactured a brand of potato-chip called "Stringfellows" and advertised it using a family disco dancing in their kitchen. The Court of Appeal held that although the advertising campaign may have led some members of the public to confuse the two, there was no damage to the plaintiff's goodwill established. Also, the plaintiff was not merchandising his name on other products: the fact that he might merchandise in the future was rejected as a basis for damage and was mere speculation.

In the Irish case of *Falcon Travel Ltd v. Owners Abroad Group plc*,[153] the former approach seems to have prevailed. There the plaintiff traded in package holidays to the public since the 1970s and had established a good reputation. The defendant was a U.K. company, also trading in holidays since the 1980s but originally they restricted themselves to the U.K. market. In 1988, the defendant moved into the Irish market, issuing brochures and opening an office. The defendant was aware of the plaintiff, but believed there would be no confusion because both businesses were very different: the plaintiff was relatively small in comparison with the defendant who were large wholesalers. In fact, a lot of confusion was caused. The plaintiff received telephone calls, correspondence and threats of legal action which should have been directed at the defendant. Furthermore, a newspaper article confused the two businesses when the defendant's customers were stranded in Turkey. The defendant argued that the plaintiff had suffered no loss, in fact they had an increased turnover. Murphy J. stated that it had to be proved that the plaintiff suffered damage. However, he appears to have decided that appropriating the plaintiff's name is sufficient damage without the need to show further actual damage.

36.7.4 Remedies

Damages to compensate for the resulting loss, such as the diversion of sales or injurious association, and an injunction to prevent any further confusion, may be available in an action for passing-off. Actual deception is not needed[154] and there is no need to prove intention to deceive,[155] but if either are proved the case will be stronger. Nominal damages may be awarded where there is no intention to deceive. In *Michelstown Co-op*

---

151 See *e.g. Drapier v. Trist* [1939] 3 All E.R. 513.

152 [1984] R.P.C. 501.

153 [1991] 1 I.R. 175.

154 *Jameson v. Dublin Distillers Co Ltd* [1900] 1 I.R. 43 at 55.

155 *Guinness Ireland Group v. Kilkenny Brewing Company* [1999] 1 I.L.R.M. 531 (H.C.); *Smithkline Beecham plc v. Antigen Pharmaceuticals Ltd* [1999] 2 I.L.R.M. 190 (H.C.).

Agricultural Society v. Goldenvale Food Products Ltd,[156] the court considered that, in general, damages would be an inadequate remedy in passing-off cases, the appropriate remedy being an injunction.

The circumstances in which a court will grant an injunction to restrain passing-off were considered by the Court of Appeal in *British Telecommunications plc v. One in a Million Ltd*.[157] The court concluded that an injunction could be granted in three types of cases:

(a) where actual passing-off is established or threatened;
(b) where the defendant is a joint-tortfeasor with another in passing-off, either actual or threatened;
(c) where the defendant has equipped himself or intends to equip another with an instrument of fraud in which case the court will intervene on a *quia timet* basis.

In *British Telecommunications plc v. One in a Million Ltd*, the defendant had registered internet domain names identical or similar to several well known business organisations, including, "bt.org." The court found that the registration of such names amounted to a representation to the public that the person registering was connected with the name and thus constituted passing-off. Additionally, it held that the registration amounted to "an instrument of fraud", which could be restrained by injunction either if the name, by reason of its similarity to that of an existing business, would inherently lead to passing-off, or even if the name would not inherently lead to passing-off, if it was produced to enable passing-off to be committed, was adapted to be used for passing-off or was likely to be used fraudulently.

In *B&S Ltd v. Irish Auto Trading Ltd*,[158] the principles of *American Cyanamid Company v. Ethicon Ltd*[159] in relation to interlocutory injunctions were adopted. Hence, the applicant must show that there is a fair question to be tried (this has proved relatively easy to satisfy in passing-off cases)[160] and the injunction will be granted or refused on the balance of convenience. It has been argued that these principles should not be strictly applied in passing-off cases. In such circumstances, the outcome of interlocutory proceedings often determines the final outcome of any dispute. Hence, it was argued, a court should consider the substance of the

156 Unreported, High Court, Costello J., December 12, 1985, approved in *Symonds Cider & English Wine Co. Ltd v. Showerings (Ireland) Ltd* [1997] 1 I.L.R.M. 481.

157 [1998] 4 All E.R. 476, [1998] F.S.R. 265; see further Thorn & Bennett, "Domain Names – Internet Warehousing" [1998] *European Intellectual Property Review* 468.

158 [1995] 2 I.L.R.M. 152.

159 [1975] A.C. 396.

160 See, *e.g. Smithkline Beecham plc v. Antigen Pharmaceuticals Ltd* [1999] 2 I.L.R.M. 190 (H.C.), where the judge identified various weaknesses in the plaintiff's case.

case at an interlocutory stage. This argument was rejected in *Symonds Cider v. Showerings (Ireland) Ltd.*[161]

It is important to remember that the tort of passing-off seeks to protect the trader and not the public. Hence, it is no defence to show that the defendant's goods or services are better or cheaper than those of the plaintiff, or that the resulting competition is good for the general public.[162]

161 [1997] 1 I.L.R.M. 481.

162 *Incorporated Law Society of Ireland v. Carroll* [1995] 3 I.R. 145.

Part VIII

COMMERCIAL DISPUTE RESOLUTION

CHAPTER 37

COMMERCIAL DISPUTE RESOLUTION

37.1 INTRODUCTION

No matter how well planned a transaction or comprehensively drafted a contract, disputes arise. Parties negotiating commercial transactions should therefore be mindful of this and should make provision for a dispute resolution mechanism in their contracts. Whether such a mechanism is invoked will depend on the nature of the dispute: if one party has breached a term of the contract, it may be too important or too costly to be left unchallenged. However, if the breach is minor, the innocent party might be best advised not to get involved in costly and time consuming proceedings.

The main forms of commercial dispute resolution are:

(i) negotiation,
(ii) arbitration,
(iii) litigation, and
(iv) ADR (alternative dispute resolution, including conciliation, mediation, and mini-trials).

37.2 NEGOTIATION

Negotiation should always be the first step in resolving a dispute. It does not incur fees or charges,[1] the details of the transaction in dispute remain private and the individual parties to the transaction remain in control of the process. However, where a negotiated settlement cannot be reached, recourse to other mechanisms may be necessary. Each method listed has its own distinct features and advantages. In this chapter, we concentrate on the use of arbitration proceedings to resolve commercial disputes, though it should be remembered that a negotiated settlement is still an option even after other dispute resolution mechanisms are set in motion.

1 Of course, where professionals, such as solicitors, are engaged in the process fees will be incurred.

37.3 ARBITRATION[2]

Arbitration is a process by which parties voluntarily refer their dispute to an impartial third person, an arbitrator, selected by them, for a decision, based on evidence and arguments to be presented before the arbitrator. The parties agree in advance that the arbitrator's determination, the award, will be final and binding upon them. Some of the salient features that distinguish arbitration from other means of dispute resolution are:

(a) it is a consensual process which offers finality;
(b) it is a private process – hearings are in private and awards are usually not published; and,
(c) it offers parties the opportunity to select their own "judge" or arbitrator, often on the basis of some expert skill or knowledge.

Arbitration has, for many years, been the main form of dispute resolution in certain fields of business activity such as, commodity sales, construction, insurance and shipping. Arbitration is said to avoid all the drawbacks of litigation and to offer the following advantages:

(a) speed;
(b) cost savings;
(c) freedom to select the arbitrator, who may have technical qualifications or trade experience;
(d) power to control the time and place of the proceedings;
(e) absence of publicity;
(f) flexible procedures; and
(g) resolution of the dispute, in the form of a final and binding award.

However, arbitration can be time consuming and costly.[3] There are opportunities to review an arbitrator's award before a court of law, hence, negativing the finality of the award, and in many circumstances, the arbitrator, having limited powers, may have to rely on the assistance of the court.[4]

---

2 See generally, Forde, *Arbitration Law and Procedure* (Dublin, Round Hall, 1994); Carrigan, *Handbook on Arbitration in Ireland* (Dublin, Law Society of Ireland, 1998); Mustill & Boyd, *The Law and Practice of Commercial Arbitration in England* (London, Butterworths, 2nd ed., 1989) and 2001 Companion; Redfern & Hunter, *Law and Practice of International Commercial Arbitration* (London, Sweet & Maxwell, 3rd ed., 1999).

3 For instance, with International Chamber of Commerce (ICC) arbitration there is an administration fee and the arbitrator's fees and expenses to be paid, and because these are calculated with reference to the amount in dispute, the total bill can be substantial: see further 37.3.3.2.

4 See 37.3.2.5. See generally, Kerr, "International Arbitration v. Litigation" [1980] *Journal of Business Law* 164.

To reinforce the extra-judicial nature of arbitration, parties may insert what is termed an "equity clause" in the arbitration agreement or state that the arbitrator is to act *ex aequo et bono*, or as *amiable compositeur*, empowering the arbitrator to decide the issues based on what is fair and equitable and not necessarily in strict accordance with the law. However, the legal effect of such clauses in domestic arbitration is unclear. In *Eagle Star Insurance Co. Ltd. v. Yuval Insurance Co.*,[5] the Court of Appeal, overruling earlier authority,[6] unanimously agreed that a clause which required an arbitrator to settle any difference according to an equitable rather than a strict legal interpretation of the provisions of their agreement was valid and of full effect: it did not oust the jurisdiction of the court. Subsequently, in *Home and Overseas Insurance Co Ltd. v. Mentor Insurance Co. (UK) Ltd*,[7] it was stated, again in the Court of Appeal, that a clause which purported to free arbitrators to decide without regard to the law and according, for example, to their own notions of what would be fair would not be a valid arbitration clause. While there is no Irish authority on the point, this later English case law clearly diminishes the extent to which the arbitrator can avoid legal technicalities and strict constructions and instead rely on his skill and expertise to decide a case. Such an approach undermines the effectiveness of the arbitral process.

In contrast, a number of institution rules recognise the use of "equity clauses" and parties might be advised, for this reason, to adopt an institutional form of arbitration,[8] conducted in a forum where equity clauses are clearly enforceable.[9] Moreover, UNCITRAL's Model Law, as adopted in Ireland by the Arbitration (International Commercial) Act 1998, allows an arbitrator this freedom in relation to international commercial arbitration.[10] In light of this trend towards the recognition of equity clauses, an Irish court might be inclined to give effect to such a clause in domestic arbitration also.

37.3.1 Types of arbitration

Arbitration can be either institutional or ad hoc; and domestic or international.

Institutional arbitration is administered by one of the many specialised arbitration institutions under their own arbitration rules. In Ireland, there is the Chartered Institute of Arbitrators; in the United Kingdom, there is the London Court of International Arbitration (LCIA); in Paris, the

5 [1978] 1 Lloyd's Rep. 357.

6 *Orion Compania Espanola de Seguros v. Belfort Maatschappij* [1962] 2 Lloyd's Rep. 257.

7 [1990] 1 W.L.R. 153.

8 See, *e.g.* ICC Arbitration Rules, 1998, Art. 17: see further 37.3.3.2.

9 *e.g.* the U.K. Arbitration Act 1996 recognises the use of "equity clauses": 1996 Act, s.46(1)(b).

10 1998 Act, s.4 and Schedule; Model Law, Art. 28(3): see further 37.3.3.1.

International Chamber of Commerce (ICC); while in the USA, there is the American Arbitration Association (AAA), to name but a few. Institutional arbitration has the advantage that there is a pre-drafted set of procedural rules under which the arbitration will be conducted and each institution provides an experienced and trained staff to administer the arbitration. However, institutional arbitration can be expensive and the rules, for example as to time limits, can be inflexible.

An *ad hoc* arbitration, on the other hand, is conducted under rules of procedure that are adopted for a specific dispute. These rules can be drawn from an international organisation, such as UNCITRAL'S Arbitration Rules 1976,[11] or drafted by the parties, the arbitration tribunal, or both, thus meeting the exact needs of the dispute.

In effect, an infrastructure for the arbitration process must be designed. Business persons who are wary of institutional arbitration because of its formality, or apparent lack of neutrality, will often prefer ad hoc arbitration, which depends entirely on the parties' goodwill. Ad hoc arbitration is time-consuming in terms of establishing the infrastructure that already exists in institutional arbitration.

---

11 These rules are used in countries throughout the world with different legal, social and economic systems, in ad hoc arbitration. They offer parties neutrality which national arbitration systems may not. The Rules do not have the force of law, rather they must be expressly adopted by the parties. A model arbitration clause is recommended in the Rules.
"Any dispute, controversy or claim arising out of or relating to this contract, or the breach, termination, or invalidity thereof, shall be settled by arbitration in accordance with the UNCITRAL Arbitration Rules as at present in force.
Note – Parties may wish to consider adding:
(a) The appointing authority shall be...... (name of institution or person);
(b) The number of arbitrators shall be...... (one or three);
(c) The place of arbitration shall be........ (town or country);
(d) The language(s) used in the arbitral proceedings shall be......"
Notable features of the Rules include the fact that:
(a) the arbitration clause must be in writing (Art. 1);
(b) any notice, including a notification of communication or proposal, is deemed to be received when it is physically delivered to the addressee or his habitual residence (Art. 2);
(c) the notice of arbitration must contain certain details (Art. 3.3);
(d) no arbitration can fail for lack of appointment or if an arbitrator cannot act: ultimately, either party can request the Secretary-General of the Permanent Court of Arbitration at the Hague to designate an appointing authority (Art. 6);
(e) the arbitration tribunal has jurisdiction to rule on objections that it has no jurisdiction and to determine the existence or the validity of a contract of which the arbitration clause forms part (Art. 21(1) and (2));
(f) the arbitration clause is severable from the contract and exists independently of it: a finding that the contract is null and void does not necessarily mean that the arbitration clause is invalid;
(g) periods of time fixed by the arbitration tribunal should not exceed 45 days, though extensions are possible (Art. 23); and
(h) the award must be in writing, dated, signed, reasoned, not published without the consent of the parties and is final (Art. 32).
For text, see www.uncitral.org

Generally, an arbitration may be termed domestic where all the relevant factors in the dispute – subject matter; domicile of the parties; place of arbitration; applicable law – converge in a single place. The more diverse these connecting factors, the more likely the arbitration will be international. Each national legal system defines what it terms as domestic and international arbitration. The Arbitration (International Commercial) Act, 1998, which adopts the UNCITRAL Model Law, states that an arbitration is international if:

(a) the parties to an arbitration agreement have, at the time of the conclusion of that agreement, their places of business in different States; or
(b) one of the following places is situated outside the State in which the parties have their places of business:
    (i) the place of arbitration if determined in, or pursuant to the arbitration agreement;
    (ii) any place where a substantial part of the obligations of the commercial relationship is to be performed or the place with which the subject-matter of the dispute is most closely connected; or
(c) the parties have expressly agreed that the subject-matter of the arbitration agreement relates to more than one country.[12]

This broad definition combines factors relating to the nationality of the parties and the nature of the dispute. The 1998 Act further provides that the Arbitration Acts 1950 and 1980 do not apply to international commercial arbitration, as defined.[13]

37.3.2 Irish domestic arbitration

The statutory basis of Irish arbitration is the Arbitration Acts 1954 and 1980.[14] The 1954 Act is the principal Act, and is based closely on the English Arbitration Act 1950 (now repealed).[15] English case law on the 1950 Act is therefore of persuasive authority, particularly where Irish

12 Model Law, Art. 1(3): see 37.3.3.1.

13 1998 Act, s.16.

14 Specific statutory arbitration schemes may also exist, *e.g.* where shareholders who object to a company's restructuring, under s.260 of the Companies Act 1963, want to have their shares bought by the company, in the absence of agreement, the price is determined by arbitration under the Companies Clauses Consolidation Act, 1854: 1963 Act, s.260(6). Most features of such statutory schemes are made subject to the 1954 Act: 1954 Act, s.48(2).

15 See 147, Dáil Debates, Col. 294 (November 3, 1954). The current U.K. legislation is the Arbitration Act 1996 which is modelled on, though not identical to, UNCITRAL's Model Law.

authority is lacking. The 1980 Act gives effect to the New York Convention[16] and the Washington Convention;[17] and amends the 1950 Act in relation to staying litigation where there is an arbitration agreement, by removing the court's discretion in this regard, and, thereby reinforcing the effectiveness of arbitration as a means of dispute resolution.

37.3.2.1 The arbitration agreement

An agreement between the parties to submit any dispute between them to arbitration is the foundation stone of modern commercial arbitration.[18] An arbitration agreement means either:

(i) a submission (*compromis*) – an agreement to submit an existing dispute to arbitration; or,
(ii) an arbitration clause (*clause compromissoire*) – an agreement to submit future disputes to arbitration.

A submission is usually a very detailed document concerning, *inter alia*, the constitution of the arbitration tribunal, and the procedure to be followed, whereas an arbitration clause often consists of a brief phrase: "All disputes, arising in connection with this contract, shall be finally settled by reference to arbitration in Dublin: Irish law shall apply."

(i) Form

While a valid oral arbitration agreement may exist at common law, the 1954 Act only applies where the agreement is in writing. Section 2(1) provides: "'arbitration agreement' means a written agreement to refer present or future differences to arbitration ..." The 1980 Act adopts this definition and provides for the possibility of an arbitration agreement being contained in an exchange of letters or telegrams.[19]

In *The St. Raphael*,[20] the Court of Appeal stated that for an agreement to be a written arbitration agreement, it was not necessary for the whole contract, including the arbitration agreement, to be in the one document; rather it was sufficient that the arbitration agreement itself was in writing and it was sufficient that there was a document that recognised the

16 See 37.3.3.3.
17 The Washington Convention on the Settlement of Investment Disputes (I.C.S.I.D.), 1965: see further Redfern & Hunter, *Law and Practice of International Commercial Arbitration* (London, Sweet & Maxwell, 3rd ed., 1999) 1-98–1-103.
18 *Bremer Vulkan Schiffbau und Maschinenfabrik v. South India Shipping Corp* [1982] A.C. 909, at 983–5.
19 1980, s.2.
20 [1985] 1 Lloyd's Rep. 403.

existence of the agreement. Also, it was stated that the agreement need not be signed. An exchange of telex communications has been held to constitute an agreement in writing.[21] Where an arbitration clause is incorporated from another document, to be effective the incorporation must be clear and express.[22]

(ii) Scope of the arbitration clause

The arbitration agreement determines the jurisdiction of the arbitrator and what disputes can be submitted to arbitration. The arbitrator must not exceed the power the parties have conferred upon him. Two questions need to be addressed in this regard:

(1) can the arbitrator decide the extent of his own jurisdiction? and,
(2) if the arbitration clause is contained in a contract, can the arbitrator decide whether that contract is void *ab initio* due to mistake or illegality, for example?

As to the first question, there is no Irish authority on the point. Under the English Arbitration Act 1950, the position was unclear.[23] In *Dalmia Dairy Industries v. National Bank of Pakistan*,[24] it was accepted that, in English law, an arbitrator cannot pronounce on his own jurisdiction, the issue of jurisdiction being ultimately one for the courts. Interestingly though, the English courts stated that an arbitrator had the power, when his jurisdiction was challenged, to enquire into the merits of the issue of whether he has jurisdiction, not as a means of making a binding conclusion (only a court can do that), but to satisfy himself, as a preliminary matter, whether he ought to continue with the arbitration or not.[25]

Any interference by a court detracts from the arbitral process as an extra-judicial means of dispute resolution. To avoid this, parties can utilise the arbitration rules of a jurisdiction,[26] or an institutional arbitration system[27] where the rules expressly empower the arbitrator to rule on his own jurisdiction.[28] In these circumstances, a party protesting that the

21 See, *e.g. Arab Africa Energy Corp. Ltd. v. Olieprodukten Nederland BV* [1983] 2 Lloyd's Rep. 419.

22 See, *e.g. Sweeney v. Mulcahy* [1993] I.L.R.M. 289 (H.C.). See also *The Rena K* [1979] Q.B. 377; *cf The Federal Bulker* [1989] 1 Lloyd's Rep. 103.

23 The position in English law has been clarified with the Arbitration Act 1996 whereby an arbitral tribunal can rule on matters concerning its own substantive jurisdiction: see the Arbitration Act 1996, s.30.

24 [1978] 2 Lloyd's Rep. 223.

25 *Brown v. Genossenschaft Oesterreichischer Waldbesitzer Holzwirtschaftsbetriebe* [1954] 1 Q.B. 8.

26 Such as the United Kingdom under the Arbitration Act 1996, s.30.

27 ICC Rules, Art. 6: see 37.3.3.2.

28 See also UNCITRAL Model Law, Art. 16 as adopted by the Arbitration (International Commercial) Act 1998.

arbitrator lacks jurisdiction, should make clear this objection and indicate that his continued participation in the process does not prejudice the lack of jurisdiction claim: failure to do so may be interpreted as a submission to arbitration.[29]

As to the second issue, historically a distinction was drawn between the *initial* and the *continued* existence of the contract. Regarding the former, the traditional view is that an arbitrator cannot make a binding award as to the initial existence of the contract.[30] If there is no contract, an arbitration clause in such a non-existent contract cannot empower the arbitrator to decide on the initial validity of the contract. However, where the issue is one of the continued existence of the contract, that is, where the contract did originally exist but for some reason (for example, repudiation, frustration, or misrepresentation) the contract comes to an end, the court uses the notion of separability of the arbitration clause from the rest of the contract, to allow the arbitrator to make a decision as to the continued existence of the contract.

Whether the arbitration clause can be severed from the main contract, thereby allowing the arbitrator to derive power from an independent arbitration contract, to determine whether the main contract still exists is essentially a matter of construction dependent on the parties' intention and the wording of the clause. The older cases did not support the notion of severance, but more recently there appears to be support for a doctrine of severance. In particular, in *Harbour Assurance Co (UK) Ltd v. Kansa General International Insurance Co Ltd*,[31] at first instance, Steyn J. stated that although there was no theoretical objection to the doctrine of separability regarding the initial existence of the contract, provided that the arbitration clause itself had not been impeached, he was compelled by authority to hold that the principle of separability could not be extended so as to enable the arbitrator to determine if the contract was void *ab initio* for illegality. However, the Court of Appeal did not feel similarly constrained by authority. It stated that an arbitration clause is usually a self-contained collateral contract and, on construction of the clause, the arbitrator could deal with the issue of illegality. This interpretation must be correct: it rightly places the emphasis on the intention of the parties, as expressed in the arbitration clause, and is a logical extension of earlier case law.

There are many cases on the meaning of particular words commonly used in arbitration clauses. For example, a formulation often used is that "all disputes *arising out of or in connection with* the contract" shall be

---

29 *The Amazona* [1989] 2 Lloyd's Rep. 130.

30 *Heyman v. Darwins Ltd* [1942] A.C. 356.

31 [1993] 1 Lloyd's Rep. 455; see further *Parkarran Ltd v. M & P Construction* [1996] 1 I.R. 83; and *Doyle v. Irish National Insurance Co plc* [1998] 1 I.R. 89, [1998] 1 I.L.R.M. 502.

submitted to arbitration. This wording has been held to cover claims concerning alleged mistake or misrepresentation as well as extra-contractual claims such as *quantum meruit* and unjust enrichment, and even tort claims connected with the contract.[32] In *Ashville Investments Ltd. v. Elmer Contractors Ltd*,[33] the court considered the term "in connection with," and found that these words were wide enough to cover claims for rectification and damages for innocent misrepresentation. In *Ethiopian Oilseeds and Pulses Export Corp. v. Rio Del Mar Foods Inc.*,[34] the court stated that the term "arising out of" must be given a wide interpretation to allow an arbitrator jurisdiction to decide on rectification of a contract. However, it should be noted that the meaning of the same phrase or formulation of words can differ from contract to contract and so the above cases can be regarded as persuasive authority, at most.[35]

(iii) Giving effect to the arbitration agreement

The inclusion of a *Scott v. Avery* clause is a useful addition to an arbitration agreement as a means of ensuring that the matter is referred to arbitration. Such a clause makes arbitration a condition precedent to litigation. It is enforceable because it does not seek to oust the jurisdiction of the courts; it merely ensures that arbitration occurs.[36]

Where, despite the existence of an arbitration clause, both parties agree to pursue their claims through the courts, the clause is overridden by this new agreement and rendered redundant within the context of the new agreement. But, where one party, in opposition to the arbitration agreement, commences litigation, the courts, at the request of the willing party, have the power to stay the litigation in order to give effect to the arbitration agreement. Under the 1954 Act, this power was discretionary,[37] but the 1980 Act removed this discretion in relation to domestic and international arbitration, making the granting of a stay mandatory in certain circumstances.

Under section 5 of the 1980 Act, where a party to an arbitration agreement commences proceedings in a court in respect of a matter subject to an arbitration agreement, the other party may, after entering an appearance but before delivering any pleadings or taking any other steps in the proceedings, apply to the court to stay the proceedings, and the court *must* order a stay unless the court is satisfied that:

32 *Woolf v. Collis Removal Services* [1947] 2 All E.R. 260.

33 [1989] Q.B. 488; [1988] 2 Lloyd's Rep. 73.

34 [1990] 1 Lloyd's Rep. 86.

35 *Ashville Investments Ltd. v. Elmer Contractors Ltd* [1989] Q.B. 488 at 494–5, [1988] 2 Lloyd's Rep. 73 at 75.

36 *Scott v. Avery* (1856) 5 H.L. Cas. 881; see further *Heyman v. Darwins* [1942] A.C. 356 at 377.

37 1954 Act, s.12.

(a) the agreement is null and void, inoperative or incapable of being performed, or,
(b) there is no dispute between the parties with regard to the matter agreed to be referred.[38]

A number of points concerning this provision are clear. The provision expressly applies to parties to an arbitration agreement and to parties claiming through or under either of the parties to the agreement. This has been held to include trustees of a bankrupt, assignees of a debt, and subsidiary and parent companies. The proceedings which are the subject of the application for a stay must be brought in "a court" and not an administrative tribunal or another arbitration. The proceedings must also have commenced. It is expressly stated that an application for a stay must be made after entering an appearance – a premature application will be refused – but before delivering any pleadings or taking any other steps in the proceedings. In *McCormack Products Ltd v. Monaghan Co-op Ltd*,[39] the applicant for a stay had obtained an interim injunction against the other party, thereby electing for litigation, and was refused a stay. In contrast, in *O'Flynn v. Bord Gais*,[40] where the defendant's solicitor wrote to the plaintiff's solicitor seeking an extension of time to submit a defence, the court held that this was not a step which would preclude a stay. The application must be made to "the court", which refers to the High Court,[41] but in *Mitchell v. Budget Travel Ltd*,[42] the Supreme Court held that the court in which the case is listed can stay the proceedings.

Nevertheless, this provision has caused some difficulty. For example, in *McCarthy & ors v. Joe Walsh Tours Ltd*,[43] the plaintiffs bought a package holiday from the defendant. The plaintiffs were not happy with the holiday and commenced proceedings in the Circuit Court for breach of the express and/or implied terms of the contract. The defendant, having entered an appearance, sought to stay the proceedings on the basis that the contract between the parties included an arbitration clause. On appeal to the High Court, the defendant's application was refused. The arbitration clause included a provision which excluded liability for personal injuries and limited liability for other claims to £5,000. The court found that this "express term" varied the defendant's liability under the implied terms of section 39 of the Sale of Goods and Supply of Services Act 1980,[44] and to

38 In *Administratia Asigurarilor de Stat v. Insurance Corporation of Ireland plc* [1990] I.L.R.M. 159, the High Court held that it had an overriding jurisdiction to refuse a stay where there are bona fide allegations of fraud.
39 [1988] I.R. 304.
40 [1982] I.L.R.M. 324.
41 Arbitration Act 1954 Act, s.2.
42 [1990] I.L.R.M. 739.
43 [1991] I.L.R.M. 813.
44 See 20.4.

be effective under section 40 of the 1980 Act, the term had to be "fair and reasonable" and brought to the specific attention of the plaintiffs, as consumers. The court found, on the facts, that the clause had not been brought to the specific attention of the plaintiffs. The court did not consider whether it was fair and reasonable. Dealing with the whole clause as one, the court found that the clause was not effective and refused the application for the stay under section 5 of the Arbitration Act 1980, on the ground that the arbitration clause was "inoperative or incapable of being performed." It has been argued that the arbitration should have taken place.[45] It is submitted that the arbitration clause and the exclusion clause could have been treated separately thereby allowing the arbitration to proceed without being bound by the exclusion clause. It would appear that the court, in reaching its decision was more concerned to protect the position of the weaker party, the plaintiff consumers, than to give effect to the arbitration clause in the defendant's standard terms of trade. Subsequently, in *Carroll v. Budget Travel & Counihans Travel*,[46] it was held that a standard arbitration clause found in a contract for the supply of holiday services is not an "express term" within the meaning of section 40 of the 1980 Act, and it was therefore irrelevant whether or not it was brought to the consumer's attention: a stay under section 5 of the 1980 Act was granted.[47]

37.3.2.2 Arbitrators and the Arbitration Tribunal

The arbitration tribunal may comprise a sole arbitrator or a panel of arbitrators.

(i) Appointment

The arbitrator(s) can be appointed by:

(a) the parties,
(b) a third party, for example, the President of the Law Society of Ireland, or,
(c) the court.

Section 14 of the 1954 Act raises a presumption in favour of a single arbitrator, but the parties can of course agree to any number of arbitrators. It should be borne in mind that the greater the number of arbitrators, the greater the arbitrators' fees.[48]

---

45 Forde, *Arbitration Law and Procedure*, (Dublin, Round Hall, 1994) p.22.

46 Unreported, High Court, Morris J., December 7 1995.

47 See generally, *e.g. Doyle v. Irish National Insurance Co plc* [1998] 1 I.R. 89, [1998] 1 I.L.R.M. 502; *Williams v. Artane Service Station Ltd* [1991] I.L.R.M. 893, *Sweeney v. Mulcahy* [1993] I.L.R.M. 289.

48 See further 1954 Act, s.17.

Section 15 provides, unless contrary intention is expressed, that where there is provision for two arbitrators, each to be chosen by each side:

(a) if one arbitrator refuses to act, is incapable or dies, the party that has chosen him can choose again, or

(b) if one party fails to choose an arbitrator, provided seven days' prior notice is served, the one appointed arbitrator can act as a sole arbitrator.

Section 16 deals with the situation where there are two arbitrators and makes provision for a secondary tribunal consisting of an umpire. This does not amount to a three-person tribunal or panel. Rather, a decision should be made by the two arbitrators, and if they are in disagreement, then by the umpire solely. Subsection (1) states that the arbitrators shall appoint an umpire immediately after they are appointed. Subsection (2) provides that if the arbitrators cannot agree, the umpire can act as sole arbitrator. Subsection (3) states that the High Court, upon application, can appoint an umpire to act as a sole arbitrator in lieu of the two arbitrators. Section 17(2) states that if there are three arbitrators, the decision of any two is binding.

The High Court, under section 18, can appoint an arbitrator or umpire where:

(a) the parties cannot agree on a sole arbitrator;
(b) the appointed arbitrator refused to act, is incapable of acting, or dies;
(c) the parties, or the arbitrators refuse to appoint an umpire or third arbitrator; or,
(d) the umpire or third arbitrator refuses to act, or is incapable of acting, or dies.

(ii) Removal or revocation of authority

The arbitrator(s) or umpire may be removed in numerous circumstances:

(a) by the agreement of the parties;[49]

(b) with the leave of the High Court;[50]

(c) the High Court can remove an arbitrator or umpire and he shall not be entitled to remuneration, if he has failed to use all "reasonable dispatch;"[51]

49 1954 Act, s.9.
50 *Ibid.*
51 1954 Act, s.24.

(d) the High Court can remove an arbitrator or umpire for misconduct (in such circumstances, the award can be set aside if improperly procured);[52] or
(e) the authority of the arbitrator can be revoked by the High Court where:

(i) the arbitrator is not or may not be impartial, or,
(ii) there are allegations of fraud.[53]

The question of what constitutes misconduct has come before the courts on numerous occasions. For example, in *State (Hegarty) v. Winter*,[54] the award was set aside on grounds of the arbitrator's misconduct because the arbitrator had visited the property, the subject of the reference, accompanied by an employee of one of the parties. In that case, the court put forward the test that there would be misconduct if the arbitrator acted in a way which would "reasonably give rise in the mind of an unprejudiced onlooker to the suspicion that justice was not being done."[55] In contrast, in *Childers Heights Housing Ltd v. Molderings*,[56] no misconduct was found where the arbitrator visited the site the subject of the reference on her own, without either party objecting. More recently, in *Tobin and Twomey Services Ltd v. Kerry Foods Ltd*,[57] the High Court confirmed that the court's discretion to remove an arbitrator is likely to be confined to cases where the arbitration cannot continue with the particular arbitrator in office either because he had shown actual or potential bias, or his conduct had given serious grounds for destroying the confidence of one or both of the parties in his ability to conduct the dispute judicially or competently.[58] Importantly, misconduct does not necessarily mean that the arbitrator has acted in any dishonest way.

(iii) Replacement

The replacement of an arbitrator or umpire may by made by:

(a) the parties expressly, or under section 15;[59] or
(b) the court under:

52 1954 Act, ss.37–38: see further 37.3.2.5(i).
53 1954 Act, s.39.
54 [1956] I.R. 320 (S.C.).
55 *Ibid*, at 336 per Maguire C.J.
56 [1987] I.L.R.M. 47.
57 [1999] 3 I.R. 483; see also *Bord na Móna v. John Sisk and Son Ltd* unreported, High Court, Blayney J., May 31, 1990.
58 See Mustill & Boyd, *The Law and Practice of Commercial Arbitration in England* (London, Butterworths, 2nd ed., 1989) p.530.
59 See 37.3.2.2(i).

(i) section 18;[60] or,
(ii) section 40, following the removal of an arbitrator or umpire by the court.

37.3.2.3 The procedure

If the parties have designed their own ad hoc arbitration or adopted an institutional arbitration, the relevant rules as to procedure will apply. There are no specific procedural rules prescribed in the general law, save the duty to observe the rules of natural justice. In particular, the legislation requires an arbitrator to act impartially.[61] For instance, in *Grangeford Structures Ltd (in liquidation) v. SH Ltd*,[62] it was held that an arbitrator is entitled to proceed with a hearing without one of the parties being in attendance if the arbitrator has given that party a reasonable opportunity to attend.

Procedures can vary from the very informal, at one extreme, to court-like proceedings at the other. The following provisions are implied into every written arbitration agreement unless a contrary intention is expressed.

Section 19 implies that the parties to the arbitration shall submit to examination by the arbitrator, on oath, and shall produce documents and do all other things required by the arbitrator. Accordingly, an arbitrator can order the discovery of documents and the administration of interrogatories;[63] and also order the inspection of property the subject of the dispute.[64] But, because dismissing a claim for want of prosecution does not facilitate the determination of the dispute, it would appear that this power is not implied by section 19(1).[65] It also seems that there is no implied power to consolidate proceedings.[66]

To support the arbitral proceedings, the High Court has power to make orders in respect of:

(a) security of costs;
(b) discovery and inspection of documents and interrogatories;
(c) the giving of evidence by affidavit;
(d) examination on oath and the issue of a request for the examination of a witness out of jurisdiction;

60 *Ibid.*
61 1954 Act, s.39.
62 [1990] I.L.R.M. 277.
63 *Kursell v. Timber Operators & Contractors Ltd* [1923] 2 K.B. 202.
64 *Vasso (Owners) v. Vasso (Owners of Cargo)* [1983] 1 W.L.R. 838.
65 *Bremer Vulkan Schiffbau und Mischinenfabrik v. South India Shipping Corp* [1982] A.C. 909.
66 *Oxford Shipping Ltd v. Nippon Yusen Kaisha* [1984] 3 All E.R. 835. *Cf.* Arbitration (International Commercial) Act 1998, s.9; see 37.3.3.1(ii).

(e) the preservation, interim custody or sale of any goods which are the subject matter of the reference;
(f) securing the amount in dispute in the reference;
(g) the detention, preservation or inspection of any property or thing subject to the reference, and authorising any person to enter upon or into any land or building, or authorising the taking of samples, or any observation to be made, or any experiment to be tried, which may be necessary or expedient for the purpose of obtaining full information or evidence; and,
(h) interim injunctions or the appointment of a receiver.[67]

37.3.2.4 The award

Section 23(1) states that the arbitrator has the power to make an award "at any time." This time can be expressly limited by agreement, of course. Under section 23(2), the High Court can extend this time. An arbitrator can only make one final award. Once the award is made, the arbitrator's jurisdiction in relation to the dispute terminates. Accordingly, section 25 provides that an arbitrator can make interim awards. This allows the arbitrator to identify preliminary matters to be dealt with, a decision on which may determine the outcome of the whole dispute without further issues being decided upon.

The award is usually retained by the arbitrator until payment of his fees: an arbitrator has a lien over the award.[68] Section 29 states that costs shall be at the arbitrator's or umpire's discretion, unless otherwise agreed. In arbitration, costs comprise:

(a) the costs of the reference, which are the costs and expenses incurred in bringing a case to arbitration; and
(b) the costs of the award, which are the arbitrator's own fees and expenses.

While an arbitrator has discretion as to who shall bear the costs of the reference and the award, and the manner in which those costs are to be paid, it has been held that this discretion should be exercised judicially.[69] In particular, an arbitrator should be slow to depart from the normal rules, such as "costs follow the event", that is, the successful party is awarded his costs. In *Vogelaar v. Callaghan*,[70] the Supreme Court had to deal with the issue of costs following long-running litigation arising from an arbitration. The arbitration arose from a dispute concerning a building contract.

67 1954 Act, s.22.
68 See further 1954 Act, s.33.
69 See, *e.g. Matheson & Co Ltd v. A Tabah & Sons* [1963] 2 Lloyd's Rep. 270 at 273.
70 Unreported, Supreme Court, July 13, 1998.

Following the arbitration, it was held that the defendant was owed £13,000 and the plaintiff was ordered to pay the defendant's costs. But, the plaintiff had offered £20,000 to settle the matter. Despite the fact that the award was less than the offer, the arbitrator still awarded the defendant his costs.[71] The plaintiff sought to have the award set aside, but the High Court remitted the matter back to the arbitrator on the basis that the arbitrator had failed to take the plaintiff's offer to settle into account and this lead to a "severe injustice."[72] The arbitrator then ordered that the defendant pay the plaintiff's cost for six of the 15 days of the arbitration. This left the plaintiff paying their own costs for nine days and the defendant's costs for the same nine days. Again, the plaintiff took proceedings before the High Court where it was held, following usual practice, that the plaintiff was not responsible for the defendant's costs because the original offer to settle of £20,000 had not been exceeded by the amount awarded. The defendant appealed unsuccessfully to the Supreme Court where it was held that the arbitrator had erred on the face of the award having regard to the express findings of the High Court.[73]

Any provision for a pre-dispute agreement as to costs is void.[74] To be enforceable, any agreement as to costs must be concluded after the dispute arises. If the award neglects to deal with costs, the parties may refer the matter to the arbitrator within 14 days to set the costs of the reference.[75] Section 34 provides, unless otherwise agreed, that an arbitrator or umpire can award simple or compound interest from the dates and at the rates and with the rests that he considers meets the justice of the case. In particular, this provision makes it clear that an arbitrator may award interest on any amount awarded by it in respect of any period up to the date of the award.[76]

The award need not be in writing, though it usually is, and it must comply with the arbitration agreement and any terms of reference. If it is signed, it should be signed by all the arbitrators. There is no general requirement that the award be reasoned.[77] Section 28 allows the amendment of the award to correct clerical errors.

Section 27 provides, unless otherwise agreed, that the award shall be final and binding. In many cases, the parties will carry out the award faithfully, but sometimes it is necessary to enlist the force of the law. There

---

71 On offers to settle see 37.4.1.1.

72 [1996] 1 I.R. 88, [1996] 2 I.L.R.M. 226.

73 Re error on the face of the award, see further 37.3.2.5(ii).

74 1954 Act, s.30.

75 1954 Act, s.31.

76 As substituted by s.17 of the Arbitration (International Commercial) Act 1998. See previously *McStay v. Asssicurzioni Generali Spa* [1991] I.L.R.M. 237.

77 See *Doyle v. County Council of Kildare* [1995] 2 I.R. 424, appealed to Supreme Court successfully on different grounds [1995] 2 I.R. 433; *Manning v. Shackleton* [1997] 2 I.L.R.M. 26 (S.C.).

is no direct, or automatic enforcement. There are two options which can be pursued to enforce domestic awards:[78]

(i) summary enforcement under section 41, by leave of the High Court, where the court enforces the award as if it was a court judgment or order, or
(ii) an action in contract on the award - this is based on the agreement to perform the award.

37.3.2.5 Court intervention

As noted above, arbitration, as an extra-judicial means of dispute resolution, is limited in the sense that recourse to judicial assistance may be needed. While it is essentially a private process between parties, the courts do intervene to enforce, support and supervise the arbitral process. We have already seen how the court gives effect to the arbitration agreement by staying litigation,[79] and by aiding in the constitution of the arbitral tribunal.[80] Furthermore, the court has complementary powers to assist the arbitration process,[81] and to enforce the award.[82]

In the early twentieth century, courts were suspicious and perhaps jealous of arbitration, and as a result tended to scrutinise, in depth, awards being challenged. More recently, however, in many jurisdictions, and in particular in relation to international commercial arbitration, there has been a move to limit the judicial review of arbitral proceedings and awards, in favour of arbitral autonomy. This move is evidenced, for example, in the Arbitration (International Commercial) Act 1998, which implements the UNCITRAL Model Law in Ireland.[83]

As early as 1930, Fitzgibbon J. noted that:

> "the trend of modern decisions has been in the direction of upholding, as far as may be reasonably possible, the awards of arbitrators and … a court should be astute, as was the case a century ago, to set aside awards upon small and technical objections …"[84]

78 Regarding enforcement of foreign awards, see 37.3.3.3.
79 See 37.3.2.1(iii).
80 See 37.3.2.2.
81 See 37.3.2.3.
82 See 37.3.2.4.
83 See Art. 34(2) of the Model Law: see further 37.3.3.1.
84 *Kingston v. Layden* [1930] I.R. 265 at 289.

While there have been no developments of a legislative nature[85] to limit the extent of judicial review regarding domestic arbitration in Ireland, courts today demonstrate a consistent reluctance to interfere in arbitral proceedings and awards.[86] McCarthy J., in the Supreme Court in *Keenan v. Shield Insurance Co.*,[87] stated:

> "It ill becomes the courts to show any readiness to interfere in such a process; if policy considerations are appropriate, as I believe they are, … then every such consideration points to the desirability of making an arbitration award final in every sense of the term."[88]

Bearing in mind this sentiment, there are four grounds under which a court has jurisdiction to intervene in the arbitral process.[89]

(i) Misconduct[90]

Where the arbitrator or umpire has misconducted himself or the proceedings, or where an arbitration or award has been improperly procured, the High Court can set aside the award under section 38. Where an award is set aside, the whole arbitration is rendered null and void. Examples of misconduct include: visiting the property the subject of the reference accompanied by an employee of one of the parties;[91] not hearing relevant evidence;[92] and not affording parties sufficient opportunity to make submissions on a relevant point.[93] But it is not misconduct to make an error of fact or of law;[94] nor to refuse to state a case to the High Court.[95]

---

85 *Cf.* the U.K. Arbitration Act 1979 (now repealed) which did away with the special case procedure and the jurisdiction to set aside an award for error of law on the face, and substituted a much more limited right of appeal on questions of law (s.1). It also allowed parties, in certain circumstances, to exclude judicial review (s.3). See now the Arbitration Act 1996, ss.1, 69, and 82.

86 There are of course modern day exceptions to this general approach. For example, in *Keenan v. Shield Insurance Co Ltd* [1988] I.R. 89, McCarthy J., at 96 stated: "*Church and General Insurance Co v. Connelly* (unreported, High Court, Costello J., May 7, 1981) … itself is an example of the type of fine tooth combing exercise which courts should not perform when it is sought to review an arbitration award."

87 [1988] I.R. 89 at 96.

88 See also Murphy J. in *Hogan v. St. Kevin's Co.* [1986] I.R. 80 at 88.

89 *Tersons Ltd v. Stevenage Development Corp.* [1965] 1 Q.B. 37 at 51.

90 See 37.3.2.2(ii).

91 *State (Hegarty) v. Winter* [1956] I.R. 320.

92 *O'Sullivan v. Joseph Woodword & Co* [1987] I.R. 255.

93 *Geraghty v. Rohan Industrial Estates Ltd* [1988] I.R. 419.

94 *Church & General Insurance Co. v. Connolly* unreported, High Court, Costello J., May 7, 1981.

95 *Stillorgan Orchard Ltd v. McLoughlin & Harvey* [1978] I.L.R.M. 128.

(ii) Error of law on the face

Where there is an error of law on the face of the award, the High Court may set aside the award, at common law,[96] or remit it, under the legislation.[97] The error must be "obvious" and "so fundamental that the courts cannot stand aside and allow it to remain unchallenged."[98] In *McStay v. Asssicurzioni Generali Spa*,[99] the Supreme Court distinguished between an "error on the face" where a general issue in dispute is submitted and an issue of law arises as a result; and an "error on the face" where a precise question of law has been submitted. In this case, the arbitration clause required, inter alia, a ruling on what interest, if any, was payable. This fell into the second class of error identified above, and the court held that because the parties had chosen arbitration to resolve this precise question of law, the decision could not be overturned, no matter how erroneous.

Pursuing a claim under this ground is dependent on the detail of the award and the documents which comprise the award: the error must be on the face of the award. Where, as is not unusual, there are no reasons given for an award, it is difficult, if not impossible, to detect an error of law on the face.[100]

(iii) Case stated[101]

Under section 35, an arbitrator or umpire may, or must if so directed by the High Court, state a question of law arising in the course of the reference, or his award, in the form of a "special case" or "case stated" for a decision by the High Court. This procedure allows the arbitrator to seek directions from the court on questions of law. Once an award has been published, it is too late to seek a case stated.[102] However, if a party has requested a case stated and the arbitrator has nevertheless proceeded to make an award without affording sufficient opportunity to apply to the court for directions, the arbitrator may have misconducted the proceedings and the award can be set aside.[103]

In *Halfdan Greig & Co. A/S v. Sterling Cable and Navigation Corp*,[104]

96 *Keenan v. Shield Insurance Co.*, [1988] I.R. 89.

97 1954 Act, s.36.

98 *Keenan v. Shield Insurance Co.*, [1988] I.R. 89 per McCarthy J. at 96.

99 [1991] I.L.R.M. 237; see also *Tobin and Twomey Services Ltd v. Kerry Foods Ltd and Kerry Group plc* [1996] 2 I.L.R.M. 1.

100 See, *e.g. Doyle v. County Council of Kildare* [1995] 2 I.R. 433 (S.C.).

101 See further Stewart, "The Special Case Stated in Arbitrations in Ireland" [1994] *Commercial Law Practitioner* 71.

102 *Hogan v. St. Kevin's Co.* [1986] I.R. 80; *cf. McStay v. Asssicurzioni Generali Spa* [1991] I.L.R.M. 237.

103 *Hogan v. St. Kevin's Co.* [1986] I.R. 80.

104 [1973] 1 Q.B. 843, (the *Lysland* case).

Lord Denning set out the factors relevant to deciding whether to state a case or not. Accordingly, where the issue is a matter of fact the arbitrator should refuse to state a case. Where the issue is a point of law, the arbitrator has a discretion in deciding whether to state a case or not. Lord Denning laid down three conditions for stating a case:

(a) the point of law should be real and substantial;
(b) the point of law should be clear-cut and capable of being accurately stated;
(c) the point of law should be of such importance that its resolution is necessary for the proper determination of the case.

It would appear that Irish courts are reluctant to interfere with the arbitral process on a point of law following the leading case of *Hogan v. St. Kevin's Co.*[105] The case involved a commercial lease under which the amount of service charge payable by the tenant was to be determined by the landlord's auditors, who were to issue certificates specifying the amount payable. The lease also provided that the certificates would be "final and binding". There was further provision in the lease for arbitration of any disputes between the parties. In 1982, a dispute arose concerning the amount of service charge payable under a number of certificates, and an accountant was appointed as arbitrator. Further, an independent solicitor was appointed to advise the arbitrator on all legal points arising in relation to the arbitration. The main issue was whether, and if so, in what circumstances was it open to the parties to go behind the certificates which were expressed in the lease to be "final and binding". The arbitrator found that the tenant could impugn the certificates, but only to a limited extent. Subsequently, the tenant sought to have this matter resolved by way of case stated. A direction to have the case stated was refused by the High Court. The High Court held that where parties had initially sought to have a matter of law resolved by arbitration, and notwithstanding the fact that the arbitrator himself has no legal qualifications, for the unsuccessful party to assert the right to substitute a decision of the High Court for that of the arbitrator, would be "unfair and unjust".[106] Accordingly, it was held that, in these special circumstances, it was inappropriate for the court to exercise its discretion to direct that a case be stated under section 35.

(iv) Power to remit

Rather than set aside the award, section 36 provides that the High Court may remit the matters referred, or any of them, to the reconsideration of the arbitrator or umpire. Where this occurs, the arbitrator or umpire has

105 [1986] I.R. 80.
106 *Ibid.* at 89.

three months from the date of order to make his award. This power can be exercised on four grounds:

(a) where there was misconduct by the arbitrator; or
(b) where there is an error on the face of the award; or
(c) where the arbitrator has made a mistake in drawing up the award and wants to have the matter remitted;[107] or
(d) where fresh evidence is discovered which probably would have had a substantial effect on the decision made.[108]

It has been held, in *King v. Thomas McKenna Ltd*[109] that the power to remit a case extends beyond the above four grounds:

> "to any case where, ..., due to mishap or misunderstanding some aspect of the dispute which has been the subject of the reference has not been considered and adjudicated upon as fully as or in the manner which the parties were entitled to expect and it would be inequitable to allow any award to take effect without some further consideration by the arbitrator."[110]

In *Portsmouth Arms Hotel v. Enniscorthy UDC*,[111] O'Hanlon J refused to remit a matter back to the arbitrator on the basis that the case did not fall within one of the four recognised categories. However, in *McCarrick v. The Gaiety (Sligo) Ltd*,[112] it was held that there was a "procedural mishap" of the type referred in *King v. Thomas McKenna Ltd* when the plaintiff failed to respond, within time, to requests from the arbitrator for written submissions, allowing the award to be remitted. The line of reasoning in *Portsmouth Arms Hotel v. Enniscorthy UDC* may be preferred because it is consistent with the court's more general non-interventionist approach to arbitral proceedings. In the meantime, a definitive ruling on the exact scope of section 36 is awaited.

(v) Excluding the court's jurisdiction

Traditionally, any agreement between the parties purporting to exclude or limit judicial review was held contrary to public policy and unenforceable.[113] Such exclusion is not sanctioned by the legislation, and in cases of serious misconduct or errors of law on the face of the award, for

107 Today, many such errors can be rectified under the "slip rule" in the 1954 Act, s.28 which allows for the correction of accidental clerical errors, but see *Mutual Shipping Corp v. Bayshore Shipping Co.*, [1985] 1 W.L.R. 625.
108 *Mennaghan v. Dublin CC* [1984] I.L.R.M. 616.
109 [1991] 2 Q.B. 480.
110 *Ibid.*, per Lord Donaldson M.R. at 491.
111 Unreported, High Court, O'Hanlon J., October 14, 1994.
112 [2001] 2 I.R. 266; [2002] 1 I.L.R.M. 55 (H.C.).
113 *Czarnikow v. Roth, Schmidt & Co* [1922] 2 K.B. 478.

example, we can expect courts to continue to intervene and exercise a supervisory jurisdiction. But otherwise, given the court's non-interventionist approach to arbitral proceedings, and similar trends in relation to international arbitration,[114] it is unclear whether an Irish court faced with an unambiguous exclusion clause would completely ignore the intentions of the parties.

37.3.3 International arbitration

There may be aspects of a national arbitration system which parties to a dispute consider undesirable – the possibilities of judicial review, extension of time limits or extensive discovery rules – and so they may turn to international arbitration to resolve their dispute.

Various bodies have devised procedures for international commercial arbitration: already mentioned are the London Court of International Arbitration (LCIA), the American Arbitration Association (AAA),[115] and the Court of Arbitration of the International Chamber of Commerce (ICC).[116] Where the parties adopt one of these systems, the arbitration is governed by the rules of that particular association or institute, and the mandatory rules of the forum where the actual arbitration takes place.[117]

Many trading centres have developed their own international arbitration facilities in an attempt to enlarge their slice of the dispute resolution cake, examples include Japan's Commercial Arbitration Association, the Hong Kong International Arbitration Centre, and the Netherland's Arbitration Institute. In 1998, the Dublin International Arbitration Centre was established. These facilities, in conjunction with the Arbitration (International Commercial) Act 1998, seeks to make Dublin an attractive venue for international commercial arbitration.[118]

37.3.3.1 Arbitration (International Commercial) Act 1998[119]

The Arbitration (International Commercial) Act 1998 incorporates the UNCITRAL Model Law on International Commercial Arbitration in Ireland,[120] and introduces some features additional to the Model Law.

UNCITRAL is the United Nations Commission on International Trade

114 See, *e.g. CBI NZ Ltd v. Badger Chiyoda* [1989] 2 N.Z.L.R. 669.
115 The A.A.A. opened its first European office in Dublin in 2001.
116 See 37.3.3.2.
117 The law which governs the substance of the dispute may, of course, be different from the law which governs the arbitration procedure.
118 481 Dáil Debates, Col. 1305-1306 (October 21, 1997); 155 Seanad Debates, Col. 770–771 (May 14, 1998).
119 The legislation came into force on May 20, 1998.
120 1998 Act, s.4. For text of Model Law see Schedule to 1998 Act. The 1998 Act also amends the 1954 and 1980 Arbitration Acts: see Part III of 1998 Act.

Law. Its functions are to prepare and promote conventions and model laws; to encourage wider acceptance of trade terms, customs and practices; disseminate information; and collaborate with other institutions responsible for the harmonisation of international trade law such as the ICC (International Chamber of Commerce), UNIDROIT (the International Institute for Unification of Private Law) and UNCTAD (the UN Commission for Trade and Development).[121] As part of this process, it has drafted a set of ad hoc arbitration rules[122] and a model arbitration law.

The Model Law was adopted by UNCITRAL in 1985. It is not an international convention, rather it is a text which countries can adopt completely, or with amendment, thus going some way to achieving uniformity of national arbitration law. To date, legislation based on the Model Law has been enacted in 40 countries, including Australia, Canada, New Zealand, and the United Kingdom.[123]

(i) Application of 1998 Act

The Arbitration (International Commercial) Act, 1998, applies to international commercial arbitration only.[124] The Arbitration Acts 1950 and 1980 do not apply to international commercial arbitration, as defined in the 1998 Act.[125]

The Model Law states that an arbitration is international if:

(a) the parties to an arbitration agreement have, at the time of the conclusion of that agreement, their places of business in different States; or
(b) one of the following places is situated outside the State in which the parties have their places of business:
  (i) the place of arbitration if determined in, or pursuant to the arbitration agreement;
  (ii) any place where a substantial part of the obligations of the commercial relationship is to be performed or the place with which the subject-matter of the dispute is most closely connected; or
(c) the parties have expressly agreed that the subject-matter of the arbitration agreement relates to more than one country.[126]

121 See 1.3.3.
122 *Supra*, note 11.
123 See, *e.g.* the U.K. Arbitration Act 1996.
124 Model Law, Art. 1(1).
125 1998, s.16.
126 Model Law, Art. 1(3).

While the UNCITRAL Model Law does not define the term "commercial", it does state in a footnote:

> "The term 'commercial' should be given a wide interpretation so as to cover matters arising from all relationships of a commercial nature, whether contractual or not. Relationships of a commercial nature include, but are not limited to, the following transactions: any trade transaction for the supply or exchange of goods or services; distribution agreement; commercial representation or agency; factoring; leasing; construction of works; consulting; engineering; licensing; investment; financing; banking; insurance; exploitation agreement or concession; joint venture or other form of industrial or business co-operation; carriage of goods or passengers by air, sea, rail or road."

(ii) Main features of arbitration under the 1998 Act

The Model Law is characterised by the principles of flexibility and arbitral freedom. The function of the court is to facilitate and support but not to interfere.[127] This contrasts sharply with the more constrained statutory regime of domestic arbitration.

The arbitration agreement must be in writing, though this is broadly defined.[128] In support of the arbitration agreement, a court must stay litigation before it unless the arbitration agreement is null, void, inoperative or incapable of being performed.[129]

Where the parties have chosen institutional arbitration, the issue of the composition of the arbitral tribunal, and the conduct of proceedings, will usually be dealt with by the institution's rules. However, in default of an agreement, under the Model Law there is a presumption of three arbitrators.[130] Where there is a failure to appoint an arbitrator, a party may apply to the court to do so.[131] An arbitrator must disclose "any circumstances likely to give rise to justifiable doubts as to his impartiality or independence." There is a procedure laid down to challenge an arbitrator for lack of impartiality or independence.[132] The Model law adopts the principle of "kompetenz-kompetenz", that is, the arbitral tribunal can rule on its own jurisdiction, including in respect of the existence and validity of the arbitration agreement.[133] Moreover, an arbitrator can decide

127 481 *Dáil Debates*, Col. 1307–1308 (October 21, 1997); 155 *Seanad Debates*, Col. 773 (May 14, 1998). Under the 1998 Act (ss.6–7) and the Model Law, the High Court can grant interim relief under Art. 9; assist in the taking of evidence under Art. 27; set aside and award under Art. 34; and recognise and enforce an award under Arts. 35 and 36.

128 Model Law, Art. 7(2).

129 Model Law, Art. 8.

130 Model Law, Art. 10.

131 Model Law, Art. 11.

132 Model Law, Arts. 12 and 13.

133 Model Law, Art. 16.

the case *ex aequo et bono* or as *amiable compositeur* if expressly authorised by the parties.[134]

The award must be in writing, signed, and, unless otherwise agreed, state reasons.[135] Judicial review of an award may be made, within three months of receiving the award, only by an application for setting aside, and, based on limited grounds including that:

(a) a party supplies evidence that a party to the agreement was incapacitated, or the agreement was not valid under the governing law;
(b) the court finds that the subject-matter of the dispute is not capable of settlement by arbitration under the applicable law;
(c) the court finds that the award is in conflict with public policy.

In addition, the 1998 Act includes a number of provisions which further enhance Ireland as a venue for international commercial arbitration. Section 8 empowers a tribunal to direct witnesses to be examined on oath or affirmation and to administer such oaths and affirmations, unless otherwise agreed by the parties. Section 9 of the 1998 Act provides that the parties to an arbitral agreement can agree to consolidate proceedings with other arbitral proceedings, or that concurrent proceedings can be held. The arbitral tribunal does not have this power, unless conferred by the parties. This provision allows related claims to be heard together, saving time and costs. For example, disputes under a main contract and sub-contracts occur frequently in the construction industry. Under section 10 of the 1998 Act, the parties to an arbitration agreement may agree on the arbitral tribunal's powers to award interest. In default of agreement, the tribunal is given wide powers to award simple or compound interest, from the dates, at the rates, and with the rests that it considers meets the justice of the case. In particular, this provision makes it clear that a tribunal may award interest on any amount awarded by it in respect of any period up to the date of the award.[136] Section 11 provides that the parties to an arbitration agreement are free to agree on how the costs of the arbitration (including the arbitrators' fees and expenses) are to be allocated and on the costs that are to be recoverable. Where there is no agreement, the tribunal can determine the costs on such basis as it thinks fit. Section 12 provides for the immunity of arbitrators, except where there is bad faith. This immunity is extended to an employee, agent or advisor of an arbitrator, to expert witnesses, and

134 Model Law, Art. 28(3).

135 Model Law, Art. 31.

136 See *McStay v. Assicurazioni Generali Spa* [1991] I.L.R.M. 237; see now 1954 Act, s.34, as substituted by s.17 of the Arbitration (International Commercial) Act 1998.

to others. Such immunity seeks to ensure the finality of arbitration awards.[137]

37.3.3.2 Court of Arbitration of the International Chamber of Commerce[138]

The ICC Court of Arbitration has been described as "the most truly international of all arbitral systems."[139] In its Rules of Arbitration, Article 1.1 states that the function of the Court of Arbitration is to provide for the settlement by arbitration of "business disputes of an international character" in accordance with these Rules.[140]

The Court of Arbitration does not itself settle disputes, but if the parties have not agreed on the arbitrator(s), the court will choose a National Committee of the ICC who, from a list of competent and suitable persons, proposes the arbitrators. The arbitration is initiated by a request for arbitration to the Secretariat of the Court. The arbitration is then conducted under the ICC Rules which:

> "provide a code that is intended to be self-sufficient in the sense that it is capable of covering all aspects of arbitrations conducted under the rules, without the need for any recourse to any municipal system of law or any application to the courts of the forum."[141]

The Arbitration Rules recommend a standard arbitration clause, in seven languages. The English version states:

> "All disputes arising out of or in connection with the present contract shall be finally settled under the Rules of Arbitration of the International Chamber of Commerce by one or more arbitrators appointed in accordance with the said Rules."[142]

Article 6.4 of the Rules empowers the arbitrator to determine questions as to his own jurisdiction, and he has jurisdiction even if the contract containing the arbitration clause is "non-existent, or null and void". There are three further distinctive characteristics of ICC arbitration:

---

137 See generally, *W v. Ireland* [1997] 2 I.R. 141.

138 See www.iccwbo.org.

139 *Bank Mallet v. GAA Development and Construction Co.* [1988] 2 Lloyd's Rep. 44 at 48 *per* Steyn J.

140 The I.C.C. administers over 500 requests for arbitration each year. In 1996, eight claimants and two respondents were Irish: see Murphy, "International Commercial Arbitration and the International Arbitration Bill, 1997" [1997] *The Bar Review* 92.

141 Per Kerr L.J. in *Bank Mallet v. Helliniki Techniki S.A.* [1984] Q.B. 291 at 304.

142 ICC Rules in force as from January 1, 1998. Parties are further recommended to stipulate in the arbitration clause itself the law governing the contract, the number of arbitrators and the place and language of the arbitration.

(i) Article 18 provides that the arbitrator is required to draw up terms of reference before proceeding with the case, in order to clarify the issues subject to the arbitration.

(ii) Before the arbitrator signs the award, under Article 27 it must be submitted in draft form to the Court of Arbitration for scrutiny, as a means of ensuring enforcement in the relevant jurisdiction: the Court may lay down modification to the award.

(iii) Under Article 30, the costs of the arbitration are covered by a deposit which the parties usually pay in equal shares to the court in advance.

An award is deemed to be made at the place of the arbitration proceedings and at the date when it is signed by the arbitrator.[143] Article 24 states that the award shall be final.

37.3.3.3 Enforcement of foreign awards – The New York Convention

The main vehicle for enforcement of foreign awards is the New York Convention on the Recognition and Enforcement of Foreign Arbitral Awards (1958), adopted in Ireland in the Arbitration Act 1980.[144] The New York Convention is designed to provide a simple and effective system for the recognition and enforcement of foreign awards and it supersedes the Geneva Protocol and Convention adopted under Part V of the 1954 Arbitration Act.[145] The New York Convention has been ratified by over 90 states.

The Convention applies to foreign awards, that is, awards made in the territory of a state other than the state where the recognition and enforcement of the award is sought.[146] In *Hiscox v. Outhwaite*,[147] where an arbitration was held in England but the award was signed in Paris, the House of Lords held, for the purposes of the New York Convention, that the award was made in Paris. This has the costly disadvantage of requiring the arbitrators to travel to the place of arbitration in order to sign the award. The 1998 Act and the UNCITRAL Model Law avoid this problem by deeming the award to be made at the place of arbitration.[148]

Article III states that each contracting State shall enforce arbitral awards in accordance with the rules set out in the Convention, thereby creating a general presumption for eligibility for enforcement.[149]

143 ICC Rules, Art. 22.
144 The Convention is re-produced in the First Schedule to the 1980 Act.
145 1980 Act, s.10; Convention, Art. VII.
146 Convention, Art. 1.1; see further 1980 Act, s.6.
147 [1991] 3 All E.R. 641.
148 Model Law, Art. 31.3.
149 1980 Act, s.9(1).

To obtain enforcement, the party must supply a duly authenticated original award or duly certified copy thereof, and the original agreement or duly certified copy thereof.[150] Enforcement can only be refused at the request of the party against whom enforcement is sought, if that person can prove, for instance, that:

(a) a party to the arbitration agreement is under some incapacity;
(b) the arbitration agreement is not valid under the law to which the parties subjected it;
(c) a party was not given proper notice of the proceedings;
(d) the award deals with matters not within the arbitration agreement;
(e) the arbitral tribunal was improperly constituted; or,
(f) the award is not yet binding on the parties or has been set aside by a competent authority.[151]

Enforcement can also be refused if the competent authority where enforcement is being sought finds that the subject-matter is not capable of settlement by arbitration or contrary to public policy under the law of that country.[152]

37.4 Litigation[153]

The disadvantages of litigation are many: it can be time-consuming (especially where an appeal is heard); it can be costly; and it lacks privacy. However, litigation does offer a final solution to a dispute, supported by the force of law, and, it may be the most appropriate means to resolve particular disputes.

When commencing litigation, a plaintiff needs to consider a number of questions.

(1) Can the plaintiff afford the litigation in terms of money and time? Despite the fact that the successful party is usually awarded costs – the losing party pays the successful party's legal costs, as well

150 Convention, Art. IV; 1980 Act, s.8.
151 Convention, Art. V; 1980 Act, s.9(2).
152 Convention Art. V(2); 1980 Act, s.9(3).
153 In 2002, a Working Group on the Jurisdiction of the Courts was established by the Courts Service. The group is to examine any necessary changes to allow for the fair, expeditious and economic administration of justice. There are three modules to the work of the Group: criminal law, civil law, and general changes in structure following modules one and two. See generally www.courts.ie.

as their own costs[154] – there is always a risk of losing. Moreover, litigation can be protracted and resource consuming.

(2) Will the litigation damage the goodwill and trading interests of the business?

(3) Is there sufficient evidence to substantiate the claim?

(4) Even if successful, will the defendant be able to meet the judgment against him?

37.4.1 The High Court

There is no specialised commercial court in Ireland, as there are in many civil law jurisdictions,[155] nor is there a separate division of the High Court which specialises in commercial disputes, as in London.[156] However, in 2002, the Committee on Court Practice and Procedure, in its 27th Interim Report,[157] recommended the establishment of a Commercial Court, and this received a broad welcome from the President of the High Court, the Courts Service and the Government.[158] Rather than establishing a "stand-alone" court, the recommendation involves creating a division of the High Court into a *de facto* Commercial Court. This Commercial Court would be staffed by judges with a particular expertise in commercial matters, who would hear cases drawn from a dedicated "commercial list". The Report envisages the establishment of a pilot Commercial Court, supported by a new Commercial Court Office, which would enable cases to proceed with speed in accordance with any new directions, rules, or electronic practices and procedures. It is suggested that the "commercial list" be restricted, at first, for example, to intellectual property and/or applications under the Arbitration (International Commercial) Act 1998, and that the type of case heard would be expanded subsequently. While such a development is to be

154 This is referred to as the rule that "costs follow the event". In general, the court order for costs covers the successful party's "party and party" costs, that is, the fees and other costs incurred by the successful party in relation to the litigation (and not, for example, general advice to the successful party, which would be a matter for the solicitor/client bill): on costs generally, see O'Callaghan, *The Law on Solicitors in Ireland* (Dublin, Butterworths, 2000) Chapter 8.

155 *E.g.* in France, there is the *tribunal commercial*: see further West et al., *The French Legal System*, (London, Butterworths, 1998) pp.76-95.

156 The Commercial Court: see Civil Procedure Rules 1998 (S.I. No. 3132 of 1998, as amended) Part 58, and Commercial Court Guide (2002) available at www.courtservice.gov.uk.

157 See the 27th Interim Report of the Committee on Court Practice and Procedure, *The Courts of e-Government – Meeting the e-Commerce Challenge: A Commercial Court in Ireland, Establishing Connections to Domestic and International Arbitration Centres,* available at www.courts.ie. See previously *First Report of the Working Group on a Courts Commission: Management and Financing of the Courts,* which suggested the establishment of a Commercial Court in the High Court (Pn 2690, 1996) p.34.

158 In an associated development, the Company Law Review Group established under the Company Law Enforcement Act 2001, in its First Report presented to the Minister for Enterprise, Trade and Employment, also recommended the establishment of a Commercial Division within the High Court.

welcomed, at the time of writing, it remains to be seen how these recommendations will be implemented.

The majority of commercial litigation is brought before the High Court. Although with the extension of the jurisdiction of the Circuit Court from IR£30,000 to €100,000 under the Courts and Court Officers Act 2002,[159] more commercial cases can be expected to come before the Circuit Court. In certain areas such as bankruptcy,[160] company law,[161] and arbitration,[162] the High Court is designated as the appropriate forum.

Procedures before the High Court are set out in the Rules of the Superior Courts (R.S.C.).[163] The R.S.C. deal with matters such as commencement of proceedings; service of summons; appearance; pleadings; payment into court; security for costs; interrogatories, discovery and inspection; trial; evidence; motion for judgment and entry of judgment; and execution.

In the remainder of this chapter, we look briefly at some procedural devices which have been developed to aid commercial litigation, before finally mentioning a further alternative to litigation: ADR.[164]

37.4.1.1 Pre-trial devices for resolving disputes

Only a small percentage of commercial cases commenced come to full trial. The majority are settled by mutual agreement or come to an end as a result of a procedural step taken by one party. There are a number of procedural devices which can be utilised to force an early conclusion.

In a claim to recover a debt or a liquidated sum, such as the price of goods delivered, the summary summons procedure may be used.[165] This procedure can be used where the matter is suitable for summary disposition without pleadings,[166] and on affidavit without the need for oral evidence.[167]

---

159 2002 Act, s.13: at the time of writing, this aspect of the legislation had not been commenced by Ministerial Order under s.1(2) of the 2002 Act. In fact, it is not clear when, if at all, this aspect of the 2002 Act will be commenced.

160 R.S.C., Ord. 76.

161 R.S.C., Ords. 74 and 75.

162 R.S.C., Ord. 56.

163 S.I. No. 15 of 1986, as amended. See Delany & McGrath, *Civil Procedures in the Superior Courts* (Dublin, Round Hall Sweet & Maxwell, 2001); Barron, *Practice and Procedure in the Master's Court* (Dublin, Round Hall Sweet & Maxwell, 2nd ed., 2001); Ó Floinn & Gannon, *Practice and Procedures in the Superior Courts* (Dublin, Butterworths, 1996).

164 Conflict of laws issues such as the jurisdiction of an Irish court over international litigation, and, the recognition and enforcement of judgments abroad, are outside the scope of this book: see Binchy, *Irish Conflict of Laws* (Dublin, Butterworths, 1988); see also Dicey and Morris, *Conflict of Laws* (London, Sweet & Maxwell, 13th ed., 2000).

165 R.S.C., Ords. 13 and 37.

166 R.S.C., Ord. 20, r.1.

167 R.S.C., Ord. 1, r.3.

It allows a plaintiff to obtain judgment against a defendant quickly in circumstances where the claim is easily quantifiable and there is no issue to be tried or the issues involved are simple and capable of being easily determined.[168]

A plaintiff may also be able to obtain judgment in default because the defendant fails to enter an appearance[169] or deliver a defence.[170] Generally, all that is required is the completion and filing of the appropriate forms: there is no hearing.

A defendant may put pressure on a plaintiff to settle by making a payment into court. The payment may be accepted in satisfaction of the claim and the proceedings ended, or if the payment is not accepted, the case will proceed to trial, where the judge will not be told of the payment until after judgment. If the amount paid into court exceeds the amount awarded to the plaintiff, the excess amount is usually paid to the defendant and the plaintiff is usually required to pay the defendant's costs from the time the payment was made.[171] Because costs escalate significantly as litigation progresses, and particularly from the time of preparation for and during the trial, a plaintiff who refuses a payment into court runs a considerable risk. The use of without prejudice offers, whereby an offer to settle is made without a payment into court, can also encourage settlement.

37.4.1.2 Mareva *injunctions*[172]

A *Mareva* injunction is a relatively new form of injunctive relief which takes its name from the case *Mareva Compania Naviera S.A. v. International Bulkcarriers S.A.*[173] At its simplest, the *Mareva* injunction is a court order freezing some or all of the respondent's assets, or ordering him not to deal with, dispose of or remove them from the court's jurisdiction. Its purpose is to prevent injustice to the applicant by ensuring that the respondent cannot remove or dissipate his assets and so frustrate any judgment made against him. It does not give the applicant any security rights over the assets, though,[174] and preferential and secured creditors maintain their position of priority in the case of insolvency, for example.

168 See further *Aer Rianta CPT v. Ryanair Ltd* [2002] 1 I.L.R.M. 381 (S.C.).

169 R.S.C., Ord. 13.

170 R.S.C., Ord. 27.

171 R.S.C., Ord. 22.

172 See Courtney, *Mareva Injunctions and Related Interlocutory Orders* (Dublin, Butterworths, 1998); Gee, *Mareva Injunctions and Anton Piller Relief* (London, Sweet & Maxwell, 4th ed., 1998); Delany, *Equity and the Law of Trusts in Ireland* (Dublin, Round Hall Sweet & Maxwell, 2nd ed., 1999) pp.505–519; Keane, *Equity and the Law of Trusts in the Republic of Ireland* (Dublin, Butterworths, 1988) pp.234–241.

173 [1975] 2 Lloyd's Rep. 509, though the first case in which such an injunction was given was *Nippon Yusen Naviera v. Karageorgis* [1975] 2 Lloyd's Rep. 509.

174 See *Capital Cameras Ltd v. Harold Line Ltd* [1991] 3 All E.R. 389.

The jurisdiction to grant a *Mareva* injunction is based on the court's general jurisdiction to make interlocutory injunctions,[175] though certain statutory jurisdictions now also exist.[176]

Before granting the injunction, usually the court will require to be satisfied that:

(i) the applicant has a substantive cause of action against the respondent;[177]
(ii) the applicant has a good arguable case or there is a substantial question to be tried;[178]
(iii) there is a risk that the respondent will try to dissipate the assets or remove the assets out of the court's jurisdiction with the intention of defeating his obligations to the applicant and frustrating the anticipated court order.[179]

Like all injunctions, the *Mareva* injunction is a discretionary order granted on the balance of convenience.[180] So as not to give the respondent advance warning, the injunction is usually granted *ex parte*. In such circumstances, the applicant is required to make a full and fair disclosure of all relevant facts.

Mareva injunctions have proved very effective and the jurisdiction to grant them has gradually extended. The injunction may be granted at any stage: before, during or after an action. A *Mareva* injunction can also be granted supporting proceedings pending, contemplated or concluded in a court of a member state of the EC.[181] Assets which can be frozen include personal property, bank accounts and land, and are not limited to assets

175 Supreme Court of Judicature (Ireland) Act 1877, s.28(8) and R.S.C., Ord. 50, r.6(1); see further *CAB v. Sweeney* [2001] 2 I.L.R.M. 81.

176 See, *e.g.* Criminal Justice Act 1994, s.24, which empowers the High Court to freeze the assets of certain defendants in criminal proceedings.

177 *Caulron v. Air Zaire* [1986] I.L.R.M. 10; *The Siskina* [1979] A.C. 210.

178 *Countyglen plc v. Carway* [1995] 1 I.R. 208 (H.C.); *O'Mahony v. Horgan* [1995] 2 I.R. 411; [1996] 1 I.L.R.M. 161 (S.C.).

179 *O'Mahony v. Horgan* [1995] 2 I.R. 411, [1996] 1 I.L.R.M. 161 (S.C.).

180 *Campus Oil Ltd v. Minister for Industry & Commerce* [1983] I.R. 88; *American Cyanamid Co v. Ethicon Ltd* [1975] 1 All E.R. 504.

181 See Council Regulation EC/44/2001 on Jurisdiction and the Recognition and Enforcement of Judgments in Civil and Commercial Matters, Art. 31, and the EC (Civil and Commercial Judgments) Regulations 2002, S.I. No. 52 of 2002. As from March 1, 2002, the above Regulation (the Brussels I Regulation) supersedes the Brussels Convention (1968) in member states of the EC other than Denmark. The Jurisdiction of Courts and Enforcement of Judgments Act 1998, shall, except as provided in Art. 68 cease to apply between member states. On granting Mareva injunctions, see 1998 Act, s.13.

within this jurisdiction.[182] The order, though directed at the respondent, also binds third parties with knowledge of it. A third party who assists in dealing with the frozen assets is in contempt of court.

A *Mareva* injunction has a profound restrictive effect on a respondent's business, and so is not usually granted against a bank.[183] To protect the respondent, the applicant will usually have to give undertakings, including an undertaking that if unsuccessful at full hearing, the applicant will pay damages to the respondent for any loss suffered as a result of the granting of the injunction; an undertaking to notify the respondent and others of the order; and an undertaking to pay third party costs in complying with the order.

The order should only cover the amount needed to satisfy the applicant's claim: a maximum amount to be frozen is set in most orders. Provision for the respondent's living expenses, legitimate trading expenses and the right to deal with any remaining assets is usually made. The order may be granted "until trial or further order", or it may be granted for a limited period of time in which case the applicant will have to apply *inter partes* for its continuance. Supporting orders include disclosure orders against the respondent or third parties to disclose information of the whereabouts of the respondent's assets, and orders which require the respondent to surrender his passport and not to leave the jurisdiction.[184]

37.4.1.3 Anton Piller *Orders*[185]

The *Anton Piller* order is an injunction that has been developed to respond to the ever-increasing problem of piracy in the sound, video and computer software industry.[186] Typically, the *Anton Piller* order is utilised where a manufacturer claims that a business rival is infringing his intellectual property rights. This injunction authorises the applicant to enter the respondent's premises, and to inspect and remove documents or assets. Its purpose is to preserve evidence which could otherwise be removed or destroyed.[187]

---

182 For examples of *Mareva* injunctions which froze assets worldwide, see *Bennett Enterprises Ltd v. Lipton* [1999] 1 I.L.R.M. 81; *Deutsche Bank Aktiengesellschaft v. Murtagh & Murtagh* [1995] 2 I.R. 122; and *Babanaft International Co. Ltd. v. Bassatne* [1990] Ch. 13, [1989] 2 W.L.R. 232. See further Courtney, "The continuing development of the Mareva Injunction in Ireland" [1999] *Commercial Law Practitioner* 39.

183 *Polly Peck International plc v. Nadir* (*No. 2*) [1992] 4 All E.R. 769.

184 Known as "*Bayer* injunctions": see *Bayer AG v. Winter* [1986] 1 All E.R. 732. See, *e.g. JN & C Ltd v. TK & JS* unreported, High Court, Kearns J., February 19, 2002.

185 Delany, *Equity and the Law of Trusts in Ireland* (Dublin, Round Hall Sweet & Maxwell, 2nd ed., 1999) p.519–527; Keane, *Equity and the Law of Trusts in the Republic of Ireland* (Dublin, Butterworths, 1988) pp.241–242.

186 See *Anton Piller K.G. v. Manufacturing Processes Ltd* [1976] Ch. 55; and *Microsoft Corp & Symantec Corp v. Brightpoint Ireland Ltd* [2001] 1 I.L.R.M. 540 (H.C.).

187 R.S.C., Ord. 50, rr.4 and 7.

The element of surprise is vital to this procedure so application is made *ex parte* on affidavit to the High Court.[188] Again, the applicant is required to make a full and fair disclosure of all relevant facts.[189] Before granting the order, the court must be satisfied that:

(i) there is a strong prima facie case on the merits;
(ii) the respondent's activities pose serious potential or actual harm to the applicant's interests; and
(iii) there must be clear evidence that the respondent possesses the items and that there is a real danger that they will be removed or destroyed before an *inter partes* application can be made.[190]

The relief is discretionary and cannot be obtained as of right. To protect the respondent from abuse of the process, the applicant is usually required to give various undertakings, which are usually incorporated in the order, including an undertaking as to damages; an undertaking to cause a writ to be issued; and an undertaking to serve the order and the writ. Furthermore, the applicant's solicitor will usually undertake:

(i) to explain the order to the respondent in everyday language;
(ii) to inform the respondent of his right to seek legal advice before allowing the execution of the order;
(iii) to make a list of all items removed and provide a copy to the respondent;[191]
(iv) not to use the items seized for any purpose other than the action without leave of the court;
(v) and, after copying documents, to return such items to the respondent's solicitor.

The order is not a court order permitting the applicant to enter premises, like a civil search warrant, rather, it is an order to the respondent "to permit" the applicant to enter the premises for the purpose of inspecting and removing documents or items. There are usually restrictions on the number of persons that can enter and at what time of the day.[192]

It has been stated that, due to its draconian nature, the order should only be used where it is essential.[193] It has been recognised that the order may be oppressive.[194] In the *Chappell Case*,[195] the European Court of Human

188 *Microsoft Corp & Symantec Corp v. Brightpoint Ireland Ltd* [2001] 1 I.L.R.M. 540 (H.C.).
189 *Ibid.*
190 *Anton Piller K.G. v. Manufacturing Processes Ltd* [1976] Ch. 55 per Ormond L.J. at 62.
191 *Microsoft Corp & Symantec Corp v. Brightpoint Ireland Ltd* [2001] 1 I.L.R.M. 540 (H.C.).
192 See *Universal Thermosensors Ltd v. Hibbon* [1992] 3 All E.R. 257.
193 Per Donaldson L.J. in *Yousif v. Salamon* [1980] 1 W.L.R. 1540 at 1544.
194 *Ibid.*
195 [1989] Eur Court H.R. Series A No.132-A, [1989] F.S.R. 617.

Rights upheld the use of *Anton Piller* orders provided they were accompanied by adequate and effective safeguards against abuse, such as requiring the applicant's solicitor or an officer of the court to execute the order, and allowing the respondent time to contact his solicitor and take the appropriate steps to challenge the execution of the order.

37.5 ADR[196]

Alternative dispute resolution includes conciliation, mediation and the use of mini-trials. Conciliation and mediation aim to achieve an amicable settlement of the dispute through the use of an independent and impartial third party. Today, the terms conciliation and mediation are used interchangeably, though a distinction can be drawn. A conciliator may seek to find common ground between the parties and encourage them to find a settlement, whereas a mediator may play a more active role in trying to bring the parties together. These methods are best suited to parties that have a close and friendly trading relationship. The advantages of such processes are that of privacy and speed. UNCITRAL and the ICC each promote their own set of Conciliation Rules, which can be adopted by parties seeking to utilise this method of dispute resolution.

A mini-trial, as the name suggests, is a form of small scale, in-house litigation. It usually involves a presentation of the issues in dispute by each party's in-house lawyers before a panel of senior executives, one from each side, who are unconnected with the dispute. Often there is a neutral chairman, such as a retired judge. Following the presentations, which are time-limited, the panel retires to negotiate a settlement. The success of this alternative to actual litigation is dependent on a willingness to settle and a realisation that either side may win. Where the parties reach a settlement, it is advisable that this settlement be incorporated in a written agreement so it can be enforced as a contract if necessary. This procedure has been successfully used in the U.S.A. to resolve some major commercial disputes.

ADR is now part of the new Civil Procedure Rules (C.P.R.) introduced in the United Kingdom in 1999.[197] For example, courts are placed under an express duty to manage cases. This includes encouraging the parties to use ADR if the courts consider it appropriate, and facilitating the use of such procedures.[198] Under the court's general power of case management, a court may take any other steps or make any order for the purpose of

196 See generally, Brown & Marriott, *ADR Principles and Practice* (London, Sweet & Maxwell, 2nd ed., 1999); York, *Practical ADR Handbook* (London, Sweet & Maxwell, 2nd ed., 1999).

197 See www.lcd.gov.uk for latest version of the Civil Procedure Rules and Practice Directions.

198 C.P.R., rule 1.4(2)(e).

managing the case;[199] this could include ordering the parties to use ADR. A party may make a written request for proceedings to be stayed while the parties try to settle the case by ADR.[200] In deciding the amount of costs to award, the court must have regard to the conduct of the parties, including in particular the effort made, if any, before and during the proceedings to try to resolve the dispute.[201] In particular, in the Commercial Court, a judge may invite parties to use ADR; parties can apply for directions as to the use of ADR; a judge may adjourn the case to enable ADR; and a judge may make an ADR Order, requiring the parties to undertake ADR.[202] To date, there has been no similar development in Ireland regarding the Rules of the Superior Court, and despite the establishment of the Centre for Dispute Resolution in 1996 in Dublin,[203] ADR has made little impact in the commercial sector. However, with the recommendation of the Committee on Court Practice and Procedure to establish a Commercial Division of the High Court,[204] it is hoped that issues such as more active case management and the combined use of ADR will be addressed in the implementation of this recommendation.

199 C.P.R., rule 3.1(2)(m).

200 C.P.R., rule 26.4(1).

201 C.P.R., rule 44.5(3)(a).

202 See Commercial Court Guide (2002) Section G on A.D.R.: available at www.courtservice.gov.uk.

203 This is a sister organisation of the Centre for Effective Dispute Resolution in London (CEDR): see www.cedr.co.uk.

204 See the 27th Interim Report of the Committee on Court Practice and Procedure, The Courts of e-Government - Meeting the e-Commerce Challenge: A Commercial Court in Ireland, Establishing Connections to Domestic and International Arbitration Centres available.

Appendix A

Terms and Conditions of Sale

CONDITIONS OF SUPPLY OF GOODS AND SERVICES DEFINITIONS

In these Conditions Customer means any person, firm, company or unincorporated association which orders, buys or licences goods or services from ABC Ltd; Goods means the goods or, where the context so admits, services which are the subject of the Order and, where the context so admits, any instalment thereof; Invoice means the invoice given or despatched to the Customer detailing the Goods and the Price; Order means the contract between ABC Ltd and the Customer (of which these Conditions form part) for the supply of goods or services by ABC Ltd to the Customer.

Price means the total price to be paid by the Customer to ABC Ltd for the supply of the Goods in accordance with these Conditions; ABC Ltd means ABC Ltd, 1 XYZ St, Dublin, Ireland.

1. Acceptance of Orders

1.1 Any quotation relating to goods or services supplied by ABC Ltd and any catalogue, mailshot or other advertisement of such goods or services shall constitute an invitation to treat only and not an offer to contract.Any order placed by a Customer with ABC Ltd for goods or services (including orders for goods On Approval) shall be accepted entirely at the discretion of ABC Ltd and, if so accepted, will only be accepted upon these Conditions.

1.2 These Conditions shall override any contrary, different or additional terms or conditions contained or referred to in a Customers order or in any other correspondence or documents from that Customer and (subject to Clause 1.5) no addition, alteration or substitution of these Conditions will bind ABC Ltd or form part of any Order unless expressly accepted in writing by a person authorised to sign on ABC Ltd's behalf.

1.3 A Customers order shall be deemed to have been accepted by ABC Ltd upon:

1.3.1 the acceptance by ABC Ltd of payment in cleared funds for the Goods;

1.3.2 despatch to the Customer of a note advising that the Customers order has been recorded and will be fulfilled once the Goods to which the advice note relates are available;

1.3.3 delivery of the Goods to the Customer or to some person authorised to collect the Goods on the Customers behalf;

1.3.4 in the case of an order for a periodical, on delivery of the first issue of the periodical to the Customer (or some person authorised to collect the same on the Customers behalf);

1.3.5 commencement by ABC Ltd of performance of the services whichever is the earliest.

1.4 Each Order which is so accepted shall constitute an individual legally binding contract between ABC Ltd and the Customer.

1.5 Where Goods include any item of software, these Conditions shall apply as varied and augmented by the appropriate ABC Ltd Software License (copies available on request) and where Goods are supplied to booksellers to whom in terms of Clause 4.2 ABC Ltd has granted trade terms, these Conditions shall apply as varied and augmented by ABC Ltd's published conditions for Trade Customers (copies available on request).

2. Delivery of Goods

2.1 Unless otherwise agreed with the Customer, ABC Ltd shall effect delivery of Goods through its distributor at the Customer's expense.

2.2 Delivery to the Customer shall be deemed to have taken place when the Goods are placed with the Customer's representative or at the address specified by the Customer.

2.3 Risk in the Goods shall pass to the Customer upon delivery to it.

2.4 ABC Ltd reserve the right to make deliveries by instalments in all cases. Where Goods are delivered by instalment, the Customer shall not be entitled to treat defective delivery in respect of one or more instalments as a repudiation of the whole of the Order nor to defer payment for any previous instalment.

2.5 Any time or date for delivery given by ABC Ltd is given in good faith but is an estimate only.

2.6 Where any periodical or looseleaf release supplied to a Customer on subscription is not received by that customer on the due date for delivery, the Customer shall not later than 14 days after receiving the next issue of that periodical or looseleaf release (time being of the essence) give notice in writing to ABC Ltd of the non-delivery of the previous issue. Failure to provide such notice within the said period shall be deemed conclusive evidence of the Customer having received and accepted the previous issue of the said periodical or looseleaf release.

3.Inspection and Acceptance of Goods

3.1 The Customer shall inspect Goods immediately upon delivery and (subject to Clause 3.2) shall within 14 days of such delivery (time being of the essence) give notice in writing to ABC Ltd of any alleged shortages in the Goods or of any damage to the Goods incurred during transit or of any other matter or thing by reason whereof the Customer alleges that the Goods are not in accordance with the Order. If the Customer shall fail to give such notice timeously, then the Goods shall be conclusively presumed to be in accordance with the Order in all respects and the Customer shall not (subject to Clause 4.1) thereafter be entitled to reject the Goods or to claim from ABC Ltd in respect of any shortage, damage or other defect in the Goods.

3.2 In the case of damage or other defect in the Goods which was not apparent on reasonable inspection, notice shall be given to ABC Ltd within 14 days after discovery of the damage or other defect and, subject to this relaxation, Clause 3.1 shall apply.

4. Goods supplied on Approval and Trade Customers

4.1 You can use the titles of your choice for up to 30 days without commitment. If for any reason you do not wish to keep a title, please return it by the date specified on the invoice in good condition and owe nothing.Please remember to pre-pack the invoice with the returned title.Otherwise please pay against the enclosed invoice which will accompany your order.

4.2 ABC Ltd may at its entire discretion grant trade terms, including discounts, to booksellers by prior arrangement. Application for the granting of trade terms should be addressed to the Sales Department, ABC Ltd, XYZ St, Dublin, Ireland.

5. Property in the Goods

5.1 Notwithstanding delivery and the passing of risk in the Goods, or any other provision of these Conditions, property in the Goods shall not pass to the Customer until ABC Ltd has received in cash or cleared funds payment in full of the Price and of all other sums which may be due by the Customer to ABC Ltd at the time the Price is so paid in full.

5.2 Until property in the Goods passes, the Customer shall keep the Goods free from any lien, charge or encumbrance and ABC Ltd may at any time require the Goods to be returned to it by the Customer and if such requirement is not met within three days ABC Ltd may retake possession of the Goods and may visit any premises of the Customer (including locked and steadfast premises) for that purpose.

5.3 Until such time as property in the Goods passes to the Customer, the Customer shall hold the same as ABC Ltd 's fiduciary agent and custodian and shall keep them separate from its property and from that of third parties and properly stored, protected and insured and identified as the property of ABC Ltd. If the Customer shall sell or otherwise dispose of or process the Goods (or any part thereof) it shall receive and hold as trustee for ABC Ltd the proceeds of such sale, disposal or process or other monies derived from or representing the Goods (or any part thereof) (including insurance proceeds) and shall keep such proceeds or other monies separate from any monies or property of the Customer and/or third parties, and shall as soon as possible after receiving the same pay such monies to ABC Ltd or into a separate account in trust for ABC Ltd.

5.4 ABC Ltd shall be entitled to sue for the Price once payment is due in terms of Clause 6.4 notwithstanding that property in the Goods has not passed to the Customer.

6. Price and Payment

6.1 The Price shall be calculated by reference to the price quoted by ABC Ltd or, where no price has been quoted (or a quoted price is no longer valid), the price listed in ABC Ltd's price list current at the date of delivery of the Order plus VAT where applicable and/or other taxes, duties and appropriate other charges and shall be specified in the Invoice.Unless otherwise agreed with the Customer, quotations are valid for 30 calendar days from the date of quotation.

6.2 Rates, prices and discounts published in catalogues, lists, mailshots, advertisements and other documents issued by ABC Ltd are subject to variation at any time without prior notice.

6.3 The Invoice shall be given or despatched by ABC Ltd to the Customer on the date of delivery or as soon as reasonably practicable thereafter provided that ABC Ltd reserves the right to despatch further Invoices to the Customer in respect of increased or other charges payable under these Conditions and not ascertainable at the time of despatch of the original Invoice.

6.4 The Price shall be paid in full by the Customer to ABC Ltd and shall be so paid on or before the date shown on the Invoice as the due date for payment unless otherwise agreed in writing between ABC Ltd and the Customer.

6.5 If the Price is not paid in full by the due date:

6.5.1 interest pursuant to the Courts Act 1981 or as otherwise determined by legislation;

6.5.2 the Customer shall reimburse to ABC Ltd (on a full indemnity basis) all costs and expenses incurred by ABC Ltd in connection with the recovery of any money due to ABC Ltd.

6.6 Without prejudice to Clause 6.5, it is hereby expressly stated that timeous payment of the Price is of the essence of the Order and if the Customer fails to make timeous payment ABC Ltd may at its option either suspend all further deliveries of Goods or performance of services under the Order or otherwise until payment is made in full or cancel the Order and subsequent Orders so far as Goods remain to be delivered or services performed thereunder.

6.7 Payments made by the Customer to ABC Ltd shall be applied by ABC Ltd to Invoices, and to Goods listed in Invoices, in such order or manner as ABC Ltd shall, at its entire discretion, think fit.

6.8 Except with the express agreement in writing of ABC Ltd, no deduction shall be made by the Customer from any payment for Goods for or on account of any matter or thing whatsoever including, but not limited to, any set-off, compensation, counterclaim or present or future taxes.

7. Warranties and Guarantee

7.1 ABC Ltd warrants that:

7.1.1 it has the right to sell the goods and has obtained all necessary rights to license them;

7.1.2 The Goods shall correspond with their description as set out in catalogues, lists, mailshots, advertisements and other documents issued by it, unless the Customer is specifically advised by ABC Ltd to the contrary prior to delivery of the Goods; and

7.1.3 where the Goods consist of or include services to be provided by ABC Ltd, such services shall be provided with due skill, care and diligence. Any verbal description of Goods or any description provided by someone other than ABC Ltd shall not form part of their description for the purposes of these warranties.

7.2 ABC Ltd guarantees that it shall free of charge either repair or, at its entire discretion, replace defective Goods PROVIDED THAT:

7.2.1 any claim is intimated to ABC Ltd by the Customer in accordance with Clause 3;

7.2.2 if so requested by ABC Ltd following intimation of a claim, the defective Goods are promptly returned to ABC Ltd;

7.2.3 the damage or other defect in the Goods complained of shall have arisen as a result of the negligence of ABC Ltd.

7.3 Alternatively to lause 7.2, ABC Ltd shall:

7.3.1 in respect of Goods which do not include the provision of services, be entitled at its entire discretion to,

7.3.2 in respect of Goods which consist of or include the provision of services, refund to the Customer, or (as the case may be) cancel the liability of the Customer to pay the Price of the defective Goods.

8. Limitation of Liability

8.1 Subject to Clause 8.4, ABC Ltd's liability under Clause 7 shall be to the exclusion of all other liability to the Customer whether contractual, tortious, delictual or otherwise for defects in the Goods or for any loss or damage caused by the Goods, and all other conditions, warranties, stipulations or other statements whatsoever concerning the Goods, whether express or implied, by statute, at common law or otherwise howsoever, are hereby excluded; in particular (but without limitation of the foregoing) except as set out at Clause 7.1, ABC Ltd grants no warranties regarding the fitness for purpose, performance, use, nature or merchantable quality of the Goods, whether express or implied, by statute, at common law or otherwise howsoever.

8.2 Subject to Clause 8.4, in no circumstances shall ABC Ltd be liable, in contract, tort (including negligence or breach of statutory duty) or otherwise howsoever and, whatever the cause thereof:

8.2.1 for any increased costs or expenses,

8.2.2 for any loss of profit, business, contracts, revenues or anticipated savings, or

8.2.3 for any special indirect or consequential damage of any nature whatsoever arising directly or indirectly out of the provision by ABC Ltd of the Goods or of any failure or defect therein, or of the performance, non-performance or delayed performance by ABC Ltd of the Order.

8.3 Subject to Clause 8.4, ABC Ltd's liability to the Customer in respect of the Order, in contract, tort (including negligence or breach of statutory duty) or howsoever otherwise arising shall be limited to the Price.

8.4 Nothing in these Conditions shall operate or be construed so as to operate to exclude or restrict:

8.4.1 the liability of ABC Ltd for death or personal injury resulting from the negligence of ABC Ltd or its servants, employees or agents;

8.4.2 the customers statutory rights are not affected.

9. Force Majeure

ABC Ltd shall not be responsible for any delay or failure to fulfill any of its obligations under the Order nor be liable for any loss or damage suffered or incurred by the Customer by reason of any delay in delivery of the Goods or any part thereof caused directly or indirectly by any act of God, war, government or parliamentary restriction, import or export regulation, strike, lockout, trade dispute, fire, theft, flooding, breakdown of plant or premises, failure of water or other supplies or any other cause whatsoever beyond the control of ABC Ltd.

10. Indemnity

The Customer shall indemnify ABC Ltd in respect of all loss, damage or injury occurring to any person, firm, company or property and against all actions, suits, claims and demands, charges or expenses in connection therewith for which ABC Ltd may become liable in respect of the Goods in the event that such loss, damage, or injury shall have been occasioned by the negligence of the Customer.

11. Copyright and restrictions on Re-sale

11.1 All copyright and other rights in the nature of copyright or any other intellectual property right whatsoever in the Goods or any materials derived therefrom (other than legal documents prepared for a particular client from a style or precedent) are reserved to the copyright owner and the Customer irrevocably acknowledges and agrees that the supply of Goods to it by ABC Ltd shall not serve to transfer any such rights.

11.2 No part of the Goods may be reproduced in any material form (including photocopying or storing it in any medium by electronic means and whether or not transiently or incidentally to some other use of the Goods) without the written permission of the copyright owner.

Warning: The doing of an unauthorised act in relation to a copyright work may result in both a civil claim for damages and criminal prosecution.

11.3 Goods are supplied to Customers subject to the condition that they shall not by way of trade or otherwise be lent, re-sold, hired out or otherwise circulated without ABC Ltd's prior written consent in any form of binding or cover other than that in which they are supplied and without a similar Condition including this Condition being imposed on any subsequent purchaser.

12. Termination

12.1 In the event of the Customer committing any breach of any term or provision of the Order (including, for the avoidance of doubt, these

Conditions), going into liquidation, having a Receiver, Examiner or other similar officer appointed over the whole or any part of its assets, becoming bankrupt or apparently insolvent or granting any trust deed or entering into any composition or similar arrangement with its creditors, or if any circumstances arise which, in the sole opinion of ABC Ltd, render any of the foregoing likely to occur then ABC Ltd shall be entitled, without notice and without any liability whatsoever, to terminate the Order forthwith and to enter the Customer's premises for the protection, removal, realisation and disposal of any of the Goods in which property shall not have passed to the Customer in accordance with these Conditions. ABC Ltd shall also be entitled to cancel all Orders or any part thereof remaining unfulfilled between ABC Ltd and the Customer and to sell to any other party or otherwise dispose of and deal with the Goods.

12.2 Termination of the Order shall not discharge any pre-existing liability of the Customer to ABC Ltd and on such termination ABC Ltd shall be entitled to recover from the Customer such loss or damage as ABC Ltd has suffered by reason of such termination.

13. General

13.1 No failure of or delay by ABC Ltd to exercise any right, power, remedy or privilege shall operate as a waiver of the same.

13.2 If any term or provision of these Conditions shall be held to be illegal or unenforceable, in whole or in part, under any enactment or rule of law, such term or provision or part shall to that extent be deemed not to form part of these Conditions but the validity and enforceability of the remainder of these Conditions shall not be affected.

13.3 Any notices or other communications required or permitted to be given by ABC Ltd to the Customer, or vice versa, under these Conditions shall be in writing and sent, in the case of notices to ABC Ltd, to the address given in these Conditions (or such other address as may be intimated to the Customer from time to time) and, in the case of notices to Customers, to that Customer's last known address. Notices and other communications shall be sent by registered post, facsimile transmission or delivered by hand and shall be deemed to have been received, in the case of registered post, at the time of delivery, on facsimile transmission, on the completion of their transmission and on delivery by hand, at the time of delivery. The Customer shall keep ABC Ltd advised of all changes of address.

13.4 The amount of any sum due by the Customer to ABC Ltd under the Order shall be sufficiently ascertained by a certificate under the hand of the Secretary or a Director or any other authorised signatory of ABC Ltd and such certificate shall be final and binding on the Customer for every purpose and, in the case of Orders between ABC Ltd and Customers to whom Goods are delivered or services provided in Scotland, ABC Ltd and the Customer consent to the registration of the Order and any such certificate for preservation and execution.

13.5 ABC Ltd shall be entitled, in its entire discretion, to alter these Conditions or any of them at any time or from time to time whether by way of variation and/or substitution and/or deletion of the subsisting Conditions and/or adding new Conditions and these Conditions as so altered shall apply to Orders whether current at the time or entered into thereafter, provided always that in the case of each Order then current one month's prior notice in writing shall be given by ABC Ltd to the Customer stating the amended Conditions of supply of goods and services and the effective date thereof.

14. Governing Law and Jurisdiction

These Conditions or any Order of which they form part shall be governed in all respects by the laws of the Republic of Ireland and ABC Ltd and the Customer each hereby irrevocably agree to submit to jurisdiction of the Irish Courts.

APPENDIX B

Effective 1st March 2000

No: 100

CONTRACT FOR SHIPMENT OF FEEDINGSTUFFS IN BULK
TALE QUALE - CIF TERMS

Date ....

SELLERS ....

INTERVENING AS BROKERS ....

BUYERS ....
have this day entered into a contract on the following terms and conditions. Wherever the word "cakes" is used, this is agreed to mean goods of the contractual description.

1. GOODS- ....
Broken cakes and/or meal in a proportion, having regard to the characteristics of the goods and methods of handling, to be taken and paid for as cakes. Goods in bulk but Buyers agree to accept up to 15% in stowage bags, such bags to be taken and paid for as cakes and any cutting to be paid for by Buyers. Sellers have the option of shipping the whole or part of the quantity in excess of 15% in bags, in which case the excess over 15% shall be delivered in bulk and Sellers shall be responsible for cutting the excess bags which remain their property.

2. QUANTITY- .... 2% more or less.
Sellers shall have the option of shipping a further 3% more or less than the contract quantity. The excess above 2% or the deficiency below 2% shall be settled on the quantity thereof at shipment at market value on the last day of discharge of the vessel at the port of destination; the value to be fixed by arbitration, unless mutually agreed. Should Sellers exercise the option to ship up to 5% more, the excess over 2% shall be paid for provisionally at contract price. The difference between the contract price and the market price calculated in accordance with the provisions of this clause, shall be adjusted in the final invoice.

3. PRICE - At ....
* per tonne of 1000 kilograms }
} gross weight, cost, insurance and freight to ....
* per ton of 1016 kilograms or 2240 lbs. }

4. BROKERAGE- .... per tonne,
to be paid by Sellers on the mean contract quantity, goods lost or not lost, contract fulfilled or not fulfilled unless such non-fulfilment is due to the successful application of the Prohibition Clause or the Force Majeure Clause. Brokerage shall be due on the day shipping documents are exchanged or, if the goods are not appropriated then the brokerage shall be due on the 30th consecutive day after the last day for appropriation or advice of shipment.

5. QUALITY-
* Warranted to contain .... at time and place of discharge.

Not less than .... % of oil and protein combined, and not more than 2.50% of sand and/or silica.
Should the whole, or any portion, not turn out equal to warranty, the goods must be taken at an allowance to be agreed or settled by arbitration as provided for below, except that for any deficiency of oil and protein there shall be allowances to Buyers at the following rates, viz: 1% of the contract price for each of the first 3 units of deficiency under the warranted percentage; 2% of the contract price for the 4th and 5th units and 3% of the contract price for each unit in excess of 5 and proportionately for any fraction thereof. When the combined content of oil and protein is warranted within a margin (as for example 40%/42%) no allowance shall be made if the analysis ascertained as herein provided be not below the minimum, but if the analysis results are below the minimum warranted the allowance for deficiency shall be computed from the mean of the warranted content.

For any excess of sand and/or silica there shall be an allowance of 1% of the contract price for each unit of excess and proportionately for any fraction thereof. Should the goods contain over 5% of sand and/or silica the Buyers shall be entitled to reject the goods, in which case the contract shall be null and void for such quantity rejected.

The goods are warranted free from castor seed and/or castor seed husk, but should the analysis show castor seed husk not exceeding 0.005%, the Buyers shall not be entitled to reject the goods, but shall accept them with the following allowances: 0.75% of contract price if not exceeding 0.001%, 1% of contract price if not exceeding 0.002%, and 1.50% of contract

* delete/specify as applicable

price if not exceeding 0.005%. Should the first analysis show the goods free from castor seed and/or castor seed husk such analysis shall be final but in the event of the first analysis showing castor seed husk to be present a second sample may be analysed at the request of either party and the mean of the two analyses shall be taken as final. Should the parcel contain castor seed husk in excess of 0.005% Buyers shall be entitled to reject the parcel, in which case the contract shall be null and void for such quantity rejected. Nevertheless, should Buyers elect to retain the parcel they shall be entitled to a further allowance for any excess over 0.005% of castor seed husk, to be settled by agreement or arbitration. For the purpose of sampling and analysis each mark shall stand as a separate shipment. The right of rejection provided by this clause shall be limited to the parcel or parcels found to be defective.

* At time of loading to be of fair average quality of the season's shipment.

* Official .... certificate of inspection, at time of loading into the ocean carrying vessel, shall be final as to quality.

* Sample, at time and place of shipment about as per sealed sample marked ...., in possession of ....; the word "about" when referring to quality shall mean the equivalent of 0.50% on contract price. Analysis as per arrival sample.

Difference in quality shall not entitle Buyers to reject except under the award of arbitrator(s) or board of appeal, as the case may be, referred to in the Arbitration Rules specified in the Arbitration Clause hereafter appearing.

Condition – Shipment in good condition. Should the goods arrive out of condition, due allowance shall be made for the time of the year in which the shipment took place. The fact of the goods so arriving shall not necessarily be sufficient proof of an improper shipment.

6. **PERIOD OF SHIPMENT**- As per bill(s) of lading dated or to be dated ....
The bill(s) of lading to be dated when the goods are actually on board. Date of the bill(s) of lading shall be accepted as proof of date of shipment in the absence of evidence to the contrary. In any month containing an odd number of days, the middle day shall be accepted as being in both halves of the month.

7. **SALES BY NAMED VESSELS**- For all sales by named vessels, the following shall apply:-
(a) Position of vessel is mutually agreed between Buyers and Sellers;
(b) The word "now" to be inserted before the word "classed" in the Shipment and Classification Clause;
(c) Appropriation Clause cancelled if sold "shipped".

8. **SHIPMENT AND CLASSIFICATION**. - Shipment from ....
Shipment to be made in good condition, direct or indirect, with or without transhipment by first class mechanically self-propelled vessel(s) suitable for the carriage of the contract goods, classed Lloyds 100A1, or equivalent class, or in accordance with the Institute Classification Clause of the Institute of London Underwriters.

9. **EXTENSION OF SHIPMENT**- The contract period for shipment, if such be 31 days or less, shall, if desired by the Shipper, be extended by an additional period of not more than 8 days, provided that the Shipper gives notice claiming extension by telegram, or telex sent not later than the next business day following the last day of the originally stipulated period. The notice need not state the number of additional days claimed, and such notice shall be passed on by Sellers to their Buyers respectively in due course after receipt. Sellers shall make an allowance to Buyers, to be deducted in the invoice from the contract price, based on the number of days by which the originally stipulated period is exceeded, as follows: for 1, 2, 3 or 4 additional days, 0.50% of the gross c.i.f. price; for 5 or 6 additional days, 1% of the gross c.i.f. price; for 7 or 8 additional days, 1.50% of the gross c.i.f. price. If, however, after having given notice to the Buyers as above, the Sellers fail to make shipment within such 8 days, then the contract shall be deemed to have called for shipment during the originally stipulated period plus 8 days, at contract price less 1.50%, and any settlement for default shall be calculated on that basis. If any allowance becomes due under this clause, the contract price shall be deemed to be the original contract price less the allowance and any other contractual differences shall be settled on the basis of such reduced price.

10. **APPROPRIATION**-
(a) Notice of Appropriation stating the vessel's name and the approximate weight shipped shall, within (i) 10 consecutive days if shipped from the U.S. Gulf and/or U.S. and/or Canadian Atlantic/Lake Ports, (ii) 14 consecutive days if shipped from any other port, from the date of the bill(s) of lading be despatched in accordance with sub-clause (e) by or on behalf of the Shipper direct to his Buyers or to the Selling Agent or Brokers named in the contract. The Non-Business Days Clause shall not apply.
(b) Notice of Appropriation stating the vessel's name and the approximate weight shipped, shall, within the period stated in sub-clause (a) above be despatched in accordance with sub-clause (e) by or on behalf of subsequent Sellers to their Buyers or to the Selling Agent or Brokers named in the contract, but if Notice of Appropriation is received by subsequent Sellers on the last day or after the period stated in sub-clause (a) from the date of the last bill of lading, their Notice of Appropriation shall be deemed to be in time if despatched:-
(1) On the same calendar day, if received not later than 1600 hours on any business day,
(2) Not later than 1600 hours on the next business day, if received after 1600 hours or on a non-business day.
(c) A Selling Agent or Brokers receiving a Notice of Appropriation shall despatch like Notice of Appropriation in accordance with the provisions of this clause. Where the Shipper or subsequent Sellers despatch the Notice of Appropriation to the Selling Agent, such Selling Agent may despatch Notice of Appropriation either direct to the Buyers or to the Brokers.
(d) The Shipper's Notice of Appropriation and every subsequent Sellers' Notice of Appropriation shall state the date or the presumed date of the bill of lading which shall be for information only and shall not be binding, but in fixing the period laid down by this clause for despatching Notices of Appropriation the actual date of the bill of lading shall prevail.
(e) Notices of Appropriation shall be despatched by telegram, telex or other method of rapid written communication, or by letter if delivered by hand on day of writing. Every such Notice of Appropriation shall be open to correction of any errors occurring in transmission, provided that the sender is not responsible for such errors, and for any previous error in transmission which has been repeated in good faith.
(f) Should the vessel arrive before receipt of the appropriation and any extra expenses be incurred thereby, such expenses shall be borne by Sellers.
(g) When a valid Notice of Appropriation has been received by Buyers, it shall not be withdrawn except with their consent.
(h) A Notice of Appropriation despatched to the Brokers named in the contract shall be considered an appropriation despatched to the Buyers.
(i) In the event of less than 95 tonnes being tendered by any one vessel Buyers shall be entitled to refund of any proved extra expenses for sampling, analysis and lighterage incurred thereby at port of discharge.

* delete/specify as applicable

(j) In the event of more than one shipment being made, each shipment shall be considered a separate contract, but the margin of the mean quantity sold shall not be affected thereby.

11. PAYMENT- .... % of invoice amount by cash in ....

* (a) In exchange for and on presentation of shipping documents;

* (b) In exchange for shipping documents on or before arrival of the vessel at destination, at Buyers' option; Sellers, however, have the option of calling upon Buyers to take up and pay for the documents on or

after...................consecutive days from the date of the bill(s) of lading.

In the event of the shipping documents not being available when called for by the Buyers or on arrival of the vessel at destination, Sellers must provide other documents or an indemnity entitling Buyers to obtain delivery of the goods and payment shall be made by Buyers in exchange for same, but such payments shall not prejudice Buyers' rights under the contract when shipping documents are eventually available. Should Sellers fail to present shipping documents or other documents or an indemnity entitling Buyers to take delivery, Buyers shall take delivery under an indemnity provided by themselves and shall pay for the documents when presented. Any reasonable extra expenses, including the costs of such indemnity or extra charges incurred by reason of the failure of Sellers to provide such documents, shall be borne by Sellers and allowed for in the final invoice but such payment shall not prejudice Buyers' rights under the contract when shipping documents are eventually available. Costs of collection shall be for account of Sellers, but if Buyers demand presentation only through a bank of their choice, in that event any additional collection costs shall be for the account of the Buyers. Any balance to be settled on rendering final invoice. **Final invoices** for monies due may be prepared by either party and shall be settled without delay. If not settled, either party may declare that a dispute has arisen which may be referred to arbitration as herein provided.

12. INTEREST- If there has been unreasonable delay in any payment interest appropriate to the currency involved shall be charged. If such charge is not mutually agreed, a dispute shall be deemed to exist which shall be settled by arbitration. Otherwise interest shall be payable only where specifically provided in the terms of the contract or by an award of arbitration. The terms of this clause do not override the parties obligation under the Payment Clause.

13. RYE TERMS- In the event of goods shipped in tankers or in oil compartments of "Oil/Ore" carriers arriving at destination damaged or out of condition, Buyers must accept delivery but shall be entitled to an allowance for deterioration calculated on a percentage based on contract price to be fixed by arbitration unless mutually agreed.

Samples shall be taken and sealed at port of discharge jointly by the Sellers and Buyers or their Representatives. In the event of Buyers receiving an allowance from Sellers under this clause, Sellers and Buyers shall give all reasonable assistance to each other in the prosecution of claims for recovery from shipowners and/or other parties. Any sum recovered under this clause shall be for the benefit of Sellers and any proved reasonable extra expense incurred by Buyers in connection with the claim are to be deducted. Buyers shall furnish Sellers on settlement of Rye Terms allowance with the usual documents required by average adjusters for preparation of average statement and return to Sellers the Policy(ies) and/or certificate(s) received from them and in addition documents for claiming against the ship or any other party, failing which Buyers shall pay such contribution to average as Sellers may be unable to recover in consequence.

14. SHIPPING DOCUMENTS- Shipping documents shall consist of:-

1. Invoice. 2. Full set(s) of on board Bill(s) of Lading and/or Ship's Delivery Order(s) and/or other Delivery Order(s) in negotiable and transferable form. Such other Delivery Order(s) if required by Buyers, to be certified by the Shipowners, their Agents or a recognised bank. 3. Policy(ies) and/or Insurance Certificate(s) and/or Letter(s) of Insurance in the currency of the contract. The Letter(s) of Insurance to be certified by a recognised bank if required by Buyers. 4. Other documents as called for under the contract. Should documents be presented with an incomplete set of bill(s) of lading or should other shipping documents be missing, payment shall be made, provided that delivery of such missing documents be guaranteed, such guarantee to be signed, if required by Buyers, by a recognised bank. Acceptance of this guarantee shall not prejudice Buyers' rights under this contract. No clerical error in the documents shall entitle Buyers to rejection or to delay payment provided that Sellers furnish at the request of Buyers a guarantee to be countersigned by a recognised bank, if required by Buyers. Sellers shall be responsible for any loss or expense incurred by Buyers on account of such error. Buyers agree to accept documents containing the Chamber of Shipping War Deviation Clause and/or other recognised official War Risk Clause.

15. DUTIES, TAXES, LEVIES, ETC.- All export duties, taxes, levies, etc., present or future, in country of origin, shall be for Sellers' account. All import duties, taxes, levies, etc., present or future, in country of destination, shall be for Buyers' account.

16. DISCHARGE- Discharge shall be as fast as the vessel can deliver in accordance with the custom of the port, but in the event of shipment being made under liner bill(s) of lading, discharge shall be as fast as the vessel can deliver in accordance with the terms of the bill(s) of lading. The cost of discharge from hold to ship's rail shall be for Sellers' account, from ship's rail overboard for Buyers' account. If documents are tendered which do not provide for discharging as above or contain contrary stipulations, Sellers shall be responsible to Buyers for all extra expenses incurred thereby. Discharge by grab(s) shall be permitted unless specifically excluded at time of contract. If shipment is effected by lash barge, then the last day of discharge shall be the day of discharging the last lash barge at the port of destination.

17. WEIGHING- Final settlement shall be made on the basis of gross delivered weights and the goods shall be weighed at time and place of discharge at port of destination herein named at Buyers' expense. Sellers have the right to superintend. If discharge is carried out by grab, the method of weighing is to be mutually agreed between Buyers and Sellers and/or their respective Agents. In case of damage the discharged weight shall be determined on the basis of an analysis made of samples of the damaged and undamaged part of the goods. Additional weight due to damage not to be paid for, unless Rye Terms apply.

18. SAMPLING AND ANALYSIS- Samples required for the purposes of the contract shall be taken in accordance with the GAFTA Sampling Rules Form No: 124 and analysis tests shall be carried out in accordance with the GAFTA Methods of Analysis in Form No: 130. Where the contract requires quality final at loading, samples shall be taken at time and place of shipment. Where the contract requires quality final at discharge, samples shall be taken at the time of discharge on or before removal from the ship or quay. The parties shall appoint superintendents, for the purposes of supervision and sampling of goods, from the GAFTA Approved Register of Superintendents.

19. INSURANCE- Sellers shall provide insurance on terms not less favourable than those set out hereunder, and as set out in detail in The Grain and Feed Trade Association Form No: 72 viz:-

(a) Risks Covered:-

Cargo Clauses (WA), with average payable, with 3% franchise or better terms	-Section 2 of Form 72
War Clauses (Cargo)	- Section 4 of Form 72
Strikes, Riots and Civil Commotions Clauses (Cargo)	- Section 5 of Form 72

* delete/specify as applicable

(b) Insurers - The insurance to be effected with first class underwriters and/or companies who are domiciled or carrying on business in the United Kingdom or who, for the purpose of any legal proceedings, accept a British domicile and provide an address for service of process in London, but for whose solvency Sellers shall not be responsible.

(c) Insurable Value - Insured amount to be for not less than 2% over the invoice amount, including freight when freight is payable on shipment or due in any event, ship and/or cargo lost or not lost, and including the amount of any War Risk premium payable by Buyers.

(d) Freight Contingency - When freight is payable on arrival or on right and true delivery of the goods and the insurance does not include the freight, Sellers shall effect insurance upon similar terms, such insurance to attach only as such freight becomes payable, for the amount of the freight plus 2%, until the termination of the risk as provided in the above mentioned clauses, and shall undertake that their policies are so worded that in the case of particular or general average claim the Buyers shall be put in the same position as if the c.i.f. value plus 2% were insured from the time of shipment.

(e) Certificates/Policies - Sellers shall give all policies and/or certificates and/or letters of insurance provided for in this contract, (duly stamped if applicable) for original and increased value (if any) for the value stipulated in (c) above. In the event of a certificate of insurance being supplied, it is agreed that such certificate shall be exchanged by Sellers for a policy if and when required, and such certificate shall state on its face that it is so exchangeable. If required by Buyers, letter(s) of insurance shall be guaranteed by a recognised bank, or by any other guarantor who is acceptable to Buyers.

(f) Total Loss - In the event of total or constructive total loss, or where the amount of the insurance becomes payable in full, the insured amount in excess of 2% over the invoice amount shall be for Sellers' account and the party in possession of the policy(ies) shall collect the amount of insurance and shall thereupon settle with the other party on that basis.

(g) Currency of Claims - Claims to be paid in the currency of the contract.

(h) War and Strike Risks/Premiums - Any premium in excess of 0.50% to be for account of Buyers. The rate of such insurance not to exceed the rate ruling in London at time of shipment or date of vessel's sailing whichever may be adopted by underwriters. Such excess premium shall be claimed from Buyers, wherever possible, with the Provisional Invoice, but in no case later than the date of vessel's arrival, or not later than 7 consecutive days after the rate has been agreed with underwriters, whichever may be the later, otherwise such claim shall be void unless, in the opinion of Arbitrators, the delay is justifiable. Sellers' obligation to provide War Risk Insurance shall be limited to the terms and conditions in force and generally obtainable in London at time of shipment.

(i) Where Sellers are responsible for allowances or other payments to Buyers under Rye Terms or other contractual terms, (and which risks are also covered by the insurance provided by Sellers), the Buyers, on receipt of settlement, shall immediately return to Sellers the insurance documents originally received from them and shall, if required, subrogate to Sellers all right of claim against the Insurers in respect of such matters.

20. PROHIBITION- In case of prohibition of export, blockade or hostilities or in case of any executive or legislative act done by or on behalf of the government of the country of origin or of the territory where the port or ports of shipment named herein is/are situate, restricting export, whether partially or otherwise, any such restriction shall be deemed by both parties to apply to this contract and to the extent of such total or partial restriction to prevent fulfilment whether by shipment or by any other means whatsoever and to that extent this contract or any unfulfilled portion thereof shall be cancelled. Sellers shall advise Buyers without delay with the reasons therefor and, if required, Sellers must produce proof to justify the cancellation.

21. FORCE MAJEURE, STRIKES, ETC- Sellers shall not be responsible for delay in shipment of the goods or any part thereof occasioned by any Act of God, strike, lockout, riot or civil commotion, combination of workmen, breakdown of machinery, fire, or any cause comprehended in the term "force majeure". If delay in shipment is likely to occur for any of the above reasons, the Shipper shall give notice to the Buyers by telegram, telex or by similar advice within 7 consecutive days of the occurrence, or not less than 21 consecutive days before the commencement of the contract period, whichever is the later. The notice shall state the reason(s) for the anticipated delay. If after giving such notice an extension to the shipping period is required, then the Shipper shall give further notice not later than 2 business days after the last day of the contract period of shipment stating the port or ports of loading from which the goods were intended to be shipped, and shipments effected after the contract period shall be limited to the port or ports so nominated. If shipment be delayed for more than 30 consecutive days, Buyers shall have the option of cancelling the delayed portion of the contract, such option to be exercised by Buyers giving notice to be received by Sellers not later than the first business day after the additional 30 consecutive days. If Buyers do not exercise this option, such delayed portion shall be automatically extended for a further period of 30 consecutive days. If shipment under this clause be prevented during the further 30 consecutive days extension, the contract shall be considered void. Buyers shall have no claim against Sellers for delay or non-shipment under this clause, provided that Sellers shall have supplied to Buyers, if required, satisfactory evidence justifying the delay or non-fulfilment.

22. NOTICES- All Notices required to be served on the parties pursuant to this contract shall be communicated rapidly in legible form. Methods of rapid communication for the purposes of this clause are defined and mutually recognised as:- either telex, or letter if delivered by hand on the date of writing, or telefax, or E-mail, or other electronic means, always subject to the proviso that if receipt of any notice is contested by the addressee, the burden of proof of transmission shall be on the sender who shall, in the case of a dispute, establish, to the satisfaction of the arbitrator(s) or board of appeal appointed pursuant to the Arbitration Clause, that the notice was actually transmitted. Any notice received after 1600 hours on a business day shall be deemed to have been received on the business day following. In case of resales all notices shall be passed on without delay by Buyers to their respective Sellers or vice versa. A notice to the Brokers or Agent shall be deemed a notice under this contract.

23. NON-BUSINESS DAYS- Saturdays, Sundays and the officially recognised and/or legal holidays of the respective countries and any days which The Grain and Feed Trade Association may declare as non-business days for specific purposes, shall be non-business days. Should the time limit for doing any act or giving any notice expire on a non-business day, the time so limited shall be extended until the first business day thereafter. The period of shipment shall not be affected by this clause.

24. PRO RATA-

(a) Should any of the above mentioned quantity form part of a larger quantity of the same or a different period of shipment of bags of the same mark, or of a similar quality, whether in bags or bulk or whether destined to more than one port, no separation or distinction shall be necessary.

(b) All loose collected, damaged goods and sweepings shall be shared by and apportioned pro-rata in kind between the various Receivers thereof at the port of discharge named in the contract, buying under contracts containing this clause. In the event of this not being practicable or any of them receiving more or less than his pro-rata share or apportionment, he shall settle with the other(s) on a pro-rata basis in cash at the market price and each Receiver shall bear his proportion of the depreciation in market value. The pro-rata statement shall be established by the Sellers or their Representatives in conjunction with the Receivers or their Representatives.

(c) The above pro-rata apportionment between Receivers shall have no bearing on the establishment of final invoices with Sellers and for the purpose of these final invoices, the total quantity of loose collected, damaged goods and sweepings shall be regarded as delivered to those Receivers who did not receive their full invoiced quantity.

(d) In the case of excess or deficiency, the difference between the invoiced and the total delivered quantity shall be settled at the market price by final invoices to be rendered by Receivers, who have received more or less than that paid for, to their immediate Sellers without taking into consideration the above pro-rata apportionment between Receivers.

(e) If an excess quantity is delivered to one or more Receiver and a deficient quantity is delivered to one or more Receiver, the excess and deficiency shall be settled between them at the market price. Final invoices shall be established with immediate Sellers for any balance resulting from this settlement.

(f) All Shippers, Sellers and Buyers of any part of such larger quantity as aforesaid under contracts containing this clause shall be deemed to have entered into mutual agreements with one another to the above effect, and to agree to submit to arbitration all questions and claims between them or any of them in regard to the execution of this clause as aforesaid in accordance with the Arbitration Clause of this contract. Sellers and Buyers shall give all reasonable assistance in execution of this clause. All Sellers shall be responsible for the settlement by the respective Buyers in accordance with this clause within a reasonable time.

(g) The market price wherever mentioned in this clause shall be the market price on the last day of discharge of the vessel in the port of destination, such price to be fixed by arbitration unless mutually agreed.

(h) In the event of this clause being brought into operation, any allowances payable in respect of condition, or quality, or under any of the other guarantees contained in this contact, shall be based upon the actual weight received by the Buyers and not on the pro-rata weight.

(i) In the event of any conflict in terms of apportionment applicable to the port of discharge the method published by The Grain and Feed Trade Association shall, where applicable, take precedence over sub-clauses (b) to (h) above.

(j) In the event that sub-clause (a) applies or that the goods subsequently become co-mingled, and that the goods were shipped by more than one Shipper and destined for one or more ports of discharge then, after the adjustment between Receivers under the terms of this clause, the Shippers shall settle pro-rata between themselves in proportion to their bill of lading quantities. Such settlements shall be made in cash and in the event of two or more discharging ports being involved, then the settlement price shall be the average of the market prices on the last day of discharge in the respective ports.

25. **DEFICIENCY**- Any deficiency on the bill of lading weight shall be paid for by Sellers, and any excess over bill of lading weight shall be paid for by Buyers, at contract price. If the goods form part of a larger quantity, the Pro-rata Clause shall apply and the provisions of this clause shall not apply and settlement shall be in accordance with the Pro-rata Clause.

26. **DEFAULT**- In default of fulfilment of contract by either party, the following provisions shall apply:-

(a) The party other than the defaulter shall, at their discretion have the right, after giving notice by letter, telegram or telex to the defaulter to sell or purchase, as the case may be, against the defaulter, and such sale or purchase shall establish the default price.

(b) If either party be dissatisfied with such default price or if the right at (a) above is not exercised and damages cannot be mutually agreed, then the assessment of damages shall be settled by arbitration.

(c) The damages payable shall be based on, but not limited to, the difference between the contract price and either the default price established under (a) above or upon the actual or estimated value of the goods, on the date of default, established under (b) above.

(d) In no case shall damages include loss of profit on any sub-contracts made by the party defaulted against or others unless the Arbitrator(s) or Board of Appeal, having regard to special circumstances, shall in his/their sole and absolute discretion think fit.

(e) Damages, if any, shall be computed on the quantity appropriated if any but, if no such quantity has been appropriated then on the mean contract quantity, and any option available to either party shall be deemed to have been exercised accordingly in favour of the mean contract quantity.

(f) Default may be declared by Sellers at any time after expiry of the contract period, and the default date shall then be the first business day after the date of Sellers' advice to their Buyers. If default has not already been declared then (notwithstanding the provisions stated in the Appropriation Clause) if notice of appropriation is not passed by the 10th consecutive day after the last day for appropriation laid down in the contract, the Seller shall be deemed to be in default and the default date shall then be the first business day thereafter.

27. **CIRCLE**- Where Sellers re-purchase from their Buyers or from any subsequent buyer the same goods or part thereof, a circle shall be considered to exist as regards the particular goods so re-purchased, and the provisions of the Default Clause shall not apply. (For the purpose of this clause the same goods shall mean goods of the same description, from the same country of origin, of the same quality, and, where applicable, of the same analysis warranty, for shipment to the same port(s) of destination during the same period of shipment). Different currencies shall not invalidate the circle. Subject to the terms of the Prohibition Clause in the contract, if the goods are not appropriated, or, having been appropriated documents are not presented, invoices based on the mean contract quantity shall be settled by all Buyers and their Sellers in the circle by payment by all Buyers to their Sellers of the excess of the Sellers' invoice amount over the lowest invoice amount in the circle. Payment shall be due not later than 15 consecutive days after the last day for appropriation, or, should the circle not be ascertained before the expiry of this time, then payment shall be due not later than 15 consecutive days after the circle is ascertained. Where the circle includes contract(s) expressed in different currencies the lowest invoice amount shall be replaced by the market price on the first day for contractual shipment and invoices shall be settled between each Buyer and his Seller in the circle by payment of the differences between the market price and the relative contract price in currency of the contract.

All Sellers and Buyers shall give every assistance to ascertain the circle and when a circle shall have been ascertained in accordance with this clause same shall be binding on all parties to the circle. As between Buyers and Sellers in the circle, the non-presentation of documents by Sellers to their Buyers shall not be considered a breach of contract. Should any party in the circle prior to the due date of payment commit any act comprehended in the Insolvency Clause of his contract, settlement by all parties in the circle shall be calculated at the closing out price as provided for in the Insolvency Clause, which shall be taken as a basis for settlement, instead of the lowest invoice amount in the circle. In this event respective Buyers shall make payment to their Sellers or respective Sellers shall make payment to their Buyers of the difference between the closing out price and the contract price.

28. **INSOLVENCY**- If before the fulfilment of this contract, either party shall suspend payments, notify any of the creditors that he is unable to meet debts or that he has suspended or that he is about to suspend payments of his debts, convene, call or hold a meeting of creditors, propose a voluntary arrangement, have an administration order made, have a winding up order made, have a receiver or manager appointed, convene, call or hold a meeting to go into liquidation (other than for re-construction or amalgamation) become subject to an Interim Order under Section 252 of the Insolvency Act 1986, or have a Bankruptcy Petition presented against him (any of which acts being hereinafter called an "Act of Insolvency") then the party committing such Act of Insolvency shall forthwith transmit by telex or telegram or by other method of rapid written communication a notice of the occurrence of such Act of Insolvency to the other party to the contract and upon proof (by either the other party to the contract or the Receiver, Administrator, Liquidator or other person representing the party committing the Act of Insolvency) that such notice was thus given within 2 business days of the occurrence of the Act of Insolvency, the contract shall be closed out at the market price ruling on the business day following the giving of the notice. If such notice be not given as aforesaid, then the other party, on learning of the occurrence of the Act of Insolvency, shall have the option of declaring the contract closed out at either the market price on the first business day after the date when such party first learnt of the occurrence of the Act of Insolvency or at the market price ruling on the first business day after the date when the Act of Insolvency occurred. In all cases the other party to the contract shall have the option of ascertaining the settlement price on the closing out of the contract by re-purchase or re-sale, and the difference between the contract price and the re-purchase or re-sale price shall be the amount payable or receivable under this contract.

29. **DOMICILE-** This contract shall be deemed to have been made in England and to be performed in England, notwithstanding any contrary provision, and this contract shall be construed and take effect in accordance with the laws of England. Except for the purpose of enforcing any award made in pursuance of the Arbitration clause of this contract, the Courts of England shall have exclusive jurisdiction to determine any application for ancillary relief, the exercise of the powers of the Court in relation to the arbitration proceedings and any dispute other than a dispute which shall fall within the jurisdiction of arbitrators or board of appeal of the Association pursuant to the Arbitration Clause of this contract. For the purpose of any legal proceedings each party shall be deemed to be ordinarily resident or carrying on business at the offices of The Grain and Feed Trade Association, England, (GAFTA) and any party residing or carrying on business in Scotland shall be held to have prorogated jurisdiction against himself to the English Courts or if in Northern Ireland to have submitted to the jurisdiction and to be bound by the decision of the English Courts. The service of proceedings upon any such party by leaving the same at the offices of The Grain and Feed Trade Association, together with the posting of a copy of such proceedings to his address outside England, shall be deemed good service, any rule of law or equity to the contrary notwithstanding.

30. **ARBITRATION-**

(a) Any dispute arising out of or under this contract shall be settled by arbitration in accordance with the Arbitration Rules, No. 125, of The Grain and Feed Trade Association, in the edition current at the date of this contract, such Rules forming part of this contract and of which both parties hereto shall be deemed to be cognisant.

(b) Neither party hereto, nor any persons claiming under either of them shall bring any action or other legal proceedings against the other of them in respect of any such dispute until such dispute shall first have been heard and determined by the Arbitrator(s) or a Board of Appeal, as the case may be, in accordance with the Arbitration Rules and it is expressly agreed and declared that the obtaining of an award from the Arbitrator(s) or a Board of Appeal, as the case may be, shall be a condition precedent to the right of either party hereto or of any persons claiming under either of them to bring any action or other legal proceedings against the other of them in respect of any such dispute.

31. **INTERNATIONAL CONVENTIONS-**

The following shall not apply to this contract:-

(a) the Uniform Law on Sales and the Uniform Law on Formation to which effect is given by the Uniform Laws on International Sales Act 1967;

(b) the United Nations Convention on Contracts for the International Sale of Goods of 1980; and

(c) the United Nations Convention on Prescription (Limitation) in the International Sale of Goods of 1974 and the amending Protocol of 1980.

(d) Incoterms

Sellers...Buyers...

Printed in England and issued by

GAFTA

(THE GRAIN AND FEED TRADE ASSOCIATION)

GAFTA HOUSE, 6 CHAPEL PLACE, RIVINGTON ST, LONDON EC2A 3SH

100/6

APPENDIX C

Effective 1st March 2000

No: 79

Gafta

Copyright
THE GRAIN AND FEED TRADE ASSOCIATION

CONTRACT FOR UNITED KINGDOM AND IRELAND GRAIN

RYE TERMS - CIF TERMS

Date ....

SELLERS ....

INTERVENING AS BROKERS ....

BUYERS ....
have this day entered into a contract on the following terms and conditions.

1. GOODS- ....

2. QUALITY-

* Warranted to contain .... at time and place of discharge.

Natural Weight.. kilograms per hectolitre, at time and place of loading/discharge.

Moisture..% Admixture..%

* **Official** .... certificate of inspection, or certification of inspection of .... at time and place of loading into the ocean carrying vessel, shall be final as to quality. The Buyers shall not be entitled to reject a tender of a higher grade of grain of the same colour and description.

* **F.A.Q.** (fair average quality) of the season's shipment at time and place of loading, to be assessed upon the basis of, and by comparison with The Grain & Feed Trade Association's (GAFTA) official F.A.Q. standard of the month during which the bill of lading is dated. In the event of no F.A.Q. Standard being established by the Association, the Arbitrator(s) shall in his/their discretion decide what is the fair average quality. An average sample of the delivery shall be taken and sealed jointly at the port of discharge by the representatives of the shipper and the representatives of the holders of the bill of lading or shipper's delivery order, and shall be forwarded immediately to the Association for the purposes of establishing the F.A.Q. standard. The expenses of such sampling and forwarding shall be paid half by the Receiver and half by the Sellers. Place of shipment under this contract shall be understood as the port or group of ports adopted by the appointed Standards Committee in making the Standard. If the difference between the delivery and the F.A.Q. Standard shall not amount to 0.50% on contract price, no allowance for quality shall be due, otherwise the Buyers shall be entitled to the full difference in value.

* **Sample**, at time and place of shipment about as per sealed sample marked .... in possession of ....; the word "about" when referring to quality shall mean the equivalent of 0.50% on contract price.

Difference in quality shall not entitle Buyers to reject except under the award of arbitrator(s) or board of appeal, as the case may be, referred to in the Arbitration Rules specified in the Arbitration Clause hereafter appearing.

Finality- Where the natural weight, analysis for moisture and admixture or analysis for warranties/guarantees is to be determined by The Grain and Feed Trade Association or their appointed Analysts, or other accepted authority agreed by both parties, instructions to proceed shall be sent by the last Buyers to the Association, Analyst or accepted authority whichever is applicable within 21 days of final discharge of the ship at the last port of destination under this contract. The certificate of The Grain and Feed Trade Association or its duly appointed analyst or accepted authority is final in respect of all warranties/guarantees. All expenses incurred to be borne half by the Sellers and half by the Buyers.

In the event of non-compliance with any of the preceding provisions of the clause claims for excess or deficiency as applicable shall be deemed to be waived and absolutely barred, unless the Arbitrator(s) or Board of Appeal referred to in the Arbitration Rules shall in his/their absolute discretion, otherwise determine.

Condition-Shipment in good condition. Should the goods arrive out of condition, due allowance shall be made for the time of the year in which the shipment took place. The fact of the goods so arriving shall not necessarily be sufficient proof of an

* delete/specify as applicable

improper shipment.

3. **SHIPMENT**- As per customary bill or bills of lading dated or to be dated .... The bill of lading to be dated when the goods are actually on board.

4. **SHIP'S CLASSIFICATION**- By first class mechanically self-propelled vessel(s) suitable for the carriage of the contract goods, classed Lloyds 100A1 or equivalent class, or in accordance with the Institute Classification Clause of the Institute of London Underwriters, excluding Tankers and Vessels which are either classified in Lloyd's Register or described in Lloyd's Shipping Index as "Ore/Oil" Vessels.

5. **PORTS OF SHIPMENT**- From ....

6. **QUANTITY** - .... tonnes, say 5% more or less. In the event of the quantity contracted for being for a full and complete cargo and/or cargoes the margin of contract quantity to be 10% more or less, excess or deficiency over 5% to be settled at the c.i.f. price on date of last bill of lading and on the quantity thereof; value to be fixed by arbitration unless mutually agreed.

7. **PRICE**- At price of .... per tonne of 1000 kilograms, shipped in bulk. Shipper has the option of shipping up to 10% in sacks or bags for stowage purposes, such sacks and bags to be taken and paid for as goods.

8. **DESTINATION**- Including insurance and freight direct or indirect to ....

9. **FREIGHT**- Freight payable on discharge, less advances for the ordinary ship's disbursements at port of loading, or ship's requirements as per Charter Party.

10. **BROKERAGE** .... per tonne, to be paid by Sellers on the mean contract quantity, goods lost or not lost, contract fulfilled or not fulfilled unless such non-fulfilment is due to the successful application of the Prohibition Clause. Brokerage shall be due on the day shipping documents are exchanged or, if the goods are not appropriated then the brokerage shall be due on the 30th consecutive day after the last day for appropriation or advice of shipment.

11. **PAYMENT**- Payment by cash in.. on presentation of and in exchange for shipping documents. If shipping documents have not been sighted at time of vessel's arrival at port of discharge, Sellers shall provide other documents (such documents to be countersigned if required by Buyers by a recognised bank) entitling Buyers to obtain delivery of the goods, and, without prejudice to Buyers' rights under the contract, payment must be made in exchange for same, provided that if such payment be made, proved additional expenses, if any, incurred by reason of such non-sighting of shipping documents shall be borne by Sellers and allowed for in final invoice. When payment is due on a non-business day, Buyers shall have the option of taking up the shipping documents on the previous business day - payment to be made not later than 12 noon. Should shipping documents be presented with an incomplete set of bill(s) of lading or should other shipping documents be missing, payment shall be made provided that delivery of such missing documents be guaranteed, such guarantee to be countersigned, if required by Buyers, by a recognised bank.
Costs of collection shall be for account of Sellers, but if Buyers demand presentation only through a bank of their choice, in that event any additional collection costs shall be for the account of Buyers.
No obvious clerical error in the documents shall entitle the Buyers to reject them or delay payment, but the Sellers shall be responsible for all loss or expense caused to Buyers by reason of such error and Sellers shall on request of Buyers furnish an approved guarantee in respect thereto.
Final Invoices for monies due may be prepared by either party and shall be settled without delay. If not settled, either party may declare that a dispute has arisen which may be referred to arbitration as herein provided.

12. **INTEREST**- If there has been unreasonable delay in any payment interest appropriate to the currency involved shall be charged. If such charge is not mutually agreed, a dispute shall be deemed to exist which shall be settled by arbitration. Otherwise interest shall be payable only where specifically provided in the terms of the contract or by an award of arbitration. The terms of this clause do not override the parties obligation under the Payment Clause.

13. **DUTIES, TAXES, LEVIES, ETC.**- Where the goods become the subject of an European Union (EC, EEC, EU) export refund in accordance with the EU regulations in force at time of export, they are not eligible for re-importation to the European Union.

14. **WAR DEVIATION**- Buyers agree to accept documents containing the Chamber of Shipping War Deviation Clauses and/or other recognised official War Risk Clause.

15. **INSURANCE**- Sellers shall provide insurance on terms not less favourable than those set out hereunder, and as set out in detail in The Grain and Feed Trade Association Form 72 viz:-
(a) Risks Covered:-

Cargo Clauses (FPA)	- Section 3 of Form 72
War Clauses (Cargo)	- Section 4 of Form 72
Strikes, Riots and Civil Commotions Clauses (Cargo)	- Section 5 of Form 72

(b) Insurers - The insurance to be effected with first class underwriters and/or companies who are domiciled or carrying on business in the United Kingdom or who, for the purpose of any legal proceedings, accept a British domicile and provide an address for service of process in London, but for whose solvency Sellers shall not be responsible.
(c) Insurable Value - Insured amount to be for not less than 2% over the invoice amount, including freight when freight is payable on shipment or due in any event, ship and/or cargo lost or not lost, and including the amount of any War Risk premium payable by Buyers.
(d) Freight Contingency - When freight is payable on arrival or on right and true delivery of the goods and the insurance does not include the freight, Sellers shall effect insurance upon similar terms, such insurance to attach only as such freight becomes

payable, for the amount of the freight plus 2%, until the termination of the risk as provided in the above mentioned clauses, and shall undertake that their policies are so worded that in the case of a particular or general average claim the Buyers shall be put in the same position as if the C.I.F. value plus 2% were insured from the time of shipment.

(e) Certificates/Policies - Sellers shall give all policies and/or certificates and/or letters of insurance provided for in this contract, (duly stamped if applicable) for original and increased value (if any) for the value stipulated in (c) above. In the event of a certificate of insurance being supplied, it is agreed that such certificate shall be exchanged by Sellers for a policy if and when required, and such certificate shall state on its face that it is so exchangeable. If required by Buyers, letter(s) of insurance shall be guaranteed by a recognised bank, or by any other guarantor who is acceptable to Buyers.

(f) Total Loss - In the event of total or constructive total loss, or where the amount of the insurance becomes payable in full, the insured amount in excess of 2% over the invoice amount shall be for Sellers' account and the party in possession of the policy(ies) shall collect the amount of insurance and shall thereupon settle with the other party on that basis.

(g) Currency of Claims - Claims to be paid in the currency of the contract.

(h) War and Strike Risks/Premiums - Any premium in excess of 0.50% to be for account of Buyers. The rate of such insurance not to exceed the rate ruling in London at time of shipment or date of vessel's sailing whichever may be adopted by underwriters. Such excess premium shall be claimed from Buyers, wherever possible, with the Provisional Invoice, but in no case later than the date of vessel's arrival, or not later than 7 consecutive days after the rate has been agreed with underwriters, whichever may be the later, otherwise such claim shall be void unless, in the opinion of Arbitrators, the delay is justifiable. Sellers' obligation to provide War Risk Insurance shall be limited to the terms and conditions in force and generally obtainable in London at time of shipment.

(i) Where Sellers are responsible for allowances or other payments to Buyers under Rye Terms or other contractual terms, (and which risks are also covered by the insurance provided by Sellers), the Buyers, on receipt of settlement, shall immediately return to Sellers the insurance documents originally received from them and shall, if required, subrogate to Sellers all right of claim against the Insurers in respect of such matters.

16. DISCHARGE- Ship to discharge according to the custom of the port.

If documents are tendered which do not provide for discharging as above, or contain contrary stipulations, Sellers to be responsible to Buyers for all extra expenses incurred thereby.

17. PRO RATA-

(a) Should any of the above mentioned quantity form part of a larger quantity of the same or a different period of shipment of bags of the same mark, or of a similar quality, whether in bags or bulk or whether destined to more than one port, no separation or distinction shall be necessary.

(b) All loose collected, damaged goods and sweepings shall be shared by and apportioned pro-rata in kind between the various Receivers thereof at the port of discharge named in the contract, buying under contracts containing this clause. In the event of this not being practicable or any of them receiving more or less than his pro-rata share or apportionment, he shall settle with the other(s) on a pro-rata basis in cash at the market price and each Receiver shall bear his proportion of the depreciation in market value. The pro-rata statement shall be established by the Sellers or their Representatives in conjunction with the Receivers or their Representatives.

(c) The above pro-rata apportionment between Receivers shall have no bearing on the establishment of final invoices with Sellers and for the purpose of these final invoices, the total quantity of loose collected, damaged goods and sweepings shall be regarded as delivered to those Receivers who did not receive their full invoiced quantity.

(d) In the case of excess or deficiency, the difference between the invoiced and the total delivered quantity shall be settled at the market price by final invoices to be rendered by Receivers, who have received more or less than that paid for, to their immediate Sellers without taking into consideration the above pro-rata apportionment between Receivers.

(e) If one or more Receivers is delivered in excess, and one or more Receivers bears a shortage, the excess and deficiency shall be settled between them at the market price. Final invoices shall be established with immediate Sellers for any balance resulting from this settlement.

(f) All Shippers, Sellers and Buyers of any part of such larger quantity as aforesaid under the contracts containing this clause shall be deemed to have entered into mutual agreements with one another to the above effect, and to agree to submit to arbitration all questions and claims between them or any of them in regard to the execution of this clause as aforesaid in accordance with the Arbitration Clause of this contract. Sellers and Buyers shall give all reasonable assistance in execution of this clause. All Sellers shall be responsible for the settlement by the respective Buyers in accordance with this clause within a reasonable time.

(g) The market price wherever mentioned in this clause shall be the market price on the last day of discharge of the vessel in the port of destination, such price to be fixed by arbitration unless mutually agreed.

(h) In the event of this clause being brought into operation, any allowances payable in respect of condition, or quality, or under any of the other guarantees contained in this contract, shall be based upon the actual weight received by the Buyers and not on the pro-rata weight.

(i) In the event of any conflict in terms of apportionment applicable to the port of discharge the method published by the Grain and Feed Trade Association shall, where applicable, take precedence over sub-clauses (b) to (h) above.

(j) In the event that sub-clause (a) applies or that the goods subsequently become co-mingled, and that the goods were shipped by more than one Shipper and destined for one or more ports of discharge then, after the adjustment between Receivers under the terms of this clause, the Shippers shall settle pro-rata between themselves in proportion to their bill of lading quantities.

Such settlements shall be made in cash and in the event of two or more discharging ports being involved, then the settlement price shall be the average of the market prices on the last day of discharge in the respective ports.

18. DEFICIENCY- Any deficiency on bill of lading weight shall be paid for by Sellers, and any excess over bill of lading weight shall be paid for by Buyers at contract price. If the goods form part of a larger quantity the Pro-rata Clause shall apply and the provisions of this clause shall not apply and settlement shall be in accordance with the Pro-rata Clause.

19. WEIGHING- The whole shipment shall be weighed at time of discharge according to the custom of the port. Sellers and

Buyers shall have the right of supervision both as to delivery and weighing.

20. ALLOWANCES-

(a) Natural Weight:
To be ascertained by The Grain and Feed Trade Association or other accepted authority and any deficiency so determined to be allowed for off the contract price in accordance with Rules No. 65 of The Grain and Feed Trade Association.

(b) Moisture - Any excess in the guaranteed maximum moisture content shall be allowed for off the contract price on the following scale:
1% for 1% up to the first 1% excess.
1.50% for 1% of the excess over the first 1% up to 2%.
2.50% for 1% of the excess over 2% up to 3%.
Fractions in proportion.
If the excess exceeds 3%, the allowance to be mutually agreed or settled by arbitration.

(c) Admixture - Any admixture of dirt and/or other foreign substance in excess of the guaranteed maximum shall be allowed for by Sellers at contract price but any grain or seed other than the grain contracted for to be reckoned as foreign substances at half their quantities. The percentage of admixture to be determined by the Grain and Feed Trade Association or its duly appointed Analysts.

21. SAMPLING AND ANALYSIS- Samples required for the purposes of the contract shall be taken in accordance with the GAFTA Sampling Rules Form No: 124 and analysis tests shall be carried out in accordance with the GAFTA Methods of Analysis in Form No: 130. Where the contract requires quality final at loading, samples shall be taken at time and place of shipment. Where the contract requires quality final at discharge, samples shall be taken at the time of discharge on or before removal from the ship or quay. The parties shall appoint superintendents, for the purposes of supervision and sampling of goods, from the GAFTA Approved Register of Superintendents.

22. RYE TERMS- Condition guaranteed on arrival (subject to any country damaged grain in the fair average quality of the Season's Crop). Slight dry warmth not injuring the grain shall not be objected to, but damage by sea-water or otherwise, shall be taken by Buyers with an allowance for deterioration (except country damaged as above), calculated on a percentage based on contract price, to be fixed by Arbitration according to the Arbitration Rules No. 125. Samples shall be taken and sealed at port of discharge jointly by the agents of the Shipper, and of the holders of the bill of lading or delivery order. In the event of Buyers receiving an allowance from Sellers under this clause, Sellers and Buyers shall give all reasonable assistance to each other in the prosecution of claim for recovery from Shipowners and/or other parties. Any sum recovered in respect of such allowance made by Sellers to Buyers under this clause shall be for the benefit of Sellers, and any proved reasonable extra expenses incurred by Buyers in connection with the claim are to be deducted.

23. PROHIBITION- In case of prohibition of export, blockade or hostilities or in case of any executive or legislative act done by or on behalf of the government of the country of origin or of the territory where the port or ports of shipment named herein is/are situate, restricting export, whether partially or otherwise, any such restriction shall be deemed by both parties to apply to this contract and to the extent of such total or partial restriction to prevent fulfilment whether by shipment or by any other means whatsoever and to that extent this contract or any unfulfilled portion thereof shall be cancelled. Sellers shall advise Buyers without delay with the reasons therefor and, if required, Sellers must produce proof to justify the cancellation.

24. LOADING STRIKES/ICE-

(a) Should shipment of the grain or any part thereof be prevented at any time during the last 28 days of guaranteed time of shipment or at any time during guaranteed contract period if such be less than 28 days, by reason of riots, strikes, lock-outs or ice at port or ports of loading or elsewhere preventing the forwarding of the goods to such port or ports, then the Shipper shall be entitled at the termination of any such occurrence aforesaid to as much time, not exceeding 28 days, for shipment from such port or ports as was left for shipment under the contract prior to the commencement of the occurrence and in the event of the time left for shipment under the contract being 14 days or less, a minimum extension of 14 days shall be allowed. In the event of further riots, strikes, lock-outs or ice occurring during the time by which the guaranteed time of shipment has been extended by reason of the operation of the provisions of the foregoing paragraph, the additional extension allowed shall be limited to the actual duration of such further riots, strikes, lock-outs or ice. In case of non-fulfilment under the above conditions the date of default shall be similarly deferred.

(b) The Shipper shall give notice by telegram or telex naming the port or ports not later than 2 business days after the last day of guaranteed time for shipment if he intends to claim an extension of time for shipment, such notice shall limit the ports for shipment after expiry of contract period to those from which an extension is claimed. All such notices shall be passed on in due course.

(c) If required by Buyers, Sellers must provide documentary evidence to establish any claim for extension under this clause.

25. DISCHARGING STRIKES/ICE - In the event of a strike or lock-out affecting the discharge of the cargo at, or ice preventing the vessel reaching the port of destination named in the contract, the terms of the "Gencon" or "Synacomex" or "Britcon" Clauses to apply. If during any of the time allowed for shipment the port of destination is inaccessible because of ice to ships of the size required under this contract, and the Sellers are unable to charter for this reason, then Sellers shall -by giving notice to Buyers - be entitled at the termination of such inaccessibility to as much time for shipment as was left for shipment prior to the commencement of the inaccessibility, with a minimum of 14 days always to be allowed for. Current charges in force at time of contract, after the date of the originally stipulated contract period of shipment to be for Buyers' account. The question of accessibility to be decided by Lloyd's Agent, if necessary.

26. EXTENSION OF SHIPMENT- The period for shipment stipulated in this contract, if 31 days or less, shall, if claimed by the Shipper, be extended for not more than 8 days, provided that the Shipper gives notice claiming extension by telegram or telex sent not later than the next business day following the last day of the originally stipulated period; the notice need not state the number of additional days claimed, and shall be passed on by intermediary Sellers to their respective Buyers in due course after receipt. If such notice be given and shipment be made within the extended period of eight days, the Sellers under their contract shall make an allowance to their Buyers, to be deducted in the invoice from the contract price, based on the number of days by which the originally stipulated period is exceeded, in accordance with the following scale: 1 to 4 days, 0.50% of the gross c.i.f. price; 5 or 6 days, 1% of the gross c.i.f. price; 7 or 8 days, 1.50% of the gross c.i.f. price; but if, notwithstanding such notice, the Shipper defaults in shipment, then the contract shall be deemed to have called for shipment during the originally stipulated period plus 8 days, at contract price less 1.50%, and any settlement for default shall be calculated on that basis.

27. APPROPRIATION- The Shipper shall advise shipment by telegram, telex or other method of rapid written communication giving approximate quantity loaded and vessel's name within 2 business days of date of bill of lading, such advice to be given by subsequent Sellers in due course after receipt.

28. PROOF OF SHIPMENT- Bill of lading to be considered proof of date of shipment in the absence of evidence to the contrary. Each shipment appropriated in whole or part fulfilment of this contract to be considered a separate contract, but each bill of lading not to be considered a separate shipment except as to the date on which it can be appropriated. In the event of more than one shipment being made each shipment to be considered a separate contract, but the margin on the mean quantity sold not to be affected thereby.

29. NOTICES-All Notices required to be served on the parties pursuant to this contract shall be communicated rapidly in legible form. Methods of rapid communication for the purposes of this clause are defined and mutually recognised as:- either telex, or letter if delivered by hand on the date of writing, or telefax, or E-mail, or other electronic means, always subject to the proviso that if receipt of any notice is contested by the addressee, the burden of proof of transmission shall be on the sender who shall, in the case of a dispute, establish, to the satisfaction of the arbitrator(s) or board of appeal appointed pursuant to the Arbitration Clause, that the notice was actually transmitted. Any notice received after 1600 hours on a business day shall be deemed to have been received on the business day following. In case of resales all notices shall be passed on without delay by Buyers to their respective Sellers or vice versa. A notice to the Brokers or Agent shall be deemed a notice under this contract.

30. NON-BUSINESS DAYS- Saturdays, Sundays and the officially recognised and/or legal holidays of the respective countries and any days which the Grain and Feed Trade Association may declare as non-business days for specific purposes, shall be non-business days. Should the time limit for doing any act or giving any notice expire on a non-business day, the time so limited shall be extended until the first business day thereafter. The period of shipment shall not be affected by this clause.

31. DEFAULT- In default of fulfilment of contract by either party, the following provisions shall apply:-

(a) The party other than the defaulter shall, at their discretion have the right, after giving notice by letter, telegram or telex to the defaulter to sell or purchase, as the case may be, against the defaulter, and such sale or purchase shall establish the default price.

(b) If either party be dissatisfied with such default price or if the right at (a) above is not exercised and damages cannot be mutually agreed, then the assessment of damages shall be settled by arbitration.

(c) The damages payable shall be based on, but not limited to, the difference between the contract price and either the default price established under (a) above or upon the actual or estimated value of the goods, on the date of default, established under (b) above.

(d) In no case shall damages include loss of profit on any sub-contracts made by the party defaulted against or others unless the Arbitrator(s) or Board of Appeal, having regard to special circumstances, shall in his/their sole and absolute discretion think fit.

(e) Damages, if any, shall be computed on the quantity appropriated but, if no such quantity has been appropriated then on the mean contract quantity, and any option available to either party shall be deemed to have been exercised accordingly in favour of the mean contract quantity.

(f) Default may be declared by Sellers at any time after expiry of the contract period, and the default date shall then be the first business day after the date of Sellers' advice to their Buyers. If default has not already been declared then (notwithstanding the provisions stated in the Appropriation Clause), if notice of appropriation is not passed by the 4th business day after the last day for appropriation laid down in the contract, the Sellers shall be deemed to be in default, and the default date shall then be the first business day thereafter.

32. CIRCLE- Where Sellers re-purchase from their Buyers or from any subsequent Buyer the same goods or part thereof, a circle shall be considered to exist as regards the particular goods so re-purchased, and the provisions of the Default Clause shall not apply. (For the purpose of this clause the same goods shall mean goods of the same description, from the same country of origin, of the same quality, and, where applicable, of the same analysis warranty, for shipment to the same port(s) of destination during the same period of shipment). Different currencies shall not invalidate the circle.

Subject to the terms of the Prohibition Clause in the contract, if the goods are not appropriated, or, having been appropriated documents are not presented, invoices based on the mean contract quantity shall be settled by all Buyers and their Sellers in the circle by payment by all Buyers to their Sellers of the excess of the Sellers' invoice amount over the lowest invoice amount in the circle. Payment shall be due not later than 15 consecutive days after the last day for appropriation, or, should the circle not be ascertained before the expiry of this time, then payment shall be due not later than 15 consecutive days after the circle is ascertained. Where the circle includes contract(s) expressed in different currencies the lowest invoice amount shall be replaced by the market price on the first day for contractual shipment and invoices shall be settled between each Buyer and his Seller in the circle by payment of the differences between the market price and the relative contract price in the currency of the contract.

All Sellers and Buyers shall give every assistance to ascertain the circle and when a circle shall have been ascertained in accordance with this clause same shall be binding on all parties to the circle.

As between Buyers and Sellers in the circle, the non-presentation of documents by Sellers to their Buyers shall not be considered a breach of contract.

Should any party in the circle prior to the due date of payment commit any act comprehended in the Insolvency Clause of this contract, settlement by all parties in the circle shall be calculated at the closing out price as provided for in the Insolvency Clause, which shall be taken as a basis for settlement, instead of the lowest invoice amount in the circle. In this event respective Buyers shall make payment to their Sellers or respective Sellers shall make payment to their Buyers of the difference between the closing out price and the contract price.

33. INSOLVENCY- If before the fulfilment of this contract, either party shall suspend payments, notify any of the creditors that he is unable to meet debts or that he has suspended or that he is about to suspend payments of his debts, convene, call or hold a meeting of creditors, propose a voluntary arrangement, have an administration order made, have a winding up order made, have a receiver or manager appointed, convene, call or hold a meeting to go into liquidation (other than for re-construction or amalgamation) become subject to an Interim Order under Section 252 of the Insolvency Act 1986, or have a Bankruptcy Petition presented against him (any of which acts being hereinafter called an "Act of Insolvency") then the party committing such Act of Insolvency shall forthwith transmit by telex or telegram or by other method of rapid written communication a notice of the occurrence of such Act of Insolvency to the other party to the contract and upon proof (by either the other party to the contract or the Receiver, Administrator, Liquidator or other person representing the party committing the Act of Insolvency) that such notice was thus given within 2 business days of the occurrence of the Act of Insolvency, the contract shall be closed out at the market price ruling on the business day following the giving of the notice. If such notice be not given as aforesaid, then the other party, on learning of the occurrence of the Act of Insolvency, shall have the option of declaring the contract closed out at either the market price on the first business day after the date when such party first learnt of the occurrence of the Act of Insolvency or at the market price ruling on the first business day after the date when the Act of Insolvency occurred.

In all cases the other party to the contract shall have the option of ascertaining the settlement price on the closing out of the contract by re-purchase or re-sale, and the difference between the contract price and the re-purchase or re-sale price shall be the amount payable or receivable under this contract.

34. DOMICILE- This contract shall be deemed to have been made in England and to be performed in England, notwithstanding any contrary provision, and this contract shall be construed and take effect in accordance with the laws of England. Except for the purpose of enforcing any award made in pursuance of the Arbitration clause of this contract, the Courts of England shall have exclusive jurisdiction to determine any application for ancillary relief, the exercise of the powers of the Court in relation to the arbitration proceedings and any dispute other than a dispute which shall fall within the jurisdiction of arbitrators or board of appeal of the Association pursuant to the Arbitration Clause of this contract. For the purpose of any legal proceedings each party shall be deemed to be ordinarily resident or carrying on business at the offices of The Grain and Feed Trade Association, (GAFTA), England, and any party residing or carrying on business in Scotland shall be held to have prorogated jurisdiction against himself to the English Courts or if in Northern Ireland to have submitted to the jurisdiction and to be bound by the decision of the English Courts. The service of proceedings upon any such party by leaving the same at the offices of The Grain and Feed Trade Association, together with the posting of a copy of such proceedings to his address outside England, shall be deemed good service, any rule of law or equity to the contrary notwithstanding.

35. ARBITRATION-

(a) Any dispute arising out of or under this contract shall be settled by arbitration in accordance with the Arbitration Rules, No. 125, of The Grain and Feed Trade Association, in the edition current at the date of this contract, such Rules forming part of this contract and of which both parties hereto shall be deemed to be cognisant.

(b) Neither party hereto, nor any persons claiming under either of them shall bring any action or other legal proceedings against the other of them in respect of any such dispute until such dispute shall first have been heard and determined by the Arbitrator(s) or a Board of Appeal, as the case may be, in accordance with the Arbitration Rules and it is expressly agreed and declared that the obtaining of an award from the Arbitrator(s) or a Board of Appeal, as the case may be, shall be a condition precedent to the right of either party hereto or of any persons claiming under either of them to bring any action or other legal proceedings against the other of them in respect of any such dispute.

36. INTERNATIONAL CONVENTIONS -

The following shall not apply to this contract:-

(a) the Uniform Law on Sales and the Uniform Law on Formation to which effect is given by the Uniform Laws on International Sales Act 1967;

(b) the United Nations Convention on Contracts for the International Sale of Goods of 1980; and

(c) the United Nations Convention on Prescription (Limitation) in the International Sale of Goods of 1974 and the amending Protocol of 1980.

(d) Incoterms

Sellers.. Buyers..

Printed in England and issued by

GAFTA

THE GRAIN AND FEED TRADE ASSOCIATION

GAFTA HOUSE, 6 CHAPEL PLACE, RIVINGTON ST, LONDON EC2A 3SH

79/6

Effective 1st March 2000

No: 79A

CONTRACT FOR UNITED KINGDOM AND IRELAND GRAIN
FOB TERMS

Date ....

SELLERS ....

INTERVENING AS BROKERS ....

BUYERS...
have this day entered into a contract on the following terms and conditions.

1. GOODS IN BULK- ....
Buyers have the option of calling for up to 10% in bags for safe stowage, such bags to be taken and paid for as Grain.

2. QUANTITY- ....tonnes,
5% more or less at Buyers' option. In the event of the quantity contracted for being for a full and complete cargo and/or cargoes the margin of contract quantity to be 10% more or less, excess or deficiency over 5% to be settled at the F.O.B. price on date of last bill of lading and on the quantity thereof; value to be fixed by arbitration unless mutually agreed. In the event of more than one shipment being made, each shipment to be considered a separate contract, but the margin on the mean quantity sold not to be affected thereby.

3. PRICE- At the price of ....
per tonne of 1000 kilograms delivered free on board Buyers' vessel(s), including trimming and/or stowage.

4. LOADING PORT- ....

Sellers have the option of declaring ....
as the loading port(s) for each period of shipment. To exercise this option, the first Sellers shall declare the

loading port(s) to their Buyers not later than 1000 hours on ....
Notice of Declaration may be passed by telephone in which case to be confirmed in writing on the same day.
The Notices Clause and the Non-Business Days Clause shall not apply to such declaration.
Where the date for declaring a port falls to be given on a non-business day (as defined in the Non-Business Days Clause) it shall be given not later than 1000 hours on the immediate preceding business day.
In case of re-sales all notices shall be despatched and passed on by any means of rapid written communication (or by telephone and confirmed by telex) on the same day if received not later than 1700 hours or not later than 1000 hours on the next business day if received after 1700 hours or on a non-business day.
A notice to the Brokers or Agent shall be deemed a notice under this contract.

5. BROKERAGE ....per tonne,
to be paid by Sellers on the mean contract quantity, contract fulfilled or not fulfilled unless such non-fulfilment is due to the successful application of the Prohibition Clause. Brokerage shall be due on the day shipping documents are exchanged or, if the goods are not delivered then the brokerage shall be due on the 30th consecutive day after the last day for delivery.

6. QUALITY-
* Warranted to contain ....

*delete/specify as applicable

Natural Weight .... kilograms per hectolitre, at time and place of loading.

Moisture... % Admixture...... ....%

* To be certified by ....
Certificate of inspection at time of loading shall be final as to quality.

* of fair average quality of the season's shipments at time and place of loading to be assessed upon the basis of, and by comparison with The Grain and Feed Trade Association's official F.A.Q. Standard of the month during which the bill of lading is dated. In the event of no F.A.Q. Standard being established by the Association, the Arbitrator(s) shall in his/their discretion decide what is the fair average quality. An average sample of the delivery shall be taken and sealed jointly at port of loading by the Representatives of the Sellers and the Representatives of the Buyers and shall be forwarded immediately to the Association for the purpose of establishing the F.A.Q. Standard. The expenses of such sampling and forwarding shall be paid half by the Sellers and half by the Buyers. Place of loading under this contract shall be understood as the port or group of ports adopted by the appointed Standards Committee in making the Standard. If the difference between the delivery and the F.A.Q. Standard shall not amount to 0.50% of contract price, no allowance for quality shall be due; otherwise Buyers shall be entitled to the full difference in value.

* at time and place of loading about as per sealed sample marked ....

in possession of ....
The word "about" shall mean the equivalent of 0.50% of the contract price.

In any assessment of allowances for quality at arbitration, due regard shall be given to any analysis under other guarantees.

7. FINALITY- Where the natural weight, analysis for moisture and admixture and/or analysis for other warranties is to be determined by The Grain and Feed Trade Association or their appointed Analysts, or other accepted authority agreed by both parties, instructions to proceed shall be sent by the last Buyers to the Association, Analyst or accepted authority whichever is applicable within 21 days of completion of loading. The certificate of The Grain and Feed Trade Association or its duly appointed Analysts or accepted authority is final in respect of all warranties/guarantees, all expenses incurred to be borne half by the Sellers and half by the Buyers.

In the event of non-compliance with any of the preceding provisions of this clause claims for excess or deficiency as applicable shall be deemed to be waived and absolutely barred, unless the Arbitrator(s) or Board of Appeal referred to in the Arbitration Rules, shall in his/their absolute discretion, otherwise determine.

8. DELIVERY PERIOD-

A. Delivery to be made in good condition during ....

.... at Buyers' call.
Vessel shall load in accordance with the custom of the port of loading at one safe berth per vessel at Sellers' option. Bill of lading shall be considered proof of date of delivery in the absence of evidence to the contrary.

B. Provided that the vessel is presented at loading port in readiness to load, Sellers shall if necessary complete loading after the contractual period, and such delivery shall be deemed to be within the contractual period, subject to the following provisions:

(a) Notwithstanding the provisions of the Nomination of Vessel's Clause the presentation shall allow at least

36/ .... consecutive hours remaining prior to the end of the contractual delivery period.

(b) The presentation must be between 0800 hours and 1700 hours on a business day.

(c) Time from 1700 hours on a Friday or a day preceding a public holiday until 0800 hours on the next working day shall not count in computing (a) above.

9. SUPERVISION- Sellers and Buyers and/or their Representatives shall have the right of supervision both as to delivery and weighing at port(s) of loading.

10. EXTENSION OF DELIVERY- The contract period of delivery shall, if desired by Buyers, be extended for not more than eight consecutive days, provided that Buyers give notice in accordance with the Notices Clause not later than the next business day following the last day of the delivery period. The notice need not state the number of additional days claimed, and such notice shall be passed on by Buyers to their Sellers respectively in due course after receipt. In this event if delivery is made within the extended period of eight days, the contract price will be increased in accordance with the number of days by which the originally stipulated period is exceeded, in accordance with the following scale:

1 to 4 days 0.50%;

***delete/specify as applicable**

5 or 6 days 1%;

7 or 8 days 1.50% of the gross F.O.B. price.

Any difference in export duties, taxes, levies etc., between those applying during the original delivery period and those applying during the period of extension shall be for the account of the Buyers; Sellers shall produce evidence of the amounts paid if required by Buyers. If any increase becomes due under this clause, the contract price shall be deemed to be the original contract price plus the increase and any other contractual differences shall be settled on the basis of such increased price. For the purpose of establishing the increased price, the calculation of extension shall commence 36/ .... consecutive hours after the vessel is presented at the loading port in readiness to load.

If however, after having given notice to Sellers as above, subject to the provisions of Clause 8B. above, Buyers fail to take delivery within such 8 days, then the contract shall be deemed to have called for delivery during the originally stipulated period plus 8 days, at contract price plus 1.50% and any settlement for default shall be calculated on that basis.

11. **NOMINATION OF VESSELS-**

(a) Nomination of Vessels

(i) The last F.O.B. Buyers shall give at least 3 clear days notice of the name of the vessel(s) and the probable readiness date; the estimated quantity required to be loaded and the name of the Ship's Agents, to be despatched by telex by the last F.O.B. Buyers by 1000 hours on a business day. The above-mentioned notice shall not become effective under the terms of this contract before the expiry of the 3 clear days notice.

(ii) Buyers shall instruct the Ship's Agents to keep the Sellers informed of any delay in the expected date of the vessel's readiness. In the event that the vessel does not present in readiness to load in compliance with the Delivery Period Clause within 5 days from the original probable readiness date, the nomination shall be deemed to have lapsed.

(b) Substitution of Vessels

Having nominated as in (a)(i) above, the last F.O.B. Buyers are entitled to substitute the last named vessel, provided that they give a notice to the Sellers of the name of the substitute vessel and any change of the Ship's Agent. The substitute vessel shall present at the loading port in readiness to load in compliance with the Delivery Period Clause no later than 5 days from the expected probable readiness date of the vessel nominated in accordance with paragraph (a)(i) above.

In the case of resales all notices shall be passed on without delay by telephone and confirmed by telex on the same day. A notice to the Brokers or Agent shall be deemed a notice under this clause. The Notices Clause and the Non-Business Days Clause shall not apply.

12. **SHIP'S CLASSIFICATION-** By first class mechanically self-propelled vessel(s) suitable for the carriage of the contract goods, classed Lloyds 100A1 or equivalent class, or in accordance with the Institute Classification Clause of the Institute of London Underwriters, excluding Tankers and Vessels which are either classified in Lloyd's Register or described in Lloyd's Shipping Index as "Ore/Oil" Vessels.

13. **PAYMENT-** Payment by cash in London on presentation of and in exchange for, bill(s) of lading or mate's receipt. No obvious clerical error in the documents shall entitle the Buyers to reject them or delay payment, but the Sellers shall be responsible for all loss or expense caused to Buyers by reason of such error and Sellers shall on request of Buyers furnish an approved guarantee in respect thereto.

Final invoices for monies due may be prepared by either party and shall be settled without delay. If not settled, either party may declare that a dispute has arisen which may be referred to arbitration as herein provided.

14. **INTEREST-** If there has been unreasonable delay in any payment interest appropriate to the currency involved shall be charged. If such charge is not mutually agreed, a dispute shall be deemed to exist which shall be settled by arbitration. Otherwise interest shall be payable only where specifically provided in the terms of the contract or by an award of arbitration. The terms of this clause do not override the parties obligation under the Payment Clause.

15. **CERTIFICATES OF ORIGIN** ....

16. **EXPORT LICENCE-** Export Licence, if required, to be obtained by Buyers.

17. **DUTIES AND TAXES ON GOODS-** All export duties and taxes, present or future, in country of origin or of the territory where the port or ports of shipment named herein is situate, shall be for Sellers' account, unless otherwise provided. E.C. Levies, Refunds etc. shall be for Buyers' account unless otherwise provided.

Where the goods become the subject of an European Union (EC, EEC, EU) export refund in accordance with the EU regulations in force at time of export, they are not eligible for re-importation to the European Union.

18. **WEIGHING** ....

19. **SAMPLING AND ANALYSIS-** Samples required for the purposes of the contract shall be taken at the time and place of shipment, in accordance with the GAFTA Sampling Rules Form No: 124 and analysis tests shall be carried

out in accordance with the GAFTA Methods of Analysis Form No:130. The parties shall appoint superintendents for the purposes of supervision and sampling of the goods from the GAFTA Approved Register of Superintendents.

20. ALLOWANCES-

(a) Natural Weight:
To be ascertained by The Grain and Feed Trade Association or other accepted authority and any deficiency so determined to be allowed for off the contract price in accordance with Rules No. 65 of The Grain and Feed Trade Association.

(b) Moisture - Any excess in the guaranteed maximum moisture content shall be allowed for off the contract price on the following scale:
1% for 1% up to the first 1% excess.
1.50% for 1% of the excess over the first 1% up to 2%.
2.50% for 1% of the excess over 2% up to 3%.
Fractions in proportion.
If the excess exceeds 3%, the allowance to be mutually agreed or settled by arbitration.

(c) Admixture - Any admixture of dirt and/or other foreign substance in excess of the guaranteed maximum shall be allowed for by Sellers at contract price but any grain or seed other than the grain contracted for to be reckoned as foreign substances at half their quantities. The percentage of admixture to be determined by The Grain and Feed Trade Association or its duly appointed Analysts.

21. INSURANCE- Marine and War Risk Insurance including strikes, riots, civil commotions and mine risk shall be effected by Buyers with first class underwriters and/or approved companies. Buyers shall supply Sellers with confirmation thereof at least 3 consecutive days prior to expected readiness of vessel(s). If Buyers fail to provide such confirmation, Sellers shall have the right to place such insurance at Buyers' risk and expense.

22. PROHIBITION- In case of prohibition of export, blockade or hostilities or in case of any executive or legislative act done by or on behalf of the government of the country of origin or of the territory where the port or ports of shipment named herein is/are situate, restricting export, whether partially or otherwise, any such restriction shall be deemed by both parties to apply to this contract and to the extent of such total or partial restriction to prevent fulfilment whether by shipment or by any other means whatsoever and to that extent this contract or any unfulfilled portion thereof shall be cancelled. Sellers shall advise Buyers without delay with the reasons therefor and, if required, Sellers must produce proof to justify the cancellation.

23. STRIKES, RIOTS, LOCK-OUTS OR ICE -

(a) Should delivery or loading of the goods or any part thereof be prevented at any time during the last 28 days of guaranteed delivery period or at any time during the guaranteed delivery period if such be less than 28 days, by reason of riots, strikes, lock-outs or ice at port(s) of loading or elsewhere preventing the forwarding of the goods to such port or ports, then the Sellers shall be entitled at the termination of such riots, strikes, lock-outs or ice to as much time, not exceeding 28 days, for delivery at such port(s) as was left for delivery under the contract prior to the outbreak of the riots, strikes, lock-outs or ice, and in the event of the time left for delivery under the contract being 14 days or less, a minimum extension of 14 days shall be allowed.

In the event of further riots, strikes, lock-outs or ice preventing delivery or loading of the goods during the time by which the guaranteed time of delivery has been extended by reason of the operation of the provisions of the foregoing paragraph, the additional extension shall be limited to the actual duration of such further riots, strikes, lock-outs or ice.

(b) Sellers shall despatch notice by telex or other rapid written communication not later than 5 business days after the commencement of the strikes, riots, lock-outs or ice or 5 business days after the commencement of the delivery period whichever is later if they intend to claim an extension of time for delivery under this clause. All such notices shall be passed on in due course.

(c) If required by Buyers, Sellers must provide documentary evidence to establish any claim for extension under this clause.

(d) In the case of non-delivery made under the above circumstances the date of default shall be similarly deferred.

24. ICE- If the ice situation at the port of delivery named in the contract prevents the ship from calling at that port, within the period of delivery, the Buyers shall be entitled at the termination of this inaccessibility to as much time as left for shipment, prior to the commencement of the inaccessibility, with a minimum of 14 days to be allowed.

The Buyers shall give notice by telex or other rapid written communication not later than the next business day after the last day of the guaranteed time of delivery if he intends to claim an extension of time for delivery. In the case of non-fulfilment under the above condition, the date of default shall be similarly deferred. The question of inaccessibility to be decided by a Lloyd's agent if required.

25. NOTICES-All Notices required to be served on the parties pursuant to this contract shall be communicated rapidly in legible form. Methods of rapid communication for the purposes of this clause are defined and mutually recognised as:- either telex, or letter if delivered by hand on the date of writing, or telefax, or E-mail, or other electronic means, always subject to the proviso that if receipt of any notice is contested by the

APPENDIX D

Standard Shipping Note

© SITPRO 1987

STANDARD SHIPPING NOTE

IMPORTANT USE THE DANGEROUS GOODS NOTE IF THE GOODS ARE CLASSIFIED AS DANGEROUS ACCORDING TO APPLICABLE REGULATIONS SEE BOX 10A

Exporter [1]

Customs reference/status [2]

Booking number [3]

Exporter's reference [4]

Port charges payable by * [5]
exporter ☐ freight forwarder ☐
other (name and address)

Forwarder's reference [6]

Freight forwarder [7]

International carrier [8]

For use of receiving authority only

Other UK transport details (e.g. ICD, terminal, vehicle bkg. ref., receiving dates) [9]

The Company preparing this note declares that, to the best of their belief, the goods have been accurately described, their quantities, weights and measurements are correct and at the time of despatch they were in good order and condition; that the goods are not classified as dangerous in any UK, IMO, ADR, RID or IATA/ICAO regulation applicable to the intended modes of transport. [10A]

Vessel/flight no. and date | Port/airport of loading [10]

Port/airport of discharge | Destination [11]

TO THE RECEIVING AUTHORITY - Please receive for shipment the goods described below subject to your published regulations and conditions (including those as to liability).

Shipping marks	Number and kind of packages; description of goods; non-hazardous special stowage requirements [12]	Receiving authority use	Gross wt (kg) of goods [13]	Cube (m^3) of goods [14]

For use of shipping company only

Total gross weight of goods

Total cube of goods

PREFIX and container/trailer number(s) [16]	Seal number(s) [16A]	Container/trailer size(s) and type(s) [16B]	Tare wt (kg) as marked on CSC plate [16C]	Total of boxes 13 and 16C [16D]

DOCK/TERMINAL RECEIPT
Received the above number of packages/containers/trailers in apparent good order and condition unless stated hereon.
RECEIVING AUTHORITY REMARKS

Haulier's name

Vehicle reg. no.

DRIVER'S SIGNATURE

SIGNATURE AND DATE

Name of company preparing this note [17]

Date

(Indicate name and telephone number of contact)

630 *Mark X as appropriate. If box 5 is not completed the company preparing this note may be held liable for payment of port charges
Non-completion of any boxes is a subject for resolution by the contracting parties

Dangerous Goods Note

DANGEROUS GOODS DECLARATION, SHIPPING NOTE & CONTAINER/VEHICLE PACKING CERTIFICATE

DANGEROUS GOODS NOTE

Exporter 1

Customs reference/status 2

Booking number 3

Exporter's reference 4

Forwarder's reference 5

Consignee 6

DSHA Notification given by: 6A

Shipper	Cargo agent	Transport operator	Shipping line

(in accordance with DSHA Regulations)

Freight forwarder 7

International carrier 8

For use of receiving authority only

Other UK transport details (e.g. ICD, terminal, vehicle bkg. ref., receiving dates) 9

Vessel — Port of Loading 10

Port of discharge — Destination 11

TO THE RECEIVING AUTHORITY
Please receive for shipment the goods described below subject to your published regulations and conditions (including those as to liability)

Shipping marks — Number and kind of packages; description of goods 12 **SPECIFY: PROPER SHIPPING NAME†, IMO HAZARD CLASS, UN No. Additional information (if applicable, see overleaf)**	Net wt (kg) 13	Gross wt (kg) 13A	Cube (m³) of goods 14

† PROPER SHIPPING NAME - TRADE NAMES ALONE ARE UNACCEPTABLE.

CONTAINER/VEHICLE PACKING CERTIFICATE
I hereby declare that the goods described above have been packed/loaded into the container/vehicle identified below in accordance with the provisions shown overleaf:-

MUST BE COMPLETED AND SIGNED FOR ALL CONTAINER/VEHICLE LOADS BY PERSON RESPONSIBLE FOR PACKING/LOADING:-

Name of company

Name/Status of declarant

Place and date

Signature of declarant

15 **DANGEROUS GOODS DECLARATION**
I hereby declare that the contents of this consignment are fully and accurately described above by the correct technical name(s) (proper shipping name(s)), that the shipment is packaged in such a manner as to withstand the ordinary risks of handling and transport by sea, having regard to the properties of the goods to be carried, and that the goods are classified, packaged, marked and labelled in accordance with the requirements of the Merchant Shipping (Dangerous Goods and Marine Pollutant) Regulations 1990 as currently amended. I further declare that, if appropriate, the goods are classified, packaged and marked to comply with the requirements of the European Agreement concerning the International Carriage of Dangerous Goods by Road (ADR) and of Annex 1 (RID) to the Uniform Rules concerning the Contract for International Carriage of Goods by Rail (CIM) or special arrangements made between the contracting parties to these Agreements.
The shipper must complete and sign box 17.

Total gross weight of goods

Total cube of goods

Prefix and container/vehicle reg. number 16	Seal number(s) 16A	Container/vehicle size & type 16B	Tare wt (kg) as marked on CSC plate 16C	Total of boxes 13A and 16C 16D

DOCK/TERMINAL RECEIPT Received the above number of packages/containers/trailers in apparent good order and condition unless stated hereon.
RECEIVING AUTHORITY REMARKS

Haulier's Name

Vehicle reg. no.

DRIVER'S SIGNATURE — SIGNATURE AND DATE

Name and telephone no. of shipper preparing this note 17

Name/status of declarant

Place and date

Signature of declarant

890 Non-completion of any boxes is a subject for resolution by the contracting parties.

LONSDALE BUSINESS FORMS LTD. (0933) 228855
SITPRO approved licensee No. 08

addressee, the burden of proof of transmission shall be on the sender who shall, in the case of a dispute, establish, to the satisfaction of the arbitrator(s) or board of appeal appointed pursuant to the Arbitration Clause, that the notice was actually transmitted. Any notice received after 1600 hours on a business day shall be deemed to have been received on the business day following. In case of resales all notices shall be passed on without delay by Buyers to their respective Sellers or vice versa. A notice to the Brokers or Agent shall be deemed a notice under this contract.

26. NON-BUSINESS DAYS- Saturdays, Sundays and the officially recognised and/or legal holidays of the respective countries and any days which The Grain and Feed Trade Association may declare as non-business days for specific purposes, shall be non-business days. Should the time limit for doing any act or giving any notice expire on a non-business day, the time so limited shall be extended until the first business day thereafter. The period of delivery shall not be affected by this clause.

27 DEFAULT- In default of fulfilment of contract by either party, the following provisions shall apply:-

(a) The party other than the defaulter shall, at their discretion have the right, after giving notice by letter, telegram or telex to the defaulter to sell or purchase, as the case may be, against the defaulter, and such sale or purchase shall establish the default price.

(b) If either party be dissatisfied with such default price or if the right at (a) above is not exercised and damages cannot be mutually agreed, then the assessment of damages shall be settled by arbitration.

(c) The damages payable shall be based on, but not limited to, the difference between the contract price and either the default price established under (a) above or upon the actual or estimated value of the goods, on the date of default, established under (b) above.

(d) In all cases the damages shall, in addition, include any proven additional expenses which would directly and naturally result in the ordinary course of events from the defaulter's breach of contract, but shall in no case include, loss of profit on any sub-contracts made by the party defaulted against or others unless the Arbitrator(s) or Board of Appeal, having regard to special circumstances, shall in his/their sole and absolute discretion think fit.

(e) Damages, if any, shall be computed on the mean contract quantity.

28. CIRCLE- Where Sellers re-purchase from their Buyers or from any subsequent Buyer the same goods or part thereof, a circle shall be considered to exist as regards the particular goods so re-purchased, and the provisions of the Default Clause shall not apply. (For the purpose of this clause the same goods shall mean goods of the same description, from the same country of origin, of the same quality, and, where applicable, of the same analysis warranty, for delivery to the same port(s) of loading during the same period of delivery). Different currencies shall not invalidate the circle.

Subject to the terms of the Prohibition Clause in the contract if the goods are not delivered invoices based on the mean contract quantity or, if the goods have been delivered invoices based on the delivered quantity, shall be settled by all Buyers and their Sellers in the circle by payment by all Buyers to their Sellers of the excess of the Sellers' invoice amount over the lowest invoice amount in the circle. Payment shall be due not later than 15 consecutive days after the last day for delivery, or, should the circle not be ascertained before the expiry of this time, then payment shall be due not later than 15 consecutive days after the circle is ascertained. Where the circle includes contract(s) expressed in different currencies the lowest invoice amount shall be replaced by the market price on the first day for contractual delivery, and invoices shall be settled between each Buyer and his Seller in the circle by payment of the differences between the market price and the relative contract price in the currency of the contract.

All Sellers and Buyers shall give every assistance to ascertain the circle and when a circle shall have been ascertained in accordance with this clause same shall be binding on all parties to the circle.

As between Buyers and Sellers in the circle, the non-presentation of documents by Sellers to their Buyers shall not be considered a breach of contract.

Should any party in the circle prior to the due date of payment commit any act comprehended in the Insolvency Clause of this contract, settlement by all parties in the circle shall be calculated at the closing out price as provided for in the Insolvency Clause, which shall be taken as a basis for settlement, instead of the lowest invoice amount in the circle. In this event respective Buyers shall make payment to their Sellers or respective Sellers shall make payment to their Buyers of the difference between the closing out price and the contract price.

29. INSOLVENCY- If before the fulfilment of this contract, either party shall suspend payments, notify any of the creditors that he is unable to meet debts or that he has suspended or that he is about to suspend payments of his debts, convene, call or hold a meeting of creditors, propose a voluntary arrangement, have an administration order made, have a winding up order made, have a receiver or manager appointed, convene, call or hold a meeting to go into liquidation (other than for re-construction or amalgamation) become subject to an Interim Order under Section 252 of the Insolvency Act 1986, or have a Bankruptcy Petition presented against him (any of which acts being hereinafter called an "Act of Insolvency") then the party committing such Act of Insolvency shall forthwith transmit by telex or telegram or by other method of rapid written communication a notice of the occurrence of such Act of Insolvency to the other party to the contract and upon proof (by either the other party to the contract or the Receiver, Administrator, Liquidator or other person representing the party committing the Act of Insolvency) that such notice was thus given within 2 business days of the occurrence of the Act of Insolvency, the contract shall be closed out at the market price ruling on the business day following the giving of the notice. If such notice be not given as aforesaid, then the other party, on learning of the occurrence of the Act of Insolvency, shall have the option of declaring the contract closed out at either the market price on the first business day after the date when such party first learnt of the occurrence of the Act of Insolvency or at the market price ruling on the first business day after the date when the Act of Insolvency occurred.

In all cases the other party to the contract shall have the option of ascertaining the settlement price on the closing out of the contract by re-purchase or re-sale, and the difference between the contract price and the re-purchase or re-sale price shall be the amount payable or receivable under this contract.

30. DOMICILE- This contract shall be deemed to have been made in England and to be performed in England, notwithstanding any contrary provision, and this contract shall be construed and take effect in accordance with the laws of England. Except for the purpose of enforcing any award made in pursuance of the Arbitration clause of this contract, the Courts of England shall have exclusive jurisdiction to determine any application for ancillary relief, the exercise of the powers of the Court in relation to the arbitration proceedings and any dispute other than a dispute which shall fall within the jurisdiction of arbitrators or board of appeal of the Association pursuant to the Arbitration Clause of this contract. For the purpose of any legal proceedings each party shall be deemed to be ordinarily resident or carrying on business at the offices of The Grain and Feed Trade Association, (GAFTA), England, and any party residing or carrying on business in Scotland shall be held to have prorogated jurisdiction against himself to the English Courts or if in Northern Ireland to have submitted to the jurisdiction and to be bound by the decision of the English Courts. The service of proceedings upon any such party by leaving the same at the offices of The Grain and Feed Trade Association, together with the posting of a copy of such proceedings to his address outside England, shall be deemed good service, any rule of law or equity to the contrary notwithstanding.

31. ARBITRATION-

(a) Any dispute arising out of or under this contract shall be settled by arbitration in accordance with the Arbitration Rules, No. 125, of The Grain and Feed Trade Association, in the edition current at the date of this contract, such Rules forming part of this contract and of which both parties hereto shall be deemed to be cognisant.

(b) Neither party hereto, nor any persons claiming under either of them shall bring any action or other legal proceedings against the other of them in respect of any such dispute until such dispute shall first have been heard and determined by the Arbitrator(s) or a Board of Appeal, as the case may be, in accordance with the Arbitration Rules and it is expressly agreed and declared that the obtaining of an award from the Arbitrator(s) or a Board of Appeal, as the case may be, shall be a condition precedent to the right of either party hereto or of any persons claiming under either of them to bring any action or other legal proceedings against the other of them in respect of any such dispute.

32. INTERNATIONAL CONVENTIONS-

The following shall not apply to this contract:-

(a) the Uniform Law on Sales and the Uniform Law on Formation to which effect is given by the Uniform Laws on International Sales Act 1967;

(b) the United Nations Convention on Contracts for the International Sale of Goods of 1980; and

(c) the United Nations Convention on Prescription (Limitation) in the International Sale of Goods of 1974 and the amending Protocol of 1980

(d) Incoterms

Sellers .... Buyers ....

Printed in England and issued by

GAFTA

(THE GRAIN AND FEED TRADE ASSOCIATION)

GAFTA HOUSE, 6 CHAPEL PLACE, RIVINGTON ST, LONDON EC2A 3SH

Appendix G

Waybill

Non-Negotiable Waybill for Combined Transport shipment or Port to Port shipment

Shipper

Waybill No.
Booking Ref.:
Shipper's Ref.:

Consignee

Notify Party/Address (It is agreed that no responsibility shall attach to the Carrier or his Agents for failure to notify of the arrival of the goods)

Place of Receipt (Applicable only when this document is used as a Combined Transport Waybill)

Vessel and Voy. No.

Place of Delivery (Applicable only when this document is used as a Combined Transport Waybill)

Port of Loading

Port of Discharge

Marks and Nos; Container Nos;	Number and kind of Packages; description of Goods	Gross Weight (kg)	Measurement (cbm)

Above particulars as declared by Shipper, but not acknowledged by the Carrier

***Total No. of Containers/Packages received by the Carrier**

Movement

Freight and Charges (indicate whether prepaid or collect):

Origin Inland Haulage Charge ... ...
Origin Terminal Handling/LCL Service Charge ... ...
Ocean Freight ... ...
Destination Terminal Handling/LCL Service Charge ...
Destination Inland Haulage Charge ... ...

Received by the Carrier from the Shipper in apparent good order and condition (unless otherwise noted herein) the total number or quantity of Containers or other packages or units indicated in the box opposite entitled "*Total No. of Containers/Packages received by the Carrier" for Carriage from the Place of Receipt or the Port of Loading, whichever applicable, to the Port of Discharge or the Place of Delivery, whichever applicable, SUBJECT TO THE TERMS OF THE CARRIER'S STANDARD BILL OF LADING TERMS AND CONDITIONS AND TARIFF FOR THE RELEVANT TRADE, WHICH ARE MUTATIS MUTANDIS APPLICABLE TO THIS WAYBILL (copies of which may be obtained from the Carrier or his agents). Except for live animals and Goods which are stated herein to be carried on deck and are so carried, these terms and conditions are warranted by the Carrier in respect of the sea portion of the Carriage to apply the Hague Rules or Hague Visby Rules, whichever would have been applicable if this Waybill were a Bill of Lading. In either case the provisions of Article III Rule 4 of the Hague Visby Rules are deemed to be incorporated herein.

The contract evidenced by this Waybill is deemed to be a contract of carriage as defined in Article 1 (b) of the Hague Rules and Hague Visby Rules. However this Waybill is not a document of title to the Goods.

Delivery will be made to the Consignee named, or his authorised agent, on production of proof of identity at the Port of Discharge or the Place of Delivery, whichever applicable. Should the Consignee require delivery to a party and/or premises other than as shown above in the "Consignee" box, then written instructions must be given by the Consignee to the Carrier or his agent. Unless the Shipper expressly waives his right to control the Goods until delivery by means of a clause on the face hereof, such instructions from the Consignee will be subject to any instruction to the contrary by the Shipper.

Unless instructed to the contrary by the Shipper prior to the commencement of Carriage and noted accordingly on the face hereof, the Carrier will, subject to the aforesaid terms and conditions, process cargo claims with the Consignee. Claims settlement, if any, shall be a complete discharge of the Carrier's liability to the Shipper. The Shipper accepts the said standard terms and conditions on his own behalf, on behalf of the Consignee and the Owner of the Goods, and authorises the Consignee to bring suit against the Carrier in his own name but as agent of the Shipper, and warrants that he has authority so to accept and authorise. The Shipper further undertakes that no claim or allegation in respect of the Goods shall be made against the Carrier by any person other than in accordance with the terms and conditions of this Waybill.

ICS
C/T W/B
April 78

This Waybill is issued subject to the CMI Uniform Rules for Sea Waybills.

Place and Date of Issue

IN WITNESS whereof this Waybill is signed.

For the Carrier:

As Agent(s) only.

Appendix F

Bill of Lading – Front

Shipper

BILL OF LADING

UK Customs Registered No.

B L No.

Shipper's Ref.

F/Agent's Ref.

Consignee (if 'Order' state Notify Party and Address)

Notify Party and Address (leave blank if stated above)

Local Vessel

From (Local port of loading)

Place of Receipt

Ocean Vessel

Port of Loading

Port of Discharge

Place of Delivery by On-Carrier*

It is agreed that no responsibility shall attach to the Carrier or his Agents for failure to notify the Consignee of the arrival of the goods.

Marks and Nos; Container No:	Number and kind of packages; description of goods	Gross Weight	Measurement

Particulars of goods are those declared by Shippers

Freight details, charges, etc.

RECEIVED the goods in apparent good order and condition and, as far as ascertained by reasonable means of checking, as specified above unless otherwise stated. The Carrier, in accordance with the provisions contained in this document, and with those of the applicable tariff conditions (copies of which are available on request).

a) undertakes to perform or to procure the performance of the entire transport from the place of acceptance to the place of delivery.

b) assumes liability as prescribed in this document for such transport.

In accepting this bill of lading the Shipper, Consignee and Owners of the goods, and the holder of this bill of lading, agree to be bound by all of its conditions, exceptions and provisions whether written, printed or stamped on the front or back hereof.

CONTAINER AND VEHICLE DEMURRAGE. Attention is drawn to the Carrier's Terms and Conditions for Container and Vehicle Demurrage which apply to this Contract and which may be obtained from the Carriers or their Agents.

Ocean Freight Paybie at

Place and date of issue

Number of Original Bs/L

In witness whereof the Master, Owner or Agent of the ship has affirmed to the number of Bills of Lading stated above, all of this tenor and date, one of which being accomplished, the others to stand void.

Number of Packages (in words)

ICS
B/L
1 Jan 72
710

* Applicable only when document used as a Through Bill of Lading

CONDITIONS CONTINUED OVERLEAF

For the Master

Bill of Lading – Back

DEFINITIONS. In the Bill of Lading both on the front and on the reverse the terms mentioned shall have the following meaning:

(a) "Carrier" includes the Master and the agents of the Carrier.

(b) "Merchant" includes the Shipper, the Consignees, the Holder of the Bill of Lading, the receiver and the Owner of the goods.

(c) "Goods" means the cargo accepted from the Shipper and includes any container, transportable tank, flat or pallet not supplied by or on behalf of the Carrier.

1. CLAUSE PARAMOUNT. IT IS MUTUALLY AGREED that this Bill of Lading shall have effect subject to the provisions of the International Convention relating to Bills of Lading dated Brussels 25th August 1924 (hereinafter called the Hague Rules), except where legislation giving effect to the Hague Rules as amended by the Protocol signed in Brussels 23rd February 1968 (hereinafter called the Hague Visby Rules) is compulsorily applicable, in which case this Bill of Lading shall have effect subject to the provisions of such legislation. Neither the Hague Rules nor the Hague Visby Rules shall apply where the goods carried hereunder are live animals or cargo which is stated on the face hereof as being carried on deck and is so carried. Provided that nothing contained in this Bill of Lading shall deprive the Carrier of any limitations of or exemptions from liability conferred on the Carrier or the ship by any statute or enactment whatsoever (whether of the United Kingdom or otherwise).

2. RESPONSIBILITY FOR CONVEYANCE, DISCHARGE AND DELIVERY

(a) The Carrier's obligations in respect of the goods shall begin when the goods are accepted at the ocean vessel's rail at the port of loading and shall continue until the goods are discharged at the ocean vessel's rail at the port of discharge. The Carrier shall not in any circumstances whatsoever be liable for any loss or delay of or damage to the goods (whether in his actual or constructive possession or not) howsoever caused occurring before they are accepted at the ocean vessel's rail at the port of loading or after they are discharged at the ocean vessel's rail at the port of discharge.

(b) Notwithstanding anything contained in Sub-Clause (a) above, where by the nature of this Bill of Lading the contract of carriage is in respect of through-transit of containerised or otherwise unitised goods from a place of acceptance to a place of delivery which are expressly stated on the face of this Bill of Lading, the Carrier shall be responsible for loss or damage of whatsoever nature and howsoever arising to the extent following but no further;

(i) with respect to such loss or damage occurring during the carriage by sea or at the sea terminal at the port of loading or the port of discharge to the extent prescribed by the Hague Rules or the Hague Visby Rules, whichever are applicable by Clause 1 above, or

(ii) with respect to such loss or damage not covered by paragraph (i) occurring during the handling, storage or carriage of the goods by a sub-contractor or agent of the Carrier or his agent in which case the liability of the Carrier shall be limited to that amount recoverable by the Carrier or his agent from the sub-contractor or agent in respect of such loss or damage for which purpose the Merchant hereby assigns and cedes to the carrier all his rights in respect thereof against such sub-contractor or agent, or

(iii) if it cannot be proved where the goods were when the loss or damage occurred, the loss or damage shall be deemed to have occurred at sea and the Carrier shall be liable to the extent prescribed by the Hague Rules.

The Carrier shall be entitled to sub-contract on any terms the whole or any part of the carriage, loading, unloading, storage, warehousing handling and all duties whatsoever undertaken by the Carrier in relation to the goods.

3. DISCHARGE AND DELIVERY. The vessel may commence discharging immediately on arrival without notice to the Consignee or any other person and notwithstanding any provision on the face hereof to notify any party which provision (if any) shall impose no obligation whatsoever on the Carrier, and discharge continuously with or without sorting the goods or separating them from other goods (whether or not such other goods are in the same ownership), irrespective of weather, by day and by night, Sundays and holidays included, any custom of the port to the contrary notwithstanding, on to quay, or into shed, warehouse, depot, hulk, lighter, premises, vehicle or any other vessel or craft as the Carrier or his Agents may determine. Delivery overside to Consignee's lighters is at the vessel's option, and, if given, is subject to the Consignee providing sufficient lighters and men to receive the goods as fast as the vessel can deliver, any custom of the port to the contrary notwithstanding. Such discharge shall constitute due delivery of the goods under this Bill of Lading. The Consignee shall bear any charges or expenses incurred by the Consignee or by the Carrier wholly or partially in respect of sorting the goods or separating them from other goods (whether in the same ownership or not) on shore or on board for any purpose whatsoever, including any charges or expenses in connection with storage on shore or afloat pending such sorting or separation, and any apportionment of such charges or expenses by the Carrier among different consignees by any method whatsoever in the discretion of the Carrier shall for the purpose of this clause be final and binding upon the Consignee.

OPTIONAL CARGO. The port of discharge for optional cargo must be declared to the vessel's Agents at the first of the optional ports named in the option not later than 48 hours before the vessel's expected arrival there, or failing such declaration the Carrier may in his absolute discretion discharge the same at the first or any optional port and such discharge shall be deemed a complete fulfilment by the Carrier of the contractual and intended voyage and all the remedies and rights of the Carrier, his servants or agents shall have effect accordingly. Any option must be for the total quantity of goods under this Bill of Lading.

4. ACKNOWLEDGMENT OF WEIGHT, QUALITY, MARKS, ETC. The Carrier, his Agents and servants shall not in any circumstances whatever be under any liability for insufficient packing or inaccuracies, obliteration or absence of marks, numbers, address or description, nor for delivery to drop marks, or quality marks or countermarks or numbers, nor for failure to notify the Consignee of the arrival of the goods, any custom of the port to the contrary notwithstanding. The Carrier is only responsible for leading marks, provided such marks are stamped or otherwise shown clearly upon the goods if uncovered or on the cases or covering in which such goods are contained, in letters at least two inches high and in such manner as should ordinarily remain legible until the end of the voyage. No acknowledgment is made as to the contents of cases, packages, barrels or containers.

4a. Any clause herein giving names of parties who desire to be notified of the arrival of the goods at destination is solely for the information of the Carrier's Agents and failure to notify shall not involve the Carrier in any responsibility or relieve the Merchant from any obligation hereunder.

5. THE CARRIER'S RIGHTS IF CONSIGNEE NOT READY. If the goods are not taken by the Consignee at the time when the vessel is entitled to call upon him to take possession, or if they are not removed from alongside the vessel without delay, the Carrier shall be at liberty, at the sole risk and expense of the Shipper, Consignee and/or Owner of the goods, to enter and land or remove the goods, or to put them into craft or store.

6. LANDING, LANDING CHARGES. The goods shall in all cases be landed by the vessel, and not by the Consignee, and the landing charges shall be payable by the Consignee against delivery. Lighterage, and expenses of weighing, measuring, valuing and counting cargo if any, at port of discharge to be paid by the Consignee of the goods, any custom or alleged custom of the port to the contrary notwithstanding.

7. VOYAGE. The vessel may at any time whatsoever sail with or without pilots, and/or tugs, adjust compasses, sail at reduced speed, be drydocked at any place, with or without cargo on board, tow or be towed and assist vessels in all situations; proceed by any route whatsoever in the Carrier's or Master's absolute discretion whether or not such route is the nearest or most direct or customary or advertised route between the ports of shipment and discharge; proceed to or stay at any port or place whatsoever and sail before or after advertised sailing dates. These liberties may be exercised at any time whatsoever whether before or after shipment or before or after proceeding towards or calling at the port of discharge, and these liberties may be exercised for any reason whatsoever including the vessel's future engagements. The exercise of any of the above liberties shall be deemed to be part of the contractual voyage.

8. DECK CARGO AND STOWAGE

(a) Notwithstanding anything contained in Sub-Clause (b) hereunder, in the case of live animals and cargo, which in this Bill of Lading is stated to be carried on deck, and is so carried, the Carrier shall be under no liability whatsoever for loss, damage or delay howsoever and whensoever occasioned.

(b) The vessel may carry goods of all kinds, dangerous or otherwise. The Carrier may stow the goods in poop, foc'sle, deckhouse, shelter deck, the passenger space, bunker space or any other covered-in space and in containers, and such goods shall be deemed for all purposes to be stowed under deck. The goods may also be stowed on deck, whether in containers or not, with or without notice to the Shipper, and if they are so carried, the Hague Rules or the Hague Visby Rules whichever are applicable by Clause 1 above, shall apply notwithstanding carriage on or under deck, and the goods and/or container shall contribute to General Average, whether carried on or under deck.

9. CARRIER'S LIBERTIES IN THE EVENT OF BLOCKADE, DELAY, ETC. In case of war, hostilities, strikes, port congestion, lock-outs, civil commotions, quarantine, ice, storms or any other cause whatsoever beyond the Carrier's control (whether any of the foregoing are actual or threatened and whether or not existing or anticipated at the commencement of the voyage) which matters or any of them in the judgment of the Master or Carrier (either of whose decision shall be absolute and binding on all parties) may result in damage to or loss of the vessel or give rise to risk of capture, seizure or detention of vessel or cargo, are likely to prejudice the interest of the vessel including her future engagements and/or her cargo whether by delay or otherwise howsoever or make it unsafe or imprudent for any reason to proceed on or continue the voyage or the Carriage by land or enter or discharge at the port or place of discharge or transhipment, or give rise to delay or difficulty in reaching, discharging at or leaving the port or place of discharge or transhipment, or the place of delivery, the Carrier shall have the following liberties any warranty or rule of law notwithstanding:–

(i) To proceed to such convenient port as the Carrier shall in his absolute discretion select and there discharge the goods.

(ii) To carry the goods back to the country of shipment and discharge them there.

(iii) To retain the goods on board the ship and/or return them to the original port of discharge in the same or substituted ship and there discharge the goods at the sole risk and expense of the Shipper/Consignee and/or Owner of the goods.

(iv) To abandon the carriage of the goods by land at such convenient place as the Carrier shall in his absolute discretion select, and discharge the goods from the container.

When the goods have been abandoned or discharged from the ship or container as herein provided they shall thereafter be at the sole risk and expense of the Consignee, and such discharge shall constitute a full performance of all the Carrier's obligations hereunder, the Carrier, Master or Agents giving immediate notice of such discharge to the Consignee of the goods so far as he is known. Full freight and charges shall be deemed to be earned hereunder, and the Carrier shall be entitled to payment for all extra expense incurred in the performance of any of the foregoing liberties for which (together with freight and charges) he shall have a lien on the goods.

10. CARRIER'S LIBERTIES IN THE EVENT OF WAR, ETC. The ship shall have liberty to comply with any orders, directions or recommendations as to departure, arrival, routes, ports of call, stoppages, destination, delivery or otherwise howsoever given by the Government of the Nation under whose flag the vessel sails or any department thereof, or by any other Government, or any department thereof, or any person acting or purporting to act with the authority of such Government or of any department thereof, or by any committee or person having under the terms of the War Risk Insurance on the ship the right to give such orders, directions or recommendations and if by reason of and in compliance with any such orders, directions or recommendations anything is done or is not done the same shall not be deemed a deviation and delivery in accordance with such orders, directions or recommendations shall be a fulfilment of the contract voyage and the freight shall be payable accordingly.

11. CONTAINERS. (i) The Carrier has no responsibility whatsoever for the functioning of reefer containers or trailers, not owned nor leased by the Carrier.

(ii) SHIPPER PACKED CONTAINERS. If a container has not been filled, packed, stuffed or loaded by the Carrier, the Carrier shall not be liable for loss of or damage to the contents and the Merchant shall indemnify the Carrier against any loss, damage, liability or expense incurred by the Carrier, if such loss, damage, liability or expense has been caused by:–

(a) The manner in which the container has been filled, packed, stuffed or loaded; or

(b) The unsuitability of the contents for carriage in containers; or

(c) The unsuitability or defective conditions of the container arising without any want of due diligence on the part of the Carrier to make the container reasonably fit for the purpose for which it is required; or

(d) The unsuitability or defective condition of the container which would have been apparent upon reasonable inspection by the Merchant at or prior to the time when the container was filled, packed, stuffed or loaded.

(iii) INSPECTION OF GOODS. The Carrier shall be entitled, but under no obligation, to open any container at any time and to inspect the contents. If it thereupon appears that the contents or any part thereof cannot safely or properly be carried or carried further either at all or without incurring any additional expense or taking any measures in relation to the container or its contents or any part thereof, the Carrier may abandon the transportation thereof and/or take any measures and/or incur any reasonable additional expense to carry or to continue the carriage or to store the same ashore or afloat under cover or in the open, at any place, which storage shall be deemed to constitute the delivery under this Bill of Lading. The Merchant shall indemnify the Carrier against any reasonable additional expenses so incurred.

(iv) REPOSITIONING OF CONTAINERS. Where containers owned or leased by the Carrier are unpacked at the Consignee's or Receiver's premises they are jointly and severally responsible for returning the empty containers with interiors brushed and clean to the port or place of discharge or to the point or place designated by the Carrier, his servants or agents within the time prescribed to them. Should a container not be returned within the prescribed time the Consignee or Receiver shall be liable for any demurrage, loss or expenses which may arise from such non-return.

(v) CONTAINER EQUIPMENT INTERCHANGE CONDITIONS Shipper and Consignee engage with Carrier to indemnify the Owner/Lessee of container (whether the Owner/Lessee of container be the Carrier or not) against all loss of or damage to any such container, and against all loss and damage occasioned by any container or any defect therein to the Owner/Lessee of container or to any third party to whom the Owner/Lessee of container may be liable by reason of such loss or damage, where such loss or damage occurs or is sustained while the container is on the premises or in the custody of the Shipper or Consignee or any Agent therefor, and howsoever such loss or damage may be caused, even if by the breach of contract, fault or negligence of the Carrier and/or the Owner/Lessee of container.

12. PORT, CUSTOMS, CONSULAR AND OTHER REGULATIONS

(a) The Shippers shall furnish all particulars necessary to enable the Bill of Lading to be made out in accordance with the prescriptions and regulations of the Port, Customs and Consular Authorities.

(b) All Consular, Health or other Certificates required to accompany the goods shall be procured by the Shipper and all detention charges or penalties accruing to the Ship or her cargo owing to the want of any such Certificate shall be borne and paid by the Shipper, Consignee and/or Owner of the goods.

(c) The Consignee and/or Owner of the goods shall bear and pay all tonnage dues, shed dues, harbour dues, customs dues and charges, wharfage charges and other dues and charges payable in respect of the goods.

(d) The Shipper, Consignee and/or Owner of the goods shall comply with the regulations and requirements of the Port, Customs and other authorities and shall bear and pay all duties, taxes, fines, imposts, expenses, loss or damage of whatever nature incurred or suffered by reason of the breach thereof or the illegal, incorrect or insufficient marking, numbering or addressing of packages or units or descriptions of their weight or contents, and shall indemnify the Carrier and his Agents and the ship and the Owner of the other cargo on board against all claims, demands, losses and expenses in respect thereof.

(e) In the event of the goods, by reason of their not being marked with the name of the country from which they are exported, or otherwise not complying with the Customs Regulations at the port of discharge, the Carrier shall be at liberty to bring back or to reship such goods to the port of shipment at the sole risk and expense of the Shipper, Consignee and/or Owners of the goods.

(f) The Collector of the port or other duly appointed official is authorised to grant a general order for the discharge of the ship immediately on the ship's arrival.

(g) Should the Carrier desire to discharge beyond usual Customs hours the Consignee shall if so required sign immediately an application for the purpose.

(h) The Carrier or his Agents may in respect of dutiable goods transhipped at the port of discharge give such undertaking as the Customs Authorities at that port require with respect to dealing with the goods at the port where duty is payable, and all charges involved or liabilities incurred shall be borne by the Shipper, Consignee and/or Owner of the goods.

13. DAMAGED PACKAGES, ETC. The Shipper, Consignee and/or Owner of the goods shall bear and pay the cost of all mending, baling and cooperage of and repairs to or replacement of packages, boxes, crates, wrappers, bags, barrels or other containers or coverings resulting from insufficiency of packing or from excepted perils.

14. TRANSHIPMENT CARGO. The Carrier acts only as a forwarding agent in arranging the carriage of the cargo prior to its loading on to and subsequent to its discharge from the ocean vessel.

15. TRANSHIPMENT AND FORWARDING. The Carrier may at any time and for any purpose whatsoever discharge the goods or any part thereof from the vessel whether before or after sailing from the port of loading and/or land to store the same either on shore or afloat, and/or tranship or forward the same by another vessel or other vessels, whether prior or subsequent to the sailing of the vessel and whether sailing from the port of receipt of the goods or from any other port and whether belonging to the Carrier or to any other persons, and/or may forward the same by any mode or method or modes or methods of conveyance whether by water, land or air or otherwise howsoever and whether under one or more bills of lading and/or other contracts of on-carriage. In any such case the responsibility of each carrier acting as such is limited to that part of the transit actually undertaken by him and the Carrier shall not be liable for any loss, damage or delay howsoever caused to the goods arising after discharge from his vessel. In respect of the storage and/or forwarding of the goods after such discharge, the Carrier acts only as forwarding agent, making contracts for such storage and/or forwarding on the terms and subject to the limitation of liability in use by the persons with whom such contracts are made. Unless the value of the goods is declared at the time of shipment and is stated hereon and extra freight as may be agreed upon is paid, the Carrier shall in no event be under any obligation to declare to the oncarrier any valuation of the goods, even though the oncarrier's contract of carriage contains a valuation or limitation of liability less than that contained in this Bill of Lading. If the goods cannot be forwarded immediately to destination, any charges incurred for storage shall be borne by the Owner of the goods. If the goods are forwarded by more than one conveyance the Consignee must take delivery of each portion immediately after arrival.

16. DANGEROUS, INFLAMMABLE, RADIOACTIVE, DAMAGING OR CONTAMINATING GOODS

(i) The Shippers undertake not to tender for transportation any goods which are of a dangerous, inflammable, radioactive or damaging or contaminating nature without previously giving written notice of their nature to the Carrier and marking the goods, and if applicable, the container, flat, trailer, etc., as required by any laws or regulations which may be applicable during the carriage.

(ii) If the requirements of Sub-Clause (i) are not complied with the Shipper shall indemnify the Carrier against all loss, damage or expense arising out of the goods being tendered for transportation or handled or carried by the Carrier.

(iii) Goods which are or at any time become dangerous [illegible] radioactive or damaging or contaminating may at any time or place be unloaded, jettisoned, destroyed or rendered harmless without compensation and the Shipper, Consignee and/or Owner of such goods shall bear and pay for all charges and expenses incurred in or in consequence of such unloading, destruction, jettisoning or rendering harmless. If the Shipper has not given notice of their nature to the Carrier under Sub-Clause (i) above the Carrier shall be under no liability to make any General Average contribution in respect of such goods.

(iv) In the event of infestation arising from cargo carried under this Bill of Lading, the Shipper and/or Owner of the goods shall indemnify the Carrier against all consequential liabilities, costs and expenses arising therefrom.

17. CLAIMS. Subject to any limits of liability under the Hague Rules or the Hague Visby Rules, whichever are applicable by Clause 1 above, the liability of the Carrier in a case of loss of or damage to or detention of the goods in circumstances involving him in responsibility shall be calculated on, and shall in no case exceed, the shipper's net invoice costs and disbursements less all charges saved. In the case of ad valorem cargo, the Carrier's responsibility shall not exceed the value of the goods declared before the time of shipment and inserted in this Bill of Lading. Where bulk goods or goods without marks, or goods with the same marks are shipped to more than one Consignee the Consignees and/or Owners of the goods shall jointly and severally bear any expense or loss in dividing the goods or parcels into pro rata quantities and any deficiency shall fall upon them in such proportion as the Carrier, his servants or agents shall decide.

The Carrier does not undertake that the goods shall arrive at the port of discharge or place of delivery at any particular time or to meet any particular market or use and the Carrier shall in no circumstances whatsoever be liable for any direct, indirect or consequential loss or damage caused by delay.

18. CALCULATION OF FREIGHT. Freight on the goods shall be deemed earned on shipment, and shall be paid vessel and/or goods lost or not lost. The freight, together with Primage and Charges, shall be due and paid to the Carrier at the port of shipment (unless otherwise agreed) at the time of shipment in the required freely transferable currency at the time of shipment calculated at the mean of the closing rates of exchange in London for the last working day of the week prior to the date when the vessel commences to load. These conditions will also apply where freight is paid at a place other than the port of shipment. The Shipper shall nevertheless remain responsible for the freight until payment is made.

Interest at 2% over the Bank of England minimum lending rate shall be paid on any freight primage and charges remaining unpaid after due date of payment. Full freight is due on damaged or unsound goods and on packages, barrels or containers received part full or empty. The freight payable hereunder has been calculated and based upon the particulars of the goods furnished by the Shipper to the Carrier. The Carrier shall be entitled at any time to open and to re-weigh or re-measure or re-value any goods and if the weight or measurement or value as furnished by the Shipper is found to be incorrect, freight shall be paid by the Shipper, Consignee and/or Owner of the goods on the excess weight or measurement or value so ascertained together with the expenses incident to re-weighing or re-measuring or re-valuing which expenses shall be considered as freight but otherwise such expenses shall be payable by the Carrier. The Shipper shall, if required by the Carrier so to do, furnish forthwith on demand to the Carrier the invoice or a true copy thereof relating to the goods. If the description or (in cases where the value has been stated) the value of the goods has been mis-stated by the Shipper, double the amount of such freight shall, if required by the Carrier, be paid (as liquidated damages) by the Shipper, Consignee and/or Owner of the goods as would have been charged if the goods had been accurately described or valued, and a certificate signed by the Carrier or his Agents shall be conclusive evidence for all purposes of the amount that would have been so charged.

19. LIEN. The Carrier his servants or agents shall have a lien on the goods and a right to sell the goods whether privately or by public auction for all freight (including additional freight payable under Clause 18) primage, dead freight, demurrage, detention charges, Salvage, General Average contributions, and for all other charges and expenses whatsoever, which are for account of the goods or of the Shipper, Consignee and/or Owner of the goods under this Bill of Lading, and for the costs and expenses of exercising such lien and of such sale and also for all previously unsatisfied debts whatsoever due to him by the Shipper, Consignee and/or Owner of the goods. Nothing in this clause shall prevent the Carrier from recovering from the Shipper, Consignee and/or Owner of the goods the difference between the amount due from them or any of them to him and the amount realised by the exercise of the rights given to the Carrier under this Clause.

20. GENERAL AVERAGE, AND SALVAGE

(a) General Average shall be payable according to York-Antwerp Rules 1974 and shall be adjusted at any port or place selected by the Carrier.

(b) In the event of accident, danger, damage or disaster before or after the commencement of the voyage, resulting from any cause whatsoever, whether due to negligence or not, for which, or for the consequence of which, the Carrier is not responsible, by statute, contract or otherwise, the goods, Shippers, Consignees and/or Owner of the goods shall contribute with the Carrier in General Average to the payment of any sacrifices, losses or expenses of a General Average nature that may be made or incurred and shall pay salvage and special charges incurred in respect of the goods.

(c) If a salving vessel is owned or operated by the Carrier, salvage shall be paid for as fully as if the said salving vessel or vessels belonged to strangers. Such deposit as the Carrier or his agents may deem sufficient to cover the estimated contribution of the goods and any salvage and special charges thereon shall, if required, be made by the goods, Shippers, Consignees and/or Owners of the goods to the Carrier before delivery.

21. BOTH TO BLAME COLLISION CLAUSE. If the ship comes into collision with another ship as a result of the negligence of the other ship and any act, neglect or default of the Master, Mariners, pilots or the servants of the Carrier in the navigation or in the management of the ship, the Owners of the goods carried hereunder will indemnify the Carrier against all loss or liability to the other non-carrying ship or her Owners in so far as such loss or liability represent loss of, or damage to, or any claim whatsoever of the Owners of the said goods, paid or payable by the other or non-carrying ship or her Owners to the Owners of the said goods and set off, recouped or recovered by the other or non-carrying ship or her Owners as part of their claim against the carrying ship or Carrier. The foregoing provisions shall also apply where the Owners, Operators or those in charge of any ship or ships or objects other than or in addition to, the colliding ships or objects are at fault in respect to a collision or contact.

22. RIGHTS AND IMMUNITIES OF ALL SERVANTS AND AGENTS OF THE CARRIER

(a) No servant or agent of the Carrier (including every independent contractor from time to time employed by the Carrier) shall in any circumstances whatsoever be under any liability whatsoever to the Shipper, Consignee, Owner of the goods, or Holder of this Bill of Lading for any loss, damage or delay of whatsoever kind arising or resulting directly or indirectly from any act, neglect or default on his part while acting in the course of or in connection with his employment and, but without prejudice to the generality of the foregoing provisions in this Clause, every exemption, limitation, condition and liberty herein contained and every right, exemption from liability, defence and immunity of whatsoever nature applicable to the Carrier or to which the Carrier is entitled hereunder shall also be available and shall extend to protect every such servant or agent of the Carrier acting as aforesaid and for the purpose of all the foregoing provisions of this Clause the Carrier is or shall be deemed to be acting as agent or trustee on behalf of and for the benefit of all persons who are or might be his servants or agents from time to time (including independent contractors as aforesaid) and all such persons shall to this extent be or be deemed to be parties to the contract in or evidenced by this Bill of Lading.

(b) The Carrier shall be entitled to be paid by the Shipper, Consignee, Owner of the goods and/or Holder of this Bill of Lading (who shall be jointly and severally liable to the Carrier therefor) on demand any sum recovered or recoverable by either such Shipper, Consignee, Owner of the goods and/or Holder of this Bill of Lading or any other from such servant or agent of the Carrier for any such loss, damage, delay or otherwise.

23. SURRENDER OF BILL OF LADING. Subject to the Law and/or custom in force at the port or place of discharge, the Bill of Lading duly endorsed must be surrendered in exchange for Delivery Order or the goods.

24. AGENCY CLAUSE. If the ship is not owned by or chartered by demise to the Company or Line by whom this Bill of Lading is issued (as may be the case notwithstanding anything that appears to the contrary) this Bill of Lading shall take effect only as a contract with the Owner or Demise Charterer, as the case may be, as Principal made through the agency of the said Company or Line who act as agents only and shall be under no personal liability whatsoever in respect thereof.

25. JURISDICTION. All claims arising under this Bill of Lading shall be determined according to English Law in England to the exclusion of the jurisdiction of the Courts of any other country unless the contrary is expressly agreed to.

26. PORTUGAL. This Bill of Lading will not be accepted for processing until it is validated by the vessel's Agents.

27. PAYMENT OF FREIGHT. Payment of ocean freight and charges to a freight forwarder, broker or anyone other than Gracechurch Container Line Ltd., or its authorised agent, shall not be deemed payment to the carrier and shall be made at payor's sole risk.

Revised November 1988

INDEX